ROMAN LITERATURE
IN TRANSLATION

THE SPIRIT OF THE CLASSICS

GREEK LITERATURE IN TRANSLATION

ROMAN LITERATURE IN TRANSLATION

SELECTED AND EDITED BY
GEORGE HOWE, P**H**.D.
University of North Carolina

AND

GUSTAVE ADOLPHUS HARRER, P**H**.D.
University of North Carolina

HARPER & BROTHERS PUBLISHERS

The Spirit of the Classics

ROMAN LITERATURE
IN TRANSLATION

Selected and Edited by

GEORGE HOWE, Ph.D.

PROFESSOR OF LATIN, UNIVERSITY OF NORTH CAROLINA

AND

GUSTAVE ADOLPHUS HARRER, Ph.D.

ASSOCIATE PROFESSOR OF LATIN, UNIVERSITY OF NORTH CAROLINA

HARPER & BROTHERS PUBLISHERS
NEW YORK AND LONDON

CONTENTS

ROMAN PURITANISM AND GREEK CULTURE

Third and Second Centuries B. C.

WORLD CONQUEST AND CIVIL WAR

Second and First Centuries B. C.

v

THE PEACE OF AUGUSTUS

End of First Century B. C. and Beginning of First Century A. D.

DESPOTISM AND SUPPRESSION

First Century

THE NEW FREEDOM

Second Century

PREFACE

THIS book of selections from Latin authors is designed as a brief presentation of the literature through the medium of English translation. Its plan embraces three items: an outline, a body of selections, and explanatory notes.

The outline, serving also as a table of contents, gives in briefest possible compass a survey of the development of the literature through its successive stages, interpreting by headings the main currents of thought, and indicating the forms in which the thought was given expression. It seeks also to suggest the essential meaning of each selection and the relation of the selection to the whole.

In the body of selections the best pieces of the literature are represented by complete units, whenever space permits, or by extended passages carefully chosen. The principle governing the selection, however, has not been that of reproducing masterpieces merely, for the book is meant to be more than an anthology. It seeks to interpret the thought of the Romans in the logical order of their experience of life. It answers the questions: What did the Romans think about in the several periods of their growth and development? How did they think about it? In what forms did they give their thinking expression? Since their experience was of course a growth and development in time, the chronological order is followed in the main, although within periods the arrangement is not allowed to become a slave to chronology. While, as a result of the principle of selection, the emphasis is placed upon masterpieces of thinking, yet masterpieces of form too are as fully illustrated as can be done in translation, since it is eminently true of the classics that the criteria of clear thinking and of form coincide.

The explanatory notes are of two sorts. At the beginning of each main division have been inserted short essays with the purpose of giving the social and political background against which the literature is to be viewed. In such brief compass it was of course impossible to sketch even in outline the political or literary history of the various periods; but the attempt has been made to supply at least the most important facts and to suggest the relation of the literature at any given moment to the broader currents of life. The second sort of notes is concerned with the identification and significance of individual authors and selections. These seek merely to point out the historical and literary position of each writer and of each passage quoted, in order that the main thought may be followed the more easily, and in order that that lack of a satisfactory explanation of the relations existing between passages which is characteristic of any book of selections may be reduced to a minimum.

The editors are indebted to many colleagues for valuable suggestions in the preparation of the manuscript. To every selection the translator's name has been appended. Grateful acknowledgment is made to Mr. James Loeb for permission to make wide use of The Loeb Classical Library, and to the following for permission to reprint copyright material: T. F. Unwin, London, for translations from Ennius in *A Literary History of Rome* by J. W. Duff, and for the translation of the Monumentum Ancyranum in *Augustus* by E. S. Shuckburgh; The Macmillan Company, New York, for the translation from Cato in *Roman Farm Management* by Fairfax Harrison; Parke Austin & Lipscomb, New York, for the translation of Cicero's Tusculan Disputations by W. H. Main in *The Greek and Latin Classics;* The University of Chicago Press and Professor F. J. Miller for his translation of Octavia in *The Tragedies of Seneca;* Professor Paul Nixon for his translations from Martial in *A Roman Wit;* Miss Georgiana W. Sargent for translations from Horace in *Horatian Echoes* by J. O. Sargent.

ROMAN PURITANISM AND GREEK CULTURE

THIRD AND SECOND CENTURIES B.C.

THE Roman people had already won an important place in the progress of civilization before their literature reached a stage worthy of consideration. Not until they came in contact with the Greek life in southern Italy and in Sicily did they lend themselves seriously to the cultivation of the fine arts. Before that time they had been busy making a state, fighting for a place in the sun, organizing, building. There are evidences of the beginnings of a native literature before the Greek contact—such as ballad songs of heroes, hymns to the gods, treaties, calendar records, etc.—but these were fostered more as necessary accompaniments of the business of life than as artistic expression, and were no doubt exceedingly crude. What direction the further development of these beginnings would have assumed, what progress would have been made, are matters of pure speculation. The determining factor for Roman literature, as well as for the other fine arts, was the Greek influence. The Greek achievements had reached and passed their zenith and stood at the disposal of all who were to follow. Not until Rome had made herself mistress of all southern Italy in the middle of the third century B.C., indeed not until the pressure of Carthage had been removed half a century later, did she find time to turn her attention to this great heritage. When she did, she found the forms ready-made, the methods and principles thoroughly established, the values fixed. The practical Roman began by translating, then passed on to adaptation to his own life, and came only gradually to the full appreciation of the possibilities of self-expression.

This transplanting of a foreign culture brought problems in its wake. Greek life was not Roman life, Greek standards differed from Roman standards, Greek aims and ambitions and enterprises did not satisfy Roman aspirations. There developed counter-currents in art, some running freely with the stream of Greek culture, some fighting against it. In general this struggle was a wholesome thing, for it enabled the Roman artist to take the benefit of the foreign culture without at the same time sacrificing his own ideas and needs. Roman literature is at all times imitative of Greek in one respect or another, but it is also a very different thing from the Greek.

I. THE TRANSPLANTING OF GREEK CULTURE

PROPHETIC DREAM OF RHEA SYLVIA [1]

ENNIUS

[From the *Annals*, Book I]

Quintus Ennius was born in 239 B.C. at Rudiæ in Calabria. He was brought to Rome by Cato, the opponent of Greek culture, was later granted citizenship, and died there in 169 B.C. By the versatility of his genius, by his feeling for beauty, by his technical mastery of poetical forms in a period characterized by crudeness, by his successful efforts in shaping a literary language, as well as by his happy choice of subjects to satisfy the Roman national taste, Ennius won for himself the name of "Father of Latin Poetry." He continued the practice, begun by his predecessor Andronicus, of translating Greek tragedies, and attempted also original tragedies on Roman subjects. He was the first to experiment with certain lyrical forms derived from the Greek. His chief contribution was the *Annals,* an epic poem narrating the history of Rome from the beginning down to his own day. Only meager fragments of his works are extant.

The prophecy in the following passage foretells the birth of Romulus and Remus.

My body hath no vital vigour left—
Methought a being fair thro' willows
    sweet
Haled me, by streams and places strange;
    and then
Alone, O sister mine, I seemed to stray,
Track my slow path, in quest of thee,
    nor yet
Held thee in heart: I found no footing
    sure.
Thereat meseemed my father's voice to
    call:
  "O daughter, thou hast tribulation first
    To bear: the river shall restore thy
    weal!"
So spake our sire, O sister, and was gone,

Nor let me look upon him though I longed
And oft upheld my hands to heaven's blue
    vault
In tears, and called him in the tones of
    love.
At length sleep left me with my pain at
    heart.
                 —J. W. DUFF.

A CHIVALROUS FOE [1]

ENNIUS

[From the *Annals*, Book VI]

The words of the following fragment are spoken by Pyrrhus, the Greek general who invaded Italy in 280 B.C. It was for such generous acts on his part that the Romans esteemed him so much more highly than they usually esteemed an enemy.

I claim no gold: bid me no ransom price:
Not hucksterers in war, but warriors,
On steel, not gold, we each must stake our
    life.
Find we in fight if Lady Fortune wills
That you or I be master. Hear my word
Withal. Since luck of battle spared the
    men,
Their freedom 'tis my fixed resolve to
    spare.
Take grant and gift: the mighty gods
    approve.
                 —J. W. DUFF.

A SOOTHSAYER [1]

ENNIUS

[From the *Telamo*]

The early Romans were extremely superstitious. Here Ennius is probably

[1] From *A Literary History of Rome,* by J. W. Duff. Copyright by T. Fisher Unwin, Ltd. Reprinted by permission.

translating from Greek tragedy, so that the ideas expressed are not necessarily Roman.

But your superstitious wizards, fortune-
tellers unabashed,
Arrant lunatics or loafers, or with wits
by beggary lashed,
Point the path out to another which
themselves they cannot see,
And for promise of a fortune fix a
drachma as the fee.
—J. W. DUFF.

MENÆCHMI [1]

PLAUTUS

The New Comedy of Menander and his school transplanted to Rome was known as *fabula palliata,* so called because the players appeared dressed in the Greek pallium. The subject matter, the setting, the characters, the form were Greek. The Romans probably began by merely trans-lating. But the Greek plays as a rule were not lively enough for Roman audiences, and the playwrights soon discovered that they could enrich them by combining material taken from two or more Greek originals. This practice was known as contamination.

The greatest representative of the *palliata* was Titus Maccius Plautus (about 254 to 184 B.C.). He was a native of Sarsina in Umbria, but came early to Rome. Because of his poverty he was under the necessity of doing manual labor as a stage-carpenter, but somehow was able to educate himself and to find time to write. He is thought to have written more than a hundred plays; extant are twenty more or less complete and fragments of another. His tendency was to depart more and more freely from his literary models in the direction of a comedy drawn from Roman life.

The Menæchmi is typical of the care-less, rollicking, fun-loving playwright.

[1] From the Loeb Classical Library, by permission.

The interest depends upon situation rather than upon character. The play is the basis of Shakespeare's *Comedy of Errors.*

DRAMATIS PERSONÆ

PENICULUS, *a parasite.*
MENÆCHMUS, *a young gentleman living in Epidamnus.*
MENÆCHMUS (Sosicles), *a young gentle-man of Syracuse.*
EROTIUM, *a courtesan.*
CYLINDRUS, *her cook.*
MESSENIO, *a slave of Menæchmus (Sos-icles).*
MAID, *in the service of Erotium.*
WIFE *of Menæchmus.*
FATHER-IN-LAW *of Menæchmus.*
A DOCTOR.

SCENE:—*Epidamnus. A street in which stand the houses of* MENÆCHMUS *and* EROTIUM.

PROLOGUE

First and foremost, spectators, I am the bearer of the very best wishes for—myself and—you. I bring you Plautus, orally, not corporally, and I pray you receive him with amiable ears. Lend me your attention and learn our argument now; I will frame it in the fewest possible words.

Now writers of comedy have this habit: they always allege that the scene of action is Athens, their object being to give the play a more Grecian air. As for me, I will report the scene as being nowhere, save where, by report, the events oc-curred. And though this argument is à la Greek, yet it is not à l'Attic but rather à la Sicilian. So much by way of ante-lude to this argument; now I will give you your rations of the argument itself, not by the peck or three peck measure, but by the very granary—such is my generosity in giving arguments!

There was a certain old merchant in Syracuse who had twin sons born to him, so much alike that their foster mother who suckled them could not distinguish them, nor even their real mother who gave them birth—so I was told, at least, by a man who had seen the boys; I myself have not seen them, and none of you is to suppose I have. When the boys were now seven years old, their father loaded a large ship with many articles of merchandise; one twin he put aboard and took away with himself to Tarentum, his place of trade, the other being left with his mother at home. At Tarentum it happened they were having a festival when he arrived. Many people had congregated, as they do at festivals; the boy strayed from his father in the crowd. A certain merchant of Epidamnus was there; this merchant picked the boy up and took him off to Epidamnus. As for the father, after he lost his son he was brokenhearted and died of grief at Tarentum a few days later.

When news of all this—how the boy was stolen and his father dead at Tarentum—got back to Syracuse to the boys' grandfather—he changed the name of this other twin. See what a deep affection he had for that other boy, the stolen one! He gave that boy's name to the one at home, calling him Menæchmus, the name of his lost brother. This was the name of the grandfather himself, too—(*confidentially*) I remember his name the more easily for having seen him vociferously dunned. To keep you from going astray later, I herewith forewarn you—both twins have the same name.

Now I must (*chuckling*) foot it back to Epidamnus so as to clarify this situation for you perfectly. If any one of you should want any business transacted for him in Epidamnus, command me freely and speak out—that is, in case you furnish the wherewithal for the transaction. For if a man has not furnished the necessary funds, it will come to nothing; if he has furnished them, it will come to—less than nothing. However, I return to the place I left, yes, and without stirring a step.

That Epidamnian I mentioned some time ago, who stole that other twin, had no children at all except his money. He adopted that kidnapped boy and gave him a wife with a dowry, and made him his heir by his own demise. For he happened one day to be going to the country after a heavy rain, and while he was trying to ford a rapid stream quite near the city, the rapids rapt the feet of the boy's abductor from beneath him and swept him off to perdition. His enormous fortune fell to his adopted son. And there it is (*pointing to house*) that this stolen twin lives.

Now that twin whose home is in Syracuse will come to-day to Epidamnus, with his servant, in search of this twin brother of his. This city (*with a wave toward the houses on the stage*) is Epidamnus, during the presentation of this play; when another play is presented it will become another town. It is quite like the way in which families, too, are wont to change their homes: now a pimp lives here, now a young gentleman, now an old one, now a poor man, a beggar, a king, a parasite, a seer.

ACT I

Enter PENICULUS, *looking dejected*

PEN. The young fellows have given me the name of Brush, the reason being that when I eat I sweep the table clean. (*With fervour*) Men that bind prisoners of war with chains and fasten shackles on runaway slaves are awful fools, at least in my opinion. Why, if the poor devil has this extra trouble on his shoulders, too, he's all the keener for escape and mischief. Why, they get out of their chains somehow. As for those in shackles, they file away the ring, or knock the rivet off with a stone. Nonsensical measures! The man you really want to keep from running off ought to be bound with (*sighing*) food and drink. A loaded table—(*smacking his lips*) tie his snout to that! Just you deal him out meat and drink to suit his pleasure and his appetite each day, and he'll never run—Lord, no! —no matter if he's done a deed for hanging. You'll keep him easily so long as you bind him with these bonds. They're such extraordinarily tenacious bonds, these belly-bands: the more you stretch 'em, the closer they cling. Here's my case —I'm going to Menæchmus here (*pointing to house*), whose bond servant I've been for many a day, going of my own accord to let him bind me. Why (*enthusiastically*), that man doesn't merely feed men, he nurtures them and re-creates them; a better doctor can't be found. Here's the sort of young fellow he is: a splendid trencherman himself, he gives you dinners fit for the festival of Ceres; piles up the courses so, erects such heaps of lovely panny things, you must stand on your couch if you want anything from off the top. (*Pauses, then sadly*) But for now these many days there has been a gap in my invitations; and all this time I've kept fast at home with my (*lingeringly*) dear ones. For not a thing do I eat or buy that isn't, oh, so dear! And now another point is—these dears I've marshalled are deserting me. (*Looking towards* MENÆCHMUS'S *house*) So here's for a call on him. But the door's opening! Aha! I see Menæchmus himself! He's coming out! (*Steps back.*)

SCENE 2

Enter MENÆCHMUS, *followed to the doorway by his wife*

MEN. (*angrily*). If you weren't mean, if you weren't stupid, if you weren't a violent virago, what you see displeases your husband would be displeasing to you, too. Now mark my words, if you act like this toward me after to-day, you shall hie yourself home to your father as a divorcee. Why, whenever I want to go out, you catch hold of me, call me back, cross-question me as to where I'm going, what I'm doing, what business I have in hand, what I'm after, what I've got, what I did when I was out. I've married a custom-house officer, judging from the way everything—all I've done and am doing—must be declared. I've pampered you too much; now then, I'll state my future policy. Inasmuch as I keep you well provided with maids, food, woollen cloth, jewellery, coverlets, purple dresses, and you lack for nothing, you (*with emphasis*) will look out for trouble if you're wise, and cease spying on your husband. (*In lower tone as his wife goes back inside*) And furthermore, that you may not watch me for nothing, I'll reward your diligence by taking a wench to dinner and inviting myself out somewhere.

PEN. (*aside, mournfully*). The fellow pretends to be abusing his wife, when he is abusing me; for if he dines out, it's certainly me, not his wife, he punishes.

MEN. (*elated*). Hurrah! By Jove, at last my lecture has driven her away from the door! Where are your married gallants? Why don't they all hurry up with gifts and congratulations for my valiant fight? (*Showing a woman's mantle worn underneath his cloak*) This mantle I just now stole from my wife inside there and (*gleefully*) it's going to a wench. This is the way to do—to cheat a cunning gaoler in such clever style! Ah, this is a beautiful job, a handsome job, a neat job, a workmanlike job! I've done the wretch out of this—(*dryly*) and done myself, too!—and it's on the road to (*glancing at* EROTIUM'S *house*) ruin. (*Pauses, then cheerfully*) I have taken booty from the enemy without loss to my allies.

PEN. (*loudly, from his retreat*). Hi, sir! Is there some share in that booty for me?

MEN. (*startled and covering mantle again*). Good Lord! Detected!

PEN. Oh no, protected! Never fear!

MEN. Who goes there?

PEN. (*stepping forward*). I.

MEN. (*vastly relieved*). Ah there, old Timeliness! Ah there, old Opportunity! Good day! (*Extends his hand.*)

PEN. (*taking it*). Good day, sir.

MEN. And what are you doing with yourself?

PEN. Shaking hands with my guardian angel.

MEN. You couldn't have arrived at a more fitting time for me.

PEN. A habit of mine; I know every juncture of timeliness.

MEN. Do you want to set your eyes on a rich treat?

PEN. What cook cooked it? I shall know if there has been a culinary slip as soon as I see the leavings.

MEN. Tell me, have you ever seen a wall painting showing the eagle making off with Catameitus, or Venus with Adonis?

PEN. Often. But what have such pictures got to do with me?

MEN. (*revealing the mantle*). Come, cast your eye on me. Do I look at all like them?

PEN. What sort of a get-up is that?

MEN. Say that I'm a splendid fellow.

PEN. (*suspiciously*). Where are we going to eat?

MEN. Just you say what I command.

PEN. (*listlessly*). I do—splendid fellow.

MEN. Won't you add something of your own?

PEN. (*with a sigh*). The jolliest sort of fellow, too.

MEN. Go on, go on!

PEN. (*indignant*). By gad, I will not go on, without knowing what good it does me. You and your wife are at odds, so I am on my guard against you all the more guardedly.

MEN. (*reassuringly*). But there's a place she's unaware of, where we can have a beautiful time and fairly burn up this day.

PEN. (*eagerly*). Come, come, then, by all means! fairly spoken! Now how soon shall I kindle the pyre? Why, the day is half dead already, dead down to its navel.

MEN. You delay yourself by interrupting me.

PEN. Knock my eye clean through its socket, Menæchmus, if I utter a single word—without your orders.

MEN. (*edging away from his house*). Come over here away from the door.

PEN. (*obeying*). All right.

MEN. (*elaborately cautious*). Here, still farther.

PEN. Very well.

MEN. (*still retreating*). Be a man—come still farther from that lioness's lair.

PEN. (*laughing*). Bravo! Gad, you certainly would make a fine charioteer, I do believe.

MEN. Why so?

PEN. You look back so often to make sure your wife is not catching up with you.

MEN. But what do you say——

PEN. I? Why, whatever you want—that's what I say and unsay.

MEN. If you happened to smell something, would the odour enable you to conjecture?

PEN. . . . The Board of Augurs should be consulted.

MEN. (*holding out the lower edge of the mantle*). Come on now, test the odour of this mantle I have. What does it smell of? (*As* PENICULUS *draws back*) Holding off?

PEN. The upper part of a woman's gown is the part to sniff; why, that part there taints the nose with an odour that's indetergible.

MEN. (*holding out another part*). Sniff here, then, Peniculus. What dainty airs you give yourself!

PEN. So I should. (*Sniffs warily.*)

MEN. Well now? What does it smell of? Answer.

PEN. A raid! a jade! a meal! I hope you have. . . .

MEN. Right you are! Yes, I'll take it to my mistress Erotium, the courtesan here (*pointing*) at once. I'll order luncheon to be prepared for us immediately, for me and you and her.

PEN. Capital!

MEN. Then we'll drink and keep drinking till the morrow's star of morn appears.

PEN. Capital! You talk to the point. (*Eyeing* EROTIUM's *door anxiously*) Shall I knock now?

MEN. Knock away. (*Maliciously, as* PENICULUS *hurries to the door*) Or, rather, wait a bit.

PEN. (*gloomily*). You've put the tankard back a mile.

MEN. Knock gently.

PEN. I dare say you fear the door is made of Samian crockery. (*About to knock lustily when the door moves.*)

MEN. (*rapturously*). Wait, wait, for Heaven's sake, wait! Look! she's coming out herself! Ah, you see the sun—is it not positively bedimmed in comparison with the brilliance of her body?

SCENE 3

Enter EROTIUM

EROT. (*fondly*). My darling Menæchmus! Good day!

PEN. What about me?

EROT. (*disdainfully*). You don't count.

PEN. (*cheerfully*). A statement that applies in the army, too—it has its supernumeraries.

MEN. I should like to have a (*with a nod at* PENICULUS) battle prepared for me at your house there to-day.

EROT. (*puzzled, then with a smile*). To-day you shall have one.

MEN. In this battle we'll both (*indicating parasite*) drink; whichever proves himself the better tankard fighter is your army: you be the judge as to—

which you're to spend the night with. (*Gazing at her amorously*) Oh, how I do hate my wife when I look at you, precious!

EROT. (*spying the fringe of the mantle*). Meanwhile you can't keep from wearing part of her wardrobe! (*Examining it*) What is this?

MEN. (*lifting his cloak*). You're arrayed and my wife's raided, rosey.

EROT. (*pleased*). Oh, of all my lovers you make me love you most, easily!

PEN. (*aside*). A courtesan is all cajolery as long as she sees something to seize upon. (*To* EROTIUM) Why, if you really loved him, you ought to have bitten his nose off by now.

MEN. (*removing his cloak*). Hold this, Peniculus; I want to make the offering I vowed.

PEN. Give it here; (*grinning at him*) but do, for heaven's sake, dance just as you are, with the mantle on, afterwards. (*Takes cloak.*)

MEN. (*irritably*) Dance? I? Lord, man, you're crazy!

PEN. Which is more so, you or I? If you won't dance, take it off, then.

MEN. (*removing mantle*). It was an awful risk I ran stealing this to-day. It's my opinion Hercules never ran such a tremendous risk when he got away with the girdle of Hippolyta. (*Handing it to* Erotium) Take it for your own, seeing you are the only living soul that likes to do what I like.

EROT. (*petting him*). That's the spirit that should inspire nice lovers.

PEN. (*aside, dryly*). At least such as are over-eager to plunge themselves into beggary.

MEN. I bought that mantle last year for my wife, and it stood me in sixteen pounds.

PEN. (*aside*). Sixteen pounds indubitably done for, according to account rendered!

MEN. Do you know what I want you to see to?

EROT. I know, I'll see to what you want.

MEN. Well, then, have luncheon prepared for the three of us at your house, and have some real delicacies purchased at the forum—(*looking amused at the intent* PENICULUS) savoury kernelets of pork, dried hammylets, half a pig's head, or something of the sort—things that make me hungry as a kite when served up to me well-done. And quickly, too!

EROT. Oh yes, by all means.

MEN. We'll go over to the forum. Soon we'll be back here; while things are cooking we'll employ the time in drinking.

EROT. Come when you wish; we'll get ready for you.

MEN. Only do hurry. (*To* PENICULUS, *unceremoniously*) Follow me, you. (*Going.*)

PEN. (*at his heels*). That I will, by Jove! Watch you and follow you, both! I wouldn't take the treasures of heaven on condition of losing you this day.

(*Exeunt.*)

EROT. (*going to her door and speaking to the maids within*). Call my cook Cylindrus out here at once.

SCENE 4

Enter CYLINDRUS

EROT. Take a basket and some money. (*Counting out some coins*) There! That's six shillings for you.

CYL. Right, ma'am.

EROT. Go and get some provisions; see you get enough for three—neither too little nor too much.

CYL. What sort of folks will they be?

EROT. I and Menæchmus and his parasite.

CYL. That makes ten already, ma'am; for a parasite easily does the duty of eight men.

EROT. I have told you about the guests; attend to the rest.

CYL. (*bustling off importantly*). Of course, ma'am. The meal is cooked; tell 'em to go in and take their places.

EROT. Come back quickly.

CYL. I'll be here directly. (*Exeunt.*)

ACT II

Half an hour has elapsed. Enter MENÆCHMUS SOSICLES *and* MESSENIO, *followed at distance by slaves with luggage.*

MEN. S. There is no pleasure sailors have, in my opinion, Messenio, greater than sighting from the deep the distant land.

MES. (*sulky*). It's a greater one, to put it plainly, if the land you see, as you near the shore, was once your own. But look here, sir, why have we come now to Epidamnus? Or are we, like the sea, to go around all the islands?

MEN. S. To hunt for my own twin brother.

MES. Well, what's to be the limit to hunting for him? This is the sixth year we've been at the job. Istrians, Spaniards, Massilians, Illyrians, the entire Adriatic, and foreign Greece and the whole coast of Italy—every section the sea washes—we've visited in our travels. If you were hunting for a needle you'd have found it long ago, I do believe, if it existed. It's a dead man we keep hunting for amongst the living; why, we should have found him long ago if he were alive.

MEN. S. Well, then, I'm hunting for someone who can prove that to me, who can say he knows my brother is dead; I'll never take up again the task of hunting for him after that. But failing that, I'll never abandon it so long as I'm alive. I alone know how dear he is to me.

MES. (*impatiently*). You're hunting for a knot in a bulrush. Why don't we go back home—that is, unless we're going to write a book of travels?

ROMAN PURITANISM AND GREEK CULTURE

MEN. S. (*sharply*). Do what you're told, eat what you're given, and beware of trouble. Don't annoy me—this business will not be conducted to suit you.

MES. (*aside, peevishly*). There you are! Talk like that shows me I'm a slave. He couldn't make the case clear more concisely. But just the same I can't keep from speaking out. (*Aloud*) Listen to me, sir, will you? By gad, when I inspect the wallet, our touring fund looks precious summerly. Unless you return home, by gad, I warrant you when your cash gives out while you're hunting for your twin, you'll certainly have a twinge. I tell you what, the sort of people you find here is this: in Epidamnus are the very worst of rakes and drinkers. And then the swindlers and sharpers that live in this city, no end to 'em! And then the harlot wenches—nowhere on earth are they more alluring, people say! This city got its name of Epidamnus for just this reason—because almost everyone that stops here gets damaged.

MEN. (*dryly*). I shall look out for that. Come, hand the wallet over to me.

MES. What do you want with it?

MEN. S. I have my fears of you now, from what you say.

MES. Fears of what?

MEN. S. Of your doing me some damage in Epidamnus. You, Messenio, are a great lover of the ladies, while I am a choleric man, of ungovernable temper; so long as I hold the money I'll guard against both dangers—a slip on your part, and resultant choler on my own.

MES. (*handing him the wallet, aggrieved*). Take it and keep it, do. Delighted that you should.

SCENE 2

Enter CYLINDRUS *with provisions*

CYL. (*stopping and examining the contents of his basket approvingly*). Good

marketing, this, and just to my taste, too. I'll set a good lunch before the lunchers. (*Looking about*) Hullo, though! There's Menæchmus! Oh, my poor back! The guests are strolling about in front of the door before I'm back with the provisions! I'll up and speak to him. (*Approaches*) Good day, Menæchmus.

MEN. S. (*surprised*). The Lord love you, my man, whoever you are!

CYL. (*surprised in turn*). Whoever? Who I am?

MEN. S. Gad! Indeed I don't know!

CYL. (*deciding he jokes*). Where are the other guests?

MEN. S. What guests are you looking for?

CYL. (*grinning*). Your parasite.

MEN. S. My parasite? (*To* MESSENIO) The fellow is certainly insane.

MES. Didn't I tell you there was no end of swindlers here?

MEN. S. What parasite of mine are you looking for, young man?

CYL. Brush.

MES. Brush? I've got that safe in the knapsack. Look!

CYL. (*paying no attention to him*). You've come here to lunch too soon, Menæchmus. I'm just getting back with the provisions.

MEN. S. (*gravely*). Answer me this, young man: how much do pigs cost here, sound pigs, for sacrifice?

CYL. (*mystified*). Two shillings.

MEN. S. Take two shillings from me; get yourself purified at my expense. For really it's quite clear you are insane—to bother an unknown man like me, whoever you are.

CYL. But I'm Cylindrus. Don't you know my name?

MEN. S. (*bored*). Whether you are Cylindrus or Pistonus, be hanged to you! I don't know you, and more than that, I have no wish to know you.

CYL. Your name is Menæchmus, at least as far as I know.

MEN. S. You talk rationally when you

call me by name. But where did you know me?

CYL. Where did I know you, when my mistress is your sweetheart Erotium here? (*Indicating house.*)

MEN. S. Not mine, by gad! And as for you, I don't know who you are.

CYL. Don't know who I am, I, who serve you your wine so often when you are drinking there?

MES. (*hotly*). Oh, blast it! Not to have a thing to smash in the fellow's head with!

MEN. S. You accustomed to serve me my wine, when I never saw or set foot in Epidamnus before this day?

CYL. You deny it?

MEN. S. Gad! Indeed I do deny it!

CYL. Don't you live in that house yonder?

MEN. S. (*wrathful*). Heaven's curse light on those that do live there!

CYL. (*aside*). He's the insane one, to be cursing his own self! (*Aloud*) Listen here, Menæchmus.

MEN. S. What is it?

CYL. If you asked my advice, sir, you'd take that two shillings you recently promised me—for, by gad, it's certainly you that are lacking in sanity, to curse your own self a moment ago—and order a porker to be brought to you, if you have any sense.

MES. Hear that! By gad, what a windy chap! He makes me tired.

CYL. (*to audience*). He often likes to joke with me this way. He's ever so humorous—when his wife's not by. (*To* MENÆCHMUS) I say, sir.

MEN. S. Well, what do you want?

CYL. (*pointing to basket*). Are these provisions you see enough for the three of you, or shall I get more, for you and the parasite and the lady?

MEN. S. What ladies, what parasites, are you talking about, man?

MES. What possesses you, to bother this gentleman?

CYL. (to MESSENIO, *irately*). What have you to do with me? I don't know you! I'm talking with this gentleman I do know.

MES. Lord, man, you're not sane; I know that for sure.

CYL. (*to* MENÆCHMUS). Well, sir, these things shall be cooked directly, I promise you, without delay. So don't wander too far from the house. (*About to go*) Anything more I can do for you?

MEN. S. Yes, go straight to the devil. (*Turns away.*)

CYL. (*vehemently*). By gad, you'd better go, meanwhile, yourself—to the couch, while I (*superbly, with a wave toward the basket*) expose these things to Vulcan's violence. I'll go inside and tell Erotium you're here, so that she may bring you in rather than leave you standing here outside. (*Exit.*)

MEN. S. Gone now, has he? By Jove! I perceive those statements of yours were no lies.

MES. Just you keep your eyes open; for I do believe some harlot wench lives there, precisely as that madman, who just now left us, said.

MEN. S. But I wonder how he knew my name?

MES. (*with an air of vastly superior wisdom*). Lord, sir, nothing wonderful in that! This is a custom harlots have: they send their artful slaves and maids down to the port; if any foreign ship comes in, they inquire where she hails from and what her owner's name is, and then they immediately affix themselves, glue themselves fast to him. Once he's seduced, they send him home a wreck. Now in that port there (*pointing to Erotium's house*) lies a pirate bark that I surely think we'd better beware of.

MEN. S. Gad, that's certainly good advice you give.

MES. (*dissatisfied*). I'll know it's good advice when you take good care, and not before.

MEN. S. (*listening*). Sh-h! Keep still

a moment! The door creaked—let's see who is coming out.

MES. (*dropping the knapsack*). Meanwhile I'll put this down. (*To the sailors, superciliously, pointing to luggage*) Kindly watch this stuff, ye ship propellers.

SCENE 3

Enter EROTIUM *into the doorway*

EROT. (*to maids within*). Leave the door so; go along, I don't want it shut. Get ready inside, look out for things, see to things, do what's necessary. (*To other maids*) Cover the couches, burn some perfumes; daintiness is what lures lovers' hearts. Attractive surroundings mean the lovers' loss and our gain. (*Looking about*) But where is that man the cook said was in front of the house? Ah yes. I see him—it's the friend I find so useful, so uncommonly helpful. And accordingly I let him quite lord it in my house as he deserves. I'll step up to him at once and give him a welcome. (*Approaching* MENÆCHMUS) Why, you darling boy, it surprises me that you should stand here outdoors when my doors are open to you and this house is more yours than your own house is. Everything is ready as you ordered and wished, and you'll meet with no delay inside. Our luncheon here has been seen to, as you ordered; you may go in and take your place when you like.

MEN. S. (*to* MESSENIO, *mystified*). To whom is this little woman talking?

EROT. (*surprised*). To you, of course.

MEN. S. What have you had to do with me, now or ever?

EROT. (*gaily, thinking he jests*). Why, bless your heart, it has pleased Venus that I should prize you as the one man of men —and not without your deserving it. For, mercy me! you alone, with all your generosity, make me prosper.

MEN. S. (*aside to* MESSENIO). This woman is certainly either insane or drunk, Messenio, to address a stranger like me so familiarly.

MES. Didn't I tell you that was the way they did here? These are mere falling leaves compared with what'll happen if we stay here the next three days; then trees will fall on you. Yes, sir, harlots are like that here—they're all silver seductresses. But you just let me have a word with her. (*To Erotium, who has been looking in at her door*) Hey there, madam! I am speaking to you.

EROT. What is it?

MES. Where did you know this gentleman?

EROT. In the same place where he has long known me, in Epidamnus.

MES. Epidamnus? When he's never set foot in this town except to-day?

EROT. Tut, tut, my smart sir! Menæchmus mine, come inside, why don't you, there's a dear. You'll find it nicer in here.

MEN. S. (*aside to Messenio*). Good Lord! Now here's this woman calling me by my right name! I certainly do wonder what in the world it all means.

MES. She's scented the wallet you have.

MEN. S. By Jove, yes, you have warned me wisely! Here, you take it. (*Hands wallet to Messenio*) Now I'll know whether it's me or my wallet she's in love with.

EROT. (*taking his arm*). Let's go in and have luncheon.

MEN. S. (*puzzled*). Very kind of you; no, thanks.

EROT. Then why did you order me to cook luncheon for you a while ago?

MEN. S. I ordered you to cook it?

EROT. Certainly, for you and your parasite.

MEN. S. What parasite, confound it? (*Aside to* MESSENIO) There's certainly something wrong with the woman's wits.

EROT. Brush, I mean.

MEN. S. What brush is that? One you clean your shoes with?

EROT. Why, the one, of course, that came with you a while ago when you brought me the mantle you stole from your wife.

MEN. S. What's this? I gave you a mantle I stole from my wife? Are you sane? (*To* MESSENIO) At any rate, this woman dreams standing up, horse fashion.

EROT. (*a little irritated*). Why is it you like to make a laughing-stock of me and deny what you did?

MEN. S. Tell me what it is I did and deny.

EROT. Giving me your wife's mantle to-day.

MEN. S. I deny it still. Why, I never had a wife, and have none now, and never from the day I was born have I put a foot within your city gate here. I lunched on board ship, then came ashore here, and met you.

EROT. (*aside, alarmed about him*). Look at that! Oh dear, this is dreadful! (*To* MENÆCHMUS) What is this ship you're telling me of?

MEN. S. (*flippantly*). A wooden affair, often battered about, often nailed, often pounded with a hammer; it's like a furrier's furniture, peg close to peg.

EROT. (*relieved by his jocularity and drawing him toward her door*). Now, now, do stop joking, there's a dear, and come along this way with me.

MEN. S. (*releasing himself*). It is some other man you are looking for, madam, not me.

EROT. I do not know you—(*playfully, as if repeating a lesson*) Menæchmus, the son of Moschus, born, so they say, in Syracuse in Sicily, where King Agathocles reigned, and after him Phintia, and thirdly Liparo, who at his death left his kingdom to Hiero, the present ruler?

MEN. S. (*more perplexed*). You are quite correct, madam.

MES. (*aside, to* MENÆCHMUS). Great

Jupiter! The woman doesn't come from there, does she, to have your history so pat?

MEN. S. By gad, I fancy I can't go on refusing her. (*Moves toward her door.*)

MES. (*alarmed*). Don't do that! You're lost, if you cross that threshold!

MEN. S. See here now, you shut up. Things are going well. I'll assent to whatever the wench says, if I can come in for entertainment here. (*Confidentially to* EROTIUM, *motioning* MESSENIO *back*) I kept contradicting you a while ago purposely, my girl; I was afraid of this fellow (*indicating* MESSENIO)—that he might inform my wife of the mantle and the luncheon. Now when you wish let's go inside.

EROT. Shall you wait any longer for the parasite?

MEN. S. Not I—I neither wait for him nor care a straw for him, nor want him admitted if he does come.

EROT. Goodness me, I'll see to that without reluctance! (*Fondling him*) But do you know what I should love you to do?

MEN. S. Whatever you wish—you have only to command me.

EROT. Take that mantle you gave me a while ago to the embroiderer, so as to have it repaired and have some trimmings I want added.

MEN. S. Right you are, by Jove! That will make it look different, too, and my wife won't recognize it on you, if she notices it on the street.

EROT. Well then, take it with you later when you leave me.

MEN. S. By all means.

EROT. Let's go in.

MEN. S. I'll follow you directly. I want another word with this fellow (*indicating* MESSENIO). (*Exit* EROTIUM.) Hullo! Messenio! Step up here.

MES. (*morose*). What's all this?

MEN. S. (*elated*). Dance a jig!

MES. What's the need of that?

MEN. S. There is need. (*Rather apologetic*) I know what you'll call me.

MES. So much the worse of you.

MEN. S. The booty's mine! Such siegeworks as I've begun! Be off as fast as you can; take those fellows (*pointing to sailors*) to an inn at once. Then see you come to meet me before sunset.

MES. You don't know those harlots, master.

MEN S. Hold your tongue, I tell you. It will hurt me, not you, if I play the fool. This woman is a fool, and a silly one; from what I've just observed, there's booty for us here. (*Exit into the house.*)

MES. (*as if to call him back*). Oh Lord! You're gone already? Lord help him! The pirate bark is towing our yacht to perdition. But I'm a silly one to expect to manage my master; he bought me to obey his orders, not to be his commander-in-chief. (*To the sailors*) Follow me, so that I can come to meet him in season as he commanded.

(*Exeunt.*)

ACT III

(*Several hours have elapsed*)

Enter PENICULUS

PEN. (*in high dudgeon*). More than thirty years I've lived, and never in all that time have I done a worse or more accursed deed than to-day when I immersed myself, poor fool, in the middle of that public meeting. While I was gaping there, Menæchmus gave me the slip, and made off to his mistress, I suppose, without caring to take me along. May all the powers above consume the fellow that first devised the holding of public meetings, to busy busy men! Shouldn't they choose men with nothing to do for that sort of thing, and fine 'em forthwith if they fail to appear at the roll call? There's a plenty of men that get edibles to eat only once a day, men

with no business on hand, men that are neither invited out nor invite anyone in to eat: they're the ones that ought to devote themselves to public meetings and assemblies. If this had been the rule, I shouldn't have lost my lunch to-day—for sure as I'm alive I believe he was willing to give me one. I'll join him; even now I have my sweet hopes of the leavings. (*Goes toward* EROTIUM'S *house as* MENÆCHMUS SOSICLES *comes into the doorway, wreathed and carrying the mantle*) But what do I see? Menæchmus coming out with a garland on! (*Grimly*) The banquet's cleared away, and, by gad, I've come just in time to see him home! (*Withdrawing*) I'll observe what the fellow's up to. Then I'll up and have a word with him.

SCENE 2

MEN. S. (*to* EROTIUM *within*). Can't you rest easy? I'll bring this back to you to-day in good season, all put in trim nicely and prettily. (*Chuckling to himself*) You'll say you haven't got this one, I warrant,—it will look so unfamiliar.

PEN. (*aside, angrily*). He's carrying the mantle to the embroiderer's, now the lunch is finished and the wine drunk, while the parasite's been shut out of doors! By heaven, I'm not the man I am if I don't avenge this injury and myself in beautiful style! You watch what I'll give you!

MEN. S. (*leaving the doorway, jubilant*). Ye immortal gods! Did ye ever in a single day bestow more blessings on any man who hoped for less? I've lunched, drunk, enjoyed the wench, and made off with this mantle whose owner will never see it more.

PEN. (*aside*). I can't quite catch what he's talking about from this hiding-place; is it about me and the part I played, now that he's stuffed himself?

MEN. S. She said I gave this to her,

yes, and stole it from my wife! Seeing she was making a mistake, I at once began to agree with her, as if I had had dealings with her; whatever she said, I'd say the same. In short, I never had a good time anywhere at less expense.

PEN. (*aside, his anger rising*). I'll up to the fellow! Oh, I'm aching for a row! (*Steps forward.*)

MEN. S. (*aside*). Who's this advancing on me?

PEN. See here, you rascal lighter than a feather, you base, villainous scoundrel, you outrage of a man, you tricky good-for-nothing! What have I ever done to you that you should spoil my life? How you sneaked off from me at the forum a while ago! You've interred the luncheon, and I not there! How did you dare do it, when I was as much its heir as you?

MEN. S. (*with dignity*). Sir, what have you to do with me, pray, that I, a perfect stranger, should meet with your abuse? (*Dangerously*) Or do you want to be given a bad time in return for this bad language?

PEN. (*groaning*). Oh Lord! You've given me that already, I perceive, good Lord, yes!

MEN. S. Pray answer me, sir, what is your name?

PEN. What? Making fun of me, as if you didn't know my name?

MEN. S. Good Lord, man, I have never seen you or known you before this day, so far as I know; but—whoever you are, this much is sure—if you want to do the decent thing, don't annoy me.

PEN. Wake up, Menæchmus!

MEN. S. Gad! why, I am awake, so far as I know.

PEN. You don't know me?

MEN. S. I should not deny it, if I did know you.

PEN. Not know you own parasite?

MEN. S. Sir, your headpiece is out of order, I perceive.

PEN. Answer me—didn't you steal that mantle from your wife to-day and give it to Erotium?

MEN. S. Lord, Lord! I neither have a wife, nor gave the mantle to Erotium, nor stole it.

PEN. Really, are you sane? (*Aside, in despair*) My business is done for! (*Aloud*) Didn't I see you come outdoors wearing the mantle?

MEN. S. Curse you! Do you think all of us follow the women, just because you do? You declare that I was wearing the mantle?

PEN. Gad, yes, of course.

MEN. S. Go to—where you belong, will you! Or else get yourself purified, you utter idiot!

PEN. (*incensed*). By the Lord, no one shall ever induce me not to tell your wife everything, just as it happened! All this abuse of yours shall fall back on yourself; you shall suffer for devouring that lunch, I promise you.

Exit PENICULUS *into house of*
MENÆCHMUS

MEN. S. (*bewildered*). What does this mean? So everyone I set eyes on tries to make a fool of me, eh? (*Listening*) But the door creaked!

SCENE 3

Enter MAID *from* EROTIUM'S *house*

MAID. Menæchmus, Erotium says she would very much like you to take this bracelet (*showing it*) to the jeweller's at the same time and add an ounce of gold to it and have it made over new.

MEN. S. (*taking it with alacrity*). Tell her I'll take care of that and whatever else she wants taken care of—anything she likes.

MAID. Do you know what bracelet this is?

MEN. S. No, only that it's gold.

MAID. It's the one you said you stole long ago on the sly from your wife's chest.

MEN. S. Good Lord, I never did!

MAID. For heaven's sake, you don't remember? Give me back the bracelet, then, if you don't remember.

MEN. S. (*thinking hard*). Wait! Yes, yes, I do remember, to be sure! Of course, this is the one I gave her.

MAID. The very one.

MEN. S. (*interestedly*). Where are those armlets I gave her along with it?

MAID. You never gave her any.

MEN. S. That's right, by gad; this was all I gave her.

MAID. Shall I say you'll take care of it?

MEN. S. (*hiding a smile*). Do. It shall be taken care of. I'll see she gets the bracelet back at the same time she gets the mantle.

MAID (*coaxingly*). Menæchmus dear, do have some earrings made for me—there's a nice man!—the pendant kind, with four shillings' worth of gold in them, so that I'll be glad to see you when you visit us.

MEN. S. (*heartily*). Surely. Give me the gold; I'll pay for the making, myself.

MAID. You furnish the gold, please do; I'll pay you back later.

MEN. S. No, no, you give me the gold; I'll pay you back later, twice over.

MAID. I haven't it.

MEN. S. Well, you give it to me when you do have it.

MAID (*turning to go*). Is there anything else, sir?

MEN. S. Say I'll take care of these things—(*aside, as maid leaves*) take care they're sold as soon as possible for what they'll bring. (*Exit* MAID.) (*Looking after her*) Gone now, has she? Gone! She's shut the door. (*Jubilant*) Well, well, all the gods do aid, augment, and love me! But I must hurry up and leave these harlot haunts while time and circumstance permit. Quick, Menæchmus! forward, march! I'll take off this garland and throw it away to the left (*does so*) so that if anyone follows me, they may think I have gone this way. (*Going in the opposite direction*) I'll go meet my servant, if I can, and let him know how bountiful the gods have been to me. (*Exit.*)

ACT IV

Enter MENÆCHMUS'S WIFE *from the house, followed by* PENICULUS

WIFE (*tempestuous*). Shall I let myself be made a fool of in such a married life as this, where my husband slyly sneaks off with everything in the house and carries it to his mistress?

PEN. Hush, hush, won't you? You shall catch him in the act now, I warrant you. Just you follow me this way. Drunk and garlanded, he was carrying to the embroiderer's the mantle he stole from you and carried from the house to-day. (*Seeing the garland*) But look here! Here is the garland he had! Now am I a liar? There! he went this way, if you want to track him. (*Looking down the street*) Yes, and by Jove, look! Splendid! He is coming back! But without the mantle!

WIFE. How shall I act toward him now?

PEN. (*dryly*). The same as always—make him miserable; that is my advice. Let's step aside here; (*drawing her back between the houses*) catch him from ambush.

SCENE 2

Enter MENÆCHMUS *in a bad temper*

MEN. What slaves we are to this consummately crazy, confoundedly chafing custom! Yes, and it's the very best men amongst us that are its worst slaves. A long train of clients—that's what they all want; whether good men or bad is immaterial; it's the wealth of the clients they consider, rather than their reputation for probity. If a man's poor and not a bad sort, he's held to be worthless; but if he's rich and is a bad sort, he's held to be an admirable client. But clients that have absolutely no regard for law, or for what is just and fair, do keep their patrons worried. They deny honest debts, are for ever at law, they're rapacious, fraudulent fellows whose money was made by usury or perjury and whose souls are centred in their lawsuits. When the day of trial is set for them, it's set for (*with increased bitterness*) their patrons, too. Up comes the case before the people, or the court, or the ædile. That's the way a certain client of mine has kept me confoundedly worried to-day, and I haven't been able to do what I wanted or have the company I wanted, he has so delayed and detained me. Before the ædiles I spoke in defence of his countless atrocities, and proposed provisos that were intricate and difficult; I had put the case more or less as was necessary to have a settlement made. But what did he do? (*Hotly*) What? Named a surety! And never have I seen any man more manifestly caught; every one of his crimes was sworn to by three witnesses of the stoutest sort. (*Pausing*) Heaven curse the man, with the way he's spoiled this day for me; yes, and curse me, too, for ever taking a look at the forum to-day! Such a splendid day as I have spoiled! A luncheon ordered, and a mistress no doubt waiting for me! At the earliest possible moment I hurried away from the forum. She's angry with me now, I suppose; (*hopefully*) my gift will mollify her—that mantle I took from my wife and brought to Erotium here.

PEN. (*triumphantly to* WIFE, *aside*). What do you say?

WIFE (*indignant*). That he's a wretch who has me for his wretched wife!

PEN. You quite hear what he says?

WIFE. Quite.

MEN. If I had any sense, I should move on and go inside where I'll have a good time. (*Passes his own house and goes towards* EROTIUM's *door*.)

PEN. (*stepping forward*). You wait! It will be a bad time, instead.

WIFE (*stepping forward on the other side*). You shall certainly pay interest on that theft, I swear you shall!

PEN. (*gleefully*). Take that!

WIFE. Did you think you could commit such outrages on the sly?

MEN. (*guileless*). What do you mean by that, my dear?

WIFE. You ask me?

MEN. Do you want me to ask him? (*Pointing to* PENICULUS.)

WIFE (*as he tries to fondle her*). None of your caresses!

PEN. (*to* WIFE). Keep at him, keep at him!

MEN. Why are you cross at me?

WIFE. You ought to know!

PEN. He does know, but he's pretending, the rascal.

MEN. What does this mean?

WIFE. A mantle——

MEN. (*worried*). A mantle?

WIFE. A mantle someone——

PEN. (*to* MENÆCHMUS). What are you frightened at?

MEN. (*trying to appear unconcerned*). Frightened? I? Not in the least.

PEN. (*triumphantly, pointing to* MENÆCHMUS's *face, which has turned pale*). Barring this: the mantle unmans you. Now none of your eating up the lunch behind my back! (*To* WIFE) Keep at the fellow!

MEN. (*aside to* PENICULUS). Keep still, won't you? (*Shakes his head at him.*)

PEN. (*loudly*). Indeed I will not keep still, by Jove! (*To* WIFE) He's shaking his head at me not to speak.

MEN. Not I, not a bit of it, by Jove! I'm not shaking my head at all, or winking at you, either.

PEN. Well, of all the cheek! To deny flatly what you see with your own eyes!

MEN. My dear, I swear by Heaven

and all that's holy—is that strong enough for you?—I did not shake my head at him.

PEN. Oh, she takes your word for that forthwith! Get back to the point.

MEN. Back to what point?

PEN. Why, to the embroiderer's shop, I should say. Go, bring back the mantle.

MEN. Mantle? What mantle?

PEN. (*disgusted at* WIFE's *tearful futility*). I say no more, seeing she doesn't remember her own affairs.

WIFE (*in tears*). Oh Heavens! I surely am an unhappy woman!

MEN. (*solicitously*). How are you unhappy? Tell me all about it. (*To* WIFE, *tenderly*) Has any one of the slaves been at fault? Do the maids or menservants talk back to you? Do speak out. They shall pay for it.

WIFE. Nonsense!

MEN. You're awfully cross. I don't quite like that.

WIFE. Nonsense!

MEN. It must be some one of the servants you're angry with.

WIFE. Nonsense!

MEN. You're not angry at me, anyhow, are you?

WIFE. There now! That's sense.

MEN. Good Lord! I haven't been at fault!

WIFE. Aha! back to your nonsense!

MEN. (*patting her*). Do tell me what troubles you, my dear.

PEN. (*scornfully*). He's soft-soaping you, the sweet thing!

MEN. (*to* PENICULUS). Can't you stop annoying me? I'm not addressing you, am I? (*Tries to caress his* WIFE.)

WIFE. Take your hand away! (*Slaps him.*)

PEN. Take that! Now be in a hurry to eat up the lunch in my absence, now get drunk and appear in front of the house with a garland on and give me the laugh!

MEN. Good heavens! I haven't eaten lunch, and I've never set foot inside this house to-day.

PEN. You deny it?

MEN. Indeed I do, gad, yes.

PEN. Well, of all the brazenness! Didn't I just now see you in front of the house wearing a garland of flowers? When you told me that my headpiece was out of order and that you didn't know me, and said you were arriving from abroad?

MEN. Why, I'm only this moment getting home after parting company with you a while ago.

PEN. (*angrily*). I know you! You didn't count on my having a way to get even with you. By gad, I've told your wife everything!

MEN. What have you told her?

PEN. Oh, I don't know; ask her yourself.

MEN. (*to his* WIFE, *bravely*). What's all this, my dear? What sort of a tale has he been relating to you? What is it? Why are you silent? Why don't you tell me what it is?

WIFE. As if you didn't know! Asking me!

MEN. Bless my soul! I shouldn't ask you if I did know.

PEN. Oh, the villain! How he plays the innocent! (*To* MENÆCHMUS) You can't conceal it; she understands the matter beautifully. I have told her the whole story, by Jove!

MEN. What does this mean?

WIFE (*with acerbity*). Since you have no sense of shame and no wish to confess of your own free will, listen, and listen closely. I'll soon let you know why I'm cross and what he told me. A mantle has been stolen from me at home.

MEN. (*indignant*). A mantle stolen from me?

PEN. See how the rascal is trying to catch you? (*To* MENÆCHMUS) It was stolen from her, not from you. Why, if it was stolen from you, it would certainly be—lost.

MEN. (*to* PENICULUS). I have nothing to do with you. (*To* WIFE) But you, what are you saying?

WIFE. A mantle, I tell you, has disappeared from the house.

MEN. Who stole it?

WIFE. Goodness me! The man who took it knows that.

MEN. Who is this man?

WIFE. A certain Menæchmus.

MEN. It's a scurvy trick, by Jove! Who is this Menæchmus?

WIFE. You yourself, I tell you.

MEN. I?

WIFE. You.

MEN. Who's my accuser?

WIFE. I am.

PEN. Yes, and I. And you took it to your mistress Erotium here, too.

MEN. I gave it away—I?

WIFE. You, you yourself, I tell you.

PEN. D'ye want us to bring on an owl, to keep saying "yoo, yoo" to you? For we've got tired of saying it by now.

MEN. (*meekly*). But I didn't give it to her out and out; I only—it's like this—I only lent it.

WIFE. Good gracious, sir! I certainly do not lend out your mantle or cloak to anyone. A woman is the proper person to give out women's clothes, a man men's. You bring that mantle back home, will you?

MEN. I'll see it's brought back.

WIFE. You will be seeing to your own comfort, I fancy; for never shall you enter the house unless you bring the mantle with you. (*Turning away abruptly*) I am going home.

PEN. (*anxiously*). What do I get for helping you in this?

WIFE (*with a sour smile*). I'll help you in return when something is stolen from your house. (*Exit into the house.*)

PEN. Oh Lord! That means never, for I have nothing in my house to lose. (*Heartily*) Be damned to you, husband and wife both! I'll hurry to the forum,

for I perceive I've plainly fallen out of the good graces of this family. (*Exit.*)

MEN. (*comfortably*). My wife thinks she has pained me by shutting me out. Just as if there wasn't another place—and a better one—where I'll be admitted. If you don't like me, I must bear it; Erotium here will like me anyway. She won't shut me out; oh no, she'll shut me in with her! Now I'll go and beg her to give me back the mantle I gave her a while ago; I'll buy her another, a better one. (*Knocking at her door*) Hullo! Anyone minding the door here? Open up and call Erotium out, someone!

SCENE 3

EROT. (*within*). Who is inquiring for me?

MEN. A man who is more his own foe than yours, dear.

Enter EROTIUM *into the doorway*

EROT. Menæchmus, love, why are you standing out here? (*Taking his arm*) Do come in.

MEN. Wait. Do you know why I've come to see you?

EROT. I know—so that we may have a nice time together.

MEN. No, you're wrong, confound it! Do give me back that mantle I gave you a while ago, there's a dear. My wife has found out about the whole business, from beginning to end. I'll buy you a mantle twice as expensive—any you choose.

EROT. (*surprised*). But I gave it to you to take to the embroiderer's just a few minutes ago, along with that bracelet you were to carry to the jeweller's to have made over.

MEN. You gave me the mantle and a bracelet—me? You'll find you never did so. Why, after giving you that mantle a while ago and going to the forum I'm just getting back; this is the first time I've seen you since then.

EROT. (*aroused*). But I see what you are up to. Just because I've put them in your hands you're attempting to do this, to cheat me.

MEN. No, heavens, no! it's not to cheat you, I ask for it—really, my wife has found out, I tell you——

EROT. (*passing over what she thinks the usual lie*). No, and I didn't beg you to give it to me in the first place; you brought it to me yourself of your own accord, made me a present of it; and now you ask it back. Very well. Take it, carry it off, wear it yourself or let your wife wear it, or for that matter lock it up in a coffer. You shall not set foot in this house after to-day, don't fool yourself. Now that you've held a good friend like me in contempt, you can bring along ready money, or else you can't lead me along like a fool. After this you just find somebody else to fool. (*Turns to go in.*)

MEN. Oh gad, now, really you're too testy! Here, here! I say! Wait! Come back! What? You won't stop? What? You aren't willing to return for my sake? (*Exit* EROTIUM, *slamming the door*.) She's gone inside! She's closed the door! Well, if I'm not getting the most exclusive reception! Neither at home nor at my mistress's, either, do they believe a word I say! I'll go and consult my friends about this and see what they think should be done.

ACT V

Enter MENÆCHMUS SOSICLES

MEN. S. What an idiot I was a while ago when I entrusted my wallet and money to Messenio! He's immersed himself in a pothouse somewhere, I suppose.

Enter the WIFE *of* MENÆCHMUS *into the doorway*

WIFE. I'll go out and see if my husband won't soon be back home. (*Seeing* MENÆCHMUS SOSICLES) Oh, why there he is! I'm saved! He is bringing back the mantle.

MEN. S. I wonder where Messenio is promenading now.

WIFE. I'll step up and welcome him with the words he deserves. (*Advancing*) Aren't you ashamed to appear in my sight with that costume, you monster?

MEN. S. (*startled*). Eh, what is it that excites you, madam?

WIFE. What! Do you dare breathe a word, do you dare speak to me, you shameless creature?

MEN. S. What, pray, is my offence, that I should not dare to speak?

WIFE. You ask me? Oh, such brazen shamelessness!

MEN. S. (*still polite*). Madam, do you not know why the ancient Greeks used to declare that Hecuba was a bitch?

WIFE (*sharply*). No, indeed, I don't.

MEN. S. Because Hecuba used to do precisely what you are doing now: she used to pour every kind of abuse on everyone she saw. So they began to call her bitch, and quite properly, too.

WIFE (*incensed*). I cannot endure this outrageous conduct of yours. Why, I'd rather live without a husband all my life than put up with the outrageous things you do.

MEN. S. And how does it concern me whether you can endure your married life, or leave your husband? Or is this the fashion here—to prattle to arriving strangers?

WIFE. Prattle? I will not put up with it any longer, I tell you. I'll get a divorce rather than tolerate your goings-on.

MEN. S. Lord, Lord! get divorced, for all I care—and stay so as long as Jove reigns!

WIFE (*examining mantle*). See here, you denied stealing this a while ago, and now you hold it, the very same one, right before my eyes. Aren't you ashamed?

MEN. S. Bravo, madam! By Jove! You are a bold, bad one with a vengeance! Do you dare tell me this was stolen from you, when another woman gave it to me so that I might get it renovated?

WIFE. Good heavens, that is—I'll send for my father this moment and I'll give him an account of your outrageous actions! (*Calling at door*) Deceo! Go look for my father—bring him here to me; say it's absolutely necessary. (*To* MENÆCHMUS SOSICLES) I'll soon lay bare your outrageous conduct!

MEN. S. Are you sane? What is this outrageous conduct of mine?

WIFE. You filched my mantle and jewellery from the house—from your own wife—and carried them off to your mistress. Isn't this perfectly true (*bitterly*) prattle?

MEN. S. Good Lord, madam, if you know of any drug I can take to enable me to endure that temper of yours, for heaven's sake name it. Who you think I am is a mystery to me; as for me, I knew you when I knew Hercules' wife's grandfather.

WIFE. You may laugh at me, but I vow you can't laugh at that man (*pointing down the street*), my father, who's coming this way. Look back there. Do you know him?

MEN. S. (*looking*). Oh yes, I knew him when I knew Calchas. I saw him on the same day I first saw you.

WIFE. You deny knowing me, you deny knowing my father?

MEN. S. Oh Lord! I'll say the same thing if you bring on your grandfather. (*Walks away.*)

WIFE. Oh dear me! that's just the way you are always acting!

SCENE 2

Enter MENÆCHMUS'S FATHER-IN-LAW *slowly and laboriously*

FATHER (*sighing wearily*). Yes, I'll step out. I'll step along as . . . fast as my age permits and the occasion demands. (*Halting*) But I know well enough how . . . easy it is for me. For I've lost my nimbleness . . . the years have taken hold of me . . . it's a heavy body I carry . . . my strength has left me. Ah, old age is a bad thing—a bad piece of freight! Yes, yes, it brings along untold tribulations when it comes; if I were to specify them all, it would be a . . . long, long story. But this is the thing that weighs on my mind and heart—what in the world has happened to make my daughter ask me, all of a sudden this way, to come to her. Not a word am I told as to what is wrong, what she wants, why she summons me. However, I have a pretty fair notion already what it's all about. She's had some squabble with her husband, I fancy. That's the way with women that try to keep their husbands under their thumbs, arrogant just because they've brought a good dowry. (*Pauses*) And the husbands often aren't blameless, either. (*Reflecting*) However, there's a limit, just the same, to what a wife should put up with; and, by Jove, a daughter never summons her father unless there's something amiss or some just cause for complaint. But I shall soon know about it, whatever it is. (*Advancing and looking about*) Ah, there she is herself in front of the house—and her husband, looking sour! It's just as I suspected. I'll have a word with her.

WIFE (*aside*). I'll go meet him. (*Advancing*) I hope you're well, father dear—very well.

FATHER. And you. Do I find all well here? Is all well, that you have me summoned? Why are you so gloomy? Yes, and why is he (*pointing to* MENÆCHMUS SOSICLES) standing aloof there, angry? You've been bickering over something or other, you two. Out with it—which is to blame? Be brief; no long words.

WIFE. I haven't been at fault at all, indeed I haven't; I'll relieve you on this point first, father. But I can't live here, I simply cannot stand it. So you must take me away from this house.

FATHER (*peevishly*). But what is the trouble?

WIFE. I'm made a laughing-stock, father!

FATHER. By whom?

WIFE. By the man you entrusted me to, my husband.

FATHER. Now look at that! A squabble! See here, how many times have I given you notice to guard against coming to me with grievances, either of you?

WIFE (*tearfully*). How can I guard against that, father dear?

FATHER (*severely*). You ask me?

WIFE. If you please.

FATHER. How many times have I explicitly told you to humour your husband and not keep watching what he does, where he goes, and what he is about?

WIFE. Well, but he makes love to this strumpet, the very next door!

FATHER. He shows excellent judgement, and he will make love to her all the more, I warrant you, to reward this diligence of yours.

WIFE. And he drinks there, too.

FATHER. Just because of you, will he drink the less there or anywhere else he pleases. Such confounded impudence! You might as well expect to keep him from accepting an invitation to dinner, or from having company at his own home. Do you expect your husbands to be your slaves? You do, and bid him sit with the maids and card wool.

WIFE (*resentfully*). I see I have brought you here, father, to defend my husband, not myself. Retained by me, you plead his case.

FATHER. If he has done anything out of the way, I shall be a great deal more severe with him than I have been with you. But inasmuch as he keeps you well supplied with jewellery and clothes, fur-nishes you with plenty of maidservants and provisions, you had better be sensible about things, my girl.

WIFE. But he filches my jewellery and mantles from my chests at home, he robs me, and carries my nicest things to strumpets on the sly!

FATHER. He does wrong, if he does that; if he doesn't, you are doing wrong to accuse an innocent man.

WIFE. Why, he has a mantle this very moment, father, and a bracelet he'd taken to her he is just now bringing back, because I found him out.

FATHER. I'll find out about this from him at once. I'll go and have a talk with the man. (*Approaching* MENÆCH-MUS SOSICLES) Speak up, Menæchmus, and let me know what you two are at odds over. Why are you so gloomy? And why is she standing aloof there, angry?

MEN. S. (*vehemently*). Whoever you are, whatever your name is, old gentleman, I call Heaven and God on high to witness——

FATHER (*surprised*). What about, concerning what conceivable thing?

MEN. S. That I have done no wrong to that woman who accuses me of having raided her house and stolen this mantle, and of having carried it off——

WIFE. He swears to that?

MEN. S. If I ever set foot inside this house, where she lives, I pray Heaven to make me the most wretched wretch on earth.

FATHER (*horrified*). Are you sane, to pray for a thing like that, or to deny that you ever put foot in this house, where you live, you utter idiot?

MEN. S. Do you, too, say I live in that house, old gentleman?

FATHER. And do you deny it?

MEN. S. By gad I do, truly!

FATHER. No, by gad, you do untruly—unless you moved away somewhere last night. (*Turning to his* WIFE) Daughter, come over here. (*She obeys.*)

Tell me—you have not moved away from here, have you?

WIFE. Where to, or why, for mercy's sake?

FATHER. Bless my soul, I don't know.

WIFE. He's making fun of you, of course. Can't you see that?

FATHER. Really now, Menæchmus, you have joked enough. Come, now, stick to the point.

MEN. S. See here, what have I got to do with you? Who are you, and where do you come from? What do I owe you, or that woman either, who is pestering me in every conceivable way?

WIFE (to her FATHER, frightened). Do you see how green his eyes are? And that greenish colour coming over his temples and forehead? How his eyes glitter! Look!

MEN. S. (aside). Seeing they declare I'm insane, what's better for me than to pretend I am insane, so as to frighten them off? (Develops alarming symptoms.)

WIFE (more frightened). How he stretches and gapes! Father, father dear, what shall I do now?

FATHER (retreating). Come over here, my child, as far as you can from him!

MEN. S. (having worked himself up properly). Euhoe! Bacchus! Bromius! Whither dost thou summon me a-hunting in the woods? I hear, but I cannot quit these regions, with that rabid bitch on watch there at my left, aye, and there behind a bald-headed goat who many a time in his life has ruined a guiltless fellow-citizen by his perjury!

FATHER (in helpless rage). Ugh! Curse you!

MEN. S. Lo! Apollo from his oracle doth bid me burn her eyes out with blazing brands!

WIFE. He'll murder me, father dear! He threatens to burn my eyes out!

FATHER (in low tone). Hey! daughter!

WIFE. What is it? What shall we do?

FATHER. How about my calling the servants here? I'll go and fetch someone to carry him away from here and tie him up at home before he makes any more trouble.

MEN. S. (aside). Now then, I'm stuck! Unless I get the start of them with some scheme, they'll be taking me off to their home. (Intercepting the old man and glaring at WIFE) Thou dost bid me, Apollo, to spare my fists in no wise upon her face, unless she doth leave my sight and—get to the devil out of here! I will do as thou biddest, Apollo! (Advancing upon her.)

FATHER. Run, run home as fast as you can before he batters you to bits!

WIFE (rushing for the door). Yes, I'm running. Do, please, keep watch of him, father dear, and don't let him leave this place! Oh, miserable woman that I am, to have to hear such words!
(Exit.)

MEN. S. Not badly, oh Apollo, did I remove that female! Now for this beastly, bewhiskered, doddering Tithonus, who calls himself the son of Cygnus —these be thy commands, that I crush his limbs and bones and joints with the same staff which he doth carry! (Advances.)

FATHER (retreating and raising his staff). You'll get hurt if you touch me, I tell you, or if you come any nearer to me!

MEN. S. I will do as thou biddest! I will take a double-edged axe, and this old man—I'll hew away his flesh, gobbet by gobbet, to the very bone!

FATHER (aside, timorously, still retreating). I must be on my guard and look out for myself, indeed I must! Really, I'm afraid he'll do me some injury, from the way he threatens me.

MEN. S. Many are thy commands, Apollo. Now thou dost bid me take yoked steeds, unbroken, fiery, and mount a chariot that I may dash to earth this aged, stinking, toothless lion. (*Mounts his chariot.*) Now am I in my car! Now do I hold the reins! Now have I goad in hand! On, steeds, on! Let the ring of your hoof-beats be heard! Let your fleetness of foot rush you rapidly on! (*Gallops about.*)

FATHER (*clutching his staff*). You threaten me with yoked steeds—me?

MEN. S. Lo, Apollo! Anew thou biddest me charge upon this man who stands here and lay him low! (*Charges; the old man raises his staff; the charioteer stops short.*) But who is this who by the hair doth tear me from the car? He revokes thy command and the edict of Apollo! (*Falls to the ground, apparently senseless.*)

FATHER. Well! Good heavens, what an acute, severe attack! Lord save us! Now this man who's gone insane—how healthy he was a little while ago! For him to have such an attack so suddenly! I'll go and summon a doctor as soon as I possibly can. (*Exit.*)

SCENE 3

MEN. S. (*getting up and looking about*). For Heaven's sake, are they out of my sight now, those two that absolutely compelled me, sound though I am, to go insane? I'd better hurry off to the ship while I can do so safely. (*To audience*) I beg you, all of you, if the old man comes back, don't tell him which way I bolted. (*Exit.*)

Enter FATHER-IN-LAW

FATHER. My loins ache me from sitting and my eyes from watching, while I waited for the doctor to come back from his calls. Finally he did manage to get away from his patients, the bore! He says he set a broken leg for Æsculapius, and put Apollo's arm in a splint, besides! So now I am wondering whether

to say I'm bringing a sawbones or a stonecutter. (*Glancing down the street.*) Just look at him mince along! (*Calling*) Quicken that ant's pace of yours!

SCENE 4

Enter a DOCTOR

DOCTOR (*ponderously*). What was the nature of his attack, did you say? State the symptoms, old gentleman. Is it a demoniacal visitation or paranoia? Inform me. Does he suffer from a lethargical habit or intercutaneous fluid?

FATHER (*sharply*). Why, I brought you just to tell me that and cure him.

DOCTOR (*lightly*). Oh, that is easy, quite easy. He shall be cured—I promise you that upon my honour.

FATHER (*distrustfully*). I want him to be cared for very carefully indeed.

DOCTOR (*reassuringly waggish*). Why, I will sigh more than six hundred times a day; that shows how I will care for him very carefully indeed for you.

FATHER (*looking down street*). Ah, there is our man himself! Let's watch what he does. (*They step back.*)

SCENE 5

Enter MENÆCHMUS

MEN. Good Lord! This has certainly proved a perverse and adverse day for me! Everything I thought I was doing on the sly has got out, thanks to that parasite who's overwhelmed me with infamy and fear—that Ulysses of mine who's brewed such a mess for his lord and master! Sure as I'm alive, I'll shuffle off that fellow's mortal coil! His? I'm a fool to call it his, when it's mine; it's my food and my money he's been reared on. I'll cut that worthy off from the breath of life! But as for the harlot, she was true to style, did only what her class always do! Because I ask her to let me carry the mantle back to my wife again, she says she has given it to me. Well! By Jove, I certainly do lead a miserable life!

FATHER (*to* DOCTOR). Do you catch what he says?

DOCTOR. He declares that he is miserable.

FATHER. I should like you to go up to him.

DOCTOR (*advancing*). Good day, Menæchmus. But, my dear man, why do you expose your arm? Are you not aware how injurious that is to one suffering from your present complaint?

MEN. (*violently*). You be hanged! (*The* DOCTOR *jumps.*)

FATHER (*aside to* DOCTOR). Do you notice anything?

DOCTOR. I should say I do. This case is beyond the powers of a wagon-load of hellebore. But see here, Menæchmus.

MEN. What d'ye want?

DOCTOR. Answer me this question: do you drink white or red wine?

MEN. Oh, go to the devil!

DOCTOR (*to* FATHER). Ah yes, now he begins to manifest the first symptoms of insanity.

MEN. Why don't you inquire whether the bread I generally eat is blood red, rose red, or saffron yellow? Whether I generally eat birds with scales, fish with feathers?

FATHER (*to* DOCTOR). Dear, dear! Do you hear how wildly he talks? Why don't you hurry up and give him a dose of something before he goes insane entirely?

DOCTOR (*to* FATHER). Now, now, one moment! I will question him still further.

FATHER. You're killing me with your talk!

DOCTOR (*to patient*). Tell me this: do you ever experience a sensation of hardness in the eyes?

MEN. What? You good-for-nothing, do you take me for a lobster?

DOCTOR. Tell me: do you ever have a rumbling of the bowels, as far as you observe?

MEN. Not after I've had a square meal; when I'm hungry, then there's a rumbling.

DOCTOR (*to* FATHER). Well, well! There's no indication of insanity in that reply. (*To* MENÆCHMUS) Do you sleep entirely through the night? Do you fall asleep readily on retiring?

MEN. I sleep through if I've paid my bills—(*angrily*) may all the powers above consume you, you inquisitive ass!

DOCTOR (*backing away*). Now the man does begin to manifest insanity! You hear him—look out for yourself!

FATHER. Oh no, to hear him now you'd think him a perfect Nestor compared with what he was a while ago. Why, a while ago he called his wife a rabid bitch.

MEN. Eh? I?

FATHER. Yes, while you were raving.

MEN. I?

FATHER. Yes, you, and you kept threatening me, too—that you would dash me to the earth with a yoked four-in-hand. I myself saw you do all this. I myself accuse you of it.

MEN. (*incensed*). Yes, and you stole the sacred crown from Jupiter's statue, I know that; and you were put in prison for it, I know that; and after getting out, you were put in the stocks and whipped, I know that; and then you murdered your father and sold your mother, that's something more I know. Do I pay you back your abuse well enough for a sane man, eh?

FATHER. For God's sake, doctor, whatever you're going to do, hurry up and do it! Don't you see the man is insane?

DOCTOR (*aside to* FATHER). Do you know what you had best do? Have him conveyed to my house.

FATHER. You advise that?

DOCTOR. By all means. There I shall

be able to care for him as I deem expedient.

FATHER. Do as you please.

DOCTOR (to MENÆCHMUS). You shall drink hellebore, I promise you, for some twenty days.

MEN. But I'll string you up and jab goads into you for thirty days.

DOCTOR (aside to FATHER). Go, summon men to convey him to my house.

FATHER. How many are needed?

DOCTOR. Considering the degree of insanity I note, four, no less.

FATHER. They shall be here soon. Keep watch of him, doctor.

DOCTOR (clearly reluctant). No, no! I shall go home so as to make the necessary preparations. You order the servants to bring him to my house.

FATHER. He'll be there soon, I promise you.

DOCTOR. I am going.

FATHER. Good-bye.   (Exeunt.)

MEN. (looking after them). Father-in-law's gone. Doctor's gone. All alone! Lord save us! What is it makes these men declare I'm insane? Why, as a matter of fact, I've never had a sick day since I was born. I'm neither insane, nor looking for fights, nor starting disputes, not I. I'm perfectly sound and regard others as sound; I recognize people, talk to them. Can it be they're insane themselves with their absurd statements that I'm insane? (Pauses.) What shall I do now? I long to go home, but my wife won't let me. And as for this place (glaring at EROTIUM's house) no one will let me in. Oh, what damnable luck! (Pauses.) Here's where I'll stay, indefinitely; I fancy I'll be let into the house at nightfall, anyhow.

SCENE 6

Enter MESSENIO

MES. (self-righteous and smug). This is your proof of a good servant who looks after his master's business, sees to it, gives it his care and consideration—when he watches over his master's business in his master's absence just as diligently as if he was present, or even more so. The chap that's got his wits in the proper place ought to think more of his back than his gullet, more of his shanks than his belly. He'd better recollect how good-for-nothings, lazy, rascally fellows, are rewarded by their masters: whippings, shackles, work in the mill, fag, famine, freezing stiff—these are the rewards of laziness. I'm badly afraid of such bad things, personally; that's why I've made up my mind to lead a good life rather than a bad one. I can stand chiding a great deal more easily—but a hiding I can't abide, myself, and I'd very much rather eat the meal than turn the mill. That's why I follow out my master's orders, attend to 'em properly and sedately; yes, indeed, I find it pays. Others can act as they think good for 'em; I'm going to be the sort of chap I should be—I must have a sense of fear, I must keep straight, so as to be on hand for master anywhere. I shan't have much to fear. The day's near when master will reward me for my service. I do my work on the principle that I think is good for my back. Here I come to meet master just as he told me, now that I've left the luggage and slaves at the inn. Now I'll knock at the door, so as to let him know I'm here, and lead him safely out of this ravine of ruination. But I'm afraid I'll be too late and find the battle over. (Goes to EROTIUM's doorway.)

SCENE 7

Enter FATHER-IN-LAW with slaves

FATHER, (to SLAVES, sternly). By heaven and earth, I charge you to be wise and heed my orders, past and present. Pick up that man (indicating

MENÆCHMUS) and carry him at once to the doctor's office—that is, unless you have no regard at all for your legs or flanks. See that none of you cares a straw for his threats. Why are you standing still? Why are you hesitating? He ought to have been hoisted up and carried off already. I'll go to the doctor's; I'll be at hand when you arrive.   (*Exit*.)

MEN. (*as the* SLAVES *dash at him*). Murder! What does this mean? What are these fellows rushing at me for, in the name of heaven? What do you want? Where are you pulling me? Where are you carrying me? (*Struggling on their shoulders*) Murder! Help, help, Epidamnians, I beg you! Save me, fellow-citizens! Let me go, I tell you!

MES. Ye immortal gods! In heaven's name, what is this my eyes behold! My master being carried off by some gang of rowdies in most outrageous fashion!

MEN. Doesn't anyone dare come to my rescue?

MES. (*running up*). I do, master,— like a regular dare-devil! (*Yelling lustily*) Oh, what an outrage, what a shame, Epidamnians! My master, a free-born visitor amongst you, to be abducted here in time of peace, in broad daylight, in your city streets! Let go of him!

MEN. For Heaven's sake, whoever you are, stand by me and don't let me be maltreated in such atrocious fashion!

MES. Not I! Stand by you I will, and defend and help you with all my heart! I won't let you be murdered, never! Better myself than you. For heaven's sake, master, pull out the eye of that chap that has you by the shoulder! (*Swinging vigorously at the nearest* SLAVES). As for these fellows here, I'm going to seed down their faces for them directly and plant my fists. By gad, you'll pay dear this day for carrying him off! Let go!

MEN. I've got this one by the eye!

MES. Leave the socket showing in his head! (*Warming up to his work*) You rascals! You robbers! You bandits!

SLAVES. Murder! Oh, for God's sake, let up!

MES. Let go, then! (*They drop* MENÆCHMUS.)

MEN. (*assisting* MESSENIO). What do you mean by touching me? (*To* MESSENIO) Comb them down with your fists! (*The* SLAVES *scatter*.)

MES. Come, clear out! Get the devil out of here! (*With a parting kick to a laggard*) There's another for you—take it as a prize for being the last to leave! (*Exeunt* SLAVES.) (*Smirking*) Oh, I measured their faces in fine style and quite to my taste. By Jove, master, I certainly did come to your aid in the nick of time just now!

MEN. Well, heaven bless you for ever and ever, young man, whoever you are. For if it hadn't been for you, I should never have lived to see the sun go down this day.

MES. Then, by Jove, master, if you did the right thing you'd set me free.

MEN. I set you free?

MES. Yes indeed, seeing I saved your life, master.

MEN. What's this? You're making a mistake, young man.

MES. Eh? A mistake?

MEN. Why, I swear by Father Jupiter I'm not your master.

MES. (*protestingly*). Oh, none of that, sir!

MEN. I'm not lying; no slave of mine ever did such a thing as you did for me.

MES. Very well, then, sir, if you say I'm not yours, let me go free.

MEN. Lord, man, be free so far as I am concerned, and go where you like.

MES. (*wild with joy*). Hail, patron mine! "Messenio, I congratulate you on your freedom!" By gad, I take your word for it! But, patron, I beseech you, don't order me about any less than when I was your slave. I intend to live with you, and when you go home I'll go with you.

MEN (*aside*). Oh no you won't.

MES. Now I'll go to the inn and fetch the luggage and cash for you. The wallet with the travelling money is duly under seal in the bag; I'll bring it here to you directly.

MEN. (*interested*). Be quick about it.

MES. I'll give it back to you intact, sir, just as you gave it to me. Wait for me here. (*Exit.*)

MEN. Well, well, how strangely strange things have happened to me to-day! Here are people saying I'm not myself and shutting me out of doors, and there's that fellow who just now said he was going to fetch me some money and that he was my slave—that saviour of mine, whom I just now set free. He says he'll bring me a wallet with money in it; if he does, I'll tell him to leave me and enjoy his freedom wherever he likes, so that he won't be coming to me for his money when he regains his sanity. (*Pauses.*) My father-in-law and the doctor said I was insane. It's a marvel to me what all this means! It seems just like a dream. (*Reflects.*) Now I will go into this harlot's house, no matter if she is in a rage with me, and see if I can't induce her to give me back the mantle to carry back home.

(*Exit into* EROTIUM'S *house.*)

SCENE 8

Enter MENÆCHMUS SOSICLES *and* MESSENIO

MEN. S. You cheeky rascal, you have the cheek to tell me you have encountered me anywhere to-day since the time I ordered you to come here and meet me?

MES. (*much aggrieved*). Why, sir, I just now rescued you when four men were carrying you off on their shoulders in front of this very house. You were yelling for all heaven and earth to help you, when I ran up and rescued you by good hard fighting, in spite of 'em. And for this, because I'd saved you, you've set me free. Then the moment I said I was going to get the money and luggage, you ran ahead as fast as you could to meet me, so as to deny what you had done!

MEN. S. So I ordered you to go free, eh?

MES. (*hopefully*). Certainly, sir.

MEN. S. (*emphatically*). Well, the most certain thing in the world is this— I had rather become a slave myself than ever free you.

SCENE 9

Enter MENÆCHMUS *from* EROTIUM'S *house*

MEN. (*to those within*). Swear it by the eyes in your head if you like, but, by the Lord, that won't make it any more true that I took the mantle and bracelet to-day, you sluts!

MES. (*gazing at him*). Ye immortal gods, what do I see?

MEN. S. What do you see?

MES. Your mirror!

MEN. S. What do you mean?

MES. (*pointing to* MENÆCHMUS). He's the very image of you! He's as like you as can be!

MEN. S. (*comparing himself with the stranger*). By Jove! He certainly is not unlike me, now that I look myself over.

MEN. (*seeing* MESSENIO). Ah there, sir, bless you—you that saved me, who-ever you are!

MES. Sir, for the love of heaven, do tell me your name, if you don't object.

MEN. Gad, man, your services to me haven't been such that I should grudge meeting your wishes. My name is Menæchmus.

MEN. S. (*startled*). Good Lord, no; it's mine!

MEN. I'm a Sicilian—a Syracusan.

MEN. S. That's my city and my country, too.

MEN. What's that you tell me?

MES. (*half to himself, as he scans* MENÆCHMUS). This is the man I know, of course; this is my master. I'm really his slave, but I fancied (*glancing at* MENÆCHMUS SOSICLES) I was his. (*To* MENÆCHMUS) I thought he was you, sir, and what's more, I made myself a nuisance to him, too. (*To* MENÆCHMUS) I beg your pardon, sir, if I said anything silly to you without realising it.

MEN. S. (*sharply*). You talk like an idiot. Do you not remember coming ashore along with me to-day?

MES. (*hurriedly*). To be sure, you're right. It's you who are my master. (*To* MENÆCHMUS) You seek another slave. (*To* MENÆCHMUS SOSICLES) Good day to you, sir. (*To* MENÆCHMUS) Good-bye to you, sir. I say this gentleman (*indicating his master*) is Menæchmus.

MEN. But I say I am.

MEN. S. (*irritated*). What yarn is this? You are Menæchmus?

MEN. So I say—the son of Moschus.

MEN. S. You are the son of my father?

MEN. No indeed, sir,—of my own: your father I have no desire to pre-empt or steal from you.

MES. (*aside, after apparently profound thought*). Ye immortal gods! Fulfil the unhoped-for hope I think I see before me! Yes, unless my mind deceives me, these two are the twin brothers! Yes, what they say about their country and father tallies exactly. I'll call my master aside. Menæchmus, sir!

MEN.
MEN. S. } What do you want?

MES. I don't want both of you, but the one that travelled on board ship with me.

MEN. I did not.

MEN. S. But I did.

MES. You're the one I want, then. (*Withdrawing*) Come over here, sir.

MEN. S. (*doing so*). Here I am. What is it?

MES. (*very sagacious and important*). That man over there is either a swindler, sir, or else he's your own twin brother. For I never did see two men more alike. No drop of water, no drop of milk, is more like another, believe me, than he's like you, yes, and you like him, sir. And then he says his country and his father's name are the same as yours. We'd better go up and question him.

MEN. S. By Jove, you have given me good advice! Thanks! Go on helping me, for God's sake! You are a free man if you find that he is my brother.

MES. I hope so.

MEN. S. And I—I hope so, too!

MES. (*stepping up to* MENÆCHMUS). Pardon me, sir. You said your name was Menæchmus, I believe.

MEN. I did indeed.

MES. This (*pointing to* MENÆCHMUS SOSICLES) gentleman's name is Menæchmus, too. You said you were born in Syracuse, in Sicily; he also was born there. You said your father's name was Moschus; so was his. Now both of you can do me a good turn, and yourselves as well.

MEN. You have earned my consent to any request you choose to make. Free though I am, I'll serve you quite as if you had bought and paid for me.

MES. I have hopes, sir, of finding that you two are twin brothers, born of one mother and one father on one day.

MEN. A strange statement! I wish you could bring to pass what you promise.

MES. I can. (*Tremendously earnest and subtle.*) But come now, both of you, and answer my questions.

MEN. Ask them when you like; I'll answer. Nothing that I know will I keep back.

Mes. Is your name Menæchmus?

Men. It is.

Mes. (*to his master*). And yours also?

Men. S. Yes.

Mes. (*to* Menæchmus). Your father was Moschus, you say?

Men. I do indeed.

Men. S. And mine too! (Messenio *scowls at him.*)

Mes. (*to* Menæchmus). Are you a Syracusan?

Men. Certainly.

Mes. (*to his master*). How about you?

Men. S. Of course I am.

Mes. Everything tallies perfectly so far. Your attention further, gentlemen. (*To* Menæchmus) What is the earliest thing you remember, tell me, in your own country?

Men. Going with my father to Tarentum, his place of trade, and then straying from my father in the crowd and being carried off.

Men. S. Lord above, preserve me!

Mes. (*with asperity*). What are you bawling out for? Keep still, won't you! (*To* Menæchmus) How old were you when your father took you away from home?

Men. Seven; you see, I was just beginning to lose my first teeth. And I never saw my father after that.

Mes. What? And how many sons did your father have then?

Men. So far as I can remember—two.

Mes. Which was the older, you or your brother?

Men. We were both of the same age.

Mes. How can that be?

Men. We were twins.

Men. S. (*unable to contain himself longer*). Oh, God has been good to me!

Mes. (*with finality*). If you interrupt, I prefer to keep still myself.

Men. S. (*contritely*). I'll keep still.

Mes. (*to* Menæchmus). Tell me, did you both have the same name?

Men. Oh no. Why, I had the same name as now, Menæchmus; he was called Sosicles then.

Men. S. (*disregarding* Messenio's *protests*). The proof's complete! I can't hold back—I must give him a hug! (*Embracing* Menæchmus) God bless you, brother, my own twin brother! I am Sosicles!

Men. (*doubtful*). How is it then, you came to be called Menæchmus?

Men. S. After word reached us that you . . . and that our father was dead, our grandfather changed my name; he gave me yours.

Men. (*still doubtful*). No doubt this was the case. But answer me this question.

Men. S. (*eagerly*). Ask it.

Men. What was our mother's name?

Men. S. Teuximarcha.

Men. (*returning his embrace heartily*). Right! To see you, so unhoped for, after all these years! Oh, God bless you!

Men. S. And you, too brother! I've searched and searched for you till this moment—and a sad, weary search it's been—and now you're found, I'm happy.

Mes. (*to his master*). This is how the wench here came to call you by his name; she mistook you for him, I suppose, when she invited you to lunch.

Men. (*reflecting, then frankly*). Well, well! The fact is, I did tell them to prepare lunch for me here to-day, unbeknown to my wife, whose mantle I stole from the house a while ago and gave to the wench here.

Men S. Is this mantle I have the one you speak of, brother? (*Showing it.*)

Men. That's the one! How did it come into your hands?

Men. S. The wench took me in here to luncheon, and said I had given it to her. Lunch I did, deuced well, and drank, and enjoyed the girl, and carried off the mantle and this piece of jewellery. (*Showing bracelet.*)

MEN. (*laughing*). By Jove! I'm glad if you're my debtor for a bit of amusement. For when she invited you in, she took you for me.

MES. (*to* MENÆCHMUS). You have no objection to my being free, as you ordered, have you, sir?

MEN. A perfectly just and reasonable request, brother. Grant it, for my sake.

MEN. S. (*to* MESSENIO). Be free.

MEN. Messenio, I congratulate you on your freedom!

MES. (*ingratiatingly*). But I need better auspices to be free for good, sirs. (*Waits for some hint of further benefits.*)

MEN. S. Now that things have turned out to our satisfaction, brother, let's both go back to our own country.

MEN. As you please, brother. I'll hold an auction here and sell all I have. In the meantime let's go inside for the present, brother.

MEN. S. By all means.

MES. Do you know what I want of you, sirs?

MEN. What?

MES. To let me be auctioneer.

MEN. You shall be.

MES. Well, then, do you want it announced at once that there'll be an auction.

MEN. Yes, a week from to-day.

MES. (*bawling*). Auction . . . of the effects of Menæchmus . . . one week from to-day in the morning, mind! . . . For sale . . . slaves, household goods, land, houses . . . everything! . . . For sale . . . your own price . . . cash down! For sale . . . even a wife, too, if any buyer appears! (*To spectators*) I don't believe the whole auction will bring him more than a mere—fifty thousand pounds. Now, spectators, fare ye well and give us your loud applause.

Exeunt omnes.

—PAUL NIXON.

PHORMIO

TERENCE

Publius Terentius Afer (about 184 to 159 B.C.) was the last of the great writers of the Græco-Roman comedy. He was brought as a slave from Africa to Rome, where he became closely associated with such men as Scipio the Younger and Lælius, who dominated the intellectual and literary circles of the time. He represents a reaction, possibly due to their influence, towards closer adherence to the Greek models. He shows little originality in plot, but is a much more careful workman than Plautus and possesses greater powers in the delineation of character.

The *Phormio* was produced in 161 B.C. The clear and logical development of the plot, the carefully drawn characters, the quieter action and the more refined language, compared with Plautus, are characteristic of the author.

DRAMATIS PERSONÆ

DEMIPHO, *an old gentleman of Athens.*
CHREMES, *his brother.*
HEGIO, *friend to Demipho.*
CRATINUS, *friend to Demipho.*
CRITO, *friend to Demipho.*
ANTIPHO, *son to Demipho.*
PHÆDRIA, *son to Chremes.*
PHORMIO, *an adventurer.*
DORIO, *a slave-dealer.*
GETA, *slave to Chremes.*
DAVUS, *a slave.*
NAUSISTRATA, *wife to Chremes.*
SOPHRONA, *nurse to Chremes' daughter.*

PROLOGUE

The Old Bard finding it impossible
To draw our Poet from the love of verse,
And bury him in indolence, attempts
By calumny to scare him from the stage;
Pretending, that in all his former plays
The characters are low, and mean the style;
Because he ne'er describ'd a mad-brain'd youth,

Who in his fits of phrenzy thought he saw
A Hind, the dogs in full cry after her;
Her too imploring and beseeching him
To give her aid.—But did he understand,
That when the piece was first produc'd,
  it ow'd,
More to the Actor, than himself, its
  safety,
He would not be thus bold to give of-
  fence.—
But if there's any one that says, or thinks,
"That had not the Old Bard assail'd him
  first
Our Poet could not have devis'd a Pro-
  logue,
Having no matter for abuse";—let such
Receive for answer, "that altho' the prize
To all advent'rers is held out in common,
The Veteran Poet meant to drive our
  Bard
From study into want: *He* therefore chose
To answer, though he would not first of-
  fend.
And had his adversary but have prov'd
A generous rival, he had had due praise.
Let him then bear these censures, and
  reflect,
Of his own slanders 'tis the due return!
But henceforth I shall cease to speak of
  him,
Altho' he ceases not himself to rail."
But now what I'd request of you, attend!
To-day I bring a new play, which the
  Greeks
Call Epidicazomenos; the Latins,
From the chief character, name Phormio;
Phormio, whom you will find a Parasite,
And the chief engine of the plot.—And
  now,
If to our Poet you are well inclin'd,
Give ear; be favourable; and be silent!
Let us not meet the same ill fortune now,
That we before encounter'd, when our
  troop
Was by a tumult driven from their place;
To which the Actor's merit, seconded
By your good-will and candour, has re-
  stor'd us.

SCENE:—*Athens. A place where four
streets meet. The houses of* DEMIPHO,
CHREMES, *and* DORIO *are on the stage.*

ACT I

Enter DAVUS *as from the Piazza*

DAVUS. Geta, my worthy friend and
  countryman,
Came to me yesterday: For some time
  past
I've ow'd him some small balance of ac-
  count:
This, he desir'd, I would make up: I
  have;
And brought it with me: For his master's
  son,
I am inform'd, has lately got a wife:
So I suppose this sum is scrap'd together
For a Bride-Gift. Alack, how hard it is,
That he, who is already poor, should still
Throw in his mite, to swell the rich man's
  heap!
What He scarce, ounce by ounce, from
  short allowance,
Sorely defrauding his own appetite,
Has spar'd, poor wretch! shall She sweep
  all at once,
Unheeding with what labour it was got.
Geta, moreover, shall be struck for more;
Another gift, when Madam's brought to
  bed;—
Another too, when Master's Birth-day's
  kept,
And they initiate him.—All this Mamma
Shall carry off, the Bantling her excuse.
But is that Geta?

Enter GETA *from* DEMIPHO'S *house*

GETA.   If a red-hair'd man
Enquire for me——
DAVUS.   No more! he's here.
GETA.   Oh, Davus!
The very man that I was going after.
DAVUS. Here, take this! (*gives a purse*)
  'tis all told; you'll find it right;
The sum I ow'd you.

GETA. Honest, worthy Davus!
I thank you for your punctuality.

DAVUS. And well you may, as men and
times go now:
Things by my troth, are come to such
a pass,
If a man pays you what he owes, you're
much
Beholden to him.—But, pray, why so
sad?

GETA. I?—You can scarce imagine in
what dread,
What danger I am in.

DAVUS. How so?

GETA. I'll tell you,
So you will keep it secret.

DAVUS. Away, fool!
The man whose faith in money you have
tried,
D'ye fear to trust with words?—And to
what end
Should I deceive you?

GETA. List then!

DAVUS. I'm all ear.

GETA. D'ye know our old man's elder
brother, Chremes?

DAVUS. Know him? Ay, sure.

GETA. You do?—And his son Phædria?

DAVUS. As well as I know you.

GETA. It so fell out,
Both the old men were forc'd to journey
forth
At the same season. He to Lemnos,
our's
Into Cilicia, to an old acquaintance
Who had decoy'd the old curmudgeon
thither
By wheedling letters, almost promising
Mountains of gold.

DAVUS. To one that had so much
More than enough already?

GETA. Prithee, peace!
Money's his passion.

DAVUS. Oh, would I had been
A man of fortune, I!

GETA. At their departure,
The two old gentlemen appointed me
A kind of governor to both their sons.

DAVUS. A hard task, Geta!

GETA. Troth, I found it so.
My angry Genius for my sins ordain'd it.
At first I took upon me to oppose:
In short, while I was trusty to th' old
man,
The young one made my shoulders an-
swer for it.

DAVUS. So I suppose: for what a foolish task
To kick against the pricks!

GETA. I then resolv'd
To give them their own way in ev'ry
thing.

DAVUS. Ay, then you made your market.

GETA. Our young spark
Play'd no mad pranks at first: But
Phædria
Got him immediately a Musick-Girl:
Fond of her to distraction! She be-
long'd
To a most avaricious sordid pimp;
Nor had we aught to give;—th' old gen-
tleman
Had taken care of That. Nought else
remain'd,
Except to feed his eyes, to follow her,
To lead her out to school, and hand her
home.
We too, for lack of other business, gave
Our time to Phædria. Opposite the
school,
Whither she went to take her lessons,
stood
A Barber's shop, wherein most commonly
We waited her return. Hither one day
Came a young man in tears: we were
amaz'd,
And ask'd the cause. Never (said he,
and wept)
Did I suppose the weight of poverty
A load so sad, so insupportable,
As it appear'd but now.—I saw but now,
Not far from hence, a miserable virgin
Lamenting her dead mother. Near the
corpse
She sat: nor friend, nor kindred, nor
acquaintance,

Except one poor old woman, was there near
To aid the funeral. I pitied her:
Her beauty too was exquisite.—In short,
He mov'd us all: And Antipho at once
Cried, "Shall we go and visit her?"—
"Why, ay,
I think so," said the other, "let us go!"
"Conduct us, if you please."—We went, arriv'd
And saw her.—Beautiful she was indeed!
More justly to be reckoned so, for she
Had no additions to set off her beauty.
Her hair dishevell'd, barefoot, woe-be-gone,
In tears, and miserably clad: that if
The life and soul of beauty had not dwelt
Within her very form, all these together
Must have extinguish'd it.—The spark, possess'd
Already with the Musick-Girl, just cried,
"She's well enough."—But our young gentleman——

DAVUS. Fell, I suppose, in love?
GETA.   In love indeed.
But mark the end! Next day, away he goes
To the old woman straight, beseeching her
To let him have the girl:—"Not she indeed!
Nor was it like a gentleman," she said,
"For him to think on't: She's a citizen,
An honest girl, and born of honest parents:—
If he would marry her indeed, by law
He might do *that;* on no account, aught else."
Our spark, distracted, knew not what to do:
At once he long'd to marry her, at once
Dreaded his absent father.
DAVUS.   Would not He,
Had he returned, have giv'n consent?
GETA.   To wed
A girl of neither family nor fortune?
Never.
DAVUS. What then?

GETA. What then! There is a Parasite,
One Phormio, a bold enterprising fellow,
Who—all the Gods confound him!—
DAVUS.   What did He?
GETA. Gave us the following counsel.—
"There's a law
That Orphan Girls should wed their next of kin,
Which law obliges too their next of kin
To marry them.—I'll say, that you're her kinsman,
And sue a writ against you. I'll pretend
To be her father's friend, and bring the cause
Before the judges. Who her father was,
Her mother who, and how she's your relation,
All this sham evidence I'll forge; by which
The cause will turn entirely in my favour.
You shall disprove no tittle of the charge;
So I succeed.—Your father will return;
Prosecute me;—what then?—the Girl's our own."

DAVUS. A pleasant piece of impudence!
GETA.   It pleas'd
Our spark at least: He put it into practice;
Came into court; and he was cast; and married.
DAVUS. How say you?
GETA.   Just as you have heard.
DAVUS.   Oh Geta,
What will become of you?
GETA.   I don't know, faith.
But only this I know, what'er chance brings,
I'll patiently endure.
DAVUS.   Why, that's well said,
And like a man.
GETA.   All my dependance is
Upon myself.
DAVUS.   And that's the best.
GETA.   I might
Beg one indeed to intercede for me,
Who may plead thus—"Nay, pardon him this once!
But if he fails again, I've not a word

To say for him."—And well if he don't add,
"When I go hence, e'en hang him!"

DAVUS.   What of him,
Gentleman-Usher to the Musick-Girl?
How goes He on?

GETA.   So, so!

DAVUS.   He has not much
To give perhaps.

GETA.   Just nothing, but mere hope.

DAVUS. His father too, is he return'd?

GETA.   Not yet.

DAVUS. And your old man, when do you
look for Him?

GETA. I don't know certainly; but I
have heard
That there's a letter from him come to
port,
Which I am going for.

DAVUS.   Would you aught else
With me, good Geta?

GETA.   Nothing, but Farewell!
                              (*Exit* DAVUS.)

Ho, Boy! what, nobody at home! (*Enter* BOY.) Take this,
And give it Dorcium. (*Gives the purse.
Exeunt severally.*)

Enter ANTIPHO *and* PHÆDRIA *from the
house*

ANT.   Is it come to this?
My father, Phædria!—my best friend!—
That I
Should tremble, when I think of his return!
When, had I not been inconsiderate,
I, as 'tis meet, might have expected him.

PHÆ. What now?

ANT.   Is that a question?
And from You,
Who know th' atrocious fault I have
committed?
Oh, that it ne'er had enter'd Phormio's
mind
To give such counsel! nor to urge me on,
In the extravagance of blind desire,

To this rash act, the source of my misfortunes!
I should not have possest her: that indeed
Had made me wretched some few days.
But then
This constant anguish had not torn my
mind,—

PHÆ. I hear you.

ANT.   —while each moment I expect
His coming to divorce me.

PHÆ.   Other men,
For lack of what they love, are miserable;
Abundance is your grievance. You're too
rich
A lover, Antipho! For your condition
Is to be wish'd and pray'd for. Now, by
heaven,
Might I, so long as you have done, enjoy
My love, it were bought cheaply with
my life.
How hard my lot, unsatisfied, unblest!
How happy yours, in full possession!—
One
Of lib'ral birth, ingenuous disposition,
And honest fame, without expence, you've
got:
The wife, whom you desir'd!—in all
things blest,
But want the disposition to believe so.
Had you, like me, a scoundrel pimp to
deal with,
Then you'd perceive—But sure 'tis in
our nature,
Never to be contented.

ANT.   Now to Me,
Phædria, 'tis You appear the happy man.
Still quite at large, free to consider still,
To keep, pursue, or quit her: I, alas,
Have so entangled and perplext myself,
That I can neither keep, nor let her
go.—
What now? isn't that our Geta, whom I
see
Running this way?—'Tis he himself—
Ah me!
How do I fear what news he brings!

Enter GETA *running*

GETA. Confusion!
A quick thought, Geta, or you're quite undone,
So many evils take you unprepar'd;
Which I know neither how to shun, nor how
To extricate myself: for this bold stroke
Of ours can't long be hid.
ANT. What's this confusion?
GETA. Then I have scarce a moment's time to think.
My master has arriv'd.
ANT. What mischief's that?
GETA. Who, when he shall have heard it, by what art
Shall I appease his anger?—Shall I speak?
'Twill irritate him.—Hold my peace?—enrage him.—
Defend myself? — Impossible! — Oh, Wretch!
Now for myself in pain, now Antipho
Distracts my mind.—But *him* I pity most;
For *him* I fear; 'tis *he* retains me here:
For, were it not for *him*, I'd soon provide
For my own safety—ay, and be reveng'd
On the old greybeard—carry something off,
And shew my master a light pair of heels.
ANT. What scheme to rob and run away is this?
GETA. But where shall I find Antipho? where seek him?
PHÆ. He mentions you.
ANT. I know not what, but doubt
That he's the messenger of some ill news.
PHÆ. Have you your wits?
GETA. I'll home: he's chiefly there.
PHÆ. Let's call him back!
ANT. Holo, you! stop!
GETA. Heyday!
Authority enough, be who you will.
ANT. Geta.
GETA. The very man I wish'd to meet!

ANT. Tell us, what news?—in one word, if you can.
GETA. I'll do it.
ANT. Speak!
GETA. This moment at the Port——
ANT. My father?
GETA. Even so.
ANT. Undone!
PHÆ. Heyday!
ANT. What shall I do?
PHÆ. What say you?
GETA. That I've seen
His father, Sir,—your Uncle.
ANT. How shall I,
Wretch that I am! oppose this sudden evil?
Should I be so unhappy, to be torn
From thee, my Phanium, life's not worth my care.
GETA. Since that's the case then, Antipho, you ought
To be the more upon your guard.
ANT. Alas!
I'm not myself.
GETA. But now you should be most so, Antipho.
For if your father should discern your fear,
He'll think you conscious of a fault.
PHÆ. That's true.
ANT. I cannot help it, nor seem otherwise.
GETA. How would you manage in worse difficulties?
ANT. Since I'm not equal to bear this, to those
I should be more unequal.
GETA. This is nothing.
Pooh, Phædria, let him go! why waste our time?
I will be gone. (*Going.*)
PHÆ. And I. (*Going.*)
ANT. Nay, prithee, stay!
What if I should dissemble?—will that do? (*Endeavouring to assume another air.*)
GETA. Ridiculous!
ANT. Nay, look at me! Will that Suffice?

GETA. Not it.

ANT. Or this?

GETA. Almost.

ANT. Or this?

GETA. Ay, now you've hit it. Do but
stick to that;

Answer him boldly; give him hit for dash,

Nor let him bear you down with angry
words.

ANT. I understand you.

GETA. "Forc'd"—"against your will"—

"By law"—"by sentence of the court"—
d'ye take me?—

But what old gentleman is that, I see

Turning the corner of the street?

ANT. 'Tis he.

I dare not face him. (*Going.*)

GETA. Ah, what is't you do?

Where d'ye run, Antipho! Stay, stay,
I say.

ANT. I know myself and my offence too
well:

To you then I commend my life and
love. (*Exit.*)

PHÆ. Geta, what now?

GETA. You shall be roundly chid;

I soundly drubb'd; or I am much deceiv'd.

But what e'en now we counsell'd Antipho.

It now behoves ourselves to practise,
Phædria.

PHÆ. Talk not of what behoves, but
say at once

What you would have me do.

GETA. Do you remember

The plea, whereon you both agreed to
rest,

At your first vent'ring on this enterprise?

"That Phormio's suit was just, sure,
equitable?

Not to be controverted."—

PHÆ. I remember.

GETA. Now then that plea! or, if it's
possible,

One better, and more plausible.

PHÆ. I'll do't.

GETA. Do you attack him first! I'll lie
in ambush,

To re-inforce you, if you give ground.

PHÆ. Well. (*They retire.*)

Enter DEMIPHO

DEM. How's this! A wife! what, Antipho! and ne'er

Ask my consent?—nor my authority—

Or, grant we pass authority, not dread

My wrath at least?—To have no sense
of shame?

Oh, impudence!—Oh, Geta, rare adviser!

GETA (*aside*). At last.

DEM. What will they say to me,

Or what excuse they will devise, I wonder.

GETA (*aside*). Oh, we have settled that
already: Think

Of something else.

DEM. Will he say this to me,—

"Against my will I did it"—"Forc'd by
law"—

I hear you: I confess it.

GETA (*aside*). Very well.

DEM. But conscious of the fraud, without a word

In answer or defence, to yield the cause

Tamely to your opponents—did the law

Force you to *that* too?

PHÆ. (*aside*). That's home.

GETA (*aside*). Give me leave!

I'll manage it.

DEM. I know not what to do:

This stroke has come so unawares upon
me,

Beyond all expectation, past belief.—

I'm so enrag'd, I can't compose my mind

To think upon it.—Wherefore ev'ry man,

When his affairs go on most swim-
mingly,

E'en then it most behoves to arm himself

Against the coming storm: loss, danger,
exile,

Returning ever let him look to meet;

His son in fault, wife dead, or daughter
sick—

All common accidents, and may have
happen'd;

That nothing should seem new or strange.
But if
Aught has fall'n out beyond his hopes,
all that
Let him account clear gain.
GETA (*aside to* PHÆDRIA). Oh, Phæ-
dria,
'Tis wonderful how much a wiser man
I am than my old master. My misfor-
tunes
I have consider'd well.—At his return
Doom'd to grind ever in the mill, beat,
chain'd,
Or set to labour in the fields;—of these
Nothing will happen new. If aught falls
out
Beyond my hopes, all that I'll count clear
gain.
But why delay t'accost th' old gentle-
man,
And speak him fair at first?

(PHÆDRIA *goes forward*)

DEM. Methinks I see
My nephew Phædria.
PHÆ. My good Uncle, welcome!
DEM. Your servant!—But where's An-
tipho?
PHÆ. I'm glad
To see you safe——
DEM. Well, well!—But answer me.
ANT. He's well, hard by.—But have af-
fairs turn'd out
According to your wishes?
DEM. Would they had!
ANT. Why, what's the matter?
DEM. What's the matter, Phædria?
You've clapp'd up a fine marriage in my
absence.
PHÆ. What! are you angry with him
about That?
GETA (*aside*). Well conterfeited!
DEM. Should I not be angry?
Let me but set eyes on him, he shall know
That his offences have converted me
From a mild father to a most severe one.
PHÆ. He has done nothing, Uncle, to
offend you.

DEM. See, all alike! the whole gang
hangs together:
Know one, and you know all.
PHÆ. Nay, 'tis not so.
DEM. One does a fault, the other's hand
at hand
To bear him out; when t'other slips, *he's*
ready:
Each in their turn!
GETA (*aside*). I' faith th' old gentle-
man
Has blunder'd on their humours to a hair.
DEM. For, were't not so, you'd not de-
fend him, Phædria.
PHÆ. If, Uncle, Antipho has done a
wrong
Or to his interest, or reputation,
I am content he suffer, as he may:
But if another, with malicious fraud,
Has laid a snare for inexperienced youth,
And triumph'd o'er it; can you lay the
blame
On us, or on the judges, who oft take
Thro' envy from the rich, or from com-
passion
Add to the poor?
GETA (*aside*). Unless I knew the cause,
I should imagine this was the truth he
spoke.
DEM. What judge can know the merits
on your side,
When you put in no plea; as he has
done?
PHÆ. He has behav'd like an ingenu-
ous youth.
When he came into court, he wanted
pow'r
To utter what he had prepar'd, so much
He was abash'd by fear and modesty.
GETA (*aside*). Oh brave!—But why,
without more loss of time,
Don't I accost th' old man? (*Going up*)
My master, welcome!
I am rejoiced to see you safe return'd.
DEM. What! my good master Governor!
your slave!
The prop! the pillar of our family!
To whom, at my departure hence, I gave
My son in charge.

GETA.   I've heard you for some time
Accuse us all quite undeservedly,
And me, of all, most undeservedly.
For what could I have done in this
   affair?
A slave the laws will not allow to plead;
Nor can he be an evidence.
DEM.   I grant it.
Nay, more—the boy was bashful—I al-
   low it.—
You but a slave.—But if she had been
   prov'd
Ever so plainly a relation, why
Needed he marry her? and why not
   rather
Give her, according to the law, a portion,
And let her seek some other for a hus-
   band?
Why did he rather bring a beggar home?
GETA.   'Twas not the thought, but
   money that was wanting.
DEM.   He might have borrow'd it.
GETA.   Have borrow'd it!
Easily said.
DEM.   If not to be had else,
On interest.
GETA.   Nay, now indeed you've hit it.
Who would advance him money in your
   life?
DEM.   Well, well, it shall not, and it
   cannot be,
That I should suffer her to live with him
As wife a single day. There is no
   cause.—
Would I might see that fellow, or could
   tell
Where he resides!
GETA.   What, Phormio!
DEM.   The girl's Patron!
GETA.   He shall be with you straight.
DEM.   Where's Antipho?
PHÆ.   Abroad.
DEM.   Go, Phædria; find him,
   bring him here.
PHÆ.   I'll go directly.   (*Exit.*)
GETA (*aside*).   Ay, to Pamphila.
                        (*Exit.*)

ACT II

Enter PHORMIO *and* GETA

PHOR.   And Antipho, you say, has slunk
   away,
Fearing his father's presence?
GETA.   Very true.
PHOR.   Poor Phanium left alone ?
GETA.   'Tis even so.
PHOR.   And the old gentleman enrag'd?
GETA.   Indeed.
PHOR.   The sum of all then, Phormio,
   rests on You:
On you, and you alone. You've bak'd
   this cake,
E'en eat it for your pains. About it
   then!
GETA.   I do beseech you.
PHOR. (*to himself*).   What if he en-
   quire?—
GETA.   Our only hope's in You.
PHOR. (*to himself*).   I have it!—Then,
Suppose he offer to return the girl?
GETA.   You urg'd us to it.
PHOR.   Ay! it shall be so.
GETA.   Assist us!
PHOR.   Let him come, Old Gentleman!
'Tis here: it is engender'd: I am arm'd
With all my counsels.
GETA.   What d'ye mean to do?
PHOR.   What would you have me do,
   unless contrive
That Phanium may remain, that Antipho
Be freed from blame, and all the old
   man's rage
Turn'd upon Me?
GETA.   Brave fellow! friend indeed!
And yet I often tremble for you, Phormio,
Lest all this noble confidence of yours
End in the stocks at last.
PHOR.   Ah, 'tis not so.
I'm an old stager too, and know my road.
How many men d'ye think I've bastina-
   doed
Almost to death? Aliens, and Citizens?
The oftener, still the safer.—Tell me
   then,
Didst ever hear of actions for assault

And batt'ry brought against me?
GETA.   How comes that?
PHOR. Because the net's not stretch'd
  to catch the hawk,
Or kite, who do us wrong; but laid for
  those,
Who do us none at all: In them there's
  profit,
In these mere labour lost. Thus other
  men
May be in danger, who have aught to
  lose;
I, the world knows, have nothing.—You
  will say,
They'll seize my person.—No, they won't
  maintain
A fellow of my stomach.—And they're
  wise,
In my opinion, if for injuries
They'll not return the highest benefit.
GETA. It is impossible for Antipho
To give you thanks sufficient.
PHOR.   Rather say,
No man sufficiently can thank his patron.
You at free cost to come! anointed,
  bath'd,
Easy and gay! while he's eat up with
  care
And charge, to cater for your entertain-
  ment!
He gnaws his heart, you laugh; eat first,
  sit first,
And see a Doubtful Banquet plac'd be-
  fore you!
GETA. Doubtful! what phrase is that?
PHOR.   Where you're in doubt,
What you shall rather chuse. Delights
  like these,
When you but think how sweet, how
  dear, they are;
Him that affords them must you not sup-
  pose
A very Deity?
GETA.   The old man's here.
Mind what you do! the first attack's the
  fiercest:
Sustain but that, the rest will be mere
  play. (*They retire.*)

Enter DEMIPHO *with* HEGIO, CRATINUS,
and CRITO

DEM. Was ever man so grossly treated,
  think ye?—
This way, Sirs, I beseech you.
GETA (*aside*).   He's enrag'd!
PHOR. (*aside*). Hist! mind your cue:
  I'll work him. (*Aloud*) Oh, ye Gods!
Does he deny that Phanium's his rela-
tion?
What, Demipho! Does Demipho deny
That Phanium is his kinswoman?
GETA.   He does.
PHOR. And who her father was he does
  not know?
GETA. No.
DEM. (*to his friends*). Here's the very
  fellow, I believe,
Of whom I have been speaking.—Fol-
  low me!
PHOR. And that he does not know, who
  Stilpho was?
GETA. No.
PHOR. Ah, because, poor thing, she's
  left in want,
Her father is unknown, and she despis'd.
What will not avarice do?
GETA.   If you insinuate
My master's avaricious, woe be to you!
DEM. Oh impudence! he dares accuse
  me first.
PHOR. As to the youth I cannot take
  offence,
If *he* had not much knowledge of him;
  since
Now in the vale of years, in want, his
  work
His livelihood, he nearly altogether
Liv'd in the country; where he held a
  farm
Under my father. I have often heard
The poor old man complain, that this his
  kinsman
Neglected him.—But what a man! A
  man
Of most exceeding virtue.
GETA.   Much at one:
Yourself and He you praise so much.

PHOR.   Away!
Had I not thought him what I've spoken
  of him,
I would not for his daughter's sake have
  drawn
So many troubles on our family,
Whom this old cuff now treats so scandal-
  ously.
GETA.   What, still abuse my absent mas-
  ter, Rascal!
PHOR.   It is no more than he deserves.
GETA.   How, villain!
DEM. (*calling*). Geta!
GETA (*pretending not to hear*). Rogue,
  Robber, Pettyfogger!
DEM.   Geta!
PHOR. (*aside*). Answer.
GETA (*turning*). Who's that?—Oh!
DEM.   Peace!
GETA.   Behind your back
All day without cessation has this knave
Thrown scurvy terms upon you, such as
  none
But men, like him, can merit.
DEM.   Well! have done
(*To* PHORMIO) Young man! permit me
  first to ask one question,
And, if you please, vouchsafe to answer
  me.—
Who was this friend of your's? Explain!
  and how
Might he pretend that I was his relation?
PHOR.   So! you fish for't, as if you didn't
  know.
DEM.   Know I!
PHOR.   Ay; you.
DEM.   Not I: You that maintain
I ought, instruct me how to recollect.
PHOR.   What! not acquainted with your
  cousin.
DEM.   Plague!
Tell me his name.
PHOR.   His name? ay!
DEM.   Well, why don't you?
PHOR. (*aside*). Confusion! I've forgot
  the name.
DEM.   What say you?
PHOR. (*aside to* GETA). Geta, if you

remember, prompt me. (*Aloud*)
  Pshaw!
I will not tell.   As if you didn't know.
You're come to try me.
DEM.   How! I try you?
GETA (*whispering*).   Stilpho.
PHOR.   What is't to me?—Stilpho.
DEM.   Whom say you?
PHOR.   Stilpho:
Did you know Stilpho, Sir?
DEM.   I neither know him;
Nor ever had I kinsman of that name.
PHOR.   How! are you not asham'd?—
  But if, poor man,
Stilpho had left behind him an estate
Of some Ten Talents——
DEM.   Out upon you!
PHOR.   Then
You would have been the first to trace
  your line
Quite from your Grandsire and Great
  Grandsire.
DEM.   True.
Had I then come, I'd have explain'd at
  large
How she was my relation: So do You!
Say, how is she my kinswoman?
GETA.   Well said!
Master, you're right. (*Aside to* PHOR-
  MIO) Take heed!
PHOR.   I have explain'd
All that most clearly, where I ought, in
  court.
If it were false, why did not then your
  son
Refute it?
DEM.   Do you tell me of my son,
Whose folly can't be spoke of, as it
  ought?
PHOR.   But You, who are so wise, go,
  seek the judge:
Ask sentence in the self-same cause
  again:
Because You're Lord alone; and have
  alone
Pow'r to obtain the judgment of the
  court
Twice in one cause.
DEM.   Although I have been wrong'd,

Yet, rather than engage in litigation,
And rather than hear You; as if she were
Indeed related to us, as the law
Ordains, I'll pay her dowry: Take her hence,
And with her take Five Minæ.

PHOR. Ha! ha! ha!
A pleasant gentleman!

DEM. Why, what's the matter?
Have I demanded anything unjust?
Sha'n't I obtain this neither, which is law?

PHOR. Is't even so, Sir?—Like a common harlot
When you've abus'd her, does the law ordain
That you should pay her hire, and whistle her off?
Or, lest a citizen thro' poverty
Bring shame upon her honour, does it order
That she be given to her next of kin
To pass her life with him? which you forbid.

DEM. Ay; to her next of kin: But why to Us;
Or wherefore?

PHOR. Oh! that matter is all settled:
Think on't no more.

DEM. Not think on't! I shall think
Of nothing else, till there's an end of this.

PHOR. Words, words!

DEM. I'll make them good.

PHOR. But, after all,
With You I have no business, Demipho!
Your Son is cast; not You: for at your age
The coupling-time is over.

DEM. Be assur'd
That all I've said, He says: Or I'll forbid
Him and this wife of his my house.

GETA (aside). He's angry.

PHOR. No; you'll think better on't.

DEM. Are you resolv'd,
Wretch that you are, to thwart me ev'ry way?

PHOR. (aside to GETA). He fears, tho'
he dissembles.

GETA (aside to PHORMIO). Well begun!

PHOR. Well; but what can't be cur'd
must be endur'd:
'Twere well, and like yourself, that we
were friends.

DEM. I! friend to you? or chuse to see,
or hear you!

PHOR. Do but agree with her, you'll
have a girl
To comfort your old age. Your years,
consider!

DEM. Plague on your comfort! take her
to yourself!

PHOR. Ah! don't be angry!

DEM. One word more, I've done.
See that you fetch away this wench, and
soon,
Or I shall turn her headlong out o' doors.
So much for Phormio!

PHOR. Offer but to touch her,
In any other manner than beseems
A gentlewoman and a citizen,
And I shall bring a swinging writ against
you.
So much for Demipho!—(Aside to GETA)
If I am wanted,
I am at home, d'ye hear.

GETA (aside to PHORMIO). I understand.
(Exit PHORMIO.)

DEM. With how much care, and what
solicitude,
My son affects me, with this wretched
match
Having embroil'd himself and me! nor
comes
Into my sight, that I might know at least
Or what he says, or thinks of this affair.
Go, you; and see if he's come home, or no.

GETA. I'm gone. (Exit.)

DEM. You see, Sirs, how this
matter stands.
What shall I do? Say, Hegio!

HEGIO. Meaning me?
Cratinus, please you, should speak first.

DEM. Say then,
Cratinus!

CRAT. Me d'ye question?

DEM. You.
CRAT. Then I,
Whatever steps are best I'd have you take.
Thus, it appears to Me. Whate'er your son
Has in your absence done, is null and void
In law and equity.—And so you'll find.
That's my opinion.
DEM. Say now, Hegio?
HEGIO. He has, I think, pronounc'd most learnedly.
But so 'tis: many men, and many minds!
Each has his fancy: Now, in my opinion,
Whate'er is done by law, can't be undone.
'Tis shameful to attempt it.
DEM. Say you, Crito!
CRITO. The case, I think, asks more deliberation.
'Tis a nice point.
HEGIO. Would you aught else with us?
DEM. You've utter'd Oracles. (*Exeunt friends.*) I'm more uncertain
Now than I was before.

Re-enter GETA

GETA. He's not return'd.
DEM. My Brother, as I hope, will soon arrive;
Whate'er advice he gives me, that I'll follow.
I'll to the Port, and ask when they expect him. (*Exit.*)
GETA. And I'll go find out Antipho, and tell him
All that has past.—But here he comes in time.

Enter ANTIPHO

ANT. (*to himself*). Indeed, indeed, my Antipho,
You're much to blame, to be so poor in spirit.
What! steal away so guilty-like? and trust
Your life and safety to the care of others?
Would They be touch'd more nearly than Yourself?

Come what come might of ev'rything beside,
Could you abandon the dear maid at home?
Could you so far deceive her easy faith,
And leave her to misfortune and distress?
Her, who plac'd all hopes in you alone?
GETA (*coming forward*). I'faith, Sir, we have thought you much to blame
For your long absence.
ANT. You're the very man
That I was looking for.
GETA. But ne'ertheless
We've mist no opportunity.
ANT. Oh, speak!
How go my fortunes, Geta? has my father
Any suspicion that I was in league
With Phormio?
GETA. Not a jot.
ANT. And may I hope?
GETA. I don't know.
ANT. Ah!
GETA. Unless that Phædria
Did all he could do for you.
ANT. Nothing new.
GETA. And Phormio, as on all occasions else,
Prov'd himself a brave fellow.
ANT. What did He?
GETA. Out-swagger'd your hot father.
ANT. Well said, Phormio!
GETA. I did the best I could, too.
ANT. Honest Geta,
I am much bounden to you all.
GETA. Thus, Sir,
Stand things at present. As yet all is calm.
Your father means to wait your uncle's coming.
ANT. For what?
GETA. For his advice, as he propos'd;
By which he will be rul'd in this affair.
ANT. How do I dread my uncle's coming, Geta,
Since by his sentence I must live or die!
GETA. But here comes Phædria.

ANT.   Where?
GETA. From his old school.
                    (*They retire.*)

Enter DORIO *and* PHÆDRIA

PHÆ. Nay, hear me, Dorio!
DOR.   Not I.
PHÆ.   But a word!
DOR. Let me alone.
PHÆ.   Pray, hear me!
DOR.   I am tir'd
With hearing the same thing a thousand
  times.
PHÆ. But what I'd say, you would be
  glad to hear.
DOR. Speak then! I hear.
PHÆ.   Can't I prevail on you
To stay but these three days?—Nay,
  where d'ye go?
DOR. I should have wonder'd had you
  said aught new.
ANT. (*aside to* GETA). This Pimp, I fear,
  will work himself no good.
GETA. I fear so too.
PHÆ.   Won't you believe
  me?
DOR. Guess.
PHÆ. Upon my honour.
DOR.   Nonsense.
PHÆ.   'Tis a kindness
Shall be repaid with interest.
DOR.   Words, words!
PHÆ. You'll be glad on't; you will, be-
  lieve me.
DOR.   Pshaw!
PHÆ. Try; 'tis not long.
DOR.   You're in the same tune still.
PHÆ. My kinsman, parent, friend.—
DOR.   Ay, talk away.
PHÆ. Can you be so inflexible, so cruel,
That neither pity, nor entreaties touch
  you?
DOR. And can You be so inconsiderate,
And so unconscionable, Phædria,
To think that you can *talk* me to your
  purpose,
And wheedle me to give the girl for
  nothing?

ANT. (*aside*). Poor Phædria!
PHÆ. (*to himself*).   Alas, he speaks
  the truth.
GETA (*aside to* ANTIPHO). How well
  they each support their characters!
PHÆ. (*to himself*). Then that this evil
  should have come upon me,
When Antipho was in the like distress!
ANT. (*coming forward*). Ha! what now,
  Phædria?
PHÆ.   Happy, happy Antipho!—
ANT.   I?
PHÆ. Who have her you love in your
  possession,
Nor e'er had plagues like these, to strug-
  gle with!
ANT. In my possession? yes, I have
  indeed,
As the old saying goes, a Wolf by the
  Ears:
For I can neither part with her, nor keep
  her.
DOR. 'Tis just my case with Him.
ANT. (*to* DORIO).   Thou thorough
  Bawd!
(*To* PHÆDRIA). What has he done?
PHÆ. Done?—The inhuman wretch
Has sold my Pamphila.
GETA.   What! Sold her!
ANT.   Sold her?
PHÆ. Yes; sold her.
DOR.   Sold her.—What
  a monstrous crime!
A wench he paid his ready money for.
PHÆ. I can't prevail upon him, to wait
  for me,
And to stave off his bargain but three
  days;
Till I obtain the money from my friends,
According to their promise.—If I do not
Pay it you then, don't wait a moment
  longer.
DOR. You stun me.
ANT.   'Tis a very little time,
For which he asks your patience, Dorio.
Let him prevail on you; your com-
  plaisance
Shall be requited doubly.
DOR.   ·   Words: mere words!

ANT. Can you then bear to see your Pamphila
Torn from this city, Phædria?—Can you, Dorio,
Divide their loves?

DOR.   Nor I, nor you.

GETA.   Plague on you!

DOR. I have, against my natural disposition,
Borne with you several months, still promising,
Whimpering, and ne'er performing anything:
Now, on the contrary, I've found a spark,
Who'll prove a ready-paymaster, no sniveler:
Give place then to your betters!

ANT.   Surely, Phædria,
There was, if I remember, a day settled
That you should pay the money down.

PHÆ.   There was.

DOR. Do I deny it?

ANT.   Is the day past?

DOR.   No.
But this has come before it.

ANT.   Infamous!
Ar'n't you asham'd of such base treachery?

DOR. Not I, while I can get by't.

GETA.   Scavenger!

PHÆ. Is this just dealing, Dorio?

DOR.   'Tis my way:
So, if you like me, use me.

ANT. Can you deceive him thus?

DOR.   Nay, Antipho,
'Tis *he* deceives *me:* he was well aware
What kind of man I was, but I believ'd
Him diff'rent. He has disappointed me,
But I am still the same to him as ever.
However, thus much I can do for him;
The Captain promis'd to pay down the money
To-morrow morning. But now, Phædria,
If you come first, I'll follow my old rule,
"The first to pay, shall be first serv'd."
Farewell.   (*Exit.*)

PHÆ. What shall I do? Unhappy that I am,
How shall I, who am almost worse than nothing,
Raise such a sum so suddenly?—Alas!
Had I prevail'd on him to wait three days,
I had a promise of it.

ANT.   Shall we, Geta,
Suffer my Phædria to be miserable?
My best friend Phædria, who but now, you said,
Assisted me so heartily?—No.—Rather
Let us, since there's need, return his kindness!

GETA. It is but just, I must confess.

ANT.   Come then;
'Tis you alone can save him.

GETA.   By what means?

ANT. Procure the money.

GETA.   Willingly: but whence?

ANT. My father is arriv'd.

GETA.   He is: what then?

ANT. A word to the wise, Geta!

GETA.   Say you so?

ANT. Ev'n so.

GETA.   By Hercules, 'tis rare advice.
Are you there with me? will it not be triumph,
So I but scape a scouring for your match,
That you must urge me to run risks for *him?*

ANT. He speaks the truth, I must confess.

PHÆ. How's that?
Am I a stranger to you, Geta?

GETA.   No:
Nor do I hold you such. But is it nothing,
That Demipho now rages at us all,
Unless we irritate him so much further,
As to preclude all hopes to pacify him?

PHÆ. Shall then another bear her hence? Ah me!
Now then, while I remain, speak to me, Antipho.
Behold me!

ANT.   Wherefore? what is it you mean?

PHÆ. Wherever she's convey'd, I'll follow her;

Or perish.

GETA. Heaven prosper your designs!— Gently, Sir, gently!

ANT. See, if you can help him.

GETA. Help him! but how?

ANT. Nay, think, invent, devise; Lest he do something we repent of, Geta!

GETA. I'm thinking. (*Pausing*) Well, then, I believe he's safe. But I'm afraid of mischief.

ANT. Never fear: We'll bear all good and evil fortune with you.

GETA. Tell me the sum you have occasion for.

PHÆ. But Thirty Minæ.

GETA. Thirty! monstrous, Phædria! She's very dear.

PHÆ. Dog-cheap.

GETA. Well, say no more. I'll get them for you.

PHÆ. O brave fellow!

GETA. Hence!

PHÆ. But I shall want it *now*.

GETA. You'll have it *now*. But Phormio must assist me in this business.

ANT. He's ready: lay what load you will upon him, He'll bear it all; for he's a friend indeed.

GETA. Let's to him quickly then!

ANT. D'ye want my help?

GETA. We've no occasion for you. Get you home To the poor girl, who's almost dead with fear; And see you comfort her.—Away! d'ye loiter?

ANT. There's nothing I would do so willingly. (*Exit.*)

PHÆ. But how will you effect this?

GETA. I'll explain That matter as we go along.—Away! (*Exeunt.*)

ACT III

Enter DEMIPHO *and* CHREMES

DEM. Well, Chremes? have you brought your daughter with you, On whose account you went to Lemnos?

CHR. No.

DEM. Why not?

CHR. Her mother grown, it seems, impatient, Perceiving that I tarried here so long, And that the girl's age brook'd not my delays, Had journey'd here, they said, in search of me, With her whole family.

DEM. Appriz'd of this, What kept you there so long then?

CHR. A disease.

DEM. How came it? what disease?

CHR. Is that a question? Old age itself is a disease.—However, The master of the ship, who brought them over, Inform'd me of their safe arr'val hither.

DEM. Have you heard, Chremes, of my son's misfortune During my absence?

CHR. Ay; and it confounds me. For to another should I tender her, I must relate the girl's whole history, And whence arises my connexion with her. You I can trust as safely as myself: But if a stranger courts alliance with me, While we're new friends, he'll hold his peace perhaps, But if he cools, he'll know too much of me. Then I'm afraid my wife should know of this; Which if she does, I've nothing else to do, But shake myself, and leave my house directly: For I've no friend at home, except myself.

DEM. I know it; and 'tis that which touches me.

Nor are there any means I'll leave untried,
Till I have made my promise to you good.

Enter GETA

GETA (*to himself*). I never saw a more
shrewd rogue than Phormio.
I came to let him know we wanted money,
With my device for getting it; and scarce
Had I related half, but he conceiv'd me.
He was o'erjoy'd; commended me; de-
manded
To meet with Demipho; and thank'd the
Gods,
That it was now the time to shew himself
As truly Phædria's friend, as Antipho's.
I bad him wait us at the Forum; whither
I'd bring th' old gentleman.—And there
he is!
But who's the furthermost? Ha! Phæ-
dria's father.
Yet what was I afraid of, Simpleton?
That I have got two dupes instead of
one?
Is it not better that my hopes are
doubled?
I'll attack him I first propos'd. If He
Answers my expectation, well: if not,
Why then have at you, Uncle!

Enter ANTIPHO

ANT. (*to himself*).   I expect
Geta's arrival presently.—But see!
Yonder's my Uncle with my father.—Ah!
How do I dread his influence!
GETA (*aside*).   I'll to them.
(*Aloud*) Oh, good Sir Chremes!
CHR.   Save you, save you, Geta!
GETA. I'm glad to see you safe arriv'd.
CHR.   I thank you.
GETA. How go affairs?
CHR.   A world of changes here,
As usual at first coming home again.
GETA. True. Have you heard of An-
tipho's affair?
CHR. The whole.
GETA.   You told him, Sir?—
'Tis monstrous, Chremes,

To be so shamefully impos'd upon!
DEM. 'Twas on that point I was just
talking with him.
GETA. And I too have turn'd it in my
thoughts,
Have found, I think, a remedy.
DEM.   How, Geta?
What remedy?
GETA.   On leaving you, by chance
I met with Phormio.
CHR.   Who is Phormio?
GETA. The girl's solicitor.
CHR.   I understand.
GETA. I thought within myself, "suppose
I sound him!"
And taking him aside, "Now prithee,
Phormio,
Why don't you try to settle this affair
By fair means rather than by foul?"
said I.
"My master is a generous gentleman,
And hates to go to law. For I assure you,
His other friends advis'd him, to a man,
To turn this girl directly out o'doors."
ANT. (*aside*). What does he mean? or
where will all this end?
GETA. "The law, you think, will give you
damages,
If he attempts to turn her out.—Alas,
He has had counsel upon that.—I'faith,
You'll have hot work, if you engage with
Him;
He's such an Orator!—But ev'n suppose
That you should gain your law-suit, after
all
The trial is not for his life, but money."
Perceiving him a little wrought upon,
And soften'd by this style of talking with
him,
"Come now," continued I, "we're all
alone.
Tell me, what money would you take in
hand
To drop your law-suit, take away the
girl,
And trouble us no farther?"
ANT. (*aside*)   Is he mad?
GETA. "For I am well convinc'd, that if
your terms

Are not extravagant and wild indeed,
My master's such a worthy gentleman,
You will not change three words between
  you."
DEM. Who
Commission'd you to say all this?
CHR.   Nay, nay,
Nothing could be more happy to effect
The point we labour at.
ANT. (*aside*).   Undone!
CHR.   Go on.
GETA. At first he rav'd.
DEM.   Why, what did he demand?
GETA. Too much: as much as came into
  his head.
CHR. Well, but the sum?
GETA.   He talk'd of a Great Talent.
DEM. Plague on the rascal! what! has he
  no shame?
GETA. The very thing I said to him.—
  "Suppose
He was to portion out an only daughter,
What could he give her more?—He
  profits little,
Having no daughter of his own; since one
Is found, to carry off a fortune from
  him."
But to be brief, and not to dwell upon
All his impertinencies, he at last
Gave me this final answer.—"From the
  first,
I wish'd," said he, "as was indeed most
  fit,
To wed the daughter of my friend my-
  self:
For I was well aware of her misfortune;
That, being poor, she would be rather
  given
In slavery, than wedlock, to the rich.
But I was forc'd, to tell you the plain
  truth,
To take a woman with some little for-
  tune,
To pay my debts: and still, if Demipho
Be willing to advance so large a sum,
As I'm to have with one I'm now en-
  gag'd to,
There is no wife I'd rather take than
  Her."

ANT. (*aside*). Whether through malice
  or stupidity,
He is rank knave or fool, I cannot tell.
DEM. What if he owes his soul?
GETA.   "I have a farm,"
Continued he, "that's mortgag'd for Ten
  Minæ."
DEM. Well, let him take her then: I'll
  pay the money.
GETA. "A house for ten more."
DEM.   Huy! huy! that's too much.
CHR. No noise! demand those ten of me.
GETA.   "My wife
Must buy a maid; some little furniture
Is also requisite; and some expence
To keep our wedding: all these articles,"
Continues he, "we'll reckon at Ten
  Minæ."
DEM. No; let him bring ten thousand
  writs against me.
I'll give him nothing. What! afford the
  villain
An opportunity to laugh at me?
CHR. Nay, but be pacified! I'll pay the
  money.
Only do you prevail upon your son
To marry her, whom we desire.
ANT. (*aside*).   Ah me!
Geta, your treachery has ruin'd me.
CHR. She's put away on my account:
  'tis just
That I should pay the money.
GETA.   "Let me know,"
Continues he, "as soon as possible,
Whether they mean to have me marry
  her;
That I may part with t'other, and be
  certain.
For t'other girl's relations have agreed
To pay the portion down immediately."
CHR. He shall be paid *this* too im-
  mediately.
Let him break off with her, and take this
  girl!
DEM. Ay, and the plague go with him!
CHR.   Luckily
It happens I've some money here; the
  rents

Of my wife's farms at Lemnos. I'll take
that;
And tell my wife that you had need of it.
(*Exeunt*.)

ANT. (*coming forward*). Geta!

GETA.   Ah, Antipho!

ANT.   What have you done?

GETA. Trick'd the old bubbles of their
money.

ANT.   Well,
Is that sufficient, think ye?

GETA.   I can't tell.
'Twas all my orders.

ANT.   Knave, d'ye shuffle
with me? (*Kicks him.*)

GETA. Plague! what d'ye mean?

ANT.   What did I mean, sirrah!
You've driven me to absolute perdition.
All pow'rs of heav'n and hell confound
you for't,
And make you an example to all villains!
Here! would you have your business duly
manag'd,
Commit it to this fellow!—What could be
More tender than to touch upon this sore,
Or even name my wife? My father's
filled
With hopes that she may be dismiss'd.—
And then
If Phormio gets the money for the por-
tion,
He to be sure must marry her.—And
what
Becomes of me then?

GETA.   He'll not marry her.

ANT. Oh, no: but when they re-demand
the money,
On my account he'll rather go to jail!

GETA. Many a tale is spoilt in telling,
Antipho.
You take out all the good and leave the
bad.
Now hear the other side.—If he receives
The money, he must wed the girl: I
grant it.
But then some little time must be allow'd
For wedding-preparation, invitation,
And sacrifices.—Meanwhile, Phædria's
friends

Advance the money they have promis'd
him:
Which Phormio shall make use of for repayment.

ANT. How so? what reason can he
give?

GETA. What reason?
A thousand.—"Since I made this fatal
bargain,
Omens and prodigies have happen'd to
me.
There came a strange black dog into my
house!
A snake fell through the tiling! a hen
crow'd!
The Soothsayer forbad it! The Diviner
Charg'd me to enter on no new affair
Before the winter.—All sufficient reasons.
Thus it shall be.

ANT.   Pray heav'n, it may!

GETA.   It shall.
Depend on me:—But here's your father.
—Go;
Tell Phædria that the money's safe.
(*Exit* ANTIPHO.)

Re-enter DEMIPHO *and* CHREMES

DEM.   Nay, peace!
I'll warrant he shall play no tricks upon
us:
I'll not part rashly with it, I assure you:
But pay it before witnesses, reciting
To whom 'tis paid, and why 'tis paid.

GETA (*aside*).   How cautious,
Where there is no occasion!

CHR.   You had need.
But haste, dispatch it while the fit's upon
him:
For if the other party should be pressing,
Perhaps he'll break with us.

GETA.   You've hit it, Sir.

DEM. Carry me to him then.

GETA.   I wait your pleasure.

CHR. When this is done, step over to my
wife,
That she may see the girl before she goes;
And tell her, to prevent her being angry,

"That we've agreed to marry her to
    Phormio,
Her old acquaintance, and a fitter match;
That we have not been wanting in our
    duty,
But given as large a portion as he ask'd."
DEM. Pshaw! what's all this to you?
CHR.   A great deal, Brother.
DEM. Is't not sufficient to have done
    your duty,
Unless the world approves it?
CHR.   I would chuse
To have the whole thing done by her
    consent:
Lest she pretend we turn'd her out
    o'doors.
DEM. Well, I can say all this to her
    myself.
CHR. A woman deals much better with
    a woman.
DEM. I'll ask your wife to do it then.
        (*Exeunt* DEMIPHO *and* GETA.)
CHR.   I'm thinking,
Where I shall find these women now.

Enter SOPHRONA

SOPH. (*to herself*).   Alas!
What shall I do, unhappy as I am?
Where find a friend? to whom disclose
    this story?
Of whom beseech assistance?—For I fear
My mistress will sustain some injury
From following my counsel: the youth's
    father,
I hear, is so offended at this marriage.
CHR. Who's this old woman, coming
    from my brother's,
Seeming so terrified?
SOPH. (*to herself*).   'Twas poverty
Compell'd me to this action: tho' I knew
This match would hardly hold together
    long,
Yet I advis'd her to it, that meanwhile
She might not want subsistence.
CHR.   Surely, surely,
Either my mind deceives me, or eyes fail
    me,
Or that's my daughter's nurse.

SOPH.   Nor can we find——
CHR. What shall I do?
SOPH.   ——her father out.
CHR.   Were't best
I should go up to her, or wait a little,
To gather something more from her dis-
    course?
SOPH. Could *he* be found, my fears were
    at an end.
CHR. 'Tis she. I'll speak with her.
SOPH.   Whose voice is that?
CHR. Sophrona!
SOPH.   Ha! my name too?
CHR.   Look this way.
SOPH. Good heav'n have mercy on us!
    Stilpho!
CHR.   No.
SOPH. Deny your own name?
CHR.   This way, Sophrona!—
A little further from that door!—this
    way!—
And never call me by that name, I charge
    you.
SOPH. What! ar'n't you then the man
    you said you were?
CHR. Hist! hist!
SOPH.   What makes you fear
    those doors so much?
CHR. I have a fury of a wife within:
And formerly I went by that false name,
Lest ye should indiscreetly blab it out,
And so my wife might come to hear of
    this.
SOPH. Ah! thus it was, that we, alas,
    poor souls,
Could never find you out here.
CHR.   Well, but tell me,
What business have you with that
    family?—
Where is your mistress and her daughter?
SOPH. Ah!
CHR.   What now? are they alive?
SOPH.   The daughter is:
The mother broke her heart with grief.
CHR.   Alas!
SOPH. And I, a poor, unknown, distress'd
    old woman,
Endeavouring to manage for the best,
Contriv'd to match the virgin to a youth,

Son to the master of this house.

CHR.   To Antipho?

SOPH. The very same.

CHR.   What! has he two wives then?

SOPH. No, mercy on us! he has none
but her.

CHR. What is the other then, who, they
pretend,

Is a relation to him?

SOPH.   This is she.

CHR. How say you?

SOPH.   It was all a mere contrivance;

That he, who was in love, might marry
her

Without a portion.

CHR.   O ye pow'rs of heaven,

How often fortune blindly brings about

More than we dare to hope for! Coming
home,

I've found my daughter, even to my wish,

Match'd to the very person I desir'd.

What we have both been labouring to
effect,

Has this poor woman all alone accomplish'd.

SOPH. But now consider what is to be
done!

The bridegroom's father is return'd: and
He,

They say, is much offended at this marriage.

CHR. Be of good comfort: there's no
danger there.

But, in the name of heav'n and earth, I
charge you,

Let nobody discover she's my daughter.

SOPH. None shall discover it from me.

CHR.   Come then!

Follow me in, and you shall hear the
rest.   (*Exeunt*.)

ACT IV

Enter DEMIPHO *and* GETA

DEM. 'Tis our own fault, that we encourage rogues,

By over-straining the due character

Of honesty and generosity.

"Shoot not beyond the mark," the proverb goes.

Was't not enough that he had done us
wrong,

But we must also throw him money too,

To live till he devised some new mischief?

GETA. Very right!

DEM.   Knavery's now its
own reward.

GETA. Very true!

DEM.   How like fools have
we behav'd!

GETA. So as he keeps his word, and takes
the girl,

'Tis well enough.

DEM.   Is that a doubt at present?

GETA. A man, you know, may change
his mind.

DEM.   How! change?

GETA. That I can't tell: but, *if perhaps*,
I say.

DEM. I'll now perform my promise to
my brother,

And bring his wife to talk to the young
woman.

You, Geta, go before, and let her know

Nausistrata will come and speak with her.
(*Exit*.)

GETA. The money's got for Phædria: all
is hush'd:

And Phanium is not to depart as yet.

What more then? where will all this end
at last?—

Alas, you're sticking in the same mire
still:

You've only chang'd hands, Geta. The
disaster,

That hung but now directly over you,

Delay perhaps will bring more heavy on
you.

You're quite beset, unless you look about.

Now then I'll home, to lesson Phanium;

That she mayn't stand in fear of
Phormio,

Nor dread this conference with Nausistrata.   (*Exit*.)

Re-enter DEMIPHO *with* NAUSISTRATA

DEM. Come then, Nausistrata, afford us now
A little of your usual art, and try
To put this woman in good humour with us:
That what is done she may do willingly.

NAU. I will.

DEM. And now assist us with your counsel,
As with your cash a little while ago.

NAU. With all my heart: and I am only sorry
That 'tis my husband's fault I can't do more.

DEM. How so?

NAU. Because he takes such little care
Of the estate my father nurs'd so well:
For from these very farms he never fail'd
To draw Two Talents by the year. But ah!
What difference between man and man!

DEM. Two Talents?

NAU. Ay—in worse times than these— and yet Two Talents.

DEM. Huy!

NAU. What, are you surpriz'd?

DEM. Prodigiously.

NAU. Would I had been a man—I'd shew——

DEM. No doubt.

NAU. ——By what means——

DEM. Nay, but spare yourself a little
For the encounter with the girl: lest she,
Flippant and young, may weary you too much.

NAU. Well, I'll obey your orders: but I see
My husband coming forth.

Enter CHREMES

CHR. Ha! Demipho!
Has Phormio had the money yet?

DEM. I paid him
Immediately.

CHR. I'm sorry for't.—(*Aside*)
My wife!

I'd almost said too much.

DEM. Why sorry, Chremes?

CHR. Nothing.—No matter.

DEM. Well, but hark ye, Chremes.
Have you been talking with the girl, and told her
Wherefore we bring your wife?

CHR. I've settled it.

DEM. Well, and what says she?

CHR. 'Tis impossible.
To send her hence.

DEM. And why impossible?

CHR. Because they're both so fond of one another.

DEM. What's that to Us?

CHR. A great deal. And besides,
I have discover'd she's related to us.

DEM. Have you your wits?

CHR. 'Tis so. I'm very serious.
Nay, recollect a little!

DEM. Are you mad?

NAU. Good now, beware of wronging a relation!

DEM. She's no relation to us.

CHR. Don't deny it.
Her father had assum'd another name,
And that deceiv'd you.

DEM. What! not know her father?

CHR. Perfectly.

DEM. Why did she misname him then?

CHR. Won't you be rul'd, nor under-stand me then?

DEM. What can I understand from nothing?

CHR. Still?

NAU. I can't imagine what this means.

DEM. Nor I.

CHR. Would you know all?—Why then, so help me heaven,
She has no nearer kindred in the world,
Than you and I.

DEM. Oh, all ye pow'rs of heaven!
Let us go to her then immediately:
I would fain know, or not know, all at once. (*Going.*)

CHR. (*stopping him*). Ah!

DEM. What's the matter?

CHR. Can't you trust me then?

DEM. Must I believe it? take it upon trust?
Well, be it so!—But what is to be done
With our friend's daughter?
CHR.   Nothing.
DEM.   Drop her?
CHR.   Ay.
DEM. And keep this?
CHR.   Ay.
DEM.   Why then, Nausistrata,
You may return. We need not trouble you.
NAU. Indeed, I think, 'tis better on all sides,
That you should keep her here, than send her hence.
For she appear'd to me, when first I saw her,
Much of a gentlewoman.   (*Exit.*)
DEM.   What means this?
CHR. Is the door shut?
DEM.   It is.
CHR.   O Jupiter!
The Gods take care of us. I've found my daughter
Married to your son.
DEM.   Ha! How could it be?
CHR. It is not safe to tell you here.
DEM.   Step in then.
CHR. But hark ye, Demipho!—I would not have
Even our very sons inform'd of this.
                              (*Exeunt.*)

Enter ANTIPHO

ANT. I'm glad, however my affairs proceed,
That Phædria's have succeeded to his mind.
How wise, to foster such desires alone,
As, altho' cross'd, are easily supplied!
Money, once found, sets Phædria at his ease;
But my distress admits no remedy.
For, if the secret's kept, I live in fear;
And if reveal'd, I am expos'd to shame.
Nor would I now return, but in the hope

Of still possessing her,—But where is Geta?
That I may learn of him, the fittest time
To meet my father.

Enter PHORMIO

PHOR. (*to himself*). I've receiv'd the money;
Paid the procurer; carried off the wench;
Who's free, and now in Phædria's possession.
One thing alone remains to be dispatch'd:
To get a respite from th' old gentlemen
To tipple some few days, which I must spend
In mirth and jollity.
ANT.   But yonder's Phormio.—
What now?
PHOR.   Of what?
ANT.   What's Phædria about?
How does he mean to take his fill of love?
PHOR. By acting your part in his turn.
ANT.   What part?
PHOR. Flying his father's presence.—
And he begs
That you'd act his, and make excuses for him:
For he intends a drinking-bout with Me.
I shall pretend to the old gentlemen
That I am going to the fair at Sunium,
To buy the servant-maid, that Geta mention'd:
Lest, finding I am absent, they suspect
That I am squandering the sum they paid me.
But your door opens.
ANT.   Who comes here?
PHOR.   'Tis Geta.

Enter GETA

GETA. O Fortune, O best Fortune, what high blessings,
What sudden, great, and unexpected joys
Hast thou show'r'd down on Antipho to-day!
ANT. (*aside*). What can this be, he's so rejoic'd about!

GETA. And from what fears deliver'd Us, his friends?
But wherefore do I loiter thus? and why
Do I not throw my cloak upon my shoulder,
And haste to find him out, that he may know
All that has happen'd?
ANT. (*to* PHORMIO). Do you comprehend
What he is talking of?
PHOR. Do you?
ANT. Not I.
PHOR. I'm just as wise as you.
GETA. I'll hurry hence
To the procurer's.—I shall find him there. (*Going.*)
ANT. Ho, Geta!
GETA. Look ye there!—Is't new or strange,
To be recall'd when one's in haste? (*Going.*)
ANT. Here, Geta!
GETA. Again? Bawl on; I'll ne'er stop. (*Going.*)
ANT. Stay, I say!
GETA. Go, and be drubb'd!
ANT. *You* shall, I promise you, Unless you stop, you Rascal!
GETA (*stopping*). Hold, hold, Geta!
Some intimate acquaintance this, be sure,
Being so free with you.—But is it he,
That I am looking for, or not?—'Tis He.
PHOR. Go up immediately.
ANT. What means all this?
GETA. O happy man! the happiest man on earth!
So very happy, that, beyond all doubt,
You are the Gods' chief fav'rite, Antipho.
ANT. Would I were! but your reason.
GETA. Isn't enough,
To plunge you over head and ears in joy?
ANT. You torture me.
PHOR. No promises! but tell us.
What are your news?
GETA. Oh, Phormio! are you here?
PHOR. I am: but why d'ye trifle?
GETA. Mind me then!
No sooner had we paid you at the Forum,

But we return'd directly home again.
Arriv'd, my master sends me to your wife.
ANT. For what?
GETA. No matter now, good Antipho.
I was just entering the women's lodging,
When up runs little Mida; catches me
Hold by the cloak behind, and pulls me back.
I turn about, and ask why he detains me.
He told me, "Nobody must see his mistress:
For Sophrona," says he, "has just now brought
Demipho's brother, Chremes, here; and He
Is talking with the women now within."
When I heard this, I stole immediately
On tip-toe towards the door; came close; stood hush;
Drew in my breath; applied my ear; and thus,
Deep in attention, catch'd their whole discourse.
ANT. Excellent, Geta!
GETA. Here I overheard
The pleasantest adventure!—On my life,
I scarce refrain'd from crying out of joy.
ANT. What?
GETA. What d'ye think?
ANT. I can't tell.
GETA. Oh! it was
Most wonderful!—most exquisite!—your uncle
Is found to be the father of your wife.
ANT. How! what?
GETA. He had a sly intrigue, it seems,
With Phanium's mother formerly at Lemnos.
PHOR. Nonsense! as if she did not know her father!
GETA. Nay, there's some reason for it, Phormio,
You may be sure.—But was it possible
For me, who stood without, to comprehend
Each minute circumstance that past within?

ANT. I have heard something of this story too.

GETA. Then, Sir, to settle your belief the more,

At last comes forth your uncle; and soon after

Returns again, and carries in your father.

Then they both said, they gave their full consent,

That you should keep your Phanium.— In a word,

I'm sent to find you out, and bring you to them.

ANT. Away with me then instantly! D'ye linger?

GETA. Not I. Away!

ANT.   My Phormio, fare you well!

PHOR. Fare you well, Antipho.
          (*Exeunt* ANTIPHO *and* GETA.)
          Well done, 'fore heaven!

I'm overjoy'd to see so much good fortune

Fallen thus unexpectedly upon them:

I've now an admirable opportunity

To bubble the old gentlemen, and ease

Phædria of all his cares about the money;

So that he need not be oblig'd to friends.

For this same money, tho' it will be given,

Will yet come from them much against the grain;

But I have found a way to force them to't.

Now then I must assume a grander air,

And put another face upon this business.

I'll hence awhile into the next bye-alley,

And pop upon them as they're coming forth.

As for the trip I talk'd of to the Fair,

I sha'n't pretend to take that journey now.   (*Exit.*)

ACT V

Enter DEMIPHO *and* CHREMES

DEM. Well may we thank the gracious Gods, good brother,

That all things have succeeded to our wish.

But now let's find out Phormio with all speed,

Before he throws away our Thirty Minæ.

Enter PHORMIO

PHOR. (*to himself*). I'll go and see if Demipho's at home,

That I may——

DEM. We were coming to you, Phormio.

PHOR. On the old score, I warrant.

DEM.   Ay.

PHOR.   I thought so.

Why should you go to Me?—Ridiculous!

Were you afraid I'd break my contract with you?

No, no! how great soe'er my poverty,

I've always shewn myself a man of honour.

CHR. (*aside to* DEMIPHO). Has not she, as I said, a liberal air?

DEM. She has.

PHOR.   And therefore I was coming, Demipho,

To let you know, I'm ready to receive

My wife whene'er you please. For I postpon'd

All other business, as indeed I ought,

Soon as I found ye were so bent on this.

DEM. Ay, but my brother has dissuaded me

From going any further in this business.

"For how will people talk of it?" says he:

"At first you might have done it handsomely;

But then you'd not consent to it; and now

After cohabitation with your son,

To think of a divorce is infamous."

In short, he urg'd almost the very things,

That you so lately charg'd me with yourself.

PHOR. You trifle with me, Gentlemen.

DEM.   How so?

PHOR. How so?—Because I cannot marry t'other,

With whom I told you I was first in treaty.

For with what face can I return to Her,
Whom I have held in such contempt?
CHR.   Tell him,
Antipho does not care to part with her.
DEM.   And my son too don't care to part
    with her:
Step to the Forum then, and give an
    order
For the repayment of our money, Phor-
    mio.
PHOR.   What! when I've paid it to my
    creditors?
DEM.   What's to be done then?
PHOR.   Give me but the wife,
To whom you have betroth'd me, and I'll
    wed her.
But if you'd rather she should stay with
    you,
The portion stays with me, good Demi-
    pho.
For 'tis not just I should be bubbled by
    you;
When, to retrieve your honour, I've re-
    fus'd
Another woman with an equal fortune.
DEM.   A plague upon your idle vapour-
    ing,
You vagabond!—D'ye fancy we don't
    know you?
You, and your fine proceedings?
PHOR.   You provoke me.
DEM.   Why, would you marry her, if
    proffer'd?
PHOR.   Try me.
DEM.   What! that my son may keep
    her privately
At your house?—That was your inten-
    tion.
PHOR.   Ha!
What say you, Sir?
DEM.   Give me my money, sirrah!
PHOR.   Give *me* my *wife*, I say.
DEM.   To justice with him!
PHOR.   To justice? Now, by heaven,
    Gentlemen,
If you continue to be troublesome——
DEM.   What will you do?
PHOR.   What will I do? Perhaps,
You think that I can only patronize

Girls without portion; but be sure of
    this,
I've some with portions too.
CHR.   What's that to Us?
PHOR.   Nothing.—I know a lady here,
    whose husband——
CHR.   Ha!
DEM.   What's the matter?
PHOR.   ——had another wife
At Lemnos.
CHR. (*aside*). I'm a dead man.
PHOR.   ——by which other
He had a daughter; whom he now brings
    up
In private.
CHR. (*aside*). Dead and buried!
PHOR.   This I'll tell her. (*Going.*)
CHR.   Don't I beseech you!
PHOR.   Oh! are you the man?
DEM.   Death! how insulting!
CHR.   We discharge you.
PHOR.   Nonsense!
CHR.   What would you more? The
    money you have got,
We will forgive you.
PHOR.   Well; I hear you now.
But what a plague d'ye mean by fooling
    thus,
Acting and talking like mere children
    with me?
"I won't; I will:—I will; I won't
    again:"—
Give, take; say, unsay: do, and then
    undo?
CHR.   Which way could he have learnt
    this?
DEM.   I don't know.
But I am sure I never mention'd it.
CHR.   Good now! amazing!
PHOR. (*aside*).   I have ruffled them.
DEM.   What! shall he carry off so large
    a sum,
And laugh at us so openly?—By heaven,
I'd rather die.—Be of good courage,
    brother!
Pluck up the spirit of a man! You see
This slip of yours is got abroad; nor
    can you

Keep it a secret from your wife. Now therefore
'Tis more conducive to your peace, good Chremes,
That we should fairly tell it her ourselves,
Than she should hear the story from another.
And then we shall be quite at liberty
To take our own revenge upon this rascal.

PHOR. (*aside*). Ha!—If I don't take care, I'm ruin'd still,
They're growing desperate, and making tow'rds me,
With a determin'd gladiatorial air.

CHR. I fear she'll ne'er forgive me.

DEM. Courage, Chremes!
I'll reconcile her to't; especially
The mother being dead and gone.

PHOR. Is this
Your dealing, Gentlemen? You come upon me
Extremely cunningly.—But, Demipho,
You have but ill consulted for your brother,
To urge me to extremities.—And you, Sir,
When you have play'd the whore-master abroad;
Having no reverence for your lady here,
A woman of condition; wronging her
After the grossest manner; come you now
To wash away your crimes with mean submission?
No.—I will kindle such a flame in her,
As, tho' you melt to tears, you sha'n't extinguish.

DEM. A plague upon him! was there ever man
So very impudent?—A knave! he ought
To be transported at the publick charge
Into some desert.

CHR. I am so confounded,
I know not what to do with him.

DEM. I know.
Bring him before a judge!

PHOR. Before a judge?
A *Lady*-judge; in here, Sirs, if you please.

DEM. Run you, and hold him, while I call the servants.

CHR. I cannot by myself: come up, and help me.

PHOR. I have an action of assault against you.

CHR. Bring it!

PHOR. Another against you too, Chremes!

DEM. Drag him away! (*Laying hold of him.*)

PHOR. (*struggling*). Is that your way with me!
Then I must raise my voice.—Nausistrata!
Come hither.

CHR. Stop his mouth!

DEM. (*struggling*). A sturdy rogue!
How strong he is!

PHOR. Nausistrata, I say.
Nausistrata!

CHR. Peace, sirrah!

PHOR. Peace, indeed!

DEM. Unless he follows, strike him in the stomach!

PHOR. Ay, or put out an eye!—But here comes one
Will give me full revenge upon you both.

Enter NAUSISTRATA

NAU. Who calls for me?

CHR. Confusion!

NAU. Pray, my dear,
What's this disturbance?

PHOR. Dumb, old Truepenny!

NAU. Who is this man?—Why don't you answer me?

PHOR. He answer you! He's hardly in his senses.

CHR. Never believe him!

PHOR. Do but go, and touch him;
He's in a shivering fit, I'll lay my life.

CHR. Nay—

NAU. But what means he then?

PHOR. I'll tell you, Madam;
Do but attend!

CHR. *Will* you believe him then?

NAU. What is there to believe, when he says nothing?

PHOR. Poor man! his fear deprives him of his wits.

NAU. I'm sure, you're not so much afraid for nothing.

CHR. What! I afraid?

PHOR. Oh, not at all!—And since You're not afraid, and what I say means nothing,
Tell it yourself.

DEM. At your desire, you rascal?

PHOR. Oh, you've done rarely for your brother, Sir!

NAU. What! won't you tell me, husband?

CHR. But——

NAU. But what?

CHR. There's no occasion for it.

PHOR. Not for You:
But for the Lady there is much occasion.
In Lemnos——

CHR. Ha! what say you?

DEM. Hold your peace!

PHOR. Without your knowledge——

CHR. Oh dear!

PHOR. He has had
Another wife.

NAU. My husband? Heaven forbid!

PHOR. 'Tis even so.

NAU. Ah me! I am undone.

PHOR. And had a daughter by her there; while You
Were left to sleep in ignorance alone.

NAU. Oh heavens!—Baseness!—Treachery!

PHOR. 'Tis fact.

NAU. Was ever anvthing more infamous?
When they're with Us, their wives forsooth, they're old.
Demipho, I appeal to You: for Him
I cannot bear to speak to.—And were these
His frequent journies, and long stay at Lemnos?
Was this the cheapness that reduc'd our rents?

DEM. That he has been to blame, Nausistrata,
I don't deny; but not beyond all pardon.

PHOR. You're talking to the dead.

DEM. It was not done
Out of aversion, or contempt to You.
In liquor, almost fifteen years ago,
He met this woman, whence he had this daughter;
Nor e'er had commerce with her from that hour.
She's dead: your only grievance is remov'd.
Wherefore I beg you'd shew your wonted goodness,
And bear it patiently.

NAU. How! bear it patiently?
Alas, I wish his vices might end here.
But have I the least hope? Can I suppose
That years will cure these rank offences in him?
E'en at that time he was already old,
If age could make him modest.—Are my years,
And beauty, think ye, like to please him more
At present, Demipho, than formerly?
In short, what ground, what reason to expect
That he should not commit the same hereafter?

PHOR. Whoever would attend the funeral
Of Chremes, now's the time!—See! That's my way.
Come on then! Provoke Phormio now, who dares!
Like Chremes, he shall fall a victim to me.
Let him get into favour, when he will!
I've had revenge sufficient. She has something
To ring into his ears his whole life long.

NAU. Have I deserv'd this?—Need I, Demipho,
Number up each particular; and say
How good a wife I've been?

DEM. I know it all.

NAU. Am I then justly treated?

DEM. Not at all.
But since reproaches can't undo what's done,
Forgive him! He begs pardon; owns his fault;
And promises to amend.—What would you more?
PHOR. But hold; before she ratifies his pardon,
I must secure myself and Phædria.—
Nausistrata, a word!—Before you give
Your answer rashly, hear me!
NAU. What's your pleasure?
PHOR. I trick'd your husband there of Thirty Minæ,
Which I have given your son; and he has paid them
To a procurer for a mistress.
CHR. How!
What say you?
NAU. Is it such a heinous crime,
For your young son, d'ye think, to have *one* mistress,
While *you* have *two* wives?—Are you not asham'd?
Have you the face to chide him? Answer me!
DEM. He shall do ev'rything you please.
NAU. Nay, nay,
To tell you plainly my whole mind at once,

I'll not forgive, nor promise anything,
Nor give an answer, till I see my son.
PHOR. Wisely resolv'd, Nausistrata.
NAU. Is That
Sufficient satisfaction for you?
PHOR. Quite.
I rest contented, well-pleas'd, past my hopes.
NAU. What is your name, pray?
PHOR. My name? Phormio:
A faithful friend to all your family,
Especially to Phædria.
NAU. Trust me, Phormio,
I'll do you all the service in my power.
PHOR. I'm much oblig'd to you.
NAU. You're worthy on't.
PHOR. Will you then even now, Nausistrata,
Grant me one favour, that will pleasure me,
And grieve your husband's sight?
NAU. With all my soul.
PHOR. Ask me to supper!
NAU. I invite you.
DEM. In then!
NAU. We will: But where is Phædria, our judge?
PHOR. He shall be with you.— (*To audience*) Farewell; clap your hands!
—GEORGE COLMAN.

II. OPPOSITION TO EASTERN INFLUENCE

The Roman never hesitated to adapt to his own needs any element whatever of a foreign civilization that appealed to him. The trait is one factor in Rome's success. In early days more or less unconsciously Etruscan influences had their effect on government, religion, the arts. Greek influence also began early. The Roman alphabet came from Cumæ, a Greek city not far from Naples. And in the fifth century it may be that Rome's first codification of her laws was a result of Greek practice. Rome used what Rome thought useful, for Rome was a city of pragmatists.

That is not to say that the Romans were always, like St. Paul's Athenians, in search of "some new thing"; far from it. They were conservatives. To the introduction of Greek literature in Latin dress they had made no objection, seeing no harm in it. The gradual growth of the identification of Roman with Greek deities had also gone on unopposed, perhaps because not realized. But after the war with Hannibal, in the second century B.C., immediate contact with Greece led to the invasion of Italy by Greek cults, Greek philosophy, and Greek education. Many of the leading Romans began to benefit by Greek culture; but many more began to see forces at work to undermine the Roman type, and opposition to foreign ways began. The demoralizing cult of Bacchus was brought to the notice of the Senate, and, because serious social and political effects were feared, it was absolutely forbidden by a decree in 186 B.C. This decree set a precedent. Less than fifty years later Chaldæan astrologers were banished from Italy. At times officials or the Senate would pay their respects to Greek philosophers and teachers, and suppress them. But there was no systematic policy of repression. Little by little the Greek, and other Eastern elements, won their way, so that by the time of Cicero in the middle of the first century B.C., and thereafter, opposition practically ceased. Only for political reasons, or because the peace was disturbed, were any foreign elements suppressed. Eastern civilizations for good and ill developed their influences unopposed.

THE RECEPTION OF MAGNA MATER

LIVY

[From Book XXXIX]

The cult of Magna Mater, or Cybele, was oriental in origin. Though unsuited to the practical unimaginative Roman of the time, it found ready acceptance under stress of war. (For Livy, see below p. 418. Livy is used for this period because the works of contemporary authors are no longer extant.)

The state was at this time suddenly occupied with a question of a religious nature, in consequence of the discovery of a prediction in the Sibylline books, which had been inspected on account of there having been so many showers of stones this year. It ran thus: "Whensoever a foreign enemy should bring war into the land of Italy, he may be driven out of Italy and conquered, if the Idæan

Mother should be brought from Pessinus to Rome." This prophecy, discovered by the decemviri, produced the greater impression upon the senate, because ambassadors also, who had carried a present to Delphi, had brought word back, that they had both obtained a favourable appearance in sacrificing to the Pythian Apollo, and that a response was delivered from the oracle, to the effect, that a much greater victory than that from the spoils of which they now brought presents, awaited the Roman people. They considered the presentiment which existed in the mind of Publius Scipio, with regard to the termination of the war, when he claimed Africa as his province, as corroborating the same anticipation. In order, therefore, that they might the more speedily put themselves in possession of victory, which was portended to them by the fates, omens, and oracles, they began to think what method could be adopted for conveying the goddess to Rome.

As yet the Roman people had none of the states of Asia in alliance with them. Recollecting, however, that formerly Æsculapius, on account of a sickness among the people, was fetched from Greece, which was not then united with them by any treaty; recollecting, also, that a friendship had already commenced between them and king Attalus, on account of the war which they waged in common against Philip, and that he would do whatever he could to oblige the Roman people, they resolved to send, as ambassadors to him, Marcus Valerius Lævinus, who had been twice consul, and had carried on operations in Greece; Marcus Cæcilius Metellus, who had been prætor; Servius Sulpicius Galba, who had been ædile; and two who had been quæstors, Caius Tremellius Flaccus and Marcus Valerius Falto. To these five quinqueremes were assigned, in order that, in a manner suitable to the dignity of the Roman people, they might visit those lands where it was important to gain respect for the Roman name. The ambassadors, on their way to Asia, having landed at Delphi, immediately approached the oracle, inquiring what hopes the deity held out to themselves and the Roman people, of accomplishing the business for which they had been sent from home. It is said that the answer given was, "that they would obtain what they were seeking by means of king Attalus. When they had conveyed the goddess to Rome, they must take care that the best man at Rome should receive her to his hospitality." They came to Pergamus to the king, who received the ambassadors graciously, and conducted them to Pessinus in Phrygia, and putting into their hands a sacred stone, which the inhabitants said was the mother of the gods, bid them convey it to Rome. Marcus Valerius Falto, who was sent in advance, brought word that the goddess was on her way, and that the most virtuous man in the state must be sought out, who might in due form receive and entertain her. . . .

In addition to these cares, they had to deliberate about the reception of the Idæan Mother; for besides that Marcus Valerius, one of the ambassadors who had come before the rest, had brought word that she would be in Italy forthwith, a recent account had arrived that she was at Tarracina. The senate was occupied with the determination of a matter of no small importance, namely, who was the most virtuous man in the state. Every one doubtless would wish for himself the victory in this contest, rather than any office of command, or any honours, which could be conferred by the suffrages of the senate or the people. Publius Scipio, son of Cneius who had fallen in Spain, a youth not yet of the age to be quæstor, they adjudged to be the best of the good men in the whole state. Though I would willingly record it for the information of posterity, had the writers who lived in the times nearest

to those events mentioned by what virtues of his they were induced to come to this determination, yet I will not obtrude my own opinion, formed upon conjecture, relative to a matter buried in the obscurity of antiquity. Publius Cornelius was ordered to go to Ostia, attended by all the matrons, to meet the goddess; to receive her from the ship himself, and, when landed, place her in the hands of the matrons to convey her away. After the ship arrived at the mouth of the Tiber, Scipio, according to the directions given him, sailed out into the open sea, and, receiving the goddess from the priests, conveyed her to the land. The chief matrons in the state received her, among whom the name of Claudia Quinta alone is worthy of remark. Her fame, which, as it is recorded, was before that time dubious, became, in consequence of her having assisted in so solemn a business, illustrious for chastity among posterity. The matrons, passing her from one to another in orderly succession, conveyed the goddess into the temple of Victory, in the Palatium, on the day before the ides of April, which was made a festival, while the whole city poured out to meet her; and, placing censers before their doors, on the way by which she was conveyed in procession, kindled frankincense, and prayed that she would enter the city of Rome willingly and propitiously. The people in crowds carried presents to the goddess in the Palatium; a lectisternium was celebrated, with games called the Megalesian.

—CYRUS EDMONDS.

THE BACCHANALIAN REVELS

LIVY

[From Book XXXIX]

The establishment of the cult of Bacchus is a second example of the Roman's imitativeness in the matter of religious practices. The mad orgies that resulted opened his eyes to his mistake, and set on foot the movement to rid himself of objectionable foreign gods.

The making inquisition concerning clandestine meetings was decreed to both the consuls. A Greek of mean condition came, first, into Etruria, not with one of the many trades which his nation, of all others the most skilful in the cultivation of the mind and body, has introduced among us, but a low operator in sacrifices, and a soothsayer; nor was he one who, by open religious rites, and by publicly professing his calling and teaching, imbued the minds of his followers with terror, but a priest of secret and nocturnal rites. These mysterious rites were, at first, imparted to a few, but afterwards communicated to great numbers, both men and women. To their religious performances were added the pleasures of wine and feasting to allure a greater number of proselytes. When wine, lascivious discourse, night, and the intercourse of the sexes had extinguished every sentiment of modesty, then debaucheries of every kind began to be practised, as every person found at hand that sort of enjoyment to which he was disposed by the passion predominant in his nature. Nor were they confined to one species of vice—the promiscuous intercourse of free-born men and women; but from this store-house of villany proceeded false witnesses, counterfeit seals, false evidences, and pretended discoveries. From the same place, too, proceeded poison and secret murders, so that in some cases, even the bodies could not be found for burial. Many of their audacious deeds were brought about by treachery, but most of them by force; it served to conceal the violence, that, on account of the loud shouting, and the noise of drums and cymbals, none of the cries uttered by the persons suffering violation or murder could be heard abroad.

The infection of this mischief, like that from the contagion of disease, spread from Etruria to Rome; where, the size of the city affording greater room for such evils, and more means of concealment, cloaked it at first; but information of it was at length brought to the consul, Postumius, principally in the following manner. Publius Æbutius, whose father had held equestrian rank in the army, was left an orphan, and his guardians dying, he was educated under the eye of his mother Duronia, and his stepfather Titus Sempronius Rutilus. Duronia was entirely devoted to her husband; and Sempronius, having managed the guardianship in such a manner that he could not give an account of the property, wished that his ward should be either made away with, or bound to compliance with his will by some strong tie. The Baccchanalian rites were the only way to effect the ruin of the youth. His mother told him, that, "during his sickness, she had made a vow for him, that if he should recover, she would initiate him among the Bacchanalians; that being, through the kindness of the gods, bound by this vow, she wished now to fulfil it; that it was necessary he should preserve chastity for ten days, and on the tenth, after he should have supped and washed himself, she would conduct him into the place of worship." There was a freedwoman called Hispala Fecenia, a noted courtesan, but deserving of a better lot than the mode of life to which she had been accustomed when very young, and a slave, and by which she had maintained herself since her manumission. As they lived in the same neighbourhood, an intimacy subsisted between her and Æbutius, which was far from being injurious either to the young man's character or property; for he had been loved and wooed by her unsolicited; and as his friends supplied his wants illiberally, he was supported by the generosity of this woman; nay, to such a length did she go under the influence of her affection, that, on the death of her patron, because she was under the protection of no one, having petitioned the tribunes and prætors for a guardian, when she was making her will, she constituted Æbutius her sole heir.

As such pledges of mutual love subsisted, and as neither kept any thing secret from the other, the young man, jokingly, bid her not be surprised if he separated himself from her for a few nights; as, "on account of a religious duty, to discharge a vow made for his health, he intended to be initiated among the Bacchanalians." On hearing this, the woman, greatly alarmed, cried out, "May the gods will more favourably!" affirming that "it would be better, both for him and her, to lose their lives than that he should do such a thing:" she then imprecated curses, vengeance, and destruction, on the head of those who advised him to such a step. The young man, surprised both at her expressions and at the violence of her alarm, bid her refrain from curses, for "it was his mother who ordered him to do so, with the approbation of his stepfather." "Then," said she, "your stepfather (for perhaps it is not allowable to censure your mother) is in haste to destroy, by that act, your chastity, your character, your hopes, and your life." To him, now surprised by such language, and inquiring what was the matter, she said (after imploring the favour and pardon of the gods and goddesses, if, compelled by her regard for him, she disclosed what ought not to be revealed), that "when in service, she had gone into that place of worship, as an attendant on her mistress; but that, since she had obtained her liberty, she had never once gone near it: that she knew it to be the receptacle of all kinds of debaucheries; that it was well known that, for two years past, no one older than twenty had been initiated there. When any person was introduced, he was delivered as a victim to the priests, who led him away to a place resounding with shouts, the sound of music, and the beating of cymbals and drums, lest his cries, while suffering violation, should be heard abroad." She then entreated and besought him to put an end to that matter in some way or other; and not to plunge himself into a situation, where he must first suffer, and afterwards commit, every thing that was abominable. Nor did she quit him until the young man gave her his promise to keep himself clear of those rites.

When he came home, and his mother made mention of such things pertaining to the ceremony as were to be performed on that day, and on the several following days, he told her that he would not perform any of them, nor did he intend to be initiated. His stepfather was present at this discourse. Immediately the woman observed, that "he could not deprive himself of the company of Hispala for ten nights; that he was so fascinated by the caresses and baneful influence of that serpent, that he retained no respect for his mother or stepfather, or even the gods themselves." His mother on one side and his stepfather on the other loading him with reproaches, drove him out of the house, assisted by four slaves. The youth on this repaired to his aunt Æbutia, told her the reason of his being turned out by his mother, and the next day, by her advice, gave information of the affair to the consul Postumius, without any witnesses of the interview. The consul dismissed him, with an order to come again on the third day following. In the mean time, he inquired of his mother-in-law Sulpicia, a woman of respectable character, "whether she knew an old matron called Æbutia, who lived on the Aventine hill?" When she had answered that "she knew her well, and that Æbutia was a woman of virtue, and of the ancient purity of morals"; he said that he required a conference with her, and that a message should be sent for her to come. Æbutia, on receiving the message, came to Sulpicia's house, and the consul, soon after, coming in, as if by accident, introduced a conversation about Æbutius, her brother's son. The tears of the woman burst forth, and she began to lament the unhappy lot of the youth: "who, after being robbed of his property by persons whom it least of all became, was then residing with her, being driven out of doors by his mother, because, being a good youth (may the gods be propitious to him), he refused to be initiated in ceremonies devoted to lewdness, as report goes."

The consul, thinking that he had made sufficient inquiries concerning Æbutius, and that his testimony was unquestionable, having dismissed Æbutia, requested his mother-in-law to send again to the Aventine, and bring from that quarter Hispala, a freedwoman, not unknown in that neighbourhood; for there were some queries which he wished to make of her. Hispala being alarmed because she was sent for by a woman of such high rank and respectable character, and being ignorant of the cause, after she saw the lictors in the porch, the multitude attending on the consul and the consul himself, was very near fainting. The consul led her into a retired part of the house, and, in the presence of his mother-in-law, told her, that "she need not be uneasy, if she could resolve to speak the truth. She might receive a promise of protection either from Sulpicia, a matron of such dignified character, or from himself. That she ought to tell him, what was accustomed to be done at the Bacchanalia, in the nocturnal orgies in the grove of Stimula." When the woman heard this, such terror and trembling of all her limbs seized her, that for a long time she was unable to speak; but recovering, at length she said, that "when she was very young, and a slave, she had been initiated, together with her mistress; but for several years past, since she had obtained her liberty, she knew nothing of what was

done there." The consul commended her so far, as not having denied that she was initiated, but charged her to explain all the rest with the same sincerity; and told her, affirming that she knew nothing further, that "there would not be the same tenderness or pardon extended to her, if she should be convicted by another person, and one who had made a voluntary confession; that there was such a person, who had heard the whole from her, and had given him a full account of it." The woman, now thinking without a doubt that it must certainly be Æbutius who had discovered the secret, threw herself at Sulpicia's feet, and at first began to beseech her, "not to let the private conversation of a freedwoman with her lover be turned not only into a serious business, but even capital charge;" declaring that "she had spoken of such things merely to frighten him, and not because she knew anything of the kind." On this Postumius, growing angry, said, "she seemed to imagine that then too she was wrangling with her gallant Æbutius, and not that she was speaking in the house of a most respectable matron, and to a consul." Sulpicia raised her, terrified, from the ground, and while she encouraged her to speak out, at the same time pacified her son-in-law's anger. At length she took courage, and, having censured severely the perfidy of Æbutius, because he had made such a return for the extraordinary kindness shown to him in that very instance, she declared that "she stood in great dread of the gods, whose secret mysteries she was to divulge; and in much greater dread of the men implicated, who would tear her asunder with their hands if she became an informer. Therefore she entreated the favour of Sulpicia, and likewise of the consul, that they would send her away to some place out of Italy, where she might pass the remainder of her life in safety." The consul desired her to be of good spirits, and said that it should be his care that she might live securely in Rome.

Hispala then gave a full account of the origin of the mysteries. "At first," she said, "those rites were performed by women. No man used to be admitted. They had three stated days in the year on which persons were initiated among the Bacchanalians, in the day-time. The matrons used to be appointed priestesses, in rotation. Paculla Minia, a Campanian, when priestess, made an alteration in every particular, as if by the direction of the gods. For she first introduced men, who were her own sons, Minucius and Herennius, both surnamed Cerrinius; changed the time of celebration, from day to night; and, instead of three days in the year, appointed five days of initiation, in each month. From the time that the rites were thus made common, and men were intermixed with women, and the licentious freedom of the night was added, there was nothing wicked, nothing flagitious, that had not been practised among them. . . . The men, as if bereft of reason, uttered predictions, with frantic contortions of their bodies; the women, in the habit of Bacchantes, with their hair dishevelled, and carrying blazing torches, ran down to the Tiber; where, dipping their torches in the water, they drew them up again with the flame unextinguished, being composed of native sulphur and charcoal. They said that those men were carried off by the gods, whom the machines laid hold of and dragged from their view into secret caves. These were such as refused to take the oath of the society, or to associate in their crimes, or to submit to defilement. Their number was exceedingly great now, almost a second state in themselves, and among them were many men and women of noble families. During the last two years it had been a rule that no person above the age of twenty should be initiated; for they sought for people of such age as made them more liable to suffer decep-

tion and personal abuse." When she had completed her information, she again fell at the consul's knees, and repeated the same entreaties, that he might send her out of the country. The consul requests his mother-in-law to clear some part of the house, into which Hispala might remove; accordingly, an apartment was assigned her in the upper part of it, of which the stairs, opening into the street, were stopped up, and the entrance made from the inner court. Thither all Fecenia's effects were immediately removed, and her domestics sent for. Æbutius, also, was ordered to remove to the house of one of the consul's clients.

When both the informers were by these means in his power, Postumius represented the affair to the senate, laying before them the whole circumstance, in due order; the information given to him at first, and the discoveries gained by his inquiries afterwards. Great consternation seized on the senators; not only on the public account, lest such conspiracies and nightly meetings might be productive of secret treachery and mischief, but, likewise, on account of their own particular families, lest some of their relations might be involved in this infamous affair. The senate voted, however, that thanks should be given to the consul because he had investigated the matter with singular diligence, and without exciting any alarm. They then commit to the consuls the holding an inquiry, out of the common course, concerning the Bacchanals and their nocturnal orgies. They order them to take care that the informers, Æbutius and Fecenia, might suffer no injury on that account; and to invite other informers in the matter, by offering rewards. They ordered that the officials in those rites, whether men or women, should be sought for, not only at Rome, but also throughout all the market towns and places of assembly, and be delivered over to the power of the consuls; and also that proclamation should be made in the city of Rome, and published through all Italy, that "no persons initiated in the Bacchanalian rites should presume to come together or assemble on account of those rites, or to perform any such kind of worship;" and above all, that search should be made for those who had assembled or conspired for personal abuse, or for any other flagitious practices. The senate passed these decrees. The consuls directed the curule ædiles to make strict inquiry after all the priests of those mysteries, and to keep such as they could apprehend, in custody until their trial; they at the same time charged the plebeian ædiles to take care that no religious ceremonies should be performed in private. To the capital triumvirs the task was assigned to post watches in proper places of the city, and to use vigilance in preventing any meetings by night. In order likewise to guard against fires, five assistants were joined to the triumvirs, so that each might have the charge of the buildings in his own separate district, on this side the Tiber.

After despatching these officers to their several employments, the consuls mounted the rostrum; and, having summoned an assembly of the people, one of the consuls, when he had finished the solemn form of prayer which the magistrates are accustomed to pronounce before they address the people, proceeded thus: "Romans, to no former assembly was this solemn supplication to the gods more suitable or even more necessary; as it serves to remind you, that these are the deities whom your forefathers pointed out as the objects of your worship, veneration, and prayers: and not those which infatuated men's minds with corrupt and foreign modes of religion, and drove them, as if goaded by the furies, to every lust and every vice. I am at a loss to know what I should conceal, or how far I ought to speak out; for I dread lest, if I leave you ignorant

in any particular, I should give room for carelessness, or if I disclose the whole, that I should too much awaken your fears. Whatever I shall say, be assured that it is less than the magnitude and atrociousness of the affair would justify: exertions will be used by us that it may be sufficient to set us properly on our guard. . . .

"Each of you, therefore, ought to pray that his kindred may have behaved with wisdom and prudence; and if lust, if madness, has dragged any of them into that abyss, to consider such a person as the relation of those with whom he has conspired for every disgraceful and reckless act, and not as one of your own. I am not secure, lest some, even of yourselves, may have erred through mistake; for nothing is more deceptive in appearance than false religion. When the authority of the gods is held out as a pretext to cover vice, fear enters our minds, lest, in punishing the crimes of men, we may violate some divine right connected therewith. Numberless decisions of the pontiffs, decrees of the senate, and even answers of the haruspices, free you from religious scruples of this character. How often in the ages of our fathers was it given in charge to the magistrates, to prohibit the performance of any foreign religious rites; to banish strolling sacrificers and soothsayers from the forum, the circus, and the city; to search for, and burn, books of divination; to abolish every mode of sacrificing that was not conformable to the Roman practice! For they, completely versed in every divine and human law, maintained, that nothing tended so strongly to the subversion of religion as sacrifice, when we offered it not after the institutions of our forefathers, but after foreign customs. This much I thought necessary to mention to you beforehand, that no vain scruple might disturb your minds when you should see us demolishing the places resorted to by the Bacchanalians, and dispersing their impious assemblies. We shall do all these things with the favour and approbation of the gods; who, because they were indignant that their divinity was dishonoured by those people's lusts and crimes, have drawn forth their proceedings from hidden darkness into the open light; and who have directed them to be exposed, not that they may escape with impunity, but in order that they may be punished and suppressed. The senate have committed to me and my colleague, an inquisition extraordinary concerning this affair. What is requisite to be done by ourselves, in person, we will do with energy. The charge of posting watches through the city, during the night, we have committed to the inferior magistrates; and, for your parts, it is incumbent on you to execute vigorously whatever duties are assigned you, and in the several places where each will be placed, to perform whatever orders you shall receive, and to use your best endeavours that no danger or tumult may arise from the treachery of the party involved in the guilt."

They then ordered the decrees of the senate to be read, and published a reward for any discoverer who should bring any of the guilty before them, or give information against any of the absent, adding, that "if any person accused should fly, they would limit a certain day upon which, if he did not answer when summoned, he would be condemned in his absence; and if any one should be charged who was out of Italy, they would allow him a longer time, if he should wish to come and make his defence." They then issued an edict, that "no person whatever should presume to buy or sell any thing for the purpose of leaving the country; or to receive or conceal, or by any means aid the fugitives." On the assembly being dismissed, great terror spread throughout the city; nor was it confined merely within the walls, or to the Roman territory, for every where throughout the whole of Italy alarm began to be felt, when letters from the guest-friends were received, concerning the decree of the senate, and what passed in the assembly, and the edict of the consuls. During the night, which succeeded the day in which the affair was made public, great numbers, attempting to fly, were seized, and brought back by the triumvirs, who had posted guards at all the gates; and informations were lodged against many, some of whom, both men and women, put themselves to death. Above seven thousand men and women are said to have taken the oath of the association. But it appeared that the heads of the conspiracy were the two Catinii, Marcus and Caius, Roman plebeians; Lucius Opiturnius, a Faliscan; and Minius Cerrinius, a Campanian: that from these proceeded all their criminal practices, and that these were the chief priests and founders of the sect. Care was taken that they should be apprehended as soon as possible. They were brought before the consuls, and, confessing their guilt, caused no delay to the ends of justice.

But so great were the numbers that fled from the city, that because the lawsuits and property of many persons were going to ruin, the prætors, Titus Mænius and Marcus Licinius, were obliged, under the direction of the senate, to adjourn their courts for thirty days, until the inquiries should be finished by the consuls. The same deserted state of the law-courts, since the persons, against whom charges were brought, did not appear to answer, nor could be found in Rome, necessitated the consuls to make a circuit of the country towns, and there to make their inquisitions and hold the trials. Those who, as it appeared, had been only initiated, and had made after the priest, and in the most solemn form, the prescribed imprecations, in which the accursed conspiracy for the perpetuation of every crime and lust was contained, but who had not themselves committed, or compelled others to commit, any of those acts to which they were bound by the oath,—all such they left in prison. But those who had forcibly committed personal defilements or murders, or were stained with the guilt of false evidence, counterfeit seals, forged wills, or other frauds, all these they punished with death. A greater number were executed than thrown into prison; indeed, the multitude of men and women who suffered in both ways, was very considerable. The consuls delivered the women, who were condemned, to their relations, or to those under whose guardianship they were, that they might inflict the punishment in private; but if there did not appear any proper person of the kind to execute the sentence, the punishment was inflicted in public. A charge was then given to demolish all the places where the Bacchanalians had held their meetings; first, in Rome, and then throughout all Italy; excepting those wherein should be found some ancient altar, or consecrated statue. With regard to the future, the senate passed a decree, "that no Bacchanalian rites should be celebrated in Rome or in Italy:" and ordered that, "in case any person should believe some such kind of worship incumbent on him, and necessary; and that he could not, without offence to religion, and incurring guilt, omit it, he should represent this to the city prætor, and the prætor should lay the business before the senate. If permission were granted by the senate, when not less than one hundred members were present, then he might perform those rites, provided that no more than five persons should be present at the sacrifice, and that they should have no common stock of money, nor any president of the ceremonies, nor priest."

Another decree connected with this was then made, on a motion of the consul, Quintus Marcius, that "the business respecting the persons who had served the consuls as informers should be proposed to the senate in its original form, when Spurius Postumius should have finished his inquiries, and returned to Rome." They voted that Minius Cerrinius, the Campanian, should be sent to Ardea, to be kept in custody there; and that a caution should be given to the magistrates of that city, to guard him with more than ordinary care, so as to prevent not only his escaping, but his having an opportunity of committing suicide. Spurius Postumius some time after came to Rome, and on his proposing the question, concerning the reward to be given to Publius Æbutius and Hispala Fecenia, because the Bacchanalian ceremonies were discovered by their exertions, the senate passed a vote, that "the city quæstors should give to each of them, out of the public treasury, one hundred thousand asses; and that the consuls should desire the plebeian tribunes to propose to the commons as soon as convenient, that the campaigns of Publius Æbutius should be considered as served, that he should not become a soldier against his wishes, nor should any censor assign him a horse at the public charge." They voted also, that "Hispala Fecenia should enjoy the privileges of alienating her property by gift or deed; of marrying out of her rank, and of choosing a guardian, as if a husband had conferred them by will; that she should be at liberty to wed a man of honourable birth, and that there should be no disgrace or ignominy to him who should marry her; and that the consuls and prætors then in office, and their successors, should take care that no injury should be offered to that woman, and that she might live in safety. That the senate wished, and thought proper, that all these things should be so ordered." All these particulars were proposed to the commons, and executed according to the vote of the senate; and full permission was given to the consuls to determine respecting the impunity and rewards of the other informers.

—W. A. M'DEVITTE.

EXPULSION OF GREEK TEACHERS

AULUS GELLIUS

[From *Attic Nights*, Book XV]

Aulus Gellius, a Roman writer of the second century after Christ, has preserved in his only extant work, *Noctes Atticæ*, an extremely miscellaneous, but often valuable collection of historical and literary material from earlier times.

The decree of the senate, quoted by him, was issued in 161 B.C., and the censors' edict in 92 B.C.

The wording of a decree of the senate on expelling philosophers from the city of Rome; also the wording of an edict of the censors, in which the men, who had begun to establish and practice training in rhetoric at Rome, were censured and suppressed.

In the consulship of C. Fannius Strabo and M. Valerius Messala a decree of the senate was passed on Latin philosophers and rhetoricians: "M. Pomponius, prætor, consulted the senate. Whereas mention has been made of philosophers and rhetoricians, on that subject the senators have decreed as follows, that M. Pomponius, prætor, should see to it and arrange, as seems good to him for the welfare of the state and his own honor, that they should not remain in Rome."

Some years after this decree of the senate, Cn. Domitius Ahenobarbus and L. Licinius Crassus, the censors, issued this edict on the suppressing of Latin rhetoricians: "It has been reported to us that there are men who have established a new kind of training, and that our youth is going to school to them; that they have granted themselves the title of Latin rhetoricians; that in their schools young men spend whole days in idleness. Our ancestors have established what they would have their children learn and to what schools they would have them go. These new teachings, which are being given against the usage and custom of our ancestors, do not meet with approval, nor do they seem right. Wherefore it has seemed necessary that, to those who conduct those schools, and to those who have been in the habit of going to them, we declare our opinion that they do not meet with our approval."

Not only in those very rude times when the people were not yet refined by Greek training were philosophers driven from the city of Rome, but while Domitian was emperor by a decree of the senate they were ejected from the city and from Italy and forbidden to return. At that time Epictetus, the philosopher, owing to that decree went from Rome to Nicopolis.

—G. A. HARRER.

III. A ROMAN PURITAN

ON AGRICULTURE [1]

CATO

Marcus Porcius Cato was born in 235 and died in 149 B.C. Cato is often spoken of

[1] From *Roman Farm Management*, by Fairfax Harrison. Copyright by the Macmillan Co. Reprinted by permission.

as Cato the Censor, or Cato the Elder, to distinguish him from the Cato of Cicero's time. He was also called the Wise. For many years he served in Rome's armies, in Italy, Spain, and Greece. Then he took a very active part in the politics of Rome. When censor he particularly distinguished himself for vehement opposition to growing luxury. To anything un-Roman he proved a fierce opponent, though as an old man he may have read Greek. Well known is his bitter hatred and fear of Carthage whose destruction he constantly sought, ending his senatorial speeches on any topic with the words, *Carthago delenda est*. In after times he always stood as the very embodiment of Roman puritanism.

The history of Roman oratory as a branch of Roman literature begins with him, since he was the first to make a practice of writing out and publishing his speeches. He made advances also in historiography over the annalists who preceded him, taking, for the first time, Latin instead of Greek for his medium, and to some extent breaking away from the limitations of the annalistic method. His precepts to his son contained practical treatises on many subjects of which only that on agriculture has survived.

Agriculture was in all periods a favorite subject of Roman authors, poets as well as writers of prose. Cato's treatise, written before 152 B.C., is the earliest extant piece of extended Latin prose, and is one of the sources from which Virgil drew for his *Georgics*. Its style is direct, without adornment, even crude; but the contents prove that its author was a practical farmer. In relation to the treatment of slaves it shows that humanitarian feelings were as yet undeveloped.

The pursuits of commerce would be as admirable as they are profitable if they were not subject to so great risks: and so, likewise, of banking, if it were always honestly conducted. For our ancestors considered, and so ordained in their laws, that, while the thief should be cast in double damages, the usurer should make four-fold restitution. From this we may judge how much less desirable a citizen they esteemed the banker than the thief. When they sought to commend an honest man, they termed him good husbandman, good farmer. This they rated the superlative of praise. Personally, I think highly of a man actively and diligently engaged in commerce, who seeks thereby to make his

fortune, yet, as I have said, his career is full of risks and pitfalls. But it is from the tillers of the soil that spring the best citizens, the stanchest soldiers; and theirs are the enduring rewards which are most grateful and least envied. Such as devote themselves to that pursuit are least of all men given to evil counsels.

And now, to get to my subject, these observations will serve as preface to what I have promised to discuss.

When you have decided to purchase a farm, be careful not to buy rashly; do not spare your visits and be not content with a single tour of inspection. The more you go, the more will the place please you, if it be worth your attention. Give heed to the appearance of the neighbourhood,—a flourishing country should show its prosperity. "When you go in, look about, so that, when needs be, you can find your way out."

Take care that you choose a good climate, not subject to destructive storms, and a soil that is naturally strong. If possible, your farm should be at the foot of a mountain, looking to the South, in a healthy situation, where labour and cattle can be had, well watered, near a good sized town, and either on the sea or a navigable river, or else on a good and much frequented road. Choose a place which has not often changed ownership, one which is sold unwillingly, that has buildings in good repair.

Beware that you do not rashly contemn the experience of others. It is better to buy from a man who has farmed successfully and built well.

When you inspect the farm, look to see how many wine presses and storage vats there are; where there are none of these you can judge what the harvest is. On the other hand, it is not the number of farming implements, but what is done with them, that counts. Where you find few tools, it is not an expensive farm to operate. Know that with a farm, as with a man, however productive it may be, if it has the spending habit, not much will be left over.

When you have arrived at your country house and have saluted your household, you should make the rounds of the farm the same day, if possible; if not, then certainly the next day. When you have observed how the field work has progressed, what things have been done, and what remains undone, you should summon your overseer the next day, and should call for a report of what work has been done in good season and why it has not been possible to complete the rest, and what wine and corn and other crops have been gathered. When you are advised on these points you should make your own calculation of the time necessary for the work, if there does not appear to you to have been enough accomplished. The overseer will report that he himself has worked diligently, but that some slaves have been sick and others truant, the weather has been bad, and that it has been necessary to work the public roads. When he has given these and many other excuses, you should recall to his attention the program of work which you had laid out for him on your last visit and compare it with the results attained. If the weather has been bad, count how many stormy days there have been, and rehearse what work could have been done despite the rain, such as washing and pitching the wine vats, cleaning out the barns, sorting the grain, hauling out and composting the manure, cleaning seed, mending the old gear, and making new, mending the smocks and hoods furnished for the hands. On feast days the old ditches should be mended, the public roads worked, briers cut down, the garden dug, the meadow cleaned, the hedges trimmed and the clippings collected and burned, the fish pond cleaned out. On such days, furthermore, the slaves' rations should be cut down as compared with what is allowed when they are working in the fields in fine weather.

When this routine has been discussed quietly and with good humor and is thoroughly understood by the overseer, you should give orders for the completion of the work which has been neglected.

The accounts of money, supplies and provisions should then be considered. The overseer should report what wine and oil has been sold, what price he got, what is on hand, and what remains for sale. Security should be taken for such accounts as ought to be secured. All other unsettled matters should be agreed upon. If anything is needed for the coming year, it should be bought; everything which is not needed should be sold. Whatever there is for lease should be leased. Orders should be given (and take care that they are in writing) for all work which next it is desired to have done on the farm or let to contract. You should go over the cattle and determine what is to be sold. You should sell the oil, if you can get your price, the surplus wine and corn, the old cattle, the worn out oxen, and the cull sheep, the wool and the hides, the old and sick slaves, and if anything else is superfluous you should sell that.

The appetite of the good farmer is to sell, not to buy.

Be a good neighbour. Do not roughly give offense to your own people. If the neighbourhood regards you kindly, you will find a readier market for what you have to sell, you will more easily get your work done, either on the place or by contract. If you build, your neighbours will aid you with their services, their cattle and their materials. If any misfortune should overtake you (which God forbid!) they will protect you with kindly interest.

If you ask me what is the best disposition to make of your estate, I would say that should you have bought a farm of one hundred *jugera* all told, in the best situation, it should be planted as follows: 1. a vineyard, if it promises a good yield, 2. an irrigated garden, 3. an osier bed, 4. an olive yard, 5. a meadow, 6. a corn field, 7. a wood lot, 8. a cultivated orchard, and 9. a mast grove.

In his youth, the farmer ought diligently to plant his land, but he should ponder before he builds. Planting does not require reflection, but demands action. It is time enough to build when you have reached your thirty-sixth year, if you have farmed your land well meanwhile. When you do build, let your buildings be proportioned to your estate, and your estate to your buildings. It is fitting that the farm buildings should be well constructed, that you should have ample oil cellars and wine vats, and a good supply of casks, so that you can wait for high prices, something which will redound to your honour, your profit and your self-respect.

Build your dwelling house in accordance with your means. If you build well in a good situation and on good property, and furnish the house suitably for country life, you will come there more often and more willingly. The farm will then be better, fewer mistakes will be made, and you will get larger crops. The face of the master is good for the land.

Plant elm trees along the roads and fence rows, so that you may have the leaves to feed the sheep and cattle, and the timber will be available if you need it. If anywhere there are banks of streams or wet places, there plant reeds; and surround them with willows that the osiers may serve to tie the vines.

It is most convenient to set out the land nearest the house as an orchard, whence fire wood and faggots may be sold and the supply of the master obtained. In this enclosure should be planted everything fitting to the land and vines should be married to the trees.

Near the house lay out also a garden with garland flowers and vegetables of all kinds, and set it about with myrtle hedges, both white and black, as well as Delphic and Cyprian laurel.

An olive farm of two hundred and forty *jugera* ought to be stocked as follows: an overseer, a housekeeper, five labourers, three ox drivers, one swineherd, one ass driver, one shepherd; in all thirteen hands: three pair of oxen, three asses with pack saddles to haul out the manure, one other ass to turn the mill, and one hundred sheep.

These are the duties of the overseer: He should maintain discipline. He should observe the feast days. He should respect the rights of others and steadfastly uphold his own. He should settle all quarrels among the hands; if any one is at fault he should administer the punishment. He should take care that no one on the place is in want, or lacks food or drink; in this respect he can afford to be generous, for he will thus more easily prevent picking and stealing.

Unless the overseer is of evil mind, he will himself do no wrong, but if he permits wrong-doing by others, the master should not suffer such indulgence to pass with impunity. He should show appreciation of courtesy, to encourage others to practise it. He should not be given to gadding or conviviality, but should be always sober. He should keep the hands busy, and should see that they do what the master has ordered. He should not think that he knows more than his master. The friends of the master should be his friends, and he should give heed to those whom the master has recommended to him. He should confine his religious practices to the cross roads altar on festival days or to his own house.

He should lend money to no man unbidden by the master, but what the master has lent he should collect. He should never lend any seed reserved for sowing, feed, corn, wine, or oil, but he should have relations with two or three other farms with which he can exchange things needed in emergency. He should state his accounts with his master frequently. He should not keep any hired men or day-hands longer than is necessary. He should not sell anything without the knowledge of the master, nor should be conceal anything from the master. He should not have any hangers-on, nor should he consult any soothsayer, fortune teller, necromancer, or astrologer. He should not spare seed in sowing, for that is bad economy. He should strive to be expert in all kinds of farm work, and, without exhausting himself, often lend a hand. By so doing, he will better understand the point of view of his hands, and they will work more contentedly; moreover, he will have less inclination to gad, his health will be better, and he will sleep more refreshingly.

First up in the morning, he should be the last to go to bed at night; and before he does, he should see that the farm gates are closed, and that each of the hands is in his own bed, that the stock have been fed. He should see that the best of care is taken of the oxen, and should pay the highest compliments to the teamsters who keep their cattle in the best condition. He should see to it that the ploughs and the plough shares are kept in good repair. Plan all the work in ample time, for so it is with farm work, if one thing is done late, everything will be late.

When it rains try to find something to do indoors. Clean up, rather than remain idle. Remember that while work may stop, expenses still go on.

The overseer should be responsible for the duties of the housekeeper. If the master has given her to you for a wife, you should be satisfied with her, and she should respect you. Require that she be not given to wasteful habits; that she does not gossip with the neighbours and other women. She should not receive visitors either in the kitchen or in her own quarters. She should not go out to parties, nor should she gad about. She should not practise religious observances, nor should she ask others to do so for her without the permission of the master or the mistress. Remember that the master practises religion for the entire household. She should be neat in appearance and should keep the house swept and garnished. Every night before she goes to bed she should see that the hearth is swept and clean. On the Kalends, the Ides, the Nones, and on all feast days, she should hang a garland over the hearth. On those days also she should pray fervently to the household gods. She should take care that she has food cooked for you and for the hands. She should have plenty of chickens and an abundance of eggs. She should diligently put up all kinds of preserves every year.

The following are the customary allowances for food: For the hands, four pecks of meal for the winter, and four and one-half for the summer. For the overseer, the housekeeper, the wagoner, the shepherd, three pecks each. For the slaves, four pounds of bread for the winter, but when they begin to cultivate the vines this is increased to five pounds until the figs are ripe, then return to four pounds.

The sum of the wine allowed for each hand per annum is eight quadrantals, or amphora, but add in the proportion as they do work. Ten quadrantals per annum is not too much to allow them to drink.

Save the wind fall olives, as much as possible as relishes for the hands. Later set aside such of the ripe olives as will make the least oil. Be careful to make them go as far as possible. When the olives are all eaten, give them fish pickles and vinegar. One peck of salt per annum is enough for each hand.

Allow each hand a smock and a cloak every other year. As often as you give out a smock or a cloak to any one, take up the old one, so that caps can be made out of it. A pair of heavy wooden shoes should be allowed every other year.

If the land is wet, it should be drained with trough shaped ditches dug three feet wide at the surface and one foot at the bottom and four feet deep. Blind these ditches with rock. If you have no rock, then fill them with green willow poles braced crosswise. If you have no poles, fill them with faggots. Then dig lateral trenches three feet deep and four feet wide in such way that the water will flow from the trenches into the ditches.

In the winter surface water should be drained off the fields. On hillsides, courses should be kept clear for the water to flow off. During the rainy season at the beginning of Autumn is the greatest risk from water. When it begins to rain all the hands should go out with picks and shovels and clear out the drains so that the water may flow off into the roads, and the crops be protected.

What is the first principle of good agriculture? To plough well. What is the second? To plough again; and the third is to manure. When you plough corn land, plough well and in good weather, lest you turn a cloddy furrow. The other things of good agriculture are to sow seed plentifully, to thin the young sprouts, and to hill up the roots with earth.

Never plough rotten land nor drive flocks or carts across it.

If care is not taken about this, the land so abused will be barren for three years.

The flocks and herds should be well supplied with litter and their feet kept clean. If litter is short, haul in oak leaves, they will serve as bedding for sheep and cattle. Beware of scab among the sheep and cattle. This comes from hunger and exposure to rain.

To prevent the oxen from wearing down their hoofs, anoint the bottom of the hoof with liquid pepper before driving them on the highroad.

Take care that during the summer the cattle drink only sweet and fresh water. Their health depends on it.

To prevent scab among sheep, make a mixture of equal parts of well strained amurca, of water in which lupine has been steeped, and of lees of good wine. After shearing, anoint all the flock with this mixture, and let them sweat profusely for two or three days. Then dip them in the sea. If you have no sea water, make salt water and dip them in that. If you will do this they will suffer no scab, they will have more and better wool, and they will not be molested by ticks.

If an ox begins to sicken, give him without delay a raw hen's egg and make him swallow it whole. The next day make him drink from a wooden bowl a measure of wine in which has been scraped the head of an onion. Both the ox and his attendant should do these things fasting and standing upright.

If a serpent shall bite an ox, or any other quadruped, take a cup of that extract of fennel which the physicians call smyrnean, and mix it with a measure of old wine. Inject this through his nostrils, and at the same time poultice the wound with hog's dung. You can treat a man the same way.

If a bone is dislocated it can be made sound by this incantation. Take a green reed four or five feet long, cut it in the middle and let two men hold the pieces against your hips. Begin then to chant as follows:

"In Alio S. F. Motas Vaeta,
Daries Dardaries Astataries Dissunapiter."

and continue until the free ends of the reed are brought slowly together in front of you. Meanwhile wave a knife above the reeds, and when they come together and one touches the other, seize them in your hand and cut them right and left.

These pieces of reed bound upon a dislocated or fractured bone will cure it.

But every day repeat the incantation, or in place of it this one:

"Huat Hanat Huat
Ista Pista Sista
Domiabo Damnaustra."

—FAIRFAX HARRISON.

CATO THE CENSOR

LIVY

[From Book XXXIX]

Livy's sketch probably follows the traditional conception of the stoical type of character of the early Republic. (For Livy, see below, p. 418.)

The censorship was the object of contention of the following candidates, Lucius Valerius Flaccus, Publius Scipio, Lucius Scipio, Cneius Manlius Vulso, and Lucius Furius Purpureo, patricians; Marcus Porcius Cato, Marcus Fulvius Nobilior, Tiberius Sempronius Longus, Marcus Sempronius Tuditanus, plebeians. But Marcus Porcius far surpassed all of them, both plebeians and patricians of the highest ranks. So great powers of mind and energy of intellect were in this man, that, no matter how lowly the position in which he was born, he appeared capable of attaining to the highest rank. No one qualification for the management of business, either public or private, was wanting to him. He was equally skilled in affairs relating to town and country. Some have been advanced to the highest honours by their knowledge of the law, others by their eloquence, some by military renown; but this man's genius was so versatile, and so well adapted to all things, that in whatever way engaged, it might be said, that nature formed him for that alone. In war, he was most

courageous, distinguishing himself highly in many remarkable battles; and, when he arrived at the highest posts, was likewise a most consummate commander. Then, in peace, if consulted on a point of law, he was the wisest counsellor; if a cause was to be pleaded, the most eloquent advocate. Nor was he one of those whose oratory was striking only during their own lives, without leaving after them any monument of it. On the contrary, his eloquence still lives, and will long live, consecrated to memory by writings of every kind. His orations are many, spoken for himself, for others, and against others; for he harassed his enemies, not only by supporting prosecutions against them, but by maintaining causes in opposition to them. Enmities in abundance gave him plenty of employment, and he never permitted them to lie dormant; nor was it easy to tell whether the nobility laboured harder to keep him down, or he to oppress the nobility. His temper, no doubt, was austere, his language bitter and unboundedly free, but his mind was never conquered by his passions, his integrity was inflexible, and he looked with contempt on popularity and riches. In spare diet, in enduring toil and danger, his body and mind were like iron; so that even old age, which brings all things to dissolution, did not break his vigour. In his eighty-sixth year he stood a trial, pleaded his own cause, and published his speech; and in his ninetieth year, he brought Servius Galba to trial, before the people.

On this occasion, when he was candidate for censorship, as in all his previous career, the nobility endeavoured to crush him. All the candidates, likewise, except Lucius Flaccus, who had been his colleague in the consulship, combined to disappoint him of the office, not merely with a view to their own success, in preference to him, or because they felt indignant at the idea of seeing a man of no family censor, but because from one who had received offence from most of them, and who wished to retaliate, they anticipated a severe censorship, that would endanger the reputations of many. For, even while soliciting, he uttered frequent menaces, and upbraided them with using their interest against him, because they dreaded an impartial and courageous execution of the duty of censor; at the same time, giving his interest to Lucius Valerius. He said, that "he was the only colleague, in conjunction with whom he could correct modern profligacy, and re-establish the ancient morals." People were so inflamed by such discourses, that, in spite of the opposition made by the nobility, they not only made Marcus Porcius censor, but gave him for his colleague Lucius Valerius Flaccus. . . .

The censors, Marcus Porcius and Lucius Valerius, while anxious curiosity was blended with fear, made their survey of the senate; they expelled seven from the senate, one of them a man of consular rank, highly distinguished by nobility of birth and honourable employments,— Lucius Quintius Flamininus. It is mentioned, as a practice instituted in the memory of our forefathers, that the censors should annex marks of censure to the names of such as they degraded from the senate. There are severe speeches of Cato, against those whom he either expelled from the senate, or degraded from the equestrian rank, but by far the most so is that against Lucius Quintius. Had he spoken in the character of prosecutor, previous to the censure, and not in that of censor after it, not even his brother Titus, if he were his colleague, could have suffered Quintius to remain in the senate. Among other charges, he objected to him, that he had, by hopes of extraordinary presents, prevailed on Philip, a Carthaginian and a catamite, to accompany him into his province of Gaul; that this youth, in order to enhance the merit of his complaisance to the consul, used frequently, in wanton squabbling, to upbraid him for having quitted Rome just before the show of gladiators. It happened, that while they were at a feast and heated with wine, a message was brought into the place of entertainment, that a Boian, of high rank, had come as a deserter with his children, and wished to see the consul, that he might in person receive his assurance of protection. He was accordingly introduced into the tent, and began to address him through an interpreter: but while he was speaking, Quintius said to his catamite, "Since you left the show of gladiators, have you a mind to see this Gaul dying?" When he had assented, but scarcely in earnest, the consul, drawing a sword that hung over his head, first struck the Gaul as he was speaking, and then, when he was running out, and imploring the protection of the Roman people, and of those present, ran him through the side.

Valerius Antias, as he was one who never read Cato's speech, and only gave credit to a tale published without authority, tells the story in another manner, but similar to this in lust and cruelty. He writes, that, at Placentia, the consul invited to an entertainment a woman of ill fame, with whom he was desperately enamoured. There, displaying his importance to this courtesan, he told her, among other matters, with what severity he had conducted the inquisitions, and how many he had then in prison under sentence of death, whom he intended to behead. Then she, being next to him on the couch, said, that having never seen an executioner perform his office, she was very desirous of seeing such a thing; on which, the indulgent lover ordered one of those wretches to be dragged to the spot, and there cut off his head. The deed of death, whether committed as the censor or as Valerius reported it, was barbarous and inhuman; that in the midst of feasting and cups, when it is customary to offer libations to the gods, and to pray for happiness, a human victim should be butchered, and the table stained with his blood, and this for the entertainment of an acknowledged wanton. In the latter part of Cato's speech, he proposes to Quintius, that if he denied this fact, and the others of which he accused him, he should give security to abide a legal trial; but if he confessed them, could he suppose, he asked him, that any one would be sorry for his disgrace; the disgrace of him who, in the midst of a feast, being intoxicated with wine and lust, had sported with the blood of a human being.

In the review of the knights, Lucius Scipio Asiaticus was degraded. In fixing the rates of taxation, also, the censor's conduct was harsh and severe to all ranks of men. People were to give account upon oath, of women's dress, and ornaments, and carriages exceeding in value fifteen thousand asses; and it was further ordered, that slaves, younger than twenty years, which, since the last survey, had been sold for ten thousand asses or more, should be estimated at ten times their value; and that, on all these articles, a tax should be laid of three denariuses for each thousand asses. The censors took away water, which belonged to the public, running or carried into any private building or field; and they demolished within thirty days all buildings or sheds, in possession of private persons, that projected into public ground. They then engaged contractors for executing national works, with the money decreed for that purpose,—for paving cisterns with stone, for cleansing the sewers where it was requisite, and forming new ones on the Aventine, and in other quarters where hitherto there had been none. Then, dividing their tasks, Flaccus built a mole at Neptunia, on the coast, and made a road through the Formian mountains. Cato purchased for the use of the people two halls, the Mænian and Titian, in the Lautumiæ, and four shops, and built

there a court of justice, which was called the Porcian. They farmed out the several branches of the revenue at the highest prices, and bargained with the contractors for the performance of the public services on the lowest terms. When the senate, overcome by the prayers and lamentations of the publicans, ordered those bargains to be revoked, and new agreements to be made, the censors, by an edict, excluded from competition the persons who had eluded the former contracts, and farmed out all the same branches at prices very little reduced. This was a remarkable censorship, and the origin of many deadly feuds: it rendered Marcus Porcius, to whom all the harshness was attributed, uneasy during the remainder of his life.

—W. A. M'DEVITTE.

CATO ON EXTRAVAGANCE

LIVY

[From Book XXXIV]

Amid the serious concerns of important wars, either scarcely brought to a close or impending, an incident intervened, trivial indeed to be mentioned, but which, through the zeal of the parties concerned, issued in a violent contest. Marcus Fundanius and Lucius Valerius, plebeian tribunes, proposed to the people the repealing of the Oppian law. This law, which had been introduced by Caius Oppius, plebeian tribune, in the consulate of Quintus Fabius and Tiberius Sempronius, during the heat of the Punic war, enacted that "no woman should possess more than half an ounce of gold, or wear a garment of various colours, or ride in a carriage drawn by horses, in a city, or any town, or any place nearer than one mile; except on occasion of some public religious solemnity." Marcus and Publius Junius Brutus, plebeian tribunes, supported the Oppian law, and declared, that they would never suffer it to be repealed; while many of the nobility stood forth to argue for and against the motion proposed. The Capitol was filled with crowds, who favoured or opposed the law; nor could the matrons be kept at home, either by advice or shame, nor even by the commands of their husbands; but beset every street and pass in the city, beseeching the men as they went down to the forum, that in the present flourishing state of the commonwealth, when the private fortune of all was daily increasing, they would suffer the women to have their former ornaments of dress restored. This throng of women increased daily, for they arrived even from the country towns and villages; and they had at length the boldness to come up to the consuls, prætors, and magistrates, to urge their request. One of the consuls, however, they found especially inexorable—Marcus Porcius Cato, who, in support of the law proposed to be repealed, spoke to this effect:

"If, Romans, every individual among us had made it a rule to maintain the prerogative and authority of a husband with respect to his own wife, we should have less trouble with the whole sex. But now, our privileges, overpowered at home by female contumacy, are, even here in the forum, spurned and trodden under foot; and because we are unable to withstand each separately, we now dread their collective body. I was accustomed to think it a fabulous and fictitious tale, that, in a certain island, the whole race of males, was utterly extirpated by a conspiracy of the women. But the utmost danger may be apprehended equally from either sex, if you suffer cabals, assemblies, and secret consultations to be held: scarcely, indeed, can I determine, in my own mind, whether the act itself, or the precedent that it affords, is of more pernicious tendency. The latter of these more particularly concerns us consuls, and the other magistrates: the former, yourselves, my fellow-citizens. For, whether the measure proposed to your consideration be profitable to the state or not, is to be determined by you, who are about to go to the vote. As to the outrageous behaviour of these women, whether it be merely an act of their own, or owing to your instigations, Marcus Fundanius and Lucius Valerius, it unquestionably implies culpable conduct in the magistrates. I know not whether it reflects greater disgrace on you, tribunes, or on the consuls: on you certainly, if you have, on the present occasion, brought these women hither for the purpose of raising tribunitian seditions; on us, if we suffer laws to be imposed on us by a secession of women, as was done formerly by that of the common people. It was not without painful emotions of shame, that I, just now, made my way into the forum through the midst of a band of women. Had I not been restrained by respect for the modesty and dignity of some individuals among them, rather than of the whole number, and been unwilling that they should be seen rebuked by a consul, I should have said to them, 'What sort of practice is this, of running out into public, besetting the streets, and addressing other women's husbands? Could not each have made the same request of her husband at home? Are your blandishments more seducing in public than in private; and with other women's husbands, than with your own? Although, if the modesty of matrons confined them within the limits of their own rights, it did not become you, even at home, to concern yourselves about what laws might be passed or repealed here.' Our ancestors thought it not proper that women should perform any, even private business, without a director; but that they should be ever under the control of parents, brothers, or husbands. We, it seems, suffer them, now, to interfere in the management of state affairs, and to introduce themselves into the forum, into general assemblies, and into assemblies of election. For, what are they doing, at this moment, in your streets and lanes? What, but arguing, some in support of the motion of the plebeian tribunes; others, for the repeal of the law? Will you give the reins to their intractable nature, and their uncontrolled passions, and then expect that themselves should set bounds to their licentiousness, when you have failed to do so? This is the smallest of the injunctions laid on them by usage or the laws, all which women bear with impatience: they long for liberty; or rather, to speak the truth, for unbounded freedom in every particular. For what will they not attempt, if they now come off victorious?

"Recollect all the institutions respecting the sex, by which our forefathers restrained their undue freedom, and by which they subjected them to their husbands; and yet, even with the help of all these restrictions, you can scarcely keep them within bounds. If, then, you suffer them to throw these off one by one, to tear them all asunder, and, at last, to be set on an equal footing with yourselves, can you imagine that they will be any longer tolerable by you? The moment they have arrived at an equality with you, they will have become your superiors. But, forsooth, they only object to any new law being made against them: they mean to deprecate, not justice, but severity. Nay, their wish is, that a law which you have admitted, established by your suffrages, and confirmed by the practice and experience of so many years to be beneficial, should now be repealed; that is, that, by abolishing one law, you should weaken all the rest. No law perfectly suits the convenience of every member of the community: the only consideration is, whether, upon the whole, it be profitable to the greater part. If, because a law proves obnoxious to a private individual, that circumstance should destroy and sweep it away, to what purpose is it for the community to enact general laws, which those, with reference to whom they were passed, could presently repeal? I should like, however, to hear what this important affair is which has induced the matrons thus to run out into public in this excited manner, scarcely restraining from pushing into the forum and the assembly of the people. Is it to solicit that their parents, their husbands, children, and brothers may be ransomed from captivity under Hannibal? By no means: and far be ever from the commonwealth so unfortunate a situation. Yet, even when such was the case, you refused this to their prayers. But it is not duty, nor solicitude for their friends; it is religion that has collected them together. They are about to receive the Idæan Mother, coming out of Phrygia from Pessinus! What motive, that even common decency will allow to be mentioned, is pretended for this female insurrection? Why, say they, that we may shine in gold and purple; that, both on festal and common days, we may ride through the city in our chariots, triumphing over vanquished and abrogated law, after having captured and wrested from you your suffrages; and that there may be no bounds to our expenses and our luxury.

"Often have you heard me complain of the profuse expenses of the women— often of those of the men; and that not only of men in private stations, but of the magistrates: and that the state was endangered by two opposite vices, luxury and avarice; those pests, which have been the ruin of all great empires. These I dread the more, as the circumstances of the commonwealth grow daily more prosperous and happy; as the empire increases; as we have now passed over into Greece and Asia, places abounding with every kind of temptation that can inflame the passions; and as we have begun to handle even royal treasures: so much the more do I fear that these matters will bring us into captivity, rather than we them. Believe me, those statues from Syracuse were brought into this city with hostile effect. I already hear too many commending and admiring the decorations of Athens and Corinth, and ridiculing the earthen images of our Roman gods that stand on the fronts of their temples. For my part I prefer these gods,—propitious as they are, and I hope will continue to be, if we allow them to remain in their own mansions. In the memory of our fathers, Pyrrhus, by his ambassador Cineas, made trial of the dispositions, not only of our men, but of our women also, by offers of presents: at that time the Oppian law, for restraining female luxury, had not been made; and yet not one woman accepted a present. What, think you, was the reason? That for which our ancestors made no provision by law on this subject: there was no luxury existing which needed to be restrained. As diseases must necessarily be known before their remedies, so passions came into being before the laws which prescribe limits to them. What called forth the Licinian law, restricting estates to five hundred acres, but the unbounded desire for enlarging estates? What the Cincian law, concerning gifts and presents, but that the plebeians had become vassals and tributaries to the senate? It is not therefore in any degree surprising, that no want of the Oppian law, or of any other, to limit the expenses of women, was felt at that time, when they refused to receive gold and purple that was thrown in their way, and offered to their acceptance. If Cineas were now to go round the city with his presents, he would find numbers of women standing in the public streets to receive them. There are some passions, the causes or motives of which I can no way account for. For that that should not be lawful for you which is permitted to another, may perhaps naturally excite some degree of shame or indignation; yet, when the dress of all is alike, why should any one of you fear, lest she should not be an object of observation? Of all kinds of shame, the worst, surely, is the being ashamed of frugality or of poverty; but the law relieves you with regard to both; since that which you have not it is unlawful for you to possess. This equalization, says the rich matron, is the very thing that I cannot endure. Why do not I make a figure, distinguished with gold and purple? Why is the poverty of others concealed under this cover of a law, so that it should be thought that, if the law permitted, they would have such things as they are not now able to procure? Romans, do you wish to excite among your wives an emulation of this sort, that the rich should wish to have what no other can have; and that the poor, lest they should be despised as such, should extend their expenses beyond their means? Be assured, that when a woman once begins to be ashamed of what she ought not to be ashamed of, she will not be ashamed of what she ought. She who can, will purchase out of her own purse; she who cannot, will ask her husband. Unhappy is the husband, both he who complies with the request, and he who does not; for what he will not give himself, he will see given by another. Now, they openly solicit favours from other women's husbands; and, what is more, solicit a law and votes. From some they obtain them; although, with regard to yourself, your property, or your children, they would be inexorable. So soon as the law shall cease to limit the expenses of your wife, you yourself will never be able to do so. Do not suppose that the matter will hereafter be in the same state in which it was before the law was made on the subject. It is safer that a wicked man should even never be accused, than that he should be acquitted; and luxury, if it had never been meddled with, would be more tolerable than it will be, now, like a wild beast, irritated by having been chained, and then let loose. My opinion is, that the Oppian law ought, on no account, to be repealed. Whatever determination you may come to, I pray all the gods to prosper it." . . . .

Although all these considerations had been urged against the motion and in its favour, the women next day poured out into public in much greater numbers, and in a body beset the doors of the tribunes who had protested against the measure of their colleagues; nor did they retire until this intervention was withdrawn. There was then no further doubt but that every one of the tribes would vote for the repeal of the law. Thus was this law annulled, in the twentieth year after it had been made.

—CYRUS EDMONDS.

WORLD CONQUEST AND CIVIL WAR

SECOND AND FIRST CENTURIES B.C.

In all the long centuries before the birth of Christ, Rome was usually engaged in war. Conquest brought about the enormous expansion from a little city with a few square miles of territory to an empire which controlled the Mediterranean. Fortune seems to have granted the Romans a very large measure of military ability and political genius. From every victorious war—and all important wars ended victoriously—Rome knew how to reap some stable benefit. By various methods, she would bind conquered cities and tribes to herself, now granting them partial, now full Roman citizenship, now entering into alliance with them. And usually the agreement resulted in lasting benefits to the conquered as well as to the conqueror. At first the process of expansion was a very slow one. From the founding of the city over 400 years passed before Rome controlled Italy. But the growth, though slow, was sound, for it stood the test of a hundred years of war which followed between Rome and Carthage. From three frightful wars, ending with the destruction of Carthage in 146 B.C., the year which also witnessed the capture of Corinth, Rome emerged as the leading power of the time.

Before the wars with Carthage Rome was an Italian power; at the close of them, she was a world power, for her victories had brought her vast territories in Sicily, Spain, Africa, which she kept. It is very doubtful whether many Romans realized that their country was engaged in an imperialistic policy until the great expansion at the defeat of Carthage. And even afterward for long there were no hasty steps made to grasp additional territory. Rather a reluctance to go forward was the rule. Rome had then grown by facing each problem of foreign relations as it arose, never objecting to warfare if necessary or advantageous at the moment. A far-reaching policy of world conquest was not a cause of her growth.

But having obtained world power, her condition and her contacts were greatly changed. Political influence in countries independent of her came to her unasked. Wealth flowed in, and more luxurious ways of living were adopted. Soon it became very plain that conquest produced these things, and easily. And so by the first century conquest, to put it bluntly, for what there was in it, for the individual commander, his army, and for the Roman state, became the vogue. The great names of Sulla, Lucullus, Pompey, Cæsar are the most significant in this era, but there were many others of less importance. And when the period ended, with the outbreak of civil war, every country around the Mediterranean belonged to Rome or was very directly under her influence.

With this outward growth had come naturally tremendous internal changes. The rise to political power of the common people is notable. Economic difficulties, agrarian problems came up again and again and were never satisfactorily solved. Decisive in its political results was the failure ultimately of the governmental forms of the Republic to adapt themselves to the controlling of an empire. In the course of time it had become the practice to send out as governors of conquered territories, which the Romans termed provinces, men of high position in the senatorial order. Their terms were often of indefinite length, and, while they were ultimately responsible to the senate, and could be tried for mal-administration, during their tenure they were practically independent of control. Their armies for the time were wholly at their beck and call, and they became a standing menace to the very existence of the government. Sulla's career, thirty years before the end of the Republic, was prophetic. With his army behind him he returned from the East and settled political affairs at Rome to suit himself. Finally the two outstanding military and political leaders of Rome, Cæsar and Pompey, met in civil war, and with the victory of Cæsar the free Republic of Rome was no more.

I. EXPANSION

Fortunately for our understanding of the period of rapid and enormous growth of the Roman Empire various of its literary products have been preserved. In keeping with an age that was materialistic, if anything, the practical spirit of the Roman had learned how to express itself, and well, in prose. At one time Cicero had stated that history did not exist as a branch of literature among the Romans—a statement which meant that, compared with Greek productions, the Roman efforts were as nothing. But the Romans had been learning from their Greek teachers and not many years passed before the publication of Cæsar's *Commentaries* and Sallust's great monographs robbed Cicero's remark of its meaning. The Roman had no longer need to fear comparisons. From Cicero's pen we have no history; but his letters and speeches furnish historical material of the first importance.

These writers were all men of affairs, intimately concerned with great public activities. Through their pages statesman, politician, military leader, governor, as well as the objective historian, speak directly. From the various angles of their interests a realistic conception can be gained of the problems, methods, and accomplishments of the time.

EXPANSION TOWARDS THE SOUTH

ROME AND JUGURTHA

SALLUST

[From the *Jugurthine War*]

Gaius Sallustius Crispus was born in 86 and died in 34 B.C. Historical writing in the disturbed Ciceronian period was confined almost entirely to the production of short monographs on contemporary incidents. Sallust brought to the task a sincere desire to narrate the truth impartially and a philosophical conception of history which was well in advance of his time. Of his productions only the *Jugurthine War* and the *Conspiracy of Catiline* are extant.

Numidia, the realm of Jugurtha, bordered on that part of Africa which had fallen to Rome on the capture of Carthage, and conflict and conquest were ultimately inevitable in the imperialistic period. Sallust's interest in the conflict with Jugurtha, which lasted from 111 to 106 B.C., is two-fold, historical and political. He does not spare the aristocratic government of the senate, but seems to foresee in its corrupt practices its ultimate downfall. He is too close to the events with which he deals to be fully aware of their bearing on the continued expansion of Rome's dominion.

Mankind unreasonably complain of their nature, that, being weak and short-lived, it is governed by chance rather than intellectual power; for, on the contrary, you will find, upon reflection, that there is nothing more noble or excellent, and that to nature is wanting rather human industry than ability or time.

The ruler and director of the life of man is the mind, which, when it pursues glory in the path of true merit, is sufficiently powerful, efficient, and worthy of honour, and needs no assistance from fortune, who can neither bestow integrity, industry, or other good qualities, nor can take them away. But if the mind, ensnared by corrupt passions, abandons itself to indolence and sensuality, when it has indulged for a season in pernicious gratifications, and when bodily strength, time, and mental vigour, have been wasted in sloth, the infirmity of nature is accused, and those who are themselves in fault impute their delinquency to circumstances.

If man, however, had as much regard

for worthy objects, as he has spirit in the pursuit of what is useless, unprofitable, and even perilous, he would not be governed by circumstances more than he would govern them, and would attain to a point of greatness, at which, instead of being mortal, he would be immortalised by glory.

As man is composed of mind and body, so, of all our concerns and pursuits, some partake the nature of the body, and some that of the mind. Thus beauty of person, eminent wealth, corporeal strength, and all other things of this kind, speedily pass away; but the illustrious achievements of the mind are, like the mind itself, immortal.

Of the advantages of person and fortune, as there is a beginning, there is also an end; they all rise and fall, increase and decay. But the mind, incorruptible and eternal, the ruler of the human race, actuates and has power over all things, yet is itself free from control.

The depravity of those, therefore, is the more surprising, who, devoted to corporeal gratifications, spend their lives in luxury and indolence, but suffer the mind, than which nothing is better or greater in man, to languish in neglect and inactivity; especially when there are so many and various mental employments by which the highest renown may be obtained.

Of these occupations, however, civil and military offices, and all administration of public affairs, seem to me, at the present time, by no means to be desired; for neither is honour conferred on merit, nor are those, who have gained power by unlawful means, the more secure or respected for it. To rule our country or subjects by force, though we may have the ability, and may correct what is wrong, is yet an ungrateful undertaking; especially as all changes in the state lead to bloodshed, exile, and other evils of discord; while to struggle in ineffectual attempts, and to gain nothing, by wearisome exertions, but public hatred, is the extreme of madness; unless when a base and pernicious spirit, perchance, may prompt a man to sacrifice his honour and liberty to the power of a party.

Among other employments which are pursued by the intellect, the recording of past events is of pre-eminent utility; but of its merits I may, I think, be silent, since many have spoken of them, and since, if I were to praise my own occupation, I might be considered as presumptuously praising myself. I believe, too, that there will be some, who, because I have resolved to live unconnected with political affairs, will apply to my arduous and useful labours the name of idleness; especially those who think it an important pursuit to court the people, and gain popularity by entertainments. But if such persons will consider at what periods I obtained office, what sort of men were then unable to obtain it, and what description of persons have subsequently entered the senate, they will think, assuredly, that I have altered my sentiments rather from prudence than from indolence, and that more good will arise to the state from my retirement, than from the busy efforts of others.

I have often heard that Quintus Maximus, Publius Scipio, and many other illustrious men of our country, were accustomed to observe, that, when they looked on the images of the ancestors, they felt their minds irresistibly excited to the pursuit of honour. Not, certainly, that the wax, or the shape, had any such influence; but, as they called to mind their forefathers' achievements, such a flame was kindled in the breasts of those eminent persons, as could not be extinguished till their own merit had equalled the fame and glory of their ancestors.

But, in the present state of manners, who is there, on the contrary, that does not rather emulate his forefathers in riches and extravagance, than in virtue and labour? Even men of humble birth, who formerly used to surpass the nobility in merit, pursue power and honour rather by intrigue and dishonesty, than by honourable qualifications; as if the prætorship, consulate, and all other offices of the kind, were noble and dignified in themselves, and not to be estimated according to the worth of those who fill them.

But, in expressing my concern and regret at the manners of the state, I have proceeded with too great freedom, and at too great length. I now return to my subject.

I am about to relate the war which the Roman people carried on with Jugurtha, King of the Numidians; first, because it was great, sanguinary, and of varied fortune; and secondly, because then, for the first time, opposition was offered to the power of the nobility; a contest which threw everything, religious and civil, into confusion, and was carried to such a height of madness, that nothing but war, and the devastation of Italy, could put an end to civil dissensions. But before I fairly commence my narrative, I will take a review of preceding particulars, in order that the whole subject may be more clearly and distinctly understood.

In the second Punic war, in which Hannibal, the leader of the Carthaginians, had weakened the power of Italy more than any other enemy since the Roman name became great, Masinissa, King of the Numidians, being received into alliance by Publius Scipio, who, from his merits was afterwards surnamed Africanus, had performed for us many eminent exploits in the field. In return for which services, after the Carthaginians were subdued, and after Syphax, whose power in Italy was great and extensive, was taken prisoner, the Roman people presented to Masinissa, as a free gift, all the cities and lands that they had captured. Masinissa's friendship for us, accordingly, remained faithful and inviolate; his reign and his life ended together. His son, Micipsa, alone suc-

ceeded to his kingdom; Mastanabal and Gulussa, his two brothers, having been carried off by disease. Micipsa had two sons, Adherbal and Hiempsal, and had brought up in his house, with the same care as his own children, a son of his brother Mastanabal, named Jugurtha, whom Masinissa, as being the son of a concubine, had left in a private station.

Jugurtha, as he grew up, being strong in frame, graceful in person, but, above all, vigorous in understanding, did not allow himself to be enervated by pleasure and indolence, but, as is the usage of his country, exercised himself in riding, throwing the javelin, and contending in the race with his equals in age; and, though he excelled them all in reputation, he was yet beloved by all. He also passed much of his time in hunting; he was first, or among the first, to wound the lion and other beasts; he performed very much, but spoke very little of himself.

Micipsa, though he was at first gratified with these circumstances, considering that the merit of Jugurtha would be an honour to his kingdom, yet, when he reflected that the youth was daily increasing in popularity, whilst he himself was advanced in age, and his children but young, he was extremely disturbed at the state of things, and revolved it frequently in his mind. The very nature of man, ambitious of power, and eager to gratify its desires, gave him reason for apprehension, as well as the opportunity afforded by his own age and that of his children, which was sufficient, from the prospect of such a prize, to lead astray even men of moderate desires. The affection of the Numidians, too, which was strong towards Jugurtha, was another cause for alarm; among whom, if he should cut off such a man, he feared that some insurrection or war might arise.

Surrounded by such difficulties, and seeing that a man, so popular among his countrymen, was not to be destroyed either by force or by fraud, he resolved, as Jugurtha was of an active disposition, and eager for military reputation, to expose him to dangers in the field, and thus make trial of fortune. During the Numantine war, therefore, when he was sending supplies of horse and foot to the Romans, he gave him the command of the Numidians, whom he despatched into Spain, hoping that he would certainly perish, either by an ostentatious display of his bravery, or by the merciless hand of the enemy. But this project had a very different result from that which he had expected. For when Jugurtha, who was of an active and penetrating intellect, had learned the disposition of Publius Scipio, the Roman general, and the character of the enemy, he quickly rose, by great exertion and vigilance, by modestly submitting to orders, and frequently exposing himself to dangers, to such a degree of reputation, that he was greatly beloved by our men, and extremely dreaded by the Numantines. He was indeed, what is peculiarly difficult, both brave in action, and wise in council; qualities, of which the one, from forethought, generally produces fear, and the other, from confidence, rashness. The general, accordingly, managed almost every difficult matter by the aid of Jugurtha, numbered him among his friends, and grew daily more and more attached to him, as a man whose advice and whose efforts were never useless. With such merits were joined generosity of disposition, and readiness of wit, by which he united to himself many of the Romans in intimate friendship.

There were at that time, in our army, a number of officers, some of low, and some of high birth, to whom wealth was more attractive than virtue or honour; men who were attached to certain parties, and of consequence in their own country; but, among the allies, rather distinguished than respected. These persons inflamed the mind of Jugurtha, of itself sufficiently aspiring, by assuring him, "that if Micipsa should die, he might have the kingdom of Numidia to himself; for that he was possessed of eminent merit, and that anything might be purchased at Rome."

When Numantia, however, was destroyed, and Scipio had determined to dismiss the auxiliary troops, and to return to Rome, he led Jugurtha, after having honoured him, in a public assembly, with the noblest presents and applauses, into his own tent; where he privately admonished him "to court the friendship of the Romans rather by attention to them as a body, than by practising on individuals; to bribe no one, as what belonged to many could not without danger be bought from a few; and adding that, if he would but trust to his own merits, glory and regal power would spontaneously fall to his lot; but, should he proceed too rashly, he would only, by the influence of his money, hasten his own ruin."

Having thus spoken, he took leave of him, giving him a letter, which he was to present to Micipsa, and of which the following was the purport: "The merit of your nephew Jugurtha, in the war against Numantia, has been eminently distinguished; a fact which I am sure will afford you pleasure. He is dear to us for his services, and we shall strive, with our utmost efforts, to make him equally dear to the senate and people of Rome. As a friend, I sincerely congratulate you; you have a kinsman worthy of yourself, and of his grandfather Masinissa."

Micipsa, when he found from the letter of the general, that what he had already heard reported was true, being moved, both by the merit of the youth, and by the interest felt for him by Scipio, altered his purpose, and endeavoured to win Jugurtha by kindnesses. He accordingly, in a short time, adopted him as his son, and made him, by his will, joint-heir with his own children.

A few years afterwards, when, being debilitated by age and disease, he perceived that the end of his life was at hand, he is said, in the presence of his friends and relations, and of Adherbal and Hiempsal, his sons, to have spoken with Jugurtha in the following manner:

"I received you, Jugurtha, at a very early age, into my kingdom, at a time when you had lost your father, and were without prospects or resources, expecting that, in return for my kindness, I should not be less loved by you than by my own children, if I should have any. Nor have my anticipations deceived me; for, to say nothing of your other great and noble deeds, you have lately, on your return from Numantia, brought honour and glory both to me and my kingdom; by your bravery, you have rendered the Romans, from being previously our friends, more friendly to us than ever; the name of our family is revived in Spain; and finally, what is most difficult among mankind, you have suppressed envy by pre-eminent merit.

"And now, since nature is putting a period to my life, I exhort and conjure you, by this right hand, and by the fidelity which you owe to my kingdom, to regard these princes, who are your cousins by birth, and your brothers by my generosity, with sincere affection; and not to be more anxious to attach to yourself strangers, than to retain the love of those connected with you by blood. It is not armies, or treasures, that form the defences of a kingdom, but friends, whom you can neither command by force nor purchase with gold; for they are acquired only by good offices and integrity. And who can be a greater friend than one brother to another? Or what stranger will you find faithful, if you are at enmity with your own family? I leave you a kingdom, which will be strong if you act honourably, but weak, if you are ill-affected to each other; for by concord even small states are increased, but by discord, even the greatest fall to nothing.

"But on you, Jugurtha, who are superior in age and wisdom, it is incumbent, more than on your brothers, to be cautious that nothing of a contrary tendency may arise; for, in all disputes, he that is the stronger, even though he receive the injury, appears, because his power is greater, to have inflicted it. And do you, Adherbal and Hiempsal, respect and regard a kinsman of such a character; imitate his virtues, and make it your endeavour to show that I have not adopted a better son than those whom I have begotten."

To this address, Jugurtha, though he knew that the king had spoken insincerely, and though he was himself revolving thoughts of a far different nature, yet replied with good feeling, suitable to the occasion. A few days afterwards Micipsa died.

When the princes had performed his funeral with due magnificence, they met together to hold a discussion on the general condition of their affairs. Hiempsal, the youngest, who was naturally violent, and who had previously shown contempt for the mean birth of Jugurtha, as being inferior on his mother's side, sat down on the right hand of Adherbal, in order to prevent Jugurtha from being the middle one of the three, which is regarded by the Numidians as the seat of honour. Being urged by his brother, however, to yield to superior age, he at length removed, but with reluctance, to the other seat.

In the course of this conference, after a long debate about the administration of the kingdom, Jugurtha suggested, among other measures, "that all the acts and decrees made in the last five years should be annulled, as Micipsa, during that period, had been enfeebled by age, and scarcely sound in intellect." Hiempsal replied, "that he was exceedingly pleased with the proposal, since Jugurtha himself, within the last three years, had been adopted as joint-heir to the throne."

This repartee sunk deeper into the mind of Jugurtha than any one imagined. From that very time, accordingly, being agitated with resentment and jealousy, he began to meditate and concert schemes, and to think of nothing but projects for secretly cutting off Hiempsal. But his plans proving slow in operation, and his angry feelings remaining unabated, he resolved to execute his purpose by any means whatsoever.

At the first meeting of the princes, of which I have just spoken, it had been resolved, in consequence of their disagreement, that the treasures should be divided among them, and that limits should be set to the jurisdiction of each. Days were accordingly appointed for both these purposes, but the earlier of the two for the division of the money. The princes, in the mean time, retired into separate places of abode in the neighbourhood of the treasury. Hiempsal, residing in the town of Thirmida, happened to occupy the house of a man, who, being Jugurtha's chief lictor, had always been liked and favoured by his master. This man, thus opportunely presented as an instrument, Jugurtha loaded with promises, and induced him to go to his house, as if for the purpose of looking over it, and provide himself with false keys to the gates; for the true ones used to be given to Hiempsal; adding, that he himself, when circumstances should call for his presence, would be at the place with a large body of men. This commission the Numidian speedily executed, and, according to his instructions, admitted Jugurtha's men in the night, who, as soon as they had entered the house, went different ways in quest of the prince; some of his attendants they killed while asleep, and others as they met them; they searched into secret places, broke open those that were shut, and filled the whole premises with uproar and tumult. Hiempsal, after a time, was found concealed in the hut of a maid-servant, where, in his alarm and ignorance of the locality, he had at first taken refuge. The Numidians, as they had been ordered, brought his head to Jugurtha.

The report of so atrocious an outrage was soon spread throughout Africa. Fear seized on Adherbal, and on all who had been subject to Micipsa. The Numidians divided into two parties, the greater number following Adherbal, but the more warlike Jugurtha; who, accordingly, armed as large a force as he could, brought several cities, partly by force and partly by their own consent, under his power, and prepared to make himself sovereign of the whole of Numidia. Adherbal, though he had sent ambassadors to Rome, to inform the senate of his brother's murder and his own circumstances, yet, relying on the number of his troops, prepared for an armed resistance. When the matter, however, came to a contest, he was defeated, and fled from the field of battle into our province, and from thence hastened to Rome.

Jugurtha, having thus accomplished his purpose, and reflecting, at leisure, on the crime which he had committed, began to feel a dread of the Roman people, against whose resentment he had no hopes of security but in the avarice of the nobility, and in his own wealth. A few days afterwards, therefore, he despatched ambassadors to Rome, with a profusion of gold and silver, whom he directed, in the first place, to make abundance of presents to his old friends, and then to procure him new ones; and not to hesitate, in short, to effect whatever could be done by bribery.

When these deputies had arrived at Rome, and had sent large presents, according to the prince's direction, to his intimate friends, and to others whose influence was at that time powerful, so remarkable a change ensued, that Jugurtha, from being an object of the greatest odium, grew into great regard and favour with the nobility; who, partly allured with hope, and partly with actual largesses, endeavoured, by soliciting the members of the senate individually, to prevent any severe measures from being adopted against him. When the ambassadors, accordingly, felt sure of success, the senate, on a fixed day, gave audience to both parties. . . .

Both parties then withdrew from the senate-house, and the senate immediately proceeded to deliberate. The partisans of the ambassadors, with a great many others, corrupted by their influence, expressed contempt for the statements of Adherbal, extolled with the highest encomiums the merits of Jugurtha, and exerted themselves as strenuously, with their interest and eloquence, in defence of the guilt and infamy of another, as they would have striven for their own honour. A few, however, on the other hand, to whom right and justice were of more estimation than wealth, gave their opinion that Adherbal should be assisted, and the murder of Hiempsal severely avenged. Of all these the most forward was Æmilius Scaurus, a man of noble birth and great energy, but factious, and ambitious of power, honour, and wealth; yet an artful concealer of his own vices. He, seeing that the bribery of Jugurtha was notorious and shameless, and fearing that, as in such cases often happens, its scandalous profusion might excite public odium, restrained himself from the indulgence of his ruling passion.

Yet that party gained the superiority in the senate, which preferred money and interest to justice. A decree was made, "that ten commissioners should divide the kingdom, which Micipsa had possessed, between Jugurtha and Adherbal." Of this commission the leading person was Lucius Opimius, a man of distinction, and of great influence at that time in the senate, from having in his consulship, on the death of Caius Gracchus and Marcus Fulvius Flaccus, prosecuted the victory over the nobility with great severity.

Jugurtha, though he had already counted Scaurus among his friends at Rome, yet received him with the most studied ceremony, and, by presents and promises, wrought on him so effectually, that he preferred the prince's interest to his own character, honour, and all other considerations. The rest of the commissioners he assailed in a similar way, and gained over most of them; by a few only integrity was more regarded than lucre. In the division of the kingdom, that part of Numidia which borders on Mauretania, and which is superior in fertility and population, was allotted to Jugurtha; of the other part, which, though better furnished with harbours and buildings, was more valuable in appearance than in reality, Adherbal became the possessor. . . . . .

When the commissioners, after dividing the kingdom, had left Africa, and Jugurtha saw that, contrary to his apprehensions, he had obtained the object of his crimes, he then, being convinced of the truth of what he had heard from his friends at Numantia, "that all things were purchasable at Rome," and being also encouraged by the promises of those whom he had recently loaded with presents, directed his views to the domain of Adherbal. He was himself bold and warlike, while the other, at whose destruction he aimed, was quiet, unfit for arms, of a mild temper, a fit subject for injustice, and a prey to fear rather than an object of it. Jugurtha, accordingly, with a powerful force, made a sudden irruption into his dominions, took several prisoners, with cattle and other booty, set fire to the buildings, and made hostile demonstrations against several places with his cavalry. He then retreated, with all his followers, into his own kingdom, expecting that Adherbal, roused by such provocation, would avenge his wrongs by force, and thus furnish a pretext for war. But Adherbal, thinking himself unable to meet Jugurtha in the field, and relying on the friendship of the Romans more than on the Numidians, merely sent ambassadors to Jugurtha to complain of the outrage; and, although they brought back but an insolent reply, yet he resolved to endure anything rather than have recourse to war, which, when he attempted it before, had ended in his defeat. By such conduct the eagerness of Jugurtha was not at all allayed; for he had now, indeed, in imagination, possessed himself of all Adherbal's dominions. He therefore renewed hostilities, not, as before, with a predatory band, but at the head of a large army which he had collected, and openly aspired to the sovereignty of all Numidia. Wherever he marched, he ravaged the towns and the fields, drove off booty, and raised confidence in his own men and dismay among the enemy.

Adherbal, when he found that matters had arrived at such a point, that he must either abandon his dominions, or defend them by force of arms, collected an army from necessity, and advanced to meet Jugurtha. Both armies took up their position near the town of Cirta, at no great distance from the sea; but, as evening was approaching, encamped without coming to an engagement. But when the night was far advanced, and twilight was beginning to appear, the troops of Jugurtha, at a given signal, rushed into the camp of the enemy, whom they routed and put to flight, some half asleep, and others resuming their arms. Adherbal, with a few of his cavalry, fled to Cirta; and, had there not been a number of Romans in the town, who repulsed his Numidian pursuers from the walls, the war between the two princes would have been begun and ended on the same day.

Jugurtha proceeded to invest the town, and attempted to storm it with the aid of mantelets, towers, and every kind of machines; being anxious, above all things, to take it before the ambassadors could arrive at Rome, who, he was informed, had been despatched thither by Adherbal

before the battle was fought. But as soon as the senate heard of their contention, three young men were sent as deputies into Africa, with directions to go to both of the princes, and to announce to them, in the words of the senate and people of Rome, "that it was their will and resolution that they should lay down their arms, and settle their disputes rather by arbitration than by the sword; since to act thus would be to the honour both of the Romans and themselves."

These deputies soon arrived in Africa, using the greater despatch, because, whilst they were preparing for their journey, a report was spread at Rome of the battle which had been fought, and of the siege of Cirta; but this report told much less than the truth. Jugurtha, having given them an audience, replied, "that nothing was of greater weight with him, nothing more respected, than the authority of the senate; that it had been his endeavour, from his youth, to deserve the esteem of all men of worth; that he had gained the favour of Publius Scipio, a man of the highest eminence, not by dishonourable practices, but by merit; that, for the same good qualities, and not from want of heirs to the throne, he had been adopted by Micipsa; but that, the more honourable and spirited his conduct had been, the less could his feelings endure injustice; that Adherbal had formed designs against his life, on discovering which, he had conteracted his malice; that the Romans would act neither justly nor reasonably, if they withheld from him the common right of nations; and, in conclusion, that he would soon send ambassadors to Rome to explain the whole of his proceedings." On this understanding, both parties separated. Of addressing Adberhal the deputies had no opportunity.

Jugurtha, as soon as he thought that they had quitted Africa, surrounded the walls of Cirta, which, from the nature of its situation, he was unable to take by assault, with a rampart and a trench; he also erected towers, and manned them with soldiers; he made attempts on the place, by force or by stratagem, day and night; he held out bribes, and sometimes menaces, to the besieged; he roused his men, by exhortations, to efforts of valour, and resorted, with the utmost perseverance, to every possible expedient.

Adherbal, on the other hand, seeing that his affairs were in a desperate condition, that his enemy was determined on his ruin, that there was no hope of succour, and that the siege, from want of provisions, could not long be protracted, selected, from among those who had fled with him to Cirta, two of his most resolute supporters, whom he induced, by numerous promises, and an affecting representation of his distress, to make their way in the night, through the enemy's lines, to the nearest point of the coast, and from thence to Rome.

The Numidians, in a few days, executed their commission; and a letter from Adherbal was read in the senate, of which the following was the purport:

"It is not through my own fault, Conscript Fathers, that I so often send requests to you; but the violence of Jugurtha compels me; whom so strong a desire for my destruction has seized, that he pays no regard either to you or to the immortal gods; my blood he covets beyond everything. Five months, in consequence, have I, the ally and friend of the Roman people, been besieged with an armed force; neither the remembrance of my father Micipsa's benefits, nor your decrees, are of any avail for my relief; and whether I am more closely pressed by the sword or by famine, I am unable to say.

"From writing further concerning Jugurtha, my present condition deters me; for I have experienced, even before, that little credit is given to the unfortunate. Yet I can perceive that his views extend further than to myself, and that he does not expect to possess, at the same time, your friendship and my kingdom; which of the two he thinks the more desirable, must be manifest to every one. For, in the first place, he murdered my brother Hiempsal; and, in the next, expelled me from my dominions; which, however, may be regarded as our own wrongs, and as having no reference to you. But now he occupies your kingdom with an army; he keeps me, whom you appointed a king over the Numidians, in a state of blockade; and in what estimation he holds the words of your ambassadors, my perils may serve to show. What then is left, except your arms, that can make an impression upon him?

"I could wish, indeed, that what I now write, as well as the complaints which I lately made before the senate, were false, rather than that my present distresses should confirm the truth of my statements. But since I am born to be an example of Jugurtha's villany, I do not now beg a release from death or distress, but only from the tyranny of an enemy, and from bodily torture. Respecting the kingdom of Numidia, which is your own property, determine as you please, but if the memory of my grandfather Masinissa is still cherished by you, deliver me, I entreat you, by the majesty of your empire, and by the sacred ties of friendship, from the inhuman hands of Jugurtha."

When this letter was read, there were some who thought that an army should be despatched into Africa, and relief afforded to Adherbal, as soon as possible; and that the senate, in the mean time, should give judgment on the conduct of Jugurtha, in not having obeyed the ambassadors. But by the partisans of Jugurtha, the same that had before supported his cause, effectual exertions were made to prevent any decree from being passed; and thus the public interest, as is too frequently the case, was defeated by private influence.

An embassy was, however, despatched

into Africa, consisting of men of advanced years, and of noble birth, and who had filled the highest offices of the state; among whom was Marcus Scaurus, already mentioned, a man who had held the consulship, and who was at that time chief of the senate. These ambassadors, as their business was an affair of public odium, and as they were urged by the entreaties of the Numidians, embarked in three days; and having soon arrived at Utica, sent a letter from thence to Jugurtha, desiring him "to come to the province as quickly as possible, as they were deputed by the senate to meet him."

Jugurtha, when he found that men of eminence, whose influence at Rome he knew to be powerful, were come to put a stop to his proceedings, was at first perplexed, and distracted between fear and cupidity. He dreaded the displeasure of the senate, if he should disobey the ambassadors; while his eager spirit, blinded by the lust of power, hurried him on to complete the injustice which he had begun. At length the evil incitements of ambition prevailed. He accordingly drew his army round the city of Cirta, and endeavoured, with his utmost efforts, to force an entrance; having the strongest hopes, that by dividing the attention of the enemy's troops, he should be able, by force or artifice, to secure an opportunity of success. When his attempts, however, were unavailing, and he found himself unable, as he had designed, to get Adherbal into his power before he met the ambassadors, fearing that, by further delay, he might irritate Scaurus, of whom he stood in great dread, he proceeded with a small body of cavalry into the Province. Yet, though serious menaces were repeated to him in the name of the senate, because he had not desisted from the siege, nevertheless, after spending a long time in conference, the ambassadors departed without making any impression upon him.

When news of this result was brought to Cirta, the Italians, by whose exertions the city had been defended, and who trusted that, if a surrender were made, they would be able, from respect to the greatness of the Roman power, to escape without personal injury, advised Adherbal to deliver himself and the city to Jugurtha, stipulating only that his life should be spared, and leaving all other matters to the care of the senate. Adherbal, though he thought nothing less trustworthy than the honour of Jugurtha, yet, knowing that those who advised could also compel him if he resisted, surrendered the place according to their desire. Jugurtha immediately proceeded to put Adherbal to death with torture, and massacred all the inhabitants that were of age, whether Numidians or Italians, as each fell in the way of his troops.

When this outrage was reported at Rome, and became a matter of discussion in the senate, the former partisans of Jugurtha applied themselves, by interrupting the debates and protracting the time, sometimes exerting their interest and sometimes quarrelling with particular members, to palliate the atrocity of the deed. And had not Caius Memmius, one of the tribunes of the people elect, a man of energy, and hostile to the power of the nobility, convinced the people of Rome that an attempt was being made, by the agency of a small faction, to have the crimes of Jugurtha pardoned, it is certain that the public indignation against him would have passed off under the protraction of the debates; so powerful was party interest, and the influence of Jugurtha's money. When the senate, however, from consciousness of misconduct, became afraid of the people, Numidia and Italy, by the Sempronian law, were appointed as provinces to the succeeding consuls, who were declared to be Publius Scipio Nasica, and Lucius Bestia Calpurnius. Numidia fell to Calpurnius, and Italy to Scipio. An army was then raised to be sent into Africa; and pay, and all other necessaries of war, were decreed for its use.

When Jugurtha received this news, which was utterly at variance with his expectations, as he had felt convinced that all things were purchasable at Rome, he sent his son, with two of his friends, as deputies to the senate, and directed them, like those whom he had sent on the murder of Hiempsal, to attack everybody with bribes. Upon the approach of these deputies to Rome, the senate was consulted by Bestia, whether they would allow them to be admitted within the gates; and the senate decreed, "that, unless they came to surrender Jugurtha's kingdom and himself, they must quit Italy within the ten following days." The consul directed this decree to be communicated to the Numidians, who consequently returned home without effecting their object.

Calpurnius, in the mean time, having raised an army, chose for his officers men of family and intrigue, hoping that whatever faults he might commit, would be screened by their influence; and among these was Scaurus, of whose disposition and character we have already spoken. There were, indeed, in our consul Calpurnius, many excellent qualities, both mental and personal, though avarice interfered with the exercise of them; he was patient of labour, of a penetrating intellect, of great foresight, not inexperienced in war, and extremely vigilant against danger and surprise.

The troops were conducted through Italy to Rhegium, from thence to Sicily, and from Sicily into Africa; and Calpurnius's first step, after collecting provisions, was to invade Numidia with spirit, where he took many prisoners, and several towns, by force of arms.

But when Jugurtha began, through his emissaries, to tempt him with bribes, and to show the difficulties of the war which he had undertaken to conduct, his mind,

corrupted with avarice, was easily altered. His accomplice, however, and manager in all his schemes, was Scaurus; who, though he had at first, when most of his party were corrupted, displayed violent hostility to Jugurtha, yet was afterwards seduced, by a vast sum of money, from integrity and honour to injustice and perfidy. Jugurtha, however, at first sought only to purchase a suspension of hostilities, expecting to be able, during the interval, to make some favourable impression, either by bribery or by interest, at Rome; but when he heard that Scaurus was co-operating with Calpurnius, he was elated with great hopes of regaining peace, and resolved upon a conference with them in person respecting the terms of it. In the mean time, for the sake of giving confidence to Jugurtha, Sextus the quæstor was despatched by the consul to Vaga, one of the prince's towns; the pretext for his journey being the receiving of corn, which Calpurnius had openly demanded from Jugurtha's emissaries, on the ground that a truce was observed through their delay to make a surrender. Jugurtha, then, as he had determined, paid a visit to the consul's camp, where, having made a short address to the council, respecting the odium cast upon his conduct, and his desire for a capitulation, he arranged other matters with Bestia and Scaurus in secret; and the next day, as if by an evident majority of voices, he was formally allowed to surrender. But, as was demanded in the hearing of the council, thirty elephants, a considerable number of cattle and horses, and a small sum of money, were delivered into the hands of the quæstor. Calpurnius then returned to Rome to preside at the election of magistrates, and peace was observed throughout Numidia and the Roman army.

When rumour had made known the affairs transacted in Africa, and the mode in which they had been brought to pass, the conduct of the consul became a subject of discussion in every place and company at Rome. Among the people there was violent indignation; as to the senators, whether they would ratify so flagitious a proceeding, or annul the act of the consul, was a matter of doubt. The influence of Scaurus, as he was said to be the supporter and accomplice of Bestia, was what chiefly restrained the senate from acting with justice and honour. But Caius Memmius, of whose boldness of spirit, and hatred to the power of the nobility, I have already spoken, excited the people by his harangues, during the perplexity and delay of the senators, to take vengeance on the authors of the treaty; he exhorted them not to abandon the public interest or their own liberty; he set before them the many tyrannical and violent proceedings of the nobles, and omitted no art to inflame the popular passions. . . .

By repeating these and similar sentiments, Memmius prevailed on the people to send Lucius Cassius, who was then prætor, to Jugurtha, and to bring him, under guarantee of the public faith, to Rome, in order that, by the prince's evidence, the misconduct of Scaurus and the rest, whom they charged with having taken bribes, might more easily be made manifest.

During the course of these proceedings at Rome, those whom Bestia had left in Numidia in command of the army, following the example of their general, had been guilty of many scandalous transactions. Some, seduced by gold, had restored Jugurtha his elephants; others had sold him his deserters; others had ravaged the lands of those at peace with us; so strong a spirit of rapacity, like the contagion of a pestilence, had pervaded the breasts of all.

Cassius, when the measure proposed by Memmius had been carried, and whilst all the nobility were in consternation, set out on his mission to Jugurtha, whom, alarmed as he was, and despairing of his fortune, from a sense of guilt, he admonished "that, since he had surrendered himself to the Romans, he had better make trial of their mercy than their power." He also pledged his own word, which Jugurtha valued not less than that of the public, for his safety. Such, at that period, was the reputation of Cassius.

Jugurtha, accordingly, accompanied Cassius to Rome, but without any mark of royalty, and in the garb, as much as possible, of a suppliant; and, though he felt great confidence on his own part, and was supported by all those through whose power or villany he had accomplished his projects, he purchased, by a vast bribe, the aid of Caius Bæbius, a tribune of the people, by whose audacity he hoped to be protected against the law, and against all harm.

An assembly of the people being convoked, Memmius, although they were violently exasperated against Jugurtha (some demanding that he should be cast into prison, others that, unless he should name his accomplices in guilt, he should be put to death, according to the usage of their ancestors, as a public enemy), yet, regarding rather their character than their resentment, endeavoured to calm their turbulence and mitigate their rage; and assured them that, as far as depended on him, the public faith should not be broken. At length, when silence was obtained, he brought forward Jugurtha, and addressed them. He detailed the misdeeds of Jugurtha at Rome and in Numidia, and set forth his crimes towards his father and brothers; and admonished the prince, "that the Roman people, though they were well aware by whose support and agency he had acted, yet desired further testimony from himself; that, if he disclosed the truth, there was great hope for him in the honour and clemency of the Romans; but if he concealed it, he would certainly not save his accomplices, but ruin himself and his hopes for ever."

But when Memmius had concluded his speech, and Jugurtha was expected to give his answer, Caius Bæbius, the tribune of the people, whom I have just noticed as having been bribed, enjoined the prince to hold his peace; and though the multitude, who formed the assembly, were desperately enraged, and endeavoured to terrify the tribune by outcries, by angry looks, by violent gestures, and by every other act to which anger prompts, his audacity was at last triumphant. The people, mocked and set at nought, withdrew from the place of assembly; and the confidence of Jugurtha, Bestia, and the others, whom this investigation had alarmed, was greatly augmented.

There was at this period in Rome a certain Numidian named Massiva, a son of Gulussa, and grandson of Masinissa, who, from having been, in the dissensions among the princes, opposed to Jugurtha, had been obliged, after the surrender of Cirta and the murder of Adherbal, to make his escape out of Africa. Spurius Albinus, who was consul with Quintus Minucius Rufus the year after Bestia, prevailed upon this man, as he was of the family of Masinissa, and as odium and terror hung over Jugurtha for his crimes, to petition the senate for the kingdom of Numidia. Albinus, being eager for the conduct of a war, was desirous that affairs should be disturbed, rather than sink into tranquillity; especially as, in the division of the provinces, Numidia had fallen to himself, and Macedonia to Minucius.

When Massiva proceeded to carry these suggestions into execution, Jugurtha, finding that he had no sufficient support in his friends, as a sense of guilt deterred some, and evil report or timidity others, from coming forward in his behalf, directed Bomilcar, his most attached and faithful adherent, to procure by the aid of money, by which he had already effected so much, assassins to kill Massiva; and to do it secretly if he could; but, if secrecy should be impossible, to cut him off in any way whatsoever. This commission Bomilcar soon found means to execute; and, by the agency of men versed in such service, ascertained the direction of his journeys, his hours of leaving home, and the times at which he resorted to particular places, and, when all was ready, placed his assassins in ambush. One of their number sprung upon Massiva, though with too little caution, and killed him; but being himself caught, he made, at the instigation of many, and especially of Albinus the consul, a full confession. Bomilcar was accordingly committed for trial, though rather on the principles of reason and justice than in accordance with the law of nations, as he was in the retinue of one who had come to Rome on a pledge of the public faith for his safety. But Jugurtha, though clearly guilty of the crime, did not cease to struggle against the truth, until he perceived that the infamy of the deed was too strong for his interest or his money. For which reason, although, at the commencement of the proceedings, he had given fifty of his friends as bail for Bomilcar, yet, thinking more of his kingdom than of the sureties, he sent him off privately into Numidia; for he feared that if such a man should be executed, his other subjects would be deterred from obeying him. A few days after, he himself departed, having been ordered by the senate to quit Italy. But, as he was going from Rome, he is said, after frequently looking back on it in silence, to have at last exclaimed, "That it was a venal city, and would soon perish, if it could but find a purchaser!"

　　　　　　　　　　　—J. S. Watson.

EXPANSION TOWARDS THE EAST

On Pompey's Command

CICERO

[From the *Manilian Law*]

Marcus Tullius Cicero was born in 106 and died in 43 B.C.

Coming from a well-to-do family of the town of Arpinum, with little political influence to assist him, Cicero won his way to the consulship, the greatest office of the state, by real ability, genius as a speaker, and honest patriotism. During his year as consul he caused the failure of Catiline's conspiracy to overthrow the government. This service Cicero regarded as his greatest to his country, and the senate gave him the honorable title of father of his country (*pater patriae*) in recognition of it. He stood apart from the first triumvirate of Pompey, Cæsar, and Crassus, which controlled Rome for a time. He acquiesced in the dictatorship of Cæsar; but after his death made a noble, if pathetic, attempt to save the Republic. The effort cost him his life at the hands of Antony's followers.

Cicero, more than any other Latin author, represents that combination of Greek learning and culture and its practical application and use in Roman thought and institutions, which characterizes the whole of Roman literature. He is not a philosopher, but rather an interpreter of philosophy. It is possible to discover Greek sources for nearly all his work, except such parts as have to do only with immediate problems of politics and the courts; but he skillfully modifies and alters what he finds to make it express more accurately the Roman life. He perfected himself especially in the art of oratory, and is reckoned the greatest master of speech of his race. By reason of the fact that he was a prolific writer of private letters, into which he poured his inmost thoughts and feelings, no man of antiquity is personally better known to us. The letters have the additional great values of covering an important period of history not otherwise known to us in detail, and of coming from the pen of one of the leading public men in an era of political upheaval.

The ever widening sphere of Rome's activity brought not only problems of war and of provincial government, but also problems of a political nature at home growing out of the foreign policy. Cicero is convinced of the wisdom of going ahead with the program of expansion, on the one hand; and on the other, he is not afraid of entrusting extraordinary power to one man. Pompey's almost limitless command against Mithridates was granted him in 66 B.C.

Though your crowded assemblies, Romans, be always a grateful sight to me; though this place appears the most conspicuous for counsel, and the most honourable for debate: yet not choice, but the way of life I have engaged in from my early youth, have hitherto excluded me from this theatre of praise, ever open to the worthy and the wise. For as till now I had not reached the age necessary to entitle me to so distinguished an honour, and as I judged nothing worthy of this tribunal, in which the most consummate genius and industry were not conspicuous; I thought it best to dedicate my whole time to the concerns of my friends. Accordingly this place has always abounded with able pleaders in the cause of the republic: and my talents, employed in the defence of private citizens, have by your suffrages been crowned with a glorious reward. For when by reason of the adjournment of the comitia, I found myself thrice chosen first prætor by all the centuries, it was easy for me thence to collect, both what your sentiments of me were, and what qualifications you required in others. Now that I am clothed with all that authority which is annexed to the offices you have honoured me with; and as my talents for business are such as the constant exercise of pleading may produce in a man of industry; be assured, that whatever authority I possess, shall be exercised in behalf of those from whom I derived it; and if my eloquence carries any weight, I will display it chiefly to those who have thought it worthy of reward. And here I think I may justly congratulate myself, that, unaccustomed as I am to harangue in this manner, and from this place, a subject presents itself, on which it is impossible not to be eloquent. I am to speak of the singular and amazing virtues of Pompey; a theme where I shall find it more difficult to know where to stop, than how to begin; and where my principal study must be, not to search for materials, but to set bounds to my oration.

But that my discourse may run back to the source of the present debate; an important and dangerous war is carried on against your tributaries and allies, by two very powerful monarchs, Mithridates and Tigranes: of whom the one being provoked, and the other not pushed after his defeat; they think a favourable opportunity offers to possess themselves of all Asia. Letters are daily brought from that quarter to the Roman knights, men of character and eminence, who have a great interest in the collection of your revenues; and on account of my near connection with their order, have thought proper to lay before me the cause of the republic, and the danger to which their own private fortunes are exposed: that in Bithynia, now a Roman province, a great number of villages are burnt down: that the kingdom of Ariobarzanes, which borders on your tributaries, is wholly in the power of your enemy: that Lucullus, after a series of great exploits, is about to relinquish that war: that his successor is but ill provided for the execution of so difficult an enterprise: and that the unanimous voice of citizens and allies, points at and demands one person for the conduct of this war, as the only man alive who strikes terror into our enemies. You see then the point in question: it now remains to consider what is fit to be done. To me it seems necessary to speak, first of the nature, then of the greatness of the war, and lastly of the choice of a general. The nature of the war is such as ought to rouse all your courage, and kindle your warmest resentment. It regards the glory of the Roman people, which your ancestors have transmitted with so much lustre in all things, but principally in the science of arms. It regards the safety of your friends and allies, in defence of which your forefathers have sustained many heavy and dangerous wars. It regards the surest and fairest revenues of the commonwealth, without which we can neither support peace with dignity, nor furnish the necessary expenses during the war. In fine, it regards the private fortunes of many illustrious citizens, whose prosperity demands your utmost attention, both on their own and the republic's account.

And because the thirst of glory, and the passion for fame, has always been stronger in you, than in any other people; you must wipe out that stain contracted in the last Mithridatic war, which has given so deep and dangerous a wound to the reputation of the Roman people: that the man who in one day, over all Asia, through so many states, by a simple courier, and the contents of a single letter, marked out the Roman citizens to butchery and destruction, has not only hitherto escaped without any suitable punishment, but now counts the twenty-third year of his reign from that period: a reign too so prosperous, that instead of seeking to hide himself in Pontus, and the fastnesses of Cappadocia, he has broke through the limits of his paternal inheritance, and riots among your tributary provinces, in the rich and fertile country of Asia. For hitherto your generals have fought in such a manner with this prince, as to carry off the trophies of victory, not victory itself. L. Sulla triumphed; L. Murena triumphed over Mithridates; both brave men, and accomplished commanders: but their triumphs were such as to leave him, after all his losses and defeats, in full possession of royalty. Nevertheless these generals deserve praise for what they did, and pardon for what they left undone; for the concerns of the commonwealth recalled Sulla, and Sulla himself recalled Murena from the prosecution of that war.

But Mithridates employed the interval that followed, not in endeavours to blot out the memory of the ancient quarrel, but in concerting measures to renew the war: and, after building and equipping vast fleets; levying great armies in all the countries whence troops could be had; and causing a report to be spread, that his design was to make war upon the people of the Bosphorus, his neighbours; he sent ambassadors from Ecbatana into Spain, to treat with the generals then at war with the republic: that obliging you to make head both by sea and land, against two mighty enemies acting in concert, and in provinces so very remote and distant from each other, you may find yourselves embarrassed by the double attack, and be reduced to the necessity of fighting for your empire. But one part of this storm, which proceeded from Sertorius and Spain, and was by far the most formidable and threatening, was dissipated by the divine conduct and singular valour of Pompey: and in the other scene of action, affairs were so managed by Lucullus, that great and illustrious commander, that his glorious successes in the beginning may be justly attributed to his prudence, not to his good fortune; whereas those later disasters, which have since befallen him, seem purely the work of chance, and are not imputable to his misconduct. But of Lucullus I will speak elsewhere, and speak in such a manner, Romans, as neither to deprive him of any due praise, nor load him with false commendations. At present, as the chief design of my speech is the honour and dignity of your empire, see what ought to be your resentments upon this occasion.

Your forefathers often engaged in a war, to revenge the insults offered to their merchants and seamen. How then ought you to be fired, when you call to mind, that in consequence of a single express, so many thousand Roman citizens were butchered in one day? Corinth, the pride and ornament of Greece, was by your ancestors doomed to utter destruction, because of the insolent behaviour of the citizens to their ambassadors: and will you suffer the tyrant to escape with impunity, by whom a consular senator of the Roman people was condemned to be bound, scourged, and put to death with the most cruel torments? Your fathers would not permit the least infringement of their privileges; and will you tamely overlook the murder of Roman citizens? These avenged even a verbal insult upon the dignity of their ambassador; and shall the blood of a Roman senator, shed in the most cruel manner, cry for no vengeance from you? Beware, citizens, beware, lest, as it was glorious for them to transmit so extensive an empire to posterity, your inability to preserve and defend it prove not infamous for you. What, to appear unconcerned when the very safety and being of your allies is at stake! Ariobarzanes, a sovereign prince, the friend and confederate of the Roman people, is expelled his dominions. Two potent kings, the inveterate foes not only of Rome, but of every state in amity and alliance with her, threaten all Asia. The provinces of Greece, and beyond the Hellespont, unable to repel the danger, look to you for aid; but without daring, or thinking it safe to name the particular general they want, because you have already put another into that commission. They see and know, as you do, that there is one man, in whom all great qualities meet; and are the more impatient to be without him, as he is so near at hand to undertake their defence: a man, whose very name and approach, though he came only vested with a naval commission, they nevertheless perceive to have checked and retarded the enemies' attempts. And because they dare not openly proclaim their desires, they silently implore you to consider them, in common with the other allied provinces, as worthy of the protection of such a hero. This request is the more reasonable, as we have lately sent them commanders, who indeed defended them from the enemy, but whose entrance into their cities differed little from taking them by storm. As to the general now in their eye, they have formerly heard, but at present find him so full of gentleness, moderation, and humanity, that happiest appears the people among whom he longest resides.

If then your ancestors, unprovoked by any injury themselves, and merely for the sake of their allies, engaged in war with Antiochus, Philip, the Ætolians, and Carthaginians: how much more ought you, irritated by a series of personal affronts, to exert yourselves warmly in a quarrel, where the dignity of your empire is united with the cause of your confederates; more especially as the fairest revenues of the republic are at stake? For the revenues of the other provinces are such as scarce to defray the expense of protecting them: but Asia is a country so opulent and fertile, that whether we regard the richness of the soil, the variety of fruits, its abundant pastures, and the multitude of commodities for exportation, it easily claims the preference to all other climates. And therefore, Romans, if you aspire either at success in war, or dignity in peace, you must not only defend this province from conquest, but even from the apprehension of being invaded. For in other affairs, the loss is felt when the disaster happens: but in what regards the revenues of a state, not only real misfortunes but the very apprehension of them is productive of mischief. For when an enemy approaches, though no irruption be yet made, the cattle are abandoned, agriculture is neglected, and commerce

stagnates. Thus all taxes, whether upon shipping, manufactures, or the fruits of the earth, necessarily cease; insomuch that the bare rumour of danger, the very apprehension of a war, often sinks the revenues of a whole year. What then may you suppose to be the situation, either of those who pay, or those who collect the public tributes, when they see themselves threatened with an invasion from two formidable monarchs? When a single incursion of the enemy's cavalry may rifle at once the revenue of an entire year? when the farmers of the taxes shall perceive, that all the people employed under them, in the forests, in the fields, in sea-ports, and in garrisons, are exposed to imminent danger? Do you imagine it possible to enjoy the labour of all these, without preserving the labourers themselves, not only from the reality, but, as I said before, from the very dread of danger?

Nor ought you to overlook the last point I proposed to mention, in speaking of the nature of the war: I mean what regards the fortunes of many Roman citizens; to which, my countrymen, your wisdom ought to pay a particular regard. For the farmers of the revenue, men of worth and rank in the republic, have conveyed all their wealth and effects into that province; and it is incumbent upon you, to bestow your utmost attention upon the preservation of their fortunes. For if we have ever considered the public tributes as the sinews of the state, sure that order of men who are employed in collecting them, may be justly looked upon as the cement and support of all the other orders. Besides, a number of active and industrious men of other denominations, whose interest you ought to take care of in their absence, are some now trading in Asia, while others have laid out their money to a great extent in that province. Humanity therefore requires you, to protect the fortunes of such a multitude of citizens; and prudence dictates, that the ruin of so many individuals cannot fail to affect the public prosperity. For it will avail but little to recover by a victory, what the officers of the revenue may have lost; because such as enjoyed the customs before, will be disabled from renewing the farm, and others will avoid engaging through fear. Besides, instructed by past misfortunes, we ought surely to keep in mind, what the same province, and the same Mithridates, taught us towards the beginning of the Asiatic war. For a number of citizens sustaining at that time great losses in Asia, we know that public credit was at a stand at Rome, from a general stoppage of payment. And indeed, where a multitude of individuals in any state suffer an entire shipwreck of their fortunes, it is impossible but others must be involved in the same calamity. Shield the commonwealth therefore from this danger, and give credit to a principle which experience must have taught you. The public credit at Rome, the circulation of money in the forum, is connected with, and dependent upon the revenues of Asia; the loss of which must infallibly draw after it the ruin of the other. Judge, then, whether you ought not to bend all your cares to the vigorous prosecution of a war, in which the glory of your empire, the safety of your allies, the principal revenues of the state, and the properties of many illustrious citizens, are connected with the defence of the republic.

Having thus finished what I had to say concerning the nature of the war, it now remains that I speak of its greatness. And this much I will venture to affirm; that it is indeed a necessary and unavoidable war, yet not so considerable as to give cause of fear. My principal endeavour therefore, on this occasion, must be, that some particulars which deserve your utmost attention, be not slightly overlooked as scarce worthy of notice. And here, that every one may be sensible how I am disposed to allow all that praise

to Lucullus, which is due to a brave citizen, a wise man, and a great general; I readily own, that at his arrival, the numerous forces of Mithridates were provided with every thing necessary or convenient; that Cyzicum, the noblest city of Asia, and the best affected to Rome, was invested and vigorously pressed by the king in person, at the head of a formidable army; and that the courage, assiduity and admirable conduct of Lucullus, freed it from the imminent danger to which it was exposed. I must add, that a strong and well appointed fleet, fitted out by Sertorius's lieutenants, who burned with desire to wreak their vengeance upon Italy, was by the same general defeated and sunk: that in numberless encounters besides, great bodies of the enemies' forces were overthrown: that Pontus, hitherto inaccessible to the Roman people, was exposed to the depredations of our legions: that Sinope and Amisus, two cities of royal residence, adorned and provided with all the means of defence, with many other towns of Pontus and Cappadocia, were taken in one march, and in one approach: that Mithridates himself, despoiled of his hereditary and paternal dominions, was forced to fly a suppliant to other kings and states: and that all these great actions were performed, without loss to our allies or diminution of our revenues. This, I think, sufficiently speaks his praise; and I believe you will readily allow, Romans, that none of the opposers of this law and measure, have so fully enlarged upon the merits of Lucullus from this place.

But now, perhaps, it will be asked, if these things are so, how can so difficult a war still remain? Let us examine into this matter a little; for the question is not without foundation. Know then, Romans, that Mithridates fled from this kingdom, just as the famed Medea is said to have escaped out of the same Pontus: whom report feigns to have scattered the limbs of her murdered brother in those places through which her father was to pass, that the care of collecting them, and paternal grief, might stay the celerity of his pursuit. Thus Mithridates, to favour his flight, left in Pontus an immense collection of gold and silver, and other valuable and costly ornaments, which he had either inherited from his ancestors, or got by plunder in the last Asiatic war, and treasured up in his own dominions. While our troops were employed in pillaging these, the person of the king escaped. Thus in the former case grief, in the latter joy, checked the eager desire of pursuit. In this flight, and under the influence of these terrors, he took refuge with Tigranes, king of Armenia, who received him kindly, roused him from his diffidence, cheered him in his distress, and restored him to some degree of hope. Lucullus followed him with his army into this prince's territories, where he found many nations ready to oppose him, from the dread they entertained of the Roman forces, though they were far from any design either to provoke or attack them. A prevalent and general persuasion had likewise taken hold of the minds of these barbarians, that the design of pillaging a rich and awful temple, had brought our armies into these parts. Thus many very powerful nations were spirited up against us, by a new kind of terror and dread. Meanwhile our troops, though they took the capital of Tigranes's kingdom, and routed the enemy in several encounters, were, nevertheless, dismayed at the distance of the provinces in which they fought, and seized with a desire to return to their own country. Here let me stop: for the issue of all was, that our soldiers discovered a greater inclination to retire, than to advance. But Mithridates had by this time revived the courage of his troops, and found his army greatly increased by multitudes that flocked to him from his own dominions, and the numerous rein-

forcements of many foreign kings and nations. This we learn from experience to be frequently the case, that the eminent distresses of princes, by the compassion they are apt to excite, raise powerful confederates in their favour, especially of such as are either monarchs themselves, or live in subjection to monarchy; because to them the name of royalty sounds great and venerable. Accordingly he was able to effect more after his defeat, than in the very height of his prosperity he durst presume to hope. For when he returned to his own kingdom, not contented with so unexpected a piece of good fortune, in recovering the possession of a country whence he thought himself expelled for ever, he even had the boldness to attack your brave and victorious army. Suffer me, Romans, in this place, after the example of the poets, who write of your affairs, to suppress the mention of our calamity: a calamity so great, that it reached the ears of Lucullus, not by any messenger escaped from the battle, but by the reports of public rumour. In this scene of distress, and amidst the heavy losses of so destructive a war, L. Lucullus, who might in some measure, perhaps have found a remedy for these evils, constrained by your orders, which, in imitation of former times, set bounds to the duration of his command, dismissed that part of the army which had completed its legal term of service, and delivered over the other to Glabrio. I designedly pass over many things; leaving it to your own conjectures to inform you how important that war is like to prove, in which, after the defeat of your former army, you are still to oppose, under the auspices of a new commander, the confederacy of two powerful kings, the renewed hostilities of resentful nations, and the entire forces of unsubdued countries.

Methinks I have said enough to prove that this war is in its nature necessary, and by its importance dangerous. Let me now speak of the choice of a general fit to command in such a war, and have charge of so great an undertaking. It were to be wished, Romans, that this state so abounded with men of courage and probity, as to make it a matter of difficulty to determine, to whom chiefly you should entrust the conduct of so important and dangerous a war. But as Pompey is universally allowed, not only to surpass the generals of the present age, but even those of antiquity, in military fame; what reason can any man assign, why he should hesitate a moment in the present choice? To me four qualifications seem requisite to form a complete general, a thorough knowledge of war, valour, authority, and good fortune. But where is the man that possesses, or indeed can be required to possess greater abilities in war, than Pompey? One that from a boy, and the exercises of the school, passed into his father's camp, and began the study of the military art, during the progress of a raging war, maintained by a furious enemy? who, before the period of childhood was elapsed, commenced a soldier under a great general? who, in the very dawn of youth, was himself at the head of a mighty army? who has fought more pitched battles, than others have maintained personal disputes; carried on more wars, than others have acquired by knowledge of reading; reduced more provinces, than others have aspired to even in thought? whose youth was trained to the profession of arms, not by precepts derived from others, but the highest offices of command; not by personal mistakes in war, but a train of important victories; not by a series of campaigns, but by a succession of triumphs? In fine, what species of war can be named, in which the fortune of the republic has not given him an opportunity of exercising himself? the civil, the African, the Transalpine, the servile, the naval; together with that of Spain, in which such a multitude of our own citizens and warlike foreigners were concerned. So many and different wars, against such a variety of foes, not only carried on, but happily terminated by this one man, sufficiently proclaim, that there is no part of military knowledge in which he is not an accomplished master. . . .

As, therefore, this war is so necessary, that it cannot be avoided; so important, that it must be managed with the utmost address: and as you may now commit it into the hands of a general, who, to the most consummate knowledge in the art of war, joins eminent courage, an illustrious reputation, and unparalleled success: will ye hesitate, Romans, to employ so favourable an opportunity, presented and put into your hands by the immortal gods, for the preservation and enlargement of your empire?

Were Pompey at this time in Rome, in the station of a private citizen, he is yet the only person fit to be chosen for the management of so great a war. But now, when with other urgent advantages, this powerful motive likewise concurs; that he is already upon the spot; that he is at the head of an army, that he can immediately join it to the forces now in those parts; what wait we for? Or why do we not, when the gods so clearly discover their pleasure, intrust likewise this royal war to the care of the man, who has already terminated so many others with the highest advantage to the state? But, Q. Catulus, a man of an illustrious character, a great lover of his country, and distinguished by the most eminent proofs of your regard; and Q. Hortensius, conspicuous by all the advantages of honour, fortune, virtue, and genius, differ from my opinion. These, I own, are men, whose sentiments have always had great weight with you, and doubtless very deservedly: but on this occasion, though some of the best and bravest men in Rome be against me, yet setting authority aside, I think we may come at the truth by reason and enquiry; the rather, because my very adversaries agree to all I have advanced, that this war is necessary, and important; and that all the great qualities requisite for conducting it are to be found in Pompey. What then is the argument of Hortensius? If all important affairs are to pass through the hands of one man, Pompey is doubtless the most deserving: but it were dangerous to trust so much power with one person. This position, refuted rather by facts than by reasoning, is now become quite stale. For you, Q. Hortensius, with that masterly and commanding eloquence which is peculiar to you, spoke fully and forcibly against Aulus Gabinius, a brave tribune; both in the senate, when his law for putting the war against the pirates into the hands of one general was brought before that assembly: and from this place, when it was proposed to the consideration of the people. But tell me, in the name of all the gods! if your authority had availed more with the Roman people, than the consideration of their own safety and true interest, should we at this day have been in possession of so much glory, or really enjoyed the sovereignty of the universe? For could we then be deemed to possess this sovereignty, when the ambassadors, prætors, and quæstors of the Roman people, were liable to an ignominious captivity? When we were deprived of all communication, either public or private, with our provinces? When navigation was so totally at a stand, that we could transact no business beyond sea, whether it regarded the interest of the whole state, or the properties of particular persons?

For was there ever a state, I speak not of the Athenians, who are said to have been once very powerful at sea; nor of the Carthaginians, renowned for their fleets and naval strength; nor of the Rhodians, the glory of whose maritime expeditions have reached even our days: but was there, I say, ever a state so inconsiderable, an island so small, that could not herself defend her own ports and territory, with some part at least of the maritime coast and region? And yet, for a continued train of years before the Gabinian law, the very people of Rome, whose reputation in sea-affairs has remained even to our day without stain, were not only divested of far the greatest part of their traffick, but were even wounded in their dignity and naval dominion. We, whose ancestors vanquished king Antiochus and Perseus at sea, and came off victorious in all naval engagements with the Carthaginians, a nation thoroughly expert and practised in maritime affairs: we, I say, were then no where a match for a band of pirates. We too, who heretofore not only guarded Italy from insults, but by the very reputation of our strength secured the quiet of our allies in all parts, however remote; insomuch that the island of Delos, distant from Rome so far as the Ægean sea, the mart of all nations, abounding in wealth, small in circumference, unprotected by walls, had yet nothing to fear: even we, these very Romans, were then not only excluded from our provinces, the maritime parts of Italy, and our harbours on the sea-coast, but durst not so much as appear on the Appian way. And yet at that very time, the magistrates of the Roman people were not ashamed to mount this tribunal, adorned by their ancestors with naval spoils, and the beaks of ships taken from the enemy.

The people of Rome were sensible, Q. Hortensius, that when you, and such as were in your way of thinking, delivered your sentiments upon the law proposed, you did it with an honest intention. And yet, in an affair that regarded the common safety, they were more swayed by a sense of their own sufferings, than a respect for your authority. Therefore one law, one man, one year, not only delivered us from that state of wretchedness and infamy, but effectually proved to all nations and people, that we were at length become the real lords of the earth and sea. On this account I cannot forbear expressing a greater indignation at the affront offered to Gabinius, shall I say, or Pompey, or, as was really the case, to both, in refusing to let Pompey have Gabinius for his lieutenant-general, though he earnestly sought and desired it? Ought the general who demanded an agreeable lieutenant to assist him in so great a war, to have been refused; when other commanders, who marched out to plunder the provinces, and pillage our allies, carried with them what lieutenant-generals they pleased? Or ought the man who proposed a law tending to secure the honour and safety of Rome and all nations, to have been excluded from sharing the glory of that general and army, whose destination was the fruit of his counsels, and effected at his personal peril? Could C. Falcidius, Q. Metellus, Q. Cœlius Latinensis, Cn. Lentulus, all of whom I mention with respect, be one year tribunes of the people, and the next appointed lieutenant-generals: and shall such a vigorous opposition be formed against Gabinius alone, who in a war carried on in consequence of his law, and by an army and general of his appointment, ought, doubtless, to have the preference to all others? But I hope the consuls will bring the affair before the senate: or if they shall decline it, or raise any difficulties, I here declare, that I myself will undertake the business; nor shall the contradictory decrees of any man, Romans, deter me, under your protection, from asserting your just rights and privileges; nor shall I regard anything but the interposition of the tribunes, which I hope will not, without repeated consideration, be exerted upon this occasion, even by those who threaten us with it. And truly, in my opinion, Romans, Aulus Gabinius, the author of the maritime war, and all that was then done, is the only person proper to act as an assistant to Pompey; because the one, by your suffrages, devolved that war upon the other; and he on whom it was devolved, undertook and brought it to a period.

It now remains that I speak to the opinion and judgment of Q. Catulus, who having put the question, that if in all emergencies you placed your hopes on Pompey alone, to whom could you have recourse in case of any disaster befalling him? he reaped the genuine fruit of his own virtue and dignity, when with unanimous voice you called out, that, in such an event, he himself was the man on whom you would rest your hopes. And indeed he is a man of such a character, that no undertaking is so great or difficult, which he cannot direct by his counsels, support by his integrity, and terminate by his valour. But in the point now before us, I entirely differ from him; because the more uncertain, and the shorter human life is, the more it behoves the commonwealth, while the gods indulge that favour, to avail herself of the virtues and talents of a great man. But it is dangerous to allow of innovations contrary to the customs and precedents of former ages. I shall not observe here, that our ancestors in peace always adhered to custom, but during war always yielded to necessity: that they were ever ready to change their measures as new emergencies required an alteration of counsels: neither shall I take notice, that two very important wars, the Carthaginian and the Spanish, were finished by one general: that two very powerful cities, Carthage and Numantia, which threatened to check the growth of our empire, were both destroyed by the same Scipio. I shall not mention the late example of C. Marius, upon whom you and your fathers thought it proper to rest your whole hopes of empire, and commit to his sole management the wars with Jugurtha, with the Teutones, and with the Cimbri. I shall only desire you to call to mind, how many things contrary to custom passed in the case of this very Pompey, with the hearty concur-rence of Catulus, who now so strenuously opposes the granting him any new powers.

For what could be more contrary to custom, than for a young man, without any public character, at a juncture dangerous to his country, to levy an army? he did levy one. To command it in person? he did command it. To conduct it with ability and success? he did with both. What could be more unprecedented, than to commit the charge of an army and province to a mere youth, whose age fell far short of that usually required in a senator? to entrust him with the government of Sicily and Africa, and the conduct of the war in those parts? He behaved notwithstanding with singular integrity, wisdom, and courage; terminated the war in Africa with success; and brought home his army victorious. Was there ever an instance of a Roman knight honoured with a triumph? yet this sight the people of Rome not only beheld, but considered as of all others the most desirable, and worthy their regard. Was it ever known, when we had two consuls of distinguished valour and renown, that a Roman knight should be sent in place of one of them, to command in a great and formidable war? Yet he was sent; and when some at that time objected in the senate, that a private man ought not to be sent in place of a consul; L. Philippus is reported to have said, that it was his opinion he should be sent, not in place of one, but of both the consuls. So well were all men persuaded of his capacity for the administration of public affairs, that, though but a youth, he was entrusted with the functions of two consuls. What could be more extraordinary, than that the senate should for his sake dispense with the laws, and suffer him to be chosen consul, before he was of an age to exercise the lowest magistracy? What could be more incredible, than that, while only a Roman knight, he should be a second time permitted to triumph by a decree of the senate? All the novelties that have happened among men, since the first memory of time, fall short of those that meet in the person of Pompey alone. And what is still more, all these numerous honours, new and extraordinary as they are, were conferred upon him by the advice of Q. Catulus, and other illustrious persons of the same dignity.

It behoves them therefore to consider, whether it may not seem unjust and presumptuous, if after having been so warmly seconded by you in the design of promoting and honouring Pompey, they should now oppose your judgment, and the authority of the Roman people, in favour of the same person: especially as you are armed with sufficient power to support your choice against all opposition; having already in spite of their endeavours to prevent it, singled out this man from amongst all your other generals to command in the war with the pirates. If you did this rashly, and without due regard to the interests of your country, they have reason to oppose their authority, and endeavour to rectify your deliberations. But if you formed a truer judgment of what was advantageous to the state; if, though opposed by them, you took the justest measures for securing the dignity of the empire, and the repose of the universe; let these rulers of the senate at length acknowledge, that both they and others ought to submit to the authority of the whole body of the Roman people. But in this Asiatic war against two powerful kings, there is not only occasion for those military talents so conspicuous in Pompey, but for many other great and eminent virtues. It is difficult in Asia, Cilicia, Syria, and other nations so remote from Rome, for a general to behave in such a manner, as that he shall think of nothing but war and conquest. And even where modesty and temperance hold some under restraint, yet nobody believes it, so great is the number of the greedy and rapacious. It is indeed impossible to express, Romans, how odious we are become among foreign nations, on account of the iniquities and oppressions of those, whom of late years we have sent to govern them. What temple in these lands have our magistrates left unprofaned? What city have they held sacred? What house has been free from their violations? Pretences are sought to attack every wealthy and opulent place, whose plunder promises to gratify the avarice of our commanders. Willingly would I debate these matters with Q. Catulus, and Q. Hortensius, men of eminent worth and dignity. For they are acquainted with the sufferings of our allies, see their distresses, and hear their complaints. Is it against the enemies of Rome, and in defence of your allies, that you send an army; or are you minded under this pretence to attack your friends and confederates? Where is the state in all Asia, that can set bounds to the ambition and avarice, I will not say of a general, or his lieutenant, but of a single tribune of the army?

Supposing therefore you should have a general who may appear capable of defeating the forces of these two powerful kings in a pitched battle; yet unless he is also one, that can refrain his hands, eyes, and thoughts, from the riches of our allies, from their wives and children, from the ornaments of their cities and temples, and from the gold and treasures of their palaces, he is by no means fit to command in an Asiatic and a regal war. Is any state suffered to enjoy tranquillity, that is known to be rich? Or was ever any state rich, which your generals permitted to remain in tranquillity? The sea-coast, O Romans, demanded Pompey, not only on account of his military glory, but likewise for his known probity and moderation of mind. The Roman people observed, that the public money from year to year enriched only a few; and that all the advantage we gained by the

empty name of a fleet was an increase of infamy from repeated losses. Are those who oppose the conferring such an extensive command upon one person, ignorant with what avaricious views, through what a profusion of bribery, and on what infamous conditions our magistrates now repair to their provinces? Insomuch that Pompey appears no less great by the contrast of their vices, than by the lustre of his own proper virtues. Therefore hesitate no longer to commit all to the care of a man, who alone of late years has so far gained the confidence of your allies, that they rejoice to see him enter their cities at the head of an army. But if you think it likewise needful, Romans, that in a point so material your choice should be backed by authorities; I can name P. Servilius, a man eminently skilled in war, and great affairs: one whose exploits by sea and land have acquired him so much reputation, that in all military deliberations, no man's opinion ought to challenge greater regard. I can name C. Curio, so distinguished by your signal favours and his own great actions, so illustrious for his matchless abilities and prudence. I can name Cn. Lentulus, in whom you have always found a capacity and talents, equal to the great honours you have conferred upon him. In fine, I can name C. Cassius, who for integrity, probity, and firmness, acknowledges no superior. Thus you see how easily, by the authority of so many great men, we can put to silence those who oppose this law.

For all these reasons, C. Manilius, I here in the first place declare my entire approbation of your law, your purpose, and your opinion: in the next place I exhort you, with the assistance of the Roman people, to continue unshaken in this purpose, and to suffer no threats nor violence to daunt you. In fact, I have no reason to doubt of your courage and firmness: and as we are supported with a greater zeal and unanimity, than was ever known in the like case before; what ground have we, either to distrust the measure itself, or our success in the prosecution of it? For my own part, whatever talents I enjoy from nature, or have acquired by application and study; whatever influence I derive from the favours of the Roman people, and the prætorian dignity wherewith they have invested me; whatever I can effect by my authority, and perserverance; I here promise and make it all over to you and my fellow-citizens, for the carrying of this point. I attest all the gods, particularly those who preside over this place and temple, and who see into the real designs of all concerned in the administration of public affairs, that I have not undertaken this part at the solicitations of any person whatever, nor with the view of ingratiating myself with Pompey, nor to procure from any one's greatness, a shelter against dangers, or an increase of honours: for as to the dangers, I shall always easily repel them by my innocence, as it becomes every virtuous man to do: and in the pursuit of honours, I shall neither trust to one man's favour, nor solicit them from this place, but endeavour to merit them by the same laborious course of life, which I have hitherto followed with your approbation. Whatever therefore I have done in this cause, Romans, I here affirm was done with a view to the good of my country: and so far have I been from pursuing any private interest, that I am sensible I have drawn much hatred upon myself, partly secret, partly open, which I might have avoided, and by which you may profit. But clothed with this honourable office, and indebted as I am to your favours, I consider it as my indispensable duty, to prefer your determinations, the dignity of the commonwealth, and the safety of our provinces and allies, to all partial and particular views of advantage.

—W. DUNCAN.

AN UPRIGHT GOVERNOR

CICERO

[From *Letters to Atticus*, Book V]

The author maintains that the lot of subject peoples is determined directly by the character of the governor.

To T. Pomponius Atticus:

Though the letter-carriers of the *publicani* are starting while I am actually travelling and on the road, and though I am still engaged on my progress, yet I thought I must snatch a moment to prevent you thinking me forgetful of your charge. So I have sat down actually on the road to write you in brief what follows, which really calls for a somewhat lengthy essay. Let me tell you, then, that with the highest possible reputation I entered, on the 31st of July, into a province in a state of desolation and lasting ruin; that I stayed three days at Laodicea, three at Apamea, the same at Synnada. It was the same tale everywhere: they could not pay the poll-tax: everybody's securities were sold: groans, lamentations, from the towns: acts of savagery worthy of some wild beast, rather than of man. In short, they are absolutely weary of their life. However, the wretched towns are somewhat relieved by my costing them nothing, nor my legates, nor quæstor, nor anyone. Let me tell you that I not only refuse to accept hay, which is customarily furnished under the Julian law, but that no one of us accepts even firewood, or anything else, except four beds and a roof to cover us; in many districts we do not accept even a roof, but remain, as a rule, under canvas. Accordingly, we are greeted by extraordinary throngs from farms, villages, houses, every sort of place. By Hercules, on my mere arrival, the justice, purity, and merciful heart of your Cicero seems to give them new life: so far has he surpassed everyone's hopes. Appius, as soon as he heard of my arrival, hurried to the most distant part of the province, right up to Tarsus: there he is holding sessions. About the Parthian not a word: but, nevertheless, some who come from those parts announce that some cavalry of ours have been cut to pieces. Bibulus even now is not so much as thinking of approaching his province. People say that he is acting thus because he wishes to leave it somewhat later. We are making all haste to the camp, which is two days' journey away.

—E. S. Shuckburgh.

Dangers of Invasion

CICERO

[From *Letters to Friends,* Book XV]

Cicero feels that the home government does not make adequate provision for the holding of what it had acquired. The letter is dated from the province of Cilicia, Asia Minor, which Cicero governed in 51-50 B.C.

To the Magistrates and Senate:

M. Tullius Cicero, son of Marcus, proconsul, greets the consuls, prætors, tribunes, and senate. If you are well, I am glad. I and the army are well.

Although I had undoubted assurance that the Parthians had crossed the Euphrates with nearly all their forces, yet, believing that more definite information could be sent you on these points by the proconsul M. Bibulus, I concluded that it was not incumbent on me to mention in a public despatch reports reaching me concerning the province of another. Having since then, however, received information on the most unquestionable authority—from legates, messengers, and despatches—whether I considered the importance of the matter itself, or the fact of not having yet heard of Bibulus's arrival in Syria, or that the conduct of

this war was almost as much my business as that of Bibulus, I came to the conclusion that it was my duty to write you word of what had reached my ears. The legates of king Antiochus of Commagene were the first to inform me that large bodies of Parthians had begun to cross the Euphrates. On the receipt of this report, as there were certain persons who thought that full credit could not be given to that sovereign, I made up my mind that I must wait for more trustworthy information. On the 18th of September, whilst marching into Cilicia at the head of my army, on the frontier between Lycaonia and Cappadocia, a despatch was handed to me from Tarcondimotus, who is considered to be the most faithful ally and the most devoted friend of the Roman people beyond Mount Taurus, announcing that Pacorus son of Orodes, the king of the Parthians, had crossed the Euphrates with a very large body of Parthian cavalry, and had pitched his camp at Tyba, and that consequently a very serious commotion had been caused in the province of Syria. On the same day a despatch on the same subject reached me from Iamblichus, phylarch of the Arabians, who is generally considered to be well-disposed and friendly to our Republic. Though I was fully aware that, on the receipt of this information, our allies were unsettled in their feelings and wavering from the expectation of political change, I yet hoped that those whom I had already visited, and who had seen the mildness and purity of my administration, had been made more devoted to the Roman people, and that Cilicia, too, would become more certainly loyal when it had once felt the advantage of my equitable rule. Acting at once from this motive, and also with a view to put down those of the Cilicians who are in arms, and to shew the enemy in Syria that the army of the Roman people, so far from retiring on receipt of that news, was actually approaching nearer, I determined to lead it right up to Mount Taurus. But if my authority has any weight with you—especially in matters which you only know by report, but which are all but passing under my eyes—I strongly urge and advise you to take measures for the defence of these provinces: it is over-late already, but better late than never. For myself, you are well aware how slenderly supplied and how imperfectly furnished with troops, in view of the expected gravity of this war, you have despatched me. And it was not from the blindness of vanity, but from a modest scruple as to refusing, that I did not decline this business. For I have never considered my danger so formidable, as to make me wish to avoid it in preference to obeying your will. But at this moment the matter is of such a nature, that unless you promptly despatch into these provinces an army on the same scale as you are wont to employ for the most important war, there is the most imminent danger of our having to give up all those provinces, on which the revenues of the Roman people depend. Again, there is this reason for your not resting any hopes on a levy in the province—that men are not numerous, and that such as there are fly in every direction at the first alarm. Again, what this class of soldier is worth in his opinion has been shewn by that gallant officer, M. Bibulus: for, though you had granted him leave to hold a levy in Asia, he has declined to do so. For auxiliaries raised from the allies, owing to the harshness and injustice of our rule, are either so weak that they can do us little service, or so disaffected to us that it seems improper to expect anything from them or trust anything to them. Both the loyalty and the forces, whatever their amount, of king Deiotarus I reckon as being at our service. Cappadocia has nothing to give. Other kings and despots are not to be relied upon either in regard to their resources or their loyalty. For myself, in spite of this short supply of soldiers, I shall certainly shew no lack of courage, nor, I hope, of prudence either. What will happen is uncertain. I pray that I may be able to secure my safety! I will certainly secure my honour.

—E. S. SHUCKBURGH.

EXPANSION TOWARDS THE NORTH

ARIOVISTUS [1]

CÆSAR

[From the *Gallic War*, Book I]

Gaius Julius Cæsar was born in 100 and was killed in 44 B.C. He was the greatest military genius and perhaps the greatest political genius that Rome produced. He became prominent at the time when Cicero was elected consul, at first for his support of Catiline for consul, and later for his speech in the senate against the death penalty for the conspirators. In 60 B.C., with Crassus and Pompey, he formed a political group, called the first triumvirate, which controlled the destinies of Rome for several years. Through it Cæsar was elected consul and then appointed to command in Gaul where he began to subdue the tribes, to create a great army devoted to himself, and to amass wealth which he freely used for political purposes. In 56 the coalition was renewed, Cæsar gained the extension of his command for five years, and in that time thoroughly subdued all Gaul to the Rhine. Meantime Crassus had lost his life in his unfortunate expedition against the Parthians in the East. Pompey at Rome and Cæsar in Gaul were left as the outstanding leaders in the state. Pompey was won over to the senatorial party which had been hostile to Cæsar since his complete estrangement from it during his consulship. Civil war was the result. Cæsar won in a series of campaigns which extended over several years. He made himself dictator, and probab'y planned a re-

[1] From the Loeb Classical Library, by permission.

organization of the constitution; but he was murdered before permanent arrangements could be made. He had, however, carried through numerous reforms of primary importance to Rome. Well known is his correction of the calendar.

It is greatly to be regretted that this foremost statesman of Rome should have left us no record from his own pen of his plans and policies, of his conceptions and ideals. We learn of his views on politics and statecraft rather from his deeds than from his books. Only his military writings have come down to us, and in them he keeps for the most part strictly to the subject in hand. They are fine examples of the historical monographs characteristic of the period, like those of Sallust; but unlike those of Sallust, they show no tendency to philosophise on politics, government and morals. His other writings included a treatise on grammar, political pamphlets, a work on astronomy, speeches and letters. Such is his genius as a military commander and his lucidity of expression as a writer, that his *Gallic War* takes rank as a unique human document.

The *Gallic War* is an account of Cæsar's activities in acquiring and consolidating new territory to the north for the Roman Republic in the years 59 to 50 B.C. Ariovistus was the most difficult opponent he encountered in the early days of the campaign; his defeat cleared the way for future successes.

Upon the conclusion of the Helvetian campaign deputies from wellnigh the whole of Gaul, the chief men of the various states, assembled in Cæsar's camp to congratulate him. They perceived, they said, that, although Cæsar had by the campaign required satisfaction of the Helvetii for past outrages suffered by the Roman people at their hands, the result had been as beneficial to the land of Gaul, as to the Roman people; for the Helvetii had left their homes at a time of exceeding prosperity with the express design of making war upon the whole of Gaul and obtaining an empire; they purposed from an ample field to select for their abode the spot which they judged to be the most convenient and the most productive in all Gaul, and to make the rest of the states tributary. The deputies asked that they might be allowed to announce—and that with Cæsar's consent— a convention of all Gaul for a certain day, for they had certain petitions which, after general agreement, they wished to ask of him. Permission was given, and they appointed a day for the convention, pledging themselves by an oath that no man should publish its proceedings save the persons authorised by their general consent.

The convention having been held and dissolved, the same chiefs of states as before returned to Cæsar with a petition that they might be allowed to discuss with him apart, in private, the question of their own and the general welfare. The petition was granted, and they all threw themselves in tears at Cæsar's feet, declaring that they were as anxious and as much concerned to prevent the publication of their utterances as to obtain their desires; for they saw that publication must expose them to the most cruel vengeance. Diviciacus the Æduan spoke on their behalf. "In all Gaul," he said, "there are two parties; in one of them the Ædui have the primacy, in the other the Arverni. For many years there was a vehement struggle between the two for the dominion; then it came about that the Arverni and the Sequani summoned the Germans to their aid for a price. About fifteen thousand of them crossed the Rhine in the first instance; then, when those fierce barbarians had got a liking for the farmlands, the civilization, and the wealth of the Gauls, more were brought over, and at the present time there are about 120,000 of them in Gaul.

"With them the Ædui and their dependents have repeatedly fought in battle: defeat has brought great disaster, the loss of all our nobility, our senate, and our knights. It is these battles and disasters that have broken the men who by their own valour, and by the courtesy and friendship of Rome, were formerly paramount in Gaul, and have obliged them to give as hostages to the Sequani the noblest men of the state, and to bind the state by oath not to require the return of the hostages, not to entreat the assistance of Rome, nor to refuse eternal submission to the sway and sovereignty of the Sequani. I am the one man of all the state of the Ædui upon whom it has not been possible to prevail to take the oath or give his children as hostages. It was for that reason that I fled from the state and came to the Senate at Rome to demand assistance, because I was the only man not bound by oath or hostages. But a worse fate has befallen the victorious Sequani than the conquered Ædui: Ariovistus, king of the Germans, has settled within their borders and seized a third part of their territory, the best in all Gaul; and now he orders them to evacuate another third, because a few months since 24,000 of the Harudes joined him, for whom he had to provide a settlement and a home. In a few years all the natives will have been driven forth from the borders of Gaul, and all the Germans will have crossed the Rhine; for there can be no comparison between the Gallic and the German territory, none between our usual scale of living and theirs. Having once conquered the forces of the Gauls in battle near Magetobriga, Ariovistus is exercising a proud and cruel tyranny, demanding as hostages the children of the greatest nobles, and perpetrating upon them all the direst forms of torture, if anything be not performed at his nod or at his pleasure. He is a passionate, a reckless barbarian: we can endure his tyrannies no longer. Unless some means of assistance is to be found in Cæsar and in the Roman people, all the Gauls must needs do just what the Helvetii have done—emigrate, to seek another habitation, other abodes far from the Germans, and risk any fortune that may befall them. If these remarks of mine be reported to Ariovistus I make no doubt that he will inflict the severest punishment on all the hostages in his keeping. You, Cæsar, by your own and your army's influence, or by your late victory, or by the name of the Roman people, can prevent the crossing of a larger host of Germans over the Rhine, and defend the whole of Gaul from the outrage of Ariovistus."

When Diviciacus had delivered this speech all who were present began with loud weeping to seek assistance from Cæsar. He noticed, however, that of all the company the Sequani alone did not act like the rest, but with head downcast stared sullenly upon the ground. He asked them, wondering, what might be the cause thereof. The Sequani made no reply, but continued in the same sullen silence. When repeated questioning could extract not a word from them, Diviciacus the Æduan made further reply. "The lot of the Sequani," he said, "is more pitiable, more grievous than that of the rest, insomuch as they alone dare not even in secret make complaint or entreat assistance, dreading the cruelty of Ariovistus as much in his absence as if he were present before them. The rest, for all their suffering, have still a chance of escape; but the Sequani, who have admitted Ariovistus within their borders, and whose towns are all in his power, must needs endure any and every torture."

When he had learnt this Cæsar comforted the Gauls with his words, promising that he would concern himself with this matter: he had, he said, great hope that by his good offices and his authority he would induce Ariovistus to put a stop to his outrages. With this speech he dissolved the convention. And straightway many considerations induced him to suppose that he must take thought and action in the matter. In the first place, he could see that the Ædui, often hailed by the Senate as brethren and kinsmen, were fast bound in slavery and subjection to the Germans, and he was aware that their hostages were with Ariovistus and the Sequani. This, considering the greatness of the Roman empire, he deemed to be an utter disgrace to himself and to the state. Next, he could see that the Germans were becoming gradually accustomed to cross over the Rhine, and that the arrival of a great host of them in Gaul was dangerous for the Roman people. Nor did he suppose that barbarians so fierce would stop short after seizing the whole of Gaul; but rather, like the Cimbri and Teutoni before them, they would break forth into the Province, and push on thence into Italy, especially as there was but the Rhone to separate the Sequani from the Roman Province. All this, he felt, must be faced without a moment's delay. As for Ariovistus himself, he had assumed such airs, such arrogance that he seemed insufferable.

He resolved, therefore, to send deputies to Ariovistus to request of him the choice of some half-way station between them for a parley, as it was his desire to discuss with him matters of state and of the highest importance to each of them. To the deputation Ariovistus made reply that if he had had need of aught from Cæsar, he would have come to him, and if Cæsar desired aught of him, he ought to come to him. Moreover, he did not venture without an army to come into those parts of Gaul which Cæsar was occupying, and he could not concentrate his army without great exertion in the matter of supply. And he found himself wondering what business Cæsar or the Roman people might have in that Gaul which he had made his own by conquest of war.

When this reply had been brought back to Cæsar he sent deputies again to him with the following message: Forasmuch as, after great kindness of treatment from Cæsar himself and from the Roman people (for it was in Cæsar's year of consulship that he had been saluted as king and friend by the Senate), he expressed his thanks to Cæsar and the Roman people by reluctance to accept the invitation to come to a parley and by thinking it needless to say or learn anything as touching their mutual concerns, Cæsar's demand of him was, first that he should not bring any further host of men across the Rhine into Gaul; second, that he should restore the hostages he held from the Ædui and grant the Sequani entire freedom to restore to the Ædui with his full consent the hostages they held; further, that he should not annoy the Ædui by outrage nor make war upon them and their allies. If he did as requested, Cæsar and the Roman people would maintain a lasting kindness and friendship towards him. If Cæsar's request were not granted, then, forasmuch as in the consulship of Marcus Messalla and Marcus Piso the Senate had decided that the governor of the Province of Gaul should protect, as far as he could do so with advantage to the state, the Ædui and other friends of the Roman people, Cæsar would not disregard the outrages suffered by the Ædui.

To this Ariovistus replied as follows: It was the right of war that conquerors dictated as they pleased to the conquered; and the Roman people also were accustomed to dictate to those whom they conquered, not according to the order of a third party, but according to their own choice. If he, for his part, did not ordain how the Roman people should exercise their own right, he ought not to be hindered by the Roman people in the enjoyment of his own right. The Ædui, having risked the fortune of war and having been overcome in a conflict of arms, had been made tributary to himself. Cæsar was doing him a serious injury, for his advance was damaging his revenues. He would not restore their ·hostages to the Ædui, nor would he make war on them nor on their allies without cause, if they stood to their agreement and paid tribute yearly; if not, they would find it of no assistance whatever to be called "Brethren of the Roman people." As for Cæsar's declaration that he would not disregard outrages suffered by the Ædui, no one had fought with Ariovistus save to his own destruction. He might join issue when he pleased: he would learn what invincible Germans, highly trained in arms, who in a period of fourteen years had never been beneath a roof, could accomplish by their valour.

At the same hour in which this message was brought back to Cæsar deputies arrived from the Ædui and the Treveri. The Ædui came to complain that the Harudes, who had lately been brought over into Gaul, were devastating their borders, and that they themselves had not been able to purchase peace from Ariovistus even by the delivery of hostages. The Treveri reported that one hundred cantons of the Suebi had settled on the banks of the Rhine, and were attempting to cross the river, under the command of two brothers, Nasua and Cimberius. At this Cæsar was exceedingly disquieted, and determined that he must make speed, for fear that, if the new company of Suebi joined the old forces of Ariovistus, resistance might be more difficult. Therefore he secured his corn-supply with all possible speed, and pushed on with forced marches to meet Ariovistus.

He had advanced a three days' march when news was brought to him that Ariovistus with all his forces was pushing on to seize Vesontio, the largest town of the Sequani, and had already advanced a three days' march from his own borders. Cæsar considered that a great effort on his part was needed to prevent this occurrence. For there was in that town an abundant supply of all things needful for war, and the place was so well fortified by nature as to afford great facilities for the conduct of a campaign. The river Dubis, with a circuit that might have been traced by compasses, surrounds wellnigh the whole town: the remaining space of not more than sixteen hundred feet, where the river breaks off, is closed in by a height of great eminence, so placed that its foundations touch the river-bank on either side. This height is surrounded by a wall to form a citadel and join it with the town. It was to this place that Cæsar pushed on with forced marches by night and day, and, seizing the town, posted a garrison in it.

During a few days' halt near Vesontio for the provision of corn and other supplies a panic arose from inquiries made by our troops and remarks uttered by Gauls and traders, who affirmed that the Germans were men of a mighty frame and an incredible valour and skill at arms; for they themselves (so they said) at meetings with the Germans had often been unable even to endure their look and the keenness of their eyes. So great was the panic, and so suddenly did it seize upon all the army, that it affected in serious fashion the intelligence and the courage of all ranks. It began first with the tribunes, the contingent-commanders, and the others who had followed Cæsar from Rome to court his friendship, without any great experience in warfare. Advancing various reasons which, according to their own statement, obliged them to depart, some sought his permission to leave; some were compelled by very shame to stay to avoid the suspicion of cowardice. They were unable to disguise their looks, or even at times to restrain their tears; they hid in their tents to complain of their own fate, or to lament in company with their friends the common danger. Everywhere throughout the camp there was signing of wills. By the cowardly utterances of such as these even men who had had long experience in the field, soldiers, centurions, and cavalry commanders, were gradually affected. Those of them who desired to be thought less timid would declare that they were not afraid of the enemy, but feared the narrow defiles and the vast forests which lay between themselves and Ariovistus, or a possible failure of proper transport for the corn-supply. Some had even gone so far as to declare to Cæsar that when he gave the order for camp to be shifted and standards advanced the soldiers would not obey, and by reason of cowardice would not move forward.

Remarking this, he convened a council of war, and summoned thereto the centurions of all grades. Then indignantly he reprimanded them, first and foremost because they thought it their business to ask or to consider in which direction or with what purpose they were being led. "Ariovistus," he said, "in my own consulship sought most eagerly the friendship of the Roman people. Why should any one conclude that he intends so recklessly to depart from his duty? For myself, I am persuaded that when my demands are made known, and the fairness of my terms understood, Ariovistus will not reject the goodwill of myself or of the Roman people. Even if, in a fit of rage and madness, he makes war, what, pray, have you to fear? Why do you despair of your own courage or of my competence? We have made trial of this foe in the time of our fathers, on the occasion when, in the defeat of the Cimbri and Teutoni by Gaius Marius, the army was deemed to have deserved no less praise than the commander himself. We have made further trial of late in Italy in the slave revolt, and yet the slaves had the practice and training which they had learnt from us to give them some measure of support. You may judge from this what profit there is in a good courage, for the very men whom you had feared without cause during a long time when they had no arms, you subsequently subdued, though they had taken up arms and won victories. Finally, these are the selfsame men with whom the Helvetii have had frequent encounters, and they have often subdued them, not only in Helvetian territory but also in Germany; yet the Helvetii have not proved a match for *our* army. If there be any who are concerned at the defeat and flight of the Gauls, they can discover for the asking that when the Gauls were worn out by the length of the campaign Ariovistus, who had kept himself for many months within his camp in the marshes, without giving a chance of encounter, attacked them suddenly when they had at last dispersed in despair of a battle, and conquered them rather by skill and stratagem than by courage. Even Ariovistus himself does not expect that our own armies can be caught by tactics for which there was a chance against unskilled barbarians. Those persons who ascribe their own cowardice to a pretended anxiety for the corn-supply or to the defiles on the route are guilty of presumption, for they appear either to despair of the commander's doing his duty or to instruct him in it. These matters are my own concern; corn is being supplied by the Sequani, the Leuci, the Lingones, and the corn-crops in the fields are already ripe; of the route you yourselves will shortly be able to judge. As for the statement that the soldiers will not obey orders nor move forward, I am not in the least concerned by that; in any cases where an army has not obeyed its general, either fortune has failed because of some actual blunder, or else some crime has been discovered and a charge of avarice has been brought home. My own blamelessness has been clearly seen throughout my life, my good fortune in the Helvetian campaign. Accordingly I intend to execute at once what I might have put off to a more distant day, and to break camp in the fourth watch of this next night, to the intent that I may perceive at once whether honour and duty, or cowardice, prevail in your minds. Even if no one else follows, I shall march with the Tenth Legion alone; I have no doubt of its allegiance, and it will furnish the commander-in-chief's escort." Cæsar had shown special favour to this legion, and he placed the greatest reliance in it because of its courage.

By the delivery of this speech the spirit of all ranks was changed in a remarkable fashion; the greatest keenness and eagerness for active service was engendered, and the Tenth Legion was the first to express thanks to Cæsar, through its tribunes, for the excellent opinion he had formed of it, and to affirm its complete readiness for active service. Then the remaining legions moved their tribunes and senior centurions to give satisfactory explanations to Cæsar that they had felt neither doubt nor panic, and had regarded it as the commander's business, not their own, to decide the plan of campaign. Their explanation was accepted, and through Diviciacus (the one person in whom Cæsar had absolute confidence) a route was found out to lead the army through open country, by a detour of more than fifty miles. In the fourth watch, as Cæsar had said, the march began. On the seventh day of continuous marching the scouts reported that the forces of Ariovistus were four-and-twenty miles away from our own.

When he learnt of Cæsar's approach Ariovistus sent deputies to him to announce that he was now ready to do what Cæsar had before demanded as touching a parley, because he had come nearer, and Ariovistus believed that he could comply without risk. Cæsar did not reject the proposal, and he was inclined to think that Ariovistus was at length returning to a proper frame of mind, inasmuch as of his own motion he proffered what he had previously refused on request. Moreover, he began to have a good hope that, in consideration of the signal benefits conferred upon him by Cæsar and the Roman people, Ariovistus would abandon his obstinacy when he knew Cæsar's demands. A day—the fifth after that—was appointed for the parley. Meanwhile there was continual sending of deputies to and fro between them; and Ariovistus demanded that Cæsar should bring no infantry with him to the parley, as he was afraid Cæsar might surround him by treachery; let each party, therefore, come with an escort of horse; otherwise he would not come at all. Cæsar did not wish the parley to be broken off upon an excuse thus interposed; at the same time he could not venture to entrust his personal safety to Gallic horse. He decided, therefore, that the best plan was to take the horses from Gallic troopers and mount upon them soldiers of the Tenth Legion, in which he had absolute confidence; thus, if there were need of action, he would have an escort of the truest friends he could find. As the order was being carried out one of the soldiers of the Tenth Legion remarked with some wit that Cæsar was doing better than his promise; for he had promised to treat the Tenth Legion as the commander-in-chief's escort, and he was making new "cavalry" of them.

There was a large plain, and in it a mound of earth of considerable size. The place was about equally distant from the camps of Cæsar and of Ariovistus. Thither, as agreed, they came for the parley. Cæsar stationed the legion which he had brought on horseback two hundred paces from the mound. The horsemen of Ariovistus halted at an equal distance. Ariovistus demanded that they should parley on horseback, and that each should bring with him to the parley ten men besides himself. When they arrived at the spot Cæsar began his speech by relating the benefits conferred upon Ariovistus by himself and by the Senate; the Senate had called him king and friend, and had sent gifts with a most lavish hand. This privilege, as he pointed out, had fallen to the lot of but few, and was usually granted in consideration of great personal services. Ariovistus, though he had no right to audience of the Senate, and no just cause of claim, had obtained the rewards in question by the favour and generosity of Cæsar and of the Senate. He proceeded to show how long-established and how just were the reasons for a close relationship between Rome and the Ædui; the frequency and the distinction of the Senate's decrees in respect of them; the manner in which, even before they had sought the friendship of Rome, the Ædui had always held the primacy of all Gaul. It was the tradition of the Roman people to desire that all its allies and friends should not only lose none of their possessions, but should enjoy increase of influence, dignity, and distinction; on the other hand, who, he asked, could endure that they should be despoiled of what they had brought with them to the friendship of the Roman people? He then made the same demands as those which he had given in his instructions to the deputies—that is to say, Ariovistus must not make war on the Ædui or on their allies; he must restore the hostages; and if he could not send back home any part of the Germans, at any rate he must not suffer any more to cross the Rhine.

To the demands of Cæsar Ariovistus replied in brief, but he dilated at length upon his own good qualities. He had crossed the Rhine, he said, not of his own desire, but upon the request and summons of the Gauls; not without great hope of great rewards had he left home and kindred; the settlements he occupied in Gaul were granted by the natives, the hostages had been given with the consent of the natives; the tribute he took was by right of war, as customarily enforced by conquerors upon conquered. He had not made war upon the Gauls, but they upon him; all the states of Gaul had come to attack him and had set up their camp against him; all their forces had been beaten and overcome by him in a single action. If they wished to try the issue again, he was prepared to fight it out again; if they wished to enjoy peace, it was unjust to refuse the payment of tribute which of their own consent they had paid hitherto. The friendship of the Roman people ought to be a distinction and a security to him, not a hindrance; and he had sought it with that hope. If through the agency of the Roman people the tribute were to be remitted and the surrendered persons withdrawn, he would refuse the friendship of the Roman people no less heartily than he had sought it. As for the host of Germans that he was bringing over into Gaul, his object was to protect himself, not to attack Gaul; and the proof thereof was that he had not come except upon request, and that his warfare had been defensive, not offensive. He had come into Gaul before the Roman people. Never heretofore had an army of the Roman people left the borders of the Province of Gaul. What did Cæsar mean? Why did he come into his sphere of occupation? This was his province of Gaul, as the other was the Roman. As it was not right to give way to him, if he made an attack on Roman territory, so likewise the Romans were unjust in obstructing him in his own jurisdiction. As for Cæsar's statement that the Ædui were called "brothers," Ariovistus was not such a barbarian, not so ignorant of affairs as not to know that neither in the last campaign against the Allobroges had the Ædui rendered assistance to the Romans, nor in the disputes of the Ædui with himself and the Sequani had they enjoyed the assistance of the Roman people. He was bound to suspect, in spite of pretended friendship, that Cæsar had an army in Gaul for the purpose of crushing him. Unless, therefore, Cæsar departed and withdrew his army from this locality, he would regard him, not as a friend, but as an enemy. And if he put Cæsar to death, he would gratify many nobles and leaders of the Roman people: this he knew for certain from themselves, by the messengers sent on behalf of all whose favour and friendship he could purchase by Cæsar's death. If, however, Cæsar departed and resigned to him the uninterrupted occupation of Gaul, he would recompense him by a great reward, and would, without any exertion or risk on his part, execute any campaigns he might wish to be carried out.

Cæsar spoke at length for the purpose of showing why he could not give up the task in hand. His own practice, he said, and the practice of the Roman people did not suffer the abandonment of allies who had deserved so well, nor did he admit that Gaul belonged to Ariovistus rather than to the Roman people. The Arverni and the Ruteni had been subdued in a campaign by Quintus Fabius Maximus: the Roman people had pardoned them, and had not formed them into a province nor imposed a tribute. If priority of time was to be the standard, then the sovereignty of the Roman people in Gaul had complete justification; if the decision of the Senate was to be observed, Gaul should be free, for after conquest of the country the Senate had willed that it should continue to observe its own laws.

During the progress of the parley Cæsar was informed that the horsemen of Ariovistus were approaching nearer the mound, riding up to our troops, and discharging stones and darts at them. Cæsar made an end of speaking, and, withdrawing to his own men, commanded them not to discharge a single dart against the enemy in reply. For, although he could see that a fight between the chosen legion and the horsemen would involve no danger, still he did not think proper, by so beating the enemy,

to make possible the report that after pledge given they had been surrounded by him during a parley. As soon as the common soldiers learnt how arrogantly at the parley Ariovistus had forbidden all Gaul to the Romans, how his horsemen had attacked our troops, and how this action had broken off the parley, the army was inspired with far greater eagerness and enthusiasm for battle.

Two days afterwards Ariovistus sent deputies to Cæsar. He desired, he said, to discuss with him the matters which they had begun to discuss together but had not settled. Let him therefore again appoint a day for a parley, or, if he did not so wish, let him send to him one of his staff. Cæsar thought there was no occasion for a parley, the more so as on the previous day the Germans could not be restrained from discharging darts upon our men. He thought it would be very dangerous to send one of his staff to him and so to expose a man to the ferocious Germans. The best plan seemed to be to send him Gaius Valerius Procillus, son of Gaius Valerius Caburus. He was a young man of exemplary courage and courtesy, and his father had been presented with the citizenship by Gaius Valerius Flaccus. Cæsar selected him because of his fidelity and his knowledge of the Gallic tongue (which from long practice Ariovistus could now use freely), and also because the Germans had in his case no reason for outrage; and with him he chose Marcus Mettius, who enjoyed the intimacy of Ariovistus. He gave them instructions that they should ascertain and bring back to him the views of Ariovistus. But when Ariovistus saw them near him in his camp he called aloud in the presence of his army, "Why come you to me? To spy?" When they tried to speak he prevented them and flung them into chains.

On the same day he advanced and pitched his camp under a hill-side six miles from Cæsar's. The next day he led his forces past the camp of Cæsar, and formed camp two miles beyond him, for the purpose of cutting Cæsar off from the corn and supplies that were to be brought up from the borders of the Sequani and the Ædui. For five days in succession Cæsar brought his own forces out in front of camp and kept them formed in line of battle, so that if Ariovistus wished to engage he might not lack the chance. On all these days Ariovistus kept his army in camp, but engaged daily in a cavalry encounter. The kind of fighting in which the Germans had trained themselves was as follows. There were six thousand horsemen, and as many footmen, as swift as they were brave, who had been chosen out of the whole force, one by each horseman for his personal protection. With them they worked in encounters; on them the horsemen would retire, and they would concentrate speedily if any serious difficulty arose; they would form round any trooper who fell from his horse severely wounded; and if it was necessary to advance farther in some direction or to retire more rapidly, their training made them so speedy that they could support themselves by the manes of the horses and keep up their pace.

When Cæsar observed that Ariovistus kept to his camp, to prevent further interruption of supplies he chose a suitable spot for a camp beyond that in which the Germans had pitched and about six hundred paces distant. Thither he marched in triple-line formation. The first and second line he ordered to keep under arms, the third to entrench a camp. The spot, as has been said, was about six hundred paces away from the enemy. Towards it Ariovistus sent some sixteen thousand light-armed troops with all the horse, as a force to frighten our men and to prevent their entrenching work. None the less Cæsar kept to his previous decision, ordering two lines to drive back the enemy, the third to com-

plete the work. When the camp was entrenched he left two legions there and a part of the auxiliaries; the remaining four he brought back to the larger camp. The next day, in accordance with his practice, Cæsar moved out his forces from both camps, and, advancing a little from the larger camp, he formed line to give the enemy a chance of battle. Perceiving that they did not even so come forth, he brought his army back to camp about noon. Then at last Ariovistus sent a part of his own forces to attack the lesser camp, and both sides fought in spirited fashion till eventide. At sunset, when many blows had been dealt and taken, Ariovistus led his forces back to camp. By questioning the prisoners why Ariovistus did not fight a decisive action, Cæsar found out the reason. It was a custom among the Germans that their matrons should declare by lots and divinations whether it was expedient or not to engage, and the matrons declared that heaven forbade the Germans to win a victory, if they fought an action before the new moon.

On the next day Cæsar left what he deemed a sufficient garrison for each camp; in front of the lesser camp, in full view of the enemy, he posted all the allied troops, intending to use them for a demonstration, because the total strength of his legionary troops was none too great in view of the enemy's numbers. He himself, with triple line deployed, advanced right up to the enemy's camp. Then at last, compelled by necessity, the Germans led their own forces out of camp and posted them at equal intervals according to their tribes, Harudes, Marcomani, Triboces, Vangiones, Nemetes, Sedusii, Suebi; and their whole line they set about with wagons and carts, to leave no hope in flight. Upon these they set their women, who with tears and outstretched hands entreated the men, as they marched out to fight, not to deliver them into Roman slavery.

Cæsar put the lieutenant-generals and the quartermaster-general each in command of a legion, that every man might have their witness of his valour. He himself took station on the right wing, having noticed that the corresponding division of the enemy was the least steady, and joined battle. Our troops attacked the enemy so fiercely when the signal was given, and the enemy dashed forward so suddenly and swiftly, that there was no time to discharge javelins upon them. So javelins were thrown aside, and it was a sword-fight at close quarters. But the Germans, according to their custom, speedily formed mass, and received the sword-attack. Not a few of our soldiers were found brave enough to leap on to the masses of the enemy, tear the shields from their hands, and deal a wound from above. The left wing of the enemy's line was beaten and put to flight, but their right wing, by sheer weight of numbers, was pressing our line hard. Young Publius Crassus, commanding our cavalry, noticed this, and as he could move more freely than the officers who were occupied in and about the line of battle, he sent the third line in support of our struggling troops.

So the battle was restored, and all the enemy turned and ran: nor did they cease in their flight until they reached the river Rhine, some five miles from that spot. There a very few, trusting to their strength, set themselves to swim across, or discovered boats and so won safety. Among these was Ariovistus, who found a skiff moored to the bank and escaped therein; all the rest our cavalry caught and slew. There were two wives of Ariovistus, one of Suebian nationality, whom he had brought with him from home; the other a woman of Noricum, sister of King Voccio, and sent by him to be married to Ariovistus in Gaul.

Both wives perished in the rout; of his two daughters one was slain, and the other taken prisoner. Gaius Valerius Procillus, bound with a threefold chain, was being dragged by his keepers in the rout, when he chanced to meet Cæsar himself pursuing the enemy with the cavalry. And indeed it brought Cæsar no less pleasure than the victory itself, to see a most distinguished member of the Province of Gaul, his own close friend and guest, snatched from the hands of the enemy and restored to himself; and to feel that fortune had in no wise lessened, by the loss of his friend, his own great pleasure and gratification. Procillus said that in his own presence the lots had been thrice consulted to see whether he should be burnt to death at once or saved for another time: to the favour of the lots he owed his safety. Marcus Mettius also was discovered and brought back to Cæsar.

When the news of this battle was carried across the Rhine, the Suebi who had come to the banks of the river began to return homewards; and when the tribes which dwell next to the Rhine perceived their panic, they pursued and slew a great number of them. Two capital campaigns were thus finished in a single summer, and Cæsar therefore withdrew his army a little earlier than the season required into winter cantonments among the Sequani, leaving Labienus in command thereof, while he himself set off for Hither Gaul to hold the assizes.

—H. J. EDWARDS.

GAULS AND GERMANS [1]

CÆSAR

[From the *Gallic War*, Book VI]

Cæsar reveals his interest in other matters than the merely military. He is an explorer as well as a soldier and statesman.

[1] From the Loeb Classical Library, by permission.

Since I have arrived at this point, it would seem to be not inappropriate to set forth the customs of Gaul and of Germany, and the difference between these nations. In Gaul, not only in every state and every canton and district, but almost in each several household, there are parties; and the leaders of the parties are men who in the judgment of their fellows are deemed to have the highest authority, men to whose decision and judgment the supreme issue of all cases and counsel may be referred. And this seems to have been an ordinance from ancient days, to the end that no man of the people should lack assistance against a more powerful neighbour; for each man refuses to allow his own folk to be oppressed and defrauded, since otherwise he has no authority among them. The same principle holds in regard to Gaul as a whole taken together; for the whole body of states is divided into two parties.

When Cæsar arrived in Gaul the leaders of one party were the Ædui, of the other the Sequani. The latter, being by themselves inferior in strength —since the highest authority from ancient times rested with the Ædui, and their dependencies were extensive—had made Ariovistus and the Germans their friends, and with great sacrifices and promises had brought them to their side. Then, by several successful engagements and the slaughter of all the Æduan nobility, they had so far established their predominance as to transfer a great part of the dependents from the Ædui to themselves, receiving from them as hostages the children of their chief men, compelling them as a state to swear that they would entertain no design against the Sequani, occupying a part of the neighbouring territory which they had seized by force, and securing the chieftaincy of all Gaul. This was the necessity which compelled Diviciacus to set forth on a journey to the Senate at Rome for the purpose of seeking aid; but he had returned without achieving his object. By the arrival of Cæsar a change of affairs was brought about. Their hostages were restored to the Ædui, their old dependencies restored, and new ones secured through Cæsar's efforts (as those who had joined in friendly relations with them found that they enjoyed a better condition and a fairer rule), and their influence and position were increased in all other respects: in result whereof the Sequani had lost the chieftaincy. To their place the Remi had succeeded; and as it was perceived that they had equal influence with Cæsar, the tribes which, by reason of ancient animosities, could in no wise join the Ædui were delivering themselves as dependents to the Remi. These tribes the Remi carefully protected, and by this means they sought to maintain their new and suddenly acquired authority. The state of things then at the time in question was that the Ædui were regarded as by far the chief state, while the Remi held the second place in importance.

Throughout Gaul there are two classes of persons of definite account and dignity. As for the common folk, they are treated almost as slaves, venturing naught of themselves, never taken into counsel. The most part of them, oppressed as they are either by debt, or by the heavy weight of tribute, or by the wrongdoing of the more powerful men, commit themselves in slavery to the nobles, who have, in fact, the rights over them as masters over slaves. Of the two classes above mentioned one consists of Druids, the other of knights. The former are concerned with divine worship, the due performance of sacrifices, public and private, and the interpretation of ritual questions; a great number of young men gather about them for the sake of instruction and hold them in great honour. In fact, it is they who decide in almost all disputes, public and private; and if any crime has been committed, or murder done, or there is any dispute about succession or boundaries, they also decide it, determining rewards and penalties: if any person or people does not abide by their decision, they ban such from sacrifice, which is their heaviest penalty. Those that are so banned are reckoned as impious and criminal; all men move out of their path and shun their approach and conversation, for fear they may get some harm from their contact, and no justice is done if they seek it, no distinction falls to their share. Of all these Druids one is chief, who has the highest authority among them. At his death, either any other who is preeminent in position succeeds, or, if there be several of equal standing, they strive for the primacy by the vote of the Druids, or sometimes even with armed force. These Druids, at a certain time of the year, meet within the borders of the Carnutes, whose territory is reckoned as the centre of all Gaul, and sit in conclave in a consecrated spot. Thither assemble from every side all that have disputes, and they obey the decisions and judgments of the Druids. It is believed that their rule of life was discovered in Britain and transferred thence to Gaul; and to-day those who would study the subject more accurately journey, as a rule, to Britain to learn it.

The Druids usually hold aloof from war, and do not pay war-taxes with the rest; they are excused from military service and exempt from all liabilities. Tempted by these great rewards, many young men assemble of their own motion to receive their training; many are sent by parents and relatives. Report says that in the schools of the Druids they learn by heart a great number of verses, and therefore some persons remain twenty years under training. And they do not think it proper to commit these utterances to writing, although in almost all other matters, and in their public and private accounts, they make use of Greek letters. I believe that they have adopted the practice for two reasons—that they do not wish the rule to become common property, nor those who learn the rule to rely on writing and so neglect the cultivation of the memory; and, in fact, it does usually happen that the assistance of writing tends to relax the diligence of the student and the action of the memory. The cardinal doctrine which they seek to teach is that souls do not die, but after death pass from one to another; and this belief, as the fear of death is thereby cast aside, they hold to be the greatest incentive to valour. Besides this, they have many discussions as touching the stars and their movement, the size of the universe and of the earth, the order of nature, the strength and the powers of the immortal gods, and hand down their lore to the young men.

The other class are the knights. These, when there is occasion, upon the incidence of a war—and before Cæsar's coming this would happen wellnigh every year, in the sense that they would either be making wanton attacks themselves or repelling such—are all engaged therein; and according to the importance of each of them in birth and resources, so is the number of liegemen and dependents that he has about him. This is the one form of influence and power known to them.

The whole nation of the Gauls is greatly devoted to ritual observances, and for that reason those who are smitten with the more grievous maladies and who are engaged in the perils of battle either sacrifice human victims or vow so to do, employing the Druids for such sacrifices. They believe, in effect, that, unless for a man's life a man's life be paid, the majesty of the immortal gods may not be appeased; and in public, as in private, life they observe an ordinance of sacrifices of the same kind. Others use figures of immense size, whose limbs, woven out of twigs, they fill with living men and set on fire, and the men perish in a sheet of flame. They believe that the execution of those who have been caught in the act of theft or robbery or some crime is more pleasing to the immortal gods; but when the supply of such fails they resort to the execution even of the innocent.

Among the gods, they most worship Mercury. There are numerous images of him; they declare him the inventor of all arts, the guide of every road and journey, and they deem him to have the greatest influence for all money-making and traffic. After him they set Apollo, Mars, Jupiter, and Minerva. Of these deities they have almost the same idea as all other nations: Apollo drives away diseases, Minerva supplies the first principles of arts and crafts, Jupiter holds the empire of the heavens, Mars controls wars. To Mars, when they have determined on a decisive battle, they dedicate as a rule whatever spoil they may take. After a victory they sacrifice such living things as they have taken, and all the other effects they gather into one place. In many states heaps of such objects are to be seen piled up in hallowed spots, and it has not often happened that a man, in defiance of religious scruple, has dared to conceal such spoils in his house or to remove them from their place, and the most grievous punishment, with torture, is ordained for such an offence.

The Gauls affirm that they are all descended from a common father, Dis, and say that this is the tradition of the Druids. For that reason they determine all periods of time by the number, not of days, but of nights, and in their observance of birthdays and the beginnings of months and years day follows night. In the other ordinances of life the main difference between them and the rest of mankind is that they do not allow their own sons to approach them openly until they have grown to an age when they can bear the burden of military service, and they count it a disgrace for a son who is still in his boyhood to take his place publicly in the presence of his father.

The men, after making due reckoning, take from their own goods a sum of money equal to the dowry they have received from their wives and place it with the dowry. Of each such sum account is kept between them and the profits saved; whichever of the two survives receives the portion of both together with the profits of past years. Men have the power of life and death over their wives, as over their children; and when the father of a house, who is of distinguished birth, has died, his relatives assemble, and if there be anything suspicious about his death they make inquisition of his wives as they would of slaves, and if discovery is made they put them to death with fire and all manner of excruciating tortures. Their funerals, considering the civilization of Gaul, are magnificent and expensive. They cast into the fire everything, even living creatures, which they believe to have been dear to the departed during life, and but a short time before the present age, only a generation since, slaves and dependents known to have been beloved by their lords used to be burnt with them at the conclusion of the funeral formalities.

Those states which are supposed to conduct their public administration to greater advantage have it prescribed by law that any one who has learnt anything of public concern from his neighbours by rumour or report must bring the information to a magistrate and not impart it to any one else; for it is recognised that oftentimes hasty and inexperienced men are terrified by false rumours, and so are driven to crime or to decide supreme issues. Magistrates conceal what they choose, and make known what they think proper for the public. Speech on state questions, except by means of an assembly, is not allowed.

The Germans differ much from this manner of living. They have no Druids to regulate divine worship, no zeal for sacrifices. They reckon among the gods those only whom they see and by whose offices they are openly assisted—to wit, the Sun, the Fire-god, and the Moon; of the rest they have learnt not even by report. Their whole life is composed of hunting expeditions and military pursuits; from early boyhood they are zealous for toil and hardship. Those who remain longest in chastity win greatest praise among their kindred; some think that stature, some that strength and sinew are fortified thereby. Further, they deem it a most disgraceful thing to have had knowledge of a woman before the twentieth year; and there is no secrecy in the matter, for both sexes bathe in the rivers and wear skins or small cloaks of reindeer hide, leaving great part of the body bare.

For agriculture they have no zeal, and the greater part of their food consists of milk, cheese, and flesh. No man has a definite quantity of land or estate of his own: the magistrates and chiefs every year assign to tribes and clans that have assembled together as much land and in such place as seems good to them, and compel the tenants after a year to pass on elsewhere. They adduce many reasons for that practice—the fear that they may be tempted by continuous association to substitute agriculture for their warrior zeal; that they may become zealous for the acquisition of broad territories, and so the more powerful may drive the lower sort from their holdings; that they may build with greater care to avoid the extremes of cold and heat; that some passion for money may arise to be the parent of parties and of quarrels. It is their aim to keep common people in contentment, when each man

sees that his own wealth is equal to that of the most powerful.

Their states account it the highest praise by devastating their borders to have areas of wilderness as wide as possible around them. They think it the true sign of valour when the neighbours are driven to retire from their lands and no man dares to settle near, and at the same time they believe they will be safer thereby, having removed all fear of a sudden inroad. When a state makes or resists aggressive war officers are chosen to direct the same, with the power of life and death. In time of peace there is no general officer of state, but the chiefs of districts and cantons do justice among their followers and settle disputes. Acts of brigandage committed outside the borders of each several state involve no disgrace; in fact, they affirm that such are committed in order to practise the young men and to diminish sloth. And when any of the chiefs has said in public assembly that he will be leader, "Let those who will follow declare it," then all who approve the cause and the man rise together to his service and promise their own assistance, and win the general praise of the people. Any of them who have not followed, after promise, are reckoned as deserters and traitors, and in all things afterwards trust is denied to them. They do not think it right to outrage a guest; men who have come to them for any cause they protect from mischief and regard as sacred; to them the houses of all are open, with them is food shared.

Now there was a time in the past when the Gauls were superior in valour to the Germans and made aggressive war upon them, and because of the number of their people and the lack of land they sent colonies across the Rhine. And thus the most fertile places of Germany round the Hercynian forest (which I see was known by report to Eratosthenes and certain Greeks, who call it the Orcynian forest) were seized by the Volcæ Tecto-sages, who settled there, and the nation maintains itself to this day in those settlements, and enjoys the highest reputation for justice and for success in war. At the present time, since they abide in the same condition of want, poverty, and hardship as the Germans, they adopt the same kind of food and bodily training. Upon the Gauls, however, the neighbourhood of our provinces and acquaintance with oversea commodities lavishes many articles of use or luxury; little by little they have grown accustomed to defeat, and after being conquered in many battles they do not even compare themselves in point of valour with the Germans.

—H. J. Edwards.

The Siege of Alesia [1]

CÆSAR

[From the *Gallic War*, Book VII]

Cæsar's conquest had been comparatively easy of accomplishment so long as the Gallic tribes had offered opposition singly. When the Gauls finally realized this, they formed a loose confederation under the leadership of Vercingetorix and made a last desperate stand at Alesia. The simplicity and objectivity with which the author describes this siege are characteristic of the whole book.

When all the horsemen had been put to flight Vercingetorix drew his forces back from their position in front of the camps and at once began the march to Alesia, a town of the Mandubii, ordering the baggage to be brought speedily out of camp and to follow close after him. Cæsar withdrew his baggage to the nearest hill and, leaving two legions to guard it, pursued as long as daylight allowed. Some three thousand of the enemy's rear-

guard were slain, and on the next day he pitched camp near Alesia. He reconnoitered the situation of the city, and as the enemy were terror-struck by the rout of their horsemen, the branch of their army on which they most relied, he urged his soldiers to the task and began the investment.

The actual stronghold of Alesia was set atop of a hill, in a very lofty situation, apparently impregnable save by blockade. The bases of the hill were washed on two separate sides by rivers. Before the town a plain extended for a length of about three miles; on all the other sides there were hills surrounding the town at a short distance, and equal to it in height. Under the wall, on the side which looked eastward, the forces of the Gauls had entirely occupied all this intervening space, and had made in front a ditch and a rough wall six feet high. The perimeter of the siege-works which the Romans were beginning had a length of eleven miles. Camps had been pitched at convenient spots, and three-and-twenty forts had been constructed on the line. In these piquets would be posted by day to prevent any sudden sortie; by night the same stations were held by sentries and strong garrisons.

When the siege-work had been started, a cavalry encounter took place in the plain which we have described above as set between hills and extending to a length of three miles. Both sides strove with the utmost vigour. When our men were distressed Cæsar sent up the Germans, and posted the legions in front of the camp to prevent any sudden inrush on the part of the enemy's footmen. With the reinforcement of the legions behind them our men's spirit was increased; the enemy were put to flight, and, hampering one another by sheer numbers, as the gates were left too narrow, were crowded together in a press. The Germans pursued most vigorously right up to the fortifications. A great slaughter ensued; some of the enemy abandoned their horses, and tried to cross the ditch and scale the wall. Cæsar ordered the legions posted in front of the rampart to advance a short distance. The Gauls inside the fortifications were in just as great a confusion as the rest; believing that the enemy were coming on them at once, they shouted the call to arms, and some in panic burst into the town. Vercingetorix ordered the gates to be shut, lest the camp should be deserted. After much slaughter and the capture of many horses the Germans retired.

Vercingetorix now made up his mind to send away all his horsemen by night, before the Romans could complete their entrenchments. His parting instructions were that each of them should proceed to his own state and impress for the campaign all men whose age allowed them to bear arms. He set forth his own claims upon them, and adjured them to have regard for his personal safety, and not to surrender to the torture of the enemy one who had done sterling service for the general liberty. He showed them that if they proved indifferent eighty thousand chosen men were doomed to perish with him. He had calculated that he had corn in short rations for thirty days, but that by economy he could hold out just a little longer. After giving these instructions he sent the horsemen silently away in the second watch, at a point where a gap was left in our works. He ordered all the corn to be brought in to his headquarters; he appointed death as the penalty for any disobedience of the order; the cattle, of which great store had been driven together by the Mandubii, he distributed man by man; he arranged that the corn should be measured out sparingly and gradually; he withdrew into the town all the force which he had posted in front of it. By such measures did he prepare for the conduct of the campaign, in anticipation of the succours from Gaul.

Cæsar had report of this from deserters and prisoners, and determined on the following types of entrenchments. He dug a trench twenty feet wide with perpendicular sides, in such fashion that the bottom thereof was just as broad as the distance from edge to edge at the surface. He set back the rest of the siege-works four hundred paces from the trench; for as he had of necessity included so large an area, and the whole of the works could not easily be manned by a ring-fence of troops, his intention was to provide against any sudden rush of the enemy's host by night upon the entrenchments, or any chance of directing their missiles by day upon our troops engaged on the works. Behind this interval he dug all round two trenches, fifteen feet broad and of equal depth; and the inner one, where the ground was level with the plain or sank below it, he filled with water diverted from the river. Behind the trenches he constructed a ramp and palisade twelve feet high; to this he added a breastwork and battlements, with large fraises projecting at the junctions of screens and ramp, to check the upward advance of the enemy; and all round the works he set turrets at intervals of eighty feet.

As it was necessary that at one and the same time timber and corn should be procured, and lines of such extent constructed, our forces, having to proceed to a considerable distance from camp, were reduced in number; and sometimes the Gauls would try to make an attempt upon our works by a sortie in force from several gates of the town. Cæsar, therefore, thought proper to make a further addition to these works, in order that the lines might be defensible by a smaller number of troops. Accordingly, trunks or very stout branches of trees were cut, and the tops thereof barked and sharpened, and continuous trenches five feet deep were dug. Into these the stumps were sunk and fastened at the bottom so that they could not be torn up, while the bough-ends were left projecting. They were in rows of five fastened and entangled together, and any one who pushed into them must impale himself on the sharpest of stakes. These they called "markers." In front of these, in diagonal rows arranged like a figure of five, pits three feet deep were dug, sloping inwards slightly to the bottom. In these, tapering stakes as thick as a man's thigh, sharpened at the top and fire-hardened, were sunk so as to project no more than four fingers' breadth from the ground; at the same time, to make all strong and firm, the earth was trodden down hard one foot from the bottom, and the remainder of the pit was covered over with twigs and brushwood to conceal the trap. Eight rows of this kind were dug, three feet apart. From its resemblance to the flower the device was called a "lily." In front of all these, logs a foot long, with iron hooks firmly attached, were buried altogether in the ground and scattered at brief intervals all over the field, and these they called "spurs."

When all these arrangements had been completed Cæsar constructed parallel entrenchments of the same kind facing the other way, against the enemy outside, following the most favourable ground that the locality afforded, with a circuit of fourteen miles. This he did to secure the garrisons of the entrenchments from being surrounded by a host, however large it might chance to be. And in order that he might not be constrained to dangerous excursions from camp, he ordered all his men to have thirty days' corn and forage collected.

While this was proceeding about Alesia, the Gauls summoned a council of chiefs and determined not to call up (according to the proposal of Vercingetorix) all who could bear arms, but to require of each chief a certain quota

from his state; for they feared that with so large a host herded together they might not be able to preserve discipline, to distinguish their several contingents, or to secure a supply of corn. Of the Ædui and their dependents, Segusiavi, Ambivareti, Aulerci Brannovices, and Blannovii, they required five-and-thirty thousand; an equal number from the Arverni, together with the Eleuteti, Cadurci, Gabali, and Vellavii, who are regularly under the sovereignty of the Arverni; from the Sequani, Senones, Bituriges, Santoni, Ruteni, and Carnutes, twelve thousand each; from the Bellovaci ten thousand, and as many from the Lemovices; eight thousand each from the Pictones, Turoni, Parisii, and Helvetii; five thousand each from the Suessiones, Ambiani, Mediomatrici, Petrocorii, Nervii, Morini, and Nitiobriges; a like number from the Aulerci Cenomani; four thousand from the Atrebates; three each from the Veliocasses, Lexovii, and Aulerci Eburovices; two each from the Raurici and the Boii; thirty thousand in all from the states touching the Ocean, commonly called by them Armoric, among whom are the Curiosolites, Redones, Ambibarii, Caletes, Osismi, Veneti, Lemovices, and Venelli. Of these the Bellovaci did not make up their quota, because they declared that they would wage war with the Romans on their own account and at their own direction, and would obey no man's command; however, when Commius made request they sent two thousand men with the rest, out of regard to their private relations with him.

This Commius, as we have before mentioned, had rendered faithful and efficient service to Cæsar in previous years in the expedition to Britain. For these good offices Cæsar had ordered his state to be exempt from taxation, had restored its rights and laws, and had made the Morini tributary to him. Yet so strong was the unanimity of Gaul as a whole for the maintenance of their liberty and the recovery of their ancient renown in war that no benefits, no memory of friendship could influence them, and all devoted themselves with heart and strength to the campaign before them. When eight thousand horsemen and about two hundred and fifty thousand footmen had been collected, the force was reviewed and a muster was taken in the country of the Ædui. Officers were appointed, and the chief command was entrusted to Commius the Atrebatian, Viridomarus and Eporedorix the Æduans, and Vercassivellaunus the Arvernian, a cousin of Vercingetorix. To them were attached a staff selected from the states, by whose counsel the campaign was to be conducted. Full of spirit and confidence, all started for Alesia; there was not a man of them all who thought the mere sight of so vast a host could be withstood, especially in a two-sided engagement, when there would be fighting with those who made a sortie from within the town, and outside the display of so vast an army of horse and foot.

However, when the day on which they had expected reinforcements of their own folk was past, and they had exhausted all their corn, and knew not what was going on in the land of the Ædui, the Gauls besieged in Alesia called a council of war to consider what would be the issue of their fortunes. Various opinions were expressed, one party voting for surrender, another for a sortie while their strength sufficed: but the speech of Critognatus should not, I think, be omitted, because of its remarkable and abominable cruelty. He was of high lineage among the Arverni, and considered to have great influence. "Of their opinion," he said, "who call a most disgraceful slavery by the name of surrender I purpose to say nothing; I hold that they should not be treated as citizens nor invited to the council. Let *my* business be with those who approve a sortie;

and in their design, by your general agreement, there seems to remain a memory of ancient courage. This is faintheartedness of yours, not courage, to be unable to endure want for a short space. It is easier to find men to fling themselves recklessly on death than men to endure pain patiently. And yet I might now have approved this view (so much weight with me has the authority of those who hold it) if I saw therein the loss of nothing but our life; but in making our decision we should have regard to the whole of Gaul, which we have aroused to our assistance. What, think ye, will be the spirit of our friends and kindred, when eighty thousand men have been slain in one spot, if they are forced to fight out the issue almost over their very bodies? Refuse to rob of your support the men who for your deliverance have disregarded their own peril; forbear by folly, recklessness, or weakmindedness of yours to lay prostrate, and subject to everlasting slavery, the whole of Gaul. Or do you doubt their faithfulness, their resolution, because they are not arrived to the day? What then? Do ye think that the Romans are daily engaged in those outer trenches for mere amusement? If it may not be that your resolve should be strengthened by messages from your friends, since every approach is blocked, yet take the Romans here to your witnesses that their coming draws nigh; and it is in fear thereof that they are busy in their works day and night. What, then, is my counsel? To do what our forefathers did in the war, in no wise equal to this, with the Cimbri and Teutones. They shut themselves into the towns, and under stress of a like scarcity sustained life on the bodies of those whose age showed them useless for war, and delivered not themselves to the enemy. And if we had not had a precedent for this, I should still have judged it a most glorious thing for the sake of liberty to set such a one and to hand it down to posterity. For wherein was that war like this? The Cimbri devastated Gaul, they brought great disaster upon us, yet they departed at length from our borders and sought other countries, leaving us our rights, laws, lands, liberty. But the Romans—what else do they seek or desire than to follow where envy leads, to settle in the lands and states of men whose noble report and martial strength they have learnt, and to bind upon them a perpetual slavery? 'Tis in no other fashion they have waged wars. And if ye know not what is afoot among distant nations, look now on Gaul close at hand, which has been reduced to a province, with utter change of rights and laws, and crushed beneath the axes in everlasting slavery."

When opinions had been expressed they determined that those who by reason of health or age were useless for war should leave the town, and that every expedient should be tried before they had recourse to the counsel of Critognatus, resolving, however, to adopt that plan, if compelled by circumstances— that is to say, the delay of reinforcements—rather than to submit to terms of surrender or of peace. The Mandubii, whose town had received them, were compelled to leave it with wives and children. When they reached the Roman lines they begged with tears and abject prayers to be received as slaves and helped with food. But Cæsar posted sentries on the rampart and prevented their admission.

Meanwhile Commius and the other leaders entrusted with the supreme command reached the neighbourhood of Alesia with all their force, and, seizing a hill outside, halted not more than a mile from our entrenchments. The day after they brought their horsemen out of camp and filled the whole of that plain which we have described as extending for a length of three miles; their force of footmen they posted a little way back from the spot, on the higher ground. There was a bird's-eye view from the town of Alesia over the plain. At sight of these reinforcements the others hastened together with mutual congratulation, and all minds were stirred to joy. So they brought out their force and halted in front of the town; they covered over the nearest trench with hurdles and filled it in with earth, and prepared for a sally and for every emergency.

Cæsar disposed the whole army on both faces of the entrenchments in such fashion that, if occasion should arise, each man could know and keep his proper station; then he ordered the cavalry to be brought out of camp and to engage. There was a view down from all the camps, which occupied the top of the surrounding ridge, and all the troops were intently awaiting the issue of the fight. The Gauls had placed archers and light-armed skirmishers here and there among the horsemen to give immediate support to their comrades if driven back and to resist the charge of our cavalry. A number of men, wounded unexpectedly by these troops, began to withdraw from the fight. When the Gauls were confident that their own men were getting the better of the battle, and saw ours hard pressed by numbers, with shouts and yells on every side—those who were confined by the entrenchments as well as the others who had come up to their assistance—they sought to inspirit their countrymen. As the action was proceeding in sight of all, and no deed, of honour or dishonour, could escape notice, both sides were stirred to courage by desire of praise and fear of disgrace. The fight lasted, and the victory was doubtful, from noon almost to sunset; then the Germans in one part of the field massed their troops of horse, charged the enemy and routed them, and when they had been put to flight the archers were surrounded and slain. Likewise, from the other parts of the field, our troops pursued the retreating enemy right up to their camp, giving them no chance of rallying. But the Gauls who had come forth from Alesia, almost despairing of victory, sadly withdrew again into the town.

After one day's interval, in the course of which they made a great number of hurdles, ladders, and grappling-hooks, the Gauls left camp silently at midnight and approached the entrenchments in the plain. Raising a sudden shout, to signify their coming to the besieged inside the town, they began to fling down the hurdles, to dislodge our men from the rampart with slings, arrows, and stones, and to carry out everything else proper to an assault. At the same moment, hearing the shout, Vercingetorix gave his troops the signal by trumpet, and led them out of the town. Our troops, as on previous days, moved each to his appointed station in the entrenchments; with slings, one-pounders, stakes set ready inside the works, and bullets, they beat off the Gauls. As the darkness made it impossible to see far, many wounds were received on both sides. A number of missiles were discharged by the artillery. Then Marcus Antonius and Gaius Trebonius, the lieutenant-generals to whom the defence of these sections had been allotted, withdrew troops from forts farther away, and sent them up to bring assistance wherever they remarked that our men were hard pressed.

While the Gauls were some distance from the entrenchment they had more advantage from the quantity of their missiles; then, when they came up closer, they were soon caught unawares on the "spurs," or they sank into the pits and were impaled, or they were shot by artillery pikes from the rampart and the turrets, and so perished on every side. Many a man was wounded, but the entrenchment was nowhere penetrated; and when daybreak drew nigh, fearing that they might be surrounded on their exposed flank by a sortie from the camps above them, they retired to their comrades. Meanwhile the inner force brought out the appliances which had been prepared by Vercingetorix for a sortie, and filled in the nearer trenches; but they lingered too long in the execution of the business, and, or ever they could get near the entrenchments, they learnt that their countrymen had withdrawn. So without success they returned to the town.

Twice beaten back with great loss, the Gauls took counsel what to do. They called in men who knew the locality well, and from them they learnt the positions and the defences of the upper camps. On the north side there was a hill, which by reason of its huge circumference our troops had been unable to include within the works; they had been obliged to lay out the camp on ground gently sloping, which put them almost at a disadvantage. This camp was held by Gaius Antistius Reginus and Gaius Caninius Rebilus, lieutenant-generals, with two legions. Having reconnoitred the locality by means of scouts, the commanders of the enemy chose out of the whole host sixty thousand men belonging to the states which had the greatest reputation for courage: they determined secretly together what should be done and in what fashion, and decided that the advance should take place at the moment when it was seen to be midday. In charge of this force they put Vercassivellaunus the Arvernian, one of the four commanders, a kinsman of Vercingetorix. He left camp in the first watch, and having almost completed his march just before dawn, he concealed himself behind the height and ordered his soldiers to rest after their night's work. When at last it was seen to be near midday he moved with speed on the camp above mentioned and at the same moment the horsemen began to advance towards the entrenchments in the plain, and the rest of the force to make a demonstration before the camp.

When from the citadel of Alesia Vercingetorix observed his countrymen, he moved out of the town, taking with him the hurdles, poles, mantlets, grappling-hooks, and all the other appliances prepared for the sally. The fight went on simultaneously in all places, and all expedients were attempted, with a rapid concentration on that section which was seen to be least strong. With lines so extensive the Roman army was strung out, and at several points defence proved difficult. The shouting which arose in rear of the fighting line did much to scare our troops, as they saw that the risk to themselves depended on the success of others; for, as a rule, what is out of sight disturbs men's minds more seriously than what they see.

Cæsar found a suitable spot from which he could see what was proceeding in each quarter. To parties distressed he sent up supports. Both sides felt that this was the hour of all others in which it was proper to make their greatest effort. The Gauls utterly despaired of safety unless they could break through the lines; the Romans anticipated an end of all toils if they could hold their own. The hardest struggle occurred by the entrenchments on the hill, whither, as we have mentioned, Vercassivellaunus had been sent. The unfavourable downward slope of the ground had great effect. Some of the enemy discharged missiles, others moved up in close formation under their shields; fresh men quickly replaced the exhausted. Earth cast by the whole body together over the entrenchments gave the Gauls a means of ascent and at the same time covered over the appliances which the Romans had concealed in the ground; and our troops had now neither arms nor strength enough.

When Cæsar learnt this, he sent Labienus with six cohorts to support them in their distress. He commanded him, if he could not hold his ground, to draw in the cohorts and fight his way out, but not to do so unless of necessity. He himself went up to the rest of the troops, and urged them not to give in to the strain, telling them that the fruit of all previous engagements depended upon that day and hour. The enemy on the inner side, despairing of success on the level ground, because of the size of the entrenchments, made an attempt to scale the precipitous parts, conveying thither the appliances they had prepared. They dislodged the defenders of the turrets by a swarm of missiles, filled in the trenches with earth and hurdles, tore down rampart and breastwork with grappling-hooks.

Cæsar first sent young Brutus with some cohorts, and then Gaius Fabius, lieutenant-general, with others; last of all, as the fight raged more fiercely, he himself brought up fresh troops to reinforce. The battle restored, and the enemy repulsed, he hastened to the quarter whither he had sent Labienus. He withdrew four cohorts from the nearest fort, and ordered part of the cavalry to follow him, part to go round the outer entrenchments and attack the enemy in rear. Labienus, finding that neither ramps nor trenches could resist the rush of the enemy, collected together eleven cohorts, which had been withdrawn from the nearest posts and by chance presented themselves, and sent messengers to inform Cæsar what he thought it proper to do. Cæsar hurried on to take part in the action.

His coming was known by the colour of his cloak, which it was his habit to wear in action as a distinguishing mark; and the troops of cavalry and the cohorts which he had ordered to follow him were noticed, because from the upper levels these downward slopes and depressions were visible. Thereupon the enemy joined battle: a shout was raised on both sides, and taken up by an answering shout from the rampart and the whole of the entrenchments. Our troops discarded their pikes and got to work with their swords. Suddenly the cavalry was noticed in the rear; other cohorts drew near. The enemy turned to flee; the cavalry met them in flight, and a great slaughter ensued. Sedulius, commander and chief of the Lemovices, was killed; Vercassivellaunus the Arvernian was captured alive in the rout; seventy-four war standards were brought in to Cæsar; of the vast host few returned safe to camp. The others beheld from the town the slaughter and rout of their countrymen, and, in despair of safety, recalled their force from the entrenchments. Directly they heard what had happened the Gauls fled from their camp. And if the troops had not been worn out by frequent reinforcing and the whole day's effort, the entire force of the enemy could have been destroyed. The cavalry were sent off just after midnight and caught up the rearguard: a great number were taken and slain, the rest fled away into the different states.

On the morrow Vercingetorix summoned a council, at which he stated that he had undertaken that campaign, not for his own occasions, but for the general liberty; and as they must yield to fortune he offered himself to them for whichever course they pleased—to give satisfaction to the Romans by his death, or to deliver him alive. Deputies were despatched to Cæsar to treat of this matter. He ordered the arms to be delivered up, the chiefs to be brought out. He himself took his seat in the entrenchments in front of the camp: the leaders were brought out to him there. Vercingetorix was surrendered, arms were thrown down. Keeping back the Ædui and the Arverni, to see if through them he could recover their states, he distributed the rest of the prisoners, one apiece to each man throughout the army, by way of plunder.

When these affairs were settled he started for the country of the Ædui and recovered the state. The Arverni sent deputies to him there who promised to carry out his commands: he required of them a great number of hostages. He sent the legions into cantonments. He restored some twenty thousand prisoners to the Ædui and the Arverni. He ordered Titus Labienus with two legions and cavalry to march off into the country of the Sequani, attaching Marcus Sempronius Rutilus to him. Gaius Fabius, the lieutenant-general, and Lucius Minucius Basilus he stationed with two legions in the country of the Remi, in order that they might suffer no damage from the neighbouring Bellovaci. Gaius Antistius Reginus he sent into the territory of the Ambivareti, Titus Sextius to the Bituriges, Gaius Caninius Rebilus to the Ruteni, with a legion apiece. Quintus Tullius Cicero and Publius Sulpicius he stationed at Cabillonum and Matisco, Æduan towns near the Arar, to secure the corn-supply. He himself decided to winter at Bibracte. When the despatches of the campaign were published at Rome a public thanksgiving of twenty days was granted.

—H. J. EDWARDS.

ON THE CONSULAR PROVINCES

CICERO

In this speech, delivered in 56 B.C. while the winning of Gaul was yet in progress, Cicero, although supporting the policy of expansion and advocating its continuance, recognizes a new element of aggression on Rome's part. It is very interesting to compare this statement of Cicero's with the interpretation which Cæsar very cleverly puts on his conquest of Gaul in his own *Commentaries*. Cæsar at most admits a defensive-offensive. Every step in advance he takes is always caused by some attack or threat of attack by Gallic tribes inimical to Rome's best interests. For Cicero, see above p. 95.

If any one of you, O conscript fathers, is waiting to see what provinces I shall propose to decree to the consuls, let him consider in his own mind what men I must think it most desirable to recall from the provinces; and then he will not have any doubt what ought to be my sentiments, when he has once seriously thought what it is absolutely inevitable that they should be. And if I were the first to deliver the opinion which I am about to state, you would in truth praise it; if I were to stand alone in it, at all events you would pardon me. Even if my opinion were to appear to you on the whole somewhat ineligible, still you would make some allowance for my just indignation. But, as the case stands at present, O conscript fathers, I feel no ordinary delight because it is so entirely for the advantage of the republic that Syria and Macedonia should be the provinces decreed to the consuls, that my own private feelings are in no respect at variance with the general good; and because also I can cite the authority of Publius Servilius, who has delivered his opinion before me, a most illustrious man, and of singular good faith and attachment both to the republic in general, and to my safety in particular. And if he, both just now, and whenever he has had any opportunity or possibility of speaking on the subject has thought it his duty to brand not only with his adverse opinion but with the greatest severity of language, Gabinius and Piso, as the two monsters who have been almost the destruction of the republic, both on other accounts, and also most especially because of their extraordinary wickedness and unseemly inhumanity towards me, with what feelings ought I myself to be actuated towards those men, —I whose safety they devoted and ruined for the gratification of their own evil passions?

But in declaring my sentiments at this time, I will not be guided by my indignation, nor will I make my speech subservient to my enmity. The same feelings which every individual among you ought to entertain towards those men, shall influence me also. My own predominant and peculiar feeling of private indignation, which, however, you have always considered as belonging to yourselves in common with me, I will put aside while delivering my opinion, and reserve for a more fitting opportunity of revenge.

There are four provinces, O conscript fathers, concerning which I understand that opinions have as yet been delivered: the two Gauls, which at present we see united under one command; and Syria; and Macedonia; which, against your will, and when you were suffering under oppression and constraint, those pernicious consuls seized on as their reward for having overturned the republic. According to the provisions of the Sempronian law, we have now to decree two to the consuls. How is it possible for us to doubt about Syria and Macedonia being these two? I say nothing of the fact that those men are holding them at present who procured them in such a way, that they did not get them till they condemned this order of ours, till they had destroyed your authority and put an end to it in the state; till they had destroyed all public credit and good faith, endangered the lasting safety of the Roman people, and harassed me and all my friends and relations in the most shameful and barbarous manner.

All these private matters, all these transactions which took place in the city, I say nothing about; though they are of such a nature that Hannibal himself never wished so much evil to the city, as those men have done. . . .

But believe me, those men will never have successors appointed to them, except when a motion shall be made in accordance with the provisions of that law by which it is unlawful for any one to interpose his veto while the debate is pending about the provinces; therefore, as this opportunity is lost, you must now wait an entire year; during which interval the calamities of the citizens, the miseries of the allies, and the impunity of the most wicked men may be extended.

But even if they were the most excellent of men, still, in my opinion, it could never be advisable to appoint a successor to Caius Cæsar. Now, concerning this matter, O conscript fathers, I shall declare my real sentiments, and I shall not be disconcerted by that interruption of my most intimate friend, who did a little while ago interrupt my speech, as you heard. That excellent man says that I ought not to be more hostile to Gabinius than to Cæsar; for that all that storm, to which I yielded, was raised by the instigation and assistance of Cæsar. And if I were in the first instance to reply that I was having regard to the common advantage, and not to my own private sufferings, could I not establish that, when I say that I am doing what I well may do according to the example of other most valiant and most illustrious citizens? Did Tiberius Gracchus (I am speaking of the father, and would that his son had never degenerated from the father's virtue!) gain such great glory because he, while tribune of the people, was the only one of the whole college who was any assistance to Lucius Scipio, though he was the bitterest possible enemy, both to him and to his brother Africanus; and did he not swear in the public assembly that he had by no means become reconciled to him, but that it seemed to him quite inconsistent with the dignity of the empire that, after the generals of the enemy had been led to prison while Scipio was celebrating his triumph, the very man also who had triumphed should be led to the same place?

Who had a greater number of enemies than Caius Marius? There were Lucius Crassus, Marcus Scaurus, (were there no more?) and all the Metelli. But those men not only forbore to recall that enemy of theirs from Gaul by their votes, but also, out of consideration for the Gallic war, they even voted him the province out of the regular order. A most important war has been waged in Gaul; very mighty nations have been subdued by Cæsar; but they are not yet established with laws, or with any fixed system of rights, or by a peace which can be very thoroughly depended on. We see that the war has been carried on, and, to say the truth, nearly brought to a conclusion; but we shall only see it all actually terminated in a successful manner, if the man who commenced it remains to follow it up to the last. If a successor is appointed to him, there is great danger that we may hear that the embers of this momentous war are again fanned into a flame and rekindled. Therefore, I, a senator, an enemy, if you please, of the man himself, feel it my duty to be, as I always have been, a friend to the republic. What if I lay aside my enmity itself for the sake of the republic, who, I should like to know, would have a right to blame me? especially as I have at all times thought that I ought to seek for the models for all my intentions and for all my actions in the conduct of the most illustrious men. . . .

Is it possible for me to be an enemy to this man, by whose letters, by whose glory, and by whose messengers my ears are every day saluted with previously unknown names of tribes, and nations, and places? I burn, believe me, O conscript fathers, (as indeed you do believe of me, and as you feel yourselves) with an incredible love for my country; which love compelled me formerly to encounter most terrible dangers which were hanging over it, at the risk of my own life; and again, when I saw every sort of weapon aimed from all quarters against my country, drove me to put myself in their way, and to expose myself singly to their blows on behalf of the whole body of citizens. And this, my ancient and perpetual disposition towards the republic, now reunites me to and reconciles me to and unites me in friendship with Caius Cæsar. In short, let men think what they please; it is impossible for me to be other than a friend to one who deserves well of his country. . . .

I admit that I was of a different opinion to Cæsar with respect to the affairs of the republic, and that I agreed with all of you: but now I am agreeing also with you with whom I felt in common before. For you,—to whom Lucius Piso does not venture to send letters respecting his exploits,—you who have condemned the letters of Gabinius with a most remarkable stigma, and an unprecedented mark of disgrace, have decreed supplications to Caius Cæsar in such number, as were never decreed before to any one in one war, and with such attending circumstances of honour as were never voted to any one at all. Why, then, need I wait for any man to act as a mediator between us, in order to reconcile me to him? This most honourable order has mediated between us; that order which is the instigator and the leader both of the public counsels and of all my own designs. I am following you, O conscript fathers, I am obeying you, I am adopting your opinions;— yours, I say, who, as long as you had no very favourable opinion of the designs of Caius Cæsar with respect to the republic, saw that I too was very little connected with him; since you changed your opinions and inclinations on account of his great achievements, you have seen me also not only the sharer of your sentiments, but also the panegyrist and advocate of them. . . .

And I who have been received in all those discussions with silent attention, now that the question is about the provinces which are to be decreed to the consuls, am interrupted; though in all the former transactions it was only a

compliment to an individual that I urged, while now I have no motive but the consideration of the war, and the general welfare of the republic. For, as for Cæsar himself, what reason can there be why he should wish any longer to remain in the province, except for the purpose of not giving over to the republic the measures which have been undertaken by him before they are completely consummated? It is the delightful nature of the country, I suppose, and the splendour of the cities, and the civilized state and accomplished habits of those nations and natives,—it is a desire for victory, it is a wish to extend the boundaries of our empire, that detains him there! What is there anywhere more severe than those countries? what more uncivilized than their towns? what more barbarous than their citizens? Moreover, what can be imagined more desirable than the victories which he has already gained, or what can be discovered beyond the ocean? Is his return to his country likely to be disagreeable to any one? Can it be so either to the people by whom he was sent on his command, or to the senate from whom he has received so many distinctions? Does time foster his wish to see his country again, or does it rather increase his forgetfulness of it? If, then, there be any one who is not attached to that man, still such an one has no reason for recalling him from his province. It is only recalling him to glory, to triumph, to receive congratulations, to receive the highest honours which the senate can bestow, to receive the thanks of the equestrian order, and to become the object of the devoted affection of the people.

But if he, out of his regard for the interests of the republic, does not hasten to the enjoyment of that extraordinary good fortune which is in store for him, preferring to remain and finish everything; what ought I to do as a senator,— I, who ought to think only of the advantage of the republic, even if his wishes were opposed to it? For I feel, O conscript fathers, that we at this time, while engaged in decreeing provinces to the consuls, ought to have a regard to the preservation of perpetual peace. For who is there who is not aware that all our other possessions are safe from all danger, and even from all suspicion of war? We have for some time seen that immense sea,—by the disturbed condition of which not only our voyages by sea were impeded, but even our cities and our military marches and roads were exposed to annoyance,—now in consequence of the valour of Cnæus Pompeius, possessed from the ocean to the very extremity of Pontus, like one vast harbour in a safe and defensible state; and as for those nations, which by their mere numbers and the immensity of their population were sufficient to overflow our provinces, we have seen some of them so thinned in numbers, and others so severely checked by that same man, that Asia, which was formerly the limit of our empire, is now itself bounded on the further side by three of our provinces. I might go on speaking of every region and of every race of men. There is no nation which is not either so far destroyed as scarcely to have any existence at all, or so utterly subdued as to be quite tranquil; or else so entirely at peace with us, as to share our exultation at our victories and at the extension of our empire.

The war with Gaul, O conscript fathers, has been carried on actively since Caius Cæsar has been our commander-in-chief; previously, we were content to act on the defensive, and to repel attacks. For our generals at all times thought it better to limit themselves to repulsing those nations, than to provoke their hostility by any attack of our own. Even that great man Caius Marius, whose godlike and amazing valour came to the assistance of the Roman people in many of its distresses and disasters, was con-

tent to check the enormous multitudes of Gauls who were forcing their way into Italy, without endeavouring to penetrate himself into their cities and dwelling-places. And lately, that partner of my labours, and dangers, and counsels, Caius Pomptinus, that most gallant man, crushed in battle a war of the Allobroges which rose up suddenly against us, and which was excited by that impious conspiracy, and defeated those tribes who had provoked us, and then he remained quiet, contented with the victory by which he had delivered the republic from alarm.

But I see that the counsels of Caius Cæsar are widely different. For he thought it his duty, not only to war against those men whom he saw already in arms against the Roman people, but to reduce the whole of Gaul under our dominion. Therefore, he fought with the greatest success against those most valiant and powerful nations, the Germans and Helvetians; and the other nations he alarmed, and drove back, and defeated, and accustomed to yield to the supremacy of the Roman people; so that those districts and those nations which were previously known to us neither by any one's letters, nor by the personal account of any one, nor even by vague report, have now been overrun and thoroughly examined by our own general, by our own army, and by the arms of the Roman people.

Hitherto, O conscript fathers, we have only known the road into Gaul. All other parts of it were possessed by nations which were either hostile to this empire, or treacherous, or unknown to us, or, at all events, savage, barbarian, and warlike;—nations which no one ever existed who did not wish to break their power and subdue: nor has any one, from the very first rise of this empire, ever carefully deliberated about our republic, who has not thought Gaul the chief object of apprehension to this empire. But still, on account of the power and vast population of those nations, we never before have had a war with all of them; we have always been content to resist them when attacked. Now, at last, it has been brought about that there should be one and the same boundary to our empire and to those nations.

Nature had previously protected Italy by the Alps, not without some special kindness of the gods in providing us with such a bulwark. For if that road had been open to the savage disposition and vast numbers of the Gauls, this city would never have been the home and chosen seat of the empire of the world. Now, indeed, they are at liberty to sink down if they please; for there is nothing beyond those lofty heights as far as the ocean itself, which can be any object of fear to Italy. But still it will be the work of one or two summers finally to bind the whole of Gaul in everlasting chains either by fear, or hope, or punishment, or reward, or arms, or laws. And if our affairs there are left in an unfinished state, and while there is still some bitterness of feeling remaining, although the enemy may be pruned back severely for the present, still they will raise their heads again some time or other, and come forth with recruited strength to renew the war. Let, then, Gaul be left in the guardianship of that man to whose valour, and good faith, and good fortune it has already been entrusted. If, in truth, he, having been distinguished by such marked kindness of Fortune, were unwilling to risk the favour of that goddess too often; if he were anxious himself to return to his country, to his household gods, to that dignity which he sees in store for him in this city, to his most charming children, and to his most illustrious son-in-law; if he were impatient to be borne in triumph as a conqueror to the Capitol, crowned with the illustrious laurel of victory; if, in short, he were apprehensive of some disaster, as no

event can now add so much glory to him as a mishap might deprive him of; still it would be your duty to insist on all those affairs being brought to a termination by the same man who has begun them so successfully. But when he has not yet satisfied his own desire for glory for the safety of the republic, and as he prefers coming at a later period to reap the rewards of his toils rather than not discharging to the full the duty which the republic has committed to him; then certainly, we, for our part, ought not to recall a general who is so eager to conduct the affairs of the republic gloriously, nor to throw into confusion and to hinder his plans for the whole Gallic war, which are now almost matured and accomplished. . . .

I am well aware, O conscript fathers, that you have decreed many extraordinary honours to Caius Cæsar; honours which are almost unprecedented. In that he has amply merited them, you have been grateful; if I add, too, that he is a man most thoroughly attached to this order of the senate, you have been wise and provident. For this order has never heaped its distinctions and kindnesses on any one who has subsequently thought any dignity preferable to that which he had obtained by your favour. For it is not possible for any one to be the leading man in this body who has preferred courting the favour of the people. But all men who have done this, have either distrusted themselves on account of their consciousness of their want of worth, or else they have been driven away from a union with this order on account of the disparagement of their merits by the rest, and so they have been almost constrained to throw themselves out of this harbour on those stormy billows. And if, after they have been tossed about on those surges, and have become wearied of their voyage amid the whims of the people, having been successful in the conduct of the affairs of the republic, they show their faces again in the senate-house, and wish to gain the favours of this most honourable order, I say that they are not only not to be repelled, but are to be received with open arms, and courted.

We are warned by the bravest man and most admirable consul who has ever existed in the memory of man, to take care that the nearer Gaul be not decreed against our will to any one after the election of those consuls who are now about to be elected, and that it be not for the future occupied for ever by these men who are the constant attackers of this order, by some turbulent system of currying favour with the mob. And although I am not indifferent to the evil consequences of such a measure, O conscript fathers, especially when warned of them by a consul of the greatest wisdom, and one who is an especial guardian of peace and tranquillity, still I think that there is an evil to be regarded with even more apprehension than that,—the evil, I mean, of diminishing the honours of most illustrious and powerful citizens, and rejecting their zeal for the maintenance of this order.

For even supposing that Caius Julius, having been distinguished by all sorts of extraordinary and unprecedented honours by the senate, were compelled to deliver up this province to one whom you would be very unwilling to see there, still I cannot possibly be induced to suspect that he would deprive that body of liberty by which he himself had had the greatest glory conferred on him. Lastly, what disposition every one will have I know not; I am aware only of what my own hopes are. I, as a senator, am bound to take care, as far as I can, that no illustrious or powerful man shall appear to have any right to feel offended with this body. These sentiments I shall express out of regard to the republic, even were I ever so great an enemy to Caius Cæsar. . . .

This is the last thing which I have to say. If I had any enmity against Caius Cæsar, still at this time I ought to consult the interests of the republic, and to reserve my hostility for another time. I might even, following the precedent of most eminent men, lay aside my enmity altogether for the sake of the republic; but as I have never entertained any enmity to him, and as the idea of having been injured by him has been extinguished by services which he has done me, I, by my opinion, O conscript fathers, if the dignity of Caius Cæsar is at stake, shall vote for the man;—if any honour to be paid to him is under discussion, I shall consult the unanimous feeling of the senate;—if the authority of your decrees is the main point to be regarded, I shall uphold the consistency of our order by voting distinctions to this same commander-in-chief;—if the everlasting consideration of the Gallic war is to be taken into account, I shall consult the interests of the republic;—if I may have respect to my own private duty, I shall show that I am not ungrateful.

And I wish, O conscript fathers, to induce you all to approve of my sentiments; but I shall not be greatly concerned if I fail to induce those men to approve of them who shielded my enemy in spite of your authority; or those who found fault with my reconciliation with their enemy, while they themselves do not hesitate to be reconciled both to my enemy and to their own.

—C. D. YONGE.

II. POLITICAL IDEAS

The course of history proves that the Romans were gifted warriors, organizers, politicians, and statesmen. They had a firm hold on realities so that in the course of centuries, by adjustment and adaptation, so characteristic of the English of the modern world, they worked out a splendid constitutional form of government. True it is that this form collapsed under the pressure of excessive wealth and a too speedy subjugation of the world; but under Augustus a new form was evolved, itself an adaptation of the old, and its success showed once again the political genius of the race.

But almost never did they theorize and speculate on government and its problems. Literary works on such a subject were not produced. To this rule Cicero is an exception. In fact only in the pages of Polybius, who in the second century B.C. wrote Rome's history, is anything similar to be found. But Polybius was a Greek, and wrote in Greek. And it is beyond question that Cicero's thorough schooling in Greek literature and Greek philosophy was an important element in the production of his works on government.

Because of his acquaintance with Greek thought, his wide knowledge of Rome's history, his first-hand contact with the machinery of government in a period of critical developments, and because of the sincerity of his patriotism, Cicero was well fitted for a study of Roman political ideas, while his splendid literary style fitted him to express them suitably. But Cicero was not a speculative philosopher, nor was he a statesman of original ideas. The reader should not expect brilliant, political theories from Cicero's works, but he may expect a valuable presentation of political forms as evolved by the Romans, and of the best of Roman ideals for the government of their city and empire.

Cicero, following a Greek analysis, looked upon the Roman state, as he would have it, as one using a mixed form of government. A monarchical element was there in the consuls, chief executives, an aristocratic element in the senate, and a democratic in the body of citizens. These elements should all have their place, and they did, in his day; but the result was not then encouraging. In his active political life Cicero often hoped and worked for a *concordia ordinum*, a harmony among the classes, quite in accordance with his ideal constitution. Possibly he came to believe that there should be some leading citizen to guide the ship of state, as Pericles in Athens, and as the younger Scipio in second century Rome. At one time certainly he hoped that Pompey might be such a leader, and that he himself would be, as Lælius to Scipio, a guide, philosopher, and friend.

Cicero thought of the state as an organism. Following Greek thought he saw in nature, in natural law, the source of human law and justice. He regards it as the proper function of a state to secure justice and provide for the well-being of its citizens.

These political ideas were set forth particularly in the *De Re Publica,* the *De Legibus,* and the *De Officiis.* They exerted no small influence on the later development of Roman law, and then both directly and indirectly on modern conceptions of law and the state. And through their study by great leaders in the church, like St. Augustine, Christian ethics have been influenced.

DEFINITION OF A STATE

CICERO

[From the *Republic*, Book I]

For Cicero, see above, p. 95.

Well, then, said Africanus, a commonwealth is a constitution of the entire people. But the people is not every association of men, however congregated, but the association of the entire number, bound together by the compact of justice, and the communication of utility. The first cause of this association is not so much the weakness of man, as a certain spirit of congregation which naturally belongs to him. For the human race is not a race of isolated individuals, wandering and solitary; but it is so constituted, that even in the affluence of all things, and without any need of reciprocal assistance, it spontaneously seeks society.

—F. Barham and C. D. Yonge.

Three Forms of Government

CICERO

[From the *Republic*, Book I]

It is necessary to presuppose these original seeds, as it were, since we cannot discover any primary establishment of the other virtues, or even of a commonwealth itself. These unions, then, formed by the principle which I have mentioned, established their head-quarters originally in certain central positions, for the convenience of the whole population; and having fortified them by natural and artificial means, they called this collection of houses a city or town, distinguished by temples and public squares. Every people, therefore, which consists of such an association of the entire multitude as I have described,— every city which consists of an assemblage of the people,—and every commonwealth which embraces every member of these associations,—must be regulated by a certain authority, in order to be permanent.

This intelligent authority should always refer itself to that grand first principle which established the commonwealth. It must be deposited in the hands of one supreme person, or entrusted to the administration of certain delegated rulers, or undertaken by the whole multitude. When the direction of all depends on one person, we call this individual a king; and this form of political constitution, a kingdom. When it is in the power of privileged delegates, the state is said to be ruled by an aristocracy; and when the people are all in all, they call it a democracy, or popular constitution. And if the tie of social affection, which originally united men in political associations for the sake of public interest, maintains its force, each of these governments is, I will not say perfect, nor, in my opinion, essentially good, but tolerable, and such that one may accidentally be better than another: either a just and wise king, or a selection of the most eminent citizens, or even the populace itself (though this is the least commendable form), may, if there be no interference of crime and cupidity, form a constitution sufficiently secure.

But in a monarchy, the other members of the state are often too much deprived of public counsel and jurisdiction; and under the rule of an aristocracy, the multitude can hardly possess its due share of liberty, since it is allowed no share in the public deliberation, and no power. And when all things are carried by a democracy, although it be just and moderate, yet its very equality is a culpable levelling, inasmuch as it allows no gradations of rank. Therefore, even if Cyrus, the king of the Persians, was a most righteous and wise monarch, I should still think that the interest of the people (for this is, as I have said before, the same as the commonwealth) could not be very effectually promoted when all things depended on the beck and nod of one individual. And though at present the people of Marseilles, our clients, are governed with the greatest justice by elected magistrates of the highest rank, still there is always in this condition of the people a certain appearance of servitude; and when the Athenians, at a certain period, having demolished their Areopagus, conducted all public affairs by the acts and decrees of the democracy alone, their state, as it no longer contained a distinct gradation of ranks, was no longer able to retain its original fair appearance.

—F. Barham and C. D. Yonge.

The Mixed Constitution

CICERO

[From the *Republic*, Book I]

Greek theory did not supply a classification which exactly fitted the Roman constitution.

Scipio. Now to return to the argument of my discourse. It appears that this extreme license, which is the only liberty in the eyes of the vulgar, is, according to Plato, such that from it as a sort of root tyrants naturally arise and spring up. For as the excessive power of an aristocracy occasions the destruction of the nobles, so this excessive liberalism of democracies brings after it the slavery of the people. Thus we find in the weather, the soil, and the animal constitution, the most favourable conditions are sometimes suddenly converted by their excess into the contrary, and this fact is especially observable in political governments; and this excessive liberty soon brings the people collectively and individually to an excessive servitude. For, as I said, this extreme liberty easily introduces the reign of tyranny, the severest of all unjust slaveries. In fact, from the midst of this unbridled and capricious populace, they elect some one as a leader in opposition to their afflicted and expelled nobles; some new chief, forsooth, audacious and impure, often insolently persecuting those who have deserved well of the state, and ready to gratify the populace at his neighbour's expense as well as his own. Then since the private condition is naturally exposed to fears and alarms, the people invest him with many powers, and these are continued in his hands. Such men, like Pisistratus of Athens, will soon find an excuse for surrounding themselves with body-guards, and they will conclude by becoming tyrants over the very persons who raised them to dignity. If such despots perish by the vengeance of the better citizens, as is generally the case, the constitution is re-established. But if they fall by the hands of bold insurgents, then the same faction succeeds them, which is only another species of tyranny. And the same revolution arises from the fair system of aristocracy, when any corruption has betrayed the nobles from the path of rectitude. Thus the power is like the ball, which is flung from hand to hand: it passes from kings to tyrants, from tyrants to the aristocracy, from them to democracy, and from these back again to tyrants and factions; and thus the same kind of government is seldom long maintained.

Since these are the facts of experience, royalty is, in my opinion, very far preferable to the three other kinds of political constitutions. But it is itself inferior to that which is composed of an equal mixture of the three best forms of government, united and modified by one another. I wish to establish in a commonwealth a royal and preeminent chief. Another portion of power should be deposited in the hands of the aristocracy, and certain things should be reserved to the judgment and wish of the multitude. This constitution, in the first place, possesses that great equality, without which men cannot long maintain their freedom;—secondly, it offers a great stability, while the particular separate and isolated forms easily fall into their contraries; so that a king is succeeded by a despot,—an aristocracy by a faction,— a democracy by a mob and confusion; and all these forms are frequently sacrificed to new revolutions. In this united and mixed constitution, however, similar disasters cannot happen without the greatest vices in public men. For there can be little to occasion revolution in a state, in which every person is firmly established in his appropriate rank, and there are but few modes of corruption into which we can fall.

But I fear, Lælius, and you, my amiable and learned friends, that if I were to dwell any longer on this argument, my words would seem rather like the lessons of a master, and not like the free conversation of one who is uniting with you in the consideration of truth. I shall therefore pass on to those things which are familiar to all, and which I have long studied. And in these matters I believe, I feel, and affirm, that of all governments, there is none which, either in its entire constitution, or the distribution of its parts, or in the discipline of its manners, is comparable to that which our fathers received from our earliest ancestors, and which they have handed down to us.

—F. Barham and C. D. Yonge.

Lawlessness Begets Tyranny

CICERO

[From the *Republic*, Book III]

Cicero realizes the distinction between democracy and Bolshevism.

Scipio. I now come to the third, or democratical, form of government, in which a considerable difficulty presents itself, because all things are there said to lie at the disposition of the people, and are carried into execution just as they please. Here the populace inflict punishments at their pleasure, and act, and seize, and keep possession, and distribute property, without let or hindrance. Can you deny, my Lælius, that this is a fair definition of a democracy, where

the people are all in all, and where the people constitute the state?

Lælius. There is no political constitution to which I more absolutely deny the name of a *commonwealth*, than that in which all things lie in the power of the multitude. If a commonwealth, which implies the welfare of the entire community, could not exist in Agrigentum, Syracuse, or Athens, when tyrants reigned over them,—if it could not exist in Rome, when under the oligarchy of the decemvirs,—neither do I see how this sacred name of commonwealth can be applied to a democracy, and the sway of the mob; because, in the first place, my Scipio, I build on your own admirable definition, that there can be no community, properly so called, unless it be regulated by a combination of rights. And, by this definition, it appears that a multitude of men may be just as tyrannical as a single despot; and it is so much the worse, since no monster can be more barbarous than the mob, which assumes the name and appearance of the people. Nor is it at all reasonable, since the laws place the property of madmen in the hands of their sane relations, that we do the very reverse in politics, and throw the property of the sane into the hands of the mad multitude.

—F. Barham and C. D. Yonge.

Rome Past and Present

CICERO

[From the *Republic*, Book V]

Cicero here gives expression to the general Roman ideal of a government based upon tradition.

Ennius has told us—

"Of men and customs mighty Rome consists";

which verse, both for its precision and its verity, appears to me as if it had issued from an oracle; for neither the men, unless the state had adopted a certain system of manners—nor the manners, unless they had been illustrated by the men—could ever have established or maintained for so many ages so vast a republic, or one of such righteous and extensive sway.

Thus, long before our own times, the force of hereditary manners of itself moulded most eminent men, and admirable citizens in return gave new weight to the ancient customs and institutions of our ancestors. But our age, on the contrary, having received the commonwealth as a finished picture of another century, but one already beginning to fade through the lapse of years, has not only neglected to renew the colours of the original painting, but has not even cared to preserve its original form and prominent lineaments.

For what now remains of those antique manners, of which the poet said that our commonwealth consisted? They have now become so obsolete and forgotten, that they are not only not cultivated, but they are not even known. And as to the men, what shall I say? For the manners themselves have only perished, through a scarcity of men; of which great misfortune we are not only called to give an account, but even, as men accused of capital offences, to a certain degree to plead our own cause in connexion with it. For it is owing to our vices, rather than to any accident, that we have retained the name of republic when we have long since lost the reality.

—F. Barham and C. D. Yonge.

The Optimates

CICERO

[From the *Defense of Sestius*]

The term optimates came to be limited in Cicero's day to a particular political party consisting principally of the conservative senators. But Cicero, playing on the word, extends it through his idealism to include all good men of every party.

There have always in this city been two kinds of men who have been ambitious of being concerned in affairs of state, and of arriving at distinction by such a course; and of these two kinds one wish to be considered popular men, and the others wish both to be, and to be considered, of the party of the best men in the state. Those whose object it was that whatever they did and whatever they said should be agreeable to the multitude, were the popular party; but those who conducted themselves in such a way as to induce all the best men to approve of their counsels, were considered of the best party.

Who then are they? Every good man. If you ask what are their numbers, they are innumerable. For if they were not, we could not stand. They are the chief men of the public council; they are those who follow their school; they are the men of the highest orders of the state, to whom the senate-house is open; they are the citizens of the municipal towns, and Roman citizens who dwell in the country; they are men engaged in business; there are even some freedmen of the best party. The number, as I have said, of this party is widely scattered in various directions; but the entire body (to prevent all mistakes) can be described and defined in a few words. All men belong to the best party, who are not guilty of any crime, nor wicked by nature, nor madmen, nor men embarrassed by domestic difficulties. Let it be laid down, then, that these men (this race, as you call them) are all those who are honest, and in their senses, and who are well off in their domestic circumstances. Those who are guided by their wishes, who consult their interests and opinions in the management of the republic, are the partisans of the best men, and are themselves accounted best men, most wise and most illustrious citizens, and chief men in the state.

What, then, is the object proposed to themselves by these directors of the republic, which they are bound to keep their eyes fixed upon, and towards which they ought to direct their course? That which is most excellent and desirable to all men in their senses, and to all good and happy men,—ease conjoined with dignity. Those who seek this are all best men; those who effect it are considered the chief leaders in and the preservers of their states. For men ought not to be so elated by the dignity of the affairs which they have undertaken to manage, as to have no regard to their ease; nor ought they to dwell with fondness on any sort of ease which is inconsistent with dignity.

And of this easy dignity these are the foundations, these are the component parts, which ought to be upheld by the chief men, and to be defended even at the hazard of their lives: religious observances, the auspices, the civil power of magistrates, the authority of the senate, the laws, the usages of one's ancestors, the courts of justice, the jurisdiction of the judges, good faith, the provinces, the allies, the glory of the empire, the whole affairs of the army, the treasury. To be the defender and advocate of all these things, numerous and important as they are, is a task to employ great courage, great ability, and great firmness. In truth, in such a vast number of citizens, there is a great multitude of those men, who either, from fear of punishment, because they are conscious of their own misdeeds, are anxious for fresh changes and revolutions in the republic; or who, on account of some innate insanity of mind, feed upon the discords and seditions of the citizens; or else who, on account of the embarrassment of their estates and circumstances,

had rather burn in one vast common conflagration, than in one which consumed only themselves. And when these men have found instigators, leaders in and promoters of their own objects and vices, their waves are stirred up in the republic, so that those men must watch who have demanded for themselves the helm of the country, and they must strive with all their skill and with all their diligence, in order that they may be able to preserve those things which I have just now called its foundations and component parts, and so keep in their course and reach that harbour of ease and dignity.

If, O judges, I were to deny that this path is rugged and difficult, and full of danger and snares, I should speak falsely; especially as I have not only been aware that it was so, but have been alive to its perils and labours more than any other man.

The republic is attacked by greater forces and more numerous bodies than those by which it is defended; because audacious and abandoned men are impelled on by a nod, and are even of their own accord excited by nature to be enemies to the republic. And somehow or other good men are slower in action, and overlooking the first beginnings of things, are at last aroused by necessity itself; so that sometimes through their very delays and tardiness of movement, while they wish to retain their ease even without dignity, they, of their own accord, lose both. But those who are desirous to be defenders of the republic, if they be fickle men, soon give up the task; if they be at all timid men, they abandon it; and those alone remain and endure everything for the sake of the republic, who are such men as your father was, O Marcus Scaurus, who resisted all seditious men, from the time of Caius Gracchus to that of Quintus Varius, whom no violence, no threats, and no unpopularity ever shook; or such as Quintus Metellus, the uncle of your mother; who when as censor he had branded a man most flourishing in the popular esteem, Lucius Saturninus, and when he had expunged a pretended Gracchus from the list of the citizens, in spite of the violence of an excited mob, and when he alone had refused to swear obedience to a law which he considered had not been legally enacted, preferred to abandon the city rather than his opinion; or, (to leave off quoting ancient examples, of which there is an abundance worthy of the glory of this empire, while yet I avoid naming any one who is now alive) such as Quintus Catulus lately was, whom neither the tempest of danger nor the breeze of honour could ever move from his straight course, either by hope or fear.

Imitate those men, I beg you in the name of the immortal gods, ye who seek for dignity, and praise, and glory. These examples are honourable; these are godlike; these are immortal; these are celebrated in fame, and are committed to the eternal recollection of our annals, and are handed down to posterity. It is a labour, I do not deny it. The dangers are great, I admit it,—

"The path of virtuous men is full of snares."

That is a most true saying.
The poet says further,—

"But to demand those honours which excite
The general envy and desire of all,
And yet to shun the toil and ceaseless care
Which can alone conduct to such a goal,
Is purest ignorance."

—C. D. YONGE.

THE FOUNDATION OF JUSTICE

CICERO

[From the *Laws*, Book I]

MARCUS. Let us, then, begin to establish the principles of justice on that supreme law, which has existed from all ages before any legislative enactments were drawn up in writing, or any political governments constituted.

QUINTUS. That will be more convenient, and more sensible with reference to the subjects of the discussion which we have determined on.

MARCUS. Shall we, then, seek for the origin of justice at its fountain-head? When we have discovered which, we shall be in no doubt to what these questions which we are examining ought to be referred.

QUINTUS. Such is the course I would advise.

ATTICUS. I also subscribe to your brother's opinion.

MARCUS. Since, then, we wish to maintain and preserve the constitution of that republic which Scipio, in those six books which I have written under that title, has proved to be the best, and since all our laws are to be accommodated to the kind of political government there described, we must also treat of the general principles of morals and manners, and not limit ourselves on all occasions to written laws; but I purpose to trace back the origin of right from nature itself, who will be our best guide in conducting the whole discussion.

ATTICUS. You will do right, and when she is our guide it is absolutely impossible for us to err.

MARCUS. Do you then grant, my Atticus, (for I know my brother's opinion already) that the entire universe is regulated by the power of the immortal Gods, that by their nature, reason, energy, mind, divinity, or some other word of clearer signification, if there be such, all things are governed and directed? for if you will not grant me this, that is what I must begin by establishing.

ATTICUS. I grant you all you can desire. But owing to this singing of birds and babbling of waters, I fear my fellow-learners can scarcely hear me.

MARCUS. You are quite right to be on your guard; for even the best men occasionally fall into a passion, and they will be very indignant if they hear you denying the first article of that notable book, entitled "The Chief Doctrines of Epicurus," in which he says "that God takes care of nothing, neither of himself nor of any other being!"

ATTICUS. Pray proceed, for I am waiting to know what advantage you mean to take of the concession I have made you.

MARCUS. I will not detain you long. This is the bearing which they have on our subject. This animal—prescient, sagacious, complex, acute, full of memory, reason, and counsel, which we call man—has been generated by the supreme God in a most transcendent condition. For he is the only creature among all the races and descriptions of animated beings who is endued with superior reason and thought, in which the rest are deficient. And what is there, I do not say in man alone, but in all heaven and earth, more divine than reason, which, when it becomes right and perfect, is justly termed wisdom?

There exists, therefore, since nothing is better than reason, and since this is the common property of God and man, a certain aboriginal rational intercourse between divine and human natures. But where reason is common, there right reason must also be common to the same parties; and since this right reason is what we call law, God and men must be considered as associated by law. Again, there must also be a communion of right where there is a communion of law. And those who have law and right thus in common, must be considered members of the same commonwealth.

And if they are obedient to the same rule and the same authority, they are even much more so to this one celestial regency, this divine mind and omnipotent deity. So that the entire universe may be looked upon as forming one vast commonwealth of gods and men. And, as in earthly states certain ranks are distinguished with reference to the relationships of families, according to a certain principle which will be discussed in its proper place, that principle, in the nature of things, is far more magnificent and splendid by which men are connected with the Gods, as belonging to their kindred and nation. . . .

Since, then, the Deity has been pleased to create and adorn man to be the chief and president of all terrestrial creatures, so it is evident, without further argument, that human nature has also made very great advances by its own intrinsic energy; that nature, which without any other instruction than her own, has developed the first rude principles of the understanding, and strengthened and perfected reason to all the appliances of science and art.

ATTICUS. Oh ye immortal Gods! to what a distance back are you tracing the principles of justice! However, you are discoursing in such a style that I will not show any impatience to hear what I expect you to say on the Civil Law. But I will listen patiently, even if you spend the whole day in this kind of discourse; for assuredly these, which perhaps you are embracing in your argument for the sake of others, are grander topics than even the subject itself for which they prepare the way.

MARCUS. You may well describe these topics as grand, which we are now briefly discussing. But of all the questions which are ever the subject of discussion among learned men, there is none which is more important thoroughly to understand than this, that man is born for justice, and that law and equity have not been established by opinion, but by nature. This truth will become still more apparent if we investigate the nature of human association and society.

For there is no one thing so like or

so equal to another, as in every instance man is to man. And if the corruption of customs, and the variation of opinions, did not induce an imbecility of minds, and turn them aside from the course of nature, no one would more nearly resemble himself than all men would resemble all men. Therefore, whatever definition we give of man, will be applicable to the whole human race. And this is a good argument that there is no dissimilarity of kind among men; because if this were the case, one definition could not include all men.

In fact, reason, which alone gives us so many advantages over beasts, by means of which we conjecture, argue, refute, discourse, and accomplish and conclude our designs, is assuredly common to all men; for the faculty of acquiring knowledge is similar in all human minds, though the knowledge itself may be endlessly diversified. By the same senses we all perceive the same objects, and those things which move the senses at all, do move in the same way the senses of all men. And those first rude elements of intelligence which, as I before observed, are the earliest developments of thought, are similarly impressed upon all men; and that faculty of speech which is the interpreter of the mind, agrees in the ideas which it conveys, though it may differ in the words by which it expresses them. And therefore there exists not a man in any nation, who, if he adopts nature for his guide, may not arrive at virtue.

Nor is this resemblance which all men bear to each other remarkable in those things only which are in accordance with right reason, but also in errors. For all men alike are captivated by pleasure, which, although it is a temptation to what is disgraceful, nevertheless bears some resemblance to natural good; for, as by its delicacy and sweetness it is delightful, it is through a mistake of the intellect adopted as something salutary.

And by an error scarcely less universal, we shun death as if it were a dissolution of nature, and cling to life because it keeps us in that existence in which we were born. Thus, likewise, we consider pain as one of the greatest evils, not only on account of its present asperity, but also because it seems the precursor of mortality. Again, on account of the apparent resemblance between renown with honour, those men appear to us happy who are honoured, and miserable who happen to be inglorious. In like manner our minds are all similarly susceptible of inquietudes, joys, desires, and fears; nor if different men have different opinions, does it follow that those who deify dogs and cats, do not labour under superstition equally with other nations, though they may differ from them in the forms of its manifestation.

Again, what nation is there which has not a regard for kindness, benignity, gratitude, and mindfulness of benefits? What nation is there in which arrogance, malice, cruelty, and unthankfulness, are not reprobated and detested? And while this uniformity of opinions proves that the whole race of mankind is united together, the last point is that a system of living properly makes men better. If what I have said meets your approbation, I will proceed; or if any doubts occur to you, we had better clear them up first.

ATTICUS. There is nothing which strikes us, if I may reply for both of us.

MARCUS. It follows, then, that nature made us just that we might share our goods with each other, and supply each other's wants. You observe in this discussion, whenever I speak of nature, I mean nature in its genuine purity, but that there is, in fact, such corruption engendered by evil customs, that the sparks, as it were, of virtue which have been given by nature are extinguished, and that antagonist vices arise around it and become strengthened.

But if, as nature prompts them to, men would with deliberate judgement, in the words of the poet, "being men, think nothing that concerns mankind indifferent to them," then would justice be cultivated equally by all. For to those to whom nature has given reason, she also has given right reason, and therefore also law, which is nothing else than right reason enjoining what is good, and forbidding what is evil. And if nature has given us law, she hath also given us right. But she has bestowed reason on all, therefore right has been bestowed on all. And therefore did Socrates deservedly execrate the man who first drew a distinction between utility and nature, for he used to complain that this error was the source of all human vices, to which this sentence of Pythagoras refers —"The things belonging to friends are common"—and that other, "Friendly equality." From whence it appears, that when a wise man has displayed this benevolence which is so extensively and widely diffused towards one who is endowed with equal virtue, then that phenomenon takes place which is altogether incredible to some people, but which is a necessary consequence, that he loves himself not more dearly than he loves his friend. For how can a difference of interests arise where all interests are similar? If there could be ever so minute a difference of interests, then there would be an end of even the nature of friendship, the real meaning of which is such, that there is no friendship at all the moment that a person prefers anything happening to himself rather than to his friend.

Now, these preliminary remarks have been put forward as a preparation for the rest of our discourse and argument, in order that you may more easily understand that nature herself is the foundation of justice. And when I have explained this a little more at large, then I will proceed to the consideration of that civil law from which all these arguments of mine are derived.

QUINTUS. Then you have not much to add, my brother, for the arguments you have already used have sufficiently proved to Atticus, or at all events to me, that nature is the fountain of justice.

ATTICUS. How could I maintain any other opinion, since you have now established these points—first, that we have been provided as we are and adorned by the gifts of the Gods; secondly, that all mankind have but one similar and common principle of living together; and, lastly, that all men are bound together by a certain natural indulgence and affection, as well as social rights? And as we have, rightly as I think, admitted the truth of these principles, how can we, with any consistency, separate from nature that law and justice which are her moral developments?

MARCUS. You are quite right, and that is the proper view of the case. But in conformity with the method of philosophers, (I do not mean the older sages of philosophy, but those modern ones, who have erected a magazine, as it were, of wisdom) those questions which were formerly discussed loosely and unconstrainedly, are now examined with strictness and distinctness. Nor will these men allow that we have done justice to the subject which we have now before us, unless we demonstrate in a dictinct discussion that right is a part of nature.

ATTICUS. You seem to have renounced your liberty in debate, my Cicero; or are you become a man who, in discussion, rather follows the authority of others, than develops his individual sentiments?

MARCUS. Not always, Atticus. But you see what the line of this present conversation is, and how the main object of this whole discussion is to strengthen the foundation of commonwealths, to establish their forces, and to benefit their population. I am, therefore, particularly anxious to avoid arguments which have not been thoroughly examined and carefully considered. Not that I expect to demonstrate my doctrine to the satisfaction of all men, for that is impossible; but I hope to do so to that of those who think that all just and honourable things deserve to be cultivated even for their own sake, and that nothing whatsoever can be properly called a good which is not intrinsically praiseworthy, or at least that there can exist no great good whatever which is not truly laudable on its own account.

All the philosophers who flourished in the old academy with Speusippus, Xenocrates, and Polemon, or those that followed Aristotle and Theophrastus, agreeing with them in doctrine, though they might differ in their method of explaining it—whether, like Zeno, they preserved the same principles, while they changed the terms of exposition,—or whether, like Aristion, they supported that difficult and arduous sect now generally scattered and confuted, which supposed that, with the exception of virtue and vice, all other things were completely equal and indifferent: all these have adopted the principles which I have been explaining. . . .

It is therefore an absurd extravagance in some philosophers to assert, that all things are necessarily just which are established by the civil laws and the institutions of nations. Are then the laws of tyrants just, simply because they are laws? Suppose the thirty tyrants of Athens had imposed certain laws on the Athenians? or, suppose again that these Athenians were delighted with these tyrannical laws, would these laws on that account have been considered just? For my own part, I do not think such laws deserve any greater estimation than that passed during our own interregnum, which ordained that the dictator should be empowered to put to death with im-

punity whatever citizens he pleased, without hearing them in their own defence.

For there is but one essential justice which cements society, and one law which establishes this justice. This law is right reason, which is the true rule of all commandments and prohibitions. Whoever neglects this law, whether written or unwritten, is necessarily unjust and wicked.

But if justice consists in submission to written laws and national customs, and if, as the same school affirms, everything must be measured by utility alone, he who thinks that such conduct will be advantageous to him will neglect the laws, and break them if it is in his power. And the consequence is, that real justice has really no existence if it have not one by nature, and if that which is established as such on account of utility is overturned by some other utility.

But if nature does not ratify law, then all the virtues may lose their sway. For what becomes of generosity, patriotism, or friendship? Where will the desire of benefiting our neighbours, or the gratitude that acknowledges kindness, be able to exist at all? For all these virtues proceed from our natural inclination to love mankind. And this is the true basis of justice, and without this not only the mutual charities of men, but the religious services of the Gods, would be at an end; for these are preserved, as I imagine, rather by the natural sympathy which subsists between divine and human beings, than by mere fear and timidity.

But if the will of the people, the decrees of the senate, the adjudications of magistrates, were sufficient to establish rights, then it might become right to rob, right to commit adultery, right to substitute forged wills, if such conduct were sanctioned by the votes or decrees of the multitude. But if the opinions and suffrages of foolish men had sufficient weight to outbalance the nature of things, then why should they not determine among them, that what is essentially bad and pernicious should henceforth pass for good and beneficial? Or why, since law can make right out of injustice, should it not also be able to change evil into good?

But we have no other rule by which we may be capable of distinguishing between a good and a bad law than that of nature. Nor is it only right and wrong which are discriminated by nature, but generally all that is honourable is by this means distinguished from all that is shameful; for common sense has impressed in our minds the first principles of things, and has given us a general acquaintance with them, by which we connect with virtue every honourable quality, and with vice all that is disgraceful. . . .

It follows that I may now sum up the whole of this argument by asserting, as is plain to every one from these positions which have already been laid down, that all right and all that is honourable is to be sought for its own sake. In truth, all virtuous men love justice and equity for what they are in themselves; nor is it like a good man to make a mistake, and love that which does not deserve their affection. Right, therefore, is desirable and deserving to be cultivated for its own sake; and if this be true of right, it must be true also of justice. What then shall we say of liberality? Is it exercised gratuitously, or does it covet some reward and recompense? If a man does good without expecting any recompense for his kindness, then it is gratuitous: if he does expect compensation, it is a mere matter of traffic. Nor is there any doubt that he who truly deserves the reputation of a generous and kind-hearted man, is thinking of his duty, not of his interest. In the same way the virtue of justice demands neither emolument nor salary, and therefore we desire it for its own sake. And the case of all the moral virtues is

the same, and so is the opinion formed of them.

Besides this, if we weigh virtue by the mere utility and profit that attend it, and not by its own merit, the one virtue which results from such an estimate will be in fact a species of vice. For the more a man refers all his actions especially to his own advantage, the further he recedes from probity; so that they who measure virtue by profit, acknowledge no other virtue than this, which is a kind of vice. For who can be called benevolent, if no one ever acts kindly for the sake of another? And where are we to find a grateful person, if those who are disposed to be so can find no benefactor to whom they can show gratitude? What will become of sacred friendship, if we are not to love our friend for his own sake with all our heart and soul, as the people say? if we are even to desert and discard him, as soon as we despair of deriving any further assistance or advantage from him. What can be imagined more inhuman than this conduct? But if friendship ought rather to be cultivated on its own account, so also for the same reason are society, equality, and justice, desirable for their own sakes. If this be not so, then there can be no such thing as justice at all; for the most unjust thing of all is to seek a reward for one's just conduct.

—F. BARHAM AND C. D. YONGE.

DUTIES OF THE INDIVIDUAL TO THE STATE [1]

CICERO

[From the *Offices*, Book II]

The typically Roman thing about the book from which this passage is taken, as well as about the passage itself, is the point of view which keeps steadily before the eyes the state rather than the indi-

[1] From the Loeb Classical Library, by permission.

vidual in a general treatise on ethics. Political conduct is the all-important matter. Ethics as a practical subject and as one which admits of discussion of man as a political animal was the only branch of philosophy which genuinely interested the Romans.

Those whom Nature has endowed with the capacity for administering public affairs should put aside all hesitation, enter the race for public office, and take a hand in directing the government; for in no other way can a government be administered or greatness of spirit be made manifest. Statesmen, too, no less than philosophers—perhaps even more so —should carry with them that greatness of spirit and indifference to outward circumstances to which I so often refer, together with calm of soul and freedom from care, if they are to be free from worries and lead a dignified and self-consistent life. This is easier for the philosophers; as their life is less exposed to the assaults of fortune, their wants are fewer; and if any misfortune overtakes them, their fall is not so disastrous. Not without reason, therefore, are stronger emotions aroused in those who engage in public life than in those who live in retirement, and greater is their ambition for success; the more, therefore, do they need to enjoy greatness of spirit and, freedom from annoying cares.

If anyone is entering public life, let him beware of thinking only of the honour it brings; but let him be sure also that he has the ability to succeed. At the same time, let him take care not to lose heart too readily through discouragement nor yet to be over-confident through ambition. In a word, before undertaking any enterprise, careful preparation must be made.

Most people think that the achievements of war are more important than those of peace; but this opinion needs to be corrected. For many men have sought occasions for war from the mere ambition for fame. This is notably the case with men of great spirit and natural ability, if they are adapted to a soldier's life and fond of warfare. But if we will face the facts, we shall find that there have been many instances of achievement in peace more important and no less renowned than in war.

However highly Themistocles, for example, may be extolled—and deservedly —and however much more illustrious his name may be than Solon's, and however much Salamis may be cited as witness of his most glorious victory—a victory glorified above Solon's statesmanship in instituting the Areopagus—yet Solon's achievement is not to be accounted less illustrious than his. For Themistocles's victory served the state once and only once; while Solon's work will be of service for ever. For through his legislation the laws of the Athenians and the institutions of their fathers are maintained. And while Themistocles could not readily point to any instance in which he himself had rendered assistance to the Areopagus, the Areopagus might with justice assert that Themistocles had received assistance from it; for the war was directed by the counsels of that senate which Solon had created. . . .

There are, therefore, instances of civic courage that are not inferior to the courage of the soldier. Nay, the former calls for even greater energy and greater devotion than the latter.

That moral goodness which we look for in a lofty, high-minded spirit is secured, of course, by moral, not by physical, strength. And yet the body must be trained and so disciplined that it can obey the dictates of judgment and reason in attending to business and in enduring toil. But that moral goodness which is our theme depends wholly upon the thought and attention given to it by the mind. And in this way, the men who in a civil capacity direct the affairs of a nation render no less important service than they who conduct its wars: by their statesmanship oftentimes wars are either averted or terminated; sometimes also they are declared. Upon Marcus Cato's counsel, for example, the Third Punic War was undertaken, and in its conduct his influence was dominant, even after he was dead. And so diplomacy in the friendly settlement is more desirable than courage in settling them on the battlefield; but we must be careful not to take that course merely for the sake of avoiding war rather than for the sake of public expediency. War, however, should be undertaken in such a way as to make it evident that it has no other object than to secure peace.

But it takes a brave and resolute spirit not to be disconcerted in times of difficulty or ruffled and thrown off one's feet, as the saying is, but to keep one's presence of mind and one's self-possession and not to swerve from the path of reason.

Now all this requires great personal courage; but it calls also for great intellectual ability by reflection to anticipate the future, to discover some time in advance what may happen whether for good or for ill, and what must be done in any possible event, and never to be reduced to having to say "I had not thought of that."

These are the activities that mark a spirit, strong, high, and self-reliant in its prudence and wisdom. But to mix rashly in the fray and to fight hand to hand with the enemy is but a barbarous and brutish kind of business. Yet when the stress of circumstances demands it, we must gird on the sword and prefer death to slavery and disgrace.

As to destroying and plundering cities, let me say that great care should be taken that nothing be done in reckless cruelty or wantonness. And it is a great man's duty in troublous times to single out the guilty for punishment, to spare the many, and in every turn of fortune to hold to a true and honourable course. For whereas there are many, as I have said before, who place the achievements of war above those of peace, so one may find many to whom adventurous, hotheaded counsels seem more brilliant and impressive than calm and well-considered measures.

We must, of course, never be guilty of seeming cowardly and craven in our avoidance of danger; but we must also beware of exposing ourselves to danger needlessly. Nothing can be more foolhardy than that. Accordingly, in encountering danger we should do as doctors do in their practice: in light cases of illness they give mild treatment; in cases of dangerous sickness they are compelled to apply hazardous and even desperate remedies. It is, therefore, only a madman who, in a calm, would pray for storm; a wise man's way is, when the storm does come, to withstand it with all the means at his command, and especially, when the advantages to be expected in case of a successful issue are greater than the hazards of the struggle.

The dangers attending great affairs of state fall sometimes upon those who undertake them, sometimes upon the state. In carrying out such enterprises, some run the risk of losing their lives, others their reputation and the good-will of their fellow-citizens. It is our duty, then, to be more ready to endanger our own than the public welfare and to hazard honour and glory more readily than other advantages.

Many, on the other hand, have been found who were ready to pour out not only their money but their lives for their country and yet would not consent to make even the slightest sacrifice of personal glory—even though the interests of their country demanded it. For example, when Callicratidas, as Spartan admiral in the Peloponnesian War, had won many signal successes, he spoiled everything at the end by refusing to listen to the proposal of those who thought he ought to withdraw his fleet from the Arginusæ and not to risk an engagement with the Athenians. His answer to them was that "the Spartans could build another fleet, if they lost that one, but he could not retreat without dishonour to himself." And yet what he did dealt only a slight blow to Sparta; there was another which proved disastrous, when Cleombrotus in fear of criticism recklessly went into battle against Epaminondas. In consequence of that the Spartan power fell.

How much better was the conduct of Quintus Maximus! Of him Ennius says:

"One man—and he alone—restored our state by delaying.
Not in the least did fame with him take precedence of safety;
Therefore now does his glory shine bright, and it grows ever brighter."

This sort of offence must be avoided no less in political life. For there are men who for fear of giving offence do not dare to express their honest opinion, no matter how excellent.

Those who propose to take charge of the affairs of government, should not fail to remember two of Plato's rules: first, to keep the good of the people so clearly in view that regardless of their own interests they will make their every action conform to that; second, to care for the welfare of the whole body politic and not in serving the interests of some one party to betray the rest. For the administration of the government, like the office of a trustee, must be conducted for the benefit of those entrusted to one's care, not of those to whom it is entrusted. Now, those who care for the interests of a part of the citizens and neglect another part, introduce into the civil service a dangerous element—dissension and party strife. The result is that some are found to be loyal supporters of the democratic, others of the aristocratic party, and few of the nation as a whole.

As a result of this party spirit bitter strife arose at Athens, and in our own country not only dissensions but also disastrous civil wars broke out. All this the citizen who is patriotic, brave, and worthy of a leading place in the state will shun with abhorrence; he will dedicate himself unreservedly to his country, without aiming at influence or power for himself; and he will devote himself to the state in its entirety in such a way as to further the interests of all. Besides, he will not expose anyone to hatred or disrepute by groundless charges, but he will surely cleave to justice and honour so closely that he will submit to any loss, however heavy, rather than be untrue to them, and will face death itself rather than renounce them.

A most wretched custom, assuredly, is our electioneering and scrambling for office. Concerning this also we find a fine thought in Plato: "Those who compete against one another," he says, "to see which of two candidates shall administer the government, are like sailors quarrelling as to which one of them shall do the steering." And he likewise lays down the rule that we should regard only those as adversaries who take up arms against the state, not those who strive to have the government administered according to their convictions. This was the spirit of the disagreement between Publius Africanus and Quintus Metellus: there was in it no trace of rancour.

Neither must we listen to those who think that one should indulge in violent anger against one's political enemies and imagine that such is the attitude of a great-spirited, brave man. For nothing is more commendable, nothing more becoming in a pre-eminently great man than courtesy and forbearance. Indeed, in a free people, where all enjoy equal rights before the law, we must school ourselves to affability and what is called "mental poise;" for if we are irritated when people intrude upon us at unseasonable hours or make unreasonable requests, we shall develop a sour, churlish temper, prejudicial to ourselves and offensive to others. And yet gentleness of spirit and forbearance are to be commended only with the understanding that strictness may be exercised for the good of the state; for without that, the government cannot be well administered. On the other hand, if punishment or correction must be administered, it need not be insulting; it ought to have regard to the welfare of the state, not to the personal satisfaction of the man who administers the punishment or reproof.

We should take care also that the punishment shall not be out of proportion to the offence, and that some shall not be chastised for the same fault for which others are not even called to account. In administering punishment it is above all necessary to allow no trace of anger. For if anyone proceeds in a passion to inflict punishment, he will never observe that happy mean which lies between excess and defect. This doctrine of the mean is approved by the Peripatetics— and wisely approved, if only they did not speak in praise of anger and tell us that it is a gift bestowed on us by Nature for a good purpose. But in reality, anger is in every circumstance to be eradicated; and it is to be desired that they who administer the government should be like the laws, which are led to inflict punishment not by wrath but by justice. . . .

Of these public services, some are of such a nature that they concern the whole body of citizens; others, that they affect individuals only. And these latter are the more productive of gratitude. If possible, we should by all means attend to both kinds of service; but we must take care in protecting the interests of individuals that what we do for them shall be beneficial, or at least not prejudicial, to the state. Gaius Gracchus inaugurated

largesses of grain on an extensive scale; this had a tendency to exhaust the exchequer. Marcus Octavius inaugurated a moderate dole; this was both practicable for the state and necessary for the commons; it was, therefore, a blessing both to the citizens and to the state.

The man in an administrative office, however, must make it his first care that every one shall have what belongs to him and that private citizens suffer no invasion of their property rights by act of the state. It was a ruinous policy that Philippus proposed when in his tribuneship he introduced his agrarian bill. However, when his law was rejected, he took his defeat with good grace and displayed extraordinary moderation. But in his public speeches on the measure he often played the demagogue, and that time viciously, when he said that "there were not in the state two thousand people who owned any property." That speech deserves unqualified condemnation, for it favoured an equal distribution of property; and what more ruinous policy than that could be conceived? For the chief purpose in the establishment of constitutional states and municipal governments was that individual property rights might be secured. For although it was by Nature's guidance that men were drawn together into communities, it was in the hope of safeguarding their possessions that they sought the protection of cities.

The administration should also put forth every effort to prevent the levying of a property tax, and to this end precautions should be taken long in advance. Such a tax was often levied in the times of our forefathers on account of the depleted state of their treasury and their incessant wars. But if any state (I say "any," for I would rather speak in general terms than forebode evils to our own; however, I am not discussing our own state but states in general)—if any state ever has to face a crisis requiring the imposition of such a burden, every effort must be made to let all the people realize that they must bow to the inevitable, if they wish to be saved. And it will also be the duty of those who direct the affairs of the state to take measures that there shall be an abundance of the necessities of life. It is needless to discuss the ordinary ways and means; for the duty is self-evident; it is necessary only to mention the matter.

But the chief thing in all public administration and public service is to avoid even the slightest suspicion of self-seeking. "I would," says Gaius Pontius, the Samnite, "that fortune had withheld my appearance until a time when the Romans began to accept bribes, and that I had been born in those days! I should then have suffered them to hold their supremacy no longer." Aye, but he would have had many generations to wait; for this plague has only recently infected our nation. And so I rejoice that Pontius lived then instead of now, seeing that he was so mighty a man! It is not yet a hundred and ten years since the enactment of Lucius Piso's bill to punish extortion; there had been no such law before. But afterward came so many laws, each more stringent than the other, so many men were accused and so many were convicted, so horrible a war was stirred up on account of the fear of what our courts would do to still others, so frightful was the pillaging and plundering of the allies when the laws and courts were suppressed, that now we find ourselves strong not in our own strength but in the weakness of others.

Panætius praises Africanus for his integrity in public life. Why should he not? But Africanus had other and greater virtues. The boast of official integrity belongs not to that man alone but to his times. When Paulus got possession of all the wealth of Macedon —and it was enormous—he brought into our treasury so much money that the spoils of a single general did away with the need for a tax on property in Rome for all time to come. But to his own house he brought nothing save the glory of an immortal name. Africanus emulated his father's example and was none the richer for his overthrow of Carthage. And what shall we say of Lucius Mummius, his colleague in the censorship? Was he one penny the richer when he had destroyed to its foundations the richest of cities? He preferred to adorn Italy rather than his own house. And yet by the adornment of Italy his own house was, as it seems to me, still more splendidly adorned.

There is, then, to bring the discussion back to the point from which it digressed, no vice more offensive than avarice, especially in men who stand foremost and hold the helm of state. For to exploit the state for selfish profit is not only immoral; it is criminal, infamous. And so the oracle, which the Pythian Apollo uttered, that "Sparta should not fall from any other cause than avarice," seems to be a prophecy not to the Lacedæmonians alone, but to all wealthy nations as well. They who direct the affairs of state, then, can win the good-will of the masses by no other means more easily than by self-restraint, and self-denial.

But they who pose as friends of the people, and who for that reason either attempt to have agrarian laws passed, in order that the occupants may be driven out of their homes, or propose that money loaned should be remitted to the borrowers, are undermining the foundations of the commonwealth: first of all, they are destroying harmony, which cannot exist when money is taken away from one party and bestowed upon another; and second, they do away with equity, which is utterly subverted, if the rights of property are not respected. For, as I said above, it is the peculiar function of the state and the city to guarantee to every man the free and undisturbed control of his own particular property. And yet, when it comes to measures so ruinous to public welfare, they do not gain even that popularity which they anticipate. For he who has been robbed of his property is their enemy; he to whom it has been turned over actually pretends that he had no wish to take it; and most of all, when his debts are cancelled, the debtor conceals his joy, for fear that he may be thought to have been insolvent; whereas the victim of the wrong both remembers it and shows his resentment openly. Thus even though they to whom property has been wrongly awarded be more in number than they from whom it has been unjustly taken, they do not for that reason have more influence; for in such matters influence is measured not by numbers but by weight. And how is it fair that a man who never had any property should take possession of lands that had been occupied for many years or even generations, and that he who had them before should lose possession of them? . . .

We must, therefore, take measures that there shall be no indebtedness of a nature to endanger the public safety. It is a menace that can be averted in many ways; but should a serious debt be incurred, we are not to allow the rich to lose their property, while the debtors profit by what is their neighbour's. For there is nothing that upholds a government more powerfully than its credit; and it can have no credit, unless the payment of debts is enforced by law. Never were measures for the repudiation of debts more strenuously agitated than in my consulship. Men of every sort and rank attempted with arms and armies to force the project through. But I opposed them with such energy that this plague was wholly eradicated from the body politic. Indebtedness was never greater; debts were never liquidated more easily or more fully; for the hope of

defrauding the creditor was cut off and payment was enforced by law. But the present victor, though vanquished then, still carried out his old design, when it was no longer of any personal advantage to him. So great was his passion for wrong-doing that the very doing of wrong was a joy to him for its own sake, even when there was no motive for it.

Those, then, whose office it is to look after the interests of the state will refrain from that form of liberality which robs one man to enrich another. Above all, they will use their best endeavours that every one shall be protected in the possession of his own property by the fair administration of the law and the courts, that the poorer classes shall not be oppressed because of their helplessness, and that envy shall not stand in the way of the rich, to prevent them from keeping or recovering possession of what justly belongs to them; they must strive, too, by whatever means they can, in peace or in war, to advance the state in power, in territory, and in revenues.

Such service calls for great men; it was commonly rendered in the days of our ancestors; if men will perform duties such as these, they will win popularity and glory for themselves and at the same time render eminent service to the state.

—WALTER MILLER.

ON GOVERNING A PROVINCE

CICERO

[From *Letters to Quintus*, Book I]

It is generally understood that the successful administration of a province rests upon honesty and justice; but it is not so generally understood that it rests also upon refinement and education. The letter contains an interesting passage showing how the Romans justified their dominion over other peoples.

To his brother Quintus:

Though I have no doubt that many messengers, and even common rumour, with its usual speed, will anticipate this letter, and that you will already have heard from others that a third year has been added to my loss and your labour, yet I thought you ought to receive from me also the news of this tiresome circumstance. For not in one, but in several of my previous letters, in spite of others having given up the idea in despair, I gave you hope of being able at an early date to quit your province, not only that I might as long as possible cheer you with a pleasurable belief, but also because I and the prætors took such pains in the matter, that I felt no misgiving as to the possibility of its being arranged. As it is, since matters have so turned out that neither the prætors by the weight of their influence, nor I by my earnest efforts, have been able to prevail, it is certainly difficult not to be annoyed, yet our minds, practised as they are in conducting and supporting business of the utmost gravity, ought not to be crushed or weakened by vexation. And since men ought to feel most vexed at what has been brought upon them by their own fault, it is I who ought in this matter to be more vexed than you. For it is the result of a fault on my part, against which you had protested both in conversation at the moment of your departure, and in letters since, that your successor was not named last year. In this, while consulting for the interests of our allies, and resisting the shameless conduct of some merchants, and while seeking the increase of our reputation by your virtues, I acted unwisely, especially as I made it possible for that second year to entail a third. And as I confess the mistake to have been mine, it lies with your wisdom and kindness to remedy it, and to see that my imprudence is turned to advantage by your careful performance of your duties. And truly, if you exert yourself in every direction to earn men's good word, not with a view to rival others, but henceforth to surpass yourself, if you rouse your whole mind and your every thought and care to the ambition of gaining a superior reputation in all respects, believe me, one year added to your labour will bring us, nay, our posterity also, a joy of many years' duration. Wherefore I begin by entreating you not to let your soul shrink and be cast down, not to allow yourself to be overpowered by the magnitude of the business as though by a wave; but, on the contrary, to stand upright and keep your footing, or even advance to meet the flood of affairs. For you are not administering a department of the state, in which fortune reigns supreme, but one in which a well-considered policy and an attention to business are the most important things. But if I had seen you receiving the prolongation of a command in a great and dangerous war, I should have trembled in spirit, because I should have known that the dominion of fortune over us had been at the same time prolonged. As it is, however, a department of the state has been entrusted to you in which fortune occupies no part, or, at any rate, an insignificant one, and which appears to me to depend entirely on your virtue and self-control. We have no reason to fear, as far as I know, any designs of our enemies, any actual fighting in the field, any revolts of allies, any default in the tribute or in the supply of corn, any mutiny in the army: things which have very often befallen the wisest of men in such a way, that they have been no more able to get the better of the assault of fortune, than the best of pilots a violent tempest. You have been granted a profound peace, a dead calm: yet if the pilot falls asleep, it may even so overwhelm him, though if he keeps awake it may give him positive pleasure. For your province consists, in the first place, of allies of a race which, of all the world, is the most civilized; and in the second place, of citizens, who, either as being *publicani*, are very closely connected with me, or, as being traders who have made money, think that they owe the security of their property to my consulship.

But it may be said that among even such men as these there occur serious disputes, many wrongful acts are committed, and hotly contested litigation is the result. As though I ever thought that you had no trouble to contend with! I know that the trouble is exceedingly great, and such as demands the very greatest prudence; but remember that it is prudence much more than fortune on which, in my opinion, the result of your trouble depends. For what trouble is it to govern those over whom you are set, if you do but govern yourself? That may be a great and difficult task to others, and indeed it is most difficult: to you it has always been the easiest thing in the world, and indeed ought to be so, for your natural disposition is such that, even without discipline, it appears capable of self-control; whereas a discipline has, in fact, been applied that might educate the most faulty of characters. But while you resist, as you do, money, pleasure, and every kind of desire yourself, there will, I am told, be a risk of your not being able to suppress some fraudulent banker or some rather over-extortionate tax-collector! For as to the Greeks, they will think, as they behold the innocence of your life, that one of the heroes of their history, or a demigod from heaven, has come down into the province. And this I say, not to induce you to act thus, but to make you glad that you are acting or have acted so. It is a splendid thing to have been three years in supreme power in Asia without allowing statue, picture, plate, napery, slave, anyone's good looks, or any offer of money—all of which are plentiful in your province—to cause you

to swerve from the most absolute honesty and purity of life. What can be imagined so striking or so desirable as that a virtue, a command over the passions, a self-control such as yours, are not remaining in darkness and obscurity, but have been set in the broad daylight of Asia, before the eyes of a famous province, and in the hearing of all nations and peoples? That the inhabitants are not being ruined by your progresses, drained by your charges, agitated by your approach? That there is the liveliest joy, public and private, wheresoever you come, the city regarding you as a protector and not a tyrant, the private house as a guest and not a plunderer?

But in these matters I am sure that mere experience has by this time taught you that it is by no means sufficient to have these virtues yourself, but that you must keep your eyes open and vigilant, in order that in the guardianship of your province you may be considered to vouch to the allies, the citizens, and the state, not for yourself alone, but for all the subordinates of your government. However, you have in the persons of your *legati* men likely to have a regard for their own reputation. Of these in rank, position, and age Tubero is first; who, I think, particularly as he is a writer of history, could select from his own Annals many whom he would like and would be able to imitate. Alienus, again, is ours, as well in heart and affection, as in his conformity to our principles. I need not speak of Gratidius: I am sure that, while taking pains to preserve his own reputation, his fraternal affection for us makes him take pains for ours also. Your quæstor is not of your own selection, but the one assigned you by lot. He is bound both to act with propriety of his own accord, and to conform to the policy and principles which you lay down. But should any one of these adopt a lower standard of conduct, you should tolerate such behaviour, if it goes no farther than a breach, in his private capacity, of the rules by which he was bound, but not if it goes to the extent of employing for gain the authority which you granted him as a promotion. For I am far from thinking, especially since the moral sentiments of the day are so much inclined to excessive laxity and self-seeking, that you should investigate every case of petty misconduct, and thoroughly examine every one of these persons; but that you should regulate your confidence by the trustworthiness of its recipient. And among such persons you will have to vouch for those whom the Republic has itself given you as companions and assistants in public affairs, at least within the limits which I have before laid down. . . .

If, however, you have found in the province itself anyone, hitherto unknown to us, who has made his way into intimacy with you, take care how much confidence you repose in him; not that there may not be many good provincials, but, though we may hope so, it is risky to be positive. For everyone's real character is covered by many wrappings of pretence and is concealed by a kind of veil: face, eyes, expression very often lie, speech most often of all. Wherefore, how can you expect to find in that class any who, while foregoing for the sake of money all from which we can scarcely tear ourselves away, will yet love you sincerely and not merely pretend to do so from interested motives? I think, indeed, it is a hard task to find such men, especially if we notice that the same persons care nothing for almost any man out of office, yet always with one consent shew affection for the prætors. But of this class, if by chance you have discovered any one to be fonder of you—for it may so happen—than of your office, such a man indeed gladly admit upon your list of friends: but if you fail to perceive that, there is no class of people

you must be more on your guard against admitting to intimacy, just because they are acquainted with all the ways of making money, do everything for the sake of it, and have no consideration for the reputation of a man with whom they are not destined to pass their lives. And even among the Greeks themselves you must be on your guard against admitting close intimacies, except in the case of the very few, if such are to be found, who are worthy of ancient Greece. As things now stand, indeed, too many of them are untrustworthy, false, and schooled by long servitude in the arts of extravagant adulation. My advice is that these men should all be entertained with courtesy, but that close ties of hospitality or friendship should only be formed with the best of them: excessive intimacies with them are not very trustworthy—for they do not venture to oppose our wishes—and they are not only jealous of our countrymen, but of their own as well. . . .

These and similar instances of your strict administration in your province we shall find difficulty in justifying, unless they are accompanied by the most perfect integrity: wherefore let there be the greatest strictness in your administration of justice, provided only that it is never varied from favour, but is kept up with impartiality. But it is of little avail that justice is administered by yourself with impartiality and care, unless the same is done by those to whom you have entrusted any portion of this duty. And, indeed, in my view there is no very great variety of business in the government of Asia: the entire province mainly depends on the administration of justice. In it we have the whole theory of government, especially of provincial government, clearly displayed: all that a governor has to do is to shew consistency and firmness enough, not only to resist favouritism, but even the suspicion of it. To this also must be added courtesy in listening to pleaders, consideration in pronouncing a decision, and painstaking efforts to convince suitors of its justice, and to answer their arguments. It is by such habits that C. Octavius has recently made himself very popular; in whose court, for the first time, the lictor did not interfere, and the marshal kept silence, while every suitor spoke as often and as long as he chose. In which conduct he would perhaps have been thought over-lax, had it not been that this laxity enabled him to maintain the following instance of severity. The partisans of Sulla were forced to restore what they had taken by violence and terrorism. Those who had made inequitable decrees, while in office, were now as private citizens forced to submit to the principles they had established. This strictness on his part would have been thought harsh, had it not been rendered palatable by many sweetening influences of courtesy. But if this gentleness were sufficient to make him popular at Rome, where there is such haughtiness of spirit, such unrestrained liberty, such unlimited licence of individuals, and, in fine, so many magistrates, so many means of obtaining protection, such vast power in the hands of the popular assembly, and such influence exercised by the senate, how welcome must a prætor's courtesy be in Asia, in which there is such a numerous body of citizens and allies, so many cities, so many communities, all hanging on one man's nod, and in which there are no means of protection, no one to whom to make a complaint, no senate, no popular assembly! Wherefore it requires an exalted character, a man who is not only equitable from natural impulse, but who has also been trained by study and the refinements of a liberal education, so to conduct himself while in the possession of such immense power, that those over whom he rules should not feel the want of any other power.

Take the case of the famous Cyrus, portrayed by Xenophon, not as in historical character, but as a model of righteous government, the serious dignity of whose character is represented by that philosopher as combined with a peculiar courtesy. And, indeed, it is not without reason that our hero Africanus used perpetually to have those books in his hands, for there is no duty pertaining to a careful and equitable government which is not to be found in them. Well, if *he* cultivated those qualities, though never destined to be in a private station, how carefully ought those to maintain them to whom power is given with the understanding that it must be surrendered, and given by laws under whose authority they must once more come? In my opinion all who govern others are bound to regard as the object of all their actions the greatest happiness of the governed. That this is your highest object, and has been so since you first landed in Asia, has been published abroad by consistent rumour and the conversation of all. It is, let me add, not only the duty of one who governs allies and citizens, but even of one who governs slaves and dumb animals, to serve the interests and advantage of those under him. In this point I notice that everyone agrees that you take the greatest pains: no new debt is being contracted by the states, while many have been relieved by you from a heavy and longstanding one. Several cities that had become delapidated and almost deserted —of which one was the most famous state in Ionia, the other in Caria, Samos and Halicarnassus—have been given a new life by you: there is no party fighting, no civil strife in the towns: you take care that the government of the states is administered by the best class of citizens: brigandage is abolished in Mysia; murder suppressed in many districts, peace is established throughout the province; and not only the robberies usual on highways and in country places, but those more numerous and more serious ones in towns and temples, have been completely stopped: the fame, fortunes, and repose of the rich have been relieved of that most oppressive instrument of prætorial rapacity—vexatious prosecution; the expenses and tribute of the states are made to fall with equal weight on all who live in the territories of those states: access to you is as easy as possible: your ears are open to the complaints of all: no man's want of means or want of friends excludes him, I don't say from access to you in public and on the tribunal, but even from your house and chamber: in a word, throughout your government there is no harshness or cruelty —everywhere clemency, mildness, and kindness reign supreme.

What an immense benefit, again, have you done in having liberated Asia from the tribute exacted by the ædiles, a measure which cost me some violent controversies! For if one of our nobles complains openly that by your edict, "No moneys shall be voted for the games," you have robbed him of 200 sestertia, what a vast sum of money would have been paid, had a grant been made to the credit of every magistrate who held games, as had become the regular custom! However, I stopped these complaints by taking up this position— what they think of it in Asia I don't know, in Rome it meets with no little approval and praise—I refused to accept a sum of money which the states had decreed for a temple and monument in our honour, though they had done so with the greatest enthusiasm in view both of my services and of your most valuable benefactions; and though the law contained a special and distinct exception in these words, "that it was lawful to receive for temple or monument;" and though again the money was not going to be thrown away, but would be employed on decorating a temple, and would thus appear to have been given to the Roman people and the immortal Gods rather than to myself—yet, in spite of its having desert,

law, and the wishes of those who offered the gift in its favour, I determined that I must not accept it, for this reason among others, namely, to prevent those, to whom such an honour was neither due nor legal, from being jealous. Wherefore adhere with all your heart and soul to the policy which you have hitherto adopted—that of being devoted to those whom the senate and people of Rome have committed and entrusted to your honour and authority, of doing your best to protect them, and of desiring their greatest happiness. Even if the lot had made you governor of Africans, or Spaniards, or Gauls—uncivilized and barbarous nations—it would still have been your duty as a man of feeling to consult for their interests and advantage, and to have contributed to their safety. But when we rule over a race of men in which civilization not only exists, but from which it is believed to have spread to others, we are bound to repay them, above all things, what we received from them. For I shall not be ashamed to go so far—especially as my life and achievements have been such as to exclude any suspicion of sloth or frivolity—as to confess that, whatever I have accomplished, I have accomplished by means of those studies and principles which have been transmitted to us in Greek literature and schools of thought. Wherefore, over and above the general good faith which is due to all men, I think we are in a special sense under an obligation to that nation, to put in practice what it has taught us among the very men by whose maxims we have been brought out of barbarism.

And indeed Plato, the fountain-head of genius and learning, thought that states would only be happy when scholars and philosophers began being their rulers, or when those who were their rulers had devoted all their attention to learning and philosophy. It was plainly this union of power and philosophy that in his opinion might prove the salvation of states. And this perhaps has at length fallen to the fortune of the whole empire: certainly it has in the present instance to your province, to have a man in supreme power in it, who has from boyhood spent the chief part of his zeal and time in imbibing the principles of philosophy, virtue, and humanity. Wherefore be careful that this third year, which has been added to your labour, may be thought a prolongation of prosperity to Asia. And since Asia was more fortunate in retaining you than I was in my endeavour to bring you back, see that my regret is softened by the exultation of the province. For if you have displayed the very greatest activity in earning honours such as, I think, have never been paid to anyone else, much greater ought your activity to be in preserving these honours. What I for my part think of honours of that kind I have told you in previous letters. I have always regarded them, if given indiscriminately, as of little value, if paid from interested motives, as worthless: if, however, as in this case, they are tributes to solid service on your part, I hold you bound to take much pains in preserving them. Since, then, you are exercising supreme power and official authority in cities, in which you have before your eyes the consecration and apotheosis of your virtues, in all decisions, decrees, and official acts consider what you owe to those warm opinions entertained of you, to those verdicts on your character, to those honours which have been rendered you. And what you owe will be to consult for the interests of all, to remedy men's misfortunes, to provide for their safety, to resolve that you will be both called and believed to be the "father of Asia."

However, to such a resolution and deliberate policy on your part the great obstacle is the *publicani:* for, if we oppose them, we shall alienate from ourselves and from the Republic an order which has done us most excellent service, and which has been brought into sympathy with the Republic by our means; if, on the other hand, we comply with them in every case, we shall allow the complete ruin of those whose interests, to say nothing of their preservation, we are bound to consult. This is the one difficulty, if we look the thing fairly in the face, in your whole government. For disinterested conduct on one's own part, the suppression of all inordinate desires, the keeping a check upon one's staff, courtesy in hearing causes, in listening to and admitting suitors—all this is rather a question of credit than of difficulty: for it does not depend on any special exertion, but rather on a mental resolve and inclination. But how much bitterness of feeling is caused to allies by that question of the *publicani* we have had reason to know in the case of citizens who, when recently urging the removal of the port-dues in Italy, did not complain so much of the dues themselves, as of certain extortionate conduct on the part of the collectors. Wherefore, after hearing the grievances of citizens in Italy, I can comprehend what happens to allies in distant lands. To conduct oneself in this matter in such a way as to satisfy the *publicani,* especially when contracts have been undertaken at a loss, and yet to preserve the allies from ruin, seems to demand a virtue with something divine in it, I mean a virtue like yours. To begin with, that they are subject to tax at all, which is their greatest grievance, ought not to be thought so by the Greeks, because they were so subject by their own laws without the Roman government. Again, they cannot despise the word *publicanus,* for they have been unable to pay the assessment according to Sulla's polltax without the aid of the publican. But that the Greek *publicani* are not more considerate in exacting the payment of taxes than our own may be gathered from the fact that the Caunii, and all the islands assigned to the Rhodians by Sulla, recently appealed to the protection of the senate, and petitioned to be allowed to pay their tax to us rather than to the Rhodians. Wherefore neither ought those to revolt at the name of a *publicanus* who have always been subject to tax, nor those to despise it who have been unable to make up the tribute by themselves, nor those to refuse his services who have asked for them. At the same time let Asia reflect on this, that if she were not under our government, there is no calamity of foreign war or internal strife from which she would be free. And since that government cannot possibly be maintained without taxes, she should be content to purchase perpetual peace and tranquillity at the price of a certain proportion of her products. . . .

But since your first year gave rise to most talk in regard to this particular complaint—I believe because the wrongdoing, the covetousness, and the arrogance of men came upon you as a surprise, and seemed to you unbearable—while your second year was much milder, because habit and reflexion, and, as I think, my letters also, rendered you more tolerant and gentle, the third ought to be so completely reformed, as not to give even the smallest ground for anyone to find fault. And here I go on to urge upon you, not by way of exhortation or admonition, but by brotherly entreaties, that you would set your whole heart, care, and thought on the gaining of praise from everybody and from every quarter. If, indeed, our achievements were only the subject of a moderate amount of talk and commendation, nothing eminent, nothing beyond the practice of others, would have been demanded of you. As it is, however, owing to the brilliancy and magnitude of the affairs in which we have been engaged, if we do not obtain the very highest reputation from your province, it seems scarcely possible for us to avoid the most violent abuse. Our position is such that all loyalists support us, but demand also and expect from us every kind of activity and virtue, while all the disloyal, seeing that we have entered upon a lasting war with them, appear contented with the very smallest excuse for attacking us. Wherefore, since fortune has allotted to you such a theatre as Asia, completely packed with an audience, of immense size, of the most refined judgment, and, moreover, naturally capable of conveying sound, so that its expressions of opinion and its remarks reach Rome, put out all your power, I beseech you, exert all your energies to appear not only to have been worthy of the part we played here, but to have surpassed everything done there by your high qualities. . . .

Farewell.

—E. S. Shuckburgh.

III. DECLINE OF THE REPUBLIC

Among the many causes of the fall of the republican form of government at Rome none was more potent than the effects of Rome's relations with her provinces. Sulla, and ultimately Cæsar, used their provinces as bases from which to launch military attacks on Rome itself. Hundreds of lesser men, governors, and all their train of subordinates, had for years used their almost unlimited powers to enrich themselves at the provincials' expense. Direct extortion, and the more indirect means of loans, sometimes forced on the natives at high interest, proved very profitable, for there was always a Roman army to assist in collection. The noble Brutus had out loans in Cicero's province Cilicia at some 48%. A saying was current that a governor must make three fortunes during his term, one to pay his debts contracted in getting the position, a second to bribe the judges who would try him for maladministration at the end of his term, and a third to live on himself. The honest governor, while not unknown, was the exception.

The effects on Roman character and consequently on the government in Rome may readily be imagined. All classes were affected. An inevitable result was loss of public spirit, the sense of duty to the state which had for ages been Rome's particular pride. Anarchy, suppressed, but breaking out again and again, followed in due course.

It was among such conditions that Julius Cæsar developed his career. He is at once an excellent illustration of the period and a direct cause of its end and the beginning of better things. After his victory in the civil war which he waged against Pompey and the Senate, he made himself supreme in the state, centering political and military powers in his dictatorship. What organization he would have worked out in detail if he had not been murdered can never be known; but it seems clear that he intended to have all important officials responsible to himself, a step which Augustus, his adopted son and ultimate successor, took in the next generation.

Cæsar was killed in March of 44 B.C. The conspirators had hoped by his death to restore the Republic; but had made no adequate plans to make their hope a reality. They had only made it possible for other dictators to rise. Cicero entered public life once more and worked heroically to unify the republican elements; but when Mark Antony with Octavius Cæsar, who had been acting on Cicero's side, and with Lepidus, governor in Gaul, formed a coalition, the second triumvirate, efforts for free government were quickly checked, and Cicero lost his life.

MISMANAGEMENT IN THE PROVINCES

SICILY UNDER VERRES

CICERO

[*Verrine Orations* I]

Verres was governor of Sicily from 73 to 71 B.C.

The political scandal here disclosed was made possible by the inadequacy of the machinery of the central government at Rome. Cicero apparently did not realize that it was symptomatic of the diseased condition of the state.

That which was above all things to be desired, O judges, and which above all things was calculated to have the greatest influence towards allaying the unpopularity of your order, and putting an end to the discredit into which your judicial decisions have fallen, appears to have been thrown in your way, and given to you not by any human contrivance, but almost by the interposition of the gods, at a most important crisis of the republic. For an opinion has now become established, pernicious to us, and pernicious to the republic, which has been the common talk of every one, not only at Rome, but among foreign nations also,—that in the courts of law as they exist at present, no wealthy man, however guilty he may be, can possibly be convicted. Now at this time of peril to your order and to your tribunals, when men are ready to attempt by harangues, and by the proposal of new laws, to increase the existing unpopularity of the senate, Caius Verres is brought to trial as a criminal, a man condemned in the opinion of every one by his life and actions, but acquitted by the enormousness of his wealth according to his own hope and boast. I, O judges, have undertaken this cause as prosecutor with the greatest good wishes and expectation on the part of the Roman people, not in order to increase the unpopularity of the senate, but to relieve it from the discredit which I share with it. For I have brought before you a man, by acting justly in whose case you have an opportunity of retrieving the lost credit of your judicial proceedings, or regaining your credit with the Roman people, and of giving satisfaction to foreign nations; a man, the embezzler of the public funds, the petty tyrant of Asia and Pamphylia, the robber who deprived the city of its rights, the disgrace and ruin of the province of Sicily. And if you come to a decision about this man with severity and a due regard to your oaths, that authority which ought to remain in you will cling to you still; but if that man's vast riches shall break down the sanctity and honesty of the courts of justice, at least I shall achieve this, that it shall be plain that it was rather honest judgment that was wanting to the republic, than a criminal to the judges, or an accuser to the criminal.

I, indeed, that I may confess to you the truth about myself, O judges, though many snares were laid for me by Caius Verres, both by land and sea, which I partly avoided by my own vigilance, and partly warded off by the zeal and kindness of my friends, yet I never seemed to be incurring so much danger, and I never was in such a state of great apprehension, as I am now in this very court of law. Nor does the expectation which people have formed of my conduct of this prosecution, nor this concourse of so vast a multitude as is here assembled, influence me (though indeed I am greatly agitated by these circumstances) so much as his nefarious plots which he is endeavouring to lay at one and the same time against me, against you, against foreign nations, against the senate, and even against the very name of senator; whose favourite saying it is that they have got to fear who have stolen only as much as is enough for themselves, but that he has stolen so much that it may

easily be plenty for many; that nothing is so holy that it cannot be corrupted, or so strongly fortified that it cannot be stormed by money. But if he were as secret in acting as he is audacious in attempting, perhaps in some particular he might some time or other have escaped our notice. But it happens very fortunately that to his incredible audacity there is joined a most unexampled folly. For as he was unconcealed in committing his robberies of money, so in his hope of corrupting the judges he has made his intentions and endeavours visible to every one. He says that once only in his life has he felt fear, at the time when he was first impeached as a criminal by me; because he was only lately arrived from his province, and was branded with unpopularity and infamy, not modern but ancient and of long standing; and, besides that, the time was unlucky, being very ill-suited for corrupting the judges. Therefore, when I had demanded a very short time to prosecute my inquiries in Sicily, he found a man to ask for two days less to make investigations in Achaia; not with any real intention of doing the same with his diligence and industry, that I have accomplished by my labour, and daily and nightly investigations. For the Achæan inquisitor never even arrived at Brundusium. I in fifty days so travelled over the whole of Sicily that I examined into the records and injuries of all the tribes and of all private individuals, so that it was easily visible to every one, that he had been seeking out a man not really for the purpose of bringing the defendant whom he accused to trial, but merely to occupy the time which ought to belong to me.

Now that most audacious and most senseless man thinks this. He is aware that I am come into court so thoroughly prepared and armed, that I shall fix all his thefts and crimes not only in your ears, but in the very eyes of all men. He sees that many senators are witnesses of his audacity; he sees that many Roman knights are so too, and many citizens, and many of the allies besides to whom he has done unmistakeable injuries. He sees also that very numerous and very important deputations have come here at the same time from most friendly cities, armed with the public authority and evidence collected by their states. And though this is the case, still he thinks so ill of all virtuous men, to such an extent does he believe the decisions of the senators to be corrupt and profligate, that he makes a custom of openly boasting that it was not without reason that he was greedy of money, since he now finds that there is such protection in money, and that he has bought (that was the hardest thing of all) the very time of his trial, in order to be able to buy everything else more easily; so that, as he could not by any possibility shirk the force of the accusations altogether, he might avoid the most violent gusts of the storm. But if he had placed any hope at all, not only in his cause, but in any honourable defence, or in the eloquence or in the influence of any one, he would not be so eager in collecting and catching at all these things; he would not scorn and despise the senatorial body to such a degree, as to procure a man to be selected out of the senate at his will to be made a criminal of, who should plead his cause before him, while he in the meantime was preparing whatever he had need of. And what the circumstances are on which he founds his hopes, and what hopes he builds on them, and what he is fixing his mind on, I see clearly. But how he can have the confidence to think that he can effect anything with the present prætor, and the present bench of judges, I cannot conceive. This one thing I know, which the Roman people perceived too when he rejected the judges, that his hopes were of that nature that he placed all his expectations of safety in his money; and that if this protection

were taken from him, he thought nothing would be any help to him.

In truth, what genius is there so powerful, what faculty of speaking, what eloquence so mighty, as to be in any particular able to defend the life of that man, convicted as it is of so many vices and crimes, and long since condemned by the inclinations and private sentiments of every one? And, to say nothing of the stains and disgraces of his youth, what other remarkable event is there in his quæstorship, that first step to honour, except that Cnæus Corbo was robbed by his quæstor of the public money? that the consul was plundered and betrayed? his army deserted? his province abandoned? the holy nature and obligations imposed on him by lot violated?—whose lieutenancy was the ruin of all Asia and Pamphylia, in which provinces he plundered many houses, very many cities, all the shrines and temples; when he renewed and repeated against Cnæus Dolabella his ancient wicked tricks when he had been quæstor, and did not only in his danger desert, but even attack and betray the man to whom he had been lieutenant, and proquæstor, and whom he had brought into odium by his crimes;—whose city prætorship was the destruction of the sacred temples and the public works, and, as to his legal decisions, was the adjudging and awarding of property contrary to all established rules and precedents. But now he has established great and numerous monuments and proofs of all his vices in the province of Sicily, which he for three years so harassed and ruined that it can by no possibility be restored to its former condition, and appears scarcely able to be at all recovered after a long series of years, and a long succession of virtuous prætors. While this man was prætor the Sicilians enjoyed neither their own laws, nor the decrees of our senate, nor the common rights of every nation. Every one in Sicily has only so much left as either escaped the notice or was disregarded by the satiety of that most avaricious and licentious man.

No legal decision for three years was given on any other ground but his will; no property was so secure to any man, even if it had descended to him from his father and grandfather, but he was deprived of it at his command; enormous sums of money were exacted from the property of the cultivators of the soil by a new and nefarious system. The most faithful of the allies were classed in the number of enemies. Roman citizens were tortured and put to death like slaves; the greatest criminals were acquitted in the courts of justice through bribery; the most upright and honourable men, being prosecuted while absent, were condemned and banished without being heard in their own defence; the most fortified harbours, the greatest and strongest cities, were laid open to pirates and robbers; the sailors and soldiers of the Sicilians, our own allies and friends, died of hunger; the best built fleets on the most important stations were lost and destroyed, to the great disgrace of the Roman people. This same man while prætor plundered and stripped those most ancient monuments, some erected by wealthy monarchs and intended by them as ornaments for their cities; some, too, the work of our own generals, which they either gave or restored as conquerors to the different states in Sicily. And he did this not only in the case of public statues and ornaments, but he also plundered all the temples consecrated in the deepest religious feelings of the people. He did not leave, in short, one god to the Sicilians which appeared to him to be made in a tolerably workmanlike manner, and with any of the skill of the ancients. I am prevented by actual shame from speaking of his nefarious licentiousness as shown in rapes and other such enormities; and I am unwilling also to increase the distress of those men who

have been unable to preserve their children and their wives unpolluted by his wanton lust. But, you will say, these things were done by him in such a manner as not to be notorious to all men. I think there is no man who has heard his name who cannot also relate wicked actions of his; so that I ought rather to be afraid of being thought to omit many of his crimes, than to invent any charges against him. And indeed I do not think that this multitude which has collected to listen to me wishes so much to learn of me what the facts of the case are, as to go over it with me, refreshing its recollection of what it already knows.

And as this is the case, that senseless and profligate man attempts to combat me in another manner. He does not seek to oppose the eloquence of any one else to me; he does not rely on the popularity, or influence, or authority of any one. He pretends that he trusts to these things; but I see what he is really aiming at; (and indeed he is not acting with any concealment). He sets before me empty titles of nobility, that is to say the names of arrogant men, who do not hinder me so much by being noble, as assist me by being notorious;—he pretends to rely on their protection; when he has in reality been contriving something else this long time. What hope he now has, and what he is endeavouring to do, I will now briefly explain to you, O judges. But first of all, remark, I beg you, how the matter has been arranged by him from the beginning. When he first returned from the province, he endeavoured to get rid of this prosecution by corrupting the judges at a great expense; and this object he continued to keep in view till the conclusion of the appointment of the judges. After the judges were appointed, because in drawing lots for them the fortune of the Roman people had defeated his hopes, and in the rejecting some my diligence had defeated his impudence, the whole attempt at bribery was abandoned. The affair was going on admirably; lists of your names and of the whole tribunal were in every one's hands. It did not seem possible to mark the votes of these men with any distinguishing mark or colour or spot of dirt; and that fellow, from having been brisk and in high spirits, became on a sudden so downcast and humbled, that he seemed to be condemned not only by the Roman people but even by himself. But lo! all of a sudden, within these few days, since the consular comitia have taken place, he has gone back to his original plan with more money, and the same plots are now laid against your reputation and against the fortunes of every one, by the instrumentality of the same people; which fact at first, O judges, was pointed out to me by a very slight hint and indication; but afterwards, when my suspicions were once aroused, I arrived at the knowledge of all the most secret counsels of that party without any mistake.

For as Hortensius the consul elect was being attended home again from the Campus by a great concourse and multitude of people, Caius Curio fell in with that multitude by chance,—a man whom I wish to name by way of honour rather than of disparagement. I will tell you what, if he had been unwilling to have it mentioned, he would not have spoken of in so large an assembly so openly and undisguisedly; which, however, shall be mentioned by me deliberately and cautiously, that it may be seen that I pay due regard to our friendship and to his dignity. He sees Verres in the crowd by the arch of Fabius; he speaks to the man, and with a loud voice congratulates him on his victory. He does not say a word to Hortensius himself, who had been made consul, or to his friends and relations who were attending on him; but he stops to speak to this man, embraces him, and bids him cast off all anxiety. "I give you notice," said he, "that you

have been acquitted by this day's comitia." And as many most honourable men heard this, it is immediately reported to me; indeed, every one who saw me mentioned it to me the first thing. To some it appeared scandalous, to others ridiculous; ridiculous to those who thought that this case depended on the credibility of the witnesses, on the importance of the charges, and on the power of the judges, and not on the consular comitia; scandalous to those who looked deeper, and who thought that this congratulation had reference to the corruption of the judge. In truth, they argued in this manner—the most honourable men spoke to one another and to me in this manner—that there were now manifestly and undeniably no courts of justice at all. The very criminal who the day before thought that he was already condemned, is acquitted now that his defender has been made consul. What are we to think then? Will it avail nothing that all Sicily, all the Sicilians, that all the merchants who have business in that country, that all public and private documents are now at Rome? Nothing, if the consul elect wills it otherwise. What! will not the judges be influenced by the accusation, by the evidence, by the universal opinion of the Roman people? No. Everything will be governed by the power and authority of one man.

I will speak the truth, O judges. This thing agitated me greatly; for every good man was speaking in this way—"That fellow will be taken out of your hands; but we shall not preserve our judicial authority much longer; for who, when Verres is acquitted, will be able to make any objection to transferring it from us?" It was a grievous thing to every one, and the sudden elation of that profligate man did not weigh with them as much as that fresh congratulation of a very honourable one. I wished to dissemble my own vexation at it; I wished to conceal my own grief of mind under a cheerful countenance, and to bury it in silence. But lo! on the very days when the prætors elected were dividing their duties by lot, and when it fell to the share of Marcus Metellus to hold trials concerning extortion, information is given me that that fellow was receiving such congratulations, that he also sent men home to announce it to his wife. And this too in truth displeased me; and yet I was not quite aware what I had so much to fear from this allotment of the prætor's duties. But I ascertained this one thing from trustworthy men from whom I received all my intelligence; that many chests full of Sicilian money had been sent by some senator to a Roman knight, and that of these about ten chests had been left at that senator's house, with the statement that they were left to be used in the comitia when I expected to be elected ædile, and that men to distribute this money among all the tribes had been summoned to attend him by night. Of whom one, who thought himself under the greatest obligations to me, came to me that same night; reports to me the speech which that fellow had addressed to them; that he had reminded them how liberally he had treated them formerly when he was candidate for the prætorship, and at the last consular and prætorian comitia; and in the second place that he had promised them immediately whatever money they required, if they could procure my rejection from the ædileship. That on this some of them said that they did not dare attempt it; that others answered that they did not think it could be managed; but that one bold friend was found, a man of the same family as himself, Quintus Verres, of the Romilian tribe, of the most perfect school of bribers, the pupil and friend of Verres's father, who promised that, if five hundred thousand sesterces were provided, he would manage it; and that there were some others who said that they would co-operate with him. And

as this was the case, he warned me beforehand with a friendly disposition, to take great care.

I was disquieted about many most important matters at one and the same moment, and with very little time to deliberate. The comitia were at hand; and at them I was to be opposed at immense expenditure of money. This trial was at hand; the Sicilian treasurers menaced that matter also. I was afraid, from apprehension about the comitia, to conduct the matters relating to the trial with freedom; and because of the trial, I was unable to attend with all my heart to my canvass. Threatening the agents of bribery was out of the question, because I saw that they were aware that I was hampered and fettered by this trial. And at this same moment I hear that notice has been given to the Sicilians by Hortensius to come to speak to him at his house; that the Sicilians behaved in that matter with a proper sense of their own liberty, and, when they understood on what account they were sent for, they would not go. In the meantime my comitia began to be held; of which that fellow thought himself the master, as he had been of all the other comitia this year. He began to run about, that influential man, with his son, a youth of engaging and popular manners, among the tribes. The son began to address and call on all the friends of his father, that is to say, all his agents for bribery; and when this was noticed and perceived, the Roman people took care with the most earnest good-will that I should not be deprived of my honour through the money of that man, whose riches had not been able to make me violate my good faith. After that I was released from that great anxiety about my canvass, I began, with a mind much more unoccupied and much more at ease, to think of nothing and to do nothing except what related to this trial. I find, O judges, these plans formed and begun to be put in execution by them, to protract the matter, whatever steps it might be necessary to take in order to do so, so that the cause might be pleaded before Marcus Metellus as prætor. That by doing so they would have these advantages; firstly, that Marcus Metellus was most friendly to them; secondly, that not only would Hortensius be consul, but Quintus Metellus also: and listen while I show you how great a friend he is to them. For he gave him a token of his good-will of such a sort, that he seemed to be giving it as a return for the suffrages of the tribes which he had secured to him. Did you think that I would say nothing of such serious matters as these? and that, at a crisis of such danger to the republic and my own character, I would consult anything rather than my duty and my dignity? The other consul elect sent for the Sicilians; some came, because Lucius Metellus was prætor in Sicily. To them he speaks in this manner; that he is the consul; that one of his brothers has Sicily for his province; that the other is to be judge in all prosecutions for extortion; and that care had been taken in many ways that there should be no possibility of Verres being injured.

I ask you, Metellus, what is corrupting the course of justice, if this is not,—to seek to frighten witnesses, and especially Sicilians, timid and oppressed men, not only by your own private influence, but by their fear of the consul, and by the power of two prætors? What would you do for an innocent man or for a relation, when for the sake of a most guilty man, entirely unconnected with you, you depart from your duty and your dignity, and allow what he is constantly saying to appear true to any one who is not acquainted with you? For they said that Verres said, that you had not been made consul by destiny, as the rest of your family had been, but by his assistance. Two consuls, therefore, and the judge are to be such because of his

will. We shall not only, says he, avoid having a man too scrupulous in investigating, too subservient to the opinion of the people, Marcus Glabrio, but we shall have this advantage also:—Marcus Cæsonius is the judge, the colleague of our accuser, a man of tried and proved experience in the decision of actions. It will never do for us to have such a man as that on the bench, which we are endeavouring to corrupt by some means or other; for before, when he was one of the judges on the tribunal of which Junius was president, he was not only very indignant at that shameful transaction, but he even betrayed and denounced it. After the first of January we shall not have this man for our judge,—we shall not have Quintus Manlius and Quintus Cornificius, two most severe and upright judges, for judges, because they will then be tribunes of the people. Publius Sulpicius, a solemn and upright judge, must enter on his magistracy on the fifth of November. Marcus Crepereius, of that renowned equestrian family and of that incorruptible character; Lucius Cassius, of a family renowned for its severity in all things, and especially as judges; Cnæus Tremellius, a man of the greatest scrupulousness and diligence;—these three men of ancient strictness of principle are all military tribunes elect. After the first of January they will not be able to act as judges. And besides this, we elect by lot a successor in the room of Marcus Metellus, since he is to preside over this trial. And so after the first of January, the prætor, and almost the whole bench of judges being changed, we shall elude the terrible threats of the prosecutor, and the great expectations entertained of this trial, and manage it according to our own will and pleasure. To-day is the fifth of August. You began to assemble at the ninth hour. This day they do not even count. There are ten days between this and the votive games which Cnæus Pompey is going to celebrate. These games will take up fifteen days; then immediately the Roman games will follow. And so, when nearly forty days have intervened, then at length they think that they shall have to answer what has been said by us; and they think that, what with speeches, and what with excuses, they will easily be able to protract the cause till the period of the games of Victory. With these the Plebeian games are connected, after which there will be either no day at all, or very few for pleading in. And so, when the accusation has got stale and cold, the matter will come all fresh before Marcus Metellus as prætor. And if I had distrusted his good faith, I should not have retained him as a judge; but now I have such an opinion of him, that I would rather this matter was brought to a close while he is judge than while he is prætor; and I would rather entrust to him his own tablet while he is on his oath, than the tablets of others when he is restrained by no such obligation.

Now, O judges, I consult you as to what you think I ought to do. For you will, in truth, without speaking, give me that advice which I understand that I must inevitably adopt. If I occupy the time which I legitimately might in speaking, I shall reap the fruit of my labour, industry, and diligence; and by this prosecution I shall make it manifest that no one in the memory of man appears ever to have come before a court of justice better prepared, more vigilant, or with his cause better got up. But while I am getting this credit for my industry, there is great danger lest the criminal may escape. What, then, is there which can be done? I think it is neither obscure nor hidden. I will reserve for another time that fruit of praise which may be derived from a long uninterrupted speech. At present I must support this accusation by documentary evidence, by witnesses, by letters of private individuals and of public bodies, and by various other kinds

of proof. The whole of this contest is between you and me, O Hortensius. I will speak openly. If I thought that you were contending with me in the matter of speaking, and of getting rid of the charges I bring against your client in this cause, I, too, would devote much pains to making an elaborate accusation, and to dilating on my charges. Now, since you have determined to contend against me with artifice, not so much in obedience to the promptings of your own nature, as from consulting his occasions and his cause, it is necessary for me to oppose conduct of that sort with prudence. Your plan is, to begin to answer me after two sets of games have been celebrated; mine is to have the adjournment over before the first games. And the result will be, that that plan of yours will be thought crafty, but this determination of mine necessary.

But as for what I had begun to say,— namely, that the contest is between you and me, this is it,—I, when I had undertaken this cause at the request of the Sicilians, and had thought it a very honourable and glorious thing for me that they were willing to make experiment of my integrity and diligence, who already knew by experience my innocence and emperance: then, when I had undertaken this business, I proposed to myself some greater action by which the Roman people should be able to see my good-will towards the republic. For that seemed to me to be by no means worthy of my industry and efforts, for that man to be brought to trial by me who had been already condemned by the judgment of all men, unless that intolerable influence of yours, and that grasping nature which you have displayed for some years in many trials, was interposed also in the case of that desperate man. But now, since all this dominion and sovereignty of yours over the courts of justice delights you so much, and since there are some men who are neither ashamed of their licentiousness and their infamy, nor weary of it, and who, as if on purpose, seem to wish to encounter hatred and unpopularity from the Roman people, I profess that I have undertaken this,—a great burden perhaps, and one dangerous to myself, but still worthy of my applying myself to it with all the vigour of my age, and all diligence. And since the whole order of the senate is weighed down by the discredit brought on it by the wickedness and audacity of a few, and is overwhelmed by the infamy of the tribunals, I profess myself an enemy to this race of men, an accuser worthy of their hatred, a persevering, a bitter adversary. I arrogate this to myself, I claim this for myself, and I will carry out this enmity in my magistracy, and from that post in which the Roman people has willed that from the next first of January I shall act in concert with it in matters concerning the republic, and concerning wicked men. I promise the Roman people that this shall be the most honourable and the fairest employment of my ædileship. I warn, I forewarn, I give notice beforehand to those men who are wont either to put money down, to undertake for others, to receive money, or to promise money, or to act as agents in bribery, or as go-betweens in corrupting the seat of judgment, and who have promised their influence or their impudence in aid of such a business, in this trial to keep their hands and inclinations from this nefarious wickedness.

Hortensius will then be consul with the chief command and authority, but I shall be ædile—that is, I shall be a little more than a private individual; and yet this business, which I promise that I am going to advocate, is of such a nature, so pleasing and agreeable to the Roman people, that the consul himself will appear in this cause, if that be possible, even less than a private individual in comparison of me. All those things shall not only be mentioned, but even, when certain matters have been explained, shall be fully discussed, which for the last ten years, ever since the office of the judge has been transferred to the senate, has been nefariously and wickedly done in the decision of judicial matters. The Roman people shall know from me why it is that when the equestrian body supplied the judges for nearly fifty years together, not even the slightest suspicion ever arose of bribes having been accepted for the purpose of influencing a decision; why it is, I say, when the judicial authority was transferred to the senatorial body, and the power of the Roman people over every one of us was taken away, Quintus Calidius, when he was condemned, said that a man of prætorian rank could not honestly be condemned at a less price than three hundred thousand sesterces; why it is that when Publius Septimius, a senator, was condemned for extortion, when Quintus Hortensius was prætor, damages were assessed against him, including money which he had received as judge to decide causes which came before him; why it is, that in the case of Caius Herennius, and in that of Caius Popillius, senators, both of whom were convicted of peculation—why it is, that in the case of Marcus Atilius, who was convicted of treason—this was made plain,—that they had all received money for the purpose of influencing their judicial decisions; why it is, that senators have been found who, when Caius Verres, as prætor of the city, gave out the lots, voted against the criminal whom they were condemning without having inquired into his case; why it is, that a senator was found who, when he was judge, took money in one and the same trial both from the defendant to distribute among the judges, and from the accuser to condemn the defendant. But how shall I adequately complain of that stain, that disgrace, that calamity of the whole senatorial order,—that this thing actually happened in the city while the senatorial order furnished the judges, that the votes of men on their oaths were marked by coloured tablets? I pledge myself that I will urge all these things with diligence and with strictness.

And what do you suppose will be my thoughts, if I find in this very trial any violation of the laws committed in any similar manner? especially when I can prove by many witnesses that Caius Verres often said in Sicily, in the hearing of many persons, "that he had a powerful friend, in confidence in whom he was plundering the province; and that he was not seeking money for himself alone, but that he had so distributed the three years of his Sicilian prætorship, that he should say he did exceedingly well, if he appropriated the gains of one year to the augmentation of his own property, those of the second year to his patrons and defenders, and reserved the whole of the third year, the most productive and gainful of all, for the judges." From which it came into my mind to say that which, when I had said lately before Marcus Glabrio at the time of striking the list of judges, I perceived the Roman people greatly moved by; that I thought that foreign nations would send ambassadors to the Roman people to procure the abrogation of the law, and of all trials, about extortion; for if there were no trials, they think that each man would only plunder them of as much as he would think sufficient for himself and his children; but now, because there are trials of that sort, every one carries off as much as it will take to satisfy himself, his patrons, his advocates, the prætor, and the judges; and that this is an enormous sum; that they may be able to satisfy the cupidity of one most avaricious man, but are quite unable to incur the expense of his most guilty victory over the laws. O trials worthy of being recorded! O splendid reputation of our order! when the allies of the Roman people are unwilling that trials for extortion should take place, which were instituted by our ancestors for the sake of the allies. Would that man ever have had a favourable hope of his own safety, if he had not conceived in his mind a bad opinion of you? on which account, he ought, if possible, to be still more hated by you than he is by the Roman people, because he considers you like himself in avarice and wickedness and perjury.

And I beg you, in the name of the immortal gods, O judges, think of and guard against this! I warn you, I give notice to you, of what I am well assured, that this most seasonable opportunity has been given to you by the favour of the gods, for the purpose of delivering your whole order from hatred, from unpopularity, from infamy, and from disgrace. There is no severity believed to exist in the tribunals, nor any scruples with regard to religion; in short, there are not believed to be any tribunals at all. Therefore we are despised and scorned by the Roman people; we are branded with a heavy and now a long standing infamy. Nor, in fact, is there any other reason for which the Roman people has with so much earnestness sought the restoration of the tribunician power: but when it was demanding that in words, it seemed to be asking for that, but in reality it was asking for tribunals which it could trust. And this did not escape the notice of Quintus Catulus, a most sagacious and honourable man, who, when Cnæus Pompeius, a most gallant and illustrious man, made a motion about the tribunician power, and when he was asked his opinion, began his speech in this manner, speaking with the greatest authority, "that the conscript fathers presided over the courts of justice badly and wickedly; but if in deciding judicial trials they had been willing to satisfy the expectations of the Roman people, men would not so greatly regret the tribunician power."

Lastly, when Cnæus Pompeius himself, when first he delivered an address to the people as consul elect, mentioned (what seemed above all things to be watched for) that he would restore the power of the tribunes, a great shout was raised at his words, and a grateful murmur pervaded the assembly. And when he had said also in the same assembly "that the provinces were depopulated and tyrannised over, that the courts of justice were become base and wicked, and that he desired to provide for and to remedy that evil," the Roman people then signified their good will, not with a shout, but with a universal uproar.

But now men are on the watch towers; they observe how every one of you behaves himself in respecting religion and in preserving the laws. They see that, ever since the passing of the law for restoring the power of the tribunes, only one senator, and he too a very insignificant one, has been condemned. And though they do not blame this, yet they have nothing which they can very much commend. For there is no credit in being upright in a case where there is no one who is either able or who endeavours to corrupt one. This is a trial in which you will be deciding about the defendant, the Roman people about you;—by the example of what happens to this man it will be determined whether, when senators are the judges, a very guilty and a very rich man can be condemned. Moreover, he is a criminal of such sort, that there is absolutely nothing whatever in him except the greatest crimes, and excessive riches; so that if he be acquitted, no other opinion can be formed of the matter except that which is the most discreditable possible. Such numerous and enormous vices as his will not be considered to have been cancelled by influence, by family connexion, by some things which may have been done well, or even by the minor vices of flattery and subserviency; in short, I will conduct the cause in this manner, I will bring forward things of such a sort, so well known, so proved by evidence, so important, and so undeniable, that no one shall venture to use his influence to obtain from you the acquittal of that man; for I have a sure path and method by which I can investigate and become acquainted with all their endeavours. The matter will be so managed by me that not only the ears but even the eyes of the Roman people shall seem to be present at all their counsels. You have in your power to remove and to eradicate the disgrace and infamy which has now for many years attached to your order. It is evident to all men, that since these tribunals have been established which we now have, there has never been a bench of judges of the same splendour and dignity as this. If anything is done wrongly in this case, all men will think not that other more capable judges should be appointed of the same order of men, which is not possible; but that another order must be sought for, from which to select the judges for the future.

On which account, in the first place, I beg this of the immortal gods, which I seem to myself to have hopes of too, that in this trial no one may be found to be wicked except him who has long since been found to be such; secondly, if there are many wicked men, I promise this to you, O judges, I promise this to the Roman people, that my life shall fail rather than my vigour and perseverance in prosecuting their iniquity. But that iniquity, if it should be committed, I promise to prosecute severely, with however much trouble and danger to myself, and whatever enmities I may bring on myself by so doing, you, O Marcus Glabrio, can guard against ever taking place by your wisdom, and authority, and diligence. Do you undertake the cause of the tribunals. Do you undertake the cause of impartiality, of integrity, of good faith and of religion. Do you undertake the cause of the senate; that, being proved worthy by its conduct in this trial, it may come into favour and popularity with the Roman people. Think who you are, and in what a situation you are placed; what you ought to give to the Roman people, what you ought to repay to your ancestors. Let the recollection of the Acilian law passed by your father occur to your mind, owing to which law the Roman people has had this advantage of most admirable decisions and very strict judges in cases of extortion. High authorities surround you which will not suffer you to forget your family credit; which will remind you day and night that your father was a most brave man, your grandfather a most wise one, and your father-in-law a most worthy man. Wherefore, if you have inherited the vigour and energy of your father Glabrio in resisting audacious men; if you have inherited the prudence of your grandfather Scævola in foreseeing intrigues which are prepared against your fame and that of your fellow-judges; if you have any share of the constancy of your father-in-law Scaurus, so that no one can move you from your genuine and deliberate opinion, the Roman people will understand that with an upright and honourable prætor, and a carefully selected bench of judges, abundance of wealth has more influence in bringing a criminal into suspicion, than in contributing to his safety.

I am resolved not to permit the prætor or the judges to be changed in this cause. I will not permit the matter to be delayed till the lictors of the consul can go and summon the Sicilians, whom the servants of the consuls elect did not influence before, when by an unprecedented course of proceeding they sent for them all; I will not permit those miserable men, formerly the allies and friends of the Roman people, now their slaves and suppliants, to lose not only their rights and fortunes by their tyranny, but to be deprived of even the power of bewailing their condition; I will not, I say, when the cause has been summed up by me, permit them after a delay of forty days has intervened, then at last to reply to me when my accusation has already fallen into oblivion through lapse of time; I will not permit the decision to be given when this crowd collected from all Italy has departed from Rome, which has assembled from all quarters at the same time on account of the comitia, of the games, and of the census. The reward of the credit gained by your decision, or the danger arising from the unpopularity which will accrue to you if you decide unjustly, I think ought to belong to you; the labour and anxiety to me; the knowledge of what is done and the recollection of what has been said by every one, to all. I will adopt this course, not an unprecedented one, but one that has been adopted before, by those who are now the chief men of our state,—the course, I mean, of at once producing the witnesses. What you will find novel, O judges, is this, that I will so marshal my witnesses as to unfold the whole of my accusation; that when I have established it by examining my witnesses, by arguments, and by my speech, then I shall show the agreement of the evidence with my accusation; so that there shall be no difference between the established mode of prosecuting, and this new one, except that, according to the established mode, when everything has been said which is to be said, then the witnesses are produced; here they shall be produced as each count is brought forward; so that the other side shall have the same opportunity of examining them, of arguing and making speeches on their evidence. If there be any one who prefers an uninterrupted speech and the old mode of conducting a prosecution without any break, he shall have it in some other trial. But for this time let him understand that what we do is done by us on compulsion, (for we only do it with the design of opposing the artifice of the opposite party by our prudence). This will be the first part of the prosecution. We say that Caius Verres has not only done many licentious acts, many cruel ones, towards Roman citizens, and towards some of the allies, many wicked acts against both gods and men; but especially that he has taken away four hundred thousand sesterces out of Sicily contrary to the laws. We will make this so plain to you by witnesses, by private documents, and by public records, that you shall decide that, even if we had abundant space and leisure days for making a long speech without any inconvenience, still there was no need at all of a long speech in this matter.

—C. D. YONGE.

ANARCHY AT HOME

THE CONSPIRACY OF CATILINE

SALLUST

Sallust's estimate of the conspiracy, which took place in the year 63 B.C., is that it was an attempt at a complete overthrow of the government. Although he may exaggerate its importance, as Cicero clearly does in his celebrated speeches against Catiline, he is right in interpreting it as one of a number of unmistakable evidences of the increasing inadequacy of the governmental machine. For Sallust, see above p. 82.

To maintain the dignity of human nature is the true ambition of man; and to that end it becomes the duty of all, who aspire to distinguish themselves from the race of inferior animals, to exert their most strenuous efforts, lest they pass their days in silence, like the herds of the field, formed by nature prone to the earth, and governed altogether by the incitements of appetite. Man is composed of mind and body, and in the exercise of both consists the energy of his nature. The mind is the directing principle; the body is subservient. The former we participate with the gods; the latter we hold in common with the brute creation. Hence the fame acquired by our intellectual powers has ever appeared to me the truest glory, far superior to all that can be achieved by mere corporeal vigour; and since the life which we enjoy is frail and transitory, it should be the endeavour of every man to extend his fame, and leave a lasting memorial of his existence. For what are all the advantages of wealth, and all the graces of form and feature? mere precarious gifts, that soon fade and moulder away. It is virtue, and virtue only, that ennobles the human character, and lives in the memory of aftertimes.

But a just estimate of our mental and bodily faculties was not easily made. Which of them was most conducive to the success of military operations, was in former times a question much agitated, and long undecided. It is evident, however, that before the undertaking of a warlike enterprise, judgment is required to concert and plan the necessary measures; vigour in the execution is equally necessary. The powers of man, in their separate functions feeble and ineffectual, demand each other's aid, and flourish by mutual assistance.

And yet we see that in the commencement of royalty (for by that title the first rulers of the world were dignified) the several kings proceeded by different exertions; some choosing to cultivate their mental faculties, while others relied on bodily vigour. But in that period men led a blameless life; each individual enjoyed his own, and with that was satisfied. In process of time, when Cyrus in Asia, and the Spartans and Athenians in Greece, began to extend their conquests over cities and nations; when the lust of dominion was a sufficient motive for the desolation of war, and the acquisition of territory swelled the conqueror's pride; then at length the dangers of the field and the intricacy of negotiations made it evident that the head, and not the sword, is the great engine of war. Were the same attention paid to the affairs of civil government; if kings and leaders of armies were as willing to display their genius in the calm seasons of peace, the rights of men would rest on a surer foundation, and the world would no longer be a scene of war and wild commotion. Dominion obtained by the powers of genius, may be supported by the same arts. But when, in the place of industry, moderation, and justice, sloth, ambition, and inordinate desires succeed, the manners of a whole people change with their condition; and the government is transferred from the hands of incapacity, to the man of superior genius.

The labours of man, whether he choose to cultivate the land, to explore the ocean, or to raise the lofty dome, agriculture, navigation, architecture, and all the arts of life, owe their success to the faculties of the mind; and yet we see in the mass of life numbers addicted to sloth and the gratifications of appetite; men uneducated and uninformed, who have passed their time like incurious travellers, of whom it may be said, the organs of bodily sensation were their delight, and their minds were no better than a burden. The life and death of all that description, I rank in the same degree; they pass away, and leave no trace behind them. He only, according to my way of thinking, can be said to live, and to answer the ends of his being, who devotes his time to some worthy employment, and either distinguishes himself by honourable deeds, or seeks the fame of excellence in some liberal art.

But the business of human life presents a variety of employments; and nature, by a secret bias, invites the industry of man to different scenes of action. To serve the commonwealth by patriot toil and vigour, is the highest glory; eloquence in the same cause deserves its rank of praise. A name may become great and eminent in peace, as well as war. The men who have performed, and the historians who have recorded generous actions, have been ever held in esteem. It is true, the fame of him who writes can never equal that of him who acts; but still to compose the history of great transactions, has ever appeared to me an arduous undertaking: first, because the style must be proportioned to the subject; and, again, because the reflections of the historian are in danger of being misconstrued. If he censures what is wrong, his objections are supposed to spring from envy and malevolence: if he describes a great and splendid virtue, and sets forth the glory of honourable deeds, every man in that case makes himself the standard by which he judges; what he fancies within the reach of his own powers, he is willing to believe, and all beyond that compass he rejects as fiction.

As to myself, I must acknowledge, that in my younger days, I felt, like many others, a strong desire to enter on the career of civil employment, but many obstacles occurred to retard me in my progress. Instead of modesty, self-denial, and virtue, I saw boldness, corruption, and rapacity, around me. A mind, like mine, as yet unpractised in wrong, was disgusted of course by this general depravity; but still entangled in the vices of the times, and young and ambitious, I was hurried away by the torrent; and, though my heart condemned the morals of those around me, I felt all the same aspiring impatience; and the love of fame, with its sure attendant envy, haunted and disturbed me. At length, however, when, after various conflicts, I escaped from all the dangers of my situation, and my spirits were restored to peace and tranquillity, I resolved to pass the rest of my life at a distance from the stage of public business: but, in that retreat, it was by no means my intention to let the hours of leisure run to waste in listless indolence. I was not willing to pass my days in agriculture, hunting, or such degrading pursuits. On the contrary, recurring to those early studies, from which vain ambition had seduced me, I formed a resolution to compose a narrative of Roman affairs, selecting for that purpose such events as seemed worthy of the notice of posterity; a task, in which I was the more willing to engage, as I could then bring to the work a mind uninfluenced by hope or fear, and perfectly free from party connexions. I shall therefore, with the strictest regard to truth, and with all possible brevity, relate the conspiracy of Catiline; this event appearing to me to rank among the most memorable and interesting, whether we consider its singular atrocity or the novelty of the dangers which it menaced. Before, however, I enter upon my narrative, it will be proper to give some account of the manners and character of the man.

Lucius Catiline was the descendant of an illustrious family. The extraordinary vigour of his body was equalled by that of his mind; but his genius was fatally bent on mischief. Intestine discord, murder and massacre, plunder and civil wars, were the delight of his youth; and in those scenes of commotion he exercised his earliest talents. His frame of body was such that he could endure hunger, cold, and watching, with a patience altogether incredible. His spirit was bold and daring; his genius subtle and various. Perfect in the arts of simulation and dissimulation; greedy after the property of others, and prodigal of his own, whatever he desired, he desired with ardour. Possessed of sufficient eloquence, his portion of wisdom was but small. Fond of the vast, the immoderate, the incredible, his spirit aimed at projects far beyond his powers.

Such being the temper of the man, it is no wonder, that, having before his eyes the late example of Sulla's usurpation, he formed a design to make himself master of the commonwealth. The measures by which he pursued the object gave him no solicitude: to be the tyrant of his country by any means, was his ardent passion. His mind, naturally fierce and impetuous, was rendered still more so by the ruin of his fortunes, and the goading reproaches of a guilty conscience; evils, which the crimes of every day augmented. The general depravity of the times was a further incentive: he saw the people corrupt and profligate, hurried on in a wild career of luxury and avarice, vices which differ in their nature, but agree in the misery of their consequences.

And here, since I have had occasion to mention the manners of the age, if I go back for a moment to review the practice of our ancestors, the digression, I trust, will not be deemed improper: it will serve to shew the spirit of the Roman government in war and peace; the system of civil and military institutions; the arts by which our ancestors founded the commonwealth, and carried it to the highest grandeur. We shall at the same time see by what fatal steps the government declined, till it fell from the noblest height to its present depth of degeneracy, and from the best and most flourishing state has now become the most weak and flagitious.

The city of Rome, as we collect from history, was founded and governed by the Trojans, who under the conduct of Æneas saved themselves from the destruction of their country, and wandered for some time from place to place in quest of a settled habitation. They were soon joined by the Aborigines, or natives of Italy; a race of men, who ran wild in the woods, and lived without any form of government, unchecked by laws, free and independent. The two nations agreed to coalesce: united within the same walls, it is wonderful how soon they became one undistinguished people, notwithstanding the diversity of their origin, their language, and their manners. The new state went on increasing in population, extending its territory, and forming wholesome regulations, insomuch that it began to assume the appearance of an opulent and flourishing colony. From that time, according to the usual course of human affairs, their growing affluence provoked the jealousy of their neighbours. Contentions ensued, and wars with different princes. The new settlers obtained little or no assistance from their allies, while the rest, struck with terror, kept aloof from the perils of war. The Romans, in the meantime, neglected nothing; intent on their internal policy, and conducting the war with vigour, they planned their military operations with judgment; they executed with dispatch, they animated one another; they gave battle to the enemy, and by their courage were able to protect their liberty, their country, and their fellow-citizens. Having at length surmounted all their difficulties, and by their valour delivered themselves from the calamities of war, they resolved to succour their allies; and thus, by conferring benefits, not by receiving them, they enlarged the circle of their friends.

They established a regular form of government, with the title of king. A select number of the wisest citizens, men indeed impaired by years, but still retaining the vigour of their mind, formed the great council of the state. They were distinguished by the title of fathers; a name derived from their advanced age; or, perhaps, from their paternal care of the commonwealth. In process of time, when the royal dignity, which was at first intended to protect the liberty of the subject, and promote the interests of the commonwealth, began to degenerate into pride and despotism, the constitution underwent a change, and two magistrates were appointed to supply the office of king for the term of a year only. The policy of the measure was, that a mere annual authority would not be sufficient to inflame the minds of men with pride and insolence. This was a period when every man stood forward in the service of his country, and when all who professed talents, discovered and exerted them. In despotic governments the able and the worthy are objects of more suspicion than the wicked and insignificant; nothing is so formidable to a tyrant as virtue.

Now civil liberty being established at Rome, the rapid progress with which the state enlarged its territory is almost incredible. The love of glory pervaded every breast. Young men, as soon as they were of age to carry arms, betook themselves to toil and labour in the camp, and in that school acquired the military art. To have burnished arms, and well-trained horses, was their pride; loose women and convivial riots had no attraction. To soldiers so formed and exercised, no labour was fatiguing; no place was rugged or difficult; the face of the enemy struck no terror: their virtue towered above all obstructions. The struggle among themselves was for glory. To assault the foe, scale the walls, and to be seen while they performed such deeds, was their ambition. In that consisted their riches; that was their highest glory; that was their true nobility. Covetous of praise and lavish of money, they panted for glory, and were indifferent about riches; a competence obtained with honour satisfied their wishes. I could here enumerate their military exploits; could mention places where they had defeated powerful armies with a very inferior force, and taken cities by assault which Nature herself had fortified; but this recital would lead me too far from my original design.

It may, however, be observed, that in the course of human affairs much is owing to chance and the circumstances of the time. Hence it happens, that the actions of men are often obscured or aggrandized, as caprice inspires, not as truth should dictate. For example, the transactions of the Athenians were, it must be acknowledged, great and noble; but surely they fall short of the splendour with which they are represented. The fact is, Athens produced a race of eloquent writers, whose genius gave such a lustre to what they related that the fame of their countrymen surpasses all the rest of the world; and the virtue of the men who figured in those times, is now seen in all the colours of eloquence, carried by the writers as high as imagination could aspire. The Romans had not those advantages: their ablest men were employed in action. They exercised the body as well as the mind. To act rather than speak, was the ambition of eminent men, and they performed what others might praise, instead of praising what others had performed.

But even that rude, unenlightened age produced a system of the best and wisest institutions. Sound morals were established in the city and the army. A spirit of union prevailed; not a symptom of avarice was seen; virtue and justice were secured as much by good inclination as by the laws. Their strife, their quarrels, and their differences were all confined to the enemy; with their fellow-citizens they knew no disunion; to distinguish themselves by superior virtue, was the only struggle. Magnificent in their temples, they were economists in their homes; and their fidelity in friendship was pure and exemplary. Their maxims for their own good and the welfare of the public were few and simple, namely, courage in war, and justice in peace. As a proof of what has been advanced, it may be observed, that in the most active campaign they had more frequent occasion to punish the soldiers who attacked the enemy without orders, or continued the battle after the signal for retreat, than the men who deserted their colours or fled from their post. In time of peace, their rule was to

secure obedience by rewards rather than by punishment; and when they received an injury, they chose rather to forgive, than to revenge.

By this wise system the republic rose to the highest pitch of grandeur; great and opulent states were reduced to subjection; powerful kings were conquered; Carthage, that formidable rival, was laid in ruins; and Rome remained mistress by land and sea. It was then that fortune began to change the scene, and throw everything into confusion. The people who had before that time endured hardship and labour, peril and adversity, began to relax; and to them repose and riches, the great objects of other nations, became a burden that broke their spirit, and extinguished their virtue. A love of money, and lust for power, took possession of every mind. These hateful passions were the source of innumerable evils. Good faith, integrity, and every virtuous principle, gave way to avarice; and in the room of moral honesty, pride, cruelty, and contempt of the gods succeeded. Corruption and venality were introduced; and everything had its price. Such were the effects of avarice. Ambition was followed by an equal train of evils; it taught men to be false and deceitful; to think one thing, and to say another; to make friendship or enmity a mere traffic for private advantage, and to set the features to a semblance of virtue, while malignity lay lurking in the heart. But at first these vices sapped their way by slow degrees, and were often checked in their progress; but spreading at length like an epidemic contagion, morals and the liberal arts went to ruin; and the government, which was before a model of justice, became the most profligate and oppressive.

In this decline of all public virtue, ambition, and not avarice, was the passion that first possessed the minds of men; and this was natural. Ambition is a vice that borders on the confines of virtue; it implies a love of glory, of power, and pre-eminence; and those are objects that glitter alike in the eyes of the man of honour, and the most unprincipled: but the former pursues them by fair and honourable means, while the latter, who finds within himself no resources of talent, depends altogether upon intrigue and fallacy for his success. Avarice, on the other hand, aims at an accumulation of riches; a passion unknown to liberal minds. It may be called a compound of poisonous ingredients; it has power to enervate the body, and debauch the best understanding; always unbounded; never satisfied; in plenty and in want equally craving and rapacious.

At length, when Lucius Sulla had by force of arms restored the commonwealth (though unfortunately the issue of his enterprise did not produce the consequences which his first intentions seemed to promise); in the commotions that followed, his soldiers, flushed with conquest, thought of nothing but plunder and depredation. One aspired to have a splendid mansion; another, to possess a landed estate: none were restrained within the bounds of moderation; all gave a loose rein to their fury, and committed the most violent outrages on their fellow-citizens. There was still another source of corruption: Sulla, in order to allure to his interest the minds of the army which he commanded in Asia, renounced the military system of our forefathers, and allowed his soldiers to riot in luxury; the consequence of which was, that the softness of those delightful regions, and a life of indolence, made the men forget the discipline of their ancestors, and relaxed their native vigour. It was in Asia that the Roman soldiers first began to yield to the seductions of wine and women; to admire statues, pictures, and sculpture; to seize them for their own use in private houses and public buildings; to pillage the temples, and to lay violent hands on everything sacred and profane

without distinction. When soldiers, thus inured to licentiousness, were flushed with victory, it cannot be matter of wonder that they left nothing to the vanquished. A series of prosperity is often too much even for the wisest and best disposed: that men corrupted should make a temperate use of their victory could not be expected. Riches became the epidemic passion; and where honours, imperial sway, and power, followed in their train, virtue lost her influence, poverty was deemed the meanest disgrace, and innocence was thought to be better than a mark for malignity of heart. In this manner riches engendered luxury, avarice, and pride; and by those vices the Roman youth were enslaved. Rapacity and confusion went on increasing; regardless of their own property, and eager to seize that of their neighbours, all rushed forward without shame or remorse, confounding everything sacred and profane, and scorning the restraint of moderation and justice.

In order to form a just idea of ancient frugality and modern luxury, let us first consider the magnificence of our buildings, our superb mansions and villas, in extent and grandeur resembling large cities: it will then be matter of curiosity to compare the temples raised by our ancestors in honour of the gods; the simplicity that appears in those venerable structures, plainly shews that our forefathers, a religious race of men, considered piety as the ornament best befitting places of worship, in the same manner as true glory was, in their estimation, the proper decoration of their houses. To those principles we must ascribe their conduct on the day of victory: they took nothing from the vanquished but the power of renewing hostilities. Is that the practice of the present times? Our victorious armies, with an abject spirit unworthy of soldiers, and with a ferocity that shocks humanity, plunder their allies, and rapaciously seize what the commanders of former times left even to their enemies. We seem to think, that to commit acts of oppression is the true use of power.

Need I mention, what to all but eye-witnesses would seem incredible? whole mountains levelled to the valley by the expense and labour of individuals, and even the seas covered with magnificent structures! To such men riches seem to be a burden: what they might enjoy with credit and advantage to themselves, they seem in eager haste to squander away in idle ostentation.

To these vices, that conspired against the commonwealth, many others may be added, such as prostitution, convivial debauchery, and all kinds of licentious pleasure. The men unsexed themselves, and the women made their persons venal. For the pleasures of the table, sea and land were ransacked; the regular returns of thirst and hunger were anticipated; the hour of sleep was left to caprice and accident; cold was a sensation not to be endured by delicate habits; luxury was the business of life, and by that everything was governed. In this scene of general depravity, the extravagance of youth exhausted whatever was left of their patrimonial stock, and their necessities urged them on to the perpetration of the most flagitious deeds. The mind, habituated to every vice, could not divest itself of passions that had taken root, and, by consequence, all were hurried down the stream of dissipation, eager to grasp whatever could administer to inordinate and wild desires.

In so vast, so populous, and so corrupt a city, which swarmed with hordes of the vile and profligate, Catiline had at his beck a band of desperate men, who served as body-guard near his person. Whoever was thoroughly debauched, and rendered infamous by a long course of adultery; whoever by his gluttony, by gaming, by his headlong passion, his lawless pleasures, and festival carousals, had ruined his for-

tune; whoever was overwhelmed with debts, contracted to pay the forfeit of his crimes; the whole gang of parricides, sacrilegious wretches, convicts, or men who lived in fear of conviction, together with the perjurer and assassin, who were nourished with the blood of their fellow-citizens; and, in short, all who felt themselves distracted by their flagitious deeds, their poverty, or the horrors of conscience; all of this description lived with Catiline in friendship and the closest familiarity. If it happened that a person of unblemished character was drawn into the vortex of Catiline and his crew, by the force of daily intercourse, and the baits thrown out to ensnare him, he soon became one of the same stamp, in nothing inferior to the rest.

To allure the youth of Rome to his party, was Catiline's main design: in the early season of life the tender mind, he well knew, was susceptible of the first impression, and consequently easily moulded to his purposes. He watched the temper of his proselytes, and studied their predominant passions. He found concubines for some, and for others horses and dogs. He spared neither his purse nor his honour, in order by any means to increase the number of his followers. . . .

The conspirators, who have been already mentioned, being assembled in convention, Catiline, though he had tampered with them separately, thought it expedient to address them in a body, in order to inflame the minds of all with new ardour, and a spirit of union. For this purpose, he withdrew with the whole party to the most retired part of the house; and, after due precaution to exclude spies and informers, he delivered the following harangue:

"If I had not abundant reason to rely with confidence on your fidelity and undaunted valour, the opportunity that now presents itself would answer no useful end, and the prospect which we have of making a radical reform of the state, would be vain and fruitless. For myself, if I thought I had now to do with weak and abject spirits, I should remain inactive, unwilling to exchange a safe and sure condition for the precarious prospect of future events. But I know you all; I know your firmness, your unshaken constancy in the worst of times. Encouraged by your fidelity and courage, I have planned a great, a glorious enterprise. Our hopes and fears are the same; our interests are interwoven with each other; the same good or evil awaits us all. We stand or fall together. Our desires and diversions are the same; we have but one will, that is our bond of union; to think alike of the commonwealth is the true source of lasting friendship.

"The cause in which we are embarked has been explained to you all in separate conferences. I burn with impatience to strike the finishing blow. The ardour that expands my bosom, is kindled by your presence to a brighter flame; but let me ask you, what must be our condition, if we have not the spirit to redress our grievances, and vindicate the rights of men? What I desire to know is the true state of the commonwealth. A few imperious demagogues have seized all power into their own hands; to those usurpers, kings, princes, and tetrarchs, crouch in subjection; they are tributary to our masters; foreign nations pay taxes to them; and as to us, wretched citizens! in what light have we been considered? The good, the virtuous, the noble, and ignoble, are all blended in one undistinguished mass; a mere vulgar herd, without interest, without place or preferment; obliged, like slaves, to bend to those, who, if a thorough reform took place, and restored the government to its true principles, would shrink and tremble before the majesty of the people. At present, everything is engrossed by a proud and insolent oligarchy; power, riches, honours, are in the hands of the few, or scantily dealt out among their creatures,

at their will and pleasure. To us they have left nothing but disgrace, contempt, and danger, the terror of prosecutions, and the pangs of griping poverty. How long, ye brave and gallant men! how long will you endure these vile indignities? Let us rouse at once; or if we must fall, let us fall nobly in one brave attempt, rather than crawl on to our graves, dragging a miserable existence under the scourge of insolent nobles, to die at last the victims of a lawless usurpation.

"But the juncture is favourable: success, I call men and gods to witness! success and victory are in our hands. We are in the vigour of life; our minds are strong and active; while, on the other hand, our enemies, enervated by sloth and luxury, droop under their infirmities, and languish in decay. To begin the attack is to conquer; events will direct and guide our future operations.

"Is there a man, who feels the energy of his nature, who in these times can look tamely on, and see the senators and the patrician order riot in such heaps of wealth, that they are able with wild profusion to cover the seas with magnificent buildings, and annihilate mountains, while we are left to pine in want and misery of heart? Shall the nobles build their splendid porticos for the purpose of making a communication between two or more palaces; and shall we in the meantime want a cottage for the reception of our household gods? Behold your tyrants at an immense expense purchasing pictures, statues, vases curiously wrought in gold and silver; see them with sudden caprice pulling down their new-built mansions, erecting others more magnificent, and in short, dissipating their riches with lavish extravagance, and yet, with all their folly, still unable to drain their coffers. And what is our case? We have beggary at home, a load of debts abroad; desolation before our eyes, and not the smallest hope of relief to assuage our misery. In a word, the breath we draw is all that is left us.

"And shall we not in these circumstances rise as one man? Behold, my friends, behold that liberty for which you long have panted; behold riches, honours, and immortal glory, all within your reach: they glitter before your eyes; they call forth to action. These are the bright rewards which fortune has in store for valour. The situation of affairs, the time, the favourable juncture, the dangers that surround you, the hard hand of poverty that weighs you down, and the splendid spoils of war, that promise joy and affluence; all these are now before you; they are strong incentives, more powerful than all the arguments I can urge. Make your own use of me; I am your general, if you will; or if you choose it, your fellow-soldier. My heart is with you; my powers of body and mind are devoted to your service. As matters stand at present, I am not without hopes of obtaining the consulship, and in that high office I propose, in conjunction with you, to concert our future measures. When I say this, I rely on your generous ardour, persuaded that you are not so abject as to pine in slavery, when you have it in your power to be the legislators of your country."

This speech was addressed to the passions of men who groaned under every kind of distress, without any means of support, and without a gleam of hope to comfort them. To such minds a convulsion in the state was an inviting prospect, the bright reward of all their labours. The majority, however, desired to be informed upon what terms they were to embark in so bold an enterprise; what was to be the recompense of their fidelity; what were their resources, and where they were to look for friends to support their cause? Catiline promised to cancel all their debts, a proscription of the rich, the honours of the magistracy, sacerdotal dignities, plunder, rapine, with all the usual perquisites of war, and whatever the insolence of victory could extort from the vanquished. . . . .

The election soon after followed, and in a full assembly of the people Cicero and Antonius were declared consuls for the year.

This event was a blow that staggered the conspirators; but Catiline, still fierce and determined, abated nothing from the violence of his temper. He continued his exertions; he strained every nerve, and provided arms at proper stations throughout Italy. The money which he was able to raise by his own credit, or that of his friends, he conveyed to the city of Fæsulæ, to be there deposited in the hands of Manlius, the man who was afterwards the first that reared the standard of rebellion.

Even in this situation of his affairs, Catiline, we are told, still had the address to gain over to his cause a number of proselytes, and among them several women, who in the prime of life had gained large sums of money by setting a price on their beauty, but in more advanced years, when the decline of their charms reduced their profits, but left their passion for luxury still in force, they continued to live in the same course of unbounded expense, and consequently contracted a load of debt. By the arts of these women, Catiline flattered himself that he should be able to cause an insurrection of the slaves, and with their assistance he resolved to set fire to the city. He had still a further use to make of his female friends: by their influence he hoped to draw their husbands into the conspiracy, or, if they refused to comply, he had no doubt but he could contrive to get them put to death. . . .

Though Catiline had thus prepared his measures, he did not lose sight of the consulship. He declared himself a candidate for the following year, still conceiving, if he succeeded, that Antonius would be an instrument in his hands.

Determined, in the meantime, not to remain inactive, he made it his business to lay snares for Cicero. The consul was never off his guard, but with consummate address was able to counteract the schemes of a wily adversary. He had no sooner entered on the consulship, than he took care to secure Fulvia in his interest, and through her he gained, by the force of promises, such an influence on Quintus Curius, who has been already mentioned, that the machinations of Catiline were discovered to him without delay. Besides this advantage, Cicero had the precaution to detach Antonius from the conspiracy. He promised by his weight and management to procure for his colleague the administration of an opulent province; and, by that prospect of preferment, engaged him to take no part with the enemies of the commonwealth. In the mean time Cicero took care to have, without parade, a number of his friends and clients near at hand to protect his person.

The day on which, according to custom, the consuls elect were declared, Catiline had the mortification of seeing all his hopes utterly defeated. His various efforts against the life of Cicero were likewise unsuccessful. In that distress, when all his secret machinations ended in confusion and disgrace, he resolved, without further hesitation, to have recourse to open arms. For that purpose, he ordered Caius Manlius to his post in Fæsulæ, to overawe that part of Etruria; to the territory of Picenum he sent a man of the name of Septimius, a native of the city of Camers, and at the same time despatched Caius Julius to guard the passes of Apulia: several others were commissioned to seize the most advantageous posts in every quarter. He himself remained at Rome, exerting his utmost industry, and concerting plans of mischief. He was still envenomed against Cicero, and never ceased to lay snares for his life. He resolved to set fire to the city, and in every quarter stationed a band of assassins. He went constantly armed, and exhorted his followers to hold themselves in readiness on the first alarm. He never rested day or night; a stranger to repose, unsubdued by toil, and never fatigued by midnight vigils.

Perceiving at length that all his labours were still ineffectual, he directed Porcius Læca to call the chiefs of the conspiracy to a meeting in the dead of night. He there expostulated with his partisans, and after severe reproaches for their want of zeal, he gave them to understand, that he had commissioned Manlius to take upon him the command of an armed force, which was already mustered; and that various other officers had been despatched to proper stations, with orders to begin the war. He added, that he wished for nothing so much as to put himself at the head of his army; but Cicero by his counsels, his activity and vigilance, continued to frustrate all his measures. To cut off the consul was, therefore, a point of the greatest moment.

The assembly remained mute, and covered with consternation, when Caius Cornelius, a Roman knight, offered to bear the murderer's poniard; and Lucius Vargunteius, a senator, declared himself ready to join in the same horrible design. They resolved that very night to collect a band of ruffians, and at the dawn of day, under pretence of paying an early visit, to proceed to the consul's house, and dispatch him on the spot, unguarded and unsuspecting. Curius took the alarm; he shuddered at the danger that threatened Cicero's life, and discovered the plot to Fulvia, who took care to give immediate intelligence to the consul. The assassins kept their appointed hour, but gained no admittance; their design proved abortive.

Manlius, in the mean time, exerted himself with his utmost vigour to raise an insurrection in Etruria. The people in that part of the country were ripe for a revolt; extreme poverty, and the sense of injuries under Sulla's usurpation, exasperated the public mind; the wretched inhabitants had been deprived of their lands, and plundered of their property; resentment was fostered in every breast, and all were loud for a revolution. The country abounded with freebooters, and all of that description the rebel chief collected in a body. At the same time he made it his business to enlist the soldiers whom Sulla had planted in different colonies; a licentious crew, who had dissipated the spoils of war in riotous expense, and were now reduced to extreme poverty.

Cicero was regularly informed of all that passed, but found himself much embarrassed by the magnitude of the danger; apprehending that it would not be in his power to traverse the machinations of the conspirators by his own private diligence, and not being' sufficiently apprized of the numbers and designs of Manlius, he resolved to open the whole affair to the senate. Public report had spread a general alarm, but the particulars were not sufficiently known.

The senate, as was usual in cases of urgent necessity, ordained by a decree, "That the consuls should take care that the state suffered no detriment." By this law, which was founded on ancient policy, and the institutions of our ancestors, the consuls were invested with extraordinary powers. They were authorized to raise new levies, and lead the armies of the republic to the field; by coercion to restrain the citizens of Rome and the allies, within due bounds; and to exercise supreme jurisdiction at home as well as in camp. When no such act has passed, the consular authority is limited by law. The acts of power above-mentioned were never known to be exercised, unless sanctioned by a declaratory law.

In the course of a few days after the decree of the fathers, Lucius Senius, a member of the senate, produced in that assembly a letter, which he said was brought to him from the city of Fæsulæ, importing that Manlius, about the sixth

of the calends of November, had taken the field at the head of a numerous army. The account was swelled, as is usual on such occasions, with a number of prodigies and reports from various quarters; with an account of conventions held in different places; that large quantities of arms were provided; and that a servile war was ready to break out in Capua and Apulia.

The senate ordered by a decree, that Quintus Marcius Rex should proceed to Fæsulæ, and Quintus Metellus Creticus to Apulia, in order to secure those parts of the country. Those two generals had been for some time waiting on the outside of the city walls, in expectation of a triumphal entry, but that honour was withheld from them by the contrivance of artful men, whose practice it was on all occasions, just or unjust, to put every thing up to sale. By the same decree of the senate, the prætor, Quintus Pompeius, and Quintus Metellus Celer, were ordered to repair to their posts; the former to command at Capua, the latter at Picenum. Both had it in commission to levy forces with all the expedition that the times required.

The senate, at the same time, passed another decree, "by which rewards were promised to whoever should give information touching the conspiracy: if a slave, he was to have his freedom, and one hundred thousand sesterces; if a freeman, double that sum, and a full indemnity." It was further ordered, that whole families of gladiators should be stationed at Capua and other municipal towns, in proportion to the strength and importance of the places. Rome was guarded by a nightwatch placed at convenient posts throughout the city, under the command of the inferior magistrates.

These preparations spread a general alarm through the city. The face of things was entirely changed. To scenes of joy and festivity, the consequence of a long peace, dismay and terror succeeded.

Hurry, bustle, and distraction, were seen in every quarter; no place was safe; distrust prevailed; no confidence among neighbours; a medley of peace and war prevailed; all were covered with confusion, and each individual formed his idea of the danger according to his doubts and fears. The panic that seized the women was still more alarming. They had until then lived secure under a great and flourishing empire, and now the horror of an approaching war threw them into consternation. In despair they raised their hands to heaven; they wept over their infant children; they ran wild through the streets inquiring for news; they trembled at every report; they forgot their taste for pleasure, their pride and luxury, anxious only for their lives, and the safety of their country.

Meanwhile Catiline abated nothing from the ferocity of his nature; He persisted in his dark designs, still meditating scenes of destruction. The vigorous measures of the senate were not sufficient to control a mind like his. He even knew that he was impeached by Lucius Paulus for an offence against the Plautian law, and he still remained unshaken and undaunted. At length, in order to varnish his character, and throw a veil over his traitorous intentions, he had the hardiness to take his seat in the senate. It was on that occasion that the consul, Marcus Tullius Cicero, apprehending, perhaps, some dangerous consequence from the presence of such a man, or else fired with indignation at the audacity of a detected traitor, delivered that noble oration, which he afterwards reduced to writing, and published to the world.

As soon as Cicero closed his speech, Catiline, who went prepared with all his arts of dissimulation, rose with a modest and dejected air, and in a softened tone implored the fathers not to give credit to false suggestions against a man descended from an illustrious family. Following the example of his ancestors, he said that on many occasions he had deserved well of the commonwealth; and from his early youth had so regulated his conduct, as to entitle himself to fair and honourable expectations. Was it probable that he, of an illustrious patrician rank, could wish to see the government overturned? or that Cicero, a new man, lately transplanted from a municipal town, could have the interest of the state more at heart than himself? He went on in a strain of bitter invective against the consul, when he was interrupted by a general clamour. The fathers with one voice pronounced him an enemy to his country, a traitor, and a parricide. By this treatment Catiline was transported beyond all bounds: he broke out with rage and fury, and "Since," he said, "I am thus encompassed by my enemies, and by this outrage driven to the last extremity, the flame which I find kindled round me, shall be extinguished in the general ruin."

Having uttered that furious menace, he rushed out of the senate, and retired to his own house. He then fell into deep reflection; he saw that Cicero was not to be assailed by stratagem, and that the midnight guards prevented his intended conflagration. In the agitation of his mind, he judged that the best step he could take, would be to augment his army, and, before the legions could be called into the field, to anticipate the measures of his enemies. Having formed this resolution, he set out in the dead of the night with a few attendants, and made the best of his way to the Manlian camp. He left directions with Lentulus, Cethegus, and such of his accomplices as he knew to be men of prompt and daring resolution, to strengthen their faction by every method in their power; if possible, to cut off the consul; and hold themselves in readiness to lay a scene of blood and massacre, to kindle a general conflagration, and involve the commonwealth in all the horrors of a destructive war. They might rely upon his firmness, and in a short time would find him at the gates of Rome with a powerful army. . . .

We are now at the point of time when the commonwealth was reduced to the most humiliating condition. She had carried her victorious arms from the rising to the setting sun: the city of Rome flourished in peace and affluence, the two great comforts of human life; and yet, in that very period, she harboured in her bosom a crew of desperate incendiaries; men determined with fatal obstinacy to overwhelm themselves and their country in one promiscuous ruin. It is worthy of notice, that after two decrees, one offering a reward to informers, and the other a free pardon to such as revolted, not a man was found to make a discovery, nor was there a single deserter from the enemy. Such was the malignity of the times; it spread like a contagion, and envenomed the minds of men against their country.

Nor was this dangerous spirit confined to the conspirators and their accomplices; it pervaded the lower class of citizens; and the rabble, with their usual levity, wished for a convulsion in the state. Nor is this to be received as matter of wonder: it is natural to men who have no means of subsistence, to view the opulent with an eye of envy; lavish of their encomiums on the leaders of faction, they traduce the good and worthy with envenomed rancour; they hate the established system, and pant for innovation; they are weary of their own condition, and hope to find relief in the distractions of their country. Tumult and sedition are to such men the season of plenty, and, in all events, poverty has nothing at stake.

There were, besides, various causes that conspired in that juncture to inflame the popular discontent. In the first place, all who had signalized themselves by their crimes; who by profusion had dissipated their substance; who were forced by their enormities to fly their country; and, in short, all the loose and abandoned, crowded in one general conflux to the city of Rome, as to the centre of corruption. To these were added the whole tribe that remembered Sulla's victory, and could name the common soldiers who rose to the dignity of senators, with a list of others who acquired immoderate riches, and lived in all the splendour of royal magnificence. All these were ready to take up arms, expecting to enrich themselves with the plunder of a civil war.

Besides these pests of society, there was at Rome a number of young men, who had been used in the country to earn a livelihood by their daily labour, but being attracted to the city by the frequency of public and private largesses, they preferred an idle life to the unprofitable labours of the field. These, and all of their stamp, hoped to find their account in public commotions. That men like these, reduced to indigence, and void of morals, yet flushed with hopes of a reform in the senate, should make the interest of the state subservient to their own private views, was a natural consequence.

There was still another party, composed of those whose fathers had been ruined by Sulla's proscriptions, and lost the rights of citizens. Their descendants hoped to find in the calamities of war a redress of grievances, and wished for nothing so much as an opportunity to assert their rights.

The city, moreover, was divided into factions, and they who did not take part with the senate, could not bear to see their country in a more flourishing condition than themselves. Dissensions between the populace and the senate had been the old inveterate canker of the commonwealth, subdued, indeed, for a considerable time; but, after an interval of many years, revived with all the violence of former rancour.

The renewal of this mischief may be traced to the consulship of Pompey and Crassus. Under their administration, the tribunes of the people recovered their ancient rights, and all the powers annexed to their office. That magistracy, in a short time, fell to the lot of young men of fierce and turbulent dispositions, who began to disturb the proceedings of the senate, and by their contentions to inflame the people against the constituted authority of the state. To strengthen their influence, they distributed largesses with unbounded generosity, and by adding liberal promises, seduced the multitude into a league against the constitution. The tribunes were elate with success, they triumphed over all opposition, and were the first men in the state. The nobles exerted themselves to stem the torrent, with pretended zeal for the dignity of the senate, but in fact to promote their own grandeur. The truth is, the men who in those times appeared on the stage of public business, had the address to gloss their designs with specious colours, some pretending to be the friends of the people; others to maintain the rights of the senate. The public good was the ostensible motive of every faction, while ambition and the love of power were the secret springs that set the whole in motion. The contention between the parties was carried on with animosity; justice and moderation were discarded, and the side that occasionally prevailed, exulted with all the pride and insolence of victory.

At length, when Pompey was sent to command against the Pirates, and afterwards to conduct the Mithridatic war, the popular party was no longer able to make head against the nobles. The reins of government were seized by a few leading men, who engrossed the honours of the magistracy, the administration of provinces, and preferment of every kind. Superior to their fellow-citizens, and above control, they lived in splendour and security, by the terror of prosecutions restraining all who presumed to take a part in public business, and, by consequence, leaving the people without a leader. In process of time, when the scene of affairs was changed, and men began to think a revolution not impracticable, the old dissension broke out with redoubled violence. The discontents of the populace rose to such a pitch, that if Catiline gained the first victory, or even left the fortune of the day undecided, the commonwealth would have been reduced to the brink of danger. The war would have continued with alternate vicissitudes, without a decisive blow to end the conflict, till both sides, enfeebled and exhausted by repeated losses, would have fallen an easy prey to some ambitious chief who stood prepared in such a crisis to usurp the supreme power, to the utter ruin of public liberty. . . .

On the following day one Lucius Tarquinius was led to the bar of the senate. This man was apprehended on his way to Catiline's army, and brought in custody to Rome. He offered to make important discoveries, if he might speak with safety under the promise of a public pardon. Being satisfied on this point by the consul, he gave an account in effect the same as Volturcius had done, stating the intended fire of the city, the massacre of the worthiest citizens, and the route by which the rebels were to advance to Rome. He added that "he was dispatched by Crassus to inform Catiline, that, so far from being discouraged by the imprisonment of Lentulus and Cethegus, with the other conspirators, he ought to expedite his march towards Rome, in order to revive the courage of his party, and rescue his friends from confinement."

As soon as the informer mentioned the name of Crassus, a man of the first consideration in the state, distinguished by his illustrious birth, his vast riches, and his power and influence, a murmur of disapprobation was heard from all quarters of the senate. Numbers pronounced the charge altogether incredible; others were of the opinion that it was not destitute of foundation, but that in such a crisis it would be more prudent to temporize, than to provoke the resentment of a great and powerful citizen. The majority of the Fathers had their private reasons for taking part with Crassus: they were under pecuniary obligations, and did not hesitate to pronounce the charge a false and malicious calumny. Upon that point they desired that the question might be put. Cicero collected the voices, and the Fathers decreed unanimously, that "the information was false and groundless, and that Tarquinius should stand committed, never to be heard again, unless he first discovered the person by whose procurement he had fabricated so vile a falsehood."

There was at that time a current opinion, that Publius Autronius was the author of the charge, under the idea that Crassus, finding himself implicated in the plot, would be a shield to protect the rest of the conspirators.

Others would have it, that Cicero suborned the witness, apprehending that Crassus might be induced, according to his custom, to undertake the defence of pernicious citizens. By involving him in the general guilt, it was supposed that his voice would be silenced. Since that time, Crassus has averred in my hearing, that he was indebted to Cicero for that dark imputation.

It must be acknowledged, that Quintus Catulus and Caius Piso were not able by their weight and influence, by entreaty, or any other inducement, to prevail on Cicero to suffer a cloud of suspicion to be thrown on Julius Cæsar by the Allobrogians, or any other witness. Those two great men were, in that juncture, the avowed enemies of Cæsar; the former, because on his return from Cisalpine Gaul, in a prosecution carried on against him for being corrupted by a bribe to pass judgment of death upon a native of the country beyond the Po, Cæsar took a decided part in that affair,

and obtained judgment against him. The mind of Catulus was embittered by his disappointment when he stood candidate for the office of high pontiff. Cæsar opposed his election; and that so young a man should enter into competitions, and be able to defeat an ancient citizen in the evening of his days, when he had almost closed the career of public honours, was a reflection that inflamed him with resentment. Their time for framing an accusation against Cæsar was not ill chosen: Cæsar, by private liberality, and a profusion of largesses, had contracted an immense load of debt, and by that circumstance gave his enemies a fair opportunity.

Cicero, however, refused to enter into their designs; but still Piso and Catulus, though they found their solicitations ineffectual, persisted in their malevolent purpose. They caballed with individuals, framing from their own invention the foulest imputations, and, to give them colour, pretending that they had all their intelligence from Volturcius and the Allobrogians. By these artifices they excited the popular odium, and made Cæsar so obnoxious, that a band of Roman knights, who had ranged themselves under arms to guard the avenues of the Temple of Concord, drew their swords, and brandished them in a menacing manner, as Cæsar went forth from the senate. By this act of violence the knights declared their detestation of the conspiracy, or, perhaps, acted with a nobler motive, to announce their ardour in the cause of their country.

The Fathers, finding ample reason to be satisfied with the testimony of the Allobrogians and Volturcius, proceeded to consider of the recompense due to them for their services. In the mean time, the freedmen and clients of Lentulus were busy in various parts of the city, with a design to collect a party of slaves and labouring men, in order to rescue their patron out of custody. Others went about the streets in quest of certain seditious declaimers, on all occasions ready incendiaries for hire, and consequently well practised in the arts of raising popular tumults. Cethegus also had his emissaries, who endeavoured to stir up, by his domestic slaves and freedmen, an abandoned crew, ever ready for any desperate mischief. They were to proceed in a body, and sword in hand set their master at liberty.

The consul, informed of all that was in agitation, disposed his guards at proper stations, as the exigence seemed to require, and without delay convened the senate. To that assembly he opened the case of the prisoners. They had been all adjudged traitors and public enemies; he now moved for a decree, to determine finally what ought to be done with men in their situation. The question being put, Decimus Junius Silanus, at that time consul elect, was the first in order to deliver his opinion. His advice was, that not only those in actual custody, but also Lucius Cassius, Publius Furius, Publius Umbranus, and Quintus Annius, as soon as taken, should all be condemned to suffer death. Julius Cæsar opposed that proposition: his speech on the occasion made such an impression on Silanus, that his resolution failed, and he went over to the opinion of Tiberius Nero, who was for strengthening the guard, and adjourning the debate for further consideration. . . .

As soon as Cato concluded, all of consular rank, and, indeed, the majority of the Fathers, went over to his opinion. They extolled his spirit and greatness of soul with the warmest applause; they fell into mutual reproaches, and accused one another of pusillanimity. The house resounded with the praises of Cato, and a decree was passed in form and substance as he proposed.

A reflection occurs in this place, which may claim some attention. The brave exploits and upright policy of the Romans have filled the page of history. After studying that page with diligence, and attending to the observations of others, I was led by curiosity to inquire what were the resources of the commonwealth, and what the principles that contributed to raise and support so vast a fabric. I was aware, that with inferior armies Rome had often made head against great and powerful nations; I knew that mighty monarchs had been obliged to yield to the superior valour of well-disciplined forces, and that the Roman legions were not to be subdued by adverse fortune. The Greeks had made the palm of eloquence their own, and the Gauls were at one time famous for a more warlike spirit.

The result of my inquiries was, that the Roman name owes all its lustre to the patriot spirit of a few great and eminent men, who by their virtue enabled poverty to cope with the wealth of nations, and inferior numbers to triumph over numerous armies. But when, after a long series of success, luxury diffused its baneful influence, and the minds of men grew torpid in ease and indolence, the commonwealth by its own inward energy was still able to stand on a solid basis, firm and unshaken by the vices of her commanders abroad, and the intrigues of her magistrates at home. But the season of public virtue has declined, and for several years Rome, like a superannuated matron, did not produce one great and eminent character.

Of late indeed, we have seen flourishing among us two illustrious citizens, both of the first order, adorned with superior talents, but different in their manners. The persons whom I have in view, are Marcus Cato and Caius Julius Cæsar. Two such characters ought not to be passed by in silence. They naturally present themselves to the historian's observation, and since the opportunity is so fair, I shall here endeavour, with all the skill I am master of, to give the prominent features of each.

In point of birth, age, and eloquence, they were nearly equal. Greatness of soul was the characteristic of both. They attained the summit of glory, but by different means. Cæsar came upon mankind by acts of friendship and public munificence: Cato stood distinguished by his moral conduct, and the integrity of his life. Humanity and benevolence were the virtues of Cæsar: severity of manners added dignity to the name of Cato. The former gained the affections of mankind by liberal donations, by generosity to his friends, and by forgiving his enemies; the latter distributed no favours, and on that reserved temper founded his glory. One was the protector of the unhappy; the other, the scourge of bad men. Cæsar was admired for the facility of his manners; Cato for his unshaken constancy. In a word, Cæsar entered on a career of vigilance, of active industry, and laborious application; he devoted his time to the interest of his friends, regardless of his own; whatever he possessed worthy of acceptance, he gave as a present; ambition was his ruling passion; he aimed at prodigious things; he desired to have the command of armies; he considered war as his element, and panted for some bright occasion, which might lay open to him the field of glory. Cato, on the other hand, was careful to observe the rules of moderation, of regular conduct, and, above all, an inflexible severity of manners. In point of riches he vied with no man; with the factious he entered into no competition; an honest emulation inspired his soul; the constant rival of the good and worthy, he struggled for the palm of courage with the brave; in simplicity of life he contended with the modest, and in a constant course of virtue, with the most pure and innocent. To be, and not to seem, was his settled principle. He disregarded popularity, and his glory rose the higher.

As soon as the senate concurred, as has been mentioned, with the sentiments of Cato, the consul thought that no time ought to be lost, and accordingly, to prevent seditious attempts during the night, which was then approaching, he ordered the triumvirs to prepare for the immediate execution of the condemned malefactors; he himself, having first disposed his guards at proper stations, conducted Lentulus to the prison. The prætors attended the rest of the conspirators.

In the jail, as you ascend on the left hand, there is a place called the Tullian dungeon, sunk about twelve feet under ground, enclosed on all sides with strong walls, and covered over with a stone arch; a dark and dismal vault, exhaling a fetid stench, the last stage of guilt and misery. Lentulus was conducted to that hideous cavern, and there strangled by the officers of justice.

Such was the dismal catastrophe of a man descended from an illustrious branch of the Cornelian family, who had been invested with the consular dignity. He closed his days by an ignominious death, the just retribution due to his crimes. Cethegus, Statilius, Gabinius, and Ceparius, suffered in like manner. . . . .

Antonius, the commander of the Roman army, was attacked by a fit of the gout, and, by consequence, unable to conduct the battle. He gave the honour of the day to Marcus Petreius, his lieutenant-general. By the directions of that officer the army was drawn up in the following order: the veterans, who had been called out to serve in the exigence of the times, were stationed in the front; the rest of the army formed their lines in the rear. Petreius rode through the ranks, calling on the men by name: he exhorted, he conjured them to exert their former courage. "You see," he said, "a band of freebooters, of robbers, and murderers, a vile collection of incendiaries almost naked and disarmed. When you advance to the charge, remember that you draw the sword in the cause of your country, your children, your altars, and your household gods." Petreius had been a military man for more than thirty years: he rose to eminence through the several gradations of tribune, præfect, lieutenant-general, and prætor, having served during all the time with the highest honour. In the several stations through which he passed, he had a fair opportunity of knowing most of the veterans; he called to mind their former conduct, and by holding to view their acts of valour, inspired them with a resolution to act in a manner worthy of themselves.

Having arranged his measures, Petreius ordered the trumpets to sound to battle. The cohorts advanced with a slow pace in regular order. Catiline's soldiers did the same. As soon as the two armies drew so near, that the light-armed troops could begin the onset by a volley of darts, both sides set up a warlike shout, and rushed on to the attack. A close engagement followed. None relied on their missive weapons; they fought sword in hand. The veterans, eager to preserve their renown in arms, advanced into the heat of the action. The rebels received them with a steady countenance. A fierce and obstinate conflict ensued. Catiline, at the head of his light-armed infantry, shewed himself in the front of the lines; he fought in the thickest ranks; he succoured all that gave ground; he supplied the place of the wounded with fresh soldiers; wherever the enemy pressed, he was ready to support the ranks; he charged in person, and enacted prodigies of valour, at once a gallant soldier and an able general.

Petreius, seeing that Catiline disputed the field with more obstinacy than he at first expected, led his prætorian cohort into the thick of the battle. The rebels were thrown into disorder, and a dreadful slaughter followed. All who resisted were put to the sword. The Roman wings, at the same time, attacked the enemy in flank. Manlius, and the commander from Fæsulæ, both fighting bravely, fell in the first onset. Catiline saw his troops routed on every side, and nothing but desolation round him. Having only a handful of his followers left, he was still determined not to forget his illustrious birth, and the dignity of his rank. He rushed among the closest ranks, and, exerting himself with fury and brave despair, fell under repeated wounds.

When the battle was ended, the fierce and obstinate spirit that animated Catiline's army, appeared manifest to view. The spot on which the soldier took his stand during the action, was covered with his body when he expired. A few, whom the prætorian cohort overpowered, were driven from their post, but they fell under honourable wounds. Catiline was found at a distance from his men, amidst heaps of slain. His breath had not quite left him: the same ferocity that distinguished him when living, was still visible in his countenance.

It may be further observed, that in his whole army not one free citizen was taken prisoner, either during the battle, or after the defeat. Determined to give no quarter, they were prodigal of their own lives. Nor could the army of the commonwealth boast of having gained a cheap victory. They paid the price of their blood. The bravest among them were either slain in the action, or carried from the field covered with wounds. Numbers went from the camp to survey the field of battle, led either by curiosity, or in search of plunder. Employed in moving the dead bodies, they found among the slain a friend, a relative, or an intimate companion. Some discovered their particular enemies stretched on the ground. The impressions made by this melancholy scene were various: mixed emotions of joy and sorrow, regret and congratulation, prevailed throughout the army.

—ARTHUR MURPHY.

THE CONFLICT BETWEEN MILO AND CLODIUS

CICERO

[From the *Defence of Milo*]

Cicero's statesmanship limited itself to solving each problem as it arose. The conflict between Milo and Clodius was only one of a number of indications that something was fundamentally wrong. The two leaders with their gangs of slaves had caused anarchy at Rome for a time by their street brawls. Finally Clodius was killed by Milo's followers in 52 B.C. Milo was brought to trial and was defended unsuccessfully by Cicero. It was later that Cicero wrote the speech given below.

When Publius Clodius had determined to distress the republic by all sorts of wickedness during his prætorship, and saw that the comitia were so delayed the year before, that he would not be able to continue his prætorship many months, as he had no regard to the degree of honour, as others have, but both wished to avoid having Lucius Paullus, a citizen of singular virtue, for his colleague, and also to have an entire year to mangle the republic; on a sudden he abandoned his own year, and transferred himself to the next year, not from any religious scruple, but that he might have, as he said himself, a full and entire year to act as prætor, that is, to overthrow the republic.

It occurred to him that his prætorship would be crippled and powerless, if Milo was consul; and, moreover, he saw that he was being made consul with the greatest unanimity of the Roman people. He betook himself to his competitors, but in such a manner that he alone managed the whole election, even against their will,—that he supported on his own shoulders, as he used to say, the whole comitia,—he convoked the tribes,—he interposed,—he erected a new Colline tribe by the enrollment of the most worthless of the citizens. In proportion as the one caused greater confusion, so did the other acquire additional power every day. When the fellow, prepared for every atrocity, saw that a most brave man, his greatest enemy, was a most certain consul, and that that was declared, not only by the conversation of the Roman people, but also by their votes, he began to act openly, and to say without disguise that Milo must be slain.

He had brought down from the Apennines rustic and barbarian slaves, whom you saw, with whom he had ravaged the public woods and Etruria. The matter was not concealed at all. In truth, he used to say undisguisedly that the consulship could not be taken from Milo, but that life could. He often hinted as much in the senate; he said it plainly in the public assembly. Besides, when Favonius, a brave man, asked him what he hoped for by giving way to such madness while Milo was alive? he answered him, that in three, or at most in four days, he would be dead. And this saying of his Favonius immediately reported to Marcus Cato, who is here present.

In the meantime, as Clodius knew— and it was not hard to know it—that Milo was forced to take a yearly, legitimate, necessary journey on the twentieth of January to Lanuvium to appoint a priest, because Milo was dictator of Lanuvium, on a sudden he himself left Rome the day before, in order (as was seen by the event) to lay an ambush for Milo in front of his farm; and he departed, so that he was not present at a turbulent assembly in which his madness was greatly missed, and which was held that very day, and from which he never would have been absent, if he had not desired to avail himself of the place and opportunity for a crime.

But Milo, as he had been that day in the senate till it was dismissed, came home, changed his shoes and his garments, waited a little, as men do, while his wife was getting ready, and then started at the time when Clodius might have returned, if, indeed, he had been coming to Rome that day. Clodius meets him unencumbered on horseback, with no carriage, with no baggage, with no Greek companions, as he was used to, without his wife, which was scarcely ever the case; while this plotter, who had taken, forsooth, that journey for the express purpose of murder, was driving with his wife in a carriage, in a heavy travelling cloak, with abundant baggage, and a delicate company of women, and maid-servants, and boys. He meets Clodius in front of his farm, about the eleventh hour, or not far from it. Immediately a number of men attack him from the higher ground with missile weapons. The men who are in front kill his driver, and when he had jumped down from his chariot and flung aside his cloak, and while he was defending himself with vigorous courage, the men who were with Clodius drew their swords, and some of them ran back towards his chariot in order to attack Milo from behind, and some, because they thought that he was already slain, began to attack his servants who were behind him; and those of the servants who had presence of mind to defend themselves, and were faithful to their master, were some of them slain, and the others, when they saw a fierce battle taking place around the chariot, and as they were prevented from getting near their master so as to succour him, when they heard Clodius himself proclaim that Milo was slain, and they thought that it was really true, they, the servants of Milo, (I am not speaking for the purpose of shifting the guilt on to the shoulders of others, but I am saying what really occurred) did, without their master either commanding it, or knowing it, or even being present to see it, what every one would have wished his servants to do in a similar case.

These things were all done, O judges, just as I have related them. The man who laid the plot was defeated; violence was defeated by violence; or, I should rather say, audacity was crushed by valour. I say nothing about what the republic, nothing about what you, nothing about what all good men gained by the result. I do not desire it to be any advantage to me to hear that he was born with such a destiny that he was unable even to save himself, without at the same time saving the republic and all of you. But if both reason has taught this lesson to learned men, and necessity to barbarians, and custom to all nations, and nature itself to the beasts, that they are at all times to repel all violence by whatever means they can from their persons, from their liberties, and from their lives, then you cannot decide this action to have been wrong, without deciding at the same time that all men who fall among thieves must perish, either by their weapons, or by your sentence.

And if he had thought that this was the law, it would have been preferable for Milo to offer his throat to Publius Clodius,—which was not attacked by him once only, nor for the first time on that day,—rather than now to be destroyed by you because he did not surrender himself then to be destroyed by him. But if there is no one of you who entertains such an opinion as that, then the question which arises for the consideration of the court is, not whether he was slain or not, which we admit, but whether he was slain legally or illegally, which is an inquiry which has often been instituted in many causes. It is quite plain that a plot was laid; and that is a thing which the senate has decided to be contrary to the laws of the republic. By whom it was laid is a question. And on this point an inquiry has been ordered to be instituted. So the senate has marked its disapproval of the fact, not of the man; and Pompeius has appointed this inquiry into the merits of the case, and not into the fact of its existence.

Does then any other point arise for the decision of the court, except this one,—which laid a plot against the other? None whatever. The case comes before you in this way, that if Milo laid a plot against Clodius, then he is not to be let off with impunity. If Clodius laid it against Milo, then we are acquitted from all guilt.

How then are we to prove that Clodius laid a plot against Milo? It is quite sufficient in the case of such a wicked, such an audacious monster as that, to prove that he had great reason to do so; that he had great hopes founded on Milo's death; that it would have been of the greatest service to him. Therefore, that maxim of Cassius, to see to whose advantage it was, may well have influence in respect of these persons. For although good men cannot be induced to commit crimes by any advantage whatever, wicked men often can by a very trifling one. And, if Milo were slain, Clodius gained this, not only that he should be prætor without having him for a consul, under whom he would not be able to commit any wickedness, but also that he should have those men for consuls while he was prætor, who, if they did not aid him, would at all events connive at all his proceedings to such an extent that he hoped he should be able to escape detection in all the frantic actions which he was contemplating; as they (so he argued to himself) would not, even if they were able to do so, be anxious to check his attempts when they considered that they were under such obligations to him; and on the other hand, if they did wish to do so, perhaps they would hardly be able to crush the audacity of that most wicked man when it got strength by its long continuance. Are you, O judges, the only persons ignorant of all this? Are you living in this city as ignorant of what passes as if you were visitors? Are your ears all abroad, do they keep aloof from all the ordinary topics of conversation of the city, as to what laws (if, indeed, they are to be called laws, and not rather firebrands to destroy the city, pestilences to annihilate the republic) that man was intending to impose on all of us, to brand on our foreheads? Exhibit, I beg you, Sextus Clodius, produce, I beg, that copy of your laws which they say that you saved from your house, and from the middle of the armed band which threatened you by night, and bore aloft, like another palladium, in order, forsooth, to be able to carry that splendid present, that instrument for discharging the duties of the tribuneship, to some one, if you could obtain his election, who would discharge those duties according to your directions. . . .

Now turn your attention to Milo. What advantages could it be to Milo that Clodius should be slain? What reason was there why Milo, I will not say should do such an action, but should even wish for his death? Oh, Clodius was an obstacle to Milo's hope of obtaining the consulship. But he was obtaining it in spite of him. Ay, I might rather say he was obtaining it all the more because Clodius was opposing him; nor in fact was I a more efficient support to him than Clodius was. The recollection, O judges, of the services which Milo had done to me and to the republic had weight with you. My entreaties and my tears, with which I perceived at that time that you were greatly moved, had weight with you; but still more weight had your own fear of the dangers which were impending. For who of the citizens was there who turned his eyes to the unrestrained prætorship of Publius Clodius, without feeling the greatest dread of a revolution? and unrestrained you saw that it would be unless you had a consul who had both courage and power to restrain him; and as the whole Roman people saw that Milo alone was that man, who could hesitate by his vote to release himself from fear, and the republic from danger?

But now, now that Clodius is removed, Milo has got to labour by more than ordinary practices to preserve his dignity. That preeminent glory, which was then attributed to him alone, and which was daily increasing in consequence of his efforts to repress the frenzy of Clodius, has been put an end to by the death of Clodius. You have gained your object of being no longer afraid of any one of the citizens; he has lost that incessant arena for his valour, that which procured him votes for the consulship, that ceaseless and ever-springing fountain of his glory. Therefore, Milo's canvass for the consulship, which could not be hindered from prospering while Clodius was alive, now, the moment he is dead, is attempted to be checked. So that the death of Clodius is not only no advantage, but is even a positive injury to Milo.

"Oh, but his hatred prevailed with him; he slew him in a passion; he slew him because he was his enemy; he acted as the avenger of his own injury; he was exacting atonement to appease his private indignation." But what will you say if these feelings, I do not say existed in a greater degree in Clodius than in Milo, but if they existed in the greatest possible degree in the former, and not at all in the latter? What will you require beyond that? For why should Milo have hated Clodius, the material and groundwork of his glory, except as far as that hatred becoming a citizen goes, with which we hate all worthless men? There was plenty of reason for Clodius to hate Milo, first, as the defender of my safety; secondly, as the repressor of his frenzy, the defeater of his arms; and lastly, also, as his prosecutor. For Clodius was liable to the prosecution of Milo, according to the provisions of the Plotian law, as long as he lived. And with what feelings do you suppose that that tyrant bore that? how great do you suppose was his hatred

towards him? and, indeed, how reasonable a hatred was it for a wicked man to entertain.

It remains for me now to urge his natural disposition and his habits of life in the defence of one, and the very same things as an accusation against the other. Clodius, I suppose, had never done anything by violence; Milo had done everything by violence. What then shall I say, O judges? When, amid the grief of all of you, I departed from the city, was I afraid of the result of a trial? was I not afraid of slaves, and arms, and violence? What, I pray you, was the first ground of my restoration, except that I had been unjustly driven out? Clodius, I suppose, had commenced a formal prosecution against me; he had named a sum as damages; he had commenced an action for high treason; and, I suppose too, I had cause to fear your decision in a cause which was an unjust one, which was my own private cause, not one which was a most righteous one, and which was, in reality, your cause, and not mine? No,—I was unwilling that my fellow-citizens, who had been saved by my prudence and by my own personal danger, should be exposed to the arms of slaves and needy citizens and convicted malefactors. For I saw—I saw, I say, this very Quintus Hortensius, the light and ornament of the republic, almost slain by the hands of slaves, while he was standing by me. In which crowd Caius Vibienus, a senator, a most excellent man, who was with Hortensius, was so maltreated that he lost his life.

When, then, was it that that assassin's dagger of his, which he had received from Catiline, rested? It was aimed at us; I would not allow you all to be exposed to it for my sake. It was prepared in treachery for Pompeius. It stained with blood, through the murder of Papirius, the very Appian road, the monument of his name; this, this same dagger, after a long interval was again turned against me; lately, as you know, it nearly murdered me close to the palace of Ancus.

What is there of Milo's conduct like all this? when all the violence that he has ever displayed has amounted to this, that he wished to prevent Publius Clodius (as he could not be brought to trial) from oppressing the city by violence. And if he wished to put him to death, what great, what repeated, and what splendid opportunities he had of doing so! Might he not have avenged himself without violating the law when he was defending his own house and his household goods from his attacks? might he not have done so when that illustrious citizen and most gallant man, Publius Sextius, his own colleague, was wounded? might he not have done so when that most excellent man, Quintus Fabricius, while carrying a bill for my restoration, was driven away, and when a most cruel slaughter was taking place in the forum? might he not have done so when the house of Lucius Cæcilius, that most upright and fearless prætor, was attacked? might he not have done so on that day on which the law concerning me was passed, and when that vast concourse of people from all parts of Italy, whom a regard for my safety had roused up, would have gladly recognised and adopted as its own the glory of that action? so that, even if Milo had performed it, the whole state would claim the praise of it as belonging to itself.

And what a time was it? A most illustrious and fearless consul, Publius Lentulus, and enemy to Clodius, the avenger of his wickedness, the bulwark of the senate, the defender of your inclinations, the patron of that general unanimity, the restorer of my safety; seven prætors, eight tribunes of the people, adversaries of him, defenders of me; Cnæus Pompeius, the prime mover of and chief agent in my return, his open enemy; whose opinion respecting my return, delivered in the most dignified and most complimentary language, the whole senate adopted; he who exhorted the whole Roman people, and, when he passed a decree concerning me at Capua, gave himself the signal to all Italy, which was eager for it, and which was imploring his good faith, to join together for the purpose of restoring me to Rome; in short, universal hatred on the part of all the citizens, was excited against him, while their minds were inflamed with as earnest a regret for me; so that if any one had slain him at that time, people's thoughts would have been, not how to procure impunity for such a man, but how to reward him sufficiently.

Nevertheless, Milo restrained himself, and twice summoned Publius Clodius before the court, but never once invited him to a trial of strength in scenes of violence. What do I say? while Milo was a private individual, and on his trial before the people, on the accusation of Publius Clodius, when an attack was made on Cnæus Pompeius, while speaking in defence of Milo, was there not then not only an admirable opportunity of, but even a reasonable pretext for slaying him? And lately when Marcus Antonius had inspired all virtuous men with the very greatest hopes of safety, and when he, being a most noble young man, had with the greatest gallantry espoused the cause of the republic, and had that beast almost in his toils in spite of his avoiding the snares of the law; what an opportunity, what a time and place was there, O ye immortal gods! And when Clodius had fled and hidden himself in the darkness of the stairs, there was a fine opportunity for Milo to slay him without incurring the slightest odium himself, and to load Antonius at the same time with the greatest glory! What? How repeatedly had he a similar chance in the comitia! when he had broken into the voting booth, and contrived to have swords drawn and stones thrown, and then on a sudden, terrified at the look of Milo, fled towards the Tiber, and you and all virtuous men prayed to heaven that Milo might take it into his head to give full scope to his valour.

If then he did not choose to slay him, when he might have done so with the gratitude of every one, is it likely that he should have chosen to do so when some people were sure to complain of it? If he did not venture to do it when he might have done so lawfully, when he had both place and time in his favour, when he might have done so with impunity, can we believe that he did not hesitate to slay him unjustly at a time and place which supplied him with no excuse for the deed, when it was at the hazard of his life? especially, O judges, when the day of contest for the greatest distinction of the state, and the day of the comitia, was at hand. At which time (for I know what a nervous thing ambition is, how vehement and how anxious is the desire for the consulship), we are afraid of everything, not only of those things which can be openly found fault with, but even of whatever can be secretly thought; we shudder at every rumour, at every idle and empty story; we look anxiously at every one's countenance, at every one's eye. For there is nothing so soft, so tender, so frail, so flexible, as the inclinations and feelings of our fellow-citizens towards us; for they are not only angry at any impropriety in the conduct of candidates, but they often even take a disgust at our virtuous actions. . . .

I see that all things up to this point are plain and consistent. That it was even desirable for Milo that Clodius should live; that for Clodius the death of Milo was the most advantageous thing possible, with reference to those objects on which he had set his heart; that he bore him the most bitter hatred, but that Milo had no such feelings towards him; that the one lived in a perpetual round of violence, that the other's habits were limited to repelling it; that Milo had been threatened by him with death, and that his death had been openly predicted by him; that no such expression had ever been heard from Milo; that the day of Milo's journey was well known to Clodius, but that Clodius's return was unknown to Milo; that the journey of the one was inevitable, and that of the other was even inconvenient to himself; that the one had openly declared that on that day he should set out from Rome, that the other had concealed the fact of his intending to return on that day; that the one had in no respect whatever changed his intention, that the other had invented a false pretence for changing his mind; that the one, if he were plotting, would naturally wish night to come on when he was near the city, while an arrival at the city by night was to be feared by the other, even if he had no apprehension of danger from this man.

Let us now consider this, which is the main point of all; for which of the two the identical spot where they did meet was the best suited for planting an ambush. But is that, O judges, a matter about which one can possibly doubt or think seriously for a moment? In front of Clodius's farm,—that farm on which, on account of those absurd erections and excavations for foundations of his, there were pretty well a thousand vigorous men employed,—on that high and raised ground belonging to his adversary, did Milo think that he should get the better in the contest, and had he with that view selected that spot above all others? Or was he rather waited for in that place by a man who had conceived the idea of attacking, because of the hopes that that particular spot suggested to him? The facts, O judges, speak for themselves; facts, which are always of the greatest weight in a cause. If you were not hearing of this transaction, but were looking at a picture of it, still it would be quite visible which of the two was the plotter, which was thinking no evil, when one of the two was driving in a chariot wrapped up in a mantle, with his wife sitting by his side. It is hard to say which was the greatest hindrance to him, his dress, or his carriage, or his wife. How could a man be less ready for battle than when he was entangled in a mantle as in a net, hampered with a carriage, and fettered as it were by his wife clinging to him? Look, on the other hand, at Clodius, first setting out from his villa; all on a sudden: why? It was evening. Why was he forced to set out at such a time? Going slowly. What was the object of that, especially at that time of night? He turns aside to the villa of Pompeius. To see Pompeius? He knew that he was near Alsium. To see the villa? He had been in it a thousand times. What, then, was his object? Delay; he wanted to waste time. He did not choose to leave the spot till Milo arrived.

Come now, compare the journey of this unencumbered bandit with all the hindrances which beset Milo. Before this time he always used to travel with his wife; now he was without her. He invariably went in a carriage; now he was on horseback. His train were a lot of Greeklings wherever he was going; even when he was hastening to the camp in Etruria; but this time there were no triflers in his retinue. Milo, who was never in the habit of doing so, did by chance have with him some musical slaves belonging to his wife, and troops of maid servants. The other man, who was always carrying with him prostitutes, worn-out debauchees both men and women, this time had no one with him except such a band that you might have thought every one of them picked men. Why, then, was he defeated? Because the traveller is not always murdered by the robber; sometimes the robber is killed by the traveller; because, although Clodius in a state of perfect prepara-

tion was attacking men wholly unprepared, still it was the case of a woman falling upon men. And, indeed, Milo was never so utterly unprepared for his violence, as not to be nearly sufficiently prepared. He was always aware how greatly it concerned the interest of Publius Clodius that he should be slain, how greatly he hated him, and how great was his daring. Wherefore, he never exposed his life to danger without some sort of protection and guard, knowing that it was threatened, and that a large price, as it were, was set upon it.

Add to this consideration all the chances; add the always uncertain result of a battle, and the common fortune of Mars, who often overthrows the man who is already exulting and stripping his enemy, and strikes him to the ground by some mean agent; and the blundering conduct of a leader who had dined and drank, and who was yawning and drowsy; who, when he had left his enemy cut off in the rear, never thought of his companions on the outskirts of his train; and then when he fell among them inflamed with anger, and despairing of saving the life of their master, he fell on that punishment which the faithful slaves inflicted on him as a retribution for their master's death. Why, then, has Milo emancipated them? He was afraid, I suppose, lest they should give information against him; lest they should be unable to bear pain; lest they should be compelled by tortures to confess that Publius Clodius was slain in the Appian road by the slaves of Milo.

What need is there of any torturer? What do you want to know? whether he was slain? He was slain. Whether he was slain lawfully or unlawfully? That is beyond the province of the torturer. For the rack can only inquire into the fact; it is the bench of judges that must decide on the law. . . .

Nor, indeed, is it without good reason that Milo's cause has always been approved of by the senate. For these wisest of men took into consideration the whole circumstances of the case; Milo's presence of mind, and vigour in defending himself. Have you forgotten, O judges, when the news of Clodius's death was still recent, the opinions and the language which was held, not only by Milo's enemies, but also by other ignorant people? They said that he would not return to Rome at all. For if he had committed the deed in a passionate and excited mood, so that he had slain his enemy while under the influence of strong hatred, they thought that he would consider the death of Publius Clodius an event of such importance, that he would bear being deprived of his country with equanimity, as he had sated his hatred in th blood of his enemy; or, if he had deliberately intended to deliver his country by the slaughter of Clodius, then they thought that he, as a brave man, would not hesitate, after having brought safety to his country at his own risk, to submit with equanimity to the laws, to carry off with himself everlasting renown, and to leave those things to us to enjoy which he had preserved for us himself.

Many also spoke of Catiline and the monsters of his train. "We shall have another Catiline breaking out. He will occupy some strong place; he will make war on his country." Wretched sometimes is the fate of those citizens who have faithfully served the republic! when men not only forget the illustrious exploits which they have performed, but even suspect them of the most nefarious designs! Therefore, all those things were false, which would certainly have turned out true, if Milo had committed any action which he could not defend with honour and truth. . . .

And if people are even now afraid of Milo, we are not now under apprehension because of the charge respecting Clodius, but we are shuddering at your suspicions,—at yours, I say, O Cnæus

Pompeius (for I address you yourself, and I speak loudly so that you may be able to hear me). If you are afraid of Milo,— if you believe that he either now cherishes wicked designs against your life, or that he ever has entertained such; if the levying of troops throughout Italy, as some of your recruiting-sergeants pretend,—if these arms,—if these cohorts in the Capitol,—if these watchmen, these sentinels,—if this picked body of youths, which is the guard of your person and your house, is all armed against an attack on the part of Milo; and if all these measures have been arranged, and prepared, and aimed against him alone,— then certainly he must be a man of great power, of incredible courage; surely it must be more than the power and resources of one single man which are attributed to him, if the most eminent of our generals is invested with a command, and all Italy is armed against this one man. But who is there that does not understand that all the diseased and feeble parts of the republic were entrusted to you, O Pompeius, that you might heal and strengthen them with your arms? And if an opportunity had been afforded to Milo, he would, doubtless, have proved to you yourself, that no man was ever more dear to another than you are to him; that he had never shunned any danger which might be of service in promoting your dignity; that he had often contended against that most foul pest on behalf of your glory; that his conduct in his tribuneship had been entirely regulated by your counsels for the protection of my safety, which was an object very dear to you; that he afterwards had been defended by you when in danger of his life, and had been assisted by you when a candidate for the prætorship; and that he had always believed that the two firmest friends whom he had were you and I,—you, as shown by the kindness of your behaviour to him, and I, secured to him by the services which he himself had done me. And if he could not convince you of this,—if that suspicion had sunk so deep in your mind that it could not possibly be eradicated; if, in short, Italy was never to have any rest from those levies, nor the city from arms, till Milo was ruined,—then no doubt, he, without hesitation, would have departed from his country, a man born to make such sacrifices and accustomed to make them; but still he would have cited you, O Magnus, as a witness in his favour, as he now does.

See, now, how various and changeable is the course of human life,—how fickle and full of revolutions is fortune; what instances of perfidy are seen in friends, how they dissemble and suit their behaviour to the occasion; when dangers beset one, how one's nearest connexions fly off, and what cowardice they show. The time will come, ay, will most certainly come,—that day will surely dawn some time or other, when you, though your affairs are all, as I trust they will be, in a really sound condition, though they may, perhaps, wear an altered appearance in consequence of some commotion of the times, such as we are all liable to (and how constantly such things happen we may know from experience),—when you, I say, may be in need of the good-will of one who is most deeply attached to you, and the good faith of a man of the greatest weight and dignity, and the magnanimity of the very bravest man that ever lived in the world. Although, who would believe that Cnæus Pompeius, a man most thoroughly versed in public law, in the usages of our ancestors, and in all the affairs of the republic, after the senate had entrusted to him the charge of taking care "that the republic suffered no injury," by which one line the consuls have always been sufficiently armed, even though no warlike weapons were given to them,—that he, I say, after having had an army and a levy of troops given to him, would wait for a legal decision to repress the designs of that man who was seeking by violence to abolish the courts of justice themselves?

It was sufficiently decided by Pompeius, quite sufficiently, that all those charges were falsely brought against Milo; when he passed a law by which, as I conceive, he was bound to be acquitted by you,—at all events, as all men allow, might legally be acquitted. But when he sits in that place, surrounded by all those bands of public guards, he declares plainly enough that he is not striking terror into you (for what could be less worthy of him than to condemn a man whom he himself might punish if guilty, both by his own authority and in strict accordance with the precedents of our ancestors?), but that he keeps them about him for the sake of protection; that you may be aware that it is allowed to you to decide with freedom according to your own opinions, in contradiction to that assembly of the people which was held yesterday.

Nor, O judges, am I at all moved by the accusation respecting Clodius, nor am I so insane, and so ignorant of, and inexperienced in, your feelings, as not to be aware what your opinions are about the death of Clodius, concerning which, if I were unwilling to do away with the accusation in the manner in which I have done away with it, still I assert that it would have been lawful for Milo to proclaim openly, with a false but glorious boast, "I have slain, I have slain, not Spurius Mælius, who fell under the suspicion of aiming at kingly power by lowering the price of corn, and by squandering his own family estate, because by that conduct he was thought to be paying too much court to the common people; not Tiberius Gracchus, who out of a seditious spirit abrogated the magistracy of his own colleague; whose slayers have filled the whole world with the renown of their name; but him ' (for he would venture to name him when he had delivered his country at his own risk) "who was detected in the most infamous adultery in the most sacred shrine, by most noble women; him, by the execution of whom the senate has repeatedly resolved that solemn religious observances required to be propitiated; him whom Lucius Lucullus, when he was examined on the point, declared on his oath that he had detected in committing unhallowed incest with his own sister; him, who by means of armed bands of slaves drove from the country that citizen whom the senate, whom the Roman people, whom all nations had declared to be the saviour of the city and of the lives of all the citizens; him, who gave kingdoms, took them away, and distributed the whole world to whomsoever he pleased; him who, after having committed numberless murders in the forum, drove a citizen of the most extraordinary virtue and glory to his own house by violence and by arms; him, to whom nothing was ever too impious to be done, whether it was a deed of atrocity or of lust; him, who burnt the temple of the nymphs, in order to extinguish the public record of the census which was committed to the public registers; lastly, him who acknowledged no law, no civil rights, no boundaries to any man's possessions,—who sought to obtain other people's estates, not by actions at law and false accusations, not by unjust claims and false oaths, but by camps, by an army, by regular standards and all the pomp of war,—who, by means of arms and soldiers, endeavoured to drive from their possessions, not only the Etrurians, for he thoroughly despised them, but even this Publius Varius, that most gallant man and most virtuous citizen, one of our judges,—who went into other people's villas and grounds with architects and surveyors, who limited his hopes of acquiring possessions by Janiculum and the Alps; him, who, when he

was unable to prevail on an estimable and gallant Roman knight, Marcus Paconius, to sell him his villa on the Prelian Lake, suddenly conveyed timber, and lime, and mortar, and tools in barques to the island, and while the owner of the island was looking at him from the opposite bank, did not hesitate to build a house on another man's land; who said to Titus Furfanius—O ye immortal gods, what a man! (for why should I mention that insignificant woman, Scantia, or that youth Aponius, both of whom he threatened with death if they did not abandon to him the possession of their villas?) but he dared to say to Furfanius, that if he did not give him as much money as he demanded, he would carry a dead body into his house, and so raise a storm of unpopularity against him; who turned his brother Appius, a man connected with me by the most faithful friendship, while he was absent, out of the possession of his farm; who determined to run a wall across the vestibule of his sister's house in such a manner, and to draw the line of foundation in such a direction, as not only to deprive his sister of her vestibule, but of all access to her house, and of her own threshold."

Although all these things appeared such as might be endured,—although he attacked with equal fury the republic, and private individuals, and men who were at a distance, and men who were near, people who had no connexion with him, and his own relations; yet somehow or other the incredible endurance of the state had by long use grown hardened and callous. But as for the things which were at hand, and were impending over you, in what manner was it possible for you either to avert them or to bear them? If he had once obtained real power,—I say nothing of our allies, of foreign nations, and kings, and tetrarchs; for you would have prayed that he might turn himself against them rather than against your possessions, your houses, and your money; money, do I say? your children, rather,—I solemnly swear he would never have restrained himself from your children and from your wives. Do you think that these things are inventions of mine? They are evident; they are notorious to every one; they are proved. Is it an invention of mine that he was about to enlist an army of slaves in the city, by whose instrumentality he might take possession of the whole republic, and of the private fortune of every one?

Wherefore, if Titus Annius, holding in his hand a bloody sword, had cried out, "Come hither, I beg of you, and listen to me, O citizens: I have slain Publius Clodius; with this sword and with this right hand I have turned aside from your necks the frenzied attacks of that man whom we were unable to restrain by any laws, and by any judicial proceedings whatever; by my single efforts has it been brought to pass that right, and equity, and laws, and liberty, and modesty, and chastity remain in this city;" would there in truth have been any reason to fear in what manner the city would receive this announcement? For now, as it is, who is there who does not approve of what has been done? who does not praise it? who does not both say and feel that of all men to whom recollection can reach back, Titus Annius has done the republic the greatest service; that of all men he has diffused the greatest joy among the Roman people, and over the whole of Italy, and throughout all nations? I cannot form a conception of what would have been the old-fashioned joy of the Roman people. Already our age has seen many, and those most illustrious victories, won by consummate generals; but not one of them has brought with it a joy that either lasted so long, or that was so excessive while it did last.

—C. D. YONGE.

THE OUTBREAK OF CIVIL WAR [1]

CÆSAR

[From the *Civil War*, Book I]

Cæsar takes advantage of a very remarkable introduction to a military narrative to make plain his own political conduct. He very skillfully defends his position, in undertaking war on the government as represented by the senate, while seeming merely to picture the unyielding attitude of the opposing faction. In the *Civil War,* Cæsar narrates the campaigns from the crossing of the Rubicon in 49 B.C. to the defeat of Pompey at Pharsalus in 48. For Cæsar, see above p. 108.

When Cæsar's dispatch had been handed to the consuls, the tribunes, with difficulty and after much wrangling, gained their permission for it to be read in the senate, but they could not obtain consent for a motion to be brought before the senate on the subject of the dispatch. The consuls bring forward a motion of the state of public affairs. The consul L. Lentulus puts pressure on the senate, and promises that he will not fail the republic if the senators are willing to express their opinions with boldness and resolution; but if they pay regard to Cæsar and try to win favour with him as they have done on previous occasions, he says that he will consider his own interests and will not obey their authority. "I too," said he, "can shelter myself under the favour and friendship of Cæsar." Scipio expresses himself in similar terms—that Pompeius is inclined not to desert the republic if the senate follows him; but if it delays and acts remissly, it will in vain solicit his aid should it wish to do so in the future.

This speech of Scipio appeared to come from the mouth of Pompeius himself, since the senate was meeting in the city and Pompeius was close at hand. Some

[1] From the Loeb Classical Library, by permission.

had expressed less rigorous views, such as M. Marcellus, who at first embarked on a speech to the effect that the question ought not to be referred to the senate till levies had been held throughout Italy and armies enrolled under whose protection the senate might venture to make such decrees as it wished safely and freely; such, too, as M. Calidius, who expressed the opinion that Pompeius should go to his own provinces in order that there might be no motive for hostilities: Cæsar, he said, was afraid lest it should be thought that Pompeius, having extorted two legions from him, was holding them back and retaining them near Rome with a view to imperilling him; such also as M. Rufus, who with a few modifications followed the opinion of Calidius. All these speakers were assailed with vehement invective by the consul L. Lentulus. He absolutely refused to put the motion of Calidius, and Marcellus, alarmed by the invectives, abandoned his proposal. Thus most of the senators, compelled by the language of the consul, intimidated by the presence of the army and by the threats of the friends of Pompeius, against their will and yielding to pressure, adopt the proposal of Scipio that Cæsar should disband his army before a fixed date, and that, if he failed to do so, he should be considered to be meditating treason against the republic. The tribunes M. Antonius and Q. Cassius intervene. The question of their intervention is immediately brought before the senate. Opinions of weighty import are expressed, and the more harsh and cruel the speech the more it is applauded by the personal enemies of Cæsar.

When the senate was dismissed in the evening all the members of the order are summoned out of the city by Pompeius. He praises the zealous and encourages them for the future; the sluggish he reproves and stimulates. Everywhere a number of reserves from the old armies of Pompeius are called out to serve by the prospect of prizes and promotion; many are summoned from the two legions handed over by Cæsar. The city and the comitium itself are filled with tribunes, centurions, reserves. All the friends of the consuls, all the adherents of Pompeius and of those whose enmity to Cæsar was of long standing, are compelled to attend the senate. By their clamorous throngs the weaker are terrified and the wavering are confirmed, while the majority are robbed of the privilege of free decision. The censor L. Piso promises to go to Cæsar, also the prætor L. Roscius, to inform him of these matters. They demand a period of six days for the execution of their purpose. Some express the opinion that envoys should be sent to Cæsar to set before him the feelings of the senate.

All these speakers encounter opposition and are confronted with speeches from the consul, from Scipio, and from Cato. Cato is goaded on by his old quarrels with Cæsar and vexation at his defeat. Lentulus is moved by the greatness of his debts, by the prospect of a military command and a province, and by the lavish bribes of rulers claiming the title of king, and boasts among his friends that he will prove a second Sulla to whom shall fall the supreme command. Scipio is stimulated by the same hope of a province and of armies, which he thinks that kinship will entitle him to share with Pompeius; also by the dread of the law courts, by the flattery of certain powerful men who had then great influence in public affairs and in the law courts, and by his own and their ostentatious character. Pompeius, urged on by Cæsar's enemies and by his desire that no one should be on the same level of dignity with himself, had completely withdrawn himself from Cæsar's friendship and become reconciled with their common enemies, most of whom he had himself imposed upon Cæsar at the time of their connexion by marriage. Stirred, too, by the discredit attaching to his diversion of two legions from their route by Asia and Syria and his appropriation of them for his own power and supremacy, he was eager that the issue should be brought to the arbitrament of war.

For these reasons everything is done in hurry and confusion. Cæsar's friends are allowed no time to inform him, nor are the tribunes given any opportunity of protesting against the peril that threatened them, nor even of retaining, by the exercise of their veto, the most fundamental of their rights, which L. Sulla had left them, but within the limit of seven days they are compelled to take measures for their own safety, whereas the most turbulent of the tribunes in earlier times had been wont to regard with apprehension the conclusion of at least eight months of administration. Recourse is had to that extreme and ultimate decree of the senate which had never previously been resorted to except when the city was at the point of destruction and all despaired of safety through the audacity of malefactors: "The consuls, the prætors, the tribunes, and all the proconsulars who are near the city shall take measures that the state incur no harm." These resolutions are recorded by decree of the senate on January 7. So on the first five days on which a meeting of the senate could be held after the date on which Lentulus entered on his consulship, except two election days, decrees of the severest and harshest character are passed affecting Cæsar's imperial command and those highly important officials, the tribunes of the people. The tribunes at once flee from the city and betake themselves to Cæsar. He was at that time at Ravenna and was awaiting a reply to his very lenient demands, in the hope that by some sense of equity a peaceable conclusion might be reached.

On the following days the senate meets outside the city. Pompeius carries out the policy which he had indicated by the mouth of Scipio. He commends the manly consistency of the senate, and sets forth the strength of his forces, showing that he has ten legions ready to hand, and, moreover, that he had ascertained for certain that the troops were ill-disposed to Cæsar and could not be persuaded to defend or follow him. Other matters are at once referred to the senate —that a levy should be held throughout Italy, that Faustus Sulla should be at once sent into Mauritania, and that a grant of money should be made to Pompeius from the treasury. A motion is also proposed that King Juba should be styled Ally and Friend. But Marcellus refuses to allow this for the present. The tribune Philippus vetoes the motion about Faustus. On the other matters decrees of the senate are recorded in writing. The provinces, two consular, the rest prætorian, are decreed to private persons. Syria falls to Scipio, Gallia to L. Domitius; Philippus and Cotta are passed over by private arrangement, nor are their lots cast into the urn. To the rest of the provinces prætors are sent. Nor do they wait, as had been the habit in previous years, for a motion to be brought before the people about their imperial command; but, wearing the scarlet military cloak, they leave Rome after offering the usual vows. The consuls quit the city, a thing which had never previously happened, and private persons have lictors in the city and the Capitol, contrary to all the precedents of the past. Levies are held throughout Italy, arms are requisitioned, sums of money are exacted from the municipal towns and carried off from the temples, and all divine and human rights are thrown into confusion.

When this was known Cæsar addresses his troops. He relates all the wrongs that his enemies had ever done him; and complains that Pompeius had been led astray and corrupted by them through jealousy and a desire to detract from his credit, though he had himself always supported and aided his honour and dignity. He complains that a new precedent had been introduced into the state whereby the right of tribunicial intervention, which in earlier years had been restored by arms, was now being branded with ignominy and crushed by arms. Sulla, he said, though stripping the tribunicial power of everything, had nevertheless left its right of intervention free, while Pompeius, who had the credit of having restored the privileges that were lost, had taken away even those that they had before. There had been no instance of the decree that the magistrates should take measures to prevent the state from suffering harm (the declaration and decision of the senate by which the Roman people are called to arms) except in the case of pernicious laws, tribunicial violence, a popular secession, or the seizure of temples and elevated positions: and he explains that these precedents of a former age had been expiated by the downfall of Saturninus and of the Gracchi. No event of this kind had occurred at the time in question or had even been thought of. He exhorts them to defend from his enemies the reputation and dignity of the commander under whose guidance they have administered the state with unfailing good fortune for nine years, fought many successful battles, and pacified the whole of Gaul and Germany. Thereupon the men of the Thirteenth Legion, which was present (he had called this out at the beginning of the disorder; the rest had not yet come together), exclaim that they are ready to repel the wrongs of their commander and of the tribunes.

Having thus learnt the disposition of the soldiery, he sets out for Ariminum with that legion, and there meets the tribunes who had fled to him. The rest of the legions he summons from their winter quarters and orders them to follow him. Thither comes the young L. Cæsar whose father was one of Cæsar's legates.

When their first greetings were over he explains—and this was the real reason of his coming—that he has a message from Pompeius to give him in a matter of private obligation. He says that Pompeius wishes to be cleared of reproach in the eyes of Cæsar, who should not censure as an affront to himself what he had done for the sake of the state. He had always placed the interests of the republic before private claims. Cæsar, too, considering his high position, should give up for the benefit of the state his partisan zeal and passion, nor be so bitterly angry with his enemies as to injure the comonwealth in the hope that he is injuring them. He adds a few other remarks of this kind, at the same time making excuses for Pompeius. The prætor Roscius lays substantially the same proposals before Cæsar, and in the same language, and makes it clear that he received them from Pompeius.

Though these proceedings seemed to have no effect in lessening the sense of wrong, nevertheless now that he had found suitable persons to convey his wishes to Pompeius he makes the request of each of them that, as they had brought him the instructions of Pompeius, they should not object to convey his demands in reply, in the hope that by a little trouble they might be able to put an end to serious disputes and free the whole of Italy from alarm. "As for myself," he said, "I have always reckoned the dignity of the republic of first importance and preferable to life. I was indignant that a benefit conferred on me by the Roman people was being insolently wrested from me, and that, robbed of my six months' command, I was being dragged back to the city, when the people had directed that I should be allowed to be a candidate in absence at the next election. Nevertheless, for the sake of the state I have borne with equanimity this infringement of my prerogative; when I sent a dispatch to the senate proposing that all should give up arms I failed to obtain even this request. Levies are being held throughout Italy, two legions which had been filched from me under the pretence of a Parthian war are being held back, the state is in arms. To what does all this tend but to my own ruin? Still I am prepared to resort to anything, to submit to anything, for the sake of the commonwealth. Let Pompeius go to his own provinces, let us disband our armies, let every one in Italy lay down his arms, let fear be banished from the state, let free elections and the whole control of the republic be handed over to the senate and the Roman people. That this may be done more easily and on definite terms and be ratified by an oath, let Pompeius himself come nearer or allow me to approach him. In this way a conference will settle all disputes."

Having received his instructions, Roscius arrives at Capua with L. Cæsar, and there finds the consuls and Pompeius, and delivers Cæsar's demands. After deliberation they reply and send him back by their hands written instructions, the main purport of which was that Cæsar should return to Gaul, quit Ariminum and disband his forces; if he did this, Pompeius would go to the Spanish provinces. Meanwhile, until a pledge was given that Cæsar would carry out his promise, the consuls and Pompeius would not interrupt their levies.

It was an unfair bargain to demand that Cæsar should quit Ariminum and return to his province while he himself retained his provinces and legions that were not his own: to wish that Cæsar's army should be disbanded while he himself continued his levies: to promise that he would go to his province and not to fix a limit of date for his departure, so that if he had not gone when Cæsar's consulship was over he would nevertheless be held guiltless of breaking his word: finally, his refusal to give an opportunity for a conference and to promise

that he would approach Cæsar tended to produce a profound despair of peace. And so he sends M. Antonius with five cohorts from Ariminum to Arretium, and himself stops at Ariminum with two cohorts and arranges to hold a levy there; he occupies Pisaurum, Fanum, and Ancona, each with one cohort.

—A. G. PESKETT.

THE DICTATORSHIP

HELPLESSNESS

CICERO

[From *Letters to Friends*, Book IV]

Cicero here voices the common feeling of the senatorial party, that under Cæsar's dictatorship they are completely shelved so far as administration of the state is concerned. For Cicero, see above p. 95.

To P. Nigidius Figulus:

Though I have for some time past been on the look-out as to what I had best write you, not only does no definite subject occur to me, but even the usual style of letter seems impossible. For of one department and habitual element in those letters, which we used to write in the days of our prosperity, the state of the times has violently deprived us, and fortune has ordained that I should be unable to write or so much as to think of anything of the sort. There only remained a certain gloomy and wretched style of letter, and one suited to the state of the times: that, too, fails me. In it there is bound to be either a promise of some assistance, or some consolation for your sorrow. I had no such promise to give: for, cast down by a similar blow of fortune, I am myself supporting my disasters by the aid of others, and it more frequently occurs to my mind to complain that I am living as I do, than to rejoice that I am alive. For although no signal injury has been inflicted upon me personally apart from others, and although it has never occurred to my mind to wish for anything in such circumstances which Cæsar has not spontaneously offered me, yet nevertheless I am being so worn out with anxieties, that I regard myself as doing wrong in the mere fact of remaining alive. For I have lost not only many very intimate associates whom either death has snatched from me, or exile torn away, but also all the friends whose affection my former defence of the Republic, accomplished with your aid, had gained for me. I am in the very midst of their shipwrecked fortunes and the confiscation of their property; and I not only hear—which in itself would have been bad enough—but I have before my very eyes the sharpest of all pangs, the actual sight of the ruin of those men by whose aid in old times I quenched that conflagration. And in the city in which I once enjoyed such popularity, influence, and glory, I am now entirely deprived of all these. I retain, indeed, Cæsar's supreme kindness: but that cannot make up for violence and a complete upset of the established order of things. Therefore, being shorn of all to which nature and taste and habit had accustomed me, I present no pleasant object either to others, as it seems to me, or to myself. For, being inclined by nature to be always actively employed in some task worthy of a man, I have now no scope, not merely for action, but even for thought. And I, who in old times was able to help men, who were either obscure or even guilty, am now unable to make even a kind promise to Publius Nigidius—the most eminent man of the day for learning and purity of character, who formerly enjoyed the highest popularity, and at any rate was a most affectionate friend to me.

Therefore from that kind of letter I am forcibly debarred. The only thing left is to console you and to put before you some considerations by which I may endeavour to distract your thoughts from your afflictions. But, if anyone ever had, you have the gift in the highest degree of consoling either yourself or another. Therefore upon that part of the subject which proceeds from profound reason and philosophy I will not touch: I will leave it entirely to you. What is becoming to a brave and wise man, what solidity of character, what a lofty mind, what a past such as yours, what studies and accomplishments, in which you have been eminent from boyhood, demand of you— that you will see for yourself. I only undertake to assure you of what I am able to gather and perceive, from being at Rome and watching affairs anxiously and with attention: it is that you will not be long in the distressing circumstances in which you are at present; but that in those, nevertheless, which I share with you, you will perhaps be permanently. I think I perceive, to begin with, that the mind of him who is all-powerful is inclined to grant your restoration. I am not writing at random. The less familiar I am with him, the more minute am I in my inquiries. It is in order that he may feel less difficulty in returning a sterner answer to those with whom he is still more angry, that he is as yet slower than he otherwise would have been in releasing you from your distressing position. His close friends, indeed, and those most liked by him, both speak and think of you with surprising kindness. Then there is in your favour the wish of the common people, or I should rather say a consensus of all classes. Even that which for the present, indeed, is most powerless of all, but which must hereafter necessarily be powerful, I mean the Republic itself, will with all the strength it may possess enforce your claim before long, believe me, upon those very men by whom it is now held in bondage.

I come round, then, to the point of

even making you a promise, which in the first instance I refrained from doing. For I will both open my arms to his most familiar friends, who are very fond of me and are much in my society, and will worm my way into his intimacy, which up to this time my scruples have closed to me, and I will at least follow up all the paths by which I shall think it possible to arrive at the object of our wishes. In all this department I will do more than I venture to write. And other things, which I know to be at your service at the hands of many, are in the highest state of preparation on my side. There is no one article of property belonging to me which I would choose to have my own rather than yours. On this point, and indeed on the whole subject, I write the less liberally, because I prefer your hoping, what I feel sure will be the case, that you will be in the enjoyment of your own again. It remains for me to beg and beseech you to keep up your spirits to the highest pitch, and not to remember those maxims only which you have learnt from other great men, but those also which you have yourself produced by your genius and industry. If you review these, you will at once hope for the best, and endure philosophically what happens, of whatsoever kind it may be. But you know this better than I, or rather anyone. For my part, whatever I understand to be your interests I will attend to with the greatest zeal and activity, and will preserve the memory of what you did for me at the saddest period of my life.

—E. S. Shuckburgh.

Home Is Exile

Cicero

[From *Letters to Friends*, Book IV]

The senators are allowed to exist as private citizens. It behooves them to be resigned to their condition.

To M. Claudius Marcellus:

I do not venture to advise a man of your consummate wisdom, nor to offer encouragement to a man of the highest spirit and the most conspicuous gallantry —certainly not to *console* him in any way whatever. For if you bear what has happened as I am told you do, I ought rather to congratulate you on your manliness than console your sorrow. But if these great disasters to the state are breaking your heart, I have no ingenuity to spare for finding consolations for you, when I cannot console myself. All that remains, therefore, for me to do is at every point so to display and guarantee my services, and to be in such a way ready to undertake whatever your friends may wish, as to shew that I hold myself your debtor not only for everything that is within my power to do, but also for what is beyond it. Nevertheless, please to consider that in what follows I have given you a warning, or (if you like) expressed an opinion, or from affection for you have been unable to refrain from saying—that you, as I do myself, should make up your mind, if there is to be a republic at all, that the first place in it is your due in everybody's judgment as well as in actual fact, though you are necessarily yielding to the circumstances of the hour: but if there is none, that after all this is the place best fitted for living even in exile. For if we are seeking freedom, what place is free from the master's hand? But if all we want is some place, no matter of what sort, what residence is pleasanter than one's own home? But believe me, even the man who now dominates everything favours men of talent: moreover, he opens his arms to high birth and lofty position, as far as circumstances and his own party needs allow. But I have said more than I intended. I return therefore to that one fact—that I am yours, and will be by the side of your friends, always provided that they *are* yours: if not, I will in any case satisfy the claims of our attachment and affection in all particulars. Good-bye.

—E. S. SHUCKBURGH.

A VICTORY OF BRUTE FORCE

CICERO

[From *Letters to Friends*, Book IV]

"Brute Force" is ever the cry of the losing side.

To M. Claudius Marcellus:

Though I am aware that as yet you have maintained a policy of a nature that I do not venture to rebuke—not that I do not myself disagree with it, but because I judge you to be a wise man, that I do not presume to prefer my views to yours—nevertheless, both the antiquity of our friendship and your eminent affection for me, which I have known from your childhood, have urged me to write to you what I believed would make for your personal security, and thought was not inconsistent with your honour. I have a vivid recollection that you were wise enough to discern the first signs of these disasters long before they occurred, and that you administered the consulship with the utmost splendour and in the most loyal spirit. But I also was conscious of this—that you were not satisfied with the policy of the civil war, nor with Pompey's forces, nor the nature of his army, and were always deeply distrustful of it: in which sentiment I think you remember that I also shared. Accordingly, you did not take much part in active service, and I always strove not to do so. For we were not fighting with the weapons with which we might have prevailed—deliberation, weight of character, and the righteousness of our cause, in all of which we had the superiority—but with muscles and brute force, in which we were not his equals. Accord-

ingly, we were beaten, or, if worth cannot really be beaten, at least we were crushed and rendered powerless. And in this no one can do otherwise than highly praise your resolution, in that with all hope of victory you cast aside all desire of keeping up the contest also; and shewed that a wise man and a good citizen takes the first steps in a civil war with reluctance, but with pleasure declines taking the last. Those who did not adopt the same course as yourself I perceive to have split up into two classes. Either they endeavoured to renew the war—and these have betaken themselves to Africa: or, like myself, they trusted themselves to the victor. Your course was a kind of compromise between the two, since you perhaps regarded the second as cowardice, the first as blind obstinacy. I confess that by most people, or I should say by everybody, your plan has been judged to be wise, by many even magnanimous and courageous. But your policy, as it seems to me at least, has a certain limit, especially as in my opinion nothing is wanting to your being able to keep your entire fortune, except your own willingness to do so. For I have gathered that there is nothing else which causes him who is all-powerful to feel any hesitation, except the fear that you would not regard it as a favour at all. As to which there is no occasion for me to say what I think, since my conduct speaks for itself. However, even if you had already made up your mind, that you preferred being absent from Rome to seeing what was repugnant to your feelings, yet you ought to have reflected that, wherever you were, you would be in the power of the man from whom you were fleeing. And even if he were likely to make no difficulty about allowing you to live in peace and freedom while deprived of property and country, you ought yet to have reflected whether you preferred living at Rome and in your own house, whatever the state of affairs, to living at

Mitylene or Rhodes. But seeing that the power of the man whom we fear is so widely extended, that it has embraced the whole world, do you not prefer being in your own house without danger to being in another man's with danger? For my part, if I must face death, I would rather do so at home and in my native country, than in a foreign and alien land. This is the sentiment of all who love you, of whom the number is as great as your eminent shining virtues deserve. We have also regard for your property, which we are unwilling to see scattered. For, though it can receive no injury destined to be lasting, because neither the present master of the Republic, nor the Republic itself, will allow it, yet I don't want to see an attack made by certain banditti upon your possessions: and who these are I would have ventured to write, had I not felt sure that you understand. Here the anxieties, nay, the copious and perpetual tears of one man, your excellent brother Gaius Marcellus, plead for your pardon: I come next him both in anxiety and sorrow, but in actual prayers am somewhat slow, because I have not the right of *entrée* to Cæsar, being myself in need of intercession. We have only the influence which the conquered have, yet in counsel and zeal we are not wanting to Marcellus. By your other relations my help is not asked. I am prepared for anything.

—E. S. SHUCKBURGH.

SUBMITTING TO NECESSITY

CICERO

[From *Letters to Friends*, Book IV]

Although Cicero reiterates complaints about the humiliating condition in which he and his colleagues find themselves, still he is capable of rising to the higher levels of the good loser.

To M. Claudius Marcellus:

Though it is only a very few days ago that I gave Quintus Mucius a letter for you written at considerable length, in which I set forth in what state of mind I thought you ought to be, and what I thought you ought to do, yet, since your freedman Theophilus was starting, of whose fidelity and affection to you I had satisfied myself, I was unwilling that he should reach you without a letter from me. On the same considerations, then, as I did in my previous letter, I again and again exhort you, to make up your mind to become a resident member of the Republic, whatever its nature may be, at the earliest possible time. You will perhaps see many things disagreeable to your feelings, but not more after all than you daily hear. Moreover, you are not the man to be affected by the sense of sight alone, and to be less afflicted when you learn the same things by the ear, which indeed are usually even magnified by imagination. But—you object—you will yourself be obliged to say something you do not feel, or to do something you do not approve. To begin with, to yield to circumstances, that is to submit to necessity, has ever been held the part of a wise man: in the next place, things are not—as matters now stand at least—quite so bad as that. You may not be able, perhaps, to say what you think: you may certainly hold your tongue. For authority of every kind has been committed to one man. He consults nobody but himself, not even his friends. There would not have been much difference if he whom we followed were master of the Republic. Can we think that the man who in a time of war, when we were all united in the same danger, consulted only himself and a certain clique of wholly incompetent persons, was likely to be more communicative in the hour of victory, than he had been when the result was still uncertain? And do you think that a man who in your consulship would never be guided by your consummate wisdom, nor, when your brother was administering the consulship under your inspiration, ever condescended to consult you two, would now, if he were in sole power, be likely to want suggestions from us?

Everything in civil war is wretched; of which our ancestors never even once had experience, while our generation has now had it repeatedly: but nothing, after all, is more wretched than victory itself, which, even if it fall to the better men, yet renders them more savage and ruthless, so that, even if they are not such by nature, they are compelled to become so by the necessity of the case. For a conqueror is forced, at the beck of those who won him his victory, to do many things even against his inclination. Were you not wont to foresee simultaneously with myself how bloody that victory was likely to be? Well, would you at that time also have absented yourself from your country for fear of seeing what you disapproved? "No," you will say, "for then I should have been in possession of wealth and my proper position." Ah, but it had been consistent with a virtue such as yours to regard your personal interests as among the most insignificant concerns, and to be more profoundly affected by those of the state. Again, what is to be the end of your present policy? For up to now your conduct is approved, and, as far as such a business admits of it, your good fortune also is commended: your conduct, because, while you engaged in the first part of the war under compulsion, you shewed your wisdom by refusing to follow it to the bitter end: your good fortune, because by an honourable retirement you have maintained both the dignity and the reputation of your character. Now, however, it is not right that you should feel any place more to your taste than your native land; nor ought you to love it less because it has lost some of its comeliness,

but rather to pity it, and not deprive it of the light of your countenance also, when already bereft of many illustrious sons. Finally, if it was the sign of high spirit not to be a supplicant to the victor, is it not perhaps a sign of pride to spurn his kindness? If it was the act of a wise man to absent himself from his country, is it not perhaps a proof of insensibility not to regret her? And, if you are debarred from enjoying a public station, is it not perhaps folly to refuse to enjoy a private one? The crowning argument is this: even if your present mode of life is more convenient, you must yet reflect whether it is not less safe. The sword owns no law: but in foreign lands there is even less scruple as to committing a crime. I am personally so anxious for your safety, that in this respect I take rank with your brother Marcellus, or at any rate come next to him. It is your business to take measures for your own interests, civil rights, life, and property.

—E. S. SHUCKBURGH.

CÆSAR AND THE LOYALISTS

CICERO

[From *Letters to Friends,* Book VI]

A more generous characterization would hardly be expected even from a follower of Cæsar. The fact that Cicero is urging his friends to adopt a policy of acceptance of the circumstances does not take away from the sincerity of his estimate of Cæsar.

To Aulus Cæcina:

I am afraid you may think me remiss in my attentions to you, which, in view of our close union resulting from many mutual services and kindred tastes, ought never to be lacking. In spite of that I fear you do find me wanting in the matter of writing. The fact is, I would have sent you a letter long ago and on frequent occasions, had I not, from expecting day after day to have some better news for you, wished to fill my letter with congratulations rather than with exhortations to courage. As it is, I shall shortly, I hope, have to congratulate you; and so I put off that subject for a letter to another time. But in this letter I think that your courage—which I am told and hope is not at all shaken—ought to be repeatedly braced by the authority of a man, who, if not the wisest in the world, is yet the most devoted to you: and that not with such words as I should use to console one utterly crushed and bereft of all hope of restoration, but as to one of whose rehabilitation I have no more doubt than I remember you had of mine. For when those men had driven me from the Republic, who thought that it could not fall while I was on my feet, I remember hearing from many visitors from Asia, in which country you then were, that you were emphatic as to my glorious and rapid restoration. If that system, so to speak, of Tuscan augury which you had inherited from your noble and excellent father did not deceive you, neither will our power of divination deceive me; which I have acquired from the writings and maxims of the greatest savants, and, as you know, by a very diligent study of their teaching, as well as by an extensive experience in managing public business, and from the great vicissitudes of fortune which I have encountered. And this divination I am the more inclined to trust, from the fact that it never once deceived me in the late troubles, in spite of their obscurity and confusion. I would have told you what events I foretold, were I not afraid to be thought to be making up a story after the event. Yet, after all, I have numberless witnesses to the fact that I warned Pompey not to form a union with Cæsar, and afterwards not to sever it. By this union I saw that the power of the senate would be broken, by its severance a civil war provoked. And yet I was very intimate with Cæsar,

and had a very great regard for Pompey, but my advice was at once loyal to Pompey and to the best interests of both alike. My other predictions I pass over; for I would not have Cæsar think that I gave Pompey advice, by which, if he had followed it, Cæsar himself would have now been a man of illustrious character in the state indeed, and the first man in it, but yet not in possession of the great power he now wields. I gave it as my opinion that he should go to Spain; and if he had done so, there would have been no civil war at all. That Cæsar should be allowed to stand for the consulship in his absence I did not so much contend to be constitutional, as that, since the law had been passed by the people at the instance of Pompey himself when consul, it should be done. The pretext for hostilities was given. What advice or remonstrance did I omit, when urging that any peace, even the most inequitable, should be preferred to the most righteous war? My advice was overruled, not so much by Pompey—for he was affected by it—as by those who, relying on him as a military leader, thought that a victory in that war would be highly conducive to their private interests and personal ambitions. The war was begun without my taking any active part in it; it was forcibly removed from Italy, while I remained there as long as I could. But honour had greater weight with me than fear: I had scruples about failing to support Pompey's safety, when on a certain occasion he had not failed to support mine. Accordingly, overpowered by a feeling of duty, or by what the loyalists would say, or by a regard for my honour—whichever you please—like Amphiaraus in the play, I went deliberately, and fully aware of what I was doing, "to ruin full displayed before my eyes." In this war there was not a single disaster that I did not foretell. Therefore, since after the manner of augurs and astrologers, I too, as a state augur, have by my previous predictions established the credit of my prophetic power and knowledge of divination in your eyes, my prediction will justly claim to be believed. Well, then, the prophecy I now give you does not rest on the flight of a bird nor the note of a bird of good omen on the left—according to the system of our augural college—nor from the normal and audible pattering of the corn of the sacred chickens. I have other signs to note; and if they are not more infallible than those, yet after all they are less obscure or misleading. Now omens as to the future are observed by me in what I may call a twofold method: the one I deduce from Cæsar himself, the other from the nature and complexion of the political situation. Cæsar's characteristics are these: a disposition naturally placable and clement—as delineated in your brilliant book of "Grievances"—and a great liking also for superior talent, such as your own. Besides this, he is relenting at the expressed wishes of a large number of your friends, which are well-grounded and inspired by affection, not hollow and self-seeking. Under this head the unanimous feeling of Etruria will have great influence on him.

Why, then,—you must ask—have these things as yet had no effect? Why, because he thinks if he grants you yours, he cannot resist the applications of numerous petitioners with whom to all appearances he has juster grounds for anger. "What hope, then," you will say, "from an angry man?" Why, he knows very well that he will draw deep draughts of praise from the same fountain, from which he has been already—though sparingly—bespattered. Lastly, he is a man very acute and farseeing: he knows very well that a man like you—far and away the greatest noble in an important district of Italy, and in the state at large the equal of any of your generation, however eminent, whether in ability or popularity or reputation among the Roman people

—cannot much longer be debarred from taking part in public affairs. He will be unwilling that you should, as you would sooner or later, have time to thank for this rather than his favour.

So much for Cæsar. Now I will speak of the nature of the actual situation. There is no one so bitterly opposed to the cause, which Pompey undertook with better intentions than provisions, as to venture to call us bad citizens or dishonest men. On this head I am always struck with astonishment at Cæsar's sobriety, fairness, and wisdom. He never speaks of Pompey except in the most respectful terms. "But," you will say, "in regard to him as a public man his actions have often been bitter enough." Those were acts of war and victory, not of Cæsar. But see with what open arms he has received us! Cassius he has made his legate; Brutus governor of Gaul; Sulpicius of Greece; Marcellus, with whom he was more angry than with anyone, he has restored with the utmost consideration for his rank. To what, then, does all this tend? The nature of things and of the political situation will not suffer, nor will any constitutional theory—whether it remains as it is or is changed—permit, first, that the civil and personal position of all should not be alike when the merits of their case are the same; and, secondly, that good men and good citizens of unblemished character should not return to a state, into which so many have returned after having been condemned of atrocious crimes.

That is my prediction. If I had felt any doubt about it I would not have employed it in preference to a consolation which would have easily enabled me to support a man of spirit. It is this. If you had taken up arms for the Republic —for so you then thought—with the full assurance of victory, you would not deserve special commendation. But if, in view of the uncertainty attaching to all wars, you had taken into consideration the possibility of our being beaten, you ought not, while fully prepared to face success, to be yet utterly unable to endure failure. I would have urged also what a consolation the consciousness of your action, what a delightful distraction in adversity, literature ought to be. I would have recalled to your mind the signal disasters not only of men of old times, but of those of our own day also, whether they were your leaders or your comrades. I would even have named many cases of illustrous foreigners: for the recollection of what I may call a common law and of the conditions of human existence softens grief. I would also have explained the nature of our life here in Rome, how bewildering the disorder, how universal the chaos: for it must needs cause less regret to be absent from a state in disruption, than from one well-ordered. But there is no occasion for anything of this sort. I shall soon see you, as I hope, or rather as I clearly perceive, in enjoyment of your civil rights. Meanwhile, to you in your absence, as also to your son who is here—the express image of your soul and person, and a man of unsurpassable firmness and excellence—I have long ere this both promised and tendered practically my zeal, duty, exertions, and labours: all the more so now that Cæsar daily receives me with more open arms, while his intimate friends distinguish me above everyone. Any influence or favour I may gain with him I will employ in your service. Be sure, for your part, to support yourself not only with courage, but also with the brightest hopes.

—E. S. Shuckburgh.

Freedom of Speech

Aulus Cæcina

[From Cicero's *Letters to Friends*, Book VI]

Aulus Cæcina was an author contemporary with Cicero and one of the latter's correspondents.

The transition from Republic to Monarchy inevitably brought up questions of individual freedom. Such restraints as existed came about more through fear than through any formal measures on the part of Cæsar.

To M. Tullius Cicero:

For my book not having been delivered to you so quickly, forgive my timidity, and pity my position. My son, I am told, was very much alarmed at the book being put in circulation, and with reason —since it does not matter so much in what spirit it was written, as in what spirit it is taken—for fear lest a stupid thing like that should stand in my light, and that too when I am still suffering for the sins of my pen. In that matter my fate has been a strange one: for whereas a slip of the pen is cured by erasure, and stupidity is punished by loss of reputation, my mistake is corrected by exile: though my greatest crime is having spoken ill of the enemy when engaged in active service. There was no one on our side, I presume, who did not pray for victory for himself; no one who, even when offering sacrifice for something else, did not breathe a wish for Cæsar's speedy defeat. If he imagines that not to be the case, he is a very fortunate man. If he does know it, and has no delusion on the subject, why be angry with a man who has written something against his views, when he has pardoned all those who offered every sort of petition to the gods against his safety?

But to return to my subject, the cause of my fear was this. I have written about you, on my honour, sparingly and timidly, not merely checking myself, but almost beating a retreat. Now everyone knows that this style of writing ought not merely to be free, but even vehement and lofty. One is thought to have a free hand in attacking another, yet you must take care not to fall into mere violence: it is not open to one to praise oneself, lest the result should be the vice of egotism: there is no other course than to praise the man, on whom any blame that you may cast is necessarily set down to weakness or jealousy. And I rather think that you will take it all the better, and think it more suited to your present position. For what I could not do in good style, it was in my power first of all not to touch upon, and, as next best, to do so as sparingly as possible. But after all I did check myself: I softened many phrases, cut out many, and a very large number I did not write down at all. Then, as in a ladder, if you were to remove some rounds, cut out others, leave some loosely fastened, you would be contriving the means of a fall, not preparing a way of ascent, just so with a writer's genius: if it is at once hampered and frustrated by so many disadvantages, what can it produce worth listening to or likely to satisfy? When, indeed, I come to mention Cæsar himself, I tremble in every limb, not from fear of his punishing, but of his criticising me. For I do not know Cæsar thoroughly. What do you think of a courage that talks thus to itself? "He will approve of this: that expression is open to suspicion." "What if I change it to this? But I fear that will be worse." Well, suppose I am praising some one: "Shan't I offend him?" Or when I am criticising some one adversely: "What if it is against his wish?" "He punishes the pen of a man engaged in a campaign: what will he do to that of a man conquered and not yet restored?"

You yourself add to my alarm, because in your Orator you shield yourself under the name of Brutus, and try to make him a party to your apology. When the universal "patron" does this, what ought I to do—an old client of yours, and now everyone's client? Amidst such misgivings therefore created by fear, and on the rack of such blind suspicion, when most of what one writes has to be adapted to what one imagines are the feelings of another, not to one's own judgment, I feel how difficult it is to come off successfully, though you have not found the same difficulty, because your supreme and surpassing genius has armed you for every eventuality. Nevertheless, I told my son to read the book to you, and then take it away, or only to give it to you on condition that you would promise to correct it, that is, if you would give it a totally new complexion.

About my journey to Asia, though the necessity for my making it was very urgent, I have obeyed your commands. Why should I urge you to exert yourself for me? You are fully aware that the time has come when my case must be decided. There is no occasion, my dear Cicero, for you to wait for my son. He is a young man: he cannot from his warmth of feeling, or his youth, or his timidity, think of all necessary measures. The whole business must rest on you: in you is all my hope. Your acuteness enables you to hit upon the measures which Cæsar likes, and which win his favour. Everything must originate with you, and be brought to the desired conclusion by you. You have great influence with Cæsar himself, very great with all his friends. If you will convince yourself of this one thing, that your duty is not merely to do what you are asked—though that is a great and important thing—but that the whole burden rests on you, you will carry it through: unless—which I don't believe—my misfortunes make me too inconsiderate, or my friendship too bold, in placing this burden upon you. But your lifelong habits suggest an excuse for both: for from your habit of exerting yourself for your friends, your intimates have come not so much to hope for that favour at your hands, as to demand it as a right. As for my book, which my son will give you, I beg that you will not let it out of your hands, or that you will so correct it as to prevent it doing me any harm.

—E. S. SHUCKBURGH.

AFTER THE IDES OF MARCH

CÆSAR LIVES ON

CICERO

[From *Letters to Atticus*, Book XIV]

Cicero has occasion to revise an earlier thought that the death of an undesirable citizen will cure the ills of the state.

To T. Pomponius Atticus:

Can it be true? Is this all that our noble Brutus has accomplished—that he should have to live at Lanuvium, and Trebonius should have to slink to his province by by-roads? That all the acts, memoranda, words, promises, and projects of Cæsar should have more validity than if he were still alive? Do you remember that on that very first day of the retreat upon the Capitol I exclaimed that the senate should be summoned into the Capitoline temple? Good heavens, what might have been effected then, when all loyalists—even semi-loyalists—were exultant, and the brigands utterly dismayed! You lay the blame on the Liberalia. What was possible at the time? Our case had long been hopeless. Do you remember that you explained that it was all over with us, if he were allowed a funeral? But he was even burnt in the forum, and a funeral oration was pronounced over him in moving terms, and a number of slaves and starvelings instigated to attack our houses with firebrands. What next! They even have the impudence to say: "You utter a word against the will of Cæsar?" These and other things like them I cannot endure, and accordingly I am thinking of wandering away "from land to land." Your land, however, is too much in the eye of the wind.

Is your sickness quite gone by this time? I rather judged so from the tone of your letter.

I return to the case of the veterans—your Tebassi, Scævae, and Frangones. Do you suppose these men feel any confidence in retaining their grants so long as our party have any footing in the state? They have found it possessed of more resolution than they expected. They, I presume, are devoted to the cause of public tranquillity rather than supporters of robbery! But when I wrote to you about Curtilius and the estate of Sextilius, I must be understood to have included Censorinus, Messalla, Plancus, Postumus, and the whole lot. It had been better to have risked destruction—which would never have befallen us—when Cæsar was killed, rather than to have lived to see this sort of thing.

Octavius arrived at Naples on the 18th of April. There Balbus called on him early next day, and on the same day came to see me at Cumæ, with the information that he intended to accept the inheritance, but that, as you say, there will be a fine scrimmage with Antony. Your business about Buthrotum is receiving, as it is bound to do, and will continue to receive my attention. You ask me whether Cluvius's legacy is reaching one hundred sestertia yet. It seems to be approaching that. At least I made eighty the first year.

My brother Quintus writes to me with heavy complaints of his son, chiefly because he is now taking his mother's part, whereas in old times when she was kind to him he was on bad terms with her. He sent me a very hot letter against him. If you know what the young man is doing, and have not yet left Rome, I wish you would write me word, and, by Hercules, on any other matter besides. I find great pleasure in your letters.

—E. S. SHUCKBURGH.

THE SEVENTH PHILIPPIC

CICERO

There come times when a lifelong advocate of peace must resort to war. It was no doubt a bitter blow for Cicero to be forced at the very end of his political career to abandon a policy for which he had always contended so vigorously. The speech is one of a number directed against Mark Antony who, after the death of Julius Cæsar, was attempting to put himself in control of the state. The name Philippic is applied to the whole group of speeches in imitation of Demosthenes' speeches against Philip of Macedon.

We are consulted to-day about matters of small importance, but still perhaps necessary, O conscript fathers. The consul submits a motion to us about the Appian road, and about the coinage; the tribune of the people one about the Luperci. And although it seems too easy to settle such matters as those, still my mind cannot fix itself on such subjects, being anxious about more important matters. For our affairs, O conscript fathers, are come to a crisis, and are in a state of almost extreme danger. It is not without reason that I have always feared, and never approved of that sending of ambassadors. And what their return is to bring us I know not; but who is there who does not see with how much languor the expectation of it affects our minds? For those men put no restraint on themselves who grieve that the senate has revived so as to entertain hopes of its former authority, and that the Roman people is united to this our order; that all Italy is animated by one common feeling; that armies are prepared, and generals ready for the armies; even already they are inventing replies for Antonius, and defending them. Some pretend that his demand is that all the armies be disbanded. I suppose then we sent ambassadors to him, not that he should submit and obey this our body, but that he should offer us conditions, impose laws upon us, order us to open Italy to foreign nations; especially while we were to leave him in safety from whom there is more danger to be feared than from any nation whatever. Others say that he is willing to give up the nearer Gaul to us, and that he will be satisfied with the further Gaul. Very kind of him! in order that from thence he may endeavour to bring not merely legions, but even nations against this city. Others say that he makes no demands now but such as are quite moderate. Macedonia he calls absolutely his own, since it was from thence that his brother Caius was recalled. But what province is there in which that firebrand may not kindle a conflagration? Therefore these same men, like provident citizens and diligent senators, say that I have sounded the charge, and they undertake the advocacy of peace. Is not this the way in which they argue? "Antonius ought not to have been irritated; he is a reckless and a bold man; there are many bad men besides him." (No doubt, and they may begin and count themselves first). And they warn us to be on our guard against them. Which conduct then is it which shows the more prudent caution; chastising wicked citizens when one is able to do so, or fearing them?

And these men speak in this way, who on account of their trifling disposition used to be considered friends of the people. From which it may be understood that they in their hearts have at all times been disinclined to a good constitution of the state, and they were not friends of the people from inclination. For how comes it to pass that those men who were anxious to gratify the people in evil things, now, on an occasion which above all others concerns the people's interests, because the same thing would also be salutary for the republic, now prefer being wicked to being friends of the people? This noble cause of which I am the advocate has made me popular, a man who (as you know) have always opposed the rashness of the people. And those men are called, or rather they call themselves, consulars; though no man is worthy of that name except those who can support so high an honour. Will you favour an enemy? Will you let him send you letters about his hopes of success? Will you be glad to produce them? to read them? Will you even give them to wicked citizens to take copies of? Will you thus raise their courage? Will you thus damp the hopes and valour of the good? And then will you think yourself a consular, or a senator, or even a citizen? Caius Pansa, a most fearless and virtuous consul, will take what I say in good part. For I will speak with a disposition most friendly to him; but I should not consider him himself a consul, though a man with whom I am most intimate, unless he was such a consul as to devote all his vigilance, and care, and thoughts to the safety of the republic.

Although long acquaintance, and habit, and a fellowship and resemblance in the most honourable pursuits, have bound us together from his first entrance into life; and his incredible diligence, proved at the time of the most formidable dangers of the civil war, showed that he was a favourer not only of my safety, but also of my dignity; still, as I said before, if he were not such a consul as I have described, I should venture to deny that he was a consul at all. But now I call him not only a consul, but the most excellent and virtuous consul within my recollection; not but that there have been others of equal virtue and equal inclination, but still they have not had an equal opportunity of displaying that virtue and inclination. But the opportunity of a time of most formidable change has been afforded to his magnanimity, and dignity, and wisdom. And that is the time when the consulship is displayed at the greatest advantage, when it governs the republic during a time which, if not desirable, is at all events critical and momentous. And a more critical time than the present, O conscript fathers, never was.

Therefore I, who have been at all times an adviser of peace, and who, though all good men always considered peace, and especially internal peace, desirable, have desired it more than all of them;—for the whole of the career of my industry has been passed in the forum and in the senate-house, and in warding off dangers from my friends; it is by this course that I have arrived at the highest honours, to moderate wealth, and at any dignity which we may be thought to have: I therefore, a nursling of peace, as I may call myself, I who, whatever I am, (for I arrogate nothing to myself), should undoubtedly not have been such without internal peace: I am speaking in peril: I shudder to think how you will receive it, O conscript fathers; but still, out of regard for my unceasing desire to support and increase your dignity, I beg and entreat you, O conscript fathers, although it may be a bitter thing to hear, or an incredible thing that it should be said by Marcus Cicero, still to receive at first, without offence, what I am going to say, and not to reject it before I have fully explained what it is;—I, who, I will say so over and over again, have always been a panegyrist, have always been an adviser of peace, do not wish to have peace with Marcus Antonius. I approach the rest of my speech with great hope, O conscript fathers, since I have now passed by that perilous point amid your silence.

Why then do I not wish for peace? Because it would be shameful; because it would be dangerous; because it cannot possibly be real. And while I explain these three points to you, I beg of you, O conscript fathers, to listen to my words with the same kindness which you usually show to me.

What is more shameful than inconsistency, fickleness, and levity, both to individuals, and to the entire senate? Moreover, what can be more inconsistent than on a sudden to be willing to be united in peace with a man whom you have lately adjudged to be an enemy, not by words, but by actions and by many formal decrees? Unless, indeed, when you were decreeing honours to Caius Cæsar, well-deserved indeed by and fairly due to him, but still unprecedented and never to be forgotten, for one single reason,—because he had levied an army against Marcus Antonius,—you were not judging Marcus Antonius to be an enemy; and unless Antonius was not pronounced an enemy by you, when the veteran soldiers were praised by your authority, for having followed Cæsar; and unless you did not declare Antonius an enemy when you promised exemptions and money and lands to those brave legions, because they had deserted him who was consul while he was an enemy.

What? when you distinguished with the highest praises Brutus, a man born under some omen, as it were, of his race and name, for the deliverance of the republic, and his army, which was waging war against Antonius on behalf of the liberty of the Roman people, and the most loyal and admirable province of Gaul, did you not then pronounce Antonius an enemy? What? when you decreed that the consuls, one or both of them, should go to the war, what war was there if Antonius was not an enemy? Why then was it that most gallant man, my own colleague and intimate friend, Aulus Hirtius the consul, has set out? And in what delicate health he is; how wasted away! But the weak state of his body could not repress the vigour of his mind. He thought it fair, I suppose, to expose to danger in defence of the Roman people that life which had been pre-

served to him by their prayers. What? when you ordered levies of troops to be made throughout all Italy, when you suspended all exemptions from service, was he not by those steps declared to be an enemy? You see manufactories of arms in the city; soldiers, sword in hand, are following the consul; they are in appearance a guard to the consul, but in fact and reality to us; all men are giving in their names, not only without any shirking, but with the greatest eagerness; they are acting in obedience to your authority. Has not Antonius been declared an enemy by such acts?

"Oh, but we have sent ambassadors to him." Alas, wretched that I am! why am I compelled to find fault with the senate whom I have always praised? Why? Do you think, O conscript fathers, that you have induced the Roman people to approve of the sending ambassadors? Do you not perceive, do you not hear, that the adoption of my opinion is demanded by them? that opinion which you, in a full house, agreed to the day before, though the day after you allowed yourselves to be brought down to a groundless hope of peace. Moreover, how shameful it is for the legions to send out ambassadors to the senate, and the senate to Antonius! Although that is not an embassy; it is a denunciation that destruction is prepared for him if he do not submit to this order. What is the difference? At all events, men's opinions are unfavourable to the measure; for all men see that ambassadors have been sent, but it is not all who are acquainted with the terms of your decree.

You must, therefore, preserve your consistency, your wisdom, your firmness, your perseverance. You must go back to the old-fashioned severity, if at least the authority of the senate is anxious to establish its credit, its honour, its renown, and its dignity, things which this order has been too long deprived of. But there was some time ago some excuse for it, as being oppressed; a miserable excuse indeed, but still a fair one; now there is none. We appeared to have been delivered from kingly tyranny; and afterwards we were oppressed much more severely by domestic enemies. We did indeed turn their arms aside; we must now wrest them from their hands. And if we cannot do so (I will say what it becomes one who is both a senator and a Roman to say), let us die. For how just will be the shame, how great will be the disgrace, how great the infamy to the republic, if Marcus Antonius can deliver his opinion in this assembly from the consular bench. For, to say nothing of the countless acts of wickedness committed by him while consul in the city, during which time he has squandered a vast amount of public money, restored exiles without any law, sold our revenue to all sorts of people, removed provinces from the empire of the Roman people, given men kingdoms for bribes, imposed laws on the city by violence, besieged the senate, and, at other times, excluded it from the senate-house by force of arms;—to say nothing, I say, of all this, do you not consider this, that he who has attacked Mutina, a most powerful colony of the Roman people—who has besieged a general of the Roman people, who is consul elect—who has laid waste the lands,—do you not consider, I say, how shameful and iniquitous a thing it would be for that man to be received into this order, by which he has been so repeatedly pronounced an enemy for these very reasons?

I have said enough of the shamefulness of such a proceeding; I will now speak next, as I proposed, of the danger of it; which, although it is not so important to avoid as shame, still offends the minds of the greater part of mankind even more.

Will it then be possible for you to rely on the certainty of any peace, when you see Antonius, or rather the Antonii, in the city? Unless, indeed, you despise Lucius; I do not despise even Caius. But, as I think, Lucius will be the dominant spirit,—for he is the patron of the five-and-thirty tribes, whose votes he took away by his law, by which he divided the magistracies in conjunction with Caius Cæsar. He is the patron of the centuries of the Roman knights, which also he thought fit to deprive of the suffrages; he is the patron of the men who have been military tribunes; he is the patron of the middle of Janus. O ye gods! who will be able to support this man's power? especially when he has brought all his dependents into the lands. Whoever was the patron of all the tribes? and of the Roman knights? and of the military tribunes? Do you think that the power of even the Gracchi was greater than that of this gladiator will be? whom I have called gladiator, not in the sense in which sometimes Marcus Antonius too is called gladiator, but as men call him who are speaking plain Latin. He has fought in Asia as a mirmillo. After having equipped his own companion and intimate friend in the armour of a Thracian, he slew the miserable man as he was flying; but he himself received a palpable wound, as the scar proves.

What will the man who murdered his friend in this way, when he has an opportunity, do to an enemy? And if he did such a thing as this for the fun of the thing, what do you think he will do when tempted by the hope of plunder? Will he not again meet wicked men in the decuries? will he not again tamper with those men who have received lands? will he not again seek those who have been banished? will he not, in short, be Marcus Antonius; to whom, on the occasion of every commotion, there will be a rush of all the profligate citizens? Even if there be no one else except those who are with him now, and these who in this body now openly speak in his favour, will they be too small in number? Especially when all the protection which we might have had from good men is lost, and when those men are prepared to obey his nod? But I am afraid, if at this time we fail to adopt wise counsels, that that party will in a short time appear too numerous for us. Nor have I any dislike to peace; only I do dread war disguised under the name of peace. Wherefore, if we wish to enjoy peace we must first wage war. If we shrink from war, peace we shall never have.

But it becomes your prudence, O conscript fathers, to provide as far forward as possible for posterity. That is the object for which we were placed in this garrison, and as it were, on this watch-tower; that by our vigilance and foresight we might keep the Roman people free from fear. It would be a shameful thing, especially in so clear a case as this, for it to be notorious that wisdom was wanting to the chief council of the world. We have such consuls, there is such eagerness on the part of the Roman people, we have such an unanimous feeling of all Italy in our favour, such generals, and such armies, that the republic cannot possibly suffer any disaster without the senate being in fault. I, for my part, will not be wanting. I will warn you, I will forewarn you, I will give you notice, I will call gods and men to witness what I do really believe. Nor will I display my good faith alone, which perhaps may seem to be enough, but which in a chief citizen is not enough; I will exert all my care, and prudence, and vigilance.

I have spoken about the danger. I will now proceed to prove to you that it is not possible for peace to be firmly cemented; for of the propositions which I promised to establish this is the last. What peace can there be between Marcus Antonius and (in the first place) the senate? with what face will he be able to look upon you, and with what eyes will you, in turn, look upon him?

Which of you does not hate him? which of you does not he hate? Come, are you the only people who hate him, and whom he hates? What? what do you think of those men who are besieging Mutina, who are levying troops in Gaul, who are threatening your fortunes? will they ever be friends to you, or you to them? Will he embrace the Roman knights? For, suppose their inclinations respecting, and their opinions of Antonius were very much concealed, when they stood in crowds on the steps of the temple of Concord, when they stimulated you to endeavour to recover your liberty, when they demanded arms, the robe of war, and war, and who, with the Roman people, invited me to meet in the assembly of the people, will these men ever become friends to Antonius? will Antonius ever maintain peace with them? For why should I speak of the whole Roman people? which, in a full and crowded forum, twice, with one heart and one voice, summoned me into the assembly, and plainly showed their excessive eagerness for the recovery of their liberty. So, desirable as it was before to have the Roman people for our comrade, we now have it for our leader.

What hope then is there that there can ever be peace between the Roman people and the men who are besieging Mutina and attacking a general and army of the Roman people? Will there be peace with the municipal towns, whose great zeal is shown by the decrees which they pass, by the soldiers whom they furnish, by the sums which they promise, so that in each town there is such a spirit as leaves no one room to wish for a senate of the Roman people? The men of Firmium deserve to be praised by a resolution of our order, who set the first example of promising money; we ought to return a complimentary answer to the Marrucani, who have passed a vote that all who evade military service are to be branded with infamy. These measures are adopted all over Italy. There is great peace between Antonius and these men, and between them and him! What greater discord can there possibly be? And in discord civil peace cannot by any possibility exist. To say nothing of the mob, look at Lucius Nasidius, a Roman knight, a man of the very highest accomplishments and honour, a citizen always eminent, whose watchfulness and exertions for the protection of my life I felt in my consulship; who not only exhorted his neighbours to become soldiers, but also assisted them from his own resources; will it be possible ever to reconcile Antonius to such a man as this, a man whom we ought to praise by a formal resolution of the senate? What? will it be possible to reconcile him to Caius Cæsar, who prevented him from entering the city, or to Decimus Brutus, who has refused him entrance into Gaul? Moreover, will he reconcile himself to, or look mercifully on the province of Gaul, by which he has been excluded and rejected? You will see everything, O conscript fathers, if you do not take care, full of hatred and full of discord, from which civil wars arise. Do not then desire that which is impossible: and beware, I entreat you by the immortal gods, O conscript fathers, that out of hope of present peace you do not lose perpetual peace.

Now what is the object of this oration? For we do not yet know what the ambassadors have done. But still we ought to be awake, erect, prepared, armed in our minds, so as not to be deceived by any civil or supplicatory language, or by any pretence of justice. He must have complied with all the prohibitions and all the commands which we have sent him, before he can demand anything. He must have desisted from attacking Brutus and his army, and from plundering the cities and lands of the province of Gaul; he must have permitted the ambassadors to go to Brutus, and led his army back on this side of the Rubicon,

and yet not come within two hundred miles of this city. He must have submitted himself to the power of the senate and of the Roman people. If he does this, then we shall have an opportunity of deliberating without any decision being forced upon us either way. If he does not obey the senate, then it will not be the senate that declares war against him, but he who will have declared it against the senate.

But I warn you, O conscript fathers, the liberty of the Roman people, which is entrusted to you, is at stake. The life and fortune of every virtuous man is at stake, against which Antonius has long been directing his insatiable covetousness, united to his savage cruelty. Your authority is at stake, which you will wholly lose if you do not maintain it now. Beware how you let that foul and deadly beast escape now that you have got him confined in chains. You too, Pansa, I warn, (although you do not need counsel, for you have plenty of wisdom yourself; but still, even the most skillful pilots receive often warnings from the passengers in terrible storms) not to allow this vast and noble preparation which you have made to fall away to nothing. You have such an opportunity as no one ever had. It is in your power so to avail yourself of this wise firmness of the senate, of this zeal of the equestrian order, of this ardor of the Roman people, as to release the Roman people from fear and danger forever. As to the matters to which your motion before the senate refers, I agree with Publius Servilius.

—C. D. Yonge.

Cicero's Policy

BRUTUS

[From Cicero's *Letters to Brutus*]

Marcus Junius Brutus was born about 79 and died in 42 B.C., when commander, wich Cassius, of the forces of the Republic which fought unsuccessfully at Philippi against Antony and Octavius Cæsar. Brutus was the friend and murderer of Cæsar, "the noblest Roman of them all," to whom Cicero dedicated a number of his treatises.

It is evident, if the following letter by Brutus is representative of the opinion of the day, that Cicero's contemporaries realized his limitations as a statesman while they admired his motives and purposes as a patriot.

To T. Pomponius Atticus:

You say in your letter that Cicero wonders at my never making any remark about his political actions. Since you ask me, under compulsion from you I will set down my sentiments. I know that Cicero does everything with the best intentions—for what could be clearer to me than his devotion to the Republic? But he, the acutest of men, appears to me in certain things to have acted with a want of—shall I call it tact or disinterestednesss?—in spite of the fact that he has not scrupled to incur the enmity of Antony at the height of his power on behalf of the Republic. I don't know what to set down on paper for you except the one thing: that the boy's ambition and unscrupulousness have been rather provoked than repressed by Cicero; and that he carries this indulgence to such a pitch that he does not abstain from abusive remarks—remarks which recoil upon himself with double force, because he put more than a single person to death, and ought rather to confess himself a murderer than to taunt Casca as he does, and because he imitates in Casca's case the conduct of Bestia. Pray, because we are not always bragging of the Ides of March, as he always has his Nones of December on his lips, is Cicero in any better position for vilifying a most glorious deed than Bestia and Clodius were for their habitual attacks upon his consulship? Our friend Cicero boasts to me that he has, though a civilian, successfully faced the war of Antony. What good is that to me, if as a price for crushing Antony succession into Antony's position is demanded, and if the avenger of that evil comes forward as the supporter of another destined to have a deeper foundation and to strike deeper roots, unless we prevent it? Granted that his present policy proceeds from fear—shall we say of tyranny, or of a tyrant, or of Antony? Well, but I feel no gratitude to one who, to avoid being the slave of a bad-tempered master, does not deprecate slavery itself—nay, rather proposes to give him a triumph and pay for his men, and by all manner of decrees instigates him not to shrink from coveting the high position of the man whose name he has adopted. Is this worthy of a consular or of a Cicero? Since I have not been allowed to be silent, you will have to read what must necessarily give you annoyance, for I am conscious myself of the pain with which I have written this to you; nor am I ignorant what your sentiments as to the situation are, and how desperate also you think the possibility of its cure. Nor, by heaven, do I blame you, Atticus. For your age, your habits, and your children make you unenterprising—a fact which I gathered also from our friend Flavius. But I return to Cicero. What is the difference between Salvidienus and him? What greater honour could he have proposed in the senate? "Cicero is afraid," you will say, "even now of the remnant of the civil war." Does anyone then, while fearing a war nearly concluded, think that neither the tyrannical power of the victorious army's commander nor the rashness of the boy is at all alarming? Or is his motive for this very action the idea that now, owing to the greatness of his power, every kind of honour must be spontaneously offered to him? How strange is the blindness of fear! While taking precautions against what you dread, actually to invite danger and to bring it upon you, though you might perhaps have avoided it altogether! We are over-fearful of death, exile, and poverty: I think that these things are the worst of evils in Cicero's eyes, and that while he has people from whom to get what he wants, and by whom to be made much of and flattered, he has no aversion to servitude, if it be but tempered by a show of respect—if there can be any respect in what is the last and most wretched degradation. Therefore, though Octavius call Cicero "father," consult him in everything, praise and thank him, nevertheless the truth will come out that words do not agree with deeds. For what can be more contrary to common sense than to regard a man as a father, who is not even reckoned as free? For my part, I set no store by these accomplishments with which I know Cicero to be better furnished than anyone else: for what good to him are the speeches on behalf of his country's liberty, the essays on dignity, death, exile, poverty, which he has composed with the utmost wealth of language? What a much truer view Philippus seems to have of those things, when he refused all compliments to his own stepson, than Cicero has, who pays them to one who has no connexion with him! Let him cease then from absolutely insulting our misfortunes by his boastful language; for what does it profit us that Antony has been conquered, if the only result of his defeat is to leave his place open to another? However, even now there is a note of uncertainty in your letter. Long live Cicero—as he

may well do—to cringe and serve! if he is not ashamed to think of his age nor his honour, nor his great past. For myself, at any rate, there is no condition of servitude, however favourable, which will deter me from waging war on the principle: that is, on royalty, unconstitutional magistracies, absolutism, and power that aims at being above the laws. Though Antony may be a good man, as you say in your letter—which, however, has never been my opinion—yet the law of our ancestors was that no one, not even a father, should be an absolute master. Unless I had been as deeply attached to you as Cicero believes that Octavius is devoted to him, I should not have written this to you. I am grieved to think that as you read this you are getting angry—for you are most affectionate to all your friends, and especially to Cicero: but assure yourself of this, that my personal good-will to Cicero is in no way modified, though my opinion is largely so, for you cannot ask a man to judge except from what seems to him to be truth in each case.

I could have wished that you had mentioned in your letter what arrangements were being made for the betrothal of our dear Attica: I might have said something to you of what I felt about the matter. I am not surprised that you are anxious about Porcia's health. Lastly, I will gladly do what you ask, for my sisters ask me the same, and I know the man and his views.

—E. S. SHUCKBURGH.

IV. LITERATURE AND PHILOSOPHY

When we turn from the political problems in which the Romans of the Ciceronian era were so deeply absorbed, we find a rather limited range of interests.

It was characteristic of the Romans always to look upon literature not so much as a thing to be cultivated for itself, or as an expression of private and personal life, but rather as an art useful in the promotion of practical affairs. Above all it was to be employed in the service of the state. This was true even of the Augustan Age, when there was no longer need or opportunity for the discussion of politics, but it was particularly true of the disturbed times that witnessed the downfall of the Republic.

Yet, even then there were a few who found other values in literature. Cicero himself devoted much of his time to the study and writing of philosophy, and understood, as no one before him had understood, the values of oratory and of poetry. Lucretius, through his didactic poem on the Epicurean system, gave a new impetus to the study of things having no immediate bearing of a practical nature but of vital concern to man in the more general problem of living. There sprang up also at this time a new school of poets who dared to experiment with lyrical forms of both the classical Greek period and the more recent Alexandrian, and who deemed their own personal experiences fit subjects for poetic expression. What they accomplished in philosophy and in poetry, though small in amount, was of a very high quality, and laid the foundations for the later work of the Augustans. It carried forward the Greek tradition and opened up new possibilities hitherto but vaguely sensed.

APOLOGY FOR PHILOSOPHY [1]

CICERO

[From the *Offices,* Book II]

Although my books have aroused in not a few men the desire not only to read but to write, yet I sometimes fear that what we term philosophy is distasteful to certain worthy gentlemen, and that they wonder that I devote so much time and attention to it.

Now, as long as the state was administered by the men to whose care she had

[1] From the Loeb Classical Library, by permission.

voluntarily entrusted herself, I devoted all my effort and thought to her. But when everything passed under the absolute control of a despot and there was no longer any room for statesmanship or authority of mine; and finally when I had lost the friends who had been associated with me in the task of serving the interests of the state, and who were men of the highest standing, I did not resign myself to grief, by which I should have been overwhelmed, had I not struggled against it; neither, on the other hand, did I surrender myself to a life of sensual pleasure unbecoming to a philosopher.

I would that the government had stood fast in the position it had begun to assume and had not fallen into the hands of men who desired not so much to reform as to abolish the constitution. For then, in the first place, I should now be devoting my energies more to public speaking than to writing, as I used to do when the republic stood; and in the second place, I should be committing to written form not these present essays but my public speeches, as I often formerly did. But when the republic, to which all my care and thought and effort used to be devoted, was no more, then, of course, my voice was silenced in the forum and in the senate. And since my mind could not be wholly idle, I thought, as I had been well-read along these lines of thought from my early youth, that the most honourable way for me to forget my sorrows would be by turning to philosophy. As a young man, I had devoted a great deal of time to philosophy as a discipline; but after I began to fill the high offices of state and devoted myself heart and soul to the public service, there was only so much time for philosophical studies as was left over from the claims of my friends and of the state; all of this was spent in reading; I had no leisure for writing.

Therefore, amid all the present most

awful calamities I yet flatter myself that I have won this good out of evil—that I may commit to written form matters not at all familiar to our countrymen but still very much worth their knowing. For what, in the name of heaven is more to be desired than wisdom? What is more to be prized? What is better for a man, what more worthy of his nature? Those who seek after it are called philosophers; and philosophy is nothing else, if one will translate the word into our idiom, than "the love of wisdom." Wisdom, moreover, as the word has been defined by the philosophers of old, is "the knowledge of things human and divine and of the causes by which those things are controlled." And if the man lives who would belittle the study of philosophy, I quite fail to see what in the world he would see fit to praise. For if we are looking for mental enjoyment and relaxation, what pleasure can be compared with the pursuits of those who are always studying out something that will tend toward and effectively promote a good and happy life? Or, if regard is had for strength of character and virtue, then this is the method by which we can attain to those qualities, or there is none at all. And to say that there is no "method" for securing the highest blessings, when none even of the least important concerns is without its method, is the language of people who talk without due reflection and who blunder in matters of the utmost importance. Furthermore, if there is really a way to learn virtue, where shall one look for it, when one has turned aside from this field of learning?

Now, when I am advocating the study of philosophy, I usually discuss this subject at greater length, as I have done in another of my books. For the present I meant only to explain why, deprived of the tasks of public service, I have devoted myself to this particular pursuit.

—WALTER MILLER.

[From the *Tusculan Disputations*,[1] Book V]

O Philosophy, thou conductor of life! thou discoverer of virtue, and expeller of vices; what had not only I myself been, but the whole life of man without you? To you we owe the origin of cities; you called together the dispersed race of men into social life; you united them together, first, by placing them near one another, then by marriages, and lastly, by the communication of speech and languages. To you we owe the invention of laws; you instructed us in morals and discipline. To you I fly for assistance; and as I formerly submitted to you in a great degree, so now I surrender up myself entirely to you. For one day well spent, and agreeably to your precepts, is preferable to an eternity of sin. Whose assistance then can be of more service to me than yours, which has bestowed on us tranquillity of life, and removed the fear of death? But philosophy is so far from being praised, as she hath deserved of man, that she is wholly neglected by most, and ill spoken of by many. Can any speak ill of the parent of life, and dare to pollute himself thus with parricide! and be so impiously ungrateful as to accuse her, whom he ought to reverence, had he been less acquainted with her? But this error, I imagine, and this darkness, has spread itself over the minds of ignorant men, from their not being able to look so far back, and from their not imagining that those by whom human life was first improved, were philosophers: for though we see philosophy to have been of long standing, yet the name must be acknowledged to be but modern.

But indeed, who can dispute the antiquity of philosophy, either in fact or name? which acquired this excellent name from the ancients, by the knowledge of the origin and causes of everything, both divine and human. Thus those seven *Sophoi*, as they were held and called by

[1] Reprinted from *Greek and Latin Classics*, by permission of Parke, Austin and Lipscomb.

the Greeks, and wise men by us: and thus Lycurgus many ages before, in whose time, before the building of this city, Homer is said to have been, as well as Ulysses and Nestor in the heroic ages, were all reported really to have been, as they were called, wise men; nor would it have been said, that Atlas supported the heavens, or that Prometheus was bound to Caucasus, nor would Cepheus, with his wife, his son-in-law, and his daughter, have been enrolled among the constellations, but that their more than human knowledge of the heavenly bodies had transferred their names into an erroneous fable. From whence, all who were exercised in the contemplation of nature, were held to be, as well as called, wise men: and that name of theirs continued to the age of Pythagoras, who is reported to have gone to Phlius, as we find it in Ponticus Heraclides, a very learned man, and a hearer of Plato's, and to have discoursed very learnedly and copiously on certain subjects, with Leon, prince of the Phliasii. Leon, admiring his ingenuity and eloquence, asked him what art he particularly professed; his answer was, that he was acquainted with no art, but that he was a philosopher. Leon, surprised at the novelty of the name, enquired what he meant by the name of philosopher, and in what they differed from other men: on which Pythagoras replied, "That the life of men seemed to him to resemble those games, which were kept with the greatest entertainment of sports, and the general concourse of all Greece. For as there were some, whose pursuit was glory, and the honour of a crown, for the performance of bodily exercises; so others were induced by the gain of buying and selling, and mere lucrative motives: but there was likewise one sort of them, and they by far the best, whose aim was neither applause, nor profit, but who came merely as spectators through curiosity, to remark what was done, and to see in what manner things were carried on there. Thus we come from another life and nature, unto this, as it were out of another city, to some much frequented mart: some slaves to glory, others to money: that there are some few, who, taking no account of any thing else, earnestly look into the nature of things: that these call themselves studious of wisdom, that is, philosophers; and as there it is more reputable to be a looker on, without making any acquisition, so in life, the contemplating on things, and acquainting yourself with them, greatly exceeds every other pursuit of life."

Nor was Pythagoras the inventor only of the name, but he enlarged also the thing itself, and, when he came into Italy after this conversation at Phlius, adorned that Greece, which is called Great Greece, both privately and publicly, with the most excellent institutions and arts; of whose discipline perhaps, I shall find another opportunity to speak. But numbers and motions, the beginning and end of things, were the subject of the ancient philosophy down to Socrates, who was a hearer of Archelaus, the disciple of Anaxagoras. These made diligent enquiry into the magnitude of the stars, their distances, courses, and all that relates to the heavens. But Socrates was the first who brought down philosophy from the heavens, placed it in cities, introduced it into families, and obliged it to examine into life and morals, good and evil. Whose several methods of disputing, together with the variety of his topics, and the greatness of his abilities, being immortalized by the memory and writings of Plato, gave rise to many sects of philosophers of different sentiments: of all which I have principally adhered to that, which, in my opinion, Socrates himself followed; to conceal my own opinion, clear others from their errors, and to discover what has the most probability in every question.

—W. H. MAIN.

PRAYER FOR PEACE

LUCRETIUS

[From Book I]

The life of the poet-philosopher Titus Lucretius Carus (about 96 to 55 B.C.) is clothed in mystery. Only legends of love potions, of madness, and of suicide have come down to us. His undertaking to write a poem on the materialistic philosophy of Epicurus was fraught with many almost insuperable difficulties, but such was his passion for his subject and the nobility of his purpose that he achieved abundant success. He is one of the very few Romans who were genuinely interested in philosophy and is an outstanding example of the peculiar Roman genius for didactic poetry. *On the Nature of Things* was his only product.

The poem opens with the following passage. Although the poem as a whole denies an intimate relation between gods and men, still so strong is epic convention that Lucretius is forced to begin with an invocation that contradicts his beliefs.

Parent of Rome! sweet Venus! source of love!
Delight of mortals and the Blest above!
Who gladst the earth, the sea, all things that lie
Beneath yon gliding spheres that beam on high;
From thee all pleasure, beauty, being, flows,
Life springs to light, and pregnant nature glows.
Thee, Goddess! thee the winds and tempests fly,
Clouds at thy presence quit the brightening sky;
The teeming Earth exerts her genial powers,
In fair profusion spreads her sweetest flowers;
The smiling seas in gentle waves appear,
And glory gilds the tranquil atmosphere.
When youthful Spring salutes the cheerful vales,
And soft Favonius wakes his balmy gales,
Pierced by thy flame, gay birds in every bower
Feel thy approach, and hail thy sacred power;
Exulting herds o'er laughing verdure play,
Rush through the rapid streams, and boundless stray.
Rapt into bliss by thy inspiring charms,
Thy sweet allurements, and thy soft alarms,
All beings burn thy pleasure to fulfil,
And wait, enraptured, on thy heavenly will.
Through seas and streams thy kindly power prevails,
O'erspreads the mountains and pervades the dales,
The bowery mansions of melodious birds,
And open pastures of rejoicing herds;
Darts through each kindling breast love's melting rage,
And all things renovates from age to age.
  Thee, whom all nature's joyous works obey,
Whose smiles from chaos called primæval day;
Thee, in whose absence every lustre dies,
All beauty vanishes and pleasure flies;—
Thee I invoke: possess me while I sing:
To Memmius' ear eternal truths I bring.
Memmius, sweet Goddess! whom thou deignst to grace
With all endowments to adorn his race;
For him, kind Deity! inspire my tongue,
Immortal beauty pour into my song.
Meanwhile, by sea, by land, bid discord cease,
And bless the world with everlasting peace.
Thou, thou alone canst peace bestow; for Mars,
Armipotent, sole arbiter of wars,
Bound by the eternal wound of love, reclines
On thy fair breast, and all his soul resigns;
With fondly-eager looks admiring lies,
And drinks celestial transport at his eyes;

Pants o'er those charms which every wish
    employ,
Tastes thy ambrosial lip, and sinks in joy.
Oh, fairest Goddess! while thy heavenly
    arms
Infold the Immortal whom thy beauty
    warms,
In melting words thy soft persuasion pour,
And peace, sweet peace, for mighty Rome
    implore!

—THOMAS BUSBY.

THE BONDAGE OF RELIGION

LUCRETIUS

[From Book I]

It was the poet's announced purpose to
devote all his powers to freeing men from
their superstitions, their fear of the gods,
and their terror of death. He was much
more interested in this application of the
theory of Epicurus than in the theory
itself.

Too long to bondage Reason was con-
    signed,
Chained by Religion, tyrant of the mind:
From heaven itself she showed her baleful
    head,
With aspect horrible and menace dread,
Frowned on mankind: but a bold Grecian
    rose,
To face her terrors, and her reign oppose.
Nor Gods could awe, nor their immortal
    fame,
Nor Jove's dread thunder, nor his forky
    flame,
In vain his purpose heavenly wrath re-
    proves,
His dauntless soul no sacred murmur
    moves.
By Nature's bounds he scorns to be con-
    fined,
And calls forth all his energy of mind;
His vivid power awakes! and soaring
    flies
Beyond the flaming portals of the skies;

In might of thought the vast expanse
    surveys,
Returns triumphant, and no man displays
What beings *may*, what being *ne'er* shall
    rise,
And where their power's eternal limit
    lies.
Hence stern Religion, our dismay before,
By him subjected, and our plague no
    more,
Humbled in turn, beneath our feet is
    driven,
And his brave victory equals us to
    heaven.
    But ah! I tremble, lest you still sup-
    pose
From Reason's elements seduction flows.
Yet at Religion, and her ruthless deeds,
What soul but shudders, and what heart
    but bleeds?
Behold fair Iphigenia's cruel doom!—
By the first chiefs of Greece, in youth-
    ful bloom,
To Death she's led! what tears of pity
    flowed,
While Dian's altar streamed with guilt-
    less blood!
The attending nymphs the holy crown
    prepare,
The sacred fillet binds her virgin hair,
Before the shrine her sire in sorrow
    stands,
The thirsty poignard lurks in priestly
    hands,
The mournful citizens are bathed in
    tears,
In silent agony the fair appears;
Now, humbly kneeling, pleads with
    streaming eyes,
And now, with piteous voice, for mercy
    cries:
That first the king a father's name she
    gave,
In vain she pleads; nor prayers, nor
    tears, can save.
Lo! from her palace and her friends she's
    torn,
Strait to the sanguine altar sanguine
    borne;

Not as when blissful Hymen wakes his
   rites
Of mutual vows and solemnized delights,
But in the roseate hour of nuptial prime
A victim falls to bigotry and crime:
A parent's hands his suppliant child de-
   stroy,
Her life the purchase of a wind for Troy.
Such mighty evils holy phrenzy brings!
Such direful outrage from religion
   springs!
   But thou, o'er whom religious fear
     prevails,
Who tremblest at the poet's fictious tales,
Dar'st thou from priestly manacles be
   free?
Dar'st thou, my Memmius, wisdom learn
   from me?
Oh! what could I invent! what idle
   themes
Of superstition, still amused with dreams,
To blast thy fortunes, rob thee of delight,
Distract thy reason, and thy soul
   affright!
And well deserved; since would man-
   kind but dare
To see in death the oblivion of their care,
In vain the baffled priests might strive
   to awe,
Their threats our laughter, and our rea-
   son law.
But now no nerve, no faculty, remains
To shake religion, and vile terror reigns:
That curse by knaves for our subjection
   given,
The terror of the eternal wrath of heaven.
       —THOMAS BUSBY.

FROM WISDOM'S CITADEL

LUCRETIUS

[From Book II]

   The idea of the false estimate of the
value of power, fame, and wealth as means
of attaining happiness is a commonplace of
Roman literature.

When the wide ocean maddening
   whirlwinds sweep,
And heave the billows of the boiling deep,
Pleased we from land the reeling bark
   survey,
And rolling mountains of the watery way.
Not that we joy another's woes to see,
But to reflect that we ourselves are free.
So the dread battle ranged in distant
   fields,
Ourselves secure, a secret pleasure yields.
But what more charming than to gain the
   height
Of true philosophy? what pure delight,
From Wisdom's citadel to view, below,
Deluded mortals, as they wandering go
In quest of happiness! ah, blindly weak!
For fame, for vain nobility they seek;
Labour for heapy treasures, night and
   day,
And pant for power and magisterial sway.
   Oh, wretched mortals, souls devoid of
     light,
Lost in the shades of intellectual night!
This transient life they miserably spend,
Strangers to Nature, and to Nature's end:
Nor see all human wants in these com-
   bined;—
A healthful body and a peaceful mind.
   But little our corporeal part requires,
To soothe our pains, and feed our just
   desires.
From simplest sources purest pleasure
   flows,
And Nature asks but pleasure and re-
   pose.
What though no sculptured boys of
   burnished gold
Around thy hall the flaming torches hold,
Gilding the midnight banquet with their
   rays,
While goblets sparkle, and while lustres
   blaze;
What though thy mansion with no silver
   shine,
Nor gold emblazon with its rich design;
No fretted arch, no painted dome, re-
   bound

The rapturous voice, and harps exulting
    sound;
Yet see the swains their gliding moments
    pass
In sweet indulgence on the tender grass,
Near some smooth limpid lapse of mur-
    muring stream,
Whose bordering oaks exclude the noon-
    tide beam.
Chiefly when Spring leads on the smiling
    hours,
And strews the brightened meads with
    opening flowers,
In grateful shades, soft seats of peace and
    health,
Calmly they lie, nor dream of needless
    wealth.
When in embroidery clad, you sumptuous
    lie
On couches blushing with the Tyrian dye,
Say, will the raging fever sooner cease
Than if you pressed the peasant's humble
    fleece?
From grandeur, then, since small the
    good that flows,
Nor noble thoughts, nor glory, wealth
    bestows,
Nor to the body true delight affords,—
What real blessings yield the shining
    hoards?
If when you see, in well-dissembled war,
Your active legions, stretching wide and
    far;
Your daring navies struggling for the day,
Or bearing to the distant seas away;—
If from these scenes religious terror fled,
Death you despised, and superstition
    dread,
'Twere well: But here if idle fears
    remain;
If mid the sound of clashing arms, they
    reign;
Force into stately palaces their way;
On princes, ministers, and nobles, prey;—
If nor the golden sceptre, nor the pride
Of Tyrian purple, bid thy fears subside;
Doubtst thou a moment, that, pursuing
    these,

Blindly we fly from pleasure, peace, and
    ease?
 As infants, wandering in the shades of
    night,
From things innoxious shrink with sore
    affright,
So we, by day, imagined evils fear,
Haunted by idle dreams, and phantoms
    drear.
These clouds terrific, which the mind
    involve,
Not Phœbus' brightest splendours can
    dissolve:
In vain around his noontide beams may
    play,
Reason alone can chase the gloom awa
            —THOMAS BUSBY.

THE PROGRESS OF MAN

LUCRETIUS

[From Book V]

To Lucretius the progress of civilization
did not present itself as a mere succession
of events, but as an evolutionary process.
Man has come a long way on his journey
from crude beginnings, and is destined to
go forward to yet greater perfection. The
thought stands out in contrast with the
general gloom that pervades the poem as
a whole.

Huge the first race of men, their limbs
    well strung,
Hardy as hardy earth from which they
    sprung;
On strong and massy bones their struc-
    ture rose,
Firm as the firmest oak that towering
    grows:
Nor heat nor cold they felt, nor weakness
    knew,
Nor from voluptuous feasts diseases
    drew;
Through long-revolving years on nature
    thrived,
And, wildly bold, in savage freedom
    lived.

No sturdy husbandmen the land prepare,
Plant the young stocks, or guide the
    shining share:
For future crops the seed no sower
    throws,
Nor dresser clips the wild luxuriant
    boughs.
What earth spontaneous gave, and sun
    and showers,
Careless they took, and propt their
    nervid powers;
Their giant energies with acorns fed,
Wild summer-apples, indurate and red:
Such in our wintry orchards sparing hang;
But larger theirs, and more abundant,
    sprang.
Earth in her primal strength these things
    bestowed,
With rich fecundity her bosom glowed;
O'er her broad surface various plenty
    reigned;
Her voluntary gifts man's hapless race
    sustained.
    Thus by her fruits the human race was
    nursed;
And springs and rivers slaked their parch-
    ing thirst;
Called them, as now the fall from pouring
    heights
The thirst-afflicted savage tribes invites.
For nightly roofs to hollow caves they
    hied,
Or with their Gods in sylvan fanes reside;
Whence a sweet spring in silvery drops
    distils,
And rolls o'er polished stones its bubbling
    rills;
O'er polished stones, and mossy greens
    they flow,
Meandering through the fertile vales
    below.
    As yet, no fire their simple food pre-
    pared;
Nor spoils of beasts their hardened bodies
    shared:
Naked among the rocks and woods they
    ran,
And hollow mountains formed the abodes
    of man.

Shelter from winds and rains in groves
    they sought,
And nature's wants supplied as nature
    taught.
    No common good they felt, no laws
    ordained,
Nor public justice private wrong re-
    strained;
What power or fortune proffered, no one
    spared;
Each his own welfare sought, nor further
    cared.
    Then Venus' fire was all the lover's
    law,
And groves and woods the consumma-
    tion saw;
Or mutual flames inspired the burning
    pair;
Or manhood's force compelled the un-
    willing fair;
Or softening presents taught her heart
    to yield;
Berries or acorns, fresh from bower or
    field.
    Bold in their native vigour—men
    pursued,
With flying feet, the fierce and savage
    brood;
With missile weapons urged the hardy
    chase;
And stones and clubs subdued the brutal
    race.
Some they hunt down, some their swift
    staves o'ertake,
Others they fled, and sought the shelter-
    ing brake.
When night o'ertook them with her sable
    shades,
Like bristly boars they pressed the grassy
    glades,
In leaves enwrapt; nor mourned the ab-
    sent light,
Nor wandered through the darkness of
    the night;
But, in soft sleep dissolved, contented
    lay,
Till rosy dawn proclaimed expected day:
For observation from their childhood
    taught,

That day the night, and night the morn-
    ing, brought.
Hence, they ne'er dreaded an eternal
    night,
But woke to hail the sure return of light:
Yet feared lest prowling beasts, that shun
    the day,
Should fall destructive on their human
    prey:
Roused from their sleep, and filled with
    timely dread
Of boars and lions, from their haunts
    they fled;
Trembling, resigned the leafy couch to
    those
Whom nature framed for their relentless
    foes.
    Yet, fewer, then, the call of death
    obeyed,—
Left the sweet light of life for endless
    shade—
Than now; though, hapless, some were
    seized, o'erpowered,
Then, by their fierce and savage foes
    devoured:
These, as the brutes their reeking bowels
    rend,
See to a living grave their flesh descend;
Wake with their piercing screams the
    affrighted skies,
And fill the woods and mountains with
    their cries:
And those who fly, the cloud of fate
    surrounds;
Pressing with trembling hands their
    throbbing wounds,
Death they implore, till gnawing worms
    consume
Their putrid flesh, and consummate their
    doom:
For, then, no healing science blessed man-
    kind,
No skilful hand the gushing wound could
    bind.
But, then, fell war no thousands swept
    away,
Hurled to destruction in a single day:
In vain the raging ocean rolls and roars;

No ships were dashed upon the rocky
    shores:
Though calm again the sinking billows
    grew,
And all their awful violence withdrew,
Yet no smooth surface, no deceitful smile,
Could the fond, thoughtless mariner be-
    guile:
No dangerous art, then, traced the briny
    path,
No floating castles braved the ocean's
    wrath.
Grim Want o'er many urged his fatal
    power;
But now to ruin Plenty hurries more.
From noxious herbs some, thoughtless,
    drew their death;
Now studied poisons urge the fleeting
    breath.
    At length they bade the bough-built
    hut aspire,
And learned the luxury of skins and fire:
Then One to One in silken bondage held,
Raised man above the savage of the field;
Connubial love a purer bliss bestowed,
And with a chaste delight the bosom
    glowed;
While, pressing to the heart his smiling
    boy,
The ennobled father felt a father's joy.
Then, by indulgence softened, men no
    more
Braved the sharp cold, rude winds unin-
    jured bore;
Hymen their fierceness tamed, and fon-
    dling arts
Of darling children humanized their
    hearts.
Then neighbourhoods grew, and social
    compacts rose;
To reason waked, no more they lived as
    foes;
To women, children, kind protection
    yield;
The softer, weaker, from the stronger
    shield.
Though not yet all by order's voice were
    swayed,
The greater part the laws of faith obeyed:

Man the approach of peace and union hailed,
And universal war no more prevailed:
Or gradual ravage, with its wide embrace,
Had, long-ere this, suppressed the human race.
　　Dumb motion now no longer things proclaimed;
By nature taught, the tongue each object named;
As infants, ere they speak, by signs express
Their simple thoughts, and all their wants confess.
For its endowments every creature feels,
To its own arms for prompt defence appeals:
Calves fiercely butt before they shed their horns;
And kids, ere age their tender heads adorns;
And lion-whelps, and pards, and boars, would fain
Exert their fangs, ere scarce their fangs they gain;
And birds of every kind are wont to try
Their fluttering pinions ere they cleave the sky.
Hence, ne'er suppose that every creature's name,
Of every kind, from one inventor came;
Could one man only all his species teach?
Could one alone by name each creature call,
And no one else by names distinguish all?
Could This to all the powers of speech aspire,
And yet no Other, too, those powers acquire?
　　Again; if others yet no language knew,
Then, tell me whence their lingual talent grew.
If none could comprehend what one expressed,
By what rare art could one instruct the rest?
Nor one alone o'er all could domineer,
Knowledge compel, and civilize by fear:

With such no reasoning could support his claims,
And force on them his catalogue of names:
Nor would their wearied patience keep its bounds,
To hear his unintelligible .sounds.
　　And is it wonderful that men, supplied
With vocal organs, and in whom reside
The powers of intellect, should names devise
For objects constantly before their eyes?
Would they of things the various natures know,
Nor appellations on those things bestow;
Since e'en the mute creation signals find,
To speak the thoughts and feelings of their mind;
Their love, their joy, their sorrow, and their ire,
And all the passions which their breasts inspire?
　　When grim Molossian mastiffs are enraged,
And by no soothing art their wrath's assuaged;
When fierce they snarl, they grin, their fangs display,
From their deep throats gruff murmurs break their way,
Unlike the sounds that rend our startled ears,
When their loud, clamorous, voice the welkin tears.
But view them when, with soft, caressing, tongue,
Gently they lick their sprawling, playful, young;
Now feign to bite, now roll them o'er and o'er,
Now, fondly gaping, threaten to devour;
But cautiously their harmless teeth employ,
And in soft whinings tell their tender joy:
Not as when left at home, they howl and cry,
Or when with trembling fear they, crouching, eye

The uplifted whip, and whimper as they
    lie. . . .
  Since, then, these creatures' dull per-
    ceptions cause
Their different notes, how clear that na-
    ture's laws
Stronger must act on intellectual man!
That sounds have varied since the world
    began;
And human speech was part of nature's
    plan!
  Let thirst of knowledge still thy mind
    inspire:
Now sings the Muse the origin of fire.
Thunder this element to earth conveyed,
When loud it rattled, and its lightnings
    played;
On their red winds the ardent vapours
    came,
And wrapped whole groves and forests in
    their flame.
For, now we see the same effect arise,
When dart the flashing terrors of the
    skies:
Or, pressed by winds, the labouring
    branches meet,
Strike, chafe, and kindle to devouring
    heat;
From tree to tree it flies, from grove to
    grove;
Climb the broad flames, and fire the
    realms above.
From friction, hence, or lightning's rage,
    might spring
The igniting cause, and fierce combustion
    bring.
  From the sun's heat men first acquired
    the art
Their viands to prepare; his rays that
    dart,
Ripening the yellow corn; that flowers
    unfold,
Play on the fruits, and change their green
    to gold,
The use of fire revealed: the wiser few
The lesson caught, and by example drew
Their fellow-men; new habits were as-
    sumed,

And savoury meats the clouded air per-
    fumed.
  Then kings arose, fair cities then
    appeared,
Armies were formed, and citadels were
    reared;
Lands were divided, separate beeves
    assigned,
As merit claimed, of body or of mind.
But chief the powers of body held the
    sway,
And strength and beauty bore the palm
    away.
Then gold was found, and men for riches
    burn,
And strength and beauty yielded in their
    turn;
The shining ore prevailed o'er old and
    young,
And gold was stronger than the brave and
    strong.
But once did reason rectify the mind,
And chase the vain delusions of mankind;
The bliss of little with content and
    health—
This were their noblest boon, their truest
    wealth.
And say, this little who should fear to
    want?
To whom this little would not fortune
    grant?
But for renown and power we every day
See mortals fling the sweets of life away:
These to their wealth a lasting base will
    give,
Then in soft ease and pleasure they will
    live.
But vain their labours, and absurd as
    vain,
Since those who anxiously aspire to gain,
Nay, who secure, high honours and estate,
(The greatest mid the wealthy and the
    great,)
But journey haplessly;—for Envy arms
Her hand with thunder, and their soul
    alarms;
Aims at their glory her destroying blow,
Their fame extinguishes, and lays them
    low.

How happier then who peacefully obey,
Than those who struggle for imperial sway!
Who prostitute their anxious, wasted, life
In sordid efforts and ambitious strife;
Climb the steep, thorny, path, where perils wait,
And Envy urges with her deadly hate;
Arms with her bolts the candidates for power,
And most delights to see her flames devour
The highest.—These let pomp and pride excite,
And drive them struggling up the dangerous height;
Let Flattery's voice their eager ear beguile,
And stimulate their never ceasing toil.
This folly still behold,—this *ancient rage,—
It maddens ours, and will the latest age.
  Those monarchs slain, the glory of their throne,
And sparkling diadem, no longer shone.
The sceptre, emblem of their regal trust,
Stained with their blood, and trodden in the dust,
Mourns its lost honours; while the rabble raise
Loud clamours, where they lately shouted praise;
Base in their power, insult the mighty dead,
And triumph o'er whom living they would dread.
  Now to the mob the varying sway returned,
And vulgar breasts with wild ambition burned:
Fired by the thirst for power, for power they strain;
Empire's the dazzling prize, and all would reign.
Wearied with jarring interests, fierce disputes,
Where each man reasons, and where each refutes;

Tired of a state where all men all assailed,
Where equity nor polity prevailed;
Where the mad Many hold the Wise in awe,
And violence usurps the throne of law;
All the fell power of anarchy deplore,
And government and order would restore;
At length the sager few a code ordain;
And, future feuds, and contests, to restrain,
Rulers elect, and check Contention's reign.
Till then, revenge o'erpaid each private wrong,
And injured justice yielded to the strong.
But violence its authors but embroils,
And on themselves their villainy recoils.
Wretched the man who lives in lawless strife;
Who bursts the sacred bonds of social life:
Though Gods and men his cunning arts deceive,
In his own bosom fear and conscience live.
Hence, oft in slumber men their guilt betray;
Oft, when their fevered mind deliriums sway,
The plots discover long concealed by time,
And tell, in broken speech, the secret crime.
  To Memmius now, inspiring Muse! disclose
Whence of the Gods our first conceptions rose:
Whence altars towns adorned; whence solemn rites,
And sacred festivals, divine delights,
And smoking hecatombs whose fumes arise,
And roll in curling volumes to the skies:
Whence the sad terror that all earth pervades,
Temples erects, and plants the sacred shades.
Nor sure too high my ardent zeal aspires;

Obvious the course, nor keen research requires.
At first creation, forms divinely bright,—
Radiant in beauty,—burst upon the sight:
Men, e'en awake, the shadows wondering saw,
Glowed as they gazed, and felt a sacred awe:
But to their dreams still grander visions came;
Visions of brighter, more gigantic frame;
Whose active limbs astonishment excite,
Clothed in the glories of supernal might.
On these bright forms their fancy sense bestowed,
Language superb, and worthy of a God.
Eternal, too, the shining phantoms seem,
Since on the sight descends a constant stream
Of images:—and then what power can harm
Such mighty beings? What their fears alarm?
And those whom mortal terrors ne'er annoy,
Peaceful must live, and perfect bliss enjoy.   .
Then, too, their shadowy wonders they display;
With wondrous ease their limbs their will obey,
Nor ever dull fatigue or lassitude betray.
  In order, too, the rolling heavens appear,
And varied seasons of the circling year:
But still the source of motion was concealed;
The Primum Mobile was unrevealed.
Hence, men to Gods creation's frame assigned,
Themselves, and all things, to their will resigned.
  Where glide the shining orbs for ever bright,
For ever rolling in refulgent light,
There they established the celestial bowers,
There fixed the mansions of the heavenly Powers;

There, where the sun and moon their fires display,
The beam nocturnal, and the flame of day;
The stars serene that shed their mingled rays,
The flying lightnings and the meteor's blaze;
The hail, the rain, the dews that float on high,
The thunder's awful bolts that threatening fly,
And all the dread commotions of the sky.
  Oh, hapless mortals! blindly-pious race!
Why with such troublous rage the Gods disgrace?
To your own age what idle fears ye taught!
On us what needless woes those fears have brought!
And still what griefs, what evils, shall supply,
What floods of tears, to our posterity!
  Strange piety the crouching head to veil!
Fondly to stocks and stones to make appeal!
To every fane with spreading arms to fly,
Fall on the earth, and in dependence lie
Before the sacred shrines! with blood to stain
The sprinkled altars, and with praises vain,
And vows on vows, the heedless Gods obtest!
Calmly all things to view, be this confest
True piety. For, when the soul surveys
The grandeur heaven's illumined dome displays;
The blue expanse, with sparkling stars o'erspread,
And sun and moon that constant courses lead;
Then doubts, that other evils had supprest,
Cloud the sad mind, and agitate the breast;

Doubts whether Gods the potent sinews
claim
Yon orbs to wield, and heavens stupen-
dous frame.
To ignorance these evils mortals owe;
From doubts what terrors spring! What
ceaseless woe!
From ignorance we doubt Creation's
birth;
The wandering stars and stationary earth;
How long the heavens great Nature will
defend;
Whether their motion and their being
end;
Or if, unfading, by the Gods they're
framed,
By everlasting energies inflamed;
In endless orbits formed to roll sublime,
And triumph o'er the ravages of Time.
   Who calmly contemplates the Blest
Abodes?
What heart but faints with terror of the
Gods?
Whose limbs so nervid not to quake, when
roll
The pealing thunders, and from pole to
pole
Thick lightnings flash? What nations,
free from fear,
Eye the blue fires, the loud explosions
hear?
Proud tyrants tremble, fears their mem-
bers thrill,
Forms of avenging Gods their fancy fill;
Lest their foul crimes have armed the
Powers on high,
And the dread day of retribution's nigh.
And o'er the seas when winds and tem-
pests roar,
And heave the rolling mountains to the
shore,
The gallant Admiral with legions armed—
And mighty elephants — with soul
alarmed,
Falls he not prostrate to the Powers
above,
To soothe their anger, and their pity
move?
Praying the blest Immortals to be kind,

And make his peace with the reluctant
wind;
Grant to his squadron soft, propitious,
gales,
And gently swell the bosom of his sails?
In vain! No prayers his tossing legions
save;
Cold death awaits them, and the Stygian
wave.
Such the contempt some hidden Power
awards
To human greatness! Such its high
regards
For rods and axes (glories of a day!)
And all the ensigns of Imperial sway!
With scornful sport it treats the gaudy
things,
And on the proudly-great its reckless
vengeance flings!
And, then, when tremors seize this
earthly ball,
And death and ruin threat to swallow all,
Should we, while all are trembling, feel
surprise
If men, their weakness see, themselves
despise;
Give to the Gods omnipotence, and place
With them the government of being and
of Space?
   Now learn that Earth disclosed her
various ores,
Lead, iron, silver, brass, and golden
stores,
When to her hills fierce fires devouring
came,
And blazing forests fed the raging flame;
Whether from heaven the wasting fury
spring,
Borne on the lightning's coruscating
wing;
Or from fierce war the devastations flow,
And woods were fired to scare the dis-
tant foe;
Or men, resolved to enlarge the fruitful
soil,
Of their green pride the encumbered
wilds despoil;
Or dauntlessly their savage tenants prest,

And with their shaggy hides themselves invest;
(For, ere with nets and dogs they snared the prey,
With fire they drove them to the light of day;
Or, with insidious pits their feet betray;)
Whether from lurid heaven's ætherial flame,
Or from mankind, the wide destruction came;
Sprang the fierce fires from art, or nature's power,
That to their roots the crackling trees devour;
Spread unrestrained through wide-extended woods;
Melt the burnt earth, and boil the hissing floods;
Then from earth's smoking veins red metals flow
Through delving channels, gliding as they glow:
When they to hardness cool, and men behold
The argent silver, and the ruddy gold;
View the rich beauty of the shining ores,
Thrown to the day from nature's latent stores;
See them the figures of their beds assume;
By fire if molten, aptly they presume
That various forms the fluid ores would take,
And pointed instruments, or edged, might make;
To hew the woods, rough timbers smooth, or cleave,
And the rude block a shapely figure give.
Silver and gold for this they wrought, and strove
The rigid nerves of stubborn brass to move:
This served their views, but those in vain they try;
Too free they yield, the needful strength deny,
Bend at the forceful stroke, or shattered fly.
Hence, harder brass the higher value bore,

And triumphed o'er either ductile ore.
But now to Gold, lead, brass, and silver, yield,
And Gold usurps the honours of the field.
Thus changing Time bids power and grandeur fly,
Exalts the humble, sinks the Proudly-High.
What once was valued, now is trod to earth,
And meanest things assume the noblest worth;
Respect from All, and admiration, claim;
New glories wear, and grace the rolls of Fame.
  And now my Memmius will perceive the source
Whence the Rude Ages learned hard iron's force.
The earliest weapons hostile mortals tried,
Hands, teeth, and nails, and broken boughs supplied:
With chasing fire the foe they next assailed;
Then the tough brass, then iron's strength prevailed.
But brass, less stubborn, and more plenteous found,
Claimed the first use—with brazen shares the ground
At first was ploughed—with brazen arms the field
Of battle blazed—brass taught the foe to yield;
Brass bade the suffering weak the strong obey,
Seized on their lands, and bore their herds away.
Then hardier iron gradual use obtained,
And brass, contemned, no more triumphant reigned:
The fertile glebe endured the iron share,
And iron gleamed in instruments of war.
  To mount the war-horse heroes first aspired,
With the left hand to guide, the art acquired;
Full on the foe, with rushing force they sprung,

And with the dexter hand the javelin
    flung,
Ere with the flying car, and mettled pair,
They swept the field, and crushed the
    ranks of war.
   First with a Pair, then Double-Pair,
    they strove;
Fixed the keen, cleaving scythe, and
    slaughtering drove.
The Libyan elephants proud Carthage
    trained,
(Those living bulwarks that their power
    sustained)
With curved probosces, and incumbent
    towers,
Their monstrous members, and their
    mountain powers;
Patient to bear the wounds of war, and
    throw
Disorder wild among the frightened foe.
Thus maddening discord art with art
    combined,
To spread destruction, and to thin man-
    kind.
   Then furious bulls were ushered to the
    war,
And tusky boars the flying squadrons
    scare;
Rush on the fallen chieftains, while before
The furious Parthians raging lions roar,
Held by their armed keepers—these in
    vain
Their anger chide, and grasp the clank-
    ing chain.
Fired with the taste of blood, they rush
    on all;
On friends and foes with curbless fury
    fall,
Shake their dread manes, and every heart
    appal.
The trembling coursers scorn the useless
    rein,
Turn from the foe, and fly the embattled
    plain:
So fierce around the roaring lions flew!
So wide their spreading, savage fury
    threw!
Some in the rear, some in the front
    assault,

Now o'er the steeds, the horsemen now,
    they vault.
In vain the struggling chief for succour
    calls,
Griped in their dreadful fold, to earth
    he falls;
There prest he lies beneath their cruel
    fangs,
Sad victim of excruciating pangs!
The bulls or toss, or crush, the helpless
    boar,
The plunging coursers and their riders
    gore,
Dash to the earth whate'er their rage
    oppose,
And now their keepers rend, and now
    their foes.
So foes and friends the bears attack, and
    death
Inflict around them with their gory teeth;
Stain with their master's blood the un-
    broken darts,
(Those broken on themselves, the gore
    that starts
From their own gaping wounds, distains)
    and all
The steeds disorder, and the chiefs appal.
Though strive the horse their fury to
    escape,
And paw the yielding earth, and wheel,
    and leap,
Vain all their efforts! nerves and sinews
    yield
The spouting gore—they drop—and thun-
    der on the field.
Thus creatures whom domestic man had
    tamed,
The battle's loud, tumultuous, rage in-
    flamed:
Tortured with wounds, no more they own
    the rein,
But, wild as winds, fly snorting from
    the plain;
Nor can the horseman's art their frantic
    fear restrain.
So joy Lucanian oxen, driven to war,
Start at the tumult, and the phrenzy
    share.
New to the battle's terrors, furious grow,

And trample down their keepers, friend
　　and foe.
　　These are of war the earliest arts;—
　　but who
Can think the inventors ne'er the effects
　　foreknew,
So sure to follow;—all the ills that rise?
Dread catalogue of human miseries!
Safer, perchance, to say these things had
　　birth
In various worlds, and not alone on
　　earth:
Obtained throughout the Universal State,
Nor here, nor there, could claim their
　　earliest date.
But not alone for victory brutes were
　　brought
Against the foe; but leaders chiefly
　　sought
Vexatious combat—though, their num-
　　bers small,
And slightly skilled in arms, they saw
　　their certain fall.
　　Their vests the shaggy spoils of beasts
　　supplied,
And thorns, inserted, held the folding
　　hide:
For Reason tells no weaving arts had
　　birth
Till iron left the bosom of the earth:
Iron the chief, the grand material proved,
Iron the treadles, shuttles, spindles,
　　moved.
Had iron still been locked from human
　　sight,
Nor these, nor rattling beams, had sprung
　　to light.
But the first wheels and distaffs Men
　　employed,
Since more inventive powers their minds
　　enjoyed
Than those of women; more they claim
　　of arts,
And all that borrows mind, or mind im-
　　parts.
But the rough peasant mocked the slender
　　toil,
Called the male spinsters to the needy
　　soil:

In softer hands the nimble shuttles
　　played,
And the smooth treadles shapelier feet
　　obeyed.
Men to superior tasks their efforts
　　turned;
For nobler arts, and hardier labours
　　burned.
　　Creative Nature, (whence all things
　　began,)
To sow, to plant, engraft, instructed
　　man:
Berries and acorns, as they fell to earth,
Giving, in season, kindred shoots to birth,
Taught him to plant; and bid the cul-
　　tured field
With fruitage teem, and fair abundance
　　yield;
Taught him to graft the tender slips, and
　　raise,
In ordered rows, the sucklings' blooming
　　sprays.
　　Then rising art to rising plenty led;
Improving earth enriching labour fed:
Wild fruits, to ripeness swelled, and sweet
　　as fair,
With mellow juice repaid the peasant's
　　care.
The mountain woods a narrower bound
　　assumed,
And vallies waved with corn, with golden
　　produce bloomed.
Then, cultivated Earth no longer wild,
Her meadows, rivers, lakes, and moun-
　　tains smiled!
Corn-fields and vineyards waked to new
　　delight
The peasant's heart, and charmed his
　　gladdened sight!
Empurpled olives hill from dale divide,
And nurturing streams through verdant
　　pastures glide:
As now with varied beauty, all around
Smile our fair farms, where Nature's
　　stores abound;
Where with the grape's the apple's sweet-
　　ness vies,
And spreading trees with clustering fruit
　　age rise.

And with their liquid lays the birds
began
To teach the ear of imitative man;
Long ere with polished notes he cheered
the plains,
Or poured his extacies in measured
strains.
And, moved by gentle gales, their mur-
m'ring sound
The tuneful reeds, soft waving, whispered
round;
To wake the hollow reed, hence, man
acquired
The melting art, and all the soul inspired.
Then sounds he learned to breathe, like
those we hear
When the soft pipe salutes the enchanted
ear;
When to the nimble fingers it replies,
And with the blended voice in sweetness
vies;
That pipe that now delights the lawns
and groves,
Where'er the solitary shepherd roves,
And speaks the dulcet language of the
Loves.
    Thus all things by degrees their use
obtain,
And by progressive skill perfection gain.
Thus Music's charms rejoiced the vocal
plains,
And cheered the banquets of the labour-
ing swains;
Their simple feast with rustic rapture
crowned,
When, stretched at ease, they pressed
the flowery ground;
With hearts at rest, indulged the leisure
hour,
By some smooth stream; or, lulled in
shady bower,
Contented lay, with peace and rosy health,
Nor tasted care, nor dreamed of needless
wealth!
Chief when the Spring on gladdened Na-
ture smiles,
Pleasure the hours of rural ease beguiles:
When laughing vallies sport their flowery
pride,

With jests and jeers the frolic moments
glide:
The jocund gambol, and the rustic song,
And the loud laugh that stops the flippant
tongue;
The rosy wreaths each honoured head
that crown,
Or from the shoulders hang in clusters
down;
The vigourous leap, the freak, the bois-
terous mirth,
The antic dance that shook their Mother
Earth;
Successive sports that still their joy pro-
long,
And still relieved by many a trolling
song;
By many a tale that age hath still in
store,
And many a trick that ne'er was played
before;
And many a tune that many a joke
succeeds,
When runs the bending lip along the
whistling reeds;
These are the sweets the rural swains
enjoyed,
These the delights that many a night
employed:
That bade the simple, easy, heart be
blest,
And robbed the drowsy midnight of its
rest.
In sports like these our wanton youth
indulge,
To listening night their amourous
thoughts divulge;
In tutored steps lead up the measured
dance,
But ne'er beyond the joys of ruder life
advance.
    While the glad mind no higher good
conceives,
The present good delight and pleasure
gives:
But doth a more exalted bliss arise?
The joy that lived till then, that moment
dies.

Hence acorns that could once the taste invite,
In time the pampered palate learned to slight.
The downy couch supplants the leafy bed,
And glossy robes to shaggy skins succeed.
Yet the first man these savage spoils that wore,
Such envy raised, his earth-born fellows tore
Quick from his back the vest his courage gained,
And with his blood his shaggy honours stained;
Their murderous hands upon the victim laid;
And death the price of his invention paid.
  Then Hides, now Gold and Purple, men delight;
No more for those, but fierce for these they fight;
And, sure, more folly we betray than those
Whose naked limbs the shivering winter froze:
While without gold and purple, we, as well,
Might all the rigours of the winds repel:
Since simplest habits will protection yield,
And richest vestments but the body shield.
  How vain, then, all the troubles, cares, and strife,
That cheat weak mortals of the sweets of life!
No limits they assign to flattering wealth,
Nor know felicity is peace and health.
Ignorant of where the bounds of pleasure lie,
Into a sea of woes they anxious fly;
Evils unceasing court, and round the world
With maddening rage the flames of war are hurled.
  At length the Sun and Moon, that wakeful roll
Their radiant orbs around the steady pole;
That to the circling skies their light display,
To cheer the silent night, or give the day;
Taught watchful man that Order governs all,
And wheels the seasons round this central ball.
  Now for defence arose embattled towers,
To castles chiefs withdrew their marshalled powers;
Lands were divided, spacious seas explored,
And civic union swayed the guardian sword:
Extending concord state with state combined,
And held in welcome bondage humankind.
Then various arts appeared, then letters sprung,
Poets exploit divine in strains diviner sung:
But deeds of ages past were all unknown,
Or but by Reason's light obscurely shone.
Custom and slow Experience knowledge brought;
(Knowledge, with all the nobler blessings fraught;)
What life improves, or fosters Virtue's cause;
Fair Agriculture, Navigation, Laws,
Cities and Public Ways, rich Vestments, Arms,
Aspiring Temples, and the immortal charms
Of Painting, Sculpture, all that man refine;
Philosophy, and Poesy divine.
  Thus Time with gradual light the mind illumes;
Thus new-born energies the soul assumes;
From art to art the brightening radiance flies,
And to their full perfection all things rise.

—THOMAS BUSBY.

ON FRIENDSHIP [1]

CICERO

Friendship is a constantly recurring motive of classical literature and a favorite theme for philosophical discussion. Compared with Aristotle's treatment of the subject, Cicero seems to be content with mere generalizations; yet he succeeds in presenting what was regarded as the fundamental question—whether friendship springs from utility or from service. For Cicero, see above p. 95.

LÆLIUS. Therefore, for a discussion of everything possible to be said on the subject of friendship, I advise you to apply to those who profess that art; all that I can do is to urge you to put friendship before all things human; for nothing is so conformable to nature and nothing so adaptable to our fortunes whether they be favourable or adverse.

This, however, I do feel first of all—that friendship cannot exist except among good men; nor do I go into that too deeply, as is done by those who in discussing this point with more than usual accuracy, and it may be correctly, but with too little view to practical results, say that no one is good unless he is wise. We may grant that; but they understand wisdom to be a thing such as no mortal man has yet attained. I, however, am bound to look at things as they are in the experience of everyday life and not as they are in fancy or in hope. Never could I say that Gaius Fabricius, Manius Curius, and Tiberius Coruncanius, whom our ancestors adjudged to be wise, were wise by such a standard as that. Therefore, let the Sophists keep their unpopular and unintelligible word to themselves, granting only that the men just named were good men. They will not do it though; they will say that goodness can be predicated only of the "wise" man.

[1] From the Loeb Classical Library, by permission.

Let us then proceed "with our own dull wits," as the saying is. Those who so act and so live as to give proof of loyalty and uprightness, of fairness and generosity; who are free from all passion, caprice, and insolence, and have great strength of character—men like those just mentioned—such men let us consider good, as they were accounted good in life, and also entitled to be called by that term because, in as far as that is possible for man, they follow Nature, who is the best guide to good living.

For it seems clear to me that we were so created that between us all there exists a certain tie which strengthens with our proximity to each other. Therefore, fellow countrymen are preferred to foreigners and relatives to strangers, for with them Nature herself engenders friendship, but it is one that is lacking in constancy. For friendship excels relationship in this, that goodwill may be eliminated from relationship while from friendship it cannot; since, if you remove goodwill from friendship, the very name of friendship is gone; if you remove it from relationship, the name relationship still remains. Moreover, how great the power of friendship is may most clearly be recognized from the fact that, in comparison with the infinite ties uniting the human race and fashioned by Nature herself, this thing called friendship has been narrowed that the bonds of affection always unite two persons only, or, at most, a few.

For friendship is nothing else than an accord in all things, human and divine, conjoined with mutual goodwill and affection, and I am inclined to think that, with the exception of wisdom, no better thing has been given to man by the immortal gods. Some prefer riches, some good health, some power, some public honours, and many prefer sensual pleasures. This last is the highest aim of brutes; the others are fleeting and unstable things and dependent less upon human foresight than upon the fickleness of fortune.

Again, there are those who place the "chief good" in virtue and that is really a noble view; but this very virtue is the parent and preserver of friendship and without virtue friendship cannot exist at all. To proceed then, let us interpret the word "virtue" by the familiar usage of our everyday life and speech, and not in pompous phrase apply to it the precise standards which certain philosophers use; and let us include in the number of good men those who are so considered—men like Paulus, Cato, Gallus, Scipio, and Philus—who satisfy the ordinary standard of life; but let us pass by such men as are nowhere to be found at all.

Therefore, among men like those just mentioned, friendship offers advantages almost beyond my power to describe. In the first place, how can life be what Ennius calls "the life worth living," if it does not repose on the mutual goodwill of a friend? What is sweeter than to have someone with whom you may dare discuss anything as if you were communing with yourself? How could your enjoyment in times of prosperity be so great if you did not have someone whose joy in them would be equal to your own? Adversity would indeed be hard to bear, without him to whom the burden would be heavier even than to yourself. In short, all other objects of desire are each, for the most part, adapted to a single end —riches, for spending; influence, for honour; public office, for reputation; pleasures, for sensual enjoyment; and health, for freedom from pain and full use of the bodily functions; but friendship embraces innumerable ends; turn where you will it is ever at your side; no barrier shuts it out; it is never untimely and never in the way. Therefore, we do not use the proverbial "fire and water" on more occasions than we use friendship. I am not now speaking of the ordinary and commonplace friendship—delightful and profitable as it is—but of that pure and faultless kind, such as was that of

the few whose friendships are known to fame. For friendship adds a brighter radiance to prosperity and lessens the burden of adversity by dividing and sharing it.

Seeing that friendship includes very many and very great advantages, it undoubtedly excels all other things in this respect, that it projects the bright ray of hope into the future, and does not suffer the spirit to grow faint or to fall. Again, he who looks upon a true friend, looks, as it were, upon a sort of image of himself. Wherefore friends, though absent, are at hand; though in need, yet abound; though weak, are strong; and—harder saying still—though dead, are yet alive; so great is the esteem on the part of their friends, the tender recollection and the deep longing that still attends them. These things make the death of the departed seem fortunate and the life of the survivors worthy of praise. But if you should take the bond of goodwill out of the universe no house or city could stand, nor would even the tillage of the fields abide. If that statement is not clear, then you may understand how great is the power of friendship and of concord from a consideration of the results of enmity and disagreement. For what house is so strong, or what state so enduring that it cannot be utterly overthrown by animosities and division?

From this it may be judged how great good there is in friendship. It is said, at any rate, that a certain learned man of Agrigentum sang in inspired strain in Greek verse that in nature and the entire universe whatever things are at rest and whatever are in motion are united by friendship and scattered by discord. And indeed this is a statement which all men not only understand but also approve. Whenever, therefore, there comes to light some signal service in undergoing or sharing the dangers of a friend, who does not proclaim it with the loudest praise? What shouts recently rang through the entire theatre during the performance of the new play, written by my guest and friend, Marcus Pacuvius, at the scene where, the king being ignorant which of the two was Orestes, Pylades, who wished to be put to death instead of his friend, declared, "I am Orestes," while Orestes continued steadfastly to assert, as was the fact, "I am Orestes!" The people in the audience rose to their feet and cheered this incident in fiction; what, think we, would they have done had it occurred in real life? In this case Nature easily asserted her own power, inasmuch as men approved in another as well done that which they could not do themselves. . . .

The oftener, therefore, I reflect on friendship the more it seems to me that consideration should be given to the question, whether the longing for friendship is felt on account of weakness and want, so that by giving and receiving favours one may get from another and in turn repay what he is unable to procure of himself; or, although this mutual interchange is really inseparable from friendship, whether there is not another cause, older, more beautiful, and emanating more directly from Nature herself. For it is love (amor), from which the word "friendship" (amicitia) is derived, that leads to the establishing of goodwill. For while it is true that advantages are frequently obtained even from those who, under a pretence of friendship, are courted and honoured to suit the occasion; yet in friendship there is nothing false, nothing pretended; whatever there is is genuine and comes of its own accord. Wherefore it seems to me that friendship springs rather from nature than from need, and from an inclination of the soul joined with a feeling of love rather than from calculation of how much profit the friendship is likely to afford. What this feeling is may be perceived even in the case of certain animals, which, up to a certain time, so love their offspring and are so loved by them, that their impulses are

easily seen. But this is much more evident in man; first, from the affection existing between children and parents, which cannot be destroyed except by some execrable crime, and again from that kindred impulse of love, which arises when once we have met someone whose habits and character are congenial with our own; because in him we seem to behold, as it were, a sort of lamp of uprightness and virtue. For there is nothing more lovable than virtue, nothing that more allures us to affection, since on account of their virtue and uprightness we feel a sort of affection even for those whom we have never seen. Is there anyone who does not dwell with some kindly affection on the memory of Gaius Fabricius and Manius Curius, though he never saw them? On the other hand, is there anyone who does not hate Tarquin the Proud, Spurius Cassius, or Spurius Mælius? Against two leaders we had bitter struggles for the empire of Italy— Pyrrhus and Hannibal; for the former, because of his uprightness, we have no great enmity; for the latter, because of his cruelty, this State will always entertain hatred. . . .

Then listen, most worthy gentlemen, to the points very frequently mentioned between Scipio and me in our discussions of friendship. Now he, indeed, used to say that nothing was harder than for a friendship to continue to the very end of life; for it often happened either that the friendship ceased to be mutually advantageous, or the parties to it did not entertain the same political views; and that frequently, too, the dispositions of men were changed, sometimes by adversity and sometimes by the increasing burdens of age. And then he would draw an illustration of this principle from the analogy of early life. "For," said he, "the most ardent attachments of boyhood are often laid aside with the boyish dress; and if continued to the time of manhood, they are broken off, sometimes by rivalry in courtship or sometimes by a contest for some advantage, in which both of the parties to the friendship cannot be successful at the same time. But should the friendship continue for a longer time, yet it is often overthrown when a struggle for office happens to arise; for while, with the generality of men, the greatest bane of friendship is the lust for money, with the most worthy men it is the strife for preferment and glory, and from this source frequently have sprung the deadliest enmities between the dearest friends."

"Then, too, disagreements of a very serious nature, and usually justifiable, arise from a demand upon friends to do something that is wrong, as, for example, to become agents of vice or abettors in violence, and when the demand is refused, however honourable the refusal, it is nevertheless charged by those to whom the compliance was denied that the laws of friendship have been disregarded; besides, those who dare demand anything and everything of a friend, by that very demand profess a willingness to do anything whatever for the sake of a friend. By their ceaseless recriminations not only are social intimacies usually destroyed, but also everlasting enmities are produced. So many dangers of this kind," he would say, "hover like evil fates over friendships, that it seems to me to require both wisdom and good luck to escape them all."

Wherefore, let us first consider, if you please, how far love ought to go in friendship. Supposing Coriolanus to have had friends, were those friends in duty bound to bear arms with him against their country? Or ought the friends of Vecellinus, or of Mælius, to have supported them in their attempts to gain regal power? As to Tiberius Gracchus, when he began to stir up revolution against the Republic, we saw him utterly deserted by Quintus Tubero and by the friends of his own age. And yet Gaius Blossius of Cumæ, a protégé of your family, Scævola, came to

me to plead for leniency, because I was present as adviser to the consuls, Lænas and Rupilius, and offered, as a reason for my pardoning him, the fact that his esteem for Tiberius Gracchus was so great he thought it was his duty to do anything that Tiberius requested him to do. Thereupon I inquired, "Even if he requested you to set fire to the Capitol?" "He never would have requested me to do that, of course," said he, "but if he had I should have obeyed." You see what an impious remark that was! And, by heavens! he did all that he said he would do, or rather even more; for he did not follow, but he directed, the infatuation of Tiberius Gracchus, and he did not offer himself as the comrade in the latter's fury, but as the leader. And so, as a result of his madness, being in fear of the special court of inquiry, he fled into Asia, joined our enemies, and paid a heavy and righteous penalty for his crimes against the Republic.

Therefore it is no justification whatever of your sin to have sinned in behalf of a friend; for, since his belief in your virtue induced the friendship, it is hard for that friendship to remain if you have forsaken virtue. But if you should resolve that it is right, either to grant our friends whatever they wish, or get from them whatever we wish, then, assuming that we were endowed with truly faultless wisdom, no harm would result. . . .

Therefore let this be ordained as the first law of friendship: Ask of friends only what is honourable; do for friends only what is honourable and without even waiting to be asked; let zeal be ever present, but hesitation absent; dare to give true advice with all frankness; in friendship let the influence of friends who are wise counsellors be paramount, and let that influence be employed in advising, not only with frankness, but, if the occasion demands, even with sternness, and let the advice be followed when given. I say this because certain men who, I am informed, are considered sages in Greece, have approved certain views, which, in my opinion, are astonishing (but there is nothing that those men will not pursue with their subtleties). Some of these men teach that too much intimacy in friendships should be avoided, lest it be necessary for one man to be full of anxiety for many; that each one of us has business of his own, enough and to spare; that it is annoying to be too much involved in the affairs of other people; but it is best to hold the reins of friendship as loosely as possible, so that we may either draw them up or slacken them at will; for, they say, an essential of a happy life is freedom from care, and this the soul cannot enjoy if one man is, as it were, in travail for many.

Again, there are others, I am told, who, with even less of human feeling, maintain (and I briefly touched on this point just now) that friendships must be sought for the sake of the defence and aid they give and not out of goodwill and affection; therefore, that those least endowed with firmness of character and strength of body have the greatest longing for friendship; and consequently, that helpless women, more than men, seek its shelter, the poor more than the rich, and the unfortunate more than those who are accounted fortunate. O noble philosophy! Why, they seem to take the sun out of the universe when they deprive life of friendship, than which we have from the immortal gods no better, no more delightful boon. For of what value is their vaunted "freedom from care"? In appearance it is indeed an alluring thing, but in reality often to be shunned. For it is inconsistent not to undertake any honourable business or course of conduct, or to lay it aside when undertaken, in order to avoid anxiety. Nay, if we continually flee from trouble, we must also flee from Virtue, who necessarily meets with some trouble in rejecting and loathing things contrary to herself, as when kindness rejects ill-will, temperance lust, and bravery cowardice. And so you may see that it is the just who are most pained at injustice, the brave at cowardice, the self-restrained at profligacy. It is, therefore, characteristic of the well-ordered mind both to rejoice at good deeds and to be pained at the reverse.

Wherefore, if distress of mind befalls a wise man (as it certainly does unless we assume that human sympathy has been rooted out of his heart), why should we remove friendship entirely from our lives in order that we may suffer no worries on its account? For when the soul is deprived of emotion, what difference is there—I do not say between man and the beasts of the field, but between man and a stock or a stone, or any such thing? Nor are we to listen to those men who maintain that virtue is hard and unyielding and is, as it were, something made of iron; whereas, in many relations of life, and especially in friendship, it is so pliable and elastic that it expands, so to speak, with a friend's prosperity and contracts with his adversity. Wherefore, that mental anguish of which I spoke and which often must be felt on a friend's account, has no more power to banish friendship from life than it has to cause us to reject virtue because virtue entails certain cares and annoyances.

But, since, as I said before, virtue knits friendship together, if there should be some exhibition of shining virtue to which a kindred spirit may attach and adjust itself, then, when that happens, love must needs spring forth. For is there anything so absurd as to delight in many inanimate things, like public office, fame, and stately buildings, or dress and personal adornment, and to take little or no delight in a sentient being endowed with virtue and capable of loving, and—if I may so term it—of loving back? For nothing gives more pleasure than the return of goodwill and the interchange of zealous service. And what if I also add, as I may fairly do, that nothing so allures and attracts anything to itself as likeness does to friendship? Then it surely will be granted as a fact that good men love and join to themselves other good men, in a union which is almost that of relationship and Nature. For there is nothing more eager or more greedy than Nature for what is like itself. Wherefore, because of this very fact, I think it should be evident, Fannius and Scævola, that the good have for the good, as if from necessity, a kindly feeling which Nature has made the fountain of friendship. But this same goodness belongs also to the generality of men. For virtue is not unfeeling, unwilling to serve, or proudly exclusive, but it is her wont to protect even whole nations and to plan the best measures for their welfare, which she certainly would not do if she disdained the affection of the common mass.

And again, it seems to me at any rate, that those who falsely assume expediency to be the basis of friendship, take from friendship's chain its loveliest link. For it is not so much the material gain procured through a friend as it is his love, and his love alone, that gives us delight; and that advantage which we derive from him becomes a pleasure only when his service is inspired by an ardent zeal. And it is far from being true that friendship is cultivated because of need; rather, is it cultivated by those who are most abundantly blessed with wealth and power and especially with virtue which is man's best defence; by those least in need of another's help; and by those most generous and most given to acts of kindness. Indeed, I should be inclined to think that it is not well for friends never to need anything at all. Wherein, for example, would my zeal have displayed itself if Scipio had never been in need of my advice or assistance either at home or abroad? It is not the case, therefore, that friendship attends upon advantage,

but, on the contrary, that advantage attends upon friendship. . . .

We now have to determine in our discussion of friendship what are the limits and, so to speak, the boundary lines of affection. On this point I observe that three views are usually advanced, none of which I approve: first, "That we should have the same feeling for our friends that we have for ourselves"; second, "That our goodwill towards our friends should correspond in all respects to their goodwill towards us," and third, "That whatever value a man places upon himself, the same value should be placed upon him by his friends." I do not agree at all with any of these views. Certainly the first one is not true which holds that "as a man feels towards himself, so should he feel towards his friend." For how many things we do for our friends that we never would do for ourselves! At one time we beg and entreat an unworthy man, and again we assail another too sharply or too loudly rail upon him— things not quite creditable in our own affairs, but exceedingly so in behalf of our friends; and there are numerous occasions when good men forgo, or permit themselves to be deprived of, many conveniences in order that their friends rather than themselves may enjoy them.

The second view limits friendship to an equal interchange of services and feelings. It surely is calling friendship to a very close and petty accounting to require it to keep an exact balance of credits and debits. I think true friendship is richer and more abundant than that and does not narrowly scan the reckoning lest it pay out more than it has received; and there need be no fear that some bit of kindness will be lost, that it will overflow the measure and spill upon the ground, or that more than is due will be poured into friendship's bin.

But worst of all is the third limitation, which is that "whatever value a man places upon himself, the same value should be placed upon him by his friends." For often in some men either the spirit is too dejected, or the hope of bettering their fortune is too faint. Therefore, it is not the province of a friend, in such a case, to have the same estimate of another that the other has of himself, but rather it is his duty to strive with all his might to arouse his friend's prostrate soul and lead it to a livelier hope and into a better train of thought. Hence some other limitation of true friendship must be fixed, after I have first stated a view which Scipio used to condemn in the strongest terms. He often said that no utterence could be found more at war with friendship than that of the man who had made this remark: "We should love as if at some time we were going to hate." And Scipio really could not, he said, be induced to adopt the commonly accepted belief that this expression was made by Bias, who was counted one of the Seven Sages; but he thought that it was the speech of some abandoned wretch, or scheming politician, or of someone who regarded everything as an instrument to serve his own selfish ends. For how will it be possible for anyone to be a friend to a man who, he believes, may be his foe? Nay, in such a case it will be necessary also for him to desire and pray that his friend may sin as often as possible and thereby give him, as it were, the more handles to lay hold of; and, again, he will be bound to feel grief, pain and envy at the good deeds and good fortune of his friends. Wherefore this maxim, whoever its author, really has the effect of destroying friendship: rather ought we to have been enjoined to exercise such care in forming friendships that we should never begin to love anyone whom we might sometime hate. Indeed, Scipio thought that, even if we had been unfortunate in our choice, we should endure it rather than plan an opportunity for a breach.

Therefore, these are the limits which I think ought to be observed, namely: when the characters of friends are blameless, then there should be between them complete harmony of opinions and inclinations in everything without any exception; and, even if by some chance the wishes of a friend are not altogether honourable and require to be forwarded in matters which involve his life or reputation, we should turn aside from the straight path, provided, however, utter disgrace does not follow; for there are limits to the indulgence which can be allowed to friendship. Nor indeed ought a man either to disregard his reputation, or to consider the goodwill of his countrymen a poor weapon in the battle of life, though to hunt after it with fawning and flattery is disgraceful; as to virtue we must by no means abjure it, for it is attended by regard.

But Scipio—and I often recur to him, my sole authority for a discourse on friendship—Scipio used to complain that men were more painstaking in all other things than in friendship; that everybody could tell how many goats and sheep he had, but was unable to tell the number of his friends; and that men took pains in getting the former, but were careless in choosing the latter, and had no certain signs, or marks, so to speak, by which to determine their fitness for friendship. We ought, therefore, to choose men who are firm, steadfast and constant, a class of which there is a great dearth; and at the same time it is very hard to come to a decision without a trial, while such trial can only be made in actual friendship: thus friendship outruns the judgement and takes away the opportunity of a trial. Hence it is the part of wisdom to check the headlong rush of goodwill as we would that of a chariot, and thereby so manage friendship that we may in some degree put the dispositions of friends, as we do those of horses, to a preliminary test. Some men often give proof in a petty money transaction how unstable they are; while others, who could not have been influenced by a trivial sum, are discovered in one that is large. But if any shall be found who think it base to prefer money to friendship, where shall we find those who do not put office, civil and military rank, high place and power, above friendship, so that when the former advantages are placed before them on one side and the latter on the other they will not much prefer the former? For feeble is the struggle of human nature against power, and when men have attained it even by the disregard of friendship they imagine the sin will be forgotten because friendship was not disregarded without a weighty cause. Therefore, true friendships are very hard to find among those whose time is spent in office or in business of a public kind. For where can you find a man so high-minded as to prefer his friend's advancement to his own? And, passing by material considerations, pray consider this: how grievous and how hard to most persons does association in another's misfortunes appear! Nor is it easy to find men who will go down to calamity's depths for a friend. Ennius, however, is right when he says:

"When Fortune's fickle the faithful friend is found;"

yet it is on these two charges that most men are convicted of fickleness: they either hold a friend of little value when their own affairs are prosperous, or they abandon him when his are adverse. Whoever, therefore, in either of these contingencies, has shown himself staunch, immovable, and firm in friendship ought to be considered to belong to that class of men which is exceedingly rare—aye, almost divine.

Now the support and stay of that unswerving constancy, which we look for in friendship, is loyalty; for nothing is constant that is disloyal. Moreover, the right course is to choose for a friend one who is frank, sociable, and sympathetic— that is, one who is likely to be influenced

by the same motives as yourself—since all these qualities conduce to loyalty; for it is impossible for a man to be loyal whose nature is full of twists and twinings; and, indeed, one who is untouched by the same influences as yourself and is naturally unsympathetic cannot be either loyal or steadfast. To this observation should be added a requirement tending to produce that steadfastness, which I have been discussing for some time: a friend must neither take pleasure in bringing charges against you nor believe them when made by others. And so, the truth of what I said in the beginning is established: "Friendship cannot exist except among good men."

For it is characteristic of the good man, whom I may also call the wise man, to maintain these two rules in friendship: first, let there be no feigning or hypocrisy; for it is more befitting a candid man to hate openly than to mask his real thoughts with a lying face; secondly, let him not only reject charges preferred by another, but also let him avoid even being suspicious and ever believing that his friend has done something wrong. To this should be added a certain affability of speech and manner, which gives no mean flavour to friendship. While unvarying seriousness and gravity are indeed impressive, yet friendship ought to be more unrestrained, genial, and agreeable, and more inclined to be wholly courteous and urbane.

But at this point there arises a certain question of some little difficulty: Are new friends who are worthy of friendship, at any time to be preferred to old friends, as we are wont to prefer young horses to old ones? The doubt is unworthy of a human being, for there should be no surfeit of friendships as there is of other things; and, as in the case of wines that improve with age, the oldest friendships ought to be the most delightful; moreover, the well-known adage is true: "Men must eat many a peck of salt together

before the claims of friendship are fulfilled." But new friendships are not to
be scorned if they offer hope of bearing
fruit like green shoots of corn that do not
disappoint us at harvest-time; yet the
old friendships must preserve their own
place, for the force of age and habit is
very great. Nay, even in the case of the
horse just now referred to, everybody,
nothing preventing, would rather use one
to which he has grown accustomed than
one that is untrained and new. And
habit is strong in the case not only of
animate, but also of inanimate things,
since we delight even in places, though
rugged and wild, in which we have lived
for a fairly long time.

But it is of the utmost importance in
friendship that superior and inferior
should stand on an equality. . . . And
this course every man should adopt and
imitate, so that if he is endowed with any
superiority in virtue, intellect, or fortune he may impart it to his relatives and
share it with his next of kin; or if, for
example, his parents are of a lowly station and his relatives are less favoured in
mind or estate than himself, he may increase the means of the one and be the
source of honour and influence to the
other; as in legends, men who have for
a long time lived the life of menials, because their lineage and family were unknown, although discovered and found
to be the sons of gods or of kings, nevertheless retain affection for the shepherds
whom for many years they regarded as
their parents. And surely such a feeling
ought to be much stronger in the case
of real and undoubted parents. For the
fruit of genius, of virtue, and, indeed, of
every excellence, imparts its sweetest
flavour when bestowed on those who are
nearest and dearest to us.

As, therefore, in the intimacy existing
between friends and relatives the superior
should put himself on a level with his inferior, so the latter ought not to grieve
that he is surpassed by the former in intellect, fortune, or position. But many of
the latter kind are continually uttering
some complaints or reproaches even, especially if they think that they have done
anything which they can speak of as an
act of duty and of friendship, involving a
certain amount of toil. A very disagreeable class of people, certainly, are those
who are ever obtruding their own services,
which ought to be kept in mind by him
for whom they were performed and should
not be mentioned by him who performed
them. As, therefore, in friendship, those
who are superior should lower themselves,
so, in a measure, should they lift up their
inferiors. For there are certain men who
render friendships disagreeable by thinking themselves slighted—a thing which
rarely happens, except in the case of
persons who think that they really deserve to be slighted; but they ought to be
relieved of such an opinion not by words
only but by action. Now, in the first
place, you must render to each friend as
much aid as you can, and, in the second
place, as much as he whom you love and
assist has the capacity to bear. For
however eminent you may be, you cannot
lead all your friends through the various
grades to the highest official rank, as
Scipio was able to do when he made
Publius Rutilius consul, though he could
not accomplish this result in the case of
his brother, Lucius Rutilius. But even
if you could bestow upon another any
honour you chose, yet you must consider
what he is able to bear.

As a rule decisions about friendships
should be formed after strength and
stability have been reached in mind and
age; nor should men who in boyhood were
devoted to hunting and games of ball,
keep as their intimates those whom they
loved at that period simply because they
were fond of the same pursuits. For on
that principle nurses and the slaves who
attended us to and from school, will, by
right of priority of acquaintance, claim
the largest share of our goodwill. I

admit that they are not to be neglected, but they are to be regarded in an entirely different way; under no other conditions can friendship remain secure. For difference of character is attended by difference of taste and it is this diversity of taste that severs friendships; nor is there any other cause why good men cannot be friends to wicked men, or wicked men to good men, except that there is the greatest possible distance between them in character and in taste.

This rule also may properly be prescribed in friendship: Let not a sort of ungoverned goodwill (as very frequently happens) hinder your friends' advantage in important matters. For indeed, if I may go back to legends, Neoptolemus could not have taken Troy if he had been willing to listen to Lycomedes, by whom he had been reared and who endeavoured with many tears to hinder him from setting out. Often, too, important duties arise which require the temporary separation of friends; and he who would hinder the discharge of those duties because he cannot easily bear his grief at the absence of his friends, is not only weak and effeminate, but, on that very account, is far from reasonable in his friendship. In brief, it is your duty on every occasion to consider carefully both what you will demand from a friend and what you will permit him to obtain when he makes a demand on you.

Furthermore, there is a sort of disaster in connexion with breaking off friendships —for now our discussion descends from the intimacies of the wise to friendships of the ordinary kind—which is sometimes unavoidable. There are often in friends outbursts of vice which affect sometimes their actual friends, sometimes strangers, yet, so that the infamy of the evil flows over on to the friends. Therefore the ties of such friendships should be sundered by a gradual relaxation of intimacy, and, as I have heard that Cato used to say, "They should be unravelled

rather than rent apart," unless there has been some outbreak of utterly unbearable wrongdoing, so that the only course consistent with rectitude and honour, and indeed the only one possible, is to effect an immediate withdrawal of affection and association.

But if, on the other hand, as usually happens, a mere change of disposition and of tastes should occur, or if a difference in political views should arise (for I am talking now, as I said a moment ago, not of friendships existing between wise men, but of those of the ordinary kind), care must be taken lest it appear, not only that friendship has been put aside, but that open hostility has been aroused. For nothing is more discreditable than to be at war with one with whom you have lived on intimate terms. . . .

In short: there is but one security and one provision against these evils and annoyances, and that is, neither to enlist your love too quickly nor to fix it on unworthy men. Now they are worthy of friendship who have within their own souls the reason for their being loved. A rare class indeed! And really everything splendid is rare, and nothing is harder to find than something which in all respects is a perfect specimen of its kind. But the majority of men recognize nothing whatever in human experience as good unless it brings some profit and they regard their friends as they do their cattle, valuing most highly those which give hope of the largest gain. Thus do they fail to attain that loveliest, most spontaneous friendship, which is desirable in and for itself; and they do not learn from their own experience what the power of such friendship is and are ignorant of its nature and extent. For everyone loves himself, not with a view of acquiring some profit for himself from his self-love, but because he is dear to himself on his own account; and unless this same feeling were transferred to friendship, the real friend would never be found; for he is, as it were, another self.

Now if it is evident in animals, whether of the air, water, or the land, and whether tame or wild, first, that they love themselves—for this feeling is born alike in every living creature—and, secondly, that they require and eagerly search for other animals of their own kind to which they may attach themselves—and this they do with a longing in some degree resembling human love—then how much more, by the law of his nature, is this the case with man who both loves himself and uses his reason to seek out another whose soul he may so mingle with his own as almost to make one out of two! . . .

Friendship was given to us by Nature as the handmaid of virtue, not as a comrade of vice; because virtue cannot attain her highest aims unattended, but only in union and fellowship with another. Such a partnership as this, whether it is, or was, or is yet to be, should be considered the best and happiest comradeship along the road to Nature's highest good. In such a partnership, I say, abide all things that men deem worthy of pursuit—honour and fame and delightful tranquillity of mind; so that when these blessings are at hand life is happy, and without them, it cannot be happy.

Since happiness is our best and highest aim, we must, if we would attain it, give our attention to virtue, without which we can obtain neither friendship nor any other desirable thing; on the other hand, those who slight virtue and yet think that they have friends, perceive their mistake at last when some grievous misfortune forces them to put their friends to the test. Therefore, I repeat the injunction, for it should be said again and again: you should love your friend after you have appraised him; you should not appraise him after you have begun to love him. But we are punished for our negligence in many things, and especially are we most grievously punished for our carelessness in the choice and treatment of our friends; for we deliberate after the event, and we do what the ancient proverb forbids—we argue the case after the verdict is found. Accordingly, after we have become involved with others in a mutual affection, either by long association or by interchange of favours, some cause of offence arises and we suddenly break the bonds of friendship asunder when it has run but half its course.

Therefore carelessness so great in regard to a relation absolutely indispensable deserves the more to be censured. For the one thing in human experience about whose advantage all men with one voice agree, is friendship; even virtue itself is regarded with contempt by many and is said to be mere pretence and display; many disdain riches, because they are content with little and take delight in meagre fare and plain dress; political honours, too, for which some have a burning desire—how many so despise them that they believe nothing more empty and nothing more inane! Likewise other things, which seem to some to be worthy of admiration, are by many thought to be of no value at all. But concerning friendship, all, to a man, think the same thing: those who have devoted themselves to public life; those who find their joy in science and philosophy; those who manage their own business free from public cares; and, finally, those who are wholly given up to sensual pleasures—all believe that without friendship life is no life at all, or at least they so believe if they have any desire whatever to live the life of free men. For it creeps imperceptibly, I know not how, into every life, and suffers no mode of existence to be devoid of its presence.

Nay, even if anyone were of a nature so savage and fierce as to shun and loathe the society of men—such, for example, as tradition tells us a certain Timon of Athens once was—yet even such a man could not refrain from seeking some person before whom he might pour out the venom of his embittered soul. Moreover, the view just expressed might best be appraised if such a thing as this could happen: suppose that a god should remove us from these haunts of men and put us in some solitary place, and, while providing us there in plenteous abundance with all material things for which our nature yearns, should take from us altogether the power to gaze upon our fellow men—who would be such a man of iron as to be able to endure that sort of a life? And who is there from whom solitude would not snatch the enjoyment of every pleasure? True, therefore, is that celebrated saying of Archytas of Tarentum, I think it was—a saying which I have heard repeated by our old men who in their turn heard it from their elders. It is to this effect: "If a man should ascend alone into heaven and behold clearly the structure of the universe and the beauty of the stars, there would be no pleasure for him in the awe-inspiring sight, which would have filled him with delight if he had had someone to whom he could describe what he had seen." Thus Nature, loving nothing solitary, always strives for some sort of support, and man's best support is a very dear friend.

But though this same Nature declares by so many utterances what she wishes, what she seeks, and what she ardently longs for, yet we somehow grow deaf and do not hearken to her voice. For varied and complex are the experiences of friendship, and they afford many causes for suspicion and offence, which it is wise sometimes to ignore, sometimes to make light of, and sometimes to endure. But there is one cause of offence which must be encountered in order that both the usefulness and loyalty of friendship may be preserved; for friends frequently must be not only advised, but also rebuked, and both advice and rebuke should be kindly received when given in a spirit of goodwill. But somehow it is true, as put by my intimate friend in his Andria:

"Complaisance gets us friends, plain speaking, hate."

A troublesome thing is truth, if it is indeed the source of hate, which poisons friendship; but much more troublesome is complaisance, which, by showing indulgence to the sins of a friend, allows him to be carried headlong away; but the greatest fault is in him who both scornfully rejects truth and is driven by complaisance to ruin.

Therefore, in this entire matter reason and care must be used, first, that advice be free from harshness, and second, that reproof be free from insult. But in showing complaisance—I am glad to adopt Terence's word, obsequium—let courtesy be at hand, and let flattery, the handmaid of vice, be far removed, as it is unworthy not only of a friend but even of a free man; for we live in one way with a tyrant and in another with a friend. Now we must despair of the safety of the man whose ears are so closed to truth that he cannot hear what is true from a friend. For there is shrewdness in that well-known saying of Cato, as there was in much that he said: "Some men are better served by their bitter-tongued enemies than by their sweet-smiling friends; because the former often tell the truth, the latter, never." And furthermore, it is absurd that men who are admonished do not feel vexation at what ought to vex them, but do feel it at what ought not; for they are annoyed, not at the sin, but at the reproof; whereas, on the contrary, they ought to grieve for the offence and rejoice at its correction.

As, therefore, it is characteristic of true friendship both to give and to receive advice and, on the one hand, to give it with all freedom of speech, but without harshness, and on the other hand, to receive it patiently, but without resentment, so nothing is to be considered a greater bane of friendship than fawning, cajolery, or flattery; for give it as many names as you choose, it deserves to be branded as a vice peculiar to fickle and falsehearted men who say everything with a view to pleasure and nothing with a view to truth. Moreover, hypocrisy is not only wicked under all circumstances, because it pollutes truth and takes away the power to discern it, but it is also especially inimical to friendship, since it utterly destroys sincerity, without which the word friendship can have no meaning. And since the effect of friendship is to make, as it were, one soul out of many, how will that be possible if not even in one man taken by himself shall there be a soul always one and the same, but fickle, changeable, and manifold? For what can be as pliant and erratic as the soul of the man who changes not only to suit another's humour and desire, but even his expression and his nod?

"He says 'nay,' and 'nay' say I; he says 'yea,' and 'yea' say I; in fine, I bade myself agree with him in everything."

This was said by Terence whom I quoted before, but he says it in the character of Gnatho; and to have such a man for a friend on any terms is a mark of inconstancy. However, there are many like Gnatho, though his superiors in birth, fortune, and reputation, who become dangerous flatterers when their insincerity is supported by their position. But by the exercise of care a fawning friend may be separated and distinguished from a true friend, just as everything pretended and false may be distinguished from what is genuine and true. A public assembly, though composed of very ignorant men, can, nevertheless, usually see the difference between a demagogue—that is, a smooth-tongued, shallow citizen—and one who has stability, sincerity and weight. . . .

Now, if on the stage, I mean on the platform, where there is the greatest opportunity for deception and disguise, truth yet prevails, provided it is made plain and brought into the light of day, what ought to be the case with friendship which is wholly weighed in the scales of truth? For in friendship, unless, as the saying is, you behold and show an open heart, you can have no loyalty or certainty and not even the satisfaction of loving and of being loved, since you do not know what true love is. And yet this flattery of which I spoke, however deadly it may be, can harm no one except him who receives and delights in it. It follows that the man who lends the readiest ear to flatterers is the one who is most given to self-flattery and is most satisfied with himself.

I grant that Virtue loves herself; for she best knows herself and realizes how lovable she is; but it is not virtue I am talking about but a reputation for virtue. For many wish not so much to be, as to seem to be, endowed with real virtue. Such men delight in flattery, and when a complimentary speech is fashioned to suit their fancy they think the empty phrase is proof of their own merits. There is nothing, therefore, in a friendship in which one of the parties to it does not wish to hear the truth and the other is ready to lie. Nor should we see any humour in the fawning parasites in comedies if there were no braggart soldiers.

"In truth did Thais send me many thanks?"

It would have been enough to answer, "Many." "Millions of them," said the parasite. The flatterer always magnifies that which the one for whose gratification he speaks wishes to be large. Wherefore, although that sort of hollow flattery influences those who court and make a bid for it, yet even stronger and steadier men should be warned to be on their guard lest they be taken in by flattery of the crafty kind.

No one, to be sure, unless he is an utter

fool, fails to detect the open flatterer, but we must exercise a watchful care against the deep and crafty one lest he steal upon us unawares. For he is very hard to recognize, since he often fawns even by opposing, and flatters and cajoles by pretending to quarrel, until at last he gives in, allowing himself to be overcome so that his dupe may appear to have seen further into the matter than himself. And yet, is there anything more discreditable than to be made a dupe? If not, then we should be all the more on our guard that it does not happen to us to have to confess:

"To-day, of all old fools that play the comic parts,
You've wheedled me the most and made your greatest dupe."

For even on the stage the silliest characters take the parts of old men lacking in foresight and easily deceived.

But in some unaccountable way I have drifted away from the friendship of faultless men—that is, men of wisdom, such wisdom I mean as is observed to fall to the lot of man—and I have rambled on to a discussion of friendships of the frivolous kind. Wherefore, let me return to the topic with which I began and finally put an end even to that.

Virtue, my dear Gaius Fannius, and you, my dear Quintus Musius, Virtue, I say, both creates the bond of friendship and preserves it. For in Virtue is complete harmony, in her is permanence, in her is fidelity; and when she has raised her head and shown her own light and has seen and recognized the same light in another, she moves towards it and in turn receives its beams; as a result love or friendship leaps into flame; for both words are derived from a word meaning "to love." But love is nothing other than the great esteem and affection felt for him who inspires that sentiment, and it is not sought because of material need or for the sake of material gain. Nevertheless, even this blossoms forth from friendship, although you did not make it your aim. . . .

For me, indeed, though he was suddenly snatched away, Scipio still lives and will always live; for it was his virtue that caused my love and that is not dead. Nor is it only in my sight and for me, who had it constantly within my reach, that his virtue lives; it will even shed its light and splendour on men unborn. No one will ever undertake with courage and hope the larger tasks of life without thinking that he must continually keep before him the memory and example of that illustrious man.

For my part, of all the blessings that fortune or Nature has bestowed on me, there is none which I can compare with Scipio's friendship. In it I found agreement on public questions; in it, counsel in private business, and in it, too, a leisure of unalloyed delight. And, so far as I was aware, I never offended him in even the most trivial point; nor did I ever hear a word from him that I could wish unsaid; there was one home for us both; we had the same fare and shared it in common, and we were together not only in our military campaigns, but also in our foreign tours and on our vacations in the country. Why need I speak of our constant devotion to investigation and to learning in which, remote from the gaze of men, we spent all our leisure time? If my recollection and memory of these things had died with him, I could not now by any means endure the loss of a man so very near and dear to me. But those experiences with him are not dead; rather they are nourished and made more vivid by my reflection and memory; and even if I were utterly deprived of the power to recall them, yet my age would of itself afford me great relief; for I cannot have much longer time to bear this bereavement; besides, every trial, which is of brief duration, ought to be endurable, even if it be severe.

This is all that I had to say about friendship; but I exhort you both so to esteem virtue (without which friendship cannot exist), that, excepting virtue, you will think nothing more excellent than friendship.

—W. A. FALCONER.

QUALIFICATIONS OF THE ORATOR

CICERO

[From *On the Orator*, Book I]

The conditions of public life in the closing days of the Republic demanded of the orator special qualifications of a very high order. Cato the Censor was credited with having defined the orator as a good man skilled in speech; to these two requisites of character and skill Cicero adds as a third a wide familiarity with the arts and sciences.

It does not escape your observation that what the Greeks call Philosophy, is esteemed by the most learned men, the originator, as it were, and parent of all the arts which merit praise; philosophy, I say, in which it is difficult to enumerate how many distinguished men there have been, and of how great knowledge, variety, and comprehensiveness in their studies, men who have not confined their labours to one province separately, but have embraced whatever they could master either by scientific investigations, or by processes of reasoning. Who is ignorant in how great obscurity of matter, in how abstruse, manifold, and subtle an art they who are called mathematicians are engaged? Yet in that pursuit so many men have arrived at excellence, that not one seems to have applied himself to the science in earnest without attaining in it whatever he desired. Who has ever devoted himself wholly to music; who has ever given himself up to the learning which they profess who are called grammarians, without compassing, in knowledge and understanding, the whole substance and matter of those sciences, though almost boundless? Of all those who have engaged in the most liberal pursuits and departments of such sciences, I think I may truly say that a smaller number of eminent poets have arisen than of men distinguished in any other branch of literature; and in the whole multitude of the learned, among whom there rarely appears one of the highest excellence, there will be found, if you will but make a careful review of our own list and that of the Greeks, far fewer good orators than good poets. This ought to seem the more wonderful, as attainments in other sciences are drawn from recluse and hidden springs; but the whole art of speaking lies before us, and is concerned with common usage and the custom and language of all men; so that while in other things that is most excellent which is most remote from the knowledge and understanding of the illiterate, it is in speaking even the greatest of faults to vary from the ordinary kind of language, and the practice sanctioned by universal reason.

Yet it cannot be said with truth, either that more are devoted to the other arts, or that they are excited by greater pleasure, more abundant hope, or more ample rewards; for to say nothing of Greece, which was always desirous to hold the first place in eloquence, and Athens, that inventress of all literature, in which the utmost power of oratory was both discovered and brought to perfection, in this very city of ours, assuredly, no studies were ever pursued with more earnestness than those tending to the acquisition of eloquence. For when our empire over all nations was established, and after a period of peace had secured tranquillity, there was scarcely a youth ambitious of praise who did not think that he must strive, with all his endeavours, to attain the art of speaking. For a time, indeed, as being ignorant of all method, and as thinking there was no course of exercise for them, or any precepts of art, they attained what they could by the single force of genius and thought. But afterward, having heard the Greek orators, and gained an acquaintance with Greek literature, and procured instructors, our countrymen were inflamed with an incredible passion for eloquence. The magnitude, the variety, the multitude of all kinds of causes, excited them to such a degree, that to that learning which each had acquired by his individual study, frequent practice, which was superior to the precepts of all masters, was at once added. There were then, as there are also now, the highest inducements offered for the cultivation of this study, in regard to public favor, wealth, and dignity. The abilities of our countrymen (as we may judge from many particulars) far excelled those of the men of every other nation. For which reason, who would not justly wonder that in the records of all ages, times, and states, so small a number of orators should be found?

But the art of eloquence is something greater, and collected from more sciences and studies than people imagine. For who can suppose that, amid the greatest multitude of students, the utmost abundance of masters, the most eminent geniuses among men, the infinite variety of causes, the most ample rewards offered to eloquence, there is any other reason to be found for the small number of orators than the incredible magnitude and difficulty of the art? A knowledge of a vast number of things is necessary, without which volubility of words is empty and ridiculous; speech itself is to be formed, not merely by choice, but by careful construction of words; and all the emotions of the mind, which Nature has given to man, must be intimately known; for all the force and art of speaking must be employed in allaying or exciting the feelings of those who listen. To this

must be added a certain portion of grace and wit, learning worthy of a well-bred man, and quickness and brevity in replying as well as attacking, accompanied with a refined decorum and urbanity. Besides, the whole of antiquity and a multitude of examples is to be kept in the memory; nor is the knowledge of laws in general, or of the civil law in particular, to be neglected. And why need I add any remarks on delivery itself, which is to be ordered by action of body, by gesture, by look, and by modulation and variation of the voice, the great power of which, alone and in itself, the comparatively trivial art of actors and the stage proves, on which though all bestow their utmost labor to form their look, voice, and gesture, who knows not how few there are, and have ever been, to whom we can attend with patience? What can I say of that repository for all things, the memory, which, unless it be made the keeper of the matter and words that are the fruits of thought and invention, all the talents of the orator, we see, though they be of the highest degree of excellence, will be of no avail? Let us, then, cease to wonder what is the cause of the scarcity of good speakers, since eloquence results from all those qualifications, in each of which singly it is a great merit to labor successfully; and let us rather exhort our children, and others whose glory and honor is dear to us, to contemplate in their minds the full magnitude of the object, and not to trust that they can reach the height at which they aim, by the aid of the precepts, masters, and exercises, that they are all now following, but to understand that they must adopt others of a different character.

In my opinion, indeed, no man can be an orator possessed of every praiseworthy accomplishment, unless he has attained the knowledge of everything important, and of all liberal arts, for his language must be ornate and copious from knowledge, since, unless there be beneath the surface matter understood and felt by the speaker, oratory becomes an empty and puerile flow of words.

—J. S. WATSON.

THE DELIGHTS OF POETRY [1]

CICERO

[From the *Defence of Archias*]

To the average Roman the chief function of literature was to serve some practical purpose. Cicero appreciated it also as an inspiration for, as well as an escape and refuge from, the labors of everyday life. The fact that he rested the defence of his client in this case on a eulogy of literature argues his expectation of a like appreciation on the part of his hearers.

Gentlemen of the Jury: Whatever talent I possess (and I realize its limitations), whatever be my oratorical experience (and I do not deny that my practice herein has not been inconsiderable), whatever knowledge of the theoretical side of my profession I may have derived from a devoted literary apprenticeship (and I admit that at no period of my life has the acquisition of such knowledge been repellent to me),—to any advantage that may be derived from all these my friend Aulus Licinius has a pre-eminent claim, which belongs to him almost of right. For if I strain my mental vision far into the past, and strive to recall the most remote memories of my boyhood, the impression which such a survey leaves with me is that it was he who first fitted my back for its burden and my feet for their destined path. If this voice of mine, trained by his precepts and his exhortation, has on some few occasions proved of service, it is my client who has put into my hands the means of succouring others and perhaps saving some, and it is to his cause,

therefore, that any power of help or protection, which it lies with me to exert, should be applied. My remarks may cause surprise; for it may be urged that the genius of the defendant is exercised in a sphere which bears no connexion with my own study and practice of oratory. But I would point out in reply that I myself have never concentrated my energies upon my professional interests to the exclusion of all others. Indeed, the subtle bond of a mutual relationship links together all arts which have any bearing upon the common life of mankind.

It may, however, be a matter for surprise in some quarters that in an inquiry dealing with statute law, in a public trial held before a specially selected prætor of the Roman people and a jury of high dignity, in the presence of a crowded audience of citizens, my speech should be made in a style out of keeping not merely with the conventions of the bar, but also with forensic language. But I crave your indulgence, an indulgence which will, I trust, cause you no inconvenience, and which is peculiarly applicable to the nature of my client's case; and I would ask you to allow me, speaking as I am on behalf of a distinguished poet and a consummate scholar, before a cultivated audience, an enlightened jury, and the prætor whom we see occupying the tribunal, to enlarge somewhat upon enlightened and cultivated pursuits, and to employ what is perhaps a novel and unconventional line of defence to suit the character of one whose studious seclusion has made him a stranger to the anxious perils of the courts. Let me but assure myself that you grant me this kind concession, and I will engage to convince you of the propriety, not only of refusing to exclude my client from the civic roll, since he is a citizen, but even of adding his name to that roll, supposing that he were not. . . .

You will no doubt ask me, Gratius, to account for the deep interest I feel in my

[1] From the Loeb Classical Library, by permission.

friend. It is because he provides refreshment for my spirit after the clamour of the courts, and repose for senses jaded by their vulgar wrangling. Do you think that I could find inspiration for my daily speeches on so manifold a variety of topics, did I not cultivate my mind with study, or that my mind could endure so great a strain, did not study too provide it with a relaxation? I am a votary of literature, and make the confession unashamed; shame belongs rather to the bookish recluse, who knows not how to apply his reading to the good of his fellows, or to manifest its fruits to the eyes of all. But what shame should be mine, gentlemen, who have made it a rule of my life for all these years never to allow the sweets of a cloistered ease or the seductions of pleasure or the enticements of repose to prevent me from aiding any man in the hour of his need? How then can I justly be blamed or censured, if it shall be found that I have devoted to literature a portion of my leisure hours no longer than others without blame devote to the pursuits of material gain, to the celebration of festivals or games, to pleasure and the repose of mind and body, to protracted banqueting, or perhaps to the gaming-board or to ball-playing! I have the better right to indulgence herein, because my devotion to letters strengthens my oratorical powers, and these, such as they are, have never failed my friends in their hour of peril. Yet insignificant though these powers may seem to be, I fully realize from what source I draw all that is highest in them. Had I not persuaded myself from my youth up, thanks to the moral lessons derived from a wide reading, that nothing is to be greatly sought after in this life save glory and honour, and that in their quest all bodily pains and all dangers of death or exile should be lightly accounted, I should never have borne for the safety of you all the brunt of many a bitter encounter, or bared my breast to

the daily onsets of abandoned persons. All literature, all philosophy, all history, abounds with incentives to noble action, incentives which would be buried in black darkness were the light of the written word not flashed upon them. How many pictures of high endeavour the great authors of Greece and Rome have drawn for our use, and bequeathed to us, not only for our contemplation, but for our emulation! These I have held ever before my vision throughout my public career, and have guided the workings of my brain and my soul by meditating upon patterns of excellence.

"But," an objector may ask, "were these great men, whose virtues are perpetuated in literature, themselves adepts in the learning which you describe in such fulsome terms?" It would be difficult to make a sweeping and categorical reply, but at the same time I have my answer ready. Many there have been, no doubt, exceptionally endowed in temperament and character, who, without any aid from culture, but only by a heaven-born light within their own souls, have been self-schooled in restraint and fortitude; I would even go so far as to say that natural gifts without education have more often attained to glory and virtue than education without natural gifts. Yet I do at the same time assert that when to a lofty and brilliant character is applied the moulding influence of abstract studies, the result is often inscrutably and unapproachably noble. Such a character our fathers were privileged to behold in the divine figure of Scipio Africanus; such were those patterns of continence and self-control, Gaius Lælius and Lucius Furius; such was the brave and venerable Marcus Cato, the most accomplished man of his day. These surely would never have devoted themselves to literary pursuits, had they not been aided thereby in the appreciation and pursuit of merit. But let us for the moment waive these solid advantages; let us assume that entertainment is the sole end of reading; even so, I think you would hold that no mental employment is so broadening to the sympathies or so enlightening to the understanding. Other pursuits belong not to all times, all ages, all conditions; but this gives stimulus to our youth and diversion to our old age; this adds a charm to success, and offers a haven of consolation to failure. In the home it delights, in the world it hampers not. Through the night-watches, on all our journeying, and in our hours of country ease, it is our unfailing companion.

But it might happen that we ourselves were without literary tastes or attainments; yet even so, it would be incumbent upon us to reverence their manifestation in others. Was there a man among us so boorish or so insensible that the recent death of Roscius did not stir his deepest emotions? He died full of years, and yet we all felt that an artist of such grace and brilliance deserved immunity from our mortal lot. Merely by the motions of his body he had won all our hearts; and shall those hearts be insensible to the inscrutable motions of the soul and the agile play of genius? How often, gentlemen, have I seen my friend Archias,—I shall presume upon your kindness, since I see you give so careful a hearing to my unconventional digression,—how often, I say, have I seen him, without writing a single letter, extemporizing quantities of excellent verse dealing with current topics! How often have I seen him, when recalled, repeat his original matter with an entire change of word and phrase. To his finished and studied work I have known such approval accorded that his glory rivalled that of the great writers of antiquity. Does not such a man deserve my affection and admiration? Should I not count it my duty to strain every nerve in his defence? And yet we have it on the highest and most learned authority that while other arts are matters of science and formula and technique, poetry depends solely upon an inborn faculty, is evoked by a purely mental activity, and is infused with a strange supernal inspiration. Rightly, then, did our great Ennius call poets "holy," for they seem recommended to us by the benign bestowal of God. Holy then, gentlemen, in your enlightened eyes let the name of poet be, inviolate hitherto by the most benighted of races! The very rocks of the wilderness give back a sympathetic echo to the voice; savage beasts have sometimes been charmed into stillness by song; and shall we, who are nurtured upon all that is highest, be deaf to the appeal of poetry? Colophon asserts that Homer is her citizen, Chios claims him for her own, Salamis appropriates him, while Smyrna is so confident that he belongs to her that she has even dedicated a shrine to him in her town; and many other cities besides engage in mutual strife for his possession. These peoples, then, are ambitious to claim, even after his death, one who was an alien, merely because he was a poet; and shall a living poet be repudiated by us, though he is ours both by inclination and by the laws? Shall we do so, in spite of the fact that a short while ago he bent all the energies of his genius to celebrating the fame and glory of the Roman people? For in his youth he wrote on the Cimbrian campaign, thereby winning the approbation of the great Gaius Marius himself, who was generally considered to be insensible to such refinements. For indeed there is no man to whom the Muses are so distasteful that he will not be glad to entrust to poetry the eternal emblazonment of his achievements. It is related that the great Athenian hero, Themistocles, when asked what recital or what voice he loved best to hear, replied, "That which bears most eloquent testimony to my prowess." On a like foundation rested the deep attachment felt by Marius towards Lucius Plotius, whose genius he thought well qualified to perpetuate his exploits. Again, my client has treated in its entirety the great and difficult theme of the war with Mithridates, pursuing all its diverse operations by land and sea, and his work sheds lustre not only on the gallant and renowned Lucius Lucullus, but also upon the fame of the Roman people. For it was the Roman people who, with Lucullus at their head, opened up the Pontus, fortified as it was not only by the resources of its monarch, but also by an advantageous situation. It was an army of the Roman people, which, under the same commander, routed with a moderate force the innumerable hordes of Armenia. And it is to the Roman people, still under the directing skill of Lucullus, that the credit belongs of having torn away and saved the friendly city of Cyzicus from all the assaults of the king, and from being swallowed up in the ravaging jaws of war. To us shall it ever be imputed with praise that under Lucullus again we crushed a hostile fleet, slew its admirals, and fought that astonishing naval battle at Tenedos. Ours, inalienably ours, are the trophies, memorials, and triumphs of that campaign; and it is the glories of the Roman people which are sounded abroad by the genius of those who laud exploits such as these.

Our great Ennius enjoyed the close affection of the elder Africanus, and so a marble statue of him is reputed to have been placed even in the tomb of the Scipios. Yet we may be sure that the panegyric he bestowed upon his patron lends adornment not only to its theme, but also to the name of the Roman people. He exalted to heaven the Cato whose great-grandson is now with us; and great glory is added thereby to the name of the Roman people. The rule holds good in every case; the glory of universal Rome borrows an added lustre from those words which distinguish the bearers of the great names of Maximus, Marcellus, or Fulvius. For this reason our ancestors admitted their author, a citizen of Rudiæ,

to the franchise; and shall we eject from our franchise one for whom many states have striven, and whom Heraclea has gained, and constituted her citizen by due process of law?

For if anyone thinks that the glory won by the writing of Greek verse is naturally less than that accorded to the poet who writes in Latin, he is entirely in the wrong. Greek literature is read in nearly every nation under heaven, while the vogue of Latin is confined to its own boundaries, and they are, we must grant, narrow. Seeing, therefore, that the activities of our race know no barrier save the limits of the round earth, we ought to be ambitious that whithersoever our arms have penetrated there also our fame and glory should extend; for the reason that literature exalts the nation whose high deeds it sings, and at the same time there can be no doubt that those who stake their lives to fight in honour's cause find therein a lofty incentive to peril and endeavour. We read that Alexander the Great carried in his train numbers of epic poets and historians. And yet, standing before the tomb of Achilles at Sigeum, he exclaimed,—"Fortunate youth, to have found in Homer an herald of thy valour!" Well might he so exclaim, for had the *Iliad* never existed, the same mound which covered Achilles' bones would also have overwhelmed his memory. Again, did not he to whom our own age has accorded the title of Great, whose successes have been commensurate with his high qualities, present with the citizenship before a mass meeting of his troops Theophanes of Mytilene, the historian of his campaigns? Were not our brave fellows, soldiers and peasants though they were, so smitten with the glamour of renown that they loudly applauded the act, feeling that they too had a share in the glory that had been shed upon their leader? Accordingly, if Archias were not legally a Roman citizen already, it would have been beyond his power, presumably, to win the gift of citizenship from some military commander. Sulla, no doubt, who gave it so freely to Spaniards and Gauls, would have refused it to the request of my client. It will be remembered that once at a public meeting some poetaster from the crowd handed up to that great man a paper containing an epigram upon him, improvised in somewhat unmetrical eligiacs. Sulla immediately ordered a reward to be paid him out of the proceeds of the sale which he was then holding, but added the stipulation that he should never write again. He accounted the diligent efforts of a poet worthy of some reward, bad though that poet was; and think you he would not have eagerly sought out my client, whose literary powers were so magnificent, and whose pen was so ready? Again, could not his own credit or the influence of the Luculli have gained him his desire from Quintus Metellus Pius, who was his intimate friend, and who had presented the citizenship to not a few? And it must be remembered that so ambitious was Metellus to have his deeds immortalized that he even deigned to lend a hearing to poets from Corduba, overladen and exotic though their style might be.

Ambition is an universal factor in life, and the nobler a man is, the more susceptible is he to the sweets of fame. We should not disclaim this human weakness, which indeed is patent to all; we should rather admit it unabashed. Why, upon the very books in which they bid us scorn ambition philosophers inscribe their names! They seek advertisement and publicity for themselves on the very page whereon they pour contempt upon advertisement and publicity. That gallant officer and gentleman, Decimus Brutus, adorned the vestibules of the temples and monuments which he raised with the poems of his friend Accius; more, the great Fulvius, who took Ennius

with him upon his Ætolian campaign, had no misgivings in dedicating to the Muses the spoils of the god of war. Surely, then, in a city where honour has been paid to the name of poet and the shrines of the Muses by generals who have scarce doffed the panoply of battle, it would ill befit a jury of peaceful citizens to disdain to pay respect to the Muses by extending protection to their bard.

And the more to incline you so to do, gentlemen of the jury, I will now proceed to open to you my heart, and confess to you my own passion, if I may so describe it, for fame, a passion overkeen perhaps, but assuredly honourable. The measures which I, jointly with you, undertook in my consulship for the safety of the empire, the lives of our citizens, and the common weal of the state, have been taken by my client as the subject of a poem which he has begun; he read this to me, and the work struck me as at once so forcible and so interesting, that I encouraged him to complete it. For magnanimity looks for no other recognition of its toils and dangers save praise and glory; once rob it of that, gentlemen, and in this brief and transitory pilgrimage of life what further incentive have we to high endeavour? If the soul were haunted by no presage of futurity, if the scope of her imaginings were bounded by the limits set to human existence, surely never then would she break herself by bitter toil, rack herself by sleepless solicitude, or struggle so often for very life itself. But deep in every noble heart dwells a power which plies night and day the goad of glory, and bids us see to it that the remembrance of our names should not pass away with life, but should endure coeval with all the ages of the future.

Are we to show so poor a spirit to the world, we, who are exposed to all the perils and toils that beset a public career, as to think that, after having lived out our allotted span without ever drawing the breath of peace and repose, all is to die along with us? Many great men have been studious to leave behind them statues and portraits, likenesses not of the soul, but of the body; and how much more anxious should we be to bequeath an effigy of our minds and characters, wrought and elaborated by supreme talent? For my part, in the very enactment of my exploits, I felt that I was sowing broadcast to reap an undying memory throughout the whole world. It may be that after death I shall be insensible to it. It may be that, as philosophers have held, some part of my being shall yet be conscious of it. Be that as it may, now at any rate I find satisfaction in the thought and in the hope.

Wherefore, gentlemen, protect, I beg of you, a man whose honour you see to be attested both by the high position of his friends, and the durability of their friendship, whose genius you can estimate at its true worth by the fact that genius itself has set a premium upon it, and the righteousness of whose cause is established by the support of the law, the authority of a municipality, the evidence of Lucullus, and the burgess-rolls of Metellus. Throughout his career he has shed glory upon you, upon your generals, and upon the history of the Roman people; he is engaged upon a work which promises to be a glorious and undying testimony to those public perils which we have recently faced together; and he belongs to a profession which has been universally held inviolable, both in act and word. I implore you therefore, gentlemen, if such high talent deserves any commendation from men, nay more, from heaven, let him rest in the assurance of your protection, and let it be seen that so far from being assailed by your displeasure, he has been assisted by your humanity.

I am sure that my statement of the case, brief and straightforward as I, true to my practice, have made it, has appealed to every one of you; and I hope that my departure from the practice and the conventions of the courts, and my digression upon the subject of my client's genius, and, in general terms, upon the art which he follows, has been welcomed by you in as generous a spirit as I am assured it has been welcomed by him who presides over this tribunal.

—N. H. WATTS.

THE POET SALUTES THE ORATOR

CATULLUS

Gaius Valerius Catullus (about 87 to about 54 B.C.) was born in Verona, but spent most of his life in Rome, a brilliant member of the younger social set and the literary circle of the biographer Cornelius Nepos. The main incident of his life and the subject of much of his poetry was his love affair with the unworthy Lesbia. He is the only Roman writer who possessed the passionate heart of the genuine lyric poet. He was one of a group scornfully dubbed "new poets" by Cicero, because they were introducing new measures and themes in imitation of the Alexandrians. Catullus is most successful, however, when he is writing from personal experience, and not on subjects borrowed from books.

The following poem may have been intended as an ironical reply to Cicero's scornful criticism of Catullus and his school.

Tully, most eloquent, most sage
  Of all the Roman race,
That deck the past or present age,
  Or future days may grace.

Oh! may Catullus thus declare
  An overflowing heart;
And, though the worst of poets, dare
  A grateful lay impart!

'Twill teach thee how thou hast surpast
　All others in thy line;
For, far as he in his is last,
　Art thou the first in thine.
—LAMB.

LESBIA'S SPARROW

CATULLUS

This and the four following poems deal
with the poet's passion for Lesbia. The
note of the happiness of love is rare—his
experience was mainly of its bitterness.

Sparrow! my nymph's delicious pleasure!
Who with thee, her pretty treasure,
Fanciful in frolic, plays
Thousand, thousand wanton ways;
And, fluttering, lays to panting rest
On the soft orbings of her breast;
Thy beak with finger-tip incites,
And dallies with thy becks and bites;
When my beauty, my desire,
Feels her darling whim inspire,
With nameless triflings, such as these,
To snatch, I trow, a tiny ease
For some keen fever of the breast,
While passion toys itself to rest;
I would that happy lady be,
And so in pastime sport with thee,
And lighten love's soft agony.
The sweet resource were bliss untold,
Dear as that apple of ripe gold,
Which, by the nimble virgin found,
Unloos'd the zone that had so fast been
　bound.
—C. A. ELTON.

KISSES

CATULLUS

Love, my Lesbia, while we live;
　Value all the cross advice
That the surly greybeards give
　At a single farthing's price.

Suns that set again may rise;
　We, when once our fleeting light,
Once our day in darkness dies,
　Sleep in one eternal night.

Give me kisses thousand-fold,
　Add to them a hundred more;
Other thousands still be told,
　Other hundreds o'er and o'er.

But, with thousands when we burn,
　Mix, confuse the sum at last,
That we may not blushing learn
　All that have between us past.

None shall know to what amount
　Envy's due for so much bliss;
None—for none shall ever count
　All the kisses we will kiss.
—LAMB.

LESBIA'S INCONSTANCY

CATULLUS

Cease from this idle fooling trade—
　Cease, wretch Catullus, all is o'er;
And what thou seest has long decay'd,
　E'en think it lost for evermore.

Of old thy suns were bright and clear,
　When thou, where'er her path was lain,
Wouldst chase the damsel, loved so dear
　As none will e'er be loved again.

Then were the sports of amorous jest
　Still urged by thee with new delight;
While she scarce chid and not repress'd—
　Oh then thy suns were truly bright!

She now rejects thee—cast her off,
　Nor weakly chase a flying fair;
Nor grieving live to be her scoff,
　But coldly steel thy mind to bear.

Damsel, farewell! Catullus stern
　Thy scorn disdains, thy love will shun;
And soon thy pride to grief shall turn,
　When left by him, and woo'd by none.

Think, wanton, what remains for thee:
Who will pursue thy lonely way?
Who in thy form will beauty see?
Whose fervent love shalt thou repay?

Whose fondling care shalt thou avow?
Whose kisses now shalt thou return?
Whose lip in rapture bite?—But thou—
Hold! Hold! Catullus, cold and stern.
—LAMB.

PARTING MESSAGE TO LESBIA

CATULLUS

Companions, who would gladly go
With me through every toil below
 To man's remotest seats:
Whether Catullus should explore
Far India, on whose echoing shore
 The eastern billow beats.

Whether he seek Hyrcania wild,
The Tartar hordes, or Arabs mild,
 Or Parthia's archer train:
Or tread that intersected isle,
Whence pouring forth the sev'n-fold Nile
 Discolours all the main.

Whether across the Alps he toil,
To view the war-ennobled soil
 Where Cæsar's trophies stand;
The Rhine that saw its Gaul's disgrace,
Or dare the painted Briton race
 In their extremest land.

Companions dear, prepared to wend
Where'er the gods may place your friend,
 And every lot to share;
A few unwelcome words receive,
And to that once-loved fair I leave
 My latest message bear.

Still let her live and still be blest,
By profligates in hundreds prest,
 Still sport in ease and wealth;
Still of those hundreds love not one,
Still cast off each by turns undone
 In fortune and in health.

But let her deem my passion o'er:
Her guilt has crushed, to bloom no more,
 The love her beauty raised;
As droops the flower, the meadow's pride,
Which springing by the furrow's side
 The passing share has grazed.
—LAMB.

THE LOVER'S PETITION

CATULLUS

If virtuous deeds, if honour ever fair,
 Pleasure the memory and console the
 mind;
And faith preserved, and pious vows that
 ne'er
 Attested heaven to deceive mankind;

Then great the bliss that waits your future
 day,
 From thy past passion for this thankless maid;
For all that tenderest love could do or say
 By thee, Catullus, has been done and
 said.

'Twas vain; false Lesbia's breast forgot
 it all.
 Why on this rack thy heart then longer
 stretch?
Cast off, undauntedly, your slothful
 thrall,
 And cease, in spite of heaven, to be a
 wretch.

'Tis hard to lay long-cherished love aside;
 'Tis hard at once. But 'tis your only
 plan;
'Tis all your hope. This love must be
 defied;
 Nor think you cannot, but assert you
 can.

Ye gods, if pity's yours, if e'er ye raise
 The wretch who sinks by hovering
 death opprest,

Oh! look on me.—If I have lived with praise,
    Root out this plague and fury from my breast;

Which, like a torpor creeping through my frame,
    Have peace and pleasure from my heart displaced.
I ask not that she should return my flame,
    Or, what e'en ye could never give, be chaste:

I ask to have my life again mine own,
    Eased of the languid load that on me weighs.
Oh! grant me this, ye gods; with this alone
    Repay my piety, and bless my days.
        —LAMB.

SIRMIO

CATULLUS

Catullus had been absent in Bithynia for a year and home seemed sweet indeed. Sirmio was the name of a peninsula in the Lago di Garda, not far from the poet's birthplace Verona.

O best of all the scatter'd spots that lie
In sea or lake,—apple of landscape's eye,—
How gladly do I drop within thy nest,
With what a sigh of full, contented rest,
Scarce able to believe my journey's o'er,
And that these eyes behold thee safe once more!
Oh where's the luxury like the smile at heart,
When the mind breathing, lays its load apart,—
When we come home again, tired out, and spread
The loosen'd limbs o'er all the wish'd-for bed!
This, this alone is worth an age of toil.
Hail, lovely Sirmio! Hail, paternal soil!

Joy, my bright waters, joy: your master's come!
Laugh every dimple on the cheek of home!
        —LEIGH HUNT.

AT HIS BROTHER'S GRAVE

CATULLUS

The brother of Catullus died and was buried in the Troad. The poet took advantage of his year in Bithynia to visit the grave and to perform the last sacred rights for the dead.

O'er many a realm, o'er many an ocean tost,
I come, my brother, to salute thy ghost!
Thus on thy tomb sad honour to bestow,
And vainly call the silent dust below.
Thou too art gone! Yes, thee I must resign,
My more than brother—ah! no longer mine.
The funeral rites to ancient Romans paid,
Duly I pay to thy lamented shade.
Take them—these tears their heart-felt homage tell;
And now—all hail for ever, and farewell!
        —HODGSON.

EPITHALAMIUM

CATULLUS

The marriage-song was usually sung by a chorus of boys and girls, but here the poet speaks throughout as leader of the chorus. It is an interesting combination of fun and superstition with the more serious view of the sanctity of marriage.

O thou, Urania's heaven-born son,
Whose loved abode is Helicon;
Whose power bestows the virgin's charms
To bless the youthful bridegroom's arms;
O Hymen! friend of faithful pairs;
O Hymen! hear our fervent prayers!

Around thy brow the chaplet bind,
Of fragrant marjoram entwined;
And bring the veil with crimson dyed,
The refuge of the blushing bride.
Come, joyous, while thy feet of snow
With yellow sandals brightly glow!

Arouse thee on this happy day;
Carol the hymeneal lay;
Raise in the strain thy silver voice,
And in the festal dance rejoice;
And brandish high the blissful sign,
The guiding torch of flaming pine.

When Venus claim'd the golden prize,
And bless'd the Phrygian shepherd's eyes;
No brighter charms his judgment sway'd
Than those that grace this mortal maid;
And every sigh and omen fair
The nuptials hail, and greet the pair.

The myrtle's sweet on Asia's ground,
Its branches fair with blossoms crown'd
Which oft the Hamadryad crew
In frolic nourish with the dew:
But not less fair, but not less sweet
Her Manlius now does Julia meet.

Then hither speed thy course to take:
Awhile the Thespian hill forsake;
Nor waste awhile the lingering hours
Reclining in Aonian bowers,
Where Aganippe's springing fount ·
Refreshes all the sacred mount.

Propitiate here the maiden's vows,
And lead her fondly to her spouse;
And firm as ivy clinging holds
The tree it grasps in mazy folds,
Let virtuous love as firmly bind
The tender passions of her mind.

Ye virgins, whom a day like this
Awaits to greet with equal bliss,
Oh! join the song, your voices raise
To hail the god ye love to praise.
O Hymen! god of faithful pairs;
O Hymen! hear our earnest prayers!

Invoked by sires, with anxious fear,
Their children's days with bliss to cheer;
By maidens, who to thee alone
Unloose the chaste, the virgin zone;
By fervid bridegrooms, whose delight
Is staid till thou hast blest the rite.

Thy influence tears, thy fond behest,
The damsel from her mother's breast;
And yields her blooming, blushing charms
To fiery man's resistless arms.
O Hymen! god of faithful pairs;
O Hymen! hear our earnest prayers!

Though wanton Venus feed the flame;
Nor grateful praise, nor virtuous fame
Can wait on those, who loose and free
Indulge a love unblest by thee.
What other god can mortals dare
With genial Hymen to compare?

No house can boast a lengthen'd race;
No heir can parents' honours grace;
They serve to deck their tombs alone,
If parents' lives thy sway disown.
What other god can mortals dare
With genial Hymen to compare?

In vain the son, if scorn'd thy band,
Seeks power or greatness in the land;
If blest by thee his natal day,
The proudest realm may own his sway.
What other god can mortals dare
With genial Hymen to compare?

Unbar the door, the gates unfold!
The bashful virgin comes.—Behold,
How red the nuptial torches glare;
How bright they shake their splendid
    hair!
Come, gentle bride!—The waning day
Rebukes thy lingering, cold delay.

We will not blame thy bashful fears,
Reluctant step, and gushing tears,
That chide the swift approach of night
To give thy bridegroom all his right.
Yet come, sweet bride!—The waning day
Rebukes thy lingering, cold delay.

Daughter of Cotta, cease to weep,
For love shall watch, and falsehood sleep.
The sun, at dawn that lifts his blaze
From ocean, and the world surveys,
Shall never look, shall never shine
On beauties that shall rival thine.

Thus blooms, amid the gay parterre,
Some wealthy owner's pride and care,
The hyacinth with colours proud,
The loveliest of the varied crowd.
Come, gentle bride!—The waning day
Rebukes thy lingering, cold delay.

Then come, sweet bride, and bless thy
    spouse,
And sanction love by nuptial vows.
At length our friendly numbers hear:
The torches high their brilliance rear,
And richly shake with glowing pride
Their golden hair.—Then come, sweet
    bride!

No profligate, no faithless swain,
No follower of the wanton train,
No rake, who joys in wild excess,
Now woos thee to his warm caress.
He ne'er will taste of welcome rest,
But pillow'd on thy tender breast.

As round the husband elm entwine
The tendrils of the clinging vine,
Thus will he woo thee still to place
Round him a fondling close embrace.
Come, gentle bride!—The waning day
Rebukes thy lingering, cold delay.

O festal couch; with garlands sweet,
What joys thy happy lord will greet!
What joys in many a sleepless night!
What joys in day's inspiring light!
Come, gentle bride!—the waning day
Rebukes thy lingering, cold delay.

Raise, boys, the beaming torches high!
She comes—but veil'd from every eye;
The deeper dyes her blushes hide:
With songs, with pæans greet the bride!

Hail, Hymen! god of faithful pairs!
Hail, Hymen! who hast heard our
    prayers!

Now pour the warm Fescennine lays,
And all the bridegroom's passion raise:
Now let his pure, his plighted hand
Throw nuts to all the youthful band,
Base emblems of the looser joys
He henceforth leaves to wanton boys.

Throw, bridegroom, throw thy nuts
    away!
Enough in joy's voluptuous day
Hast thou beguiled thy youthful time;
But now thy manhood's riper prime
Let pure, let bless'd Thalassus sway:
Then throw thy mystic nuts away.

'Tis whisper'd that the wanton's charms
Will yet allure thee to her arms:
Oh! let no shameless rival's pride
Degrade and pain thy gentle bride.
Hail, Hymen! god of faithful pairs!
Hail, Hymen, who hast heard our prayers!

Unloved, unwedded youths and boys
May freely sport in wanton joys:
Let him, that's blest by wedlock's rite,
In wedlock seek his sole delight.
Hail, Hymen, god of faithful pairs!
Hail, Hymen, who hast heard our prayers!

And let no coldness damp his fire,
Fair bride, nor coyness check desire.
Oh! make his heart less sweet confess
All lawless love, than thy caress.
Hail, Hymen! god of faithful pairs!
Hail, Hymen! who hast heard our
    prayers!

Till dotage, with enfeebling sway,
Shall tremble in thy temples grey;
And shake the brow, as if it meant
To nod perpetual assent.
Hail, Hymen! god of faithful pairs!
Hail, Hymen! who hast heard our
    prayers!

Let not the threshold, omen blest!
Be with thy golden slipper prest;
But swiftly spring with lightness o'er,
And swiftly pass the polish'd door.
Hail, Hymen! god of faithful pairs!
Hail, Hymen! who hast heard our
    prayers!

See, on the Tyrian couch reclining,
The bridegroom for thy summons pin-
    ing:
By thee are all his senses fired;
By thee is all his frame inspired.
Hail, Hymen; god of faithful pairs!
Hail, Hymen! who hast heard our
    prayers!

As warm as thine, his passion's heat,
As strong his rapturous pulses beat;
Nay, fiercer flames must still pervade
The bridegroom than the timid maid.
Hail, Hymen! god of faithful pairs!
Hail, Hymen! who hast heard our
    prayers!

Purple-robed boy, whose pleasing care
Has been to lead the lingering fair,
Release her arm:—By others led
She now ascends the bridal bed.
Hail, Hymen! god of faithful pairs!
Hail, Hymen! who hast heard our
    prayers!

Ye chaster matrons, who have known
One honour'd husband's love alone,
Of truth in years long virtuous tried,
'Tis yours to place the lovely bride.
Hail, Hymen! god of faithful pairs!
Hail! Hymen! who hast heard our
    prayers!

Now haste, young bridegroom, swiftly
    haste;
The bride is in the chamber placed:
Inspiring blushes warmly streak
The fairness of her snowy cheek.
So mix'd with poppies' crimson glow
The white parthenium's flow'rets blow.

Nor is thy form, by heaven above!
Unworthy such a fair one's love.
Venus in rival charms array'd
The manly youth and tender maid.
Haste, bridegroom, haste!—One western
    ray,
Still faintly lingering, chides delay.

Needs not to chide; thou swift hast sped.
Propitious Venus bless thy bed!
For sanction'd passion, solemn rites,
On thee bestow thy wish'd delights:
Not lust perverted, shame supprest,
The pure desires that warm thy breast.

Whoe'er the number would define
Of sports and joys that shall be thine,
He first must count the grains of sand
That spread the Erythræan strand,
And every star and twinkling light
That stud the glistening arch of night.

Oh, boundless be your love's excess,
And soon our hopes let children bless!
Let not this ancient honour'd name
Want heirs to guard its future fame;
Nor any length of years assign
A limit to the glorious line.

Soon may we see a baby rest
Upon its lovely mother's breast;
Which, feebly playful, stretching out
Its little arms to those about,
With lips apart a tiny space,
Is laughing in its father's face.

Let young Torquatus' look avow
All Manlius' features in his brow;
That those, who know him not, may
    trace
The knowledge of his noble race;
And by his lineal brow declare
His lovely mother chaste as fair.

Then shall maternal virtue claim
As splendid praise, as pure a name
To deck her child, as erst was known
To young Telemachus alone,

Whom, then of all most fair and chaste,
Penelope with honour graced.

Now close the doors, ye maiden friends;
Our sports, our rite, our service ends.
With you let virtue still reside,
O bridegroom brave, and gentle bride!
And youth its lusty hours employ
Inconstant love and ardent joy.

—LAMB.

ATYS

CATULLUS

Catullus projects himself into the state
of mind of a frenzied worshipper of the
Phrygian goddess Cybele and pictures the
feelings of such a man at the moment
when he regains his senses after his self-
mutilation. The oriental coloring, as
finely done as it is rare in the literature,
is a suitable accompaniment to the wild
acts of the fanatic.

Atys o'er the distant waters, driving in
his rapid bark,
Soon with foot of wild impatience touch'd
the Phrygian forest dark,
Where amid the awful shades possess'd
by mighty Cybele,
In his zealous frenzy blind,
And wand'ring in his hapless mind,
With flinty knife he gave to earth the
weights that stamp virility.
Then as the widow'd being saw its
wretched limbs bereft of man,
And the unaccustom'd blood that on the
ground polluting ran,
With snowy hand it snatch'd in haste the
timbrel's airy round on high,
That opens with the trumpet's blast thy
rites, Maternal Mystery;
And upon its whirling fingers, while the
hollow parchment rung,
Thus in outcry tremulous to its wild com-
panions sung:—
"Now come along, come along with me,
Worshippers of Cybele,

To the lofty groves of the deity!
Ye vagabond herds that bear the name
Of the Dindymenian dame!
Who seeking strange lands, like the ban-
ish'd of home,
With Atys, with Atys distractedly roam;
Who your limbs have unmann'd in a des-
perate hour,
With a frantic disdain of the Cyprian
power;
Who have carried my sect through the
dreadful salt sea,
Rouse, rouse your wild spirits career-
ingly!
No delay, no delay,
But together away,
And follow me up to the Dame all-com-
pelling,
To her high Phrygian groves, and her
dark Phrygian dwelling,
Where the cymbals they clash, and the
drums they resound,
And the Phrygian's curved pipe pours
its mourning around;
Where the ivy-crown'd priestesses toss
with their brows,
And send the shrill howl through their
deity's house;
Where they shriek, and they scour, and
they madden about,—
'Tis there we go bounding in mystical
rout."
No sooner had spoken
This voice half-broken,
When suddenly from quivering tongues
arose the universal cry.
The timbrels with a boom resound, the
cymbals with a clash reply,
And up the verdant Ida with a quicken'd
step the chorus flew,
While Atys with the timbrels' smite the
terrible procession drew;
Raging, panting, wild, and witless,
through the sullen shades it broke,
Like the fierce, unconquer'd heifer burst-
ing from her galling yoke;
And on pursue the sacred crew, till at the
door of Cybele,

Faint and fasting, down they sink, in
pale immovability:
The heavy sleep—the heavy sleep—
grows o'er their failing eyes,
And lock'd in dead repose the rabid
frenzy lies.
But when the Sun look'd out with eyes
of light,
Found the firm earth, wild seas, and
skies of morning white,
  Scaring the lingering shades
  With echo-footed steeds,
Sleep took his flight from Atys, hurrying
To his Pasithea's arms on tremulous
wing;
And the poor dreamer woke, oppress'd
with sadness,
To memory woke, and to collected mad-
ness.—
Struck with its loss, with what it was,
and where,
Back trod the wretched being in despair
To the sea-shore, and stretching forth
its eye
O'er the wide waste of waters and of sky,
Thus to its country cried with tears of
misery:—
"My country, oh my country, parent
state,
Whom like a very slave and runagate,
Wretch that I am, I left for wilds like
these,
This wilderness of snows and matted
trees,
To house with shivering beasts and
learn their wants,
A fierce intruder on their sullen haunts,—
Where shall I fancy thee? Where cheat
mine eye
With tricking out thy quarter in the sky?
Fain, while my wits a little space are free,
Would my poor eye-balls strain their
points on thee!
Am I then torn from home and far away!
Doom'd through these woods to trample
day by day,
Far from my kindred friends and native
soil,

The mall, the race, and wrestlers bright
with oil?
Ah wretch, bewail, bewail; and think for
this
On all thy past variety of bliss.
I was the charm of life, the social spring,
First in the race, and brightest in the
ring:
Warm with the stir of welcome was my
home;
And when I rose betimes, my friends
would come
Smiling and pressing in officious scores,
Thick as the flowers that hang at lovers'
doors:—
And shall I then a minist'ring madman be
To angry gods? A howling devotee?—
A slave to bear what never senses can,—
Half of myself, sexless,—a sterile man?
And must I feel, with never-varied woes,
The o'erhanging winter of these moun-
tain snows,
Skulking through ghastly woods for ever-
more,
Like the lean stag, or the brute vagrant
boar?
Ah me! ah me! Already I repent;
E'en now, e'en now I feel my shame and
punishment!"
As thus with rosy lips the wretch grew
loud,
Startling the ears of heaven's imperial
crowd,
The Mighty Mistress o'er her lion yoke
Bow'd in her wrath,—and loosening as
she spoke
The left-hand savage, scatterer of herds,
Roused his fell nature with impetuous
words.
"Fly, ruffian, fly, indignant and amain,
And scare this being, who resists my
reign,
Back to the horror-breathing woods
again.
Lash thee, and fly and shake with sinewy
might
Thine ireful hair, and as at dead of night
Fill the wild echoes with rebellowing
fright."

Threatening she spoke, and loosed the
vengeance dire,
Who gathering all his rage and glaring
fire,
Starts with a roar, and scours beneath
her eyes,
Scattering the splinter'd bushes as he
flies:
Down by the sea he spies the wretch at
last,
And springs precipitous:—the wretch as
fast,

Flies raving back into his living grave,
And there for ever dwells, a savage and
a slave.
O Goddess! Mistress! Cybele! dread
name!
O mighty power! O Dindymenian dame!
Far from my home thy visitations
be:
Drive others mad, not me:
Drive others into impulse wild, and fierce
insanity.

—LEIGH HUNT.

THE PEACE OF AUGUSTUS

END OF FIRST CENTURY B.C. AND BEGINNING OF FIRST CENTURY A.D.

IN contrast with the conspiracies, civil wars, and proscriptions of the Ciceronian period, the outstanding political characteristic of the succeeding decades was the restoration of peace by Augustus. The Republic had finally worn itself out, and in its place was established monarchy. Republican forms were retained, republican formulæ continued to be used, but the old freedom and the widespread participation in public affairs had gone forever. The state was now controlled by an emperor and his armies.

In such circumstances men's thoughts and pursuits of necessity were directed into new channels. Politics, with its accompaniments of controversy and oratory, was no longer attractive or profitable as a subject for writing; even history was not altogether safe, since it opened up old sores that should be allowed to heal. Practical affairs were in the hands of the ruler, and, so long as he proved wise and capable, were best left there. Men turned more and more to the world of the imagination and to their private lives for the material of their literary expression. The time of Cicero had been an era of prose, that of Augustus was an era of poetry.

The wise Augustus set about many reforms in his efforts to revive the state from its exhaustion. Whether directly under his influence or indirectly through his example and through his advisers, or whether because of their own convictions, the men of letters attached themselves to the emperor's program and accomplished more than any other agency in bringing about general acceptance of the new régime. They busied themselves with turning their eyes upon the past to discover the qualities of character that had made Rome so great; they sang the glories of peace and the praises of the ruling house; they inculcated lessons in the appreciation of the beautiful and inspired men to the rebuilding of what had been destroyed; they encouraged the peaceful pursuits of agriculture and pictured the glories of Italian landscape; they promoted the revival of old customs; they realized fully for the first time the meaning of Rome as a great nation instead of as a city-state; and with their interpretation of Rome's mission in society they set aflame the pride of the people in their splendid enterprise. It was the great outpouring of the Roman genius.

On the formal side there was much variety. Epic reached its supremacy in Virgil, satire and lyric in Horace, and elegy in Tibullus, Propertius, and Ovid. Some success seems to have been achieved also in dramatic poetry, but no representative play has come down to us by which we may judge. There are no finer examples of the pastoral and the didactic than the *Eclogues* and the *Georgics* of Virgil. The sole important piece of prose was Livy's history, and this takes rank with the best in Roman Literature.

It was an age that fostered in every way possible the production of poetry. Patrons like Mæcenas and Pollio not only encouraged poets by suggestions and helpful criticism, but made it possible for them to devote themselves to writing by providing them with the means of livelihood. The new public library put at the disposal of writers the literature of the past, and public recitations, instituted now for the first time, provided them with a public. The profession of writing, especially of writing poetry, received full recognition, and a poet became now an artist rather than an artisan.

I. ESTABLISHMENT OF EMPIRE

The death of Julius Cæsar speedily plunged the empire into anarchy and civil war once more. At first Octavius, heir and adopted son of Cæsar, supported Cicero and the consuls in an attempt to save the state from the domination of Antony. This situation soon ended when Antony, Octavius, and Lepidus formed the combination known as the second triumvirate which signalized its assumption of power by the murder of Cicero in 43 B.C. The next year the triumvirate defeated the last forces of the Republic under Brutus and Cassius at Philippi. Thereupon Antony and Octavius with Lepidus a negligible third, divided the empire between them. Antony took the East, Octavius took the West, including Italy. This settlement could not be permanent; but for some ten years, during which each leader had wars to wage in his part of the empire, peace was maintained between them. Finally, civil war broke out once more, and at Actium in 31 B.C. Octavius won a victory which soon gave him undisputed control of the Roman world.

Rome was exhausted by the series of civil wars which had extended over a period of twenty years. Peace was longed for by all citizens, and by the leadership of Octavius they believed it could be secured. Without opposition he was then enabled to reform the constitution. Using the old form of government as a basis both because of its worth and to satisfy the conservative feelings of the Romans, Octavius essentially changed the Republic to a constitutional monarchy. In theory he was himself an official of the state, his military powers being an expansion of the powers granted Pompey in the East a generation before, and his executive authority being centered largely in the tribunician power, an expansion of the age-old position of tribune. Augustus, as he was now called, in fact publicly declared that he had restored the Republic. However, with the army entirely at his disposal, there was never any doubt where power actually lay. In Tacitus' phrase, there were still the same names of offices. But consul, prætor, senate still had a very real part to play, though subordinate to the ruler. Emperor he really was; but the term he preferred was *princeps,* chief citizen of the state. From that term the government is known as the principate. Augustus had done wisely in not openly establishing monarchy. Time justified him, for the structure whose foundations he laid withstood the shocks and storms of many centuries.

Achievements of the First Emperor [1]

AUGUSTUS

Gaius Julius Cæsar Octavianus Augustus was born in 63 B.C. and died in 14 A.D. When not yet twenty years of age, at the death of Julius Cæsar, whose adopted son and heir he was, he made himself a leader in the state by the support of many of the dictator's veterans. On the conclusion of the civil wars he reformed the constitution and by general consent was made head of the state. During his long rule the empire enjoyed peace and economic prosperity, while literature and the arts flourished.

Augustus was himself a serious and appreciative patron of letters and an author of no little distinction. But, with the exception of a few quotations from his letters preserved in later authors, only one of his writings is extant, the *Res Gestae divi Augusti.* A plain, unadorned account of the achievements of his career, a kind of official autobiography, it is of historical significance not only for the information it gives, but also because it comes from the pen of the first emperor and gives his interpretations of events as he would have Rome understand them. He represents the victory over Brutus and Cassius as the

[1] From *Augustus,* by E. S. Shuckburgh. Copyright by T. Fisher Unwin, Ltd. Reprinted by permission.

avenging of his father's murder, and he considers his reform of the constitution as a restoring of the Republic. This document Augustus caused to be inscribed on bronze tablets which were placed beside the door of his tomb. The original has not survived; but a copy in the Greek and Latin languages cut on the walls of the temple of Rome and Augustus at Ancyra, Asia Minor, has preserved it to modern times.

When I was nineteen I collected an army on my own account and at my own expense, by the help of which I restored the republic to liberty, which had been enslaved by the tyranny of a faction; for which services the Senate, in complimentary decrees, added my name to the roll of their House in the consulship of Gaius Pansa and Aulus Hirtius, giving me at the same time consular precedence in voting; and gave me the imperium. It ordered me as pro-prætor "to see along with the consuls that the republic suffered no damage." Moreover, in the same year, both consuls having fallen, the people elected me consul and a triumvir for revising the constitution.

Those who killed my father I drove into exile, after a legal trial, in punishment of their crime, and afterwards when these same men rose in arms against the republic I conquered them twice in a pitched battle.

I had to undertake wars by land and sea, civil and foreign, all over the world, and when victorious I spared surviving citizens. Those foreign nations, who could safely be pardoned, I preferred to preserve rather than exterminate. About 500,000 Roman citizens took the military oath to me. Of these I settled out in colonies or sent back to their own towns, after their terms of service were over, considerably more than 300,000; and to them all I assigned lands purchased by myself or money in lieu of lands. I captured 600 ships, not counting those below the rank of triremes.

I twice celebrated an ovation, three times curule triumphs, and was twenty-one times greeted as Imperator. Though the Senate afterwards voted me several triumphs I declined them. I frequently also deposited laurels in the Capitol after performing the vows which I had taken in each war. For successful operations performed by myself or by my legates under my auspices by land and sea, the Senate fifty-three times decreed a supplication to the immortal gods. The number of days during which, in accordance with a decree of the Senate, supplication was offered amounted to 890. In my triumphs there were led before my chariot nine kings or sons of kings. I had been consul thirteen times at the writing of this, and am in the course of the thirty-seventh year of my tribunician power.

The Dictatorship offered me in my presence and absence by the Senate and people in the consulship of Marcus Marcellus and Lucius Arruntius I declined to accept. I did not refuse at a time of very great scarcity of corn the commissionership of corn supply, which I administered in such a way that within a few days I freed the whole people from fear and danger. The consulship—either yearly or for life—then offered to me I declined to accept.

In the consulship of M. Vinicius and Q. Lucretius, and P. and Cn. Lentulus, and of Paulus Fabius Maximus and Q. Tubero, when the Senate and the people of Rome unanimously agreed that I should be elected overseer of the laws and morals, with unlimited powers and without a colleague, I refused every office offered me which was contrary to the customs of our ancestors. But what the Senate at that time wished me to manage, I carried out in virtue of my tribunician power, and in this office I five times received at my own request a colleague from the Senate.

I was one of the triumvirate for the re-establishment of the constitution for ten consecutive years. I have been *princeps senatus* up to the day on which I write this for forty years. I am Pontifex Maximus, Augur, one of the fifteen commissioners for religion, one of the seven for sacred feasts, an Arval Brother, a *sodalis Titius*, a fetial.

In my fifth consulship I increased the number of the patricians by order of people and Senate. I three times made up the roll of the Senate, and in my sixth consulship I took a census of the people with M. Agrippa as my colleague. I performed the *lustrum* after an interval of forty-one years; in which the number of Roman citizens entered on the census roll was 4,063,000. A second time with consular imperium I took the census by myself in the consulship of Gaius Censorinus and Gaius Asinius, in which the number of Roman citizens entered on the roll was 4,223,000. I took a third census with consular imperium, my son Tiberius Cæsar acting as my colleague, in the consulship of Sextus Pompeius and Sextus Appuleius, in which the number of Roman citizens entered on the census roll was 4,937,000. By new laws passed I recalled numerous customs of our ancestors that were falling into desuetude in our time, and myself set precedents in many particulars for the imitation of posterity.

The Senate decreed that vows should be offered for my health by consuls and priests every fifth year. In fulfilment of these vows the four chief colleges of priests or the consuls often gave games in my lifetime. Also individually and by townships the people at large always offered sacrifices at all the temples for my health.

By a decree of the Senate my name was included in the ritual of the Salii; and it was ordained by a law that my person should be sacred and that I should have the tribunician power for the term of my natural life. I refused to become Pontifex Maximus in succession to my colleague during his life, though the people offered me that sacred office formerly held by my father. Some years later I accepted that sacred office on the death of the man who had availed himself of the civil disturbance to secure it; such a multitude flocking to my election from all parts of Italy as is never recorded to have come to Rome before, in the consulship of P. Sulpicius and C. Valgius.

The Senate consecrated an altar to Fortuna Redux, near the temple of Honour and Virtue, by the Porta Capena, for my return, on which it ordered the Vestal Virgins to offer a yearly sacrifice on the day on which in the consulship of Q. Lucretius and M. Vinucius I returned to the city from Syria, and gave that day the name *Augustalia* from my cognomen. By a decree of the Senate at the same time part of the prætors and tribunes of the plebs, along with the consul Q. Lucretius and leading nobles, were despatched into Campania to meet me—an honour that up to this time has been decreed to no one else. When I returned to Rome from Spain and Gaul after successful operations in those provinces, in the consulship of Tiberius Nero and Publius Quintilius, the Senate voted that an altar to Pax Augusta should be consecrated for my return on the Campus Martius, upon which it ordered the magistrates and priests and Vestal Virgins to offer an annual sacrifice.

Whereas the Ianus Quirinus, which our ancestors ordered to be closed when peace throughout the whole dominions of the Roman people by land and sea had been obtained by victories, is recorded to have been only twice shut before my birth since the foundation of the city, the Senate three times voted its closure during my principate.

My sons Gaius and Lucius Cæsar, whom fortune snatched from me in their early manhood, in compliment to me, the Senate and Roman people designated consuls in their fifteenth year with a proviso that they should enter on that office after an interval of five years. From the day of their assuming the *toga virilis* the Senate decreed that they should take part in public business. Moreover, the Roman equites in a body gave each of them the title of *Princeps Iuventutis,* and presented them with silver shields and spears.

To the Roman plebs I paid 300 sesterces per head in virtue of my father's will; and in my own name I gave 400 apiece in my fifth consulship from the sales of spoils of war; and a second time in my tenth consulship out of my own private property I paid a bounty of 400 sesterces per man, and in my eleventh consulship I measured out twelve distributions of corn, having purchased the grain from my own resources. In the twelfth year of my tribunician power, for a third time I gave a bounty of 400 sesterces a head. These largesses of mine affected never less than 250,000 persons. In the eighteenth year of my tribunician power and my twelfth consulship I gave 320,000 of the urban plebs sixty denarii a head. In the colonies of my soldiers, in my fifth consulship I gave from the sale of spoils of war 1000 sesterces a head; and among such settlers the number who received that triumphal largess amounted to about 120,000 men. In my thirteenth consulship I gave 60 denarii apiece to the plebeians then in receipt of public corn; they amounted to somewhat more than 200,000 persons.

The money for the lands, which in my fourth consulship, and afterwards in the consulship of M. Crassus and Cn. Lentulus the augur, I assigned to the soldiers, I paid to the municipal towns. The amount was about 600,000,000 sesterces, which I paid for lands in Italy, and about 260,000,000 which I disbursed for lands in the provinces.

I was the first and only one within the memory of my own generation to do this of all who settled colonies in Italy and the provinces. And afterwards in the consulship of Tib. Nero and Cn. Piso, and again in the consulship of C. Antistius and D. Lælius, and of C. Calvisius and L. Pasienus, and of L. Lentulus and M. Messalla, and of L. Caninius and Q. Fabricius, to the soldiers, whom after their terms of service I sent back to their own towns, I paid good service allowances in ready money; on which I expended 400,000,000 sesterces as an act of grace.

I four times subsidised the *ærarium* from my own money, the sums which I thus paid over to the commissioners of the treasury amounting to 150,000,000 sesterces. And in the consulship of M. Lepidus and L. Arruntius, to the military treasury, which was established on my initiative for the payment of their good service allowance, to the soldiers who had served twenty years or more, I contributed from my own patrimony 170,000,000 sesterces.

From and after the year of the consulship of Gnæus and Publius Lentulus, whenever the payments of the revenues were in arrears, I paid into the treasury from my own patrimony the taxes, whether due in corn or money, sometimes of 100,000 persons, sometimes of more.

I built the curia and the chalcidicum adjoining it, and the temple of Apollo on the Palatine with its colonnades, the temple of the divine Julius, the Lupercal, the colonnade at the Flaminian circus, which I allowed to be called Octavia, from the name of the builder of the earlier one on the same site, the state box at the Circus Maximus, the temples of Jupiter Feretrius and of Jupiter Tonans on the Capitol, the temple of Quirinus, the temples of Minerva and of Juno the Queen, and of Jupiter Liberalis on the Aventine, the temple of the Lares at the head of the *Via Sacra,* the temple of the divine Penates in the Velia, the temple of Youth, the temple of the Magna Mater on the Palatine.

The Capitolium and the Pompeian

theatre—both very costly works—I restored without any inscription of my own name. Water-conduits in many places that were decaying from age I repaired; and I doubled the acqueduct called the Aqua Marcia, by turning a new spring into its channel.

The Forum Iulium and the basilica, which was between the temple of Castor and the temple of Saturn, works begun and far advanced by my father, I completed; and when the same basilica was destroyed by fire, I began its reconstruction on an extended plan, to be inscribed with the names of my sons, and in case I do not live to complete it I have ordered it to be completed by my heirs.

In my sixth consulship, I repaired eighty-two temples of the gods in the city in accordance with a decree of the Senate, none being omitted which at that time stood in need of repair. In my seventh consulship I constructed the Flaminian road from the city to Ariminum, and all the bridges except the Mulvian and Minucian.

On ground belonging to myself I built a temple to Mars Ultor and the Forum Augustum, with money arising from sale of spoils of war. I built a theatre adjoining the temple of Apollo, on ground for the most part purchased from private owners, to be under the name of my son-in-law Marcus Marcellus. Offerings from money raised by sale of war-spoil I consecrated in the temple of Apollo, and in the temple of Vesta, and in the temple of Mars Ultor, which cost me about 100,000,000 sesterces. Thirty-five thousand pounds of gold, crown money contributed by the municipia and colonies of Italy for my triumphs, I refunded in my fifth consulship, and subsequently, as often as I was greeted Imperator, I refused to receive crown money, though the municipia and colonies had decreed it with as much warmth as before.

I three times gave a show of gladiators in my own name, and five times in the name of my sons and grandsons; in which shows about 10,000 men contended. I twice gave the people a show of athletes collected from all parts of the world in my own name, and a third time in the name of my grandson. I gave games in my own name four times, as representing other magistrates twenty-three times. In behalf of the quindecimviri, and as master of the college, with M. Agrippa as colleague, I gave the Secular games in the consulship of C. Furnius and C. Silanus. In my thirteenth consulship, I gave for the first time games of Mars which, since that time, the consuls have given in successive years. I gave the people wild-beast hunts, of African animals, in my own name and that of my sons and grandsons, in the circus and forum, and the amphitheatres twenty-six times, in which about 3,500 animals were killed.

I gave the people the spectacle of a naval battle on the other side of the Tiber, in the spot where now is the grove of the Cæsars, the ground having been hollowed out to a length of 1,800 feet, and a breadth of 1,200 feet, in which thirty beaked ships, triremes or biremes, and a still larger number of smaller vessels contended. In these fleets, besides the rowers, there fought about three thousand men.

In the temples of all the states of the province of Asia, I replaced the ornaments after my victory, which he with whom I had fought had taken into his private possession from the spoliation of the temples. There were about eighty silver statues of me, some on foot, some equestrian, some in chariots, in various parts of the city. These I removed, and from the money thus obtained I placed golden offerings in the temple of Apollo in my own name and in the name of those who had honoured me by the statues.

I cleared the sea of pirates. In that war I captured about 30,000 slaves, who had run away from their masters, and had borne arms against the republic, and handed them back to their owners to be punished. The whole of Italy took the oath to me spontaneously, and demanded that I should be the leader in the war in which I won the victory off Actium. The provinces of the Gauls, the Spains, Africa, Sicily, Sardinia, took the same oath. Among those who fought under my standards were more than seven hundred Senators, eighty-three of whom had been, or have been since, consuls up to the time of my writing this, 170 members of the sacred colleges.

I extended the frontiers of all the provinces of the Roman people, which were bordered by tribes that had not submitted to our Empire. The provinces of the Gauls, and Spains and Germany, bounded by the Ocean from Gades to the mouth of the river Elbe, I reduced to a peaceful state. The Alps, from the district near the Adriatic to the Tuscan sea, I forced to remain peaceful without waging unprovoked war with any tribe. My fleet sailed through the Ocean from the mouth of the Rhine towards the rising sun, up to the territories of the Cimbri, to which point no Roman had penetrated, up to that time, either by land or sea. The Cimbri, and Charydes, and Semnones and other peoples of the Germans, belonging to the same tract of country, sent ambassadors to ask for the friendship of myself and the Roman people. By my command and under my auspices, two armies were marched into Æthiopia and Arabia, called Felix, nearly simultaneously, and large hostile forces of both these nations were cut to pieces in battle, and a large number of towns were captured. Æthiopia was penetrated as far as the town Nabata, next to Meroe. Into Arabia the army advanced into the territories of the Sabæi as far as the town of Mariba.

I added Egypt to the Empire of the Roman people. When I might have made the greater Armenia a province after the assassination of its king Artaxes, I preferred, on the precedent of our ancestors, to hand over the kingdom to Tigranes, son of King Artavasdes, grandson of King Tigranes, by the hands of Tiberius Nero, who was then my stepson. The same nation being afterwards in a state of revolt and rebellion, I handed over to the government of King Ariobarzanes, son of Artabazus, king of the Medes, after it had been reduced by my son Gaius; and after his death to his son Artavasdes, upon whose assassination I sent Tigranes, a member of the royal family of the Armenians, into that kingdom. I recovered all the provinces on the other side of the Adriatic towards the East and Cyrenæ, which were by this time for the most part held by various kings, and before them Sicily and Sardinia which had been overrun by an army of slaves.

I settled colonies of soldiers in Africa, Sicily, Macedonia, both the Spains, Achaia, Asia, Syria, Gallia Narbonensis, Pisidia. Italy has twenty-eight colonies established under my auspices, which have in my lifetime become very densely inhabited and places of great resort.

A large number of military standards, which had been lost under other commanders, I recovered, after defeating the enemy, from Spain and Gaul and the Dalmatians. I compelled the Parthians to restore the spoils and standards of three Roman armies, and to seek as suppliants the friendship of the Roman people. These standards I laid up in the inner shrine belonging to the temple of Mars Ultor.

The tribes of the Pannonii, which before I was *princeps* an army of the Roman people never reached, having been subdued by Tiberius Nero, who was then my stepson and legate, I added to the Empire of the Roman people, and I extended the frontier of Illyricum to the bank of the river Danube. And when an army of the Daci crossed to the south of that river it was conquered and put to flight under my auspices; and subsequently my army being led across the Danube, forced the tribes of the Daci to submit to the orders of the Roman people.

To me there were often sent embassies of kings from India who had never been seen in the camp of any Roman general. By embassadors the Bastarnæ and the Scythians and the kings of the Sarmatians, who live on both sides of the river Don, and the king of the Albani and of the Hiberi and of the Medes, sought our friendship.

Kings of the Parthians—Tiridates, and afterwards Phrates, son of King Phrates —fled to me for refuge; of the Medes Artavasdes; of the Adiabeni Artaxares; of the Britons Dumnobellaunus and Tim . . . ; of the Marcomanni and Suebi . . . Phrates, king of the Parthians, son of Orodes, sent all his sons and grandsons to me in Italy, not because he had been overcome in war, but seeking our friendship by means of his own sons as pledges. And a very large number of other nations experienced the good faith of the Roman people while I was *princeps,* with whom before that time there had been no diplomatic or friendly intercourse.

The nations of the Parthians and the chief men of the Medes by means of embassies sought and accepted from me kings of those peoples—the Parthians Vonones, son of King Phrates, grandson of King Orodes; the Medes Ariobarzanes, son of King Artavasdes, grandson of King Ariobarzanes.

In my sixth and seventh consulships, when I had extinguished the flames of civil war, having by universal consent become possessed of the sole direction of affairs, I transferred the republic from my power to the will of the Senate and people of Rome. For which good service on my part I was by decree of the Senate called by the name of Augustus, and the door-posts of my house were covered with laurels in the name of the state, and a civic crown was fixed up over my door, and a golden shield was placed in the Curia Iulia, which it was declared by its inscription the Senate and people of Rome gave me in recognition of valour, clemency, justice, piety. After that time I took precedence of all in rank, but of power I had nothing more than those who were my colleagues in the several magistracies.

While I was administering my thirteenth consulship, the Senate and equestrian order and the Roman people with one consent greeted me as FATHER OF MY COUNTRY, and decreed that it should be inscribed in the vestibule of my house, and in the Senate house, and in the Forum Augustum, and under the chariot which was there placed in my honour in accordance with a senatorial decree.

When I wrote this I was in my seventy-sixth year.

—E. S. Shuckburgh.

II. THE EPIC OF ROME'S DESTINY: VIRGIL'S ÆNEID

Publius Vergilius Maro was born of peasant stock in the village of Andes near Mantua in 70 B.C. In his boyhood he gained at first hand an experience of farm life and a knowledge of nature which proved of inestimable value to him in his later career. His training was received at the schools of neighboring towns, then in Rome, and later under the Epicurean philosopher Siro near Naples. His life was the quiet life of the student and man of letters, spent partly in Rome but mainly in the neighborhood of Naples. He died in 19 B.C. at Brundisium.

Virgil was the finest product of the system of patronage which flourished in the time of Augustus. His early activity as a poet fell under the influence of Pollio and Mæcenas, and was devoted to themes that sprang directly from the farm life of his youth—pastoral poems known as the *Eclogues* or *Bucolics,* and the didactic poem called the *Georgics.* The *Æneid,* the product of his maturer years, is said to have been written at the request of Augustus, who encouraged poetry not only for its own sake, but also as a means of moral, religious, and political reform. There are extant also a number of other poems whose genuineness has long been the subject of controversy.

The view of epic as history, exemplified by Ennius in his *Annals* and again by Nævius in his *Punic War,* was still looked upon as the proper view even in the Augustan Age. Epic, like most other forms of literature, was a servant of the state, and could best perform this function by reciting the achievements of the past and glorifying the heroes of Rome. It was also an appropriate vehicle for celebrating the deeds of contemporary leaders, for making secure their place in song and story, and for bolstering up their following and their policies. There can be little doubt that the pressure of such ideas was brought to bear upon Virgil when he undertook his great task.

But Virgil skillfully found a means of satisfying these demands without at the same time suffering his work to be made subject to the limitations which history imposes upon the imagination and the defects which inevitably result from the lack of a unified theme. He chose the mythological type of subject, the story of a legendary hero. But by assigning to that hero the definite mission of founding Rome, by interpreting the meaning and consequences of the hero's deeds, by portraying his character as the embodiment of Roman ideals, and by actually weaving into the narrative through devices of prophecy and the like many of the great events and personages of Roman history, he gave the poem as a whole a vivid coloring of the historical and the patriotic. By choosing as his hero a mythical ancestor of the Cæsars he was able also to sing the praises of the emperor.

As Æneas had a mission among men, so Rome had a mission among peoples. It was Rome's task to bring order out of confusion, to unify the conflicting elements of the Mediterranean civilization, to establish peace, and to secure the supremacy of law. She was to rule the world through law. This is still our general understanding of the part Rome played in the progress of civilization, and it is in the *Æneid* that we find its clearest presentation.

The story of the poem is briefly as follows. Æneas, an exile from Troy at the time of its destruction by the Greeks, flees under guidance of the gods with his son and father and a small company of refugees. Gradually the divine plan of the founding of a new empire in Italy is unfolded to him, and he journeys on from place to place seeking his destined goal. After many adventures on land and sea, at the court of Dido the Carthaginian queen, and in Sicily, he comes to Italy. Before entering upon the second phase of his great task, he visits Hades to consult his father, who had died on the journey, in order to obtain guidance for his future career. Returning to the upper world, he first makes peaceable overtures to the native king Latinus and is cordially received. But a local prince, Turnus, seeing in Æneas a rival for the hand of the king's daughter, betrothed to himself, and a foreign invader of his country, stirs up war against him. Epic battles follow, the tide of fortune shifting now this way, now that. The fighting finally resolves itself into a duel between the two leaders, and with the slaying of Turnus by Æneas the story ends.

ÆNEAS AT CARTHAGE

[From Book I]

The opening of the *Æneid,* like that of Homer's *Odyssey,* plunges the reader *in medias res.* The first book gives the account of the hero's landing in Africa and of his reception by Dido; in the two following books Æneas himself tells the story of the antecedent circumstances.

Arms and the man I sing, who forc'd by fate,
And haughty Juno's unrelenting hate;
Expell'd and exil'd, left the Trojan shore,
Long labours both by sea and land he bore;
And in the doubtful war, before he won
The Latian realm, and built the destin'd town:
His banish'd gods restor'd to rites divine,
And settl'd sure succession in his line:
From whence the race of Alban fathers come,
And the long glories of majestic Rome.
  O! Muse, the causes and the crimes relate,
What goddess was provok'd, and whence her hate;
For what offence the queen of heav'n began
To persecute so brave, so just a man!
Involv'd his anxious life in endless cares,
Expos'd to wants, and hurry'd into wars!
Can heav'nly minds such high resentment show,
Or exercise their spite in human woe?
  Against the Tiber's mouth, but far away,
An ancient town was seated on the sea:
A Tyrian colony, the people made
Stout for the war, and studious of their trade,
Carthage the name, belov'd by Juno more
Than her own Argos, or the Samian shore.
Here stood her chariot, here, if heav'n were kind,
The seat of awful empire she design'd.
Yet she had heard an ancient rumour fly,
(Long cited by the people of the sky)
That times to come should see the Trojan race
Her Carthage ruin, and her tow'rs deface:

Nor thus confin'd, the yoke of sov'reign sway,
Should on the necks of all the nations lay.
She ponder'd this, and fear'd it was in fate,
Nor could forget the war she wag'd of late,
For conqu'ring Greece against the Trojan state.
Besides long causes working in her mind,
And secret seeds of envy lay behind.
Deep graven in her heart, the doom remain'd
Of partial Paris, and her form disdain'd:
The grace bestow'd on ravish'd Ganymed,
Electra's glories, and her injur'd bed.
Each was a cause alone, and all combin'd
To kindle vengeance in her haughty mind.
For this, far distant from the Latian coast,
She drove the remnants of the Trojan host:
And sev'n long years th' unhappy wand'ring train,
Were toss'd by storms, and scatter'd through the main.
Such time, such toil requir'd the Roman name,
Such length of labour for so vast a fame.
  Now scarce the Trojan fleet with sails and oars
Had left behind the fair Sicilian shores:
Ent'ring with cheerful shouts the wat'ry reign,
And ploughing frothy furrows in the main:
When lab'ring still, with endless discontent,
The queen of heav'n did thus her fury vent.
"Then am I vanquish'd, must I yield," said she,
"And must the Trojans reign in Italy?
So fate will have it, and Jove adds his force,
Nor can my pow'r divert their happy course.
Could angry Pallas, with revengeful spleen,

The Grecian navy burn, and drown the men?
She for the fault of one offending foe,
The bolts of Jove himself presum'd to throw:
With whirlwinds from beneath she toss'd the ship,
And bare expos'd the bosom of the deep:
Then, as an eagle gripes the trembling game,
The wretch yet hissing with her father's flame,
She strongly seiz'd, and with a burning wound,
Transfix'd and naked, on a rock she bound.
But I, who walk in awful state above,
The majesty of heav'n, the sister-wife of Jove,
For length of years my fruitless force employ
Against the thin remains of ruin'd Troy.
What nations now to Juno's pow'r will pray,
Or off'rings on my slighted altars lay?"
  Thus rag'd the goddess, and with fury fraught,
The restless regions of the storms she sought.
Where in a spacious cave of living stone,
The tyrant Æolus from his airy throne,
With pow'r imperial curbs the struggling winds,
And sounding tempests in dark prisons binds.
This way, and that, th' impatient captives tend,
And pressing for release, the mountains rend.
High in his hall, th' undaunted monarch stands,
And shakes his sceptre, and their rage commands:
Which did he not, their unresisted sway
Would sweep the world before them in their way:
Earth, air and seas through empty space would roll,
And heav'n would fly before the driving soul.
In fear of this the father of the gods
Confin'd their fury to those dark abodes,
And lock'd 'em safe within, oppress'd with mountain loads:
Impos'd a king with arbitrary sway,
To loose their fetters, or their force allay.
To whom the suppliant queen her pray'rs addrest,
And thus the tenor of her suit express'd:
  "O Æolus! for to thee the king of heav'n
The pow'r of tempests, and of winds has giv'n:
Thy force alone their fury can restrain,
And smooth the waves, or swell the troubl'd main:
A race of wand'ring slaves, abhorr'd by me,
With prosp'rous passage cut the Tuscan sea:
To fruitful Italy their course they steer,
And for their vanquish'd gods design new temples there.
Raise all thy winds, with night involve the skies,
Sink or disperse my fatal enemies.
Twice sev'n, the charming daughters of the main,
Around my person wait, and bear my train:
Succeed my wish, and second my design,
The fairest, Deiopeia, shall be thine,
And make thee father of a happy line."
  To this the god:—" 'Tis yours, O queen! to will
The work, which duty binds me to fulfil.
These airy kingdoms, and this wide command,
Are all the presents of your bounteous hand;
Yours is my sov'reign grace, and as your guest,
I sit with gods at their celestial feast,
Raise tempests at your pleasure, or subdue,
Dispose of empire, which I hold from you."

He said, and hurl'd against the mountain side
His quiv'ring spear, and all the god apply'd.
The raging winds rush through the hollow wound,
And dance aloft in air, and skim along the ground:
Then settling on the sea, the surges sweep,
Raise liquid mountains, and disclose the deep.
South, east, and west, with mix'd confusion roar,
And roll the foaming billows on the shore.
The cables crack, the sailors' fearful cries
Ascend; and sable night involves the skies,
And heav'n itself is ravish'd from their eyes.
Loud peals of thunder from the poles ensue,
Then flashing fires the transient light renew;
The face of things a frightful image bears,
And present death in various forms appears.
Struck with unusual fright, the Trojan chief,
With lifted hands and eyes, invokes relief.
"And thrice and four times happy those," he cried,
"That under Ilian walls before their parents died.
Tydides, bravest of the Grecian train,
Why could not I by that strong arm be slain,
And lie by noble Hector on the plain:
Or great Sarpedon in those bloody fields,
Where Simois rolls the bodies and the shields
Of heroes, whose dismember'd hands yet bear
The dart aloft, and clench the pointed spear?"
Thus while the pious prince his fate bewails,

Fierce Boreas drove against his flying sails,
And rent the sheets; the raging billows rise,
And mount the tossing vessel to the skies:
Nor can the shiv'ring oars sustain the blow,
The galley gives her side, and turns her prow:
While those astern descending down the steep,
Through gaping waves behold the boiling deep.
Three ships were hurried by the southern blast,
And on the secret shelves with fury cast.
Those hidden rocks th' Ausonian sailors knew,
They call'd them altars, when they rose in view,
And show'd their spacious backs above the flood.
Three more, fierce Eurus in his angry mood
Dash'd on the shallows of the moving sand,
And in mid ocean left them moor'd a-land.
Orontes' barque that bore the Lycian crew,
(A horrid sight) ev'n in the hero's view,
From stem to stern, by waves was overborn,
The trembling pilot from his rudder torn,
Was headlong hurl'd, thrice round the ship was tost,
Then bulg'd at once, and in the deep was lost;
And here and there above the waves were seen
Arms, pictures, precious goods, and floating men.
The stoutest vessel to the storm gave way,
And suck'd through loosen'd planks the rushing sea.
Ilioneus was her chief: Aletes old,
Achates faithful, Abas young and bold,

Endur'd not less; their ships, with gaping
    seams,
Admit the deluge of the briny streams.
    Meantime imperial Neptune heard the
    sound
Of raging billows breaking on the ground:
Displeas'd, and fearing for his wat'ry
    reign,
He rear'd his awful head above the main:
Serene in majesty, then roll'd his eyes
Around the space of earth, and seas, and
    skies.
He saw the Trojan fleet dispers'd, dis-
    tress'd,
By stormy winds and wintry heav'n op-
    press'd.
Full well the god his sister's envy knew,
And what her aims and what her arts
    pursue:
He summon'd Eurus and the western
    blast,
And first an angry glance on both he
    cast:
Then thus rebuk'd: "Audacious winds!
    from whence
This bold attempt, this rebel insolence?
Is it for you to ravage seas and land,
Unauthoriz'd by my supreme command?
To raise such mountains on the troubled
    main?
Whom I—But first 'tis fit, the billows to
    restrain,
And then you shall be taught obedience
    to my reign.
Hence, to your lord my royal mandate
    bear,
The realms of ocean and the fields of air
Are mine, not his; by fatal lot to me
The liquid empire fell, and trident of
    the sea.
His pow'r to hollow caverns is confin'd,
There let him reign, the jailor of the
    wind:
With hoarse commands his breathing
    subjects call,
And boast and bluster in his empty hall."
He spoke, and while he spoke he smooth'd
    the sea,

Dispell'd the darkness, and restor'd the
    day:
Cymothoe, Triton, and the sea-green
    train
Of beauteous nymphs, the daughters of
    the main,
Clear from the rocks the vessels with
    their hands;
The god himself with ready trident
    stands,
And opes the deep and spreads the mov-
    ing sands;
Then heaves them off the shoals, where'er
    he guides
His finny coursers, and in triumph rides,
The waves unruffle, and the sea subsides.
As when in tumults rise the ignoble crowd,
Mad are their motions, and their tongues
    are loud;
And stones and brands in rattling vollies
    fly,
And all the rustic arms that fury can
    supply;
If then some grave and pious man appear,
They hush their noise, and lend a lis-
    t'ning ear;
He soothes with sober words their angry
    mood,
And quenches their innate desire of
    blood:
So when the father of the flood appears,
And o'er the seas his sov'reign trident
    rears,
Their fury fails; he skims the liquid
    plains,
High on his chariot, and with loosen'd
    reins,
Majestic moves along, and awful peace
    maintains.
The weary Trojans ply their shatter'd
    oars,
To nearest land, and make the Libyan
    shores.
    Within a long recess there lies a bay,
An island shades it from the rolling sea,
And forms a port secure for ships to ride,
Broke by the jutting land on either side:
In double streams the briny waters glide.
Betwixt two rows of rocks, a sylvan scene

Appears above, and groves for ever green:
A grot is form'd beneath, with mossy
    seats,
To rest the Nereids, and exclude the
    heats:
Down through the crannies of the living
    walls
The crystal streams descend in mur-
    m'ring falls.
No haulsers need to bind the vessels here,
Nor bearded anchors, for no storms they
    fear.
Sev'n ships within this happy harbour
    meet,
The thin remainders of the scatter'd fleet.
The Trojans worn with toils, and spent
    with woes,
Leap on the welcome land, and seek their
    wish'd repose.
First, good Achates, with repeated strokes
Of clashing flints, their hidden fire pro-
    vokes;
Short flame succeeds a bed of wither'd
    leaves,
The dying sparkles in their fall receives:
Caught into life, in fiery fumes they rise,
And, fed with stronger food, invade the
    skies.
The Trojans, dropping wet, or stand
    around
The cheerful blaze, or lie along the
    ground;
Some dry their corn infected with the
    brine,
Then grind with marbles, and prepare to
    dine.
Æneas climbs the mountain's airy brow,
And takes a prospect of the seas below:
If Capys thence, or Antheus he could
    spy,
Or see the streamers of Caicus fly:
No vessels were in view; but, on the
    plain,
Three beamy stags command a lordly
    train
Of branching heads, the more ignoble
    throng
Attend their stately steps, and slowly
    graze along.

He stood, and while secure they fed be-
    low,
He took the quiver and the trusty bow
Achates us'd to bear, the leaders first
He laid along and then the vulgar
    pierc'd;
Nor ceas'd his arrows, till the shady plain
Sev'n mighty bodies with their blood
    distain.
For the sev'n ships he made an equal
    share,
And to the port return'd triumphant from
    the war.
The jars of gen'rous wine (Acestes' gift,
When his Trinacrian shores the navy
    left),
He set abroach, and for the feast pre-
    par'd,
In equal portions with the ven'son shar'd.
Thus while he dealt it round, the pious
    chief,
With cheerful words allay'd the common
    grief:
"Endure and conquer, Jove will soon dis-
    pose
To future good our past and present
    woes.
With me the rocks of Scylla you have
    tried,
Th' inhuman Cyclops and his den defied.
What greater ills hereafter can you bear?
Resume your courage, and dismiss your
    care.
An hour will come, with pleasure to re-
    late
Your sorrows past, as benefits of fate.
Through various hazards and events we
    move
To Latium and the realms foredoom'd by
    Jove,
Call'd to the seat (the promise of the
    skies)
Where Trojan kingdoms once again may
    rise.
Endure the hardships of your present
    state,
Live and reserve yourselves for better
    fate."

These words he spoke, but spoke not
    from his heart;
His outward smiles conceal'd his inward
    smart:
The jolly crew, unmindful of the past,
The quarry share, their plenteous dinner
    haste;
Some strip the skin, some portion out the
    spoil,
The limbs yet trembling in the cauldrons
    boil:
Stretch'd on the grassy turf, at ease they
    dine,
Restore their strength with meat, and
    cheer their souls with wine.
Their hunger thus appeas'd, their care
    attends
The doubtful fortune of their absent
    friends;
Alternate hopes and fears their minds
    possess,
Whether to deem 'em dead or in distress.
Above the rest, Æneas mourns the fate
Of brave Orontes, and th' uncertain state
Of Gyas, Lycus, and of Amycus:
The day, but not their sorrows ended
    thus.
When, from aloft, almighty Jove surveys
Earth, air, and shores, and navigable seas,
At length on Libyan realms he fix'd his
    eyes,
Whom, pond'ring thus on human miseries,
When Venus saw, she with a lovely look,
Not free from tears, her heav'nly sire
    bespoke.
"O king of gods and men, whose awful
    hand
Disperses thunder on the seas and land,
Disposes all with absolute command:
How could my pious son thy pow'r in-
    cense,
Or what, alas! is vanquish'd Troy's of-
    fence?
Our hope of Italy not only lost
On various seas, by various tempests
    tost,
But shut from ev'ry shore, and barr'd
    from ev'ry coast.
You promis'd once a progeny divine,

Of Romans rising from the Trojan line,
In after-times should hold the world in
    awe,
And to the land and ocean give the law.
How is your doom revers'd, which eas'd
    my care,
When Troy was ruin'd in that cruel war?
Then fates to fates I could oppose; but
    now,
When fortune still pursues her former
    blow,
What can I hope? What worse can still
    succeed?
What end of labours has our will de-
    creed?
Antenor, from the midst of Grecian hosts,
Could pass secure, and pierce th' Illyrian
    coasts:
Where rolling down the steep, Timavus
    raves,
And through nine channels disembogues
    his waves.
At length he founded Padua's happy seat,
And gave his Trojans a secure retreat:
There fix'd their arms, and there renew'd
    their name,
And there in quiet rules, and crown'd
    with fame:
But we, descended from your sacred
    line,
Entitled to your heav'n, and rites divine,
Are banish'd earth, and for the wrath of
    one,
Remov'd from Latium, and the promis'd
    throne.
Are these our sceptres? these our due
    rewards?
And is it thus that Jove his plighted faith
    regards?"
To whom the father of immortal race,
Smiling with that serene indulgent face,
With which he drives the clouds, and
    clears the skies,
First gave a holy kiss, then thus replies:
"Daughter, dismiss thy fears: to thy
    desire
The fates of thine are fix'd, and stand
    entire.

Thou shalt behold thy wish'd Lavinian
    walls,
And, ripe for heav'n, when fate Æneas
    calls,
Then shalt thou bear him up, sublime,
    to me;
No councils have revers'd my firm decree:
And lest new fears disturb thy happy
    state,
Know, I have search'd the mystic rolls of
    fate:
Thy son (nor is th' appointed season far)
In Italy shall wage successful war;
Shall tame fierce nations in the bloody
    field,
And sov'reign laws impose, and cities
    build.
Till, after ev'ry foe subdued, the sun
Thrice through the signs his annual race
    shall run:
This is his time prefix'd. Ascanius then,
Now call'd Iulus, shall begin his reign.
He thirty rolling years the crown shall
    wear,
Then from Lavinium shall the seat trans-
    fer,
And, with hard labour, Alba Longa build,
The throne with his succession shall be
    fill'd;
Three hundred circuits more, then shall
    be seen,
Ilia the fair, a priestess and a queen;
Who full of Mars, in time, with kindly
    throws,
Shall at a birth two goodly boys disclose.
The royal babes a tawny wolf shall drain,
Then Romulus his grandsire's throne
    shall gain;
Of martial tow'rs the founder shall be-
    come,
The people Romans call, the city Rome.
To them no bounds of empire I assign,
Nor term of years to their immortal line.
Ev'n haughty Juno, who with endless
    broils
Earth, seas, and heav'n, and Jove himself
    turmoils;
At length aton'd, her friendly pow'r shall
    join,

To cherish and advance the Trojan line.
The subject world shall Rome's dominion
    own,
And prostrate shall adore the nation of
    the gown.
An age is ripening in revolving fate,
When Troy shall overturn the Grecian
    state;
And sweet revenge her conqu'ring sons
    shall call,
To crush the people that conspir'd her
    fall.
Then Cæsar from the Julian stock shall
    rise,
Whose empire ocean, and whose fame the
    skies
Alone shall bound: whom, fraught with
    eastern spoils,
Our heav'n, the just reward of human
    toils,
Securely shall repay with rites divine;
And incense shall ascend before his sa-
    cred shrine.
Then dire debate and impious war shall
    cease,
And the stern age be soften'd into peace:
Then banish'd faith shall once again
    return,
And vestal fires in hallow'd temples burn,
And Remus with Quirinus shall sustain
The righteous laws, and fraud and force
    restrain.
Janus himself before his fane shall wait,
And keep the dreadful issues of his gate,
With bolts and iron bars: within remains
Imprison'd fury, bound in brazen chains:
High on a trophy rais'd of useless arms
He sits, and threats the world with vain
    alarms."
He said, and sent Cyllenius with com-
    mand
To free the ports, and ope the Punic land
To Trojan guests, lest, ignorant of fate,
The queen might force them from her
    town and state.
Down from the steep of heav'n Cyllenius
    flies,
And cleaves with all his wings the yield-
    ing skies:

Soon on the Libyan shore descends the
    god,
Performs his message, and displays his
    rod;
The surly murmurs of the people cease,
And as the fates requir'd they give the
    peace.
The queen herself suspends the rigid
    laws,
The Trojans pities, and protects their
    cause.
    Meantime, in shades of night Æneas
    lies;
Care seiz'd his soul, and sleep forsook his
    eyes.
But when the sun restor'd the cheerful
    day,
He rose, the coast and country to survey,
Anxious and eager to discover more:
It look'd a wild uncultivated shore;
But whether human kind, or beasts alone
Possess'd the new-found region, was un-
    known.
Beneath a ledge of rocks his fleet he
    hides;
Tall trees surround the mountain's shady
    sides;
The bending brow above a safe retreat
    provides.
Arm'd with two pointed darts, he leaves
    his friends,
And true Achates on his steps attends.
Lo, in the deep recesses of the wood,
Before his eyes his goddess mother
    stood;
A huntress in her habit and her mien,
Her dress a maid, her air confess'd a
    queen.
Bare were her knees, and knots her gar-
    ments bind;
Loose was her hair, and wanton'd in the
    wind;
Her hand sustain'd a bow, a quiver hung
    behind.
She seem'd a virgin of the Spartan blood;
With such array Harpalice bestrode
Her Thracian courser, and outstripp'd
    the rapid flood.

"Ho! strangers! have you lately seen,"
    she said,
"One of my sisters, like myself array'd,
Who cross'd the lawn, or in the forest
    stray'd?
A painted quiver at her back she bore,
Varied with spots, a lynx's hide she wore,
And at full cry pursued the tusky boar."
Thus Venus; thus her son replied again:
"None of your sisters have we heard or
    seen,
O virgin! or what other name you bear
Above that stile; O more than mortal
    fair!
Your voice and mien celestial birth be-
    tray!
If, as you seem, the sister of the day;
Or one at least of chaste Diana's train,
Let not an humble suppliant sue in vain;
But tell a stranger, long in tempest toss'd,
What earth we tread, and who commands
    the coast?
Then on your name shall wretched mor-
    tals call,
And offer'd victims at your altars fall."
"I dare not," she replied, "assume the
    name
Of goddess, or celestial honours claim;
For Tyrian virgins bows and quivers
    bear,
And purple buskins o'er their ankles wear.
Know, gentle youth, in Libyan lands you
    are,
A people rude in peace, and rough in
    war.
The rising city which from far you see
Is Carthage, and a Tyrian colony.
Phœnician Dido rules the growing state,
Who fled from Tyre to shun her broth-
    er's hate:
Great were her wrongs, her story full of
    fate,
Which I will sum in short. Sichæus
    known
For wealth, and brother to the Punic
    throne,
Possess'd fair Dido's bed; and either
    heart
At once was wounded with an equal dart.

Her father gave her, yet a spotless maid;
Pygmalion then the Tyrian sceptre
    sway'd;
One who contemn'd divine and human
    laws.
Then strife ensued, and cursed gold the
    cause.
The monarch, blinded with desire of
    wealth,
With steel invades his brother's life by
    stealth;
Before the sacred altar made him bleed;
And long from her conceal'd the cruel
    deed;
Some tale, some new pretence he daily
    coin'd,
To soothe his sister, and delude her mind.
At length, in dead of night, the ghost
    appears
Of her unhappy lord: the spectre stares,
And with erected eyes his bloody bosom
    bares.
The cruel altars, and his fate he tells,
And the dire secret of his house reveals.
Then warns the widow, and her house-
    hold gods,
To seek a refuge in remote abodes.
Last, to support her in so long a way,
He shows her where his hidden treasure
    lay.
Admonish'd thus, and seiz'd with mortal
    fright,
The queen provides companions of her
    flight:
They meet, and all combine to leave the
    state,
Who hate the tyrant, or who fear his
    hate.
They seize a fleet, which ready rigg'd
    they find;
Nor is Pygmalion's treasure left behind.
The vessels, heavy laden, put to sea
With prosp'rous winds; a woman leads
    the way.
I know not, if by stress of weather
    driv'n,
Or was their fatal course dispos'd by
    heav'n!

At last they landed, where from far
    your eyes
May view the turrets of new Carthage
    rise:
There bought a space of ground, which
    Byrsa call'd
From the bull's hide, they first inclos'd,
    and wall'd.
But whence are you, what country
    claims your birth?
What seek you, strangers, on our Libyan
    earth?"
    To whom, with sorrow streaming from
    his eyes,
And deeply sighing, thus her son replies:
"Could you with patience hear, or I
    relate,
O nymph! the tedious annals of our fate!
Through such a train of woes if I should
    run,
The day would sooner than the tale be
    done!
From ancient Troy, by force expell'd, we
    came,
If you by chance have heard the Trojan
    name:
On various seas, by various tempests
    toss'd,
At length we landed on your Libyan
    coast:
The good Æneas am I call'd, a name,
While fortune favour'd, not unknown to
    fame:
My household gods, companions of my
    woes,
With pious care I rescued from our foes;
To fruitful Italy my course was bent,
And from the king of heav'n is my
    descent.
With twice ten sail I cross'd the Phrygian
    sea;
Fate and my mother goddess led the way.
Scarce sev'n, the thin remainder of my
    fleet,
From storms preserv'd, within your har-
    bour meet:
Myself distress'd, an exile, and unknown,
Debarr'd from Europe, and from Asia
    thrown,

In Libyan deserts wander thus alone."
His tender parent could no longer bear,
But, interposing, sought to soothe his
care.
"Whoe'er you are, not unbelov'd by
heav'n,
Since on our friendly shore your ships
are driv'n,
Have courage: to the gods permit the
rest,
And to the queen expose your just re-
quest.
Now take this earnest of success for
more:
Your scatter'd fleet is join'd upon the
shore;
The winds are chang'd, your friends from
danger free,
Or I renounce my skill in augury.
Twelve swans behold in beauteous order
move,
And stoop with closing pinions from
above;
Whom late the bird of Jove had driv'n
along,
And through the clouds pursued the scat-
t'ring throng;
Now all united in a goodly team,
They skim the ground, and seek the quiet
stream.
As they with joy returning clap their
wings,
And ride the circuit of the skies in rings;
Not otherwise your ships, and ev'ry
friend,
Already hold the port, or with swift sails
descend.
No more advice is needful, but pursue
The path before you, and the town in
view."
Thus having said, she turn'd, and made
appear
Her neck refulgent, and dishevell'd hair;
Which, flowing from her shoulders
reach'd the ground,
And widely spread ambrosial scents
around:
In length of train descends her sweeping
gown,
And by her graceful walk the queen of
love is known.
The prince pursued the parting deity
With words like these: "Ah, whither
dost thou fly?
Unkind and cruel, to deceive your son
In borrow'd shapes, and his embrace to
shun;
Never to bless my sight but thus un-
known,
And still to speak in accents not your
own."
Against the goddess these complaints he
made,
But took the path, and her commands
obey'd.
They march obscure, for Venus kindly
shrouds
With mists their persons, and involves
in clouds;
That thus unseen their passage none
might stay,
Or force to tell the causes of their way.
This part perform'd, the goddess flies
sublime,
To visit Paphos, and her native clime;
Where garlands ever green and ever fair,
With vows are offer'd, and with solemn
pray'r;
A hundred altars in her temple smoke,
A thousand bleeding hearts her pow'r
invoke.
They climb the next ascent, and look-
ing down,
Now at a nearer distance view the town:
The prince with wonder sees the stately
tow'rs,
Which late were huts and shepherds'
homely bow'rs;
The gates and streets; and hears from
ev'ry part
The noise and busy concourse of the
mart.
The toiling Tyrians on each other call,
To ply their labour: some extend the
wall,
Some build the citadel; the brawny
throng
Or dig, or push unwieldy stones along.

Some for their dwellings choose a spot of ground,
Which first design'd with ditches they surround.
Some laws ordain, and some attend the choice
Of holy senates, and elect by voice.
Here some design a mole, while others there
Lay deep foundations for a theatre:
From marble quarries mighty columns hew,
For ornaments of scenes, and future view.
Such is their toil, and such their busy pains,
As exercise the bees in flow'ry plains;
When winter past, and summer scarce begun,
Invites them forth to labour in the sun.
Some lead their youth abroad, while some condense
Their liquid store, and some in cells dispense.
Some at the gate stand ready to receive
The golden burden, and their friends relieve.
All with united force combine to drive
The lazy drones from the laborious hive;
With envy stung, they view each other's deeds;
The fragrant work with diligence proceeds.
"Thrice happy you, whose walls already rise,"
Æneas said, and view'd with lifted eyes,
Their lofty tow'rs; then entering at the gate,
Conceal'd in clouds (prodigious to relate),
He mix'd unmark'd among the busy throng,
Borne by the tide, and pass'd unseen along.
Full in the center of the town there stood,
Thick set with trees, a venerable wood:
The Tyrians landed near this holy ground,
And digging here, a prosp'rous omen found:

From under earth a courser's head they drew,
Their growth and future fortune to foreshew:
This fated sign their foundress Juno gave,
Of a soil fruitful, and a people brave.
Sidonian Dido here with solemn state
Did Juno's temple build and consecrate;
Enrich'd with gifts, and with a golden shrine,
But more the goddess made the place divine.
On brazen steps the marble threshold rose,
And brazen plates the cedar beams inclose:
The rafters are with brazen cov'rings crown'd,
The lofty doors on brazen hinges sound.
What first Æneas in this place beheld
Reviv'd his courage, and his fear expell'd.
For while, expecting there the queen, he rais'd
His wond'ring eyes, and round the temple gaz'd;
Admir'd the fortune of the rising town,
The striving artists, and their art's renown;
He saw in order painted on the wall,
Whatever did unhappy Troy befall;
The wars that fame around the world had blown,
All to the life, and ev'ry leader known.
There Agamemnon, Priam here he spies,
And fierce Achilles, who both kings defies.
He stopp'd, and weeping said, "O friend! ev'n here
The monuments of Trojan woes appear!
Our known disasters fill ev'n foreign lands:
See there, where old unhappy Priam stands!
Ev'n the mute walls relate the warrior's fame,
And Trojan griefs the Tyrians' pity claim."
He said: his tears a ready passage find,
Devouring what he saw so well design'd,
And with an empty picture fed his mind.

For there he saw the fainting Grecians
    yield,
And here the trembling Trojans quit the
    field,
Pursued by fierce Achilles through the
    plain,
On his high chariot driving o'er the slain.
The tents of Rhesus next his grief renew,
By their white sails betray'd to nightly
    view.
And wakeful Diomede, whose cruel sword
The sentries flew, nor spar'd their slum-
    b'ring lord,
Then took the fiery steeds, ere yet the
    food
Of Troy they taste, or drink the Xan-
    thian flood.
Elsewhere he saw where Troilus defied
Achilles, and unequal combat tried.
Then where the boy disarm'd, with
    loosen'd reins,
Was by his horses hurried o'er the plains:
Hung by the neck and hair, and dragg'd
    around,
The hostile spear yet sticking in his
    wound,
With tracks of blood inscrib'd the dusty
    ground.
Meantime the Trojan dames, oppress'd
    with woe,
To Pallas' fane in long procession go,
In hopes to reconcile their heav'nly foe:
They weep, they beat their breasts, they
    rend their hair,
And rich embroider'd vests for presents
    bear:
But the stern goddess stands unmov'd
    with pray'r.
Thrice round the Trojan walls Achilles
    drew
The corpse of Hector, whom in fight he
    slew.
Here Priam sues; and there for sums
    of gold
The lifeless body of his son is sold.
So sad an object, and so well express'd,
Drew sighs and groans from the griev'd
    hero's breast:
To see the figure of his lifeless friend,

And his old sire his helpless hand extend.
Himself he saw amidst the Grecian train,
Mix'd in the bloody battle on the plain.
And swarthy Memnon in his arms he
    knew,
His pompous ensigns, and his Indian
    crew.
Penthesilea there, with haughty grace,
Leads to the wars an Amazonian race:
In their right hands a pointed dart they
    wield,
The left for ward sustains the lunar
    shield.
Athwart her breast a golden belt she
    throws,
Amidst the press alone provokes a thou-
    sand foes,
And dares her maiden arms to manly
    force oppose.
    Thus while the Trojan prince employs
    his eyes,
Fix'd on the walls with wonder and sur-
    prise,
The beauteous Dido, with a num'rous
    train,
And pomp of guards, ascends the sacred
    fane.
Such on Eurotas' banks, or Cynthus'
    height,
Diana seems; and so she charms the sight,
When in the dance the graceful goddess
    leads
The quire of nymphs, and overtops their
    heads.
Known by her quiver and her lofty mien,
She walks majestic, and she looks their
    queen:
Latona sees her shine above the rest,
And feeds with secret joy her silent
    breast.
Such Dido was; with such becoming
    state,
Amidst the crowd she walks serenely
    great.
Their labour to her future sway she
    speeds,
And passing with a gracious glance pro-
    ceeds;

Then mounts the throne, high plac'd be-
fore the shrine;
In crowds around, the swarming people
join.
She takes petitions, and dispenses laws,
Hears and determines ev'ry private cause.
Their tasks in equal portions she divides,
And where unequal, there by lots decides.
Another way by chance Æneas bends
His eyes, and unexpected sees his friends:
Antheus, Sergestus grave, Cloanthus
strong,
And at their backs a mighty Trojan
throng,
Whom late the tempest on the billows
toss'd,
And widely scatter'd on another coast.
The prince, unseen, surpriz'd with wonder
stands,
And longs with joyful haste to join their
hands:
But doubtful of the wish'd event, he
stays,
And from the hollow cloud his friend
surveys:
Impatient till they told their present
state,
And where they left their ships, and what
their fate;
And why they came, and what was their
request:
For these were sent commission'd by the
rest,
To sue for leave to land their sickly men,
And gain admission to the gracious queen.
Ent'ring, with cries they fill'd the holy
fane;
Then thus with lowly voice Ilioneus
began:
"O queen, indulg'd by favour of the gods
To found an empire in these new abodes;
To build a town, with statutes to restrain
The wild inhabitants beneath thy reign;
We wretched Trojans, toss'd on ev'ry
shore,
From sea to sea, thy clemency implore:
Forbid the fires our shipping to deface,
Receive th' unhappy fugitives to grace,
And spare the remnant of a pious race.

We come not with design of wasteful
prey,
To drive the country, force the swains
away;
Nor such our strength, nor such is our
desire:
The vanquish'd dare not to such thoughts
aspire.
A land there is, Hesperia nam'd of old,
The soil is fruitful, and the men are bold;
Th' Œnotrians held it once by common
fame,
Now call'd Italia, from the leader's name:
To that sweet region was our voyage
bent,
When winds, and ev'ry warring element,
Disturb'd our course, and far from sight
of land,
Cast our torn vessels on the moving
sand:
The sea came on; the south with mighty
roar
Dispers'd and dash'd the rest upon the
rocky shore.
Those few you see escap'd the storm, and
fear,
Unless you interpose, a shipwreck here;
What men, what monsters, what inhuman
race,
What laws, what barb'rous customs of
the place,
Shut up a desert shore to drowning men,
And drive us to the cruel seas again!
If our hard fortune no compassion draws,
Nor hospitable rites, nor human laws,
The gods are just, and will revenge our
cause.
Æneas was our prince, a juster lord,
Or nobler warrior, never drew a sword;
Observant of the right, religious of his
word.
If yet he lives, and draws this vital air,
Nor we his friends of safety shall despair,
Nor you, great queen, these offices repent,
Which he will equal, and perhaps aug-
ment.
We want not cities, nor Sicilian coasts,
Where king Acestes Trojan lineage boasts.
Permit our ships a shelter on your shores,

Refitted from your woods with planks
   and oars;
That if our prince be safe, we may renew
Our destin'd course, and Italy pursue.
But if, O best of men, the fates ordain
That thou art swallow'd in the Libyan
   main:
And if our young Iulus be no more,
Dismiss our navy from the friendly
   shore;
That we to good Acestes may return,
And with our friends our common losses
   mourn."
Thus spoke Ilioneus; the Trojan crew
With cries and clamours his request
   renew.
The modest queen awhile, with downcast
   eyes,
Ponder'd the speech; then briefly thus
   replies:
   "Trojans, dismiss your fears: my cruel
   fate,
And doubts attending an unsettled state,
Force me to guard my coast from foreign
   foes:
Who has not heard the story of your
   woes?
The name and fortune of your native
   place,
The fame and valour of the Phrygian
   race?
We Tyrians are not so devoid of sense,
Nor so remote from Phœbus' influence.
Whether to Latian shores your course is
   bent,
Or driv'n by tempests from your first
   intent,
You seek the good Acestes' government,
Your men shall be receiv'd, your fleet
   repair'd,
And sail, with ships of convoy for your
   guard:
Or would you stay, and join your friendly
   pow'rs,
To raise and to defend the Tyrian tow'rs,
My wealth, my city, and myself are
   yours.
And would to heav'n the storm you felt
   would bring

On Carthaginian coasts your wand'ring
   king.
My people shall, by my command, explore
The ports and creeks of ev'ry winding
   shore;
And towns, and wilds, and shady woods,
   in quest
Of so renown'd and so desir'd a guest."
Rais'd in his mind the Trojan hero stood,
And long'd to break from out his ambient
   cloud;
Achates found it, and thus urg'd his way:
"From whence, O goddess-born, this long
   delay?
What more can you desire, your welcome
   sure,
Your fleet in safety, and your friends
   secure?
One only wants, and him we saw in vain
Oppose the storm, and swallow'd in the
   main.
Orontes in his fate our forfeit paid,
The rest agrees with what your mother
   said."
Scarce had he spoken, when the cloud
   gave way,
The mists flew upward, and dissolv'd in
   day.
The Trojan chief appear'd in open sight,
August in visage, and serenely bright.
His mother goddess, with her hands
   divine,
Had form'd his curling locks, and made
   his temples shine;
And giv'n his rolling eyes a sparkling
   grace,
And breathed a youthful vigour on his
   face;
Like polish'd iv'ry, beauteous to behold,
Or Parian marble, when enchas'd in gold:
Thus radiant from the circling cloud he
   broke,
And thus with manly modesty he spoke:
   "He whom you seek am I; by tempests
   toss'd,
And sav'd from shipwreck on your Libyan
   coast;
Presenting, gracious queen, before your
   throne,

A prince that owes his life to you alone,
Fair majesty, the refuge and redress
Of those whom fate pursues, and wants
    oppress.
You, who your pious offices employ
To save the relics of abandon'd Troy,
Receive the shipwreck'd on your friendly
    shore,
With hospitable rites relieve the poor:
Associate in your town a wand'ring train,
And strangers in your palace entertain.
What thanks can wretched fugitives
    return,
Who scatter'd through the world in exile
    mourn?
The gods (if gods to goodness are in-
    clin'd)
If acts of mercy touch their heav'nly
    mind;
And more than all the gods, your gen'rous
    heart,
Conscious of worth, requite its own
    desert!
In you this age is happy, and this earth;
And parents more than mortal gave you
    birth.
While rolling rivers into seas shall run,
And round the space of heav'n the radiant
    sun;
While trees the mountain-tops with shades
    supply,
Your honour, name, and praise shall never
    die.
Whate'er abode my fortune has assign'd,
Your image shall be present in my mind."
Thus having said, he turn'd with pious
    haste,
And joyful his expecting friends em-
    brac'd:
With his right hand Ilioneus was grac'd,
Sergestus with his left; then to his breast
Cloanthus and the noble Gyas press'd;
And so by turns descended to the rest.
    The Tyrian queen stood fix'd upon
        his face,
Pleas'd with his motions, ravish'd with
    his grace;
Admir'd his fortunes, more admir'd the
    man;

Then recollected stood, and thus began:
    "What fate, O goddess-born, what
        angry pow'rs
Have cast you shipwreck'd on our barren
    shores?
Are you the great Æneas known to fame,
Who from celestial seed your lineage
    claim!
The same Æneas whom fair Venus bore
To fam'd Anchises on th' Idean shore?
It calls into my mind, though then a
    child,
When Teucer came from Salamis exil'd;
And sought my father's aid to be restor'd:
My father Belus then with fire and sword
Invaded Cyprus, made the region bare,
And conqu'ring, finish'd the successful
    war.
From him the Trojan siege I understood,
The Grecian chiefs, and your illustrious
    blood.
Your foe himself the Dardan valour
    prais'd,
And his own ancestry from Trojans rais'd.
Enter, my noble guest, and you shall
    find,
If not a costly welcome, yet a kind:
For I myself, like you, have been dis-
    tress'd,
Till heav'n afforded me this place of rest.
Like you an alien in a land unknown,
I learn to pity woes so like my own."
She said, and to the palace led her guest,
Then offer'd incense, and proclaim'd a
    feast.
Nor yet less careful for her absent friends,
Twice ten fat oxen to the ships she sends;
Besides a hundred boars, a hundred
    lambs,
With bleating cries attend their milky
    dams.
And jars of gen'rous wine, and spacious
    bowls,
She gives, to cheer the sailors' drooping
    souls.
Now purple hangings clothe the palace
    walls,
And sumptuous feasts are made in splen-
    did halls:

On Tyrian carpets, richly wrought, they
  dine,
With loads of massy plate the sideboards
  shine.
And antique vases all of gold emboss'd,
(The gold itself inferior to the cost)
Of curious work, where on the sides were
  seen
The fights and figures of illustrious men,
From their first founder to the present
  queen.

—JOHN DRYDEN.

THE TRAGEDY OF DIDO

[From Book IV]

The episode of Dido supplies the romantic cause for the wars of later times
between Rome and Carthage. The conduct of the hero, however, is not to be
judged by modern romantic standards.
The poet pictures Æneas as true to his
divine mission in the face of great temptation. Loyalty to God is a matter of in-
finitely greater importance than loyalty
to Dido.

The rosy morn was risen from the
  main,
And horns and hounds awake the princely
  train:
They issue early through the city gate,
Where the more wakeful huntsmen ready
  wait,
With nets, and toils, and darts, beside
  the force
Of Spartan dogs, and swift Massylian
  horse:
The Tyrian peers and officers of state,
For the slow queen, in antechambers
  wait:
Her lofty courser, in the court below
(Who his majestic rider seems to know),
Proud of his purple trappings, paws the
  ground,
And champs his golden bit, and spreads
  the foam around.

The queen at length appears: on either
  hand,
The brawny guards in martial order
  stand.
A flow'r'd cymar with golden fringe she
  wore,
And at her back a golden quiver bore:
Her flowing hair a golden caul restrains:
A golden clasp the Tyrian robe sustains.
Then young Ascanius, with a sprightly
  grace,
Leads on the Trojan youth to view the
  chase.
But far above the rest in beauty shines
The great Æneas, when the troop he
  joins;
Like fair Apollo, when he leaves the frost
Of wintry Xanthus, and the Lycian coast,
When to his native Delos he resorts,
Ordains the dances, and renews the
  sports;
Where painted Scythians, mixed with
  Cretan bands,
Before the joyful altars join their hands:
Himself, on Cynthus walking, sees below
The merry madness of the sacred show.
Green wreaths of bays his length of hair
  enclose:
A golden fillet binds his awful brows:
His quiver sounds.—Not less the prince
  is seen
In manly presence, or in lofty mien.
  Now had they reached the hills, and
  storm'd the seat
Of savage beasts in dens, their last
  retreat.
The cry pursues the mountain-goats:
  they bound
From rock to rock, and keep the craggy
  ground:
Quite otherwise the stags, a trembling
  train,
In herds unsingled scour the dusty plain,
And a long chase, in open view, maintain.
The glad Ascanius, as his courser guides,
Spurs through the vale, and these and
  those outrides.
His horse's flanks and sides are forced
  to feel

The clanking lash, and goring of the steel.
Impatiently he views the feeble prey,
Wishing some nobler beast to cross his
way,
And rather would the tusky boar attend,
Or see the tawny lion downward bend.
  Meantime the gath'ring clouds obscure
the skies:
From pole to pole the forky lightning
flies;
The rattling thunders roll; and Juno
pours
A wintry deluge down, and sounding
show'rs.
The company, dispersed, to coverts ride,
And seek the homely cots, or mountain's
hollow side.
The rapid rains, descending from the
hills,
To rolling torrents raise the creeping
rills.
The queen and prince, as Love or For-
tune guides,
One common cavern in her bosom hides.
Then first the trembling earth the signal
gave;
And flashing fires enlighten all the cave,
Hell from below, and Juno from above,
And howling nymphs, were conscious to
their love.
From this ill-omen'd hour, in time arose
Debate and death, and all succeeding
woes.
  The queen, whom sense of honour
could not move,
No longer made a secret of her love,
But called it marriage, by that specious
name
To veil the crime, and sanctify that
shame.
  The loud report through Libyan cities
goes.
Fame, the great ill, from small beginnings
grows—
Swift from the first; and ev'ry movement
brings
New vigour to her flights, new pinions to
her wings.
Soon grows the pigmy to gigantic size;

Her feet on earth, her forehead in the
skies.
Enraged against the gods, revengeful
Earth
Produced her, last of the Titanian birth—
Swift is her walk, more swift her winged
haste—
A monstrous phantom, horrible and vast.
As many plumes as rise her lofty flight,
So many piercing eyes enlarge her sight:
Millions of op'ning mouths to Fame be-
long;
And ev'ry mouth is furnished with a
tongue;
And round with list'ning ears the flying
plague is hung.
She fills the peaceful universe with cries:
No slumbers ever close her wakeful eyes:
By day, from lofty tow'rs her head she
shows,
And spreads through trembling crowds
disastrous news;
With court informers' haunts, and royal
spies;
Things done relates; not done she feigns;
and mingles truth with lies.
Talk is her bus'ness; and her chief delight
To tell of prodigies, and cause affright.
She fills the people's ears with Dido's
name,
Who, "lost to honour and the sense of
shame,
Admits into her throne and nuptial bed
A wand'ring guest, who from his country
fled:
Whole days with him she passes in de-
lights,
And wastes in luxury long winter nights,
Forgetful of her fame, and royal trust,
Dissolv'd in ease, abandoned to her lust."
The goddess widely spreads the loud
report,
And flies at length to King Iarbas' court.
When first possess'd with this unwelcome
news,
Whom did he not of men and gods
accuse?
This prince, from ravish'd Garamantis
born,

A hundred temples did with spoils adorn,
In Ammon's honour, his celestial sire,
A hundred altars fed with wakeful fire;
And, through his vast dominions, priests
ordain'd,
Whose watchful care these holy rites
maintain'd.
The gates and columns were with gar-
lands crown'd,
And blood of victim beasts enriched the
ground.
  He, when he heard a fugitive could
move
The Tyrian princess, who disdain'd his
love,
His breast with fury burn'd, his eyes
with fire—
Mad with despair, impatient with de-
sire—
Then on the sacred altars pouring wine,
He thus with pray'rs implored his sire
divine:
"Great Jove, propitious to the Moorish
race,
Who feast on painted beds, with off'rings
grace
Thy temples, and adore thy pow'r divine
With blood of victims, and with sparkling
wine;
Seest thou not this? or do we fear in
vain
Thy boasted thunder, and thy thought-
less reign?
Do thy broad hands the forky lightnings
lance?
Thine are the bolts, or the blind work of
chance?
A wand'ring woman builds within our
state
A little town, bought at an easy rate;
She pays me homage (and my grants
allow
A narrow space of Libyan land to
plough);
Yet, scorning me, by passion blindly led,
Admits a banish'd Trojan to her bed!
And now this other Paris, with his train
Of conquer'd cowards, must in Afric
reign!

(Whom, what they are, their looks and
garb confess,
Their locks with oil perfumed, their
Lydian dress.)
He takes the spoil, enjoys the princely
dame;
And I, rejected I, adore an empty name!"
  His vows, in haughty terms, he thus
preferr'd,
And held his altar's horns: the mighty
thund'rer heard,
Then cast his eyes on Carthage, where he
found
The lustful pair in lawless pleasure
drown'd,
Lost in their loves, insensible of shame,
And both forgetful of their better fame.
He calls Cyllenius; and the god attends,
By whom this menacing command he
sends:
"Go mount the western winds, and cleave
the sky;
Then, with a swift descent, to Carthage
fly:
There find the Trojan chief, who wastes
his days
In slothful riot and inglorious ease,
Nor minds the future city, giv'n by fate.
To him this message from my mouth
relate:
Not so fair Venus hoped, when twice she
won
Thy life with pray'rs; nor promised such
a son.
Hers was a hero, destined to command
A martial race, and rule the Latian land;
Who should his ancient line from Teucer
draw;
And on the conquer'd world impose his
law.
If glory cannot move a mind so mean,
Nor future praise from fading pleasure
wean,
Yet why should he defraud his son of
fame,
And grudge the Romans their immortal
name?
What are his vain designs? what hopes
he more

From his long ling'ring on a hostile shore,
Regardless to redeem his honour lost,
And for his race to gain th' Ausonian coast?
Bid him with speed the Tyrian court forsake:
With this command the slumb'ring warrior wake."

Hermes obeys; with golden pinions binds
His flying feet, and mounts the western winds:
And, whether o'er the seas or earth he flies,
With rapid force they near him down the skies.
But first he grasps within his awful hand
The mark of sov'reign pow'r, his magic wand:
With this he draws the ghosts from hollow graves;
With this he drives them down the Stygian waves;
With this he seals in sleep the wakeful sight,
And eyes, though closed in death, restores to light.
Thus arm'd, the god begins his airy race,
And drives the racking clouds along the liquid space;
Now sees the top of Atlas, as he flies,
Whose brawny back supports the starry skies—
Atlas, whose head, with piney forests crown'd,
Is beaten by the wind—with foggy vapours bound.
Snows hide his shoulders: from beneath his chin
The founts of rolling streams their race begin:
A beard of ice on his large breast depends.—
Here, poised upon his wings, the god descends:
Then, rested thus, he from the tow'ring height
Plunged downward with precipitated flight,
Lights on the seas, and skims along the flood.
As waterfowl, who seek their fishy food,
Less, and yet less, to distant prospect show:
By turns they dance aloft, and dive below:
Like these, the steerage of his wings he plies,
And near the surface of the water flies,
Till, having pass'd the seas, and cross'd the sands,
He clos'd his wings, and stoop'd on Libyan lands,
Where shepherds once were housed in homely sheds;
Now tow'rs within the clouds advance their heads.
Arriving there, he found the Trojan prince
New ramparts raising for the town's defence.
A purple scarf, with gold embroider'd o'er
(Queen Dido's gift) about his waist he wore;
A sword, with glitt'ring gems diversified,
For ornament, not use, hung idly by his side.
Then thus, with winged words, the god began,
Resuming his own shape—"Degenerate man!
Thou woman's property! what mak'st thou here,
These foreign walls and Tyrian tow'rs to rear,
Forgetful of thy own? All-pow'rful Jove
Who sways the world below and heav'n above,
Has sent me down with this severe command:
What means thy ling'ring in the Libyan land?
If glory cannot move a mind so mean,
Nor future praise from flitting pleasure wean,
Regard the fortunes of thy rising heir:

The promised crown let young Ascanius wear,
To whom the Ausonian sceptre, and the state
Of Rome's imperial name, is owed by Fate."
So spoke the god: and, speaking, took his flight,
Involved in clouds; and vanished out of sight.
  The pious prince was seized with sudden fear:
Mute was his tongue, and upright stood his hair.
Revolving in his mind the stern command,
He longs to fly, and loathes the charming land.
What should he say? or how should he begin?
What course, alas! remains, to steer between
Th' offended lover and the pow'rful queen?
This way, and that, he turns his anxious mind,
And all expedients tries, and none can find.
Fix'd on the deed, but doubtful of the means—
After long thought, to this advice he leans:
Three chiefs he calls, commands them to repair
The fleet, and ship their men, with silent care:
Some plausible pretence he bids them find,
To colour what in secret he design'd.
Himself, meantime, the softest hours would choose,
Before the love-sick lady heard the news;
And move her tender mind, by slow degrees,
To suffer what the sov'reign pow'r decrees:
Jove will inspire him, when, and what to say.—

They hear with pleasure, and with haste obey.
  But soon the queen perceives the thin disguise:
(What arts can bind a jealous woman's eyes?)
She was the first to find the secret fraud,
Before the fatal news was blazed abroad.
Love the first motions of the lover hears,
Quick to presage, and ev'n in safety fears.
Nor impious Fame was wanting, to report
The ships repair'd, the Trojans' thick resort,
And purpose to forsake the Tyrian court.
Frantic with fear, impatient of the wound,
And impotent of mind, she roves the city round.
Less wild the Bacchanalian dames appear,
When, from afar, their nightly god they hear,
And howl about the hills, and shake the wreathy spear.
At length she finds the dear perfidious man;
Prevents his form'd excuse, and thus began:
"Base and ungrateful! could you hope to fly,
And undiscover'd 'scape a lover's eye?
Nor could my kindness your compassion move,
Nor plighted vows, nor dearer bands of love?
Or is the death of a despairing queen
Not worth preventing, though too well foreseen?
Ev'n when the wintry winds command your stay,
You dare the tempests, and defy the sea.
False, as you are, suppose you were not bound
To lands unknown, and foreign coasts to sound;
Were Troy restored, and Priam's happy reign,
Now durst you tempt, for Troy, the raging main?

See whom you fly! am I the foe you
  shun?
Now, by these holy vows, so late begun,
By this right hand (since I have nothing
  more
To challenge, but the faith you gave
  before),
I beg you by these tears too truly shed,
By the new pleasures of our nuptial bed;
If ever Dido, when you most were kind,
Were pleasing in your eyes, or touch'd
  your mind:
By these my pray'rs, if pray'rs may yet
  have place,
Pity the fortunes of a falling race!
For you I have provoked a tyrant's hate,
Incensed the Libyan and the Tyrian
  state;
For you alone I suffer in my fame,
Bereft of honour, and exposed to shame!
Whom have I now to trust, ungrateful
  guest?
(That only name remains of all the rest!)
What have I left? or whither can I fly?
Must I attend Pygmalion's cruelty,
Or till Iarbas shall in triumph lead
A queen, that proudly scorn'd his prof-
  fer'd bed!
Had you deferr'd, at least, your hasty
  flight,
And left behind some pledge of our
  delight,
Some babe to bless the mother's mournful
  sight,
Some young Æneas to supply your place,
Whose features might express his father's
  face;
I should not then complain to live bereft
Of all my husband, or be wholly left."
Here paused the queen. Unmoved he
  holds his eyes,
By Jove's command; nor suffer'd love to
  rise,
Though heaving in his heart; and thus
  at length replies:
"Fair queen, you never can enough repeat
Your boundless favours, or I own my
  debt;

Nor can my mind forget Eliza's name,
While vital breath inspires this mortal
  frame.
This only let me speak in my defence—
I never hoped a secret flight from hence,
Much less pretended to the lawful claim
Of sacred nuptials, or a husband's name.
For if indulgent heav'n would leave me
  free,
And not submit my life to Fate's decree,
My choice would lead me to the Trojan
  shore,
Those relics to review, their dust adore,
And Priam's ruin'd palace to restore.
But now the Delphian oracle commands,
And Fate invites me to the Latian lands.
That is the promised place to which I
  steer;
And all my vows are terminated there.
If you, a Tyrian and a stranger born,
With walls and tow'rs a Libyan town
  adorn,
Why may not we—like you, a foreign
  race—
Like you, seek shelter in a foreign place?
As often as the night obscures the skies
With humid shades, or twinkling stars
  arise,
Anchises' angry ghost in dreams appears,
Chides my delay, and fills my soul with
  fears:
And young Ascanius justly may complain,
Defrauded of his fate and destined reign.
Ev'n now the herald of the gods ap-
  pear'd—
Waking I saw him, and his message
  heard.
From Jove he came commission'd,
  heav'nly bright
With radiant beams, and manifest to
  sight:
(The sender and the sent I both attest)
These walls he enter'd, and those words
  express'd:
Fair queen, oppose not what the gods
  command:
Forced by my fate, I leave your happy
  land."
  Thus while he spoke, already she began

With sparkling eyes to view the guilty
man,
From head to foot surveyed his person
o'er,
Nor longer these outrageous threats
forbore:
"False as thou art, and more than false,
forsworn!
Not sprung from noble blood, nor god-
dess-born,
But hewn from harden'd entrails of a
rock!
And rough Hyrcanian tigers gave thee
suck!
Why should I fawn? What have I worse
to fear?
Did he once look, or lent a list'ning ear,
Sigh'd when I sobb'd, or shed one kindly
tear?
All symptoms of a base ungrateful mind,
So foul, that which is worse 'tis hard to
find.
Of man's injustice why should I com-
plain?
The gods, and Jove himself, behold in
vain
Triumphant treason: yet no thunder
flies;
Nor Juno views my wrongs with equal
eyes:
Faithless is earth, and faithless are the
skies!
Justice is fled, and truth is now no more!
I saved the shipwreck'd exile on the
shore:
With needful food his hungry Trojans
fed;
I took the traitor to my throne and bed:
Fool that I was!—'tis little to repeat
The rest—I stored and rigg'd his ruin'd
fleet.
I rave, I rave! A god's command he
pleads,
And makes heav'n accessory to his deeds.
Now Lycian lots, and now the Delian
god,
Now Hermes is employed from Jove's
abode,

To warn him hence; as if the peaceful
state
Of heav'nly pow'rs were touch'd with
human fate!
But go! thy flight no longer I detain—
Go! seek thy promised kingdom through
the main!
Yet, if the heav'ns will hear my pious
vow,
The faithless waves, not half so false as
thou,
Or secret sands, shall sepulchres afford
To thy proud vessels, and their perjured
lord.
Then shalt thou call on injured Dido's
name:
Dido shall come in a black sulph'ry flame,
When death has once dissolved her mor-
tal frame—
Shall smile to see the traitor vainly weep:
Her angry ghost, arising from the deep,
Shall haunt thee waking, and disturb thy
sleep.
At least my shade thy punishment shall
know;
And Fame shall spread the pleasing news
below."
    Abruptly here she stops—then turns
away
Her loathing eyes, and shuns the sight of
day.
Amazed he stood, revolving in his mind
What speech to frame, and what excuse
to find.
Her fearful maids their fainting mistress
led,
And softly laid her on her iv'ry bed.
    But good Æneas, though he much de-
sired
To give that pity which her grief re-
quired—
Though much he mourn'd, and labour'd
with his love—
Resolved at length, obeys the will of
Jove;
Reviews his forces: they with early care
Unmoor their vessels, and for sea pre-
pare.
The fleet is soon afloat, in all its pride;

And well-caulk'd galleys in the harbour
    ride.
Then oaks for oars they fell'd; or, as
    they stood,
Of its green arms despoil'd the growing
    wood,
Studious of flight. The beach is cover'd
    o'er
With Trojan bands that blacken all the
    shore:
On ev'ry side are seen, descending down,
Thick swarms of soldiers, loaden from the
    town.
Thus, in battalia, march imbodied ants,
Fearful of winter, and of future wants,
T'nvade the corn, and to their cells
    convey
The plunder'd forage of their yellow prey.
The sable troops, along their narrow
    tracks,
Scarce bear the weighty burdens on their
    backs:
Some set their shoulders to the pond'rous
    grain;
Some guard the spoil, some lash the
    lagging train;
All ply their sev'ral tasks, and equal toil
    sustain.
What pangs the tender breast of Dido
    tore,
When, from the tow'r, she saw the cover'd
    shore,
And heard the shouts of sailors from afar,
Mix'd with the murmurs of the wat'ry
    war!
All-powerful Love! what changes canst
    thou cause
In human hearts, subjected to thy laws!
Once more her haughty soul the tyrant
    bends:
To pray'rs and mean submissions she
    descends.
No female arts or aids she left untried,
Nor counsels unexplored, before she died.
"Look, Anna! look! the Trojans crowd
    the sea;
They spread their canvass, and their
    anchors weigh.

The shouting crew their ships with gar-
    lands bind,
Invoke the sea-gods, and invite the wind.
Could I have thought this threat'ning
    blow so near,
My tender soul had been forewarn'd to
    bear.
"But do not you my last request deny:
With yon perfidious man your int'rest
    try,
And bring me news, if I must live or die.
You are his fav'rite: you alone can find
The dark recesses of his inmost mind:
In all his trusted secrets you have part,
And know the soft approaches to his
    heart.
Haste then, and humbly seek my haughty
    foe;
Tell him, I did not with the Grecians go,
Nor did my fleet against his friends
    employ,
Nor swore the ruin of unhappy Troy,
Nor moved with hands profane his
    father's dust:
Why should he then reject a suit so just?
Whom does he shun, and whither would
    he fly?
Can he this last, this only pray'r deny?
Let him at least his dang'rous flight
    delay,
Wait better winds, and hope a calmer sea.
The nuptials he disclaims I urge no more:
Let him pursue the promised Latian shore.
A short delay is all I ask him now—
A pause of grief, an interval from wo,
Till my soft soul be temper'd to sustain
Accustom'd sorrows, and inured to pain.
If you in pity grant this one request,
My death shall glut the hatred of his
    breast."
This mournful message pious Anna bears,
And seconds, with her own, her sister's
    tears:
But all her arts are still employ'd in vain:
Again she comes, and is refused again.
His harden'd heart nor pray'rs nor
    threat'nings move:
Fate, and the god, had stopp'd his ears
    to love.

As, when the winds their airy quarrel try,
Jostling from ev'ry quarter of the sky,
This way and that the mountain oak they bend;
His boughs they shatter, and his branches rend;
With leaves and falling mast they spread the ground;
The hollow valleys echo to the sound:
Unmoved, the royal plant their fury mocks,
Or, shaken, clings more closely to the rocks:
Far as he shoots his tow'ring head on high,
So deep in earth his fix'd foundations lie.
No less a storm the Trojan hero bears,
Thick messages and loud complaints he hears,
And bandied words, still beating on his ears.
Sighs, groans, and tears, proclaim his inward pains;
But the firm purpose of his heart remains.
The wretched queen, pursued by cruel Fate,
Begins at length the light of heav'n to hate,
And loathes to live. Then dire portents she sees,
To hasten on the death her soul decrees—
Strange to relate! for when, before the shrine,
She pours in sacrifice the purple wine,
The purple wine is turn'd to putrid blood;
And the white offer'd milk converts to mud.
This dire presage, to her alone reveal'd,
From all, and ev'n her sister, she conceal'd.
A marble temple stood within the grove,
Sacred to death, and to her murder'd love;
That honour'd chapel she had hung around
With snowy fleeces, and with garlands crown'd:

Oft, when she visited this lonely dome,
Strange voices issued from her husband's tomb:
She thought she heard him summon her away,
Invite her to his grave, and chide her stay.
Hourly 'tis heard, when, with a boding note,
The solitary screech-owl strains her throat,
And, on a chimney's top or turret's height,
With songs obscene disturbs the silence of the night.
Besides, old prophecies augment her fears;
And stern Æneas in her dreams appears,
Disdainful as by day: she seems, alone,
To wander in her sleep, through ways unknown,
Guideless and dark; or in a desert plain,
To seek her subjects, and to seek in vain—
Like Pentheus, when, distracted with his fear,
He saw two suns, and double Thebes appear;
Or mad Orestes, when his mother's ghost
Full in his face infernal torches toss'd,
And shook her snaky locks: he shuns the sight,
Flies o'er the stage, surprised with mortal fright;
The Furies guard the door, and intercept his flight.
Now, sinking underneath a load of grief,
From death alone she seeks her last relief:
The time and means resolved within her breast,
She to her mournful sister thus address'd
(Dissembling hope, her cloudy front she clears,
And a false vigour in her eyes appears):
"Rejoice!" she said. "Instructed from above,
My lover I shall gain, or lose my love.

Nigh rising Atlas, next the falling sun,
Long tracts of Ethiopian climates run:
There a Massylian priestess I have found,
Honour'd for age, for magic arts re-
nown'd:
Th' Hesperian temple was her trusted
care;
'Twas she supplied the wakeful dragon's
fare.
She poppy-seeds in honey taught to steep,
Reclaim'd his rage, and sooth'd him into
sleep.
She watched the golden fruit. Her
charms unbind
The chains of love, or fix them on the
mind:
She stops the torrents, leaves the channel
dry,
Repels the stars, and backward bears the
sky.
The yawning earth rebellows to her call;
Pale ghosts ascend, and mountain ashes
fall.
Witness, ye gods, and thou my better
part,
How loath I am to try this impious art!
Within the secret court, with silent care,
Erect a lofty pile, exposed in air:
Hang, on the topmost part, the Trojan
vest,
Spoils, arms, and presents, of my faith-
less guest.
Next, under these, the bridal bed be
placed,
Where I my ruin in his arms embraced.
All relics of the wretch are doom'd to fire:
For so the priestess and her charms re-
quire."
Thus far she said, and further speech
forbears.
A mortal paleness in her face appears:
Yet the mistrustless Anna could not find
The secret fun'ral in these rites design'd;
Nor thought so dire a rage possess'd her
mind.
Unknowing of a train conceal'd so well,
She fear'd no worse than when Sichæus
fell:

Therefore obeys. The fatal pile they
rear,
Within the secret court, exposed in air.
The cloven holms and pines are heap'd
on high,
And garlands on the hollow spaces lie.
Sad cypress, vervain, yew, compose the
wreath,
And ev'ry baleful green denoting death.
The queen, determined to the fatal deed,
The spoils and sword he left in order
spread,
And the man's image on the nuptial bed.
And now (the sacred altars placed
around)
The priestess enters, with her hair un-
bound,
And thrice invokes the pow'rs below the
ground.
Night, Erebus, and Chaos, she proclaims,
And threefold Hecate, with her hundred
names,
And three Dianas: next she sprinkled
round,
With feign'd Avernian drops, the hallow'd
ground;
Culls hoary simples, found by Phœbe's
light,
With brazen sickles reap'd at noon of
night;
Then mixes baleful juices in the bowl,
And cuts the forehead of a new-born foal,
Robbing the mother's love.—The des-
tined queen
Observes, assisting at the rites obscene:
A leaven'd cake in her devoted hands
She holds; and next the highest altar
stands:
One tender foot was shod, her other bare;
Girt was her gather'd gown, and loose her
hair.
Thus dress'd, she summon'd, with her
dying breath,
The heav'ns and planets, conscious of her
death;
And ev'ry pow'r, if any rules above,
Who minds or who revenges injured love.
'Twas dead of night, when weary
bodies close

Their eyes in balmy sleep and soft
    repose:
The winds no longer whisper through the
    woods,
Nor murm'ring tides disturb the gentle
    floods.
The stars in silent order moved around;
And Peace, with downy wings, was
    brooding on the ground.
The flocks and herds, and party-coloured
    fowl,
Which haunt the woods or swim the
    weedy pool,
Stretch'd on the quiet earth, securely lay,
Forgetting the past labours of the day.
All else of Nature's common gift partake:
Unhappy Dido was alone awake.
Nor sleep nor ease the furious queen can
    find:
Sleep fled her eyes, as quiet fled her mind.
Despair, and rage, and love, divide her
    heart;
Despair and rage had some, but love the
    greater part.
    Then thus she said within her secret
    mind:
"What shall I do? what succour can I
    find?
Become a suppliant to Iarbas' pride,
And take my turn to court and be denied?
Shall I with this ungrateful Trojan go,
Forsake an empire, and attend a foe?
Himself I refuged, and his train relieved—
'Tis true—but am I sure to be received?
Can gratitude in Trojan souls have place?
Laomedon still lives in all his race!
Then shall I seek alone the churlish crew,
Or with my fleet their flying sails pursue?
What force have I but those, whom scarce
    before
I drew reluctant from their native shore?
Will they again embark at my desire,
Once more sustain the seas, and quit their
    second Tyre?
Rather with steel thy guilty breast invade,
And take the fortune thou thyself hast
    made.
Your pity, sister, first seduced my mind,
Or seconded too well what I design'd.

These dear-bought pleasures had I never
    known—
Had I continued free, and still my own—
Avoiding love, I had not found despair,
But shared with savage beasts the com-
    mon air.
Like them, a lonely life I might have led,
Not mourn'd the living, nor disturb'd the
    dead."
These thoughts she brooded in her anxious
    breast.—
On board, the Trojan found more easy
    rest.
Resolved to sail, in sleep he pass'd the
    night;
And order'd all things for his early flight.
    To whom once more the winged god
    appears:
His former youthful mien and shape he
    wears,
And with this new alarm invades his ears:
"Sleep'st thou, O goddess-born? and canst
    thou drown
Thy needful cares so near a hostile town,
Beset with foes; nor hear'st the western
    gales
Invite thy passage, and inspire thy sails?
She harbours in her heart a furious hate
(And thou shalt find the dire effects too
    late),
Fix'd on revenge, and obstinate to die.
Haste swiftly hence, while thou hast
    pow'r to fly.
The sea with ships will soon be cover'd
    o'er,
And brazen firebrands kindle all the shore.
Who knows what hazards thy delay may
    bring?
Woman's a various and a changeful
    thing."
Thus Hermes in the dream; then took
    his flight,
Aloft in air unseen, and mix'd with night.
    Twice warn'd by the celestial mes-
    senger,
The pious prince arose with hasty fear;
Then roused his drowsy train without
    delay:

"Haste to your banks! your crooked
    anchors weigh,
And spread your flying sails, and stand
    to sea!
A god commands: he stood before my
    sight,
And urged us once again to speedy flight.
O sacred pow'r! what pow'r soe'er thou
    art,
To thy bless'd orders I resign my heart.
Lead thou the way; protect thy Trojan
    bands,
And prosper the design thy will com-
    mands."
He said: and drawing forth his flaming
    sword,
His thund'ring arm divides the many-
    twisted cord.
An emulating zeal inspires his train:
They run; they snatch; they rush into
    the main.
With headlong haste they leave the desert
    shores,
And brush the liquid seas with lab'ring
    oars.
    Aurora now had left her saffron bed,
And beams of early light the heav'ns
    o'erspread,
When, from a tow'r, the queen, with
    wakeful eyes,
Saw day point upward from the rosy
    skies.
She look'd to seaward: but the sea was
    void,
And scarce in ken the sailing ships
    descried.
Stung with despite, and furious with
    despair,
She struck her trembling breast, and tore
    her hair.
"And shall the ungrateful traitor go," she
    said,
"My land forsaken, and my love be-
    tray'd?
Shall we not arm? not rush from ev'ry
    street,
To follow, sink, and burn his perjured
    fleet?

Haste! haul my galleys out! pursue the
    foe!
Bring flaming brands! set sail, and
    quickly row!
What have I said? Where am I? Fury
    turns
My brain; and my distemper'd bosom
    burns.
Then, when I gave my person and my
    throne,
This hate, this rage, had been more timely
    shown.
See now the promised faith, the vaunted
    name,
The pious man, who, rushing through the
    flame,
Preserved his gods, and to the Phrygian
    shore
The burden of his feeble father bore!
I should have torn him piecemeal;—
    strew'd in floods
His scatter'd limbs, or left exposed in
    woods—
Destroy'd his friends and son—and from
    the fire
Have set the reeking boy before the sire.
Events are doubtful which on battle wait;
Yet where's the doubt to souls secure of
    fate?
My Tyrians, at their injured queen's
    command,
Had tossed their fires amid the Trojan
    band;
At 'once extinguish'd all the faithless
    name;
And I myself, in vengeance of my shame,
Had fall'n upon the pile, to mend the
    fun'ral flame.
Thou Sun, who view'st at once the world
    below!
Thou Juno, guardian of the nuptial vow!
Thou Hecate, hearken from thy dark
    abodes!
Ye furies, fiends, and violated gods!
All pow'rs invoked with Dido's dying
    breath,
Attend her curses, and avenge her death!
If so the Fates ordain, and Jove com-
    mands,

Th' ungrateful wretch should find the Latian lands,
Yet let a race untamed, and haughty foes,
His peaceful entrance with dire arms oppose:
Oppress'd with numbers in th' unequal field,
His men discouraged, and himself expell'd,
Let him for succour sue from place to place,
Torn from his subjects, and his son's embrace.
First let him see his friends in battle slain,
And their untimely fate lament in vain:
And when, at length, the cruel war shall cease,
On hard conditions may he buy his peace:
Nor let him then enjoy supreme command;
But fall, untimely, by some hostile hand,
And lie unburied on the barren sand!
These are my pray'rs, and this my dying will:
And you, my Tyrians, ev'ry curse fulfil.
Perpetual hate and mortal wars proclaim
Against the prince, the people, and the name.
These grateful off'rings on my grave bestow;
Nor league, nor love, the hostile nations know!
Now, and from hence in ev'ry future age,
When rage excites your arms, and strength supplies the rage,
Rise some avenger of our Libyan blood,
With fire and sword pursue the perjured brood—
Our arms, our seas, our shores, opposed to theirs—
And the same hate descend on all our heirs!"
  This said, within her anxious mind she weighs
The means of cutting short her odious days.
Then to Sichæus' nurse she briefly said,

(For, when she left her country, hers was dead),
"Go, Barce, call my sister. Let her care
The solemn rites of sacrifice prepare:
The sheep, and all th' atoning off'rings, bring;
Sprinkling her body from the crystal spring
With living drops: then let her come; and thou
With sacred fillets bind thy hoary brow.
Thus will I pay my vows to Stygian Jove,
And end the cares of my disastrous love;
Then cast the Trojan image on the fire;
And, as that burns, my passion shall expire."
  The nurse moves onward with officious care,
And all the speed her aged limbs can bear.
But furious Dido, with dark thoughts involved,
Shook at the mighty mischief she resolved.
With livid spots distinguish'd was her face;
Red were her rolling eyes, and discomposed her pace:
Ghastly she gazed; with pain she drew her breath;
And nature shiver'd at approaching death.
  Then swiftly to the fatal place she pass'd,
And mounts the fun'ral pile with furious haste:
Unsheaths the sword the Trojan left behind
(Not for so dire an enterprise design'd).
But when she view'd the garments loosely spread,
Which once he wore, and saw the conscious bed,
She paused, and, with a sigh, the robes embraced;
Then on the couch her trembling body cast,
Repress'd the ready tears, and spoke her last:

"Dear pledges of my love, while heav'n
    so pleased,
Receive a soul, of mortal anguish eased.
My fatal course is finished; and I go,
A glorious name, among the ghosts below.
A lofty city by my hands is raised;
Pygmalion punish'd, and my lord ap-
    peased.
What could my fortune have afforded
    more,
Had the false Trojan never touch'd my
    shore?"
Then kiss'd the couch; and "must I die,"
    she said,
"And unrevenged? 'tis doubly to be dead!
Yet ev'n this death with pleasure I re-
    ceive:
On any terms, 'tis better than to live.
These flames, from far, may the false
    Trojan view;
These boding omens his base flight pur-
    sue!"
She said, and struck: deep enter'd in her
    side
The piercing steel, with reeking purple
    died:
Clogg'd in the wound the cruel weapon
    stands;
The spouting blood came streaming on
    her hands.
Her sad attendants saw the deadly
    stroke,
And with loud cries the sounding palace
    shook.
Distracted from the fatal sight they fled,
And through the town the dismal rumour
    spread.
First from the frighted court the yell
    began;
Redoubled, thence from house to house it
    ran:
The groans of men, with shrieks, laments,
    and cries
Of mixing women, mount the vaulted
    skies.
Not less the clamour, than if—ancient
    Tyre,
Or the new Carthage, set by foes on
    fire—

The rolling ruin, with their loved abodes,
Involved the blazing temples of their
    gods.
Her sister hears; and, furious with
    despair,
She beats her breasts, and rends her
    yellow hair,
And, calling on Eliza's name aloud,
Runs breathless to the place, and breaks
    the crowd.
"Was all that pomp of wo for this pre-
    pared,
These fires, this fun'ral pile, these altars
    rear'd?
Was all this train of plots contrived,"
    said she,
"All only to deceive unhappy me?
Which is the worst? Didst thou in death
    pretend
To scorn thy sister, or delude thy friend?
Thy summon'd sister and thy friend had
    come:
One sword had served us both, one com-
    mon tomb.
Was I to raise the pile, the pow'rs invoke,
Not to be present at the fatal stroke?
At once thou hast destroy'd thyself and
    me,
Thy town, thy senate, and thy colony!
Bring water! bathe the wound: while I
    in death
Lay close my lip to hers, and catch the
    flying breath."
This said, she mounts the pile with eager
    haste,
And in her arms the gasping queen em-
    braced:
Her temples chafed; and her own gar-
    ments tore,
To stanch the streaming blood, and
    cleanse the gore.
Thrice Dido tries to raise her drooping
    head,
And, fainting, thrice fell grov'ling on the
    bed;
Thrice op'd her heavy eyes, and saw the
    light,
But, having found it, sicken'd at the
    sight,

And closed her lids at last in endless
   night.
Then Juno, grieving that she should
   sustain
A death so ling'ring, and so full of pain,
Sent Iris down, to free her from the strife
Of lab'ring nature, and dissolve her life.
For, since she died, not doom'd by
   heav'n's decree,
Or her own crime, but human casualty,
And rage of love, that plunged her in
   despair,
The sisters had not cut the topmost hair,
Which Proserpine and they can only
   know;
Nor made her sacred to the shades below.
Downward the various goddess took her
   flight,
And drew a thousand colours from the
   light;
Then stood above the dying lover's head,
And said, "I thus devote thee to the
   dead.
This off'ring to th' infernal gods I bear."
Thus while she spoke, she cut the fatal
   hair,
The struggling soul was loosed, and life
   dissolved in air.

                —JOHN DRYDEN.

VISION OF ROME'S DESTINY

[From Book VI]

   Arrived in the promised land of Italy,
Æneas visits the underworld to seek guidance for his future conduct. The poet
makes use of the supernatural to picture,
through prophecy, the glorious destiny of
Rome. He avails himself also of the opportunity to eulogize the reigning house
of Cæsar. The doctrine of immortality
is in direct contradiction to the teachings
of Lucretius and to the belief of many
of his contemporaries.

                Arrived at last,
The prince, with living water, sprinkled
   o'er

His limbs and body; then approach'd the
   door,
Possess'd the porch, and on the front
   above
He fix'd the fatal bough, required by
   Pluto's love.
These holy rites perform'd, they took
   their way,
Where long extended plains of pleasure
   lay.
The verdant fields with those of heav'n
   may vie,
With ether vested, and a purple sky—
The blissful seats of happy souls below:
Stars of their own, and their own suns,
   they know.
Their airy limbs in sports they exercise,
And, on the green, contend the wrestler's
   prize.
Some, in heroic verse, divinely sing:
Others in artful measures lead the ring.
The Thracian bard, surrounded by the
   rest,
There stands conspicuous in his flowing
   vest.
His flying fingers, and harmonious quill,
Strike sev'n distinguish'd notes, and sev'n
   at once they fill.
Here found they Teucer's old heroic race,
Born better ties and happier years to
   grace.
Assaracus and Ilus here enjoy
Perpetual fame, with him who founded
   Troy.
The chief beheld their chariots from afar,
Their shining arms, and coursers train'd
   to war.
Their lances fix'd in earth—their steeds
   around,
Free from their harness, graze the flow'ry
   ground.
The love of horses which they had, alive,
And care of chariots, after death survive.
Some cheerful souls were feasting on the
   plain;
Some did the song, and some the choir,
   maintain,
Beneath a laurel shade, where mighty Po

Mounts up to woods above, and hides his head below.
Here patriots live, who, for their country's good,
In fighting fields, were prodigal of blood:
Priests of unblemish'd lives here make abode,
And poets worthy their inspiring god;
And searching wits, of more mechanic parts,
Who graced their age with new-invented arts;
Those who to worth their bounty did extend,
And those who knew that bounty did commend,
The heads of these with holy fillets bound,
And all their temples were with garlands crown'd.
　To these the Sibyl thus her speech address'd,
And first to him surrounded by the rest—
(Tow'ring his height, and ample was his breast)
"Say, happy souls! divine Musæus! say,
Where lives Anchises, and where lies our way
To find the hero, for whose only sake
We sought the dark abodes, and cross'd the bitter lake?"
To this the sacred poet thus replied:
"In no fix'd place the happy souls reside.
In groves we live, and lie on mossy beds,
By crystal streams, that murmur through the meads:
But pass yon easy hill, and thence descend;
The path conducts you to your journey's end."
This said, he led them up the mountain's brow,
And showed them all the shining fields below.
They wind the hill, and through the blissful meadows go.
But old Anchises, in a flow'ry vale,
Review'd his muster'd race, and took the tale—

Those happy spirits which, ordain'd by Fate,
For future being and new bodies wait—
With studious thought observed th' illustrious throng,
In Nature's order as they pass'd along—
Their names, their fates, their conduct, and their care,
In peaceful senates, and successful war.
He, when Æneas on the plain appears,
Meets him with open arms, and falling tears.
"Welcome," he said, "the gods' undoubted race!
O long expected to my dear embrace!
Once more 'tis giv'n me to behold your face!
The love and pious duty which you pay
Have pass'd the perils of so hard a way.
'Tis true, computing times, I have believed
The happy day approach'd; nor, are my hopes deceived.
What length of lands, what oceans have you pass'd,
What storms sustain'd, and on what shores been cast!
How have I fear'd your fate! but fear'd it most
When love assail'd you on the Libyan coast."
To this the filial duty thus replies:
"Your sacred ghost, before my sleeping eyes,
Appear'd, and often urged this painful enterprise.
After long tossing on the Tyrrhene sea,
My navy rides at anchor in the bay.
But reach your hand, oh parent shade! nor shun
The dear embraces of your longing son!"
He said: and falling tears his face bedew:
Then thrice around his neck his arms he threw;
And thrice the flitting shadow slipp'd away,
Like winds, or empty dreams that fly the day.
Now, in a secret vale, the Trojan sees

A sep'rate grove, through which a gentle breeze
Plays with a passing breath, that whispers through the trees:
And, just before the confines of the wood,
The gliding Lethe leads her silent flood.
About the boughs an airy nation flew,
Thick as the humming bees, that hunt the golden dew
In summer's heat; on tops of lilies feed,
And creep within their bells, to suck the balmy seed:
The winged army roams the field around;
The rivers and the rocks remurmur to the sound.
Æneas wond'ring stood, then ask'd the cause
Which to the stream the crowding people draws.
Then thus the sire: "The souls that throng the flood
Are those to whom, by Fate, are other bodies owed.
In Lethe's lake they long oblivion taste,
Of future life secure, forgetful of the past.
Long has my soul desired this time and place,
To set before your sight your glorious race,
That this presaging joy may fire your mind
To seek the shores by destiny design'd."—
"O father! can it be, that souls sublime
Return to visit our terrestrial clime,
And that the gen'rous mind, released by death,
Can covet lazy limbs, and mortal breath?"
Anchises then, in order, thus begun
To clear those wonders to his godlike son:
"Know, first, that heav'n, and earth's compacted frame,
And flowing waters, and the starry flame,
And both the radiant lights, one common soul
Inspires and feeds—and animates the whole.
This active mind, infused through all the space,
Unites and mingles with the mighty mass.
Hence men and beasts the breath of life obtain,
And birds of air, and monsters of the main.
Th' ethereal vigour is in all the same;
And ev'ry soul is fill'd with equal flame—
As much as earthy limbs, and gross allay
Of mortal members subject to decay,
Blunt not the beams of heav'n and edge of day.
From this coarse mixture of terrestrial parts,
Desire and fear by turns possess their hearts,
And grief, and joy: nor can the grovelling mind,
In the dark dungeon of the limbs confined,
Assert the native skies, or own its heav'nly kind:
Nor death itself can wholly wash their stains;
But long-contracted filth ev'n in the soul remains.
The relics of invet'rate vice they wear;
And spots of sin obscene in ev'ry face appear.
For this are various penances enjoin'd;
And some are hung to bleach upon the wind,
Some plunged in waters, others purged in fires,
Till all the dregs are drain'd, and all the rust expires.
All have their manes, and those manes bear:
The few, so cleansed, to these abodes repair,
And breathe, in ample fields, the soft Elysian air.
Then are they happy, when by length of time
The scurf is worn away of each committed crime;
No speck is left of their habitual stains;
But the pure ether of the soul remains.
But, when a thousand rolling years are past

(So long their punishments and penance
    last),
Whole droves of minds are, by the
    driving god,
Compell'd to drink the deep Lethean
    flood,
In large forgetful draughts to steep the
    cares
Of their past labours and their irksome
    years,
That, unrememb'ring of its former pain,
The soul may suffer mortal flesh again."
Thus having said, the father spirit leads
The priestess and his son through swarms
    of shades,
And takes a rising ground, from thence
    to see
The long procession of his progeny.
"Survey," pursued the sire, "this airy
    throng,
As, offer'd to the view, they pass along.
These are th' Italian names, which Fate
    will join
With ours, and graft upon the Trojan
    line.
Observe the youth who first appears in
    sight,
And holds the nearest station to the light,
Already seems to snuff the vital air,
And leans just forward on a shining spear:
Sylvius is he, thy last begotten race,
But first in order sent, to fill thy place—
An Alban name, but mix'd with Dardan
    blood:
Born in the covert of a shady wood,
Him fair Lavinia, thy surviving wife,
Shall breed in groves to lead a solitary
    life.
In Alba he shall fix his royal seat,
And, born a king, a race of kings beget:—
Then Procas, honour of the Trojan name,
Capys, and Numitor, of endless fame.
A second Sylvius after these appears—
Sylvius Æneas, for thy name he bears—
For arms and justice equally renown'd.
How great they look! how vigorously they
    wield
Their weighty lances, and sustain the
    shield!

But they, who crown'd with oaken
    wreaths appear,
Shall Gabian walls and strong Fidenæ
    rear;
Nomentum, Bola, with Pometia found;
And raise Collatian tow'rs on rocky
    ground.
All these shall then be towns of mighty
    fame,
Though now they lie obscure, and lands
    without a name.
See Romulus the great, born to restore
The crown that once his injured grand-
    sire wore.
This prince a priestess of our blood shall
    bear;
And like his sire in arms he shall appear.
Two rising crests his royal head adorn:
Born from a god, himself to godhead
    born,
His sire already signs him for the skies,
And marks his seat amid the deities.
Auspicious chief! thy race, in times to
    come,
Shall spread the conquests of imperial
    Rome—
Rome, whose ascending tow'rs shall
    heav'n invade,
Involving earth and ocean in her shade;
High as the mother of the gods in place,
And proud, like her, of an immortal race,
Then, when in pomp she makes the
    Phrygian round,
With golden turrets on her temples
    crown'd:
A hundred gods her sweeping train
    supply;
Her offspring all, and all command the
    sky.
Now fix your sight, and stand intent, to
    see
Your Roman race, and Julian progeny.
There mighty Cæsar waits his vital hour,
Impatient for the world, and grasps his
    promised pow'r.
But next behold the youth of form
    divine—
Cæsar himself, exalted in his line—
Augustus, promised oft, and long foretold,

Sent to the realm that Saturn ruled of
    old;
Born to restore a better age of gold.
Afric and India shall his pow'r obey;
He shall extend his propagated sway
Beyond the solar year, without the starry
    way,
Where Atlas turns the rolling heav'ns
    round,
And his broad shoulders with their lights
    are crown'd.
At his foreseen approach, already quake
The Caspian kingdoms and Mæotian lake.
Their seers behold the tempest from afar;
And threat'ning oracles denounce the war.
Nile hears him knocking at his sev'nfold
    gates,
And seeks his hidden spring, and fears
    his nephew's fates.
Nor Hercules more lands or labours knew,
Not though the brazen-footed hind he
    slew,
Freed Erymanthus from the foaming
    boar,
And dipp'd his arrows in Lernæan gore;
Nor Bacchus, turning from his Indian
    war,
By tigers drawn triumphant in his car,
From Nysa's top descending on the plains,
With curling vines around his purple
    reins.
And doubt we yet through dangers to
    pursue
The paths of honour, and a crown in
    view?
But what's the man, who from afar ap-
    pears,
His head with olive crown'd, his hand a
    censer bears?
His hoary beard and holy vestments bring
His lost idea back: I know the Roman
    king.
He shall to peaceful Rome new laws
    ordain,
Call'd from his mean abode, a sceptre to
    sustain.
Him Tullus next in dignity succeeds,
An active prince, and prone to martial
    deeds.

He shall his troops for fighting fields pre-
    pare,
Disused to toils, and triumphs of the war.
By dint of sword his crown he shall in-
    crease,
And scour his armour from the rust of
    peace.
Whom Ancus follows, with a fawning air,
But vain within, and proudly popular.
Next view the Tarquin kings, th' aveng-
    ing sword
Of Brutus, justly drawn, and Rome re-
    stored.
He first renews the rods and axe severe,
And gives the consuls royal robes to wear.
His sons, who seek the tyrant to sustain,
And long for arbitrary lords again,
With ignominy scourged in open sight,
He dooms to death deserved, asserting
    public right.
Unhappy man! to break the pious laws
Of Nature, pleading in his children's
    cause!
Howe'er the doubtful fact is understood,
'Tis love of honour, and his country's
    good:
The consul, not the father, sheds the
    blood.
Behold Torquatus the same track pursue;
And, next, the two devoted Decii view—
The Drusian line, Camillus loaded home
With standards well redeem'd, and for-
    eign foes o'ercome.
The pair you see in equal armour shine,
Now, friends below, in close embraces
    join;
But, when they leave the shady realms of
    night,
And, clothed in bodies, breathe your
    upper light,
With mortal hate each other shall pursue:
What wars, what wounds, what slaughter,
    shall ensue!
From Alpine heights the father first
    descends;
His daughter's husband in the plain
    attends:
His daughter's husband arms his eastern
    friends.

Embrace again, my sons! be foes no more;
Nor stain your country with her children's gore!
And thou, the first, lay down thy lawless claim,
Thou, of my blood, who bear'st the Julian name!
Another comes, who shall in triumph ride,
And to the capitol his chariot guide,
From conquer'd Corinth, rich with Grecian spoils.
And yet another, famed for warlike toils,
On Argos shall impose the Roman laws,
And, on the Greeks, revenge the Trojan cause;
Shall drag in chains their Achillean race;
Shall vindicate his ancestors' disgrace,
And Pallas, for her violated place.
Great Cato there, for gravity renown'd,
And conqu'ring Cossus goes with laurels crown'd.
Who can omit the Gracchi, who declare
The Scipios' worth, those thunderbolts of war,
The double bane of Carthage? Who can see
Without esteem for virtuous poverty,
Severe Fabricius, or can cease t' admire
The ploughman consul in his coarse attire?
Tired as I am, my praise the Fabii claim;
And thou, great hero, greatest of thy name,
Ordain'd in war to save the sinking state,
And, by delays, to put a stop to fate!
Let others better mould the running mass
Of metals, and inform the breathing brass,
And soften into flesh a marble face;
Plead better at the bar; describe the skies,
And when the stars ascend, and when they rise.
But, Rome! 'tis thine alone, with awful sway,
To rule mankind, and make the world obey.
Disposing peace and war thy own majestic way;

To tame the proud, the fetter'd slave to free:
These are imperial arts, and worthy thee."
He paused—and, while with wond'ring eyes they view'd
The passing spirits, thus his speech renew'd:
"See great Marcellus! how, untired in toils,
He moves with manly grace, how rich with regal spoils!
He, when his country (threaten'd with alarms)
Requires his courage and his conqu'ring arms,
Shall more than once the Punic bands affright;
Shall kill the Gaulish king in single fight;
Then to the capitol in triumph move:
And the third spoils shall grace Feretrian Jove."
Æneas here beheld, of form divine
A godlike youth in glitt'ring armour shine,
With great Marcellus keeping equal pace:
But gloomy were his eyes, dejected was his face.
He saw, and, wond'ring, ask'd his airy guide,
What and of whence was he, who press'd the hero's side.
"His son, or one of his illustrious name?
How like the former, and almost the same!
Observe the crowds that compass him around:
All gaze, and all admire, and raise a shouting sound:
But hov'ring mists around his brows are spread;
And night, with sable shades, involves his head."
"Seek not to know," the ghost replied with tears,
"The sorrows of thy sons in future years.
This youth (the blissful vision of a day)
Shall just be shown on earth, and snatch'd away.

The gods too high and raised the Roman
state,
Were but their gifts as permanent as
great.
What groans of men shall fill the Martian
Field!
How fierce a blaze his flaming pile shall
yield!
What fun'ral pomp shall floating Tiber
see,
When, rising from his bed, he views the
sad solemnity!
No youth shall equal hopes of glory give,
No youth afford so great a cause to
grieve.
The Trojan honour, and the Roman
boast,
Admired when living, and adored when
lost!
Mirror of ancient faith in early youth!
Undaunted worth, inviolable truth!
No foe, unpunish'd, in the fighting field
Shall dare thee, foot to foot, with sword
and shield,
Much less in arms oppose thy matchless
force,
When thy sharp spurs shall urge thy
foaming horse.
Ah! couldst thou break through Fate's
severe decree!
A new Marcellus shall arise in thee!
Full canisters of fragrant lilies bring,
Mix'd with the purple roses of the spring:
Let me with fun'ral flow'rs his body
strow:
This gift which parents to their children
owe,
This unavailing gift, at least, I may
bestow!"
Thus having said, he led the hero round
The confines of the bless'd Elysian
ground;
Which when Anchises to his son had
shown,
And fired his mind to mount the promised
throne,
He tells the future wars ordain'd by Fate:
The strength and customs of the Latin
state;

The prince, and people; and forearms
his care
With rules, to push his fortune, or to bear.
Two gates the silent house of Sleep
adorn:
Of polish'd iv'ry this, that of transparent
horn:
True visions through transparent horn
arise;
Through polish'd iv'ry pass deluding lies.
Of various things discoursing as he pass'd,
Anchises hither bends his steps at last.
Then, through the gate of iv'ry he dis-
miss'd
His valiant offspring, and divining guest.
Straight to the ships Æneas took his way,
Embark'd his men, and skimm'd along
the sea,
Still coasting, till he gain'd Caieta's bay.
At length on oozy ground his galleys
moor:
Their heads are turn'd to sea, their
sterns to shore.

—JOHN DRYDEN.

THE OUTBREAK OF WAR

[From Book VII]

Æneas has sought to establish a settlement on Italian soil by peaceful means,
but the attitude of the native peoples who
looked upon him as an intruder made war
a necessity. Whatever the causes of wars
may be, their actual outbreak, according
to Virgil, is due to trivial misunderstand-
ings and falsehood. If the ugly passions
of leaders could be controlled, wars might
be avoided.

But jealous Juno, from Pachynus'
height,
As she from Argos took her airy flight,
Beheld, with envious eyes, this hateful
sight.
She saw the Trojan and his joyful train
Descend upon the shore, desert the main,
Design a town, and, with unhoped success,

Th' ambassadors return with promised
    peace.
Then, pierced with pain, she shook her
    haughty head,
Sigh'd from her inward soul, and thus
    she said:
"O hated offspring of my Phrygian foes!
O fates of Troy, which Juno's fates
    oppose!
Could they not fall unpitied on the plain,
But, slain, revive, and, taken, 'scape
    again?
When execrable Troy in ashes lay,
Through fires and swords and seas they
    forced their way.
Then vanquish'd Juno must in vain con-
    tend,—
Her rage disarm'd, her empire at an end!
Breathless and tired, is all my fury spent?
Or does my glutted spleen at length
    relent?
As if 'twere little from their town to
    chase,
I through the seas pursued their exiled
    race;
Engaged the heav'ns, opposed the stormy
    main:
But billows roar'd and tempests raged in
    vain.
What have my Scyllas and my Syrtes
    done,
When these they overpass, and those
    they shun?
On Tiber's shores they land, secure of
    fate,
Triumphant o'er the storms and Juno's
    hate!
Mars could in mutual blood the Centaurs
    bathe;
And Jove himself gave way to Cynthia's
    wrath,
Who sent the tusky boar to Calydon:
(What great offence had either people
    done?)
But I, the consort of the Thunderer,
Have waged a long and unsuccessful war,
With various arts and arms in vain have
    toil'd,

And by a mortal man at length am
    foil'd!
If native pow'r prevail not, shall I doubt
To seek for needful succour from with-
    out?
If Jove and heav'n my just desires deny,
Hell shall the pow'r of heav'n and Jove
    supply.
Grant that the Fates have firm'd, by their
    decree,
The Trojan race to reign in Italy:
At least I can defer the nuptial day,
And, with protracted wars, the peace
    delay:
With blood the dear alliance shall be
    bought,
And both the people near destruction
    brought.
So shall the son-in-law and father join,
With ruin, war, and waste of either line.
O fatal maid! thy marriage is endow'd
With Phrygian, Latian, and Rutulian
    blood!
Bellona leads thee to thy lover's hand:
Another queen brings forth another
    brand,
To burn with foreign fires another land!
A second Paris, diff'ring but in name,
Shall fire his country with a second
    flame."
    Thus having said, she sinks beneath the
    ground,
With furious haste, and shoots the
    Stygian sound,
To rouse Alecto from th' infernal seat
Of her dire sisters, and their dark retreat.
This fury, fit for her intent, she chose;
One who delights in wars and human
    woes.
Ev'n Pluto hates his own misshapen race;
Her sister Furies fly her hideous face;
So frightful are the forms the monster
    takes,
So fierce the hissings of her speckled
    snakes.
Her Juno finds, and thus inflames her
    spite:
"O virgin daughter of eternal night,
Give me this once thy labour, to sustain

My right, and execute my just disdain.
Let not the Trojans, with a feign'd pretence
Of proffer'd peace, delude the Latian prince:
Expel from Italy that odious name,
And let not Juno suffer in her fame.
'Tis thine to ruin realms, o'erturn a state,
Between the dearest friends to raise debate,
And kindle kindred blood to mutual hate.
Thy hand o'er towns the fun'ral torch displays,
And forms a thousand ills ten thousand ways.
Now shake, from out thy fruitful breast, the seeds
Of envy, discord, and of cruel deeds:
Confound the peace establish'd, and prepare
Their souls to hatred, and their hands to war."
Smear'd as she was with black Gorgonean blood,
The Fury sprang above the Stygian flood:
And on her wicked wings, sublime through night,
She to the Latian palace took her flight;
There sought the queen's apartment, stood before
The peaceful threshold, and besieged the door.
Restless Amata lay, her swelling breast
Fired with disdain for Turnus dispossess'd,
And the new nuptials of the Trojan guest.
From her black bloody locks the Fury shakes
Her darling plague, the fav'rite of her snakes:
With her full force she threw the pois'nous dart,
And fix'd it deep within Amata's heart,
That, thus envenom'd, she might kindle rage,
And sacrifice to strife her house and husband's age.
Unseen, unfelt, the fiery serpent skims
Between her linen and her naked limbs,

His baneful breath inspiring as he glides.
Now like a chain around her neck he rides,
Now like a fillet to her head repairs,
And with his circling volumes folds her hairs.
At first the silent venom slid with ease,
And seized her cooler senses by degrees;
Then, ere th' infected mass was fired too far,
In plaintive accents she began the war,
And thus bespoke her husband: "Shall," she said,
"A wand'ring prince enjoy Lavinia's bed?
If Nature plead not in a parent's heart,
Pity my tears, and pity her desert.
I know, my dearest lord, the time will come
You would, in vain, reverse your cruel doom:
The faithless pirate soon will set to sea,
And bear the royal virgin far away!
A guest like him, a Trojan guest before,
In show of friendship sought the Spartan shore,
And ravish'd Helen from her husband bore.
Think on a king's inviolable word;
And think on Turnus, her once plighted lord.
To this false foreigner you give your throne,
And wrong a friend, a kinsman, and a son.
Resume your ancient care; and, if the god
Your sire, and you, resolve on foreign blood,
Know all are foreign, in a larger sense,
Not born your subjects, or derived from hence.
Then, if the line of Turnus you retrace,
He springs from Inachus of Argive race."
But when she saw her reasons idly spent,
And could not move him from his fix'd intent,
She flew to rage; for now the snake possess'd

Her vital parts, and poison'd all her
    breast.
She raves, she runs with a distracted pace,
And fills, with horrid howls, the public
    place.
And, as young striplings whip the top
    for sport,
On the smooth pavement of an empty
    court;
The wooden engine flies and whirls about,
Admired, with clamours, of the beardless
    rout;
They lash aloud; each other they provoke,
And lend their little souls at ev'ry stroke:
Thus fares the queen; and thus her fury
    blows
Amid the crowd, and kindles as she goes.
Nor yet content, she strains her malice
    more,
And adds new ills to those contrived
    before:
She flies the town, and, mixing with the
    throng
Of madding matrons, bears the bride
    along,
Wand'ring through woods and wilds, and
    devious ways,
And with these arts the Trojan match
    delays.
She feign'd the rites of Bacchus; cried
    aloud,
And to the buxom god the virgin vow'd.
"Euoi! O Bacchus!" thus began the
    song;
And "Euoi!" answer'd all the female
    throng.
"O virgin worthy thee alone!" she cried;
"O worthy thee alone!" the crew replied.
"For thee she feeds her hair, she leads
    thy dance,
And with thy winding ivy wreathes her
    lance."
Like fury seized the rest: the progress
    known,
All seek the mountains, and forsake the
    town:
All, clad in skins of beasts, the javelin
    bear,

Give to the wanton winds their flowing
    hair;
And shrieks and shoutings rend the
    suff'ring air.
The queen herself, inspired with rage
    divine,
Shook high above her head a flaming
    pine,
Then roll'd her haggard eyes around the
    throng,
And sang, in Turnus' name, the nuptial
    song:
"Io! ye Latian dames, if any here
Hold your unhappy queen, Amata, dear;
If there be here," she said, "who dare
    maintain
My right, nor think the name of mother
    vain;
Unbind your fillets, loose your flowing
    hair,
And orgies and nocturnal rites prepare."
Amata's breast the Fury thus invades,
And fires with rage, amid the sylvan
    shades.
Then, when she found her venom spread
    so far,
The royal house embroil'd in civil war,
Raised on her dusky wings, she cleaves
    the skies,
And seeks the palace where young Turnus
    lies.
His town, as fame reports, was built of
    old
By Danae, pregnant with almighty gold,
Who fled her father's rage, and, with a
    train
Of following Argives, through the stormy
    main,
Driven by the southern blasts, was fated
    here to reign.
    'Twas Ardua once: now Ardea's name
    it bears;
Once a fair city, now consumed with
    years.
Here, in his lofty palace, Turnus lay,
Between the confines of the night and
    day,
Secure in sleep.—The Fury laid aside

Her looks and limbs, and with new methods tried
The foulness of th' infernal form to hide.
Propp'd on a staff, she takes a trembling mien;
Her face is furrow'd, and her front obscene;
Deep-dinted wrinkles on her cheek she draws;
Sunk are her eyes, and toothless are her jaws;
Her hoary hair with holy fillets bound,
Her temples with an olive wreath are crown'd.
Old Chalybe, who kept the sacred fane
Of Juno, now she seem'd, and thus began,
Appearing in a dream, to rouse the careless man:
"Shall Turnus then such endless toil sustain
In fighting fields, and conquer towns in vain?
Win, for a Trojan head to wear the prize,
Usurp thy crown, enjoy thy victories?
The bride and sceptre, which thy blood has bought,
The king transfers; and foreign heirs are sought!
Go now, deluded man, and seek again
New toils, new dangers, on the dusty plain!
Repel the Tuscan foes; their city seize;
Protect the Latians in luxurious ease!
This dream all-pow'rful Juno sends: I bear
Her mighty mandates; and her words you hear.
Haste! arm your Ardeans; issue to the plain;
With faith to friend, assault the Trojan train:
Their thoughtless chiefs, their painted ships that lie
In Tiber's mouth, with fire and sword destroy.
The Latian king, unless he shall submit,
Own his old promise, and his new forget—

Let him, in arms, the pow'r of Turnus prove,
And learn to fear whom he disdains to love.
For such is heav'n's command."—The youthful prince
With scorn replied, and made this bold defence:
"You tell me, mother, what I knew before,
The Phrygian fleet is landed on the shore.
I neither fear nor will provoke the war:
My fate is Juno's most peculiar care.
But time has made you dote, and vainly tell
Of arms imagined in your lonely cell.
Go! be the temple and the gods your care:
Permit to men the thought of peace and war."
    These haughty words Alecto's rage provoke;
And frighted Turnus trembled as she spoke.
Her eyes grow stiffen'd, and with sulphur burn,
Her hideous looks and hellish form return:
Her curling snakes with hissings fill the place,
And open all the furies of her face:
Then, darting fire from her malignant eyes,
She cast him backward as he strove to rise,
And, ling'ring, sought to frame some new replies.
High on her head she rears her twisted snakes:
Her chains she rattles, and her whip she shakes;
And, churning bloody foam, thus loudly speaks:
"Behold whom time has made to dote, and tell
Of arms, imagined in her lonely cell;
Behold the Fates' infernal minister!
War, death, destruction, in my hand I bear."

Thus having said, her smould'ring torch, impress'd
With her full force, she plunged into his breast.
Aghast he waked; and starting from his bed,
Cold sweat, in clammy drops, his limbs o'erspread.
"Arms! arms!" he cries: "my sword and shield prepare!"
He breathes defiance, blood and mortal war.
So, when with crackling flames a caldron fries,
The bubbling waters from the bottom rise:
Above the brims they force their fiery way;
Black vapours climb aloft, and cloud the day.
   The peace polluted thus, a chosen band
He first commissions to the Latian land,
In threat'ning embassy; then raised the rest,
To meet in arms th' intruding Trojan guest,
To force the foes from the Lavinian shore,
And Italy's endanger'd peace restore.
Himself alone an equal match, he boasts,
To fight the Phrygian and Ausonian hosts.
The gods invoked, the Rutuli prepare
Their arms, and warm each other to the war.
His beauty these, and those his blooming age,
The rest his house, and his own fame engage.
   While Turnus urges thus his enterprise,
The Stygian Fury to the Trojans flies;
New frauds invents, and takes a steepy stand,
Which overlooks the vale with wide command;
Where fair Ascanius and his youthful train
With horns and hounds a hunting match ordain,

And pitch their toils around the shady plain.
The Fury fires the pack; they snuff, they vent,
And feed their hungry nostrils with the scent.
'Twas of a well-grown stag, whose antlers rise
High o'er his front, his beams invade the skies.
From this light cause, th' infernal maid prepares
The country churls to mischief, hate, and wars.
   The stately beast the two Tyrridæ bred,
Snatch'd from his dam, and the tame youngling fed.
Their father Tyrrheus did his fodder bring;
Tyrrheus, chief ranger to the Latian king:
Their sister Sylvia cherish'd with her care
The little wanton, and did wreathes prepare
To hang his budding horns, with ribands tied
His tender neck, and comb'd his silken hide,
And bathed his body. Patient of command
In time he grew, and growing used to hand,
He waited at his master's board for food;
Then sought his savage kindred in the wood,
Where grazing all the day, at night he came
To his known lodgings, and his country dame.
This household beast, that used the woodland grounds,
Was view'd at first by the young hero's hounds,
As down the stream he swam, to seek retreat
In the cool waters, and to quench his heat.
Ascanius, young, and eager of his game,

Soon bent his bow, uncertain in his aim:
But the dire fiend the fatal arrow guides,
Which pierced his bowels through his panting sides.
The bleeding creature issues from the floods,
Possess'd with fear, and seeks his known abodes,
His old familiar hearth, and household gods.
He falls; he fills the house with heavy groans,
Implores their pity, and his pain bemoans.
Young Sylvia beats her breast, and cries aloud
For succour from the clownish neighbourhood:
The churls assemble; for the fiend, who lay
In the close woody covert, urged their way.
One with a brand yet burning from the flame,
Arm'd with a knotty club another came:
Whate'er they catch or find, without their care,
Their fury makes an instrument of war.
Tyrrheus, the foster-father of the beast,
Then clench'd a hatchet in his horny fist,
But held his hand from the descending stroke,
And left his wedge within the cloven oak,
To whet their courage, and their rage provoke.
And now the goddess, exercised in ill,
Who watch'd an hour to work her impious will,
Ascends the roof, and to her crooked horn,
Such as was then by Latian shepherds borne,
Adds all her breath. The rocks and woods around,
And mountains, tremble at th' infernal sound.
The sacred lake of Trivia from afar,
The Veline fountains, and sulphureous Nar,
Shake at the baleful blast, the signal of the war.
Young mothers wildly stare, with fear possess'd,
And strain their helpless infants to their breast.
The clowns, a boist'rous, rude, ungovern'd crew,
With furious haste to the loud summons flew.
The pow'rs of Troy, then issuing on the plain,
With fresh recruits their youthful chief sustain:
Nor theirs a raw and unexperienced train,
But a firm body of embattled men.
At first, while fortune favour'd neither side,
The fight with clubs and burning brands was tried:
But now, both parties reinforced, the fields
Are bright with flaming swords and brazen shields.
A shining harvest either host displays,
And shoots against the sun with equal rays.
Thus, when a black-brow'd gust begins to rise,
White foam at first on the curl'd ocean fries;
Then roars the main, the billows mount the skies;
Till, by the fury of the storm full blown,
The muddy bottom o'er the clouds is thrown.
First Almon falls, old Tyrrheus eldest care,
Pierced with an arrow from the distant war:
Fix'd in his throat the flying weapon stood,
And stopp'd his breath, and drank his vital blood.
Huge heaps of slain around the body rise:
Among the rest, the rich Galesus lies;
A good old man, while peace he preach'd in vain,
Amid the madness of th' unruly train:

Five herds, five bleating flocks his
    pastures fill'd;
His lands a hundred yoke of oxen till'd.
Thus, while in equal scales their fortune
    stood,
The Fury bathed them in each other's
    blood;
Then, having fix'd the fight, exulting flies,
And bears fulfill'd her promise to the
    skies.
To Juno thus she speaks: "Behold; 'tis
    done,
The blood already drawn, the war begun;
The discord is complete; nor can they
    cease
The dire debate, nor you command the
    peace.
Now, since the Latian and the Trojan
    brood
Have tasted vengeance, and the sweets
    of blood,
Speak, and my pow'r shall add this office
    more:
The neighb'ring nations of th' Ausonian
    shore
Shall hear the dreadful rumour from afar,
Of arm'd invasion, and embrace the war."
Then Juno thus: "The grateful work is
    done,
The seeds of discord sow'd, the war
    begun:
Frauds, fears, and fury have possess'd the
    state,
And fix'd the causes of a lasting hate.
A bloody Hymen shall th' alliance join
Between the Trojan and Ausonian line:
But thou with speed to night and hell
    repair;
For not the gods, nor angry Jove, will
    bear
Thy lawless wand'ring walks in upper
    air.
Leave what remains to me." Saturnia
    said:
The sullen fiend her sounding wings dis-
    play'd,
Unwilling left the light, and sought the
    nether shade.

               —JOHN DRYDEN.

AT THE SITE OF ROME

[From Book VIII]

Faced with the prospect of war, Æneas
goes out to seek allies. He comes to the
city of Evander, located on the site afterwards to be occupied by Rome. The
episode is a fine example of Virgil's interest in the historical and religious origins
of Rome, and of his skill in weaving such
material into the main narrative. A passage like this must have caused a patriotic
thrill in every Roman heart.

The Trojans mount their ships; they
    put from shore,
Borne on the waves, and scarcely dip an
    oar.
Shouts from the land give omen to their
    course,
And the pitch'd vessels glide with easy
    force.
The woods and waters wonder at the
    gleam
Of shields, and painted ships that stem
    the stream.
One summer's night and one whole day
    they pass
Between the greenwood shades, and cut
    the liquid glass.
The fiery sun had finish'd half his race,
Look'd back and doubted in the middle
    space,
When they from far beheld the rising
    tow'rs,
The tops of sheds, and shepherds' lowly
    bow'rs,
Thin as they stood, which, then, of
    homely clay,
Now rise in marble, from the Roman
    sway.
These cots (Evander's kingdom, mean
    and poor)
The Trojan saw, and turn'd his ships to
    shore.
'Twas on a solemn day: th' Arcadian
    states,
The king and prince, without the city
    gates,

Then paid their off'rings in a sacred grove
To Hercules, the warrior son of Jove.
Thick clouds of rolling smoke involve the skies;
And fat of entrails on his altar fries.
   But, when they saw the ships that stemm'd the flood,
And glitter'd through the covert of the wood,
They rose with fear, and left th' unfinish'd feast,
Till dauntless Pallas reassured the rest
To pay the rites. Himself without delay
A jav'lin seized, and singly took his way,
Then gain'd a rising ground, and call'd from far:
"Resolve me, strangers, whence and what you are;
Your bus'ness here, and bring you peace or war?"
High on the stern Æneas took his stand,
And held a branch of olive in his hand,
While thus he spoke: "The Trojans and their chief
Bring holy peace, and beg the king's relief."
Struck with so great a name, and all on fire,
The youth replies: "Whatever you require
Your fame exacts. Upon our shores descend,
A welcome guest, and, what you wish, a friend."
He said, and, downward hastening to the strand,
Embraced the stranger prince, and join'd his hand.
Conducted to the grove, Æneas broke
The silence first, and thus the king bespoke:
"Best of the Greeks! to whom, by fate's command,
I bear these peaceful branches in my hand—
Undaunted I approach you, though I know

Your birth is Grecian, and your land my foe;
From Atreus though your ancient lineage came,
And both the brother kings your kindred claim;
Yet, my self-conscious worth, your high renown,
Your virtue, through the neighb'ring nations blown,
Our fathers' mingled blood, Apollo's voice,
Have led me hither, less by need than choice.
Our father Dardanus, as fame has sung,
And Greeks acknowledge, from Electra sprung;
Electra from the loins of Atlas came—
Atlas, whose head sustains the starry frame.
Your sire is Mercury, who long before
On cold Cyllene's top fair Maia bore.
Maia the fair, on fame if we rely,
Was Atlas' daughter, who sustains the sky.
Thus from one common source our streams divide:
Ours is the Trojan, yours th' Arcadian side.
Raised by these hopes, I sent no news before,
Nor ask'd your leave, nor did your faith implore;
But come, without a pledge, my own ambassador.
The same Rutulians, who with arms pursue
The Trojan race, are equal foes to you.
Our host expell'd, what further force can stay
The victor troops from universal sway?
Then will they stretch their pow'r athwart the land,
And either sea from side to side command.
Receive our offer'd faith, and give us thine:
Ours is a gen'rous and experienced line:

We want not hearts nor bodies for the war:
In councils cautious, and in fields we dare."
He said: and while he spoke, with piercing eyes
Evander view'd the man with vast surprise—
Pleased with his action, ravish'd with his face;
Then answer'd briefly, with a royal grace:
"O valiant leader of the Trojan line,
In whom the features of thy father shine!
How I recall Anchises! how I see
His motions, mien, and all my friend, in thee!
Long though it be, 'tis fresh within my mind,
When Priam to his sister's court design'd
A welcome visit, with a friendly stay,
And through th' Arcadian kingdom took his way.
Then, pass'd a boy, the callow down began
To shade my chin, and call me first a man.
I saw the shining train with vast delight;
And Priam's goodly person pleased my sight:
But great Anchises, far above the rest,
With awful wonder fired my youthful breast.
I long'd to join, in friendship's holy bands,
Our mutual hearts, and plight our mutual hands.
I first accosted him: I sued, I sought,
And, with a loving force, to Pheneus brought.
He gave me, when at length constrain'd to go,
A Lycian quiver and a Gnossian bow,
A vest embroider'd, glorious to behold,
And two rich bridles, with their bits of gold,
Which my son's coursers in obedience hold.
The league you ask, I offer, as your right;

And, when tomorrow's sun reveals the light,
With swift supplies you shall be sent away.
Now celebrate, with us, this solemn day,
Whose holy rites admit no long delay.
Honour our annual feast; and take your seat,
With friendly welcome, at a homely treat."
Thus having said, the bowls (removed for fear)
The youths replaced, and soon restored the cheer.
On sods of turf he set the soldiers round:
A maple throne, raised higher from the ground,
Received the Trojan chief; and, o'er the bed,
A lion's shaggy hide, for ornament, they spread.
The loaves were served in canisters; the wine
In bowls; the priest renew'd the rites divine:
Broil'd entrails are their food, and beef's continued chine.
But, when the rage of hunger was repress'd,
Thus spoke Evander to his royal guest:
"These rites, these altars, and this feast, O king,
From no vain fears or superstition spring,
Or blind devotion, or from blinder chance,
Or heady zeal, or brutal ignorance:
But, saved from danger, with a grateful sense,
The labours of a god we recompense.
See, from afar, yon rock that mates the sky,
About whose feet such heaps of rubbish lie;
Such indigested ruin; bleak and bare,
How desert now it stands, exposed in air!
'Twas once a robber's den, enclosed around
With living stone, and deep beneath the ground

The monster Cacus, more than half a
    beast,
This hold, impervious to the sun, pos-
    sess'd.
The pavement ever foul with human
    gore;
Heads, and their mangled members, hung
    the door.   .
Vulcan this plague begot: and, like his
    sire,
Black clouds he belch'd, and flakes of
    livid fire.
Time, long expected, eased us of our load,
And brought the needful presence of a
    god.
Th' avenging force of Hercules, from
    Spain,
Arrived in triumph, from Geryon slain:—
Thrice lived the giant, and thrice lived
    in vain.
His prize, the lowing herds, Alcides drove
Near Tiber's banks, to graze the shady
    grove.
Allured with hope of plunder, and intent
By force to rob, by fraud to circumvent,
The brutal Cacus, as by chance they
    stray'd,
Four oxen thence, and four fair kine
    convey'd.
And, lest the printed footsteps might be
    seen,
He dragg'd them backwards to his rocky
    den.
The tracks averse a lying notice gave,
And led the searcher backward from the
    cave.
Meantime the herdsman hero shifts his
    place,
To find fresh pasture, and untrodden
    grass.
The beasts, who miss'd their mates, fill'd
    all around
With bellowings; and the rocks restored
    the sound.
One heifer, who had heard her love com-
    plain,
Roar'd from the cave, and made the
    project vain.

Alcides found the fraud: with rage he
    shook,
And toss'd about his head his knotted
    oak.
Swift as the winds, or Scythian arrow's
    flight,
He climb'd, with eager haste, th' aerial
    height.
Then first we saw the monster mend his
    pace:
Fear in his eyes, and paleness in his
    face,
Confess'd the god's approach. Trem-
    bling he springs,
As terror had increased his feet with
    wings;
Nor staid for stairs; but down the depth
    he threw
His body: on his back the door he drew
(The door, a rib of living rock; with
    pains
His father hew'd it out, and bound with
    iron chains):
He broke the heavy links, the mountain
    closed,
And bars and levers to his foe opposed.
The wretch had hardly made his dungeon
    fast;
The fierce avenger came with bounding
    haste;
Survey'd the mouth of the forbidden
    hold;
And here and there his raging eyes he
    roll'd.
He gnash'd his teeth; and thrice he com-
    pass'd round
With winged speed the circuit of the
    ground.
Thrice at the cavern's mouth he pull'd
    in vain,
And, panting, thrice desisted from his
    pain.
A pointed flinty rock, all bare and black,
Grew gibbous from behind the moun-
    tian's back:
Owls, ravens, all ill omens of the night,
Here built their nests, and hither wing'd
    their flight.

The leaning head hung threat'ning o'er
the flood,
And nodded to the left. The hero stood
Averse, with planted feet, and, from the
right,
Tugg'd at the solid stone with all his
might.
Thus heav'd, the fix'd foundations of the
rock
Gave way: heav'n echo'd at the rattling
shock.
Tumbling, it choked the flood: on either
side
The banks leap backward, and the
streams divide:
The sky shrunk upward with unusual
dread;
And trembling Tiber dived beneath his
bed.
The court of Cacus stands reveal'd to
sight;
The cavern glares with new-admitted
light.
So the pent vapours, with a rumbling
sound,
Heave from below, and rend the hollow
ground;
A sounding flaw succeeds; and, from on
high,
The gods with hate behold the nether
sky:
The ghosts repine with violated night,
And curse th' invading sun, and sicken
at the sight.
The graceless monster, caught in open
day,
Enclosed, and in despair to fly away,
Howls horrible from underneath, and
fills
His hollow palace with unmanly yells.
The hero stands above, and from afar
Plies him with darts, and stones, and
distant war.
He, from his nostrils and huge mouth,
expires
Black clouds of smoke, amid his father's
fires,
Gath'ring, with each repeated blast, the
night,

To make uncertain aim, and erring sight.
The wrathful god then plunges from
above,
And, where in thickest waves the sparkles
drove,
There lights; and wades through fumes,
and gropes his way,
Half singed, half stifled, till he grasps
his prey.
The monster, spewing fruitless flames, he
found;
He squeezed his throat; he writhed his
neck around,
And in a knot his crippled members
bound;
Then, from their sockets, tore his burning
eyes.
Roll'd on a heap, the breathless robber
lies.
The doors, unbarr'd, receive the rushing
day;
And thorough lights disclose the ravish'd
prey.
The bulls, redeem'd, breathe open air
again.
Next, by his feet, they drag him from
his den.
The wond'ring neighbourhood, with glad
surprise,
Beheld his shagged breast, his giant size,
His mouth that flames no more, and his
extinguish'd eyes.
From that auspicious day, with rites
divine,
We worship at the hero's holy shrine.
Potitius first ordain'd these annual vows:
As priests, were added the Pinarian
house,
Who raised this altar in the sacred shade,
Where honours, ever due, for ever shall
be paid.
For these deserts, and this high virtue
shown,
Ye warlike youths, your heads with gar-
lands crown:
Fill high the goblets with a sparkling
flood;
And with deep draughts invoke our com-
mon god."

This said, a double wreath Evander twined;
And poplars black and white his temples bind.
Then brims his ample bowl. With like design
The rest invoke the gods with sprinkled wine.
   Meantime the sun descended from the skies,
And the bright ev'ning star began to rise.
And now the priests, Potitius at their head,
In skins of beasts involved, the long procession led:
Held high the flaming tapers in their hands,
As custom had prescribed their holy bands;
Then with a second course the tables load,
And with full chargers offer to the god.
The Salii sing, and 'cense his altar round
With Saban smoke, their heads with poplar bound—
One choir of old, another of the young,
To dance, and bear the burden of the song.
The lay records the labours, and the praise,
And all th' immortal acts of Hercules:
First, how the mighty babe, when swathed in bands,
The serpents strangled with his infant hands;
Then, as in years and matchless force he grew,
Th' Œchalian walls, and Trojan, overthrew.
Besides, a thousand hazards they relate,
Procured by Juno's and Eurystheus' hate.
"Thy hands, unconquer'd hero, could subdue
The cloud-born Centaurs, and the monster crew.
Nor thy resistless arm the bull withstood,
Nor he, the roaring terror of the wood.
The tripled porter of the Stygian seat,
With lolling tongue, lay fawning at thy feet,
And, seized with fear, forgot his mangled meat.
Th' infernal waters trembled at thy sight;
Thee, god! no face of danger could affright;
Not huge Typhœus, nor th' unnumber'd snake,
Increased with hissing heads, in Lerna's lake.
Hail, Jove's undoubted son! an added grace
To heav'n and the great author of thy race!
Receive the grateful off'rings which we pay,
And smile propitious on thy solemn day!"
In numbers thus they sung: above the rest,
The den and death of Cacus crown the feast.
The woods to hollow vales convey the sound;
The vales to hills; and hills the notes rebound.
   The rites perform'd, the cheerful train retire.
Between young Pallas and his aged sire
The Trojan pass'd, the city to survey;
And pleasing talk beguiled the tedious way.
The stranger cast around his curious eyes,
New objects viewing still with new surprise;
With greedy joy inquires of various things,
And acts and monuments of ancient kings.
Then thus the founder of the Roman tow'rs:
"These woods were first the seat of sylvan pow'rs,
Of nymphs and fauns, and savage men who took
Their birth from trunks of trees and stubborn oak.
Nor laws they knew, nor manners, nor the care

Of lab'ring oxen, nor the shining share,
Nor arts of gain, nor what they gain'd
  to spare.
Their exercise the chase: the running
  flood
Supplied their thirst; the trees supplied
  their food.
Then Saturn came, who fled the pow'r of
  Jove,
Robb'd of his realms, and banish'd from
  above.
The men, dispersed on hills, to towns he
  brought,
And laws ordain'd, and civil customs
  taught,
And Latium call'd the land where safe
  he lay
From his unduteous son, and his usurp-
  ing sway.
With his mild empire, peace and plenty
  came;
And hence the golden times derived their
  name.
A more degen'rate and discolour'd age
Succeeded this, with avarice and rage.
Th' Ausonians then, and bold Sicanians,
  came;
And Saturn's empire often changed the
  name.
Then kings—gigantic Tybris, and the
  rest—
With arbitrary sway the land oppress'd:
For Tiber's flood was Albula before,
Till, from the tyrant's fate, his name it
  bore.
I last arrived, driv'n from my native
  home
By fortune's pow'r, and fate's resistless
  doom.
Long toss'd on seas, I sought this happy
  land,
Warn'd by my mother-nymph, and call'd
  by heav'n's command."
  Thus, walking on, he spoke, and show'd
  the gate
Since call'd Carmental by the Roman
  state;
Where stood an altar, sacred to the name
Of old Carmenta, the prophetic dame,
Who to her son foretold th' Ænean race,
Sublime in fame, and Rome's imperial
  place;—
Then shows the forests, which, in after-
  times,
Fierce Romulus, for perpetrated crimes,
A sacred refuge made;—with this the
  shrine
Where Pan below the rock had rites
  divine;
Then tells of Argus' death, his murder'd
  guest,
Whose grave and tomb his innocence at-
  test.
Thence, to the steep Tarpeian rock he
  leads—
Now roof'd with gold, then thatch'd with
  homely reeds—
A rev'rent fear (such superstition reigns
Among the rude) ev'n then possess'd the
  swains.
Some god, they knew—what god, they
  could not tell—
Did there amid the sacred horror dwell.
Th' Arcadians thought him Jove: and
  said they saw
The mighty thund'rer with majestic awe,
Who shook his shield, and dealt his bolts
  around,
And scatter'd tempests on the teeming
  ground.
Then saw two heaps of ruins (once they
  stood
Two stately towns, on either side the
  flood),
Saturnia's and Janiculum's remains;
And either place the founder's name
  retains.
Discoursing thus together, they resort
Where poor Evander kept his country
  court.
They view'd the ground of Rome's liti-
  gious hall
(Once oxen low'd, where now the lawyers
  bawl):
Then, stooping, through the narrow gate
  they press'd,
When thus the king bespoke his Trojan
  guest:

"Mean as it is, this palace, and this door,
Received Alcides, then a conqueror.
Dare to be poor: accept our homely food,
Which feasted him; and emulate a god."
Then underneath a lowly roof he led
The weary prince and laid him on a bed;
The stuffing leaves with hides of bears
    o'erspread.
               —JOHN DRYDEN.

THE FIGHT OF ÆNEAS AND TURNUS

[From Book XII]

War is a matter of kings, not of peoples;
it should be settled by those responsible
in Homeric combat hand to hand.

Both armies from their bloody work
    desist,
And, bearing backward, form a spacious
    list.
The Trojan hero, who received from
    fame
The welcome sound, and heard the cham-
    pion's name,
Soon leaves the taken works and mounted
    walls;
Greedy of war where greater glory calls,
He springs to fight, exulting in his force;
His jointed armour rattles in the course.
Like Eryx, or like Athos, great he shows,
Or father Appennine, when, white with
    snows,
His head divine obscure in clouds he
    hides,
And shakes the sounding forest on his
    sides.
    The nations overaw'd, surcease the
    fight;
Immovable their bodies, fix'd their sight;
Ev'n death stands still; nor from above
    they throw
Their darts, nor drive their batt'ring-
    rams below.
In silent order either army stands,
And drop their swords, unknowing, from
    their hands.

Th' Ausonian king beholds, with won-
    d'ring sight,
Two mighty champions match'd in single
    fight,
Born under climes remote, and brought
    by fate
With swords to try their title to the state.
    Now, in closed field, each other from
    afar
They view; and, rushing on, begin the
    war.
They launch their spears; then hand to
    hand they meet.
The trembling soil resounds beneath their
    feet:
Their bucklers clash; thick blows descend
    from high,
And flakes of fire from their hard helmets
    fly.
Courage conspires with chance; and both
    engage
With equal fortune yet, and mutual rage.
    As, when two bulls for their fair female
    fight
In Sila's shades, or on Taburnus' height,
With horns adverse they meet: the
    keeper flies:
Mute stands the herd; the heifers roll
    their eyes,
And wait th' event—which victor they
    shall bear,
And who shall be the lord to rule the
    lusty year:
With rage of love the jealous rivals burn,
And push for push, and wound for wound
    return.
Their dewlaps gored, their sides are
    laved in blood:
Loud cries and roaring sounds rebellow
    through the wood.
Such was the combat in the listed ground;
So clash their swords, and so their shields
    resound.
    Jove sets the beam: in either scale
    he lays
The champions' fate, and each exactly
    weighs.
On this side, life, and lucky chance
    ascends:

Loaded with death, that other scale descends.
Raised on the stretch, young Turnus aims a blow
Full on the helm of his unguarded foe:
Shrill shouts and clamours ring on either side,
As hopes and fears their panting hearts divide.
But all in pieces flies the traitor sword,
And, in the middle stroke, deserts his lord.
Now 'tis but death or flight: disarm'd he flies,
When in his hand an unknown hilt he spies.
Fame says that Turnus, when his steeds he join'd,
Hurrying to war, disorder'd in his mind,
Snatch'd the first weapon which his haste could find.
'Twas not the fated sword his father bore,
But that his charioteer Metiscus wore.
This, while the Troans fled, the toughness held:
But vain against the great Vulcanian shield.
The mortal-temper'd steel deceived his hand:
The shiver'd fragments shone amid the sand.
  Surprised with fear, he fled along the field,
And now forthright, and now in orbits wheel'd:
For here the Trojan troops the list surround,
And there the pass is closed with pools and marshy ground.
Æneas hastens, though with heavier pace—
His wound, so newly knit, retards the chase,
And oft his trembling knees their aid refuse,
Yet, pressing foot by foot, his foe pursues.
  Thus, when a fearful stag is closed around

With crimson toils, or in a river found,
High on a bank the deep-mouth'd hound appears,
Still op'ning, following still, where'er he steers;
The persecuted creature, to and fro,
Turns here and there, to 'scape his Umbrian foe:
Steep is the ascent, and, if he gains the land,
The purple death is pitch'd along the strand:
His eager foe, determin'd to the chase,
Stretch'd at his length, gains ground at ev'ry pace:
Now to his beamy head he makes his way,
And now he holds, or thinks he holds his prey:
Just at the pinch, the stag springs out with fear:
He bites the wind, and fills his sounding jaws with air:
The rocks, the lakes, the meadows, ring with cries;
The mortal tumult mounts, and thunders in the skies.
  Thus flies the Daunian prince, and, flying, blames
His tardy troops, and, calling by their names,
Demands his trusty sword. The Trojan threats
The realm with ruin, and their ancient seats
To lay in ashes, if they dare supply,
With arms or aid, his vanquish'd enemy.
Thus menacing, he still pursues the course
With vigour, though diminish'd of his force.
Ten times already, round the listed place,
One chief had fled, and t'other giv'n the chase:
No trivial prize is play'd; for, on the life
Or death of Turnus, now depends the strife.
  Within the space an olive tree had stood,
A sacred shade, a venerable wood,

For vows to Faunus paid, the Latins'
    guardian god.
Here hung the vests, and tablets were
    engraved,
Of sinking mariners from shipwreck
    saved.
With heedless hands the Trojans fell'd
    the tree,
To make the ground enclosed for combat
    free.
Deep in the root, whether by fate or
    chance,
Or erring haste, the Trojan drove his
    lance;
Then stoop'd, and tugg'd with force im-
    mense, to free
Th' encumber'd spear from the tenacious
    tree:
That, whom his fainting limbs pursued
    in vain,
His flying weapon might from far attain.
   Confused with fear, bereft of human
    aid,
Then Turnus to the gods, and first to
    Faunus, pray'd:
"O Faunus! pity! and thou, mother
    Earth,
Where I, thy foster-son, received my
    birth,
Hold fast the steel! If my religious
    hand
Your plant has honour'd, which your foes
    profaned,
Propitious hear my pious pray'r!" He
    said,
Nor with successless vows invoked their
    aid.
Th' incumbent hero wrench'd, and pull'd,
    and strain'd;
But still the stubborn earth the steel
    detain'd.
Juturna took her time; and, while in
    vain
He strove, assumed Metiscus' form again,
And, in that imitated shape, restored
To the despairing prince his Daunian
    sword.
The queen of love—who, with disdain and
    grief,

Saw the bold nymph afford this prompt
    relief—
T' assert her offspring with a greater
    deed,
From the tough root the ling'ring weapon
    freed.
   Once more erect, the rival chiefs ad-
    vance:
One trusts the sword, and one the pointed
    lance;
And both resolved alike to try their fatal
    chance.
   Meantime imperial Jove to Juno spoke,
Who from a shining cloud beheld the
    shock:
"What new arrest, O queen of heav'n!
    is sent
To stop the Fates now lab'ring in th'
    event?
What further hopes are left thee to
    pursue?
Divine Æneas (and thou know'st it too)
Foredoom'd, to these celestial seats is due.
What more attempts for Turnus can be
    made,
That thus thou ling'rest in this lonely
    shade?
Is it becoming of the due respect
And awful honour of a god elect,
A wound unworthy of our state to feel,
Patient of human hands, and earthly
    steel?
Or seems it just the sister should restore
A second sword, when one was lost before,
And arm a conquer'd wretch against his
    conqueror?
For what, without thy knowledge and
    avow,
Nay more, thy dictate, durst Juturna do?
At last, in def'rence to my love, forbear,
To lodge within thy soul this anxious
    care:
Reclined upon my breast, thy grief un-
    load:—
Who should relieve the goddess but the
    god?
Now all things to their utmost issue tend,
Push'd by the Fates to their appointed
    end.

While leave was giv'n thee, and a lawful
hour
For vengeance, wrath, and unresisted
pow'r,
Toss'd on the seas thou couldst thy foes
distress,
And, driv'n ashore, with hostile arms
oppress;
Deform the royal house; and, from the
side
Of the just bridegroom, tear the plighted
bride:
Now cease at my command." The thun-
d'rer said;
And, with dejected eyes, this answer Juno
made:
"Because your dread decree too well I
knew,
From Turnus and from earth unwilling
I withdrew.
Else should you not behold me here,
alone,
Involved in empty clouds, my friends
bemoan,
But, girt with vengeful flames, in open
sight,
Engaged against my foes in mortal fight.
'Tis true, Juturna mingled in the strife
By my commands, to save her brother's
life.
At least to try; but (by the Stygian
lake—
The most religious oath the gods can
take)
With this restriction, not to bend the
bow,
Or toss the spear, or trembling dart to
throw.
And now resign'd to your superior might,
And tired with fruitless toils, I loath the
fight.
This let me beg (and this no fates with-
stand)
Both for myself and for your father's
land,
That, when the nuptial bed shall bind
the peace,
(Which I, since you ordain, consent to
bless)

The laws of either nation be the same;
But let the Latins still retain their name,
Speak the same language which they
spoke before,
Wear the same habits which their grand-
sires wore.
Call them not Trojans: perish the renown
And name of Troy, with that detested
town.
Latium be Latium still; let Alba reign,
And Rome's immortal majesty remain."
Then thus the founder of mankind
replies,
(Unruffled was his front, serene his eyes):
"Can Saturn's issue, and heaven's other
heir,
Such endless anger in her bosom bear?
Be mistress, and your full desires obtain;
But quench the choler you foment in vain.
From ancient blood th' Ausonian people
sprung,
Shall keep their name, their habit, and
their tongue:
The Trojans to their customs shall be
tied.
I will myself their common rites provide.
The natives shall command, the foreigners
subside.
All shall be Latium; Troy without a
name;
And her lost sons forget from whence
they came.
From blood so mix'd a pious race shall
flow,
Equal to gods, excelling all below.
No nation more respect to you shall pay,
Or greater off'rings on your altars lay."
Juno consents, well pleased that her
desires
Had found success, and from the cloud
retires.
The peace thus made, the thund'rer
next prepares
To force the wat'ry goddess from the
wars.
Deep in the dismal regions void of light,
Three daughters, at a birth, were born to
Night;

These their brown mother, brooding on
her care,
Endued with windy wings, to flit in air,
With serpents girt alike, and crown'd with
hissing hair.
In heav'n the Diræ call'd, and still at
hand,
Before the throne of angry Jove they
stand,
His ministers of wrath, and ready still
The minds of mortal men with fears to
fill,
Whene'er the moody sire, to wreak his
hate
On realms or towns deserving of their
fate,
Hurls down diseases, death, and deadly
care,
And terrifies the guilty world with war.
One sister plague of these from heav'n
he sent
To fright Juturna with a dire portent.
The pest comes whirling down: by far
more slow,
Springs the swift arrow from the Parthian
bow,
Or Cydon yew, when, traversing the skies,
And drench'd in pois'nous juice, the pure
destruction flies.
With such a sudden, and unseen a flight,
Shot through the clouds the daughter of
the Night.
Soon as the field enclosed she had in view,
And from afar her destined quarry
knew—
Contracted, to the boding bird she turns,
Which haunts the ruin'd piles and hol-
low'd urns,
And beats about the tombs with nightly
wings,
Where songs obscene on sepulchres she
sings.
Thus lessen'd in her form, with frightful
cries
The Fury round unhappy Turnus flies,
Flaps on his shield, and flutters o'er his
eyes.
A lazy chillness crept along his blood;

Choked was his voice; his hair with
horror stood.
Juturna from afar beheld her fly,
And knew th' ill omen, by her screaming
cry,
And stridor of her wing. Amazed with
fear,
Her beauteous breast she beat, and rent
her flowing hair.
"Ah me!" she cries—" in this unequal
strife,
What can thy sister more to save thy life?
Weak as I am, can I alas! contend
In arms with that inexorable fiend?
Now, now I quit the field! forbear to
fright
My tender soul, ye baleful birds of night!
The lashing of your wings I know too
well,
The sounding flight, and fun'ral screams
of hell!
These are the gifts you bring from
haughty Jove,
The worthy recompense of ravish'd love!
Did he for this exempt my life from
fate?
O hard conditions of immortal state!
Though born to death, not privileged
to die,
But forced to bear imposed eternity!
Take back your envious bribes, and let
me go
Companion to my brother's ghost below!
The joys are vanish'd: nothing now re-
mains
Of life immortal, but immortal pains.
What earth will open her devouring
womb
To rest a weary goddess in the tomb?"
She drew a length of sighs; nor more she
said,
But in her azure mantle wrapp'd her
head,
Then plunged into her stream, with deep
despair;
And her last sobs came bubbling up in
air.
  Now stern Æneas waves his weighty
spear

Against his foe, and thus upbraids his
fear:
"What farther subterfuge can Turnus
find?
What empty hopes are harbour'd in his
mind?
'Tis not thy swiftness can secure thy
flight:
Not with their feet, but hands, the valiant
fight.
Vary thy shape in thousand forms, and
dare
What skill and courage can attempt in
war;
Wish for the wings of winds, to mount
the sky;
Or hid within the hollow earth to lie!"
The champion shook his head, and made
this short reply:
"No threats of thine my manly mind can
move:
'Tis hostile heav'n I dread, and partial
Jove."
He said no more, but, with a sigh, re-
press'd
The mighty sorrow in his swelling breast.
Then, as he roll'd his troubled eyes
around,
An antique stone he saw, the common
bound
Of neighb'ring fields, and barrier of the
ground—
So vast, that twelve strong men of modern
days
Th' enormous weight from earth could
hardly raise.
He heaved it at a lift, and, poised on
high,
Ran stagg'ring on against his enemy,
But so disorder'd, that he scarcely knew
His way, or what unwieldy weight he
threw.
His knocking knees are bent beneath the
load;
And shiv'ring cold congeals his vital
blood.
The stone drops from his arms, and, fall-
ing short
For want of vigour, mocks his vain effort.

And as, when heavy sleep has closed the
sight,
The sickly fancy labours in the night:
We seem to run; and, destitute of force,
Our sinking limbs forsake us in the
course:
In vain we heave for breath; in vain we
cry:
The nerves, unbraced, their usual strength
deny;
And on the tongue the falt'ring accents
die:
So Turnus fared: whatever means he
tried,
All force of arms, and points of art
employ'd,
The fury flew athwart, and made th'
endeavour void.
    A thousand various thoughts his soul
confound:
He stared about; nor aid nor issue
found:
His own men stop the pass; and his own
walls surround.
Once more he pauses, and looks out again,
And seeks the goddess charioteer in vain.
Trembling he views the thund'ring chief
advance.
And brandishing aloft the deadly lance:
Amazed he cow'rs beneath his conqu'ring
foe,
Forgets to ward, and waits the coming
blow.
Astonish'd while he stands, and fix'd with
fear,
Aim'd at his shield he sees th' impending
spear.
    The hero measured first, with narrow
view,
The destined mark; and, rising as he
threw,
With its full swing the fatal weapon flew.
Not with less rage the rattling thunder
falls,
Or stones from batt'ring engines break
the walls:
Swift as a whirlwind, from an arm so
strong,

The lance drove on, and bore the death along.
Nought could his sev'nfold shield the prince avail,
Nor aught, beneath his arms, the coat of mail:
It pierced through all, and with a grisly wound
Transfix'd his thigh and doubled him to ground.
With groans the Latins rend the vaulted sky:
Woods, hills, and valleys, to the voice reply.
  Now low on earth the lofty chief is laid,
With eyes cast upwards, and with arms display'd,
And, recreant, thus to the proud victor pray'd:
"I know my death deserved, nor hope to live:
Use what the gods and thy good fortune give.
Yet think, oh! think, if mercy may be shown
(Thou hadst a father once, and hast a son),
Pity my sire, now sinking to the grave;
And, for Anchises' sake, old Daunus save!
Or, if thy vow'd revenge pursue my death,
Give to my friends my body void of breath!
The Latian chiefs have seen me beg my life:

Thine is the conquest, thine the royal wife:
Against a yielded man, 'tis mean ignoble strife."
  In deep suspense the Trojan seemed to stand,
And, just prepared to strike, repress'd his hand.
He roll'd his eyes, and ev'ry moment felt
His manly soul with more compassion melt;
When, casting down a casual glance, he spied
The golden belt that glitter'd on his side,
The fatal spoil which haughty Turnus tore
From dying Pallas, and in triumph wore;
Then roused anew to wrath, he loudly cries
(Flames while he spoke came flashing from his eyes):
"Traitor! dost thou—dost thou to grace pretend,
Clad, as thou art, in trophies of my friend?
To his sad soul a grateful off'ring go!
'Tis Pallas—Pallas gives this deadly blow!"
He raised his arm aloft, and, at the word,
Deep in his bosom drove the shining sword.
The streaming blood distain'd his arms around;
And the disdainful soul came rushing through the wound.

—JOHN DRYDEN.

III. THE JOYS OF PEACE

The agricultural problem had become an acute one long before the time of Virgil. The accumulation of vast estates by the rich, the extension of tenant-farming, the increasing use of slave labor by large landholders, the devastations and confiscations incident to war, the increase of wealth and luxury, the securing by conquest of new sources of food supply, had all contributed to the neglect of what had formerly been a most important industry of Italy. Under the régime of Augustus a move was set on foot to build it up anew into some semblance of its old position of leadership. The interest in agriculture had always been one of the keenest among the Romans, and the new peace fostered such a policy. It quickly became a commonplace among the Augustan poets to contrast the glories of country life with the turmoil of the city. But to Virgil the theme was far more than a mere convention of poetry. It had been the very substance of his early life, he knew its toil and its rewards thoroughly, and he could bring to it a deep and genuine love and enthusiasm. His shepherd songs, the *Eclogues,* though artificial and consciously modelled after the *Idylls* of Theocritus, nevertheless display in unforgetable phrases his close kinship with the soil and his appreciation of the simple life of the country. But it was in his *Georgics* that he gave himself whole-heartedly to the subject and through his knowledge and sympathy metamorphosed a didactic material into the most exquisite poetry.

THE SHEPHERD'S GRATITUDE

VIRGIL

[*Eclogue* I]

Virgil introduces into his pastoral poems, much more freely than his model Theocritus did, allusions to personal affairs and to contemporary happenings of the outside world. This poem is an allegory in which Virgil, represented as Tityrus, gives expression to the poet's gratitude to Augustus for restoring to him property which had been confiscated for the benefit of veteran soldiers of the civil wars.

MELIBŒUS. Stretched in the shadow of
    the broad beech, thou
Rehearsest, Tityrus, on the slender pipe
Thy woodland music. We our fatherland
Are leaving, we must shun the fields we
    love:
While, Tityrus, thou, at ease amid the
    shade,
Bidd'st answering woods call Amaryllis
    'fair.'

TITYRUS. O Melibœus! 'Tis a god that
    made
For me this holiday: for god I'll aye
Account him; many a young lamb from
    my fold
Shall stain his altar. Thanks to him, my
    kine
Range, as thou seest them: thanks to
    him, I play
What songs I list upon my shepherd's
    pipe.
M. For me, I grudge thee not; I marvel
    much:
So sore a trouble is in all the land.
Lo! feeble *I* am driving hence my goats—
Nay *dragging*, Tityrus, one, and that with
    pain.
For, yearning here amidst the hazel-
    stems,
She left her twin kids—on the naked
    flint
She left them; and I lost my promised
    flock.
This evil, I remember, oftentimes,
(Had not my wits been wandering) oaks
    foretold
By heaven's hand smitten: oft the wicked
    crow
Croaked the same message from the rifted
    holm.
—Yet tell me, Tityrus, of this "God" of
    thine.
T. The city men call *Rome* my folly
    deemed
Was e'en like this of ours, where week
    by week
We shepherds journey with our weanling
    flocks.
So whelp to dog, so kid (I knew) to dam
Was likest: and I judged great things by
    small.
But o'er all cities this so lifts her head,
As doth o'er osiers lithe the cypress tree.
M. What made thee then so keen to
    look on Rome?
T. Freedom: who marked, at last, my
    helpless state:
Now that a whiter beard than that of
    yore

Fell from my razor: still she marked, and
    came
(All late) to help me—now that all my
    thought
Is Amaryllis, Galatea gone.
While Galatea's, I despaired, I own,
Of freedom, and of thrift. Though from
    my farm
Full many a victim stept, though rich
    the cheese
Pressed for yon thankless city: still my
    hand
Returned not, heavy with brass pieces,
    home.
M. I wondered, Amaryllis, whence that
    woe,
And those appeals to heav'n: for whom
    the peach
Hung undisturbed upon the parent tree.
Tityrus was gone! Why, Tityrus, pine
    and rill,
And all these copses, cried to thee, "Come
    home!"
T. What could I do? I could not step
    from out
My bonds; nor meet, save there, with
    Pow'rs so kind.
There, Meliboeus, I beheld that youth
For whom each year twelve days my
    altars smoke.
Thus answered he my yet unanswered
    prayer;
"Feed still, my lads, your kine, and yoke
    your bulls."
M. Happy old man! Thy lands are yet
    thine own!
Lands broad enough for thee, although
    bare stones
And marsh choke every field with reedy
    mud.
Strange pastures shall not vex thy teem-
    ing ewes,
Nor neighboring flocks shed o'er them
    rank disease.
Happy old man! Here, by familiar
    streams
And holy springs, thou'lt catch the leafy
    cool.

Here, as of old, yon hedge, thy boundary
    line,
Its willow-buds a feast for Hybla's bees,
Shall with soft whisperings woo thee to
    thy sleep.
Here, 'neath the tall cliff, shall the
    vintager
Sing carols to the winds: while all the
    time
Thy pets, the stockdoves, and the turtles
    make
Incessantly their moan from aery elms.
T. Aye, and for this shall slim stags
    graze in air,
And ocean cast on shore the shrinking
    fish;
For this, each realm by either wandered
    o'er,
Parthians shall Arar drink, or Tigris
    Gauls;
Ere from this memory shall fade that
    face!
M. And we the while must thirst on
    Libya's sands,
O'er Scythia roam, and where the Cretan
    stems
The swift Oaxes; or, with Britons, live
Shut out from all the world. Shall I e'er
    see,
In far-off years, my fatherland? the turf
That roofs my meagre hut? see, wonder-
    ing last,
Those few scant cornblades that are
    realms to me?
What! must rude soldiers hold these fal-
    lows trim?
That corn barbarians? See what comes
    of strife,
Poor people—where we sowed, what
    hands shall reap!
Now, Meliboeus, pr'thee graft thy pears,
And range thy vines! Nay on, my she-
    goats, on,
Once happy flock! For never more
    must I,
Outstretched in some green hollow, watch
    you hang
From tufted crags, far up: no carols
    more

I'll sing: nor, shepherded by me, shall ye
Crop the tart willow and the clover-
  bloom.
T. Yet here, this one night, thou may'st
  rest with me,
Thy bed green branches. Chestnuts soft
  have I
And mealy apples, and our fill of cheese.
Already, see, the far-off chimneys smoke,
And deeper grow the shadows of the hills.
—C. S. CALVERLEY.

DAWN OF THE GOLDEN AGE

VIRGIL

[Eclogue IV]

From fairly early times the *Fourth
Eclogue* was looked upon as a pagan
prophecy of the coming of Christ, and is
still frequently called the *Messianic
Eclogue.* The golden age pictured is the
happy era of peace under Augustus, which
coincides with the period into which Christ
was born.

Muses of Sicily, a loftier song
Wake we! Some tire of shrubs and
  myrtles low.
Are woods our theme? Then princely be
  the woods.

Come are those last days that the
  Sibyl sang:
The ages' mighty march begins anew.
Now comes the virgin, Saturn reigns
  again:
Now from high heaven descends a won-
  drous race.
Thou on the newborn babe—who first
  shall end
That age of iron, bid a golden dawn
Upon the broad world—chaste Lucina,
  smile:
Now thy Apollo reigns. And, Pollio,
  thou
Shalt be our prince, when he that grander
  age

Opens, and onward roll the mighty
  moons:
Thou, trampling out what prints our
  crimes have left,
Shalt free the nations from perpetual
  fear.
While he to bliss shall waken; with the
  Blest
See the Brave mingling, and be seen of
  them,
Ruling that world o'er which his father's
  arm shed peace.—

On thee, child, everywhere shall earth,
  untilled,
Show'r, her first baby-offerings, vagrant
  stems
Of ivy, foxglove, and gay briar, and bean;
Unbid the goats shall come big-uddered
  home,
Nor monstrous lions scare the herded
  kine.
Thy cradle shall be full of pretty flowers:
Die must the serpent, treacherous poison-
  plants
Must die; and Syria's roses spring like
  weeds.

But, soon as thou canst read of hero-
  deeds
Such as thy father wrought, and under-
  stand
What is true worth: the champaign day
  by day
Shall grow more yellow with the waving
  corn;
From the wild bramble purpling then
  shall hang
The grape; and stubborn oaks drop
  honeydew.
Yet traces of that guile of older days
Shall linger; bidding men tempt seas in
  ships,
Gird towns with walls, cleave furrows in
  the land.
Then a new Tiphys shall arise, to man
New argosies with heroes: then shall be
New wars; and once more shall be bound
  for Troy

A mightier Achilles. After this,
When thou hast grown and strengthened
    into man,
The pilot's self shall range the seas no
    more;
Nor, each land teeming with the wealth
    of all,
The floating pines exchange their mer-
    chandise.
Vines shall not need the pruning-hook,
    nor earth
The harrow: ploughmen shall unyoke
    their steers.
Nor then need wool be taught to counter-
    feit
This hue and that. At will the meadow
    ram
Shall change to saffron, or the gorgeous
    tints
Of Tyre, his fair fleece; and the grazing
    lamb
At will put crimson on. So grand an age
Did those three Sisters bid their spindles
    spin;
Three, telling with one voice the change-
    less will of Fate.

    Oh draw—the time is all but present—
    near
To thy great glory, cherished child of
    heaven,
Jove's mighty progeny! And lo! the
    world,
The round and ponderous world, bows
    down to thee;
The earth, the ocean-tracts, the depths of
    heaven.
Lo! nature revels in the coming age.
Oh! may the evening of my days last on,
May breath be mine, till I have told thy
    deeds!
Not Orpheus then, not Linus, shall out-
    sing
Me: though each vaunts his mother or
    his sire,
Calliopea this, Apollo that.
Let Pan strive with me, Arcady his judge;
Pan, Arcady his judge, shall yield the
    palm.

Learn, tiny babe, to read a mother's
    smile:
Already ten long months have wearied
    her.
Learn, tiny babe. Him, who ne'er knew
    such smiles,
Nor god nor goddess bids to board or
    bed.
              —C. S. CALVERLEY.

INVOCATION OF THE RURAL POWERS

VIRGIL

[From the *Georgics*, Book I]

This prayer to Augustus suggests the
later idea of deification and the divine
right of kings.

What makes a plenteous harvest, when
    to turn
The fruitful soil, and when to sow the
    corn;
The care of sheep, of oxen, and of kine;
The birth and genius of the frugal bee,
I sing, Mæcenas, and I sing to thee.
    Ye deities! who fields and plains pro-
    tect,
Who rule the seasons, and the year di-
    rect;
Bacchus and fostering Ceres, powers
    divine,
Who gave us corn for mast, for water
    wine:
Ye fawns, propitious to the rural swains,
Ye nymphs, that haunt the mountains and
    the plains,
Join in my work, and to my numbers
    bring
Your needful succour, for your gifts I
    sing.
And thou, whose trident struck the teem-
    ing Earth,
And made a passage for the courser's
    birth;
And thou, for whom the Cæan shore sus-
    tains

The milky herds, that graze the flowery plains;
And thou, the shepherds' tutelary god,
Leave for a while, O Pan! thy lov'd abode:
And, if Arcadian fleeces be thy care,
From fields and mountains to my song repair.
Inventor, Pallas, of the fattening oil,
Thou founder of the plough and plough-man's toil;
And thou, whose hands the shroud-like cypress rear;
Come, all ye gods and goddesses that wear
The rural honours, and increase the year.
You, who supply the ground with seeds of grain;
And you, who swell those seeds with kindly rain:
And chiefly thou, whose undertermin'd state
Is yet the business of the gods' debate;
Whether in after-times to be declar'd
The patron of the world, and Rome's peculiar guard,
Or o'er the fruits and seasons to preside,
And the round circuit of the year to guide;
Powerful of blessings, which thou strew'st around,
And with thy goddess mother's myrtle crown'd.
Or wilt thou, Cæsar, choose the watery reign,
To smooth the surges, and correct the main?
Then mariners, in storms, to thee shall pray,
Ev'n utmost Thule shall thy power obey;
And Neptune shall resign the fasces of the sea.
The watery virgins for thy bed shall strive,
And Tethys all her waves in dowry give.
Or wilt thou bless our summers with thy rays,
And seated near the Balance, poise the days:

Where in the void of Heaven a space is free,
Betwixt the Scorpion and the Maid, for thee.
The Scorpion, ready to receive thy laws,
Yields half his region, and contracts his claws.
Whatever part of Heaven thou shalt obtain,
For let not Hell presume of such a reign;
Nor let so dire a thirst of empire move
Thy mind, to leave thy kindred gods above.
Though Greece admires Elysium's blest retreat,
Though Proserpine affects her silent seat,
And, importun'd by Ceres to remove,
Prefers the fields below to those above.
But thou, propitious Cæsar! guide my course,
And, to my bold endeavours, add thy force.
Pity the poet's and the ploughman's cares,
Interest thy greatness in our men's affairs,
And use thyself betimes to hear and grant our prayers.
—JOHN DRYDEN.

LABOR OMNIA VINCIT

VIRGIL

[From the *Georgics,* Book I]

Virgil delights to sing the dignity of common labor. To him rural life was no mere pastime, a retreat from the fret and bustle of the city, but a life of hard work. But hard work was a wholly worthy thing and brought its own rewards of real happiness. It was a lesson much needed by his contemporaries.

Nor yet the ploughman, nor the labour-ing steer,
Sustain alone the hazards of the year;

But glutton geese, and the Strymonian
  crane,
With foreign troops, invade the tender
  grain:
And towering weeds malignant shadows
  yield;
And spreading succory chokes the rising
  field.
The sire of gods and men, with hard
  decrees,
Forbids our plenty to be bought with
  ease:
And wills that mortal men, inur'd to toil,
Should exercise, with pains, the grudging
  soil.
Himself invented first the shining share,
And whetted human industry by care:
Himself did handycrafts and arts ordain,
Nor suffer'd sloth to rust his active reign.
Ere this, no peasant vex'd the peaceful
  ground,
Which only turfs and greens for altars
  found:
No fences parted fields, nor marks nor
  bounds
Distinguish'd acres of litigious grounds:
But all was common, and the fruitful
  Earth
Was free to give her unexacted birth.
Jove added venom to the viper's brood,
And swell'd, with raging storms, the
  peaceful flood:
Commission'd hungry wolves t' infest the
  fold,
And shook from oaken leaves the liquid
  gold:
Remov'd from human reach the cheerful
  fire,
And from the rivers bade the wine re-
  tire:
That studious need might useful arts
  explore:
From furrow'd fields to reap the foodful
  store;
And force the veins of clashing flints t'
  expire
The lurking seeds of their celestial fire.
Then first o'er seas the hollow'd alder
  swam;

Then sailors quarter'd Heaven, and found
  a name
For every fix'd and every wandering star:
The Pleiads, Hyads, and the Northern
  Car.
Then toils for beasts, and lime for birds
  were found,
And deep-mouth'd dogs did forest-walks
  surround:
And casting-nets were spread in shallow
  brooks,
Drags in the deep, and baits were hung
  on hooks.
Then saws were tooth'd, and sounding
  axes made
(For wedges first did yielding wood in-
  vade);
And various arts in order did succeed.
(What cannot endless labour, urg'd by
  need?)
  First Ceres taught, the ground with
    grain to sow,
And arm'd with iron shares the crooked
  plough,
When now Dodonian oaks no more sup-
  ply'd
Their mast, and trees their forest-fruit
  deny'd.
Soon was his labour doubled to the
  swain,
And blasting mildews blackened all his
  grain.
Tough thistles chok'd the fields, and kill'd
  the corn,
And an unthrifty crop of weeds was
  born.
Then burs and brambles, an unbidden
  crew
Of graceless guests, th' unhappy field
  subdue:
And oats unblest, and darnel domineers,
And shoots its head above the shining
  ears.
So that unless the land with daily care
Is exercis'd, and with an iron war
Of rakes and harrows the proud foes ex-
  pell'd,
And birds with clamours frighted from
  the field;

Unless the boughs are lopp'd that shade
the plain,
And Heaven invok'd with vows for fruit-
ful rain,
On other crops you may with envy look,
And shake for food the long abandon'd
oak.
—JOHN DRYDEN.

SWORDS AND PLOUGHSHARES

VIRGIL

[From the *Georgics*, Book I]

This and the following passages from
the *Georgics* are digressions from the
main theme of agriculture. It was by
means of such digressions that Virgil, like
Lucretius, lifted his subject from the level
of a practical manual to the plane of
poetry.

The Sun reveals the secrets of the sky;
And who dares give the source of light
the lie?
The change of empires often he declares,
Fierce tumults, hidden treasons, open
wars.
He first the fate of Cæsar did foretell,
And pity'd Rome, when Rome in Cæsar
fell,
In iron clouds conceal'd the public light;
And impious mortals fear'd eternal night.
Nor was the fact foretold by him alone:
Nature herself stood forth, and seconded
the Sun.
Earth, air, and seas, with prodigies were
sign'd,
And birds obscene, and howling dogs
divin'd.
What rocks did Ætna's bellowing mouth
expire
From her torn entrails; and what floods
of fire!
What clanks were heard, in German skies
afar,
Of arms and armies rushing to the war!
Dire earthquakes rent the solid Alps
below,
And from their summits shook th' eternal
snow:
Pale spectres in the close of night were
seen;
And voices heard of more than mortal
men,
In silent groves, dumb sheep and oxen
spoke,
And streams ran backward, and their
beds forsook:
The yawning Earth disclos'd th' abyss
of Hell:
The weeping statues did the wars fore-
tell;
And holy sweat from brazen idols fell.
Then rising in his might, the king of
floods
Rush'd through the forests, tore the lofty
woods;
And rolling onward, with a sweepy sway,
Bore houses, herds, and labouring hinds
away.
Blood sprang from wells, wolves howl'd
in towns by night,
And boding victims did the priests af-
fright.
Such peals of thunder never pour'd from
high,
Nor forky lightnings flash'd from such
a sullen sky.
Red meteors ran across th' ethereal space;
Stars disappear'd, and comets took their
place.
For this, th' Emathian plains once more
were strew'd
With Roman bodies, and just Heaven
thought good
To fatten twice those fields with Roman
blood.
Then, after length of time, the labouring
swains,
Who turn the turfs of those unhappy
plains,
Shall rusty piles from the plough'd furrows take,

And over empty helmets pass the rake,
Amaz'd at antique titles on the stones,
And mighty relics of gigantic bones.
    Ye homeborn deities, of mortal birth!
Thou, father Romulus, and mother Earth,
Goddess unmov'd, whose guardian arms
    extend
O'er Tuscan Tiber's course, and Roman
    towers defend;
With youthful Cæsar your joint powers
    engage,
Nor hinder him to save the sinking age.
O! let the blood, already spilt, atone
For the past crimes of curst Laomedon!
Heaven wants thee there; and long the
    gods, we know,
Have grudg'd thee, Cæsar, to the world
    below:
Where fraud and rapine, right and wrong
    confound!
Where, impious arms from every part re-
    sound,
And monstrous crimes in every shape are
    crown'd.
The peaceful peasant to the wars is
    prest;
The fields lie fallow in inglorious rest;
The plain no pasture to the flock affords,
The crooked scythes are straighten'd into
    swords:
And there Euphrates her soft offspring
    arms,
And here the Rhine rebellows with
    alarms;
The neighbouring cities range on several
    sides,
Perfidious Mars long plighted leagues di-
    vides,
And o'er the wasted world in triumph
    rides.
So four fierce coursers starting to the
    race,
Scour through the plain, and lengthen
    every pace:
Nor reins, nor curbs, nor threatening
    cries they fear,
But force along the trembling charioteer.
                    —JOHN DRYDEN.

THE PRAISES OF ITALY

VIRGIL

[From the *Georgics,* Book II]

But neither Median woods, (a plenteous
    land)
Fair Ganges, Hermus rolling golden sand,
Nor Bactria, nor the richer Indian fields,
Nor all the gummy stores Arabia yields;
Nor any foreign earth of greater name,
Can with sweet Italy contend in fame.
No bulls, whose nostrils breathe a living
    flame,
Have turn'd our turf, no teeth of ser-
    pents here
Were sown, an armed host, an iron crop
    to bear.
But fruitful vines, and the fat olive's
    freight,
And harvest heavy with their fruitful
    weight,
Adorn our fields; and on the cheerful
    green,
The grazing flocks and lowing herds are
    seen.
The warrior horse, here bred, is taught to
    train:
There flows Clitumnus through the flow-
    ery plain;
Whose waves for triumphs, after pros-
    perous war,
The victim ox and snowy sheep prepare.
Perpetual spring our happy climate sees;
Twice breed the cattle, and twice bear
    the trees;
And summer suns recede by slow degrees.
    Our land is from the rage of tigers
    freed,
Nor nourishes the lion's angry seed;
Nor poisonous aconite is here produc'd,
Or grows unknown, or is, when known,
    refus'd.
Nor in so vast a length our serpents glide,
Or rais'd on such a spiry volume ride.
    Next add our cities of illustrious name,
Their costly labour, and stupendous
    frame:

Our forts on steepy hills, that far below
See wanton streams in winding valleys
 flow.
Our twofold seas, that, washing either
 side,
A rich recruit of foreign stores provide.
Our spacious lakes; thee, Larius, first;
 and next
Benacus, with tempestuous billows vext.
Or shall I praise thy ports, and mention
 make
Of the vast mound that binds the Lucrine
 lake;
Or the disdainful sea, that, shut from
 thence,
Roars round the structure, and invades
 the fence;
There, where secure the Julian waters
 glide,
Or where Avernus' jaws admit the Tyr-
 rhene tide;
Our quarries deep in Earth were fam'd of
 old
For veins of silver, and for ore of gold;
Th' inhabitants themselves their coun-
 try grace;
Hence rose the Marsian and Sabellian
 race;
Strong-limb'd and stout, and to the wars
 inclin'd,
And hard Ligurians, a laborious kind;
And Volscians, arm'd with iron-headed
 darts,
Besides an offspring of undaunted hearts,
The Decii, Marii, great Camillus came
From hence, and greater Scipio's double
 name:
And mighty Cæsar, whose victorious arms
To farthest Asia carry fierce alarms;
Avert unwarlike Indians from his Rome;
Triumph abroad, secure our peace at
 home.
 Hail, sweet Saturnian soil! of fruitful
 grain
Great parent, greater of illustrious men,
For thee my tuneful accents will I raise,
And treat of arts disclos'd in ancient
 days:

Once more unlock for thee the sacred
 spring,
And old Ascræan verse in Roman cities
 sing.

    —JOHN DRYDEN.

SPRING

VIRGIL

[From the *Georgics*, Book II]

Be not seduc'd with wisdom's empty
 shows,
To stir the peaceful ground when Boreas
 blows.
When winter frosts constrain the field
 with cold,
The fainty root can take no steady hold.
But when the golden spring reveals the
 year,
And the white bird returns, whom ser-
 pents fear;
That season deem the best to plant thy
 vines,
Next that, is when autumnal warmth de-
 clines;
Ere heat is quite decay'd, or cold begun,
Or Capricorn admits the winter Sun.
 The spring adorns the woods, renews
 the leaves,
The womb of Earth the genial seed re-
 ceives.
For then almighty Jove descends, and
 pours
Into his buxom bride his fruitful showers:
And, mixing his large limbs with hers, he
 feeds
Her birth with kindly juice, and fosters
 teeming seeds.
Then joyous birds frequent the lonely
 grove,
And beasts, by Nature stung, renew
 their love.
Then fields the blades of bury'd corn dis-
 close,
And, while the balmy western spirit
 blows,

Earth to the breath her bosom dares expose.
With kindly moisture then the plants abound,
The grass securely springs above the ground;
The tender twig shoots upward to the skies,
And on the faith of the new Sun relies.
The swerving vines on the tall elms prevail,
Unhurt by southern showers or northern hail.
They spread their gems the genial warmth to share,
And boldly trust the buds in open air.
In this soft season (let me dare to sing)
The world was hatch'd by Heaven's imperial king:
In prime of all the year, and holydays of spring.
Then did the new creation first appear;
Nor other was the tenour of the year:
When laughing Heaven did the great birth attend,
And eastern winds their wintry breath suspend:
Then sheep first saw the Sun in open fields;
And savage beasts were sent to stock the wilds:
And golden stars flew up to light the skies,
And man's relentless race from stony quarries rise.
Nor could the tender, new creation bear
Th' excessive heats or coldness of the year;
But, chill'd by winter, or by summer fir'd,
The middle temper of the spring requir'd,
When warmth and moisture did at once abound,
And Heaven's indulgence brooded on the ground.

—JOHN DRYDEN.

HAPPY THE MAN

VIRGIL

[From the *Georgics*, Book II]

O happy, if he knew his happy state!
The swain, who, free from business and debate,
Receives his easy food from Nature's hand,
And just returns of cultivated land!
No palace, with a lofty gate, he wants,
T' admit the tides of early visitants,
With eager eyes devouring, as they pass,
The breathing figures of Corinthian brass;
No statues threaten from high pedestals;
No Persian arras hides his homely walls,
With antic vests; which, through their shady fold,
Betray the streaks of ill-dissembled gold.
He boasts no wool, whose native white is dy'd
With purple poison of Assyrian pride.
No costly drugs of Araby defile
With foreign scents the sweetness of his oil.
But easy quiet, a secure retreat,
A harmless life that knows not how to cheat,
With homebred plenty the rich owner bless,
And rural pleasures crown his happiness.
Unvex'd with quarrels, undisturb'd with noise,
The country king his peaceful realm enjoys:
Cool grots, and living lakes, the flowery pride
Of meads, and streams that through the valley glide,
And shady groves that easy sleep invite,
And after toilsome days a soft repose at night.
Wild beasts of nature in his woods abound;
And youth, of labour patient, plough the ground,
Inur'd to hardship, and to homely fare,

Nor venerable age is wanting there,
In great examples to the youthful train;
Nor are the gods ador'd with rites profane.
From hence Astrea took her flight, and here
The prints of her departing steps appear.
Ye sacred Muses, with whose beauty fir'd,
My soul is ravish'd, and my brain inspir'd;
Whose priest I am, whose holy fillets wear,
Would you your poet's first petition hear:
Give me the ways of wandering stars to know:
The depths of Heaven above, and Earth below.
Teach me the various labours of the Moon,
And whence proceed th' eclipses of the Sun.
Why flowing tides prevail upon the main,
And in what dark recess they shrink again,
What shakes the solid earth, what cause delays
The summer nights, and shortens winter days.
But if my heavy blood restrain the flight
Of my free soul, aspiring to the height
Of Nature and unclouded fields of light;
My next desire is, void of care and strife,
To lead a soft, secure, inglorious life:
A country cottage near a crystal flood,
A winding valley, and a lofty wood.
Some god conduct me to the sacred shades,
Where bacchanals are sung by Spartan maids,
Or lift me high to Hemus' hilly crown;
Or in the plains of Tempe lay me down:
Or lead me to some solitary place,
And cover my retreat from human race.
Happy the man, who, studying Nature's laws,
Through known effects can trace the secret cause.
His mind possessing in a quiet state,

Fearless of Fortune, and resign'd to Fate.
And happy too is he, who decks the bowers
Of sylvans, and adores the rural powers:
Whose mind, unmov'd, the bribes of courts can see;
Their glittering baits and purple slavery.
Nor hopes the people's praise, nor fears their frown,
Nor when contending kindred tear the crown,
Will set up one, or pull another down.
Without concern he hears, but hears from far,
Of tumults and descents, and distant war:
Nor with a superstitious fear is aw'd,
For what befals at home, or what abroad.
Nor envies he the rich their heapy store,
Nor his own peace disturbs, with pity for the poor.
He feeds on fruits, which, of their own accord,
The willing ground and laden trees afford.
From his lov'd home no lucre him can draw;
The senate's bad decrees he never saw;
Nor heard, at bawling courts, corrupted law.
Some to the seas and some to camps resort,
And some with impudence invade the court.
In foreign countries others seek renown;
With wars and taxes others waste their own,
And houses burn, and household gods deface,
To drink in bowls which glittering gems enchase:
To loll on couches, rich with cytron steds,
And lay their guilty limbs on Tyrian beds;
This wretch in earth entombs his golden ore,
Hovering and brooding on his bury'd store.
Some patriot fools to popular praise aspire

Of public speeches, which worse fools
    admire;
While from both benches, with redoubled
    sounds,
Th' applause of lords and commoners
    abounds.
Some through ambition, or through thirst
    of gold,
Have slain their brothers, or their coun-
    try sold;
And leaving their sweet homes, in exile
    run
To lands that lie beneath another sun.
    The peasant, innocent of all these ills,
With crooked ploughs the fertile fallows
    tills;
And the round year with daily labour
    fills.
And hence the country-markets are
    supply'd:
Enough remains for household charge
    beside:
His wife and tender children to sustain,
And gratefully to feed his dumb deserv-
    ing train.
Nor cease his labours, till the yellow field
A full return of bearded harvest yield:
A crop so plenteous as the land to load,
O'ercome the crowded barns, and lodge
    on ricks abroad.
Thus every several season is employ'd:
Some spent in toil, and some in ease
    enjoy'd.
The yeaning ewes prevent the springing
    year;
The laded boughs their fruits in autumn
    bear:
'Tis then the vine her liquid harvest
    yields,
Bak'd in the sunshine of ascending fields.
The winter comes, and then the falling
    mast
For greedy swine provides a full repast.
Then olives, ground in mills, their fatness
    boast,
And winter fruits are mellow'd by the
    frost.
His cares are eas'd with intervals of bliss;

His little children climbing for a kiss,
Welcome their father's late return at
    night;
His faithful bed is crown'd with chaste
    delight.
His kine, with swelling udders, ready
    stand,
And, lowing for the pail, invite the milk-
    er's hand.
His wanton kids, with budding horns
    prepar'd,
Fight harmless battles in his homely
    yard:
Himself in rustic pomp, on holidays,
To rural powers a just oblation pays;
And on the green his careless limbs
    displays.
The hearth is in the midst; the herdsmen,
    round
The cheerful fire, provoke his health in
    goblets crown'd.
He calls on Bacchus, and propounds the
    prize;
The groom his fellow-groom at buts
    defies;
And bends his bows, and levels with his
    eyes,
Or, stript for wrestling, smears his limbs
    with oil,
And watches with a trip his foe to foil.
Such was the life the frugal Sabines led;
So Remus and his brother god were bred:
From whom th' austere Etrurian virtue
    rose,
And this rude life our homely fathers
    chose.
Old Rome from such a race deriv'd her
    birth,
(The seat of empire, and the conquer'd
    Earth;)
Which now on seven high hills triumphant
    reigns,
And in that compass all the world con-
    tains.
Ere Saturn's rebel son usurp'd the skies,
When beasts were only slain for sacrifice;
While peaceful Crete enjoy'd her ancient
    lord;

Ere sounding hammers forg'd th' inhuman sword;
Ere hollow drums were beat, before the
   breath
Of brazen trumpets rung the peals of
   death;
The good old god his hunger did assuage
With roots and herbs, and gave the
   golden age.
              —JOHN DRYDEN.

THE SIMPLE LIFE

TIBULLUS

[From Book I]

Albius Tibullus (about 54 to 19 B.C.)
was of equestrian rank and possessed of
sufficient means to be independent. Of
the details of his life little is known. Like
the other Augustan elegists, though following in general the Alexandrians as
his models, he draws his material directly
from his own experience. Indeed the personal subjective character of all Roman
elegy is that which gives it a distinction
not attained by the Greek writers of the
same form. Tibullus writes only of love,
and the whole product of his pen fills but
part of a very small collection of elegies
that has come down to us under his name.
The poet's ideal is "love in a cottage."
The pastoral note in elegy is peculiar to
Tibullus.

Their piles of golden ore let others heap,
   And hold their countless roods of cul-
      tured soil,
Whom neighbouring foes in constant ter-
      ror keep—
   The weary victims of unceasing toil.

Let clang of arms and trumpet's blast
      dispel
   The balmy sleep their hearts in vain
      desire;
At home in poverty and ease I'd dwell,
   My heart aye gleaming with a cheerful
      fire.

In season due I'd plant the pliant vine,
   With skilful hand my swelling apples
      rear;
Nor fail, blest Hope! but still to me
      consign
   Rich fruits and vats abrim with rosy
      cheer.

For the lone stump afield I still revere,
   Or ancient stone, whence flowery gar-
      lands nod,
In cross-roads set: the first-fruits of the
      year
   I duly offer to the peasant's god.

O fair-haired Ceres! let the spiky crown,
   Culled from my field, adorn thy shrine-
      door aye;
Amid my orchards red Priapus frown,
   And with his threatening bill the birds
      dismay.

Guards of a wealthy once, now poor,
      domain,
   Ye Lares! still my gift your wardship
      cheers;
A fatted calf did then your altars stain,
   To purify innumerable steers.

A lambkin now—a meagre offering—
   From the few fields that still I reckon
      mine,
Shall fall for you while rustic voices sing:
   "Oh grant the harvest, grant the gen-
      erous wine!"

Now I can live content on scanty fare,
   Nor for long travels do I bear the will;
'Neath some tree's shade I'd shun the
      Dog's fierce glare,
   Beside the waters of a running rill.

Nor let me blush the while to wield the
      rake,
   Or with the lash the laggard oxen ply;
The straggling lamb within my bosom
      take,
   Or kid, by heedless dam left lone to
      die.

Spare my small flock, ye thieves and
    wolves! away
    Where wealthier cotes an ampler booty
      hold;
I for my swain lustrations yearly pay,
    And soothe with milk the Goddess of
      the fold.

Then smile, ye gods! nor view with high
    disdain
    The frugal gifts clean earthen bowls
      convey;
Such earthen vessels erst the ancient
    swain
    Moulded and fashioned from the plas-
      tic clay.

The wealth and harvest-stores my sires
    possessed
    I covet not: few sheaves will yield me
      bread;
Enough; reclining on my couch to rest,
    And stretch my limbs upon the wonted
      bed.

How sweet to lie and hear the wild winds
    roar,
    While to our breast the lovèd one we
      strain;
Or, when the cold South's sleety torrents
    pour,
    To sleep secure, lulled by the plashing
      rain!

This lot be mine: let him be rich, 'tis fair,
    Who braves the wrathful sea and
      tempests drear:
Oh, rather perish gold and gems than
    e'er
    One fair one for my absence shed a
      tear!

Dauntless, Messala, scour the earth and
    main
    To deck thy home with warfare's
      spoils; 'tis well:
Me here a lovely maiden's bonds enchain,
    At her hard door, a sleepless sentinel.

Delia, I court not praise, if mine thou be;
    Let men cry lout and clown, I'll bear
      the brand;
In my last moments let me gaze on thee,
    And dying, clasp thee with my falter-
      ing hand!

Thou'lt weep to see me laid upon the bier,
    That will too soon the flames' mad fury
      feel;
Thou'lt mingle kisses with the bitter tear,
    For thine no heart of stone, no breast
      of steel.

Nor only thou wilt weep; no youth, no
    maid,
    With tearless eye, will from my tomb
      repair:
But, Delia, vex not thou thy lover's
    shade;
    Thy tender cheeks, thy streaming
      tresses spare!

Love's joys be ours while still the Fates
    allow,
    Soon death will come with darkly-
      mantled head;
Dull age creeps on, and love-cup or love-
    vow
    Becomes no forehead when its snows
      are shed.

Then let us worship Venus while we may,
    With brow unblushing, burst the bolted
      door
And join with rapture in the midnight
    fray,
    Your leader I—Love's soldier proved
      of yore.

Hence flags and trumpets! me ye'll never
    lure;
    Bear wounds and wealth to warriors
      bent on gain:
I, in my humble competence secure,
    Shall wealth and poverty alike disdain.
             —JAMES CRANSTOUN.

WAR AND PEACE

TIBULLUS

[From Book I]

The love poets were made the objects of reproach because they kept themselves entirely apart from all activities of public life and were interested only in their own passion. Peace was a theme to be celebrated by all men, but avoidance of war for personal comfort met only with scorn. The lover hates war not because of what it is, but because it separates him from his mistress.

Who was the man first forged the fatal blade?
    Oh! cruel he and of an iron soul!
Then war and carnage first made gory raid,
    Opening a shorter way to life's drear goal.

Yet blameless he: we've turned to woe, I ween,
    The weapons formed to slay the savage beast.
'Tis gold's to blame: no wars had ever been
    While still the beechen platter graced the feast.

Man reared nor towers nor forts: from all alarms
    Swains slept secure, while roamed their flocks around:
Would then I'd lived, nor known of baneful arms,
    Nor heard with quivering heart the trumpet's sound.

I'm dragged to war, and now, perchance, some foe
    Bears the dread shaft that's doomed to pierce my side;
Save! ye paternal gods who watched me grow
    And gambol at your feet, an infant pride.

Blush not ye're fashioned from an ancient tree,
    So were ye in my grandsire's loved domain;
Then faith was fair, and offerings poor but free
    Were yours, dear hearth-gods, in your humble fane.

And ye were blessed if vintage ever flowed,
    Or spiky garland girt your holy brow;
The swain gave cakes, while maiden hands bestowed
    Pure honeycomb, when ye had heard his vow.

Drive hence the brazen shaft, and from my sty
    A pig to you, dear gods, shall be consigned;
While, robed in white, brow myrtle-wreathed, I'll hie
    Behind you bearing baskets myrtle-twined.

Still smile on me, let valiant breasts assail
    And smite down hostile chiefs along the line;
Here let me drink and hear the soldier's tale,
    And see him sketch his battle-fields with wine.

Ah me! why court dark death in war? all round
    It creeps unseen and silent, ever near:
Below, no crops—no vines—but the fierce hound
    And the grim boatman of the Stygian mere.

And there with sunken chaps and half-burnt hair
    By the dark lake the wan-faced tenants roam;
Far happier he who with his own may share

In age and competence the joys of
  home.

He tends his sheep, his son the lambs,
    and aye
  His loving wife her weary husband
    cheers.
So may I live and see my hair grow grey,
  And tell, when old, the deeds of early
    years.

Peace dwell with us! fair Peace and none
    before
  Yoked to the curvèd plough the sturdy
    steer;
Peace reared the vine—with vine-juice
    filled the store
  With which the sire his loving son
    might cheer.

Flourish in peace the mattock and the
    share,
  While rust in darkness rots the war-
    rior's arms—
And jolly swains from groves in waggons
    bear
  Their wives and children back to smil-
    ing farms.

Then rage the wars of Love: her tresses
    rent
  The maiden mourns, and weeps o'er
    broken doors,
And tender cheeks all bruised, till, peni-
    tent,
  The victor e'en his ruthlessness de-
    plores.

Love sits and fills with taunts the angry
    pair,
  The tricksome elf enjoying all the
    scene—
Ah! steel and stone the man who'd strike
    the fair;
  The gods are wroth at such a deed, I
    ween.

Enough, if he should tear her silken vest,
  Or spoil the wreaths that round her
    tresses creep,

Or move her heart to tears: oh! four
    times blest
  Is he whose ire can make a maiden
    weep!

Let savage warriors wield the sword and
    spear,
  But keep aloof from gentle damsel's
    door;
Come, bounteous Peace! still hold the
    wheaten ear,
  And from thy joyous lap rich fruits
    outpour.
                            —JAMES CRANSTOUN.

A RURAL FESTIVAL

TIBULLUS

[From Book II]

We cleanse the fruits and fields: be mute
    each tongue:
  This rite our fathers did of old ordain.
Come, Bacchus, come! thy horns with
    clusters hung!
  Come, Ceres, crowned with ears of
    golden grain!

Let soil and tiller keep this feast alway,
  Suspend the share—be no hard labour
    here;
Unchain the yoke; at well-filled stalls
    to-day
  'Tis meet with garlands ye should
    crown the steer.

Let rapt devotion reign, nor woman dare
  To ply the spindle while we pay the
    rite;
Hence far and from the altars all repair,
  Who've sought the joys of Venus
    yesternight.

Chaste things please heaven: with
    raiment pure attend:
  Make clean your hands with water
    from the spring;

See the doomed lamb the blazing mound
ascend,
   White crowds with olive chaplets
following.

Gods of our sires! we lustrate hind and
plain,
   Drive from our confines every cause of
bale;
May ne'er unfruitful blades deceive the
swain,
   Nor fleet-foot wolves his helpless lambs
assail.

Then the sleek rustic, cheered with hopes
benign,
   Large fagots on his blazing hearth will
pile,
And crowds of born-thralls—comfort's
surest sign—
   Play round the Lar, and make twig
bowers the while.

My prayers are heard: the auspicious
entrails, see!
   Declare the rural gods of peaceful
mind;
Now bring the smoked Falernian jars for
me
   Of ancient date: the Chian casks
unbind.

Pass round the wine; on this glad morn
be gay;
   To reel and stagger now be held no
shame;
Let each one drink Messala's health
to-day,
   Each tongue resound the absent hero's
name.

Famed for thy triumphs over Aquitaine,
   Shedding great glory o'er thy bearded
sires!
Oh come, Messala! aid me in the strain
   Which homage to the vernal powers
inspires.

The fields and rural gods are now my
theme,
   Who made our sires for acorns cease
to roam,
Taught them to build their log-huts beam
by beam,
   And thatch with leafy boughs their
humble home.

They trained the steer the bended yoke
to bear,
   Placed wheels beneath the cart, and,
by degrees,
Weaned man primeval from his savage
fare,
   And bade the orchards smile with
fruitful trees.

Then fertile gardens drank the watering
wave—
   Then first the purple fruitage of the
vine,
Pressed by fair feet, immortal nectar
gave;
   Then water first was blent with generous wine.

The fields bear harvests, when the Dog-
star's heat
   Bids earth each year her golden honours shed;
And in spring's lap bees gather honey
sweet,
   And fill their combs from many a floral
bed.

Returning from the plough, the weary
swain
   First sang his rustic lays in measured
tread,
And, supper o'er, tried on oat-pipe some
strain
   To play before his gods brow-chapleted.

He, vermil-stained, great Bacchus! first
made bold
   To lead the untutored chorus on the
floor,

And (valued prize!) from forth a numerous fold
  Received a goat to swell his household store.

Young hands first strung spring flow'rets in the fields,
  And with a wreath the ancient gods arrayed;
Here its soft fleece the tender lambkin yields,
  To form a task for many a tender maid.

Hence wool and distaffs fill the housewife's room,
  And nimble thumbs deft spindles keep in play;
Hence maidens sing and ply the busy loom,
  Hence rings the web beneath the driven lay.

Great Cupid, too, 'tis said, was born and nursed
  'Mong sheep and cattle and unbroken mares;
There with unskilful bow he practised first—
  Now with a skilful hand the weapon bears.

Not cattle now, as heretofore, his prey,
  But blooming maids and men of stalwart frame;
He robs the youth, and makes the greybeard say,

At scornful maiden's threshold, words of shame.

Yea, led by love, alone the maiden steals
  'Mid sleeping guards, to her fond lover bound,
Breathless with fear her way on tiptoe feels—
  Her fingers groping through the darkness round.

O wretched they who drain love's bitter draughts!
  O happy they who 'neath his smiles abide!
Hie to our feast, blest Boy! but leave thy shafts,
  And far away thy flaming torches hide.

Swains! laud and call him to your flocks aloud,
  But to yourselves in silence and alone,
Or loud and free—now rave the jocund crowd,
  And the curved pipe outpours its Phrygian tone.

Sport on! Night yokes her steeds: with nimble tread
  The golden stars behind her chariot wheel;
Then silent sleep, with tawny wings outspread,
  And gloom-wrapt dreams, behind them tottering steal.
  —JAMES CRANSTOUN.

IV. THE POET LAUREATE: HORACE

Quintus Horatius Flaccus was born at Venusia in southern Italy in 65 B.C. His father, a freedman, gave him the best schooling the town afforded, and then accompanied him to Rome to attend him while he pursued his studies further under the best teachers of the capital. Horace tells us that he owes the best things in his training to the common sense and wise guidance of his uneducated father. After his military experience under Brutus at Philippi in 42 B.C. he returned to Rome and supported himself as a quæstor's clerk. He was introduced to Mæcenas by Virgil and received from him the celebrated Sabine farm, which afforded him sufficient independence to free him for the writing of poetry. He died in 8 B.C.

Horace may be called the poet laureate of the Augustan court not because of any formal appointment to such a position, but because better than any other writer of the time he gave expression to the ideas current among persons of the court and on occasion wrote official poems by request. In the early days of his career he had been an ardent republican, but later he accepted the new régime and gradually became one of its most eloquent promoters.

The principle of contrast is probably the secret of the intimacy of the two great protégés of Mæcenas, Virgil and Horace—the former serious, mystic, withdrawn, and the latter fun-loving, matter-of fact, and a keen observer of contemporary life. Horace's *Epodes* and *Satires* reveal the critical bent of his mind and his fine sense of humor. His *Odes,* graceful and quite perfect in phrasing, treat of a great variety of subjects of .common experience—of love and wine, of friendship, of nature, of the gods, of the virtues. The *Epistles* are the product of his maturity, when he had become mellowed by long experience and found his happiness in meditation on philosophical and literary themes.

THE PRAISES OF AUGUSTUS

AUGUSTUS REGENT

[*Odes* I, 12]

Horace gives Augustus full credit for the happy era of peace and prosperity enjoyed during his administration. The contrast with the preceding period of civil wars heightened the appreciation of the value of peace. Of the many poems singing the praises of the emperor only three are given here.

Clio, what man, what hero, or what God
  Shall wake thy lyre—thy flute with sweetness thrill;
Whose name shall playful echo send abroad
  In whispers from her hill?

Whether on Helicon's umbrageous side,
  Or Pindus' height, or Hæmus' peak of snow,
Whence suddenly, self-woo'd, the forests glide
  As Orpheus' numbers flow.

And by the art his goddess mother gave,
  He bids the rivers pause, the winds delay;
The oaks as in gigantic strength they wave
  Hear and his lute obey.

Father Supreme, of earth and ocean King—
  Ruler of all things human and divine—
Guide of the world, whose praises can I sing
  Before I utter thine?

None greater than thyself has sprung from thee;
  None like, none second to thy pow'r is found;
Yet Pallas next, thy wondrous progeny,
  Is after thee renown'd.

Victorious Bacchus, how can I abstain
  To laud thy name? Or thine, thou virgin foe
Of the fierce forest tribes? Or thine refrain,
  Lord of the fatal bow?

Alcides sing I,—and each royal twin,—
  The wild-steed tamer and the arm of might;—
When on the mariners their stars begin
  To pour their silver light,

Down from the cliffs the showers of spray distil,
  The winds are lulled, the clouds obedient flee;
The mountain waves, subservient to their will,
  Sink down upon the sea.

Shall Romulus, or Numa's tranquil reign,
  Afford the fittest theme to celebrate?—
Shall Tarquin's haughty rule awake the
    strain,
    Or Cato's noble fate?

To Regulus, the Scauri and (of life
    Too prodigal on Cannæ's bloody
    field)
Paulus, and old Fabricius, verses rife
  With grace their fame shall yield.

Stern poverty and the ancestral farm
  Trained these, and Curius rough with
    tangled hair,
For war; and nerved Camillus' mighty
    arm
  The battle's toil to dare.

As spreads a tree, so grows Marcellus'
    fame
  With every year; the Julian orb afar
Gleams bright, as when the moonbeam's
    lambent flame
  Outshines each minor star.

Father and guardian of the human race—
  Offspring of Saturn—thine by destiny,
Great Cæsar's charge. Thou art su-
    preme; his place
  Second to none but thee:—

Whether when Parthia threatened with
    her hosts
  Fair Latium, their repulse his triumph
    gained;
Or India's tribes, or hordes from China's
    coasts
  His mighty hand restrained.

On thy behalf still may he rule the world;
  Shake with thy ponderous car the
    worlds above!
By thee th' avenging bolts of heaven be
    hurled
  On each polluted grove.
          —WILLIAM DOWE.

THE PEACE OF AUGUSTUS

[Odes IV, 5]

God-given guardian of Quirinus' sons,
  The sacred Senate holds thy promise
    dear;
Return, return; too long his absence runs
  Who spake of brief delay and is not
    here.

Restore to Rome the radiance of that
    face
  Which, smiling on us like the budding
    year,
Can lend to gracious day a novel grace,
  And gift the sunshine with a warmer
    cheer:

For as some mother hungering for her
    son—
  Fast bound beyond the far Carpa-
    thean swell
By jealous gales till all the year be done,
  In exile from the home that loves him
    him well,—

Calls him with vows and prayers and
    augur's art,
  Her eyes still set toward the sinuous
    sand,
So from a grateful people's faithful heart
  A cry for Cæsar echoes through the
    land.

For safe the cattle range the peaceful
    mead,—
  Ceres the mead and glad Abundance
    bless;
O'er bloodless seas the flying galleys
    speed;
  And faith is fearful of unfaithfulness.

Our homes are pure and happy, every
    one;
  Good laws, good customs cleanse our
    leprosies;
The father's face is imaged in the son;
  Immediate vengeance follows hard on
    vice.

Who recks of dwellers in the Scythian
    snows?
  Who dreads the Mede? Who fears, if
    Cæsar reign,
Yon savage brood the Teuton forest
    knows?
  Or who is troubled for the war with
    Spain?

Each sees the sun down in his native
    glen,
  There wedding widower elm and tender
    vine;
Then blithely hies him homeward, and
    again
  Crowns his glad cup and bids thee bless
    the wine.

Thee with all prayer, with all libation
    thee,
  Thee in the number of his Lares set
He worships; so Hellenic piety
  To Castor and Alcides paid its debt.

Good chief, with years of joy thy coun-
    try dower!
  Thus at the dawn of days not yet be-
    gun
Dry-lipped we pray; and thus in wassail
    hour
  When couched in ocean sleeps the
    weary sun.

                —T. R. CLARK.

THE RESTORER[1]

[*Odes* IV, 15]

On siege and battlefield I mused,
  Of martial themes I wished to sing,
But Phœbus chid—my lyre refused
  To speak, and mute was every string;
He bade me furl my little sails,
Nor rashly tempt Tyrrhenian gales.

[1] Reprinted from J. O. Sargent, *Horatian
Echoes*, by permission of Miss Georgiana W.
Sargent.

'Tis thine, O Cæsar, to restore
  To wasted fields their wealth of corn;
And standards that we lost of yore,—
  From haughty Parthia's columns
    torn,—
Bring back in triumph to our shrine,
Of Jupiter Capitoline.

Beneath thy sway we live in peace,
  The double gates of Janus close,
Outbursts of vagrant license cease,
  And all is order and repose;
Thy hand that stays the people's crimes
Restores the arts of olden times;

Arts which have spread the Latin name,
  Increased the might of Italy,
Founded the empire's matchless fame
  And all embracing majesty,
Till they have spanned the earth's extent
From sunset to the Orient.

While we have Cæsar at our head,
  Serene custodian of the State,
No civil fury shall we dread,
  Nor feuds that cities desolate;
The rage that fires barbarian hordes
Shall never sharpen Roman swords.

Not they who dwell upon its banks
  And the deep Danube's waters drink,
No faithless Parthian's quivered ranks
  No natives of the Tanaïs' brink,
No tribes about the Larian lake,
The Julian edicts dare to break.

These themes I leave; the lot be mine
  On common and on festal days,
With Bacchus' gifts of flowers and wine,
  To mingle my congenial lays,—
And while our wives and children share
In offerings of peace and prayer,

We'll, like our fathers, celebrate—
  In songs that blend with Lydian pipes—
The men in simple virtues great,
  Our captains of the ancient types;
Anchises, Troy, our themes shall be,
And genial Venus' progeny.
              —J. O. SARGENT.

THE CENTURY SONG

After ten years of the rule of Augustus the new age was celebrated by elaborate games and ceremonies. Among the latter was the singing of a choral ode by boys and girls. That Horace was chosen to write the song indicates an official recognition of him as poet laureate.

O Phœbus, and O forest-queen Diana,
Ye the twin lustrous ornament of heaven,
Though ever holy, in this time most hallowed,
    Be most benign to prayer!

For duly now, as Sibyl verse enjoins us,
Pure youths, with chosen virgins linked in chorus,
To Powers divine o'er the Seven Hills presiding,
    Uplift the solemn hymn.

O Sun, the nurturer, in bright chariot leading
Day into light to hide it under shadow,
Born still the same, yet other, mayst thou never
    See aught more great than Rome!

Blest Ilithyia, mild to watch o'er mothers,
And aid the timely coming of the new-born,
Whether thou rather wouldst be as Lucina
    Or Genetalis hailed,

Goddess as each, mature our offspring; prosper
The law that guards the sanctity of marriage,
And may it give new blossom and new fruitage
    To the grand parent-stem!

So that as each eleventh solemnial decade
Round to its close, this sacred feast renewing,

In song and sport, assembled Rome may hallow
    Three days and joyful nights.

And ye, O Parcæ, who have sung prophetic
Truths, which, once said, the sure events determine,
Fixed as divine decrees,—a glorious future
    Join to the glorious past.

Fertile in fruits and flocks, let Earth maternal
With spiked corn-wreath crown the brow of Ceres;
Pure from all taint let airs and dews of heaven
    Nourish the new-born life.

Mild, all thine arrows sheathed within the quiver,
Hear thy boy-suppliants, merciful Apollo;
Hear thy girl-votaries, crescent-crowned Luna,
    Queen of the clustered stars.

If Rome be your work—if beneath your safeguard
A band of wanderers, Ilion's scanty remnant,
Ordained to change their cities and their Lares,
    Have held this Tuscan land—

They, unto whom, through Troy that blazed unharming,
Pure-souled Æneas, his lost land's survivor,
Opened free path, and heritage more ample
    Than aught relinquished gave;

Gods, grant to docile youth worth's upright manners—
Gods, grant to placid age worth's calm contentment—

Grant to the Roman race growth, power,
    and riches,
  And all that can adorn!

Bless him who nears with milk-white
    steers your altars,
Whose blood flows bright from Venus and
    Anchises;
Still every foe in battle may he conquer,
  And after conquest spare.

Awed by our arms, and by the Alban
    lictors,
Now the Mede owns our power on land
    and ocean;
Now Ind and Scythia, she of late so
    haughty,
  To Rome for pardon sue.

Now Faith and Peace, and antique Shame
    and Honor
Flock fearless back, and Virtue long-
    neglected;
And with them comes their sure com-
    panion Plenty,
  Rich with o'erflowing horn.

May he adorned with fulgent bow—the
    Augur,
Phœbus, the darling of the nine
    Camenæ—
He the mild Healer, lifting the sore
    burden
  That weighs down weary limbs—

If shrines in Palatine he views with
    favor,
The coming lustre bless, and link it on-
    ward
To those yet brighter, through all time
    prolonging
  Rome and the Latian race.

And oh, may she who holds the sacred
    hill-tops
Of Aventine and Algidus, Diana,
To the Fifteen, and to her own young
    vot'ries,
  Lend an approving ear!

So we, the choir of Dian and of Phœbus,
Versed in their praise, take home with us
    hope certain
That, heard by Jove and each divine Im-
    mortal,
  These words are felt in heaven.
          —BULWER-LYTTON.

ROMAN VIRTUES

SIMPLICITY

[Odes III, 1]

Augustus wisely made use of his men
of letters to aid him in his measures of
reform. A large proportion of Horace's
Odes is devoted to the celebration of those
virtues which he regarded as forming the
very foundation of the state. Of those
given below five are from a series written
more or less officially in his capacity as
court poet, but themes of like nature are
to be found throughout his work.

I loathe an uninitiate ear!
  Hush! Let the Muses' minion raise
  A psalm unsung in elder days
For youths and maids alone to hear.

Kings keep their subject flocks in awe;
  Themselves to Jove obedience owe,
  Triumphant o'er his Titan foe,
And nodding universal law.

And man than man in planted lands
  Is richer; one in right of birth
  Seeks office, one pleads moral worth,
And one the clients he commands:

But destiny assigns in turn
  To king and clown impartial doom;
  And every name hath ample room
To jostle in her ballot urn.

A naked sword the guilty keep
  Poised overhead: to tempt their taste
  Sicilian feasts their science waste;
Nor harp nor song-bird summon sleep.

Sleep undisdainful of the herd,
  Sweet sleep in lowly cots abides,
  And in the shade of river sides,
And dells of Tempe zephyr-stirred.

Who asks the needful, nothing more,
  Him no tumultuous seas appal;
  He frets not, though Arcturus fall,
Or Hædus rise in wild uproar;

Though fields deny the promised gain,
  And vines be beaten down of hail,
  And orchards tell a piteous tale
Of parching stars, and frost, and rain.

Invading earthworks leave a dearth
  Of ocean for the scaly race,
  Where builders' gangs usurp its space
To house a master tired of earth.

But fear and menace dog his track,
  Albeit from tower to tower he flits;
  Black care in brazen galleys sits,
Care clings behind the horseman's back.

Then why, since souls with sorrow rent
  Not Phrygian stone, Falernian jars,
  Or wear of purples bright as stars,
Or Achæmenian balms content,

Why build—to win but envy thus—
  A pillared mansion huge and strange?
  Or why my Sabine vale exchange
For riches more laborious?
          —T. R. CLARK.

Endurance and Faithfulness

[Odes III, 2]

Go, teach our sturdy youth the trade of
  war,
And to sustain the mean estate and poor,
His school the camp, until the harassed
  Mede
To terror turn before his spear and steed,
To take the inclement sky, till from the
  town
The warring emperor's dame with sighs
  look down,

And royal maid may gaze with sighs,
  and say:
"O grant my lord, unskilled in war's
  array,
Cross not with yonder lion in the fray,
With angry-chafing ravin as he goes
O'er fields of carnage to amaze his foes."
How blest is he who for his country dies,
Since death pursues the coward as he
  flies!
The youth in vain would fly from Fate's
  attack,
With trembling knees, and Terror at his
  back;
Though Fear should lend him pinions like
  the wind,
Yet swifter fate will seize him from be-
  hind.
  Virtue repulsed yet knows not to re-
    pine;
But shall with unattainted honour shine;
Nor stoops to take the staff, nor lays it
  down,
Just as the rabble please to smile or
  frown.
  Virtue that spurns on upward pinions
    bound
The crowd low-thoughted, and the humid
  ground,
Virtue, to crown her favourites, loves to
  try
Some new unbeaten passage to the sky;
Where Jove a seat among the gods will
  give
To those who die for meriting to live.
  Next, faithful Silence hath a sure re-
    ward;
Within our breast be every secret barr'd!
He who betrays his friend shall never be
Under one roof, or in one ship with me:
For who with traitors would his safety
  trust,
Lest with the wicked, Heaven involve the
  just?
And though the villain 'scape a while, he
  feels
Slow vengeance, like a bloodhound, at
  his heels.
          —JONATHAN SWIFT.

STEADFASTNESS

[From *Odes* III, 3]

The righteous man of purpose fixed and
    strong
  Scorns the depraved commands
Of angry Faction clamouring for wrong,
Nor fears the Despot's frown. Not Aus-
    ter's roar
Whitening the restless wave on Adria's
    shore,
  Not the red thunder hurled
  From Jove's avenging hands
Can shake his solid will. Unmoved he
    stands
Erect amid the ruins of a world.
Thus rose Alcides to the flaming skies:
Thus Leda's son to those Divine abodes
Where couched among th' Immortals
    Cæsar lies
Drinking with purpled lip the nectar of
    the Gods.
Thus Bacchus clomb to Jove's Olympian
    throne
Drawn by wild tigers, ivy garlanded:
Thus, strong and true, Rome's mighty
    founder sped,
Wafted by steeds of Mars to Heaven,
    not Acheron.
        —STEPHEN DeVERE.

WISDOM

[From *Odes* III, 4]

Force lacking judgment falls by its own
    weight:
Force held in rein the gods to high estate
  Advance, but hate the soul
    Whose strength makes any guilt its
      goal.

The hundred-handed Gyas to my view
Bears witness, and ill-famed Orion too,
  Who Dian sought to stain,
    And fell by maiden's arrow slain.

Earth sorrows as she folds her monsters
    deep,
And mourns her sons by lightning's blaz-
    ing sweep
  To Orcus hurled: fleet flame
    Has failed to gnaw through Ætna's
      frame;

And, sentry set o'er guilt, the warder bird
From lustful Tityos hath never stirred;
  And weight of countless chains
    Pirithous from love restrains.
        —J. H. DEAZELEY.

COURAGE

[*Odes* III, 5]

Jove rules the skies, his thunder wielding:
Augustus Cæsar, thou on earth shalt be
  Enthroned a present Deity;
Britons and Parthian hordes to Rome
    their proud necks yielding.

Woe to the Senate that endures to see
(O fire extinct of old nobility!)
The soldier dead to honour and to pride
  Ingloriously abide
Grey-headed mate of a Barbarian bride,
Freeman of Rome beneath a Median
    King:

Woe to the land that fears to fling
Its curse, not ransom, to the slave
Forgetful of the shield of Mars,
Of Vesta's unextinguished flame,
Of Roman garb, of Roman name;
The base unpitied slave who dares
From Rome his forfeit life to crave:
In vain;—Immortal Jove still reigns on
    high:
Still breathes in Roman hearts the Spirit
    Liberty.

With warning voice of stern rebuke
Thus Regulus the Senate shook:
He saw, prophetic, in far days to come,

The heart corrupt, and future doom of
  Rome.
"These eyes," he cried, "these eyes have
  seen
Unbloodied swords from warriors torn,
And Roman standards nailed in scorn
  On Punic shrines obscene;
Have seen the hands of free-born men
Wrenched back and bound; th' un-
  guarded gate;
And fields our war laid desolate
By Romans tilled again.
What! will the gold-enfranchised slave
Return more loyal and more brave?
  Ye heap but loss on crime!
The wool that Cretan dyes distain
Can ne'er its virgin hue regain;
And valour fallen and disgraced
Revives not in a coward breast
  Its energy sublime.
The stag released from hunter's toils
From the dread sight of man recoils.
Is he more brave than when of old
He ranged his forest free? Behold
In him your soldier! He has knelt
To faithless foes; he too has felt
The knotted cord; and crouched beneath
  Fear, not of shame, but Death,

"He sued for peace, tho' vowed to **war:**
Will such men, girt in arms once more,
Dash headlong on the Punic shore?
No! they will buy their craven lives
With Punic scorn and Punic gyves.
O mighty Carthage, rearing high
Thy fame upon our infamy,
A city, aye, an empire built
On Roman ruins, Roman guilt."

From the chaste kiss, and wild embrace
Of wife and babes he turned his face,
  A man self-doomed to die;
Then bent his manly brow, in scorn,
Resolved, relentless, sad, but stern,
  To earth, all silently;
Till counsel never heard before
Had nerved each wavering Senator;
Till flushed each cheek with patriot
  shame,

And surging rose the loud acclaim;—
Then, from his weeping friends, in haste,
To exile and to death he passed.

He knew the tortures that Barbaric hate
Had stored for him. Exulting in his fate
  With kindly hand he waved away
  The crowds that strove his course to
    stay.

He passed from all, as when in days of
  yore,
  His judgment given, thro' client throngs
    he pressed
  In glad Venafrian fields to seek his
    rest,
Or Greek Tarentum on the Southern
  shore.

       —STEPHEN DeVERE.

PURITY

[Odes I, 22]

Fuscus, the man of upright life and pure,
Needeth nor javelin nor bow of Moor,
Nor arrows tipped with venom deadly-
  sure.
  Loading his quiver;

Whether o'er Afric's burning sands he
  rides,
Or frosty Caucasus' bleak mountain-sides,
Or wanders lonely, where Hydaspes
  glides,
  That storied river.

For as I strayed along the Sabine wood,
Singing my Lalage in careless mood,
Lo, all at once a wolf before me stood,
  Then turned and fled:

Creature so huge did warlike Daunia
  ne'er
Engender in her forests' wildest lair,
Not Juba's land, parched nurse of lions,
  e'er
  Such monster bred.

Place me where no life-laden summer
    breeze
Freshens the meads, or murmurs 'mongst
    the trees,
Where clouds oppress, and withering
    tempests freeze
    From shore to shore.

Place me beneath the sunbeam's fiercest
    glare,
On arid sands, no dwelling anywhere,
Still Lalage's sweet smile, sweet voice
    even there
    I will adore.
            —THEODORE MARTIN.

CONTENTMENT

THE GOLDEN MEAN

[*Odes* II, 10]

Horace's idea of contentment, as indicated in the poems below, is that of a
golden mean. He would advocate a simple life, but not one wholly devoid of certain comforts and luxuries necessary to
peace of mind. His opposition to great
wealth and to the fame that comes of high
position leaves out of the reckoning the
opportunities for service which they offer.
His thought is fixed upon what one gets
from them rather than upon what one
may give through them. But in the main
he is fighting the general laxity of morals
which was the accompaniment of luxurious
living, and is holding up as a standard the
ideals of the simple life of the good old
days.

You better sure shall live, not evermore
    Trying high seas; nor, while sea's rage
      you flee,
Pressing too much upon ill-harboured
    shore.

    The golden mean who loves, lives
    safely free

From filth of foreworn house, and quiet
    lives,
    Releas'd from court, where envy needs
      must be.

The wind most oft the hugest pine tree
    grieves:
    The stately towers come down with
      greater fall:
The highest hills the bolt of thunder
    cleaves.

    Evil haps do fill with hope, good haps
      appal
With fear of change, the courage well
    prepar'd:
    Foul winters, as they come, away they
      shall.

Though present times, and past with evils
    be snar'd,
    They shall not last: with cithern silent
      muse
Apollo wakes, and bow hath sometime
    spar'd.

    In hard estate, with stout shows, valour
      use,
The same man still, in whom wisdom pre-
    vails;
In too full wind draw in thy swelling
    sails.
            —PHILIP SIDNEY.

MODERATION IN ALL THINGS

[*Satires* I, 1]

How comes it, say, Mæcenas, if you can,
That none will live like a contented man
Where choice or chance directs, but each
    must praise
The folk who pass through life by other
    ways?
"Those lucky merchants!" cries the sol-
    dier stout,
When years of toil have well-nigh worn
    him out:

What says the merchant, tossing o'er the
    brine?
"Yon soldier's lot is happier, sure, than
    mine:
One short, sharp shock, and presto! all
    is done:
Death in an instant comes, or victory's
    won."
The lawyer lauds the farmer, when a
    knock
Disturbs his sleep at crowing of the cock:
The farmer, dragged to town on business,
    swears
That only citizens are free from cares.
I need not run through all: so long the
    list,
Fabius himself would weary and desist:
So take in brief my meaning: just sup-
    pose
Some God should come, and with their
    wishes close:
"See, here am I, come down of my mere
    grace
To right you: soldier, take the merchant's
    place!
You, counsellor, the farmer's! go your
    way,
One here, one there! None stirring? all
    say nay?
How now? you won't be happy when you
    may."
Now, after this, would Jove be aught to
    blame
If with both cheeks he burst into a flame,
And vowed, when next they pray, they
    shall not find
His temper easy, or his ear inclined?
  Well, not to treat things lightly
    (though for me,
Why truth may not be gay, I cannot see:
Just as, we know, judicious teachers coax
With sugar-plum or cake their little folks
To learn their alphabet):—still, we will
    try
A graver tone, and lay our joking by.
The man that with his plough subdues
    the land,
The soldier stout, the vintner sly and
    bland,

The venturous sons of ocean, all declare
That with one view the toils of life they
    bear,
When age has come, and labour has
    amassed
Enough to live on, to retire at last:
E'en so the ant (for no bad pattern she),
That tiny type of giant industry,
Drags grain by grain, and adds it to the
    sum
Of her full heap, foreseeing cold to come:
Yet she, when winter turns the year to
    chill,
Stirs not an inch beyond her moulded hill,
But lives upon her savings: you, more
    bold,
Ne'er quit your gain for fiercest heat or
    cold:
Fire, ocean, sword, defying all, you strive
To make yourself the richest man alive.
Yet where's the profit, if you hide by
    stealth
In pit or cavern your enormous wealth?
"Why, once break in upon it, friend, you
    know,
And, dwindling piece by piece, the whole
    will go."
But, if 'tis still unbroken, what delight
Can all that treasure give to mortal
    wight?
Say, you've a million quarters on your
    floor:
Your stomach is like mine: it holds no
    more:
Just as the slave who 'neath the bread-
    bag sweats
No larger ration than his fellows gets.
What matters it to reasonable men
Whether they plough a hundred fields or
    ten?
"But there's a pleasure, spite of all you
    say,
In a large heap from which to take
    away."
If both contain the modicum we lack,
Why should your barn be better than my
    sack?
You want a draught of water: a mere urn,

Perchance a goblet, well would serve your turn:
You say, "The stream looks scanty at its head;
I'll take my quantum where 'tis broad instead."
But what befalls the wight who yearns for more
Than Nature bids him? down the waters pour,
And whelm him, bank and all; while he whose greed
Is kept in check, proportioned to his need,
He neither draws his water mixed with mud,
Nor leaves his wife behind him in the flood.
　But there's a class of persons, led astray
By false desires, and this is what they say:
"You cannot have enough: what you possess,
That makes your value, be it more or less."
What answer would you make to such as these?
Why, let them hug their misery if they please,
Like the Athenian miser, who was wont
To meet men's curses with a hero's front:
"Folks hiss me," said he, "but myself I clap
When I tell o'er my treasures on my lap."
So Tantalus catches at the waves that fly
His thirsty palate—Laughing, are you? why?
Change but the name, of you the tale is told:
You sleep, mouth open, on your hoarded gold;
Gold that you treat as sacred, dare not use,
In fact, that charms you as a picture does.
Come, will you hear what wealth can fairly do?
'Twill buy you bread, and vegetables too,
And wine, a good pint measure: add to this
Such needful things as flesh and blood would miss.
But to go mad with watching, nights and days
To stand in dread of thieves, fires, runaways
Who filch and fly,—in these if wealth consist,
Let me rank lowest on the paupers' list.
　"But if you suffer from a chill attack,
Or other chance should lay you on your back,
You then have one who'll sit by your bed-side,
Will see the needful remedies applied,
And call in a physician, to restore
Your health, and give you to your friends once more."
Nor wife nor son desires your welfare: all
Detest you, neighbors, gossips, great and small.
What marvel if, when wealth's your one concern,
None offers you the love you never earn?
Nay, would you win the kinsmen Nature sends
Made ready to your hand, and keep them friends,
'Twere but lost labour, as if one should train
A donkey for the course by bit and rein.
　Make then an end of getting: know, the more
Your wealth, the less the risk of being poor;
And, having gained the object of your quest,
Begin to slack your efforts and take rest;
Nor act like one Ummidius (never fear,
The tale is short, and 'tis the last you'll hear),
So rich, his gold he by the peck would tell,
So mean, the slave that served him dressed as well;

E'en to his dying day he went in dread
Of perishing for simple want of bread,
Till a brave damsel, of Tyndarid line
The true descendant, clove him down the
    chine.
    "What? would have me live like some
    we know,
Mænius or Nomentanus?" There you go!
Still in extremes! in bidding you forsake
A miser's ways, I say not, Be a rake.
'Twixt Tanais and Visellius' sire-in-law
A step there is, and broader than a straw.
Yes, there's a mean in morals: life has
    lines,
To north and south of which all virtue
    pines.
    Now to resume our subject: Why, I
    say,
Should each man act the miser in his way,
Still discontented with his natural lot,
Still praising those who have what he
    has not?
Why should he waste with very spite, to
    see
His neighbour has a milkier cow than he,
Ne'er think how much he's richer than
    the mass,
But always strive this man or that to
    pass?
In such a contest, speed we as we may,
There's some one wealthier ever in the
    way.
So from their base when vying chariots
    pour,
Each driver presses on the car before,
Wastes not a thought on rivals overpast;
But leaves them to lag on among the
    last.
Hence comes it that the man is rarely
    seen
Who owns that his a happy life has been,
And, thankful for past blessings, with
    good will
Retires, like one who has enjoyed his fill.
Enough: you'll think I've rifled the scru-
    tore
Of blind Crispinus, if I prose on more.
        —JOHN CONINGTON.

ON LUXURY

[*Odes* II, 15]

These kingly piles the acres take
    Once ploughed. The ponds dug round
    us gain
Bounds wider than the Lucrine lake.
    For elms, we plant the unwedded plane.

Myrtles abound, and violet beds,
    And every flower, that yields a scent,
O'er olive-ground its perfume sheds,
    That whilome brought its lord a rent.

Dense laurel shade shall stop the rays
    Of summer. Ah! not such the rule
Of Romulus, nor Cato's ways
    Too rude, nor all the elder school.

Romans were poor: but yet they made
    Rome greatly rich. No measuring then
With ten-foot rod the colonnade
    Tow'rd the cool North, for private men.

The common turf, that grew at large,
    Those ancient laws bade all respect,
But freely at the public charge
    With stone our towns and temples
    decked.
        —W. E. GLADSTONE.

TRUE HAPPINESS

[*Odes* II, 16]

Quiet! the trembling Merchant cries,
    Into Egean Seas driven far:
When the Moon winks, and he descri⌣
    No guiding star.
Quiet! In war the Thracian bold;
    Quiet! the Medes with quivers dight;
Not to be bought with gems, nor gold,
    Nor purple bright.
For 'tis not wealth, nor armed troops,
    Can tumults of the mind remove,
And cares, which about fretted roofs
    Hover above.

His little's much, whose thrifty board
  Shines with a salt that was his sire's:
Who easie sleeps nor fears disturb,
  Nor base desires.
Why in short life eternal care?
  Why changing for another Sun?
Who having shun'd his native air,
  Himself could shun?
Take horse, rude Care will ride behind;
  Embarque, into thy ship she crouds:
Fleeter than stags, and the East-wind
  Chasing the Clouds.
Let minds of any joy possest,
  Sweeten with that whatever gall
Is mixt. No soul that ere was blest,
  Was blest in all.
The fam'd Achilles timeless dy'd,
  Old Tithon did his bliss outlive,
And Chance, what she to thee deny'd
  To me may give.
A hundred flocks about thee bleat,
  And fair Sicilian heifers low;
To thee large neighing mares curvete:
  In scarlet thou,
Twice-dipt, art clad. Indulgent fate
  Gave me a grange; a versing vein;
A heart which (injur'd) cannot hate
  But can disdain.
                    —RICHARD FANSHAWE.

THE VANITY OF RICHES

[*Odes* II, 18]

My ceiling shows not brave
  With gold or ivories;
No marble architrave
  On quarried pillars lies,
Which utmost Libya gave.

No despot did devise
  On me, a stranger heir,
His royal treasuries;
  No dames of birth prepare
For me Laconian dyes.

Pure faith is all my store,
  Faith, and so rich a vein

Of poet power and lore
  That wealth itself is fain
To seek this humble door.

I ask not Heaven to send
  Aught else; I never pressed
For more, my puissant friend,
  Who am entirely blessed
One Sabine farm to tend.

To-morrow ousts to-day;
  Young moons grow large and less;
Death dogs thy steps; but aye
  On marble palaces,
O fool, thy fancies stray,

Who, reckless of the tomb,
  Dost build, and 'mid the roar
Of Baian surf presume
  On the great sea, whose shore
Yields not ambition room.

What, shall this lust of gain
  Not even the landmarks keep
Which that is thine contain?
  This avarice o'er leap
Thy client's scant domain?

Thence the poor exiles fare,
  Husband and wife; and, strained
To their sad bosoms, bear
  Young babes all squalor-stained,
And gods, their father's care.

Natheless no other hall
  More surely shalt thou find,
Thou gilded prodigal,
  Than that by Death designed,
The greediest of us all.

What would'st thou? Earth's embrace
  Impartial shall enfold
King's son and peasant base:—
  Prometheus' guile and gold
From Charon gained no grace.

Proud Tantalus, he wears
  He and his race, the chains

Of Death, who needs no prayers
To lighten of their pains
The world's worn labourers.

—T. R. CLARK.

THE POWER OF GOLD

[*Odes* III, 16]

A tower of brass held Danae immured;—
Strong oaken doors and watch-dog's mid-
night bay
'Gainst love too bold the royal maid
secured;
But Jove and Venus smiled
Mocking her Sire, for gold will work its
way
Through guarded gates and sentinels be-
guiled.

Gold cleaves the fortress and the rock
With force more potent than the thun-
der's shock.
The Argive augur, sold
By his false wife, Eriphyle, for gold,
Died with his sons. The man of
Macedon •
Subdued with bribes proud kings in arms
arrayed:
And Menas, won
By Roman gold, a Roman fleet betrayed.

Mæcenas! knighthood's boast! thou
knowest how
Like thee I shrank from lifting of my
brow
Above my peers. To him whose modest
thrift
Denies itself, Heaven sends its ampler
gift.
Naked I fly the standard of the great,
And seek the ranks of those who nought
desire,
More honoured thus despising vulgar
state
Than if I should my bursting garners fill
With rich Apulia's grain heaped daily
higher,

Sitting 'mid worthless wealth, a beggar
still.

Enough for me my little wood, my
spring
Where Zephyr's cooling wing
Fans the crisp stream; my garden plot
Whose promised crop deceiveth not:—
The Afric despot knows no happier lot.

What though Calabrian bees for me
No honey filch from flower or tree—
What though no Gallic flocks increase
For me their wealth of snowy fleece—
What though no Formian vine
Ripens not in my bin its mellowing wine—
Content I live; not rich; yet free
From harsh unfortunate penury:
If more I claimed thou would'st not more
refuse.

True riches mean not revenues:
Care clings to wealth: the thirst for
more
Grows as our fortunes grow. I stretch
my store
By narrowing my wants; far wealthier
thus
Than if the treasures of Alatteus
And Phrygia's plains were mine. We
are not poor
While nought we seek. Happiest to
whom high Heaven
Enough—no more—with sparing hand
has given.

—STEPHEN DEVERE.

ORIENTALISM

THE FALL OF CLEOPATRA

[*Odes* I, 37]

This cry of triumph is inspired not only
by the thought of the removal of an
enemy, but also by the feeling that Cleo-
patra's death was a definite check put upon
the further invasion into Roman civilization of the undermining influences of the
Orient.

Drink we now, and dancing round,
Press with footsteps free the ground;
Pour we now the rosy wine,
And, in honour of the gods,
Comrades, in their own abodes
Pile we the banquet on each holy shrine.

Sin it were ere now to pour
Forth the cellar's generous store;
While the haughty queen of Nile,
With her base and scurvy crew,
Dared unbridled to pursue
Wild hopes, and drunk with Fortune's
favouring smile,

Madly dreamed the Capitol
Soon should totter to its fall,
And the Empire's self should die;
But her spirit quailed awhile,
When of all the ships of Nile
From Rome's avenging fires scarce one
could fly.

Then assailed her stricken soul
Frenzied with the wassail bowl
Terrors true, and wild despair,
When (as falcon from above
Pounces on the timorous dove,
Or hunters o'er Hæmon's snow the hare)

Oar and sail incessant plying
As he marked her galleys flying,
Cæsar urged her headlong race:
Deeming that his wondrous prize
Soon would gladden Roman eyes,
And bound in chains his haughty tri-
umph grace.

Nobly she to death resigned,
Not with woman's shrinking mind,
Gazed upon the deadly knife;
Nor within some friendly creek
Basely lurking, did she seek
To save from death a now dishonoured
life.

On her prostrate Citadel
Dared her dauntless eye to dwell:
Firm of purpose, calm she stood,

Holding with unflinching grasp,
To her breast applied the asp,
Whose venom dire she drank through all
her blood.

Sternly resolute she died;
Nor could stoop her royal pride,
That, reserved to swell a show,
She a Woman and a Queen,
Should be led like captive mean
Through streets of Rome to grace her
conquering foe.
—EARL OF DERBY.

PERSIAN LUXURY

[*Odes* I, 38]

Boy, I hate their empty shows,
Persian garlands I detest,
Bring not me the late-blown rose,
Lingering after all the rest.
Plainer myrtle pleases me,
Thus outstretched beneath my vine;
Myrtle more becoming thee
Waiting with thy master's wine.
—W. COWPER.

THE SHIP OF STATE

[*Odes* I, 14]

This poem is generally regarded as an
allegory, and may be taken as a confession on the part of the poet of his change
of heart in matters political.

O Ship! new billows sweep thee out
Seaward. What wilt thou? hold the port,
be stout.
See'st not? thy mast
How rent by stiff south-western blast,

Thy side, of rowers how forlorn?
Thine hull, with groaning yards, with
rigging torn,
Can ill sustain
The fierce, and ever fiercer main;

Thy gods, no more than sails entire,
From whom yet once thy need might aid
require,
O Pontic pine,
The first of woodland stocks is thine,

Yet race and name are but as dust,
Not painted sterns give storm-tost sea-
men trust.
Unless thou dare
To be the sport of storms, beware.

Of old at best a weary weight,
A yearning care and constant strain of
late,
O shun the seas
That gird those glittering Cyclades.
—W. E. GLADSTONE.

DEDICATION OF APOLLO

[Odes I, 31]

The official poet must needs speak when
the emperor dedicates a temple to the god
who is the object of his special worship.
Horace turns the utterance into a characteristic plea for simplicity and contentment.

What asks the Poet, who adores
Apollo's virgin shrine,
What asks he, as he freely pours
The consecrating wine?

Not the rich grain, that waves along
Sardinia's fertile land,
Nor the unnumbered herds, that throng
Calabria's sultry strand;

Not gold, nor ivory's snowy gleam,
The spoil of far Cathay,
Nor fields, which Liris, quiet stream,
Gnaws silently away.

Let Fortune's favoured sons the vine
Of fair Campania hold;
The merchant quaff the rarest wine
From cups of gleaming gold;

For to the gods the man is dear
Who scathelessly can brave,
Three times or more in every year,
The wild Atlantic wave.

Let olives, endive, mallows light
Be all my fare; and health
Give thou, Latöus, so I might
Enjoy my present wealth!

Give me but these, I ask no more,
These, and a mind entire—
An old age, not unhonoured, nor
Unsolaced by the lyre!
—THEODORE MARTIN.

THE POET

HIS CAREER

[From the *Epistles* II, 2]

With the possible exception of Ovid no
Roman poet tells us so much about his
life and personality as Horace. His was
a remarkable career—from a nobody to
the intimate of kings. With it all, he retained his charming naturalness of outlook, resisting all temptations to snobbery,
honoring his simple father as the best
influence in his life, asking no more than
he merited, and giving genuine gratitude
for what fortune had bestowed upon him.

At Rome I had my schooling, and was
taught
Achilles' wrath, and all the woes it
brought;
At classic Athens, where I went ere long,
I learnt to draw the line 'twixt right and
wrong,
And search for truth, if so she might be
seen,
In academic groves of blissful green;
But soon the stress of civil strife removed
My adolescence from the scenes it loved,
And ranged me with a force that could
not stand
Before the might of Cæsar's conquering
hand.

Then when Philippi turned me all adrift
A poor plucked fledgeling, for myself to
    shift,
Bereft of property, impaired in purse,
Sheer penury drove me into scribbling
    verse:
But now, when times are altered, having
    got
Enough, thank heaven, at least to boil
    my pot,
I were the veriest madman if I chose
To write a poem rather than to doze.
  Our years keep taking toll as they
    move on;
My feasts, my frolics are already gone,
And now, it seems, my verses must go
    too:
Bestead so sorely, what's a man to do?
                    —JOHN CONINGTON.

PRECEPT AND EXAMPLE

[From the *Satires* I, 4]

  But if I still seem personal and bold,
Perhaps you'll pardon, when my story's
    told.
When my good father taught me to be
    good,
Scarecrows he took of living flesh and
    blood.
Thus, if he warned me not to spend but
    spare
The moderate means I owe to his wise
    care,
'Twas, "See the life that son of Albius
    leads!
Observe that Barrus, vilest of ill weeds!
Plain beacons these for heedless youth,
    whose taste
Might lead them else a fair estate to
    waste:"
If lawless love were what he bade me
    shun,
"Avoid Scetanius' slough," his words
    would run:
"Wise men," he'd add, "the reasons will
    explain

Why you should follow this, from that
    refrain:
For me, if I can train you in the ways
Trod by the worthy folks of earlier days,
And, while you need direction, keep your
    name
And life unspotted, I've attained my aim:
When riper years have seasoned brain
    and limb,
You'll drop your corks, and like a Triton
    swim."
'Twas thus he formed my boyhood: if he
    sought
To make me do some action that I ought,
"You see your warrant there," he'd say,
    and clench
His words with some grave member of
    the bench:
So too with things forbidden: "can you
    doubt
The deed's a deed an honest man should
    scout.
When, just for this same matter, these
    and those,
Like open drains, are stinking 'neath your
    nose?"
Sick gluttons of a next-door funeral hear,
And learn self-mastery in the school of
    fear:
And so a neighbor's scandal many a time
Has kept young minds from running into
    crime.
  Thus I grew up, unstained by serious
    ill,
Though venial faults, I grant you, haunt
    me still:
Yet items I could name retrenched e'en
    there
By time, plain speaking, individual care;
For, when I chance to stroll or lounge
    alone,
I'm not without a Mentor of my own:
"This course were better: that might help
    to mend
My daily life, improve me as a friend:
There some one showed ill-breeding: can
    I say
I might not fall into the like one day?"
So with closed lips I ruminate, and then

In leisure moments play with ink and
pen:
For that's an instance, I must needs
avow,
Of those small faults I hinted at just
now:
Grant it your prompt indulgence, or a
throng
Of poets shall come up, some hundred
strong,
And by mere numbers, in your own
despite,
Force you, like Jews, to be our proselyte.
—JOHN CONINGTON.

POET AND PATRON

[From the *Satires* I, 6]

Now on myself, the freedman's son, I
touch,
The freedman's son, by all contemned as
such,
Once, when a legion followed my com-
mand,
Now, when Mæcenas takes me by the
hand.
But this and that are different: some
stern judge
My military rank with cause might
grudge,
But not your friendship, studious as
you've been
To choose good men, not pushing, base,
or mean.
In truth, to luck I care not to pretend,
For 'twas not luck that mark'd me for
your friend:
Virgil at first, that faithful heart and
true,
And Varius after, named my name to
you.
Brought to your presence, stammeringly
I told
(For modesty forbade me to be bold)
No vaunting tale of ancestry of pride,
Of good broad acres and sleek nags to
ride,

But simple truth: a few brief words you
say,
As is your wont, and wish me a good day.
Then, nine months after, graciously you
send,
Desire my company, and hail me friend.
O, 'tis no common fortune, when one
earns
A friend's regard, who man from man
discerns,
Not by mere accident of lofty birth
But by unsullied life, and inborn worth!
Yet, if my nature, otherwise correct,
But with some few and trifling faults is
flecked,
Just as a spot or mole might be to blame,
Upon some body else of comely frame,
If none can call me miserly and mean
Or tax my life with practices unclean,
If I have lived unstained and unreproved
(Forgive self-praise), if loving and be-
loved,
I owe it to my father, who, though poor,
Passed by the village school at his own
door,
The school where great tall urchins in a
row,
Sons of great tall centurions, used to go,
With slate and satchel on their backs, to
pay
Their monthly quota punctual to the day,
And took his boy to Rome, to learn the
arts
Which knight or senator to his imparts.
Who'er had seen me, neat and more than
neat,
With slave behind me, in the crowded
street,
Had surely thought a fortune fair and
large,
Two generations old, sustained the
charge.
Himself the true tried guardian of his
son,
Whene'er I went to class, he still made
one.
Why lengthen out the tale? he kept me
chaste,
Which is the crown of virtue, undisgraced

In deed and name: he feared not lest one
day
The world should talk of money thrown
away,
If after all I plied some trade for hire,
Like him, a tax-collector, or a crier:
Nor had I murmured: as it is, the score
Of gratitude and praise is all the more.
No: while my head's unturned, I ne'er
shall need
To blush for that dear father, or to plead
As men oft plead, 'tis Nature's fault, not
mine,
I came not of a better, worthier line.
Not thus I speak, not thus I feel: the
plea
Might serve another, but 'twere base in
me.
Should Fate this moment bid me to go
back
O'er all my length of years, my life
retrack
To its first hour, and pick out such
descent
As man might wish for e'en to pride's
content,
I should rest satisfied with mine, nor
choose
New parents, decked with senatorial
shoes,
Mad, most would think me, sane, as
you'll allow,
To waive a load ne'er thrust on me till
now.
More gear 'twould make me get without
delay,
More bows there'd be to make, more calls
to pay,
A friend or two must still be at my side,
That all alone I might not drive or ride,
More nags would want their corn, more
grooms their meat,
And waggons must be bought, to save
their feet.
Now on my bobtailed mule I jog at ease,
As far as e'en Tarentum, if I please,
A wallet for my things behind me tied,
Which galls his crupper, as I gall his side,

And no one rates my meanness, as they
rate
Yours, noble Tillius, when you ride in
state
On the Tiburtine road, five slaves en
suite,
Wineholder and et-ceteras all complete.
'Tis thus my life is happier, man of
pride,
Than yours and that of half the world
beside.
When the whim leads, I saunter forth
alone,
Ask how are herbs, and what is flour a
stone,
Lounge through the Circus with its crowd
of liars,
Or in the Forum, when the sun retires,
Talk to a soothsayer, then go home to
seek
My frugal meal of fritter, vetch, and
leek:
Three youngsters serve the food: a slab
of white
Contains two cups, one ladle, clean and
bright:
Next, a cheap basin ranges on the shelf,
With jug and saucer of Campanian delf:
Then off to bed, where I can close my
eyes
Not thinking how with morning I must
rise
And face grim Marsyas, who is known
to swear
Young Novius' looks are what he cannot
bear.
I lie a-bed till ten: then stroll a bit,
Or read or write, if in a silent fit,
And rub myself with oil, not taken
whence
Natta takes his, at some poor lamp's
expense.
So to the field and ball; but when the
sun
Bids me go bathe, the field and ball I
shun:
Then eat a temperate luncheon, just to
stay

A sinking stomach till the close of day,
Kill time in-doors, and so forth.   Here
      you see
A careless life, from stir and striving free,
Happier (O be that flattering unction
      mine!)
Than if three quæstors figured in my
      line.
                        —JOHN CONINGTON.

AS A SOLDIER

[From *Odes* II, 7]

O, oft with me in troublous times
      Involved, when Brutus warred in
      Greece,
Who gives you back to your own clime
      And your own gods, a man of peace,
Pompey, the earliest friend I knew,
      With whom I oft cut short the hours
With wine, my bright hair bathed in dew
      Of Syrian oils, and wreathed with
      flowers?
With you I shared Philippi's rout,
      Unseemly parted from my shield,
When Valour fell, and warriors stout
      Were tumbled on the inglorious field:
But I was saved by Mercury,
      Wrapped in thick mist, yet trembling
      sore,
While you to that tempestuous sea
      Were swept by battle's tide once more.
                        —JOHN CONINGTON.

TITLE TO FAME

[*Odes* III, 30]

Now have I reared a monument more
      durable than brass,
And one that doth the royal scale of
      pyramids surpass,
Nor shall defeated Aquilo destroy, nor
      soaking rain,
Nor yet the countless tide of years, nor
      seasons in their train.

Not all of me shall die: my praise shall
      grow, and never end
While pontiff and mute vestal shall the
      Capitol ascend,
And so a mighty share of me shall
      Libitina foil.
Where bellows headstrong Aufidus, where,
      on his arid soil,
King Daunus ruled a rural folk, of me
      it shall be told
That, grown from small to great, I first
      of all men subtly wrought
Æolian strains to unison with our Italian
      thought.
So take thine honours earned by deeds;
      and graciously do thou,
Melpomene, with Delphic bays adorn thy
      poet's brow.
                        —W. E. GLADSTONE.

THE POET'S CONVERSION

[*Odes* I, 34]

One that has seldom worshipped; one
      that strays
      As to a mad sect too much given, and
      lore
      So falsely called, now set my sails once
      more
      Backward, to follow in rejected ways.
For he, the cloud-dividing lightning's
      blaze
      Not through the region cloud, as wont
      before,
      Divided, but with thundering horses
      o'er
      The serene skies his winged car con-
      veys;

Whereon the huge earth shuddered at the
      sound,
      And wandering streams, and Tænarus'
      seat abhorred,
      And Styx, and Atlas at Creation's
      bound;
It shook me too: The high, He changes
      them,

And from the cloud withdraws all is
  obscured,
And plucks from brow to brow the
  diadem.
                              —M. JOURDAIN.

LITERARY CRITICISM

APOLOGY FOR SATIRE

[From the *Satires* I, 4]

Satire as a distinct branch of poetry
is the only one claimed by the Romans
as their own invention. As they developed
it, it was a running commentary, mainly
ethical in spirit, on the common vices,
great and trivial, of contemporary society.
Its weapon was ridicule. Horace defines
it as "telling the truth in jest." In his
hands it is not mere destructive criticism,
but it advocates constructively better
standards and points ways of attaining
them. Horace is usually gentle, though at
times he can be quite stinging, and laughs
with us as well as at us. He often includes
himself among those at whom his shafts
are aimed. In the following passage, he
lays no claim to the name of poetry for
his satires; he regards them only as metrical "talks." The writing of satire is
justified by social conditions which call
for criticism.

Cratinus, Aristophanes, and all
The elder comic poets, great and small,
If e'er a worthy in those ancient times
Deserved peculiar notice for his crimes,
Adulterer, cut-throat, ne'er-do-well, or
  thief,
Portrayed him without fear in strong
  relief.
From these, as lineal heir, Lucilius
  springs,
The same in all points save the tune he
  sings,
A shrewd keen satirist, yet somewhat
  hard
And rugged, if you view him as a bard.
For this was his mistake: he liked to
  stand,
One leg before him, leaning on one hand,
Pour forth two hundred verses in an hour,
And think such readiness a proof of
  power.
When like a torrent he bore down, you'd
  find
He left a load of refuse still behind:
Fluent, yet indolent, he would rebel
Against the toil of writing, writing well,
Not writing much; for that I grant you.
  See,
Here comes Crispinus, wants to bet with
  me,
And offers odds: "A meeting, if you
  please:
Take we our tablets each, you those, I
  these:
Name place, and time, and umpires: let
  us try
Who can compose the faster, you or I."
Thank Heaven, that formed me of un-
  fertile mind,
My speech not copious, and my thoughts
  confined!
But you, be like the bellows, if you
  choose,
Still puffing, puffing, till the metal fuse,
And vent your windy nothings with a
  sound
That makes the depth they come from
  seem profound.
  Happy is Fannius, with immortals
  classed,
His bust and bookcase canonized at last,
While, as for me, none reads the things I
  write.
Loath as I am in public to recite,
Knowing that satire finds small favour,
  since
Most men want whipping, and who want
  it, wince.
Choose from the crowd a casual wight,
  'tis seen
He's place-hunter or miser, vain or mean:
One raves of others' wives: one stands
  agaze
At silver dishes: bronze is Albius' craze:
Another barters goods the whole world
  o'er,

From distant east to furthest western
    shore,
Driving along like dust-cloud through the
    air
To increase his capital or not impair:
These, one and all, the clink of metre
    fly,
And look on poets with a dragon's eye.
"Beware! he's vicious: so he gains his
    end,
A selfish laugh, he will not spare a friend:
Whate'er he scrawls, the mean malignant
    rogue
Is all alive to get it into vogue:
Give him a handle, and your tale is
    known
To every giggling boy and maundering
    crone."
A weighty accusation! now, permit
Some few brief words, and I will answer
    it:
First, be it understood, I make no claim
To rank with those who bear a poet's
    name:
'Tis not enough to turn out lines com-
    plete,
Each with its proper quantum of five
    feet;
Colloquial verse a man may write like me,
But (trust an author) 'tis not poetry.
No; keep that name for genius, for a soul
Of Heaven's own fire, for words that
    grandly roll.
Hence some have questioned if the Muse
    we call
The Comic Muse be really one at all:
Her subject ne'er aspires, her style ne'er
    glows,
And, save that she talks metre, she talks
    prose.
"Aye, but the angry father shakes the
    stage,
When on his graceless son he pours his
    rage,
Who, smitten with the mistress of the
    hour,
Rejects a well-born wife with ample
    dower,

Gets drunk, and (worst of all) in public
    sight
Reels with a blazing flambeau while 'tis
    light."
Well, could Pomponius' sire to life return,
Think you he'd rate his son in tones less
    stern?
So then 'tis not sufficient to combine
Well-chosen words in a well-ordered line,
When, take away the rhythm, the self-
    same words
Would suit an angry father off the
    boards.
Strip what I write, or what Lucilius
    wrote,
Of cadence and succession, time and note,
Reverse the order, put those words
    behind
That went before, no poetry you'll find:
But break up this, "When Battle's brazen
    door
Blood boltered Discord from its fasten-
    ings tore,"
'Tis Orpheus mangled by the Mænads:
    still
The bard remains, unlimb him as you
    will.
    Enough of this: some other time we'll
    see
If Satire is or is not poetry:
To-day I take the question, if 'tis just
That men like you should view it with
    distrust.
Sulcius and Caprius promenade in force,
Each with his papers, virulently hoarse,
Bugbears to robbers both: but he that's
    true
And decent living may defy the two.
Say, you're first cousin to that goodly
    pair
Cælius and Birrus, and their foibles
    share:
No Sulcius nor yet Caprius here you see
In your unworthy servant: why fear me?
No books of mine on stall or counter
    stand,
To tempt Tigellius' or some clammier
    hand,

Nor read I save to friends, and that when
    pressed,
Not to chance auditor or casual guest.
Others are less fastidious; some will air
Their last production in the public
    square:
Some choose the bath-room, for the walls
    all round
Make the voice sweeter and improve the
    sound:
Weak brains, to whom the question ne'er
    occurred
If what they do be vain, ill-timed, absurd.
"But you give pain: your habit is to
    bite,"
Rejoins the foe, "of set deliberate spite."
Who broached that slander? of the men
    I know,
With whom I live, have any told you so?
He who maligns an absent friend's fair
    fame,
Who says no word for him when others
    blame,
Who courts a reckless laugh by random
    hits,
Just for the sake of ranking among wits,
Who feigns what he ne'er saw, a secret
    blabs,
Beware him, Roman! that man steals or
    stabs!
Oft you may see three couches, four on
    each,
Where all are wincing under one man's
    speech,
All, save the host: his turn too comes at
    last,
When wine lets loose the humour shame
    held fast:
And you, who hate malignity, can see
Nought here but pleasant talk, well-bred
    and free.
I, if I chance in laughing vein to note
Rufillus' civet and Gargonius' goat,
Must I be toad or scorpion? Look at
    home:
Suppose Petillius' theft, the talk of Rome,
Named in your presence, mark how you
    defend

In your accustomed strain your absent
    friend:
"Petillius? yes, I know him well: in truth
We have been friends, companions, e'en
    from youth:
A thousand times he's served me, and I
    joy
That he can walk the streets without
    annoy:
Yet 'tis a puzzle, I confess, to me
How from that same affair he got off
    free."
Here is the poison-bag of malice, here
The gall of fell detraction, pure and
    sheer:
And these, I swear, if man such pledge
    may give,
My pen and heart shall keep from, while
    I live.

             —JOHN CONINGTON.

LUCILIUS

[Satires I, 10]

Horace's great forerunner in satire had
been Lucilius (about 180 to 103 B.C.),
a brilliant independent critic of men and
manners, of literature, politics, and philosophy in the time of Lælius and the
younger Scipio. In such universal esteem was he held by Romans of later days
that Horace's criticism of his defects of
style brought upon him the censure of the
critics for having dared to find fault with
the Father of Satire.

Yes, I did say that, view him as a bard,
Lucilius is unrhythmic, rugged, hard.
Lives there a partisan so weak of brain
As to join issue on a fact so plain?
But that he had a gift of biting wit,
In the same page I hastened to admit.
Now understand me: that's a point con-
    fessed;
But he who grants it grants not all the
    rest:
For, were a bard a bard because he's
    smart,

Laberius' mimes were products of high
  art.
'Tis not enough to make your reader's
  face
Wear a broad grin, though that too has
  its place:
Terseness there wants, to make the
  thought ring clear,
Nor with a crowd of words confuse the
  ear:
There wants a plastic style, now grave,
  now light,
Now such as bard or orator would write,
And now the language of a well-bred
  man,
Who masks his strength, and says not
  all he can:
And pleasantry will often cut clean
  through
Hard knots that gravity would scarce
  undo.
On this the old comedians rested: hence
They're still the models of all men of
  sense,
Despite Tigellius and his ape, whose
  song
Is Calvus and Catullus all day long.
  "But surely that's a merit quite unique,
His gift of mixing Latin up with Greek."
Unique, you lags in learning? what? a
  knack
Caught by Pitholeon with his hybrid
  clack?
"Nay, but the mixture gives the style
  more grace,
As Chian, plus Falernian, has more race."
Come, tell me truly: is this rule applied
To verse-making by you, and nought be-
  side,
Or would you practise it, when called to
  plead
For poor Petillius, at his direst need?
Forsooth, you choose that moment, to
  disown
Your old forefathers, Latin to the bone,
And while great Pedius and Corvinus
  strain
Against you in pure Latin lungs and
  brain,

Like double-tongued Canusian, try to
  speak
A piebald speech, half native and half
  Greek!
  Once when, though born on this side of
  the sea,
I tried my hand at Attic poetry,
Quirinus warned me, rising to my view
An hour past midnight, just when dreams
  are true:
"Seek you the throng of Grecian bards to
  swell?
Take sticks into a forest just as well."
So, while Alpinus spills his Memnon's
  blood,
Or gives his Rhine a headpiece of brown
  mud,
I toy with trifles such as this, unmeet
At Tarpa's grave tribunal to compete,
Or, mouthed by well-graced actors, be
  the rage
Of mobs, and hold possession of the
  stage.
  No hand can match Fundanius at a
  piece
Where slave and mistress clip an old
  man's fleece:
Pollio in buskins chants the deeds of
  kings:
Varius outsoars us all on Homer's wings:
The Muse that loves the woodland and
  the farm
To Virgil lends her gayest, tenderest
  charm.
For me, this walk of satire, vainly tried
By Atacinus and some few beside,
Best suits my gait: yet readily I yield
To him who first set footstep on that field,
Nor meanly seek to rob him of the bay
That shows so comely on his locks of
  grey.
  Well, but I called him muddy, said
  you'd find
More sand than gold in what he leaves
  behind.
And you, sir Critic, does your finer sense
In Homer mark no matter for offence?
Or e'en Lucilius, our good-natured friend,

Sees he in Accius nought he fain would
mend?
Does he not laugh at Ennius' halting
verse,
Yet own himself no better, if not worse?
And what should hinder me, as I peruse
Lucilius' works, from asking, if I choose,
If fate or chance forbade him to attain
A smoother measure, a more finished
strain,
Than he (you'll let me fancy such a man)
Who anxious only to make sense and
scan,
Pours forth two hundred verses ere he
sups,
Two hundred more, on rising from his
cups?
Like to Etruscan Cassius' stream of song,
Which flowed, men say, so copious and
so strong
That, when he died, his kinsfolk simply
laid
His works in order, and his pyre was
made.
No; grant Lucilius arch, engaging, gay;
Grant him the smoothest writer of his
day;
Lay stress upon the fact that he'd to
seek
In his own mind what others find in
Greek;
Grant all you please, in turn you must
allow,
Had fate postponed his life from then to
now,
He'd prune redundancies, apply the file
To each excresence that deforms his style,
Oft in the pangs of labour scratch his
head,
And bite his nails, and bite them, till
they bled.
Oh! yes! believe me, you must draw
your pen
Not once nor twice but o'er and o'er again
Through what you've written, if you
would entice
The man that reads you once to read you
twice,
Not making popular applause your cue,

But looking to fit audience, although few.
Say, would you rather have the things
you scrawl
Doled out by pedants for their boys to
drawl?
Not I: like hissed Arbuscula, I slight
Your hooting mobs, if I can please a
knight.
　Shall bug Pantilius vex me? shall I
choke
Because Demetrius needs must have his
joke
Behind my back, and Fannius, when he
dines
With dear Tigellius, vilifies my lines?
Mæcenas, Virgil, Varius, if I please
In my poor writings these and such as
these,
If Plotius, Valgius, Fuscus will commend,
And good Octavius, I've achieved my end.
You, noble Pollio (let your friend dis-
claim
All thought of flattery when he names
your name),
Messala and his brother, Servius too,
And Bibulus, and Furnius kind and true,
With others whom, despite their sense
and wit
And friendly hearts, I purposely omit;
Such I would have my critics; men to
gain
Whose smiles were pleasure, to forego
them pain.
Demetrius and Tigellius, off! go pule
To the bare benches of your ladies'
school!
　Hallo there, youngster! take my book,
you rogue,
And write this in, by way of epilogue.
　　　　　　　　—JOHN CONINGTON.

ON THE DRAMA

[From the *Art of Poetry*]

Horace's purpose is not, like Aristotle's,
to inquire into the essential nature of
various forms of poetry, but rather to reduce established practice to clearly formu-

lated rules. It is interesting that he places his emphasis on dramatic poetry, although he himself produced nothing in that branch and although Roman opinion was generally agreed in giving epic the highest place.

Now listen, dramatists, and I will tell
What I expect, and all the world as well.
If you would have your auditors to stay
Till curtain-rise and plaudit end the play,
Observe each age's temper, and impart
To each the grace and finish of your art.
Note first the boy who just knows how
    to talk
And feels his feet beneath him in his
    walk:
He likes his young companions, loves a
    game,
Soon vexed, soon soothed, and not two
    hours the same.
    The beardless youth, at last from tutor
    freed,
Loves playing—field and tennis, dog and
    steed:
Pliant as wax to those who lead him
    wrong,
But all impatience with a faithful tongue;
Imprudent, lavish, hankering for the
    moon,
He takes things up and lays them down
    as soon.
    His nature revolutionized, the man
Makes friends and money when and how
    he can:
Keen-eyed and cool, though on ambition
    bent,
He shuns all acts of which he may repent.
    Grey hairs have many evils: without
    end
The old man gathers what he dares not
    spend,
While, as for action, do he what he will,
'Tis all half-hearted, spiritless and chill:
Inert, irresolute, his neck he cranes
Into the future, grumbles, and complains,
Extols his own young years with peevish
    praise,
But rates and censures these degenerate
    days.

Years, as they come, bring blessings in
    their train;
Years, as they go, take blessings back
    again:
Yet haste or chance may blink the obvious
    truth,
Make youth discourse like age, and age
    like youth:
Attention fixed on life alone can teach
The traits and adjuncts which pertain to
    each.
    Sometimes an action on the stage is
    shown,
Sometimes 'tis done elsewhere, and there
    made known.
A thing when heard, remember, strikes
    less keen
On the spectator's mind than when 'tis
    seen.
Yet 'twere not well in public to display
A business best transacted far away,
And much may be secluded from the eye
For well-graced tongues to tell of by and
    by.
Medea must not shed her children's
    blood,
Nor savage Atreus cook man's flesh for
    food,
Nor Philomel turn bird or Cadmus snake,
With people looking on and wide awake.
If scenes like these before my eyes be
    thrust,
They shock belief and generate disgust.
    Would you your play should prosper
    and endure?
Then let it have five acts, nor more nor
    fewer.
Bring in no god save as a last resource,
Nor make four speakers join in the dis-
    course.
    An actor's part the chorus should
    sustain
And do their best to get the plot in train:
And whatsoe'er between the acts they
    chant
Should all be apt, appropriate, relevant.
Still let them give sage counsel, back the
    good,

Attemper wrath, and cool impetuous
     blood,
Praise the spare meal that pleases but
     not sates,
Justice, the law, and peace with unbarred
     gates,
Conceal all secrets, and the gods implore
To crush the proud and elevate the poor.
     Not trumpet-tongued, as now, nor
         brass-belayed,
The flute was used to lend the chorus aid:
Simple and slight and moderately loud,
It charmed the ears of not too large a
     crowd,
Which, frugal, rustic, primitive, severe,
Flocked in those early days to see and
     hear.
     Then, when the city gained increase of
         land,
And wider walls its waxing greatness
     spanned,
When the good Genius, frolicsome and
     gay,
Was soothed at festivals with cups by
     day,
Change spread to scenic measures:
     breadth, and ease,
And freedom unrestrained were found in
     these:
For what (said men) should jovial rustic,
     placed
At random 'mid his betters, know of
     taste?
     So graceful dance went hand in hand
         with song,
And robes of kingly splendour trailed
     along:
So by the side of music words upgrew,
And eloquence came rolling, prompt and
     new:
Shrewd in things mundane, wise in things
     divine,
Its voice was like the voice of Delphi's
     shrine.
     The aspiring bard who served the
         tragic muse,
A paltry goat the summit of his views,
Soon brought in Satyrs from the woods,
     and tried

If grave and gay could flourish side by
     side,
That the spectator, feasted to his fill,
Noisy and drunk, might ne'ertheless sit
     still.
     Yet, though loud laugh and frolic jest
         commend
Your Satyr folk, and mirth and morals
     blend,
Let not your heroes doff their robes of
     red
To talk low language in a homely shed,
Nor, in their fear of crawling, mount too
     high,
Catching at clouds and aiming at the sky.
Melpomene, when bidden to be gay,
Like matron dancing on a festal day,
Deals not in idle banter, nor consorts
Without reserve with Satyrs and their
     sports.
     In plays like these I would not deal
         alone
In words and phrases trite and too well
     known,
Nor, stooping from the tragic height, drop
     down
To the low level of buffoon and clown,
As though pert Davus, or the saucy jade
Who sacks the gold and jeers the gull
     she made,
Were like Silenus, who, though quaint
     and odd,
Is yet the guide and tutor of a god.
A hackneyed subject I would take and
     treat
So deftly, all should hope to do the feat,
Then, having strained and struggled,
     should concede
To do the feat were difficult indeed.
So much may order and arrangement do
To make the cheap seem choice, the
     threadbare new.
Your rustic Fauns, methinks, should have
     a care
Lest people deem them bred in city air;
Should shun the cant of exquisites, and
     shun
Coarse ribaldry no less and blackguard
     fun.

For those who have a father or a horse
Or an estate will take offence of course,
Nor think they're bound in duty to admire
What gratifies the vetch-and-chestnut-buyer.
The Iambic foot is briefly thus defined:
Two syllables, a short with long behind:
Repeat it six times o'er, so quick its beat,
'Tis trimeter, three measures for six feet:
At first it ran straight on; but, years ago,
Its hearers begged that it would move more slow;
On which it took, with a good-natured air,
Stout spondees in, its native rights to share,
Yet so that none should ask it to resign
The sixth, fourth, second places in the line.
But search through Attius' trimeters, or those
Which Ennius took such pleasure to compose,
You'll rarely find it: on the boards they groan,
Laden with spondees, like a cart with stone,
And brand our tragedy with want of skill
Or want of labour, call it what you will.
What then? false rhythm few judges can detect,
And Roman bards of course are all correct.
What shall a poet do? make rules his sport,
And dash through thick and thin, through long and short?
Or pick his steps, endeavour to walk clean,
And fancy every mud-stain will be seen?
What good were that, if though I mind my ways
And shun all blame, I do not merit praise?
My friends, make Greece your model when you write,
And turn her volumes over day and night.

"But Plautus pleased our sires, the good old folks;
They praised his numbers, and they praised his jokes."
They did: 'twas mighty tolerant in them
To praise where wisdom would perhaps condemn;
That is, if you and I and our compeers
Can trust our tastes, our fingers, and our ears,
Know polished wit from horse-play, and can tell
What verses do, and what do not, run well.
Thespis began the drama: rumour says
In travelling carts he carried round his plays,
Where actors, smeared with lees, before the throng
Performed their parts with gesture and with song.
Then Æschylus brought in the mask and pall,
Put buskins on his men to make them tall,
Turned boards into a platform, not too great,
And taught high monologue and grand debate.
The elder Comedy had next its turn,
Nor small the glory it contrived to earn:
But freedom passed into unbridled spite,
And law was soon invoked to set things right:
Law spoke: the chorus lost the power to sting,
And (shame to say) thenceforth refused to sing.
Our poets have tried all things; nor do they
Deserve least praise, who follow their own way,
And tell in comedy or history-piece
Some story of home growth, not drawn from Greece.
Nor would the land we love be now more strong
In warrior's prowess than in poet's song,

Did not her bards with one consent de-
cline
The tedious task, to alter and refine.
Dear Pisos! as you prize old Numa's
blood,
Set down that work, and that alone, as
good,
Which, blurred and blotted, checked and
counterchecked,
Has stood all tests, and issued forth
correct.
—JOHN CONINGTON.

COMMENTS ON LIFE

INVITATION TO THE COUNTRY

[*Odes* I, 17]

Swift-footed Faunus oft delights to roam
From snow-clad peaks of Arcady, and
find
Here in my soft Lucretilis a home,
   Where in sequestered brake
   Safe from hot suns and pitiless wind
From ledge to ledge my nimble young-
lings climb,
Nipping fresh Arbutus and fragrant
Thyme,
Fearless of prowling wolf or venomed
snake,
   While from Ustica's vale profound
The polished rocks the Wood-god's pipe
resound.

   The gods protect me. They approve
   My piety; my song they love.
   Haste, Tyndaris, haste! partake my
   store
   Of rural honours brimming o'er
   From plenteous horn. This cool
   retreat
   Shall guard thee from the Dog-star's
   heat.
Here that white hand the Teian lyre shall
strike;
That sweet voice sing the old Greek
melody

Of him, the wand'ring Prince beloved
alike
   By that true wife, Penelope,
And Circe glittering as a summer sea.

   Tyndaris! 'neath the arching vine
   Lift to thy lips the Lesbian wine,
   An innocent draught! Not here
   shall Mars
   And Bacchus wage their customed
   wars;
   Not here shall jealous Cyrus dare
   To rend thy guiltless robe, or tear
   The clinging garland from thy hair.
   —STEPHEN DEVERE.

JOYS OF THE COUNTRY

[From *Epodes* II]

Happy the man, in busy schemes un-
skilled,
   Who, living simply, like our sires of
   old,
Tills the few acres which his father tilled,
   Vexed by no thoughts of usury or gold.

The shrilling clarion ne'er his slumber
mars,
   Nor quails he at the howl of angry seas;
He shuns the forum with its wordy jars,
   Nor at a great man's door consents to
   freeze.

The tender vine-shoots, budding into life,
   He with the stately poplar-tree doth
   wed,
Lopping the fruitless branches with his
knife,
   And grafting shoots of promise in their
   stead;

Or in some valley, up among the hills,
   Watches his wandering herds of lowing
   kine,
Or fragrant jars with liquid honey fills,
   Or shears his silly sheep in sunny shine;

Or when Autumnus o'er the smiling land
  Lifts up his head with rosy apples
    crowned,
Joyful he plucks the pears, which erst his
    hand
  Graffed on the stem they're weighing
    to the ground;

Plucks grapes in noble clusters purple-
    dyed,
  A gift for thee, Priapus, and for thee,
Father Sylvanus, where thou dost preside,
  Warding his bounds beneath thy sacred
    tree.

Now he may stretch his careless limbs to
    rest,
  Where some old ilex spreads its sacred
    roof;
Now in the sunshine lie, as likes him best,
  On grassy turf or close elastic woof.

And streams the while glide on with
    murmurs low,
  And birds are singing 'mong the
    thickets deep,
And fountains babble, sparkling as they
    flow,
  And with their noise invite to gentle
    sleep.

But when grim winter comes, and o'er his
    grounds
  Scatters its biting snows with angry
    roar,
He takes the field, and with a cry of
    hounds
  Hunts down into the toils the foaming
    boar;

Or seeks the thrush, poor starveling, to
    ensnare,
  In filmy net with bait delusive stored,
Entraps the travelled crane, and timorous
    hare,
  Rare dainties these to glad his frugal
    board.

Who amid joys like these would not forget
  The pangs which love to all its victims
    bears,
The fever of the brain, the ceaseless fret,
  And all the heart's lamentings and
    despairs?

But if a chaste and blooming wife, beside,
  His cheerful home with sweet young
    blossoms fills,
Like some stout Sabine, or the sunburnt
    bride
  Of the lithe peasant of the Apulian
    hills,

Who piles the hearth with logs well dried
    and old
  Against the coming of her wearied lord,
And, when at eve the cattle seek the fold,
  Drains their full udders of the milky
    hoard;

And bringing forth from her well-tended
    store
  A jar of wine, the vintage of the year,
Spreads an unpurchased feast,—oh then,
    not more
  Could choicest Lucrine oysters give me
    cheer,

Or the rich turbot, or the dainty char,
  If ever to our bays the winter's blast
Should drive them in its fury from afar;
  Nor were to me a welcomer repast

The Afric hen or the Ionic snipe,
  Than olives newly gathered from the
    tree,
That hangs abroad its clusters rich and
    ripe,
  Or sorrel, that doth love the pleasant
    lea,

Or mallows wholesome for the body's
    need,
  Or lamb foredoomed upon some festal
    day
In offering to the guardian gods to bleed,
  Or kidling which the wolf hath marked
    for prey.

What joy, amidst such feasts, to see the
    sheep,
  Full of the pasture, hurrying home-
      wards come,
To see the wearied oxen, as they creep,
  Dragging the upturned ploughshare
      slowly home!

Or, ranged around the bright and blazing
    hearth,
  To see the hinds, a house's surest
      wealth,
Beguile the evening with their simple
    mirth,
  And all the cheerfulness of rosy health!
      —THEORDORE MARTIN.

TOWN AND COUNTRY

[From the *Satires* II, 6]

Should someone be unwise enough to
    praise
Arellius' toilsome wealth, he straightway
    says:
  "One day a country mouse in his poor
    home
Received an ancient friend, a mouse from
    Rome:
The host, though close and careful, to a
    guest
Could open still: so now he did his best.
He spares not oats or vetches: in his
    chaps
Raisins he brings and nibbled bacon-
    scraps,
Hoping by varied dainties to entice
His town-bred guest, so delicate and nice,
Who condescended graciously to touch
Thing after thing, but never would take
    much,
While he, the owner of the mansion, sate
On threshed-out straw, and spelt and
    darnels ate.
At length the townsman cries: 'I wonder
    how
You can live here, friend, on this hill's
    rough brow:

Take my advice, and leave these ups and
    downs,
This hill and dale, for humankind and
    towns.
Come now, go home with me; remember,
    all
Who live on earth are mortal, great and
    small:
Then take, good sir, your pleasure while
    you may;
With life so short, 'twere wrong to lose a
    day.'
This reasoning made the rustic's head
    turn round;
Forth from his hole he issues with a
    bound,
And they two make together for their
    mark,
In hopes to reach the city during dark.
The midnight sky was bending over all,
When they set foot within a stately hall,
Where couches of wrought ivory had been
    spread
With gorgeous coverlets of Tyrian red,
And viands piled up high in baskets lay,
The relics of a feast of yesterday.
The townsman does the honours, lays his
    guest
At ease upon a couch with crimson
    dressed,
Then nimbly moves in character of host,
And offers in succession boiled and roast;
Nay, like a well-trained slave, each wish
    prevents,
And tastes before the tit-bits he presents.
The guest, rejoicing in his altered fare,
Assumes in turn a genial diner's air,
When hark! a sudden banging of the
    door:
Each from his couch is tumbled on the
    floor:
Half dead, they scurry round the room,
    poor things,
While the whole house with barking
    mastiffs rings.
Then says the rustic: 'It may do for
    you,
This life, but I don't like it; so adieu:

THE PEACE OF AUGUSTUS

Give me my hole, secure from all alarms,
I'll prove that tares and vetches still have
    charms.' "
          —JOHN CONINGTON.

FOUNTAIN OF BANDUSIA

[Odes III, 13]

O well, whose waters are as glass to shine,
  Bandusia, worthy vintage to be shed,
  And not without a flower visited,
A kid with swelling brow to-morrow is
    thine,
Whose horns to war and wantonness
    destine.
  In vain; in vain, for his dark blood
    shall spread,
  Child of the frolic fold, in thy chill
    bed;
When the hot Dog-star's hours to rage
    incline,
They pierce thee not, that profferest
    pleasant cold
  To flocks that range, and labour-weary
    bulls;
Thou too from all time forward shalt be
    told
Great among wells of name, by me that
    sing
The ilex shadowing thy stone-bound
    spring
  Whence issues all the tumult of thy
    pools.
          —M. JOURDAIN.

CARPE DIEM

[Odes I, 11]

Strive not, Leuconoe, to know what end
The gods above to me or thee will send:
Nor with astrologers consult at all,
That thou mayst better know what can
    befall;
Whether thou liv'st more winters, or thy
    last
Be this, which Tyrrhen waves 'gainst
    rocks do cast.

Be wise! Drink free, and in so short a
    space
Do not protracted hopes of life embrace:
Whilst we are talking, envious time doth
    slide;
This day's thine own; the next may be
    denied.
          —THOMAS HAWKINS.

ENJOY YOUR YOUTH

[Odes II, 11]

What the Cantabrian stout, or Scythian
    think
Divided with opposed Adria's brink,
Quintus Hirpinus, do not thou enquire;
Nor for life's use, which little doth desire,
Be thou too careful: smooth-faced youth
    apace
Doth backward fly, and with it beauty's
    grace,
Dry aged hoariness with furrows deep,
Dispelling amorous fires and gentle sleep.
The summer flowers keep not their native
    grace,
Nor shines the bright moon with a con-
    stant face.
Why dost thou tire thy mind, subordinate
Unto the counsels of eternal fate?
Why under this high plane or pine-tree's
    shade
In discomposèd manner, careless laid,
Our hoary hair perfumed with fragrant
    rose,
And odours, which Assyria doth disclose,
Do we, anointed, not to drink prepare?
Free Bacchus dissipates consuming care:
But oh! what boy Falernian wine's hot
    rage
Will soon for me, with gliding stream,
    assuage?
Ah, who retirèd Lyde will require,
Hither to come? Boy, with her ivory lyre
Bid her make haste, and hair to tie not
    shame
In careless knot, like a Laconian dame.
          —THOMAS HAWKINS.

LIFE IS SHORT

[*Odes* II, 3]

When life is hard, your soul possess
  In calm serene; when times are fair,
  Refrain from triumph's haughty air,
For Dellius, death will come no less

If length of days be wholly spanned
  With grief, or if as glad hours laugh
You lie in quiet meads and quaff
Falernum's wine of choicest brand;

Where lofty pines and poplars white
  Their boughs in friendly shade entwine
  Together, and with winding line
The brooklet babbles in its flight.

Here call for wine and nard and bloom
  Of roses fading all too fast,
  While youth remains and fortunes last
And Fate still spares the thread of doom.

The lawns you buy you must forsake,
  That home by tawny Tiber's wave;
  The growing stores for which you slave
In heirship will another take.

What boots your wealth or long descent
  From Inachus? As well to lie
  A lowly beggar 'neath the sky
For any ruth in Death's intent.

One bourn constrains us all; for all
  The lots are shaken in the urn,
  Whence, soon or late, will fall our turn
Of exile's barge without recall.
                    —J. H. DEAZELEY.

DEATH INEVITABLE

[*Odes* II, 14]

The whirling Year, ah, Friend! the
      whirling Year
    Rolls on apace,
And soon shall Wrinkles plough thy
      withered Face:

In vain you waste your breath,
  No Prayers can stay nor Vows defer
The swift approach of Age, and con-
      quering Death:

No, tho' ten thousand Oxen stain'd his
      Shrines
    With sacred Blood,
Should'st thou appease th' inexorable
      God:
  He opens, and he shuts the grave;
  Geryon's triple Soul confines,
And stubborn Gyges with the Stygian
      Wave:

That fatal Wave that must be pass'd by
      all,
    The Rich, the Poor
Are doomed alike to view the Stygian
      shore;
    The Knaves and Fools, the Wise and
      Just,
    The Kings as well as Clowns must fall;
And undistinguished lie with meaner
      Dust:

In vain we all retreat from dangerous
      War,
    And live in ease;
In vain we shun the Rage of angry Seas;
    The burning Fevers Autumn brings,
    In vain we fly, and idly fear
The Plagues that South-winds bear on
      sickly Wings.

For all the Stygian Waves are doomed to
      pass;
    We all must go
And view Cocytus' wand'ring Streams
      below:
    We all must see the lasting Chains
    That hold curst Danaus his Race,
And Sisyphus condemned to endless
      Pains.

Thy Children must be left, thy Lands and
      House,
    Thy pleasing Wife,
That happy Comfort and Delight of Life;

Of all the Trees thy hands restor'd,
None but the Cypress' hated Boughs
Shall follow their short-lived decaying
    Lord.

The Wines you keep so close thy worthier
        Heir
    Shall soon possess,
And waste 'midst wanton Luxury and
        Ease;
    Much nobler Wine the squand'ring
        Youth
Shall spill, and costlier Feasts prepare,
Than ever pleas'd a Pampered Abbot's
        Tooth.
                        —THOMAS CREECH.

IN PRAISE OF WINE

[Odes III, 21]

Co-eval mine of Manlius' year,
    Or be thy content woe or wit,
    Or feuds by lovers' frenzy lit,
Or, gentle jar, be slumber here,

With whatsoever purpose sealed
    A Massic meet for golden days
    Thou guardest; come; Corvinus prays
For mellower wine 'tis ours to yield.

Not he so rude as spurn the bowl,
    Deep though he drink of Plato's well,—
    That bowl which many a time, they tell,
Hath warmed old Cato's honest soul.

Thou hast a pleasing pang for breasts
    Obdurate, wringing from the wise
    Their deep designs and secret sighs
Revealed to Bacchus, God of jests.

Hope to the hopeless, pride again
    And prowess to the trodden down
    Thou lendest, till he mocks the frown
Of monarchs and the swords of men.

Liber, the Queen of happy love,
    And Graces slow to sever, they

Shall watch with thee the taper's ray
Till Phœbus fright the stars above.
                        —T. R. CLARK.

TO A FLIRT

[Odes I, 5]

What slender youth, bedew'd with liquid
        odours,
Courts thee on roses in some pleasant
        cave,
Pyrrha? For whom bind'st thou
    In wreaths thy golden hair,
    Plain in thy neatness? O how oft shall
        he
    On faith and changed gods complain,
        and seas
    Rough with black winds, and storms
    Unwonted shall admire!
Who now enjoys thee credulous, all gold,
Who always vacant, always amiable,
    Hopes thee, of flattering gales
    Unmindful. Hapless they
T' whom thou untried seem'st fair. Me
        in my vow'd
Picture, the sacred wall declares to have
        hung
    My dank and dropping weeds
    To the stern God of the sea.
                        —JOHN MILTON.

THE RECONCILIATION

[Odes III, 9]

HOR.   Whilst, Lydia, I was lov'd of
            thee,
        And 'bout thy ivory neck no youth
            did fling
        His arms more acceptably free,
I   thought me richer than the
            Persian king.

LYD.   Whilst Horace lov'd no mistress
            more,

Nor after Chloe did his Lydia
    sound;
  In name I went all names before,
The Roman Ilia was not more
    renown'd.

HOR.   'Tis true, I'm Thracian Chloe's I,
Who sings so sweet, and with such
    cunning plays,
    As, for her, I'd not fear to die,
So fate would give her life, and
    longer days.

LYD.   And I am mutually on fire
With   gentle   Calais,   Thurine
    Ornith's son,
    For whom I doubly would ex-
    pire,
So fate would let the boy a long
    thread run.

HOR.   But say old love return should
    make,
And us disjoin'd force to her
    brazen yoke;
    That I bright Chloe off should
    shake,
And to left Lydia now the gate
    stood ope?

LYD.   Though he be fairer than a star;
Thou lighter than the bark of any
    tree,
    And than rough Adria angrier
    far;
Yet would I wish to love, live, die
    with thee.
        —BEN JONSON.

WINTER

[*Odes* I, 9]

Behold yon mountain's hoary height
  Made higher with new mounts of snow;
Again behold the winter's weight
  Oppress the lab'ring woods below:
And streams, with icy fetters bound,
Benumb'd and crampt to solid ground.

With well-heap'd logs dissolve the cold,
  And feed the genial hearth with fires,
Produce the wine that makes us bold,
  And sprightly wit and love inspires:
For what hereafter shall betide,
God, if 'tis worth his care, provide.

Let him alone, with what he made,
  To toss and turn the world below;
At his command the storms invade;
  The winds by his commission blow;
Till with a nod he bids them cease,
And then the calm returns, and all is
    peace.

To-morrow and her works defy,
  Lay hold upon the present hour,
And snatch the pleasures passing by,
  To put them out of fortune's power:
Nor love, nor love's delights disdain;
Whate'er thou get'st to-day, is gain.

Secure those golden early joys,
  That youth unsour'd with sorrows
    bears,
Ere with'ring time the taste destroys,
  With sickness and unwiedly years.
This is the time to be possest;
The best is but in season best.

Th' appointed hour of promis'd bliss,
  The pleasing whisper in the dark,
The half unwilling willing kiss,
  The laugh that guides thee to the mark,
When the kind nymph would coyness
    feign,
And hides but to be found again;
These, these are joys the gods for youth
    ordain.

        —JOHN DRYDEN.

SPRING [1]

[*Odes* I, 4]

Hard Winter melts; the welcome Spring
    again
  Comes back, and in her train

[1] Reprinted from J. O. Sargent, *Horatian Echoes*, by permission of Miss Georgiana W. Sargent.

The West wind, and the laid-up keels once
  more
Are launched from the dry shore.
No longer do the herds the stalls de-
  sire,
Nor husbandman his fire;
The meadows that but now were white
  with frost
Their pallid hues have lost.
In dance by Cytherean Venus led,
  With the moon overhead,
Joined with the Nymphs the sister
  Graces beat
The earth with rhythmic feet,
While at the Cyclops' ponderous forge the
  light
Makes swarthy Vulcan bright.
Now round the tresses that with unguents
  shine
  Green myrtles we may twine,
Or flowers with which from icy fetters
  freed
  Earth garnishes the mead.

Now is the time to make in shady groves
  The offerings Pan loves,
Whether he may demand a lamb or bid
  Oblation of a kid.
Pale Death before them stalks impartially
  Whether the portals be
Of peasant or of prince—hovel or tower
  Alike all feel his power.
O happy Sestius! Life's little span
  Forbids long hope to man;
Thy sunny day impending night invades,
  Thee wait the fabled shades,
And Pluto's narrow house; where, once
  thou go,
  No more by lucky throw
Of dice wilt thou in banquet hall recline
  King of the realms of wine;
No tender Lycidas will love inspire,
  Whose charms thou dost admire,—
Whom rival youths regard with jealous
  eye,
  And maids will by and by.
                        —J. O. SARGENT.

V. MYTH AND LEGEND

STORIES FROM MYTHOLOGY: OVID

Publius Ovidius Naso (43 B.C. to about 18 A.D.), a native of Sulmo in the eastern part of central Italy, began his career as a brilliant and successful poet of pleasure, but was forced by imperial command to bring it to a close in disgrace and exile. He was a prolific writer of elegy and of narrative poems on mythological subjects. He is credited also with a tragedy which has not survived. His best known titles are *The Loves, The Art of Love, Letters of Heroines, The Calendar, Metamorphoses, The Lament,* and *Letters from the Pontus.* He brings into play more than any other Roman poet a penetrating insight into human nature; his wit and humor, even if flippant and cynical, make him at all times interesting; he is a supreme master of metrical expression.

PYRRHA AND DEUCALION

[From the *Metamorphoses*, Book I]

In his *Metamorphoses* Ovid undertook and carried to successful completion the immense task of re-telling practically all the stories of Greek mythology, and many from Roman legend, that yielded to narrative treatment. The complete work is the most exhaustive manual of mythology extant, a manual made rich and entertaining by the poet's vivid imagination and his unusual powers in dramatic narration.

A mountain of stupendous height there
  stands
Betwixt th' Athenian and Bœotian lands,
The bound of fruitful fields, while fields
  they were,
But then a field of waters did appear:
Parnassus is its name; whose forky rise

Mounts thro' the clouds, and mates the lofty skies.

High on the summit of this dubious cliff,
Deucalion wafting, moor'd his little skiff.
He with his wife were only left behind
Of perish'd man; they two were human kind.
The mountain nymphs, and Themis they adore,
And from her oracles relief implore.
The most upright of mortal men was he;
The most sincere, and holy woman, she.

  When Jupiter, surveying Earth from high,
Beheld it in a lake of water lie,
That where so many millions lately liv'd,
But two, the best of either sex, surviv'd;
He loos'd the northern wind; fierce Boreas flies
To puff away the clouds, and purge the skies:
Serenely, while he blows, the vapours driv'n
Discover Heav'n to Earth, and Earth to Heav'n.
The billows fall, while Neptune lays his mace
On the rough sea, and smooths its furrow'd face.
Already Triton at his call appears
Above the waves; a Tyrian robe he wears;
And in his hand a crooked trumpet bears.
The sovereign bids him peaceful sounds inspire,
And give the waves the signal to retire.
His writhen shell he takes; whose narrow vent
Grows by degrees into a large extent;
Then gives it breath; the blast with doubling sound,
Runs the wide circuit of the world around:
The Sun first heard it, in his early east,
And met the rattling echoes in the west.
The waters list'ning to the trumpet's roar,
Obey the summons, and forsake the shore.
A thin circumference of land appears;

And Earth, but not at once, her visage rears,
And peeps upon the seas from upper grounds;
The streams, but just contain'd within their bounds,
By slow degrees into their channels crawl;
And Earth increases, as the waters fall.
In longer time the tops of trees appear,
Which mud on their dishonour'd branches bear.
  At length the world was all restor'd to view;
But desolate, and of a sickly hue:
Nature beheld herself, and stood aghast,
A dismal desert, and a silent waste.

  Which when Deucalion, with a piteous look,
Beheld, he wept, and thus to Pyrrha spoke;
"Oh wife, oh sister, oh of all thy kind
The best, and only creature left behind,
By kindred, love, and now by dangers join'd;
Of multitudes, who breath'd the common air,
We two remain: a species in a pair:
The rest the seas have swallow'd; nor have we
Ev'n of this wretched life a certainty.
The clouds are still above; and while I speak,
A second deluge o'er our heads may break.
Should I be snatcht from hence, and thou remain,
Without relief, or partner of thy pain,
How couldst thou such a wretched life sustain?
Should I be left, and thou be lost, the sea,
That bury'd her I love, should bury me.
Oh could our father his old arts inspire,
And make me heir of his informing fire,
That so I might abolish'd man retrieve
And perish'd people in new souls might live!
But Heav'n is pleas'd, nor ought we to complain,

That we, th' examples of mankind, remain."

He said; the careful couple join their tears;

And then invoke the gods with pious prayers.

Thus, in devotion having eas'd their grief,

From sacred oracles they seek relief;

And to Cephisus' brook their way pursue:

The stream was troubled, but the ford they knew;

With living waters, in the fountain bred,

They sprinkle first their garments, and their head,

Then took the way, which to the temple led.

The roofs were all defil'd with moss and mire,

The desert altars void of solemn fire.

Before the gradual, prostrate they ador'd:

The pavement kiss'd; and thus the saint implor'd.

"O righteous Themis! if the pow'rs above

By pray'rs are bent to pity, and to love;

If human miseries can move their mind;

If yet they can forget, and yet be kind;

Tell how we may restore, by second birth,

Mankind, and people desolated Earth."

Then thus the gracious goddess, nodding, said;

"Depart, and with your vestments veil your head:

And stooping lowly down, with loosen'd zones,

Throw each behind your backs, your mighty mother's bones."

Amaz'd the pair, and mute with wonder, stand,

'Till Pyrrha first refus'd the dire command.

"Forbid it Heav'n," said she, "that I should tear

Those holy relics from the sepulchre."

They ponder'd the mysterious words again,

For some new sense; and long they sought in vain:

At length Deucalion clear'd his cloudy brow,

And said, "The dark enigma will allow

A meaning, which if well I understand,

From sacrilege will free the god's command:

This Earth our mighty mother is, the stones

In her capacious body are her bones:

These we must cast behind." With hope, and fear,

The woman did the new solution hear:

The man diffides in his own augury,

And doubts the gods; yet both resolve to try.

Descending from the mount, they first unbind

Their vest, and veil'd they cast the stones behind;

The stones (a miracle to mortal view,

But long tradition makes it pass for true)

Did first the rigour of their kind expel,

And suppled into softness as they fell;

Then swell'd, and swelling, by degrees grew warm,

And took the rudiments of human form;

Imperfect shapes: in marble such are seen,

When the rude chisel does the man begin;

While yet the roughness of the stone remains,

Without the rising muscles, and the veins.

The sappy parts, and next resembling juice,

Were turn'd to moisture, for the body's use:

Supplying humours, blood, and nourishment;

The rest, too solid to receive a bent,

Converts to bones; and what was once a vein,

Its former name and nature did retain.

By help of pow'r divine, in little space,

What the man threw, assum'd a manly face;

And what the wife, renew'd the female race.

Hence we derive our nature; born to bear

Laborious life; and harden'd into care.

—JOHN DRYDEN.

NARCISSUS

[From the *Metamorphoses,* Book III]

There stands a fountain in a darksome
   wood,
Nor stain'd with falling leaves nor rising
   mud;
Untroubled by the breath of winds it
   rests,
Unsully'd by the touch of men or beasts;
High bow'rs of shady trees above it grow,
And rising grass and cheerful greens
   below.
Pleas'd with the form and coolness of the
   place,
And over-heated by the morning chase,
Narcissus on the grassy verdure lies:
But whilst within the crystal fount he
   tries
To quench his heat, he feels new heat
   arise.
For, as his own bright image he survey'd,
He fell in love with the fantastic shade;
And o'er the fair resemblance hung un-
   mov'd,
Nor knew, fond youth! it was himself he
   lov'd.
The well-turned neck and shoulders he
   descries,
The spacious forehead, and the sparkling
   eyes;
The hands that Bacchus might not scorn
   to show,
And hair that round Apollo's head might
   flow;
With all the purple youthfulness of face,
That gently blushes in the wat'ry glass.
By his own flames consum'd the lover lies,
And gives himself the wound by which he
   dies.
To the cold water oft he joins his lips,
Oft catching at the beauteous shade he
   dips
His arms, as often from himself he slips.
Nor knows he who it is his arms pursue
With eager clasps, but loves he knows
   not who.
   What could, fond youth, this helpless
      passion move?

What kindled in thee this unpity'd love?
Thy own warm blush within the water
   glows,
With thee the colour'd shadow comes and
   goes,
Its empty being on thyself relies;
Step thou aside, and the frail charmer
   dies.
   Still o'er the fountain's wat'ry gleam
      he stood,
Mindless of sleep, and negligent of food;
Still view'd his face, and languish'd as he
   view'd.
At length he rais'd his head, and thus
   began
To vent his grief, and tell the woods his
   pain.
"You trees," says he, "and thou surround-
   ing grove,
Who oft have been the kindly scenes of
   love,
Tell me, if e'er within your shades did lie
A youth so tortur'd, so perplex'd as I?
I, who before me see the charming fair,
Whilst there he stands, and yet he stands
   not there:
In such a maze of love my thoughts are
   lost:
And yet no bulwark'd town, nor distant
   coast,
Preserve the beauteous youth from being
   seen,
No mountains rise, nor oceans flow be-
   tween.
A shallow water hinders my embrace;
And yet the lovely mimic wears a face
That kindly smiles, and when I bend to
   join
My lips to his, he fondly bends to mine.
Hear, gentle youth, and pity my com-
   plaint;
Come from thy well, thou fair inhabitant.
My charms an easy conquest have ob-
   tain'd
O'er other hearts, by thee alone disdain'd.
But why should I despair? I'm sure he
   burns
With equal flames, and languishes by
   turns.

Whene'er I stand, he offers at a kiss,
And when my arms I stretch, he stretches his.
His eyes with pleasure on my face he keeps,
He smiles my smiles, and when I weep he weeps.
Whene'er I speak, his moving lips appear
To utter something which I cannot hear.
  "Ah, wretched me! I now begin too late
To find out all the long-perplex'd deceit;
It is myself I love, myself I see;
The gay delusion is a part of me.
I kindle up the fires by which I burn,
And my own beauties from the well return.
Whom should I court? how utter my complaint?
Enjoyment but produces my restraint,
And too much plenty makes me die for want.
How gladly would I from myself remove!
And at a distance set the thing I love.
My breast is warm'd with such unusual fire,
I wish him absent whom I most desire.
And now I faint with grief; my fate draws nigh;
In all the pride of blooming youth I die:
Death will the sorrows of my heart relieve.
Oh might the visionary youth survive,
I should with joy my latest breath resign!
But oh! I see his fate involv'd in mine."
  This said, the weeping youth again return'd
To the clear fountain, where again he burn'd;
His tears defac'd the surface of the well,
With circle after circle, as they fell:
And now the lovely face but half appears,
O'er-run with wrinkles, and deform'd with tears.
"Ah, whither," cries Narcissus, "dost thou fly?
Let me still feed the flame by which I die;

Let me still see, though I'm no further blest."
Then rends his garment off, and beats his breast;
His naked bosom reddens with the blow,
In such a blush as purple clusters show,
Ere yet the Sun's autumnal heats refine
Their sprightly juice, and mellow it to wine.
The glowing beauties of his breast he spies,
And with a new redoubled passion dies.
As wax dissolves, as ice begins to run,
And trickle into drops before the Sun;
So melts the youth, and languishes away,
His beauty withers, and his limbs decay;
And none of those attractive charms remain,
To which the slighted Echo su'd in vain.
  She saw him in his present misery,
Whom, spite of all her wrongs, she griev'd to see.
She answer'd sadly to the lover's moan,
Sigh'd back his sighs, and groan'd to ev'ry groan:
"Ah youth! belov'd in vain," Narcissus cries;
"Ah youth! belov'd in vain," the nymph replies.
"Farewell," says he; the parting sound scarce fell
From his faint lips, but she reply'd "Farewell."
Then on th' unwholesome earth he gasping lies,
Till death shuts up those self-admiring eyes.
To the cold shades his flitting ghost retires,
And in the Stygian waves itself admires.
  For him the Naiads and the Dryads mourn,
Whom the sad Echo answers in her turn;
And now the sister nymphs prepare his urn:
When, looking for his corpse, they only found
A rising stalk, with yellow blossoms crown'd. —JOSEPH ADDISON.

PYRAMUS AND THISBE

[From the *Metamorphoses*, Book IV]

In Babylon, where first her queen, for
state,
Rais'd walls of brick magnificently great,
Liv'd Pyramus and Thisbe, lovely pair!
He found no eastern youth his equal
there,
And she beyond the fairest nymph was
fair.
A closer neighbourhood was never known,
Though two the houses, yet the roof was
one.
Acquaintance grew, th' acquaintance they
improve
To friendship, friendship ripen'd into
love:
Love had been crown'd, but impotently
mad,
What parents could not hinder, they
forbad.
For with fierce flames young Pyramus
still burn'd,
And grateful Thisbe flames as fierce re-
turn'd.
Aloud in words their thoughts they dare
not break,
But silent stand; and silent looks can
speak.
The fire of love, the more it is supprest,
The more it glows, and rages in the
breast.
    When the division-wall was built, a
chink
Was left, the cement unobserv'd to shrink.
So slight the cranny, that it still had
been
For centuries unclos'd, because unseen.
But oh! what thing so small, so secret
lies,
Which 'scapes, if form'd for love, a lover's
eyes?
Ev'n in this narrow chink they quickly
found
A friendly passage for a trackless sound.
Safely they told their sorrows, and their
joys,

In whisper'd murmurs, and a dying noise.
By turns to catch each other's breath they
strove,
And suck'd in all the balmy breeze of
love.
Oft as on diff'rent sides they stood, they
cry'd,
"Malicious wall, thus lovers to divide!
Suppose, thou should'st awhile to us give
place
To lock, and fashion in a close embrace:
But if too much to grant so sweet a bliss,
Indulge at least the pleasure of a kiss.
We scorn ingratitude: to thee, we know,
This conveyance of our minds we owe."
    Thus they their vain petition did re-
new
Till night, and then they softly sigh'd
adieu.
But first they strove to kiss, and that was
all;
Their kisses dy'd untasted on the wall.
Soon as the morn had o'er the stars
prevail'd,
And, warm'd by Phœbus, flow'rs their
dews exhale,
The lovers to their well-known place
return,
Alike they suffer, and alike they mourn.
At last their parents they resolve to
cheat,
(If to deceive in love be call'ed deceit)
To steal by night from home, and thence
unknown
To seek the fields, and quit th' unfaithful
town.
But, to prevent their wand'ring in the
dark,
They both agree to fix upon a mark;
A mark, that could not their designs
expose:
The tomb of Ninus was the mark they
chose.
There they might rest secure beneath the
shade,
Which boughs, with snowy fruit en-
cumber'd, made:
A wide-spread mulberry its rise had took

Just on the margin of a gurgling brook.
Impatient for the friendly dusk they stay,
And chide the slowness of departing day;
In western seas down sunk at last the
    light.
From western seas uprose the shades of
    night.
The loving Thisbe ev'n prevents the hour,
With cautious silence she unlocks the
    door,
And veils her face, and marching thro'
    the gloom
Swiftly arrives at th' assignation-tomb.
For still the fearful sex can fearless
    prove;
Boldly they act, if spirited by love.
When lo! a lioness rush'd o'er the plain,
Grimly besmear'd with blood of oxen
    slain:
And what to the dire sight new horrours
    brought,
To slake her thirst the neighb'ring spring
    she sought.
Which, by the Moon, when trembling
    Thisbe spies,
Wing'd with her fear, swift as the wind,
    she flies;
And in a cave recovers from her fright,
But dropt her veil, confounded in her
    flight.
When sated with repeated draughts, again
The queen of beasts scour'd back along
    the plain,
She found the veil, and mouthing it all
    o'er,
With bloody jaws the lifeless prey she
    tore.
    The youth, who could not cheat his
    guards so soon,
Late came, and noted by the glimmering
    Moon
Some savage feet, now printed on the
    ground,
His cheeks turn'd pale, his limbs no
    vigour found:
But when, advancing on, the veil he spy'd
Distain'd with blood, and ghastly torn,
    he cry'd,

"One night shall death to two young
    lovers give,
But she deserv'd unnumber'd years to
    live!
'Tis I am guilty, I have thee betray'd,
Who came not early, as my charming
    maid.
Whatever slew thee, I the cause remain;
I nam'd, and fix'd the place where thou
    wast slain.
Ye lions from your neighb'ring dens re-
    pair,
Pity the wretch, this impious body tear!
But cowards thus for death can idly cry;
The brave still have it in their pow'r to
    die."
Then to th' appointed tree he hastes
    away,
The veil first gather'd, though all rent it
    lay:
The veil all rent yet still endears,
He kiss'd and kissing, wash'd it with
    his tears.
"Tho' rich," he cry'd, "with many a
    precious stain,
Still from my blood a deeper tincture
    gain."
Then in his breast his shining sword he
    drown'd,
And fell supine, extended on the ground.
As out again the blade he dying drew,
Out spun the blood, and streaming up-
    wards flew.
So if a conduit-pipe e'er burst you saw,
Swift spring the gushing waters thro' the
    flaw:
Then spouting in a bow, they rise on high,
And a new fountain plays amid the sky.
The berries, stain'd with blood, began to
    show
A dark complexion, and forgot their
    snow;
While fatten'd with the flowing gore, the
    root
Was doom'd for ever to a purple fruit.
    Meantime poor Thisbe fear'd, so long
    she stay'd,
Her lover might suspect a perjur'd maid.

Her fright scarce o'er, she strove the
youth to find
With ardent eyes, which spoke an ardent
mind.
Already in his arms, she hears him sigh
At her destruction, which was once so
nigh.
The tomb, the tree, but not the fruit
she knew;
The fruit she doubted for its alter'd
hue.
Still as she doubts, her eyes a body found
Quiv'ring in death, and gasping on the
ground.
She started back, the red her cheeks
forsook,
And ev'ry nerve with thrilling horrours
shook.
So trembles the smooth surface of the
seas,
If brush'd o'er gently with a rising breeze.
But when her view her bleeding love
confess'd,
She shriek'd, she tore her hair, she beat
her breast.
She rais'd the body, and embrac'd it
round,
And bath'd with tears unfeign'd the gap-
ing wound.
Then her warm lips to the cold face
apply'd;
"And is it thus, ah! thus we meet?" she
cry'd:
"My Pyramus! whence sprung the cruel
fate?
My Pyramus!—ah! speak, ere 'tis too
late.
I, thy own Thisbe, but one word implore,
One word thy Thisbe never ask'd before."
At Thisbe's name, awak'd, he open'd
wide
His dying eyes; with dying eyes he try'd
On her to dwell, but clos'd them slow,
and dy'd.
  The fatal cause was now at last ex-
plor'd,
Her veil she knew, she saw his sheathless
sword:

"From thy own hand thy ruin thou hast
found,"
She said; "but love first taught that hand
to wound.
Ev'n I for thee as bold a hand can show,
And love, which shall as true direct the
blow.
I will against the woman's weakness
strive,
And never thee, lamented youth, survive.
The world may say, I caus'd, alas! thy
death,
But saw thee breathless, and resign'd my
breath.
Fate, tho' it conquers, shall no triumph
gain,
Fate, that divides us, still divides in vain.
Now, both our cruel parents, hear my
pray'r;
My pray'r to offer for us both I dare;
Oh! see our ashes in one urn confin'd,
Whom Love at first, and Fate at last has
join'd.
The bliss, you envy'd, is not our request;
Lovers when dead, may sure together rest.
Thou, tree, where now one lifeless lump
is laid,
Ere long o'er two shalt cast a friendly
shade.
Still let our loves from thee be under-
stood,
Still witness in thy purple fruit our
blood."
She spoke, and in her bosom plung'd the
sword
All warm and reeking from its slaughter'd
lord.
  The pray'r, which dying Thisbe had
preferr'd,
Both gods, and parents, with compassion
heard.
The whiteness of the mulberry soon fled,
And, ripening, sadden'd in a dusky
red:
While both their parents their lost chil-
dren mourn,
And mix their ashes in one golden urn.
                    —LAWRENCE EUSDEN.

PERSEUS AND ANDROMEDA

[From the *Metamorphoses,* Book IV]

Now Æolus had with strong chains con-
 fin'd,
And deep imprison'd ev'ry blust'ring
 wind,
The rising Phosphor with a purple light
Did sluggish mortals to new toils invite.
His feet again the valiant Perseus plumes,
And his keen sabre in his hand resumes:
Then nobly spurns the ground, and up-
 ward springs,
And cuts the liquid air with sounding
 wings.
O'er various seas and various lands he
 past,
Till Æthiopia's shore appear'd at last.
Andromeda was there, doom'd to atone
By her own ruin follies not her own:
And if injustice in a god can be,
Such was the Libyan god's unjust decree.
Chain'd to a rock she stood; young Per-
 seus stay'd
His rapid flight, to view the beauteous
 maid.
So sweet her frame, so exquisitely fine,
She seem'd a statue by a hand divine,
Had not the wind her waving tresses
 show'd,
And down her cheeks the melting sorrows
 flow'd.
Her faultless form the hero's bosom fires;
The more he looks, the more he still
 admires.
Th' admirer almost had forgot to fly,
And swift descended, fluttering from on
 high.
"O! virgin, worthy no such chains to
 prove,
But pleasing chains in the soft folds of
 love;
Thy country, and thy name," he said,
 "disclose,
And give a true rehearsal of thy woes."
 A quick reply her bashfulness refus'd,
To the free converse of a man unus'd.
Her rising blushes had concealment found

From her spread hands, but that her
 hands were bound.
She acted to her full extent of pow'r,
And bath'd her face with a fresh, silent
 show'r.
But by degrees in innocence grown bold,
Her name, her country, and her birth
 she told:
And how she suffer'd for her mother's
 pride,
Who with the Nereids once in beauty
 vy'd.
Part yet untold, the seas began to roar,
And mounting billows tumbled to the
 shore.
Above the waves a monster rais'd his
 head,
His body o'er the deep was widely
 spread:
Onward he flounc'd; aloud the virgin
 cries;
Each parent to her shrieks in shrieks
 replies:
But she had deepest cause to rend the
 skies.
Weeping, to her they cling; no sign
 appears
Of help, they only lend their helpless
 tears.
"Too long you vent your sorrows,"
 Perseus said,
"Short is the hour, and swift the time of
 aid.
In me the son of thund'ring Jove behold,
Got in a kindly show'r of fruitful gold.
Medusa's snaky head is now my prey,
And thro' the clouds I boldly wing my
 way.
If such desert be worthy of esteem,
And, if your daughter I from death
 redeem,
Shall she be mine? Shall it not then be
 thought
A bride, so lovely, was too cheaply
 bought?
For her my arms I willingly employ,
If I may beauties, which I save, enjoy."
The parents eagerly the terms embrace:

For who would slight such terms in such
a case?
Nor her alone they promise, but beside,
The dowry of a kingdom with the bride.
    As well-rigg'd galleys, which slaves,
sweating, row,
With their sharp beaks the whiten'd ocean
plough;
So when the monster mov'd, still at his
back
The furrow'd waters left a foamy track.
Now to the rock he was advanc'd so nigh,
Whirl'd from a sling a stone the space
would fly.
Then, bounding, upwards the brave Per-
seus sprung,
And in mid air on hovering pinions hung.
His shadow quickly floated on the main;
The monster could not his wild rage
restrain,
But at the floating shadow leap'd in
vain.
As when Jove's bird a speckled serpent
spies,
Which in the shine of Phœbus basking
lies,
Unseen, he souses down, and bears away,
Truss'd from behind, the vainly-hissing
prey.
To writhe his neck and labour nought
avails,
Too deep th' imperial talons pierce his
scales.
Thus the wing'd hero now descends, now
soars,
And at his pleasure the vast monster
gores.
Full in his back, swift-stooping from
above,
The crooked sabre to its hilt he drove.
The monster rag'd, impatient of the pain,
First bounded high, and then sunk low
again.
Now, like a savage boar, when chaf'd
with wounds,
And bay'd with opening mouths of hungry
hounds,
He on the foe turns with collected might,
Who still eludes him with an airy flight;

And wheeling round, the scaly armour
tries
Of his thick sides; his thinner tail now
plies:
Till from repeated strokes out-gush'd a
flood,
And the waves redden'd with the stream-
ing blood.
At last the dropping wings, befoam'd
all o'er,
With flaggy heaviness their master bore:
A rock he spy'd, whose humble head was
low,
Bare at an ebb, but cover'd at a flow.
A ridgy hold he, thither flying, gain'd,
And with one hand his bending weight
sustain'd;
With th' other vigorous blows he dealt
around,
And the home-thrusts th' expiring mon-
ster own'd.
In deaf'ning shouts the glad applauses
rise,
And peal on peal runs rattling thro' the
skies.
The saviour-youth the royal pair confess,
And with heav'd hands their daughter's
bride-groom bless.
The beauteous bride moves on, now
loos'd from chains,
The cause, and sweet reward of all the
hero's pains.
           —THOMAS EUSDEN.

THE RAPE OF PROSERPINE

[From the *Metamorphoses,* Book V]

Near Enna's walls a spacious lake is
spread,
Fam'd for the sweetly-singing swans it
bred;
Pergusa is its name: and never more
Were heard, or sweeter, on Cayster's
shore.
Woods crown the lake; and Phœbus ne'er
invades
The tufted fences, or offends the shades:

Fresh fragrant breezes fan the verdant
    bow'rs,
And the moist ground smiles with
    enamel'd flow'rs.
The cheerful birds their airy carols sing,
And the whole year is one eternal spring.
  Here, while young Proserpine, among
    the maids,
Diverts herself in these delicious shades;
While like a child with busy speed and
    care
She gathers lilies here, and vi'lets there;
While first to fill her little lap she strives,
Hell's grizly monarch at the shade
    arrives;
Sees her thus sporting on the flow'ry
    green,
And loves the blooming maid, as soon as
    seen.
His urgent flame impatient of delay,
Swift as the thought he seiz'd the beaute-
    ous prey,
And bore her in his sooty car away.
The frighted goddess to her mother cries,
But all in vain, for now far off she flies.
Far she behind her leaves her virgin
    train;
To them too cries, and cries to them in
    vain.
And while with passion she repeats her
    call,
The vi'lets from her lap, and lilies fall:
She misses them, poor heart! and makes
  . new moan;
Her lilies, ah! are lost, her vi'lets gone.
  O'er hills, the ravisher, and valleys
    speeds,
By name encouraging his foamy steeds;
He rattles o'er their necks the rusty reins,
And ruffles with the stroke their shaggy
    manes.
O'er lakes he whirls his flying wheels,
    and comes
To the Palici breathing sulph'rous fumes.
And thence to where the Bacchiads of
    renown
Between unequal havens built their town;
Where Arethusa, round th' imprison'd
  sea,

Extends her crooked coast to Cyane;
The nymph who gave the neighb'ring
    lake a name,
Of all Sicilian nymphs the first in fame.
She from the waves advanc'd her beaute-
    ous head,
The goddess knew, and thus to Pluto
    said;
"Farther thou shalt not with the virgin
    run;
Ceres unwilling, canst thou be her son?
The maid should be by sweet persuasion
    won.
Force suits not with the softness of the
    fair;
For, if great things with small I may
    compare,
Me Anapis once lov'd; a milder course
He took, and won me by his words, nor
    force."
  Then stretching out her arms, she stopt
    his way;
But he, impatient of the shortest stay,
Throws to his dreadful steeds the
    slacken'd rein,
And strikes his iron sceptre through the
    main;
The depths profound thro' yielding waves
    he cleaves,
And to Hell's centre a free passage leaves;
Down sinks his chariot, and his realms
    of night
The god soon reaches with a rapid flight.
        —ARTHUR MAYNWARING.

NIOBE

[From the *Metamorphoses*, Book VI]

Swift thro' the Phrygian towns the
    rumour flies,
And the strange news each female tongue
    employs:
Niobe, who before she married knew
The famous nymph, now found the story
    true;
Yet, unreclaimed by poor Arachne's fate,
Vainly above the gods assum'd a state.

Her husband's fame, their family's descent,
Their pow'r, and rich dominion's wide extent,
Might well have justify'd a decent pride;
But not on these alone the dame rely'd:
Her lovely progeny that far excell'd,
The mother's heart with vain ambition swell'd:
The happiest mother not unjustly styl'd,
Had no conceited thoughts her tow'ring fancy fill'd.

For once a prophetess, with zeal inspir'd,
Their slow neglect to warm devotion fir'd;
Thro' ev'ry street of Thebes who ran possess'd,
And thus in accents wild her charge express'd:
"Haste, haste, ye Theban matrons, and adore,
With hallow'd rites, Latona's mighty pow'r;
And to the heav'nly twins that from her spring,
With laurel crown'd, your smoking incense bring."
Straight the great summons ev'ry dame obey'd,
And due submission to the goddess paid:
Graceful, with laurel chaplets dress'd they came,
And offer'd incense in the sacred flame.

Meanwhile, surrounded with a courtly guard,
The royal Niobe in state appear'd;
Attir'd in robes embroider'd o'er with gold,
And mad with rage, yet lovely to behold:
Her comely tresses, trembling as she stood,
Down her fine neck with easy motion flow'd;
Then, darting round a proud disdainful look,
In haughty tone her hasty passion broke,
And thus began; "What madness this, to court

A goddess, founded merely on report?
Dare ye a poor pretended pow'r invoke,
While yet no altars to my godhead smoke?
Mine, whose immediate lineage stands confess'd
From Tantalus, the only mortal guest
That e'er the gods admitted to their feast.
A sister of the Pleiads gave me birth;
And Atlas, mightiest mountain upon Earth,
Who bears the globe of all the stars above,
My grandsire was, and Atlas sprung from Jove.
The Theban towns my majesty adore,
And neighb'ring Phrygia trembles at my pow'r:
Rais'd by my husband's lute, with turrets crown'd,
Our lofty city stands secur'd around.
Within my court, where'er I turn my eyes,
Unbounded treasures to my prospect rise:
With these my face I modestly may name,
As not unworthy of so high a claim;
Seven are my daughters of a form divine,
With seven fair sons, an indefective line.
Go, fools! consider this; and ask the cause
From which my pride its strong presumption draws:
Consider this; and then prefer to me
Cæus the Titan's vagrant progeny;
To whom, in travail, the whole spacious earth
No room afforded for her spurious birth.
Not the least part in earth, in Heav'n, or seas,
Would grant your out-law'd goddess any ease:
Till pitying hers, from his own wand'ring case,
Delos, the floating island, gave a place.
There she a mother was, of two at most;
Only the seventh part of what I boast.
My joys are all beyond suspicion fix'd,
With no pollutions of misfortune mix'd;
Safe on the basis of my pow'r I stand,
Above the reach of Fortune's fickle hand.

Lessen she may my inexhausted store,
And much destroy, yet still must leave
    me more.
Suppose it possible that some may die
Of this my numerous lovely progeny;
Still with Latona I might safely vie:
Who, by her scanty breed, scarce fit to
    name,
But just escapes the childless woman's
    shame.
Go then, with speed your laurel'd heads
    uncrown,
And leave the silly farce you have begun."
    The tim'rous throng their sacred rites
      forbore,
And from their heads the verdant laurel
    tore;
Their haughty queen they with regret
    obey'd,
And still in gentle murmurs softly pray'd.
    High on the top of Cynthus' shady
      mount,
With grief the goddess saw the base
    affront;
And, the abuse revolving in her breast,
The mother her twin-offspring thus
    addrest:
    "Lo I, my children, who with comfort
      knew
Your godlike birth, and thence my glory
    drew;
And thence have claim'd precedency of
    place
From all but Juno of the heav'nly race,
Must now despair, and languish in dis-
    grace.
My godhead question'd, and all rites
    divine,
Unless you succour, banish'd from my
    shrine.
Nay more, the imp of Tantalus has flung
Reflexions with her vile paternal tongue;
Has dar'd prefer her mortal breed to
    mine,
And call'd me childless; which, just Fate,
    may she repine!"
    When to urge more the goddess was
      prepar'd,

Phoebus in haste replies, "Too much
    we've heard,
And ev'ry moment's lost, while vengeance
    is deferr'd."
Diana spoke the same. Then both en-
    shroud
Their heav'nly bodies in a sable cloud;
And to the Theban tow'rs descending
    light,
Through the soft yielding air direct their
    flight.
    Without the wall there lies a cham-
      paign ground,
With even surface, far extending round,
Beaten and level'd, while it daily feels
The trampling horse, and chariot's grind-
    ing wheels.
Part of Niobe's young rival breed,
Practising there to ride the manag'd
    steed,
Their bridles boss'd with gold, were
    mounted high
On stately furniture of Tyrian dye.
Of these, Ismenos, who by birth had been
The first fair issue of the fruitful queen,
Just as he drew the rein to guide his
    horse
Around the compass of the circling course,
Sigh'd deeply, and the pangs of smart
    express'd,
While the shaft stuck engorg'd within his
    breast:
And, the reins dropping from his dying
    hand,
He sunk quite down, and tumbled on the
    sand.
Sipylus next the rattling quiver heard,
And with full speed for his escape pre-
    par'd.
As when the pilot from the black'ning
    skies
A gath'ring storm of wintry rain descries,
His sails unfurl'd, and crowded all with
    wind,
He strives to leave the threat'ning cloud
    behind:
So fled the youth; but an unerring dart
O'ertook him, quick discharg'd, and sped
    with art;

Fix'd in his neck behind, it trembling
stood,
And at his throat display'd the point be-
smear'd with blood.
Prone, as his posture was, he tumbled
o'er,
And bath'd his courser's mane with
streaming gore.
Next at young Phædimus they took their
aim,
And Tantalus, who bore his grandsire's
name:
These, when their other exercise was
done,
To try the wrestler's oily sport begun:
And, straining ev'ry nerve, their skill ex-
press'd
In closest grapple, joining breast to
breast:
When from the bending bow an arrow
sent,
Join'd as they were, thro' both their
bodies went:
Both groan'd, and writhing both their
limbs with pain,
They fell together bleeding on the plain;
Then both their languid eyeballs faintly
roll,
And thus together breathe away their
soul.
With grief Alphenor saw their doleful
plight,
And smote his breast, and sicken'd at the
sight;
Then to their succour ran with eager
haste.
And, fondly griev'd, their stiff'ning limbs
embrac'd;
But in the action falls: a thrilling dart,
By Phœbus guided, pierc'd him to the
heart.
This, as they drew it forth, his midriff
tore,
Its barbed point the fleshy fragments
bore,
And let the soul gush out in streams of
purple gore.
But Damasichthon, by a double wound,

Beardless, and young, lay gasping on the
ground.
Fix'd in his sinewy ham, the steely point
Stuck thro' his knee, and pierc'd the nerv-
ous joint:
And, as he stoop'd to tug the painful dart,
Another struck him in a vital part;
Shot through his wezon, by the wing it
hung,
The life-blood forc'd it out, and darting
upward sprung.
Ilioneus, the last, with terrour stands,
Lifting in pray'r his unavailing hands;
And, ignorant from whom his griefs arise,
"Spare me, O all ye heav'nly pow'rs," he
cries:
Phœbus was touch'd too late, the sound-
ing bow
Had sent the shaft, and struck the fatal
blow;
Which yet but gently gor'd his tender
side,
So by a slight and easy wound he dy'd.
Swift to the mother's ears the rumour
came,
And doleful sighs the heavy news pro-
claim;
With anger and surprise inflam'd by
turns,
In furious rage her haughty stomach
burns:
First she disputes th' effects of heav'nly
pow'r,
Then at their daring boldness wonders
more;
For poor Amphion with sore grief dis-
trest,
Hoping to soothe his cares by endless rest,
Had sheath'd a dagger in his wretched
breast.
And she, who toss'd her high disdainful
head,
When thro' the streets in solemn pomp
she led
The throng that from Latona's altar fled,
Assuming state beyond the proudest
queen,
Was now the miserablest object seen.

Prostrate among the clay-cold dead she
  fell,
And kiss'd an undistinguish'd last fare-
  well.
Then, her pale arms advancing to the
  skies,
"Cruel Latona! triumph now," she cries.
"My grieving soul in bitter anguish
  drench,
And with my woes your thirsty passion
  quench;
Feast your black malice at a price thus
  dear,
While the sore pangs of sev'n such deaths
  I bear.
Triumph, too cruel rival, and display
Your conqu'ring standard; for you've won
  the day.
Yet I'll excel; for yet, though sev'n are
  slain,
Superior still in number I remain."
Scarce had she spoke; the bow-string's
  twanging sound
Was heard, and dealt fresh terrours all
  around;
Which all, but Niobe alone, confound.
Stunn'd, and obdurate by her load of
  grief,
Insensible she sits, nor hopes relief.
  Before the funeral biers, all weeping
  sad,
Her daughters stood, in vests of sable
  clad.
When one, surpris'd, and stung with sud-
  den smart,
In vain attempts to draw the sticking
  dart:
But to grim death her blooming youth
  resigns,
And o'er her brothers' corpse her dying
  head reclines.
This to assuage her mother's anguish
  tries,
And, silenc'd in the pious action, dies;
Shot by a secret arrow, wing'd with death,
Her falt'ring lips but only gasp'd for
  breath.
One, on her dying sister, breathes her
  last;

Vainly in flight another's hopes are plac'd:
This hiding, from her fate a shelter
  seeks;
That trembling stands, and fills the air
  with shrieks.
And all in vain; for now all six had found
Their way to death, each by a diff'rent
  wound.
The last with eager care the mother
  veil'd,
Behind her spreading mantle close con-
  ceal'd,
And with her body guarded, as a shield.
"Only for this, this youngest, I implore,
Grant me this one request, I ask no more;
O grant me this!" she passionately cries:
But while she speaks, the destin'd virgin
  dies.
  Widow'd, and childless, lamentable
  state!
A doleful sight, among the dead she sate;
Harden'd with woes, a statue of despair,
To ev'ry breath of wind unmov'd her
  hair;
Her cheek still redd'ning, but its colour
  dead,
Faded her eyes, and set within her head.
No more her pliant tongue its motion
  keeps,
But stands congeal'd within her frozen
  lips.
Stagnate, and dull, within her purple
  veins,
Its current stopp'd, the lifeless blood re-
  mains.
Her feet their usual offices refuse,
Her arms and neck their graceful gestures
  lose:
Action and life from ev'ry part are gone,
And ev'n her entrails turn to solid stone;
Yet still she weeps, and whirl'd by stormy
  winds,
Borne thro' the air her native country
  finds;
There fix'd, she stands upon a bleaky hill,
There yet her marble cheeks eternal tears
  distil.

  —SAMUEL CROXALL.

DÆDALUS AND ICARUS

[From the *Metamorphoses*, Book VIII]

In tedious exile now too long detain'd,
Dædalus languish'd for his native land:
The sea foreclos'd his flight; yet thus he
said;
"Though earth and water in subjection
laid,
O cruel Minos, thy dominion be,
We'll go through air; for sure the air is
free."
Then to new arts his cunning thought
applies,
And to improve the work of nature tries.
A row of quills in gradual order plac'd,
Rise by degrees in length from first to
last;
As on a cliff th' ascending thicket grows,
Or different reeds the rural pipe compose.
Along the middle runs a twine of flax,
The bottom stems are join'd by pliant
wax.
Thus, well compact, a hollow bending
brings
The fine composure into real wings.
　His boy, young Icarus, that near him
stood,
Unthinking of his fate, with smiles
pursu'd
The floating feathers, which the moving
air
Bore loosely from the ground, and wafted
here and there;
Or with the wax impertinently play'd,
And with his childish tricks the great
design delay'd.
　The final master-stroke at last impos'd,
And now the neat machine completely
clos'd;
Fitting his pinions on, a flight he tries,
And hung self-balanc'd in the beaten
skies.
Then thus instructs his child: "My boy,
take care
To wing your course along the middle air;
If low, the surges wet your flagging
plumes;

If high, the Sun the melting wax con-
sumes:
Steer between both: nor to the northern
skies,
Nor south Orion, turn your giddy eyes:
But follow me: let me before you lay
Rules for the flight, and mark the path-
less way."
Then teaching, with a fond concern, his
son,
He took the untry'd wings, and fix'd them
on;
But fix'd with trembling hands, and as
he speaks,
The tears roll gently down his aged
cheeks:
Then kiss'd, and in his arms embrac'd
him fast,
But knew not this embrace must be the
last.
And mounting upward, as he wings his
flight,
Back on his charge he turns his aching
sight;
As parent birds, when first their callow
care
Leave the high nest to tempt the liquid
air.
Then cheers him on, and oft, with fatal
art,
Reminds the stripling to perform his part.
　These, as the angler at the silent brook,
Or mountain-shepherd leaning on his
crook,
Or gaping ploughman, from the vale
descries,
They stare, and view them with religious
eyes,
And straight conclude them gods; since
none, but they,
Through their own azure skies could find
a way.
Now Delos, Paros, on the left are seen,
And Samos, favour'd by Jove's haughty
queen;
Upon the right, the isle Lebynthos nam'd,
And fair Calymne for its honey fam'd.
When now the boy, whose childish
thoughts aspire

To loftier aims, and make him ramble
    higher,
Grown wild, and wanton, more em-
    bolden'd flies
Far from his guide, and soars among the
    skies,
The soft'ning wax, that felt a nearer sun,
Dissolv'd apace, and soon began to run.
The youth in vain his melting pinions
    shakes;
His feathers gone, no longer air he takes.
"Oh! father, father," as he strove to cry,
Down to the sea he tumbled from on high,
And found his fate; yet still subsists by
    fame,
Among those waters that retain his name.
    The father, now no more a father,
    cries,
"Ho, Icarus! where are you?" as he flies;
Where shall I seek my boy?" he cries
    again,
And saw his feathers scatter'd on the
    main.
Then curs'd his art; and funeral rites
    conferr'd,
Naming the country from the youth
    interr'd.
              —SAMUEL CROXALL.

BAUCIS AND PHILEMON

[From the *Metamorphoses*, Book VIII]

Heav'n's pow'r is infinite: earth, air, and
    sea,
The manufactured mass, the making
    pow'r obey:
By proof to clear your doubt; in Phrygian
    ground
Two neighb'ring trees, with walls en-
    compass'd round,
Stand on a mod'rate rise, with wonder
    shown,
One a hard oak, a softer linden one:
I saw the place, and them, by Pittheus
    sent
To Phrygian realms; my grandsire's
    government.

Not far from thence is seen a lake, the
    haunt
Of coots, and of the fishing cormorant:
Here Jove with Hermes came; but in
    disguise
Of mortal men conceal'd their deities;
One laid aside his thunder, one his rod;
And many toilsome steps together trod:
For harbour at a thousand doors they
    knock'd,
Not one of all the thousand but was
    lock'd.
At last a hospitable house they found,
A homely shed; the roof, not far from
    ground,
Was thatch'd with reeds and straw, to-
    gether bound.
    There Baucis and Philemon liv'd, and
    there
Had liv'd long marry'd, and a happy
    pair:
Now old in love, though little was their
    store,
Inur'd to want, their poverty they bore,
Nor aim'd at wealth, professing to be
    poor.
For master, or for servant here to call,
Was all alike, where only two were all.
Command was none, where equal love
    was paid,
Or rather both commanded, both obey'd.
    From lofty roofs the gods repuls'd
    before,
Now stooping, enter'd through the little
    door:
The man (their hearty welcome first ex-
    press'd)
A common settle drew for either guest,
Inviting each his weary limbs to rest.
But ere they sat, officious Baucis lays
Two cushions stuff'd with straw, the seat
    to raise;
Coarse, but the best she had: then rakes
    the load
Of ashes from the hearth, and spreads
    abroad
The living coals; and, lest they should
    expire,

With leaves and bark she feeds her infant
    fire:
It smokes; and then with trembling breath
    she blows,
Till in a cheerful blaze the flames arose.
With brush-wood, and with chips she
    strengthens these,
And adds at last the boughs of rotten
    trees.
The fire thus form'd, she sets the kettle
    on,
(Like burnish'd gold the little seether
    shone)
Next took the coleworts which her hus-
    band got
From his own ground, (a small well-
    water'd spot;)
She stripp'd the stalks of all their leaves;
    the best
She cull'd, and them with handy care she
    drest.
High o'er the hearth a chine of bacon
    hung;
Good old Philemon siez'd it with a prong,
And from the sooty rafter drew it down,
Then cut a slice, but scarce enough for
    one;
Yet a large portion of a little store,
Which for their sakes alone he wish'd
    were more.
This in the pot he plung'd without delay,
To tame the flesh, and drive the salt
    away.
The time between, before the fire they
    sat,
And shorten'd the delay by pleasing chat.
    A beam there was, on which a beechen
    pail
Hung by the handle, on a driven nail:
This fill'd with water, gently warm'd,
    they set
Before their guests; in this they bath'd
    their feet,
And after with clean towels dry'd their
    sweat.
This done, the host produc'd the genial
    bed,
Shallow the feet, the borders, and the
    stead,

Which with no costly coverlet they
    spread,
But coarse old garments; yet such robes
    as these
They laid alone at feasts, on holidays.
The good old housewife, tucking up her
    gown,
The table sets; th' invited gods lie down.
The trivet-table of a foot was lame,
A blot which prudent Baucis overcame,
Who thrust beneath the limping leg a
    sherd,
So was the mended board exactly rear'd:
Then rubb'd it o'er with newly gather'd
    mint,
A wholesome herb, that breath'd a grate-
    ful scent.
Pallas began the feast, where first was
    seen
The party-colour'd olive, black and green:
Autumnal cornels next in order serv'd,
In lees of wine well pickled, and pre-
    serv'd.
A garden-salad was the third supply,
Of endive, radishes, and succory:
Then curds and cream, the flow'r of coun-
    try fare,
And new-laid eggs, which Baucis' busy
    care
Turn'd by a gentle fire, and roasted rare.
All these in earthenware were serv'd to
    board;
And next in place an earthen pitcher,
    stor'd
With liquor of the best the cottage could
    afford.
This was the table's ornament and pride,
With figures wrought: like pages at his
    side
Stood beechen bowls; and these were
    shining clean,
Varnish'd with wax without, and lin'd
    within.
By this the boiling kettle had prepar'd,
And to the table sent the smoking lard;
On which with eager appetite they dine,
A sav'ry bit, that serv'd to relish wine:
The wine itself was suiting to the rest,

Still working in the must, and lately
press'd.
The second course succeeds like that
before,
Plums, apples, nuts, and of their wintry
store
Dry figs, and grapes, and wrinkled dates
were set
In canisters, t' enlarge the little treat:
All these a milk-white honey-comb sur-
round,
Which in the midst the country banquet
crown'd:
But the kind hosts their entertainment
grace
With hearty welcome, and an open face:
In all they did, you might discern with
ease
A willing mind, and a desire to please.
   Meantime the beechen bowls went
round, and still,
Though often empty'd, were observ'd to
fill;
Fill'd without hands, and of their own
accord
Ran without feet, and danc'd about the
board.
Devotion seiz'd the pair, to see the feast
With wine, and of no common grape,
increas'd;
And up they held their hands, and fell to
pray'r,
Excusing, as they could, their country
fare.
One goose they had, ('twas all they could
allow)
A wakeful sentry, and on duty now,
Whom to the gods for sacrifice they
vow:
Her with malicious zeal the couple
view'd;
She ran for life, and limping they
pursu'd:
Full well the fowl perceiv'd their bad
intent,
And would not make her master's com-
pliment;
But persecuted, to the Pow'rs she flies,

And close between the legs of Jove she
lies:
He with a gracious ear the suppliant
heard,
And sav'd her life; the what he was
declar'd,
And own'd the god. "The neighbour-
hood," said he,
"Shall justly perish for impiety;
You stand alone exempted; but obey
With speed, and follow where we lead
the way:
Leave these accurs'd; and to the moun-
tain's height
Ascend; nor once look backward in your
flight."
   They haste, and what their tardy feet
deny'd,
The trusty staff (their better leg) sup-
ply'd.
An arrow's flight they wanted to the top,
And there secure, but spent with travel,
stop;
Then turn their now-no-more-forbidden
eyes;
Lost in a lake the floated level lies:
A watery desert covers all the plains,
Their cot alone, as in an isle, remains.
Wond'ring with weeping eyes, while they
deplore
Their neighbours' fate, and country now
no more,
Their little shed, scarce large enough for
two,
Seems from the ground, increas'd in
height and bulk, to grow.
A stately temple shoots within the skies,
The crotches of their cot in columns rise:
The pavement polish'd marble they be-
hold,
The gates with sculpture grac'd, the spires
and tiles of gold.
   Then thus the sire of gods, with looks
serene:
"Speak thy desire, thou only just of men;
And thou, O woman, only worthy found
To be with such a man in marriage
bound."

Awhile they whisper; then to Jove address'd,
Philemon thus prefers their joint request:
"We crave to serve before your sacred shrine,
And offer at your altar rites divine;
And since not any action of our life
Has been polluted with domestic strife;
We beg one hour of death, that neither she
With widow'd tears may live to bury me,
Nor weeping I, with wither'd arms, may bear
My breathless Baucis to the sepulchre."
  The godheads sign their suit. They run the race
In the same tenour all th' appointed space;
Then, when their hour was come, while they relate
These past adventures at the temple gate,
Old Baucis is by old Philemon seen
Sprouting with sudden leaves of sprightly green:
Old Baucis look'd where old Philemon stood,
And saw his lengthen'd arms a sprouting wood:
New roots their fasten'd feet begin to bind,
Their bodies stiffen in a rising rind;
Then, ere the bark about their shoulders grew,
They give and take at once their last adieu.
At once, "Farewell, O faithful spouse," they said;
At once th' incroaching rinds their closing lips invade.
Ev'n yet an ancient Tyanæan shows
A spreading oak, that near a linden grows;
The neighbourhood confirm the prodigy,
Grave men, not vain of tongue, or like to lie.
I myself saw the garlands on their boughs,
And tablets hung for gifts of granted vows,

And off'ring fresher up, with pious pray'r,
"The good," said I, "are God's peculiar care,
And such as honour Heav'n, shall heav'nly honour share."
                                —JOHN DRYDEN.

ORPHEUS AND EURYDICE

[From the *Metamorphoses*, Book X]

Thence, in his saffron robe, for distant Thrace,
Hymen departs, through air's unmeasur'd space;
By Orpheus call'd, the nuptial pow'r attends,
But with ill-omen'd augury descends:
Nor cheerful look'd the god, nor prosp'rous spoke,
Nor blaz'd his torch, but wept in hissing smoke.
In vain they whirl it round, in vain they shake,
No rapid motion can its flames awake.
  With dread these inauspicious signs were view'd,
And soon a more disastrous end ensu'd;
For as the bride, amid the Naiad train,
Ran joyful sporting o'er the flow'ry plain,
A venom'd viper bit her as she pass'd;
Instant she fell, and sudden breath'd her last.
  When long his loss the Thracian had deplor'd,
Not by superior pow'rs to be restor'd;
Inflam'd by love, and urg'd by deep despair,
He leaves the realms of light, and upper air;
Daring to tread the dark Tenarian road,
And tempt the shades in their obscure abode;
Through gliding spectres of th' interr'd to go,
And phantom people of the world below;
Persephone he seeks, and him who reigns
O'er ghosts, and Hell's uncomfortable plains.

Arriv'd, he, tuning to his voice his strings,
Thus to the king and queen of shadows
    sings.
  "Ye pow'rs, who under Earth your
    realms extend,
To whom all mortals must one day
    descend;
If here 'tis granted sacred truth to tell,
I come not curious to explore your Hell;
Nor come to boast (by vain ambition
    fir'd)
How Cerberus at my approach retir'd.
My wife alone I seek; for her lov'd sake
These terrours I support, this journey
    take.
She, luckless wand'ring, or by fate mis-
    led,
Chanc'd on a lurking viper's crest to
    tread;
The vengeful beast, inflam'd with fury,
    starts,
And through her heel his deathful venom
    darts.
Thus was she snatch'd untimely to her
    tomb;
Her growing years cut short, and spring-
    ing bloom.
Long I my loss endeavour'd to sustain,
And strongly strove, but strove, alas! in
    vain:
At length I yielded, won by mighty Love;
Well known is that omnipotence above!
But here, I doubt, his unfelt influence
    fails;
And yet a hope within my heart prevails,
That here, ev'n here, he has been known
    of old;
At least if truth be by tradition told;
If fame of former rapes belief may find,
You both by love, and love alone were
    join'd.
Now by the horrours which these realms
    surround;
By the vast chaos of these depths pro-
    found;
By the sad silence which eternal reigns
O'er all the waste of these wide-stretch-
    ing plains,
Let me again Eurydice receive,

Let Fate her quick-spun thread of life
    re-weave.
All our possessions are but loans from
    you,
And soon, or late, you must be paid your
    due:
Hither we haste to human-kind's last seat,
Your endless empire, and our sure retreat.
She too, when ripen'd years she shall
    attain,
Must, of avoidless right, be yours again:
I but the transient use of that require,
Which soon, too soon, I must resign
    entire.
But if the destinies refuse my vow,
And no remission of her doom allow;
Know, I'm determin'd to return no more;
So both retain, or both to life restore."
  Thus, while the bard melodiously com-
    plains,
And to his lyre accords his vocal strains,
The very bloodless shades attention keep,
And silent, seem compassionate to weep;
Ev'n Tantalus his flood unthirsty views,
Nor flies the stream, nor he the stream
    pursues;
Ixion's wond'ring wheel its whirl sus-
    pends,
And the voracious vulture, charm'd
    attends;
No more the Belides their toil bemoan,
And Sisyphus, reclin'd, sits list'ning on
    his stone.
  Then first ('tis said) by sacred verse
    subdu'd,
The Furies felt their cheeks with tears
    bedew'd;
Nor could the rigid king, or queen of
    Hell,
Th' impulse of pity in their hearts repel.
  Now, from a troop of shades that last
    arriv'd
Eurydice was call'd, and stood reviv'd:
Slow she advanc'd, and halting seem'd
    to feel
The fatal wound, yet painful in her heel.
Thus he obtains the suit so much desir'd,
On strict observance of the terms re-
    quir'd:

For if, before he reach the realms of air,
He backward cast his eyes to view the fair,
The forfeit grant, that instant, void is made,
And she for ever left a lifeless shade.
 Now through the noiseless throng their way they bend,
And both with pain the rugged road ascend;
Dark was the path, and difficult, and steep,
And thick with vapours from the smoky deep.
They well nigh now had pass'd the bounds of night,
And just approach'd the margin of the light,
When he, mistrusting lest her steps might stray,
And gladsome of the glimpse of dawning day,
His longing eyes, impatient, backward cast,
To catch a lover's look, but look'd his last;
For, instant dying, she again descends,
While he to empty air his arm extends.
Again she dy'd, nor yet her lord reprov'd;
What could she say, but that too well he lov'd?
One last farewell she spoke, which scarce he heard;
So soon she dropt, so sudden disappear'd.
 All stunn'd he stood, when thus his wife he view'd
By second fate, and double death subdu'd:
Not more amazement by that wretch was shown,
Whom Cerberus beholding turn'd to stone;
Nor Olenus could more astonish'd look,
When on himself Lethea's fault he took,
His beauteous wife, who too secure had dar'd
Her face to vie with goddesses compar'd:

Once join'd by love, they stand united still,
Turn'd to contiguous rocks on Ida's hill.
 Now to repass the Styx in vain he tries:
Charon averse, his pressing suit denies.
Sev'n days entire, along th' infernal shores,
Disconsolate, the bard Eurydice deplores;
Defil'd with filth his robe, with tears his cheeks,
No sustenance but grief, and cares, he seeks:
Of rigid fate incessant he complains,
And Hell's inexorable gods arraigns.
This ended, to high Rhodope he hastes,
And Hæmus' mountain, bleak with northern blasts.
 And now his yearly race the circling Sun
Had thrice complete through wat'ry Pisces run,
Since Orpheus fled the face of womankind,
And all soft union with the sex declin'd.
Whether his ill success this change had bred,
Or binding vows made to his former bed;
Whate'er the cause, in vain the nymphs contest,
With rival eyes to warm his frozen breast:
For ev'ry nymph with love his lays inspir'd,
But ev'ry nymph repuls'd, with grief retir'd.

    —WILLIAM CONGREVE.

ATALANTA

[From the *Metamorphoses*, Book X]

Perhaps thou may'st have heard a virgin's name,
Who still in swiftness swiftest youths o'ercame.
Wond'rous! that female weakness should out-do
A manly strength; the wonder yet is true.
'Twas doubtful, if her triumphs in the field

Did to her form's triumphant glories
yield;
Whether her face could with more ease
decoy
A crowd of lovers, or her feet destroy.
For once Apollo she implor'd to show
If courteous fates a consort would allow:
"A consort brings thy ruin," he reply'd;
"O! learn to want the pleasures of a
bride!
Nor shalt thou want them to thy wretched
cost,
And Atalanta living shall be lost."
With such a rueful fate th' affrighted
maid
Sought green recesses in the woodland
glade;
Nor sighing suitors her resolve could
move,
She bade them show their speed, to show
their love.
He only, who could conquer in the race,
Might hope the conquer'd virgin to em-
brace;
While he, whose tardy feet had lagg'd
behind,
Was doom'd the sad reward of death to
find.
Though great the prize, yet rigid the de-
cree,
But blind with beauty, who can rigour
see?
Ev'n on those laws the fair they rashly
sought,
And danger in excess of love forgot.
　　There sat Hippomenes, prepar'd to
blame
In lovers such extravagance of flame.
"And must," he said, "the blessing of a
wife
Be dearly purchas'd by a risk of life?"
But when he saw the wonders of her face,
And her limbs naked, springing to the
race,
(Her limbs, as exquisitely turn'd as mine,
Or if a woman thou, might vie with
thine,)
With lifted hands he cry'd, "Forgive the
tongue

Which durst, ye youths, your well-tim'd
courage wrong.
I knew not that the nympth, for whom
you strove,
Deserv'd th' unbounded transports of
your love."
He saw, admir'd, and thus her spotless
frame
He prais'd, and praising, kindled his own
flame.
A rival now to all the youths who run,
Envious, he fears they should not be
undone.
"But why," reflects he, "idly thus is
shown
The fate of others, yet untry'd my own?
The coward must not in love's aid de-
pend;
The god was ever to the bold a friend."
Meantime the virgin flies, or seems to
fly,
Swift as a Scythian arrow cleaves the
sky:
Still more and more the youth her charms
admires,
The race itself t' exalt her charms con-
spires.
The golden pinions, which her feet adorn,
In wanton flutt'rings by the wind are
borne.
Down from her head the long, fair
tresses flow
And sport with lovely negligence below.
The waving ribbands, which her buskins
tie,
Her snowy skin with waving purple dye;
As crimson veils in palaces display'd,
To the white marble lend a blushing
shade.
Not long he gaz'd, yet while he gaz'd, she
gain'd
The goal, and the victorious wreath ob-
tain'd.
The vanquish'd sigh, and, as the law
decreed,
Pay the dire forfeit, and prepare to bleed.
　　Then rose Hippomenes, not yet afraid,
And fix'd his eyes full on the beauteous
maid.

"Where is," he cry'd, "the mighty conquest won,
To distance those, who want the nerves to run?
Here prove superior strength, nor shall it be
Thy loss of glory, if excell'd by me.
High my descent, near Neptune I aspire,
For Neptune was grand-parent to my sire.
From that great god the fourth myself I trace,
Nor sink my virtues yet beneath my race.
Thou, from Hippomenes o'ercome, may'st claim
An envy'd triumph, and a deathless fame."
  While thus the youth the virgin pow'r defies,
Silent she views him still with softer eyes.
Thoughts in her breast a doubtful strife begin,
If 'tis not happier now to lose, than win.
"What god, a foe to beauty, would destroy
The promis'd ripeness of this blooming boy?
With his life's danger does he seek my bed?
Scarce am I half so greatly worth," she said:
"Nor has his beauty mov'd my breast to love,
And yet, I own, such beauty well might move.
'Tis not his charms, 'tis pity would engage
My soul to spare the greenness of his age:
What, that heroic courage fires his breast,
And shines through brave disdain of fate confest?
What, that his patronage by close degrees
Springs from the imperial ruler of the seas?
Then add the love, which bids him undertake
The race, and dare to perish for my sake.
Of bloody nuptials, heedless youth, beware!
Fly, timely fly from a too barb'rous fair.

At pleasure choose; thy love will be repaid
By a less foolish, and more beauteous maid.
But why this tenderness, before unknown?
Why beats and pants my breast for him alone?
His eyes have seen his num'rous rivals yield;
Let him too share the rigour of the field,
Since, by their fates untaught, his own he courts,
And thus with ruin insolently sports.
Yet for what crime shall he his death receive?
Is it a crime with me to wish to live?
Shall his kind passion his destruction prove?
Is this the fatal recompense of love?
So fair a youth, destroy'd, would conquest shame,
And nymphs eternally detest my fame.
Still why should nymphs my guiltless fame upbraid?
Did I the fond adventurer persuade?
Alas! I wish thou wouldst the course decline,
Or that my swiftness was excell'd by thine.
See! what a virgin's bloom adorns the boy!
Why wilt thou run, and why thyself destroy?
Hippomenes! Oh that I ne'er had been
By those bright eyes unfortunately seen!
Ah! tempt not thus a swift, untimely fate;
Thy life is worthy of the longest date.
Were I left wretched, did the galling chain
Of rigid gods not my free choice restrain,
By thee alone I could with joy be led
To taste the raptures of a nuptial bed."
  Thus she disclos'd the woman's secret heart,
Young, innocent, and new to Cupid's dart.
Her thoughts, her words, her actions wildly rove,

With love she burns, yet knows not that
  'tis love.
  Her royal sire now with the murm'ring
    crowd
Demands the race impatiently aloud.
Hippomenes then with true fervour
  pray'd,
"My bold attempt let Venus kindly aid.
By her sweet pow'r I felt this am'rous
  fire,
Still may she succour whom she did in-
  spire."
A soft, unenvious wind, with speedy care,
Wafted to Heav'n the lover's tender
  pray'r.
Pity, I own, soon gain'd the wish'd con-
  sent,
And all th' assistance he implor'd I lent.
The Cyprian lands, though rich, in rich-
  ness yield
To that, surnam'd the Tamasenian field.
That field of old was added to my shrine,
And its choice products consecrated mine.
A tree there stands, full glorious to be-
  hold,
Gold are the leaves, the crackling
  branches gold.
It chanc'd, three apples in my hand I
  bore,
Which newly from the tree I sportive
  tore;
Seen by the youth alone, to him I
  brought
The fruit, and when, and how to use it,
  taught.
The signal sounding by the king's com-
  mand,
Both start at once, and sweep th' im-
  printed sand.
So swiftly mov'd their feet, they might
  with ease,
Scarce moisten'd, skim along the glassy
  seas;
Or with a wond'rous levity be borne
O'er yellow harvests of unbending corn.
Now fav'ring peals resound from ev'ry
  part,
Spirit the youth, and fire his fainting
  heart.

"Hippomenes!" they cry'd, "thy life
  preserve,
Intensely labour, and stretch ev'ry nerve.
Base fear alone can baffle thy design,
Shoot boldly onward, and the goal is
  thine."
'Tis doubtful whether shouts, like these,
  convey'd
More pleasures to the youth, or to the
  maid.
When a long distance oft she could have
  gain'd,
She check'd her swiftness, and her feet
  restrain'd:
She sigh'd, and dwelt, and languish'd on
  his face,
Then with unwilling speed pursu'd the
  race.
O'er-spent with heat, his breath he faintly
  drew,
Parch'd was his mouth, nor yet the goal
  in view,
And the first apple on the plain he threw.
The nymph stopp'd sudden at th' unusual
  sight,
Struck with the fruit so beautifully bright.
Aside she starts, the wonder to behold,
And eager stoops to catch the rolling
  gold.
Th' observant youth past by, and scour'd
  along,
While peals of joy rung from th' ap-
  plauding throng.
Unkindly she corrects the short delay,
And to redeem the time fleets swift
  away,
Swift, as the lightning, or the northern
  wind,
And far she leaves the panting youth
  behind.
Again he strives the flying nymph to hold
With the temptation of the second gold:
The bright temptation fruitlessly was
  tost,
So soon, alas! she won the distance lost.
Now but a little interval of space
Remain'd for the decision of the race.
"Fair author of the precious gift," he said,
"Be thou, O goddess, author of my aid!"

Then of the shining fruit the last he drew,
And with his full-collected vigour threw:
The virgin still the longer to detain,
Threw not directly, but across the plain.
She seem'd awhile perplex'd in dubious
　thought,
If the far-distant apple should be sought:
I lur'd her backward mind to seize the
　bait,
And to the massy gold gave double
　weight.
My favour to my votary was show'd,
Her speed I lessen'd, and increas'd her
　load.
But lest, though long, the rapid race be
　run
Before my longer, tedious tale is done,
The youth the goal, and so the virgin won.
　　　　　　　—Lawrence Eusden.

STORIES OF EARLY ROME

Value of the Past [1]

LIVY

[The *Preface*]

Titus Livius was born at Padua in 59
B.C., and died there in 17 A.D. For the
greater part of his life he lived quietly
at Rome, a teacher and a writer. Though
in spirit a Republican, he won the favor
and friendship of the emperor Augustus.
He is the only prominent writer of prose
of the Augustan age. Of his general
history of Rome from its foundation to
his own day only portions have come down
to us. The first sections of it furnish us
with most of what is known about the
early times, and even the literary movements of the period of the Republic before
Cicero have to be sketched in from his
work. Fortunately, Livy is much more
than a mere chronicler of political and
military events and institutions; he seeks
to narrate also the development of Roman
culture. He brings to his task a philosoph-

[1] From The Loeb Classical Library, by permission.

ical training and a mastery of the art of
narration.

Livy will not stand comparison with
Thucydides, the great Athenian historian,
in scientific method or accuracy; but in a
clear arrangement of large masses of historic material, in a style that is spirited,
and in an appreciation of the glorious
past of Republican Rome so vivid that
through his pages Rome still lives, he has
his reward.

The conception of history as a guide in
public morality is characteristic of the
point of view of Roman historians and
biographers. Their concentration upon
this phase of it accounts in part for certain sorts of carelessness in their treatment of history as a record.

Whether I am likely to accomplish
anything worthy of the labour, if I
record the achievements of the Roman
people from the foundation of the city, I
do not really know, nor if I knew would
I dare to avouch it; perceiving as I do
that the theme is not only old but hackneyed, through the constant succession
of new historians, who believe either that
in their facts they can produce more au-
thentic information, or that in their style
they will prove better than the rude attempts of the ancients. Yet, however
this shall be, it will be a satisfaction to
have done myself as much as lies in me to
commemorate the deeds of the foremost
people of the world; and if in so vast a
company of writers my own reputation
should be obscure, my consolation would
be the fame and greatness of those whose
renown will throw mine into the shade.
Moreover, my subject involves infinite
labour, seeing that it must be traced back
above seven hundred years, and that proceeding from slender beginnings it has so
increased as now to be burdened by its
own magnitude; and at the same time I
doubt not that to most readers the earliest
origins and the period immediately succeeding them will give little pleasure, for
they will be in haste to reach these

modern times, in which the might of a people which has long been very powerful is working its own undoing. I myself, on the contrary, shall seek in this an additional reward for my toil, that I may avert my gaze from the troubles which our age has been witnessing for so many years, so long at least as I am absorbed in the recollection of the brave days of old, free from every care which, even if it could not divert the historian's mind from the truth, might nevertheless cause it anxiety.

Such traditions as belong to the time before the city was founded, or rather was presently to be founded, and are rather adorned with poetic legends than based upon trustworthy historical proofs, I purpose neither to affirm nor to refute. It is the privilege of antiquity to mingle divine things with human, and so to add dignity to the beginnings of cities; and if any people ought to be allowed to consecrate their origins and refer them to a divine source, so great is the military glory of the Roman People that when they profess that their Father and the Father of their Founder was none other than Mars, the nations of the earth may well submit to this also with as good a grace as they submit to Rome's dominion. But to such legends as these, however they shall be regarded and judged, I shall, for my own part, attach no great importance. Here are the questions to which I would have every reader give his close attention—what life and morals were like; through what men and by what policies, in peace and in war, empire was established and enlarged; then let him note how, with the gradual relaxation of discipline, morals first gave way, as it were, then sank lower and lower, and finally began the downward plunge which has brought us to the present time, when we can endure neither our vices nor their cure.

What chiefly makes the study of history wholesome and profitable is this, that you behold the lessons of every kind of experience set forth as on a conspicuous monument; from these you may choose for yourself and for your own state what to imitate, from these mark for avoidance what is shameful in the conception and shameful in the result. For the rest, either love of the task I have set myself deceives me, or no state was ever greater, none more righteous or richer in good examples, none ever was where avarice and luxury came into the social order so late, or where humble means and thrift were so highly esteemed and held in honour. For true it is that the less men's wealth was, the less was their greed. Of late, riches have brought in avarice, and excessive pleasures the longing to carry wantonness and licence to the point of ruin for oneself and of universal destruction.

But complaints are sure to be disagreeable, even when they shall perhaps be necessary; let the beginning, at all events, of so great an enterprise have none. With good omens rather would we begin, and, if historians had the same custom which poets have, with prayers and entreaties to the gods and goddesses, that they might grant us to bring to a successful issue the great task we have undertaken.

—B. O. FOSTER.

FROM THE ASHES OF TROY

PROPERTIUS

[Elegies IV, 1]

Sextus Propertius was born in Umbria about 49 and died about 15 B.C. Apart from the fact that he was of equestrian rank and was a member of the Mæcenas circle, almost nothing is known of his life. He prided himself on being the Roman Callimachus. There is a certain obscurity in his work which may be attributed to the Alexandrian influence, but it is a truer explanation of his lack of clearness to say that his powers of expression were not equal to the richness of his imagination and the depth of his feeling. He revived the practice of the Alexandrians of employing elegy on themes drawn from myth and legend as well as on the subject of his own personal experience as a lover.

Whether the Romans derived the thought of Rome as a continuation of Troy from the vague suggestions of the Greek poets, or were prompted to trace their origin back to Phrygian ancestors because of the universal fascination which a lost cause ever exercises upon later peoples, their poets certainly found in it an inspiration for the expression of their patriotism. Rome as the symbol of eternity was as familiar an idea to them as it is to us.

Stranger, that place—whate'er you see—
  where stands imperial Rome,
Was hill and grass before Æneas left his
  Phrygian home;
And where to Phœbus, god of fleets,
  towers sacred Palatine,
Along the mountain-pastures lay Evan-
  der's exiled kine.
To the gods of clay they formed, these
  golden temples grew apace;
Then shrines—the work of artless hands
  —were reckoned no disgrace.
From the bare rock was wont to thunder
  forth Tarpeian Jove,
And Tiber greeted on his way our oxen in
  the grove.
Up yonder steps, where Remus' humble
  cottage stands on high,
One hearth was all the empire of the
  Twins in days gone by.
Yon lofty senate-house, agleam with
  peers in purple braid,
Once held our rustic fathers, all in shaggy
  skins arrayed.
Gathered then the old Quirites, warned
  by neatherd's bugle harsh;
Ofttimes there the chosen "Hundred"
  held their council in the marsh.
Above the vaulted theatre no bellying
  canvas hung:

No saffron perfume o'er the stage its
  pleasant odor flung.
None cared to seek for foreign gods, what
  time, with souls intent,
The people o'er their native rites in fear
  and trembling bent;
But yearly they with kindled hay showed
  Pales honor due,
Even as with horse's blood we now her
  lustral rites renew.
Poor Vesta then rejoiced in asses crowned
  with wheaten bread,
And meagre offerings to her shrine by
  starveling steers were led.
With fatted pigs the small cross-roads
  they cleansed, and simple swains
Offered the entrails of a lamb to the Pan-
  pipe's rustic strains.
The skin-clad yeoman swung his bristly
  thongs, and thus began
The rites of lewd Lupercus of the ancient
  Fabian Clan.
The soldier rude ne'er went to war in
  gleaming armor drest:
A charred stake was all he had to shield
  his naked breast.
First of his camps the hooded Lygmon
  planted on the wold;
The greater part of Tatius' reign was
  spent amid the fold.
Hence the Titii sprung, the Ramnes bold,
  and Luceres, sons of toil;
Hence our founder drave his four white
  steeds in triumph o'er the soil.

Bovillæ, now a suburb, then was far
  from Rome, I trow,
And the journey to Fidenæ was a weary
  way to go;
Powerful then was Alba, sprung from portent of the milk-white sow,
Gabii then a mighty city, though a roof-
  less ruin now.
Naught ancestral has the Roman nursling
  left him save the name,
Yet feels he not ashamed to boast the
  wolf his foster-dame.
'Twas better, Troy, your banished gods
  ye sent to Latium's shore;

Lo! with what omens hitherward the
    Dardan vessel bore!
Even then the augury was fair, that many
    a wily foe
Bursting from forth the wooden horse
    could never work her woe,
When to the son's neck clung the sire,
    all-trembling, and the flame
Those filial shoulders feared to scorch,
    though mantling round it came.

Then followed valiant Decius, followed
    Brutus stern and true.
And Venus' self her Cæsar's arms bore
    o'er the ocean blue—
The arms that soon with victory should
    wreathe renascent Troy;
A happy land received thy gods, Iulus,
    favored boy!
If the trembling Sibyl's tripod on
    Avernus did divine
The fields should be for Remus cleansed
    on holy Aventine;
Or if the Trojan maiden's strain, late
    ratified in sooth,
Thundered forth to sacred Priam, bore
    the sacred stamp of truth:

"List thee, thou shalt fall, O Troy!—in
    Rome, O Troy; thou'lt re-arise;
How many a weary woe by sea and land
    before thee lies!
Turn the horse, oh! fell your conquest,
    Greeks! the Ilian land shall live;
Arms to these crumbling ashes yet great
    Jupiter shall give."

O she-wolf sent of Mars, best nurse of
    all our fortunes thou,
How vast the walls that from thy milk
    have grown around us now!
Those walls I fain, in this my strain,
    would sing with words of love;
Oh! woe is me, the melody should all so
    lowly prove!
Yet ne'er the less each rill of song from
    humble breast of mine
That e'er shall flow, my loved land, my
    country, shall be thine!

Let Ennius wreathe around his rhymes a
    chaplet rudely wrought,
O Bacchus! give to me the leaves from
    thine own ivy sought,
That Umbria glory in my strains—proud
    Umbria, the home
Of him who'll bear the name of the
    Callimachus of Rome.
Let all who view those lofty towers, high-
    climbing o'er the valleys,
Measure them by the bard, and say:
    "There genius filled his chalice."

Give ear, O Rome! for thee I sing—
    for thee my strains arise;
Ye citizens, give omens fair! Heaven
    crown mine enterprise!
I sing of sacred rites and days and an-
    cient names of places;
On to the goal, my gallant steed, though
    difficult the race is!
        —JAMES CRANSTOUN.

THE FOUNDING OF ROME [1]

LIVY

[From Book I]

By the time of Augustus the story of
Æneas as the founder of Rome had gained
sufficient currency to justify Virgil in
choosing it as the subject of his epic and
Livy in making it the starting-point of his
history. The Romans were under the
necessity of filling in the period between
Æneas and Romulus with myths of their
own invention. Livy so marvellously described legend, myth, and the historic
deeds of the forefathers, that in his work
they were canonized not only for the
Augustan age, but for all time.

The first four of the extracts which follow belong to the early days of Rome
about which fact and fancy were often
intermingled in the writings of historians
as well as poets. The story of Virginia
may be historical. At least it is typical

[1] From The Loeb Classical Library, by permission.

of the early struggles between Romans of high and low estate, and represents truly old Roman standards of morality. In the last selection Livy tells the story of Rome's defeat by Hannibal at the battle of Lake Trasimene in 217 B.C.

First of all, then, it is generally agreed that when Troy was taken vengeance was wreaked upon the other Trojans, but that two, Æneas and Antenor, were spared all the penalties of war by the Achivi, owing to long-standing claims of hospitality, and because they had always advocated peace and the giving back of Helen. They then experienced various vicissitudes. Antenor, with a company of Eneti who had been expelled from Paphlagonia in a revolution and were looking for a home and a leader—for they had lost their king, Pylæmenes, at Troy—came to the inmost bay of the Adriatic. There, driving out the Euganei, who dwelt between the sea and the Alps, the Eneti and Trojans took possession of those lands. And in fact the place where they first landed is called Troy, and the district is therefore known as Trojan, while the people as a whole are called the Veneti. Æneas, driven from home by a similar misfortune, but guided by fate to undertakings of greater consequence, came first to Macedonia; thence was carried, in his quest of a place of settlement, to Sicily; and from Sicily laid his course towards the land of Laurentum. This place too is called Troy. Landing there, the Trojans, as men who, after their all but immeasurable wanderings, had nothing left but their swords and ships, were driving booty from the fields, when King Latinus and the Aborigines, who then occupied that country, rushed down from their city and their fields to repel with arms the violence of the invaders. From this point the tradition follows two lines. Some say that Latinus, having been defeated in the battle, made a peace with Æneas, and

later an alliance of marriage. Others maintain that when the opposing lines had been drawn up, Latinus did not wait for the charge to sound, but advanced amidst his chieftains and summoned the captain of the strangers to a parley. He then inquired what men they were, whence they had come, what mishap had caused them to leave their home, and what they sought in landing on the coast of Laurentum. He was told that the people were Trojans and their leader Æneas, son of Anchises and Venus; that their city had been burnt, and that, driven from home, they were looking for a dwelling-place and a site where they might build a city. Filled with wonder at the renown of the race and the hero, and at his spirit, prepared alike for war or peace, he gave him his right hand in solemn pledge of lasting friendship. The commanders then made a treaty, and the armies saluted each other. Æneas became a guest in the house of Latinus: there the latter, in the presence of his household gods, added a domestic treaty to the public one, by giving his daughter in marriage to Æneas. This event removed any doubt in the minds of the Trojans that they had brought their wanderings to an end at last in a permanent and settled habitation. They founded a town, which Æneas named Lavinium, after his wife. In a short time, moreover, there was a male scion of the new marriage, to whom his parents gave the name of Ascanius.

War was then made upon Trojans and Aborigines alike. Turnus was king of the Rutulians, and to him Lavinia had been betrothed before the coming of Æneas. Indignant that a stranger should be preferred before him, he attacked, at the same time, both Æneas and Latinus. Neither army came off rejoicing from that battle. The Rutulians were beaten: the victorious Aborigines and Trojans lost their leader Latinus. Then Turnus and the Rutulians, discouraged at their situation, fled for succour to the opulent and powerful Etruscans and their king Mezentius, who held sway in Cære, at that time an important town. Mezentius had been, from the very beginning, far from pleased at the birth of the new city; he now felt that the Trojan state was growing much more rapidly than was altogether safe for its neighbours, and readily united his forces with those of the Rutulians. Æneas, that he might win the good-will of the Aborigines to confront so formidable an array, and that all might possess not only the same rights but also the same name, called both nations Latins; and from that time on the Aborigines were no less ready and faithful than the Trojans in the service of King Æneas. Accordingly, trusting to this friendly spirit of the two peoples, which were growing each day more united, and, despite the power of Etruria, which had filled with the glory of her name not only the lands but the sea as well, along the whole extent of Italy from the Alps to the Sicilian Strait, Æneas declined to defend himself behind his walls, as he might have done, but led out his troops to battle. The fight which ensued was a victory for the Latins: for Æneas it was, besides, the last of his mortal labours. He lies buried, whether it is fitting and right to term him god or man, on the banks of the river Numicus; men, however, call him Jupiter Indiges.

Ascanius, Æneas' son, was not yet ripe for authority; yet the authority was kept for him, unimpaired, until he arrived at manhood. Meanwhile, under a woman's regency, the Latin State and the kingdom of his father and his grandfather stood unshaken—so strong was Lavinia's character—until the boy could claim it. I shall not discuss the question—for who could affirm for certain so ancient a matter—whether this boy was Ascanius, or an elder brother, born by Creusa while Ilium yet stood, who accompanied his father

when he fled from the city, being the same whom the Julian family call Iulus and claim as the author of their name. This Ascanius, no matter where born, or of what mother—it is agreed in any case that he was Æneas' son—left Lavinium, when its population came to be too large, for it was already a flourishing and wealthy city for those days, to his mother, or stepmother, and founded a new city himself below the Alban Mount. This was known from its position, as it lay stretched out along the ridge, by the name of Alba Longa. From the settlement of Lavinium to the planting of the colony at Alba Longa was an interval of some thirty years. Yet the nation had grown so powerful, in consequence especially of the defeat of the Etruscans, that even when Æneas died, and even when a woman became its regent and a boy began his apprenticeship as king, neither Mezentius and his Etruscans nor any other neighbours dared to attack them. Peace had been agreed to on these terms, that the River Albula, which men now call the Tiber, should be the boundary between the Etruscans and the Latins. Next Silvius reigned, son of Ascanius, born, as it chanced, in the forest. He begat Æneas Silvius, and he Latinus Silvius. By him several colonies were planted, and called the Ancient Latins. Thereafter the cognomen Silvius was retained by all who ruled at Alba. From Latinus came Alba, from Alba Atys, from Atys Capys, from Capys Capetus, from Capetus Tiberinus. This last king was drowned in crossing the River Albula, and gave the stream the name which has been current with later generations. Then Agrippa, son of Tiberinus, reigned, and after Agrippa Romulus Silvius was king, having received the power from his father. Upon the death of Romulus by lightning, the kingship passed from him to Aventinus. This king was buried on that hill, which is now a part of the city of Rome, and gave his name to the hill. Proca ruled next. He begat Numitor and Amulius; to Numitor, the elder, he bequeathed the ancient realm of the Silvian family. Yet violence proved more potent than a father's wishes or respect for seniority. Amulius drove out his brother and ruled in his stead. Adding crime to crime, he destroyed Numitor's male issue; and Rhea Silvia, his brother's daughter, he appointed a Vestal under pretence of honouring her, and by consigning her to perpetual virginity, deprived her of the hope of children.

But the Fates were resolved, as I suppose, upon the founding of this great city, and the beginning of the mightiest of empires, next after that of Heaven. The Vestal was ravished, and having given birth to twin sons, named Mars as the father of her doubtful offspring, whether actually so believing, or because it seemed less wrong if a god were the author of her fault. But neither gods nor men protected the mother herself or her babes from the king's cruelty; the priestess he ordered to be manacled and cast into prison, the children to be committed to the river. It happened by singular good fortune that the Tiber having spread beyond its banks into stagnant pools afforded nowhere any access to the regular channel of the river, and the men who brought the twins were led to hope that being infants they might be drowned, no matter how sluggish the stream. So they made shift to discharge the king's command, by exposing the babes at the nearest point of the overflow, where the fig-tree Ruminalis—formerly, they say, called Romularis—now stands. In those days this was a wild and uninhabited region. The story persists that when the floating basket in which the children had been exposed was left high and dry by the receding water, a she-wolf, coming down out of the surrounding hills to slake her thirst, turned her steps towards the cry of the infants, and with her teats gave them suck so

gently, that the keeper of the royal flock found her licking them with her tongue. Tradition assigns to this man the name of Faustulus, and adds that he carried the twins to his hut and gave them to his wife Larentia to rear. Some think that Larentia, having been free with her favours, had got the name of "she-wolf" among the shepherds, and that this gave rise to this marvellous story. The boys, thus born and reared, had no sooner attained to youth than they began—yet without neglecting the farmstead or the flocks—to range the glades of the mountains for game. Having in this way gained both strength and resolution, they would now not only face wild beasts, but would attack robbers laden with their spoils, and divide up what they took from them among the shepherds, with whom they shared their toils and pranks, while their band of young men grew larger every day.

They say that the Palatine was even then the scene of the merry festival of the Lupercalia which we have today, and that the hill was named Pallantium, from Pallanteum, an Arcadian city, and then Palatium. There Evander, an Arcadian of that stock, who had held the place many years at the time of which I am writing, is said to have established the yearly rite, derived from Arcadia, that youths should run naked about in playful sport, doing honour to Lycæan Pan, whom the Romans afterwards called Inuus. When the young men were occupied in this celebration, the rite being generally known, some robbers who had been angered by the loss of their plunder laid an ambush for them, and although Romulus successfully defended himself, captured Remus and delivered up their prisoner to King Amulius, even lodging a complaint against him. The main charge was that the brothers made raids on the lands of Numitor, and pillaged them, with a band of young fellows which they had got together, like an invading enemy. So Remus was given up to Numitor to be punished. From the very beginning Faustulus had entertained the suspicion that they were children of the royal blood that he was bringing up in his house; for he was aware both that infants had been exposed by order of the king, and that the time when he had himself taken up the children exactly coincided with that event. But he had been unwilling that the matter should be disclosed prematurely, until opportunity offered or necessity compelled. Necessity came first; accordingly, driven by fear, he revealed the facts to Romulus. It chanced that Numitor too, having Remus in custody, and hearing that the brothers were twins, had been reminded, upon considering their age and their far from servile nature, of his grandsons. The inquiries he made led him to the same conclusion, so that he was almost ready to acknowledge Remus. Thus on every hand the toils were woven about the king. Romulus did not assemble his company of youths—for he was not equal to open violence—but commanded his shepherds to come to the palace at an appointed time, some by one way, some by another, and so made his attack upon the king; while from the house of Numitor came Remus, with another party which he had got together, to help his brother. So Romulus slew the king. At the beginning of the fray Numitor exclaimed that an enemy had invaded the city and attacked the palace, and drew off the active men of the place to serve as an armed garrison for the defence of the citadel; and when he saw the young men approaching, after they had dispatched the king, to congratulate him, he at once summoned a council, and laid before it his brother's crimes against himself, the parentage of his grandsons, and how they had been born, reared, and recognised. He then announced the tyrant's death, and declared himself to be responsible for it. The brothers advanced with their band through the midst of the crowd, and hailed their grandfather king, whereupon such a shout of assent arose from the entire throng as confirmed the new monarch's title and authority.

The Alban state being thus made over to Numitor, Romulus and Remus were seized with the desire to found a city in the region where they had been exposed and brought up. And in fact the population of Albans and Latins was too large; besides, there were the shepherds. All together, their numbers might easily lead men to hope that Alba would be small, and Lavinium small, compared with the city which they should build. These considerations were interrupted by the curse of their grandsires, the greed of kingly power, and by a shameful quarrel which grew out of it, upon an occasion innocent enough. Since the brothers were twins, and respect for their age could not determine between them, it was agreed that the gods who had those places in their protection should choose by augury who should give the new city its name, who should govern it when built. Romulus took the Palatine for his augural quarter, Remus the Aventine. Remus is said to have been the first to receive an augury, from the flight of six vultures. The omen had been already reported when twice that number appeared to Romulus. Thereupon each was saluted king by his own followers, the one party laying claim to the honour from priority, the other from the number of the birds. They then engaged in a battle of words and, angry taunts leading to bloodshed, Remus was struck down in the affray. The commoner story is that Remus leaped over the new walls in mockery of his brother, whereupon Romulus in great anger slew him, and in menacing wise added these words withal, "So perish whoever else shall leap over my walls!" Thus Romulus acquired sole power, and the city, thus founded, was called by its founder's name.

—B. O. FOSTER.

THE RAPE OF THE SABINE WOMEN [1]

LIVY

[From Book I]

Rome was now strong enough to hold her own in war with any of the adjacent states; but owing to the want of women a single generation was likely to see the end of her greatness, since she had neither prospect of posterity at home nor the right of intermarriage with her neighbours. So, on the advice of the senate, Romulus sent envoys round among all the neighbouring nations to solicit for the new people an alliance and the privilege of intermarrying. Cities, they argued, as well as all other things, take their rise from the lowliest beginnings. As time goes on, those which are aided by their own worth and by the favour of Heaven achieve great power and renown. They said they were well assured that Rome's origin had been blessed with the favour of Heaven, and that worth would not be lacking; their neighbours should not be reluctant to mingle their stock and their blood with the Romans, who were as truly men as they were. Nowhere did the embassy obtain a friendly hearing. In fact men spurned, at the same time that they feared, both for themselves and their descendants, that great power which was then growing up in their midst; and the envoys were frequently asked, on being dismissed, if they had opened a sanctuary for women as well as for men, for in that way only would they obtain suitable wives. This was a bitter insult to the young Romans, and the matter seemed certain to end

[1] From The Loeb Classical Library, by permission.

in violence. Expressly to afford a fitting time and place for this, Romulus, concealing his resentment, made ready solemn games in honour of the equestrian Neptune, which he called Consualia. He then bade proclaim the spectacle to the surrounding peoples, and his subjects prepared to celebrate it with all the resources within their knowledge and power, that they might cause the occasion to be noised abroad and eagerly expected. Many people—for they were also eager to see the new city—gathered for the festival, especially those who lived nearest, the inhabitants of Cænina, Crustumium, and Antemnæ. The Sabines, too, came with all their people, including their children and wives. They were hospitably entertained in every house, and when they had looked at the site of the city, its walls, and its numerous buildings, they marvelled that Rome had so rapidly grown great. When the time came for the show, and people's thoughts and eyes were busy with it, the preconcerted attack began. At a given signal the young Romans darted this way and that, to seize and carry off the maidens. In most cases these were taken by the men in whose path they chanced to be. Some, of exceptional beauty, had been marked out for the chief senators, and were carried off to their houses by plebeians to whom the office had been entrusted. One, who far excelled the rest in mien and loveliness, was seized, the story relates, by the gang of a certain Thalassius. Being repeatedly asked for whom they were bearing her off, they kept shouting that no one should touch her, for they were taking her to Thalassius, and this was the origin of the wedding-cry. The sports broke up in a panic, and the parents of the maidens fled sorrowing. They charged the Romans with the crime of violating hospitality, and invoked the gods to whose solemn games they had come, deceived in violation of religion and honour. The stolen maidens were no more hopeful of their plight, nor less indignant. But Romulus himself went amongst them and explained that the pride of their parents had caused this deed, when they had refused their neighbours the right to intermarry; nevertheless the daughters should be wedded and become co-partners in all the possessions of the Romans, in their citizenship and, dearest privilege of all to the human race, in their children; only let them moderate their anger, and give their hearts to those to whom fortune had given their persons. A sense of injury had often given place to affection, and they would find their husbands the kinder for this reason, that every man would earnestly endeavour not only to be a good husband, but also to console his wife for the home and parents she had lost. His arguments were seconded by the wooing of the men, who excused their act on the score of passion and love, the most moving of all pleas to a woman's heart.

The resentment of the brides was already much diminished at the very moment when their parents, in mourning garb and with tears and lamentations, were attempting to rouse their states to action. Nor did they confine their complaints to their home towns, but thronged from every side to the house of Titus Tatius, king of the Sabines; and thither, too, came official embassies, for the name of Tatius was greatest in all that country. . . .

The Romans and the Sabines renewed their battle in the valley that lies between the two hills. But the advantage rested with the Romans. Then the Sabine women, whose wrong had given rise to the war, with loosened hair and torn garments, their woman's timidity lost in a sense of their misfortune, dared to go amongst the flying missiles, and rushing in from the side, to part the hostile forces and disarm them of their anger, beseeching their fathers on this side, on that their husbands, that fathers-in-law and

sons-in-law should not stain themselves with impious bloodshed, nor pollute with parricide the suppliants' children, grandsons to one party and sons to the other. "If you regret," they continued, "the relationship that unites you, if you regret the marriage-tie, turn your anger against us; we are the cause of the war, the cause of wounds, and even death to both our husbands and our parents. It will be better for us to perish than to live, lacking either of you, as widows or as orphans." It was a touching plea, not only to the rank and file, but to their leaders as well. A stillness fell on them, and a sudden hush. Then the leaders came forward to make a truce, and not only did they agree on peace, but they made one people out of the two. They shared the sovereignty, but all authority was transferred to Rome.

—B. O. FOSTER.

THE HORATII [1]

LIVY

[From Book I]

It chanced that there were in each of these armies triplet brothers, not ill-matched either in age or in physical prowess. That they were Horatii and Curiatii is generally allowed, and scarcely any other ancient tradition is better known; yet, in spite of the celebrity of the affair, an uncertainty persists in regard to the names—to which people, that is, the Horatii belonged, and to which the Curiatii. The writers of history are divided. Still, the majority, I find, call the Roman brothers Horatii, and theirs is the opinion I incline to adopt. To these young men the kings proposed a combat in which each should fight for his own city, the dominion to belong with the side

[1] From The Loeb Classical Library, by permission.

where the victory should rest. No objection was raised, and time and place were agreed on. Before proceeding with the battle, a treaty was made between the Romans and the Albans, providing that the nation whose citizens should triumph in this contest should hold undisputed sway over the other nation. . . .

When the treaty had been established, the brothers armed themselves, in accordance with the agreement. On either side the soldiers urged on their champions. They reminded them that their fathers' gods, their native land, their parents, and all their countrymen, whether at home or with the army, had their eye only on their swords and their right hands. Eager for the combat, as well owing to their native spirit as to the shouts of encouragement which filled their ears, the brothers advanced into the space between the two lines of battle. The two armies were drawn up, each in front of its own camp, no longer in any immediate danger, but their concern as great as ever; and no wonder, since empire was staked on those few men's valour and good fortune! Alert, therefore, and in suspense, they concentrated their attention upon this unpleasing spectacle. The signal was given, and with drawn steel, like advancing battle-lines, the six young men rushed to the charge, breathing the courage of great armies. Neither side thought of its own danger, but of the nation's sovereignty or servitude, and how from that day forward their country must experience the fortune they should themselves create. The instant they encountered, there was a clash of shields and a flash of glittering blades, while a deep shudder ran through the onlookers, who, as long as neither side had the advantage, remained powerless to speak or breathe. Then, in the hand-to-hand fight which followed, wherein were soon exhibited to men's eyes not only struggling bodies and the play of the sword and shield, but also bloody wounds, two of the Romans fell, fatally wounded, one upon the other, while all three of the Albans were wounded. At the fall of the Romans a shout of joy burst from the Alban army, while the Roman levies now bade farewell to all their hopes; but not to their anxiety, for they were horror-stricken at the plight of the single warrior whom the three Curiatii had surrounded. He happened to have got no hurt, and though no match for his enemies together, was ready to fight them one at a time. So, to divide their attack, he fled, thinking that each of them would pursue him with what speed his wounds permitted. He had already run some little distance from the spot where they had fought, when, looking back, he saw that they were following at wide intervals and that one of them had nearly overtaken him. Facing about, he ran swiftly up to his man, and while the Alban host were calling out to the Curiatii to help their brother, Horatius had already slain him, and was hastening, flushed with victory, to meet his second antagonist. Then with a cheer, such as is often drawn from partisans by a sudden turn in a contest, the Romans encouraged their champion, and he pressed on to end the battle. And so, before the third Curiatius could come up—and he was not far off—Horatius dispatched the second. They were now on even terms, one soldier surviving on each side, but in hope and vigour they were far from equal. The one, unscathed and elated by his double victory, was eager for a third encounter. The other dragged himself along, faint from his wound and exhausted with running! He thought how his brothers had been slaughtered before him, and was a beaten man when he faced his triumphant foe. What followed was no combat. The Roman cried exultantly, "Two victims I have given to the shades of my brothers: the third I will offer up to the cause of this war, that Roman may rule Alban." His adversary could barely hold up his shield. With a downward thrust Horatius buried his sword in the Alban's throat, and despoiled him where he lay. The Romans welcomed their hero with jubilations and thanksgivings, and their joy was all the greater that they had come near despairing. The burial of their dead then claimed the attention of the two armies,—with widely different feelings, since one nation was exalted with imperial power, the other made subject to a foreign sway. The graves may still be seen where each soldier fell: two Roman graves in one spot, nearer Alba; those of the three Albans towards Rome, but separated, just as they had fought.

Before they left the field Mettius asked, in pursuance of the compact, what Tullius commanded him to do, and the Roman ordered him to hold his young men under arms, saying that he should employ their services, if war broke out with the Veientes. The armies then marched home. In the van of the Romans came Horatius, displaying his triple spoils. As he drew near the Porta Capena he was met by his unwedded sister, who had been promised in marriage to one of the Curiatii. When she recognized on her brother's shoulders the military cloak of her betrothed, which she herself had woven, she loosed her hair and, weeping, called on her dead lover's name. It enraged the fiery youth to hear his sister's lamentations in the hour of his own victory and the nation's great rejoicing. And so, drawing his sword and at the same time angrily upbraiding her, he ran her through the body. "Begone," he cried, "to your betrothed, with your ill-timed love, since you have forgot your brothers, both the dead and the living, and forgot your country! So perish every Roman woman who mourns a foe!"

Horrid as this deed seemed to the Fathers and the people, his recent service was an off-set to it; nevertheless he was seized and brought before the king for trial. The king, that he might not take upon himself the responsibility for so stern and unpopular a judgment, and for the punishment which must follow sentence, called together the council of the people and said: "In accordance with the law I appoint duumvirs to pass judgment upon Horatius for treason." The dread formula of the law ran thus: "Let the duumvirs pronounce him guilty of treason; if he shall appeal from the duumvirs, let the appeal be tried; if the duumvirs win, let the lictor veil his head; let him bind him with a rope to a barren tree; let him scourge him either within or without the pomerium." By the terms of this law duumvirs were appointed. They considered that they might not acquit, under that act, even one who was innocent, and having given a verdict of guilty, one of them pronounced the words, "Publius Horatius, I adjudge you a traitor; go, lictor, bind his hands." The lictor had approached and was about to fit the noose. Then Horatius, at the prompting of Tullus, who put a merciful construction upon the law, cried, "I appeal!" And so the appeal was tried before the people. What influenced men most of all in that trial was the assertion of Publius Horatius, the father, that his daughter had been justly slain; otherwise he should have used a father's authority and have punished his son, himself. He then implored them not to make him childless whom they had beheld a little while before surrounded by a goodly offspring. So saying, the old man embraced the youth, and pointing to the spoils of the Curiatii set up in the place which is now called "the Horatian Spears," he exclaimed, "This man you saw but lately advancing decked with spoils and triumphing in his victory; can you bear, Quirites, to see him bound beneath a fork and scourged and tortured? Hardly could Alban eyes endure so hideous a sight. Go, lictor, bind the hands which but now, with sword and shield, brought imperial power to the

Roman people! Go, veil the head of the liberator of this city! Bind him to a barren tree! Scourge him within the pomerium, if you will—so it be amidst yonder spears and trophies of our enemies —or outside the pomerium—so it be amongst the graves of the Curiatii! For whither can you lead this youth where his own honours will not vindicate him from so foul a punishment?" The people could not withstand the father's tears, or the courage of Horatius himself, steadfast in every peril; and they acquitted him, more in admiration of his valour than from the justice of his cause. And so, that the flagrant murder might yet be cleansed away, by some kind of expiatory rite, the father was commanded to make atonement for his son at the public cost. He therefore offered certain piacular sacrifices, which were thenceforward handed down in the Horatian family, and, erecting a beam across the street, to typify a yoke, he made his son pass under it, with covered head. It remains to this day, being restored from time to time at the state's expense, and is known as "the Sister's Beam." Horatia's tomb, of hewn stone, was built on the place where she had been struck down.

—B. O. FOSTER.

HORATIUS AT THE BRIDGE [1]

LIVY

[From Book II]

When the enemy appeared, the Romans all, with one accord, withdrew from their fields into the City, which they surrounded with guards. Some parts appeared to be rendered safe by their walls, others by the barrier formed by the river Tiber. The bridge of piles almost

[1] From The Loeb Classical Library, by permission.

afforded an entrance to the enemy, had it not been for one man, Horatius Cocles; he was the bulwark of defence on which that day depended the fortune of the City of Rome. He chanced to be on guard at the bridge when Janiculum was captured by a sudden attack of the enemy. He saw them as they charged down on the run from Janiculum, while his own people behaved like a frightened mob, throwing away their arms and quitting their ranks. Catching hold first of one and then of another, blocking their way and conjuring them to listen, he called on gods and men to witness that if they forsook their post it was vain to flee; once they had left a passage in their rear by the bridge, there would soon be more of the enemy on the Palatine and the Capitol than on Janiculum. He therefore warned and commanded them to break down the bridge with steel, with fire, with any instrument at their disposal; and promised that he would himself receive the onset of the enemy, so far as it could be withstood by a single body. Then, striding to the head of the bridge, conspicuous amongst the fugitives who were clearly seen to be shirking the fight, he covered himself with his sword and buckler and made ready to do battle at close quarters, confounding the Etruscans with amazement at his audacity. Yet were there two who were prevented by shame from leaving him. These were Spurius Larcius and Titus Herminius, both famous for their birth and their deeds. With these he endured the peril of the first rush and the stormiest moment of the battle. But after a while he forced even these two to leave him and save themselves, for there was scarcely anything left of the bridge, and those who were cutting it down called to them to come back. Then, darting glances of defiance around at the Etruscan nobles, he now challenged them in turn to fight, now railed at them collectively as slaves of haughty kings, who, heedless of their own liberty, were come to overthrow the liberty of others. They hesitated for a moment, each looking to his neighbour to begin the fight. Then shame made them attack, and with a shout they cast their javelins from every side against their solitary foe. But he caught them all upon his shield, and, resolute as ever, bestrode the bridge and held his ground; and now they were trying to dislodge him by a charge, when the crash of the falling bridge and the cheer which burst from the throats of the Romans, exulting in the completion of their task, checked them in mid-career with a sudden dismay. Then Cocles cried, "O Father Tiberinus, I solemnly invoke thee; receive these arms and this soldier with propitious stream!" So praying, all armed as he was, he leaped down into the river, and under a shower of missiles swam across unhurt to his fellows, having given proof of valour which was destined to obtain more fame than credence with posterity. The state was grateful for so brave a deed; a statue of Cocles was set up in the comitium, and he was given as much land as he could plough around in one day. Private citizens showed their gratitude in a striking fashion, in the midst of his official honours, for notwithstanding their great distress everybody made him some gift proportionate to his means, though he robbed himself of his own ration.

—B. O. FOSTER.

VIRGINIA [1]

LIVY

[From Book III]

This outrage was followed by another, committed in Rome, which was inspired by lust and was no less shocking in its

[1] From The Loeb Classical Library, by permission.

consequences than that which had led, through the rape and the death of Lucretia, to the expulsion of the Tarquinii from the City and from their throne; thus not only did the same end befall the decemvirs as had befallen the kings, but the same cause deprived them of their power. Appius Claudius was seized with the desire to debauch a certain maiden belonging to the plebs. The girl's father, Lucius Virginius, a centurion of rank, was serving on Algidus, a man of exemplary life at home and in the army. His wife had been brought up in the same principles, and his children were being trained in them. He had betrothed his daughter to the former tribune Lucius Icilius, an active man of proven courage in the cause of the plebeians. She was a grown girl, remarkably beautiful, and Appius, crazed with love, attempted to seduce her with money and promises. But finding that her modesty was proof against everything, he resolved on a course of cruel and tyrannical violence. He commissioned Marcus Claudius, his client, to claim the girl as his slave, and not to yield to those who demanded her liberation, thinking that the absence of the maiden's father afforded an opportunity for the wrong. As Virginia was entering the Forum—for there, in booths, were the elementary schools—the minister of the decemvir's lust laid his hand upon her, and calling her the daughter of his bond-woman and herself a slave, commanded her to follow him, and threatened to drag her off by force if she hung back. Terror made the maiden speechless, but the cries of her nurse imploring help of the Quirites quickly brought a crowd about them. The names of Virginius her father and of her betrothed Icilius were known and popular. Their acquaintance were led to support the girl out of regard for them; the crowd was influenced by the shamelessness of the attempt. She was already safe from violence, when the claimant protested that there was no occasion for the people to become excited; he was proceeding lawfully, not by force. He then summoned the girl to court. She was advised by her supporters to follow him, and they went before the tribunal of Appius. The plaintiff acted out a comedy familiar to the judge, since it was he and no other who had invented the plot: The girl had been born, said Marcus, in his house, and had thence been stealthily conveyed to the home of Virginius and palmed off upon him as his own; he had good evidence for what he said, and would prove it even though Virginius himself were judge, who was more wronged than he was; meanwhile it was right that the hand-maid should follow her master. The friends of the girl said that Virginius was absent on the service of the state; he would be at hand in two days' time if he were given notice of the matter; it was unjust that a man should be involved in litigation about his children when away from home; they therefore requested Appius to leave the case open until the father arrived, and in accordance with the law he had himself proposed, grant the custody of the girl to the defendants, nor suffer a grown maiden's honour to be jeopardized before her freedom should be adjudicated.

Appius prefaced his decision by saying that it was evident how much he favoured liberty from the very law which the friends of Virginius made the pretext for their claim; but the law would afford liberty a sure protection only if it varied neither with causes nor with persons; for in the case of others who were claimed as free, the demand was legal, since any one might bring an action: in the case of one who was under the authority of a father there was no one else to whom the master ought to yield the custody; accordingly he decreed that the father should be summoned, and that meanwhile the claimant should not relinquish his right, but should take the girl in charge

and guarantee that she should be produced at the coming of him who was called her father.

Against the injustice of the decree, though many murmured their disapproval, there was not a single man who dared to stand out; when Publius Numitorius, the girl's great-uncle, and her lover, Icilius, arrived on the scene. When a path had been opened for them through the throng, since the crowd believed that the intervention of Icilius would be particularly effectual in resisting Appius, the lictor cried that the case had been decided, and as Icilius began to protest, attempted to thrust him aside. Even a placid nature would have been incensed by so violent an insult. "You must use iron to rid yourself of me, Appius," he cried, "that you may carry through in silence what you desire should be concealed. This maiden I am going to wed; and I intend that my bride shall be chaste. So call together all your colleagues' lictors too; bid them make ready rods and axes: the promised wife of Icilius shall not pass the night outside her father's house. No! If you have taken from the Roman plebs the assistance of the tribunes and the right of appeal, two citadels for the defence of liberty, it has not therefore been granted to your lust to lord it over our children and our wives as well! Vent your rage upon our backs and our necks: let our chastity at least be safe. If that shall be assailed, I will call on the Quirites here present to protect my bride, Virginius will invoke the help of the soldiers in behalf of his only daughter, and all of us will implore the protection of gods and men; nor shall you ever make good that threat of yours without shedding our blood. I ask you, Appius, to consider earnestly whither you are going. Let Virginius decide what to do about his daughter, when he comes; but of one thing he may rest assured: if he yields to this man's claim, he will have to seek a husband for her. As for me, in defence of the freedom of my bride I will sooner die than prove disloyal."

The crowd was deeply moved and a conflict appeared to be imminent. The lictors had surrounded Icilius, but had nevertheless gone no further than to threaten him, since Appius declared that it was not a question of Virginia's defence by Icilius, but of a turbulent fellow, who even now breathed the spirit of the tribunate, seeking an opportunity to stir up strife. He would furnish him no excuse for it that day; but that he might know now that the concession had not been made to his own wantonness but to the absent Virginius, to the name of father, and to liberty, he would not pronounce judgment that day nor deliver a decision; he would request Marcus Claudius to waive his right and suffer the girl to remain at large until the morrow; but unless the father should appear the next day, he gave notice to Icilius and to those like Icilius that the proposer of his law would not fail to support it, nor the decemvir be wanting in firmness; and in any case he should not call together his colleagues' lictors to repress the instigators of sedition, but rest content with his own.

The time for accomplishing the wrong having been postponed, the girl's supporters went apart by themselves, and decided that first of all the brother of Icilius and the son of Numitorius, active young men, should proceed straight to the City gate and make all possible haste to the camp, to summon Virginius; for the maiden's safety turned on her protector's being at hand in time. They set out the moment they got their orders, and galloping their horses, carried the message through to the father. When the claimant of the girl pressed Icilius to furnish the sureties required of her guarantor, and Icilius said that it was precisely that which he was considering (though he was doing his best to consume time, that the messengers who had been dispatched to the camp might get a start on the way), the people began on every side to raise their hands, and every man of them to indicate his readiness to go bail for Icilius. And Icilius said, with tears in his eyes, "I am grateful to you; to-morrow I will use your services; of sureties I now have enough." So Virginia was surrendered, on the security of her kinsmen. Appius waited a little while, that he might not appear to have sat for this case only, and when nobody applied to him—for all other matters were forgotten in men's concern over this,—he went to his house and wrote to his colleagues in camp that they should grant no furlough to Virginius, and should even detain him in custody. His base design was too late, as it deserved to be; Virginius had already got his leave, and had set out in the fore-part of the night, nor was it until early the next morning that the letters for detaining him were delivered, to no purpose.

But in the City, as the citizens at break of day were standing in the Forum, agog with expectation, Virginius, dressed in sordid clothes and leading his daughter, who was also meanly clad and was attended by a number of matrons, came down into the market-place with a vast throng of supporters. He then began to go about and canvass people, and not merely to ask their aid as a favour, but to claim it as his due, saying that he stood daily in the battle-line in defence of their children and their wives; that there was no man of whom more strenuous and courageous deeds in war could be related—to what end, if despite the safety of the City those outrages which were dreaded as the worst that could follow a city's capture must be suffered by their children? Pleading thus, as if in a kind of public appeal, he went about amongst the people. Similar appeals were thrown out by Icilius; but the women who attended them were more moving, as they wept in silence, than any words. In the face of all these things Appius hardened his heart—so violent was the madness, as it may more truly be called than love, that had overthrown his reason —and mounted the tribunal. The plaintiff was actually uttering a few words of complaint, on the score of having been balked of his rights the day before through partiality, when, before he could finish his demand, or Virginius be given an opportunity to answer, Appius interrupted him. The discourse with which he led up to his decree may perhaps be truthfully represented in some one of the old accounts, but since I can nowhere discover one that is plausible, it seems my duty to set forth the naked fact, upon which all agree, that he adjudged Virginia to him who claimed her as his slave. At first everybody was rooted to the spot in amazement at so outrageous a proceeding, and for a little while after the silence was unbroken. Then, when Marcus Claudius was making his way through the group of matrons to lay hold upon the girl, and had been greeted by the women with wails and lamentations, Virginius shook his fist at Appius and cried, "It was to Icilius, Appius, not to you that I betrothed my daughter; and it was for wedlock, not dishonour, that I brought her up. Would you have men imitate the beasts of the field and the forest in promiscuous gratification of their lust? Whether these people propose to tolerate such conduct I do not know: I cannot believe that those who have arms will endure it."

The claimant of the maiden was being forced back by the ring of women and supporters who surrounded her, when silence was commanded by a herald; and the decemvir, crazed with lust, declared that he knew, not only from the abusive words uttered by Icilius the day before and the violence of Virginius, which he could prove by the testimony of the Roman People, but also from definite information, that all through the night meetings had been held in the City to promote sedition. Accordingly, having been aware of the approaching struggle, he had come down into the Forum with armed men, not that he might do violence to any peaceable citizen, but to coerce, conformably to the dignity of his office, those who would disturb the nation's peace. "You will therefore," he cried, "best be quiet! Go, lictor, remove the mob and open a way for the master to seize his slave!" When he had wrathfully thundered out these words, the crowd parted spontaneously and left the girl standing there, a prey to villainy. Then Virginius, seeing no help anywhere, said, "I ask you, Appius, first to pardon a father's grief if I have somewhat harshly inveighed against you; and then to suffer me to question the nurse here, in the maiden's presence, what all this means, that if I have been falsely called a father, I may go away with a less troubled spirit." Permission being granted, he led his daughter and the nurse apart, to the booths near the shrine of Cloacina, now known as the "New Booths," and there, snatching a knife from a butcher, he exclaimed, "Thus, my daughter, in the only way I can, do I assert your freedom!" He then stabbed her to the heart, and, looking back to the tribunal, cried, " 'Tis you, Appius, and your life I devote to destruction with this blood!" The shout which broke forth at the dreadful deed roused Appius, and he ordered Virginius to be seized. But Virginius made a passage for himself with his knife wherever he came, and was also protected by a crowd of men who attached themselves to him, and so reached the City gate. Icilius and Numitorius lifted up the lifeless body and showed it to the people, bewailing the crime of Appius, the girl's unhappy beauty, and the necessity that had constrained her father. After them came the matrons crying aloud, "Was it on these terms that children were brought into the world? Were these the rewards of chastity?"—with such other complaints as are prompted at a time like this by a woman's anguish, and are so much the more pitiful as their lack of self-control makes them the more give way to grief. The men, and especially Icilius, spoke only of the tribunician power; of the right of appeal to the people which had been taken from them; and of their resentment at the nation's wrongs. . . .

But Virginius begged them rather to pity himself and his daughter, and to hearken, not to the entreaties of the Claudian family, whose province it was to tyrannize over the plebs, but instead to those of Virginia's relations, the three plebeian tribunes, who had been appointed to help the plebs but were themselves imploring the plebs to protect and comfort them. Men found more reason in his tears. And so Appius, cut off from hope, did not wait for the appointed day to come, but killed himself.

Immediately thereafter, Publius Numitorius caused the arrest of Spurius Oppius, who stood next in point of unpopularity, because he had been in the City when the unjust verdict was pronounced by his colleague. Yet a wrong which Oppius committed was more responsible for men's bitterness towards him than the one which he failed to prevent. A witness was produced who, after enumerating his twenty-seven campaigns, during which he had eight times received special decorations, which he wore in full sight of the people, tore open his tunic and exhibited his back, scored by the rods, professing that if the defendant could name any crime of which he had been guilty, he would suffer him without complaining, private citizen though he was, to vent his rage upon him a second time. Oppius too was led to prison, and before the day of trial he there put an end to his life. The property of Claudius and that of Oppius was confiscated by the tribunes. Their colleagues in the decemvirate went into exile, and their possessions were forfeited. Marcus Claudius also, the claimant of Virginia, was cited and condemned, but at the instance of Virginius himself the extreme penalty was remitted; and being allowed to depart, he went into exile at Tibur. And so the manes of Virginia, who was more fortunate after her death than she had been while alive, after ranging through so many houses in quest of vengeance, were finally at peace; for no guilty man remained.

—B. O. FOSTER.

THE BATTLE OF LAKE TRASIMENE

LIVY

[From Book XXII]

At the first approach of spring, Hannibal moved out of his winter quarters; having been foiled before, in his attempt to pass over the Apennine, by the intolerable severity of the cold, and exposed, during his stay in quarters, to the utmost degree of apprehension and danger. For, when the Gauls, whom the hopes of spoil and pillage had allured to his standard, perceived, that, instead of their carrying off booty from the lands of others, their own had become the seat of war, and were burthened with the winter residence of both the contending armies, they turned upon Hannibal the enmity which they had harboured against the Romans; and many plots were formed against him, by their chiefs, from the effects of which he was preserved, by their treacherously betraying one another, and discovering their designs, through the same inconstancy of temper which led them to conspire against him. He guarded himself also against their plots, by frequent disguises; changing sometimes his dress, sometimes the covering of his head.

However, his fears, on this account, were his principal motives for leaving his winter quarters earlier than usual. In the meantime, at Rome, Cnæus Servilius entered on the office of consul, on the Ides of March. He proposed to the senate to take under consideration the state of the commonwealth; whereupon the clamour against Caius Flaminius was renewed. "They created," they said, "two consuls, yet had but one. For what legal authority, what auspices, did the other possess? These the magistrates carried with them from home, from their own tutelar gods; and those of the public, the Latin festival being celebrated, the sacrifices on the Alban mount performed, and vows duly offered in the Capitol. Setting out in a private capacity, he could not carry the auspices with him, neither could he take them new, and for the first time, in a foreign soil." Their apprehensions were increased by reports of prodigies, brought from various places at once. In Sicily, a number of arrows, and in Sardinia, the truncheon of a horseman, which he held in his hand, as he was going the rounds of the watch on the walls of Sulci, took fire, as was said; many fires were seen blazing on the shore; two shields sweated blood; several soldiers were struck by lightning; and the sun's orb appeared to be contracted. At Præneste, red hot stones fell from the sky. At Arpi, bucklers were seen in the air, and the sun fighting with the moon. At Capena, two moons appeared in the day-time. At Cære, the streams of water were mixed with blood; and even the fountain of Hercules was tinged with bloody spots. In the district of Antium, while people were reaping, bloody ears of corn fell into a basket. At Falerii, the sky seemed to be rent asunder with a very wide cleft, and through the opening a strong light burst forth; the divining tickets, without any apparent cause, were diminished in size, and one fell out, which had

this inscription, "Mars brandishes his spear." About the same time, at Rome, the statue of Mars, on the Appian road, and the images of the wolves, sweated. At Capua, the sky appeared as if on fire, and the moon as falling amongst rain. Afterwards, prodigies of lesser note were credited: that, with some people, goats were converted into sheep; that a hen turned into a male, and a cock into a female. The consul, laying before the senate all these matters, as reported, and bringing the authors of the reports into the senate-house, proposed to their consideration the affairs of religion. They decreed, that those prodigies should be expiated, some with the greater, some with the lesser victims; and that a supplication for three days should be performed at all the shrines; that, when the decemvirs should have inspected the books, all other particulars should be conducted in such manner as the gods should declare, in their oracles, to be agreeable to them. By the direction of the decemvirs, it was decreed, that, first, a golden thunderbolt, of fifty pounds' weight, should be made as an offering to Jupiter; and that offerings of silver should be presented to Juno and Minerva; that sacrifices of the greater victims should be offered to Juno Regina, on the Aventine, and to Juno Sospita, at Lanuvium; that the matrons, contributing such sums of money as might be convenient to each, should carrry an offering to Juno Regina, to the Aventine, and celebrate a lectisternium to her: and that even the descendants of freed women should make a contribution, in proportion to their abilities, out of which an offering should be made to Feronia. When these orders were fulfilled, the decemvirs sacrificed, with the greater victims, in the Forum at Ardea: and, lastly, so late as the month of December, sacrifices were offered at the temple of Saturn in Rome, and a lectisternium was ordered; on which occasion the couches were laid out by senators, and also a public banquet. Proclamation was likewise made through the city, of a feast of Saturn, to be celebrated during a day and a night, and the people were commanded to keep that day as a festival, and to observe it for ever.

While the consul was employed at Rome in endeavouring to procure the favour of the gods, and in levying troops, Hannibal, having set out from his winter quarters, and hearing that the consul Flaminius had already arrived at Arretium, notwithstanding that another road, less difficult, but longer, was pointed out to him, yet chose a shorter one through marshes, which, at the time, were overflowed by the river Arnus, to an unusual height. He ordered the Spaniards and Africans, the main strength of his veteran troops, to march in the van, with their baggage between their divisions; that, in case they should be obliged to halt, they might not be at a loss for a supply of necessaries; then the Gauls to follow, so that they should compose the centre of the line, and the cavalry to march in the rear; and after them Mago, with the light-armed Numidians, as a rear guard, to prevent the troops from straggling; and particularly, to restrain the Gauls, if weary of the labour, or of the length of the journey, as people of that nation want firmness to support such fatigues, from attempting either to slip away, or to stay behind. The troops in the van, though almost swallowed in mud, and frequently plunging entirely under water, yet followed their standards wherever their guides led the way, in spite of the deep gulphs formed by the river, and the steepness of their banks. But the Gauls could neither support themselves on their feet, nor, when they fell, raise themselves out of the gulphs; for they were destitute of spirits to support their bodies, and of hope, to support their spirits; while some, with difficulty, dragged on their enfeebled limbs,

others, whose spirits were exhausted by the long fatigue, having once fallen, lay there, and died among the cattle, of which great numbers also perished. But what, beyond everything else, utterly overpowered them, was the want of sleep, which they had now endured for four days and three nights; when, all places being covered by the waters, so that no dry spot could be found on which they might stretch their wearied limbs, they threw their baggage into the water in heaps, on the top of which they laid themselves down. The heaps of cattle, which lay dead in abundance along the whole course of their march, afforded them, in their necessity, a temporary bed, as they looked for no further accommodation for sleeping, than something raised above the water. Hannibal himself, having a complaint in his eyes, occasioned, at first, by the unwholesome weather of the spring, when changes are frequent from heat to cold, rode on the only elephant which he had remaining, in order to keep himself as high as he could above the water; but, at length, the want of sleep, the damps of the night, and the air of the marshes, so disordered his head, that, as he had neither place, nor time, to make use of remedies, he lost one of his eyes.

At length, after great numbers of men and cattle had perished miserably, he got clear of the marshes; and, on the first dry ground at which he arrived, pitched his camp. Here, from scouts, whom he had sent forward, he learned, with certainty, that the Roman army lay round the walls of Arretium. He then employed the utmost diligence in enquiring into the disposition and the designs of the consul, the nature of the several parts of the country, the roads, and the sources from which provisions might be procured, and every other circumstance requisite to be known. As to the country, it was one of the most fertile in Italy; the Etrurian plains, which lie between

Fæsulæ and Arretium, abounding with corn and cattle, and plenty of everything useful. The consul was inflated with presumption since his former consulate, and too regardless, not only of the laws and the dignity of the senate, but even of the gods. This head-strong self-sufficiency, natural to his disposition, Fortune had cherished, by the prosperous course of success which she had granted him, in his administration of affairs, both civil and military. There was, therefore, sufficient reason to suppose, that without regarding the sentiments of gods or men, he would act on all occasions with presumption and precipitancy; and the Carthaginian, in order the more effectually to dispose him to follow the bias of his natural imperfection, resolved to irritate and exasperate him. With this view, leaving the enemy on his left, and pointing his route towards Fæsulæ, he marched through the heart of Etruria, ravaging the country, and exhibiting to the consul, at a distance, a view of the greatest devastations that could be effected by fire and sword. Flaminius, even had the enemy lain quiet, would not have been content to remain inactive; but now, seeing the property of the allies plundered and destroyed before his eyes, and thinking that on him would fall the disgrace of Hannibal's over-running the middle of Italy, and marching, without opposition, to attack the very walls of Rome; notwithstanding that every other member of his council recommended salutary, rather than specious measures; that he should wait the arrival of his colleague, when they might enter on the business with joint forces, and with united spirit and judgment; and that, in the mean time, the enemy should be restrained from his unbounded license in plundering, by means of the cavalry and light auxiliaries; he burst away from the council in a rage, and displayed, at once, the signals both for marching and fighting. "We must lie here, then," said he,

"under the walls of Arretium, because here is our native city and our household gods; let Hannibal slip out of our hands, ravage Italy, and, after wasting and burning all the rest, arrive at the walls of Rome; nor stir from hence until the senate summons Caius Flaminius from Arretium, as formerly Camillus from Veii." While he upbraided them in this manner, he, at the same time, ordered the standards to be raised with speed; and he himself having mounted on horseback, his horse, by a sudden plunge, displaced him from his seat, and threw him over his head. All present were greatly dismayed by such an inauspicious omen, at the opening of the campaign; and, to add to their uneasiness, an account was brought, that there was one of the standards which could not be pulled out of the ground, though the standard-bearer endeavoured it with his utmost strength. The consul, turning to the messenger, said, "Do you also bring a letter from the senate, forbidding me to act? Go, bid them dig up the standard, if fear has so benumbed their hands, that they cannot pull it out." The army then began to march, while the principal officers, besides, that, in their own judgments, they were averse to the design, were terrified at the two prodigies; but the generality of the soldiers rejoiced at the presumptuous conduct of the general; for they looked no farther than the confidence which he displayed, and never examined the grounds on which it was founded.

Hannibal, the more to exasperate the enemy, and provoke him to seek revenge for the sufferings of his allies, desolated, with every calamity of war, the whole tract of country between the city of Cortona and the lake Trasimenus. And now the army had arrived at a spot, formed by nature for an ambuscade, where the Trasimenus approaches closest to the Cortonian mountains. Between them is only a very narrow road, as if room had been designedly left for that purpose; farther on, the ground opens to somewhat a greater width, and, beyond that, rises a range of hills. On these, he formed a camp in open view where he himself, with the African and Spanish infantry only, was to take post. The Balearians, and other light-armed troops, he drew round behind the mountains, and posted the cavalry near the entrance of the defile, where they were commodiously covered by some rising grounds; with design, that as soon as the Romans entered the pass, the cavalry should take possession of the road, and thus the whole space be shut up, between the lake and the mountains. Flaminius, though he arrived at the lake about sunset, took no care to examine the ground, but, next morning, before it was clear day, passed through the narrow way, and when the troops began to spread into the wider ground, they saw only that party of the enemy which fronted them; those in ambush on their rear, and over their heads, quite escaped their notice. The Carthaginian, having now gained the point at which he aimed, the enemy being pent up between the mountains and the lake, and surrounded by his troops, immediately gave the signal for the whole to charge at once. They accordingly poured down, every one by the shortest way he could, and the surprise was the more sudden and alarming to the Romans, because a mist, rising from the lake, lay thicker on the low grounds than on the mountains; and the parties of the enemy, seeing each other distinctly enough from the several eminences, were the better able to run down together. The Romans, before they could discover with their eyes, learned, from the shouts raised on all sides, that they were surrounded; and the attack began on their front and flank, before they could properly form a line, and get ready their arms, and draw their swords.

In the midst of the general consterna-tion, the consul, perilous as the conjuncture was, shewed abundance of intrepidity, restored, as well as the time and place would allow, the ranks, which were disordered by the men turning themselves about to all the various shouts, and wherever he could come, or be heard, encouraged, and charged them to stand steady, and to fight; telling them, that "they must not expect to get clear of their present situation, by vows and prayers to the gods, but by strength and courage. By the sword, men opened a way through the midst of embattled foes; and, in general, the less fear, the less danger." But such was the noise and tumult, that neither his counsel nor commands could be heard; and so far were the soldiers from knowing each his own standard, his rank, and post, that scarcely had they sufficient presence of mind to take up their arms, and get them ready for fighting; and many, while they were rather encumbered than defended by them, were overpowered by the enemy. Besides, the darkness was so great, that they had more use of their ears than of their eyes. The groans of the wounded, the sound of blows on men's bodies or armour, and the confused cries of threatening and terror, drew their eyes and attention from one side to another. Some, attempting to fly, were stopped by running against a party engaged in fight; others, returning to the fight, were driven back by a body of runaways. At length, after they had made many fruitless essays in every quarter, and inclosed, as they were, by the mountains and lake on the sides, by the enemy's forces on the front and rear, they evidently perceived that there was no hope of safety but in their own valour and their weapons, every one's own thoughts then supplied the place of command and exhortation to exertion, and the action began anew with fresh vigour; but the troops were not marshalled according to the distinct bodies of the different orders of soldiers, nor so disposed, that the van-guard should fight before the standards, and the rest of the troops behind them; or that each soldier was in his own legion, or cohort, or company: chance formed their bands, and every man's post in the battle, either before or behind the standards, was fixed by his own choice. So intense was the ardour of the engagement, so eagerly was their attention occupied by the fight, that not one of the combatants perceived a great earthquake, which, at the time, overthrew large portions of many of the cities of Italy, turned rapid rivers out of their courses, carried up the sea into the rivers, and by the violence of the convulsion, levelled mountains.

They fought for near three hours, and furiously in every part. But round the consul the battle was particularly hot and bloody: for the ablest of the men attended him, and he himself was briskly active in supporting his troops, wherever he saw them pressed, and in need of assistance; and, as he was distinguished above others by his armour, the enemy pointed their utmost efforts against him, while his own men defended him with equal vigour. At length, an Insubrian horseman (his name was Decario) knowing his face, called out to his countrymen, "Behold, this is the consul, who cut to pieces our legions, and depopulated our country and city. I will now offer this victim to the shades of my countrymen, who lost their lives in that miserable manner"; and then, giving spurs to his horse, he darted through the thickest of the enemy, and, after first killing his armour-bearer, who threw himself in the way of the attack, ran the consul through with his lance. He then attempted to spoil him of his arms, but the veterans, covering the body with their shields, drove him back. This event first caused a great number of the troops to fly; and now, so great was their panic, that neither lake nor mountain stopped them:

through every place, however narrow or steep, they ran with blind haste, and arms, and men, were tumbled headlong in promiscuous disorder. Great numbers, finding no room for farther flight, pushed into the water in the shallow edges of the lake, and plunged themselves in in such a manner, that only their heads and shoulders were above water. Some, the violence of their fears impelled to make the desp rate attempt of escaping by swimming: but this proving impracticable, on account of the great extent of the lake, they either exhausted their strength, and were drowned in the deep, or, after fatiguing themselves to no purpose, made their way back with the utmost difficulty, to the shallows, and were there slain, wherever they appeared, by the enemy's horsemen wading into the water. About six thousand of the van-guard, bravely forcing their way through the opposite enemy, got clear of the defile, and knowing nothing of what was passing behind them, halted on a rising ground, where they could only hear the shouting, and the din of arms, but could not see, by reason of the darkness, nor judge, with any certainty, what was the fortune of the battle. At length, after the victory was decided, the increasing heat of the sun dispelling the mist, and the day clearing up, the prospect was opened, and the mountains and plains shewed the desperate condition of their affairs, and the shocking carnage of the Roman army: wherefore, lest, on their being seen at a distance, the cavalry should be sent against them, they hastily raised their standards, and hurried away with all possible speed. Next day, when, besides their other distresses, they were threatened with the extremity of hunger, Maharbal, who, with the whole body of cavalry, had overtaken them during the night, pledging his faith, that if they surrendered their arms, he would suffer them to depart with single garments, they delivered themselves into his hands. But this capitulation Hannibal observed with Punic sincerity, and threw them into chains.

Such was the memorable fight at the Trasimenus, and the severe blow there received by the Romans, remarkable among the few disasters of the kind which the nation has ever undergone. Of the Romans, fifteen thousand were slain in the field; ten thousand, who fled, and dispersed themselves through every part of Etruria, made their way afterwards, by different roads, home to the city. Of the enemy, one thousand five hundred perished in the fight, and a great many afterwards of their wounds. By some writers, the loss of men on both sides is represented as vastly greater: for my part, besides that I wish to avoid the magnifying of any particular beyond the reality, an error to which writers are in general too prone, I think it reasonable to give the preference to the authority of Fabius, who lived in the very time of this war. Hannibal dismissed, without ransom, such of the prisoners as were natives of Latium, and threw the Romans into chains; he then ordered that the bodies of his own men should be collected, from among the heaps of the enemy, and buried; directing, at the same time, that the body of Flaminius should be sought for, with intention to honour him with a funeral; but after a most diligent search, it could not be found. As soon as the first news of this disaster arrived at Rome, the people, in great terror and tumult, crowded together into the Forum. The matrons, running up and down through the streets, asked every one who came in their way, what sudden calamity was said to have happened; in what state was the army; at length, after a crowd, not less numerous than that of a full assembly of the people, had collected in the Comitium, and about the senate-house, calling on the magistrates for information, a little before sunset, Marcus Pomponius, the praetor, told them, "We have been defeated in a great battle." Though nothing more particular was heard from him, yet the people, catching up rumours, one from another, returned to their houses with accounts, that, "the consul was slain, together with a great part of his army; that few survived, and that these were either dispersed through Etruria, or taken by the enemy." Every kind of misfortune, which had ever befallen vanquished troops, was now pictured in the anxious minds of those, whose relations had served under the consul Caius Flaminius, while they were ignorant of the fate of their friends, and had no positive information on which they could found either hope or fear. During the next, and several succeeding days, a multitude, composed of rather more women than men, stood round the gates, watching for the arrival, either of their friends, or of some who might give intelligence concerning them; and whenever any person came up, they crowded about him with eager enquiries; nor could they be prevailed on to retire, especially from such as were of their acquaintance, until they had examined minutely into every particular. Then, when they did separate from about the persons who brought information, might be seen their countenances expressive of various emotions, according as the intelligence, which each received, was pleasing or unfavourable; and numbers, surrounding them, returned to their houses, offering either congratulations or comfort. Among the women, particularly, the effects both of joy or grief were very conspicuous; one, as we are told, meeting, unexpectedly, at the very gate, her son returning safe, expired at the sight of him: another, who sat in her house, overwhelmed with grief, in consequence of a false report of her son's death, on seeing that son returning, died immediately, through excess of joy. The praetors, during several days, kept the senate assembled in their house, from the rising to the setting of the sun, deliberating by what commander, or with what forces, opposition could be made to the victorious Carthaginians.

—George Baker.

VI. THE LOVER

Elegy is one of the few branches of literature in which the Romans may justly claim to have attained a higher point of excellence than did the Greeks before them. It was of course a Greek invention, and practically all its uses, themes, and motives are to be found in one place or another in the Greek product. But in this case no particular Greek poet was accepted by the Romans as a model and no one Greek employment of the form was taken as defining its scope. Rather, Roman elegy is a combination of all the leading themes and motives appearing in both the elegy of Greek classical times and in that of the Alexandrian period. Yet, it is the latter rather than the former which determined the nature of the Roman product, in so far at least as it is mainly the erotic type and is a personal and subjective expression of the poet's own experience. The high quality of excellence attained by the Roman poets was due to their spontaneity, their genuineness of feeling, their ability to picture the actual life of at least one phase of contemporary society. Even when conscious imitation is practised, as in Propertius, still so true is the poet's emotion, so real is his passion, that he goes far beyond his purpose of imitation.

It is possible to trace a steady development through the works of the canon of elegists listed by Ovid. Gallus, a contemporary and intimate friend of Virgil, seems to have been a close imitator of Alexandrian elegy, confining himself to the erotic and overloading it with learning and mythological allusion. Tibullus sang also of love, but in clear simple style, with genuine feeling, and entirely free from the defects of Alexandrianism. Propertius, the most passionate lover of them all, widened the field of elegy considerably by the addition of the ætiological story and by the introduction of certain new motives later elaborated into types by Ovid. Finally, Ovid perfected the mechanics of the verse, dealt with every conceivable phase of the subject of love—from the personal complaint of the lover to fictitious letters from mythological heroines and a formal didactic exposition of love as an art,—made a theme hitherto treated seriously a plaything of his wit, and employed the form on totally new subject matter.

BEAUTY UNADORNED

PROPERTIUS

[*Elegies* I, 2]

For Propertius, see above, p. 419.

Why to walk forth, sweet life, thy tresses
    braid?
Why in the Coan garb's thin folds
    array'd?
Why with Orontes' myrrh thy locks
    imbue?
Thy beauty's price enhance by foreign
    show?
Why Nature's charms with purchas'd
    lustre hide,
Nor let thy limbs disclose their genuine
    pride?
Trust me thy face wants no cosmetic's
    aid;
Love's naked god abhors the dressing
    trade:
O, mark what blooms the painted earth
    displays,

How of themselves best climb the ivy-
  sprays,
How in lone caves arbutus lovelier grows,
Through untaught channels how the
  streamlet flows,
How native gems deckt shores sponta-
  neous yield,
And sweeter notes by untamed birds are
  trill'd!
  Leucippus' daughter, beauteous Phœbe,
  fired
Young Castor's bosom, with no gauds
  attired;
And her fair sister Hilaira too,
As unadorn'd, delighted Pollux' view.
No ostentatious ornaments could boast
Evenus' offspring, on her native coast;
When once the nymph the cause of dis-
  cord proved
'Twixt Idas, and the god who fondly
  loved.
Nor Hippodamia, when the stranger's car
In triumph bore away the virgin fair,
By beauties borrow'd from the shores of
  art,
Subdued to love her Phrygian husband's
  heart;
No jewels heighten'd her bright face, that
  show'd
Such tints as in Apelles' pictures glow'd.
These heroines strove not various loves to
  win,
Enough for them by chastity to shine;
Yet sure in virtue thou canst vie with
  these;
She wants no charms, who can one lover
  please.
  Since thine is all that Phœbus can
  inspire,
Thine fond Calliope's Aonian lyre,
Thine the choice gift of pleasing speech,
  my fair,
Thine all that's Beauty's, all that's Wis-
  dom's care;
'Tis surely thine to gild my life with joy,
But ne'er let odious pomp thy thoughts
  employ!
                              —JOHN NOTT.

IN THE FOREST

PROPERTIUS

[*Elegies* I, 18]

If the course of true love ran smooth,
there would be no elegy. Elegy celebrates
the darker side of the passion, is full of
complaints and fears.

Lonesome these glooms, and peaceful to
  lorn swains;
Along th' unpeopled grove bland Zephyr
  reigns:
Here may we dare our secret griefs to tell,
For desert rocks these griefs will ne'er
  reveal.
  Whence, O my Cynthia! shall I date
  thy scorn?
When was it first that Cynthia bade me
  mourn?
I, who late bore a happy lover's name,
Now see my passion doom'd to fatal
  shame!
Why treat me thus? what spell subverts
  thy love?
Say, does some rival nymph thy hatred
  move?
As to my home no stranger fair has borne
Her steps; so may'st thou, credulous!
  return:
And though to thee their sting my sor-
  rows owe,
Not so resentful shall my anger flow,
That thou shouldst e'er grow frantic with
  despair,
And thy swoll'n eyes the recent tear
  declare.
Say, does neglect my change of love
  proclaim?
And do no vows breathe forth my am'rous
  flame?
Witness, thou beech! (if trees make love
  their care,)
And by Arcadia's god, thou pine! held
  dear;
How your green shades my song has vocal
  made,

And Cynthia's name your letter'd rinds
display'd:
Say, do my cares spring from thy wrongs
alone?
Those cares, which only to mute doors
are known!
Fearful I want thy dictates to obey,
Nor loudly murmur'd at thy haughty
sway:
For this, ye gelid rocks! ye founts divine!
In these wild haunts is sleepless torment
mine;
For this! I'm doom'd, alone to tuneful
choirs
To sing whate'er my tender woe inspires.
　　But true, or faithless, be my Cynthia
　　found;
Cynthia's sweet name let woods and hills
resound!

—JOHN NOTT.

CUPID

PROPERTIUS

[*Elegies* II, 12]

In descriptive passages Roman poets
often follow representations of their subjects in painting and sculpture instead of
the inventions of their own imagination.

Had he not hands of rare device, whoe'er
　　First painted Love in figure of a boy?
He saw what thoughtless beings lovers
were,
　　Who blessings lose, whilst lightest cares
　　employ.

Nor added he those airy wings in vain,
　　And bade through human hearts the
　　godhead fly;
For we are tost upon a wavering main;
　　Our gale, inconstant, veers around the
　　sky.

Nor, with cause, he grasps those barbed
darts,
　　The Cretan quiver o'er his shoulder
　　cast:

Ere we suspect a foe, he strikes our
hearts;
　　And those inflicted wounds for ever
　　last.

In me are fixed those arrows, in my
breast;
　　But sure his wings are shorn, the boy
　　remains;
For never takes he flight, nor knows he
rest;
　　Still, still I feel him warring through
　　my veins.

In these scorched vitals dost thou joy to
dwell?
　　Oh shame! to others let thy arrows
　　flee;
Let veins untouched with all thy venom
swell;
　　Not me thou torturest, but the shade
　　of me.

Destroy me—who shall then describe the
fair?
　　This my light Muse to thee high Glory
　　brings:
When the nymph's tapering fingers, flowing hair,
　　And eyes of jet, and gliding feet she
　　sings.

—JOHN NOTT.

THE LOVER'S DEATH

PROPERTIUS

[*Elegies* II, 13a]

The thought of death as the final separation of lovers is a commonplace of elegy.
To Propertius, however, it seems to have
been more than a mere conventional motive. It was no doubt a very real fear to
one who was far from robust in health
and consequently given to moods of deep
depression.

Then, soon as night o'ershades my dying
  eyes,
    Hear my last charge; let no procession
    trail
Its lengthened pomp, to grace my
  obsequies,
    No trump with empty moan my fate
    bewail.

Let not the ivory stand my bier sustain,
    Nor on embroidered vests my corse
    recline;
Nor odour-breathing censers crowd the
  train:
    The poor-man's mean solemnities be
    mine.

Enough of state—enough, if of my
  verse
    Three slender rolls be borne with pious
    care:
No greater gift, attendant on my hearse,
    Can soothe the breast of hell's imperial
    fair.

But thou, slow-following, beat thy naked
  breast,
    Nor weary faint with calling on the
    dead:
Be thy last kisses to my cold lips prest,
    While alabaster vases unguents shed.

When flames the pyre, and I am embers
  made,
    My relics to an earthen shell convey:
Then plant a laurel, which the tomb may
  shade,
    Where my quenched ashes rest, and
    grave the lay:

"What here a heap of shapeless ashes
  lies,
    Was once the faithful slave of Love
    alone:"
Then shall my sepulchre renowned arise
    As the betrothed Achilles' blood-
    stained stone.

And thou, whene'er thou yieldest thus to
  fate,
    Oh dear one! seek the memorable way
Already trod; the mindful stones await
    Thy second coming, and for thee they
    stay.

Meantime, whilst life endures, oh, warned
  beware
    Lest thou the buried lover should'st
    despise:
Some conscious spark e'en mouldering
  ashes share:
    The senseless clay is touched by
    injuries.

Ah! would some kinder Fate while yet I
  lay
    In cradled sleep, had bid me breathe
    my last!
What boots the breath of our precarious
  day?
    Nestor is dead, his three long ages
    past.

On Ilium's rampart had the Phrygian
  spear
Abridged his age, and sent a swifter
  doom:
He ne'er had seen his sons' untimely bier,
    Nor cried, "Oh, death! why art thou
    slow to come?"

Thou thy lost friend shalt many a time
  deplore;
And love may ever last for those who die:
Witness Adonis, when the ruthless boar
    Smote in the Idalian brake his snowy
    thigh:

'Tis said, that Venus wept her lover lost,
    Trod the dank soil, and spread her
    streaming hair:
Thou too in vain would'st call upon my
  ghost:
    These mouldered bones are dumb to
    thy despair.

—JOHN NOTT.

A ROMAN MATRON TO HER HUSBAND

PROPERTIUS

[*Elegies* IV, 11]

This has been called the "queen of elegies." It represents a typical Roman matron as wife and mother speaking from her grave to those who remain to mourn her. It reads as if it might have been intended for a sepulchral inscription.

O Paulus! vex my grave with tears no
    more;
  No prayers unlock the portals of the
    tomb;
When once the dead have trod the in-
    fernal floor,
  Barred stand the adamantine doors of
    doom.

Though the dark hall's dread king would
    hear thy prayer,
  'Twere vain: deaf shores will drink
    thy tears the while.
Prayers move high heaven; but, pay the
    boatman's fare,
  The drear gate closes on the shadowy
    pile.

So sang the mournful trumpets when my
    head
  Sank on the bier before the ruthless
    fires.
What then availed me Paulus' bridal bed,
  And cars triumphal of my valiant sires?

What all the pledges of my fair renown?
  Though flowed Rome's noblest blood
    in all my veins,
Say, did it mitigate the Parcæ's frown?
  Lo! now five fingers lift my poor
    remains.

O darkness of the damned! O sullen
    mere!
  And every wave that clogs my tangled
    feet!

Though all too young, yet blameless came
    I here:
  My tender shade may Pluto mildly
    treat.

Or, if as judge an Æacus preside,
  With urn before him, in the realms
    below,
His jury let him draw, and then decide
  My destiny for endless weal or woe.

The seat of judgment let his brothers
    share,
  And the Eumenides, with hearts of
    steel,
Stand in the listening court by Minos'
    chair.
  Rest Sisyphus; be still Ixion's wheel.

Drink, wave-mocked Tantalus; nor snap
    to-day
  At shade, fell hound! hush, bars and
    chains of gloom;
I'll plead; if falsely, on my shoulders lay
  The urn's eternal toil—the Sister's
    doom.

If e'er ancestral trophies earned renown,
  Numantia's realms my father's deeds
    proclaim;
Like bays my mother's line, the Libos,
    crown;
  Each house on well-won titles rests its
    fame.

I doffed the maiden's dress: I was a
    bride;
  The matron's coif confined my braided
    hair;
Too soon, O Paulus! doomed to leave
    thy side;
  I was but thine, my tombstone shall
    declare.

Witness, our sires, whose ashes Rome
    reveres,
  Beneath whose names shorn Afric
    wails her fall,

Who, with the splendor of your conquering spears,
  Smote Spain, Antiochus, proud Hannibal,

And Perseus, boasting the vast soul that
gushed
In his great sire Achilles, and the might
Of that still greater ancestor, who crushed
  Thy pride, Avernus, and thy realms of
night!

Ne'er censor bent the law to screen my
shame;
  Your heart was aye the shrine of honor
fair;
No slur I brought upon your stainless
name;
  Your house was noble—I the pattern
there.

Years changed me not; a blameless life I
spent;
  From wedlock to its close our fame
secure;
Nature my blood with inborn virtue
blent;
  No fears could make my guileless heart
more pure.

Though harsh the verdict of the urn, yet
ne'er
  My presence shall the purest virgin
shame;
Not Claudia, crowned Cybebe's priestess
rare,
  Who with her girdle led the laggard
Dame,

Or her whose linen robe—when Vesta
sought
  The intrusted fires—bade living flames
arise.
I ne'er to thee, sweet mother, sorrow
brought;
  What, save my fate, wouldst thou have
otherwise?

My meed—a mother's tears, the city's
woe;
  Even Cæsar's sorrow consecrates my
bier;
Rome saw the mighty god a-weeping go,
  And mourn his daughter's worthy
sister-peer.

Though young, the matron's honored
robe I wore;
  Death from no barren dwelling bore
his prize;
My boys! my solace when I live no more,
  Ye held me in your hands and closed
my eyes.

Twice had my brother filled the curule
chair,
  A consul ere his sister's days were run.
Thy censor-sire in mind, sweet daughter,
bear;
  Uphold his honor; wed, like me, but
one.

With offspring prop our line: the bark's
afloat;
  I gladly go, so many mourn my doom;
A wife's last triumph, and of fairest note,
  Is fame's sweet incense rising o'er her
tomb.

Paulus, our pledges I commend to thee,
  Burnt in my bones, still breathes a
mother's care.
Discharge a mother's duties, then for me;
  For now thy shoulders all their load
must bear.

Kiss them, and kiss them for their
mother; dry
  Their childish tears; thine all the burden now.
Ne'er let them see thee weep or hear thee
sigh,
  But with a smile thy sorrow disavow.

Enough that thou the weary nights
shouldst moan,
  And woo my semblance back in visions
vain;

Yet whisper to my portrait when alone,
    As if the lips could answer thee again.

If e'er these halls should own another
    queen,
    And a new mother fill your mother's
      bed,
My children, ne'er let frowning look be
    seen,
    But honor her your father chose to
      wed.

So shall your manners win her tender
    grace,
    And surely she will love for love
      return;
Nor praise too much your mother to her
    face,
    For fear her breast with jealous feel-
      ings burn.

But should my image still his thoughts
    engage,
    And Paulus dower my dust with love
      so rare,
Oh! learn to watch your father's failing
    age,
    And shield his weary, widowed heart
      from care!

Heaven add to yours the years I hoped
    in store,
    And may your lives my aged Paulus
      cheer!
'Tis well: I ne'er the robes of mourning
    wore,
    And all my children gathered round my
      bier.

My cause is pled. Each weeping witness,
    rise,
    Since death's rewards life's losses well
      repay.
Heaven waits the pure in heart: be mine
    the prize
    To soar triumphant to the realms of
      day.

        —JAMES CRANSTOUN.

LOVE IS THE GOD OF PEACE

PROPERTIUS

[*Elegies* III, 5]

Propertius's defence of his service under the banner of Love is very much like
that of Tibullus.

Love is the God of peace: we lovers know
But love's hard combats, and a mistress-
    foe:
Not gold's devouring want my soul has
    curst;
Not from a jewelled cup I slake my
    thirst;
I plough not wide Campania's mellowed
    soil,
Nor for thy brass in ships, oh Corinth!
    toil:
Ah! hapless clay that erst Prometheus
    pressed,
Moulding a rash and unforeseeing breast:
The skill, that knit the frame, o'erlooked
    the heart:
An upright reasoning soul escaped his
    art.
Nor tost by winds we roam the troubled
    flood,
Link foe to foe, and restless pant for
    blood.
Fool! not on Acheron thy wealth shall
    float,
All naked drifting in the infernal boat.
The conqueror with the captive skims
    the tide,
And chained Jugurtha sits at Marius'
    side:
Robed Crœsus shares the tattered Irus'
    doom,
And owns that death the best, which soon
    shall come.
Me in youth's flower could Helicon
    entrance,
My hands with Muses linked in mazy
    dance:
Me has it charmed to bathe my soul in
    wine,
And vernal roses round my temples
    twine:

When irksome age hath stolen on love's
    delight,
And strewn my sable locks with sprinkled
    white:
Then may it please to search in Nature's
    ways,
And learn what God the world's vast
    fabric sways;
How dawns the rising east and fades
    again;
How the round moon repairs her crescent
    wane;
How winds the salt sea sweep, and the
    eastern blast
The billows warps, and clouds their
    ceaseless waters cast.
Whether a day shall come, when head-
    long, hurled
Shall fall the tottering pillars of the
    world;
Why drinks the purpling bow the rainy
    cloud;
Why Pindus' summits reel in earthquake
    bowed;
Why shines the sun's wheeled orb with
    umbered light.
His golden coursers palled in morning
    night;
Why turns Bootes slow his starry wain,
Why sparkling throng the Pleiads' clus-
    tered train;
Why bounded roll the deepening ocean's
    tides;
Why the full year in parted seasons
    glides;
If under earth Gods judge, and giants
    rave;
Tisiphone's fierce ringlets snaky wave;
Furies Alcmæon scourge, and Phineus
    hungering crave,
Thirst burn in streams, wheels whirl,
    rocks backward leap,
Or hell's dark mouth three-headed
    Cerberus keep:
If Tityos' straitened limbs nine acres
    press;
Or fables mock man's credulous wretch-
    edness

Through long tradition's age: nor terror's
    strife
Survive the pyre:—be such my close of
    life.
Go ye who list, the Parthian overcome,
Bring Crassus' wrested standards back to
    Rome.

—JOHN NOTT.

TO A JANITOR

OVID

[Amores I, 6]

The note of sincerity in the elegy of
Tibullus and Propertius gives place to
one of mock seriousness in that of Ovid.
The behavior of lovers affords him an excellent opportunity for the free play of
his wit and humor. He represents himself as the lover in order to give greater
reality to the situations on which he comments. For Ovid, see above p. 393.

O Janitor bound with hard iron—a truly
    unworthy fate!—
Turn back on its hinges the portal, and
    open the stubborn gate!
A little thing I entreat you; you need
    not open it wide;
Grant only a narrow passage, I'll slip
    through turning my side.
Long time have I been a good lover, and
    loving has wasted my frame,
Has rendered the whole of my body
    attenuate for such a game.
And Cupid it is who has taught me with
    sure and unfaltering feet
By wardens who watch in the night-time
    on silent tiptoe to retreat.
There once was a time, I admit it, when
    phantoms did fill me with fright,
A time when I wondered at any who
    ventured the darkness of night;
But Venus and mischievous Cupid but
    mocked me and laughed in my ear,
And Cupid said, whispering lightly, "You
    too shall be free from all fear."

My heart was straight pierced with his
arrow—no shades that inhabit the
night,
No arms uplifted to slay me can beget
any feeling of fright!
Only thee do I fear now and flatter, so
stubborn, unyielding thou art!
Thou only the thunderbolt wieldest can
penetrate into my heart.
But look!—and the better to see it, unlock the pitiless door—
Behold how the door has been moistened
by tears I can hold back no more!
Once trembling and naked thou stoodest
awaiting the lash of the whip:
For thee once I plead with thy mistress
with earnest and eloquent lip.
Is therefore the pleading I did then, with
power to save even thee,
Now become unavailing—shame on
thee!—to win a slight favor for me?
A grateful return do thou render! Be not
stubborn and hard, I implore.
The season of night-time is speeding:
away with the bar from the door!
Away with the bar!—so I'll wish thee
release from the janitor's chain,
Nor slave-like to be ever drinking the
waters of infinite pain!
Alas, my pleading is futile! Iron-
hearted the janitor hears;
The door stands solid and rigid, an oak
of an hundred years.
Closed gates belong rather to cities be-
sieged by a merciless foe;
But this is a peaceful season—what
weapons, pray, frighten thee so?
If a lover is thus to be treated, for a
foe what remains there in store?
The season of night-time is speeding:
away with the bar from the door!
I come unattended by soldiers, I bear
neither sword, spear, nor shield:
If Love, cruel love, were not with me,
I'd be all alone in the field.
And Love, though I fervently wished it, I
cannot dismiss from my heart:
Life itself would I rather surrender than
bid cruel Love to depart!

Three comrades are all that attend me
—a chaplet of flowers above,
And wine, just a little to warm me, in
addition to these only Love.
Would any be fearful to meet them?
What are they that thou tremblest
before?
The season of night-time is speeding:
away with the bar from the door!
Perchance it is sleep makes thee stubborn, my words gives the unfeeling
breeze—
May that sleep which has deafened thy
hearing make thee grovel in dust on
thy knees!
Wert wakeful enough, I remember, ev'n
late as the stars of midnight,
When first in a former encounter I sought
to escape thy keen sight.
Thou holdest perhaps at this moment a
mistress confessing her thine—
Alas, have thou pity upon me! Far
richer thy lot is than mine!
Could I but enjoy thy fortune, I'd wel-
come thy chains and thy floor!
The season of night-time is speeding:
away with the bar from the door!
But hark! Does my hearing deceive me?
The creak of the hinge of the gate?
The rattle of doors that are turning?
A sign of a happier fate?
Deceived! It was only a fancy, or else
but a stirring of wind—
Alas, cruel wind, thou hast carried all
hope far away from my mind!
If thou, mighty Boreas, remember thy
mistress was stolen of yore,
Come hither, I pray thee, come hither,
beat down with thy blast this door!
Through all of the city is silence, and
glistens with dew the wet floor:
The season of night-time is speeding:
away with the bar from the door!
Else I in a twinkling will arm me, with
fire and sword will I come—
Already I carry my torchlight—to humble the pride of this home.
For love and the wine and the darkness
urge nothing of self-restraint,

But night is the time for the shameless,
nor Love neither Bacchus is faint.
In vain have I all things attempted, entreaty and warnings of fate,
But truly art thou moved by nothing.
More obdurate thou than thy gate!
Unworthy art thou to watch over the
home of my sweet lady fair:
A keeper thou art of a dungeon, the
gloom of a prison thy care!
Already the star of the morning is setting in motion his wheels,
The bird of the dawn is now calling
each one from the sleep that he
steals.
But thou, little chaplet of flowers, unhappily torn from my head,
Lie there on this pitiless threshold till
morning discover thee dead.
And when on the morrow my lady shall
find thee all withered and pale,
Be proof of my long loyal vigil, of pleading and pain sans avail.
To thee, though thou meritest nothing, a
word of farewell do I give—
Thy fame for refusing a lover I promise
in verses shall live.
And ye, fare ye well, cruel doorposts, ye
doors of unyielding oak staves,
With him who sits ever to guard you ye
are but his own fellowslaves.

—GEORGE HOWE.

EVERY LOVER IS A SOLDIER

OVID

[From *Amores* I, 9]

Here is a new turn given to the usual
defence of the lover—not that there are
good reasons why he should not be a
soldier, but that he is already one, under
the standard of Cupid.

All lovers are campaigners, and Cupid
has his wars:
Yes, Atticus, all lovers are genuine sons
of Mars.

Your soldier must be youthful, your lover
be the same—
Old soldiers are a pity, old lovers are a
shame;
Your general chooses soldiers ready to do
and dare,
Your pretty girl a lover with strength
and pluck to spare;
Both spend all night on duty; the soldier
stands before
The quarters of his general, the lover
guards her door;
The soldier makes long marches, but
whereso'er you send
A girl, be sure her lover will track her
to the end;
No mountain peak can stop him, he'll
find a way to go
Through roaring winter torrents, through
sleet and drifting snow;
Although he be no sailor you'll never hear
him say,
"I see a storm is coming," " 'tis quite too
rough today."
A lover or a soldier—what others would
you find
Unmoved by cold and darkness, by driving sleet or wind?

· · · ·

Who think of Love as slothful will find
'tis otherwise;
Love is the soul of action, the soul of
enterprise.

—KIRBY FLOWER SMITH.

DIDO TO ÆNEAS

OVID

[*Heroides* VII]

It is possible that Propertius in his
Roman Matron to her Husband furnished
to Ovid the suggestion for his *Heroines*.
The book consists of a series of fictitious
letters by certain heroines of mythology
who write to complain of desertion by
their lovers.

So, on Mæander's banks, when death is
   nigh,
The mournful swan sings her own elegy.
Not that I hope (for, oh, that hope were
   vain!)
By words your lost affection to regain:
But, having lost whate'er was worth my
   care,
Why should I fear to lose a dying prayer?
'Tis then resolv'd poor Dido must be left,
Of life, of honour, and of love bereft!
While you, with loosen'd sails and vows,
   prepare
To seek a land, that flies the searcher's
   care.
Nor can my rising towers your flight re-
   strain,
Nor my new empire, offer'd you in vain.
Built walls you shun, unbuilt you seek;
   that land
Is yet to conquer; but you this command.
Suppose you landed where your wish de-
   sign'd,
Think what reception foreigners would
   find.
What people is so void of common sense,
To vote succession from a native prince?
Yet there new sceptres and new loves you
   seek;
New vows to plight, and plighted vows to
   break.
When will your towers the height of Car-
   thage know?
Or when your eyes discern such crowds
   below?
If such a town and subjects you could see,
Still would you want a wife, who lov'd
   like me,
For, oh, I burn, like fires with incense
   bright:
Not holy tapers flame with purer light:
Æneas is my thoughts' perpetual theme;
Their daily longing, and their nightly
   dream.
Yet he's ungrateful and obdurate still:
Fool that I am to place my heart so ill!
Myself I cannot to myself restore:
Still I complain, and still I love him more.
Have pity, Cupid, on my bleeding heart,

And pierce thy brother's with an equal
   dart.
I rave: nor canst thou Venus' offspring
   be,
Love's mother could not bear a son like
   thee.
From harden'd oak, or from a rock's cold
   womb,
At least thou art from some fierce tigress
   come;
Or on rough seas, from their foundation
   torn,
Got by the Winds and in a tempest born:
Like that which now thy trembling sail-
   ors fear;
Like that whose rage should still detain
   thee here.
Behold how high the foamy billows ride!
The wind and waves are on the juster
   side.
To winter weather and a stormy sea
I'll owe, what rather I would owe to thee.
Death thou deserv'st from Heaven's
   avenging laws;
But I'm unwilling to become the cause.
To shun my love, if thou wilt seek thy
   fate,
'Tis a dear purchase, and a costly hate.
Stay but a little, till the tempest cease,
And the loud winds are lull'd into a peace.
May all thy rage, like theirs, unconstant
   prove!
And so it will, if there be power in love.
Know'st thou not yet what dangers ships
   sustain?
So often wreck'd, how dar'st thou tempt
   the main?
Which were it smooth, were every wave
   asleep,
Ten thousand forms of Death are in the
   deep.
In that abyss the gods their vengeance
   store,
For broken vows of those who falsely
   swore.
There winged storms on sea-born Venus
   wait,
To vindicate the justice of her state.
Thus I to thee the means of safety show;

And, lost myself, would still preserve my
    foe.
False as thou art, I not thy death design:
O rather live, to be the cause of mine!
Should some avenging storm thy vessel
    tear,
(But Heaven forbid my words should
    omen bear)
Then in thy face thy perjur'd vows would
    fly;
And my wrong'd ghost be present to thy
    eye.
With threatening looks think thou be-
    hold'st me stare,
Gasping my mouth, and clotted all my
    hair.
Then, should fork'd lightning and red
    thunder fall,
What could'st thou say, but I deserv'd
    'em all?
Lest this should happen, make not haste
    away;
To shun the danger will be worth thy
    stay.
Have pity on thy son, if not on me:
My death alone is guilt enough for thee.
What has his youth, what have thy gods
    deserv'd,
To sink in seas, who were from fires pre-
    serv'd?
But neither gods nor parent dost thou
    bear;
Smooth stories all to please a woman's
    ear,
False as the tale of thy romantic life.
Nor yet am I thy first deluded wife:
Left to pursuing foes Creusa stay'd,
By thee, base man, forsaken and be-
    tray'd.
This, when thou told'st me, struck my
    tender heart,
That such requital follow'd such desert.
Nor doubt I but the gods, for crimes
    like these,
Seven winters kept thee wandering on the
    seas.
Thy starv'd companions, cast ashore, I
    fed,
Thyself admitted to my crown and bed.

To harbour strangers, succour the dis-
    trest,
Was kind enough; but, oh, too kind the
    rest!
Curst be the cave which first my ruin
    brought,
Where, from the storm, we common shel-
    ter sought!
A dreadful howling echo'd round the
    place:
The mountain nymphs, thought I, my
    nuptials grace.
I thought so then, but now too late I
    know
The Furies yell'd my funerals from below.
O Chastity and violated Fame,
Exact your dues to my dead husband's
    name!
By death redeem my reputation lost,
And to his arms restore my guilty ghost.
Close by my palace, in a gloomy grove,
Is rais'd a chapel to my murder'd love;
There, wreath'd with boughs and wool,
    his statue stands,
The pious monument of artful hands.
Last night, methought, he call'd me from
    the dome,
And thrice, with hollow voice cry'd,
    "Dido, come."
She comes; thy wife thy lawful summons
    hears;
But comes more slowly, clogg'd with con-
    scious fears.
Forgive the wrong I offer'd to thy bed;
Strong were his charms, who my weak
    faith misled.
His goddess mother, and his aged sire
Borne on his back, did to my fall con-
    spire.
Oh! such he was, and is, that, were he
    true,
Without a blush I might his love pursue.
But cruel stars my birth-day did attend;
And as my fortune open'd, it must end.
My plighted lord was at the altar slain,
Whose wealth was made my bloody
    brother's gain.
Friendless, and follow'd by the murder-
    er's hate,

To foreign countries I remov'd my fate;
And here, a suppliant, from the natives' hands
I bought the ground on which my city stands,
With all the coast that stretches to the sea;
Ev'n to the friendly port that shelter'd thee:
Then rais'd these walls, which mount into the air,
At once my neighbours' wonder, and their fear.
For now they arm; and round me leagues are made,
My scarce-establish'd empire to invade.
To man my new-built walls I must prepare,
An helpless woman, and unskill'd in war.
Yet thousand rivals to my love pretend;
And for my person would my crown defend:
Whose jarring votes in one complaint agree,
That each unjustly is disdain'd for thee.
To proud Hyarbas give me up a prey;
(For that must follow, if thou goest away.)
Or to my husband's murderer leave my life,
That to the husband he may add the wife.
Go then, since no complaints can move thy mind:
Go, perjur'd man, leave thy gods behind.
Touch not those gods, by whom thou art forsworn,
Who will in impious hands no more be borne:
Thy sacreligious worship they disdain,
And rather would the Grecian fires sustain.
Perhaps my greatest shame is still to come,
And part of thee lies hid within my womb.
The babe unborn must perish by thy hate,
And perish guiltless in his mother's fate.

Some god, thou say'st, thy voyage does command;
Would the same god had barr'd thee from my land!
The same, I doubt not, thy departure steers,
Who kept thee out at sea so many years;
While thy long labours were a price so great,
As thou to purchase Troy would'st not repeat.
But Tyber now thou seek'st, to be at best,
When there arriv'd, a poor precarious guest.
Yet it deludes thy search: perhaps it will
To thy old age lie undiscover'd still.
A ready crown and wealth in dower I bring,
And, without conquering, here thou art a king.
Here thou to Carthage may'st transfer thy Troy:
Here young Ascanius may his arms employ;
And, while we live secure in soft repose,
Bring many laurels home from conquer'd foes.
By Cupid's arrows, I adjure thee, stay;
By all the gods, companions of thy way.
So may thy Trojans, who are yet alive,
Live still, and with no future fortune strive;
So may thy youthful son old age attain,
And thy dead father's bones in peace remain:
As thou hast pity on unhappy me,
Who knew no crime, but too much love for thee.
I am not born from fierce Achilles' line,
Nor did my parents against Troy combine.
To be thy wife if I unworthy prove,
By some inferior name admit my love.
To be secur'd of still possessing thee,
What would I do, and what would I not be!
Our Libyan coasts their certain seasons know,

When free from tempests passengers may
go:
But now with northern blasts the billows
roar,
And drive the floating sea-weed to the
shore.
Leave to my care the time to sail away;
When safe, I will not suffer thee to
stay.
Thy weary men would be with ease con-
tent;
Their sails are tatter'd, and their masts
are spent.
If by no merit I thy mind can move,
What thou deny'st my merit, give my
love.
Stay, till I learn my loss to undergo;
And give me time to struggle with my
woe.
If not, know this, I will not suffer long;
My life's too loathsome, and my love too
strong.
Death holds my pen and dictates what I
say,
While cross my lap the Trojan sword I
lay.
My tears flow down: the sharp edge cuts
their flood,
And drinks my sorrows that must drink
my blood.
How well thy gift does with my fate
agree!
My funeral pomp is cheaply made by
thee.
To no new wounds my bosom I display:
The sword but enters where Love made
the way.
But thou, dear sister, and yet dearer
friend,
Shalt my cold ashes to their urn attend.
Sichæus' wife let not the marble boast,
I lost that title, when my fame I lost.
This short inscription only let it bear:
"Unhappy Dido lies in quiet here.
The cause of death, and sword by which
she dy'd,
Æneas gave: the rest her arm supply'd."
—JOHN DRYDEN.

THE PRECEPTOR OF LOVE

OVID

[From the *Art of Love*, Book I]

The lover of Roman elegy came to look
upon himself as peculiarly fitted by experience to give instruction to others in
the art of love. Tibullus and Propertius
give only hints of this point of view; Ovid
comes out boldly with the announcement,
at the beginning of a textbook on the
subject, that he is the expert and supreme
master.

In Cupid's school whoe'er would take
degree,
Must learn his rudiments by reading me.
Seamen with sailing arts their vessels
move;
Art guides the chariot: Art instructs to
love.
Of ships and chariots others know the
rule;
But I am master in Love's mighty school.
Cupid indeed is obstinate and wild,
A stubborn god; but yet the god's a
child:
Easy to govern in his tender age,
Like fierce Achilles in his pupillage:
That hero, born for conquest, trembling
stood
Before the Centaur, and receiv'd the rod.
As Chiron mollify'd his cruel mind
With art, and taught his warlike hands
to wind
The silver strings of his melodious lyre:
So Love's fair goddess does my soul
inspire,
To teach her softer arts; to sooth the
mind,
And smooth the rugged breasts of
human-kind.
Yet Cupid and Achilles each with scorn
And rage were fill'd; and both were
goddess-born.
The bull, reclaim'd and yok'd, the
burthen draws;
The horse receives the bit within his
jaws;

And stubborn Love shall bend beneath
    my sway,
Though struggling oft he strives to
    disobey.
He shakes his torch, he wounds me with
    his darts;
But vain his force, and vainer are his
    arts.
The more he burns my soul, or wounds
    my sight,
The more he teaches to revenge the spite.
  I boast no aid the Delphian god
    affords,
Nor auspice from the flight of chattering
    birds;
Nor Clio nor her sisters have I seen;
As Hesiod saw them on the shady green:
Experience makes my work; a truth so
    try'd
You may believe; and Venus be my
    guide.

—JOHN DRYDEN.

THE EXILE

OVID

[Tristia IV, 8]

The reasons for Ovid's banishment are
not understood. His exile served to change
completely his outlook on life. The flip-
pancy, the fine spirit of fun and playful-
ness fell away, and in their place grew up
an attitude of bitterness and despair
which colored everything he wrote after
his departure from Rome.

Now the swan's plumes are o'er my tem-
    ples shed;
White age my sable hair has silvery
    spread:
Frail years creep on: a life inert is near;
Now scarce erect my frame infirm I rear:
Now were it fit, some term to toil as-
    signed,
No fear should vex solicitous my mind:
That I should reap my ever favourite
    ease,

And my soft leisure with light studies
    please,
Haunt my small house, my ancient home
    and board,
And patrimonial fields, that miss their
    lord,
While a loved wife, dear children, should
    enfold
My neck, and in my country I grew old.
Thus had I hoped to steal my life away,
Not undeserving of this mild decay:
The Gods thought otherwise: o'er sea
    and land
They drove me to this bleak Sarmatian
    strand
In hollow docks the shattered ships re-
    cline;
Lest, in mid-ocean, split the starting
    pine;
Lest faint he fall, and shame his palm-
    crowned speed,
The languid race-horse crops the grassy
    mead:
The veteran soldier, active now no more,
Hangs by his old fireside the arms he
    bore:
So, while in tardy age my powers decline,
The wand of free dismissal should be
    mine.
'Twas time no more to breathe a foreign
    air,
Nor to a Scythian spring in thirst repair;
But to wide gardens, (such I had) re-
    treat,
Or seek the face of men in Rome's en-
    livening street.
This, for no thoughts the future could
    divine,
This soft old age I hoped would have
    been mine.
The fates withstood: my early years they
    blessed,
And bade calamity weigh down the rest.
Ten lustres, free from moral stain, are
    fled:
In life's worst stage misfortune bows my
    head.
The goal of ease just opening to my view,

A dreadful shock my chariot wheels
    o'erthrew:
Ah! madman! have I forced from HIM a
    frown,
Than whom the world no milder heart
    has known?
And do my crimes that clemency exceed?
Yet life is spared me for my error's deed.
Ah me! a life beneath the Northern
    pole;
Left to the Euxine's waves that blacken-
    ing roll:
Had Delphos' cave, Dodona's oak, in
    strain
Prophetic warned me, I had deemed them
    vain.

But nought so strong, though adamant
    its frame,
As that its strength repels Jove's rushing
    flame:
Nor aught so high, above misfortune's
    rod,
But lies beneath the o'er-ruling arm of
    God.
What though my fault, in part, these
    miseries drew,
Too hard a doom from angry heaven I
    rue.
Warned by my fate, HIS gracious favour
    prize,
Who sits vicegerent of the Deities.

—C. A. ELTON.

VII. FABLES: PHÆDRUS

Phædrus was a freedman, possibly of
Augustus, who is thought to have written
his *Fables* in the reign of Tiberius (14
to 37). Fables of this type were written
at least as early as the sixth century B.C.
Those of Æsop were widely popular
among the Greeks, and served as models
for later imitators. The collection by
Phædrus is the earliest now in existence.

THE PURPOSE OF FABLE-WRITING

[From the *Prologue*]

What from the founder Æsop fell,
In neat familiar verse I tell:
Twofold's the genius of the page,
To make you smile and make you
    sage.
But if the critics we displease,
By wrangling brutes and talking trees,
Let them remember, ere they blame,
We're working neither sin nor shame;
'Tis but a play to form the youth
By fiction, in the cause of truth.

—CHRISTOPHER SMART.

THE WOLF AND THE LAMB

[*Fables* I, 1]

By thirst incited; to the brook
The Wolf and Lamb themselves betook.
The Wolf high up the current drank,
The Lamb far lower down the bank.
Then, bent his rav'nous maw to cram,
The Wolf took umbrage at the Lamb.
"How dare you trouble all the flood,
And mingle my good drink with mud?"
"Sir," says the Lambkin, sore afraid,
"How should I act, as you upbraid?
The thing you mention cannot be,
The stream descends from you to me."
Abashed by facts, says he, "I know
'Tis now exact six months ago
You strove my honest fame to blot"—
"Six months ago, sir, I was not."
"Then 'twas th' old ram thy sire," he
    cried,
And so he tore him, till he died.
    To those this fable I address
Who are determined to oppress,
And trump up any false pretence,
But they will injure innocence.

—CHRISTOPHER SMART.

The Dog in the River

[Fables I, 4]

The churl that wants another's fare
Deserves at least to lose his share.
  As through the stream a Dog conveyed
A piece of meat, he spied his shade
In the clear mirror of the flood,
And thinking it was flesh and blood,
Snapped to deprive him of the treat:—
But mark the glutton's self-defeat,
Missed both another's and his own,
Both shade and substance, beef and bone.
  —Christopher Smart.

The Man and the Weasel

[Fables I, 22]

A Weasel, by a person caught,
And willing to get off, besought
The man to spare. "Be not severe
On him that keeps your pantry clear
Of those intolerable mice."
"This were," says he, "a work of price,
If done entirely for my sake,
And good had been the plea you make:
But since, with all these pains and care,
You seize yourself the dainty fare
On which those vermin used to fall,
And then devour the mice and all,
Urge not a benefit in vain."
This said, the miscreant was slain.
  The satire here those chaps will own,
Who, useful to themselves alone,
And bustling for a private end,
Would boast the merit of a friend.
  —Christopher Smart.

The Dog and the Wolf

[Fables III, 6]

I will as briefly as I may,
The sweets of liberty display.
  A Wolf half famished, chanced to see
A Dog, as fat as dog could be:

For one day meeting on the road,
They mutual compliments bestowed:
"Prithee," says Isgrim, faint and weak,
"How came you so well fed and sleek?
I starve, though stronger of the two."
"It will be just as well with you,"
The Dog quite cool and frank replied,
"If with my master you'll abide."
"For what?" "Why merely to attend,
And from night thieves the door defend."
"I gladly will accept the post,
What! shall I bear with snow and frost
And all this rough inclement plight,
Rather than have a home at night,
And feed on plenty at my ease?"
"Come, then, with me"—the Wolf agrees.
But as they went the mark he found,
Where the Dog's collar had been bound:
"What's this, my friend?" "Why, noth-
      ing." "Nay,
Be more explicit, sir, I pray."
"I'm somewhat fierce and apt to bite,
Therefore they hold me pretty tight,
That in the day-time I may sleep,
And night by night my vigils keep.
At eveningtide they let me out,
And then I freely walk about:
Bread comes without a care of mine.
I from my master's table dine;
The servants throw me many a scrap,
With choice of pot-liquor to lap;
So, I've my bellyful, you find."
"But can you go where you've a mind?"
"Not always, to be flat and plain."
"Then, Dog, enjoy your post again,
For to remain this servile thing,
Old Isgrim would not be a king."
  —Christopher Smart.

Æsop at Play

[Fables III, 13]

As Æsop was with boys at play,
And had his nuts as well as they,
A grave Athenian, passing by,
Cast on the sage a scornful eye,
As on a dotard quite bereaved:

Which, when the moralist perceived,
(Rather himself a wit professed
Than the poor subject of a jest)
Into the public way he flung
A bow that he had just unstrung:
"There solve, thou conjurer," he cries,
"The problem, that before thee lies."
The people throng; he racks his brain,
Nor can the thing enjoined explain.
At last he gives it up—the seer

Thus then in triumph made it clear:
"As the tough bow exerts its spring,
A constant tension breaks the string;
But if 'tis let at seasons loose,
You may depend upon its use."
   Thus recreative sports and play
Are good upon a holiday,
And with more spirit they'll pursue
The studies which they shall renew.
          —CHRISTOPHER SMART.

DESPOTISM AND SUPPRESSION

FIRST CENTURY A.D.

THE extravagant hopes of the return of a golden age, which enthusiasm for Augustus and his policy had raised, were naturally not possible of fulfillment. The new form of government indeed worked splendidly in Italy and the provinces, and few among the Italians or provincials could have been found to wish for any change, for they learned that peace, prosperity, and protection of life and property were all but guaranteed them. It was in Rome, the capital, that friction developed. There was the emperor and there the senate. The emperor was himself chosen from this class, and set over it. From it of course would come his successor. Hence inevitably an emperor of suspicious disposition might be inclined to see a rival and possible supplanter in any prominent senator. Then, too, because of the exalted position of the emperor, there soon arose a class of people who by a policy of flattery hoped to advance their fortunes under imperial favor. On the other hand, probably partly as a reaction against flattery and partly from an inherited republicanism, a small group of irreconcilables, heart and soul opposed to the Imperial régime, developed. There was, no doubt, a class which favored the principate and yet would preserve an independence of thought on questions of policy before the senate; but able and fortunate indeed was the senator who could successfully maintain such a position and his self respect under the eye of a Caligula or a Nero. And lucky the emperor who was blessed with popularity, tact, and common-sense enough to steer a safe course amid conditions always potentially so dangerous.

The conditions of the time were reflected in the literature, which was strongly influenced by them, particularly so because from the senatorial class, or from people associated with it, came many of the writers. Those who wished to present their own ideas tended to confine themselves to topics not at all, or but remotely, connected with politics, while those who would write of state and emperor regularly did so in flattering vein. The publication of independent studies on history and government was rather too hazardous to be popular. In fact the works of some who indulged in free speech were suppressed and their authors removed by enforced suicide. Under such conditions literature of the first rank could not and did not develop, and therefore it is often necessary to refer to writers of the second century in regard to the history of the first.

I. REALIZATION OF POLITICAL CONDITIONS

THE HISTORIAN: TACITUS

Cornelius Tacitus was born about 55 and died about 120. He entered the senatorial career and advanced through the usual preliminary offices to the consulship, and ultimately to the honorable post of proconsul of Asia. He was a leader of the bar at Rome, and in his legal work was at times associated with Pliny, his intimate friend.

The historical works of Tacitus, the *Annals* and the *Histories,* form a continuation of Livy's history, carrying the narrative forward to cover the first century of the Empire. Because of the attitude of the tyrannical Domitian, Tacitus was compelled to wait until he was well advanced in years before giving expression to his estimate of the characters and the deeds of the emperors and to his bitterness over the loss of individual freedom under the Cæsars. His first productions were three short pieces in preparation for the greater works to follow—a dialogue on the decay of oratory, a life of his father-in-law Agricola, and a sketch of Germany and the German tribes.

As Livy was the historian of the Roman Republic, so was Tacitus for the first century of the Empire, and there was none to rival him. He had not the scientific accuracy of Thucydides, nor the full flowing periods of Livy. He preferred a short sentence, and the biting epigram of which he was a master. He excelled in the presenting of historic scenes with dramatic intensity, and in the psychological study of character. The actors on the stage of history, their thoughts, and plans, and moods, and characters interested him tremendously, more than did the problems and conditions of the times.

THE BEGINNINGS OF DESPOTISM

[From The *Annals*, Book I]

Tacitus traces the beginnings of the despotism that prevailed in the first century back to the establishment of the Empire by Augustus, which had been welcomed as the dawn of a golden age.

IN the beginning, Rome was ruled by Kings. Lucius Brutus established liberty and the Consulship. The Dictatorship was resorted to in emergencies. The authority of the Decemvirs lasted for only two years; that of the Military Tribunes with Consular Powers for no long period. The tyrannies of Cinna and of Sulla were short-lived; the ascendency of Pompeius and Crassus passed quickly on to Cæsar, the swords of Lepidus and Antonius made way before Augustus: who under the title of "Princeps" took the whole world, worn out by civil conflict, under Imperial rule.

The story of ancient Rome, in her triumphs and reverses, has been related by illustrious writers; nor were men of genius wanting to tell of Augustus and his times, until the rising spirit of sycophancy bid them beware. The histories of Tiberius and Caius, of Claudius and Nero, were either falsified through fear, if written during their life-time; or composed under feelings of fresh hatred after their fall. I purpose, therefore, to write shortly of Augustus and his end, and then narrate the reigns of Tiberius and his successors; unmoved, as I have no reason to be moved, by either hatred or partiality.

When the last army of the Republic had fallen with Brutus and Cassius on the field; when Sextus Pompeius had been crushed in Sicily; and when the deposition of Lepidus, followed by the death of Antonius, had left Augustus sole leader of the Julian party, he laid aside the title of Triumvir, assumed the Consulship, and professed himself content with the Tribunitian Power for the protection of the plebs. But when he had won the soldiery by bounties, the populace by cheap corn, and all classes alike by the sweets of peace, he rose higher and higher by degrees, and drew into his own hands all the functions of the Senate, the magistrates and the laws. And there was no one to oppose; for the most ardent patriots had fallen on the field, or in the proscriptions; and the rest of the nobles, advanced in wealth and place in proportion to their servility, and drawing profit out of the new order of affairs, preferred the security of the present to the hazards of the past.

Nor did the provinces resent the change; for the rule of the Senate and the People had become odious to them from the contests between the great leaders, and the greed of the magistrates, against whom the laws, upset by force, by favour, and, in fine, by bribery, were powerless to protect them.

Meanwhile Augustus, as buttresses to his rule, advanced Claudius Marcellus, his sister's son, to the priesthood and Curule Ædileship, while yet a lad; and bestowed the honour of two Consulships on Marcus Agrippa—a man of ignoble birth, but a stout soldier, and partner in his victories. When Marcellus died, he took Agrippa as his son-in-law; and distinguished his two step-sons, Tiberius Nero and Claudius Drusus, with Imperatorial titles, though as yet there was no lack of heirs in his own family.

For he had adopted the two sons of Agrippa, Gaius and Lucius, into the family of the Cæsars; and before they assumed the manly gown, had caused them to be styled "Chiefs of the Youth," and to be designated Consuls—honours which he had affected to decline, but had most ardently coveted for them. But first Agrippa died; then the two Cæsars were cut off—whether by an untimely fate, or through the machinations of their step-mother Livia—the younger of them on his way to join the Spanish army, the elder when returning wounded from Armenia. Tiberius was now the sole surviving step-son of Augustus; for his brother Drusus had perished long before. On him therefore all hopes were centred. He was adopted as a son, made colleague in the "Imperium," admitted to share the Tribunitian Power, and exhibited to all the armies: his mother no longer intriguing for him in secret, but affording him open encouragement.

For Livia had acquired such an ascendency over Augustus in his old age, that he cast out on the island of Planasia his only surviving grandson, Agrippa Postumus: an uncultured youth, no doubt, with nothing but brute bodily strength to recommend him, but one who had never been found guilty of any open misdemeanour. And yet so anxious was Augustus to strengthen his position that he appointed Germanicus, the son of Drusus, to command of the eight legions on the Rhine, and ordered his adoption by Tiberius, although Tiberius had a young son of his own.

All wars had now ceased except that against the Germans; and even that was being continued rather to wipe out the disgrace of the loss of Quintilius Varus and his legions, than from the desire to extend the empire, or for any profitable end. Tranquillity reigned at home; the magistrates were called by their old names; the younger generation had been born since Actium, the elder, for the most part, during the course of the Civil Wars: how many were there left who had beheld the Republic?

Thus a revolution had been accomplished. The old order had passed away; everything had suffered change. The days of equality were gone: men looked to the Prince for his commands, having no anxiety for the present, so long as Augustus was of the age, and had the strength, to keep himself, his house and the public peace secure. But when he advanced in years, when his health and strength failed, and his approaching end gave birth to new hopes, some few discoursed idly on the blessings of liberty; many dreaded war; some longed for it.

But the greater number pulled to pieces the characters of their future masters with comments such as these:— Agrippa, they said, was a savage, exasperated by contumelious treatment; he had neither the years nor the experience to bear the weight of empire. Tiberius Nero was of ripe age, and a tried warrior: but he had all the old pride of the Claudii in his blood; and, however carefully suppressed, many indications of a cruel temper had escaped him. He had been brought up from infancy in a reigning house; Consulships and Triumphs had been heaped upon him in his youth: even during the years of exile which he had spent in Rhodes, under pretence of retreat, he had done nothing but brood over his resentments, or practise hypocrisy and solitary debauch. And then there was his mother, with all the ungovernable passions of her sex: they would have to serve a woman, and two striplings into the bargain, who would begin by oppressing the commonwealth, and end by rending it in sunder.

Amid speculations such as these, the health of Augustus began to fail. Some suspected foul play on the part of his wife. For a rumour had got abroad that Augustus, some months before, with the privity of a few special friends, and with Fabius Maximus as sole companion, had journeyed to Planasia to see Agrippa. It was said that many tears had been shed, many signs of affection exchanged, between the two; and hopes were raised that the young man might be restored to his grandfather's home. The secret of this visit, it was reported, had been betrayed by Maximus to his wife Marcia, and by her to Livia. This had come to the ears of Augustus; and when Maximus died not long after (whether by his own hand or not was a matter of doubt), Marcia had been overheard lamenting

at his funeral, and blaming herself for her husband's death.

Be that as it may, Tiberius had scarcely reached Illyricum when he was recalled in haste by message from his mother. Whether on arriving at Nola he found Augustus still alive, or already dead, was never known. For Livia had placed a strict guard upon the palace and its approaches; favourable bulletins were issued from time to time; until, when every necessary precaution had been taken, it was announced in one and the same breath that Augustus was dead, and that Tiberius was in possession of the government.

The opening crime of the new reign was the murder of Agrippa Postumus. He was taken by surprise, and was unarmed; yet the centurion, though a determined man, had some difficulty in despatching him. Tiberius made no communication on the subject to the Senate. His father, he pretended, had left orders with the officer in charge to put Agrippa to death as soon as he himself should breathe his last. Now Augustus, no doubt, had said many harsh things about the young man's character, and had caused the Senate to decree his banishment; but he never hardened himself so far as to put any of his own family to death, nor is it credible that he should have slain his grandson to secure a step-son's safety. It is more probable that this hurried murder of a youth detested equally by Tiberius and by Livia, was the work of both; the former moved by fear, the latter by her hatred as a step-mother.

When the centurion reported, according to military custom, that he had executed the order, Tiberius replied that he had never given any such order; and that the man would have to answer to the Senate for his conduct. When this was known to Sallustius Crispus, who was in the secret—it was he who had sent the written instructions to the

Tribune—he was afraid the charge would be shifted on to his own shoulders, in which case, whether he should tell the truth or not, he would be in equal peril. He therefore warned Livia that the secrets of the palace, the private advice of friends, and the services of the soldiery, were things not to be published abroad: —Tiberius must not weaken the powers of the Principate by referring everything to the Senate. The condition of Imperial rule was this: that every one should be accountable to one man, and to one only.

Meanwhile all at Rome—Consuls, Senators, and Knights—were plunging into servitude. Men bearing the most illustrious names were the foremost with false professions; composing their features so as not to show too much pleasure at the death of the one prince, or too little at the accession of the other; blending tears with their smiles, and flattery with their lamentations. The Consuls, Sextus Pompeius and Sextus Appuleius, were the first to take the oath of allegiance, which they in turn administered to Seius Strabo and Gaius Turranius— the former Commandant of the Prætorian Cohorts, the latter, Superintendent of the corn-market. Then came the Senate, the soldiers, and the people. For Tiberius left all initiative with the Consuls, as though the old Republic were still standing, and as if he himself had not made up his mind to assume the Empire: even the edict by which he summoned the Senate he only put forth in virtue of the Tribunitian authority conferred on him in the lifetime of Augustus.

The edict itself was short, and moderate in tone:— He desired to take their advice as to the honours to be paid his father; he himself would not leave the body, nor undertake any other public duty. And yet, no sooner was Augustus dead, than he had given the password to the Prætorians as their commander; he had surrounded himself with guards and sentinels and all the paraphernalia of a court; he was escorted by soldiers to the Forum and to the Senate-house, and he had issued a proclamation to the army as though he were already Emperor: nowhere did he show hesitation save in his language to the Senate.

His chief reason for this attitude was his fear of Germanicus. That prince had many legions under his command, and a vast force of allies; he was the darling of the people; and it might be that he would prefer possession to expectation. Tiberius had regard also to public opinion. He wanted men to believe that he had been chosen and called to power by his countrymen, rather than that he had crept into it through the intrigues of a wife, or as the adopted son of a dotard. It transpired afterward that this air of hesitation was assumed deliberately, for the purpose of fathoming the feelings of the leading men; for Tiberius would distort a word or a look into an offence, and treasure it up in his memory.

At the first meeting of the Senate, Tiberius permitted no business to be transacted except that relating to the obsequies of Augustus. The testament was carried in by the Vestal Virgins. Tiberius and Livia were appointed heirs. Livia was to be adopted into the Julian house, and to receive the title of "Augusta." His grandsons and great-grandsons came next in the succession; in the third rank were many names of distinction, mostly those of personal enemies, inserted in a spirit of vain-glory, with an eye to the approbation of posterity. The amount bequeathed was not above the scale of a private fortune; but a sum of forty-three and a half million sesterces was left to the people and to the plebs. Each soldier of the Prætorian Cohorts was to receive one thousand sesterces; the soldiers of the Urban Cohorts five hundred; the legionaries, and the members of the Cohorts raised from Roman citizens, three hundred sesterces apiece.

The question of funeral honours was then considered. The most outstanding proposals were that of Gallus Asinius, that the procession should pass through the Triumphal Gate; and that of Lucius Arruntius, that the titles of the laws passed by the deceased, and the names of nations which he had conquered, should be borne before the body. To these Messalla Valerius added that the oath of allegiance to Tiberius should be renewed every year; and when challenged by Tiberius to say whether that motion had been made at his instigation, he replied that no man had prompted him: nor would he follow any counsel but his own in public matters, even though he might give offence thereby. Such was the only form of flattery still left untried!

It was carried by acclamation that the body should be borne to the pyre by Senators; an honour which Tiberius waived, in a tone of arrogant condescension. And to the people he issued a proclamation, praying them not to think of burning the body in the Forum, rather than at its appointed resting-place in the Campus Martius, nor to repeat the disturbances caused by excess of affection at the obsequies of the Immortal Julius.

On the funeral day, the troops were drawn up on guard, amid the derision of those who had themselves beheld or had heard their elders describe the day when Rome, unripe as yet for slavery, had struck that ill-fated blow for freedom— the day when some regarded the assassination of Cæsar as a foul crime, others as a most glorious achievement: whereas now an aged emperor, after a long lease of power, and after providing his heirs with resources against the Commonwealth, had need of a guard of soldiers to keep order over his grave!

There followed much talk about Augustus. People idly marvelled that he had died upon the same day as that on which he had first entered on power; in the same house, in the very room, at Nola, in which his father Octavius had breathed his last. They dwelt upon the number of his consulships, equal to those of Valerius Corvus and Gaius Marius put together; they recounted how the Tribunitian Power had been continued to him for thirty-seven years; how the title of "Imperator" had been conferred upon him one-and twenty times: how other distinctions had been heaped on him, or invented in his honour.

Reflecting men discussed his career in various tones of praise or blame. Some maintained:—That he had been forced into civil war by regard for his father's memory, and by the exigencies of public affairs, which left no room for law: and civil war was a thing which none could bring about or carry on clean-handed. He had made many concessions to Antonius, many also to Lepidus, in order to secure vengeance on his father's murderers; but when the latter became old and lethargic, and the former lost himself in debauch, no resource was left for the distracted country but the rule of one man. Yet even so, Augustus had not set up his government as King or Dictator, but under the name of "Princeps.' Under his rule, the frontiers had been pushed forward to the Ocean or to distant rivers; the provinces, the armies, and the fleets of the Empire had been brought into communication with one another. Justice had been dispensed at home; consideration had been shown to the allies; the city itself had been sumptuously adorned: and, if some few acts of violence had been committed, it had been in order to secure the general tranquillity.

On the other side it was said:—The pleas of filial duty and political necessity were but pretexts. It was lust of power which had prompted Augustus to attract the veterans by bribes, to collect an army while he was still a stripling and without office, to tamper with the troops of the Consul, and to affect sympathy with the

Pompeian party. After that, by virtue of a decree of the Senate, he had usurped the Prætorship, with its military and judicial powers; and when Hirtius and Pansa were slain in battle—whether or no those generals were so slain: or had died, the latter, of a poisoned wound, the former, at the hands of his own soldiers treacherously set on by Octavianus—he had assumed command of both armies; he had forced the Senate to make him Consul against its will, and having received an army to oppose Antonius, had turned it against his own country: the proscriptions, the confiscations, were measures which not even their perpetrators could approve. The deaths of Brutus and Cassius, indeed, might be deemed a tribute of vengeance to his father; though even so it were right for private hatred to give way before the public good. But he had tricked Sextus Pompeius by a pretence of peace, and Lepidus under the guise of friendship; later on, he had entrapped Antonius by the treaties of Tarentum and Brundisium, and by giving him his own sister in marriage—a treacherous alliance which Antonius had paid for with his blood. Peace, no doubt, had followed, but it was a peace stained with blood: there had been the disasters of Lollius and Varus abroad; at home, the executions of a Varro, an Egnatius, and a Iulus.

Nor was his private life spared:—He had torn Livia, when pregnant, from her husband, going through the farce of consulting the augurs whether she could rightfully marry without waiting for the child to be born; he had permitted the extravagance of a Quintus Tedius and a Vedius Pollio. And lastly, there was Livia: a very scourge to the Commonwealth as a mother, no less a scourge to the house of the Cæsars as a step-mother. What honours were left for the Gods, when Augustus ordained temples and images to be set up to himself as to a Deity, with Flamens and Priests to wor-

ship him? Even in adopting Tiberius as his successor, he had not been moved by affection, or by care for the public good; but having sounded the depths of that proud and cruel nature, he had sought to win glory for himself by contrast with an execrable successor.

For many years before, when Augustus was asking the Senate to confer anew the Tribunitian Power on Tiberius, though he spoke of him in terms of compliment, he had let fall some observations about his bearing, his manners and style of living, which under guise of apology bore all the character of a reproach.

—G. G. RAMSAY.

MUTINY ON THE RHINE

[From the *Annals,* Book I]

The government of the provinces continued under the Empire to be a serious problem. Such a revolt as that pictured here from the early part of the reign of Tiberius led on more than one occasion to the overthrow of the prince and the seating on the throne of a new emperor chosen by the armies.

About the same time, and from identical causes, disturbances broke out in the armies of the Rhine; and with all the greater violence, in proportion to their greater numbers. They indulged the hope also that Germanicus Cæsar, unable to brook a master over him, would lend himself to the legions: they were strong enough, they thought, to carry all before them. There were two armies on the banks of the Rhine. The Upper army, as it was called, was under the Legate Gaius Silius; Aulus Cæcina had command of the Lower: both alike were under the supreme command of Germanicus, who was at that time occupied in taking the census in the provinces of Gaul.

The army of Silius hesitated, watching the result of the movement elsewhere;

but the Lower army broke out in open mutiny. The movement began with the men of the 21st and 5th legions, who carried along with them the 1st and the 20th; all these four being at that time encamped together in the territory of the Ubii, with little or no work to occupy them. No sooner had the news of the death of Augustus arrived, than the town-bred recruits who had been raised in the city not long before, accustomed to license, and impatient of all labour, filled the simple minds of their comrades with the idea that the time had now come for the veterans to press for an early discharge, the younger soldiers for more pay, for all alike to demand some relief from their irksome duties, and wreak vengeance on the centurions for their brutality. And such talk was not confined to single agitators, like Percennius in the Pannonian army, nor addressed to trembling soldiers, looking anxiously around to armies more powerful than themselves. The spirit of sedition found many tongues and many voices:—The fortunes of Rome were in their own hands; it was by their victories that the Empire was extended, it was from their name that Emperors derived their titles.

Unnerved by the general frenzy, the Legate made no attempt at resistance. In one moment, an infuriated mob rushed with drawn swords upon the centurions— the objects, from time immemorial, of the soldiers' hatred, and the first victims of their violence. The men threw them down and beat them, sixty of them setting upon each centurion, so as to match the number of the centuries; then having belaboured and mangled them, they cast them out, many already dead, upon the entrenchments, or into the river. One of them called Septimius took refuge on the tribunal, and threw himself down before Cæcina's feet; but so determined was the demand made for him, that he was given up to death. One young man of spirit, called Cassius Chærea, who after-

wards acquired notoriety as one of the murderers of Gaius Cæsar, cut his way, sword in hand, through the armed mob which blocked his path.

The Tribunes, and the Commandant of the camp, now lost all authority. The men distributed among themselves all sentry and picket duty, and other matters of immediate urgency. To those who best understood the temper of the soldiery, nothing showed more clearly the serious and uncompromising character of the movement than this, that everything was done in concert, nothing at the prompting of a few; all rose to fury, or sunk into silence, like one man: with such uniformity and regularity that it seemed to be at the word of command.

Meantime Germanicus, as we have said, was taking the census in Gaul when he heard of the death of Augustus. He was the son of Drusus, brother of Tiberius; the grandson of Augusta; and his wife Agrippina, by whom he had several children, was the grand-daughter of Augustus. But he was disquieted by the secret hatred which both his uncle and his grandmother bore him: a hatred which was all the more bitter that it sprang from unworthy reasons. For the memory of his father Drusus was much cherished by the Roman people; and it was the popular belief that if he had succeeded to power, he would have restored the Republic. Germanicus had become the object of the same favour, and the same hopes; for his unassuming character, and his rare affability of manner, presented a strong contrast to the haughty looks and dark language of Tiberius. And besides all this, feminine rancours were at work. For Livia regarded Agrippina with a true step-mother's hatred; and Agrippina herself was somewhat passionate and imperious in temper, though her faults were all redeemed by her chastity and her devotion to her husband.

But the fact that Germanicus stood near to the succession only caused him to exert himself all the more strenuously for Tiberius. He took the oath of allegiance himself, and then administered it to the neighbouring tribes, and to the communities of Belgium. On hearing of the mutiny, he hurried back at once. The men met him outside the camp, their eyes cast down to the ground as if in penitence. As he passed within the lines, a babel of murmurs might be heard. Some seized his hand as if to kiss it, and then thrust his fingers into their mouths to let him feel their toothless gums; others pointed to their bodies bowed down with age. Perceiving the crowd about him to be without order, he bid them form up in maniples; they replied that they could hear him better as they were. Next, he ordered the standards to the front, so that the cohorts at least might be distinguished from one another; reluctantly they obeyed. Beginning with expressions of reverence to Augustus, he passed on to speak of the victories and triumphs of Tiberius, dwelling especially upon his splendid achievements in Germany, along with those same legions; he extolled the unanimity of Italy, the loyalty of the Gallic provinces:—Nowhere was there disturbance or disaffection. He was listened to in silence, or with slight murmurs of dissent.

He then touched on the mutiny:—Where was now their military subordination? he asked, where their old pride in discipline? Whither had they driven forth their Tribunes and their centurions? At this, with one consent, they bared their bodies, and pointed reproachfully to the marks of wounds and stripes. With a confused roar, they denounced the cost of exemptions, the smallness of their pay, the severity of their labours: naming one by one the making of earthworks and ditches, the collecting of fodder, timber and firewood, and every other kind of necessary work, or work devised to keep the camp from idleness. Fiercest of all was the clamour of the veterans. Counting up their thirty or more years of service, they implored him to find some remedy for their troubles: not to let them perish in the same round of toil, but to vouchsafe to them some limit to so arduous a service, and with repose, a competence.

Some even demanded of Germanicus the money bequeathed by Augustus, adding words of happy augury towards himself, signifying that, if he aimed at empire, they would back him up in the attempt. At this he leaped down headlong from the tribunal, as though himself infected with their crime; but the men thrust their arms in his way, threatening him with violence unless he returned. At that he drew his sword, raised it in the air, and exclaiming that he would rather die than play the traitor, he was in the act of plunging it into his breast, when the bystanders seized his arm, and held it back by force. Some voices from the densely packed crowd behind, and even, what almost passes belief, individual men coming close up to him, urged him to strike on; and one soldier called Calusidius offered him a drawn sword, adding:—It was sharper than his own. Infuriated as the men were, they thought this a cruel and inhuman speech; and during the pause which followed, Germanicus was hurried off by his friends into his tent.

A consultation was now held as to what should be done. Word came that the men were preparing to send envoys to bring over the Upper Army to the movement; that the town of the Ubii had been marked out for destruction; and that the troops, having once tasted plunder, would make a raid into Gaul. The alarm was heightened by the fact that the enemy were aware of the mutiny, and by the likelihood that they would make an incursion into Gaul if the riverbank were left unguarded; yet if they called out the auxiliary and allied forces against the seceding legions, they would be embarking on civil war. An unbending attitude was hazardous; to give way was ignominious: whether all or nothing were conceded, the Commonwealth would be in equal jeopardy. After all due consideration, it was resolved to write a letter in the Emperor's name granting discharge after twenty years' service; partial release to men of sixteen years' service, who should be kept under a standard of their own, and relieved of all duty except that of fighting; the sum claimed as legacies to be paid in full, and to twice the amount.

The soldiers felt that these terms were concocted for the emergency, and demanded their instant fulfilment. Accordingly the discharges were made out by the Tribunes at once; the payments in cash were to be deferred till the troops should return to their respective winter quarters. But as the men of the 5th and 21st legions refused to move till the money was paid in their present summer quarters, Germanicus had to make up the amount from the privy purses of himself and his staff. The 1st and 20th legions were conducted back to the country of the Ubii by the Legate Cæcina; when might be seen the disgraceful spectacle of the treasure-chests taken from Germanicus being conveyed among the standards and the eagles. Germanicus himself proceeded to the Upper Army, where the oath of allegiance was taken without hesitation by the 2nd, 13th, and 16th legions. The 14th hesitated for a moment; so the money and the discharge was granted to them unasked.

Meantime, in the country of the Chauci, a movement had begun among the veterans of the disaffected legions stationed there on outpost duty; but it was suppressed for the moment by the summary execution of two soldiers, on the order of Manius Ennius, Prefect of the camp. Salutary as this example was, the Prefect had exceeded his authority in ordering it; and as the trouble grew worse, he took to flight. Discovered and dragged from his hiding-place, he drew upon audacity for his protection:— To do violence to him, he declared, would be to lay hands, not on the Prefect of the camp, but on their General Germanicus—nay, upon the Emperor Tiberius himself. Having thus overawed the men who stood in his way, he seized the standard, headed with it towards the river, and proclaiming that all who left the ranks should be treated as deserters, he brought the force back to their winter quarters, disaffected indeed, but not in open mutiny.

Meanwhile the envoys from the Senate reached Germanicus on his return to the altar of the Ubii. Two legions were wintering there, the 1st and 20th, together with the recently discharged veterans under a standard of their own. Uneasy and conscience-stricken, a terror seized upon them that the envoys had come with orders from the Senate to cancel the concessions extorted by the mutiny; and with the usual tendency of a mob to fasten a charge, however false, on some one's shoulders, they laid the blame of the decree on Munatius Plancus, a Consular, who was at the head of the embassy. In the dead of night, they called for their standard, which was in the house of Germanicus. Mobbing the door of the house, they forced it open, dragged Germanicus from his bed, and compelled him to give up the standard under fear of death.

Later on, as they were parading along the camp-roads, they encountered the envoys, who having heard the uproar were on their way to the quarters of Germanicus. They loaded them with insults, and were on the point of murdering them—more particularly Plancus, who thought it beneath his dignity to take flight. The only refuge open to him was the camp of the 1st legion. Embracing the standards and the eagle, he sought to protect himself by their sacred character; but had not the standard-bearer Calpurnius prevented the men from proceeding to extremities, there would have been witnessed in a Roman camp a sight scarce ever seen even among our enemies—that of a Legate of the Roman people staining the altars of the Gods with his blood. At last, when day dawned, and it became impossible to distinguish soldiers from officers, and to discover what had happened, Germanicus ordered Plancus to be brought to him, and took him up on to the tribunal. Upbraiding the soldiers for their infatuation—now reviving, he declared, not so much from their own passions as through the wrath of the Gods—he explained to them the purpose of the mission; spoke with eloquence and sorrow of the rights of envoys, of the grievous and undeserved peril of Plancus, and of the disgrace thereby brought upon the legion; and having thus cowed rather than quieted the assemblage, he sent off the envoys under an escort of auxiliary cavalry.

At this perilous juncture, Germanicus was much blamed for not proceeding to the army of the Upper Rhine, which was still loyal, and would have afforded aid against the mutineers:—Mischief enough, and more than enough, had been done by discharges and bounties and other weak concessions. If he had no regard for his own life, why leave his little son and his wife, and his yet unborn child, among an infuriated soldiery, who had violated every human right? He should send these, at least, back in safety to their grandfather and their country. For a while he hesitated; and Agrippina would not listen to such counsels, protesting that she was of the blood of Augustus, and could face danger like the rest of her race. At last, tearfully embracing his wife, now great with child, and the son she had borne him, he prevailed on her to depart. And now the long sad line of women moved away; the General's wife a fugitive, carrying her little boy in her arms; her friends' wives dragging themselves after her, and weeping as they went: not less sorrowful were the friends that were left behind.

This spectacle, these wailings, more like those of a captured city than of a camp commanded by a Cæsar, drew towards them the eyes and the ears of even the common soldiers. Coming forth from their tents, What are these sounds of weeping? they ask; What this dismal procession? A company of high-born ladies—with no centurion, not even a soldier, for an escort; with none of the state or retinue that befit the wife of an Imperator—going forth to the Treveri, to seek protection at the hand of strangers!

A feeling of shame and pity came over them at the sight. They remembered her father Agrippa, her grandfather Augustus, and her father-in-law Drusus; they thought of her notable fertility, her incomparable purity; then of her infant son, born in camp, and brought up in the soldiers' quarters, to whom, in soldier fashion, they had given the name of "Little Boots" because to please the men he used to wear boots like those of the legionaries. But what moved them most of all was a feeling of jealousy towards the Treveri; so they threw themselves in the way, and implored her to come back and remain with them; some going after Agrippina herself, the greater number turning back to Germanicus. Stung to the quick with grief and indignation, he thus addressed the throng around him: Neither wife nor son are dearer to me than my father and my country; but my father is safe in his Imperial Majesty, and the other armies of Rome will protect the Empire. My wife and children, whom I would freely offer up to death for your glory, I am now removing from your rage; that whatever crime you may yet be meditating may be wiped out by my blood alone, and that you may not add to your guilt by the slaughter of the great-grand-son of Augustus, the murder of the daughter-in-law of Tiberius. For of what insolence, of what impiety, have you not been guilty, during these past days? What name shall I give to this concourse? Am I to call you soldiers?—you who have besieged the son of your Emperor with arms and entrenchments? Or citizens—you who have trampled under foot the authority of the Senate; who have disregarded rights accorded even to enemies; who have done violence to the sacred person of an envoy, and the law of nations? The Divine Julius quelled a mutiny by one word: styling those who broke their oath of fealty "Quirites." The Divine Augustus, by one look, made the legions at Actium quail before him. Though I be not such as they, yet am I sprung from them; and it were a strange and unworthy thing if soldiers from Spain, or Syria, were to scorn my commands. And will you, the men of the 1st legion, who received your standard from Tiberius; and you of the 20th—you who shared in his many battles, whom he enriched with so many rewards—will you thus notably repay your General? Is this the word I am to carry to my father, at a time when he is receiving from other provinces no news but what is good? How his own recruits, his own veterans, are not content with discharge and bounties; how here, and here alone, centurions are being murdered, Tribunes cast out, envoys beleaguered, camp and river stained with blood? And that I am in the midst of enemies, holding my life at their mercy!

Why, O why, did you, unthinking friends, on that first day of assembling, hold back the steel which I was ready to plunge into my breast? A better and kindlier act was his who offered to me this sword! For I should have fallen then with no guilty knowledge of outrages by my army; and you would have

chosen for yourselves a General, to leave my death indeed unpunished, but to avenge Varus and his three legions. For may the Gods grant that the Belgians—ready as they are to offer themselves—may not have the honour and glory of restoring the Roman name, and of conquering the tribes of Germany! O! may thy spirit, Divine Augustus, that has now been received into Heaven; may thy image, O my father Drusus, and thy memory, in the hearts of these same soldiers, alive once more to a sense of shame and honour, wash out this stain, and turn this fury between fellow-citizens to the destruction of our foes! And you also: you whose looks, whose hearts, I see to be other than they were: if you would render obedience to your General; if you would restore to the Senate their envoys, to me my wife and child: withdraw from the contagion! Put forth from you the breeders of sedition! Thus only will you make fast your penitence, thus firmly bind your loyalty.

This speech turned the soldiers into suppliants. Humbly acknowledging the justice of these reproaches, they implored Germanicus to punish the guilty, to forgive those who had been led astray, and to lead them out against the enemy; they entreated him to recall his wife, and to let the legions have their foster-child back again, rather than hand him over as a hostage to the Gauls. Germanicus excused Agrippina from returning because of her lying-in, now near at hand, and the wintry season; but he would let his son come back: the rest they must do themselves.

At this they hurried away like new men, and dragged the ring-leaders in chains before Gaius Cætronius, the Legate of the 1st legion, who judged the culprits and passed sentence upon them one by one in the following fashion. In front stood the legions, with swords drawn; the accused was put up to view by the Tribune on a raised platform. If the men shouted "Guilty," he was thrown headlong down, and cut to pieces. The troops delighted in the slaughter, as though they were thereby absolving themselves; and Cæsar allowed it to go on, since in this way, without any order from him, the severity and odium alike were laid upon the same shoulders. The example thus set was followed by the veterans, who were despatched soon afterwards to Rætia, under pretence of protecting that province from an attack threatened by the Suevi; but in reality, to remove them from a camp whose grim associations reminded them not only of their crime, but also of the rigour with which it had been repressed. Germanicus then revised the list of centurions. Each was called up in turn, and stated his name, rank, and country; his period of service; his acts of gallantry, and his decorations, if he had any. If men and officers commended him for energy and integrity, he was permitted to retain his rank. If they agreed in declaring him corrupt or cruel, he was discharged from the service.

Things having thus been settled for the moment, a trouble no less formidable remained because of the defiant attitude of the 5th and 21st legions, who were in camp at a place called Vetera, sixty miles away. These men had been the first to mutiny; they had committed the worst excesses; and now, neither awed by the punishment of their comrades, nor moved by their repentance, they remained as intractable as ever. Germanicus accordingly prepared to despatch a flotilla down the Rhine with a force of legionaries and allied troops, determined to fight it out if his authority were disputed.

At Rome, meanwhile, the news of the outbreak in the German army had arrived before the issue of the troubles in Illyricum was known. The city was in a panic; and men censured Tiberius in this fashion:—He was befooling the poor helpless Senate and people with his pretences of hesitation, at the moment when the legions were in revolt, and needed something more than the authority of two youths, new to command, to put them down. He should have gone himself, and confronted them with the Imperial presence: they would have given way before a prince of ripe experience, himself the final arbiter of rewards and punishments. Augustus, in extreme old age, had been able to pay repeated visits to Germany; was Tiberius, in the prime of life, to sit still in the Senate-house, carping at the speeches of the Fathers? Precautions enough had been taken to secure the servility of the capital: it was time that something was done to soothe the army, and reconcile it to a state of peace.

Talk like this made no impression upon Tiberius; he was resolved not to quit the capital, nor to expose himself and the Commonwealth to risk. He was distracted by many opposing considerations: —Of the two armies, the German was the more powerful, the Pannonian the nearer to Rome; the former had the resources of Gaul behind it, Italy lay at the mercy of the latter. Which of the two should he visit first? Whichever he put last, would be a-flame at the indignity. In sending a son to each, he put both on an equality; yet without compromising his own dignity, which gained in reverence from the distance. Then again, the young men might be excused for referring some points to their father, and if the troops resisted Drusus or Germanicus, they might be crushed or conciliated by himself: but if they were to flout their Emperor, what resource was left?

For all that, however, he made as though he were always on the point of starting; he selected his staff, collected his baggage, and had ships made ready; then pleading various excuses of weather, business, and what not, he hoodwinked the shrewdest for a time; the populace for a while longer; longest of all, the Provinces.

Meantime Germanicus had collected his army, and had everything ready for taking vengeance upon the rebels. Thinking, nevertheless, that he should still give them time to take the matter into their own hands, according to the example lately set, he sent on a letter to Cæcina, informing him of his approach with a strong force, and announcing that unless the guilty were punished before he came, he would put all indiscriminately to the sword. This despatch Cæcina read privately to the eagle- and standard-bearers, and to the best affected among the men, urging them to save the honour of the corps as well as their own lives. In time of peace, he remarked, cases are judged upon their merits; when it comes to fighting, innocent and guilty fall alike.

These men sounded those whom they thought the likeliest; and having satisfied themselves that the majority were loyal, fixed a time, at the suggestion of the Legate, for falling upon the most obnoxious and prominent agitators. At a given signal, they burst into their tents, and cut them down unawares, none but those in the secret knowing how the slaughter had begun, or where it was to end.

Never was there a conflict in any civil war like to this. There was no battle; there were no opposing camps: men who had messed together by day, and slept together by night, rose out of the same beds, divided themselves into sides, and fell upon each other. The shouts, the wounds, and the blood, every one could see or hear; but no cause for it could be seen: chance ruled all. Some loyal men were slain with the rest; for the worst offenders had taken up their arms on discovering against whom the attack was aimed. There was no Legate, no Tribune, to control; every man had free license to glut his vengeance to the full. Germanicus entered the camp soon after-

wards; and declaring, with many tears, that this was a massacre, and no remedy, he ordered the bodies to be burned.

The minds of the soldiers being still set on blood, a longing seized them to march against the enemy as an atonement for their madness; as though there were no other way to appease the spirits of their comrades than to expose their guilty breasts to honourable wounds. Falling in with their ardour, Germanicus threw a bridge across the Rhine, and passed a force of twelve thousand legionaries over the river, together with twenty-six cohorts and eight squadrons of the allies, who had never wavered in their allegiance.

The Germans were not far off. They had rejoiced to see our attention taken up, first by the holiday on the death of Augustus, and afterwards by the mutiny. A rapid march brought Germanicus to the Cæsian forest, where he crossed the lines laid out by Tiberius and encamped upon the works, his front and his rear protected by entrenchments, his flanks by barricades of trees. He had next to traverse a dense forest country, having two routes to choose from—one the shorter and usual route, the other more difficult and unfrequented, and for that reason unguarded by the enemy. Selecting the longer of the two, he pushed on with all speed; for his scouts had brought word that the Germans were to hold a festival that night, with games and banqueting. Cæcina was sent on with some light cohorts to clear a way through the forest; the legions followed at some little distance. A bright starry night favoured the enterprise. On reaching the Marsian villages, he drew his posts all round them. The enemy were already in bed, or sprawling upon the tables, suspecting no danger; there were no sentries set in front; all was carelessness and confusion: for they had no thought of battle, and even such quiet as they were enjoying was but the feeble and relaxed repose of drunkenness.

To extend the area of his ravages, Germanicus divided his eager troops into four columns, and laid waste fifty miles of country with fire and sword. No pity was shown to either age or sex. Things sacred and profane alike—even the most famous temple of the tribe, that of the Goddess called Tanfana—were levelled to the ground; and as our men had fallen on the enemy when half-asleep, unarmed or dispersed, they had sustained no loss.

The news of this massacre roused the Bructeri, the Tubantes, and the Usipetes, who beset the forest passes by which the army had to return. Apprised of this, Germanicus arranged his retreat alike for marching and for fighting. The auxiliary cohorts, with part of the cavalry, led the way; then came the 1st legion. In the middle was the baggage, guarded on the left flank by the 21st, on the right by the 5th legions; the 20th protected the rear, and behind came the rest of the allies.

The enemy bided their time till the force was stretching out through the pass; then making feint attacks upon the front and flanks, they fell with their full force upon the rear. The light cohorts were being thrown into confusion by the dense masses of the Germans, when Germanicus rode up to the 20th:—"Now is the time," he shouted, "to wipe out all memory of the mutiny! Forward! quick forward! and turn your shame into glory!" Inflamed by these words, the 20th burst through the enemy's line with one dash, and drove them back with great slaughter into the open; at the same moment the van emerged from the pass, and threw up entrenchments for a camp. From this point onward the march was undisturbed. Rendered confident by their recent successes, and forgetting past occurrences, the troops settled down into their winter quarters.

The news of these events caused Ti-

berius no less anxiety than satisfaction. He was pleased that the mutiny had been got under; but he was annoyed that Germanicus should have gained the good-will of the soldiers by gifts of money, and by shortening the term of service. He was jealous also of his military success. Nevertheless, he brought his exploits before the notice of the Senate, and said much in his praise, though in language too carefully studied for effect to create an impression of sincerity. His satisfaction with Drusus, and at the ending of the movement in Illyricum, he expressed in fewer words; but they were more earnest and sincere. And he extended to the Pannonian army all the concessions which Germanicus had granted to the other.

—G. G. Ramsay.

The Purpose of History

[From the *Annals*, Book III]

Tacitus has the same conception of the ethical function of history as his predecessor Livy.

It is no part of my purpose to set forth every motion that was made in the Senate, but only such as were either very honourable or specially disgraceful in their character. For I deem it to be the chief function of history to rescue merit from oblivion, and to hold up before evil words and evil deeds the terror of the reprobation of posterity. And in those days, so deep, so foul, was the taint of flattery, that not only men of leading in the state —men who could only maintain their illustrious position by subserviency—but also the whole body of Consulars, many of prætorian rank, and even many ordinary senators, would rise in the Senate and outbid one another in making fulsome and extravagant proposals. Tradition tells how Tiberius, every time that he left the Senate-house, would exclaim in Greek, "O men meet for slavery!" For even he, enemy of public freedom as he was, felt disgust at such abject and all-enduring servility.

—G. G. RAMSAY.

FREEDOM OF SPEECH

[From the *Annals*, Book IV]

The genuine freedom of oral and written speech enjoyed under the Republic had given place to specious flattery and degrading servility under the Empire. Tacitus himself under the tyrant Domitian preferred silence.

The writer of ancient history finds few to criticise him; it concerns no one if he praise too warmly the armies of Carthage or of Rome. But there are many living now whose ancestors suffered punishment, or incurred disgrace, under Tiberius; and even if the families concerned have died out, there are those who deem an attack upon vices akin to their own to be an attack upon themselves. Even glory and virtue have their enemies; for when placed too close to their opposites they wear an aspect of rebuke. But I must return from this digression.

In this year Cremutius Cordus was impeached upon a novel charge, now heard for the first time—that he had commended Marcus Brutus in his History, and called Gaius Cassius "The last of the Romans." The accusers, Satrius Secundus and Pinarius Natta, were both clients of Sejanus; which fact, as well as the evident displeasure with which Tiberius listened to the defence, proved fatal to the accused. Having made up his mind to die, Cremutius spoke as follows: "My words, Conscript Fathers, are arraigned; so innocent am I of any evil deed. Yet these words were not uttered against the Emperor, or his father, the persons to whom the law of Majesty applies: my offence is that I

have praised Brutus and Cassius, men whose deeds have been recorded by many, whom none have named without respect. Titus Livius, a writer pre-eminent for eloquence and candour, eulogised Gnæus Pompeius so warmly that Augustus called him 'a Pompeian': but this caused no interruption in their friendship. He speaks of Scipio and Afranius, of this same Cassius, this Brutus, never as raiders and parricides—the names men give them now—but often as distinguished men. Asinius Pollio gives a noble account of them in his history; Messalla Corvinus used to call Cassius 'his own Imperator'; and yet both lived on wealthy and honoured to the end. When Marcus Cicero wrote a book in which he lauded Cato to the skies, what else did the Dictator Cæsar do but write a speech in answer, as though he were pleading before a judge? The letters of Antonius, the speeches of Brutus, contain the most bitter abuse of Augustus, as false as it is foul; men read the poems of Bibaculus and Catullus, which are full of insults to the Cæsars; yet the Divine Julius, the Divine Augustus, bore these things and passed them by. Whether in this more to praise their forbearance, or their wisdom, I know not: for the insult which goes unnoticed dies; to resent it, is to accord it recognition.

I say nothing of the Greeks, who tolerated not liberty only, but license, or at the most, paid back words with words; and men have always been free to speak uncensured of those whom Death has placed beyond the reach of hate or favour. Am I, forsooth, in arms, with Cassius and Brutus, upon the plains of Philippi, or inflaming the people to civil war by my harangues? Is the case not rather this: that just as these men are known to us by their statues—statues respected even by their conqueror—so in like manner, though dead for more than seventy years, they still hold their place upon the page of history? For posterity awards to every man the honour that is his due; and if I be now condemned, men will remember not Cassius and Brutus only, but me also."

Cremutius then left the Senate-house, and put an end to himself by starvation. His books, by order of the Senate, were burned by the Ædiles. And yet they were saved; hidden away for a time, they were again put forth. Hence one cannot but smile at the dulness of those who believe that the authority of to-day can extinguish men's memories tomorrow. Nay rather, they who penalise genius do but extend its power: whether they be foreign tyrants, or imitators of foreign tyranny, they do but reap dishonour for themselves, and glory for their victims.

—G. G. RAMSAY.

TYRANNY BEGETS TYRANTS

[From the *Annals*, Book VI]

Tyranny is not necessarily the result of a ruler's character. It is often forced upon the ruler by the very system of government of which he is the head.

At Rome, meanwhile, the seeds of future blood-shed were being sown. Lælius Balbus had brought a charge of treason against Acutia, formerly wife of Publius Vitellius; but when she was convicted, and it was proposed to vote a reward to the accuser, Junius Otho, a tribune of the Plebs, interposed his veto: the quarrel thus raised between the two resulting in Otho's banishment. Next, Albucilla, who was notorious for her amours, and had been the wife of Satrius Secundus, one of the informers against Sejanus, was accused of impiety towards Tiberius: Gnæus Domitius, Vibius Marsus, and Lucius Arruntius being named as her lovers and accomplices. Of the noble birth of Domitius, I have already spoken; Marsus also belonged to an ancient and illustrious family, and was a man of high attainments. It appeared from the papers laid before the Senate that Macro had himself presided at the examination of the witnesses, and the torture of the slaves; but as Tiberius wrote no letter against the accused persons, the suspicion arose that Macro, taking advantage of the Emperor's weakness, and perhaps even without his knowledge, had trumped up a series of false charges to gratify his well-known hatred of Arruntius.

So the lives of Domitius and Marsus were prolonged; the former set about preparing for his defence, the latter made as though he had resolved upon starvation. But when the friends of Arruntius implored him to delay and temporise, he replied as follows:— The rule of honour, he said, was not the same for all. He had had enough of life: the one thing he had to repent of was that he had endured to live on to old age amid perils and mockeries, always in anxiety, always the object of some great man's hatred. It had been Sejanus for a time, it was now Macro; and his only crime was that he could not tolerate iniquity. He might doubtless live through the few remaining days of Tiberius: but how could he escape from the stripling who was to come after? If the possession of power had perforce deranged and transformed Tiberius, with all his experience of affairs, was it likely that Gaius Cæsar would do better, with Macro to point the way? The lad was scarce out of his teens, ignorant of everything, or instructed only in what was evil; and Macro had been chosen to crush Sejanus as the greater villain of the two, having committed crimes more numerous, more disastrous to the State than he. He could foresee days of still grosser servitude; and he was making his escape from future as well as from present evils.

Uttering these words in the manner of an inspired prophet, he opened his veins. What follows will show how well Arruntius did to die.

—G. G. RAMSAY.

THE DEATH OF SENECA

[From the *Annals,* Book XV]

To believers in Stoicism suicide seemed a proper means of escape from a life which had nothing further to offer. Scenes like that here described were frequently enacted under the regime of the early Cæsars.

Then came the death of Annæus Seneca, which gave great joy to Nero; not that he had any clear evidence of his guilt, but because he could now do by the sword what he had failed to do by poison. The sole witness against him was Natalis, and his evidence only came to this, that he had been sent to see Seneca when he was ill, and to complain of his refusing to see Piso:— It would be better, he had said, for such old friends to keep up their habits of intercourse. To this Seneca had replied: — Frequent meetings and conversations would do neither of them any good, but his own welfare depended on Piso's safety. Gavius Silvanus, Tribune of a Prætorian Cohort, was ordered to take the report of this incident to Seneca, and to ask him, Whether he admitted the correctness of the question of Natalis, and of his own answer to it? Either by chance or purposely, it happened that Seneca was returning on that day from Campania, and had halted at a suburban villa four miles from Rome. Thither, towards evening the Tribune proceeded; and having surrounded the house with soldiers, he delivered the Emperor's message to Seneca when he was at table with his wife Pompeia Paulina and two friends. Seneca's reply was:—Natalis had been sent to complain on behalf of Piso that he was not permitted to visit him; and

he had tendered in excuse the state of his health and his love of quiet. As to his reason for regarding the welfare of a private individual as of more value than his own safety, he had had none. He was not a man addicted to flattery: and that no one knew better than Nero himself, who had more often found him too free than too servile in his utterances.

On receiving this report from the Tribune in the presence of Poppæa and Tigellinus, who formed the Emperor's inner council of cruelty, Nero asked, Was Seneca preparing to put an end to himself? The Tribune declared that, He had observed no sign of alarm or dejection in Seneca's face or language. He was therefore ordered to go back and tell him he must die.

Fabius Rusticus states that the Tribune did not return by the same road by which he came, but that he went out of his way to see Fænius the Perfect; and having shown him Cæsar's order, asked him, Should he obey it? and that Fænius, with that fatal weakness which had come over them all, told him to execute his orders. For Silvanus himself was one of the conspirators, and he was now adding one more crime to those which he had conspired to avenge. But he spared his own eyes and tongue, sending in one of the centurions to announce to Seneca that his last hour was come.

Seneca, undismayed, asked for his will; but this the centurion refused. Then turning to his friends, he called them to witness that, Being forbidden to requite them for their services, he was leaving to them the sole, and yet the noblest, possession that remained to him—the pattern of his life. If they bore that in mind, they would win for themselves a name for virtue as the reward of their devoted friendship. At one moment he would check their tears with conversation; at another he would brace up their courage by high-strung language of rebuke, asking, Where was now their philosophy? Where was that attitude towards the future which they had rehearsed for so many years? To whom was Nero's cruelty unknown? What was left for one who had murdered his mother and his brother but to slay his guardian and teacher also?

Having discoursed thus as if to the whole company, he embraced his wife, and abating somewhat of his tone of high courage, he implored her to moderate her grief, and not cling to it for ever:— Let contemplation of her husband's life of virtue afford her noble solace in her bereavement.

She, however, announced her resolve to die with him; and called on the operator to do his part. Seneca would not thwart her noble ambition; and he loved her too dearly to expose her to insult after he was gone. "I have pointed out to thee," he said "how thou mayest soothe thy life; but if thou prefer a noble death, I will not begrudge thee the example. Let us both share the fortitude of thus nobly dying: but thine shall be the nobler end."

A single incision with the knife opened the arm of each; but as Seneca's aged body, reduced by spare living, would scarcely let the blood escape, he opened the veins of his knees and ankles also. Worn out at last by the pain, and fearing to break down his wife's courage by his suffering, or to lose his own self-command at the sight of hers, he begged her to move into another chamber. But even in his last moments his eloquence did not fail; he called his secretaries to his side, and dictated to them many things which being published in his own words I deem it needless to reproduce.

Nero however had no personal dislike to Paulina; and not wishing to add to his character for cruelty, he ordered her death to be stayed. So at the bidding of the soldiers, the slaves and freedmen tied up her arms, and stopped the flow of blood; perhaps she was unconscious.

But with that alacrity to accept the worst version of a thing which marks the vulgar, some believed that so long as she thought Nero would be implacable, she clutched at the glory of sharing her husband's death; but that when the hope of a reprieve presented itself, the attractions of life proved too strong for her. She lived on for a few years more, worthily cherishing her husband's memory; but the pallor of her face and limbs showed how much vitality had gone out of her.

Meanwhile Seneca, in the agonies of a slow and lingering death, implored Statius Annæus, his tried and trusted friend and physician, to produce a poison with which he had long provided himself, being the same as that used for public executions at Athens. The draught was brought and administered, but to no purpose; the limbs were too cold, the body too numb, to let the poison act. At last, he was put into a warm bath; and as he sprinkled the slaves about him he added—This libation is to Jupiter the Liberator! He was then carried into the hot vapour-bath, and perished of suffocation. His body was burnt without any funeral ceremony, in accordance with instructions about his end which he had inserted in his will in the heyday of his wealth and power.

Report had it that Subrius Flavus had made a secret plot with some centurions, not unknown to Seneca, to slay Piso himself as soon as he should have assisted in the assasination of Nero, and offer the Empire to Seneca, as though selected for the sovereignty by men innocent of the murder, on the score of his eminent virtues. And indeed a saying of Flavus got abroad that as for the disgrace of the thing, it would make but little difference to remove a lyrist and put a tragedian in his place: for as Nero sang to the lyre, so did Piso sing in tragic character.

—G. G. RAMSAY.

THE RESULTS OF DESPOTISM

[From the *Histories*, Book I]

The beginning of the *Histories* offered the author an opportunity to summarize the tendencies of half a century of monarchy. Tacitus afterwards added the *Annals* in order to treat the history of that period in greater detail.

I propose to begin my narrative with the second consulship of Servius Galba, in which Titus Vinius was his colleague. Many historians have dealt with the 820 years of the earlier period beginning with the foundation of Rome, and the story of the Roman Republic has been told with no less ability than truth. After the battle of Actium, when the interests of peace were served by the centralization of all authority in the hands of one man, there followed a dearth of literary ability, and at the same time truth suffered more and more, partly from ignorance of politics, which were no longer a citizen's concern, partly from the growing taste for flattery or from hatred of the ruling house. So between malice on one side and servility on the other the interests of posterity were neglected. But historians find that a tone of flattery soon incurs the stigma of servility and earns for them the contempt of their readers, whereas people readily open their ears to the criticisms of envy, since malice makes a show of independence. Of Galba, Otho, and Vitellius, I have known nothing either to my advantage or my hurt. I cannot deny that I originally owed my position to Vespasian, or that I was advanced by Titus and still further promoted by Domitian; but professing, as I do, unbiassed honesty, I must speak of no man either with hatred or affection. I have reserved for my old age, if life is spared to me, the reigns of the sainted Nerva and of the Emperor Trajan, which afford a richer and withal a safer theme: for it is the rare fortune of these days

that a man may think what he likes and say what he thinks.

The story I now commence is rich in vicissitudes, grim with warfare, torn by civil strife, a tale of horror even during times of peace. It tells of four emperors slain by the sword, three civil wars, an even larger number of foreign wars and some that were both at once: successes in the East, disaster in the West, disturbance in Illyricum; disaffection in the provinces of Gaul, the conquest of Britain and its immediate loss, the rising of the Sarmatian and Suebic tribes. It tells how Dacia had the privilege of exchanging blows with Rome, and how a pretender claiming to be Nero almost deluded the Parthians into declaring war. Now too Italy was smitten with new disasters, or disasters it had not witnessed for a long period of years. Towns along the rich coast of Campania were submerged or buried. The city was devastated by fires, ancient temples were destroyed, and the Capitol itself was fired by Roman hands. Sacred rites were grossly profaned, and there were scandals in high places. The sea swarmed with exiles and the island cliffs were red with blood. Worse horrors reigned in the city. To be rich or well-born was a crime: men were prosecuted for holding or refusing office: merit of any kind meant certain ruin. Nor were the informers more hated for their crimes than for their prizes: some carried off a priesthood or the consulship as their spoil, others won offices and influence in the imperial household: the hatred and fear they inspired worked universal havoc. Slaves were bribed against their masters, freedmen against their patrons, and, if a man had no enemies, he was ruined by his friends.

However the period was not so utterly barren as to yield no examples of heroism. There were mothers who followed their sons, and wives their husbands into exile: one saw here a kinsman's courage and there a son-in-law's devotion: slaves obstinately faithful even on the rack: distinguished men bravely facing the utmost straits and matching in their end the famous deaths of older times. Besides these manifold disasters to mankind there were portents in the sky and on the earth, thunderbolts and other premonitions of good and evil, some doubtful, some obvious. Indeed never has it been proved by such terrible disasters to Rome or by such clear evidence that Providence is concerned not with our peace of mind but rather with vengeance for our sin.

—W. H. FYFE.

IMPERIAL SUCCESSION

[From the *Histories*, Book I]

No policy for the choice of the successor to the throne had ever been definitely formulated; but the practice of the early emperors had led to the general acceptance of the principle of dynastic succession. The method which the author credits Galba with having proposed was that actually in effect at the time Tacitus was writing, and with such happy results that there can be no doubt that it met with his approval.

Galba is said to have taken Piso's hand and addressed him as follows: "Were I a private citizen, and were I to adopt you in the presence of the Priests by the usual formality of a curial statute, it would be an honour for me to introduce into my family a descendant of Cnæus Pompeius and of Marcus Crassus, and for you it would be a distinction to all to add to your noble ancestry the glories of the Sulpician and Lutatian houses. As it is, I have been called by the consent of gods and men to be an emperor. Your distinguished qualities and your patriotism have persuaded me to offer to you peacefully and quietly the throne for which our ancestors fought on the field of battle, and which I too won by war.

In so doing I am following the precedent set by the sainted Augustus, who raised to the rank next himself first his nephew Marcellus, then his son-in-law Agrippa, then his daughter's sons, and finally his stepson Tiberius Nero. However, while Augustus looked for a successor in his own family, I have searched throughout the country. Not that I lack either kinsmen or supporters, but it was by no favour of birth that I myself came to the throne, and, to prove my policy in this matter, consider how I have passed over not only my own relatives but yours. . . .

"If the vast bulk of this empire could stand and keep its balance without a guiding hand, the Republic might well have dated its birth from me. As it is, things have long ago come to such a pass that neither I in my old age can give the Roman people any better gift than a good successor, nor you in your prime anything better than a good emperor. Under Tiberius, Caligula, and Claudius, Rome was the heirloom of a single family. There is a kind of liberty in the free choice we have begun to exercise. Now that the Julian and Claudian houses are extinct, by the plan of adoption the best man will always be discovered. Royal birth is the gift of fortune, and is but valued as such. In adoption we can use a free judgment, and if we wish to choose well, the voice of the country points the way. Think of Nero, swollen with the pride of his long line of royal ancestry. It was not Vindex with a powerless province at his back, nor I with a single legion that freed Rome's shoulders of that burden: it was his own cruelty and profligacy. And that was before there was any precedent for the conviction of an emperor.

"We have been called to the throne by the swords of those who thought us worthy. Our high state will not escape the eye of envy. You may be sure of that. But there is no reason for you to feel alarm because in this world-wide up-heaval a couple of legions have not yet settled down. I myself did not succeed to a safe and peaceful throne, and, when once the news of your adoption is spread, I shall cease to be charged with my advanced age, which is now the only fault they find in me. The rascals will always miss Nero: you and I have got to see that good citizens do not miss him too.

"A longer sermon would ill befit the time and I have fulfilled my purpose, if I have done right in choosing you. The soundest and easiest criterion of right and wrong policy is to consider what you would have approved or condemned in another emperor. For Rome is not like the nations which are ruled by kings, where one house is supreme and the rest are slaves. Your future subjects are men who cannot endure the extremes either of bondage or of freedom."

Galba spoke these words and more to the same effect in the tone of one creating an emperor: the rest addressed Piso as though he were emperor already.

—W. H. FYFE.

THE EMPIRE AND THE PROVINCES

[From the *Histories*, Book IV]

The idea that Rome confers a benefit upon the provinces for which they should be willing to pay is in harmony with Cicero's conception of the proper relation of Rome and her provinces. But the century that had elapsed since Cicero had brought about great changes in the extent to which provincials might take part in the governing of the Empire.

Cerialis next summoned the Treviri and Lingones, and addressed them as follows: "Unpractised as I am in public speaking, for it is only on the field that I have asserted the superiority of Rome, yet since words have so much weight with you, and since you distinguish good and bad not by the light of facts but by what

agitators tell you, I have decided to make a few remarks, which, as the war is practically over, are likely to be more profitable to the audience than to ourselves. Roman generals and officers originally set foot in your country and the rest of Gaul from no motives of ambition, but at the call of your ancestors, who were worn almost to ruin by dissension. The Germans whom one party summoned to their aid had forced the yoke of slavery on allies and enemies alike. You know how often we fought against the Cimbri and the Teutons, with what infinite pains and with what striking success our armies have undertaken German wars. All that is notorious. And to-day it is not to protect Italy that we have occupied the Rhine, but to prevent some second Ariovistus making himself master of All Gaul. Do you imagine that Civilis and his Batavi and the other tribes across the Rhine care any more about you than their ancestors cared about your fathers and grandfathers? The Germans have always had the same motives for trespassing into Gaul—their greed for gain and their desire to change homes with you. They wanted to leave their marshes and deserts, and to make themselves masters of this magnificently fertile soil and of you who live on it. Of course they use specious pretexts and talk about liberty. No one has ever wanted to enslave others and play the tyrant without making use of the very same phrases.

"Tyranny and warfare were always rife throughout the length and breadth of Gaul, until you accepted Roman government. Often as we have been provoked, we have never imposed upon you any burden by right of conquest, except what was necessary to maintain peace. Tribes cannot be kept quiet without troops. You cannot have troops without pay; and you cannot raise pay without taxation. In every other respect you are treated as our equals. You frequently command our legions yourselves: you govern this and other provinces yourselves. We have no exclusive privileges. Though you live so far away, you enjoy the blessings of a good emperor no less than we do, whereas the tyrant only oppresses his nearest neighbours. You must put up with luxury and greed in your masters, just as you put up with bad crops or excessive rain, or any other natural disaster. Vice will last as long as mankind. But these evils are not continual. There are intervals of good government, which make up for them. You cannot surely hope that the tyranny of Tutor and Classicus would mean milder government, or that they will need less taxation for the armies they will have to raise to keep the Germans and Britons at bay. For if the Romans were driven out—which Heaven forbid—what could ensue save a universal state of intertribal warfare? During eight hundred years, by good fortune and good organization, the structure of empire has been consolidated. It cannot be pulled down without destroying those who do it. And it is you who would run the greatest risk of all, since you have gold and rich resources, which are the prime causes of war. You must learn, then, to love and foster peace and the city of Rome in which you, the vanquished, have the same rights as your conquerors. You have tried both conditions. Take warning, then, that submission and safety are better than rebellion and ruin."

—W. H. FYFE.

THE DRAMATIST

OCTAVIA [1]

PSEUDO-SENECA

The *Octavia* is the only tragedy on a Roman subject that has come down to us.

[1] From *The Tragedies of Seneca* by F. J. Miller, copyright by The University of Chicago Press. Reprinted by permission.

Although tradition credits Seneca with its authorship, there are a number of considerations which have led to the conclusion now generally accepted that the play should be assigned to some other poet of the same period. The dramatist transfers the tyranny of the times from the public to the domestic stage. The contemporaneous conflict of opinion on monarchical government is represented not only in plot and counterplot, but also in the debates between the emperor and the philosopher on the duties and responsibilities of a king.

DRAMATIS PERSONÆ

OCTAVIA, *stepsister and wife of Nero.*
NURSE *of Octavia.*
POPPÆA, *mistress and afterward wife of Nero.*
GHOST OF AGRIPPINA, *mother of Nero, slain by him.*
NERO, *Emperor of Rome.*
SENECA, *former tutor of Nero, and later one of his chief counselors.*
PREFECT OF ROMAN SOLDIERS.
MESSENGER.
CHORUS OF ROMANS, *sympathetic with Octavia.*
CHORUS *attached to the interests of the court.*
   The scene is laid throughout in different apartments of the palace of Nero, and is concerned with the events of the year 62 A.D.

ACT I

OCTAVIA: Now doth the flushing dawn from heaven drive
The wandering stars; the sun mounts into sight
With radiant beams, and brings the world once more
The light of day. Up, then, my heavy soul,
With grievous cares o'erburdened, and resume
Thy woe; out-wail the sea-bred Halcyons,
And those sad birds of old Pandion's house;
For this thy lot is heavier far than theirs.

O mother, constant source of tears to me,
Hear now thy woeful daughter's sad
    complaints,
If aught of sense remains among the
    shades.
Oh, that the grizzly Clotho long ago,
With her own hand had clipt my thread
    of life!
Through blinding tears I saw thy bleeding
    wounds,
Thy features sprinkled with defiling
    blood.
Oh, light of day, abhorrent to my eyes!
From that dread hour I hate the day's
    pure light
More than the night's dark gloom; for
    daily now
Must I endure a cruel stepdame's rule,
Must daily bear her hateful looks and
    words.
She, she the baleful fury fiend it was
Who at my marriage rites bore torches lit
With hellish fires; 'twas she who wrought
    thy death,
O wretched father, whom but yesterday
The whole world owned as lord on land
    and sea;
To whom the Briton bowed, though ne'er
    before
Had he a Roman master known or owned.
Alas, my father, by thy wife's fell plots
Thou liest low, and I and all thy house
Like captives groan beneath the tyrant's
    sway.

(Exit to her chamber)

NURSE (*entering*): Who stands in won-
    der, smitten by the gloss
And splendor of a princely court, amazed
At sight of easy-won prosperity,
Let him behold how, at the stroke of fate,
The house of Claudius is overthrown,
To whose control the world was subjugate,
Whose rule an ocean, long to sway un-
    known,
Obeyed, and bore our ships with subject
    will.
Lo, he, who first the savage Britons
    curbed,

And filled an unknown ocean with his
    fleet,
And passed in safety 'mid barbaric
    tribes—
By his own wife's impiety was slain.
And she is destined by her son to fall,
Whose hapless brother lies already slain
By poison's hand, whose sister-wife alone
Is left to mourn. Nor may she hide her
    grief,
By bitter wrath impelled to speak. She
    shuns
Her cruel lord's society, and, fired
With equal hate, with mutual loathing
    burns.
Our pious faithfulness in vain consoles
Her grieving heart; her cruel woes reject
Our aid; the noble passion of her soul
Will not be ruled, but grows on ills re-
    newed.
Alas, my fears forebode some desperate
    deed,
Which may the gods forbid!
OCTAVIA (*heard speaking from within
    her chamber*): O fate of mine, that
    can no equal know!
Thy woes, Electra, were no match for
    these;
For thou couldst soothe with tears the
    grief thou hadst
For thy dear father's fall; thou couldst
    avenge
The murder by thy brother's ready hand,
Who by thy piety was saved from death,
And whom thy faith concealed. But me
    base fear
Forbids to weep my parents reft away
By cruel fate; forbids to weep the death
Of him, my brother, who my sole hope
    was,
My fleeting comfort of so many woes.
And now, surviving but to suffer still,
I live, the shadow of a noble name.
NURSE: Behold, the voice of my sad
    foster-child
Falls on my list'ning ears. Slow steps of
    age,
Why haste ye not within her chamber
    there?

(Starts to enter the chamber, but is met by OCTAVIA *coming forth)*

OCTAVIA: Within thy bosom let me weep, dear nurse,
Thou ever trusty witness of my grief.

NURSE: What day shall free thee from thy woes, poor child?

OCTAVIA: The day that sends me to the Stygian shades.

NURSE: May heaven keep such dark omens far away!

OCTAVIA: 'Tis not thy prayers, but fate that shapes my life.

NURSE: But God will bring thy life to better days.
Do thou but be appeased, and win thy lord
With mild obedience.

OCTAVIA: I'll sooner tame
The savage lion's heart, the tiger's rage,
Than curb that brutal tyrant's cruel soul.
He hates all sons of noble blood, and gods
And men he sets at naught; nor can he bear
That high estate to which along the paths
Of shameful crime his impious mother led;
For though it shames him now, ungrateful one,
To hold the scepter which his mother gave;
And though by death he has requited her:
Still will the glory of the empire won
Belong to her for centuries to come.

NURSE: Restrain these words that voice thy raging heart,
And check thy tongue's too rash and thoughtless speech.

OCTAVIA: Though I should bear what may be borne, my woes,
Save by a cruel death, could not be ended.
For, since my mother was by murder slain,
And my father taken off by crime most foul,
Robbed of my brother, overwhelmed with woe,

Oppressed with sadness, by my husband scorned,
Degraded to the level of my slave,
I find this life no more endurable.
My heart doth tremble, not with fear of death,
But slander base, employed to work my death.
Far from my name and fate be that foul blot.
For death itself—Oh, 'twould be sweet to die;
For 'tis a punishment far worse than death,
To live in contact with the man I loathe,
To see the tyrant's face all passion puffed,
And fierce with rage, to kiss my deadliest foe.
That I should fear his nod, obey his will,
My grief, resentful, will not suffer me,
Since by his hand my brother was destroyed,
Whose kingdom he usurps, and boasts himself
The author of that shameful deed.   How oft
Before my eyes does that sad image come,
My brother's ghost, when I have gone to rest,
And sleep has closed my eyelids faint with tears!
Now in his weakling hand he brandishes
The smoking torch, and violently assails
His brother to his face; now, trembling sore,
He flees for refuge to my sheltering arms.
His foe pursues, and, as his victim clings
Convulsively to me, he thrusts his sword
With murderous intent through both our sides.
Then, all a-tremble, do I start awake,
And in my waking sense renew my fear.
Add to these cares a rival, arrogant,
Who queens it in the spoils of this our house;
At whose behest the mother was enticed
To that fell ship which should have carried her

To Orcus' depths; but when o'er ocean's waves
She triumphed, he, than ocean's waves more harsh
And pitiless, despatched her with the sword.
Amid such deeds, what hopes of peace have I?
O'erblown with hate, triumphant, doth my rival
Within my very chamber's hold defy me;
With deadly malice doth she blaze against me,
And as the price of her adulterous sweets,
Doth she demand that he, my husband, give
My life, his lawful wife's, in sacrifice.
Oh, rise thou, father, from the gloomy shades,
And help thy daughter who invokes thine aid;
Or else cleave wide the earth to Stygian depths,
And let me plunge at last to shelter there.

NURSE: In vain dost thou invoke thy father's soul,
Poor child, in vain; for there among the shades
He little thinks upon his offspring here;
Who, when in life, unto his own true son
Preferred the offspring of another's blood,
And to himself in most incestuous bonds
And rites unhallowed joined his brother's child.
From this foul source has flowed a stream of crime:
Of murder, treachery, the lust of power,
The thirst for blood. Thy promised husband fell,
A victim slain to grace that wedding feast,
Lest, joined with thee, he should too mighty grow.
Oh, monstrous deed! Silanus, charged with crime,
Was slain to make a bridal offering,
And stained the household gods with guiltless blood.

And then this alien comes. Oh, woe is me,
And by his mother's wiles usurps the house,
Made son-in-law and son to the emperor,
A youth of temper most unnatural,
To impious crime inclined, whose passion's flame
His mother fanned, and forced thee at the last
In hated wedlock into his embrace.
Emboldened by this notable success,
She dared to dream of wider sovereignty.
What tongue can tell the changing forms of crime,
Her impious hopes, her cozening treacheries,
Who seeks the throne along the ways of sin?
Then Piety with trembling haste withdrew,
And Fury through the empty palace halls
With baleful tread resounded, and defiled
The sacred images with Stygian brands.
All holy laws of nature and of heaven
In mad abandon did she set at naught.
She mingled deadly poison for her lord,
And she herself by the impious mandate fell
Of her own son. Thou too dost lifeless lie,
Poor youth, forever to be mourned by us,
Ill-starred Britannicus, so late, in life,
The brightest star of this our firmament,
The prop and stay of our imperial house;
But now, Oh, woe is me, a heap of dust,
Of unsubstantial dust, a flitting shade.
Nay, even thy stepmother's cruel cheeks
Were wet with tears, when on the funeral pyre
She placed thy form and saw the flames consume
Thy limbs and face fair as the wingèd god's.

OCTAVIA: Me, too, he must destroy—or fall by me.

NURSE: But nature has not given thee strength to slay.

OCTAVIA: Yet anger, anguish, pain, distress of soul,
The ecstasy of grief will give me strength.
NURSE: Nay, by compliance, rather, win thy lord.
OCTAVIA: That thus he may restore my brother slain?
NURSE: That thou thyself mayst go unscathed of death;
That thou by thine own offspring mayst restore
Thy father's falling house.
OCTAVIA: This princely house
Expects an heir, 'tis true; but not from me,
For I am doomed to meet my brother's fate.
NURSE: Console thy heart with this, that thou art dear
Unto the populace, who love thee well.
OCTAVIA: That thought doth soothe, but cannot cure my grief.
NURSE: Their power availeth much.
OCTAVIA: The prince's more.
NURSE: He will regard his wife.
OCTAVIA: My foe forbids.
NURSE: But she is scorned by all.
OCTAVIA: Yet loved by him.
NURSE: She is not yet his wife.
OCTAVIA: But soon will be,
And mother of his child, his kingdom's heir.
NURSE: The fire of youthful passion glows at first
With heat impetuous; but soon abates,
And vanishes like flickering tongues of flame.
Unhallowed love cannot for long endure;
But pure and lasting is the love inspired
By chaste and wifely faith. She who has dared
To violate thy bed, and hold so long
Thy husband's heart in thrall, herself a slave,
Already trembles lest his fickle love
Shall thrust her forth and set a rival there.
Subdued and humble, even now she shows
How deep and real her fear; for her, indeed,

Shall wingèd Cupid, false and fickle god,
Abandon and betray. Though face and form
Be passing fair, though beauty vaunt herself,
And boast her power, still are her triumphs brief,
Her joys a passing dream.
           Nay, Juno's self,
Though queen of heaven, endured such grief as thine,
When he, her lord, and father of the gods,
Stole from her side to seek in mortal forms
The love of mortal maids. Now, in his need,
He dons the snowy plumage of a swan;
Now hornèd seems, like a Sidonian bull;
And now a glorious, golden shower falls,
And rests within the arms of Danae.
Nor yet is Juno's sum of woe complete:
The sons of Leda glitter in the sky
In starry splendor; Bacchus proudly stands
Beside his father on Olympus' height;
Divine Alcides hath to Hebe's charms
Attained, and fears stern Juno's wrath no more.
Her very son-in-law hath he become
Whom once she hated most. Yet in her heart
Deep down she pressed her grief, and wisely won,
By mild compliance to his wayward will,
Her husband's love again. And now the queen,
Secure at last from rivalry, holds sway
Alone, within the Thunderer's heart. No more,
By mortal beauty smitten, does he leave
His royal chambers in the vaulted sky.
Thou, too, on earth, another Juno art,
The wife and sister of our mighty lord.
Then be thou wise as she, make show of love,
And hide thy crushing sorrows with a smile.
OCTAVIA: The savage seas shall sooner mate with stars,

And fire with water, heav'n with gloomy
hell,
Glad light with shades, and day with
dewy night,
Than shall my soul in amity consort
With his black heart, most foul and im-
pious:
Too mindful I of my poor brother's ghost.
And Oh, that he who guides the heavenly
worlds,
Who shakes the realms of earth with
deadly bolts,
And with his dreadful thunders awes our
minds,
Would whelm in fiery death this mur-
derous prince.
Strange portents have we seen: the comet
dire,
Shining with baleful light, his glowing
train
Far gleaming in the distant northern sky,
Where slow Bootes, numb with arctic
frosts,
Directs his ponderous wagon's endless
rounds.
The very air is tainted by the breath
Of this destructive prince; and for his
sake
The stars, resentful, threaten to destroy
The nations which so dire a tyrant rules.
Not such a pest was impious Typhon
huge,
Whom earth, in wrath and scorn of
heaven, produced.
This scourge is more destructive far than
he.
He is the bitter foe of gods and men,
Who drives the heavenly beings from
their shrines,
And from their native land the citizens;
Who from his brother took the breath of
life,
And drained his mother's blood.
              And does he live,
This guilty wretch, and draw his tainted
breath?
O Jove, thou high-exalted father, why
Dost thou so oft with thy imperial hand
Thy darts invincible at random hurl?

Why from his guilty head dost thou with-
hold
Thy hand of vengeance? Oh, that he
might pay
For all his crimes the fitting penalty,
This son of deified Domitius,
This Nero, heartless tyrant of the world,
Which he beneath the yoke of bondage
holds,
This moral blot upon a noble name!
NURSE: Unworthy he to be thy mate, I
know;
But, dearest child, to fate and fortune
yield,
Lest thou excite thy savage husband's
wrath.
Perchance some god will come to right
thy wrongs,
And on thy life some happier day will
dawn.
OCTAVIA: That may not be. Long since,
our ill-starred house
Has groaned beneath the heavy wrath of
heaven.
That wrath at first my hapless mother
felt,
Whom Venus cursed with lust insatiate;
For she, with heedless, impious passion
fired,
Unmindful of her absent lord, of us
Her guiltless children, and the law's re-
straints,
In open day another husband wed.
To that fell couch avenging Fury came
With streaming locks and serpents inter-
twined,
And quenched those stolen wedding fires
in blood.
For with destructive rage, on murder
bent,
She fired the prince's heart; and at his
word,
Ah, woe is me, my ill-starred mother fell,
And, dying, doomed me to perpetual grief.
For after her in quick succession came
Her husband and her son; and this our
house,
Already falling, was to ruin plunged.

NURSE: Forbear with pious tears to re-
new thy grief,
And do not so disturb thy father's shade,
Who for his rage has bitterly atoned.

CHORUS (*sympathetic with* OCTAVIA):
False prove the rumor that of late
To our ears has come! May its vaunted
threats
Fall fruitless out and of no avail!
May no new wife invade the bed
Of our royal prince; may Octavia, born
Of the Claudian race, maintain her right
And bear us a son, the pledge of peace,
In which the joyful world shall rest,
And Rome preserve her glorious name.
Most mighty Juno holds the lot
By fate assigned—her brother's mate;
But this our Juno, sister, wife
Of our august prince, why is she driven
From her father's court? Of what avail
Her faith, her father deified,
Her love and spotless chastity?
We, too, of our former master's fame
Have been unmindful, and his child
At the hest of cringing fear betrayed.
Not so of old: then Rome could boast
Of manly virtue, manly blood.
There lived a race of heroes then
Who curbed the power of haughty kings
And drove them forth from Rome; and
thee,
O maiden, slain by thy father's hand,
Lest thou shouldst in slavery's bonds be
held,
And lest foul lust its victorious will
Should work on thee, did well avenge.
Thee, too, a bloody war avenged,
O chaste Lucretia; for thou,
By the lust of an impious tyrant stained,
With wretched hand didst seek to cleanse
Those stains by thy innocent blood.
Then Tullia with her guilty lord,
Base Tarquin, dared an impious deed,
Whose penalty they paid; for she
Over the limbs of her murdered sire,
A heartless child, drove cruel wheels,
And left his corpse unburied there.
Such deeds of dire impiety

Our age has known, our eyes have seen,
When the prince on the mighty Tyrrhene
deep
In a fatal bark his mother sent,
By guile ensnared.
The sailors at his bidding haste
To leave the peaceful harbor's arms;
And soon the rougher waves resound
Beneath their oars, and far away
Upon the deep the vessel glides;
When suddenly the reeling bark
With loosened beams yawns open wide,
And drinks the briny sea.
A mighty shout to heaven goes,
With women's lamentations filled,
And death stalks dire before the eyes
Of all. Each seeks to save himself.
Some naked cling upon the planks
Of the broken ships and fight the floods,
While others swimming seek the shore.
But most, alas! a watery death
By fate awaits. Then did the queen
In mad despair her garments rend;
Her comely locks she tore, and tears
Fell streaming down her grieving cheeks.
At last, with hope of safety gone,
With wrath inflamed, by woes o'ercome,
"Dost thou, O son, make this return,"
She cried, "for that great boon I gave?
Such death I merit, I confess,
Who bore such monstrous child as thou,
Who gave to thee the light of day,
And in my madness raised thee high
To Cæsar's name and Cæsar's throne.
Oh, rise from deepest Acheron,
My murdered husband, feast thine eyes
Upon my righteous punishment;
For I brought death to thee, poor soul,
And to thy son. See, see, I come,
Deep down to meet thy grieving shade;
And there, as I have merited,
Shall I unburied lie, o'erwhelmed
By the raging sea." E'en as she spoke,
The lapping waves broke o'er her lips,
And deep she plunged below. Anon
She rises from the briny depths,
And, stung by fear of death, she strives
With frenzied hands to conquer fate;
But, spent with fruitless toil at last,

She yields and waits the end. But lo,
In hearts which in trembling silence
    watch,
Faith triumphs over deadly fear,
And to their mistress, spent and wan
With fruitless buffetings, they dare
To lend their aid with cheering words
And helping hands.
                            But what avails
To escape the grasp of the savage sea?
By the sword of the son is she doomed to
    die,
Whose monstrous deed posterity
Will scarce believe. With rage and grief
Inflamed, he raves that still she lives,
His mother, snatched from the wild sea's
    jaws,
And doubles crime on impious crime.
Bent on his wretched mother's death,
He brooks no tarrying of fate.
His willing creatures work his will,
And in the hapless woman's breast
The fatal sword is plunged; but she
To that fell minister of death
Appeals with dying tongue: "Nay here,
Here rather strike the murderous blow,
Here sheathe thy sword, deep in the womb
Which such a monster bore."
So spake the dying queen, her words
And groans commingling. So at last
Through gaping wounds her spirit fled
In grief and agony.

Act II

SENECA (*alone*): Why hast thou, potent
    Fate, with flattering looks,
Exalted me, contented with my lot,
That so from this great height I might
    descend
With heavier fall, and wider prospect see
Of deadly fears? Ah, better was I, hid
Far from the stinging lash of envy's
    tongue,
Amid the lonely crags of Corsica.
There was my spirit free to act at will,
Was master of itself, had time to think
And meditate at length each favorite
    theme.

Oh, what delight, than which none greater
    is,
Of all that mother nature hath produced,
To watch the heavens, the bright sun's
    sacred rounds,
The heavenly movements and the chang-
    ing night,
The moon's full orb with wandering stars
    begirt,
The far-effulgent glory of the sky!
And is it growing old, this structure vast,
Doomed to return to groping nothing-
    ness?
Then must that final doomsday be at
    hand,
That shall by heaven's fall o'erwhelm a
    race
So impious, that thus the world may see
A newer race of men, a better stock,
Which once the golden reign of Saturn
    knew.
Then virgin Justice, holy child of heaven,
In mercy ruled the world; the race of men
Knew naught of war, the trumpet's savage
    blare,
The clang of arms; not yet were cities
    hedged
With ponderous walls; the way was free
    to all,
And free to all the use of everything.
The earth, untilled, spread wide her fertile
    lap,
The happy mother of a pious stock.
Then rose another race of sterner mold;
Another yet to curious arts inclined,
But pious still; a fourth of restless mood,
Which lusted to pursue the savage beasts,
To draw the fishes from their sheltering
    waves
With net or slender pole, to snare the
    birds,
To force the headstrong bullocks to en-
    dure
The bondage of the yoke, to plow the
    earth
Which never yet had felt the share's deep
    wound,
And which in pain and grief now hid her
    fruits

Within her sacred bosom's safer hold.
Now deep within the bowels of the earth
Did that debased, unfilial age intrude;
And thence it dug the deadly iron and
gold,
And soon it armed its savage hands for
war.
It fixed the bounds of realms, constructed
towns,
Fought for its own abodes, or threat'ning
strove
To plunder those of others as a prize.
Then did abandoned Justice, heavenly
maid,
In terror flee the earth, the bestial ways
Of men, their hands with bloody slaughter
stained,
And, fixed in heaven, now shines among
the stars.
Then lust of war increased, and greed for
gold,
Throughout the world; and luxury arose,
That deadliest of evils, luring pest,
To whose fell powers new strength and
force were given
By custom long observed, and precedent
Of evil into worser evil led.
This flood of vice, through many ages
dammed,
In ours has burst its bounds and over-
flowed.
By this dire age we're fairly over-
whelmed—
An age when crime sits regnant on the
throne,
Impiety stalks raging, unrestrained;
Foul lust, with all unbridled power, is
queen,
And luxury long since with greedy hands
Has snatched the boundless riches of the
world,
That she with equal greed may squander
them.

(*Enter* NERO, *followed by a* PREFECT)

But see, with frenzied step and savage
mien,
The prince approaches. How I fear his
will.

NERO (*to* PREFECT): Speed my com-
mands: send forth a messenger
Who straight shall bring me here the
severed heads
Of Plautus and of Sulla.
PREFECT: Good, my lord;
Without delay I'll speed me to the camp.
(*Exit*)
SENECA: One should not rashly judge
against his friends.
NERO: Let him be just whose heart is
free from fear.
SENECA: But mercy is a sovereign cure
for fear.
NERO: A ruler's part is to destroy his
foes.
SENECA: A ruler's better part, to save
his friends.
NERO: A mild old man's advice is fit for
boys.
SENECA: Still more does hot young man-
hood need the rein—
NERO: I deem that at this age we're wise
enough.
SENECA: That on thy deed the heavenly
gods may smile.
NERO: Thou fool, shall I fear gods my-
self can make?
SENECA: Fear this the more, that so
great power is thine.
NERO: My royal fortune grants all things
to me.
SENECA: But trust her cautiously; she
may deceive.
NERO: A fool is he who does not what
he may.
SENECA: To do, not what he may, but
ought, wins praise.
NERO: The crowd spurns sluggish men.
SENECA: The hated, slays.
NERO: Yet swords protect a prince.
SENECA: Still better, faith.
NERO: A Cæsar should be feared.
SENECA: And more be loved.
NERO: But men must fear.
SENECA: Enforced commands are
hard.
NERO: Let them obey our laws.
SENECA: Make better laws—

NERO: I'll be the judge.

SENECA: Which all men may approve.

NERO: The sword shall force respect.

SENECA: May heaven forbid!

NERO: Shall I then tamely let them seek my blood,
That suddenly despised and unavenged,
I may be taken off? Though exiled far,
The stubborn spirits are not broken yet
Of Plautus and of Sulla. Still their rage
Persistent spurs their friends to seek my death;
For still have they the people's love in Rome,
Which ever nourishes the exile's hopes.
Then let the sword remove my enemies;
My hateful wife shall die and follow him,
That brother whom she loves. The high must fall.

SENECA: How fair a thing it is to be the first
Among great men, to think for fatherland,
To spare the weak, to hold the hand of power
From deeds of blood, to give wrath time to think,
Give rest to a weary world, peace to the age.
This is the noblest part; by this high path
Is heaven sought. So did Augustus first,
The father of his country, gain the stars,
And as a god is worshiped at the shrines.
Yet he was long by adverse fortune tossed
On land and sea, in battle's deadly chance,
Until his father's foes he recompensed.
But fortune hath to thee in peaceful guise
Bent her divinity; with unstained hand
Hath she the reins of government bestowed,
And given world-dominion to thy nod.
Sour hate is overcome, and in its stead
Is filial harmony; the senate, knights,
All orders yield obedience to thy will;
For in the father's judgment and the prayers
Of humbler folk, thou art the arbiter
Of peace, the god of human destinies,
Ordained to rule the world by right divine.
Thy country's father thou. This sacred name
Doth suppliant Rome beseech thee to preserve,
And doth commend her citizens to thee.

NERO: It is the gift of heaven that haughty Rome,
Her people, and her senate bow to me,
And that my terror doth extort those prayers
And servile words from their unwilling lips.
To save the citizens! seditious men,
Who ever 'gainst their land and prince conspire,
Puffed up with pride of race—sheer madness that,
When all my enemies one word of mine
Can doom to death. Base Brutus raised his hand
To slay that prince from whom he had his all;
And he, who never 'mid the shock of arms
Had been o'ercome, the world's great conqueror,
Who trod, a very Jove, the lofty paths
Of honor, he was slain by impious hands—
Of *citizens!* What streams of blood hath Rome,
So often rent by civil strife, beheld!
That very saint of thine, Augustus' self,
Who, as thou said'st but now, did merit heaven
By piety—how many noble men
Did he destroy, in lusty youth, in age,
At home, abroad, when, spurred by mortal fear,
They fled their household gods and that fell sword
Of the Triumvirate, consigned to death
Upon those mindful tablets' fatal lists.
The grieving parents saw their severed heads
Upon the rostra set, but dared not weep

Their hapless sons; the forum reeked
    with blood,
And gore down all those rotting faces
    dripped.
Nor this the end of slaughter and of
    death:
Long did the plains of grim Philippi feed
The ravenous birds and prowling beasts
    of prey;
While ships and men, in deadly conflict
    met,
Beneath Sicilia's waters were engulfed.
The whole world trembled with the shock
    of arms;
And now, when all was lost, with fleeing
    ships,
That mighty leader sought the distant
    Nile,
Doomed soon himself to perish there.
    And thus,
Once more incestuous Egypt drank the
    blood
Of Rome's great captains. Now his flit-
    ting shade
Is hovering there; and there is civil strife,
So long and impious, at last interred.
Now did the weary victor sheathe his
    sword,
All blunted with the savage blows he
    gave,
And held his empire with the rein of
    fear.
He lived in safety 'neath the ample shield
Of loyal guards; and when his end was
    come,
The pious mandate of his son proclaimed
Him god, and at the temples' sacred
    shrines
Was he adored. So shall the stars expect
My godhead too, if first I seize and slay
With sword relentless all who bear me
    hate,
And on a worthy offspring found my
    house.
SENECA: But she will fill thy house with
    noble sons,
That heaven-born glory of the Claudian
    stock,
Who by the will of fate was wed to thee,

As Juno to her brother Jove was given.
NERO: A child of hers would stain my
    noble line,
For she herself was of a harlot born;
And more—her heart was never linked to
    me.
SENECA: In tender years is faith not
    manifest,
When love, by shame o'ercome, conceals
    its fires.
NERO: This I myself long trusted, but in
    vain,
Though she was clearly of unloving heart,
And every look betrayed her hate of me.
At length, in angry grief, I sought re-
    venge;
And I have now a worthy wife obtained,
In race and beauty blessed, before whose
    charms
Minerva, Venus, Juno—all would bow.
SENECA: But honor, wifely faith, and
    modesty—
These should the husband seek, for these
    alone,
The priceless treasures of the heart and
    soul,
Remain perpetual; but beauty's flower
Doth fade and languish with each pass-
    ing day.
NERO: On her has heaven all its charms
    bestowed,
And fate has given her from her birth
    to me.
SENECA: But love will fail; do not too
    rashly trust.
NERO: Shall he give way, that tyrant of
    the skies,
Whom Jove, the Thunderer, cannot re-
    move,
Who lords it over savage seas, the realms
Of gloomy Dis, and draws the gods to
    earth?
SENECA: 'Tis by our human error that
    we paint
Love as a god, wingèd, implacable,
And arm his sacred hands with dart and
    bow,
Assign him blazing torches, count him
    son

Of fostering Venus and of Vulcan. Nay,
But love is of the heart's compelling
power,
A fond and cozening passion of the soul;
Of hot youth is it born, and in the lap
Of ease and luxury, 'midst fortune's joys,
Is fostered. But it sickens straight and
dies
When you no longer feed and fondle it.

NERO: I deem the primal source of life
is this,
The joy of love; and it can never die,
Since by sweet love, which soothes e'en
savage breasts,
The human race is evermore renewed.
This god shall bear for me the wedding
torch,
And join me with Poppæa in his bonds.

SENECA: The people's grief could scarce
endure to see
That marriage, nor would piety permit.

NERO: Shall I alone avoid what all may
do?

SENECA: The state from loftiest souls
expects the best.

NERO: I fain would see if, broken by my
power,
This rashly cherished favor will not yield.

SENECA: 'Tis best calmly to obey the
state.

NERO: Ill fares the state, when commons govern kings.

SENECA: They justly chafe who pray
without avail.

NERO: When prayers do not avail, should
force be sought?

SENECA: Rebuffs are hard.

NERO: 'Tis wrong to force a prince.

SENECA: He should give way.

NERO: Then rumor counts him forced.

SENECA: Rumor's an empty thing.

NERO: But harmful too.

SENECA: She fears the strong.

NERO: But none the less maligns.

SENECA: She soon can be o'ercome. But
let the youth,
The faith and chastity of this thy wife,
The merits of her sainted sire prevail
To turn thee from thy will.

NERO: Have done at last,
For wearisome has thy insistence grown;
One still may do what Seneca condem..s.
And I myself have now too long delayed
The people's prayers for offspring to the
throne.
Tomorrow's morn her wedding day shall
prove,
Who bears within her womb my pledge
of love.

(Exeunt)

ACT III

GHOST OF AGRIPPINA (*bearing a flaming
torch*): Through cloven earth from
Tartarus I come,
To bring in bloody hands this torch of
hell
To light these cursed rites; with such
dire flames
Let this Poppæa wed my son, which soon
His mother's grief and vengeful hand
shall turn
To funeral fires. And ever 'mid the
shades
My impious murder in my memory
dwells,
A heavy weight upon my grieving soul
Still unavenged; for, Oh, ingratitude
He gave me in return for all my gifts,
E'en for the gift of empire did he give
A murderous ship designed to work my
death.
I would have wept my comrades' plight,
and more,
My son's most cruel deed: no time for
tears
Was given, but even higher did he heap
His sum of crime. Though I escaped the
sea,
I felt the keen sword's thrust, and with
my blood
The very gods defiling, poured my soul
In anguish forth. But even yet his hate
Was not appeased. Against my very
name

The tyrant raged; my merits he obscured;
My statues, my inscriptions, honors—all,
On pain of death he bade to be destroyed
Throughout the world—that world my hapless love,
To my own direful punishment, had given
To be by him, an untried boy, controlled.
And now my murdered husband's angry ghost
Shakes vengeful torches in my guilty face,
Insistent, threat'ning; blames his death on me,
His murdered son, and loud demands that now
The guilty cause be given up. Have done:
He shall be given, and that right speedily.
Avenging furies for his impious head
Are planning even now a worthy fate:
Base flight and blows, and fearful sufferings,
By which the raging thirst of Tantalus
He shall surpass; the cruel, endless toil
Of Sisyphus; the pain that Tityus feels,
And the dread, racking anguish of the wheel
On which Ixion's whirling limbs are stretched.
Let gold and marble deck his palace walls;
Let armèd guards protect him; let the world
Be beggared that its treasures vast may flow
Into his lap; let suppliant Parthians bend
To kiss his hands, and bring rich offerings:
The day and hour will come when for his crimes
His guilty soul shall full atonement make,
When to his enemies he shall be given,
Deserted and destroyed and stripped of all.
Oh, to what end my labors and my prayers?
Why did thy frenzied madness, O my son,
And fate impel thee to such depths of crime

That e'en thy mother's wrath, whom thou didst slay,
Is all too small to match her sufferings?
Oh, would that, ere I brought thee forth to light,
And suckled thee, my vitals had been rent
By savage beasts! Then senseless, innocent,
And mine wouldst thou have perished; joined to me
Wouldst thou forever see the quiet seats
Of this abode of souls, thy mighty sire,
And grandsires too, those men of glorious name,
Whom now perpetual shame and grief await
Because of thee, thou monster, and of me.
But why delay in hell to hide my face,
Since I have proved a curse to all my race?   (*Vanishes*)
OCTAVIA (*to the* CHORUS *in deprecation of their grief because of her divorce*):
    Restrain your tears; put on a face of joy,
As on a festal day, lest this your love
And care for me should stir the royal wrath,
And I be cause of suffering to you.
This wound is not the first my heart has felt;
Far worse have I endured; but all shall end,
Perchance in death, before this day is done.
No more upon my brutal husband's face
Shall I be forced to look; that hateful couch,
Long since consigned to slavish uses, base,
I shall behold no more.
For now Augustus' sister shall I be,
And not his wife. But Oh, be far from me
All cruel punishments and fear of death.
Poor, foolish girl! and canst thou hope for this?
Bethink thee of his former sins—and hope.

Nay, he has spared thy wretched life till
　now,
That thou mayst at his marriage altars
　fall.
But why so often turn thy streaming
　eyes
Upon thy home? Now speed thy steps
　away,
And leave this bloody prince's hall for
　aye.
CHORUS: Now dawns at last the day we
　long have feared
And talked of. Lo, our Claudia, driven
　forth
By cruel Nero's threats, leaves that abode
Which even now Poppæa calls her own;
While we must sit and grieve with slug-
　gish woe,
By heavy fear oppressed.
Where is that Roman people's manhood
　now,
Which once the pride of mighty leaders
　crushed,
Gave righteous laws to an unconquered
　land,
Gave powers at will to worthy citizens,
Made peace and war, fierce nations over-
　came,
And held in dungeons dark their captive
　kings?
Behold, on every side our eyes are grieved
By this Poppæa's gleaming statues joined
With Nero's images—a shameful sight.
Come, overturn them with indignant
　hands,
Too like in feature to her living face.
And her we'll drag from off that royal
　couch;
And then, with flaming brand and deadly
　sword,
Attack the princely palace of her lord.

ACT IV

NURSE (to POPPÆA, who appears, dis-
　traught, coming out of her chamber):
　Why dost thou from thy husband's
　chamber come,

Dear child, with hurried step and
　troubled face?
Why dost thou seek a lonely place to
　weep?
For surely has the day we long have
　sought
With prayers and promised victims come
　at last.
Thou hast thy Cæsar, firmly joined to
　thee
By ties of marriage, whom thy beauty
　won,
Whom Venus gave to thee in bonds of
　love,
Though Seneca despised and flouted her.
How beautiful, upon the banquet couch
Reclining in the palace, didst thou seem!
The senate viewed thy beauty in amaze
When thou didst offer incense to the gods,
And sprinkle wine upon the sacred
　shrines,
Thy head the while with gauzy purple
　veiled.
And close beside thee was thy lord him-
　self;
Amid the favoring plaudits of the crowd
He walked majestic, in his look and mien
Proclaiming all his pride and joy in thee.
So did the noble Peleus lead his bride
Emerging from the ocean's snowy foam,
Whose wedding feast the heavenly gods
　adorned,
With equal joy the sea divinities.
What sudden cause has clouded o'er thy
　face?
Tell me, what mean thy pallor and thy
　tears!
POPPÆA: Dear nurse, this night I had a
　dreadful dream;
And even now, as I remember it,
My mind is troubled and my senses fail.
For when the joyful day had sunk to rest,
And in the darkened sky the stars ap-
　peared,
I lay asleep within my Nero's arms.
But that sweet sleep I could not long
　enjoy;
For suddenly a grieving crowd appeared

To throng my chamber—Roman matrons
they,
With hair disheveled and loud cries of
woe.
Then 'midst the oft-repeated, strident
blasts
Of trumpets, there appeared my hus-
band's mother,
And shook before my face with threat'n-
ing mien
A bloody torch. Compelled by present
fear,
I followed her; when suddenly the earth
Seemed rent asunder to its lowest depths.
Headlong to these I plunged, and even
there
In wonder I beheld my wedding couch,
Whereon I sank in utter weariness.
Then with a throng of followers I saw
My son and former husband drawing
near.
Straightway Crispinus hastened to my
arms,
And on my lips his eager kisses fell:
When suddenly within that chamber
burst
My lord the king with frantic, hurrying
steps,
And plunged his sword into that other's
throat.
A mighty terror seized me, and at last
It roused me from my sleep. I started up
With trembling limbs and wildly beating
heart.
Long was I speechless from that haunting
fear,
Until thy fond affection gave me tongue.
Why do the ghosts of Hades threaten me?
Or why did I behold my husband's blood?
NURSE: All things which occupy the
waking mind,
Some subtle power, swift working, weaves
again
Into our web of dreams. Small wonder
then,
Thy sleeping thoughts were filled with
marriage beds
And husbands, when thy newly mated
lord

Held thee in his embrace. Does it seem
strange
That thou shouldst dream tonight of
sounds of woe,
Of breasts hard beaten and of streaming
hair?
Octavia's departure did they mourn
Within her brother's and her father's
house.
The torch which thou didst follow, borne
aloft
By Agrippina's hand, is but a sign
That hate shall win for thee a mighty
name.
Thy marriage couch, in realms infernal
seen,
Portends a lasting state of wedded joy.
Since in Crispinus' neck the sword was
sheathed,
Believe that no more wars thy lord shall
wage,
But hide his sword within the breast of
peace.
Take heart again, recall thy joys, I pray,
Throw off thy fears, and to thy couch
return.
POPPÆA: Nay, rather will I seek the
sacred shrines,
And there make sacrifice unto the gods,
That they avert these threats of night and
sleep,
And turn my terrors all upon my foes.
Do thou pray for me and the gods
implore
That in this happy state I may endure.

(*Exeunt* POPPÆA AND NURSE)

CHORUS (*of Roman women in sympathy
with* POPPÆA): If babbling rumor's
tales of Jove,
His secret joys in mortal love,
Are true, he once, in plumage dressed,
Was to the lovely Leda pressed;
And as a savage bull he bore
Europa from her native shore:
But should he once thy form, Poppæa, see,
He would leave his shining stars to dwell
with thee.
· For thou than Leda many fold

Art fairer, or that maid of old
Whom Jove embraced in showers of
gold.
Let Sparta boast her lovely dame,
Who, as his prize, to Paris came:
Though Helen's beauty drove the world
to arms,
She still must yield to our Poppæa's
charms.

(*Enter* MESSENGER)

But who comes here with hurried step and
wild?
What tidings bears he in his heaving
breast?
MESSENGER: Whoever guards our noble
prince's house,
Let him defend it from the people's rage.
Behold, the prefects lead their men in
haste,
To save the city from the furious mob
Whose reckless passion grows, unchecked
by fear.
CHORUS: What is the madness that in-
flames their hearts?
MESSENGER: The people for their loved
Octavia
Are wild with rage and grief; and now in
throngs
Are rushing forth in mood for any deed.
CHORUS: What are they bent to do, or
with what plan?
MESSENGER: To give Octavia back her
father's house,
Her brother's bed, and her due share of
empire.
CHORUS: But these Poppæa holds as
Nero's wife.
MESSENGER: 'Tis even she 'gainst whom
the people's rage
Burns persistent, and to reckless deeds
Is driven headlong on.   Whate'er they
see,
Of noble marble wrought, or gleaming
bronze,
The hated image of Poppæa's face,
They cast it to the earth with wanton
hands

And crushing bars.   The shattered parts
they drag
Along the streets, and with insulting heel
Deep in the filthy mud they trample them.
These savage deeds are mingled with such
words
As I should fear to utter in your ears.
Soon will they hedge the royal house with
flames,
Unless the prince his new-made wife give
up
To sate the people's wrath, and then re-
store
To noble Claudia her father's house.
That he himself may know these
threatened deeds, .
I'll haste to tell him as the prefect bade.
(*Exit*)
CHORUS: Why vainly strive against the
powers above?
For Cupid's weapons are invincible.
Your puny fires by those fierce flames
he'll dim
By which he oft has quenched the bolts
of Jove,
And brought the Thunderer captive from
the sky.
For this offense you shall dire forfeit pay,
E'en with your blood; for hot of wrath is
he,
And may not be o'ercome.   At his com-
mand
Did fierce Achilles strike the peaceful
lyre;
He forced the Greeks and Agamemnon
proud
To do his will.   Illustrious cities, too,
And Priam's realm he utterly destroyed.
And now my mind in fear awaits to see
What Cupid's cruel penalties will be.

ACT V

NERO (*seated in a room of his palace*):
Too slow my soldiers' hands, too
mild my wrath,
When citizens have dared such crimes as
these.

Those torches that they kindled 'gainst
their prince
Their blood shall quench; and Rome,
who bore such men,
Shall be bespattered with her people's
gore.
Yet death is far too light a punishment
For such atrocities; this impious mob
Shall suffer worse than death. But she,
my wife
And sister, whom I hate with deadly fear,
For whose sole sake the people rage at me,
Shall give her life at last to sate my grief,
And quench my anger in her flowing
blood.
Soon shall my flames enwrap the city's
walls,
And in the ruins of her falling homes
The people shall be buried; squalid want,
Dire hunger, grief—all these shall they
endure.
Too fat upon the blessings of our age
Has this vile mob become, and know not
how
To bear our clemency and relish peace;
But, rash and reckless, are they ever
borne
By shifting tides of passion to their hurt.
They must be held in check by suffering,
Be ever pressed beneath the heavy yoke,
Lest once again they dare assail the
throne,
And to the august features of my wife
Dare lift again their vulgar eyes. O'er-
awed
By fear of punishment must they be
taught
To yield obedience to their prince's nod.
But here I see the man whose loyalty
Has made him captain of my royal guards.

(*Enter* PREFECT)

PREFECT: The people's rage by slaughter of a few,
Who most resistance made, is overcome.
NERO: Is that enough? Was that my
word to thee?
"Is overcome?" Where then is my revenge?

PREFECT: The guilty leaders of the mob
are dead.
NERO: Nay, but the mob itself, which
dared to assail
My house with flames, to dictate laws to
me,
To drag my noble wife from off my bed,
And with unhallowed hands and angry
threats
To affront her majesty—are they un-
scathed?
PREFECT: Shall angry grief decide their
punishment?
NERO: It shall—whose fame no future
age shall dim.
PREFECT: Which neither wrath nor fear
shall moderate?
NERO: She first shall feel my wrath who
merits it.
PREFECT: Tell whom thou mean'st. My
hand shall spare her not.
NERO: My wrath demands my guilty
sister's death.
PREFECT: Benumbing horror holds me
in its grasp.
NERO: Wilt not obey my word?
PREFECT: Why question that?
NERO: Because thou spar'st my foe.
PREFECT: A woman, foe?
NERO: If she be criminal.
PREFECT: But what her crime?
NERO: The people's rage.
PREFECT: But who can check their rage?
NERO: The one who fanned its flame.
PREFECT: But who that one?
NERO: A woman she, to whom an evil
heart
Hath nature given, a soul to fraud in-
clined.
PREFECT: But not the power to act.
NERO: That she may be
Without the power to act, that present
fear
May break her strength, let punishment
at once,
Too long delayed, crush out her guilty
life.
Have done at once with argument and
prayers,

And do my royal bidding: let her sail
To some far distant shore and there be slain,
That thus at last my fears may be at rest.
(*Exeunt*)

CHORUS (*attached to* OCTAVIA): Oh,
  dire and deadly has the people's love
To many proved, which fills their swelling sails
With favoring breeze, and bears them out to sea;
But soon its vigor languishes and dies,
And leaves them to the mercy of the deep.
The wretched mother of the Gracchi wept
Her murdered sons, who, though of noble blood,
Far famed for eloquence and piety,
Stout-hearted, learnèd in defense of law,
Were brought to ruin by the people's love
And popular renown. And Livius, thee
To equal fate did fickle fortune give,
Who found no safety in thy lictors' rods,
No refuge in thy home. But grief forbids
To tell more instances. This hapless girl,
To whom but now the citizens decreed
The restoration of her fatherland,
Her home, her brother's couch, is dragged away
In tears and misery to punishment,
With citizens consenting to her death!
Oh, blessèd poverty, content to hide
Beneath the refuge of a lowly roof!
For lofty homes, to fame and fortune known,
By storms are blasted and by fate o'erthrown!

(*Enter* OCTAVIA *in the custody of the palace guards, who are dragging her roughly out into the street.*)

OCTAVIA: Oh, whither do ye hurry me? What fate
Has that vile tyrant or his queen ordained?
Does she, subdued and softened by my woes,
Grant me to live in exile? Or, if not,
If she intends to crown my sufferings
With death, why does her savage heart begrudge
That I should die at home? But now, alas,
I can no longer hope for life; behold,
My brother's bark, within whose treacherous hold
His mother once was borne; and now for me,
Poor wretch, his slighted sister-wife, it waits.
No more has right a place upon the earth,
Nor heavenly gods. Grim Fury reigns supreme.
Oh, who can fitly weep my evil plight?
What nightingale has tongue to sing my woes?
Would that the fates would grant her wings to me!
Then would I speed away on pinions swift,
And leave my grievous troubles far behind,
Leave these unholy haunts of savage men,
There, all alone, within some forest wide,
Among the swaying branches would I sit,
And let my grieving spirit weep its fill.

CHORUS: The race of men is by the fates controlled,
And none may hope to make his own secure;
And o'er the ever-shifting ways of life
The day which most we fear shall come to us.
But comfort now thy heart with thought of those
Of thine own house who suffered ill, and ask:
In what has fortune been more harsh to thee?
Thee first I name, Agrippa's noble child,
The famous mother of so many sons,
Great Cæsar's wife, whose name throughout the world
In flaming glory shone, whose teeming womb
Brought forth so many hostages of peace:
E'en thee did exile wait, and cruel chains,

Blows, bitter anguish, and at last a death
Of lingering agony. And Livia, thou,
Though fortunate in husband and in sons,
Didst walk the way of sin—and punish-
    ment.
And Julia, too, endured her mother's
    fate;
For, though no evil deed was charged to
    her,
She fell a victim to the sword at last.
What could not once thy mighty mother
    do
Who ruled supreme the house of Claudius,
By him beloved, and in her son secure?
Yet she at last was subject to a slave,
And fell beneath a brutal soldier's sword.
For what exalted heights of royalty
Might not our Nero's mother once have
    hoped?
Mishandled first by vulgar sailors' hands,
Then slain and mangled by the bungling
    sword,
She lay the victim of her cruel son.

OCTAVIA: Me, too, the tyrant to the
    world of shades
Is sending. Why delay? Then speed my
    death.
For fate hath made me subject to your
    power.
I pray the heavenly gods—what wouldst
    thou, fool?
Pray not to gods who show their scorn
    of thee.
But, O ye gods of hell, ye furies dire,
Who work your vengeance on the crimes
    of men,
And thou, my father's restless spirit, come
And bring this tyrant fitting punishment.

(To her guards)

The death you threaten has no terrors
    now
For me. Go, set your ship in readiness,
Unfurl your sails, and let your pilot seek
The barren shores of Pandataria.

(Exit OCTAVIA *with guards)*

CHORUS: Ye gentle breezes and ye
    zephyrs mild,

Which once from savage Dian's altar
    bore
Atrides' daughter in a cloud concealed,
This child of ours, Octavia, too, we pray,
Bear far away from these too cruel woes,
And set her in the fane of Trivia.
For Aulis is more merciful than Rome,
The savage Taurian land more mild than
    this:
There hapless strangers to their gods they
    feed,
But Rome delights to see her children
    bleed.

—F. J. MILLER.

THE SATIRIST

A COUNCIL OF STATE

JUVENAL

[From *Satires* IV]

Decimus Junius Juvenalis, the last of
the great satirists, was born about 55 at
Aquinum in Latium and died shortly after
130. He trained himself in declamation,
had some military experience and occupied municipal offices, and late in life was
banished on account of criticism of an
actor who was a favorite at the court.
The total product of his pen seems to
have consisted of the sixteen satires still
extant. The keynote of his writings is
moral indignation over the vices of the
times, and the tone one of deep seriousness.

The satirist is under no obligation to
be true to historical fact. It matters not
at all whether Domitian did actually summon a council of state to debate the manner of serving a fish, if only it be true
that he used his council of state for matters of like trivialness and that his coun-
cillors obeyed out of fear or flattery.

When the last Flavius, drunk with fury,
    tore
The prostrate world, which bled at every
    pore,

And Rome beheld, in body as in mind,
A bald-pate Nero rise, to curse mankind;
It chanced, that where the fane of Venus
    stands,
Reared on Ancona's coast by Grecian
    hands,
A turbot, wandering from the Illyrian
    main,
Fill'd the wide bosom of the bursting
    seine.
Monsters so bulky, from its frozen stream,
Mæotis renders to the solar beam,
And pours them, fat with a whole win-
    ter's ease,
Through the bleak Euxine, into warmer
    seas.
    The mighty draught the astonished
        boatman eyes,
And to the Pontiff's table dooms his
    prize:
For who would dare to sell it? who to
    buy?
When the coast swarmed with many a
    practiced spy,
Mud-rakers, prompt to swear the fish
    had fled
From Cæsar's ponds, ingrate! where long
    it fed,
And thus recaptured, claimed to be re-
    stored
To the dominion of its ancient lord!
Nay, if Palphurius may our credit gain,
Whatever rare or precious swims the
    main,
Is forfeit to the crown, and you may seize
The obnoxious dainty, when and where
    you please.
This point allowed, our wary boatman
    chose
To give—what, else, he had not failed to
    lose.
    Now were the dogstar's sickly fervors
        o'er,
Earth, pinched with cold, her frozen
    livery wore;
The old began their quartan fits to fear,
And wintry blasts deformed the beaute-
    ous year,

And kept the turbot sweet: yet on he
    flew,
As if the sultry South corruption blew.—
And now the lake, and now the hill he
    gains,
Where Alba, though in ruins, still main-
    tains
The Trojan fire, which, but for her, were
    lost,
And worships Vesta, though with less of
    cost.
    The wondering crowd, that gathered to
        survey
The enormous fish, and barred the fisher's
    way,
Satiate, at length retires; the gates un-
    fold!—
Murmuring, the excluded senators behold
The envied dainty enter:—On the man
To great Atrides pressed, and thus began:
    "This, for a private table far too great,
Accept, and sumptuously your Genius
    treat:
Haste to unload your stomach, and
    devour
A turbot, destined to this happy hour.
I sought him not;—he marked the toils
    I set,
And rushed, a willing victim, to my net."
    Was flattery e'er so rank! yet he grows
        vain,
And his crest rises at the fulsome strain.
When to divine, a mortal power we raise,
He looks for no hyperboles in praise.
    But when was joy unmixed? no pot is
        found,
Capacious of the turbot's ample round:
In this distress, he calls the chiefs of
    state,
At once the objects of his scorn and hate,
In whose pale cheeks distrust and doubt
    appear,
And all a tyrant's friendship breeds of
    fear.
    Scarce was the loud Liburnian heard
        to say,
"He sits," ere Pegasus was on his way;
Yes:—the new bailiff of the affrighted
    town,

(For what were Præfects more?) had
snatched his gown,
And rushed to council: from the ivory
chair,
He dealt out justice with no common
care;
But yielded oft to those licentious times,
And where he could not punish, winked
at crimes.

Then old, facetious Crispus tript along,
Of gentle manners, and persuasive
tongue:
None fitter to advise the lord of all,
Had that pernicious pest, whom thus we
call,
Allowed a friend to soothe his savage
mood,
And give him counsel, wise at once and
good.
But who shall dare this liberty to take,
When, every word you hazard, life's at
stake?
Though but of stormy summers, showery
springs—
For tyrants' ears, alas! are ticklish things.
So did the good old man his tongue re-
strain;
Nor strove to stem the torrent's force in
vain.
Not one of those, who, by no fears de-
terred,
Spoke the free soul, and truth to life
preferred.
He temporized—thus fourscore summers
fled,
Even in that court, securely, o'er his
head.

Next him, appeared Acilius hurrying
on,
Of equal age—and followed by his son;
Who fell, unjustly fell, in early years,
A victim to the tyrant's jealous fears:
But long ere this were hoary hairs become
A prodigy, among the great, at Rome;
Hence, had I rather owe my humble
birth,
Frail brother of the giant brood, to earth.
Poor youth! in vain the ancient sleight
you try;

In vain, with frantic air, and ardent eye,
Fling every robe aside, and battle wage
With bears and lions, on the Alban stage.
All see the trick: and, spite of Brutus'
skill,
There are who count him but a driveler
still;
Since, in his days, it cost no mighty pains
To outwit a prince, with much more
beard than brains.

Rubrius, though not, like these, of
noble race,
Followed with equal terror in his face;
And, laboring with a crime too foul to
name,
More, than the pathic satirist, lost to
shame.

Montanus' belly next, and next appeared
The legs, on which that monstrous pile
was reared.

Crispinus followed, daubed with more
perfume,
Thus early! than two funerals consume.
Then bloodier Pompey, practiced to be-
tray,
And hesitate the noblest lives away.
Then Fuscus, who in studious pomp at
home,
Planned future triumphs for the Arms of
Rome.
Blind to the event! those arms, a differ-
ent fate,
Inglorious wounds, and Dacian vultures,
wait.

Last, sly Veiento with Catullus came,
Deadly Catullus, who, at beauty's name
Took fire, although unseen: a wretch,
whose crimes
Struck with amaze even those prodigious
times.
A base, blind parasite, a murderous lord,
From the bridge-end raised to the council-
board;
Yet fitter still to dog the traveler's heels,
And whine for alms to the descending
wheels!
None dwelt so largely on the turbot's
size,

Or raised with such applause his wonder-
ing eyes;
But to the left (O, treacherous want of
sight)
He poured his praise;—the fish was on
the right!
Thus would he at the fencer's matches
sit,
And shout with rapture, at some fancied
hit;
And thus applaud the stage-machinery,
where
The youths were rapt aloft, and lost in
air.
 Nor fell Veiento short:—as if possest
With all Bellona's rage, his laboring
breast
Burst forth in prophecy: "I see, I see
The omens of some glorious victory!
Some powerful monarch captured!—lo,
he rears,
Horrent on every side, his pointed spears!
Arviragus hurled from the British car:
The fish is foreign, foreign is the war."
 Proceed, great seer, and what remains
untold,
The turbot's age and country next un-
fold;
So shall your lord his fortunes better
know,
And where the conquest waits and who
the foe.
 The emperor now the important ques-
tion put,
"How say ye, Fathers, *shall the fish be
cut?*"
"O, far be that disgrace," Montanus
cries;
"No, let a pot be formed, of amplest size,
Within whose slender sides the fish, dread
sire,
May spread his vast circumference en-
tire!
Bring, bring the tempered clay, and let
it feel
The quick gyrations of the plastic
wheel:—
But, Cæsar, thus forewarned, make no
campaign,

Unless your potters follow in your train!"
 Montanus ended; all approved the
plan,
And all, the speech, so worthy of the
man!
Versed in the old court luxury, he knew
The feasts of Nero, and his midnight
crew;
Where oft, when potent draughts had
fired the brain,
The jaded taste was spurred to gorge
again.—
And, in my time, none understood so
well
The science of good eating: he could tell,
At the first relish, if his oysters fed
On the Rutupian, or the Lucrine bed;
And from a crab, or lobster's color, name
The country, nay, the district, whence it
came.
 Here closed the solemn farce. The
Fathers rise.
And each submissive, from the presence
hies:—
Pale, trembling wretches, whom the chief,
in sport,
Had dragged, astonished, to the Alban
court;
As if the stern Sicambri were in arms,
Or the fierce Chatti threatened new
alarms;
As if ill news by flying posts had come,
And gathering nations sought the fall of
Rome!
O! that such scenes (disgraceful at the
most)
Had all those years of cruelty engrost,
Through which his rage pursued the
great and good,
Unchecked, while vengeance slumbered
o'er their blood!
And yet he fell!—for when he changed
his game,
And first grew dreadful to the vulgar
name,
They seized the murderer, drenched with
Lamian gore,
And hurled him, headlong, to the infernal
shore!   —WILLIAM GIFFORD.

THE FLATTERER

ADDRESS TO NERO

LUCAN

[From the *Pharsalia*, Book I]

Marcus Annæus Lucanus, nephew of the younger Seneca, was born in Corduba, Spain, in 39, and because of his connection with the conspiracy of Piso, was compelled to commit suicide in 65. He was a prolific writer of prose and verse, but the only extant work is the epic poem on the war between Cæsar and Pompey entitled *Pharsalia*. It is an extreme example of the Roman idea that recorded history furnishes material suitable to epic. Lucan sides with the cause of Pompey, interpreting the war as a conflict between liberty and tyranny.

It would appear that Lucan experienced a complete change of heart in his relation to Nero. Whether his early attitude of admiration is mere flattery or sincere conviction, certain it is that later passages in the same poem reveal only contempt and hatred for Nero and all that he stands for.

But if our fates severely have decreed
No way but this for Nero to succeed;
If only thus our heroes can be gods,
And Earth must pay for their divine
    abodes;
If Heaven could not the thunderer
    obtain,
Till giants' wars made room for Jove to
    reign,
'Tis just, ye gods, nor ought we to
    complain:
Opprest with death though dire Pharsalia
    groan,
Though Latian blood the Punic ghosts
    atone;
Though Pompey's hapless sons renew the
    war,
And Munda view the slaughter'd heaps
    from far;
Though meagre famine in Perusia reign,

Though Mutina with battles fill the
    plain;
Though Leuca's isle, and wide Ambracia's
    bay,
Record the rage of Actium's fatal day;
Though servile hands are arm'd to man
    the fleet,
And on Sicilian seas the navies meet;
All crimes, all horrours, we with joy
    regard,
Since thou, O Cæsar, art the great reward.
    Vast are the thanks thy grateful Rome
    should pay
To wars, which usher in thy sacred
    sway.
When, the great business of the world
    achiev'd,
Late by the willing stars thou art
    receiv'd,
Through all the blissful seats the news
    shall roll,
And Heaven resound with joy from pole
    to pole.
Whether great Jove resign supreme
    command,
And trust his sceptre to thy abler hand;
Or if thou choose the empire of the day,
And make the Sun's unwilling steeds
    obey;
Auspicious if thou drive the flaming
    team,
While Earth rejoices in thy gentler
    beam;
Wher'er thou reign, with one consenting
    voice,
The Gods and Nature shall approve thy
    choice.
But oh! whatever be thy godhead great,
Fix not in regions too remote thy seat;
Nor deign thou near the frozen Bear to
    shine,
Nor where the sultry southern stars
    decline;
Less kindly thence thy influence shall
    come,
And thy blest rays obliquely visit Rome.
Press not too much on any part the
    sphere:

Hard were the task thy weight divine to
    bear;
Soon would the axis feel th' unusual load,
And groaning bend beneath th' incum-
    bent god:
O'er the mid orb more equal shalt thou
    rise,
And with a juster balance fix the skies.
Serene for ever be that azure space,
No blackening clouds the purer Heaven
    disgrace,
Nor hide from Rome her Cæsar's radiant
    face.
Then shall mankind consent in sweet
    accord,
And warring nations sheath the wrathful
    sword;
Peace shall the world in friendly leagues
    compose,
And Janus' dreadful gates for ever close.
To me thy present godhead stands
    confest,
Oh let thy sacred fury fire my breast!
So thou vouchsafe to hear, let Phœbus
    dwell
Still uninvok'd in Cyrrha's mystic cell;
By me uncall'd, let sprightly Bacchus
    reign,
And lead the dance on Indian Nysa's
    plain.
To thee, O Cæsar, all my vows belong;
Do thou alone inspire the Roman song.
           —NICHOLAS ROWE.

THE ENEMY ENVIED

MARTIAL

[*Epigrams* VII, 5]

Marcus Valerius Martialis was born
about 40 in Bilbilis, Spain. He came to
Rome to make his fortune, lived there in
a garret, and eked out a miserable existence by "writing verses while you wait,"
by flattering the rich, and by the sale of
his books of epigrams. Later he returned
to Spain, where he died in 104. The
peculiar Roman gift for satire took on
new life in the hands of Martial, "father
of the epigram." The extant collection
of fifteen books is a monument to the
keenness of his observation of life, to his
unusual power of seeing through the disguises of affectation, and to his remarkable gift for summing up the real meaning of a person or of a situation within
the limits of a single sentence. He was
not above the vices of his day, nor did
he make any pretense of being a moralist.
Yet he deemed it his peculiar province to
direct the shafts of his wit at every form
of sham and insincerity, even if occasionally he himself might be accused of being
guilty of the things which he attacked.

As illustrated in this and the following
six pieces, Martial turned his cleverness
to practical account by employing it in
the service of flattery. It would seem
that his many attempts to win Domitian's
favor met with but indifferent success.

If with thee, Cæsar, the desires take place
Of people, senate, all the Roman race,
Thy presence graciously to them afford,
At their impatient suit, return their lord.
Rome her foe envies, that they thee de-
    tain,
Though many laurels she thereby doth
    gain;
That barb'rous nations see her prince so
    near,
Enjoy that face which they do so much
    fear.
           —ANON.

UNITED IN LOYALTY

MARTIAL

[*Epigrams* VII, 7]

Mid polar ice and Peucian snows,
Where with the hoof hard Ister glows;
And rebel Rhine, with broken horn,
Still bids thee awe, and still adorn,
The kingdoms of a faithless race,
That spurn thy guidance and thy grace;
O earth's controller unconfined,

Propitious parent of mankind!
Far from our vows thou canst not be:
Our heads and hearts are full of thee.
Nay, all our eyes thou holdest so,
That not the vasty Circus know
What paragons pretend to shine,
A Tigris or a Passerine.
—JAMES ELPHINSTON.

COMMEND ME TO THE THUNDERER

MARTIAL

[Epigrams VII, 99]

May'st thou the prince still gracious to
    thee find,
And Rome, no less than Egypt, ever kind;
If, when in court, my verses thou dost
    hear
(For sometimes Cæsar deigns to them an
    ear),
Thou me afford'st this free and candid
    praise,
This man's a glory, Cæsar, to thy days,
Yields not to Marsus, Pedo, or the best,
This is enough; to Cæsar leave the rest.
—ANON.

RESTORER AND FOUNDER

MARTIAL

[Epigrams VIII, 80]

Our fathers' deeds, Cæsar, thou dost re-
    vive,
Preserve the grayest ages still alive;
The antiquated Latian games renew,
The fight with simple fists, thy sands do
    show;
Temples, though old, their honour thou
    maintain'st,
The mean, for th' sake of richer, not dis-
    dain'st.
Thus while thou new dost build, the old
    restore,
We owe thee for thy own, and all before.
—ANON.

THE INDEBTEDNESS OF THE GODS

MARTIAL

[Epigrams IX, 3]

If thou shouldst challenge what is due to
    thee
From heaven, and its creditor wouldst
    be;
If public sale should be cried through
    the spheres,
And th' gods sell all to satisfy arrears,
Atlas will bankrupt prove, nor one
    ounce be
Reserv'd for Jupiter to treat with thee.
What canst thou for the Capitol receive?
Or for the honour of the laurel-wreath?
Or what will Juno give thee for her
    shrine?
Pallas I pass, she waits on thee and thine.
Alcides, Phœbus, Pollux I slip by,
And Flavia's temple neighb'ring on the
    sky.
Cæsar, thou must forbear and trust the
    heaven:
Jove's chest has not enough to make all
    even.
—FLETCHER.

THE VOTIVE GOOSE

MARTIAL

[Epigrams IX, 31]

In northern climes, amid sublime alarms,
This bird a Velius vow'd for Cæsar's
    arms.
Not twice four times her course did Luna
    stray,
When Mars his vot'ry call'd his vow to
    pay.
The gander joyous pealed his fun'ral
    knell,
And on the sacred fire spontaneous fell.
Eight wondrous coins he dropt from out
    his bill:

These from his bowels he did late distil.
Who now with silver, not with blood,
  atones;
The happy unavail of iron knows.
      —JAMES ELPHINSTON.

SECOND PLACE FOR JUPITER

MARTIAL

[*Epigrams* IX, 91]

If that a diverse invitation came
At once in Jove's and in great Cæsar's
  name,
Though that the stars were near, Rome
  more remote,
The gods in answer should have this my
  vote,
"Go, seek another that Jove's guest would
  be,
My Jupiter on earth hath fetter'd me."
      —FLETCHER.

THE COURT GOSSIP

AN ECCENTRIC EMPEROR [1]

SUETONIUS

[From the *Deified Claudius*]

Gaius Suetonius Tranquillus was born about 75 and died about 160. Suetonius, secretary to the emperor Hadrian, was a voluminous writer in the field of biography, the history of culture, and language and literature. His chief interest lay in biography, a branch in which he produced several series of lives. Except for fragments, some of them of considerable length, we possess only the *Lives of the Twelve Cæsars,* a work of primary importance for the history of the first century of the Empire. So great was Suetonius' popularity and influence that

[1] From The Loeb Classical Library, by permission.

his form and method, including even its tendency to preserve the trivial gossip as of equal value with the historical and with the interpretation of character, determined the course of historical writing for some time to come.

The peculiarities of Claudius, who ruled the Empire from 41 to 54, are set forth by means of a succession of anecdotes illustrating certain generally accepted qualities of the man. Suetonius as a rule contents himself with this method, seldom making a serious attempt to read the secrets of character beneath the anecdotes. In this way he often loses sight of contemporaneous circumstances impelling a character to action, and frequently assigns motives of a personal sort to deeds which may have been dictated by public policy.

He gave frequent and grand dinner parties, as a rule in spacious places, where six hundred guests were often entertained at one time. He even gave a banquet close to the outlet of the Fucine Lake and was well-nigh drowned, when the water was let out with a rush and deluged the place. He always invited his own children to dinner along with the sons and daughters of distinguished men, having them sit at the arms of the couches as they ate, after the old time custom. When a guest was suspected of having stolen a golden bowl the day before, he invited him again the next day, but set before him an earthenware cup.

He was eager for food and drink at all times and in all places. Once when he was holding court in the forum of Augustus and had caught the savour of a meal which was preparing for the Salii in the temple of Mars hard by, he left the tribunal, went up where the priests were, and took his place at their table. He hardly ever left the dining-room until he was stuffed and soaked; then he went to sleep at once, lying on his back with his mouth open, and a feather was put down his throat to relieve his stomach.

He slept but a little at a time, for he was usually awake before midnight; but he would sometimes drop off in the daytime while holding court and could hardly be roused when the advocates raised their voices for the purpose. He was immoderate in his passion for women, but wholly free from unnatural vice. He was greatly devoted to gaming, even publishing a book on the art, and he actually used to play while driving, having the board so fitted to his carriage as to prevent his game from being disturbed.

That he was of a cruel and bloodthirsty disposition was shown in matters great and small. He always exacted examination by torture and the punishment of parricides at once and in his presence. When he was at Tibur and wished to see an execution in the ancient fashion, no executioner could be found after the criminals were bound to the stake. Whereupon he sent to fetch one from the city and continued to wait for him until nightfall. At any gladiatorial show, either his own or another's, he gave orders that even those who fell accidentally should be slain, in particular the net-fighters, so that he could watch their faces as they died. When a pair of gladiators had fallen by mutually inflicted wounds, he at once had some little knives made from both their swords for his use. He took such pleasure in the combats with wild beasts and of those that fought at noonday, that he would go down to the arena at daybreak and after dismissing the people for luncheon at midday, he would keep his seat and in addition to the appointed combatants, he would for trivial and hasty reasons match others, even of the carpenters, the assistants, and men of that class, if any automatic device, or pageant, or anything else of the kind, had not worked well. He even forced one of his pages to enter the arena just as he was, in his toga.

But there was nothing for which he was so notorious as timidity and suspicion. Although in the early days of his reign, as we have said, he made a display of simplicity, he never ventured to go to a banquet without being surrounded by guards with lances and having his soldiers wait upon him in place of the servants; and he never visited a man who was ill without having the patient's room examined beforehand and his pillows and bed-clothing felt over and shaken out. Afterwards he even subjected those who came to pay their morning call to search, sparing none of the strictest examination. Indeed, it was not until late, and then reluctantly, that he gave up having women and young boys and girls grossly mishandled, and the cases for pens and styles taken from every man's attendant or scribe. When Camillus began his revolution, he felt sure that Claudius could be intimidated without resorting to war; and in fact when he ordered the emperor in an insulting, threatening, and impudent letter to give up his throne and betake himself to a life of privacy and retirement, Claudius called together the leading men and asked their advice about complying.

He was so terror-stricken by unfounded reports of conspiracies that he had tried to abdicate. When, as I have mentioned before, a man with a dagger was caught near him as he was sacrificing, he summoned the senate in haste by cries and loudly and tearfully bewailed his lot, saying that there was no safety for him anywhere; and for a long time he would not appear in public. His ardent love for Messalina too was cooled, not so much by her unseemly and insulting conduct, as through fear of danger, since he believed that her paramour Silius aspired to the throne. On that occasion he made a shameful and cowardly flight to the camp, doing nothing all the way but ask whether his throne was secure.

No suspicion was too trivial, nor the inspirer of it too insignificant, to drive him on to precaution and vengeance, once a slight uneasiness entered his mind. One of two parties to a suit, when he made his morning call, took Claudius aside, and said that he had dreamed that he was murdered by someone; then a little later pretending to recognize the assassin, he pointed out his opponent, as he was handing his petition. The latter was immediately seized, as if caught red-handed, and hurried off to execution. It was in a similar way, they say, that Appius Silanus met his downfall. When Messalina and Narcissus had put their heads together to destroy him, they ageed on their parts and the latter rushed into his patron's bed-chamber before day-break in pretended consternation, declaring that he had dreamed that Appius had made an attack on the emperor. Then Messalina, with assumed surprise, declared that she had had the same dream for several successive nights. A little later, as had been arranged, Appius, who had received orders the day before to come at that time, was reported to be forcing his way in, and as if this were proof positive of the truth of the dream, his immediate accusation and death were ordered. And Claudius did not hesitate to recount the whole affair to the senate next day and to thank the freedman for watching over his emperor's safety even in his sleep.

He was conscious of his tendency to wrath and resentment and excused both in an edict; he also drew a distinction between them, promising that the former would be short and harmless and the latter not without cause. After sharply rebuking the people of Ostia, because they had sent no boats to meet him when he entered the Tiber, and in such bitter terms that he wrote that they had reduced him to the rank of a commoner, he suddenly forgave them and all but apologised. He repulsed with his own hand men who approached him in public at unseasonable times. He also banished

a quæstor's clerk without a hearing, as well as a senator of prætorian rank, although they were blameless: the former for going too far in pleading a suit against him before he became emperor; the latter, because he had fined the tenants of Claudius's estates for violating the law forbidding the selling of cooked victuals, and had whipped his bailiff when he remonstrated. And with the same motive he took from the ædiles the regulation of the cook-shops.

He did not even keep quiet about his own stupidity, but in certain brief speeches he declared that he had purposely feigned it under Gaius, because otherwise he could not have escaped alive and attained his present station. But he convinced no one, and within a short time a book was published, the title of which was "The Elevation of Fools" and its thesis, that no one feigned folly.

Among other things men have marvelled at his absent-mindedness and blindness. When he had put Messalina to death, he asked shortly after taking his place at the table why the empress did not come. He caused many of those whom he had condemned to death to be summoned the very next day to consult with him or game with him, and sent a messenger to upbraid them for sleepy-heads when they delayed to appear. When he was planning his unlawful marriage with Agrippina, in every speech that he made he constantly called her his daughter and nursling, born and brought up in his arms. Just before his adoption of Nero, as if it were not bad enough to adopt a stepson when he had a grown-up son of his own, he publicly declared more than once that no one had ever been taken into the Claudian family by adoption.

In short, he often showed such heedlessness in word and act that one would suppose that he did not know or care to whom, with whom, when, or where he was speaking. When a debate was going on about the butchers and vintners, he cried out in the House: "Now, pray, who can live without a snack," and then went on to describe the abundance of the old taverns to which he himself used to go for wine in earlier days. He gave as one of his reasons for supporting a candidate for the quæstorship, that the man's father had once given him cold water when he was ill and needed it. Once when a witness had been brought before the senate, he said: "This woman was my mother's freedwoman and tirewoman, but she always regarded me as her patron; I mention this because there are still some in my household now who do not look on me as patron." When the people of Ostia made a public petition to him, he flew into a rage on the very tribunal and bawled out that he had no reason for obliging them; that he was surely free if anyone was. In fact every day, and almost every hour and minute, he would make such remarks as these: "What! do you take me for a Telegenius?" "Scold me, but hands off!" and many others of the same kind which would be unbecoming even in private citizens, not to mention a prince who lacked neither eloquence nor culture, but on the contrary constantly devoted himself to liberal pursuits.

He began to write history in his youth with the encouragement of Titus Livius and the direct help of Sulpicius Flavus. But when he gave his first reading to a large audience, he had difficulty in finishing, since he more than once threw cold water on his own performance. For at the beginning of the reading the breaking down of several benches by a fat man raised a laugh, and even after the disturbance was quieted, Claudius could not keep from recalling the incident and renewing his guffaws. Even while he was emperor he wrote a good deal and gave constant recitals through a professional reader. He began his history with the death of the dictator Cæsar, but passed to a later period and took a fresh start

at the end of the civil war, realising that he was not allowed to give a frank or true account of the earlier times, since he was often taken to task both by his mother and his grandmother. He left two books of the earlier history, but forty-one of the later. He also composed an autobiography in eight books, lacking rather in good taste than in style, as well as a "Defence of Cicero against the Writings of Asinius Gallus," a work of little learning. Besides this he invented three new letters and added them to the alphabet, maintaining that they were greatly needed; he published a book on their theory when he was still in private life, and when he became emperor had no difficulty in bringing about their general use. These characters may still be seen in numerous books, in the daily gazette, and in inscriptions on public buildings.

—J. C. ROLFE.

AN IMPERIAL ARTIST [1]

SUETONIUS

[From the *Nero*]

It will probably never be possible to form a fair judgment of Nero as an artist. It may be that he possessed unusual abilities; but all accounts of his activities are so colored by the Roman prejudice against participation by a gentleman in public performances of all sorts that a true estimate is out of the question. The Romans never wholly outgrew the notion that the making of art products, including even poetry itself, was but a form of manual labor belittling to the dignity of a man of high station.

Having gained some knowledge of music in addition to the rest of his early education, as soon as he became emperor

[1] From The Loeb Classical Library, by permission.

he sent for Terpnus, the greatest master of the lyre in those days, and after listening to him sing after dinner for many successive days until late at night, he little by little began to practice himself, neglecting none of the exercises which artists of that kind are in the habit of following, to preserve or strengthen their voices. For he used to lie upon his back and hold a leaden plate on his chest, purge himself by the syringe and by vomiting, and deny himself fruits and all foods injurious to the voice. Finally encouraged by his progress, although his voice was weak and husky, he began to long to appear on the stage, and every now and then in the presence of his intimate friends he would quote a Greek proverb meaning "Hidden music counts for nothing." And he made his debut at Naples, where he did not cease singing until he had finished the number which he had begun, even though the theatre was shaken by a sudden earth-quake shock. In the same city he sang frequently and for several successive days. Even when he took a short time to rest his voice, he could not keep out of sight but went to the theatre after bathing and dined in the orchestra with the people all about him, promising them in Greek, that when he had wetted his whistle a bit, he would ring out something good and loud. He was greatly taken too with the rhythmic applause of some Alexandrians who had flocked to Naples from a fleet that had lately arrived, and summoned more men from Alexandria. Not content with that, he selected some young men of the order of the knights and more than five thousand sturdy young commoners, to be divided into groups and learn the Alexandrian styles of applause (they called them "the bees," "the roof-tiles," and "the bricks"), and to ply them vigorously whenever he sang. These men were noticeable for their thick hair and fine apparel; their left hands were bare and without rings,

and the leaders were paid four hundred thousand sesterces each.

Considering it of great importance to appear in Rome as well, he repeated the contest of the Neronia before the appointed time, and when there was a general call for his "divine voice," he replied that if any wished to hear him, he would favour them in the gardens; but when the guard of soldiers which was then on duty seconded the entreaties of the people, he gladly agreed to appear at once. So without delay he had his name added to the list of the lyre-players who entered the contest, and casting his own lot into the urn with the rest, he came forward in his turn, attended by the prefects of the Guard carrying his lyre, and followed by the tribunes of the soldiers and his intimate friends. Having taken his place and finished his preliminary speech, he announced through the ex-consul Cluvius Rufus that "he would sing Niobe"; and he kept at it until late in the afternoon, putting off the award of the prize for that event and postponing the rest of the contest to the next year, to have an excuse for singing oftener. But since even that seemed too long to wait, he did not cease to appear in public from time to time. He even thought of taking part in private performances among the professional actors, when one of the prætors offered him a million sesterces. He also put on the mask and sang tragedies representing gods and heroes and even heroines and goddesses, having the masks fashioned in the likeness of his own features or those of the women of whom he chanced to be enamoured. Among other themes he sang "Canace in Labor," "Orestes the Matricide," "The Blinding of Œdipus" and the "Frenzy of Hercules." At the last named performance they say that a young recruit, seeing the emperor in mean attire and bound with chains, as the subject required, rushed forward to lend him aid.

From his earliest years he had a special

passion for horses and talked constantly about the games in the Circus, though he was forbidden to do so. Once when he was lamenting with his fellow pupils the fate of a charioteer of the "Greens," who was dragged by his horses, and his preceptor scolded him, he told a lie and pretended that he was talking of Hector. At the beginning of his reign he used to play every day with ivory chariots on a board, and he came from the country to all the games, even the most insignificant, at first secretly, and then so openly that no one doubted that he would be in Rome on that particular day. He made no secret of his wish to have the number of the prizes increased, and in consequence more races were added and the performance was continued to a late hour, while the managers of the troupes no longer thought it worth while to produce their drivers at all except for a full day's racing. He soon longed to drive a chariot himself and even to show himself frequently in public; so after a trial exhibition in his gardens before his slaves and the dregs of the populace, he gave all an opportunity of seeing him in the Circus Maximus, one of his freedmen dropping the napkin from the place usually occupied by the magistrates.

Not content with showing his proficiency in these arts at Rome, he went to Achaia, as I have said, influenced especially by the following consideration. The cities in which it was the custom to hold contests in music had adopted the rule of sending all the lyric prizes to him. These he received with the greatest delight, not only giving audience before all others to the envoys who brought them, but even inviting them to his private table. When some of them begged him to sing after dinner and greeted his performance with extravagant applause, he declared that "the Greeks were the only ones who had an ear for music and that they alone were worthy of his efforts." So he took ship without delay and immediately on arriving at Cassiope made a preliminary appearance as a singer at the altar of Jupiter Cassius, and then went the round of all the contests.

To make this possible, he gave orders that even those which were widely separated in time should be brought together in a single year, so that some had even to be given twice, and he introduced a musical competition at Olympia also, contrary to custom. To avoid being distracted or hindered in any way while busy with these contests, he replied to his freedman Hellius, who reminded him that the affairs of the city required his presence, in these words: "However much it may be your advice and your wish that I should return speedily, yet you ought rather to counsel me and to hope that I may return worthy of Nero."

While he was singing no one was allowed to leave the theatre for the most urgent reasons. And so it is said that some women gave birth to children there, while many who were worn out with listening and applauding, secretly leaped from the wall, since the gates at the entrance were closed, or feigned death and were carried out as if for burial. The trepidation and anxiety with which he took part in the contests, his keen rivalry of his opponents and his awe of the judges, can hardly be credited. As if his rivals were of quite the same station as himself, he used to show respect to them and try to gain their favour, while he slandered them behind their backs, sometimes assailed them with abuse when he met them, and even bribed those who were especially proficient.

Before beginning, he would address the judges in the most deferential terms, saying that he had done all that could be done, but the issue was in the hands of Fortune; they however, being men of wisdom and experience, ought to exclude what was fortuitous. When they bade him take heart, he withdrew with greater confidence, but not even then without anxiety, interpreting the silence and modesty of some as sullenness and ill-nature, and declaring that he had his suspicions of them.

In competition he observed the rules most scrupulously, never daring to clear his throat and even wiping the sweat from his brow with his arm. Once indeed, during the performance of a tragedy, when he had dropped his sceptre but quickly recovered it, he was terribly afraid that he might be excluded from the competition because of his slip, and his confidence was restored only when his accompanist swore that it had passed unnoticed amid the delight and applause of the people. When the victory was won, he made the announcement himself; and for that reason he always took part in the contests of the heralds. To obliterate the memory of all other victors in the games and leave no trace of them, their statues and busts were all thrown down by his order, dragged off with hooks, and cast into privies.

He also drove a chariot in many places, at Olympia even a ten-horse team, although in one of his own poems he had criticised Mithridates for just that thing. But after he had been thrown from the car and put back in it, he was unable to hold out and gave up before the end of the course; but he received the crown just the same. On his departure he presented the entire province with freedom and at the same time gave the judges Roman citizenship and a large sum of money. These favours he announced in person on the day of the Isthmian Games, standing in the middle of the stadium.

Returning from Greece, since it was at Naples that he had made his first appearance, he entered the city with white horses through a part of the wall which had been thrown down, as is customary with victors in the sacred games. In like manner he entered Antium, then Albanum, and finally Rome; but at Rome he rode in the chariot which Augustus had used in his triumphs in days gone by, and wore the purple robe and a Greek cloak adorned with stars of gold, bearing on his head the Olympic crown and in his right hand the Pythian, while the rest were carried before him with inscriptions telling where he had won them and against what competitors, and giving the titles of the songs or the subject of the plays. His car was followed by his claque as by the escort of a triumphal procession, who shouted that they were the attendants of Augustus and the soldiers of his triumph. Then through the arch of the Circus Maximus, which was thrown down, he made his way across the Velabrum and the Forum to the Palatine and the temple of Apollo. All along the route victims were slain, the streets were sprinkled from time to time with perfume, while birds, ribbons, and sweetmeats were showered upon him. He placed the sacred crowns in his bedchambers around his couches, as well as statues representing him in the guise of a lyre-player; and he had a coin too struck with the same device. So far from neglecting or relaxing his practice of the art after this, he never addressed the soldiers except by letter or in a speech delivered by another, to save his voice; and he never did anything for amusement or in earnest without an elocutionist by his side, to warn him to spare his vocal organs and hold a handkerchief to his mouth. To many men he offered his friendship or announced his hostility, according as they applauded him lavishly or grudgingly.

—J. C. ROLFE.

II. SALVATION THROUGH STOICISM

The times of Nero witnessed a revival of interest in philosophy, and nearly all the writers of that day were carefully trained in the doctrines of Stoicism. That system of ethics seemed to offer the intellectuals an escape from the extravagances and suppressions to which they were subjected under despotic rulers. With its doctrine that freedom springs from within and is not dependent upon the outward circumstances of life, it held out a peculiarly effective consolation to those who were suffering from the loss of political liberty. Harmony with nature and nature's law could be achieved even by men out of harmony with the conditions in which their lives were cast. No power could thwart ambition if the highest ambition was to be realized in personal character.

THE PHILOSOPHER'S SECLUSION [1]

SENECA

[*Epistles to Lucilius* VIII]

Lucius Annæus Seneca, often called Seneca the Younger to distinguish him from his father of the same name who was also a man of letters, was born at Corduba in Spain about 4 B.C. As tutor of the young Nero he gained an ascendancy over him which later assured Seneca the practical control of the government during the first part of Nero's administration. Later, accused of participation in a conspiracy against the emperor, he fell into disfavor and was finally forced to commit suicide in the year 65. His philosophical writings took the form of moral essays, some of them in the guise of letters, on Stoic themes. He wrote also a number of tragedies based directly upon the material used by the Greek tragedians, but altered so as to become

[1] From The Loeb Classical Library, by permission.

the vehicle of his own philosophical views. They exerted a powerful influence, both in respect of technique and of matter, on the English dramatic literature of the Elizabethan period.

Seneca, like Cicero, found in philosophy a refuge from public life. The experience of both of them was such as to beget an appreciation of the delights of such withdrawal. The thought, however, is a commonplace of philosophical literature.

To Lucilius:

"Do you bid me," you say, "shun the throng, and withdraw from men, and be content with my own conscience? Where are the counsels of your school, which order a man to die in the midst of active work?" As to the course which I seem to you to be urging on you now and then, my object in shutting myself up and locking the door is to be able to help a greater number. I never spend a day in idleness; I appropriate even a part of the night for study. I do not allow time for sleep but yield to it when I must, and when my eyes are wearied with waking and ready to fall shut, I keep them at their task. I have withdrawn not only from men, but from affairs, especially from my own affairs; I am working for later generations, writing down some ideas that may be of assistance to them. There are certain wholesome counsels, which may be compared to prescriptions of useful drugs; these I am putting into writing; for I have found them helpful in ministering to my own sores, which, if not wholly cured, have at any rate ceased to spread.

I point other men to the right path, which I have found late in life, when wearied with wandering. I cry out to them: "Avoid whatever pleases the throng: avoid the gifts of Chance! Halt before every good which Chance brings to you, in a spirit of doubt and fear; for it is the dumb animals and fish that are deceived by tempting hopes. Do you call these things the 'gifts' of Fortune? They are snares. And any man among you who wishes to live a life of safety will avoid, to the utmost of his power, these limed twigs of her favour, by which we mortals, most wretched in this respect also, are deceived; for we think that we hold them in our grasp, but they hold us in theirs. Such a career leads us into precipitous ways, and life on such heights ends in a fall. Moreover, we cannot even stand up against prosperity when she begins to drive us to leeward; nor can we go down, either, 'with the ship at least on her course,' or once for all; Fortune does not capsize us,—she plunges our bows under and dashes us on the rocks.

"Hold fast, then, to this sound and wholesome rule of life; that you indulge the body only as far as is needful for good health. The body should be treated more rigorously, that it may not be disobedient to the mind. Eat merely to relieve your hunger; drink merely to quench your thirst; dress merely to keep out the cold; house yourself merely as a protection against personal discomfort. It matters little whether the house be built of turf, or of variously coloured imported marble; understand that a man is sheltered just as well by a thatch as by a roof of gold. Despise everything that useless toil creates as an ornament and an object of beauty. And reflect that nothing except the soul is worthy of wonder; for to the soul, if it be great, naught is great."

When I commune in such terms with myself and with future generations, do you not think that I am doing more good than when I appear as counsel in court, or stamp my seal upon a will, or lend my assistance in the senate, by word or action, to a candidate? Believe me, those who seem too busied with nothing are busied with the greater tasks; they are dealing at the same time with things mortal and things immortal.

But I must stop, and pay my customary contribution, to balance this letter. The payment shall not be made from my own property; for I am still conning Epicurus. I read to-day, in his works, the following sentence: "If you would enjoy real freedom, you must be the slave of Philosophy." The man who submits and surrenders himself to her is not kept waiting; he is emancipated on the spot. For the very service of Philosophy is freedom.

It is likely that you will ask me why I quote so many of Epicurus's noble words instead of words taken from our own school. But is there any reason why you should regard them as sayings of Epicurus and not common property? How many poets give forth ideas that have been uttered, or may be uttered, by philosophers! I need not touch upon the tragedians and our writers of national drama; for these last are also somewhat serious, and stand half-way between comedy and tragedy. What a quantity of sagacious verses lie buried in the mime! How many of Publilius's lines are worthy of being spoken by buskin-clad actors, as well as by wearers of the slipper! I shall quote one verse of his, which concerns philosophy, and particularly that phase of it which we were discussing a moment ago, wherein he says that the gifts of Chance are not to be regarded as part of our possessions:

"Still alien is whatever you have gained
By coveting."

I recall that you yourself expressed this idea much more happily and concisely:

"What Chance has made yours is not really yours."

And a third, spoken by you still more happily, shall not be omitted:

"The good that could be given, can be removed."

I shall not charge this up to the expense account, because I have given it to you from your own stock. Farewell.
—R. M. GUMMERE.

THE GOD WITHIN US [1]

SENECA

[Epistles to Lucilius XLI]

The strength of the appeal that Stoicism made to the Romans consisted in the emphasis it placed upon character as the determining factor in life.

To Lucilius:
You are doing an excellent thing, one which will be wholesome for you, if, as you write me, you are persisting in your effort to attain sound understanding; it is foolish to pray for this when you can acquire it from yourself. We do not need to uplift our hands towards heaven, or to beg the keeper of a temple to let us approach his idol's ear, as if in this way our prayers were more likely to be heard. God is near you, he is with you, he is within you. That is what I mean, Lucilius: a holy spirit indwells within us, one who marks our good and bad deeds, and is our guardian. As we treat this spirit, so are we treated by it. Indeed, no man can be good without the help of God. Can one rise superior to fortune unless God helps him to rise? He it is that gives noble and upright counsel. In each good man

"A god doth dwell, but what god know we not."

[1] From the Loeb Classical Library, by permission.

If ever you have come upon a grove that is full of ancient trees which have grown to an unusual height, shutting out a view of the sky by a veil of pleached and intertwining branches, then the loftiness of the forest, the seclusion of the spot, and your marvel at the thick unbroken shade in the midst of the open spaces, will prove to you the presence of deity. Or if a cave, made by the deep crumbling of the rocks, holds up a mountain on its arch, a place not built with hands but hollowed out into such spaciousness by natural causes, your soul will be deeply moved by a certain intimation of the existence of God. We worship the sources of mighty rivers; we erect altars at places where great streams burst suddenly from hidden sources; we adore springs of hot water as divine, and consecrate certain pools because of their dark waters or their immeasurable depth. If you see a man who is unterrified in the midst of dangers, untouched by desires, happy in adversity, peaceful amid the storm, who looks down upon men from a higher plane, and views the gods on a footing of equality, will not a feeling of reverence for him steal over you? Will you not say: "This quality is too great and too lofty to be regarded as resembling this petty body in which it dwells? A divine power has descended upon that man." When a soul rises superior to other souls, when it is under control, when it passes through every experience as if it were of small account, when it smiles at our fears and at our prayers, it is stirred by a force from heaven. A thing like this cannot stand upright unless it be propped by the divine. Therefore, a greater part of it abides in that place from whence it came down to earth. Just as the rays of the sun do indeed touch the earth but still abide at the source from which they are sent; even so the great and hallowed soul, which has come down in order that we may have a nearer knowledge of divinity, does indeed associate with us, but still cleaves to its origin; on that source it depends, thither it turns its gaze and strives to go, and it concerns itself with our doings only as a being superior to ourselves.

What, then, is such a soul? One which is resplendent with no external good, but only with its own. For what is more foolish than to praise in a man the qualities which come from without? And what is more insane than to marvel at characteristics which may at the next instant be passed on to someone else? A golden bit does not make a better horse. The lion with gilded mane, in process of being trained and forced by weariness to endure the decoration, is sent into the arena in quite a different way from the wild lion whose spirit is unbroken; the latter, indeed, bold in his attack, as nature wished him to be, impressive because of his wild appearance,—and it is his glory that none can look upon him without fear,—is favoured in preference to the other lion, that languid and guilded brute.

No man ought to glory except in that which is his own. We praise a vine if it makes the shoots teem with increase, if by its weight it bends to the ground the very poles which hold its fruit; would any man prefer to this vine one from which golden grapes and golden leaves hang down? In a vine the virtue peculiarly its own is fertility; in man also we should praise that which is his own. Suppose that he has a retinue of comely slaves and a beautiful house, that his farm is large and large his income; none of these things is in the man himself; they are all on the outside. Praise the quality in him which cannot be given or snatched away, that which is the peculiar property of the man. Do you ask what this is? It is soul, and reason brought to perfection in the soul. For man is a reasoning animal. Therefore, man's highest good is attained, if he has

fulfilled the good for which nature designed him at birth. And what is it which this reason demands of him? The easiest thing in the world,—to live in accordance with his own nature. But this is turned into a hard task by the general madness of mankind; we push one another into vice. And how can a man be recalled to salvation, when he has none to restrain him, and all mankind to urge him on? Farewell.

—R. M. GUMMERE.

ON PEACE OF MIND

SENECA

[*Dialogues* IX]

Peace of mind is to be attained by first discovering one's relation to one's fellowmen and to the state, and then by playing the man under whatever limitations that relation imposes. Withdrawal from life is a dream of the philosopher, but life is not a dream. Seneca was a philosopher, but he was also a practical man of affairs and a typical Roman.

SERENUS. When I examine myself, Seneca, some vices appear on the surface, and so that I can lay my hands upon them, while others are less distinct and harder to reach, and some are not always present, but recur at intervals: and these I should call the most troublesome, being like a roving enemy that assails one when he sees his opportunity, and who will neither let one stand on one's guard as in war, nor yet take one's rest without fear as in peace. The position in which I find myself more especially (for why should I not tell you the truth as I would to a physician), is that of neither being thoroughly set free from the vices which I fear and hate, nor yet quite in bondage to them: my state of mind, though not the worst possible, is a particularly discontented and sulky one: I am neither ill nor well. It is of no use for you to tell me that all virtues are weakly at the outset, and that they acquire strength and solidity by time, for I am well aware, that even those which do but help our outward show, such as grandeur, a reputation for eloquence, and everything that appeals to others, gain power by time. But those which afford us real strength and those which do but trick us out in a more attractive form, require long years before they gradually are adapted to us by time. But I fear that custom, which confirms most things, implants this vice more and more deeply in me. Long acquaintance with both good and bad people leads one to esteem them all alike. What this state of weakness really is, when the mind halts between two opinions without any strong inclination towards either good or evil, I shall be better able to show you piecemeal than all at once. I will tell you what befalls me, you must find out the name of the disease. I have to confess the greatest possible love of thrift; I do not care for a bed with gorgeous hangings, nor for clothes brought out of a chest, or pressed under weights and made glossy by frequent manglings, but for common and cheap ones, that require no care either to keep them or to put them on. For food I do not want what needs whole troops of servants to prepare it and admire it, nor what is ordered many days before and served up by many hands, but something handy and easily come at, with nothing far-fetched or costly about it, to be had in every part of the world, burdensome neither to one's fortune nor one's body, not likely to go out of the body by the same path by which it came in. I like a rough and unpolished homebred servant, I like my servant born in my house: I like my country-bred father's heavy silver plate stamped with no maker's name: I do not want a table that is beauteous with dappled spots, or known to all the town by the number of fashionable people to whom it has successively belonged, but one which stands merely for use, and which causes no guest's eye to dwell upon it with pleasure or to kindle at it with envy. While I am well satisfied with this, I am reminded of the clothes of a certain schoolboy, dressed with no ordinary care and splendour, of slaves bedecked with gold and a whole regiment of glittering attendants. I think of houses too, where one treads on precious stones, and where valuables lie about in every corner, where the very roof is brilliantly painted, and a whole nation attends and accompanies an inheritance on the road to ruin. What shall I say of waters, transparent to the very bottom, which flow round the guests, and banquets worthy of the theatre in which they take place? Coming as I do from a long course of dull thrift, I find myself surrounded by the most brilliant luxury, which echoes around me on every side: my sight becomes a little dazzled by it: I can lift up my heart against it more easily than my eyes. When I return from seeing it I am a sadder, though not a worse man, I cannot walk amid my own paltry possessions with so lofty a step as before, and silently there steals over me a feeling of vexation, and a doubt whether that way of life may not be better than mine. None of these things alter my principles, yet all of them disturb me. At one time I would obey the maxims of our school and plunge into public life, I would obtain office and become consul, not because the purple robe and lictor's axes attract me, but in order that I may be able to be of use to my friends, my relatives, to all my countrymen, and indeed to all mankind. Ready and determined, I follow the advice of Zeno, Cleanthes, and Chrysippus, all of whom bid one take part in public affairs, though none of them ever did so himself: And then, as soon as something disturbs my mind, which is not used to receiving shocks, as soon as something occurs which is either disgraceful, such as often occurs in all men's lives, or which does not proceed quite easily, or when subjects of very little importance require me to devote a great deal of time to them, I go back to my life of leisure, and, just as even tired cattle go faster when they are going home, I wish to retire and pass my life within the walls of my house. "No one," I say, "that will give me compensation worth such a loss shall ever rob me of a day. Let my mind be contained within itself and improve itself: let it take no part with other men's affairs, and do nothing which depends on the approval of others: let me enjoy a tranquillity undisturbed by either public or private troubles." But whenever my spirit is roused by reading some brave words, or some noble example spurs me into action, I want to rush into the law courts, to place my voice at one man's disposal, my services at another's, and try to help him even though I may not succeed, or to quell the pride of some lawyer who is puffed up by ill-deserved success: but I think, by Hercules, that in philosophical speculation it is better to view things as they are, and to speak of them on their own account, and as for words, to trust to things for them, and to let one's speech simply follow whither they lead. "Why do you want to construct a fabric that will endure for ages? Do you not wish to do this in order that posterity may talk of you: yet you were born to die, and a silent death is the least wretched. Write something therefore in a simple style, merely to pass the time, for your own use, and not for publication. Less labour is needed when one does not look beyond the present." Then again, when the mind is elevated by the greatness of its thoughts, it becomes ostentatious in its use of words, the loftier its aspirations, the more loftily it desires to express them, and its speech rises to the dignity of its subject. At such times I forget my mild and moderate determination and soar higher than is my wont, using a language that is not my own. Not to multiply examples, I am in all things attended by this weakness of a well-meaning mind, to whose level I fear that I shall be gradually brought down, or, what is even more worrying, that I may always hang as though about to fall, and that there may be more the matter with me than I myself perceive: for we take a friendly view of our own private affairs, and partiality always obscures our judgment. I fancy that many men would have arrived at wisdom had they not believed themselves to have arrived there already, had they not purposely deceived themselves as to some parts of their character, and passed by others with their eyes shut: for you have no grounds for supposing that other people's flattery is more ruinous to us than our own. Who dares to tell himself the truth? Who is there, by however large a troop of caressing courtiers he may be surrounded, who in spite of them is not his own greatest flatterer? I beg you therefore, if you have any remedy by which you could stop this vacillation of mine, to deem me worthy to owe my peace of mind to you. I am well aware that these oscillations of mind are not perilous and that they threaten me with no serious disorder: to express what I complain of by an exact simile, I am not suffering from a storm, but from sea-sickness. Take from me, then, this evil, whatever it may be, and help one who is in distress within sight of land.

SENECA. I have long been silently asking myself, my friend Serenus, to what I should liken such a condition of mind, and I find that nothing more closely resembles it than the conduct of those who, after having recovered from a long and serious illness, occasionally experience slight touches and twinges, and, although they have passed through the final stages of the disease, yet have suspicions that it has not left them, and though in perfect health yet hold out their pulse to be felt by the physician, and whenever they feel warm suspect that the fever is returning. Such men, Serenus, are not unhealthy, but they are not accustomed to being healthy; just as even a quiet sea or lake nevertheless displays a certain amount of ripple when its waters are subsiding after a storm. What you need, therefore, is not any of those harsher remedies to which allusion has been made, not that you should in some cases check yourself, in others be angry with yourself, in others sternly reproach yourself, but that you should adopt that which comes last in the list, have confidence in yourself, and believe that you are proceeding on the right path, without being led aside by the numerous divergent tracks of wanderers which cross it in every direction, some of them circling about the right path itself. What you desire, to be undisturbed, is a great thing, nay, the greatest thing of all, and one which raises a man almost to the level of a god. The Greeks call this calm steadiness of mind *euthymia*, and Democritus's treatise upon it is excellently written: I call it peace of mind: for there is no necessity for translating so exactly as to copy the words of the Greek idiom: the essential point is to mark the matter under discussion by a name which ought to have the same meaning as its Greek name, though perhaps not the same form. What we are seeking, then, is how the mind may always pursue a steady, unruffled course, may be pleased with itself, and look with pleasure upon its surroundings, and experience no interruption of this joy, but abide in a peaceful condition without being ever either elated or depressed: this will be "peace of mind." Let us now consider in a general way how it may be attained: then you may apply as much as you choose of the universal remedy

to your own case. Meanwhile we must drag to light the entire disease, and then each one will recognize his own part of it: at the same time you will understand how much less you suffer by your self-depreciation than those who are bound by some showy declaration which they have made, and are oppressed by some grand title of honour, so that shame rather than their own free will forces them to keep up the pretence. The same thing applies both to those who suffer from fickleness and continual changes of purpose, who always are fondest of what they have given up, and those who merely yawn and dawdle: add to these those who, like bad sleepers, turn from side to side, and settle themselves first in one manner and then in another, until at last they find rest through sheer weariness: in forming the habits of their lives they often end by adopting some to which they are not kept by any dislike of change, but in the practice of which old age, which is slow to alter, has caught them living: add also those who are by no means fickle, yet who must thank their dulness, not their consistency for being so, and who go on living not in the way they wish, but in the way they have begun to live. There are other special forms of this disease without number, but it has but one effect, that of making people dissatisfied with themselves. This arises from a distemperature of mind and from desires which one is afraid to express or unable to fulfil, when men either dare not attempt as much as they wish to do, or fail in their efforts and depend entirely upon hope: such people are always fickle and changeable, which is a necessary consequence of living in a state of suspense: they take any way to arrive at their ends, and teach and force themselves to use both dishonourable and difficult means to do so, so that when their toil has been in vain they are made wretched by the disgrace of failure, and do not regret having longed for what was wrong, but having longed for in vain. They then begin to feel sorry for what they have done, and afraid to begin again, and their mind falls by degrees into a state of endless vacillation, because they can neither command nor obey their passions, of hesitation, because their life cannot properly develop itself, and of decay, as the mind becomes stupefied by disappointments. All these symptoms become aggravated when their dislike of a laborious misery has driven them to idleness and to secret studies, which are unendurable to a mind eager to take part in public affairs, desirous of action and naturally restless, because, of course, it finds too few resources within itself: when therefore it loses the amusement which business itself affords to busy men, it cannot endure home, loneliness, or the walls of a room, and regards itself with dislike when left to itself. Hence arises that weariness and dissatisfaction with oneself, that tossing to and fro of a mind which can nowhere find rest, that unhappy and unwilling endurance of enforced leisure. In all cases where one feels ashamed to confess the real cause of one's suffering, and where modesty leads one to drive one's sufferings inward, the desires pent up in a little space without any vent choke one another. Hence comes melancholy and drooping of spirit, and a thousand waverings of the unsteadfast mind, which is held in suspense by unfulfilled hopes, and saddened by disappointed ones: hence comes the state of mind of those who loathe their idleness, complain that they have nothing to do, and view the progress of others with the bitterest jealousy: for an unhappy sloth favours the growth of envy, and men who cannot succeed themselves wish every one else to be ruined. This dislike of other men's progress and despair of one's own produces a mind angered against fortune, addicted to complaining of the age in which it lives,

to retiring into corners and brooding over its misery until it becomes sick and weary of itself: for the human mind is naturally nimble and apt at movement: it delights in every opportunity of excitement and forgetfulness of itself, and the worse a man's disposition the more he delights in this, because he likes to wear himself out with busy action, just as some sores long for the hands that injure them and delight in being touched, and the foul itch enjoys anything that scratches it. Similarly I assure you that these minds, over which desires have spread like evil ulcers, take pleasure in toils and troubles, for there are some things which please our body while at the same time they give it a certain amount of pain, such as turning oneself over and changing one's side before it is wearied, or cooling oneself in one position after another. It is like Homer's Achilles, lying first upon its face, then upon its back, placing itself in various attitudes, and, as sick people are wont, enduring none of them for long, and using changes as though they were remedies. Hence men undertake aimless wanderings, travel along distant shores, and at one time at sea, at another by land, try to soothe that fickleness of disposition which always is dissatisfied with the present. "Now let us make for Campania: now I am sick of rich cultivation: let us see wild regions, let us thread the passes of Bruttii and Lucania: yet amid this wilderness one wants something of beauty to relieve our pampered eyes after so long dwelling on savage wastes: let us seek Tarentum with its famous harbour, its mild winter climate, and its district, rich enough to support even the great hordes of ancient times. Let us now return to town: our ears have too long missed its shouts and noise: it would be pleasant also to enjoy the sight of human bloodshed." Thus one journey succeeds another, and one sight is changed for another. As Lucretius says:—

"Thus every mortal from himself doth flee;"

but what does he gain by so doing if he does not escape from himself? he follows himself and weighs himself down by his own most burdensome companionship. We must understand, therefore, that what we suffer from is not the fault of the places but of ourselves: we are weak when there is anything to be endured, and cannot support either labour or pleasure, either one's own business or any one else's for long. This has driven some men to death, because by frequently altering their purpose they were always brought back to the same point, and had left themselves no room for anything new. They had become sick of life and of the world itself, and as all indulgences palled upon them they began to ask themselves the question, "How long are we to go on doing the same thing?"

You ask me what I think we had better make use of to help us to support this ennui. "The best thing," as Athenodorus says, "is to occupy oneself with business, with the management of affairs of state and the duties of a citizen: for as some pass the day in exercising themselves in the sun and in taking care of their bodily health, and athletes find it most useful to spend the greater part of their time in feeding up the muscles and strength to whose cultivation they have devoted their lives; so too for you who are training your mind to take part in the struggles of political life, it is far more honourable to be thus at work than to be idle. He whose object is to be of service to his countrymen and to all mortals, exercises himself and does good at the same time when he is engrossed in business and is working to the best of his ability both in the interests of the public and of private men. But," continues he, "because innocence is hardly safe among such furious ambitions and so many men who turn one aside from the right path, and

it is always sure to meet with more hindrance than help, we ought to withdraw ourselves from the forum and from public life, and a great mind even in a private station can find room wherein to expand freely. Confinement in dens restrains the springs of lions and wild creatures, but this does not apply to human beings, who often effect the most important works in retirement. Let a man, however, withdraw himself only in such a fashion that wherever he spends his leisure his wish may still be to benefit individual men and mankind alike, both with his intellect, his voice, and his advice. The man that does good service to the state is not only he who brings forward candidates for public office, defends accused persons, and gives his vote on questions of peace and war, but he who encourages young men in well-doing, who supplies the present dearth of good teachers by instilling into their minds the principles of virtue, who seizes and holds back those who are rushing wildly in pursuit of riches and luxury, and, if he does nothing else, at least checks their course —such a man does service to the public though in a private station. Which does the most good, he who decides between foreigners and citizens (as prætor peregrinus), or, as prætor urbanus, pronounces sentence to the suitors in his court at his assistant's dictation, or he who shows them what is meant by justice, filial feeling, endurance, courage, contempt of death and knowledge of the gods, and how much a man is helped by a good conscience? If then you transfer to philosophy the time which you take away from the public service, you will not be a deserter or have refused to perform your proper task. A soldier is not merely one who stands in the ranks and defends the right or the left wing of the army, but he also who guards the gates— a service which, though less dangerous, is no sinecure—who keeps watch, and takes charge of the arsenal: though all these are bloodless duties, yet they count as military service. As soon as you have devoted yourself to philosophy, you will have overcome all disgust at life: you will not wish for darkness because you are weary of the light, nor will you be a trouble to yourself and useless to others: you will acquire many friends, and all the best men will be attracted towards you: for virtue, in however obscure a position, cannot be hidden, but gives signs of its presence: any one who is worthy will trace it out by its footsteps: but if we give up all society, turn our backs upon the whole human race, and live communing with ourselves alone, this solitude without any interesting occupation will lead to a want of something to do: we shall begin to build up and to pull down, to dam out the sea, to cause waters to flow through natural obstacles, and generally to make a bad disposal of the time which Nature has given us to spend: some of us use it grudgingly, others wastefully; some of us spend it so that we can show a profit and loss account, others so that they have no assets remaining: than which nothing can be more shameful. Often a man who is very old in years has nothing beyond his age by which he can prove that he has lived a long time."

To me, my dearest Serenus, Athenodorus seems to have yielded too completely to the times, to have fled too soon: I will not deny that sometimes one must retire, but one ought to retire slowly, at a foot's pace, without losing one's ensigns or one's honour as a soldier: those who make terms with arms in their hands are more respected by their enemies and more safe in their hands. This is what I think ought to be done by virtue and by one who practises virtue: if Fortune get the upper hand and deprive him of the power of action, let him not straightway turn his back to the enemy, throw away his arms, and run away seeking for a hiding-place, as if there were any place whither Fortune could not pursue him, but let him be more sparing in his acceptance of public office, and after due deliberation discover some means by which he can be of use to the state. He is not able to serve in the army: then let him become a candidate for civic honours: must he live in a private station? then let him be an advocate: is he condemned to keep silence? then let him help his countrymen with silent counsel. Is it dangerous for him even to enter the forum? then let him prove himself a good comrade, a faithful friend, a sober guest in people's houses, at public shows, and at wine-parties. Suppose that he has lost the status of a citizen; then let him exercise that of a man: our reason for magnanimously refusing to confine ourselves within the walls of one city, for having gone forth to enjoy intercourse with all lands and for professing ourselves to be citizens of the world is that we may thus obtain a wider theatre on which to display our virtue. Is the bench of judges closed to you, are you forbidden to address the people from the hustings, or to be a candidate at elections? then turn your eyes away from Rome, and see what a wide extent of territory, what a number of nations present themselves before you. Thus, it is never possible for so many outlets to be closed against your ambition that more will not remain open to it: but see whether the whole prohibition does not arise from your own fault. You do not choose to direct the affairs of the state except as consul or prytanis or meddix or sufes: what should we say if you refused to serve in the army save as general or military tribune? Even though others may form the first line, and your lot may have placed you among the veterans of the third, do your duty there with your voice, encouragement, example, and spirit: even though a man's hands be cut off, he may find means to help his side in a battle, if he stands his ground and cheers on his comrades. Do something of that sort yourself: if Fortune removes you from the front rank, stand your ground nevertheless and cheer on your comrades, and if somebody stops your mouth, stand nevertheless and help your side in silence. The services of a good citizen are never thrown away: he does good by being heard and seen, by his expression, his gestures, his silent determination, and his very walk. As some remedies benefit us by their smell as well as by their taste and touch, so virtue even when concealed and at a distance sheds usefulness around. Whether she moves at her ease and enjoys her just rights, or can only appear abroad on sufferance and is forced to shorten sail to the tempest, whether it be unemployed, silent, and pent up in a narrow lodging, or openly displayed, in whatever guise she may appear, she always does good. What? do you think that the example of one who can rest nobly has no value? It is by far the best plan, therefore, to mingle leisure with business, whenever impediments or the state of public affairs forbid one's leading an active life: for one is never so cut off from all pursuits as to find no room left for honourable action.

Could you anywhere find a more miserable city than that of Athens when it was being torn to pieces by the thirty tyrants? they slew thirteen hundred citizens, all the best men, and did not leave off because they had done so, but their cruelty became stimulated by exercise. In the city which possessed that most reverend tribunal, the Court of the Areopagus, which possessed a Senate, and a popular assembly which was like a Senate, there met daily a wretched crew of butchers, and the unhappy Senate House was crowded with tyrants. A state in which there were so many tyrants that they would have been enough to form a bodyguard for one, might surely have rested from the struggle; it seemed impossible for men's minds even to conceive hopes of recovering their liberty, nor could they see any hope for a remedy for such a mass of evil: for whence could the unhappy state obtain all the Harmodiuses it would need to slay so many tyrants? Yet Socrates was in the midst of the city, and consoled its mourning Fathers, encouraged those who despaired of the republic, by his reproaches brought rich men, who feared that their wealth would be their ruin, to a tardy repentance of their avarice, and moved about as a great example to those who wished to imitate him, because he walked a free man in the midst of thirty masters. However, Athens herself put him to death in prison, and Freedom herself could not endure the freedom of one who had treated a whole band of tyrants with scorn: you may know, therefore, that even in an oppressed state a wise man can find an opportunity for bringing himself to the front, and that in a prosperous and flourishing one wanton insolence, jealousy, and a thousand other cowardly vices bear sway. We ought, therefore, to expand or contract ourselves according as the state presents itself to us, or as Fortune offers us opportunities: but in any case we ought to move and not to become frozen still by fear: nay, he is the best man who, though peril menaces him on every side and arms and chains beset his path, nevertheless neither impairs nor conceals his virtue: for to keep oneself safe does not mean to bury oneself. I think that Curius Dentatus spoke truly when he said that he would rather be dead than alive: the worst evil of all is to leave the ranks of the living before one dies: yet it is your duty, if you happen to live in an age when it is not easy to serve the state, to devote more time to leisure and to literature. Thus, just as though you were making a perilous voyage, you may from time to time put into harbour, and set yourself free from public business without waiting for it to do so.

We ought, however, first to examine our own selves, next the business which we propose to transact, next those for whose sake or in whose company we transact it.

It is above all things necessary to form a true estimate of oneself, because as a rule we think that we can do more than we are able: one man is led too far through confidence in his eloquence, another demands more from his estate than it can produce, another burdens a weakly body with some toilsome duty. Some men are too shamefaced for the conduct of public affairs, which require an unblushing front: some men's obstinate pride renders them unfit for courts: some cannot control their anger, and break into unguarded language on the slightest provocation: some cannot rein in their wit or resist making risky jokes: for all these men leisure is better than employment: a bold, haughty and impatient nature ought to avoid anything that may lead it to use a freedom of speech which will bring it to ruin. Next we must form an estimate of the matter which we mean to deal with, and compare our strength with the deed we are about to attempt: for the bearer ought always to be more powerful than his load: indeed, loads which are too heavy for their bearer must of necessity crush him: some affairs also are not so important in themselves as they are prolific and lead to much more business, which employments, as they involve us in new and various forms of work, ought to be refused. Neither should you engage in anything from which you are not free to retreat: apply yourself to something which you can finish, or at any rate can hope to finish: you had better not meddle with those operations which grow in importance, while they are being transacted, and which will not stop where you intended them to stop.

In all cases one should be careful in one's choice of men, and see whether they be worthy of our bestowing a part of our life upon them, or whether we shall waste our own time and theirs also: for some even consider us to be in their debt because of our services to them. Athenodorus said that "he would not so much as dine with a man who would not be grateful to him for doing so:" meaning, I imagine, that much less would he go to dinner with those who recompense the services of their friends by their table, and regard courses of dishes as donatives, as if they over-ate themselves to do honour to others. Take away from these men their witnesses and spectators: they will take no pleasure in solitary gluttony. You must decide whether your disposition is better suited for vigorous action or for tranquil speculation and contemplation, and you must adopt whichever the bent of your genius inclines you for. Isocrates laid hands upon Ephorus and led him away from the forum, thinking that he would be more usefully employed in compiling chronicles; for no good is done by forcing one's mind to engage in uncongenial work: it is vain to struggle against Nature. Yet nothing delights the mind so much as faithful and pleasant friendship: what a blessing it is when there is one whose breast is ready to receive all your secrets with safety, whose knowledge of your actions you fear less than your own conscience, whose conversation removes your own anxieties, whose advice assists your plans, whose cheerfulness dispels your gloom, whose very sight delights you! We should choose for our friends men who are, as far as possible, free from strong desires: for vices are contagious, and pass from a man to his neighbour, and injure those who touch them. As, therefore, in times of pestilence we have to be careful not to sit near people who are infected and in whom the disease is raging, because by so doing, we shall run into danger and catch the plague from their very breath; so, too, in choosing our friends' dispositions, we must take care to select those who are as far as may be unspotted by the world; for the way to breed disease is to mix what is sound with what is rotten. Yet I do not advise you to follow after or draw to yourself no one except a wise man: for where will you find him whom for so many centuries we have sought in vain? in the place of the best possible man take him who is least bad. You would hardly find any time that would have enabled you to make a happier choice than if you could have sought for a good man from among the Platos and Xenophons and the rest of the produce of the brood of Socrates, or if you had been permitted to choose one from the age of Cato: an age which bore many men worthy to be born in Cato's time (just as it also bore many men worse than were ever known before, planners of the blackest crimes: for it needed both classes in order to make Cato understood: it wanted both good men, that he might win their approbation, and bad men, against whom he could prove his strength): but at the present day, when there is such a dearth of good men, you must be less squeamish in your choice. Above all, however, avoid dismal men who grumble at whatever happens, and find something to complain of in everything. Though he may continue loyal and friendly towards you, still one's peace of mind is destroyed by a comrade whose mind is soured and who meets every incident with a groan.

Let us now pass on to the consideration of property, that most fertile source of human sorrows: for if you compare all the other ills from which we suffer—deaths, sicknesses, fears, regrets, endurance of pains and labours—with those miseries which our money inflicts upon us, the latter will far outweigh all the others. Reflect, then, how much less a grief it is never to have had any money than to have lost it: we shall thus understand that the less poverty has to lose, the less torment it has with which to afflict us: for you are mistaken if you suppose that the rich bear their losses with greater spirit than the poor: a wound causes the same amount of pain to the greatest and the smallest body. It was a neat saying of Bion's, "that it hurts bald men as much as hairy men to have their hairs pulled out:" you may be assured that the same thing is true of rich and poor people, that their suffering is equal: for their money clings to both classes, and cannot be torn away without their feeling it: yet it is more endurable, as I have said, and easier not to gain property than to lose it, and therefore you will find that those upon whom Fortune has never smiled are more cheerful than those whom she has deserted. Diogenes, a man of infinite spirit, perceived this, and made it impossible that anything should be taken from him. Call this security from loss, poverty, want, necessity, or any contemptuous name you please: I shall consider such a man to be happy, unless you find me another who can lose nothing. If I am not mistaken, it is a royal attribute among so many misers, sharpers, and robbers, to be the one man who cannot be injured. If any one doubts the happiness of Diogenes, he would doubt whether the position of the immortal gods was one of sufficient happiness, because they have no farms or gardens, no valuable estates let to strange tenants, and no large loans in the money market. Are you not ashamed of yourself, you who gaze upon riches with astonished admiration? Look upon the universe: you will see the gods quite bare of property, and possessing nothing though they give everything. Do you think that this man who has stripped himself of all fortuitous accessories is a pauper, or one like to the immortal gods? Do you call Demetrius, Pompeius's freedman, a happier man, he who was not ashamed to be richer than Pompeius, who was daily furnished with a list of the number of his slaves, as a general is with that of his army, though he had long deserved that all his riches should consist of a pair of underlings, and a roomier cell than the other slaves? But Diogenes's only slave ran away from him, and when he was pointed out to Diogenes, he did not think him worth fetching back. "It is a shame," he said, "that Manes should be able to live without Diogenes, and that Diogenes should not be able to live without Manes." He seems to me to have said, "Fortune, mind your own business: Diogenes has nothing left that belongs to you. Did my slave run away? nay, he went away from me as a free man." A household of slaves requires food and clothing: the bellies of so many hungry creatures have to be filled: we must buy raiment for them, we must watch their most thievish hands, and we must make use of the services of people who weep and execrate us. How far happier is he who is indebted to no man for anything except for what he can deprive himself of with the greatest ease! Since we, however, have not such strength of mind as this, we ought at any rate to diminish the extent of our property, in order to be less exposed to the assaults of fortune: those men whose bodies can be within the shelter of their armour, are more fitted for war than those whose huge size everywhere extends beyond it, and exposes them to wounds: the best amount of property to have is that which is enough to keep us from poverty, and which is yet not far removed from it.

We shall be pleased with this measure of wealth if we have previously taken pleasure in thrift, without which no riches are sufficient, and with which none are insufficient, especially as the remedy is always at hand, and poverty itself by calling in the aid of thrift can convert itself into riches. Let us accustom ourselves to set aside mere outward show, and to measure things by their uses, not by their ornamental trappings: let our hunger be tamed by food, our thirst quenched by drinking, our lust confined within needful bounds; let us learn to use our limbs, and to arrange our dress and way of life according to what was approved of by our ancestors, not in imitation of new-fangled models: let us learn to increase our continence, to repress luxury, to set bounds to our pride, to assuage our anger, to look upon poverty without prejudice, to practise thrift, albeit many are ashamed to do so, to apply cheap remedies to the wants of nature, to keep all undisciplined hopes and aspirations as it were under lock and key, and to make it our business to get our riches from ourselves and not from Fortune. We never can so thoroughly defeat the vast diversity and malignity of misfortune with which we are threatened as not to feel the weight of many gusts if we offer a large spread of canvas to the wind: we must draw our affairs into a small compass, to make the darts of Fortune of no avail. For this reason, sometimes slight mishaps have turned into remedies, and more serious disorders have been healed by slighter ones. When the mind pays no attention to good advice, and cannot be brought to its senses by milder measures, why should we not think that its interests are being served by poverty, disgrace, or financial ruin being applied to it? one evil is balanced by another. Let us then teach ourselves to be able to dine without all Rome to look on, to be the slaves of fewer slaves, to get clothes which fulfil their original purpose, and to live in a smaller house. The inner curve is the one to take, not only in running races and in the contests of the circus, but also in the race of life; even literary pursuits, the most becoming thing for a gentleman to spend money upon, are only justifiable as long as they are kept within bounds. What is the use of possessing numberless books and libraries, whose titles their owner can hardly read through in a lifetime? A student is overwhelmed by such a mass, not instructed, and it is much better to devote yourself to a few writers than to skim through many. Forty thousand books were burned at Alexandria: some would have praised this library as a most noble memorial of royal wealth, like Titus Livius, who says that it was "a splendid result of the taste and attentive care of the kings." It had nothing to do with taste or care, but was a piece of learned luxury, nay, not even learned, since they amassed it, not for the sake of learning, but to make a show, like many men who know less about letters than a slave is expected to know, and who uses his books not to help him in his studies but to ornament his dining-room. Let a man, then, obtain as many books as he wants, but none for show. "It is more respectable," say you, "to spend one's money on such books than on vases of Corinthian brass and paintings." Not so: everything that is carried to excess is wrong. What excuses can you find for a man who is eager to buy bookcases of ivory and citrus wood, to collect the works of unknown or discredited authors, and who sits yawning amid so many thousands of books, whose backs and titles please him more than any other part of them? Thus in the houses of the laziest of men you will see the works of all the orators and historians stacked upon book-shelves reaching right up to the ceiling. At the present day a library has become as necessary an appendage to a house as a hot and cold bath. I would excuse them straightway if they really were carried away by an excessive zeal for literature; but as it is, these costly works of sacred genius, with all the illustrations that adorn them, are merely bought for display and to serve as wall-furniture.

Suppose, however, that your life has become full of trouble, and that without knowing what you were doing you have fallen into some snare which either public or private Fortune has set for you, and that you can neither untie it nor break it: then remember that fettered men suffer much at first from the burdens and clogs upon their legs: afterwards, when they have made up their minds not to fret themselves about them, but to endure them, necessity teaches them to bear them bravely, and habit to bear them easily. In every station of life you will find amusements, relaxations, and enjoyments; that is, provided you be willing to make light of evils rather than to hate them. Knowing to what sorrows we were born, there is nothing for which Nature more deserves our thanks than for having invented habit as an alleviation of misfortune, which soon accustoms us to the severest evils. No one could hold out against misfortune if it permanently exercised the same force as at its first onset. We are all chained to Fortune: some men's chain is loose and made of gold, that of others is tight and of meaner metal: but what difference does this make? we are all included in the same captivity, and even those who have bound us are bound themselves, unless you think that a chain on the left side is lighter to bear: one man may be bound by public office, another by wealth: some have to bear the weight of illustrious, some of humble birth: some are subject to the commands of others, some only to their own: some are kept in one place by being banished thither, others by being elected to the priesthood. All life is slavery: let each man therefore reconcile himself to his lot, complain of it as little as possible, and lay hold of whatever good lies within his reach. No condition can be so wretched that an impartial mind can find no compensation in it. Small sites, if ingeniously divided, may be made use of for many different purposes, and arrangement will render ever so narrow a room habitable. Call good sense to your aid against difficulties: it is possible to soften what is harsh, to widen what is too narrow, and to make heavy burdens press less severely upon one who bears them skilfully. Moreover, we ought not to allow our desires to wander far afield, but we must make them confine themselves to our immediate neighbourhood, since they will not endure to be altogether locked up. We must leave alone things which either cannot come to pass or can only be effected with difficulty, and follow after such things as are near at hand and within reach of our hopes, always remembering that all things are equally unimportant, and that though they have a different outward appearance, they are all alike empty within. Neither let us envy those who are in high places: the heights which look lofty to us are steep and rugged. Again, those whom unkind fate has placed in critical situations will be safer if they show as little pride in their proud position as may be, and do all they are able to bring down their fortunes to the level of other men's. There are many who must needs cling to their high pinnacle of power, because they cannot descend from it save by falling headlong: yet they assure us that their greatest burden is being obliged to be burdensome to others, and that they are nailed to their lofty post rather than raised to it: let them then, by dispensing justice, clemency, and kindness with an open and liberal hand, provide themselves with assistance to break their fall, and looking forward to this maintain their position more hopefully. Yet nothing sets us free from these alternations of hope and fear so well as always fixing some limit to our successes, and not allowing Fortune to choose when to stop our career, but to halt of our own accord long before we apparently need do so. By acting thus certain desires will rouse up our spirits, and yet being confined within bounds, will not lead us to embark on vast and vague enterprises.

These remarks of mine apply only to imperfect, commonplace, and unsound natures, not to the wise man, who needs not to walk with timid and cautious gait: for he has such confidence in himself that he does not hesitate to go directly in the teeth of Fortune, and never will give way to her. Nor indeed has he any reason for fearing her, for he counts not only chattels, property, and high office, but even his body, his eyes, his hands, and everything whose use makes life dearer to us, nay, even his very self, to be things whose possession is uncertain; he lives as though he had borrowed them, and is ready to return them cheerfully whenever they are claimed. Yet he does not hold himself cheap, because he knows that he is not his own, but performs all his duties as carefully and prudently as a pious and scrupulous man would take care of property left in his charge as trustee. When he is bidden to give them up, he will not complain of Fortune, but will say, "I thank you for what I have had possession of: I have managed your property so as largely to increase it, but since you order me, I give it back to you and return it willingly and thankfully. If you still wish me to own anything of yours, I will keep it for you: if you have other views, I restore into your hands and make restitution of all my wrought and coined silver, my house and my household. Should Nature recall what she previously entrusted us with, let us say to her also: 'Take back my spirit, which is better than when you gave it me: I do not shuffle or hang back. Of my own free will I am ready to return what you gave me before I could think: take me away.'" What hardship can there be in returning to the place from whence one came? a man cannot live well if he knows not how to die well. We must, therefore, take away from this commodity its original value, and count the breath of life as a cheap matter. "We dislike gladiators," says Cicero, "if they are eager to save their lives by any means whatever: but we look favourably upon them if they are openly reckless of them." You may be sure that the same thing occurs with us: we often die because we are afraid of death. Fortune, which regards our lives as a show in the arena for her own enjoyment, says, "Why should I spare you, base and cowardly creature that you are? you will be pierced and hacked with all the more wounds because you know not how to offer your throat to the knife: whereas you, who receive the stroke without drawing away your neck or putting up your hands to stop it, shall both live longer and die more quickly." He who fears death will never act as becomes a living man: but he who knows that this fate was laid upon him as soon as he was conceived will live according to it, and by this strength of mind will gain this further advantage, that nothing can befall him unexpectedly: for by looking forward to everything which can happen as though it would happen to him, he takes the sting out of all evils, which can make no difference to those who expect it and are prepared to meet it: evil only comes hard upon those who have lived without giving it a thought and whose attention has been exclusively directed to happiness. Disease, captivity, disaster, conflagration, are none of them unexpected: I always knew with what disorderly company Nature had associated me. The dead have often been wailed for in my neighbourhood: the torch and taper have often been borne past my door before the bier of one who has died before his time: the crash of falling buildings has often resounded by my side: night has snatched away many of those with whom I have become intimate in the forum, the Senate-house, and in society, and has sundered the hands which were joined in friendship: ought I to be surprised if the dangers which have always been circling round me at last assail me? How large a part of mankind never thinks of storms when about to set sail? I shall never be ashamed to quote a good saying because it comes from a bad author. Publilius, who was a more powerful writer than any of our other playwrights, whether comic or tragic, whenever he chose to rise above farcical absurdities and speeches addressed to the gallery, among many other verses too noble even for tragedy, let alone for comedy, has this one:—

"What one hath suffered may befall us all."

If a man takes this into his inmost heart and looks upon all the misfortunes of other men, of which there is always a great plenty, in this spirit, remembering that there is nothing to prevent their coming upon him also, he will arm himself against them long before they attack him. It is too late to school the mind to endurance of peril after peril has come. "I did not think this would happen," and "Would you ever have believed that this would have happened?" say you. But why should it not? Where are the riches after which want, hunger, and beggary do not follow? what office is there whose purple robe, augur's staff, and patrician reins have not as their accompaniment rags and banishment, the brand of infamy, a thousand disgraces, and utter reprobation? what kingdom is there for which ruin, trampling under foot, a tyrant and a butcher are not ready at hand? nor are these matters divided by long periods of time, but there is but the space of an hour between sitting on the throne ourselves and clasping the knees of some one else as suppliants. Know then that every station of life is transitory, and that what has ever happened to anybody may happen to you also. You are wealthy: are you wealthier than Pompeius? Yet when Gaius, his old relative and new host, opened Cæsar's house to him in order that he might close his own, he lacked both bread and water: though he owned so many rivers which both rose and discharged themselves within his dominions, yet he had to beg for drops of water: he perished of hunger and thirst in the palace of his relative, while his heir was contracting for a public funeral for one who was in want of food. You have filled public offices: were they either as important, as unlooked for, or as all-embracing as those of Sejanus? Yet on the day on which the Senate disgraced him, the people tore him to pieces: the executioner could find no part left large enough to drag to the Tiber, of one upon whom gods and men had showered all that could be given to man. You are a king: I will not bid you go to Crœsus for an example, he who while yet alive saw his funeral pile both lighted and extinguished, being made to outlive not only his kingdom but even his own death, nor to Jugurtha, whom the people of Rome beheld as a captive within the year in which they had feared him. We have seen Ptolemæus King of Africa, and Mithridates King of Armenia, under the charge of Gaius's guards: the former was sent into exile, the latter chose it in order to make his exile more honourable. Among such continual topsy-turvy changes, unless you expect that whatever can happen will happen to you, you give adversity power against you, a power which can be destroyed by any one who looks at it beforehand.

The next point to these will be to take care that we do not labour for what is vain, or labour in vain: that is to say, neither to desire what we are not able to obtain, nor yet, having obtained our desire too late and after much toil to discover the folly of our wishes: in other words, that our labour may not be without result, and that the result may not be unworthy of our labour: for as a rule

sadness arises from one of these two things, either from want of success or from being ashamed of having succeeded. We must limit the running to and fro which most men practise, rambling about houses, theatres, and market-places. They mind other men's business, and always seem as though they themselves had something to do. If you ask one of them as he comes out of his own door, "Whither are you going?" he will answer, "By Hercules, I do not know: but I shall see some people and do something." They wander purposelessly seeking for something to do, and do, not what they have made up their minds to do, but what has casually fallen in their way. They move uselessly and without any plan, just like ants crawling over bushes, which creep up to the top and then down to the bottom again without gaining anything. Many men spend their lives in exactly the same fashion, which one may call a state of restless indolence. You would pity some of them when you see them running as if their house was on fire: They actually jostle all whom they meet, and hurry along themselves and others with them, though all the while they are going to salute some one who will not return their greeting, or to attend the funeral of some one whom they did not know: they are going to hear the verdict on one who often goes to law, or to see the wedding of one who often gets married: they will follow a man's litter, and in some places will even carry it: afterwards returning home weary with idleness, they swear that they themselves do not know why they went out, or where they have been, and on the following day they will wander through the same round again. Let all your work, therefore, have some purpose, and keep some object in view: these restless people are not made restless by labour, but are driven out of their minds by mistaken ideas: for even they do not put themselves in motion without any hope: they are excited by the outward appearance of something, and their crazy mind cannot see its futility. In the same way every one of those who walk out to swell the crowd in the streets, is led round the city by worthless and empty reasons; the dawn drives him forth, although he has nothing to do, and after he has pushed his way into many men's doors, and saluted their nomenclators one after the other, and been turned away from many others, he finds that the most difficult person of all to find at home is himself. From this evil habit comes that worst of all vices, talebearing and prying into public and private secrets, and the knowledge of many things which it is neither safe to tell nor safe to listen to.

It was, I imagine, following out this principle that Democritus taught that "he who would live at peace must not do much business either public or private," referring of course to unnecessary business: for if there be any necessity for it we ought to transact not only much but endless business, both public and private; in cases, however, where no solemn duty invites us to act, we had better keep ourselves quiet: for he who does many things often puts himself in Fortune's power, and it is safest not to tempt her often, but always to remember her existence, and never to promise oneself anything on her security. I will set sail unless anything happens to prevent me, I shall be prætor if nothing hinders me, my financial operations will succeed unless anything goes wrong with them. This is why we say that nothing befalls the wise man which he did not expect—we do not make him exempt from the chances of human life, but from its mistakes, nor does everything happen to him as he wished it would, but as he thought it would: now his first thought was that his purpose might meet with some resistance, and the pain of disappointed wishes must affect a man's mind less severely if he has not been at all events confident of success.

Moreover, we ought to cultivate an easy temper, and not become over fond of the lot which fate has assigned to us, but transfer ourselves to whatever other condition chance may lead us to, and fear no alteration either in our purposes or our position in life, provided that we do not become subject to caprice, which of all vices is the most hostile to repose: for obstinacy, from which Fortune often wrings some concession, must needs be anxious and unhappy, but caprice, which can never restrain itself, must be more so. Both of these qualities, both that of altering nothing, and that of being dissatisfied with everything, are enemies to repose. The mind ought in all cases to be called away from the contemplation of external things to that of itself: let it confide in itself, rejoice in itself, admire its own works; avoid as far as may be those of others, and devote itself to itself; let it not feel losses, and put a good construction even upon misfortunes. Zeno, the chief of our school, when he heard the news of a shipwreck, in which all his property had been lost, remarked, "Fortune bids me follow philosophy in lighter marching order." A tyrant threatened Theodorus with death, and even with want of burial. "You are able to please yourself," he answered, "my half pint of blood is in your power: for, as for burial, what a fool you must be if you suppose that I care whether I rot above ground or under it." Julius Kanus, a man of peculiar greatness, whom even the fact of his having been born in this century does not prevent our admiring, had a long dispute with Gaius, and when as he was going away that Phalaris of a man said to him, "That you may not delude yourself with any foolish hopes, I have ordered you to be executed," he answered, "I thank you, most excellent prince." I am not sure what he meant: for many ways of explaining his conduct occur to me. Did he wish to be reproachful, and to show him how great his cruelty must be if

death became a kindness? or did he upbraid him with his accustomed insanity?
for even those whose children were put to
death, and whose goods were confiscated,
used to thank him: or was it that he
willingly received death, regarding it as
freedom? Whatever he meant, it was a
magnanimous answer. Some one may
say, "After this Gaius might have let him
live." Kanus had no fear of this: the
good faith with which Gaius carried out
such orders as these was well known. Will
you believe that he passed the ten intervening days before his execution without
the slightest despondency? it is marvellous how that man spoke and acted, and
how peaceful he was. He was playing at
draughts when the centurion in charge of
a number of those who were going to be
executed bade him join them: on the
summons he counted his men and said to
his companion, "Mind you do not tell a
lie after my death, and say that you
won;" then, turning to the centurion, he
said, "You will bear me witness that I
am one man ahead of him." Do you
think that Kanus played upon that
draught-board? nay, he played with it.
His friends were sad at being about to
lose so great a man: "Why," asked he,
"are you sorrowful? you are enquiring
whether our souls are immortal, but I
shall presently know." Nor did he up to
the very end cease his search after truth,
and raised arguments upon the subject
of his own death. His own teacher of
philosophy accompanied him, and they
were not far from the hill on which the
daily sacrifice to Cæsar our god was
offered, when he said, "What are you
thinking of now, Kanus, or what are your
ideas?" "I have decided," answered
Kanus, "at that most swiftly-passing
moment of all to watch whether the spirit
will be conscious of the act of leaving the
body." He promised, too, that if he made
any discoveries, he would come round to
his friends and tell them what the condition of the souls of the departed might be.

Here was peace in the very midst of the
storm: here was a soul worthy of eternal
life, which used its own fate as a proof
of truth, which when at the last step of
life experimented upon his fleeting breath,
and did not merely continue to learn until
he died, but learned something even from
death itself. No man has carried the life
of a philosopher further. I will not
hastily leave the subject of a great man,
and one who deserves to be spoken of
with respect: I will hand thee down to all
posterity, chief among the many victims
of Gaius.

Yet we gain nothing by getting rid of
all personal causes of sadness, for sometimes we are possessed by hatred of the
human race. When you reflect how rare
simplicity is, how unknown innocence,
how seldom faith is kept, unless it be to
our advantage, when you remember such
numbers of successful crimes, so many
equally hateful losses and gains of lust,
and ambition so impatient even of its own
natural limits that it is willing to purchase distinction by baseness, the mind
seems as it were cast into darkness, and
shadows rise before it as though the
virtues were all overthrown and we were
no longer allowed to hope to possess them
or benefited by their possession. We
ought therefore to bring ourselves into
such a state of mind that all the vices of
the vulgar may not appear hateful to us,
but merely ridiculous, and we should
imitate Democritus rather than Heracli-
tus. The latter of these, whenever he
appeared in public, used to weep, the
former to laugh: the one thought all
human doings to be follies, the other
thought them to be miseries. We must
take a higher view of all things, and bear
with them more easily: it better becomes
a man to scoff at life than to lament over
it. Add to this that he who laughs at
the human race deserves better of it than
he who mourns for it, for the former
leaves it some good hopes of improve-
ment, while the latter stupidly weeps over

what he has given up all hopes of mending. He who after surveying the universe cannot control his laughter shows, too, a greater mind than he who cannot restrain his tears, because his mind is only affected in the slightest possible degree, and he does not think that any part of all this apparatus is either important, or serious, or unhappy. As for the several causes which render us happy or sorrowful, let every one describe them for himself, and learn the truth of Bion's saying, "That all the doings of men were very like what he began with, and that there is nothing in their lives which is more holy or decent than their conception." Yet it is better to accept public morals and human vices calmly without bursting into either laughter or tears; for to be hurt by the sufferings of others is to be for ever miserable, while to enjoy the sufferings of others is an inhuman pleasure, just as it is a useless piece of humanity to weep and pull a long face because some one is burying his son. In one's own misfortunes, also, one ought so to conduct oneself as to bestow upon them just as much sorrow as reason, not as much as custom requires: for many shed tears in order to show them, and whenever no one is looking at them their eyes are dry, but they think it disgraceful not to weep when every one does so. So deeply has this evil of being guided by the opinion of others taken root in us, that even grief, the simplest of all emotions, begins to be counterfeited.

There comes now a part of our subject which is wont with good cause to make one sad and anxious: I mean when good men come to bad ends; when Socrates is forced to die in prison, Rutilius to live in exile, Pompeius and Cicero to offer their necks to the swords of their own followers, when the great Cato, that living image of virtue, falls upon his sword and rips up both himself and the republic, one cannot help being grieved that Fortune should bestow her gifts so unjustly: what, too,

can a good man hope to obtain when he sees the best of men meeting with the worst fates. Well, but see how each of them endured his fate, and if they endured it bravely, long in your heart for courage as great as theirs; if they died in a womanish and cowardly manner, nothing was lost: either they deserved that you should admire their courage, or else they did not deserve that you should wish to imitate their cowardice: for what can be more shameful than that the greatest men should die so bravely as to make people cowards. Let us praise one who deserves such constant praises, and say, "The braver you are the happier you are! You have escaped from all accidents, jealousies, diseases; you have escaped from prison: the gods have not thought you worthy of ill-fortune, but have thought that fortune no longer deserved to have any power over you," but when one shrinks back in the hour of death and looks longingly at life, we must lay hands upon him. I will never weep for a man who dies cheerfully, nor for one who dies weeping: the former wipes away my tears, the latter by his tears makes himself unworthy that any should be shed for him. Shall I weep for Hercules because he was burned alive, or for Regulus because he was pierced by so many nails, or for Cato because he tore opens his wounds a second time? All these men discovered how at the cost of a small portion of time they might obtain immortality, and by their deaths gained eternal life.

It also proves a fertile source of troubles if you take pains to conceal your feelings and never show yourself to any one undisguised, but, as many men do, live an artificial life, in order to impose upon others: for the constant watching of himself becomes a torment to a man, and he dreads being caught doing something at variance with his usual habits, and, indeed, we never can be at our ease if we imagine that every one who looks at us is weighing our real value: for many things occur which strip people of their disguise, however reluctantly they may part with it, and even if all this trouble about oneself is successful, still life is neither happy nor safe when one always has to wear a mask. But what pleasure there is in that honest straightforwardness which is its own ornament, and which conceals no part of its character! Yet even this life, which hides nothing from any one, runs some risk of being despised; for there are people who disdain whatever they come close to: but there is no danger of virtue's becoming contemptible when she is brought near our eyes, for it is better to be scorned for one's simplicity than to bear the burden of unceasing hypocrisy. Still, we must observe moderation in this matter, for there is a great difference between living simply and living slovenly. Moreover, we ought to retire a great deal into ourselves: for association with persons unlike ourselves upsets all that we had arranged, rouses the passions which were at rest, and rubs into a sore any weak or imperfectly healed place in our minds. Nevertheless we ought to mix up these two things, and to pass our lives alternately in solitude and among throngs of people; for the former will make us long for the society of mankind, the latter for that of ourselves, and the one will counteract the other: solitude will cure us when we are sick of crowds, and crowds will cure us when we are sick of solitude. Neither ought we always to keep the mind strained to the same pitch, but it ought sometimes to be relaxed by amusement. Socrates did not blush to play with little boys, Cato used to refresh his mind with wine after he had wearied it with application to affairs of state, and Scipio would move his triumphal and soldierly limbs to the sound of music, not with a feeble and halting gait, as is the fashion now-a-days, when we sway in our very walk with more than womanly weakness, but dancing as men were wont in

the days of old on sportive and festal occasions, with manly bounds, thinking it no harm to be seen so doing even by their enemies. Men's minds ought to have relaxation: they rise up better and more vigorous after rest. We must not force crops from rich fields, for an unbroken course of heavy crops will soon exhaust their fertility, and so also the liveliness of our minds will be destroyed by unceasing labour, but they will recover their strength after a short period of rest and relief: for continuous toil produces a sort of numbness and sluggishness. Men would not be so eager for this, if play and amusement did not possess natural attractions for them, although constant indulgence in them takes away all gravity and all strength from the mind: for sleep, also, is necessary for our refreshment, yet if you prolong it for days and nights together it will become death. There is a great difference between slackening your hold of a thing and letting it go. The founders of our laws appointed festivals, in order that men might be publicly encouraged to be cheerful, and they thought it necessary to vary our labours with amusements, and, as I said before, some great men have been wont to give themselves a certain number of holidays in every month, and some divide every day into play-time and work-time. Thus, I remember that great orator Asinius Pollio would not attend to any business after the tenth hour: he would not even read letters after that time for fear some new trouble should arise, but in those two hours used to get rid of the weariness which he had contracted during the whole day. Some rest in the middle of the day, and reserve some light occupation for the afternoon. Our ancestors, too, forbade any new motion to be made in the Senate after the tenth hour. Soldiers divide their watches, and those who have just returned from active service are allowed to sleep the whole night undisturbed. We must humour our minds and grant them rest from time to time, which acts upon them like food, and restores their strength. It does good also to take walks out of doors, that our spirits may be raised and refreshed by the open air and fresh breeze: sometimes we gain strength by driving in a carriage, by travel, by change of air, or by social meals and a more generous allowance of wine: at times we ought to drink even to intoxication, not so as to drown, but merely to dip ourselves in wine: for wine washes away troubles and dislodges them from the depths of the mind, and acts as a remedy to sorrow as it does to some diseases. The inventor of wine is called Liber, not from the license which he gives to our tongues, but because he liberates the mind from the bondage of cares, and emancipates it, animates it, and renders it more daring in all that it attempts. Yet moderation is wholesome both in freedom and in wine. It is believed that Solon and Arcesilaus used to drink deep. Cato is reproached with drunkenness: but whoever casts this in his teeth will find it easier to turn this reproach into a commendation than to prove that Cato did anything wrong: however, we ought not to do it often, for fear the mind should contract evil habits, though it ought sometimes to be forced into frolic and frankness, and to cast off dull sobriety for a while. If we believe the Greek poet, "it is sometimes pleasant to be mad:" again, Plato always knocked in vain at the door of poetry when he was sober; or, if we trust Aristotle, no great genius has ever been without a touch of insanity. The mind cannot use lofty language, above that of the common herd, unless it be excited. When it has spurned aside the commonplace environments of custom, and rises sublime, instinct with sacred fire, then alone can it chant a song too grand for mortal lips: as long as it continues to dwell within itself it cannot rise to any pitch of splendour: it must break away from the beaten track, and

lash itself to frenzy, till it gnaws the curb and rushes away bearing up its rider to heights whither it would fear to climb when alone.

I have now, my beloved Serenus, given you an account of what things can preserve peace of mind, what things can restore it to us, what can arrest the vices which secretly undermine it: yet be assured, that none of these is strong enough to enable us to retain so fleeting a blessing, unless we watch over our vacillating mind with intense and unremitting care.
—AUBREY STEWART.

THE FREEDOM OF THE WISE MAN

PERSIUS

[From *Satires* V]

Aulus Persius Flaccus was born in 34 at Volaterræ in Etruria and died in 62. From the time of Lucilius on philosophical topics had been fit themes for satire. The six satires of Persius are merely lectures in satiric form on certain doctrines of Stoicism. Their moral earnestness foreshadows Juvenal, while their phraseology and general method are reminiscent of Horace.

In the following passage Persius argues that the state has not the power, with all its despotism, to destroy or bestow freedom. Freedom is a thing of the spirit, not of political circumstance.

Countless the various species of mankind,
Countless the shades which separate mind from mind;
No general object of desire is known;
Each has his will, and each pursues his own;
With Latian wares, one roams the Eastern main,
To purchase spice, and cummin's blanching grain;
Another, gorged with dainties, swilled with wine,

Fattens in sloth, and snores out life, supine;
This loves the Campus; that, destructive play;
And those in wanton dalliance melt away:—
But when the knotty gout their strength has broke,
And their dry joints crack like some withered oak,
Then they look back, confounded and aghast,
On the gross days in fogs and vapours past;
With late regret the waste of life deplore,
No purpose gained, and time, alas! no more.
 But you, my friend, whom nobler views delight,
To pallid vigils give the studious night;
Cleanse youthful breasts from every noxious weed,
And sow the tilth with Cleanthean seed.
There seek, ye young, ye old, secure to find
That certain end which stays the wavering mind;
Stores, which endure, when other means decay,
Through life's last stage, a sad and cheerless way.
 "Right; and to-morrow this shall be our care."
Alas! to-morrow, like to-day, will fare.
 "What! is one day, forsooth, so great a boon?"
But when it comes (and come it will too soon),
Reflect, that yesterday's to-morrow's o'er.—
Thus "one to-morrow! one to-morrow! more,"
Have seen long years before them fade away;
And still appear no nearer than to-day!
So while the wheels on different axles roll,
In vain (though governed by the selfsame pole)
The hindmost to o'ertake the foremost tries:
Fast as the one pursues the other flies!
Freedom, in truth, it steads us much to have:
Not that by which each manumitted slave,
Each Publius, with his tally, may obtain
A casual dole of coarse and damaged grain.
—O souls! involved in Error's thickest shade,
Who think a Roman with one turn is made!
Look on this paltry groom, this Dama here,
Who at three farthings would be prized too dear;
This blear-eyed scoundrel, who your husks would steal,
And outface truth to hide the starving meal;
Yet—let his master twirl this knave about,
And Marcus Dama in a trice steps out!
Amazing! Marcus surety?—yet distrust!
Marcus your judge?—yet fear a doom unjust!
Marcus avouch it?—then the fact is clear.
The writings!—set your hand, good Marcus, here.
 This is mere liberty—a name alone:
Yet this is all the cap can make your own.
"Sure, there's no other. All mankind agree
That those who live without control are free:
I live without control; and therefore hold
Myself more free than Brutus was of old."
 Absurdly put; a Stoic cries, whose ear,
Rinsed with sharp vinegar, is quick to hear:
True;—all who live without control are free;
But that you live so, I can ne'er agree.
 "No? From the Prætor's wand when I withdrew,
Lord of myself, why, might I not pursue

My pleasure unrestrained, respect still
  had
To what the rubric of the law forbad?"
   Listen—but first your brows from
    anger clear,
And bid your nose dismiss that rising
  sneer;
Listen while I the genuine truth impart,
And root those old wives' fables from
  your heart.
   It was not, is not the "Prætor's wand,"
To gift a fool with power, to understand
The nicer shades of duty, and educe,
From short and rapid life, its end and
  use;
The laboring hind shall sooner seize the
  quill,
And strike the lyre with all a master's
  skill.
Reason condemns the thought, with mien
  severe,
And drops this maxim in the secret ear,
"Forbear to venture, with preposterous
  toil,
On what, in venturing, you are sure to
  spoil."
In this plain sense of what is just and
  right
The laws of nature and of man unite;
That Inexperience should some caution
  show,
And spare to reach at what she does not
  know.
   Prescribe you hellebore! without the
   skill
To weigh the ingredients, or compound
  the pill?—
Physic, alarmed, the rash attempt with-
  stands,
And wrests the dangerous mixture from
  your hands.
   Should the rude clown, skilled in no
   star to guide
His dubious course, rush on the trackless
  tide,
Would not Palemon at the fact exclaim,
And swear the world had lost all sense
  of shame!

   Say, is it yours, by wisdom's steady
   rays,
To walk secure through life's entangled
  maze?
Yours to discern the specious from the
  true,
And where the gilt conceals the brass
  from view?
Speak, can you mark, with some appro-
  priate sign,
What to pursue, and what, in turn, de-
  cline?
Does moderation all your wishes guide
And temperance at your cheerful board
  preside?
Do friends your love experience? are your
  stores
Now dealt with closed and now with open
  doors,
As fit occasion calls?　Can you restrain
The eager appetite of sordid gain?
Nor feel, when in the mire a doit you
  note,
Mercurial spittle gurgle in your throat?
   If you can say, and truly, "These are
   mine,
And This I can:" suffice it.　I decline
All farther question; you are wise and
  free,
No less by Jove's than by the law's de-
  cree.
   But if, good Marcus, you who formed
   so late
One of our batch, of our enslaved estate,
Beneath a specious outside, still retain
The foul contagion of your ancient strain;
If the sly fox still burrow in some part,
Some secret corner, of your tainted heart;
I straight retract the freedom which I
  gave,
And hold your Dama still, and still a
  slave!
   Reason concedes you nothing.　Let us
   try.
Thrust forth you're finger.　"See."　O,
  heavens, awry!
Yet what so trifling?—But, though altars
  smoke,

Though clouds of incense every god in-
voke,
In vain you sue, one drachm of Right to
find,
One scruple, lurking in the foolish mind.
Nature abhors the mixture; the rude
clown
As well may lay his spade and mattock
down,
And with light foot and agile limbs pre-
pare
To dance three steps with soft Bathyllus'
air!
   "Still I am free." You! subject to the
sway
Of countless masters, Free! What *datum*,
pray,
Supports your claim? Is there no other
yoke
Than that which, from your neck, the
Prætor broke!
"Go, bear these scrapers to the bath with
speed;
What! loitering, knave?"—Here's servi-
tude indeed!
Yet you unmoved the angry sounds would
hear;
You own no duty, and can know no fear.
But if within you feel the strong control—
If stormy passions lord it o'er your soul,
Are you more free than he whom threat-
enings urge
To bear the strigils and escape the
scourge?
   'Tis morn; yet sunk in sloth you snor-
ing lie.
"Up! up!" cries Avarice, "and to business
hie;
Nay, stir." I will not. Still she presses,
"Rise!"
I can not. "But you must and shall,"
she cries.
And to what purpose? "This a question!
Go,
Bear fish to Pontus, and bring wines from
Co;
Bring ebon, flax, whate'er the East sup-
plies,

Musk for perfumes, and gums for sacri-
fice:
Prevent the mart, and the first pepper
take
From the tired camel ere his thirst he
slake.
Traffic forswear, if interest intervene"—
But Jove will overhear me.—"Hold, my
spleen!
O dolt; but, mark—that thumb will bore
and bore
The empty salt (scraped to the quick
before)
For one poor grain, a vapid meal to mend,
If you aspire to thrive with Jove your
friend!"
   You rouse (for who can truths like
these withstand?),
Victual your slaves, and urge them to the
strand.
Prepared in haste to follow; and, ere now,
Had to the Ægean turned your vent'rous
prow,
But that sly Luxury the process eyed,
Waylaid your desperate steps, and, taunt-
ing, cried,
   "Ho, madman, whither, in this hasty
plight?
What passion drives you forth? what
furies fright?
Whole urns of hellebore might hope in
vain
To cool this high-wrought fever of the
brain.
What! quit your peaceful couch, renounce
your ease,
To rush on hardships, and to dare the
seas!
And while a broken plank supports your
meat,
And a coiled cable proves your softest
seat,
Suck from squab jugs that pitchy scents
exhale,
The seaman's beverage, sour at once and
stale!
And all for what? that sums, which now
are lent,

At modest five, may sweat out twelve
    per cent!—
"O rather cultivate the joys of sense,
And crop the sweets which youth and
    health dispense;
Give the light hours to banquets, love,
    and wine:
These are the zest of life, and these are
    mine!
Dust and a shade are all you soon must
    be:
Live, then, while yet you may. Time
    presses.—See!
Even while I speak, the present is be-
    come
The past, and lessens still life's little
    sum."
    Now, sir, decide; shall this, or that,
    command?
Alas, the bait, displayed on either hand,
Distracts your choice:—but ponder as
    you may,
Of this be sure; both, with alternate
    sway,
Will lord it o'er you, while, with slavish
    fears,
From side to side your doubtful duty
    veers.
    Nor must you, though in some auspi-
    cious hour
You spurn your mandate, and resist their
    power,
At once conclude their future influence
    vain: —
With struggling hard the dog may snap
    his chain:
Yet little freedom from the effort find,
If, as he flies, he trails its length behind.
"Yes, I am fixed; to Love a long adieu!—
Nay, smile not, Davus; you will find it
    true."
So, while his nails, gnawn to the quick,
    yet bled,
The sage Chærestratus, deep-musing,
    said.—
"Shall I my virtuous ancestry defame.
Consume my fortune, and disgrace my
    name,
While, at a harlot's wanton threshold laid,

Darkling, I whine my drunken serenade!"
    'Tis nobly spoken:—Let a lamb be
    brought
To the Twin Powers that this deliverance
    wrought.
    "But—if I quit her, will she not com-
    plain?
Will she not grieve? Good Davus, think
    again."
Fond trifler! you will find her "grief" too
    late;
When the red slipper rattles round your
    pate,
Vindictive of the mad attempt to foil
Her potent spell, and all-involving toil.
Dismissed, you storm and bluster: hark!
    she calls,
And, at the word, your boasted manhood
    falls.
"Mark, Davus; of her own accord, she
    sues!
Mark, she invites me! Can I now re-
    fuse?"
Yes, Now and Ever. If you left her door
Whole and entire, you must return no
    more.
    Right. This is He, the man whom I
    demand;
This, Davus; not the creature of a wand
Waved by some foolish lictor.—And is he,
This master of himself, this truly free,
Who marks the dazzling lure Ambition
    spreads,
And headlong follows where the meteor
    leads?
"Watch the nice hour, and on the scramb-
    ling tribes
Pour, without stint, your mercenary
    bribes,
Vetches and pulse; that, many a year
    gone by,
Graybeards, as basking in the sun they
    lie,
May boast how much your Floral Games
    surpast,
In cost and splendor, those they witnessed
    last!"
A glorious motive! And on Herod's day,
When every room is decked in meet array,

And lamps along the greasy windows
spread,
Profuse of flowers, gross, oily vapors
shed;
When the vast tunny's tail in pickle
swims,
And the crude must foams o'er the
pitcher's brims;
You mutter secret prayers, by fear devised,
And dread the sabbaths of the cir-
cumcised!
Then a cracked egg-shell fills you with
affright,
And ghosts and goblins haunt your sleepless night.
Last, the blind priestess, with her
sistrum shrill,
And Galli, huge and high, a dread instill

Of gods, prepared to vex the human
frame
With dropsies, palsies, ills of every name,
Unless the trembling victim champ, in
bed,
Thrice every morn, on a charmed garlic-
head.
Preach to the martial throng these lofty
strains,
And lo! some chief more famed for bulk
than brains,
Some vast Vulfenius, blessed with lungs
of brass,
Laughs loud and long at the scholastic
ass;
And, for a clipt cent-piece, sets, by the
tale,
A hundred Greek philosophers to sale!
—WILLIAM GIFFORD.

III. TURNING TO THE PAST

In the second half of the first century,
the men of letters, forced out of contemporary interests, became more and more
absorbed in a study of the past. This resulted in an ever increasing respect for
the days and ways of the Republic, and
though there were dangers in contrasting
those times of freedom with the present
state of affairs, they could safely choose
their subjects from the earlier history and
treat them as glorious episodes in the
development of Rome. There grew up
an odd contradiction in their attitude—a
tendency on the one hand to look down,
as from a superior height of attainment,
upon their republican forerunners, and
on the other a sincere admiration for their
achievements, not only in politics, but also
in literature. Quintilian and Tacitus
could write the praises of the Ciceronian
style, yet there was a general feeling that
the style developed by Seneca was a distinct advance over the cumbersome
periods of the earlier writing. The more
remote past of myth, as at all times in
the course of their literature, so now too
claimed the attention of those who preferred to deal neither with the present
nor with the republican history of Rome.

LEADERS OF THE REPUBLIC: LUCAN

STOIC CHARACTER

[From the *Pharsalia*, Book II]

Cato came to be regarded by the Romans
of later generations as the standing example of perfect character. The Roman
ideal demands the sort of patriotism that
gives without stint and at the same time
an obstinacy of will that makes a near
approach to Puritanism and selfishness.
For Lucan, see above p. 504.

For when he saw the fatal factions arm,
The coming war, and Rome's impending
harm;
Regardless quite of every other care,
Unshorn he left his loose neglected hair;
Rude hung the hoary honours of his head,
And a foul growth his mournful cheeks
o'erspread.
No stings of private hate his peace infest,
Nor partial favour grew upon his breast;
But, safe from prejudice, he kept his
mind

Free, and at leisure to lament mankind.
Nor could his former love's returning
    fire,
The warmth of one connubial wish in-
    spire,
But strongly he withstood the just desire.
These were the stricter manners of the
    man,
And this the stubborn course in which
    they ran:
The golden mean unchanging to pursue,
Constant to keep the purpos'd end in
    view;
Religiously to follow Nature's laws,
And die with pleasure in his country's
    cause,
To think he was not for himself design'd,
But born to be of use to all mankind.
To him 'twas feasting, hunger to repress;
And home-spun garments were his costly
    dress:
No marble pillars rear'd his roof on high,
'Twas warm, and kept him from the
    winter sky:
He sought no end of marriage, but in-
    crease,
Nor wish'd a pleasure, but his country's
    peace:
That took up all the tenderest parts of
    life,
His country was his children and his wife.
From justice' righteous lore he never
    swerv'd,
But rigidly his honesty preserv'd.
On universal good his thoughts were bent,
Nor knew what gain, or self-affection
    meant;
And while his benefits the public share,
Cato was always last in Cato's care.
                    NICHOLAS ROWE.

APOSTROPHE TO BRUTUS

[From the *Pharsalia*, Book VII]

Brutus is described by Lucan in accordance with the conception of his character
and rôle in history which remained ever
after fixed in literature.

Say thou! thy sinking country's only
    prop,
Glory of Rome, and liberty's last hope;
What helm, O Brutus! could, amidst the
    crowd,
Thy sacred undistinguish'd visage shroud?
Where fought thy arm that day! But
    ah! forbear!
Nor rush unwary on the pointed spear;
Seek not to hasten on untimely fate,
But patient for thy own Emathia wait:
Nor hunt fierce Cæsar on this bloody
    plain,
To-day thy steel pursues his life in vain.
Somewhat is wanting to the tyrant yet,
To make the measure of his crimes com-
    plete;
As yet he has not every law defy'd,
Nor reach'd the utmost heights of daring
    pride.
Ere long thou shalt behold him Rome's
    proud lord,
And ripen'd by ambition for thy sword;
Then, thy griev'd country vengeance shall
    demand,
And ask the victim at thy righteous hand.
                    —NICHOLAS ROWE.

THE TOMB OF POMPEY

[From the *Pharsalia*, Book VIII]

The author was at pains throughout
his poem to portray Pompey as an epic
hero. The historical Pompey was a serious stumbling-block in his way. It was
by such devices as the one in this passage
that he was able to give the desired impression without doing violence to recorded fact.

But soon behold! the bolder youth re-
    turns,
While, half consum'd, the smouldering
    carcass burns;
Ere yet the cleansing fire had melted
    down
The fleshy muscles, from the firmer bone.
He quench'd the relics in the briny wave,
And hid them, hasty, in a narrow grave:

Then with a stone the sacred dust he
binds,
To guard it from the breath of scattering
winds:
And lest some heedless mariner should
come,
And violate the warrior's humble tomb,
Thus with a line the monument he keeps,
"Beneath this stone the once great
Pompey sleeps."
Oh Fortune! can thy malice swell so
high?
Canst thou with Cæsar's every wish
comply?
Must he, thy Pompey once, thus meanly
lie?
But oh! forbear, mistaken man, forbear!
Nor dare to fix the mighty Pompey there:
Where there are seas, or air, or earth, or
skies,
Where'er Rome's empire stretches, Pom-
pey lies:
Far be the vile memorial then convey'd!
Nor let this stone the partial gods up-
braid.
Shall Hercules all Œta's heights demand,
And Nysa's hill, for Bacchus only, stand;
While one poor pebble is the warrior's
doom,
That fought the cause of liberty and
Rome?
If fate decrees he must in Egypt lie,
Let the whole fertile realm his grave
supply:
Yield the wide country to his awful shade,
Nor let us bear on any part to tread,
Fearful to violate the mighty dead.
But if one stone must bear the sacred
name,
Let it be fill'd with long records of fame.
There let the passenger, with wonder,
read,
The pirates vanquish'd, and the ocean
freed;
Sertorius taught to yield; the Alpine war;
And the young Roman knight's triumphal
car;
With these, the mighty Pontic king be
plac'd,

And every nation of the vanquish'd east:
Tell with what loud applause of Rome,
he drove
Thrice his glad wheels to Capitolian Jove:
Tell too, the patriot's greatest, best re-
nown,
Tell, how the victor laid his empire down,
And chang'd his armour for the peaceful
gown.
But ah! what marbles to the task suffice!
Instead of these, turn, Roman, turn thy
eyes;
Seek the known name our Fasti us'd to
wear,
The noble mark of many a glorious year:
The name that wont the trophy's arch to
grace,
And e'en the temples of the gods found
place:
Decline thee lowly, bending to the ground,
And there that name, that Pompey may
be found.

—NICHOLAS ROWE.

CATO AND AMMON

[From the *Pharsalia*, Book IX]

The general population of Rome was
exceedingly superstitious, but the attitude
of Cato represents fairly that of the more
highly educated classes from the time of
Cicero on.

Before the temple's entrance, at the gate,
Attending crowds of eastern pilgrims
wait:
These from the horned god expect relief:
But all give way before the Latian chief.
His host, (as crowds are superstitious
still)
Curious of fate, of future good and ill,
And fond to prove prophetic Ammon's
skill,
Entreat their leader to the god would go,
And from his oracle Rome's fortunes
know:
But Labienus chief the thought approv'd,
And thus the common suit to Cato mov'd:

"Chance, and the fortune of the way,"
he said,
"Have brought Jove's sacred counsels to
our aid:
This greatest of the gods, this mighty
chief,
In each distress shall be a sure relief;
Shall point the distant dangers from afar,
And teach the future fortunes of the war.
To thee, O Cato! pious! wise! and just!
Their dark decrees the cautious gods shall
trust!
To thee their fore-determin'd will shall
tell:
Their will has been thy law, and thou
hast kept it well.
Fate bids thee now the noble thought
improve;
Fate brings thee here, to meet and talk
with Jove.
Inquire betimes, what various chance
shall come
To impious Cæsar and thy native Rome;
Try to avert, at least, thy country's
doom.
Ask if these arms our freedom shall re-
store:
Or else, if laws and right shall be no more.
Be thy great breast with sacred knowledge
fraught,
To lead us in the wandering maze of
thought:
Thou, that to virtue ever wert inclin'd,
Learn what it is, how certainly defin'd,
And leave some perfect rule to guide
mankind."
　　Full of the god that dwelt within his
breast,
The hero thus his secret mind express'd,
And in-born truths reveal'd; truths which
might well
Become e'en oracles themselves to tell.
　　"Where would thy fond, thy vain in-
quiry go?
What mystic fate, what secret would'st
thou know?
Is it a doubt if death should be my doom,
Rather than live till kings and bondage
come,

Rather than see a tyrant crown'd in
Rome?
Or would'st thou know if, what we value
here,
Life, be a trifle hardly worth our care?
What by old age and length of days we
gain,
More than to lengthen out the sense of
pain?
Or if this world, with all its forces join'd,
The universal malice of mankind,
Can shake or hurt the brave and honest
mind?
If stable virtue can her ground main-
tain,
Whilst fortune feebly threats and frowns
in vain?
If truth and justice with uprightness
dwell,
And honesty consist in meaning well?
If right be independent of success,
And conquest cannot make it more or
less?
Are these, my friend, the secrets thou
would'st know,
These doubts for which to oracles we go?
'Tis known, 'tis plain, 'tis already told,
And horned Ammon can no more unfold.
From God deriv'd, to God by nature
join'd,
We act the dictates of his mighty mind:
And though our priests are mute, and
temples still,
God never wants a voice to speak his will.
When first we from the teeming womb
were brought,
With in-born precepts then our souls were
fraught,
And then the Maker his new creatures
taught.
Then when he form'd and gave us to be
men,
He gave us all our useful knowledge then.
Canst thou believe, the vast Eternal Mind
Was e'er to Syrts and Libyan sands con-
fin'd?
That he would choose this waste, this
barren ground,
To teach the thin inhabitants around.

And leave his truth in wilds and deserts
    drown'd?
Is there a place that God would choose
    to love
Beyond this earth, the seas, yon Heaven
    above,
And virtuous minds, the noblest throne
    for Jove?
Why seek we further then? Behold
    around,
How all thou seest does with the God
    abound,
Jove is alike in all, and always to be
    found.
Let those weak minds, who live in doubt
    and fear,
To juggling priests for oracles repair;
One certain hour of death to each decreed,
My fix'd, my certain soul from doubt
    has freed.
The coward and the brave are doom'd to
    fall;
And when Jove told this truth, he told
    us all."
So spoke the hero; and, to keep his word,
Nor Ammon, nor his oracle explor'd;
But left the crowd at freedom to believe
And take such answers as the priest
    should give.
          —NICHOLAS ROWE.

ORATORS OF THE REPUBLIC [1]

TACITUS

[From the *Dialogue on Orators*]

The importance of oratory in Roman
life was due to the fact that it was almost
the only channel through which a man
could pass to a public career of service
to the state. It was further the best means
of publicity in an age that lacked the
printing press. Since appointment under
the Empire had taken the place of popular election under the Republic, and since
despotism tended to suppress the freedom
of speech, oratory had fallen upon evil
days. For Tacitus, see above p. 461.

[1] From The Loeb Classical Library, reprinted
by permission.

In the good old days, every man's son,
born in wedlock, was brought up not in
the chamber of some hireling nurse, but
in his mother's lap, and at her knee. And
that mother could have no higher praise
than that she managed the house and
gave herself to her children. Again,
some elderly relative would be selected
in order that to her, as a person who had
been tried and never found wanting,
might be entrusted the care of all the
youthful scions of the same house; in the
presence of such an one no base word
could be uttered without grave offence,
and no wrong deed done. Religiously
and with the utmost delicacy she regulated not only the serious tasks of her
youthful charges, but their recreations
also and their games. It was in this
spirit, we are told, that Cornelia, the
mother of the Gracchi, directed their up-
bringing, Aurelia that of Cæsar, Atia of
Augustus: thus it was that these mothers
trained their princely children. The object of this rigorous system was that the
natural disposition of every child, while
still sound at the core and untainted, not
warped as yet by any vicious tendencies,
might at once lay hold with heart and
soul on virtuous accomplishments, and
whether its bent was towards the army,
or the law, or the pursuit of eloquence,
might make that its sole aim and its all-
absorbing interest.

Nowadays, on the other hand, our children are handed over at their birth to
some silly little Greek serving-maid, with
a male slave, who may be any one, to
help her,—quite frequently the most
worthless member of the whole establishment incompetent for any serious service.
It is from the foolish tittle-tattle of such
persons that the children receive their
earliest impressions, while their minds are
still pliant and unformed; and there is
not a soul in the whole house who cares
a jot what he says or does in the presence
of its lisping little lord. Yes, and the
parents themselves make no effort to

train their little ones in goodness and self-control; they grow up in an atmosphere of laxity and pertness, in which they come gradually to lose all sense of shame, and all respect both for themselves and for other people. Again, there are the peculiar and characteristic vices of this metropolis of ours, taken on, as it seems to me, almost in the mother's womb,—the passion for play-actors, and the mania for gladiatorial shows and horse-racing; and when the mind is engrossed in such occupations, what room is left over for high pursuits? How few are to be found whose home-talk runs to any other subjects than these? What else do we overhear our younger men talking about whenever we enter their lecture-halls? And the teachers are just as bad. With them, too, such topics supply material for gossip with their classes more frequently than any others; for it is not by the strict administration of discipline, or by giving proof of their ability to teach that they get pupils together, but by pushing themselves into notice at morning calls and by the tricks of toadyism.

I pass by the first rudiments of education, though even these are taken too lightly: it is in the reading of authors, and in gaining a knowledge of the past, and in making acquaintance of things and persons and occasions that too little solid work is done. Recourse is had instead to the so-called rhetoricians. As I mean to speak in the immediate sequel of the period at which this vocation first made its way to Rome, and of the small esteem in which it was held by our ancestors, I must advert to the system which we are told was followed by those orators whose unremitting industry and daily preparation and continuous practice in every department of study are referred to in their own published works. You are of course familiar with Cicero's "Brutus," in the concluding portion of which treatise—the first part contains a review of the speakers of former days—he gives an account of

his own first beginnings, his gradual progress, and what I may call his evolutions as an orator. He tells us how he studied civil law with Q. Mucius, and thoroughly absorbed philosophy in all its departments as a pupil of Philo the Academic and Diodotus the Stoic; and not being satisfied with the teachers who had been accessible to him at Rome, he went to Greece, and travelled also through Asia Minor, in order to acquire a comprehensive training in every variety of knowledge. Hence it comes that in Cicero's works one may detect the fact that he was not lacking in a knowledge of mathematics, of music, of linguistics—in short, in any department of the higher learning. Yes, Cicero was quite at home in the subtleties of dialectic, in the practical lessons of ethical philosophy, in the changes and origins of natural phenomena. Yes, my good friends, that is the fact: it is only from a wealth of learning, and a multitude of accomplishments, and a knowledge that is universal that his marvellous eloquence wells forth like a mighty stream. The orator's function and activity is not, as is the case with other pursuits, hemmed in all round within narrow boundaries. He only deserves the name who has the ability to speak on any and every topic with grace and distinction of style, in a manner fitted to win conviction appropriately to the dignity of his subject-matter, suitably to the case in hand, and with resulting gratification to his audience.

This was fully understood by the men of former days. They were well aware that, in order to attain the end in view, the practice of declamation in the schools of rhetoric was not the essential matter, —the training merely of tongue and voice in imaginary debates which had no point of contact with real life. No, for them the one thing needful was to stock the mind with those accomplishments which deal with good and evil, virtue and vice, justice and injustice. It is this that forms the subject-matter of oratory. Speaking broadly, in judicial oratory our argument turns upon fair dealing, in the oratory of debate upon advantage, in eulogies upon moral character, though these topics quite frequently overlap. Now it is impossible for any speaker to treat them with fullness, and variety, and elegance, unless he has made a study of human nature, of the meaning of goodness and the wickedness of vice, and unless he has learnt to appreciate the significance of what ranks neither on the side of virtue nor on that of vice. This is the source from which other qualifications also are derived. The man who knows what anger is will be better able either to work on or to mollify the resentment of a judge, just as he who understands compassion, and the emotions by which it is aroused, will find it easier to move him to pity. If your orator has made himself familiar with these branches by study and practice, whether he has to address himself to a hostile or a friendly or a grudging audience, whether his hearers are ill-humoured or apprehensive, he will feel their pulse, and will handle them in every case as their character requires, and will give the right tone to what he has to say, keeping the various implements of his craft lying ready to hand for any and every purpose. There are some with whom a concise, succinct style carries most conviction, one that makes the several lines of proof yield a rapid conclusion: with such it will be an advantage to have paid attention to dialectic. Others are more taken with a smooth and steady flow of speech, drawn from the fountain-head of universal experience: in order to make an impression upon these we shall borrow from the Peripatetics their stock arguments, suited and ready in advance for either side of any discussion. Combativeness will be the contribution of the Academics, sublimity that of Plato, and charm that of Xenophon; nay, there will be nothing amiss in a speaker taking over even some of the excellent aphorisms of Epicurus and Metrodorus, and applying them as the case may demand. It is not a professional philosopher that we are delineating, nor a hangeron of the Stoics, but the man who, while he ought thoroughly to absorb certain branches of study, should also have a bowing acquaintance with them all. That is the reason why the orators of former days made a point of acquiring a knowledge of civil law, while they received a tincture also of literature, music, and mathematics. In the cases that come one's way, what is essential in most instances, indeed almost invariably, is legal knowledge, but there are often others in which you are expected to be well versed also in the subjects just mentioned.

Do not let any one argue in reply that it is enough for us to be coached in some straightforward and clearly defined issue in order to meet the case immediately before us. To begin with, the use we make of what belongs to ourselves is quite different from our use of what we take on loan: there is obviously a wide gulf between owning what we give out and borrowing it from others. In the next place, breadth of culture is an ornament that tells of itself even when one is not making a point of it: it comes prominently into view where you would least expect it. This fact is fully appreciated not only by the learned and scholarly portion of the audience, but also by the rank and file. They cheer the speaker from the start, protesting that he has been properly trained, that he has gone through all the points of good oratory, and that he is, in short, an orator in the true sense of the word: and such an one cannot be, as I maintain, and never was any other than he who enters the lists of debate with all the equipment of a man of learning, like a warrior taking the field in full armour. Our clever speakers of to-day, however, lose sight of this ideal to such an extent that one can detect in their pleadings the shameful and discreditable blemishes even of our everyday speech. They know nothing of statute-law, they have no hold of the decrees of the senate, they go out of their way to show contempt for the law of the constitution, and as for the pursuit of philosophy and the sages' saws they regard them with downright dismay. Eloquence is by them degraded, like a discrowned queen, to a few commonplaces and cramped conceits. She who in days of yore reigned in the hearts of men as the mistress of all the arts, encircled by a brilliant retinue, is now curtailed and mutilated, shorn of all her state, all her distinction, I had almost said all her freedom, and is learnt like any vulgar handicraft.

This then I take to be the first and foremost reason why we have degenerated to such an extent from the eloquence of the orators of old. If you want witnesses, what weightier evidence can I produce than Demosthenes among the Greeks, who is said to have been one of Plato's most enthusiastic students? Our own Cicero tells us too—I think in so many words—that anything he accomplished as an orator he owed not to the workshops of the rhetorician, but to the spacious precincts of the Academy. . . .

Since I have given what seems to be a sufficient account of the first beginnings and the germs of ancient oratory, by setting forth the branches on which the orators of former days were wont to base their training and instruction, I shall now proceed to take up their practical exercises. And yet theory itself involves practice, and it is impossible for any one to grasp so many diverse and abstruse subjects, unless his theoretical knowledge is re-inforced by practice, his practice by natural ability, and his ability by experience of public speaking. The inference is that there is a certain identity between the method of assimilating what you express and that of expressing what you have assimilated. But if any one thinks this a dark saying, and wants to separate theory from practice, he must at least admit that the man whose mind is fully furnished with such theoretical knowledge will come better prepared to the practical exercises which are commonly regarded as the distinctive training of the orator.

Well then, in the good old days the young man who was destined for the oratory of the bar, after receiving the rudiments of a sound training at home, and storing his mind with liberal culture, was taken by his father, or his relations, and placed under the care of some orator who held a leading position at Rome. The youth had to get the habit of following his patron about, of escorting him in public, of supporting him at all his appearances as a speaker, whether in the law courts or on the platform, hearing also his word-combats at first hand, standing by him in his duellings, and learning, as it were, to fight in the fighting-line. It was a method that secured at once for the young students a considerable amount of experience, great self-possession, and a goodly store of sound judgment: for they carried on their studies in the light of open day, and amid the very shock of battle, under conditions in which any stupid or ill-advised statement brings prompt retribution in the shape of the judge's disapproval, taunting criticism from your opponent—yes, and from your own supporters expressions of dissatisfaction. So it was a genuine and unadulterated eloquence that they were initiated in from the very first; and though they attached themselves to a single speaker, yet they got to know all the contemporary members of the bar in a great variety of both civil and criminal cases. Moreover a public meeting gave them the opportunity of noting marked divergences of taste, so that they could easily detect what commended itself in the case of each individual speaker, and what on the other hand failed to please. In this way they could command, firstly, a teacher, and him the best and choicest of his kind, one who could show forth the true features of eloquence, and not a weak imitation; secondly, opponents and antagonists, who fought with swords, not with wooden foils; and thirdly, an audience always numerous and always different, composed of friendly and unfriendly critics, who would not let any points escape them, whether good or bad. For the oratorical renown that is great and lasting is built up, as you know, quite as much among the opposition benches as on those of one's own side; indeed, its growth in that quarter is sturdier, and takes root more firmly. Yes, under such instructors the young man who is the subject of this discourse, the pupil of real orators, the listener in the forum, the close attendant on the law courts, trained to his work in the school of other people's efforts, who got to know his law by hearing it cited every day, who became familiar with the faces on the bench, who made the practice of public meetings a subject of constant contemplation, and who had many opportunities of studying the vagaries of the popular taste,—such a youth, whether he undertook to appear as prosecutor or for the defence, was competent right away to deal with any kind of case, alone and unaided. Lucius Crassus was only eighteen when he impeached Gaius Carbo, Cæsar twenty when he undertook the prosecution of Dolabella, Asinius Pollio twenty-one when he attacked Gaius Cato, and Calvus not much older when he prosecuted Vatinius. The speeches they delivered on those occasions are read to this day with admiration.

But nowadays our boys are escorted to the schools of the so-called "professors of rhetoric,"—persons who came on the scene just before the time of Cicero but failed to find favour with our forefathers, as is obvious from the fact that the censors Crassus and Domitius ordered them to shut down what Cicero calls their "school of shamelessness." They are escorted, as I was saying, to these schools,

of which it would be hard to say what is most prejudicial to their intellectual growth, the place itself, or their fellow-scholars, or the studies they pursue. The place has nothing about it that commands respect,—no one enters it who is not as ignorant as the rest; there is no profit in the society of the scholars, since they are all either boys or young men who are equally devoid of any feeling of responsibility whether they take the floor or provide an audience; and the exercises in which they engage largely defeat their own objects. You are of course aware that there are two kinds of subject-matter handled by these professors, the deliberative and the disputatious. Now while, as regards the former, it is entrusted to mere boys, as being obviously of less importance and not making such demands on the judgment, the more mature scholars are asked to deal with the latter,—but, good heavens! what poor quality is shown in their themes, and how unnaturally they are made up! Then in addition to the subject-matter that is so remote from real life, there is the bombastic style in which it is presented. And so it comes that themes like these: "the reward of the king-killer," or "the outraged maid's alternatives," or "a remedy for the plague," or "the incestuous mother," and all the other topics that are treated every day in the school, but seldom or never in actual practice, are set forth in magniloquent phraseology. . . . Great oratory is like a flame: it needs fuel to feed it, movement to fan it, and it brightens as it burns.

At Rome too the eloquence of our forefathers owed its development to the same conditions. For although the orators of to-day have also succeeded in obtaining all the influence that it would be proper to allow them under settled, peaceable, and prosperous political conditions, yet their predecessors in those days of unrest and unrestraint thought they could accomplish more when, in the general ferment and without the strong hand of a single ruler, a speaker's political wisdom was measured by his power of carrying conviction to the unstable populace. This was the source of the constant succession of measures put forward by champions of the people's rights, of the harangues of state officials who almost spent the night on the hustings, of the impeachments of powerful criminals and hereditary feuds between whole families, of schisms among the aristocracy and never-ending struggles between the senate and the commons. All this tore the commonwealth in pieces, but it provided a sphere for the oratory of those days and heaped on it what one saw were vast rewards. The more influence a man could wield by his powers of speech, the more readily did he attain to high office, the further did he, when in office, outstrip his colleagues in the race for precedence, the more did he gain favour with the great, authority with the senate, and name and fame with the common people. These were the men who had whole nations of foreigners under their protection, several at a time; the men to whom state officials presented their humble duty on the eve of their departure to take up the government of a province, and to whom they paid their respects on their return; the men who, without any effort on their own part, seemed to have prætorships and consulates at their beck and call; the men who even when out of office were in power, seeing that by their advice and authority they could bend both the senate and the people to their will. With them moreover it was a conviction that without eloquence it was impossible for any one either to attain to a position of distinction and prominence in the community, or to maintain it: and no wonder they cherished this conviction, when they were called on to appear in public even when they would rather not, when it was not enough to move a brief resolution in the senate, unless one made good one's

opinion in an able speech, when persons who had in some way or other incurred odium, or else were definitely charged with some offence, had to put in an appearance in person, when moreover evidence in criminal trials had to be given not indirectly or by affidavit, but personally and by word of mouth. So it was that eloquence not only led to great rewards, but was also a sheer necessity; and just as it was considered great and glorious to have the reputation of being a good speaker, so, on the other hand, it was accounted discreditable to be inarticulate and incapable of utterance.

Thus it was a sense of shame quite as much as material reward that gave them an incentive. They wanted to be ranked with patrons rather than with poor dependents; they could not bear to let inherited connections pass into the hands of strangers; and they had to avoid the reputation for apathy and incompetence that would either keep them from obtaining office or make their official careers a failure. I wonder if you have seen the ancient records which are still extant in the libraries of collectors, and which are even now being compiled by Mucianus: they have already been arranged and edited in eleven volumes, I think, of Proceedings and five of Letters. They make it clear that Gnæus Pompeius and Marcus Crassus rose to power not only as warriors and men of might, but also by their talent for oratory; that the Lentuli and the Metelli and the Luculli and the Curios and all the great company of our nobles devoted great care and attention to these pursuits; and that in their day no one attained to great influence without some gift of eloquence.

There was a further advantage in the high rank of the persons who were brought to trial and the importance of the interests involved, factors which are also in a great degree conducive to eloquence. For it makes a good deal of difference whether you are briefed to speak about a case of theft, or a rule of procedure, and the provisional order of a magistrate, or about electioneering practices, the robbery of a province, and the murder of fellow-citizens. It is better, of course, that such horrors should not occur at all, and we must regard that as the most enviable political condition in which we are not liable to anything of the kind. Yet when these things did happen, they furnished the orators of the day with ample material. Hand in hand with the importance of the theme goes the growing ability to cope with it, and it is a sheer impossibility for any one to produce a great and glorious oration unless he has found a theme to correspond. It is not, I take it, the speeches which he composed in the action brought against his guardians that give Demosthenes his name and fame, nor does Cicero rest his claims to greatness as an orator on his defence of Publius Quintius or Licinius Archias. No, it was a Catiline, a Milo, a Verres, an Antonius that made his reputation for him. I do not mean that it was worth the country's while to produce bad citizens, just in order that our orators might have an ample supply of material; but let us bear in mind the point at issue, as I keep urging you to do, realising that our discourse is dealing with an art which comes to the front more readily in times of trouble and unrest. We all know that the blessings of peace bring more profit and greater happiness than the horrors of war; yet war produces a larger number of good fighters than peace. It is the same with eloquence. The oftener it takes its stand in the lists, the more numerous the strokes it gives and receives, the more powerful the opponents and the more keenly contested the issues it deliberately selects, in like proportion does eloquence carry its head higher and more erect before the eyes of men, deriving ever greater lustre from the very hazards it encounters. For men are naturally prone,

while courting security for themselves, to admire whatever has an element of risk.

I pass on to the organization and procedure of the old law-courts. It may nowadays have become more practical, but all the same the forum as it then was provided a better training-ground for oratory. There was no obligation on any speaker to complete his pleading within an hour or two at most; adjournments were always in order; as regards a time-limit, each man was a law to himself; and no attempt was made to define either how many days the case was to take or how many counsel were to be employed in it. It was Gnæus Pompeius who, in his third consulship, first introduced limitations in regard to these matters. He may be said to have curbed eloquence with bit and bridle, without however concelling the provision that everything should be done in court, according to law, and before a prætor. The best proof you can have of the greater importance of the cases dealt with by the prætors in former days is the fact that actions before the centumviral court, which are now considered to outrank all others, used to be so much overshadowed by the prestige of other tribunals that there is not a single speech, delivered before that court, that is read to-day, either by Cicero, or by Cæsar, or by Brutus, or by Cælius, or by Calvus, or in fact by any orator of rank. The only exceptions are the speeches of Asinius Pollio entitled "For Urbinia's Heirs," and yet these are just the ones which he delivered well on in the middle of the reign of Augustus, when in consequence of the long period of peace, and the unbroken spell of inactivity on the part of the commons and of peaceableness on the part of the senate, by reason also of the working of the great imperial system, a hush had fallen upon eloquence, as indeed it had upon the world at large.

My next point will perhaps strike you as trivial and ridiculous, but I shall make it, even if only to excite your ridicule. Take those gowns into which we squeeze ourselves when we chat with the court, a costume that shackles movement, do we ever reflect how largely responsible they are for the orator's loss of dignity? Or think of the recitation-halls and record-offices in which pretty well most cases are nowadays despatched, have they not also greatly contributed to the emasculation of eloquence? Why, just as with blood-horses it takes a roomy track to show their mettle, so orators need a spacious field in which to expatiate without let or hindrance, if their eloquence is not to lose all its strength and pith. Moreover, painstaking preparation and the anxious effort for stylistic finish are found after all to do more harm than good. The judge often asks when you are going to come to the point, and you are bound to make a start as soon as he puts the question. Just as often he tells counsel to stop (so that evidence may be led and witnesses examined). All the time the speaker has only two or three for an audience, and the hearing goes forward in what is a scene of desolation. But your public speaker can't get along without "hear, hear," and the clapping of hands. He must have what I may call his stage. This the orators of former times could command day by day, when the forum was packed by an audience at the same time numerous and distinguished, when persons who had to face the hazard of a public trial could depend on being supported by shoals of clients and fellow-tribesmen, and by deputations also from the country towns; half Italy, in fact, was there to back them. These were the days when the people of Rome felt that in quite a number of cases they had a personal stake in the verdict. We know on good authority that both the impeachment and the defence of a Cornelius, a Scaurus, a Milo, a Bestia, a Vatinius brought the whole community

together *en masse:* so that it would have been impossible for even the most frigid of speakers not to be enkindled and set on fire by the mere clash of partisan enthusiasm. That is why the quality of the published orations that have come down to us is so high that it is by these more than by any others that the speakers who appeared on either side actually take rank.

Think again of the incessant public meetings, of the privilege so freely accorded in inveighing against persons of position and influence,—yes, and of the glory you gained by being at daggers drawn with them, in the days when so many clever speakers could not let even a Scipio alone, or a Sulla, or a Pompeius, and when, taking a leaf out of the book of stage-players, they made public meetings also the opportunity of launching characteristically spiteful tirades against the leading men of the state: how all this must have inflamed the able debater and added fuel to the fire of his eloquence!

The art which is the subject of our discourse is not a quiet and peaceable art, or one that finds satisfaction in moral worth and good behaviour: no, really great and famous oratory is a foster-child of license, which foolish men called liberty, an associate of sedition, a goad for the unbridled populace. It owes no allegiance to any. Devoid of reverence, it is insulting, off-hand, and overbearing. It is a plant that does not grow under a well-regulated constitution. Does history contain a single instance of any orator at Sparta, or at Crete, two states whose political system and legislation were more stringent than any other on record? It is equally true to say that in Macedonia and in Persia eloquence was unknown, as indeed it was in all states that were content to live under a settled government. Rhodes has had some orators, Athens a great many: in both communities all power was in the hands of the populace—that is to say, the untutored democracy. The crowd ruled the roost. Likewise at Rome, so long as the constitution was unsettled, so long as the country kept wearing itself out with factions and dissensions and disagreements, so long as there was no peace in the forum, no harmony in the senate, no restraint in the courts of law, no respect for authority, no sense of propriety on the part of the officers of state, the growth of eloquence was doubtless sturdier, just as untilled soil produces certain vegetation in greater luxuriance. But the benefit derived from the eloquence of the Gracchi did not make up for what the country suffered from their laws, and too dearly did Cicero pay by the death he died for his renown in oratory.

In the same way what little our orators have left them of the old forensic activities goes to show that our civil condition is still far from being ideally perfect. Does any one ever call us lawyers to his aid unless he is either a criminal or in distress? Does any country town ever ask for our protection except under pressure either from an aggressive neighbor or from internal strife? Are we ever retained for a province where robbery and oppression have not been at work? Yet surely it were better to have no grievances than to need to seek redress. If a community could be found in which nobody ever did anything wrong, orators would be just as superfluous among saints as doctors among those that need no physician. Just as the healing art, I repeat, is very little in demand and makes very little progress in countries where people enjoy good health and strong constitutions, so oratory has less prestige and smaller consideration where people are well behaved and ready to obey their rulers. What is the use of long arguments in the senate, when good citizens agree so quickly? What is the use of one harangue after another on public platforms, when it is not the ignorant multitude that decides a political issue, but a monarch who is the incarnation of wisdom? What is the use of taking a prosecution on one's own shoulders when misdeeds are so few and so trivial, or of making oneself unpopular by a defence of inordinate length, when the defendant can count on a gracious judge meeting him half-way. Believe me, my friends, you will have all the eloquence that the times require: if you had lived in bygone days, or if the orators who rouse our admiration had lived to-day,—if some deity, I say, had suddenly made you change places in your lives and epochs, you would have attained to their brilliant reputation for eloquence just as surely as they would show your restraint and self-control. As things are, since it is impossible for anybody to enjoy at one and the same time great renown and great repose, let every one make the most of the blessings his own times afford without disparaging any other age.

—WILLIAM PETERSON.

HANNIBAL CROSSING THE ALPS

SILIUS ITALICUS

[From the *Punica*, Book III]

Silius Italicus (about 25 to 101) withdrew from a successful public career, in which he had reached the consulship, to devote himself to elaborating an epic poem on the historical subject of the second Punic war. He seems to have been the author also of a metrical abridgement of the *Iliad*.

Beyond the Pyrenean's lofty bound,
Through blackening forests shagged with
    pine around,
The Carthaginian passed; and, fierce,
    explored
The Volcan champaign with his wasting
    sword.
Then trod the threatening banks, with
    hastening force,

Where Rhone high-swelling rolls its
sweeping course.
From Alpine heights, and steep rocks,
capped with snow,
Gushes the Rhone, where Gaul is
stretched below,
Cleaves with a mighty surge the foaming
plain,
And with broad torrent rushes in the
main.
Swollen Arar mingles slow its lingering
tide,
That, silent gliding, scarcely seems to
glide:
Caught in the headlong whirlpool,
breaks away,
Snatched through the plains, and start-
ing from delay;
Plunged in the deep the hurried stream
is tost,
And in the greater flood its name is lost.
Alert the troops the bridgeless current
brave,
With head and neck upraised above the
wave,
Secure their steely swords; or firm di-
vide,
With sinewy arms, the strong and bois-
terous tide.
The war-steed, bound on rafts, the river
treads;
Nor the vast elephant retarding dreads
To tempt the ford; while scattered earth
they strow
O'er the hid planks, that hide the stream
below.
Loosed from the banks the gradual cord
extends,
And on the flood the unconscious beast
descends.
As the trooped quadrupeds, down-sliding
slow,
Launched on the stream that, quivering,
dashed, below;
Beneath the incumbent weight, with
starting tide,
The rapid Rhone poured back on every
side:

Tossed its white eddies on the frothy
strand,
And, sullen, murmured on its chafing
sand.
Now stretched the onward host their
long array
Through the Tricastine plains; and
wound their way
O'er smooth ascents, and where Vocon-
tia yields
The level champaign of her verdant
fields.
Athwart their easy march Druentia
spread
The devastation of its torrent bed:
Turbid with stones and trunks of trees,
descends
The Alpine stream; the ashen forests
rends;
Rolls mountain fragments, crumbling to
the shock,
And beats with raving surge the chan-
nelled rock.
Of nameless depth its ever-changing bed
Betrays the fording warrior's faithless
tread;
The broad and flat pontoon is launched
in vain,
High swells the flood with deluges of
rain;
Snatched with his arms the staggering
soldier slides,
And mangled bodies toss in gulfy tides.
But now, the o'erhanging Alps, in pros-
pect near,
Efface remembered toils in future fear.
While with eternal frost, with hailstones
piled,
The ice of ages grasps those summits
wild.
Stiffening with snow the mountain soars
in air,
And fronts the rising sun, unmelted by
the glare.
As the Tartarean gulf, beneath the
ground,
Yawns to the gloomy lake in hell's pro-
found;

So high earth's heaving mass the air invades,
And shrouds the heaven with intercepting shades.
No Spring, no Summer strews its glories here,
Lone Winter dwells upon these summits drear;
And guards his mansion round the endless year,
Mustering from far around his grisly form
Black rains, and hailstone showers, and clouds of storm.
Here in their wrathful kingdom whirlwinds roam,
And the blasts struggle in their Alpine home.
The upward sight a swimming darkness shrouds,
And the high crags recede into the clouds.
First Hercules those untried heights explored,
And 'midst the aerial hills, adventurous, soared;
The Gods beheld him cleave through many a cloud,
While sinking rocks beneath his footsteps bowed:
And striving, leave the vanquished steeps below,
Where never foot had touched the eternal snow.
Did Taurus, piled on Athos, pierce the skies;
And Mimas, heaved on Rhodope, arise;
Hæmus its steepy mass on Othrys roll;
And Pelion, reared on Ossa, shade the pole;
Mountain on mountain would in vain be hurled,
And lessening shrink beside the Alpine world.
A lingering holy dread the soldier bound;
His step hung doubtful, as on sacred ground:
It seemed that Nature's self the access denied;

That their invading arms the Gods defied.
But no rude Alp, no terror of the scene,
Moved Hannibal, undaunted and serene:
Indignant sadness only changed his brow;
As with exhorting words he quickened now
Their languid hopes, and hearts: "What shame were ours,
Tired with the favour of the heavenly Powers;
Sick of our long success, those glorious bays
That crowned the labour of our well-fought days;
To turn our recreant backs on mountain snows,
And slothful yield, where only rocks are foes!
Oh! now my friends, e'en now, believe, ye climb
Despotic Rome's proud walls, and tread, sublime,
The Capitol of Jove! thus, thus we gain
The prize of toil, and Tiber owns our chain."
He spoke; nor they delayed: the troops he drew
Up the steep hills, their promised spoil in view:
Transgressed the Herculean road, and made first known
Tracks yet untrodden and a path their own:
Where inaccessible the desert rose,
He burst a passage through forbidden snows;
He, first, the opposing ridge ascending tried,
And bade the unconquerable cliff subside;
Cheered on the lingering troops; and, beckoning high,
Stood on the crag, and shouted from the sky.
Oft, where the slippery path belied the tread,

And concrete frost the whitening cliff
bespread;
Through the reluctant ice his arm ex-
plored
The upward track, that opened to his
sword.
Oft the thawed surface from the footstep
shrank;
Sucked in the absorbing gulf the war-
riors sank;
Or from high ridge the mass of rush-
ing snow
In humid ruin whelmed the ranks below.
On dusky wings the west-wind swept the
heaven;
Dull in their face the snowy whirls were
driven;
Now from their empty grasp the arms
are torn,
And sudden on the howling whirlwind
borne;
Snatched on the blast, the wrested weap-
ons fly,
And wheel in airy eddies round the sky.
When, striving o'er the ascent, the height
they gain
With planted foot, increasing toils re-
main:
Yet other heights their upward view sur-
prise,
And opening mountains upon mountains
rise.
No joy results from breathless efforts
past;
The plains are won, yet still the moun-
tains last:
Repeated summits fright their aching
eyes,
While one white heap of frost in circling
prospect lies.
Thus in mid-sea, the mariner explores,
With fruitless longing, the receded
shores:
When no fresh wind, with spirit-stirring
gale,
Bends the tall mast, or fills the flagging
sail;
O'er boundless deeps his eyes exhausted
rove,

And rest relieved upon the skies above.
O'er jagged heights, and icy fragments
rude,
Thus climb they, 'midst the mountain
solitude;
And from the rocky summits, haggard,
show
Their half-wild visage, clotted thick with
snow.
Continual drizzlings of the drifting air
Scar their rough cheeks, and stiffen in
their hair.
Now poured from craggy dens, a head-
long force,
The Alpine hordes hang threatening on
their course;
Track the known thickets, beat the
mountain snow,
Bound o'er the steeps, and hovering hem
the foe.
Here changed the scene; the snows were
crimsoned o'er,
The hard ice trickled to the tepid gore.
With pawing hoof **the courser** delved the
ground,
And rigid frost his clinging fetlock
bound:
Nor yet his slippery fall the peril ends;
The fracturing ice the bony socket rends.
Twelve times they **measured** the long
light of day,
And night's black gloom, and urged
through wounds their way;
Till on the topmost ridge their camp
was flung,
High o'er the steepy crags, in airy dis-
stance, hung.

—THOMAS ROSS.

GREEK LEGEND

MEDEA AND JASON

VALERIUS FLACCUS

[From the *Argonautica*, Book VIII]

Practically nothing is known of Gaius
Valerius Flaccus except that he lived and

wrote in the times of Vespasian. His epic poem called *Argonautica* gives evidence of power in the analysis and delineation of character, an ability characteristic of many of the writers of the latter part of the first century.

Romantic love as a theme for literature is rare in Greek and Roman poetry. Valerius Flaccus was influenced, as Virgil had been before him, by Apollonius of Rhodes, who is unique among the ancients in his treatment of the motive.

Trembling within her chamber walls, afraid
Of her own deeds, remained the Colchian maid.
The threats and furies of her father rise
In flitting vision to her wandering eyes:
No more the azure deeps inflict dismay,
And no far land to her is far away.
Whate'er the bark, whate'er the ocean be,
She pants to climb the deck, nor fears the sea.
Then on her virgin fillets she bestowed
A last, last kiss; while tears in torrents flowed:
Clung with fond arms round that deserted bed;
And rent her cheeks and hair: for, ere she fled,
The traces of her ancient dream again
Rose wildering on her melancholy brain.
On the prest couch her grovelling form she throws,
And, thus exclaiming, breathes her parting woes.
"Oh did my father these embraces give,
And fondly bless the wretched fugitive!
Oh could'st thou, most revered Æetes! see
Those streaming tears! for not more loved is he;
No—trust me, father! not more dear than thee!
Oh! that the swelling waves might close above,
And I might perish with the man I love!

My prayers I leave thee: may thy reign endure
To long old age, in placid rest secure:
And other children, oh my father! be
Worthier thy trust, and kinder far than me!"
She said; and drew from caskets, fraught with death,
Drugs prized by Jason to his latest breath:
The magic poisons intricate inrolled
Within her virgin vesture's bosom fold;
With these her jewelled necklace, artful, stored,
And in her mantle wrapped the murderous sword.
Then forth she leaped; as if the Furies urged
Her haste, and with their twisted serpents scourged.
So with scared foot the flying Ino leaps,
Clasping the unheeded babe, among the deeps:
With vain pursuit the husband stretches o'er
The isthmus sands, and raging stamps the shore.
The hero, first, had sought the grove; and stood,
Urged by his anxious hopes, amidst the wood,
Shrouded in shade; yet, seen from far, the grace
Of heavenly beauty flushed his youthful face.
As, while his comrades through the thicket strayed,
The Latmian hunter rested in the shade,
Worthy to draw a goddess from the sky;
And lo! the moon, with crescent veiled, drew nigh.
So, through the mists of overshadowing night,
The bloom of Jason breathed its rosy light;
And, gentle as the moon, amid the grove
Stole the soft form of his expected Love.
Behold! as, trembling, light, on flitting wings

The dove, in darkness, 'gainst the passer
    springs;
So flew Medea, panting with her fears,
To Jason's arms, and he soft-whispering
    cheers
The enfolded maid: and "oh!" he sooth-
    ing cried,
"Oh! of my sacred home the future
    pride!
Thou, virgin, thou alone art worthy
    found
Of all our wanderings, the wide seas
    around;
I ask no fleece; enough if o'er the sea
My vessel waft a prize so fair as thee!
But, since thou canst, let this kind gift
    increase
Thy rich deservings: grant the golden
    fleece.
The precious hide must grace our tasked
    return;
For this my friends in zealous glory
    burn."
  He said: and soft with suppliant kisses
    pressed
Her finger-tips: sobs heaved the virgin's
    breast;
And, with new grief, she cried: "for thy
    dear sake
From country and from realm my flight
    I take:
I speak not as a queen; my sceptre now
Is fallen; the slave of an enamoured
    vow!
Keep then the faith which thou hast
    vowed to me,
The first soft oath, thou knowest, was
    breathed from thee;
Those oaths the Gods have witnessed
    from on high;
The stars behold us from the silent sky.
With thee I tempt the seas: with thee
    explore
Whatever ocean, and whatever shore.
But let me not, on this ill-omened day,
Be torn a culprit from thy arms away;
Nor dragged, with blushes, to my par-
    ents' eyes;
Forbid the shame, ye pitying Deities!

Forbid it, oh my guest!" In bounding
    haste
She rushed, all frantic, through the
    briery waste.
Close at her side the watchful hero
    pressed,
And pitying saw the struggles of her
    breast.
When through the gloom the youth a
    flame surveyed,
And a fierce light shone quivering
    through the shade,
"Whence glows the reddening Heaven?"
    he, trembling, cries;
"What dismal star is gleaming from the
    skies?"
The Virgin answered: "Lo! before thy
    gaze
Askance the dragon's eyes terrific blaze;
And brandished thus, athwart the bur-
    nished air,
From his keen crest the lightning splen-
    dours glare.
Me only he discerns; in fawning mood,
Crouching, with softened hiss he craves
    his food.
Say now if thou wilt tear the spoil from
    high,
While on his foe is bent that watchful
    eye;
Or shall my art his glance in slumber
    shade,
And, first, the serpent at thy feet be
    laid!"
  Silent he stood: the magic maid im-
    pressed
So deep a horror on his heaving breast.
The Colchian princess lifts her hands in
    air,
And scatters towards the stars her
    streaming hair.
While chanted rhymes barbaric cadence
    keep,
Her moving lips invoke the Sire of sleep:
  "Hear, mighty Sleep! the Colchian
    virgin's call!
Where'er thou lingerest on this earthly
    ball.

I bid thee haste from all beneath the
pole,
And rush collected on the serpent's soul!
Oft have I poured thy horn's oblivious
dew
To still the rapid lightning, as it flew:
The surging seas; the turbid clouds on
high;
The sparkling stars, and meteors of the
sky.
I call thee now in all thy mightiest
power:
Come like thy brother death, in this
momentous hour.
Guard of the golden fleece! let sleep al-
lay
Thy restless watching: turn thine eyes
away.
At length 'tis time: what treachery canst
thou fear,
The Colchian maid, thy own Medea,
near?
Myself will guard the grove, and watch
the while;
Then let repose thy long, long toils be-
guile."
  He not relaxed his weary folds; but
feared
The rest permitted, and by toil en-
deared:
Yet slumbering felt the cloud of slumber
creep,
And from the branches shook the balm
of sleep.
The Colchian maid her foaming venoms
threw,
And waved the bough, immersed in
Lethe's dew:
With chanted rhyme she lulls his droop-
ing eyes,
With hand and tongue the Stygian charm
she plies;
And still persists: till whelming slum-
ber holds
The burning wrath that writhes his
struggling folds.
He falls his crest: he droops his languid
head;

And lies, beyond the fleece, in trailing
volumes spread:
Like refluent Po, or Nile of sevenfold
train,
Or Alpheus winding o'er Hesperia's
plain.
But when Medea saw the folds unwound,
And her loved dragon grovelling on the
ground;
Cast at her length, her clasping arms she
threw;
And, "Ah! not such thou met'st Medea's
view,
When yesternight thy opening jaws I
fed,
With honeyed cates, and medicated
bread.
How moveless is thy weight! how slow
thy breath!
At least my hand is guiltless of thy
death.
Unhappy serpent! when in evil day
Thy eyes no glittering fleece beneath
the bough survey.
Yield to the God; and seek a happier lot
In other groves, the faithless maid for-
got.
Nor may thy well-known hiss thy flight
pursue
From sea to sea; my keen remorse renew.
But thou, oh Jason! tremble at delay:
Haste, snatch the fleece, and bear thy
prize away.
By my pernicious arts, my injured sire
Has seen his brazen-footed bulls expire;
Spell-doomed by me the earth-born
giants bled;
Stretched at thy feet the dragon bows his
head;
Now may I hope the crown of guilt is
won;
Now all is finished; now my crimes are
done."
  Then, while he questioned how, with
grappling hold,
To reach the elm-tree top, that waved
with gold;
  "On, on," she cried; "and o'er the
dragon's mail

With firm-pressed foot the height as-
    cending scale."
He lingered not; but at the maid's be-
    hest,
With firm set heel the bulky serpent
    pressed;
And to the ærial elm ascending clung,
On whose tall boughs the hide resplend-
    ent hung:
Like fiery clouds, that flush with ruddy
    glare,
Or Iris, gliding through the purple air;
When loosely girt her dazzling mantle
    flows,
And 'gainst the sun in arching colours
    glows.
Exulting Jason grasped the shining hide,
His last of labours, and his envied pride.
Slow from the groaning branch the fleece
    was rent;
Of Phryxus' flight the splendid monument
For years long past: the tree reluctant
    bends,
And sudden darkness o'er its top de-
    scends.
    Emerging from the wood, they took
    their way
Through plains that glanced beneath
    the gleaming ray,
To where the river opened in a bay.
His limbs and back are wrapt in shaggy
    gold,
His left arm mantled in the glistening
    fold:
So from Nemea's den Alcides strode,
The lion's yellow spoil around his shoul-
    ders flowed.
Now, where his friends their destined
    station hold,
He breaks the darkness, garmented in
    gold:
The Thracians shout: instinctive Argo
    glides
Swift to the bank; self-moving through
    the tides.
With steps impetuous Jason trod the
    shore;
The fleece of downy gold he sent before.

Then, with the maid, who shrank in
    wondering fear,
Leaped on the deck, and couched his
    quivering spear.
Dread horrors now the parents' ears af-
    fright,
Their fated house, the virgin's fraud, and
    flight:
In sudden arms the brother blazed along,
And the moved city poured its gathering
    throng:
While, nerved with anguish of indignant
    rage,
Æetes flew, forgetful of his age.
With bristling spears in vain the shores
    are lined;
The darted vessel flies before the wind.
Distracted on the shore the mother
    stands,
And towards the boundless ocean spreads
    her hands.
The sister, every mother, every bride,
Hang round her steps, and hover o'er the
    tide:
Thy sweet companions, oh deluded fair!
The partners of thy virgin sports are
    there:
Wild, starting from the rest, the mother
    flies
And fills the air with shrieks and agonies:
    "Stay thy rash flight! and from the
    distant main,
For oh! thou canst, my daughter! turn
    again!
Whither depart? the vessel backward
    steer;
Thy friends, thy still fond father, wait
    thee here.
Here is thy own hereditary sway:
Then why to Greece, in trusting rash-
    ness, stray?
What place to thee will Grecian maids
    resign;
A foreign virgin, say, what claims are
    thine?
Is this the house? are these the wedding
    ties?
Is this the day to bless my aged eyes?
Oh! might I with a vulture's talons rend

That robber's cheeks! His very deck
    ascend;
And, audible, in clear and piercing
    strain,
Demand my daughter at his hands
    again?
The Albanian monarch's bride the maid
    should be;
No compact, Jason! had we joined with
    thee:
No amorous theft did Pelias' lips com-
    mand;
No rape of virgins from our Colchian
    strand.
Thine be the golden fleece! unenvied,
    thine!—
Nay more—our temple's treasures we
    resign.
But why these wild unjust reproaches
    give?
She is, herself, the willing fugitive:
So glows her breast to guilty love re-
    signed;
How every truth comes thronging on my
    mind!
Since the Thessalian vessel touched the
    shore,
Thy food, sad maid! thy pastime pleased
    no more;
Thy colour paled; thou would'st in mur-
    murs speak;
The flushing red came wandering o'er
    thy cheek;
And the gay smile, that flashed its tran-
    sient grace,
But shone reflected from another's face.
Why was the dreadful mischief not dis-
    closed?
Then Jason were our son: nor thou ex-
    posed
To shameful flight; or I at least had
    known
To share a crime which now is all thy
    own;
Had shared thy wanderings o'er the
    boundless sea,
And trod Thessalia's distant soil with
    thee:

In what far town that cruel stranger
    dwell,
Had I been with thee, it had then been
    well!"

    She spoke, in loud and passionate la-
    ment:
With shrieks the shrilling air the sister
    rent:
Alike the damsels to the winds exclaim,
With empty words, and call the nymph
    by name:
But thee, far off, the ocean gales convey,
And thy fates waft thee on the destined
    way.

—WHYTE.

HYPSIPYLE'S LAMENT

STATIUS

[From the *Thebais*, Book V]

Publius Papinius Statius (about 60 to
about 96) was the author of an epic poem
entitled *Thebais* and of a fragment of
another entitled *Achilleis*. He wrote also
a number of occasional poems on contemporary incidents and persons collected
under the title *Silvæ*. He was one of a
group of poets who secured their standing
under Domitian by methods of gross flattery.

As now Hypsipyle, the serpent slain,
Sees her lost infant on the spacious
    plain,
Upon a distant eminence she spy'd
The with'ring grass with drops of slaugh-
    ter dy'd:
Hither in haste the beauteous mourner
    flies,
And soon, too soon the killing object
    eyes.
In vain from words she seeks a short
    relief,
In vain in tears to vent her swelling
    grief;
Short of its course the pearly current
    hung,

And to the roof inactive cleaves the
tongue.
One while she kisses his discolour'd
cheeks,
Then thro' his limbs life's luke-warm
passage seeks
In vain, his face and breast misplac'd,
are drown'd
In blood, and the whole body seems one
wound.
As when the bird, whose nest in search
of food
Some serpent climb'd, and crush'd the
tender brood,
Returning, finds her clam'rous infants
gone,
And blood and scatter'd feathers left
alone,
She drops the meat, and spurns the nest
away;
The grove responsive echoes to her lay.
Soon as the wretch had in her lap with
care
Repos'd his limbs, and dry'd them with
her hair,
Her voice, releas'd from sad excess of
grief,
A passage found, and thus she sought
relief.
"O thou, whose form and features oft
have brought
My own dear offspring's image to my
thought,
Whose soft caresses could alone abate
The pangs of exile and a servile state:
Say, whence these wounds? what god
could thus disgrace
Thy faultless figure, and thy charms ef-
face?
I left thee fresh in life, in beauty gay,
Engag'd in pleasure, and amus'd with
play.
Where now are all those sweet attempts
to speak,
The sparkling eye and rose-resembling
cheek?
Where are those artful smiles, that lisp-
ing tone

To me address'd, and known to me
alone?
How to procure thee slumbers did I toil,
And talk of Argo, and thy native soil!
How have I press'd thee in my folding
arms,
And gaz'd and doated on thy budding
charms?
Thus sooth'd, I could forget I was a
slave;
To thee my breast, another's right, I
gave:
Now ready to thy mouth descends again
The middle current, but descends in vain.
Nor were there omens wanting to dis-
close
His fate, and warn me of impending
woes:
Amidst the dusky horrours of the night
The Cyprian goddess stood confest to
sight.
But why should I the fatal act disclaim,
And to the guiltless gods transfer the
blame?
My speedy death shall for the crime
atone,
'Tis thus decreed, nor seek I death to
shun.
Say, could I thus forget my precious
care,
While, urg'd by vain ambition, I declare
My daring country's fortune and my
own,
And court the transient blazes of re-
nown?
Lemnos, no more against thy queen ex-
claim,
Our guilt is equal, our disgrace the same.
If this entreaty merits your regard,
If my past service claims this small re-
ward,
Lead me, O quickly to the serpent lead,
Or with your swords absolve my impious
deed.
Oh! never may these eyes behold again
The sire, or injur'd partner of his reign:
Tho' (what can scarcely merit your be-
lief)
My own would equal her severest grief.

Ere from these hands she take th' ungrateful load,
Th' ungrateful load, unhappily bestow'd,
May yawning earth a sudden passage rend,
And let me thro' the dark abyss descend."

—W. L. Lewis.

The Abode of Sleep

STATIUS

[From the *Thebais*, Book X]

Far on the confines of the western main,
Where Æthiopia bounds her wide domain,
There stands a grove, that casts a shade afar,
Impenetrable to the brightest star,
Beneath whose hollow rocks a cave descends
Of depth immense, and in the mountain ends.
Here all-disposing Nature fix'd th' abode
Of Somnus, and secur'd the drowsy god.
Sloth, who scarce knows an interval from sleep,
Rest motionless, and dark Oblivion keep
Eternal sentry at the gloomy gate:
There listless Ease, and awful Silence sate
With close-contracted wings, and, still as Death,
Repel the winds, and hush each murmur's breath:
No rustling foliage here is heard to move,
No feather'd songsters warble through the grove;
No lightnings glare, no crashing thunders roar,
No foamy waves, rebounding from the shore.
The neighb'ring stream along the valley glides,
And rolls between the rocks his noiseless tides.

The sable herds and flocks from food abstain,
Or only graze, recumbent on the plain:
Nor stops th' infection here, but spreads around,
And withers herbs just springing from the ground.
Within, a thousand statues of the god
Were grav'd by Vulcan.—Here was seen to nod
Pleasure, with overacted joys oppress'd,
And healthful toil, ne'er physick'd into rest.
There Love from am'rous cares a respite stole,
And Bacchus snor'd o'er a half-finish'd bowl.
Deep, deep within, Death, his half-brother, lies,
His face was void of terror, clos'd his eyes.
Beneath the dew-bespangled cavern lay
The god himself and dos'd his cares away.
The roof was verdant; his own poppies spread
A carpet soft, and swell'd the rising bed.
His mouth, half-shut, breathes soporific steams,
And his warm vests exhale the vap'ry streams.
One hand sustains his head; the horn drops down,
Unheeded, from his other torpid grown.
A thousand various dreams attend their chief,
Truths mix'd with falsehood, joys alloy'd with grief:
The sons of darkness these, and night's black hosts,
On earth they lie, or cleave to beams and posts.
Some slender glimm'rings faintly shine between,
And serve to make the gloom more clearly seen.

—W. L. Lewis.

IV. SATIRIZING THE PRESENT

THE BANQUET OF THE NEWLY RICH [1]

PETRONIUS

[From the *Satyricon*]

Petronius, the author of the *Satyricon*, is now generally identified with the arbiter of taste of the court of Nero. The date of his birth is not known; the manner of his death by suicide in the year 66 is fully described by Tacitus in his *Annals*. His book is the first example in literature of the novel of manners. It narrates the adventures of certain more or less educated unscrupulous roustabouts on a journey in southern Italy. It is in the form of Menippean satire, that is, a somewhat haphazard mixture of prose and verse. In order to obtain an objective view of urban society for the purpose of satirizing it, the author puts the narrative in the mouth of Encolpius, a freedman from a provincial town. Only fragments of the work are extant.

The hero describes a dinner of a certain vulgar untutored Trimalchio, who, having amassed a fortune, sets about aping the fashionable society of the capital in accordance with his conception of it.

At last then we sat down, and boys from Alexandria poured water cooled with snow over our hands. Others followed and knelt down at our feet, and proceeded with great skill to pare our hangnails. Even this unpleasant duty did not silence them, but they kept singing at their work. I wanted to find out whether the whole household could sing, so I asked for a drink. A ready slave repeated my order in a chant not less shrill. They all did the same if they were asked to hand anything. It was more like an actor's dance than a gentleman's dining-room. But some rich and tasty whets for the appetite were brought on; for every one had now

sat down except Trimalchio, who had the first place kept for him in the new style. A donkey in Corinthian bronze stood on the side-board, with panniers holding olives, white in one side, black in the other. Two dishes hid the donkey; Trimalchio's name and their weight in silver was engraved on their edges. There were also dormice rolled in honey and poppy-seed, and supported on little bridges soldered to the plate. Then there were hot sausages laid on a silver grill, and under the grill damsons and seeds of pomegranate.

While we were engaged with these delicacies, Trimalchio was conducted in to the sound of music, propped on the tiniest of pillows. A laugh escaped the unwary. His head was shaved and peered out of a scarlet cloak, and over the heavy clothes on his neck he had put on a napkin with a broad stripe and fringes hanging from it all round. On the little finger of his left hand he had an enormous gilt ring, and on the top joint of the next finger a smaller ring which appeared to me to be entirely gold, but was really set all round with iron cut out in little stars. Not content with this display of wealth, he bared his right arm, where a golden bracelet shone, and an ivory bangle clasped with a plate of bright metal. Then he said, as he picked his teeth with a silver quill, "It was not convenient for me to come to dinner yet, my friends, but I gave up all my pleasure; I did not like to stay away any longer and keep you waiting. But you will not mind if I finish my game?" A boy followed him with a table of terebinth wood and crystal pieces, and I noticed the prettiest thing possible. Instead of black and white counters they used gold and silver coins. Trimalchio kept passing every kind of remark as he played, and we were still busy with the hors d'œuvres, when a tray was brought in with a basket on it, in which there was a hen made of wood, spreading out her wings as they do when they are sitting. The music grew loud: two slaves at once came up and began to hunt in the straw. Peahen's eggs were pulled out and handed to the guests. Trimalchio turned his head to look, and said, "I gave orders, my friends, that peahen's eggs should be put under a common hen. And upon my oath I am afraid they are hard-set by now. But we will try whether they are still fresh enough to suck." We took our spoons, half-a-pound in weight at least, and hammered at the eggs, which were balls of fine meal. I was on the point of throwing away my portion. I thought a peachick had already formed. But hearing a practised diner say, "What treasure have we here?" I poked through the shell with my finger, and found a fat becafico rolled up in spiced yolk of egg.

Trimalchio had now stopped his game, and asked for all the same dishes, and in a loud voice invited any of us, who wished, to take a second glass of mead. Suddenly the music gave the sign, and the light dishes were swept away by a troop of singing servants. An entrée-dish happened to fall in the rush, and a boy picked it up from the ground. Trimalchio saw him, and directed that he should be punished by a box on the ear, and made to throw down the dish again. A chairman followed and began to sweep out the silver with a broom among the other rubbish. The two long-haired Ethiopians with little wine-skins, just like the men who scatter sand in an amphitheatre, came in and gave us wine to wash our hands in, for no one offered us water.

We complimented our host on his arrangements. "Mars loves a fair field," said he, "and so I gave orders that every one should have a separate table. In that way these filthy slaves will not make us so hot by crowding past us."

Just then some glass jars carefully fastened with gypsum were brought on, with labels tied to their necks, inscribed, "Falernian of Opimius's vintage, 100 years in the bottle." As we were poring over the labels Trimalchio clapped his hands and cried, "Ah me, so wine lives longer than miserable man. So let us be merry. Wine is life. I put on real wine of Opimius's year. I produced some inferior stuff yesterday, and there was a much finer set of people to dinner." As we drank and admired each luxury in detail, a slave brought in a silver skeleton, made so that its limbs and spine could be moved and bent in every direction. He put it down once or twice on the table so that the supple joints showed several attitudes, and Trimalchio said appropriately: "Alas for us poor mortals, all that poor man is is nothing. So we shall all be, after the world below takes us away. Let us live then while it goes well with us."

After we had praised this outburst a dish followed, not at all of the size we expected; but its novelty drew every eye to it. There was a round plate with the twelve signs of the Zodiac set in order, and on each one the artist had laid some food fit and proper to the symbol; over the Ram ram's-head pease, a piece of beef on the Bull, kidneys over the Twins, over the Crab a crown, an African fig over the Lion, a barren sow's paunch over Virgo, over Libra a pair of scales with a muffin on one side and a cake on the other, over Scorpio a small sea-fish, over Sagittarius a bull's-eye, over Capricornus a lobster, over Aquarius a goose, over Pisces two mullets. In the middle lay a honeycomb on a sod of turf with the green grass on it. An Egyptian boy took bread round in a silver chafing-dish. . . .

Trimalchio himself too ground out a tune from the musical comedy "Assafœtida" in a most hideous voice. We came to such an evil entertainment rather depressed. "Now," said Trimalchio, "let us have dinner. This is sauce for dinner." As he spoke, four dancers ran up in time with the music and took off the top part of the dish. Then we saw in the well of it fat fowls and sow's bellies, and in the middle a hare got up with wings to look like Pegasus. . . . Trimalchio was delighted with the trick he had played us, and said, "Now, Carver." The man came up at once, and making flourishes in time with the music pulled the dish to pieces; you would have said that a gladiator in a chariot was fighting to the accompaniment of a water-organ. Still Trimalchio kept on in a soft voice, "Oh, Carver, Carver." I thought this word over and over again must be part of a joke, and I made bold to ask the man who sat next to me this very question. He had seen performances of this kind more often. "You see the fellow who is carving his way through the meat? Well, his name is Carver. So whenever Trimalchio says the word, you have his name, and he has his orders."

I was now unable to eat any more, so I turned to my neighbor to get as much news as possible. I began to seek for far-fetched stories, and to inquire who the woman was who kept running about everywhere. "She is Trimalchio's wife Fortunata," he said, "and she counts her money by the bushel. And what was she a little while ago? You will pardon me if I say that you would not have taken a piece of bread from her hand. Now without why or wherefore she is queen of Heaven, and Trimalchio's all in all. In fact, if she tells him that it is dark at high noon, he will believe it. He is so enormously rich that he does not know himself what he has; but this lynx-eyed woman has a plan for everything, even where you would not think it. She is temperate, sober, and prudent, but she has a nasty tongue, and henpecks him on his own sofa. Whom she likes, she likes; whom she dislikes, she dislikes. Trimalchio has estates wherever a kite can fly in a day, is a millionaire of millionaires. There is more plate lying in his steward's

room than other people have in their whole fortunes. And his slaves! My word! I really don't believe that one out of ten of them knows his master by sight. Why he can knock any of these young louts into a nettle-bed if he chooses. You must not suppose either that he buys anything. Everything is home-grown: wool, citrons, pepper; you can have cock's milk for the asking. Why, his wool was not growing of fine enough quality. He bought rams from Tarentum and sent them into his flocks with a smack behind. He had bees brought from Athens to give him Attic honey on the premises; the Roman-born bees incidentally will be improved by the Greeks. Within the last few days, I may say, he has written for a cargo of mushroom spawn from India. . . . But do not look down on the other freedmen who are his friends. They are very juicy people. That one you see lying at the bottom of the end sofa, has his eight hundred thousand. He was quite a nobody. A little time ago he was carrying loads of wood on his back. People do say—I know nothing, but I have heard—that he pulled off a goblin's cap and found a fairy hoard. If God makes presents I am jealous of nobody. Still, he shows the marks of his master's fingers, and has a fine opinion of himself. So he has just put up a notice on his hovel: 'This attic, the property of Caius Pompeius Diogenes, to let from the 1st of July, the owner having purchased a house.' That person there too who is lying in the freedman's place is well pleased with himself. I do not blame him. He had his million in his hands, but he has had a bad shaking. I believe he cannot call his hair his own. No fault of his I am sure; there is no better fellow alive; but it is the damned freedmen who have pocketed everything. You know how it is: the company's pot goes off the boil, and the moment business takes a bad turn your friends desert you. You see him in this state: and what a fine trade he drove! He was an undertaker. He used to dine like a prince: boars cooked in a cloth, wonderful sweet things, game, chefs and confectioners! There used to be more wine spilt under the table than many a man has in his cellars. He was a fairy prince, not a mortal. When his business was failing, and he was afraid his creditors might guess that he was going bankrupt, he advertised a sale in this fashion: "Caius Julius Proculus will offer for sale some articles for which he has no further use."

—MICHAEL HESELTINE.

A PRACTICAL EDUCATION [1]

PETRONIUS

[From the *Satyricon*]

The controversy over the value of the study of literature in the scheme of education is at least as old as Petronius.

I have another boy who is no scholar, but very inquiring, and can teach you more than he knows himself. So on holidays he generally comes home, and is quite pleased whatever you give him. I bought the child some books with red-letter headings in them a little time ago. I want him to have a smack of the law in order to manage the property. Law has bread and butter in it. He has dipped quite deep enough into literature. If he is restless, I mean to have him learn a trade, a barber or an auctioneer, or at least a barrister, something that he can carry to the grave with him. So I drum it into him every day: 'Mark my words, Primigenius, whatever you learn, you learn for your own good. Look at Phileros, the barrister: if he had not worked, he would not be keeping the wolf from the door to-day. It is not so long since he used to carry things round

[1] From The Loeb Classical Library, reprinted by permission.

on his back and sell them, and now he makes a brave show even against Norbanus. Yes, education is a treasure, and culture never dies.'

—MICHAEL HESELTINE.

THE CONNOISSEUR [1]

PETRONIUS

[From the *Satyricon*]

To the newly rich sound appreciation of art is as simple a matter as the adequate acquisition of historical and mythological learning.

The cook too was rewarded with a drink and a silver crown, and was handed the cup on a Corinthian dish. Agamemnon began to peer at the dish rather closely, and Trimalchio said, "I am the sole owner of genuine Corinthian plate." I thought he would declare with his usual effrontery that he had cups imported direct from Corinth. But he went one better: "You may perhaps inquire," said he, "how I come to be alone in having genuine Corinthian stuff: the obvious reason is that the name of the dealer I buy from is Corinthus. But what is real Corinthian, unless a man has Corinthus at his back? Do not imagine that I am an Ignoramus. I know perfectly well how Corinthian plate was first brought into the world. At the fall of Ilium, Hannibal, a trickster and a great knave, collected all the sculptures, bronze, gold, and silver, into a single pile, and set light to them. They all melted into one amalgam of bronze. The workmen took bits out of this lump and made plates and entrée dishes and statuettes. That is how Corinthian metal was born, from all sorts lumped together, neither one kind nor the other. You will forgive me if I say that personally I prefer glass; glass at least does not smell. If it were not so breakable I should prefer it to gold; as it is, it is so cheap. But there was once a workman who made a glass cup that was unbreakable. So he was given an audience of the Emperor with his invention; he made Cæsar give it back to him and then threw it on the floor. Cæsar was as frightened as could be. But the man picked up his cup from the ground: it was dinted like a bronze bowl; then he took a little hammer out of his pocket and made the cup quite sound again without any trouble. After doing this he thought he had himself seated on the throne of Jupiter, especially when Cæsar said to him: 'Does anyone else know how to blow glass like this?' Just see what happened. He said not, and then Cæsar had him beheaded. Why? Because if his invention were generally known we should treat gold like dirt. Myself I have a great passion for silver. I own about a hundred four-gallon cups engraved with Cassandra killing her children, and they lying there dead in the most life-like way. I have a thousand jugs which Mummius left to my patron, and on them you see Dædalus shutting Niobe into the Trojan horse. And I have got the fights between Hermeros and Petraites on my cups, and every cup is a heavy one; for I do not sell my connoisseurship for any money."

—Michael Heseltine.

Trimalchio's Tombstone [1]

PETRONIUS

[From the *Satyricon*]

Trimalchio is at one with the average Roman in his desire for an elaborate tombstone which shall secure for him the benefits of earthly immortality.

[1] From The Loeb Classical Library, reprinted by permission.

Then he looked at Habinnas and said, "Now tell me, my dear friend: you will erect a monument as I have directed? I beg you earnestly to put up round the feet of my statue my little dog, and some wreaths, and bottles of perfume, and all the fights of Petraites, so that your kindness may bring me a life after death; and I want the monument to have a frontage of one hundred feet and to be two hundred feet in depth. For I should like to have all kinds of fruit growing round my ashes, and plenty of vines. It is quite wrong for a man to decorate his house while he is alive, and not to trouble about the house where he must make a longer stay. So above all things I want added to the inscription, 'This monument is not to descend to my heir.' I shall certainly take care to provide in my will against any injury being done to me when I am dead. I am appointing one of the freedmen to be caretaker of the tomb and prevent the common people from running up and defiling it. I beg you to put ships in full sail on the monument, and me sitting in official robes on my official seat, wearing five gold rings and distributing coin publicly out of a bag; you remember that I gave a free dinner worth two denarii a head. I should like a dining-room table put in too, if you can arrange it. And let me have the whole people there enjoying themselves. On my right hand put a statue of dear Fortunata holding a dove, and let her be leading a little dog with a waistband on; and my dear little boy, and big jars sealed with gypsum, so that the wine may not run out. And have a broken urn carved with a boy weeping over it. And a sundial in the middle, so that anyone who looks at the time will read my name whether he likes it or not. And again, please think carefully whether this inscription seems to you quite appropriate: 'Here lieth Caius Pompeius Trimalchio, freedman of

Mæcenas. The degree of Priest of Augustus was conferred upon him in his absence. He might have been attendant on any magistrate in Rome, but refused it. God-fearing, gallant, constant, he started with very little and left thirty millions. He never listened to a philosopher. Fare thee well, Trimalchio: and thou too, passer-by.' "

After saying this, Trimalchio began to weep floods of tears. Fortunata wept, Habinnas wept, and then all the slaves began as if they had been invited to his funeral, and filled the dining-room with lamentation. I had even begun to lift up my voice myself, when Trimalchio said, "Well, well, if we know we must die, why should we not live? As I hope for your happiness, let us jump into a bath. My life on it, you will never regret it. It is as hot as a furnace." "Very true, very true," said Habinnas, "making two days out of one is my chief delight." And he got up with bare feet and began to follow Trimalchio, who was clapping his hands.

—MICHAEL HESELTINE.

THE LOST ARTS [1]

PETRONIUS

[From the *Satyricon*]

At every period men locate the golden age in the past. The writers of the first century have so much to say about the decay of this, that, and the other thing, that Petronius is prompted to satirize the whole point of view.

I began to draw on his knowledge about the age of the pictures, and about some of the stories which puzzled me, and at the same time to discuss the decadence of the age, since the fine arts had died, and painting, for instance, had left

[1] From The Loeb Classical Library, reprinted by permission.

no trace of its existence behind. "Love of money began this revolution," he replied. "In former ages virtue was still loved for her own sake, the noble arts flourished, and there were the keenest struggles among mankind to prevent anything being long undiscovered which might benefit posterity. So Democritus extracted the juice of every plant on earth, and spent his whole life in experiments to discover the virtues of stones and twigs. Eudoxos grew old on the top of a high mountain in order to trace the movements of the stars and the sky, and Chrysippus three times cleared his wits with hellebore to improve his powers of invention. If you turn to sculptors, Lysippus died of starvation as he brooded over the lines of a single statue, and Myron, who almost caught the very soul of men and beasts in bronze, left no heir behind him. But we are besotted with wine and women, and cannot rise to understand even the arts that are developed; we slander the past, and learn and teach nothing but vices. Where is dialectic now, or astronomy? Where is the exquisite way of wisdom? Who has ever been to a temple and made an offering in order to attain to eloquence, or to drink of the waters of philosophy? They do not even ask for good sense or good health, but before they even touch the threshold of the Capitol, one promises an offering if he may bury his rich neighbor, another if he may dig up a hid treasure, another if he may make thirty millions in safety. Even the Senate, the teachers of what is right and good, often promise a thousand pounds in gold to the Capitol, and decorate even Jupiter with pelf, that no one need be ashamed of praying for money. So there is nothing surprising in the decadence of painting, when all the gods and men think an ingot of gold more beautiful than anything those poor crazy Greeks, Apelles and Phidias, ever did."

MICHAEL HESELTINE.

An Explanation [1]

MARTIAL

[*Epigrams* IV, 65]

For Martial, see above, p. 505.

Philænis weeps with just one eye.
   Queer, is it not?
You wish you knew the reason why?
   That's all she's got.
                    —Paul Nixon.

To Lupus [1]

MARTIAL

[*Epigrams* XI, 18]

You gave me a farm—so you called it,
      at least,
   In a sort of rhetorical turn—
But I'm forced to relate that the total
      estate
   Doesn't hold as much dirt as an urn.

A grove of Diana, you told me, I think
   Was a notable sight on the place:
But beyond one poor beet, overcome by
      the heat,
   Of grove I deny there's a trace.

The wing of a cricket would cover that
      farm,
   And an overfed ant with the gout
Couldn't find enough crops to tickle his
      chops
   To last till the sun flickered out.

Moreover that garden you bragged so
      about
   Proves a worm-eaten rose with one leaf,
And the lawn's yield of grass doesn't
      greatly surpass
   Its produce of gravy and beef.

[1] From *A Roman Wit*, by Paul Nixon, reprinted by permission of the author.

A cucumber hasn't got room to lie
      straight,
   And a snake's bound to live there in
      pieces.
A grasshopper hopped just one day and
      then stopped—
   Starved to death, with its stomach in
      creases.

A mole is the sole agriculturist there,
   And he's hardly got room to turn
      round.
Why, a mushroom can't spread, or a
      flower wave its head
   Sans trespass on my neighbor's ground.

An undergrown mouse when he gets at
      that farm
   Makes it look as though hit by the
      plague,
And my whole crop of hay was carried
      away
   By a thrush hardly out of the egg.

A statue of Pan—minus head, legs, and
      trunk—
   Casts its shade over all the domain;
And the shell of a clam, without sign of
      a jam,
   My harvest complete can contain.

Now pardon, my friend, if my praise has
      been faint—
   We can seldom express what we feel:
So I merely will add that I'd be mighty
      glad
   To swap farm for a thirty-cent meal.
                    —Paul Nixon.

Tailor Bills [1]

MARTIAL

[*Epigrams* II, 58]

You laughed at my toga, friend Zoilus,
      as worn,
   While the new one you wore fairly
      shone.

I forgot to remark, overcome by your
    scorn:
"My toga, though worn, is my own."
      —PAUL NIXON.

A MISUNDERSTANDING [1]

MARTIAL

[*Epigrams* II, 41]

"O smile, maiden, smile, if you care to be
    wise,"
  The Pelignian bard, I think, said.
If you dream, though, this counsel to all
    girls applies,
  Get the notion right out of your head.

Even though he meant all girls he
    would'nt mean you,
  For you know you're no girl now,
    Maxime:
Why, you've got but three teeth, if
    you've got more than two;
  And they're pitch-covered bone, it
    would seem.

In your mirror and me put unwavering
    trust;
  Dread a smile as rouged Lais dreads
    rain,
As Priscus, the dandy, dreads wind and
    the dust,
  As Sabella the sun on her stain.

Andromache's, Hecuba's look wouldn't
    do.
  Why, for you it's too merry by half.
Keep from comedies, banquets; be sure
    and eschew
  Doubtful jokes that might tempt you
    to laugh.

Always sit by some mother who's mourn-
    ing a son,
  By a wife as her loved husband dies.

[1] From *A Roman Wit*, by Paul Nixon, reprinted by permission of the author.

Go only to tragedies: gayety shun,
  And weep, maiden, weep, if you're wise.
      —PAUL NIXON.

THE BEAU [1]

MARTIAL

[*Epigrams* III, 63]

You are everywhere thought just too
    lovely to live.
  You must be: I hear and believe it.
But, Cotilus, pray be so good as to say
  What's a lovely man, as you conceive
    it?

"Well, a lovely man must have his hair
    combed and curled,
  Of perfumes he mustn't be chary,
Must hum the last strain from the Nile
    and from Spain,
  Must dance well and mustn't be hairy.

"He must linger all day by some lady
    friend's chair,
  With murmured remarks must regale
    her,
Must get billets doux and respond to
    them, too;
  Must be firm and precise with his
    tailor.

"He must always be posted on every
    intrigue
  And must whirl in the gay social
    vortex;
Each family tree through all years A.U.C.
  He must know from medulla to cortex."

That will do! This will make a man
    lovely, you say?
  I'm not in position to doubt it—
But when I want to pass for a thorough-
    bred ass
  I can see how I'd best set about it.
      —PAUL NIXON.

FROM THE WEST [1]

MARTIAL

[*Epigrams* III, 38]

Why, hullo, Sextus! Left the farm?
　　Well, here's a how-do-do!
What rustic hope or horoscope
　　Fills Rome with chaps like you?

How's that? You'll be a Cicero?
　　Surprising legal bent?
Poor C—, you knew. Just his thought,
　　too.
　　But he can't make his rent.

Indeed! You'll be a poet, then?
　　Make Virgil's verses seem flat?
See those poor coots in cast-off suits?
　　They're Virgils all—*verb. sat.*

Oho! You'll sponge on plutocrats?
　　My boy, you're rather late.
Just three men say they're fed that way;
　　The rest are losing weight.

You want advice? You're bound to stay?
　　No scruples, then, but pluck.
And with a share of *savoir faire*
　　You may exist—with luck.
　　　　　　　—PAUL NIXON.

A TOTAL ABSTAINER [1]

MARTIAL

[*Epigrams* IV, 69]

Though you serve richest wines,
Paulus, Rumor opines
　　That they poisoned your four wives, I
　　think.
It's of course all a lie;
None believes less than I—
　　No, I really don't care for a drink.
　　　　　　　—PAUL NIXON.

[1] From *A Roman Wit*, by Paul Nixon, reprinted by permission of the author.

THERMOMETRICAL [1]

MARTIAL

[*Epigrams* V, 79]

A full dozen times, Zoilus, during a meal
　　You arise and make slaves change
　　your clothes.
You perspire, you observe, and when
　　damp fear the breeze,—
　　No matter how lightly it blows.
Don't I, too, perspire, since I'm dining
　　with you,
　　And sit at your right as a rule?
No, a poor man is not so affected by
　　heat—
　　I own but one suit and keep cool.
　　　　　　　—PAUL NIXON.

NOR A LENDER BE [*]

MARTIAL

[*Epigrams* II, 44]

I can't buy a toga, a slave, or some books
　　To give to my study a tone,
　　　　But an old friend of mine
　　　　In the 12 p. c. line
　　At once fears requests for a loan.

By way of prevention he'll seem most
　　distrait
　　When I meet him and stop to converse;
　　　　In soliloquy he—
　　　　But he means it for me—
　　Will lament the sad state of his purse.

"Four thousand due Phœbus, Philetas
　　owed ten,
　　And Secundus, well, seven, at best—
　　　　Eh-eh, what did you say?
　　　　Yes, it *is* a fine day—
　　And I haven't a cent in my chest."

It's mean to refuse one a loan when it's
　　asked:
　　To do so before is too much.

Friend, Sextus, it's shrewd
But it's frightfully rude
To preclude the bare chance of a touch.
—PAUL NIXON.

TO LAWYER POSTUMUS [1]

MARTIAL

[*Epigrams* VI, 19]

It's no case of murder, or poison, or rape
That I've paid you to plead, my dear
sir:
It's there in your notes;
I want my three goats
That a near neighbor stole, I aver.

The proof of this claim's what the judge
wants to hear:
Kindly let Mithridatic wars drop.
The Cannæ defeat
And Punic deceit
In this case seem rather *de trop.*

On Marius, Sulla, and Mucius, I think,
We've dined long enough *table d'hôte:*
Save some of your strength
And struggle at length
To flavor your discourse with goat.
—PAUL NIXON.

THE SHOPPER [1]

MARTIAL

[*Epigrams* IX, 59]

For hours without stopping
Mamurra goes shopping
Where golden Rome's grand bazaar
lies:
Comely slaves he inspects,
Pointing out their defects
As he quite eats them up with his eyes.

[1] From *A Roman Wit,* by Paul Nixon, reprinted by permission of the author.

His taste far surpasses
The taste of the masses:
Their best girls he tells them to show,
And upstairs in the mart
Studies slaves set apart,
Unprofaned by the gaze of the low.

He then, satiated,
Has tables uncrated;
Iv'ry stands from top shelves bids them
get:
A tortoise shell chair,
Thrice measured with care,
He groans is too small for his set.
He appeared to be telling
Corinthian by smelling;
In Myron's art flaws he descried;
Sighed on finding a spot
In a crystalline pot;
Ordered ten agate jars laid aside.

Over old bowls he lingered;
Their chasing he fingered;
Then asked to see cups Mentor
wrought.
After counting the gems
On their handles he hems—
And would like to see ear-rings, he
thought.
Then the jewel shops he haunted,
Real sardonyx wanted,
And priced one as big as a dome.
Now the day being spent,
He bought two cups—one cent—
Tucked them under his arm and walked
home.
—PAUL NIXON.

MAN'S INHUMANITY TO MAN [1]

MARTIAL

[*Epigrams* VIII, 14]

That your trees may be bold
When the weather grows cold;

That their buds may be nipped by no
    breeze,
  In hot-houses faced
  To the south they're encased
And enjoy the warm sunlight at ease.
In a cell I am bunked
With one window—defunct;
  If he slept there old Boreas would
    sneeze.
  If this is the best
  That you'll do for a guest,
Why, the next time I'll visit your
    trees.
                        —PAUL NIXON.

OUTCLASSED [1]

MARTIAL

[Epigrams X, 79]

Torquatus four miles from the city
  Owns a country seat costly and grand:
Four miles from the city Otillus
  Bought a cot and an acre of land.

Torquatus reared baths of rich marble;
  You'd think they were built for a club:
Otillus installed then, undaunted,
  A superfine second-hand tub.

Torquatus had laurel groves planted;
  Each tree was well-leaved and full
    grown:
As soon as he saw them Otillus
  Had a hundred of fine acorns sown.

Torquatus was next chosen consul:
  Otillus was boss of his ward
And inwardly felt more than certain
  That now poor Torquatus was floored.

I fear it will end like the fable
  Where the undergrown frog had a
    thirst
To rival the ox in dimensions:
  There's danger Otillus will burst.
                        —PAUL NIXON.

[1] From *A Roman Wit*, by Paul Nixon, reprinted by permission of the author.

THE ANTIQUARY [1]

MARTIAL

[Epigrams VIII, 6]

The antiques of old Auctus will bore me
    to death:
  I prefer ware of clay from Saguntum.
  Of his pedigree'd plate
  Wondrous tales he'll relate:
If you thirst till he's through you'll
    affront'm.

"On Laomedon's board were these goblets
    you see,
  Bestowed for his walls on Apollo:
  With that bowl that dire day
  Rhœtus entered the fray—
A Lapith's head left this deep hollow.

"You have read of the cups Nestor
    owned: these are they.
  You can see where his thumb's worn
    'em brighter.
  And Achilles (II. IX)
  Filled this tankard with wine
Of a kind that would make his friends
    tighter.

"With this beaker at Carthage Æneas was
    pledged
  By his hostess, the beautiful Dido"—
  When he's got you enthused,
  Then from jars Priam used
He pours wine that you'd hate to give
    Fido.
                        —PAUL NIXON.

TO SEPTICIANUS [1]

MARTIAL

[Epigrams XI, 107]

You've returned me my book all unrolled
    to the end:
  That you've read it is visibly shown.

I know it. It's true. I believe and
commend—
That's the way I've read four of your
own.
—PAUL NIXON.

TO QUINTUS [1]

MARTIAL

[*Epigrams* IX, 53]

Your birthday I wished to observe with
a gift;
You forbade and your firmness is
known.
Every man to his taste:
I remark with some haste,
May the third is the date of my own.
—PAUL NIXON.

UN MÉDECIN MALGRÉ EUX [1]

MARTIAL

[*Epigrams* I, 30]

Diaulus now's a body snatcher,
Though a surgeon once.
His clientele, however, left him—
It's for them he hunts.
—PAUL NIXON.

A FAIR FIELD FOR SATIRE

JUVENAL

[From *Satires* I]

The excuse for satire is always the
same, that the abundance of material is
responsible. Juvenal makes the same explanation that Horace did. Details of
course differ; the public recitations of
poets, new in Horace's time, had not then
become the insufferable bore they were
later. For Juvenal, see above p. 500.

[1] From *A Roman Wit*, by Paul Nixon, reprinted by permission of the author.

Oh! heavens—while thus hoarse Codrus
perseveres
To force his Theseid on my tortured
ears,
Shall I not once attempt "to quit the
score,"
Always an auditor, and nothing more!
Forever at my side, shall this rehearse
His elegiac, that his comic verse,
Unpunished? shall huge Telephus, at will,
The livelong day consume, or, huger still,
Orestes, closely written, written, too
Down the broad marge and yet—no end
in view!
Away, away!—None knows his home
so well
As I the grove of Mars, and Vulcan's
cell,
Fast by the Æolian rocks!—How the
Winds roar,
How ghosts are tortured on the Stygian
shore,
How Jason stole the golden fleece, and
how
The Centaurs fought on Othrys' shaggy
brow;
The walks of Fronto echo round and
round—
The columns trembling with the eternal
sound,
While high and low, as the mad fit in-
vades,
Bellow the same trite nonsense through
the shades.
I, too, can write—and, at a pedant's
frown,
Once poured my fustian rhetoric on the
town:
And idly proved that Sulla, far from
power,
Had passed, unknown to fear, the tran-
quil hour:—
Now I resume my pen; for, since we meet
Such swarms of desperate bards in every
street,
'Tis vicious clemency to spare the oil,
And hapless paper they are sure to spoil.
But why I choose, adventurous, to re-
trace

The Aururcan's route, and, in the ar-
duous race,
Follow his burning wheels, attentive hear,
If leisure serve, and truth be worth your
ear.
When the soft eunuch weds, and the bold
fair
Tilts at the Tuscan boar, with bosom
bare;
When one that oft, since manhood first
appeared,
Has trimmed the exuberance of his sound-
ing beard,
In wealth outvies the senate; when a vile,
A slave-born, slave-bred, vagabond of the
Nile,
Crispinus, while he gathers now, now
flings
His purple open, fans his summer rings;
And, as his fingers sweat beneath the
freight,
Cries, "Save me—from a gem of greater
weight!"
'Tis hard a less adventurous course to
choose,
While folly plagues, and vice inflames the
Muse.
   For who so slow of heart, so dull of
brain,
So patient of the town, as to contain
His bursting spleen, when, full before
his eye,
Swings the new chair of lawyer Matho by,
Crammed with himself! then, with no less
parade,
That caitiff's, who his noble friend be-
trayed,
Who now, in fancy, prostrate greatness
tears,
And preys on what the imperial vulture
spares!
Whom Massa dreads, Latinus, trembling,
plies
With a fair wife, and anxious Carus buys!
   When those supplant thee in thy
dearest rights,
Who earn rich legacies by active nights;
Those, whom (the shortest, surest way to
rise)

The widow's itch advances to the skies!—
Not that an equal rank her minions
hold;
Just to their various powers, she metes
her gold,
And Proculeius mourns his scanty share,
While Gillo triumphs, hers and nature's
heir!
And let him triumph! 'tis the price of
blood:
While, thus defrauded of the generous
flood,
The color flies his cheek, as though he
prest,
With unsuspecting foot, a serpent's crest;
Or stood engaged at Lyons to declaim,
Where the least peril is the loss of fame.
   Ye gods!—what rage, what phrensy
fires my brain,
When that false guardian, with his splen-
did train,
Crowds the long street, and leaves his
orphan charge
To prostitution, and the world at large!
When by a juggling sentence damned in
vain,
(For who, that holds the plunder, heeds
the pain?)
Marius to wine devotes his morning hours,
And laughs, in exile, at the offended
Powers:
While, sighing o'er the victory she won,
The Province finds herself but more un-
done!
   And shall I feel, that crimes like these
require
The avenging strains of the Venusian
lyre,
And not pursue them? shall I still repeat
The lengendary tales of Troy and Crete;
The toils of Hercules, the horses fed
On human flesh by savage Diomed,
The lowing labyrinth, the builder's flight,
And the rash boy, hurl'd from his airy
height?
When, what the law forbids the wife to
heir,
The adulterer's Will may to the wittol
bear,

Who gave, with wand'ring eye and vacant
  face,
A tacit sanction to his own disgrace;
And, while at every turn a look he stole,
Snored, unsuspected, o'er the treacherous
  bowl!
  When he presumes to ask a troop's
    command,
Who spent on horses all his father's land,
While, proud the experienced driver to
  display,
His glowing wheels smoked o'er the
  Appian way:—
For there our young Automedon first
  tried
His powers, there loved the rapid car to
  guide;
While great Pelides sought superior bliss,
And toyed and wantoned with his master-
  miss.
  Who would not, reckless of the swarm
    he meets,
Fill his wide tablets, in the public streets,
With angry verse? when, through the
  midday glare,
Borne by six slaves, and in an open chair,
The forger comes, who owes this blaze
  of state
To a wet seal and a fictitious date;
Comes, like the soft Mæcenas, lolling by,
And impudently braves the public eye!
Or the rich dame, who stanched her hus-
  band's thirst
With generous wine, but—drugged it
  first!
And now, more dext'rous than Locusta,
  shows
Her country friends the beverage to com-
  pose,
And, midst the curses of the indignant
  throng,
Bear, in broad day, the spotted corpse
  along.
  Dare nobly, man! if greatness be thy
    aim,
And practice what may chains and exile
  claim:
On Guilt's broad base thy towering for-
  tunes raise,

For virtue starves on—universal praise!
While crimes, in scorn of niggard fate,
  afford
The ivory couches, and the citron board,
The goblet high-embossed, the antique
  plate,
The lordly mansion, and the fair estate!
  O! who can rest—who taste the sweets
    of life,
When sires debauch the son's too greedy
  wife;
When males to males, abjuring shame, are
  wed,
And beardless boys pollute the nuptial
  bed!
No: Indignation, kindling as she views,
Shall, in each breast, a generous warmth
  infuse,
And pour, in Nature and the Nine's de-
  spite,
Such strains as I, or Cluvienus, write!
  E'er since Deucalion, while, on every
    side,
The bursting clouds upraised the whelm-
  ing tide,
Reached in his little skiff, the forked hill,
And sought, at Themis' shrine, the Im-
  mortals' will;
When softening stones grew warm with
  gradual life,
And Pyrrha brought each male a virgin
  wife:
Whatever passions have the soul possest,
Whatever wild desires inflamed the breast,
Joy, Sorrow, Fear, Love, Hatred, Trans-
  port, Rage,
Shall form the motley subject of my page.
                    —WILLIAM GIFFORD.

ROME A GREEK CITY

JUVENAL

[From *Satires* III]

In imperial times Rome had her problem of the melting-pot. Among the fortune hunters of all races attracted to the
capital of the world none was so cunning,

so versatile, so successful as the Greek. The Roman, often outstripped in the competition, felt that that which was his by rights was gradually slipping away from him.

The nation by the great, admired, carest,
And hated, shunned by me, above the rest,
No longer now, restrained by wounded pride,
I haste to show (nor thou my warmth deride),
I cannot rule my spleen, and calmly see,
A Grecian capital, in Italy!
Grecian? O no! with this vast sewer compared,
The dregs of Greece are scarcely worth regard:
Long since, the stream that wanton Syria laves
Has disembogued its filth in Tiber's waves,
Its language, arts; o'erwhelmed us with the scum
Of Antioch's streets, its minstrel, harp, and drum.
Hie to the Circus! ye who pant to prove
A barbarous mistress, an outlandish love;
Hie to the Circus! there, in crowds they stand,
Tires on their head, and timbrels in their hand.
Thy rustic Mars the Trechedipna wears,
And on his breast, smeared with ceroma, bears
A paltry prize, well pleased; while every land,
Sicyon, and Amydos, and Alaband,
Tralles and Samos and a thousand more,
Thrive on his indolence and daily pour
Their starving myriads forth: hither they come,
And batten on the genial soil of Rome;
Minions, then lords, of every princely dome!
A flattering, cringing, treacherous, artful race,

Of torrent tongue, and never-blushing face;
Which shifts to every form, and shines in all:
Grammarian, painter, augur, rhetorician,
Rope-dancer, conjurer, fiddler, physician,
All trades his own your hungry Greekling counts;
And bid him mount the sky—the sky he mounts!
You smile—was't a barbarian, then, that flew?
No, 'twas a Greek; 'twas an Athenian, too!
—Bear with their state who will: for I disdain
To feed their upstart pride, or swell their train:
Slaves, that in Syrian lighters stowed, so late,
With figs and prunes (an inauspicious freight),
Already see their faith preferred to mine,
And sit above me! and before me sign!—
That on the Aventime I first drew air,
And, from the womb, was nursed on Sabine fare,
Avails me not! our birthright now is lost,
And all our privilege, an empty boast!
For lo! where versed in every soothing art,
The wily Greek assails his patron's heart,
Finds in each dull harangue an air, a grace,
And all Adonis in a Gorgon face;
Admires the voice that grates upon the ear,
Like the shrill scream of amorous chanticleer;
And equals the crane neck, the narrow chest,
To Hercules, when, straining to his breast
The giant son of Earth, his every vein
Swells with the toil, and more than mortal pain.
We too can cringe as low, and praise as warm,
But flattery from the Greeks alone can charm.

See! they step forth, and figure to the
    life,
The naked nymph, the mistress, or the
    wife,
So just, you view the very woman there,
And fancy all beneath the girdle bare!
No longer now, the favourites of the
    stage
Boast their exclusive power to charm the
    age:
The happy art with them a nation shares,
Greece is a theatre, where all are players.
For lo! their patron smiles,—they burst
    with mirth;
He weeps—they droop, the saddest souls
    on earth;
He calls for fire—they court the mantle's
    heat;
'Tis warm, he cries—and they dissolve in
    sweat.
Ill-matched!—secure of victory they
    start,
Who, taught from youth to play a bor-
    rowed part,
Can, with a glance, the rising passion
    trace,
And mould their own, to suit their
    patron's face;
At deeds of shame their hands admiring
    raise,
And mad debauchery's worst excesses
    praise.
    Besides, no bound their raging lust
    restrains,
All ties it breaks, all sanctity profanes;
Wife, virgin-daughter, son unstained be-
    fore—
And, where these fail, they tempt the
    grandam hoar:
They notice every word, haunt every ear,
Your secrets learn, and fix you theirs
    from fear.
    Turn to their schools:—yon gray pro-
    fessor see,
Smeared with the sanguine stains of
    perfidy!
That tutor most accursed his pupil sold!
That Stoic sacrificed his friend to gold!
A true-born Grecian! littered on the coast,

Where the Gorgonian hack a pinion lost.
    Hence, Romans, hence! no place for
    you remains,
Where Diphilus, where Erimanthus
    reigns;
Miscreants, who, faithful to their native
    art,
Admit no rival in a patron's heart:
For let them fasten on his easy ear,
And drop one hint, one secret slander
    there,
Sucked from their country's venom, or
    their own,
That instant they possess the man alone;
While we are spurned, contemptuous,
    from the door,
Our long, long slavery thought upon no
    more.

            —WILLIAM GIFFORD.

THE NEW WOMAN

JUVENAL

[From *Satires* VI]

Juvenal had little sympathy with the
growing movement making for the greater
freedom of women. He could see only
vicious motives behind their actions and
only disastrous results to society.

    Some faults, though small, no husband
    yet can bear:
'Tis now the nauseous cant, that none is
    fair,
Unless her thoughts in Attic terms she
    dress;
A mere Cecropian of a Sulmoness!
All now is Greek: in Greek their souls
    they pour,
In Greek their fears, hopes, joys;—what
    would you more?
In Greek they clasp their lovers. We
    allow
These fooleries to girls: but thou, O thou,
Who tremblest at the verge of eighty-
    eight,
To Greek it still!—'tis now a day too late.

Foh! how it savors of the dregs of lust,
When an old hag, whose blandishments
   disgust,
Affects the infant lisp, the girlish squeak,
And mumbles out, "My life!" "My
   soul!" in Greek. . . .
   Women support the Bar; they love the
   law,
And raise litigious questions for a straw;
They meet in private, and prepare the
   Bill,
Draw up the Instructions with a lawyer's
   skill,
Suggest to Celsus where the merits lie,
And dictate points for statement or reply.
   Nay, more, they fence! who has not
   marked their oil,
Their purple rugs for this preposterous
   toil?
Room for the lady—lo! she seeks the list,
And fiercely tilts at her antagonist,
A post! which, with her buckler, she pro-
   vokes,
And bores and batters with repeated
   strokes;
Till all the fencer's art can do she shows,
And the glad master interrupts her blows.
O worthy, sure, to head those wanton
   dames,
Who foot it naked at the Floral games;
Unless, with nobler daring, she aspire,
And tempt the arena's bloody field—for
   hire!
   What sense of shame is to that female
   known,
Who envies our pursuits, and hates her
   own?
Yet would she not, though proud in arms
   to shine
(True woman still), her sex for ours re-
   sign. . . .
   But she is more intolerable yet,
Who plays the critic when at table set;
Calls Virgil charming, and attempts to
   prove
Poor Dido right, in venturing all for love.
From Maro, and Mæonides, she quotes
The striking passages, and, while she
   notes

Their beauties and defects, adjusts her
   scales,
And accurately weighs which bard prevails.
The astonished guests sit mute: grammarians yield,
Loud rhetoricians, baffled, quit the field;
Even auctioneers and lawyers stand
   aghast,
And now a woman speaks!—So thick and
   fast,
The wordy shower descends, that you
   would swear
A thousand bells were jangling in your
   ear,
A thousand basins clattering. Vex no
   more
Your trumpets and your timbrels, as of
   yore,
To ease the laboring moon; her single
   yell
Can drown their clangor, and dissolve the
   spell.
            —WILLIAM GIFFORD.

THE VANITY OF HUMAN WISHES

JUVENAL

[From *Satires* X]

   This is ever a favorite theme of the
moralist. Juvenal's treatment of it is
more like that of an essayist than of a
satirist. It is inspired not by direct observations of life, as in Horace, but by
reading and meditation on abstractions.

In every clime, from Ganges' distant
   stream
To Gades, gilded by the western beam,
Few, from the clouds of mental error free,
In its true light or good or evil see.
For what, with reason, do we seek or
   shun?
What plan, how happily soe'er begun,
But, finished, we our own success lament,
And rue the pains, so fatally misspent?—
To headlong ruin see whole houses driven,

Cursed with their prayers, by too indulgent heaven!
Bewildered thus by folly or by fate,
We beg pernicious gifts in every state,
In peace, in war. A full and rapid flow
Of eloquence, lays many a speaker low:
Even strength itself is fatal; Milo tries
His wondrous arms, and—in the trial dies!
But avarice wider spreads her deadly snare,
And hoards amassed with too successful care,
Hoards, which o'er all paternal fortunes rise,
As o'er the dolphin towers the whale in size.
For this, in other times, at Nero's word,
The ruffian bands unsheathed the murderous sword,
Rushed to the swelling coffers of the great,
Chased Lateranus from his lordly seat,
Besieged too-wealthy Seneca's wide walls,
And closed, terrific, round Longinus' halls:
While sweetly in their cocklofts slept the poor,
And heard no soldier thundering at their door.
The traveler, freighted with a little wealth,
Sets forth at night, and wins his way by stealth:
Even then, he fears the bludgeon and the blade,
And starts and trembles at a rush's shade;
While, void of care, the beggar trips along,
And, in the spoiler's presence, trolls his song.
The first great wish, that all with rapture own,
The general cry, to every temple known,
Is, gold, gold, gold!—"and let, allgracious Powers,
The largest chest the Forum boasts be ours!"

Yet none from earthen bowls destruction sip:
Dread then the draught, when, mantling, at your lip,
The goblet sparkles, radiant from the mine,
And the broad gold inflames the ruby wine.
And do we, now, admire the stories told
Of the two Sages, so renowned of old;
How this forever laughed, whene'er he stepped
Beyond the threshold; that, forever wept?
But all can laugh:—the wonder yet appears,
What fount supplied the eternal stream of tears!
Democritus, at every step he took,
His sides with unextinguished laughter shook,
Though, in his days, Abdera's simple towns
No fasces knew, chairs, litters, purple gowns.—
What! had he seen, in his triumphal car,
Amid the dusty Cirque, conspicuous far,
The Prætor perched aloft, superbly dress'd
In Jove's proud tunic, with a trailing vest
Of Tyrian tapestry, and o'er him spread
A crown, too bulky for a mortal head,
Borne by a sweating slave, maintained to ride
In the same car, and mortify his pride!
Add now the bird, that, with expanded wing,
From the raised sceptre seems prepared to spring;
And trumpets here; and there the long parade
Of duteous friends, who head the cavalcade;
Add, too, the zeal of clients robed in white,
Who hang upon his reins, and grace the sight,
Unbribed, unbought—save by the dole, at night!

Yes, in those days, in every varied scene,
The good old man found matter for his spleen:
A wondrous sage! whose story makes it clear
That men may rise in folly's atmosphere,
Beneath Bœotian fogs, of soul sublime,
And great examples to the coming time.—
He laughed aloud to see the vulgar fears,
Laughed at their joys, and sometimes at their tears:
Secure the while, he mocked at Fortune's frown,
And when she threatened, bade her hang or drown!
Superfluous then, or fatal, is the prayer,
Which to the Immortals' knees we fondly bear.
  Some, Power hurls headlong from her envied height,
Some, the broad tablet, flashing on the sight,
With titles, names: the statues, tumbled down,
Are dragged by hooting thousands through the town;
The brazen cars torn rudely from the yoke,
And, with the blameless steeds, to shivers broke—
Then roar the flames! the sooty artist blows,
And all Sejanus in the furnace glows;
Sejanus, once so honored, so adored,
And only second to the world's great lord,
Runs glittering from the mould, in cups and cans,
Basins and ewers, plates, pitchers, pots, and pans.
  "Crown all your doors with bay, triumphant bay!
Sacred to Jove, the milk-white victim slay,
For lo! where great Sejanus by the throng,
A joyful spectacle! is dragged along.

What lips! what cheeks! ha, traitor!—for my part,
I never loved the fellow—in my heart."
"But tell me; Why was he adjudged to bleed?
And who discovered? and who proved the deed?"
"Proved!—a huge, wordy letter came to-day
From Capreæ." Good! what think the people? They!
They follow fortune, as of old, and hate,
With their whole souls, the victim of the state.
Yet would the herd, thus zealous, thus on fire,
Had Nurscia met the Tuscan's fond desire,
And crushed the unwary prince, have all combined,
And hailed Sejanus, Master of Mankind!
For since their votes have been no longer bought,
All public care has vanished from their thought;
And those who once, with unresisted sway,
Gave armies, empire, everything, away,
For two poor claims, have long renounced the whole,
And only ask—the Circus and the Dole.
  "But there are more to suffer." "So I find;
A fire so fierce for one was ne'er designed.
I met my friend Brutidius, and I fear,
From his pale looks, there's danger near.
What if this Ajax, in his phrensy, strike,
Suspicious of our zeal, at all alike!"
"True: fly we then, our loyalty to show;
And trample on the carcass of his foe,
While yet exposed on Tiber's banks it lies"—
"But let our slaves be there," another cries:
"Yes; let them (lest our ardor they forswear,
And drag us, pinioned, to the Bar) be there."

Thus of the favorite's fall the converse ran,
And thus the whisper passed from man to man.
Lured by the splendor of his happier hour,
Would'st thou possess Sejanus' wealth and power;
See crowds of suppliants at thy levee wait,
Give this to sway the army, that the state;
And keep a prince in ward, retired to reign
O'er Capreæ's crags, with his Chaldean train?
Yes, yes, thou would'st (for I can read thy breast)
Enjoy that favor which he once possess'd,
Assume all offices, grasp all commands,
The Imperial Horse, and the Prætorian Bands,
'Tis nature, this; even those who want the will,
Pant for the dreadful privilege to kill:
Yet what delight can rank and power bestow,
Since every joy is balanced by its woe!
Still would'st thou choose the favorite's purple, say?
Or, thus forewarned, some paltry hamlet sway?
At Gabii, or Fidenæ, rules propound,
For faulty measures, and for wares unsound;
And take the tarnished robe and petty state,
Of poor Ulubræ's ragged magistrate?—
You grant me then, Sejanus grossly erred,
Nor knew what prayer his folly had preferred:
For when he begged for too much wealth and power,
Stage above stage, he raised a tottering tower,
And higher still, and higher; to be thrown,

With louder crash, and wider ruin, down! . . .
But (for 'tis good our humble hope to prove),
That thou may'st, still, ask something from above,
Thy pious offerings to the temple bear,
And, while the altars blaze, be this thy prayer.
O Thou, who know'st the wants of human kind,
Vouchsafe me health of body, health of mind;
A soul prepared to meet the frowns of fate,
And look undaunted on a future state;
That reckons death a blessing, yet can bear
Existence nobly, with its weight of care;
That anger and desire alike restrains,
And counts Alcides' toils, and cruel pains,
Superior far to banquets, wanton nights,
And all the Assyrian monarch's soft delights!
Here, bound, at length, thy wishes. I but teach
What blessings man, by his own powers, may reach.
The path to peace is virtue. We should see,
If wise, O Fortune, naught divine in thee:
But we have deified a name alone,
And fixed in heaven thy visionary throne!

—WILLIAM GIFFORD.

THE MILITARY CASTE

JUVENAL

[Satires XVI]

In early times the boastful soldier had been a fit theme for jest, but under the militaristic regime of the Empire the superior position occupied by the soldier became a matter for more serious thought on the part of mere civilians.

Who can recount the advantages that
 wait,
Dear Gallus, on the Military State?—
For let me once, beneath a lucky star,
Faint as I am at heart, and new to
 war,
But join the camp, and that ascendant
 hour
Shall lord it o'er my fate with happier
 power,
Than if a line from Venus should com-
 mend
My suit to Mars, or Juno stand my
 friend!
 And first, of benefits which all may
 share:
'Tis somewhat—that no citizen shall
 dare
To strike you, or, though struck, return
 the blow:
But waive the wrong; nor to the Prætor
 show
His teeth dashed out, his face deformed
 with gore,
And eyes no skill can promise to restore!
 A Judge, if to the camp your plaints
 you bear,
Coarse shod, and coarser greaved, awaits
 you there:
By antique law proceeds the cassocked
 sage,
And rules prescribed in old Camillus'
 age;
To wit, Let soldiers seek no foreign
 bench,
Nor plead to any charge without the
 trench.
O nicely do centurions sift the cause,
When buff-and-belt-men violate the
 laws!
And ample, if with reason we complain,
Is, doubtless, the redress our injuries
 gain!
Even so:—but the whole legion are our
 foes,
And, with determined aim, the award
 oppose.
"These sniveling rogues take special
 pleasure still

To make the punishment outweigh the
 ill."
So runs the cry; and he must be possest
Of more, Vigellius, than thy iron breast,
Who braves their anger, and, with ten
 poor toes,
Defies such countless hosts of hobnailed
 shoes.
 Who so untutored in the ways of
 Rome,
Say, who so true a Pylades, to come
Within the camp?—no; let thy tears be
 dried,
Nor ask that kindness, which must be
 denied,
For, when the Court exclaims, "Your
 witness, here!"
Let that firm friend, that man of men,
 appear,
And testify but what he saw and heard;
And I pronounce him worthy of the
 beard
And hair of our forefathers! You may
 find
False witnesses against an honest hind,
Easier than true (and who their fears
 can blame?),
Against a soldier's purse, a soldier's
 fame!
 But there are other benefits, my friend,
And greater, which the sons of war at-
 tend:
Should a litigious neighbor bid me yield
My vale irriguous, and paternal field;
Or from my bounds the sacred landmark
 tear,
To which, with each revolving spring, I
 bear,
In pious duty to the grateful soil,
My humble offerings, honey, meal, and
 oil;
Or a vile debtor my just claims with-
 stand,
Deny his signet, and abjure his hand;
Term after Term I wait, till months be
 past,
And scarce obtain a hearing at the last.
Even when the hour is fixed, a thousand
 stays

Retard my suit, a thousand vague delays:
The cause is called, the witnesses attend,
Chairs brought, and cushions laid—and
there an end!
Cæditius finds his cloak or gown too hot,
And Fuscus slips aside to seek the pot;
Thus, with our dearest hopes the judges
sport,
And when we rise to speak, dismiss the
Court!
But spear-and-shield-men may command
the hour;
The time to plead is always in their
power;
Nor are their wealth and patience worn
away,
By the slow drag-chain of the law's
delay.
  Add that the soldier, while his father
  lives,

And he alone, his wealth bequeaths or
gives;
For what by pay is earned, by plunder
won,
The law declares, vests solely in the son.
Coranus therefore sees his hoary sire,
To gain his Will, by every art, aspire!—
He rose by service; rank in fields ob-
tained,
And well deserved the fortune which
he gained.
And every prudent chief must, sure, de-
sire,
That still the worthiest should the most
acquire;
That those who merit, their rewards
should have,
Trappings, and chains, and all that decks
the brave.
                              —WILLIAM GIFFORD.

V. EDUCATION OF THE PUBLIC MAN: QUINTILIAN

A general system of public education such as exists in America today was not known in the Roman Empire. To be sure some cities seem to have maintained school by taxation, and in some places a group of parents would establish a school for their children. Undoubtedly many of the poor taught their children what they could at home, and many of the rich engaged private tutors. Among all classes it is quite certain that knowledge of the "three Rs" was widespread.

Higher education, true to the practical spirit of the Romans, aimed to prepare for a public career. It was pursued under teachers to whom the students would pay a fee. The emperors, beginning with Vespasian, provided for a few professors of the higher branches at Rome.

Following a development from the time of the Republic special stress was laid on oratory. Although there was no longer the possibility of influencing the policy of the state by persuasive speech before the people, and though, as one consequence of the Imperial form of government, the art of oratory was on the decline, yet there was within a narrower range need of ability to speak in law-court and in senate. In the senatorial class too, and for that class the higher education was largely intended, there was considerable demand for speeches in praise of the emperor.

It was with reference to the education of the ruling classes that writers in the first century produced their treatises. Their ideal product was still, as in the days of Cato, "a good man skilled in speaking." To this end they regarded as among the essentials wide and careful reading in great Greek and Latin authors, both for subject matter and for details of style of value to a speaker. There was also much memorizing and reciting of speeches, much analysis of style and language, and much attention to even the minutiæ of figures of speech. In fact here the emphasis was too great, for it led to an affected, artificial style even in speeches of the law-court. Great attention was given to developing the student's ability to debate by the assignment of special topics or questions on which all possible arguments were to be prepared. The method could develop keenness of mind; but the topics assigned had nothing to do with the life of the state, and at best would deal with some historical subject. For example this question was proposed: What would have happened if Hannibal had marched on Rome immediately after his victory at Cannæ?

To balance these criticisms it should be stated that the first and second centuries produced many able senators, great jurists, wise administrators, and a few writers of the first rank. Many of these men undoubtedly were trained in the formal schooling of their day, and to it must have owed some part of their success.

Marcus Fabius Quintilianus was born in Spain about 35 and died in Italy about 95. Quintilian as professor of oratory at Rome exerted a powerful influence on the writers and men of public life in the latter part of the first century and the beginning of the second. Late in life he published an epoch-making book on education. Its very title, *Institutio Oratoria,* reveals the point of view that characterizes the whole system of Roman education, which looked upon the orator as its final and highest product. The book is valuable not only as an excellent treatise on pedagogy, but also for its sane critical judgments on the literatures of Greece and Rome. Quintilian takes Cicero as the model of Latin style, and withholds his approval from the rhetorical peculiarities of Silver Latin which culminated in the affectations of Seneca.

THE TRAINING OF THE CHILD [1]

[From *The Training of the Orator,* Book I]

The aim of education is to produce the perfect orator; the perfect orator must be first of all a perfect man; education must therefore begin with infancy. The point is emphasized by Quintilian because in his day there was prevalent a tendency on the part of well-to-do parents to relieve themselves of the care of children by turning

[1] From The Loeb Classical Library, reprinted by permission.

them over completely to more or less uneducated slaves.

Above all see that the child's nurse speaks correctly. The ideal, according to Chrysippus, would be that she should be a philosopher; failing that he desired that the best should be chosen, as far as possible. No doubt the most important point is that they should be of good character; but they should speak correctly as well. It is the nurse that the child first hears, and her words that he will first attempt to imitate. And we are by nature most tenacious of childish impressions, just as the flavour first absorbed by vessels when new persists, and the colour imparted by dyes to the primitive whiteness of wool is indelible. Further it is the worst impressions that are most durable. For, while what is good readily deteriorates, you will never turn vice into virtue. Do not therefore allow the boy to become accustomed even in infancy to a style of speech which he will subsequently have to unlearn.

As regards parents, I should like to see them as highly educated as possible, and I do not restrict this remark to fathers alone. We are told that the eloquence of the Gracchi owed much to their mother Cornelia, whose letters even to-day testify to the cultivation of her style. Lælia, the daughter of Gaius Lælius, is said to have reproduced the elegance of her father's language, in her own speech, while the oration delivered before the triumvirs by Hortensia, the daughter of Quintus Hortensius, is still read and not merely as a compliment to her sex. And even those who have not had the fortune to receive a good education should not for that reason devote less care to their son's education; but should on the contrary show all the greater diligence in other matters where they can be of service to their children. . . .

Still if it should prove impossible to secure the ideal nurse, the ideal companions, or the ideal *pædagogus,* I would insist that there should be one person at any rate attached to the boy who has some knowledge of speaking and who will, if any incorrect expression should be used by nurse or *pædagogus* in the presence of the child under their charge, at once correct the error and prevent its becoming a habit. But it must be clearly understood that this is only a remedy, and that the ideal course is that indicated above. . . .

Some hold that boys should not be taught to read till they are seven years old, that being the earliest age at which they can derive profit from instruction and endure the strain of learning. . . . Those however who hold that a child's mind should not be allowed to lie fallow for a moment are wiser. Chrysippus, for instance, though he gives the nurses a three years' reign, still holds the formation of the child's mind on the best principles to be a part of their duties. . . .

I am not however so blind to differences of age as to think that the very young should be forced on prematurely or given real work to do. Above all things we must take care that the child, who is not yet old enough to love his studies, does not come to hate them and dread the bitterness which he has once tasted, even when the years of infancy are left behind. His studies must be made an amusement: he must be questioned and praised and taught to rejoice when he has done well: sometimes too, when he refuses instruction, it should be given to some other to excite his envy, at times also he must be engaged in competition and should be allowed to believe himself successful more often than not, while he should be encouraged to do his best by such rewards as may appeal to his tender years. . . .

At any rate I am not satisfied with the course (which I note is usually adopted) of teaching small children the names and order of the letters before their shapes. Such a practice makes them slow to recognise the letters, since they do not pay attention to their actual shape, preferring to be guided by what they have already learned by rote. It is for this reason that teachers, when they think that they have sufficiently familiarized their young pupils with the letters written in their usual order, reverse that order or rearrange it in every kind of combination, until they learn to know the letters from their appearance and not from the order in which they occur. It will be best therefore for children to begin by learning their appearance and names just as they do with men. The method, however, to which we have objected in teaching the alphabet, is unobjectionable when applied to syllables. I quite approve on the other hand of a practice which has been devised to stimulate children to learn by giving them ivory letters to play with, as I do of anything else that may be discovered to delight the very young, the sight, handling and naming of which is a pleasure.

As soon as the child has begun to know the shapes of the various letters, it will be no bad thing to have them cut as accurately as possible upon a board, so that the pen may be guided along the grooves. Thus mistakes such as occur with wax tablets will be rendered impossible; for the pen will be confined between the edges of the letters and will be prevented from going astray. Further by increasing the frequency and speed with which they follow these fixed outlines we shall give steadiness to the fingers, and there will be no need to guide the child's hand with our own. The art of writing well and quickly is not unimportant for our purpose, though it is generally disregarded by persons of quality. Writing is of the utmost importance in the study which we have under consideration and by its means alone can true and deeply rooted proficiency be obtained. But a sluggish pen delays our thoughts, while an unformed and illiterate hand cannot be deciphered, a circumstance which necessitates another wearisome task, namely the dictation of what we have written to a copyist. We shall therefore at all times and in all places, and above all when we are writing private letters to our friends, find a gratification in the thought that we have not neglected even this accomplishment.

As regards syllables, no short cut is possible: they must all be learnt, and there is no good in putting off learning the most difficult; this is the general practice, but the sole result is bad spelling. Further we must beware of placing a blind confidence in a child's memory. It is better to repeat syllables and impress them on the memory and, when he is reading, not to press him to read continuously or with greater speed, unless indeed the clear and obvious sequence of letters can suggest itself without its being necessary for the child to stop to think. The syllables once learnt, let him begin to construct words with them and sentences with the words. You will hardly believe how much reading is delayed by undue haste. If the child attempts more than his powers allow, the inevitable result is hesitation, interruption and repetition, and the mistakes which he makes merely lead him to lose confidence in what he already knows. Reading must therefore first be sure, then connected, while it must be kept slow for a considerable time, until practice brings speed unaccompanied by error. For to look to the right, which is regularly taught, and to look ahead depends not so much on precept as on practice; since it is necessary to keep the eyes on what follows while reading out what precedes, with the resulting difficulty that the at-

tention of the mind must be divided, the eyes and voice being differently engaged. It will be found worth while, when the boy begins to write out words in accordance with the usual practice, to see that he does not waste his labour in writing out common words of everyday occurrence. He can readily learn the explanations or *glosses*, as the Greeks call them, of the more obscure words by the way and, while he is still engaged on the first rudiments, acquire what would otherwise demand special time to be devoted to it. And as we are still discussing minor details, I would urge that the lines, which he is set to copy, should not express thoughts of no significance but convey some sound moral lesson. He will remember such aphorisms even when he is an old man, and the impression made upon his unformed mind will contribute to the formation of his character. He may also be entertained by learning the sayings of famous men and above all selections from the poets, poetry being more attractive to children. For memory is most necessary to an orator, as I shall point out in its proper place, and there is nothing like practice for strengthening and developing it. And at the tender age of which we are now speaking, when originality is impossible, memory is almost the only faculty which can be developed by the teacher.

—H. E. BUTLER.

CULTURE AND VOCATION [1]

[From *The Training of the Orator*, Book I]

The standard even for a practical education is to be fixed not solely on the basis of utility, but on the basis of the ideal of perfection for which one strives.

I will now proceed briefly to discuss the remaining arts in which I think boys ought to be instructed before being

[1] From The Loeb Classical Library, reprinted by permission.

handed over to the teacher of rhetoric: for it is by such studies that the course of education described by the Greeks as ἐγκύκλιος παιδεία or general education will be brought to its full completion.

For there are other subjects of education which must be studied simultaneously with literature. These being independent studies are capable of completion without a knowledge of oratory, while on the other hand they cannot by themselves produce an orator. The question has consequently been raised as to whether they are necessary for this purpose. What, say some, has the knowledge of the way to describe an equilateral triangle on a given straight line got to do with pleading in the law-courts or speaking in the senate? Will an acquaintance with the names and intervals of the notes of the lyre help an orator to defend a criminal or direct the policy of his country? They will perhaps produce a long list of orators who are most effective in the courts but have never sat under a geometrician and whose understanding of music is confined to the pleasure which their ears, like those of other men, derive from it. To such critics I reply, and Cicero frequently makes the same remark in his Orator, that I am not describing any orator who actually exists or has existed, but have in my mind's eye an ideal orator, perfect down to the smallest detail. For when the philosophers describe the ideal sage who is to be consummate in all knowledge and a very god incarnate, as they say, they would have him receive instruction not merely in the knowledge of things human and divine, but would also lead him through a course of subjects, which in themselves are comparatively trivial, as for instance the elaborate subtleties of formal logic: not that acquaintance with the so-called "horn" or "crocodile" problems can make a man wise, but because it is important that he should never trip even in the small-

est trifles. So too the teacher of geometry, music or other subjects which I could class with these, will not be able to create the perfect orator (who like the philosopher ought to be a wise man), but none the less these arts will assist in his perfection. I may draw a parallel from the use of antidotes and other remedies applied to the eyes or to wounds. We know that these are composed of ingredients which produce many and sometimes contrary effects, but mixed together they make a single compound resembling no one of its component parts, but deriving its peculiar properties from all: so too dumb insects produce honey, whose taste is beyond the skill of man to imitate, from different kinds of flowers and juices. Shall we marvel then, if oratory, the highest gift of providence to man, needs the assistance of many arts, which, although they do not reveal or intrude themselves in actual speaking, supply hidden forces and make their silent presence felt? "But," it will be urged, "men have proved fluent without their aid." Granted, but I am in quest of an orator. "Their contribution is but small." Yes, but we shall never attain completeness, if minor details be lacking. And it will be agreed that though our ideal of perfection may dwell on a height that is hard to gain, it is our duty to teach all we know, that achievement may at least come somewhat nearer the goal. But why should our courage fail? The perfect orator is not contrary to the laws of nature, and it is cowardly to despair of anything that is within the bounds of possibility.

—H. E. BUTLER.

SPECIAL APTITUDES [1]

[From *The Training of the Orator*, Book II]

Special aptitudes should receive due recognition; but to limit one's training to

[1] From The Loeb Classical Library, reprinted by permission.

those matters for which one shows liking and ability at a particular stage is to fail to lead one beyond his early limitations to the mastery of things which are worth while even though difficult.

It is generally and not unreasonably regarded as the sign of a good teacher that he should be able to differentiate between the abilities of his respective pupils and to know their natural bent. The gifts of nature are infinite in their variety, and mind differs from mind almost as much as body from body. This is clear from a consideration of the orators themselves, who differ in style to such an extent that no one is like another, in spite of the fact that numbers have modelled their style on that of their favorite authors. Many again think it useful to direct their instruction to the fostering of natural advantages and to guide the talents of their pupils along the lines which they instinctively tend to follow. Just as an expert gymnast, when he enters a gymnasium full of boys, after testing body and mind in every way, is able to decide for what class of athletic contest they should be trained, even so, they say, a teacher of oratory after careful observation of a boy's stylistic preferences, be they for terseness and polish, energy, dignity, charm, roughness, brilliance or wit, will so adapt his instructions to individual needs that each pupil will be pushed forward in the sphere for which his talents seem specially to design him; for nature, when cultivated, goes from strength to strength, while he who runs counter to her bent is ineffective in those branches of the art for which he is less suited and weakens the talents which he seemed born to employ. Now, since the critic who is guided by his reason is free to dissent even from received opinions, I must insist that to my thinking this view is only partially true. It is undoubtedly necessary to note the individual gifts of each boy,

and no one would ever convince me that it is not desirable to differentiate courses of study with this in view. One boy will be better adapted for the study of history, another for poetry, another for law, while some perhaps had better be packed off to the country. The teacher of rhetoric will distinguish such special aptitudes, just as our gymnast will turn one pupil into a runner, another into a boxer or wrestler or an expert at some other of the athletic accomplishments for which prizes are awarded at the sacred games. But on the other hand, he who is destined for the bar must study not one department merely, but must perfect himself in all the accomplishments which his profession demands, even though some of them may seem too hard for him when he approaches them as a learner. For if natural talent alone were sufficient, education might be dispensed with. Suppose we are given a pupil who, like so many, is of depraved tastes and swollen with his own conceit; shall we suffer him to go his own sweet way? If a boy's disposition is naturally dry and jejune, ought we not to feed it up or at any rate clothe it in fairer apparel? For, if in some cases it is necessary to remove certain qualities, surely there are others where we may be permitted to add what is lacking. Not that I would set myself against the will of nature. No innate good quality should be neglected, but defects must be made good and weaknesses made strong. When Isocrates, the prince of instructors, whose works proclaim his eloquence no less than his pupils testify to his excellence as a teacher, gave his opinion of Ephorus and Theopompus to the effect that the former needed the spur and the latter the curb, what was his meaning? Surely not that the sluggish temperament of the one and the headlong ardour of the other alike required modification by instruction, but rather that each would gain from an admixture of the qualities of the other.

In the case of weaker understandings, however, some concession must be made and they should be directed merely to follow the call of their nature, since thus they will be more effective in doing the only thing that lies in their power. But if we are fortunate enough to meet with richer material, such as justifies us in the hope of producing a real orator, we must leave no oratorical virtue uncared for. For though he will necessarily have a natural bent for some special department of oratory, he will not feel repelled by the others, and by sheer application will develop his other qualities until they equal those in which he naturally excels. The skilled gymnast will once again provide us with a parallel: if he undertakes to train a pancratiast, he will not merely teach him how to use his fists or his heels, nor will he restrict his instructions to the holds in wrestling, giving special attention to certain tricks of this kind, but will train him in every department of the science. Some will no doubt be incapable of attaining proficiency in certain exercises; these must specialise on those which lie within their powers. For there are two things which he must be most careful to avoid: first, he must not attempt the impossible, secondly, he must not switch off his pupil from what he can do well to exercises for which he is less well suited. But if his pupil is like the famous Nicostratus, whom we saw when he was old and we were boys, he will train him equally in every department of the science and will make him a champion both in boxing and wrestling, like Nicostratus himself who won the prize for both contests within a few days of each other. And how much more important is the employment of such methods where our future orator is concerned! It is not enough to be able to speak with terseness, subtlety or vehemence, any more than it would be for a singing master to excel in the upper, middle or lower register only, or in particular sections of these registers alone. Eloquence is like a harp and will never reach perfection, unless all its strings be taut and in tune.

—H. E. BUTLER.

THE CHOICE OF WORDS [1]

[From *The Training of the Orator,* Book VIII]

Advice to the effect that words are not an end in themselves but a means to an end was very much needed in Quintilian's day.

This does not, however, mean that we should devote ourselves to the study of words alone. For I am compelled to offer the most prompt and determined resistance to those who would at the very portals of this enquiry lay hold of the admissions I have just made and, disregarding the subject matter which, after all, is the backbone of any speech, devote themselves to the futile and crippling study of words in a vain desire to acquire the gift of elegance, a gift which I myself regard as the fairest of all the glories of oratory, but only when it is natural and unaffected. Healthy bodies, enjoying a good circulation and strengthened by exercise, acquire grace from the same source that gives them strength, for they have a healthy complexion, firm flesh and shapely thews. But, on the other hand, the man who attempts to enhance these physical graces by the effeminate use of depilatories and cosmetics, succeeds merely in defacing them by the very care which he bestows on them. Again, a tasteful and magnificent dress, as the Greek poet tells us, lends added dignity to its wearer: but effeminate and luxurious apparel fails to adorn the body and merely reveals the foulness of the mind. Similarly, a translucent and iridescent style

[1] From The Loeb Classical Library, reprinted by permission.

merely serves to emasculate the subject which it arrays with such pomp of words. Therefore I would have the orator, while careful in his choice of words, be even more concerned about his subject matter. For, as a rule, the best words are essentially suggested by the subject matter and are discovered by their own intrinsic light. But to-day we hunt for these words as though they were hiding themselves and striving to elude our grasp. And thus we fail to realise that they are to be found in the subject of our speech, and seek them elsewhere, and, when we have found them, force them to suit their context. It is with a more virile spirit that we should pursue eloquence, who, if only her whole body be sound, will never think it her duty to polish her nails and tire her hair.

The usual result of over-attention to the niceties of style is the deterioration of our eloquence. The main reason for this is that those words are best which are least far-fetched and give the impression of simplicity and reality. For those words which are obviously the result of careful search and even seem to parade their self-conscious art fail to attain the grace at which they aim and lose all appearance of sincerity because they darken the sense and choke the good seed by their own luxuriant overgrowth. For in our passion for words we paraphrase what might be said in plain language, repeat what we have already said at sufficient length, pile up a number of words where one would suffice, and regard allusion as better than directness of speech. So, too, all directness of speech is at a discount, and we think no phrase eloquent that another could conceivably have used. We borrow figures and metaphors from the most decadent poets, and regard it as a real sign of genius that it should require a genius to understand our meaning. And yet Cicero long since laid down this rule in the clearest of language, that the worst fault in speaking

is to adopt a style inconsistent with the idiom of ordinary speech and contrary to the common feeling of mankind. But nowadays our rhetoricians regard Cicero as lacking both polish and learning; we are far superior, for we look upon everything that is dictated by nature as beneath our notice, and seek not for the true ornaments of speech, but for meretricious finery, as though there were any real virtue in words save in their power to represent facts. And if we have to spend all our life in the laborious effort to discover words which will at once be brilliant, appropriate and lucid, and to arrange them with exact precision, we lose all the fruit of our studies. And yet we see the majority of modern speakers wasting their time over the discovery of single words and over the elaborate weighing and measurement of such words when once discovered. Even if the special aim of such a practice were always to secure the best words, such an ill-starred form of industry would be much to be deprecated, since it checks the natural current of our speech and extinguishes the warmth of imagination by the delay and loss of self-confidence which it occasions. For the orator who cannot endure to lose a single word is like a man plunged in griping poverty. On the other hand, if he will only first form a true conception of the principles of eloquence, accumulate a copious supply of words by wide and suitable reading, apply the art of arrangement to the words thus acquired, and finally, by continual exercise, develop strength to use his acquisitions so that every word is ready at hand and lies under his very eyes, he will never lose a single word. For the man who follows these instructions will find that facts and words appropriate to their expression will present themselves spontaneously. But it must be remembered that a long course of preliminary study is necessary and that the requisite ability must not merely be acquired, but carefully stored for use; for the anxiety devoted to the search for words, to the exercise of the critical faculty and the power of comparison is in its place while we are learning, but not when we are speaking. Otherwise, the orator who has not given sufficient attention to preliminary study will be like a man who, having no fortune, lives from hand to mouth. If, on the other hand, the powers of speech have been carefully cultivated beforehand, words will yield us ready service, not merely turning up when we search for them, but dwelling in our thoughts and following them as the shadow follows the body. There are, however, limits even to this form of study; for when our words are good Latin, full of meaning, elegantly and aptly arranged, why should we labour further? And yet there are some who are never weary of morbid self-criticism, who throw themselves into an agony of mind almost over separate syllables, and even when they have discovered the best words for their purpose look for some word that is older, less familiar, and less obvious, since they cannot bring themselves to realise that when a speech is praised for its words, it implies that its sense is inadequate. While, then, style calls for the utmost attention, we must always bear in mind that nothing should be done for the sake of words only, since words were invented merely to give expression to things: and those words are the most satisfactory which give the best expression to the thoughts of our mind and produce the effect which we desire on the minds of the judges. Such words will assuredly be productive of a style that will both give pleasure and awaken admiration; and the admiration will be of a kind far other than that which we bestow on portents, while the pleasure evoked by the charm will have nothing morbid about it, but will be praiseworthy and dignified.

—H. E. BUTLER.

STUDY AND WRITING [1]

[From *The Training of the Orator,* Book X]

Quintilian's common sense constantly brings him out in strong relief against the contemporary background of affectation.

The condemnation which I have passed on such carelessness in writing will make it pretty clear what my views are on the luxury of dictation which is now so fashionable. For, when we write, however great our speed, the fact that the hand cannot follow the rapidity of our thoughts gives us time to think, whereas the presence of our amanuensis hurries us on, and at times we feel ashamed to hesitate or pause, or make some alteration, as though we were afraid to display such weakness before a witness. As a result our language tends not merely to be haphazard and formless, but in our desire to produce a continuous flow we let slip positive improprieties of diction, which show neither the precision of the writer nor the impetuosity of the speaker. Again, if the amanuensis is a slow writer, or lacking in intelligence, he becomes a stumbling-block, our speed is checked, and the thread of our ideas is interrupted by the delay or even perhaps by the loss of temper to which it gives rise. Moreover, the gestures which accompany strong feeling, and sometimes even serve to stimulate the mind, the waving of the hand, the contraction of the brow, the occasional striking of the forehead or side, and those which Persius notes when he describes a trivial style as one that

"Thumps not the desk nor smacks of
    bitten nails,"

all these become ridiculous, unless we are alone. Finally, we come to the most important consideration of all, that the ad-

[1] From The Loeb Classical Library, reprinted by permission.

vantages of privacy are lost when we dictate. Everyone, however, will agree that the absence of company and deep silence are most conducive to writing, though I would not go so far as to concur in the opinion of those who think woods and groves the most suitable localities for the purpose, on the ground that the freedom of the sky and the charm of the surroundings produce sublimity of thought and wealth of inspiration. Personally I regard such an environment as a pleasant luxury rather than a stimulus to study. For whatever causes us delight must necessarily distract us from the concentration due to our work. The mind cannot devote its undivided and sincere attention to a number of things at the same time, and wherever it turns its gaze it must cease to contemplate its appointed task. Therefore, the charm of the woods, the gliding of the stream, the breeze that murmurs in the branches, the song of birds, and the very freedom with which our eyes may range, are mere distractions, and in my opinion the pleasure which they excite is more likely to relax than to concentrate our attention. Demosthenes took a wiser view; for he would retire to a place where no voice was to be heard, and no prospect greeted the sight, for fear that his eyes might force his mind to neglect its duty. Therefore, let the burner of the midnight oil seclude himself in the silence of night, within closed doors, with but a solitary lamp to light his labours. But for every kind of study, and more especially for night work, good health and its chief source, simple living, are essential; for we have fallen into the habit of devoting to relentless labour the hour which nature has appointed for rest and relaxation. From those hours we must take only such time as is superfluous for sleep, and will not be missed. For fatigue will make us careless in writing, and the hours of daylight are amply sufficient for one who has no other distractions. It is

only the busy man who is driven to encroach on the hours of darkness. Nevertheless, night work, so long as we come to it fresh and untired, provides by far the best form of privacy.

But although silence and seclusion and absolute freedom of mind are devoutly to be desired, they are not always within our power to attain. Consequently we must not fling aside our book at once, if disturbed by some noise, and lament that we have lost a day: on the contrary, we must make a firm stand against such inconveniences, and train ourselves so to concentrate our thoughts as to rise superior to all impediments to study. If only you direct all your attention to the work which you have in hand, no sight or sound will ever penetrate to your mind. If even casual thoughts often occupy us to such an extent that we do not see passers-by, or even stray from our path, surely we can obtain the same result by the exercise of our will. We must not give way to pretexts for sloth. For unless we make up our mind that we must be fresh, cheerful and free from all other care when we approach our studies, we shall always find some excuse for idleness. Therefore, whether we be in a crowd, on a journey, or even at some festive gathering, our thoughts should always have some inner sanctuary of their own to which they may retire. Otherwise what shall we do when we are suddenly called upon to deliver a set speech in the midst of the forum, with lawsuits in progress on every side, and with the sound of quarrels and even casual outcries in our ears, if we need absolute privacy to discover the thoughts which we jot down upon our tablets? It was for this reason that Demosthenes, the passionate lover of seclusion, used to study on the seashore amid the roar of the breakers that they might teach him not to be unnerved by the uproar of the public assembly.

There are also certain minor details

which deserve our attention, for there is nothing too minute for the student. It is best to write on wax owing to the facility which it offers for erasure, though weak sight may make it desirable to employ parchment by preference. The latter, however, although of assistance to the eye, delays the hand and interrupts the stream of thought owing to the frequency with which the pen has to be supplied with ink. But whichever we employ, we must leave blank pages that we may be free to make additions when we will. For lack of space at times gives rise to a reluctance to make corrections, or, at any rate, is liable to cause confusion when new matter is inserted. The wax tablets should not be unduly wide; for I have known a young and over-zealous student write his compositions at undue length, because he measured them by the number of lines, a fault which persisted, in spite of frequent admonition, until his tablets were changed, when it disappeared. Space must also be left for jotting down the thoughts which occur to the writer out of due order, that is to say, which refer to subjects other than those in hand. For sometimes the most admirable thoughts break in upon us which cannot be inserted in what we are writing, but which, on the other, it is unsafe to put by, since they are at times forgotten, and at times cling to the memory so persistently as to divert us from some other line of thought. They are therefore best kept in store.

—H. E. BUTLER.

THE NEW FREEDOM

SECOND CENTURY

There can be no doubt that the self-centered and suspicious character of the emperor Domitian, whose rule extended from 81 to 96 A.D., was a continual threat against the lives of prominent members of the ruling classes of Rome. Some were put to death, and nearly all driven to a servile attitude or to a careful policy of silence and inaction. No wonder then that at the accession of Nerva, men felt that they were seeing the dawn of a new era. The pages of melancholy Tacitus and of genial Pliny alike reflect the horror of the old and the hope for the new. But it is not to be thought that any essential differences in the form of government involving any diminution of the emperor's powers were introduced. Trajan certainly exercised as much authority as Domitian. Nor was there thought of discarding or annulling the acts of Domitian in the governing of the empire, for the records show that Trajan often confirmed them.

The new era, however, was a very real thing to men of the time. It grew out of a new relation, a new feeling, between emperor and senate. After the murder of Domitian, Nerva succeeded to the throne. He gained his place neither by dynastic succession, nor by the sword of the army, but by the deliberate choice of the senate itself. Nerva was an old man no longer possessed of the vigor necessary to rule the Empire. The idea of adopting as his son and ultimate successor a tried and capable administrator was conceived, and, on the advice of leading senators and with the consent of the senate as a body, Nerva adopted Trajan. The policy of adoption then successfully inaugurated was continued for several following reigns and played no small part in making possible the happiness of the succeeding century. The senate then had actually and freely chosen its emperor. It is noteworthy that there was no talk of a restoration of the Republic, as had at times occurred in years past. That is to say, the senate had come to realize the necessity for Imperial rule. Time had done its work in teaching this fact, and also had conveniently removed the irreconcilables, and had brought in new blood even from the provinces. The senate was now prepared to work with and under the presidency of any reasonable man. Nerva and Trajan responded to this attitude, publicly treated the senate with honor, and the individual senators with respect. The splendid tact of Trajan, which brings Augustus to mind, undoubtedly had much to do with the ensuing era of good feeling. He would have the senate really function as under Augustus, and it showed appreciation by unprecedented loyalty.

This was the period which Tacitus hailed as "a rarely happy time when a man thinks what he likes, and says what he thinks." To men of letters this realization, with the general feeling of relief and hope, gave great encouragement. The result was the enriching of Roman literature by two works of real genius, the historical books of Tacitus and the satires of Juvenal, and by the respectable writings of Pliny and of Suetonius.

But these were the final products in literature of the true Roman spirit. With the reign of Hadrian, successor to Trajan, set in a literary period of archaism which clearly marked a decline in originality. The same reign, however, saw the beginning of a great development in the science of law.

I. APPRECIATION OF THE NEW ORDER

THE CONTRAST [1]

TACITUS

[From the *Agricola*]

The reign of Nerva witnessed a marked literary revival, which was the result of the increased freedom of individual writers to deal with matters of public interest from which they had been excluded for the better part of a century. For Tacitus, see above p. 461.

To hand down to posterity the works and ways of famous men was our father's custom: our age has not yet abandoned it even now, indifferent though it be to its own children, whenever, at least, some great and notable virtue has dominated and overpowered the vice common alike to small states and great—misapprehension of integrity and jealousy.

But in our fathers' times, just as the doing of deeds worth recording was natural and more obvious, so also there was inducement then to the brightest spirits to publish such records of virtue. Partisanship was not the motive or ambition: a good conscience was its own reward; nay, many men even counted it not presumption, but self-respect, to narrate their own lives. A Rutilius, a Scaurus, could do so without falling short of belief or provoking a sneer; so true is it that virtues are best appreciated in those ages which most readily give them birth; but to-day, even though the man whose life I am about to write is already gone, I ought to have craved an indulgence which I should not have needed, had invective been my purpose; so harsh is the spirit of our age, so cynical towards virtue.

It is recorded that when Rusticus Aru-

lenus extolled Thrasea Pætus, when Herennius Senecio extolled Helvidius Priscus, their praise became a capital offence, so that persecution fell not merely on the authors themselves but on the very books: to the public hangman, in fact, was given the task of burning in the courtyard of the Forum the memorials of our noblest characters.

They imagined, no doubt, that in those flames disappeared the voice of the people, the liberty of the Senate, the conscience of mankind; especially as the votaries of Philosophy also were expelled, and all liberal culture exiled, in order that nowhere might anything of good report present itself to men's eyes.

Assuredly we have furnished a signal proof of our submissiveness; and even as former generations witnessed the utmost excesses of liberty, so have we the extremes of slavery; wherein our "Inquisitors" have deprived us even of the give and take of conversation. We should have lost memory itself as well as voice, had forgetfulness been as easy as silence.

Now at last heart is coming back to us: from the first, from the very outset of this happy age, Nerva has united things long incompatible, Empire and liberty; Trajan is increasing daily the happiness of the times; and public confidence has not merely learned to hope and pray, but has received security for the fulfilment of its prayers and even the substance thereof. Though it is true that from the nature of human frailty cure operates more slowly than disease, and as the body itself is slow to grow and quick to decay, so also it is easier to damp men's spirits and their enthusiasm than to revive them: nay, listlessness itself has a certain subtle charm, and the languor we hate at first we learn to love: what else were possible? For the term

[1] From The Loeb Classical Library, reprinted by permission.

of fifteen years, a large space in human life, chance and change have been cutting off many among us; others, and the most energetic, have perished by the Emperor's ferocity; while the few who remain have outlived not merely their neighbours but, so to say, themselves; for out of their prime have been blotted fifteen years, during which mature men reached old age and old men the very bounds almost of decrepitude, and all without opening their lips.

But after all I shall not regret the task of recording our former slavery and testifying to our present blessings, albeit with unpractised and stammering tongue.
—MAURICE HUTTON.

RELEASE FROM TYRANNY [1]

PLINY

[Letters, VIII, 14]

Gaius Plinius Cæcilius Secundus, known as Pliny the Younger, was born at Comum in the year 62. He owed much in his training to the example and guidance of his uncle, Pliny the Elder, author of the *Natural History*, and to the instruction of Quintilian. He entered the public career, climbed to the consulship, and later became governor of Bithynia. In the public business he displayed special ability in matters of finance. Rich, and generous with his riches, he became interested in various forms of philanthropy, which he practised by methods altogether modern. He died about 114.

Pliny is a worthy representative of the better class among the Roman nobility at the beginning of the second century. His *Letters* show him sober, industrious, a good man and a clever, but with little imagination. They give pleasing pictures of society in marked contrast with those found in the satires of the cynical Juvenal. Unlike Cicero, he collected, arranged, and published his letters himself; indeed, there

[1] From The Loeb Classical Library, reprinted by permission.

can be little doubt that they were written for publication in the first instance. They exhibit nothing of the rambling method of the private letter. Rather, they are short essays, each, as a rule, dealing with but a single theme, and having a more or less formal introduction and conclusion.

Pliny finds the most pronounced change among the many that resulted from the new freedom to be the restoration of the senate to its proper place in the government of the Empire.

To Aristo:

As you are equally versed in civil and constitutional law, which latter includes the procedure of the Senate, I am particularly desirous to have your opinion, whether or no I made a mistake in the House the other day. This I request for my better instruction, not as to what is passed (for that is now too late), but as regards questions of the same nature that may hereafter arise.

I can fancy your replying, "Why do you ask, what you ought to have known?" But our servitude under a former reign cast a cloud of oblivion and ignorance over all branches of useful knowledge, and not excluding even the usages of the Senate; for who is so tamespirited as to desire to learn an art of which he will be debarred the exercise? Besides, it is not easy to retain the knowledge one has acquired, without putting it in practice. Thus Liberty at her return found us ignorant and inexperienced; and kindled by her charms, we are sometimes impelled to action, ere we know how to act.

But in the olden time it was an established rule that Romans should learn from their elders, not only by precept, but by example, the principles on which they themselves should one day act, and which they should in their turn transmit to the younger generation. Hence they were inured from boyhood to service in camp, that by being accustomed to obey, they might learn to command, and by following others, be trained to play the leader. And hence, on becoming candidates for office, they used to stand in the senate-house doors, and were spectators, before they were members of the Council of State. The father of each youth served as his instructor, or, if he had none, some person of years and dignity supplied the place of a father. Thus they were taught by that surest method of instruction, example, how far the right of proposing any law to the Senate extended, what privileges a senator had in delivering his opinion; the powers of senators who are magistrates, and the independence of the rest; where it is proper to yield, and where to stand firm; how long to speak, and when to be silent; how to distinguish conflicting motions, and how to discuss an amendment. In a word, they learnt by this means the whole conduct of a senator.

It is true, indeed, I myself served in the army as a young man; but it was at a time when courage was suspected, and cowardice at a premium; when the generals were without authority, and the soldiers without awe; when there was neither command nor obedience; when our whole military system was relaxed, disordered, and actually turned upside down—in short, when it was better to forget than to remember its lessons. I likewise went as a spectator to the Senate, but a Senate that was mute and fearful; since it was dangerous to speak one's real sentiments, and infamous to profess any others. What satisfaction in learning, or indeed what could be learnt, when the Senate was convened either for utter idleness or for business the most criminal; when they were kept sitting either for cruel or ridiculous purposes; and when their resolutions were never serious, though often tragical? On becoming a senator, and a partaker of these miseries, I both witnessed and endured them for many years; which so broke and damped my spirits, that they have not even yet been able fully to recover themselves. It is but a short time (for every period is shorter, the happier it is) since we could take any pleasure in knowing the rights and duties of our station, or in putting that knowledge into practice. . . . Farewell.

—MELMOTH-HUTCHINSON.

AN ENLIGHTENED PRINCE

ON COMPLIMENTING THE PRINCE [1]

PLINY

[*Letters*, VI, 27]

Upon his elevation to the consulship in the year 100, Pliny delivered a speech of thanks to Trajan. The speech, known as the *Panegyric,* is the only one of many by the author which is still extant. In the following letter he is hard put to it to explain away by sophistries its obvious and fulsome flattery.

To Severus

You desire me to consider what turn you should give to your speech in honour of the Emperor, upon your being appointed consul. It is easy to find, but not easy to select, topics of encomium, for this prince's virtues supply them in abundance. However, I will write, or (what I prefer) indicate my views to you in person, only I must first lay my grounds for hesitating before you.

I doubt whether I should advise you to do as I did on the same occasion. When I was consul elect, I refrained from all that customary panegyric which, though not adulation, might yet bear the semblance of it. Not that I affected an intrepid freedom; but as well knowing the sentiments of our amiable prince, and that the highest praise I could offer to him would be to show the world I was

[1] From The Loeb Classical Library, reprinted by permission.

under no necessity of paying him any. When I reflected what honours had been heaped upon the very worst of his predecessors, nothing, I imagined, could more distinguish a prince of his real virtues from these infamous Emperors, than to eulogise him in a different manner. And this point I did not omit or slur over in my speech, lest it might be suspected I passed over his glorious acts, not out of judgment, but forgetfulness.

Such was the method I then observed; but I am sensible the same measures are neither agreeable, nor indeed suitable to all alike. Besides, the propriety of doing or omitting a thing depends not only upon persons, but time and circumstances; and as the late actions of our illustrious Prince afford materials for panegyric, no less just than recent and magnificent, I doubt (as I said before) whether I should persuade you to act in this case as I did myself. In this, however, I am clear, that it was proper to offer to your consideration the plan I pursued. Farewell.

—MELMOTH-HUTCHINSON.

A VISIT TO THE PRINCE [1]

PLINY

[*Letters*, VI, 31]

A century under monarchical government had wrought a great change, since Cicero's day under the dictatorship of Cæsar, in the attitude of men towards one in a position of supreme power.

To Cornelianus

I received lately the most exquisite entertainment imaginable at Centumcellæ (as it is called), whither our Emperor had summoned me to his privy council. Could anything indeed afford a higher pleasure than to see the sovereign exer-

cising his justice, his wisdom, and his affability, and that in retirement, where they are laid most open to view? Various were the cases brought before him, which showed under several aspects the virtues of the judge. That of Claudius Ariston came on first. He is an Ephesian nobleman, of great munificence and unambitious popularity; having thus aroused the envy of persons his opposites in character, they had spirited up an informer against him; such being the facts, he was honourably acquitted. . . .

Thus you see how honourably and seriously we spent our days, which however were followed by the most agreeable recreations. We were every day invited to Cæsar's supper, which, for a prince, was a modest repast; there we were either entertained with interludes, or passed the night in the most pleasing conversation. On the last day he sent each of us presents at our departure, so unremitting is the benevolence of Cæsar! As for myself, I was not only charmed with the dignity of the proceedings, the honour paid to the assessors, the ease and unreserved freedom of the conversation, but with the place itself.

Here is a villa, surrounded by the most verdant meadows, and overhanging a bay of the coast where they are at this moment constructing a harbour. The left-hand mole of this port is protected by immensely solid masonry; the right is now being completed. An island is rising in the mouth of the harbour, which will break the force of the waves when the wind blows shorewards, and afford passage to ships on either side. Its construction is highly worth seeing; huge stones are transported hither in a broad-bottomed vessel, and being sunk one upon the other, are fixed by their own weight, gradually accumulating in the manner, as it were, of a rampart. It already lifts its rocky back above the ocean, while the waves which beat upon it, being tossed to an immense height,

[1] From The Loeb Classical Library, reprinted by permission.

roar prodigiously, and whiten all the sea round. To these stones are added wooden piles, which in time will give it the appearance of a natural island. This port will be, and already is, named after its great author, and will prove of infinite benefit, by affording a haven to ships on a long stretch of harbourless coast. Farewell.

—MELMOTH-HUTCHINSON.

II. MEN AND BOOKS: PLINY

LITERARY FRIENDS

SILIUS ITALICUS [1]

[Letters, III, 7]

The thought that most frequently presents itself to Pliny in the contemplation of men distinguished in any walk of life is the desirability of earthly immortality together with the industry necessary to attain it.

To Caninius Rufus

I am just now informed that Silius Italicus has starved himself to death, at his villa near Naples. Having been afflicted with an imposthume, which was deemed incurable, he grew weary of life under such uneasy circumstances, and therefore put an end to it with the most determined courage. He had been extremely fortunate through the whole course of his days, excepting only the loss of his younger son; however, that was made up to him in the satisfaction of seeing his elder, who is of a more amiable character, attain the consular dignity, and of leaving him in a very flourishing situation. He suffered in his reputation in the time of Nero, having been suspected of forwardly joining in some of the informations which were carried on in the reign of that prince; but he made use of his intimacy with Vitellius, with great discretion and humanity. He acquired much honour by his administration of the government of Asia; and by his proved behaviour after his retirement from business, cleared his character

[1] From The Loeb Classical Library, reprinted by permission.

from that stain which his former intrigues had thrown upon it.

He lived among the nobility of Rome without power, and consequently without envy. He was highly respected and much sought after, and though he was bedridden, his chamber was always thronged with visitors, who came not merely out of regard to his rank. He spent his time in philosophical discussion, when not engaged in writing verses; these he sometimes recited, in order to try the sentiments of the public, but he discovered in them more industry than genius. Lately owing to declining years, he entirely quitted Rome, and lived altogether in Campania, from whence even the accession of the new Emperor did not draw him. A circumstance which I mention as well to the honour of the prince, who permitted such a liberty, as of Italicus, who was not afraid to take it.

He carried his taste for objects of *virtù* so far as to incur reprehension for greedy buying. He had several villas in the same districts, and the last purchase was always the chief favourite, to the neglect of the rest. They were all furnished with large collections of books, statues and portraits, which he more than enjoyed, he even adored; above all the portrait of Virgil, whose birthday he celebrated with more solemnity than his own, especially at Naples, where he used to approach his tomb with as much reverence as if it had been a temple.

In this tranquillity he lived to the seventy-sixth year of his age, with a delicate, rather than a sickly, constitution.

It is remarkable, that as he was the last person upon whom Nero conferred the consular office, so he was the last to die of all those who had been raised by him to that dignity; and again, that the last survivor of Nero's consuls was the one in whose year of office that prince was killed. When I consider this, I cannot forbear lamenting the transitory condition of mankind. Is there anything in nature so short and limited as human life, even in its most extended period? Does it not seem to you, my friend, but yesterday that Nero was upon the throne? and yet not one of all those who were consuls in his reign now remains! But why should I wonder at a circumstance so common? Lucius Piso (the father of that Piso who was infamously assassinated by Valerius Festus in Africa) used to say he did not see one person in the Senate whom he had called upon to speak on the motion before the house when he was consul.

Such multitudes, however strong their vitality, are swept away in so short a space! I am therefore so far from thinking those historic tears of Xerxes need any apology, that in my judgment the story does honour to his character, which informs us, that when this prince had attentively surveyed his immense army, he could not refrain from weeping at the thought that so many thousand lives would so soon be extinct. Let us strive the more earnestly therefore to lengthen out our span of life—life that is poured out like water and falls as the leaf—if not by action (the means to which lie in another's power), yet in any case by study and research; and since it is not granted us to live long, let us transmit to posterity some memorial that we *have* at least *lived*. I well know, you want not any incitement to virtue; but the warmth of my affection for you inclines me to forward you in the course you already pursue; as I have often found myself encouraged by your generous exhortations. "Good is the contention," when friends thus strive who shall animate each other most in their pursuit of immortal fame. Farewell.
—MELMOTH-HUTCHINSON.

AN EXHORTATION TO PUBLISH [1]

[*Letters*, V, 10]

To Suetonius Tranquillus

It is time you should acquit the promise my hendecasyllabic verses gave to our common friends, of your works. The world is every day impatiently inquiring after them, and there is already some danger of their being served with an order to "produce documents." I am myself a good deal backward in publishing, but your slowness and hesitancy are more than a match for even mine. You must hasten your hand, however, otherwise the severity of my satiric verses may perhaps extort from you those self-same writings which the blandishments of my softer Muse could not obtain. Your work is already arrived to that degree of perfection, that the file can only weaken, not polish it. Allow me then the pleasure of seeing your title-page, and hearing that books of my dear Tranquillus are being copied out, sold, and read. It is but fair, and agreeable to our mutual friendship, that I should reap from you the same pleasure you enjoy from me. Farewell.
—MELMOTH-HUTCHINSON.

A NOBLE COMMERCE [1]

[*Letters*, VII, 20]

A number of Pliny's letters are addressed to the historian Tacitus. His admiration and affection for him are evident. We do not know to what extent Tacitus reciprocated, but we do know that on more than one occasion he applied to

[1] From The Loeb Classical Library, reprinted by permission.

Pliny for information to be used in his histories.

To Tacitus

I have perused your oration, and with all the attention I was master of have marked the passages where I think alteration or excision advisable. For 'tis my habit to speak truth, and yours to hear it gladly—very naturally, since none are more patient of censure than those who have the best claim to applause.

I now expect in return your observations upon the speech of mine which I sent you. How agreeable, how noble is such a commerce! and how am I pleased with the thought, that posterity, if it shall at all concern itself with us, will not cease to recount in what harmony, what openness, what mutual confidence we lived together! It will be an instance as remarkable as it is uncommon, that two persons nearly of the same age and official rank, and of some literary reputation (for since I join myself with you, I am obliged to speak of your merit with reserve) should thus foster each other's studies. When I was a very young man, and you already in the prime of your glory and renown, I longed to follow your steps, and to be both really and reputedly "next, but with many a length between," to yourself.

There were at that time many celebrated geniuses in Rome; but you of all others (owing to a similarity in our dispositions) appeared to me the easiest and the most worthy object of my imitation. I am the more rejoiced to find that whenever oratory is the topic of conversation, we are always mentioned together, and that my name comes up as soon as anyone talks of you. There are some who prefer you to me, as others, on the contrary, give me the advantage; but I care not in what order we are placed, so that we are united; for in my estimation, whoever is next to you stands before everybody else. You cannot but have remarked that in wills (unless in the case of particular friendship to either of us), we are named side by side, and the legacies bequeathed to us are the same in value. Since therefore we are thus closely linked together by our pursuits, manners, reputation, and even by those last instances of human judgment, should all this not tend to enflame us mutually with the most ardent affection? Farewell.

—MELMOTH-HUTCHINSON.

AN INCIDENT FOR HISTORY [1]

[*Letters*, VII, 33]

Pliny does not go so far in his request of the historian as Cicero did, who appealed to a contemporary writer to overstep the limits of strict truth in order to make his achievements stand out in large proportions.

To Tacitus

I strongly presage (and I am persuaded not falsely) that your histories will be immortal. I ingenuously own therefore, I so much the more covet a place in them. If we are generally careful to have our faces taken by the best artists, ought we not to desire that our actions may be celebrated by an author like yourself? In view to this, I acquaint you with the following affair, which though it cannot have escaped your attention, as it is mentioned in the journals of the public, still I acquaint you with it, that you may be the more sensible how agreeable it will be to me, that my action, greatly heightened by the hazard which attended it, should receive an additional lustre from the testimony of so bright a genius.

The Senate had appointed Herennius Senecio and myself as counsel for the province of Bætica, in their prosecution of Bæbius Massa. He was convicted;

[1] From The Loeb Classical Library, reprinted by permission.

and the House ordered his effects to be placed under official custody. Senecio, having learnt that the consuls were about to sit to hear complaints, came to me, and proposed that with the same unanimity with which we had conducted the prosecution enjoined on us, we should lodge an application with the consuls, that they would not suffer Massa's effects to be dissipated by those whose duty it was to guard them. I answered, "As we were appointed counsel in this cause by the Senate, you had better consider whether we have not done our part, now the Senate's inquiry is over." "You are at liberty," said he, "to prescribe what bounds you please to yourself, who have no particular connections with the province, except what arise from your late services to them; but it is not so with me, who was born there, and enjoyed the post of Quæstor among them." If such, I told him, was his determined resolution, I was ready to attend him, that whatever resentment should be the consequence of this affair, it might not fall singly upon himself.

We went to the consuls; Senecio spoke what was proper to the occasion, to which I subjoined some remarks. We had scarce ended, when Massa, complaining that Senecio had not acted from loyalty to his clients but bitter animosity against himself, desired leave to prosecute him for high treason. The whole assembly was struck with consternation. I immediately rose up; "Most noble consuls," said I, "I am afraid that Massa has tacitly charged me with betrayal of my client's interests, since he has not asked leave to prosecute me likewise." This speech was instantly caught up, and soon afterwards was the talk of the town. The late Emperor Nerva (who while still a subject remarked every worthy action which passed in public) wrote a most impressive letter to me, congratulating not only me, but the age, which had been vouchsafed an example so much in the spirit (as he was pleased to call it) of the ancients.

But be my action what it may, 'tis yours to heighten and spread the lustre of it; not that I require you to exceed the bounds of reality. For History ought not to depart from the truth, and the truth is all the praise that virtuous actions need. Farewell.

—MELMOTH-HUTCHINSON.

FAME [1]

[*Letters*, IX, 23]

To Maximus

It has frequently happened, as I have been pleading before the centumviri, that those judges, after having preserved as long as possible the gravity and solemnity suitable to their character, have at length as though overcome and compelled, suddenly risen up with one consent to applaud me. I have often likewise gained as much glory in the Senate, as my utmost wishes could desire: but I never was touched with a more sensible pleasure than by an account which I lately received from Cornelius Tacitus. He informed me, that at the last Circensian games, he sat next to a Roman knight, who, after much discourse had passed between them upon various points of learning, asked him if he was an Italian or a provincial? Tacitus replied, "Your acquaintance with literature must have informed you who I am." "Ay!" said the knight, "Pray then is it Tacitus or Pliny I am talking with?" I cannot express how highly I am pleased to find, that our names, as if they were rather the proper appellatives of letters than of men, are ascribed to literature itself; and that those very pursuits render us known to those, who would be ignorant of us by any other means.

An accident of the same nature hap-

[1] From The Loeb Classical Library, reprinted by permission.

pened to me a few days ago. Fabius Rufinus, a person of distinguished merit, was placed next to me at table; and above him a fellow-townsman of his, who was just then come to Rome for the first time. Rufinus desired his friend to take notice of me, and fell to expatiating upon the subject of my eloquence; to whom the other immediately replied, "That must undoubtedly be Pliny." To own the truth, I look upon these instances as a very considerable recompense of my labours. Had Demosthenes reason to be pleased with the old woman of Athens crying out on recognizing him "There goes Demosthenes!" and may I not be allowed to congratulate myself upon the extensive reputation my name has acquired? Yes, my friend, I will rejoice in it. and without scruple own that I do. As I only mention the judgment of others concerning me, not the opinion I conceive of myself, I am not afraid of incurring the censure of vanity; especially from you, who, as you envy no man's reputation, so you are particularly zealous for mine. Farewell.

—MELMOTH-HUTCHINSON.

PUBLIC RECITATIONS [1]

[*Letters*, I, 13]

The practice of public recitations by men of letters had been established in the Augustan age for the purpose of encouraging literature by providing it a wider audience than the manuscript books could secure. It was not long before abuses of one sort or another, such as the removal of all restrictions as to those who merited a public hearing, the substitution of politeness in place of worth as the motive for attendance, hired applause, and the like, crept in to make them little more than a farce. Pliny still takes them quite seriously.

[1] From The Loeb Classical Library, reprinted by permission.

To Sosius Senecio

This year has proved extremely fertile in poetical productions: during the whole month of April, scarce a day has passed wherein we have not been entertained with the recital of some poem. It is a pleasure to me to find, notwithstanding there seems to be so little disposition in the public to attend assemblies of this kind, that literary pursuits still flourish, and men of genius are not discouraged from producing their performances. The greater part of the audience which is collected upon these occasions seat themselves in the ante-chambers; spend the time of the recitation in talk and send in every now and then to inquire whether the author is come in, whether he has read the preface, or whether he has almost finished the piece. Not till then, and even then with the utmost deliberation, they just look in, and withdraw again before the end, some by stealth, and others without ceremony. It was not thus in the time of our ancestors. It is reported that Claudius Cæsar, one day hearing a noise as he walked on the Palatine, inquired the occasion of it, and being informed that Nonianus was reciting a composition of his, went immediately to the place, and surprised the author with his presence. But now, were one to bespeak the company even of the most idle man living, and remind him of the appointment ever so often, or ever so 'long beforehand, either he would avoid it, or, if not, would complain of having *lost a day;* and for no other reason, but because he had *not* lost it. So much the rather do *those* authors deserve our encouragement and applause, who have resolution to persevere in their studies, and exhibit their performances, notwithstanding this indolence or pride of their audience. For my own part, I scarce ever refuse to be present upon such occasions. Though, to say truth, the authors have generally been my friends; as indeed there are few friends of learning who are not. It is this has kept me in town longer than I intended. I am now however at liberty to withdraw to my retirement, and write something myself: but without any intentions of reciting in my turn. I would not have it thought that I rather *lent* than gave my attendance; for in these, as in all other good offices, the obligation ceases the moment you seem to expect a return. Farewell.

—MELMOTH-HUTCHINSON.

MINERVA AND DIANA [1]

[*Letters*, I, 6]

To Cornelius Tacitus

Certainly you will laugh (and laugh you may) when I tell you that your old acquaintance is turned sportsman, and has taken three noble boars. What! (methinks I hear you say with astonishment) Pliny!—*Even he.* However, I indulged at the same time my beloved inactivity, and whilst I sat at my nets, you would have found me, not with spear and dart, but pen and tablets by my side. I mused and wrote, being resolved if I returned with my hands empty, at least to come home with my pocket-book full. Believe me, this manner of studying is not to be despised; you cannot conceive how greatly exercise contributes to enliven the imagination. Besides the sylvan solitude with which one is surrounded, and the very silence which is observed on these occasions, strongly incline the mind to meditation. For the future therefore let me advise you, whenever you hunt, to take along with you your tablets, as well as your basket and bottle: for be assured you will find Minerva as fond of roaming the hills as Diana. Farewell.

—MELMOTH-HUTCHINSON.

[1] From The Loeb Classical Library, reprinted by permission.

TOWN AND COUNTRY [1]

[*Letters*, I, 9]

To Minicius Fundanus

One cannot but be surprised, that take any single day in Rome, the reckoning comes out right, or at least seems to do so; and yet, if you take them in the lump, the reckoning comes out wrong. Ask anyone how he has been employed today? he will tell you, perhaps, "I have been at the ceremony of assuming the *manly robe;* this friend invited me to a betrothal, this to a wedding; that desired me to attend the hearing of his cause; one begged me to be witness to his will; another called me to sit as co-assessor." These are offices which, on the day one is engaged in them, appear necessary; yet they seem *bagatelles* when reckoned as your daily occupation—and far more so, when you have quitted Rome for the country. *Then* one is apt to reflect, How many days have I spent on trifles! At least it is a reflection which frequently comes across me at Laurentum, after I have been employing myself in my studies, or even in the necessary care of the animal machine (for the body must be repaired and supported, if we would preserve the mind in all its vigour). In that peaceful retreat, I neither hear nor speak anything of which I have occasion to repent. I suffer none to repeat to me the whispers of malice; nor do I censure any man, unless myself, when I am dissatisfied with my compositions. There I live undisturbed by rumour, and free from the anxious solicitudes of hope or fear, conversing only with myself and with my books. True and genuine life! pleasing and honourable repose! More, perhaps, to be desired than the noblest employments! Thou solemn sea and solitary shore, best and most retired scene for contemplation, with how many noble thoughts have you inspired me! Snatch then, my friend, as I have, the first occasion of leaving the noisy town with all its very empty pursuits, and devote your days to study or even resign them to sloth: for as my ingenious friend Atilius pleasantly said, "It is better to do nothing than to be *doing* of *nothing.*" Farewell.

—MELMOTH-HUTCHINSON.

THE ELDER PLINY'S LIFE AND WORKS [1]

[*Letters*, III, 5]

Of the tremendous product of the Elder Pliny's pen only his *Natural History,* a general encyclopedia of the arts and sciences, is now extant.

To Bæbius Macer

It is with much pleasure I find you are so constant a reader of my uncle's works, as to wish to have a complete collection of them; and for that purpose desire me to send you an account of all the treatises he wrote. I will fill the place of an index and even acquaint you with the order in which they were composed: for that, too, is a sort of information not at all unacceptable to men of letters.

The first book he published was a treatise concerning the *Art of using a javelin on horseback:* this he wrote when he commanded a troop of horse, and is drawn up with equal accuracy and judgment. *The life of Pomponius Secundus,* in two volumes: Pomponius had a very great affection for him, and he thought he owed this tribute to his memory. *The history of the wars in Germany,* in twenty books, in which he gave an account of all the campaigns we were engaged in against that nation. A dream which he had when he served in the army in Germany, first suggested to him the design of this work. The phantom of Drusus Nero (who extended his conquests very far into that country, and there lost his life) appeared to him in his sleep, and

[1] From The Loeb Classical Library, reprinted by permission.

conjured him not to suffer his memory to be buried in oblivion. He has left us likewise *The student,* in three books, divided into six volumes, owing to their length. In this work he takes the orator from his cradle and leads him on till he has carried him up to the highest point of perfection in this art. In the last years of Nero's reign, when the tyranny of the times made it dangerous to engage in studies of a more free and elevated spirit, he published *Linguistic queries,* in eight books; *A Continuation,* in one book, of the thirty books of Aufidius Bassus' history; and thirty-seven books of a *Natural History:* this is a work of great compass and learning, and as full of variety as nature herself.

You will wonder how a man so engaged as he was, could find time to compose such a number of books; and some of them too upon abstruse subjects. But your surprise will rise still higher, when you hear, that for some time he engaged in the profession of an advocate, that he died in his fifty-sixth year, that from the time of his quitting the bar to his death he was engaged and trammelled by the execution of the highest posts, and by the friendships of his sovereigns. But he had a quick apprehension, incredible zeal, and a wakefulness beyond compare. He always began to work at midnight when the August festival of Vulcan came round; not for the good omen's sake, but for the sake of study; in winter generally at one in the morning, but never later than two, and often at midnight. No man ever slept more readily, insomuch that he would sometimes, without retiring from his book, take a short sleep, and then pursue his studies.

Before day-break he used to wait upon Vespasian; who likewise chose that season to transact business. When he had finished the affairs which that emperor committed to his charge, he returned home again to his studies. After a short and light repast at noon (agreeably to the good old custom of our ancestors) he would frequently in the summer, if he was disengaged from business, repose himself in the sun; during which time some author was read to him, from whence he made extracts and observations, as indeed this was his constant method whatever book he read: for it was a maxim of his that "no book was so bad but some profit might be gleaned from it." When this basking was over, he generally went into the cold bath, and as soon as he came out of it, just took a slight refreshment, and then reposed himself for a little while. Then, as if it had been a new day, he immediately resumed his studies till dinner-time, when a book was again read to him, upon which he would make some running notes. I remember once, his reader having pronounced a word wrong, somebody at the table made him repeat it again; upon which my uncle asked his friend if he understood it? Who acknowledging that he did; "why then," said he, "would you make him go back again? We have lost by this interruption of yours above ten lines:" so chary was this great man of time! In summer he always rose for supper by day-light; and in winter as soon as it was dark; and this was a sort of binding law with him.

Such was his manner of life amidst the noise and hurry of the town; but in the country his whole time was devoted to study without intermission, excepting only while he bathed. But in this exception I include no more than the time he was actually in the bath; for all the while he was rubbed and wiped, he was employed either in hearing some book read to him, or in dictating himself. In his journeys, as though released from all other cares, he found leisure for this sole pursuit. A shorthand writer, with book and tablet, constantly attended him in his chariot, who, in the winter, wore a particular sort of warm gloves, that the sharpness of the weather might not occasion any interruption to his studies; and for the same reason my uncle always used a sedan chair in Rome. I remember he once reproved me for walking; "You might," said he, "not have lost those hours"; for he thought all was time lost that was not given to study. By this extraordinary application he found time to write so many volumes, besides one hundred and sixty which he left me, consisting of a kind of common-place, written on both sides, in a very small character; so that one might fairly reckon the number considerably more. I have heard him say that when he was comptroller of the revenue in Spain, Larcius Licinius offered him four hundred thousand sesterces for these manuscripts: and yet they were not then quite so numerous.

When you reflect upon the books he has read, and the volumes he has written, are you not inclined to suppose that he never was an official or a courtier? On the other hand, when you are informed how painstaking he was in his studies, are you not disposed to think that he read and wrote too little? For, on one side, what obstacles would not the business of a court throw in his way? And on the other, what is it that such intense application might not perform? I cannot but smile therefore when I hear myself called a studious man, who in comparison to him am a mere loiterer. But why do I mention myself, who am diverted from these pursuits by numberless duties both public and private? Where is he, among those whose whole lives are spent in study, who must not blush under the consciousness of being but a sluggard and a dreamer, compared with this great scholar?

I have run out my letter, I perceive, beyond the extent I at first designed, which was only to inform you, as you desired, what treatises he has left behind him. But I trust this will not be less acceptable to you than the books themselves, as it may possibly not only raise your curiosity to read his works, but your emulation to copy his example by some attempts of the same nature. Farewell.

—MELMOTH-HUTCHINSON.

ENDOWING A SCHOOL [1]

[*Letters*, IV, 13]

There is nothing new in the method of giving a dollar for every dollar raised from other sources.

To Cornelius Tacitus

I rejoice that you are safely arrived in Rome; for though I am always desirous to see you, I am more particularly so now. I purpose to continue a few days longer at my Tusculum estate in order to finish a little work which I have upon my hands. For I am afraid, should I put a stop to this design, now that it is so nearly completed, I should find it difficult to resume it. Meanwhile, that I may strike while the iron is hot, I send this letter, like an *avant-courier*, to request a favour of you, which I mean shortly to ask in person. But before I inform you what my request is, I must let you into the occasion of it.

Being lately at my native place, a young lad, son to one of my fellow-townsmen, made me a visit. "Do you go to school?" I asked him. "Yes," said he. "And where?" He told me, "At Milan." "And why not here?" "Because" (said his father, who was present, and had in fact brought the boy with him), "we have no teachers." "How is that?" said I; "surely it nearly concerns you who are fathers" (and very opportunely several of the company were so) "that your sons should receive their education here, rather than any where else. For where can they be placed more agreeably than in

[1] From The Loeb Classical Library, reprinted by permission.

their own country, or be maintained in more modest habits and at less expense, than at home and under the eye of their parents? Upon what very easy terms might you, by a general contribution, procure teachers, if you would only apply towards raising a salary for them what you now spend on your sons' lodging, journeys, and whatever a man has to pay for when abroad (which means, paying for everything). Why, I, who have as yet no children myself, am ready to give a third part of any sum you shall think proper to raise for this purpose, for the benefit of our Commonwealth, whom I regard as a daughter or a parent. I would take upon myself the whole expense, were I not apprehensive that my benefaction might hereafter be abused and perverted to private ends; as I have observed to be the case in several places where teachers are engaged by the local authorities. The single means to prevent this mischief is, to leave the choice of the professors entirely in the breast of the parents, who will be so much the more careful to determine properly, as they shall be obliged to share the expense of maintaining them. For though they may be careless in disposing of another's bounty, they will certainly be cautious how they apply their own; and will see that none but those who deserve it shall receive my money, when they must at the same time receives theirs too. Let my example then encourage you to unite heartily in this design; and be assured the greater the sum my share shall amount to, the more agreeable it will be to me. You can undertake nothing more advantageous to your children, nor more acceptable to your country. They will by this means receive their education where they receive their birth, and be accustomed from their infancy to inhabit and affect their native soil. May you be able to procure professors of such distinguished abilities, that the neighbouring towns shall be glad to draw their learning from hence; and as you now send your children to foreigners for education, may foreigners hereafter flock hither for their instruction."

I thought proper thus to lay open to you the rise of this affair, that you might be the more sensible how agreeable it will be to me, if you undertake the office I request. I entreat you, therefore, with all the earnestness a matter of so much importance deserves, to look out, amongst the great numbers of men of letters which the reputation of your genius brings to you, teachers to whom we may apply for this purpose; but it must be understood that I cannot make a binding agreement with any of them. For I would leave it entirely free to the parents to judge and choose as they shall see proper: all the share I pretend to claim is, that of contributing my care and my money. If therefore any one shall be found who relies upon his own talents, he may repair thither; but under the proviso that the said reliance is all he can count upon, so far as I am concerned. Farewell.
—MELMOTH-HUTCHINSON.

THE ERUPTION OF VESUVIUS [1]

[*Letters,* VI, 16]

The description given in this and the following letter of the external appearance of things and of the conduct of the people on the occasion of the terrible eruption of Vesuvius in the year 79, which destroyed the flourishing cities of Pompeii and Herculaneum, was followed closely by Bulwer Lytton in his *Last Days of Pompeii.*

To Tacitus

Your request that I would send you an account of my uncle's end, so that you may transmit a more exact relation of it

[1] From The Loeb Classical Library, reprinted by permission.

to posterity, deserves my acknowledgements; for if his death shall be celebrated by your pen, the glory of it, I am aware, will be rendered for ever deathless. For notwithstanding he perished, as did whole peoples and cities, in the destruction of a most beautiful region, and by a misfortune memorable enough to promise him a kind of immortality; notwithstanding he has himself composed many and lasting works; yet I am persuaded, the mentioning of him in your immortal writings, will greatly contribute to eternize his name. Happy I esteem those, whom Providence has gifted with the ability either to do things worthy of being written, or to write in a manner worthy of being read; but most happy they, who are blessed with both talents: in which latter class my uncle will be placed both by his own writings and by yours. The more willingly do I undertake, nay, solicit, the task you set me.

He was at that time with the fleet under his command at Misenum. On the 24th of August, about one in the afternoon, my mother desired him to observe a cloud of very unusual size and appearance. He had sunned himself, then taken a cold bath, and after a leisurely luncheon was engaged in study. He immediately called for his shoes and went up an eminence from whence he might best view this very uncommon appearance. It was not at that distance discernible from what mountain this cloud issued, but it was found afterwards to be Vesuvius. I cannot give you a more exact description of its figure, than by resembling it to that of a pine-tree, for it shot up a great height in the form of a trunk, which extended itself at the top into several branches; because, I imagine, a momentary gust of air blew it aloft, and then failing, forsook it; thus causing the cloud to expand laterally as it dissolved, or possibly the downward pressure of its own weight produced this effect. It was at one moment white, at another dark and spotted, as if it had carried up earth or cinders.

My uncle, true savant that he was, deemed the phenomenon important and worth a nearer view. He ordered a light vessel to be got ready, and gave me the liberty, if I thought proper, to attend him. I replied I would rather study; and, as it happened, he had himself given me a theme for composition. As he was coming out of the house he received a note from Rectina, the wife of Bassus, who was in the utmost alarm at the imminent danger (his villa stood just below us, and there was no way to escape but by sea); she earnestly entreated him to save her from such deadly peril. He changed his first design and what he began with a philosophical, he pursued with an heroical turn of mind. He ordered large galleys to be launched, and went himself on board one, with the intention of assisting not only Rectina, but many others; for the villas stand extremely thick upon that beautiful coast. Hastening to the place from whence others were flying, he steered his direct course to the point of danger, and with such freedom from fear, as to be able to make and dictate his observations upon the successive motions and figures of that terrific object.

And now cinders, which grew thicker and hotter the nearer he approached, fell into the ships, then pumice-stones too, with stones blackened, scorched, and cracked by fire, then the sea ebbed suddenly from under them, while the shore was blocked up by landslips from the mountains. After considering a moment whether he should retreat, he said to the captain who was urging that course, "Fortune befriends the brave; carry me to Pomponianus." Pomponianus was then at Stabiæ, distant by half the width of the bay (for, as you know, the shore, insensibly curving in its sweep, forms here a receptacle for the sea). He had already embarked his baggage; for though

at Stabiæ the danger was not yet near, it was full in view, and certain to be extremely near, as soon as it spread; and he resolved to fly as soon as the contrary wind should cease. It was full favourable, however, for carrying my uncle to Pomponianus. He embraces, comforts, and encourages his alarmed friend, and in order to soothe the other's fears by his own unconcern, desires to be conducted to a bathroom; and after having bathed, he sate down to supper with great cheerfulness, or at least (what is equally heroic) with all the appearance of it.

In the meanwhile Mount Vesuvius was blazing in several places with spreading and towering flames, whose refulgent brightness the darkness of the night set in high relief. But my uncle, in order to soothe apprehensions, kept saying that some fires had been left alight by the terrified country people, and what they saw were only deserted villas on fire in the abandoned district. After this he retired to rest, and it is most certain that his rest was a most genuine slumber; for his breathing, which, as he was pretty fat, was somewhat heavy and sonorous, was heard by those who attended at his chamber-door. But the court which led to his apartment now lay so deep under a mixture of pumice-stones and ashes, that if he had continued longer in his bedroom, egress would have been impossible. On being aroused, he came out, and returned to Pomponianus and the others, who had sat up all night. They consulted together as to whether they should hold out in the house, or wander about in the open. For the house now tottered under repeated and violent concussions, and seemed to rock to and fro as if torn from its foundations. In the open air, on the other hand, they dreaded the falling pumice-stones, light and porous though they were; yet this, by comparison, seemed the lesser danger of the two; a conclusion which my uncle arrived at by balancing reasons, and the others by balancing fears. They tied pillows upon their heads with napkins; and this was their whole defence against the showers that fell round them.

It was now day everywhere else, but there a deeper darkness prevailed than in the most obscure night; relieved, however, by many torches and divers illuminations. They thought proper to go down upon the shore to observe from close at hand if they could possibly put out to sea, but they found the waves still run extremely high and contrary. There my uncle having thrown himself down upon a disused sail, repeatedly called for, and drank, a draught of cold water; soon after, flames, and a strong smell of sulphur, which was the forerunner of them, dispersed the rest of the company in flight; him they only aroused. He raised himself up with the assistance of two of his slaves, but instantly fell; some unusually gross vapour, as I conjecture, having obstructed his breathing and blocked his windpipe, which was not only naturally weak and constricted, but chronically inflamed. When day dawned again (the third from that he last beheld) his body was found entire and uninjured, and still fully clothed as in life; its posture was that of a sleeping, rather than a dead man.

Meanwhile my mother and I were at Misenum. But this has no connection with history, and your inquiry went no further than concerning my uncle's death. I will therefore put an end to my letter. Suffer me only to add, that I have faithfully related to you what I was either an eye-witness of myself, or heard at the time, when report speaks most truly. You will select what is most suitable to your purpose; for there is a great difference between a letter, and an history; between writing to a friend, and writing for the public. Farewell.
—MELMOTH-HUTCHINSON.

ESCAPE FROM VESUVIUS [1]

[Letters, VI, 20]

To Cornelius Tacitus

The letter which, in compliance with your request, I wrote to you concerning the death of my uncle, has raised, you say, your curiosity to know not only what terrors, but what calamities I endured when left behind at Misenum (for there I broke off my narrative).

"Though my shock'd soul recoils, my tongue shall tell."

My uncle having set out, I gave the rest of the day to study—the object which had kept me at home. After which I bathed, dined, and retired to short and broken slumbers. There had been for several days before some shocks of earthquake, which the less alarmed us as they are frequent in Campania; but that night they became so violent that one might think that the world was not being merely shaken, but turned topsy-turvy. My mother flew to my chamber; I was just rising, meaning on my part to awaken her, if she was asleep. We sat down in the forecourt of the house, which separated it by a short space from the sea. I know not whether I should call it courage or inexperience—I was not quite eighteen—but I called for a volume of Livy, and began to read, and even went on with the extracts I was making from it, as if nothing were the matter. Lo and behold, a friend of my uncle's who was just come to him from Spain, appears on the scene; observing my mother and me seated, and that I have actually a book in my hand, he sharply censures her patience and my indifference; nevertheless I still went on intently with my author.

It was now six o'clock in the morning, the light still ambiguous and faint. The buildings around us already tottered, and though we stood upon open ground, yet as the place was narrow and confined, there was certain and formidable danger from their collapsing. It was not till then we resolved to quit the town. The common people follow us in the utmost consternation, preferring the judgment of others to their own (wherein the extreme of fear resembles prudence), and impel us onwards by pressing in a crowd upon our rear. Being got outside the houses, we halt in the midst of a most strange and dreadful scene. The coaches which we had ordered out, though upon the most level ground, were sliding to and fro, and could not be kept steady even when stones were put against the wheels. Then we beheld the sea sucked back, and as it were repulsed by the convulsive motion of the earth; it is certain at least the shore was considerably enlarged, and now held many sea-animals captive on the dry sand. On the other side, a black and dreadful cloud bursting out in gusts of igneous serpentine vapour now and again yawned open to reveal long fantastic flames, resembling flashes of lightning but much larger.

Our Spanish friend already mentioned now spoke with more warmth and instancy: "If your brother—if your uncle," said he, "is yet alive, he wishes you both may be saved; if he has perished, it was his desire that you might survive him. Why therefore do you delay your escape?" We could never think of our own safety, we said, while we were uncertain of his. Without more ado our friend hurried off, and took himself out of danger at the top of his speed.

Soon afterwards, the cloud I have described began to descend upon the earth, and cover the sea. It had already begirt the hidden Capreæ, and blotted from sight the promontory of Misenum. My mother now began to beseech, exhort, and command me to escape as best I might; a young man could do it; she

burdened with age and corpulency, would die easy if only she had not caused my death. I replied, I would not be saved without her, and taking her by the hand, I hurried her on. She complies reluctantly and not without reproaching herself for retarding me. Ashes now fall upon us, though as yet in no great quantity. I looked behind me; gross darkness pressed upon our rear, and came rolling over the land after us like a torrent. I proposed while we yet could see, to turn aside, lest we should be knocked down in the road by the crowd that followed us and trampled to death in the dark. We had scarce sat down, when darkness overspread us, not like that of a moonless or cloudy night, but of a room when it is shut up, and the lamp put out. You could hear the shrieks of women, the crying of children, and the shouts of men; some were seeking their children, others their parents, others their wives or husbands, and only distinguishing them by their voices; one lamenting his own fate, another that of his family; some praying to die, from the very fear of dying; many lifting their hands to the gods; but the greater part imagining that there were no gods left anywhere, and that the last and eternal night was come upon the world.

There were even some who augmented the real perils by imaginary terrors. Newcomers reported that such or such a building at Misenum had collapsed or taken fire—falsely, but they were credited. By degrees it grew lighter; which we imagined to be rather the warning of approaching fire (as in truth it was) than the return of day: however, the fire stayed at a distance from us: then came darkness, and a heavy shower of ashes; we were obliged every now and then to rise and shake them off, otherwise we should have been buried and even crushed under their weight. I might have boasted that amidst dangers so appalling, not a sigh or expression of fear escaped from me, had not my support been founded in that miserable, though strong consolation, that all mankind were involved in the same calamity, and that I was perishing with the world itself.

At last this dreadful darkness was attenuated by degrees to a kind of cloud or smoke, and passed away; presently the real day returned, and even the sun appeared, though lurid as when an eclipse is in progress. Every object that presented itself to our yet affrighted gaze was changed, covered over with a drift of ashes, as with snow. We returned to Misenum, where we refreshed ourselves as well as we could, and passed an anxious night between hope and fear; though indeed with a much larger share of the latter, for the earthquake still continued, and several enthusiastic people were giving a grotesque turn to their own and their neighbours' calamities by terrible predictions. Even then, however, my mother and I, notwithstanding the danger we had passed, and that which still threatened us, had no thoughts of leaving the place, till we should receive some tidings of my uncle.

And now, you will read this narrative, so far beneath the dignity of a history, without any view of transferring it to your own; and indeed you must impute it to your own request, if it shall appear scarce worthy of a letter. Farewell.
—MELMOTH-HUTCHINSON.

VIRGINIUS RUFUS [1]

[Letters, II, 1]

To Voconius Romanus

Rome has not for many years beheld so striking and memorable a spectacle as was lately exhibited in the public funeral of Virginius Rufus, one of her greatest citizens, and no less fortunate than illustrious. For he lived thirty years after

[1] From The Loeb Classical Library, reprinted by permission.

achieving fame, he read his actions in the pages of poets and historians, and thus made one among his survivors. He was thrice raised to the dignity of Consul, that he who refused to be the first of princes, might at least be the highest of subjects. He escaped the resentment of those emperors to whom his virtues had rendered him suspect, and even odious, and left the best, the most amicable of princes firmly seated on the throne, as if providence had purposely preserved him to receive the honour of this public funeral. He arrived, in full tranquillity and universally revered, to the eighty-fourth year of his age, still enjoying robust health, excepting only a paralytic disorder in his hands, which however was attended with no pain. His passage to death, alone, was severe and tedious; but even this was matter for praise. As he was rehearsing his speech of thanks to the Emperor, who had raised him to the consulship, a volume, which chanced to be inconveniently large for him to hold, escaped by its sheer weight the grasp that his age and his upright posture doubly enfeebled. In hastily endeavouring to recover it, he missed his footing on the smooth slippery pavement; fell down, and broke his hip-bone; which fracture, as it was unskillfully set at first, and having besides the infirmities of age to contend with, could never be brought to unite again.

The funeral obsequies paid to the memory of this great man have done honour to the Emperor, to the present age, and also to Eloquence herself. The consul Cornelius Tacitus pronounced his funeral oration: for the series of his felicities was crowned by the applause of the most eloquent of orators. He died full of years and of glory, as illustrious by the honours he refused, as by those he accepted. Still, however, he will be missed and lamented by us, as the bright model of a bygone age; especially by myself, who not only admired him as a patriot, but loved him as a friend. We were not only natives of the same province, and of neighbouring towns, but our estates were contiguous. Besides, he was also left guardian to me, and treated me with the affection of a parent. Whenever I offered myself as a candidate for any employment, he constantly honoured me with his support; though he had long since renounced friendly services of this nature, he would always hasten from his rural retirement to attend my formal entry upon an office. At the time when it is customary for the priests to nominate such as they judge worthy to be received into their sacred office, he constantly proposed me. Even in his last sickness, being apprehensive he might be named one of the five commissioners appointed by the senate to reduce the public expenses, he fixed upon me, young as I am, to carry his excuses, in preference to so many other friends of superior age and dignity; and in a very obliging manner assured me, that had he a son of his own, he would nevertheless have employed me in that office.

Thus I am constrained to lament his death, as if it were immature, and pour out the fullness of my grief in the bosom of my friend; if indeed it be permissible to grieve at all upon this occasion, or to call that event *death*, which to *such* a man, is rather to be looked upon as the period of his mortality, than of his life. For he lives and will continue to live for ever; and his fame will be spread farther by the recollection and the tongues of men now that he is removed from their sight.

I had many other things to write to you, but my mind is so entirely taken up with this subject, that I cannot call it off to any other. Virginius is constantly in my thoughts; the vain but lively impressions of him are continually before my eyes, and I am for ever fondly imagining that I hear him, converse with him, and embrace him. There are, perhaps,

and possibly hereafter will be, some few Romans who may rival him in virtue; but not one, I am persuaded, that will ever equal him in glory. Farewell.
—MELMOTH-HUTCHINSON.

ARRIA'S LIFE AND DEATH [1]

[*Letters*, III, 16]

To Nepos

Methinks I have observed, that amongst the actions and sayings of distinguished persons in either sex, those which have been most celebrated have not always been the most illustrious; and I am confirmed in this opinion by a conversation I had yesterday with Fannia. This lady is granddaughter to that celebrated Arria, who gave her husband not only consolation, but an example, in the hour of death. She informed me of several particulars relating to Arria, not less heroical than this famous action of hers, though not so well known; which I am persuaded will raise your admiration as much when you read, as they did mine when I heard them.

Arria's husband, Cæcina Pætus, and her son, were both at the same time attacked with a seemingly mortal illness, of which the son died. This youth, who had a most beautiful person and was as modest as he was beautiful, had endeared himself to his parents no less by his other claims on their affection than by his relation to them. His mother managed his funeral so privately that Pætus did not know of his death, nay, more, whenever she came into his bed-chamber, she pretended her son was better; and as often as he inquired after his health, would answer that he had rested well, or had eaten with an appetite. When she found that she could no longer restrain her grief, but her tears were gushing out,

[1] From The Loeb Classical Library, reprinted by permission.

she would leave the room, and having given vent to her passion, return again with dry eyes and a serene countenance, as if she had dismissed every pang of bereavement at her entrance. The action was, no doubt, truly noble, when drawing the dagger she plunged it in her breast, and then presented it to her husband with that ever-memorable, I had almost said that divine expression, "It does not hurt, my Pætus." It must however be considered, when she spoke and acted thus, she had the prospect of immortal glory before her eyes to encourage and support her. But was it not something much greater, without the view of such powerful motives, to hide her tears, to conceal her grief, and cheerfully play the mother when she was so no more?

Scribonianus had taken up arms in Illyria against Claudius, but being slain, Pætus, who was of his party, was brought prisoner to Rome. When they were going to put him on board a ship, Arria besought the soldiers that she might be permitted to go with him: "Of course," said she, "you mean to give a consular, as he is, a few slaves to wait upon him at his table and toilet; but if you will take me, I alone will perform their whole duties." This favour, however, she could not obtain; upon which she hired a small fishing-vessel, and pursued that great ship in a mere cockle-shell. At her return to Rome, she met the wife of Scribonianus in the emperor's palace, who had turned evidence for the prosecution: "What," said she, "am I to suffer you to address me, who saw your husband murdered even in your very arms, and yet survived him?" An expression which plainly shews, that the noble manner in which she put an end to her life, was no unpremeditated effect of sudden passion.

When, too, Thrasea, who married her daughter, was dissuading her from her purpose of destroying herself, and among other arguments which he used, said to her, "Would you then advise your daughter to die with me, if my life were to be taken from me?" "Most certainly I would," she replied, "if she had lived as long and in as much harmony with you as I have with my Pætus." This answer greatly heightened the alarm of her family, and made them observe her for the future more narrowly; which, when she perceived, "you are wasting your trouble," said she, "you can oblige me to die a painful death, but you cannot prevent me from dying." She had scarce said this, when she sprang from her chair, and running her head with the utmost violence against the wall, she fell down, in appearance dead. But being brought to herself, "I told you," said she, "if you would not suffer me to take the easy path to death, I should make my way to it through some more difficult passage."

Now, is there not, my friend, something much greater in all this, than the so-much-talked-of "Pætus, it is not painful," to which these actions led the way? and yet this last is the favourite topic of fame, while all the former are passed over in profound silence. Whence we must infer, what I observed in the beginning of my letter, that the most famous actions are not always the most noble. Farewell.

—MELMOTH-HUTCHINSON.

GHOST STORIES [1]

[Letters, VII, 27]

To Sura

The present recess from business affords you leisure to give, and me to receive, instruction. I am extremely desirous therefore to know your sentiments concerning spectres, whether you believe they actually exist and have their own proper shapes and a measure of divinity, or are only the false impressions of a terrified imagination?

[1] From The Loeb Classical Library, reprinted by permission.

What particularly inclines me to give credit to their existence, is a story which I heard of Curtius Rufus. When he was in low circumstances and unknown in the world, he attended the newly-made governor of Africa into that province. One afternoon as he was walking in the public portico he was extremely daunted with the figure of a woman which appeared to him, of a size and beauty more than human. She told him that she was the tutelar Genius that presided over Africa, and was come to inform him of the future events of his life:—that he should go back to Rome, where he should hold office, and return to that province invested with the proconsular dignity, and there should die. Every circumstance of this prophecy was actually accomplished. It is said farther, that upon his arrival at Carthage, as he was coming out of the ship, the same figure accosted him upon the shore. It is certain, at least, that being seized with a fit of illness, though there were no symptoms in his case that led his attendants to despair, he instantly gave up all hope of recovery; judging, it should seem, of the truth of the future part of the prediction, by that which had already been fulfilled; and of the misfortune which threatened him, by the success which he had experienced.

To this story, let me add another as remarkable as the former, but attended with circumstances of greater horror; which I will give you exactly as it was related to me. There was at Athens a large and spacious, but ill-reputed and pestilential house. In the dead of the night a noise, resembling the clashing of iron, was frequently heard, which, if you listened more attentively, sounded like the rattling of fetters; at first it seemed at a distance, but approached nearer by degrees; immediately afterward a phantom appeared in the form of an old man, extremely meagre and squalid, with a long beard and bristling hair, rattling the gyves on his feet and hands. The poor inhabitants consequently passed sleepless nights under the most dismal terrors imaginable. This, as it broke their rest, threw them into distempers, which, as their horrors of mind increased, proved in the end fatal to their lives. For even in the day time, though the spectre did not appear, yet the remembrance of it made such a strong impression upon their imaginations that it still seemed before their eyes, and their terror remained when the cause of it was gone. By this means the house was at last deserted, as being judged by everybody to be absolutely uninhabitable; so that it was now entirely abandoned to the ghost. However, in hopes that some tenant might be found who was ignorant of this great calamity which attended it, a bill was put up, giving notice that it was either to be let or sold.

It happened that Athenodorus the philosopher came to Athens at this time, and reading the bill ascertained the price. The extraordinary cheapness raised his suspicion; nevertheless, when he heard the whole story, he was so far from being discouraged, that he was more strongly inclined to hire it, and, in short, actually did so. When it grew towards evening, he ordered a couch to be prepared for him in the fore-part of the house, and after calling for a light, together with his pen and tablets, he directed all his people to retire within. But that his mind might not, for want of employment, be open to the vain terrors of imaginary noises and apparitions, he applied himself to writing with all his faculties. The first part of the night passed with usual silence, then began the clanking of iron fetters; however, he neither lifted up his eyes, nor laid down his pen, but closed his ears by concentrating his attention. The noise increased and advanced nearer, till it seemed at the door, and at last in the chamber. He looked round and saw the apparition exactly as it had been described to him: it stood before him, beckoning with the finger. Athenodorus made a sign with his hand that it should wait a little, and bent again to his writing, but the ghost rattling his chains over his head as he wrote, he looked round and saw it beckoning as before. Upon this he immediately took up his lamp and followed it. The ghost slowly stalked along, as if encumbered with its chains; and having turned into the court-yard of the house, suddenly vanished. Athenodorus being thus deserted, marked the spot with a handful of grass and leaves. The next day he went to the magistrates, and advised them to order that spot to be dug up. There they found bones commingled and intertwined with chains; for the body had mouldered away by long lying in the ground, leaving them bare, and corroded by the fet-ters. The bones were collected, and buried at the public expense; and after the ghost was thus duly laid the house was haunted no more.

This story I believe upon the affirma-tion of others; I can myself affirm to others what I now relate. I have a freedman named Marcus, who has some tincture of letters. One night, his younger brother, who was sleeping in the same bed with him, saw, as he thought, somebody sitting on the couch, who put a pair of shears to his head, and actually cut off the hair from the very crown of it. When morning came, they found the boy's crown was shorn, and the hair lay scattered about on the floor. After a short interval, a similar occurrence gave credit to the former. A slave-boy of mine was sleeping amidst several others in their quarters, when two persons clad in white came in (as he tells the story) through the windows, cut off his hair, as he lay, and withdrew the same way they entered. Daylight revealed that this boy too had been shorn, and that his hair was likewise spread about the room. Nothing remarkable followed, unless it were that I escaped prosecution; prose-cuted I should have been, if Domitian (in whose reign these things happened) had lived longer. For an information lodged by Carus against me was found in his scrutore. Hence it may be con-jectured, since it is customary for accused persons to let their hair grow, that this cutting of my servants' hair was a sign I should defeat the peril that hung over me.

I beg, then, you will apply learning to this question. It merits your prolonged and profound consideration; and I am not myself an unworthy recipient of your abounding knowledge. And though you should, after your manner, argue on both sides; yet I hope you will throw your weightiest reasons into one scale, lest you should dismiss me in suspense and uncer-tainty, whereas I consult you on purpose to determine my doubts. Farewell.

—MELMOTH-HUTCHINSON.

THE SAME WINE FOR ALL [1]

[*Letters*, II, 6]

To Avitus

It would be a long story, and of no importance, were I to recount too parti-cularly by what accident I (who am not at all fond of society) supped lately with a person, who in his own opinion lives in splendour combined with economy; but according to mine, in a sordid but expen-sive manner. Some very elegant dishes were served up to himself and a few more of the company; while those which were placed before the rest were cheap and paltry. He had apportioned in small flagons three different sorts of wine; but you are not to suppose it was that the guests might take their choice: on the contrary, that they might not choose at all. One was for himself and me; the next for his friends of a lower order (for,

[1] From The Loeb Classical Library, reprinted by permission.

you must know, he measures out his friendship according to the degree of quality); and the third for his own freed-men and mine. One who sat next me took notice of this, and asked me if I approved of it. "Not at all," I told him. "Pray, then," said he, "what is your method on such occasions?" "Mine, " I returned, "is, to give all my company the same fare; for when I make an invitation, it is to sup, not to be censored. Every man whom I have placed on an equality with myself by admitting him to my table, I treat as an equal in all particulars." "Even freed-men?" he asked. "Even them," I said; "for on these occasions I regard them not as freed-men, but boon companions." "This must put you to great expense," says he. I assured him not at all; and on his asking how that could be, I said: "Why you must know my freed-men don't drink the same wine I do—but *I* drink what *they* do."

And certainly if a man is wise enough to moderate his own gluttony, he will not find it so very chargeable a thing to entertain all his visitors in general as he does himself. Restrain and, so to speak, humble that failing, if you would be an economist in good earnest. You will find your own temperance a much better method of saving expenses, than affronts to other people.

What is my drift in all this, do you ask? Why, to hinder a young man of your excellent disposition from being imposed upon by the self-indulgence which prevails at some men's tables, under the guise of frugality. And whenever any folly of this nature falls within my observation, I shall, in consequence of that affection I bear you, point it out to you as an example which you ought to shun. Remember therefore, nothing is more to be avoided than this modern conjunction of self-indulgence and meanness; qualities superlatively odious when existing in distinct characters, but still more odious where they meet together in the same person. Farewell.

—Melmoth-Hutchinson.

III.   ROMANS AND CHRISTIANS

Concerning the early history of Christianity no Latin writer of the first century has anything to say. All the more significant then for the Roman point of view are the brief passages from the works of Tacitus and Pliny, and the regulations of the emperors Trajan and Hadrian in the first quarter of the second century.

These records, which are here presented in full, bring out clearly certain facts; the wide spread of Christianity in the East, the unpopularity of the Christians in some sections among the non-Christian peoples, the decision of the Roman government to treat confessed Christians as worthy of death because disloyal to the state. Difficulties had arisen from a simple, and yet fundamental, difference in point of view. The government demanded of the provincials formal worship of the Roman gods, not as an act of religion, but as a sign of loyal allegiance to the Roman state. The Christian, no matter how loyal to Rome he might be, could not bring himself to bow down and worship strange gods, even though a mere form of homage alone was demanded. Hence arose Rome's belief that Christians were disloyal. A traitor was always worthy of death in a Roman's eyes. Finding, however, that the Christians engaged in no acts of hostility against the state, a policy was adopted not to hunt them down; but, if they were openly accused in court on the initiative of individual provincials and were convicted by their own admission of being Christian, they were to be put to death.

THE BURNING OF ROME

TACITUS

[From The *Annals*, Book XV]

While Tacitus has no sympathy with the early Christians, and in fact was not at pains to inform himself thoroughly about them, still his sense of fairness does not allow him to acquiesce in Nero's effort to place the responsibility for crimes like the burning of Rome on their shoulders. Whatever the cause of the great fire of the year 64, it furnished the occasion for the first persecution, which was not therefore the result of any systematic plan for the suppression of the new religion. For Tacitus, see above, p. 461.

And now came a calamitous fire— whether it was accidental or purposely contrived by the Emperor, remains uncertain: for on this point authorities are divided—more violent and more destructive than any that ever befell our city. It began in that part of the Circus which adjoins the Palatine and Cælian hills. Breaking out in shops full of inflammable merchandise, it took hold and gathered strength at once; and being fanned by the wind soon embraced the entire length of the Circus, where there were no mansions with protective walls, no temple-enclosures, nor anything else to arrest its course. Furiously the destroying flames swept on, first over the level ground, then up the heights, then again plunging into the hollows, with a rapidity that oustripped all efforts to cope with them, the ancient city lending itself to their progress by its narrow tortuous streets and its misshapen blocks of buildings. The shrieks of panic-stricken women; the weakness of the aged, and the helplessness of the young; the efforts of some to save themselves, of others to help their neighbours; the hurrying of those who dragged their sick along, the lingering of those who waited for them— all made up a scene of inextricable confusion.

Many persons, while looking behind them, were enveloped from the front or from the side; or having escaped to the nearest place of safety, found this too in possession of the flames, and even places which they had thought beyond their reach in the same plight with the rest. At last, not knowing where to turn, or what to avoid, they poured into the roads or threw themselves down in the fields: some having lost their all, not having even food for the day; others, though with means of escape open to them, preferred to perish for love of the dear ones whom they could not save. And none dared to check the flames; for there were many who threatened and forced back those who would extinguish them, while others openly flung in torches, saying that they had their orders;—whether it was really so, or only that they wanted to plunder undisturbed.

At this moment Nero was at Antium. He did not return to the city until the flames were approaching the mansion which he had built to connect the Palatine with the Gardens of Mæcenas; nor could they be stopped until the whole Palatine, including the palace and everything around it, had been consumed. Nero assigned the Campus Martius and the Agrippa monuments for the relief of the fugitive and houseless multitude. He threw open his own gardens also, and put up temporary buildings for the accommodation of the destitute; he brought up provisions from Ostia and the neighbouring towns; and he reduced the price of corn to three sesterces the peck. But popular as these measures were, they aroused no gratitude; for a rumour had got abroad that at the moment when the city was in flames Nero had mounted upon a stage in his own house, and by way of likening modern calamities to ancient, had sung the tale of the sack of Troy.

Not until the sixth day was the fire got under, at the foot of the Esquiline hill, by demolishing a vast extent of buildings, so as to present nothing but the ground, and as it were the open sky, to its continued fury. But scarcely had the alarm subsided, or the populace recovered from their despair, when it burst out again in the more open parts of the city; and though here the loss of life was less, the destruction of temples and porticoes of pleasure was still more complete. And the scandal attending this new fire was the greater that it broke out in the property owned by Tigellinus, in the Æmilian quarter; the general belief being that Nero had the ambition to build a new city to be called after his own name. For of the fourteen regions into which Rome was divided only four remained intact. Three were burnt to the ground; in the other seven, nothing remained save a few fragments of ruined and half-burnt houses.

To count up the number of mansions, of tenements, and of temples that were destroyed would be no easy matter. Among the oldest of the sacred buildings burnt was that dedicated by Servius Tullius to the Moon, and the Great Altar and fane raised by Evander to the Present Hercules. The temple vowed by Romulus to Jupiter, the Stayer of Flight; the Royal palace of Numa; the Temple of Vesta, with the Household Gods of the Roman people, were all destroyed; added to these were the treasures won in numerous battles, and masterpieces of Greek art, as well as ancient and genuine monuments of Roman genius which were remembered by the older generation amid all the splendour of the restored city, and which could never be replaced. Some noted that the nineteenth of July, the day on which the fire began, was also the day on which the Senonian Gauls had taken and burnt the city; others were so curious in their calculations as to discover that the two burnings were separated from one

another by exactly the same number of years, of months, and of days.

Nero profited by the ruin of his country to erect a palace in which the marvels were not to be gold and jewels, the usual and common-place objects of luxury, so much as lawns and lakes and mock-wildernesses, with woods on one side and open glades and vistas on the other. His engineers and masters-of-works were Severus and Celer; men who had the ingenuity and the impudence to fool away the resources of the Empire in the attempt to provide by Art what Nature had pronounced impossible.

For these men undertook to dig a navigable canal, along the rocky shore and over the hills, all the way from Lake Avernus to the mouths of the Tiber. There was no other water for supplying such a canal than that of the Pontine marshes; and even if practicable, the labour would have been prodigious, and no object served. But Nero had a thirst for the incredible, and traces of his vain attempt to excavate the heights adjoining Lake Avernus are to be seen to this day.

The parts of the city unoccupied by Nero's palace were not built over without divisions, or indiscriminately, as after the Gallic fire, but in blocks of regular dimensions, with broad streets between. A limit was placed to the height of houses; open spaces were left; and colonnades were added to protect the fronts of tenements, Nero undertaking to build these at his own cost, and to hand over the building sites, cleared of rubbish, to the proprietors. He offered premiums also, in proportion to the rank and means of the owners, on condition of mansions or tenements being completed within a given time; and he assigned the marshes of Ostia for the reception of the rubbish, which was taken down the Tiber in the same vessels which had brought up the corn. Certain parts of the houses were to be built without beams, and of solid stone, Gabian or Alban, those stones being impervious to fire. Then as water had often been improperly intercepted by individuals, inspectors were appointed to secure a more abundant supply, and over a larger area, for public use; owners were required to keep appliances for quenching fire in some open place; party walls were forbidden, and every house had to be enclosed within walls of its own.

These useful measures added greatly to the appearance of the new city; and yet there were not wanting persons who thought that the plan of the old city was more conducive to health, as the narrow streets and high roofs were a protection against the rays of the sun, which now beat down with double fierceness upon broad and shadeless thoroughfares.

Such were the measures suggested by human counsels; after which means were taken to propitiate the Gods. The Sibylline books were consulted, and prayers were offered, as prescribed by them, to Vulcan, to Ceres, and to Proserpine. Juno was supplicated by the matrons, in the Capitol first, and afterwards at the nearest point upon the sea, from which water was drawn to sprinkle the temple and image of the Goddess; banquets to the Goddesses and all-night festivals were celebrated by married women.

But neither human aid, nor imperial bounty, nor atoning-offerings to the Gods, could remove the sinister suspicion that the fire had been brought about by Nero's order. To put an end therefore to this rumour, he shifted the charge on to others, and inflicted the most cruel tortures upon a body of men detested for their abominations, and popularly known by the name of Christians. This name came from one Christus, who was put to death in the reign of Tiberius by the Procurator Pontius Pilate; but though checked for the time, the detestable superstition broke out again, not in Judea only, where the mischief began, but even in Rome, where every horrible and shameful iniquity, from every quarter of the world, pours in and finds a welcome.

First those who acknowledged themselves of this persuasion were arrested; and upon their testimony a vast number were condemned, not so much on the charge of incendiarism as for their hatred of the human race. Their death was turned into a diversion. They were clothed in the skins of wild beasts, and torn to pieces by dogs; they were fastened to crosses, or set up to be burned, so as to serve the purpose of lamps when daylight failed. Nero gave up his own gardens for this spectacle; he provided also Circensian games, during which he mingled with the populace, or took his stand upon a chariot, in the garb of a charioteer. But guilty as these men were and worthy of direst punishment, the fact that they were being sacrificed for no public good, but only to glut the cruelty of one man, aroused a feeling of pity on their behalf.

Meanwhile Italy was ransacked for contributions. The provinces and allied peoples were rifled, as well as the states which are called "free." Even the Gods had to submit to being plundered. The temples in the city were despoiled, and emptied of the gold consecrated at triumphs, or vowed by past generations in times of panic or prosperity. As for Asia and Achaia, not offerings only, but the very images of the Gods were carried off by Acratus and Secundus Carrinas, who were sent out to those provinces for the purpose. The former was a freedman ready for any kind of villany; the latter was a man whose lips were tinged with Greek learning, but who had no real culture in his heart.

We are told that Seneca craved leave to withdraw to a remote country retreat to avoid the odium of such sacrilege; on this being denied him he pretended to be suffering from some muscular ailment, and shut himself up in his own chamber. Other accounts say that Nero ordered poison to be administered to him by one of his own freedmen, called Cleonicus; but that Seneca escaped the trap, either by the man's avowal, or by his own precaution in adopting a simple diet of natural fruits, and slaking his thirst from running water.

—G. G. RAMSAY.

THE STATE AND THE CHRISTIANS

PLINY

[*Letters*, X, 96]

At the time Pliny made this report to the emperor (about 112 A.D.), he was governor of the province of Bithynia, the Northern section of Asia Minor. The account is the earliest by a Roman of the Christians and their practices. Although Pliny may fail to understand their point of view, he leaves no doubt whatever of his honest desire to deal fairly with them. For Pliny, see above, p. 598.

To the Emperor Trajan

It is a rule, Sir, which I inviolably observe, to refer myself to you in all my doubts; for who is more capable of guiding my uncertainty or informing my ignorance? Having never been present at any trials of the Christians, I am unacquainted with the method and limits to be observed either in examining or punishing them. Whether any difference is to be made on account of age, or no distinction allowed between the youngest and the adult; whether repentance admits to a pardon, or if a man has been once a Christian it avails him nothing to recant; whether the mere profession of Christianity, albeit without crimes, or only the crimes associated therewith are punishable—in all these points I am greatly doubtful.

In the meanwhile, the method I have observed towards those who have been

---

denounced to me as Christians is this: I interrogated them whether they were Christians; if they confessed it I repeated the question twice again, adding the threat of capital punishment; if they still persevered, I ordered them to be executed. For whatever the nature of their creed might be, I could at least feel no doubt that contumacy and inflexible obstinacy deserved chastisement. There were others also possessed with the same infatuation, but being citizens of Rome, I directed them to be carried thither.

These accusations spread (as is usually the case) from the mere fact of the matter being investigated and several forms of the mischief came to light. A placard was put up, without any signature, accusing a large number of persons by name. Those who denied they were, or ever had been, Christians, who repeated after me an invocation to the Gods, and offered adoration, with wine and frankincense, to your image, which I had ordered to be brought for that purpose, together with those of the Gods, and who finally cursed Christ—none of which acts, it is said, those who are really Christians can be forced into performing—these I thought it proper to discharge. Others who were named by that informer at first confessed themselves Christians, and then denied it. True, they had been of that persuasion but they had quitted it, some three years, others many years, and a few as much as twenty-five years ago. They all worshipped your statue and the images of the Gods, and cursed Christ.

They affirmed, however, the whole of their guilt, or their error, was, that they were in the habit of meeting on a certain fixed day before it was light, when they sang in alternate verses a hymn to Christ, as to a god, and bound themselves by a solemn oath, not to any wicked deeds, but never to commit any fraud, theft or adultery, never to falsify their word, nor deny a trust when they should be called upon to deliver it up; after which it was their custom to separate, and then re-assemble to partake of food—but food of an ordinary and innocent kind. Even this practice, however, they had abandoned after the publication of my edict, by which, according to your orders, I had forbidden political associations. I judged it so much the more necessary to extract the real truth, with the assistance of torture, from two female slaves, who were styled *deaconnesses:* but I could discover nothing more than depraved and excessive superstition.

I therefore adjourned the proceedings, and betook myself at once to your counsel. For the matter seemed to me well worth referring to you,— especially considering the numbers endangered. Persons of all ranks and ages, and of both sexes, are, and will be, involved in the prosecution. For this contagious superstition is not confined to the cities only, but has spread through the villages and rural districts; it seems possible, however, to check and cure it. 'Tis certain at least that the temples, which had been almost deserted, begin now to be frequented; and the sacred festivals, after a long intermission, are again revived; while there is a general demand for sacrificial animals, which for some time past have met with but few purchasers. From hence it is easy to imagine what multitudes may be reclaimed from this error, if a door be left open to repentance.
—Melmoth-Hutchinson.

The Emperor's Reply [1]

TRAJAN

[Pliny's *Letters*, X, 97]

Acknowledgment of the gods of the Roman state amounted to evidence of allegiance to the Roman government. Trajan, Emperor from 98 to 117, is willing to

[1] From The Loeb Classical Library, reprinted by permission.

make every concession possible, but feels that he must insist upon such acknowledgment, not for religious reasons but for reasons of state. This rescript to Pliny contains the outlines of the policy followed by the government towards Christianity for more than a century thereafter.

To Pliny

The method you have pursued, my dear Pliny, in sifting the cases of those denounced to you as Christians is extremely proper. It is not possible to lay down any general rule which can be applied as the fixed standard in all cases of this nature. No search should be made for these people; when they are denounced and found guilty they must be punished; with the restriction, however, that when the party denies himself to be a Christian, and shall give proof that he is not (that is, by adoring our Gods) he shall be pardoned on the ground of repentance, even though he may have formerly incurred suspicion. Informations without the accuser's name subscribed must not be admitted in evidence against anyone, as it is introducing a very dangerous precedent, and by no means agreeable to the spirit of the age.
—Melmoth-Hutchinson.

Hadrian's Decision

HADRIAN

The policy which Trajan had initiated in dealing with the Christians his successor Hadrian, emperor from 117 to 138, probably adopted. In the following rescript to Minicius Fundanus, governor of Asia about 124, the emperor emphasizes the point that public, not anonymous, accusations alone will be heard in Roman courts, and that false charges will be severely punished.

I received a letter from your illustrious predecessor Serenus Gratianus, and I do not wish to leave his inquiry unanswered, lest innocent men be troubled and false accusers seize occasion for robbery.

If the provincials are clearly willing to appear in person to substantiate suits against Christians, if, that is, they come themselves before your judgment seat to prefer their accusations, I do not forbid them to prosecute. But I do not permit them to make mere entreaties and protestations. Justice demands that if any one wishes to bring an accusation, you should make due legal enquiry into the charge. If such an accusation be brought and it be proved that the accused men have done anything illegal, you will punish them as their misdeeds deserve. But, in Heaven's name, take the very greatest care that if a man prosecute any one of these men by way of false accusation you visit the accuser, as his wickedness deserves, with severer penalties.

—BERNARD W. HENDERSON.

INDEX OF AUTHORS AND TITLES